Rick Steves®

WINDSOR PUBLIC LIBRARY

3 2503 13266 2870

ENGLAND

DATE

CONTENTS

Welcome to Rick Steves' Europe

Travel is intensified living—maximum thrills per minute and one of the last great sources of legal adventure. Travel is freedom. It's recess, and we need it.

I discovered a passion for European travel as a teen and have been sharing it ever since—through my tours, public television and radio shows, and travel guidebooks. Over the years, I've taught thousands of travelers how to best enjoy Europe's blockbuster sights—and experience "Back Door" discoveries that most tourists miss.

This book offers you a balanced mix of England's biggies (Big Ben and Stonehenge) and more intimate locales (windswept Roman lookouts and nearly edible Cotswolds villages). And it's selective: There are dozens of hikes in the Lake District; I recommend only the best ones. My self-guided museum tours and city walks give insight into the country's vibrant history and today's living, breathing culture.

I advocate traveling simply and smartly. Take advantage of my money- and time-saving tips on sightseeing, transportation, and more. Try local, characteristic alternatives to expensive hotels and restaurants. In many ways, spending more money only builds a thicker wall between you and what you traveled so far to see.

We visit England to experience it—to become temporary locals. Thoughtful travel engages us with the world, as we learn to appreciate other cultures and new ways to measure quality of life.

Judging from the positive feedback I receive from readers, this book will help you enjoy a fun, affordable, and rewarding vacation—whether it's your first trip or your tenth.

Have a brilliant holiday! Happy travels!

Rick Steves

ENGLAND

From the grandeur and bustle of London, to the pastoral countryside that inspired Wordsworth, to some of the quaintest towns you'll ever experience, England delights. Stand in a desolate field and ponder an ancient stone circle. Strike up a conversation just to hear the Queen's English. Bite into a scone smothered with clotted cream, sip a cup of tea, and wave your pinky as if it's a Union Jack.

England, with a population of 55 million, is the center of the United Kingdom in every way: home to four out of five UK citizens, the seat of government, the economic power-house, the center of higher learning, and the cultural heart.

All of this is contained in a hilly land about the size of Louisiana (50,350 square miles), occupying the southern two-thirds of the isle of Britain. Scotland is to the north, the English Channel and France are to the south, and Wales is to the west. England's highest mountain (Scafell Pike in the Lake District) is 3,206 feet, a foothill by American standards. Fed by ocean air, the climate is mild, with a chance of cloudy, rainy weather nearly any day of the year.

South England, including London, has always had more people and more money than the north. Blessed with roll-ing hills, wide plains, and the Thames River, in the past this region was rich with farms, and its rivers flowed with trade. Then and now, high culture flourished in London, today a thriving metropolis of eight million people.

North England is known for the country's most beautiful

Bustling London offers nonstop entertainment while England's countryside provides a tranquil retreat.

landscapes. Its hilly terrain yields poor soil, so the traditional economy of the region was based on livestock (grazing cows and sheep). In the 19th century, North England was dotted with belching smokestacks as its major cities became centers for coal and iron mining, and manufacturing. Now its working-class cities and ports (such as Liverpool) are experiencing a comeback, buoyed by tourism, vibrant arts scenes, and higher employment.

England's economy can stand alongside many much larger nations. The country boasts high-tech industries (software, chemicals, aviation), international banking, and textile manufacturing, and is a major exporter of beef. England is an urban, industrial, and post-industrial colossus, yet its farms, villages, and people are down-to-earth.

You can trace England's illustrious history by roaming the countryside. Prehistoric peoples built the mysterious stone circles of Stonehenge and Avebury. Then came the Romans, who built Hadrian's Wall and the baths at Bath. Viking invaders left their mark in York, and the Normans built the Tower of London. As England Christianized and unified, the grand cathedrals of Salisbury, Wells, and Durham arose.

Next came the castles and palaces of the English monarchs (Windsor) and the Shakespeare sights from the era of

Britain's Pub Hub

In Britain, a pub is a home-away-from-home. Spend some time in one and you'll have your finger on the pulse of the community. These cozy hangouts are extended living rooms, where locals and travelers alike can eat, drink, get out of the rain, watch a sporting event, and meet other people.

Britain's pubs are also national treasures, with great cultural value and rich history, not to mention good beer and grub. Crawling between classic pubs is more than a tipsy night out—it's bona fide sightseeing. Each offers a glimpse—and a taste—of traditional British culture.

Pubs' odd names often go back hundreds of years. Because many medieval pub-goers were illiterate, pubs were simply named for the picture hung outside (e.g., The Crooked Stick, The Queen's Arms—meaning her coat of arms).

The Golden Age for pub-building was in the late Victorian era (c. 1880–1905). In this class-conscious time, pubs were divided by screens (now mostly gone), allowing the wealthy to drink in a more refined setting. Pubs were really "public houses," featuring nooks (snugs) for groups and clubs to meet, friends and lovers to rendezvous, and families to get out of the house at night.

Pubs are neighborhood hangouts with a personality, a quaint name, and a cozy or even elegant setting.

Fancy, late-Victorian pubs often come with heavy embossed wallpaper ceilings, decorative tile work, fine-etched glass, ornate carved stillions (the big central hutch for storing bottles and glass), and even urinals equipped with a place to set your glass. The "former-bank pubs" represent a more modern trend in pub-building: As banks increasingly go electronic, they're moving out of lavish, high-rent old buildings. ▶▶▶

▶▶▶ Many of these former banks are being refitted as pubs with elegant bars and freestanding stillions, which provide a fine centerpiece.

Pubs usually serve traditional dishes, such as "bangers and mash" (sausages and mashed potatoes) and roast beef with Yorkshire pudding, but you're just as likely to find pasta, curried dishes, and quiche.

And, of course, there's the number-one reason people have always flocked to pubs: beer. The British take great pride in their brews. Many Brits think that drinking beer cold and carbonated, as Americans do, ruins the taste. Most pubs will have lagers (cold, refreshing, American-style beer), ales (amber-colored, cellar-temperature beer), bitters (hop-flavored ale, perhaps the most typical British beer), and stouts (dark and somewhat bitter, like Guinness). At pubs, long-handled pulls are used to pull the traditional, rich-flavored "real ales" up from the cellar. These are the connoisseur's favorites: fermented naturally, varying from sweet to bitter, often with a hoppy or nutty flavor. Short-handled pulls mean colder, fizzier, mass-produced, and less interesting keg beers. Mild beers are sweeter, with a creamy malt flavoring. Irish cream ale is a smooth, sweet experience. Try the draft cider (sweet or dry)...carefully.

Like in days past, people go to a pub to be social. If that's your aim, stick by the bar (rather than a table) and people will assume you're in the mood to talk. Go pubbing in the

Pubs offer hearty food (such as bangers and mash), various ales and beer, and friendly service.

evening for a lively time, or drop during the quiet late morning (fro 11:00) for some lunchtime grub.

No matter what time of day, a visit to a historic pub is an enriching experience. Slow down, try a local beer, and make yourself at home. You'll likely gain a broader perspective, some interesting stories, and maybe even a new friend or two. ∎

Elizabeth I (Stratford-upon-Avon). In following centuries, tiny England became a maritime empire (the *Cutty Sark* at Greenwich) and the world's first industrial power (Iron-bridge Gorge). England's Romantic poets were inspired by the unspoiled nature and time-passed villages of the Lake District and the Cotswolds.

In the 20th century, the gritty urban culture of 1960s Liverpool gave the world the Beatles. London is a world in itself, with monuments (Big Ben), museums (the British Museum), royalty (Buckingham Palace), theater, and night-life, throbbing with the beat of the global community.

The English people have a worldwide reputation (or stereotype) for being cheerful, courteous, and well-mannered. Cutting in line is very gauche. On the other hand, English soccer fans can be notorious hooligans. The English are not known for being physically demonstrative (hugging and kiss-ing), but they love to talk. And when times get tough, they persevere with a stiff upper lip, dry wit, and a "keep calm and carry on" attitude.

England is set apart from its fellow United Kingdom countries (Scotland, Wales, and Northern Ireland) by its ethnic makeup. Traditionally, those countries had Celtic roots, while the English mixed in Saxon and Norman blood. In the 20th century, England welcomed many Scots, Welsh, and Irish as low-wage workers. More recently, it's become

Changing the world: Ironbridge Gorge started the Industrial Revolu-tion, while Liverpool gave birth to the Beatles.

Cosmopolitan London celebrates cultural festivals. The Houses of Parliament honor centuries of tradition.

home to immigrants from former colonies of its worldwide empire—particularly from India, Pakistan, Bangladesh, the Caribbean, and Africa—and to many workers from poorer Eastern European countries. These days it's not a given that every "English" person speaks English.

This is the current English paradox. England—the birthplace and center of the extended worldwide family of nearly one billion English speakers—is losing its traditional Englishness. Where Scotland, Wales, and Northern Ireland have their own parliaments and cultural movements to preserve their local languages and customs, England does not. Politically, there is no "English" party in the UK Parliament; England must depend on the decisions of the UK government at large. Many English people don't really think of themselves as "English"—more as "Brits," a part of the wider UK.

Today, England races forward as a leading global player. Whether the UK's departure from the European Union ("Brexit") speeds up or slows down England's progress, the result is sure to be interesting. With its rich heritage, lively present, and momentous future, England is a culturally diverse land in transition. Catch it while you can.

England's Top Destinations

There's so much to see in England and so little time. This overview breaks the country's top destinations into must-see sights (to help first-time travelers plan their trip) and worth-it sights (for those with extra time or special interests). I've also suggested a minimum number of days to allow per destination.

SCOTLAND

**PLACES COVERED
IN THIS BOOK**

▲▲▲ Must See
▲▲ Try Hard to See
▲ Worthwhile

DURHAM
& N.E. ENGLAND

LAKE
DISTRICT

*Irish
Sea*

NORTH
YORKSHIRE

*North
Sea*

BLACKPOOL

YORK

50 Kilometers
50 Miles

LIVERPOOL

IRONBRIDGE
GORGE

WARWICK
& COVENTRY

STRATFORD-
UPON-AVON

WALES

ENGLAND

THE
COTSWOLDS

OXFORD

WINDSOR &
CAMBRIDGE

*Celtic
Sea*

BATH

AVEBURY,
STONEHENGE &
SALISBURY

GLASTONBURY
& WELLS

LONDON

DARTMOOR

PORTSMOUTH

CANTERBURY

DOVER
& S.E.
ENGLAND

CORNWALL

English Channel

BRIGHTON

11

MUST-SEE DESTINATIONS

Three cities—cosmopolitan London, aristocratic Bath, and historic York—offer an excellent sampler of the best that England has to offer.

▲▲▲London (3-4 days)
London has world-class museums (British Museum, National Gallery, and many more), bustling markets, and cutting-edge architecture sharing the turf with the Tower of London and St. Paul's Cathedral. Simply getting around is memorable—from double-decker buses and Thames river boats to chatty cabs and the hardworking Tube. Enjoy London's cuisine scene, parks, grand squares, and palaces. Live theater takes center stage at night.

▲▲▲Bath (2 days)
Bath is a genteel Georgian showcase city, built around an ancient Roman bath. Its glorious abbey, harmonious architecture, engaging walking tours, and small-town feel make it a good candidate for your first stop in England. Fun day trips include Bristol, Wells, Glastonbury, Stonehenge, and more.

▲▲▲York (1-2 days)
This walled medieval town has a grand Gothic cathedral (with a divine evensong) and fine museums (Viking, Victorian, and railway). Classy restaurants hide out in the atmospheric old center, with its "snickelway" passages and colorful Shambles shopping lane.

London's Tower Bridge; Bath's riverside setting and ancient Roman Baths museum; York's Castle Museum portrays a bygone era.

WORTH-IT DESTINATIONS

You can weave any of these destinations—rated ▲ or ▲▲—into your itinerary. They're listed in the order they appear in this book. It's easy to add some destinations based on proximity (if you're going to the Cotswolds, Stratford-upon-Avon is next door), but out-of-the-way places (such as Cornwall or Hadrian's Wall) can also merit the journey, depending on your time and interests.

▲▲Windsor and Cambridge (1-2 days)
Good day trips from London include Windsor, starring the Queen's impressive home-sweet-castle. Cambridge, one of England's best university towns, features the stunning King's College Chapel and Wren Library.

▲Canterbury (1 day)
The pleasant town, with England's top church, became a pilgrimage site after Archbishop Thomas Becket was martyred here. Today the town's lively, compact core attracts more pedestrians and shoppers than pilgrims.

▲Dover and Southeast England (1-2 days)
Dover hosts an imposing castle, famous White Cliffs, and grand Channel views. Nearby are the lush Sissinghurst Gardens, the hill town of Rye, and the historic site of the Battle of Hastings.

▲Brighton (1 day)
The flamboyant beach resort on England's south coast, with its amusement pier, Royal Pavilion, and viewpoint tower, makes a fun stop. Nearby are the chalky cliffs at Beachy Head, good for a drive or hike.

Canterbury's fancy Christ Church Gate; the White Cliffs of Dover; a sunny day at Brighton beach; the gothic King's College Chapel at Cambridge

Visiting the Historic Dockyard in Portsmouth; entry to Tintagel Castle; Cornwall's tiny Mousehole harbor; wild ponies at Dartmoor National Park

A double arch supports Wells Cathedral; Avebury's vast stone circle is free to wander.

▲Portsmouth (1 day)
The revitalized shipbuilding city has top nautical sights (famous ships and naval museums) at the Historic Dockyard, plus Roman ruins and the stately Arundel Castle nearby.

▲Dartmoor (1 day)
This mysterious, desolate, moor-cloaked national park has wild ponies, hiking paths, and an ancient stone circle.

▲Cornwall (1 day)
The feisty western peninsula, littered with prehistoric ruins, sports the seaside resort towns of Penzance and St. Ives, the scenically windblown Penwith Peninsula, King Arthur's supposed Tintagel Castle, and the tip of England at Land's End.

▲▲Glastonbury and Wells (1 day)
Little Glastonbury has a mystical New Age vibe, with its Holy Grail and King Arthur lore. The enjoyable town of Wells has an ingeniously fortified cathedral. Both towns are easy to visit from Bath.

▲▲Avebury, Stonehenge, and Salisbury (1 day)
For spine-tingling stone circles, see famed Stonehenge (worth ▲▲▲ on its own) and the larger, less touristy Avebury. Nearby is Salisbury and its striking cathedral.

▲▲Oxford (1 day)

The stately but youthful university town, with historic colleges and a host of esteemed literary alumni, has Blenheim Palace —one of England's best—on its doorstep.

▲▲The Cotswolds (1-2 days)

These quaint villages—the cozy market town of Chipping Campden, popular Stow-on-the-Wold, and the handy transit hub Moreton-in-Marsh—are scattered over a hilly countryside, which can be fun to explore on foot, by bike, or by car.

▲Stratford-upon-Avon (half-day to 1 day)

Shakespeare's pretty hometown, featuring residences that belonged to the Bard and his loved ones, is the top venue for performances of his plays.

▲Warwick and Coventry (half-day to 1 day)

Warwick, England's best medieval castle, has impressive fortifications and fun demonstrations. The inspiring town of Coventry, nearly destroyed in World War II, built its new St. Michael's Cathedral amid the bombed-out ruins of the old one.

▲Ironbridge Gorge (half-day to 1 day)

Boasting the planet's first iron bridge, this unassuming village was the birthplace of the Industrial Revolution, with sights and museums that tell the earth-changing story.

▲Liverpool (half-day to 1 day)

The rejuvenated port city is the Beatles' hometown, with a host of related sights (including the homes of John and Paul), museums, and pub-and-club nightlife.

▲Blackpool (half-day)

England's tackiest, fun-loving beach resort has amusement piers, roller-coaster rides, and a long beach, offering a chance to mix with the English working class at play.

▲▲The Lake District (2 days)

This peaceful idyllic region, dotted with lakes, hills, and sheep, is known for its enjoyable hikes, joyrides, time-passed valleys, and William Wordsworth and Beatrix Potter sights.

Blenheim Palace—one of Europe's finest; falconer at Warwick Castle; namesake bridge at Ironbridge Gorge; hiking the Lake District; Liverpool's iconic Cavern Club; ambling through a charming Cotswolds village

▲North Yorkshire (half-day)
In this pastoral region of hills and moors, drivers can choose among ruined abbeys, a castle, a POW camp museum, and the salty seaside towns of Whitby and tiny Staithes.

▲Durham and Northeast England (1-2 days)
The youthful workaday town has a magnificent cathedral, plus (nearby) an open-air museum, the Roman remains of Hadrian's Wall, Holy Island, and Bamburgh Castle.

Ancient Rome meets ancient Britain at Hadrian's Wall (top) and the Vindolanda Fort & Museum (above); pintsize Staithes dots the North Yorkshire coast.

Planning Your Trip

To plan your trip, you'll need to design your itinerary—choosing where and when to go, how you'll travel, and how many days to spend at each destination. For my best advice on sightseeing, accommodations, restaurants, and transportation, see the Practicalities chapter.

DESIGNING AN ITINERARY

As you read this book and learn your options...

Choose your top destinations.

My recommended itinerary (on the next page) gives you an idea of how much you can reasonably see in 20 days, but you can adapt it to fit your own interests and time frame.

If you enjoy big cities, you could easily spend a week in London. If villages beckon, linger in the Cotswolds. York and Bath are inviting, walkable towns with fascinating sights. Nature lovers get wonderfully lost in the Lake District and Dartmoor.

History buffs can choose their era: prehistoric (Stonehenge, Avebury), ancient Roman (Bath, Hadrian's Wall), religious (Canterbury), medieval (York, Warwick Castle), Industrial Revolution (Ironbridge Gorge), or royal (Tower of London, Windsor, Blenheim).

Literary fans make a pilgrimage to Stratford (Shakespeare), Bath (Austen), and the Lake District (Wordsworth and Potter). Beatles fans from here, there, and everywhere head to Liverpool. For amusement pier fun, stroll the arcades at the coastal resorts of Brighton or Blackpool.

England's Best Three-Week Trip by Car

This 20-day itinerary covers the top sights in England.

With More Time: You can easily combine this 20-day itinerary with my 11-day "South England Drive" (see page 24). Start with the south itinerary, ending in Bath. Then continue with Day 4 of the main itinerary (Avebury and Blenheim to Oxford).

Decide when to go.

July and August are peak season—with long days, the best weather, and a busy schedule of tourist fun. May and June can be lovely anywhere. Spring and fall offer decent weather and smaller crowds.

Winter travelers face few crowds and soft room prices (except in London), but sightseeing hours are shorter and the weather is reliably bad. In the countryside, some attractions open only on weekends or close entirely. While rural charm falls with the leaves, city sightseeing is fine. For weather specifics, see the climate chart in the appendix.

Day	Plan	Sleep in
1	Arrive in London, connect to Bath	Bath
2	Sightsee Bath	Bath
3	Pick up car, visit Stonehenge, Wells, and Glastonbury	Bath
4	Avebury, Blenheim Palace	Oxford
5	Oxford, evening to Cotswolds	Chipping Campden
6	Explore Cotswolds	Chipping Campden
7	More Cotswolds (plus evening in Stratford if you've booked a play)	Chipping Campden
8	Stratford, Warwick Castle, to Ironbridge Gorge	Ironbridge Gorge
9	Ironbridge Gorge, then Liverpool	Liverpool
10	To Lake District, visiting South Lake District en route to Keswick	Keswick area
11	Explore North Lake District (hikers may want an extra day)	Keswick area
12	Visit Hadrian's Wall, then to Durham	Durham
13	Visit North Yorkshire, drop car in York	York
14	York	York
15	Morning train to London	London
16	Sightsee London	London
17	London	London
18	Day trips: Windsor, Cambridge, Brighton, or Canterbury/Dover	London
19	London or another day trip	London
20	Whew!	

Connect the dots.

Link your destinations into a logical route. Determine which cities you'll fly into and out of. Begin your search for transatlantic flights at Kayak.com.

Decide if you'll travel by car or public transportation or both. A car is helpful for exploring countryside destinations, but is useless in big cities. Some travelers rent a car on site for a day or two, and use public transportation for the rest. Trains are faster and more expensive than buses (which don't run as often on Sundays).

For approximate travel times between destinations, study

South England Drive

South England is best by car and worth a full week or more. Consider this 11-day trip from Canterbury to Cornwall to Bath. To meld this trip with my longer England itinerary, see page 22.

Day	Plan	Sleep in
1	Arrive in London, take the train to Canterbury	Canterbury
2	See Canterbury, pick up car, visit Dover	Canterbury
3	Drive to the Battle of Hastings site and Beachy Head	Brighton
4	Brighton and Portsmouth	Portsmouth
5	Finish Portsmouth and head to Salisbury	Salisbury
6	See Stonehenge early, then drive to Dartmoor	Dartmoor
7	Dartmoor National Park	Dartmoor
8	Visit Cornwall, then Penzance	Penzance
9	Explore the Penwith Peninsula	Penzance
10	Drive north to Tintagel and Glastonbury	Wells
11	Wells and Bath	Bath

Without a Car: While less ideal, it's possible to see most of the south by train or bus. Do the southeast sights (Canterbury, Dover, Brighton) as day trips from London. Skip Dartmoor and reach Penzance and Cornwall by train (and tour the peninsula via minibus from Penzance). Then visit Wells and Glastonbury by bus from Bath.

Best Three-Week Trip by Public Transportation

This 21-day itinerary connects England's top destinations by train and bus, with minibus tour options along the way. Keep in mind that bus service can be scarce on Sundays (particularly around the Cotswolds and Stratford).

Day	Plan	Sleep in
1	Arrive in London, connect to Bath by train or bus (1.5 hours)	Bath
2	Sightsee Bath	Bath
3	Stonehenge and Avebury by minibus day tour	Bath
4	To Oxford by train (1.5 hours)	Oxford
5	Blenheim Palace by bus (1 hour roundtrip)	Oxford
6	To Cotswolds by train to Moreton-in-Marsh (2.5 hours), then bus to Chipping Campden	Chipping Campden
7	Explore Cotswolds	Chipping Campden
8	Bus to Stratford (0.5 hours)	Stratford
9	Train to Liverpool (3 hours)	Liverpool
10	To Lake District by train to Penrith, then bus to Keswick (about 3 hours)	Keswick area
11	Explore North Lake District	Keswick area
12	To Hadrian's Wall by bus to Penrith, train to Haltwhistle (2 hours), then explore the wall by shuttle bus or taxi	Haltwhistle area or Durham
13	To Durham by train from Hexham (1 hour), then Beamish Museum by bus (1 hour roundtrip)	Durham
14	To York by train (1 hour)	York
15	York	York
16	Morning train to London (2 hours)	London
17	Sightsee London	London
18	London	London
19	Day trips: Windsor, Cambridge, Brighton, or Canterbury/Dover	London
20	London or another day trip	London
21	Whew!	

With Less Time: I'd skip places where public transportation is particularly sparse or time-consuming (such as Hadrian's Wall).

Expect a mix of sun and clouds, whether on the canals in Canterbury or the top-of-the-world Lake District.

the driving chart (see the Practicalities chapter) or train schedules (www.nationalrail.co.uk or www.bahn.com).

If traveling beyond England, consider taking the Eurostar train (for instrance, to Paris) or a budget flight; check Skyscanner.com for flights within Europe.

Write out a day-by-day itinerary.

Figure out how many destinations you can comfortably fit in your time frame. Don't overdo it—few travelers wish they'd hurried more. Allow enough days per stop (see estimates in "England's Top Destinations," earlier). Minimize one-night stands, especially consecutive ones. It can be worth taking a late-afternoon drive or train ride to get settled into a town for two nights.

Include sufficient time for transportation; it'll take you a half-day to get between most destinations. Staying in a home base (like London or Bath) and making day trips can be more time-efficient than changing locations and hotels.

Take sight closures into account. Avoid visiting a town on the one day a week its must-see sights are closed. Check if any holidays or festivals fall during your trip— these attract crowds and can close sights (for the latest, visit England's tourist website, www.visitbritain.com).

Give yourself some slack. Every trip, and every traveler, needs downtime for doing laundry, picnic shopping, people-watching, and so on. Pace yourself. Assume you will return.

Trip Costs per Person

Run a reality check on your dream trip. You'll have major transportation costs in addition to daily expenses.

Flight: A round-trip flight from the US to London costs about $900-1,500, depending on where you fly from and when.

Public Transportation: For a three-week trip, allow $600 for second-class trains ($850 for first class), $60 for buses, and $30 for the London Tube. A BritRail England pass is a good value; buy it before you go.

Car Rental: Allow roughly $250 per week, not including tolls, gas, parking, and insurance.

AVERAGE DAILY EXPENSES PER PERSON

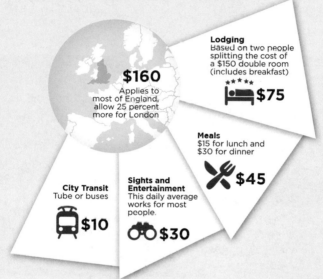

$160
Applies to most of England, allow 25 percent more for London

Lodging
Based on two people splitting the cost of a $150 double room (includes breakfast)
★★★★★
$75

Meals
$15 for lunch and $30 for dinner
$45

City Transit
Tube or buses
$10

Sights and Entertainment
This daily average works for most people.
$30

Budget Tips

Cut your daily expenses by taking advantage of the deals you'll find throughout England and mentioned in this book.

City transit passes (for multiple rides or all-day usage) decrease your cost per ride. For example, it's smart to get an Oyster card in London.

Avid sightseers buy combo-tickets or passes that cover multiple museums. If a town doesn't offer deals, limit yourself to the sights you most want to see, and seek out free experiences and sights (offered even in London).

Some businesses—especially hotels and walking-tour companies—offer discounts to my readers (look for the RS% symbol in the hotel listings ▶▶▶

Rick Steves England

▶▶▶ in this book).

Book your rooms directly with the hotel. Some hotels offer a discount if you pay in cash and/or stay three or more nights (check online or ask). Rooms cost less outside of peak season (July and August). And even seniors can sleep cheap in hostels (some have double rooms) for as little as $30 per person. Or check Airbnb-type sites for deals.

It's no hardship to eat cheap in England. You can get tasty, inexpensive meals at pubs, cafeterias, chain restaurants, ethnic eateries, and fish-and-chips joints. Some upscale restaurants offer early-bird dinner specials. And groceries sell ready-made sandwiches. Cultivate the art of picnicking in atmospheric settings.

When you splurge, choose an experience you'll remember, such as an elegant afternoon tea or a splashy London musical. Minimize souvenir shopping—how will you get it all home? Focus instead on collecting wonderful memories. ■

Welcoming B&Bs in the Lake District; a London musical performance; London's colorful Borough Market.

BEFORE YOU GO

You'll have a smoother trip if you tackle a few things ahead of time. For more information on these topics, see the Practicalities chapter (and www.ricksteves.com, which has helpful tips and travel talks).

Make sure your passport is valid. If it's due to expire within six months of your ticketed date of return, you need to renew it. Allow up to six weeks to renew or get a passport (www.travel.state.gov).

Arrange your transportation.
Book your international flights early. Figure out your main form of transportation within England: It's worth thinking about buying train tickets online in advance, getting a rail pass, renting a car, or booking cheap British flights. (You can wing it once you're there, but it may cost more.)

Book rooms well in advance, especially if your trip falls during peak season or any major holidays or festivals.

Reserve or buy tickets ahead for must-see plays, special tours, or sights. If there's a show you're set on seeing in London or Stratford, you can buy tickets before you go. When you're in London, you can save time in line by buying Fast Track tickets for some popular sights. At Stonehenge, you'll need reservations to go inside the stone circle. To tour the interiors of the Lennon and McCartney homes in Liverpool, reserve ahead.

Consider travel insurance. Compare the cost of the

insurance to the cost of your potential loss. Check whether your existing insurance (health, homeowners, or renters) covers you and your possessions overseas.

Call your bank. Alert your bank that you'll be using your debit and credit cards in Europe. Ask about transaction fees, and get the PIN number for your credit card. You don't need to bring pounds for your trip; you can withdraw currency from cash machines in Europe.

Use your smartphone smartly. Sign up for an international service plan to reduce your costs, or rely on Wi-Fi in Europe instead. Download any apps you'll want on the road, such as maps, transit schedules, and Rick Steves Audio Europe (see sidebar).

Rip up this book! Turn chapters into mini guidebooks: Break the book's spine and use a utility knife to slice apart chapters, keeping gummy edges intact. Reinforce the chapter spines with clear wide tape; use a heavy-duty stapler; or make or buy a cheap cover (see the Travel Store at www.ricksteves.com), swapping out chapters as you travel.

Pack light. You'll walk with your luggage more than you think. Bring a single carry-on bag and a daypack. Use the packing checklist in the appendix as a guide.

Rick's Free Video Clips and Audio Tours

Travel smarter with these free, fun resources:

Rick Steves Classroom Europe, a powerful tool for teachers, is also useful for travelers. This video library contains over 400 short clips excerpted from my public television series. Enjoy these videos as you sort through options for your trip and to better understand what you'll see in Europe. Check it out at Classroom.RickSteves.com (just enter a topic in the search bar to find everything I've filmed on a subject).

Rick Steves Audio Europe, an app for Apple and Android devices, makes it easy to download my audio tours and listen to them offline as you travel. For this book (look for the 🎧), these audio tours cover sights and neighborhoods in London. The app also offers insightful interviews from my public radio show with experts from Europe and around the globe. Find it in your app store or at RickSteves.com/AudioEurope.

Travel Smart

If you have a positive attitude, equip yourself with good information (this book), and expect to travel smart, you will.

Read—and reread—this book. To have an "A" trip, be an "A" student. Note opening hours of sights, closed days, crowd-beating tips, and whether reservations are required or advisable. Check the latest at www.ricksteves.com/update.

Be your own tour guide. As you travel, get up-to-date info on sights, reserve tickets and tours, reconfirm hotels and travel arrangements, and check transit connections. Visit local tourist information offices. Upon arrival in a new town, lay the groundwork for a smooth departure; confirm the train, bus, or road you'll take when you leave.

Outsmart thieves. Pickpockets abound in crowded places where tourists congregate. Treat commotions as smokescreens for theft. Keep your cash, credit cards, and passport secure in a money belt tucked under your clothes; carry only a day's spending money in your front pocket. Don't set valuable items down on counters or café tabletops, where they can be quickly stolen or easily forgotten.

Minimize potential loss. Keep expensive gear to a minimum. Bring photocopies or take photos of important documents (passport and cards) to aid in replacement if they're lost or stolen.

Guard your time and energy. Taking a taxi can be a good value if you're too tired to tackle public transit. To avoid long lines, follow my crowd-beating tips, such as making advance reservations, or sightseeing early or late.

Be flexible. Even if you have a well-planned itinerary, expect changes, strikes, closures, sore feet, bad weather, and so on. Your Plan B could turn out to be even better.

Connect with the culture. Interacting with locals carbonates your experience. Enjoy the friendliness of the English people. Ask questions; most locals are happy to point you in their idea of the right direction. Set up your own quest for the friendliest pub, grandest cathedral, best musical, or silliest name for a sweet treat. When an opportunity pops up, make it a habit to say "yes."

England...here you come!

London, gaze up at mighty Big Ben, and see the Houses of Parliament in action. Cruise the Thames River, and take a spin on the London Eye. Hobnob with poets' tombstones in Westminster Abbey, and visit with Leonardo, Botticelli, and Rembrandt in the National Gallery. Enjoy Shakespeare in a replica of the Globe Theatre and marvel at a glitzy, fun musical at a modern-day theater. Whisper across the dome of St. Paul's Cathedral, then rummage through our civilization's attic at the British Museum. And sip your tea with pinky raised and clotted cream dribbling down your scone.

PLANNING YOUR TIME

The sights of London alone could easily fill a trip to England. It's a great one-week getaway. But on a three-week tour of England, I'd give London three busy days. You won't be able to see everything, so don't try. You'll keep coming back to London. After dozens of visits myself, I still enjoy a healthy list of excuses to return. If you're flying in to one of London's airports, consider starting your trip in Bath and making London your English finale. Especially if you hope to enjoy a play or concert, a night or two of jet lag is bad news.

Here's a suggested three-day schedule:

Day 1

Use my Westminster Walk to link the following sights:

9:00	Be in line at Westminster Abbey (opens at 9:30, closed Sun), to tour the place with fewer crowds.
11:00	Visit the Churchill War Rooms.
13:00	Eat lunch at the Churchill War Rooms café or nearby, or grab a later lunch near Trafalgar Square.
15:00	Visit the National Gallery and any nearby sights that interest you (National Portrait Gallery or St. Martin-in-the-Fields Church)
Evening	Dinner and a play in the West End.

Day 2

8:30	Take a double-decker hop-on, hop-off London sightseeing bus tour (from Victoria Station or Green Park).
10:00	Hop off at Trafalgar Square and walk briskly to Buckingham Palace to secure a spot to watch the Changing of the Guard.
11:00	Buckingham Palace (guards usually change May-July

LONDON

London is more than 600 square miles of urban jungle—a world in itself and a barrage on all the senses. On my first visit, I felt extremely small. The city's museums and landmarks are just the beginning. It's the L.A., DC, and N.Y.C. of Britain—a living, breathing, thriving organism...a coral reef of humanity.

London has changed dramatically in recent years, and many visitors are surprised to find how "un-English" it is. ESL (English as a second language) seems like the city's first language, as native Brits are now a minority in major parts of the city that once symbolized white imperialism. London is a city of eight million separate dreams, inhabiting a place that tolerates and encourages them. Arabs have nearly bought out the area north of Hyde Park. Chinese takeouts outnumber fish-and-chips shops. Eastern Europeans pull pints in British pubs, and Italians express your espresso. Many hotels are run by people with foreign accents (who hire English chambermaids), while outlying suburbs are home to huge communities of Indians and Pakistanis.

The city, which has long attracted tourists, seems perpetually at your service, with an impressive slate of sights, entertainment, and eateries, all linked by a great transit system. With just a few days here, you'll get no more than a quick splash in this teeming human tidal pool. But with a good orientation, you'll find London manageable and fun. You'll get a sampling of the city's top sights, history, and cultural entertainment, and a good look at its ever-changing human face.

Blow through the city on the open deck of a double-decker orientation tour bus, and take a pinch-me-I'm-in-London walk through the West End. Ogle the crown jewels at the Tower of

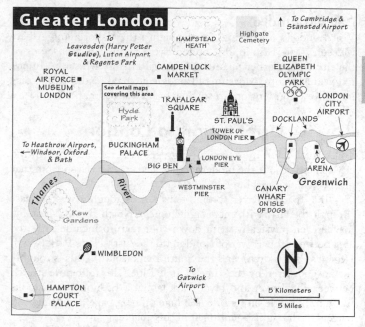

daily at 11:00, Aug-April Sun-Mon, Wed, and Fri—
confirm online).

14:00   After lunch, tour the British Museum.

16:00   Tour the British Library.

Evening   Choose from a play, concert, or walking tour, or do some shopping at one of London's elegant department stores (Harrod's, Liberty, and Fortnum & Mason are open until 20:00 or 21:00 except on Sun).

Day 3

9:00   Tower of London (crown jewels first, then Beefeater tour and White Tower; note that the Tower opens at 10:00 Sun-Mon).

12:00   Grab a picnic, catch a boat at Tower Pier, and have lunch on the Thames while cruising to Blackfriars Pier.

13:00   Tour St. Paul's Cathedral and climb its dome for views (cathedral closed Sun except for worship).

15:00   Walk across Millennium Bridge to the South Bank to visit the Tate Modern, Shakespeare's Globe, or other sights.

Evening   Catch a play at Shakespeare's Globe, or see the other suggestions under Days 1 and 2.

Day 4 (or more)

Visit London's remaining top-tier sights: the Victoria and Albert Museum, Tate Britain, or London Eye. Or you can choose one of the city's many other museums (Natural History Museum, Imperial War Museum, Museum of London, etc.); take a day trip, cruising to Kew Gardens or Greenwich; or hit a street market.

Orientation to London

To grasp London more comfortably, see it as the old town in the city center without the modern, congested sprawl. (Even from that perspective, it's still huge.)

The Thames River (pron. "tems") runs roughly west to east through the city, with most sights on the North Bank. Mentally, maybe even physically, trim down your map to include only the area between the Tower of London (to the east), Hyde Park (west), Regent's Park (north), and the South Bank (south). This is roughly the area bordered by the Tube's Circle Line. This four-mile stretch between the Tower and Hyde Park (about a 1.5-hour walk) looks like a milk bottle on its side (see map on next page), and holds 80 percent of the sights mentioned in this chapter.

The sprawling city becomes much more manageable if you think of it as a collection of neighborhoods.

Central London: This area contains Westminster and what Londoners call the West End. The Westminster district includes Big Ben, Parliament, Westminster Abbey, and Buckingham Palace—the grand government buildings from which Britain is ruled. Trafalgar Square, London's gathering place, has many major museums. The West End is the center of London's cultural life, with bustling squares: Piccadilly Circus and Leicester Square host cinemas, tourist traps, and nighttime glitz. Soho and Covent Garden are thriving people zones with theaters, restaurants, pubs, and boutiques. And Regent and Oxford streets are the city's main shopping zones.

North London: Neighborhoods in this part of town—including Bloomsbury, Fitzrovia, and Marylebone—contain such major sights as the British Museum and the overhyped Madame Tussauds Waxworks. Nearby, along busy Euston Road, is the British Library, plus a trio of train stations (one of them, St. Pancras International, is linked to Paris by the Eurostar "Chunnel" train).

The City: Today's modern financial district, called simply "The City," was a walled town in Roman times. Gleaming skyscrapers are interspersed with historical landmarks such as St. Paul's Cathedral, legal sights (Old Bailey), and the Museum of London. The Tower of London and Tower Bridge lie at The City's eastern border.

East London: Just east of The City is the East End—the

London's Neighborhoods

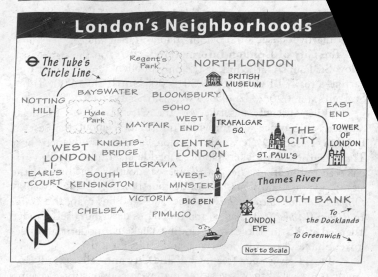

The Tube's Circle Line →

Regent's Park

NORTH LONDON

BRITISH MUSEUM

NOTTING HILL

BAYSWATER

BLOOMSBURY

SOHO

Hyde Park

MAYFAIR

WEST END

TRAFALGAR SQ.

EAST END

TOWER OF LONDON

WEST LONDON

KNIGHTS-BRIDGE

CENTRAL LONDON

THE CITY

ST. PAUL'S

BELGRAVIA

EARL'S COURT

SOUTH KENSINGTON

WEST-MINSTER

Thames River

VICTORIA

BIG BEN

SOUTH BANK

CHELSEA

PIMLICO

LONDON EYE

To → the Docklands

To Greenwich →

Not to Scale

former stomping ground of Cockney ragamuffins and Jack the Ripper, and now an increasingly gentrified neighborhood of hipsters, "pop-up" shops, and an emerging food scene.

The South Bank: The South Bank of the Thames River offers major sights (Tate Modern, Shakespeare's Globe, London Eye, Imperial War Museum) linked by a riverside walkway. Within this area, Southwark (SUTH-uck) stretches from the Tate Modern to London Bridge. Pedestrian bridges connect the South Bank with The City and Trafalgar Square.

West London: This huge area contains neighborhoods such as Mayfair, Belgravia, Pimlico, Chelsea, South Kensington and Notting Hill. It's home to London's wealthy and has many trendy shops and enticing restaurants. Here you'll find a range of museums (Victoria and Albert Museum, Tate Britain, and last) top hotel recommendations, live green expanses of Hyde Park

Outside the Center and/or Manhattan, is farther is southeast of Lo Hampton Cour London is the

TOURIST II

It's amazing
formation
office
m

ter tickets; others are run by Transport for London (TFL) and primarily focused on providing public-transit advice.

The City of London Information Centre, on the street just below St. Paul's Cathedral, is the only publicly funded—and impartial—"real" TI (Mon-Sat 9:30-17:30, Sun 10:00-16:00; Tube: St. Paul's, tel. 020/7332-1456, www.visitthecity.co.uk).

While officially a service of The City (London's financial district), this office also provides information about the rest of London. It sells Oyster cards, London Passes, and advance "Fast Track" sightseeing tickets (all described later). It also stocks various free publications: *London Planner* (a monthly that lists all the sights, events, and hours), walking-tour brochures, the biweekly *Official London Theatre Guide*, a free Tube and bus map, the *Guide to River Thames Boat Services*, and brochures describing self-guided themed walks in The City (including Dickens, modern architecture, Shakespeare, film locations, and walks for kids).

The TI gives out a free map of The City and sells several city-wide maps; ask if they have a free map with coupons for discounts on sights. Skip their theater box office; you're better off booking direct.

Visit London, which serves the greater London area, doesn't have an office you can visit in person—but does have an information-packed website (www.visitlondon.com).

Fast Track Tickets: To skip the ticket-buying queues at certain London sights, you can buy Fast Track tickets (sometimes called "priority pass" tickets) in advance—and they're typically cheaper than tickets sold right at the sight. These are particularly smart for the Tower of London (a voucher you exchange for a ticket at the Tower's group ticket window), The Shard, and Madame Tussauds Waxworks, all of which get very busy in high season. They're available through various sales outlets (including the City of London TI, souvenir stands, and faux TIs scattered throughout London).

London Pass This pass, which covers many big sights and lets you skip some lines, is très expensive but potentially worth the investment for very busy sightseers who will be using it on consecutive days. Among the many sights it includes are the Tower of London, Westminster Abbey, Churchill War Rooms, and Windsor Castle. Buy it online, think through what you'll cover, and audioguides at many places are covered, and tailor the card to your sightseeing plans, days at less

LONDON

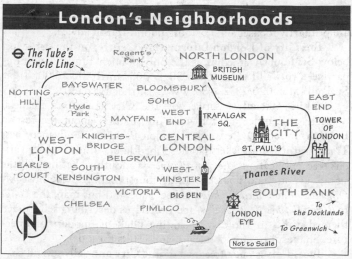

London's Neighborhoods

⊖ *The Tube's Circle Line*

Regent's Park

NORTH LONDON

BRITISH MUSEUM

NOTTING HILL

BAYSWATER

Hyde Park

BLOOMSBURY

SOHO

MAYFAIR

WEST END

TRAFALGAR SQ.

EAST END

TOWER OF LONDON

WEST LONDON

KNIGHTS-BRIDGE

CENTRAL LONDON

THE CITY

ST. PAUL'S

EARL'S COURT

SOUTH KENSINGTON

BELGRAVIA

WEST-MINSTER

Thames River

VICTORIA

BIG BEN

SOUTH BANK

CHELSEA

PIMLICO

LONDON EYE

To the Docklands

To Greenwich

Not to Scale

N

former stomping ground of Cockney ragamuffins and Jack the Ripper, and now an increasingly gentrified neighborhood of hipsters, "pop-up" shops, and an emerging food scene.

The South Bank: The South Bank of the Thames River offers major sights (Tate Modern, Shakespeare's Globe, London Eye, Imperial War Museum) linked by a riverside walkway. Within this area, Southwark (SUTH-uck) stretches from the Tate Modern to London Bridge. Pedestrian bridges connect the South Bank with The City and Trafalgar Square.

West London: This huge area contains neighborhoods such as Mayfair, Belgravia, Pimlico, Chelsea, South Kensington, and Notting Hill. It's home to London's wealthy and has many trendy shops and enticing restaurants. Here you'll find a range of museums (Victoria and Albert Museum, Tate Britain, and more), my top hotel recommendations, lively Victoria Station, and the vast green expanses of Hyde Park and Kensington Gardens.

Outside the Center: The Docklands, London's version of Manhattan, is farther east than the East End. Historic Greenwich is southeast of London and across the Thames. Kew Gardens and Hampton Court Palace are southwest of London. To the north of London is the Warner Bros. Studio Tour for Harry Potter fans.

TOURIST INFORMATION

It's amazing how hard it can be to find unbiased sightseeing information and advice in London. You'll see "Tourist Information" offices advertised everywhere, but most are private agencies that make a big profit selling tours and advance sightseeing and/or theater tickets; others are run by Transport for London (TFL) and are primarily focused on providing public-transit advice.

The City of London Information Centre, on the street just below St. Paul's Cathedral, is the only publicly funded—and impartial—"real" TI (Mon-Sat 9:30-17:30, Sun 10:00-16:00; Tube: St. Paul's, tel. 020/7332-1456, www.visitthecity.co.uk).

While officially a service of The City (London's financial district), this office also provides information about the rest of London. It sells Oyster cards, London Passes, and advance "Fast Track" sightseeing tickets (all described later). It also stocks various free publications: *London Planner* (a monthly that lists all the sights, events, and hours), walking-tour brochures, the biweekly *Official London Theatre Guide*, a free Tube and bus map, the *Guide to River Thames Boat Services,* and brochures describing self-guided themed walks in The City (including Dickens, modern architecture, Shakespeare, film locations, and walks for kids).

The TI gives out a free map of The City and sells several city-wide maps; ask if they have a free map with coupons for discounts on sights. Skip their theater box office; you're better off booking direct.

Visit London, which serves the greater London area, doesn't have an office you can visit in person—but does have an information-packed website (www.visitlondon.com).

Fast Track Tickets: To skip the ticket-buying queues at certain London sights, you can buy Fast Track tickets (sometimes called "priority pass" tickets) in advance—and they're typically cheaper than tickets sold right at the sight. These are particularly smart for the Tower of London (a voucher you exchange for a ticket at the Tower's group ticket window), The Shard, and Madame Tussauds Waxworks, all of which get very busy in high season. They're available through various sales outlets (including the City of London TI, souvenir stands, and faux TIs scattered throughout touristy areas).

London Pass: This pass, which covers many big sights and lets you skip some lines, is expensive but potentially worth the investment for extremely busy sightseers who will be using it on consecutive days. Among the many sights it includes are the Tower of London, Westminster Abbey, Churchill War Rooms, and Windsor Castle, as well as many temporary exhibits and audioguides at otherwise "free" biggies. Think through your sightseeing plans, study their website to see what's covered, and do the math before you buy. Note: Adding an Oyster card to your order is a needless complication; it's easier to buy them on arrival (£75/1 day, £99/2 days, £125/3 days, £169/6 days, £199/10 days; days are calendar days rather than 24-hour periods; comes with 180-page guidebook, also sold at major train stations and airports, tel. 020/7293-0972, www.londonpass.com).

ARRIVAL IN LONDON

For more information on getting to or from London, see "London Connections" at the end of this chapter.

By Train: London has nine major train stations, all connected by the Tube (subway). All have ATMs, and many of the larger stations also have shops, fast food, exchange offices, and luggage storage. From any station, you can ride the Tube or taxi to your hotel.

By Bus: The main intercity bus station is Victoria Coach Station, one block southwest of Victoria train/Tube station.

By Plane: London has six airports. Most tourists arrive at Heathrow or Gatwick airport, although flights from elsewhere in Europe may land at Stansted, Luton, Southend, or London City airport.

HELPFUL HINTS

Theft Alert: Wear a money belt and keep your wallet in your front pocket. The Artful Dodger is alive and well in London. Be on guard, particularly on public transportation and in places crowded with tourists, who, considered naive and rich, are targeted. The Changing of the Guard scene is a favorite for thieves. More than 7,500 purses are stolen annually at Covent Garden alone.

Pedestrian Safety: Cars drive on the left side of the road—which can be as confusing for foreign pedestrians as for foreign drivers. Before crossing a street, I always look right, look left, then look right again just to be sure. While Londoners are champion jaywalkers, you shouldn't try it; jaywalking is treacherous when you're disoriented about which direction traffic is coming from.

Medical Problems: Local hospitals have good-quality 24-hour emergency care centers, where any tourist who needs help can be seen by a doctor. Your hotel has details. St. Thomas' Hospital, immediately across the river from Big Ben, has a fine reputation.

Sunday Sightseeing: On Sundays, the Houses of Parliament, City Hall, and Old Bailey are closed and the neighborhood called The City is dead. Westminster Abbey and St. Paul's are open for worship but closed to sightseers (the Diamond Jubilee Galleries at the Abbey is closed). Most big stores open late (11:30) and close early (18:00). Most street markets flourish but Portobello Road and Borough markets are closed. Many theaters are quiet, as most actors take today off—Shakespeare's Globe is an exception.

"Free" Museums: Many of London's great museums don't charge admission—though they do suggest a donation (typically £5).

Advance Tickets: Buying tickets online in advance is always smart if you don't mind sticking to a schedule. You'll generally save a few pounds per sight and can skip the ticket-buying line once you arrive—though you may need to wait in a security line or pick up your ticket at the sight.

You must book ahead for The Making of Harry Potter: Warner Bros. Studio Tour. For summer, weekends, and holiday periods, consider booking ahead (or risk wasting time in long lines) for the following London sights: Westminster Abbey, the Houses of Parliament, the Churchill War Rooms, St. Paul's Cathedral, the Tower of London, and the London Eye.

Getting Your Bearings: London is well-signed, with thoughtfully designed, pedestrian-focused maps all over town—especially handy when exiting Tube stations. In this sprawling city—where predictable grid-planned streets are relatively rare—it's also smart to use a good map. For suggestions, see page 909.

Festivals: For one week in February and another in September, fashionistas descend on the city for **London Fashion Week** (www.londonfashionweek.co.uk). The famous **Chelsea Flower Show** blossoms in late May (book ahead for this popular event at www.rhs.org.uk/chelsea). During the annual **Trooping the Colour** in June, there are military bands and pageantry, and the Queen's birthday parade (www.qbp.army.mod.uk). Tennis fans pack the stands at the **Wimbledon Tennis Championship** in late June to early July (www.wimbledon.com), and partygoers head for the **Notting Hill Carnival** in late August.

Traveling in Winter: London dazzles year-round, so consider visiting in winter, when airfares and hotel rates are generally cheaper and there are fewer tourists. For ideas on what to do, see the "Winter Activities in London" article at www.ricksteves.com/winteracts.

Useful Apps: Mapway's free **Tube Map London Underground** and **Bus Times London** (www.mapway.com) apps show the easiest way to connect Tube stations and provide bus stops and route information. When you are online, the apps provide live updates about delays, closures, and time estimates for your journey. The handy **Citymapper** app for London covers every mode of public transit in the city. And **Time Out London**'s free app has reviews and listings for theater, museums, and movies. See page 909 for mapping app suggestions.

Bookstores: Located between Covent Garden and Leicester Square, the very good **Stanfords Travel Bookstore** stocks a huge selection of guidebooks (including current editions of my titles), travel-related novels, maps, and gear (Mon-Sat 9:00-20:00, Sun 11:30-18:00, 7 Mercer Walk, Tube: Leicester Square, tel. 020/7836-1321, www.stanfords.co.uk).

Two impressive **Waterstones** bookstores have the biggest collection of travel guides in town: on Piccadilly (Mon-Sat 9:00-22:00, Sun 12:00-18:30, café, great views from top-floor bar, 203 Piccadilly, tel. 0843-290-8549) and on Trafalgar Square (Mon-Sat 9:00-21:00, Sun 12:00-18:00, Costa Café on second floor, tel. 020/7839-4411).

Daunts Books, in a church-like Edwardian building, is a North London staple known for arranging books by geography, regardless of subject or author (Mon-Sat 9:00-19:30, Sun 11:00-18:00, 83 Marylebone High Street, Tube: Baker Street, tel. 020/7724-2295, www.dauntbooks.co.uk).

Foyles' flagship store is a world of books (and literary events), between Soho and Covent Garden (Mon-Sat 9:00-21:00, Sun 11:30-18:00, 107 Charing Cross Road, tel. 020/7437-5660, www.foyles.co.uk).

Baggage Storage: Train stations have left-luggage counters, where each bag is scanned (just like at the airport); expect up to 45-minute waits (£12.50/24 hours per item, most stations open daily 7:00-23:00). You can also store bags at the airports (similar rates and hours, www.left-baggage.co.uk).

GETTING AROUND LONDON

To travel smart in a city this size, you must get comfortable with public transportation. London's excellent taxis, buses, and subway (Tube) system can take you anywhere you need to go—a blessing for travelers' precious vacation time, not to mention their feet. And, as the streets become ever more congested, the key is to master the Tube.

For more information about public transit (bus and Tube), the best source is the helpful *Welcome to London* brochure, which includes both a Tube map and a handy schematic map of the best bus routes (available free at TIs, museums, and hotels).

For specific directions on how to get from point A to point B on London's transit, detailed transit maps, updated prices, and general information, check www.tfl.gov.uk, or call the info line at 0343-222-1234.

Tickets and Cards

London's is one of the most expensive public transit systems in the world, so for most tourists, the Oyster card transit pass is better than individual tickets. Here's the lowdown.

The transit system has nine zones, but almost all tourist sights

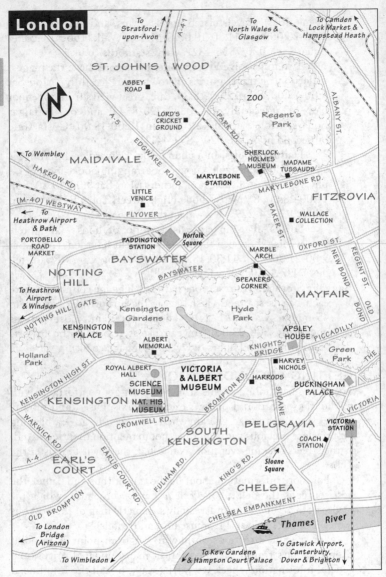

London

To Stratford-upon-Avon

To North Wales & Glasgow

To Camden Lock Market & Hampstead Heath

ST. JOHN'S WOOD

ABBEY ROAD

ZOO

Regent's Park

A-41

A-5

PARK RD.

ALBANY ST.

LORD'S CRICKET GROUND

SHERLOCK HOLMES MUSEUM

MADAME TUSSAUDS

To Wembley

MAIDAVALE

HARROW RD.

EDGWARE ROAD

MARYLEBONE STATION

MARYLEBONE RD.

FITZROVIA

(M-40) WESTWAY

LITTLE VENICE

FLYOVER

BAKER ST.

WALLACE COLLECTION

To Heathrow Airport & Bath

PORTOBELLO ROAD MARKET

PADDINGTON STATION

Norfolk Square

MARBLE ARCH

OXFORD ST.

NEW BOND ST.

REGENT ST.

OLD BOND ST.

BAYSWATER

BAYSWATER

SPEAKERS' CORNER

MAYFAIR

NOTTING HILL

To Heathrow Airport & Windsor

NOTTING HILL GATE

Kensington Gardens

Hyde Park

KENSINGTON PALACE

ALBERT MEMORIAL

APSLEY HOUSE

PICCADILLY

Holland Park

KENSINGTON HIGH ST.

ROYAL ALBERT HALL

SCIENCE MUSEUM

VICTORIA & ALBERT MUSEUM

KNIGHTS-BRIDGE

HARVEY NICHOLS

Green Park

THE

NAT. HIS. MUSEUM

HARRODS

BROMPTON RD.

SLOANE ST.

BUCKINGHAM PALACE

WARWICK RD.

KENSINGTON

CROMWELL RD.

SOUTH KENSINGTON

BELGRAVIA

VICTORIA

VICTORIA STATION

EARL'S COURT

A-4

EARLS COURT RD.

FULHAM RD.

KING'S RD.

Sloane Square

COACH STATION

OLD BROMPTON

To London Bridge (Arizona)

To Wimbledon

CHELSEA

CHELSEA EMBANKMENT

Thames River

To Kew Gardens & Hampton Court Palace

To Gatwick Airport, Canterbury, Dover & Brighton

are within Zones 1 and 2, so those are the prices I've listed. For more information, visit www.tfl.gov.uk/tickets.

Individual Tickets: Paper tickets for the Tube are ridiculously expensive (£5 per Tube ride). At every Tube station, tickets are sold at easy-to-use self-service machines (hit "Adult Single" and enter your destination). Tickets are valid only on the day of purchase. But unless you're literally taking only one Tube ride your entire visit, you'll save money (and time) by buying an Oyster card.

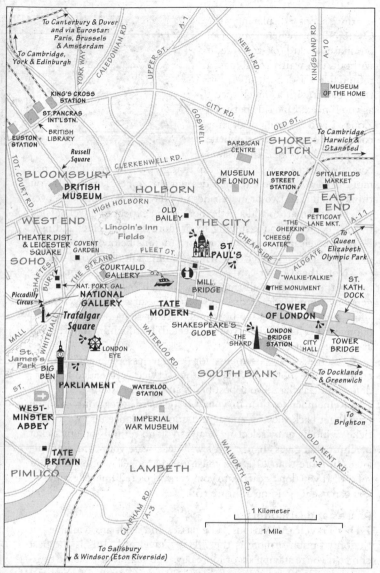

Oyster Card: A pay-as-you-go Oyster card allows you to ride the Tube, buses, Docklands Light Railway (DLR), and Overground (mostly suburban trains) for about half the rate of individual tickets. To use the card, simply touch it against the yellow card reader at the turnstile or entrance. It flashes green and the fare is automatically deducted. (You must also tap your card again to "touch out" as you exit the Tube, but not buses.)

Buy the card at any Tube station ticket machine, or look for nearby shops displaying the Oyster logo, where you can purchase a card or add credit without the wait. You'll pay a refundable £5 deposit up front, then load it with as much credit as you'll need. One ride between Zones 1 and 2 during peak time costs £2.90; off peak is a little cheaper (£2.40/ride). The system

comes with an automatic price cap that guarantees you'll never pay more than £7 in one day for rides within Zones 1 and 2. If you think you'll take two or more rides in a day, £7 of credit will cover you, but it's smart to add a little more if you expect to travel outside the city center. If you're staying six or more days, consider adding a 7-Day Travelcard to your Oyster card (details below). For a three-day visit, I get an Oyster card with £20 of credit, for a total of £25.

Note that Oyster cards are not shareable among companions taking the same ride; all travelers need their own. If your balance gets low, simply add credit—or "top up"—at a ticket machine or shop. You can always see how much credit remains on your card (along with a list of where you've traveled) by touching it to the pad at any ticket machine.

You'll see advertisements for "contactless payment" using a credit card or mobile device, but that service is intended for residents, not travelers—your best bet is an Oyster card.

Remember to turn in your Oyster card after your last ride (you'll get back the £5 deposit and unused balance up to £10) at a ticket window or by selecting "Pay as you go refund" on any ticket machine that gives change. This will deactivate your card. For balances of more than £10, you must go to a ticket window for your refund. If you don't deactivate your card, the credit never expires—you can use it again on a future trip.

Passes and Discounts

7-Day Travelcard: Various Tube passes and deals are available but the only option of note is the 7-Day Travelcard. This is the best choice if you're staying six or more days and plan to use public transit a lot (£35.10 for Zones 1-2; £64.20 for Zones 1-6). For most travelers, the Zone 1-2 pass works best. Heathrow Airport is in Zone 6, but there's no need to buy the Zones 1-6 version if that's the only ride outside the city center you plan to take—instead you can pay a small supplement to cover the difference. You can add the 7-Day Travelcard to your Oyster card, or purchase the paper version at any National Rail train station.

Families: A paying adult can take up to four kids (ages 10 and under) for free on the Tube, Docklands Light Railway (DLR), Overground, and buses. Kids ages 11-15 get a discount. Explore other child and student discounts at www.tfl.gov.uk/tickets—or ask a Tube station employee.

River Cruises: A Travelcard gives you a 33 percent discount on most Thames cruises (described later under "Tours in London: By Cruise Boat"). The Oyster card gives you roughly a 10 percent discount on Thames Clippers (including the Tate Boat museum ferry).

By Tube

London's subway system is called the Tube or Underground (but never "subway," which, in Britain, refers to a pedestrian underpass).

The Tube is one of this planet's great people-movers and usually the fastest long-distance transport in town (runs Mon-Sat about 5:00-24:00, Sun about 7:00-23:00; Central, Jubilee, Northern, Piccadilly, and Victoria lines also run Fri-Sat 24 hours). Two other commuter rail lines are tied into the network and use the same tickets: the Docklands Light Railway (called DLR) and the Overground. The new Crossrail system will eventually cut through central London connecting Heathrow with Paddington, Bond, and Liverpool Street Tube stations on the Elizabeth line before continuing to the city's outlying eastern neighborhoods.

Get your bearings by studying a map of the system, free at any station, or download a transit app (described earlier). Each line has a name (such as Circle, Northern, or Bakerloo) and two directions (indicated by the end-of-the-line stops). Find the line that will take you to your destination, and figure out roughly which direction (north, south, east, or west) you'll need to go to get there.

At the Tube station, there are two ways to pass through the turnstile. With an Oyster card, touch it flat against the turnstile's

yellow card reader, both when you enter and exit the station. With a paper ticket or paper Travelcard, feed it into the turnstile, reclaim it, and hang on to it—you'll need it later.

Find your train by following signs to your

line and the (general) direction it's headed (such as Central Line: Eastbound). Since some tracks are shared by several lines, double-check before boarding: Make sure your destination is one of the stops listed on the sign at the platform. Also, check the electronic signboards that announce which train is next, and make sure the destination (the end-of-the-line stop) is the direction you want. Some trains, particularly on the Circle and District lines, split off for other directions, but each train has its final destination marked above its windshield and on the side of the cars.

Trains run about every 3-10 minutes. (The Victoria line brags that it's the most frequent anywhere, with trains coming every 100 seconds at peak time.) A general rule of thumb is that it takes 30 minutes to travel six Tube stops (including walking time within stations), or roughly 5 minutes per stop.

When you leave the system, "touch out" with your Oyster card at the electronic reader on the turnstile, or feed your paper ticket into the turnstile (it will eat your now-expired ticket). With a paper Travelcard, it will spit out your still-valid card. Check maps and signs for the most convenient exit.

The system can be fraught with construction delays and break-downs. Pay attention to signs and announcements explaining nec-essary detours. Rush hours (8:00-10:00 and 16:00-19:00) can be packed and sweaty. If one train is stuffed—and another is coming in three minutes—it may be worth a wait to avoid the sardine rou-tine. Also, the cars closer to the middle of the train are generally more crowded, so if you anticipate crowds, stand closer to the ends of the platform. I've often scored a seat on an otherwise packed train using this simple strategy. (But note that at a few shorter sta-tions, the doors of the cars at the very start and end of the train can't open—listen for announcements and move closer to the mid-dle of the platform if necessary.)

For help, check out the "Plan a Journey" feature at www.tfl.gov.uk.

Tube Etiquette and Tips

- When your train arrives, stand off to the side and let riders exit before you board.
- When the car is jam-packed, avoid using the hinged seats near the doors of some trains—they take up valuable standing space.
- If you're blocking the door when the train stops, step out of the car and off to the side, let others off, then get back on.
- Talk softly in the cars. Listen to how quietly Londoners com-municate and follow their lead.
- On escalators, stand on the right and pass on the left. But note that in some passageways or stairways, you might be directed

to walk on the left (the direction Brits go when behind the wheel).

- Discreet eating and drinking are fine; drinking alcohol and smoking are banned.
- Be zipped up to thwart thieves.
- Carefully check exit options before surfacing to street level. Signs point clearly to nearby sights—you'll save lots of walking by choosing the right exit.

By Bus

If you figure out the bus system, you'll swing like Tarzan through the urban jungle of London (see sidebar for a list of handy routes). Get in the habit of hopping buses for quick little straight shots, even just to get to a Tube stop. However, during bump-and-grind rush hours (8:00-10:00 and 16:00-19:00), you'll usually go faster by Tube.

You can't buy single-trip tickets for buses, and you can't use cash to pay when boarding. Instead, you must have an Oyster card, a paper Travelcard, or a one-day Bus & Tram Pass (£5, can buy on day of travel only—not beforehand, from ticket machine in any Tube station). If you're using your Oyster card, any bus ride in downtown London costs £1.50 (capped at £4.50/day).

The first step in mastering London's bus system is learning how to decipher the bus-stop signs. The accompanying photo shows a typical sign listing the buses (the N91, N68, etc.) that come by here and their destinations (Oakwood, Old Coulsdon, etc.). In the first column, find your destination on the list—e.g., to Paddington (Tube and rail station). In the next column, find a bus that goes there—the #23 (routes marked "N" are night-only). In the final column, a letter within a circle (e.g., "H") tells you exactly which nearby bus stop to use. Find your stop on the accompanying bus-stop map, then make your way to that stop—you'll know it's yours because it will have the same letter on its pole.

O		
Oakwood ⇌	N91	
Old Coulsdon	N68	Aldwych
Old Ford	N8	Oxford Circus
Old Kent Road Canal Bridge	53, N381	
	453	
	N21	
Old Street ⇌	243	Aldwych
Orpington ⇌	N47	
Oxford Circus	Any bus	
	N18	

P		
Paddington ⇌	23, N15	
Palmers Green	N29	
Park Langley	N3	
Peckham	12	
	N89, N343	
	N136	
	N381	
Penge Pawleyne Arms	176	
	N3	
Petts Wood	N47	
Pimlico Grosvenor Road	24	
Plaistow Greengate	N15	
Plumstead	53	
Plumstead Common	53	
Ponders End	N279	

LONDON

Handy Bus Routes

The best views are upstairs on a double-decker. Check the bus stop closest to your hotel—it might be convenient to your sightseeing plans. Here are some of the most useful routes:

Route #9: High Street Kensington to Knightsbridge (Harrods) to Hyde Park Corner to Trafalgar Square to Aldwych (Somerset House).

Route #11: Victoria Station to Westminster Abbey to Trafalgar Square to St. Paul's and Liverpool Street Station and the East End.

Route #15: Trafalgar Square to St. Paul's to Tower of London (occasionally with heritage "Routemaster" old-style double-decker buses).

Routes #23 and #159: Paddington Station (#159 begins at Marble

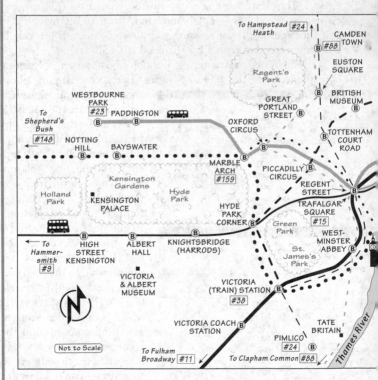

Arch) to Oxford Circus to Piccadilly Circus to Trafalgar Square; from there, #23 heads east to St. Paul's and Liverpool Street Station, while #159 heads to Westminster and the Imperial War Museum. In addition, several buses (including #6, #12, and #139) also make the corridor run between Marble Arch, Oxford Circus, Piccadilly Circus, and Trafalgar Square.

Route #24: Pimlico to Victoria Station to Westminster Abbey to Trafalgar Square to Euston Square, then all the way north to Camden Town (Camden Lock Market) and Hampstead Heath.

Route #38: Victoria Station to Hyde Park Corner to Piccadilly Circus to British Museum.

Route #88: Tate Britain to Westminster Abbey to Trafalgar Square to Piccadilly Circus to Oxford Circus to Great Portland Street Station (Regent's Park), then north to Camden Town.

Route #148: Westminster Abbey to Victoria Station to Notting Hill and Bayswater (by way of the east end of Hyde Park and Marble Arch).

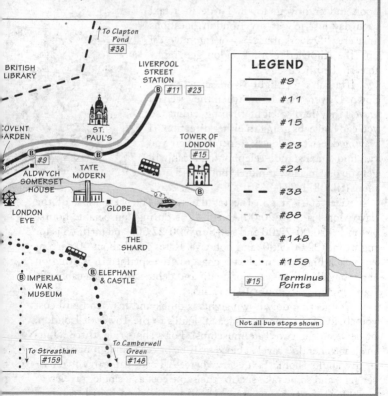

When your bus approaches, it's wise to hold your arm out to let the driver know you want on. Hop on and confirm your destination with the driver (often friendly and helpful).

As you board, touch your Oyster card to the card reader, or show your paper Travelcard or Bus & Tram Pass to the driver. Unlike on the Tube, there's no need to show or tap your card when you hop off. On the older heritage "Routemaster" buses without card readers (used on the #15 route on summer weekends), you simply take a seat, and the conductor comes around to check cards and passes.

To alert the driver that you want to get off, press one of the red buttons (on the poles between the seats) before your stop.

By Taxi

London is the best taxi town in Europe. Big, black, carefully regulated cabs are everywhere—there are about 25,000 of them.

I've never met a crabby cabbie in London. They love to talk, and they know every nook and cranny in town. I ride in a taxi each day just to get my London questions answered. Drivers must pass a rigorous test on "The Knowledge" of London geography to earn their license.

If a cab's top light is on, just wave it down. Drivers flash lights when they see you wave. They have a tight turning radius, so you can hail cabs going in either direction. If waving doesn't work, ask someone where you can find a taxi stand. Telephoning a cab will get you one in a few minutes, but costs a little more (tel. 0871-871-8710).

Rides start at £3. The regular tariff #1 covers most of the day (Mon-Fri 5:00-20:00), tariff #2 is during "unsociable hours" (Mon-Fri 20:00-22:00 and Sat-Sun 5:00-22:00), and tariff #3 is for nighttime (22:00-5:00) and holidays. Rates go up about 40 percent with each higher tariff. Extra charges are explained in writing on the cab wall. All cabs accept credit and debit cards. Tip a cabbie by rounding up (maximum 10 percent).

Connecting downtown sights is quick and easy, and will cost you about £8-12 (for example, St. Paul's to the Tower of London, or between the two Tate museums). For a short ride, three adults in a cab generally travel at close to Tube prices—and groups of four or five adults should taxi everywhere. All cabs can carry five passengers, and some take six, for the same cost as a single traveler.

Don't worry about meter cheating. Licensed British cab meters come with a sealed computer chip and clock that ensures you'll get the correct tariff. The only way a cabbie can cheat you is by taking a needlessly long route. Don't, however, take a cab in bad traffic—especially to a destination efficiently served by the Tube.

If you overdrink and ride in a taxi, be warned: Taxis charge up to £60 for "soiling" (a.k.a., pub puke).

By Uber

Uber faces legal challenges in London and may not be operating when you visit. If Uber is running, it can be much cheaper than a taxi and is a handy alternative if there's a long line for a taxi or if no cabs are available. Uber drivers generally don't know the city as well as regular cabbies, and they don't have the access to some fast lanes that taxis do. Still, if you like using Uber, it can work great here.

By Car

If you have a car, stow it—you don't want to drive in London. An £11.50 **congestion charge** is levied on any private car entering the city center during peak hours (Mon-Fri 7:00-18:00, no charge Sat-Sun and holidays). You can pay the fee either online or by phone (www.cclondon.com, from within the UK call 0343/222-2222, from outside the UK call 011-44-20/7649-9122, phones answered Mon-Fri 8:00-22:00, Sat 9:00-15:00, be ready to give the vehicle registration number and country of registration). There are painfully stiff penalties for late payments.

By Boat

It's easy to connect downtown London sights between Westminster and the Tower of London by boat (see page 57).

By Bike

London operates a citywide bike-rental program similar to ones in other major European cities, and new bike lanes are still cropping up around town. Still,  London isn't (yet) ideal for biking. Its network of designated bike lanes is far from complete, and the city's many one-way streets (not to mention the need to bike on the "wrong" side) can make biking here a bit more challenging. If you're accustomed to urban biking, it can be a good option for connecting your sightseeing stops, but if you're just up for a joyride, stick to London's large parks.

Santander Cycles, intended for quick point-to-point trips, are fairly easy to rent and a giddy joy to use. These cruisers have big, cushy seats, a bag rack with elastic straps, and three gears. Approximately 750 bike-rental stations are scattered throughout the city. To rent a bike, you'll pay an access fee (£2/day). The first 30 minutes are free; if you keep the bike for longer, you'll be charged £2 for every additional 30-minute period. Maps showing docking stations are available at major Tube stations, at www.tfl.gov.uk, and via the free app.

Helmets are not provided, so ride carefully. Stay to the far-left side of the road and watch closely at intersections for *left*-turning cars. Be aware that in most parks (including Hyde Park/Kensington Gardens) only certain paths are designated for bike use—you can't ride just anywhere. Maps posted at park entrances identify bike paths, and non-bike paths are generally clearly marked.

Some bike tour companies also rent bikes (for details, see their listings later in this chapter).

Tours in London

🎧 To sightsee on your own, download my free Rick Steves Audio Europe app with **audio tours** that illuminate some of London's top sights and neighborhoods, including my Westminster Walk, Historic London: The City Walk, and tours of the British Museum, British Library, and St. Paul's Cathedral (see sidebar on page 30 for details).

BY HOP-ON, HOP-OFF DOUBLE-DECKER BUS

London is full of hop-on, hop-off bus companies competing for your tourist pound. I've focused on the two companies I like the most: **Original** and **Big Bus.** Both offer essentially the same tours of the city's sightseeing highlights—an experience rated ▲▲▲.

These once-over-lightly bus tours drive by all the famous sights, providing a stress-free way to get your bearings and see the biggies: Piccadilly Circus, Trafalgar Square, Big Ben, St. Paul's, the Tower of London, Marble Arch, Victoria Station, and elsewhere. With a good guide, decent traffic, and nice weather, I'd sit back and enjoy the entire tour. (If traffic is bad or you don't like your guide, you can hop off and try the next departure.)

Each company offers at least one route with live (English-only) guides, and a second (sometimes slightly different route) with recorded, dial-a-language narration. In addition to the overview tours, both Original and Big Bus include the Thames River boat trip by City Cruises (between Westminster and the Tower of London) and several walking tours. Employees for both companies will

---

Combining a London Bus Tour and the Changing of the Guard

For a grand and efficient intro to London, consider catching an 8:30 departure of a hop-on, hop-off overview bus tour, riding most of the loop (which takes just over 1.5 hours, depending on traffic). Hop off just before 10:00 at Trafalgar Square (Cockspur Street, stop "S") and walk briskly to Buckingham Palace to find a spot to watch the Changing of the Guard ceremony at 11:00.

---

try hard to sell you tickets and Fast Track admissions to various sights in London. Review your sightseeing plan carefully in advance so you can take advantage of offers that will save you time or money, but skip the rest.

Pick up a map from any flier rack or from one of the countless salespeople, and study the color-coded system. Sunday morning—when traffic is light and many museums are closed—is a fine time for a tour. Traffic is at its peak around lunch and during the evening rush hour (around 17:00).

Buses run daily about every 10-15 minutes in summer and every 10-20 minutes in winter, starting at about 8:30. The last full loop usually leaves Victoria Station at around 20:00 in summer, and 17:00 in winter.

You can buy tickets online in advance, from drivers, or from staff at street kiosks (credit cards accepted at kiosks at major stops such as Victoria Station; the standard tickets are typically valid 24 hours in summer, 48 hours in winter).

Original London Sightseeing Bus Tour

They offer two versions of their basic highlights loop, both marked with a yellow triangle (confirm version with the driver before boarding): **The Original Tour** (T1, live guide) and the **City Sightseeing Tour** (T2, same route but with recorded narration and a kids' soundtrack option). Other routes include the orange-triangle **British Museum Tour** (T5, connecting the museum and King's Cross neighborhoods with central London), and the blue-triangle **Royal Borough Tour** (T4, high-end shopping and regal hangouts). All routes are covered by the same ticket (£32, RS%—£6 discount with this book, limit four discounts per book, they'll rip off the corner of this page—raise bloody hell if the staff or driver won't honor this discount; www.theoriginaltour.com).

Big Bus London Tours

For £37 (cheaper online), you get the same basic overview tours: Red buses come with a live guide, while the blue route has a recorded narration and a one-hour longer path that goes around Hyde Park. These pricier Big Bus tours tend to have more departures—meaning shorter waits for those hopping on and off (tel. 020/7808-6753, www.bigbustours.com).

BY BUS OR CAR
London by Night Sightseeing Tour

Various companies offer a 1- to 2-hour circuit, but after hours, with no extras (e.g., walks, river cruises), at a lower price. While the narration can be lame, the views at twilight are grand—though note that it stays light until late on summer nights, and London just doesn't do floodlighting as well as, say, Paris. **Golden Tours** buses depart at 19:00 and 20:00 from their offices on Buckingham Palace Road (£28, tel. 020/7630-2028; www.goldentours.com). **See London By Night** buses offer live English guides and daily departures from Green Park (next to the Ritz Hotel) at 19:30, 20:00, 20:30, 21:15, 21:45, and 22:15; Oct-March at 19:30 and 21:20 only (£28.50, tel. 020/7183-4744, www.seelondonbynight.com). For a memorable and economical evening, munch a scenic picnic dinner on the top deck. (There are plenty of takeaway options near the various stops.)

Driver-Guides

These guides have cars or a minibus (particularly helpful for travelers with limited mobility), and also offer walking-only tours: **Janine Barton** (£390/half-day, £575/day, day tours outside of London start at £625 depending on the distance, registered Blue Badge guide, tel. 020/7402-4600, www.seeitinstyle.synthasite. com, jbsiis@aol.com); **Mike Dickson** (£345/half-day, £535/day, overnights also possible, registered Blue Badge guide; mobile 07769/905-811, michael.dickson5@btinternet.com); and **David Stubbs** (£375 for 1-3 people, £395 for 4-6 people, £415 for 7-8, also does tours to the Cotswolds, Stonehenge, Stratford, Windsor Castle, and Bath; mobile 07775-888-534, www.londoncountrytours. co.uk, info@londoncountrytours.co.uk).

ON FOOT

Top-notch local guides lead (sometimes big) groups on walking tours—worth ▲▲—through specific slices of London's past. Look for brochures at TIs or ask at hotels. *Time Out,* the weekly entertainment guide, lists some, but not all, scheduled walks. Check with the various tour companies by phone or online to get their full picture.

To take a walking tour, simply show up at the announced location and pay the guide. Then enjoy two chatty hours of Dickens,

Harry Potter, the Plague, Shakespeare, street art, The Beatles, Jack the Ripper, or whatever is on the agenda.

London Walks

Just perusing this leading company's fascinating lineup opens me up to dimensions of London I never considered, and inspires me to stay longer. Their extensive daily schedule is online, as well as in a white *London Walks* brochure (most reliably found in the Café in the Crypt, below Trafalgar Square's St. Martin-in-the-Fields church). Their two-hour walks are led by top-quality professional guides ranging from archaeologists to actors (£12, cash only, walks offered year-round, private tours available, tel. 020/7624-3978, www.walks.com).

London Walks also offers day trips into the countryside, a good option for those with limited time (£20 plus £15-70 for transportation and admission costs, cash only: Stonehenge/Salisbury, Oxford/Cotswolds, Cambridge, Bath, and so on). These are economical in part because everyone gets group discounts for transportation and admissions.

Sandemans New London "Free Royal London Tour"

This company offers tours covering the basic London sights in a youthful, light, and irreverent way that can be both entertaining and fun, but it's misleading to call them "free," as tips are expected. Given that London Walks offers daily tours at a reasonable price, taking this "free" tour makes no sense to me (daily at 10:00, 11:00, and 13:00; meet at Covent Garden Piazza by the Apple Store, Tube: Covent Garden). Sandemans also offers guided tours for a charge, including a Pub Crawl (£10, nightly at 19:30, meet at Brewmaster, 37 Cranbourn Street, Tube: Leicester Square, www.neweuropetours.eu).

Beatles Walks

Fans of the still-Fab Four can take one of three Beatles walks (London Walks has two that run 5 days/week; for more on Beatles sights, see page 103).

Jack the Ripper Walks

Each walking tour company seems to make most of its money with "haunted" and Jack the Ripper tours. While almost no hint of the dark and scary London of Jack the Ripper's time survives, guides do a good job of spinning the story.

Two reliably good two-hour tours start every night at the Tower Hill Tube station exit. **London Walks** leaves nightly at 19:30, plus Saturdays at 15:00 (£12, pay at the start, tel. 020/7624-3978, www.jacktheripperwalk.com). **Ripping Yarns,** which leaves nightly at 18:30, is guided by off-duty Yeoman Warders—the Tower of London "Beefeaters" (£8, pay at end, mobile 07813-559-

301, www.jack-the-ripper-tours.com). After taking both, I found the London Walks tour more entertaining, informative, and with a better route (along quieter, once hooker-friendly lanes, with less traffic), starting at Tower Hill and ending at Liverpool Street Station. Groups can be huge for both, and one group can be nearly on top of another, but there's always room—just show up.

Private Walks with Local Guides

Standard rates for London's registered Blue Badge guides are about £165-200 for four hours and £270 or more for nine hours (tel. 020/7611-2545, www.guidelondon.org.uk or www. britainsbestguides.org). I know and like these fine local guides: **Sean Kelleher,** an engaging storyteller who knows his history (tel. 020/8673-1624, mobile 07764-612-770, sean@seanlondonguide. com); **Britt Lonsdale,** who's great with families (£265/half-day, £365/day, tel. 020/7386-9907, mobile 07813-278-077, brittl@ btinternet.com); **Joel Reid,** an imaginative guide who breathes life into the major sights but also loves sharing off-the-beaten-track London (mobile 07887-955-720, joelyreid@gmail.com); and two others who work in London when they're not on the road leading my Britain tours: **Tom Hooper** (mobile 07986-048-047, tomh1@ btinternet.com) and **Gillian Chadwick** (£300/day, mobile 07889-976-598, gillychad@hotmail.co.uk). If you have a particular interest, London Walks (see earlier) can book one for your exact focus (£215/half-day).

BY BIKE

Many of London's best sights can be laced together with a pleasant pedal through its parks.

London Bicycle Tour Company

Three tours leave from their base next to the Imperial War Museum, south of the Thames (all are £27). Sunday is the best, as there is less car traffic; optional helmets are included. The following tour times are for peak season (April-Oct); times are different for off-season, when you need to book ahead (**Classic Tour**—daily at 10:30, 8 miles, 3 hours, includes Westminster, Buckingham Palace, Covent Garden, and St. Paul's; **Love London Tour**—daily at 14:30, 8 miles, 3 hours, includes Westminster, Buckingham Palace, Hyde Park, Soho, and Covent Garden; **Old Town Tour**—Sat-Sun at 14:00, 9 miles, 3.5 hours, includes south side of the river to Tower Bridge, the East End, The City, and St. Paul's). They also rent bikes (£3.50/hour, £20/day; office open daily 9:30-18:00, shorter hours Nov-March, 74 Kennington Road, tel. 020/7928-6838, www.londonbicycle.com).

Fat Tire Bike Tours

These bike tours cover the highlights of downtown London, on two different itineraries (RS%—£2 discount with this book): **Royal London** (£26, daily at 11:00 in peak season, also at 15:30 in summer, 7 miles, 4 hours, meet at Queensway Tube station; includes Parliament, Buckingham Palace, Hyde Park, and Trafalgar Square) and **River Thames** (£48, nearly daily in summer at 10:30, 4.5 hours, reservations required, meet just outside Southwark Tube Station; includes London Eye, St. Paul's, Tower of London, and London Bridge). Their guiding style is light, mixing history with humor (must reserve ahead for kids' bikes, off-season tours also available, mobile 078-8233-8779, www.fattiretours.com/london). They also offer a range of walking tours that include a fish-and-chips dinner, a beer-tasting pub tour, and theater packages.

BY CRUISE BOAT

London offers many made-for-tourist cruises, most on slow-moving, open-top boats accompanied by entertaining commentary (an experience worth ▲▲). Several companies offer essentially the same trip. Generally speaking, you can either do a **short city-center cruise** by riding a boat 30 minutes from Westminster Pier to Tower Pier (particularly handy if you're interested

in visiting the Tower of London anyway), or take a **longer cruise** that includes a peek at the East End, riding from Westminster all the way to Greenwich (save time by taking the Tube back).

Each company runs cruises daily, about twice hourly, from morning until dark; many reduce frequency off-season. Boats come and go from various docks in the city center. The most popular places to embark are Westminster Pier (at the base of Westminster Bridge across the street from Big Ben) and London Eye Pier (also known as Waterloo Pier, across the river).

A one-way trip within the city center costs about £11; going all the way to Greenwich costs about £3 more. Most companies charge around £4 more for a round-trip ticket. Others sell hop-on, hop-off day tickets (around £19). But I'd rather savor a one-way cruise, then zip home by Tube.

You can buy tickets at kiosks on the docks; always ask about discounts (they vary by company). With a Travelcard, you get a 33 percent discount off most cruises; the Oyster card can often be used as payment but nets you a discount only on Thames Clippers.

Thames Boat Piers

Thames boats (both tour and commuter boats) stop at these piers in the town center and beyond. While Westminster Pier is the most popular, it's not the only dock in town. Consider all the options (listed from west to east, as the Thames flows—see the color maps in the back of this book).

Millbank Pier (North Bank): At the Tate Britain museum, used primarily by the Tate Boat ferry service (express connection to Tate Modern at Bankside Pier).

Westminster Pier (North Bank): Near the base of Big Ben, offers round-trip sightseeing cruises and lots of departures in both directions (though the Thames Clippers boats don't stop here). Nearby sights include Parliament and Westminster Abbey.

London Eye Pier (a.k.a. **Waterloo Pier,** South Bank): At the base of the London Eye; good, less-crowded alternative to Westminster, with many of the same cruise options (Waterloo Station is nearby).

Embankment Pier (North Bank): Near Covent Garden, Trafalgar Square, and Cleopatra's Needle (the obelisk on the Thames). This pier is used mostly for special boat trips, such as some RIB (rigid inflatable boats) and lunch and dinner cruises.

Festival Pier (South Bank): Next to the Royal Festival Hall, just downstream from the London Eye.

Blackfriars Pier (North Bank): In The City, not far from St. Paul's.

Bankside Pier (South Bank): Directly in front of the Tate Modern and Shakespeare's Globe.

London Bridge Pier (a.k.a. **London Bridge City Pier,** South Bank): Near the HMS *Belfast.*

Tower Pier (North Bank): At the Tower of London, at the east edge of The City and near the East End.

St. Katharine's Pier (North Bank): Just downstream from the Tower of London.

Canary Wharf Pier (North Bank): At the Docklands, London's new "downtown."

Greenwich, Kew Gardens, and **Hampton Court Piers:** These outer London piers may also come in handy.

You can purchase drinks and overpriced snacks on board. Budget travelers can pack a picnic for the cruise.

The three dominant companies are **City Cruises** (handy 45-minute cruise from Westminster Pier to Tower Pier; www.citycruises.com), **Thames River Services** (fewer stops, classic boats, friendlier and more old-fashioned feel; www.thamesriverservices.co.uk), and **Circular Cruise** (full cruise takes about an hour, operated by Crown River Services, www.circularcruise.london). I'd skip the **London Eye**'s River Cruise from London Eye Pier, as it's more expensive and shorter. The speedy **Thames Clippers** (described below) are designed more for no-nonsense transport than lazy sightseeing.

To compare all of your options in one spot, head to Westminster Pier, which has a row of kiosks for all of the big outfits.

Cruising Downstream, to Greenwich: Both **City Cruises** and **Thames River Services** head from Westminster Pier to Greenwich. The cruises are usually narrated by the captain, with most commentary given on the way to Greenwich. The companies' prices are the same, though their itineraries are slightly different ('Thames River Services makes only one stop en route and takes an hour, while City Cruises makes two stops and adds about 15 minutes). The **Thames Clippers** boats, described below, are cheaper and faster (about 20-55 minutes to Greenwich), but have no commentary and no up-top seating.

Cruising Upstream, to Kew Gardens and Hampton Court Palace: Thames River Boats leave for Kew Gardens from Westminster Pier (£15 one-way, £22 round-trip, discounts with Travelcard, 2-4/day depending on season, 1.5 hours, boats sail April-Oct, about half the trip is narrated, www.thamesriverboats.co.uk). Most boats continue on to Hampton Court Palace for an additional £4 (and another 1.5 hours).

Commuting by Clipper

The sleek, 220-seat catamarans used by **Thames Clippers** are designed for commuters rather than sightseers. Think of the boats as express buses on the river—they zip through London every 20-30 minutes, stopping at most of the major docks en route. They're fast: roughly 20-30 minutes from Embankment to Tower, 10 more minutes to Docklands/Canary Wharf, and 15 more minutes to Greenwich. The boats are less pleasant for joyriding than the cruises described earlier, with no commentary and no open deck up top (the only outside access is on a crowded deck at the exhaust-choked back of the boat, where you're jostling for space to take photos). Any one-way ride in Central London (roughly London Eye to Tower Pier) costs £8.60; a one-way ride to East London (Canary Wharf and Greenwich) is £10, and a River Roamer all-day ticket costs £19.80 (discounts online and with Travelcard and Oyster card, www.thamesclippers.com).

Thames Clippers also offers two express trips. The **Tate Boat** ferry service, which directly connects the Tate Britain (Millbank Pier) and the Tate Modern (Bankside Pier), is made for art lovers (£8.60 one-way, covered by River Roamer day ticket; buy ticket at kiosks or self-service machines before boarding or use Oyster card;

London at a Glance

▲▲▲**Westminster Abbey** Britain's finest church and the site of royal coronations and burials since 1066. **Hours:** Abbey—Mon-Fri 9:30-16:30, Wed until 19:00, Sat 9:00-16:00 (Sept-April until 14:00); Diamond Jubilee Galleries—Mon-Fri 10:00-16:00, Sat 9:30-15:30; closed Sun except for worship. See page 64.

▲▲▲**Churchill War Rooms** Underground WWII headquarters of Churchill's war effort. **Hours:** Daily 9:30-18:00, July-Aug until 19:00. See page 73.

▲▲▲**National Gallery** Remarkable collection of European paintings (1250-1900), including Leonardo, Botticelli, Velázquez, Rembrandt, Turner, Van Gogh, and the Impressionists. **Hours:** Daily 10:00-18:00, Fri until 21:00. See page 79.

▲▲▲**British Museum** The world's greatest collection of artifacts of Western civilization, including the Rosetta Stone and the Parthenon's Elgin Marbles. **Hours:** Daily 10:00-17:30, Fri until 20:30 (select galleries only). See page 92.

▲▲▲**British Library** Fascinating collection of important literary treasures of the Western world. **Hours:** Mon-Thu 9:30-20:00, Fri until 18:00, Sat until 17:00, Sun 11:00-17:00. See page 99.

▲▲▲**St. Paul's Cathedral** The main cathedral of the Anglican Church, designed by Christopher Wren, with a climbable dome and daily evensong services. **Hours:** Mon-Sat 8:30-16:30, closed Sun except for worship. See page 104.

▲▲▲**Tower of London** Historic castle, palace, and prison housing the crown jewels and a witty band of Beefeaters. **Hours:** Tue-Sat 9:00-17:30, Sun-Mon from 10:00; Nov-Feb closes one hour earlier. See page 112.

▲▲▲**Victoria and Albert Museum** The best collection of decorative arts anywhere. **Hours:** Daily 10:00-17:45, Fri until 22:00 (select galleries only). See page 132.

▲▲**Houses of Parliament** Famous for Big Ben and occupied by the Houses of Lords and Commons. **Hours:** When Parliament is in session, generally open Oct-late July Mon-Thu, closed Fri-Sun and during recess late July-Sept. Guided tours offered year-round on Sat and most weekdays during recess. See page 69.

▲▲**Trafalgar Square** The heart of London, where Westminster, The City, and the West End meet. See page 77.

▲▲**National Portrait Gallery** A *Who's Who* of British history, featuring portraits of this nation's most important historical figures. **Hours:** Daily 10:00-18:00, Fri until 21:00. See page 83.

▲▲**Covent Garden** Vibrant people-watching zone with shops, cafés, street musicians, and an iron-and-glass arcade that once hosted a produce market. See page 85.

▲▲**Changing of the Guard at Buckingham Palace** Hour-long spectacle at Britain's royal residence. **Hours:** May-July daily at 11:00, Aug-April Sun-Mon, Wed, and Fri. See page 89.

▲▲**London Eye** Enormous observation wheel, dominating—and offering commanding views over—London's skyline. **Hours:** Daily 10:00-20:30 or later, Sept-May 11:00-18:00. See page 119.

▲▲**Imperial War Museum** Exhibits examining military conflicts from the early 20th century to today. **Hours:** Daily 10:00-18:00. See page 121.

▲▲**Tate Modern** Works by Monet, Matisse, Dalí, Picasso, and Warhol displayed in a converted powerhouse complex. **Hours:** Daily 10:00-18:00, Fri-Sat until 22:00. See page 122.

▲▲**Shakespeare's Globe** Timbered, thatched-roof reconstruction of the Bard's original "wooden O." **Hours:** Theater complex, museum, and actor-led tours generally daily 9:00-17:30; April-Oct generally morning theater tours only. Plays are also staged here. See page 123.

▲▲**Tate Britain** Collection of British painting from the 16th century through modern times, including works by Blake, the Pre-Raphaelites, and Turner. **Hours:** Daily 10:00-18:00. See page 126.

▲▲**Natural History Museum** A Darwinian delight, packed with stuffed creatures, engaging exhibits, and enthralled kids. **Hours:** Daily 10:00-18:00. See page 136.

▲▲**Greenwich** Seafaring borough just east of the city center, with *Cutty Sark* tea clipper, Royal Observatory, other maritime sights, and a pleasant market. **Hours:** Most sights open daily 10:00-17:00. See page 137.

▲▲**Kew Gardens** Greenhouses, an arboretum, and many gardens hosting diverse plants from around the world. **Hours:** Mon-Thu 10:00-19:00, Fri-Sun until 20:00, closes earlier Sept-March. See page 141.

▲▲**Hampton Court Palace** The opulent digs of Henry VIII. **Hours:** Daily 10:00-18:00, Nov-March until 16:30. See page 142.

for frequency and times, see www.tate.org.uk/visit/tate-boat). The **O2 Express** runs only on nights when there are events at the O2 arena (departs from London Eye Pier, can sell out in advance).

Westminster Walk

Just about every visitor to London strolls along historic Whitehall from Big Ben to Trafalgar Square. This self-guided walk gives meaning to that touristy ramble (most of the sights you'll see are described in more detail later). Under London's modern traffic and big-city bustle lie 2,000 fascinating years of history. You'll get a whirlwind tour as well as a practical orientation to London. ⌖ You can download a free, extended audio version of this walk; see page 30.

Start halfway across ❶ **Westminster Bridge** for that "Wow, I'm really in London!" feeling. Get a close-up view of the **Houses of Parliament** and **Big Ben** (floodlit at night). Downstream you'll see the **London Eye,** the city's giant Ferris wheel. Down the stairs to Westminster Pier are boats to the Tower of London and Greenwich (downstream) or Kew Gardens (upstream).

En route to Parliament Square, you'll pass a ❷ **statue of Boadicea,** the Celtic queen who unsuccessfully resisted Roman invaders in AD 60. Julius Caesar was the first Roman general to cross the Channel, but even he was weirded out by the island's strange inhabitants, who worshipped trees, sacrificed virgins, and went to war painted blue. Later, Romans subdued and civilized them, building roads and making this spot on the Thames—"Londinium"—a major urban center.

You'll find four red phone booths lining the north side of ❸ **Parliament Square** along Great George Street—great for a phone-box-and-Big-Ben photo op.

Wave hello to Winston Churchill and Nelson Mandela in Parliament Square. To Churchill's right is the historic **Westminster Abbey,** with its two stubby, elegant towers. The white building (flying the Union Jack) at the far end of the square houses Britain's **Supreme Court.**

Head north up Parliament Street, which turns into ❹ **Whitehall,** and walk toward Trafalgar Square. You'll see the thought-provoking ❺ **Cenotaph** in the middle of the boulevard, reminding passersby of the many Brits who died in the last century's world wars. To visit the **Churchill War Rooms,** take a left before the Cenotaph, on King Charles Street.

Continuing on Whitehall, stop at the barricaded and guarded ❻ **#10 Downing Street** to see the British "White House," the traditional home of the prime minister since the position was created in the early 18th century. Break the bobby's boredom and ask him

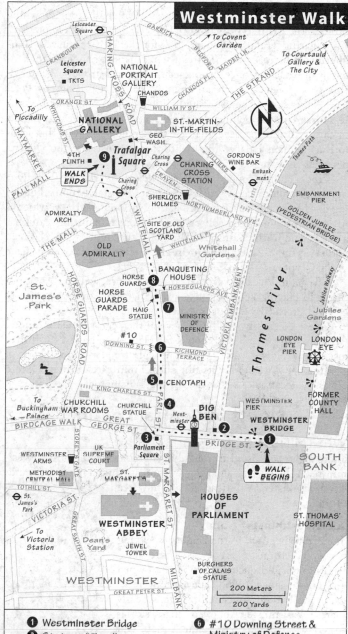

Westminster Walk

Leicester Square
GARRICK
BEDFORD
MAIDEN LN.
To Covent Garden
To Courtauld Gallery & The City
CRANBOURN
Leicester Square
TKTS
CHARING CROSS ROAD
NATIONAL PORTRAIT GALLERY
CHANDOS
CHANDOS PL.
THE STRAND
To Piccadilly
WHITCOMB ST.
ORANGE ST.
WILLIAM IV ST.
NATIONAL GALLERY
ST.-MARTIN-IN-THE-FIELDS
GEO. WASH.
HAYMARKET
4TH PLINTH
9 Trafalgar Square
VILLIERS
GORDON'S WINE BAR
Charing Cross
CHARING CROSS STATION
Embankment
Thames Path
EMBANKMENT PIER
PALL MALL
WALK ENDS
Charing Cross
CRAVEN
SHERLOCK HOLMES
NORTHUMBERLAND AVE.
GOLDEN JUBILEE (PEDESTRIAN BRIDGE)
ADMIRALTY ARCH
THE MALL
SITE OF OLD SCOTLAND YARD
WHITEHALL PL.
Whitehall Gardens
OLD ADMIRALTY
WHITEHALL
VICTORIA EMBANKMENT
Thames River
Jubilee Walkway
St. James's Park
HORSE GUARDS ROAD
HORSE GUARDS
8
BANQUETING HOUSE
HORSEGUARDS AVE.
Jubilee Gardens
HORSE GUARDS PARADE
HAIG STATUE
7
MINISTRY OF DEFENCE
LONDON EYE PIER
LONDON EYE
#10
DOWNING ST.
6
RICHMOND TERRACE
FORMER COUNTY HALL
To Buckingham Palace
KING CHARLES ST.
5 CENOTAPH
Churchill War Rooms
CHURCHILL WAR ROOMS
CHURCHILL STATUE
PARL. ST.
4
Westminster
BIG BEN
WESTMINSTER PIER
BIRDCAGE WALK
GREAT GEORGE ST.
2
WESTMINSTER BRIDGE
1
WESTMINSTER ARMS
UK SUPREME COURT
3
Parliament Square
BRIDGE ST.
WALK BEGINS
SOUTH BANK
METHODIST CENTRAL HALL
STOREY'S GATE
GREAT SMITH ST.
ST. MARGARET'S
HOUSES OF PARLIAMENT
ST. THOMAS' HOSPITAL
St. James's Park
TOTHILL ST.
VICTORIA ST.
WESTMINSTER ABBEY
ST. MARGARET ST.
To Victoria Station
Dean's Yard
JEWEL TOWER
WESTMINSTER
BURGHERS OF CALAIS STATUE
MILLBANK
GREAT PETER ST.

200 Meters
200 Yards

1 Westminster Bridge
2 Statue of Boadicea
3 Parliament Square
4 Walking along Whitehall
5 Cenotaph
6 #10 Downing Street & Ministry of Defence
7 Banqueting House
8 Horse Guards
9 Trafalgar Square

a question. The huge building across Whitehall from Downing Street is the **Ministry of Defence** (MOD), the "British Pentagon."

Nearing Trafalgar Square, look for the 17th-century ❼ **Banqueting House** across the street, which is just about all that remains of what was once the biggest palace in Europe—Whitehall Palace. If you visit, you can enjoy its ceiling paintings by Peter Paul Rubens, and the exquisite hall itself. Also take a look at the ❽ **Horse Guards** behind the gated fence. For 200 years, soldiers in cavalry uniforms have guarded this arched entrance that leads to Buckingham Palace. These elite troops constitute the Queen's personal bodyguard.

The column topped by Lord Nelson marks ❾ **Trafalgar Square,** London's central meeting point. The stately domed building on the far side of the square is the **National Gallery,** which is filled with the national collection of European paintings, and has a classy café in the Sainsbury Wing. To the right of the National Gallery is the 1722 **St. Martin-in-the-Fields Church** and its Café in the Crypt.

To get to Piccadilly from Trafalgar Square, walk up Cockspur Street to Haymarket, then take a short left on Coventry Street to colorful **Piccadilly Circus** (see map on page 86).

Near Piccadilly, you'll find several theaters. **Leicester Square** (with its half-price TKTS booth for plays—see page 149) thrives just a few blocks away. Walk through trendy **Soho** (north of Shaftesbury Avenue) for its fun pubs. From Piccadilly or Oxford Circus, you can take a taxi, bus, or the Tube home.

Sights in Central London

WESTMINSTER

These sights are listed in roughly geographical order from Westminster Abbey to Trafalgar Square, and are linked in my self-guided Westminster Walk (earlier) and my free 🎧 audio tour.

▲▲▲Westminster Abbey

The greatest church in the English-speaking world, Westminster Abbey is where England's kings and queens have been crowned and buried since 1066. Like a stony refugee camp huddled outside St. Peter's Pearly Gates, Westminster Abbey has many stories to tell. To experience the church more vividly, take a live tour, or attend evensong or an organ concert.

Cost and Hours: £23, £5 more for timed-

LONDON

entry ticket to worthwhile Queen's Diamond Jubilee Galleries, family ticket available, cheaper online; Abbey—Mon-Fri 9:30-16:30, Wed until 19:00 (main church only), Sat 9:00-16:00 (Sept-April until 14:00), guided tours available; Queen's Galleries—Mon-Fri 10:00-16:00, Sat 9:30-15:30; Cloister—Mon-Sat 8:00-18:00; closed Sun to sightseers but open for services; last entry one hour before closing; Tube: Westminster or St. James's Park, tel. 020/7222-5152, www.westminster-abbey.org.

Timed-Entry Tickets: Avoid long ticket-buying lines (especially in summer) by buying a timed-entry ticket on the Abbey's website (don't buy tickets from copycat websites; use the official ".org" site). If you choose to add the Queen's Galleries, book that entry about an hour after you'll start your Abbey visit.

When to Go: It's most crowded every day at midmorning and all day Saturdays and Mondays. Visit early, during lunch, or late to avoid tourist hordes. Weekdays after 14:30 are less congested; come late and stay for the 17:00 evensong.

Church Services and Music: Mon-Fri at 7:30 (prayer), 8:00 and 12:30 (communion), 17:00 evensong (on Wed it's spoken, not sung); Sat at 8:00 (communion), 9:00 (prayer), 15:00 (evensong; May-Aug it's at 17:00); Sun services generally come with more music: at 8:00 (communion), 10:00 (sung Matins), 11:15 (sung Eucharist), 15:00 (evensong), 18:30 (evening service). Services are free to anyone, though visitors who haven't paid church admission aren't allowed to linger afterward. Free organ recitals are usually held Sun at 17:45 (30 minutes). Things can change, so get the latest info for your particular day from posted signs or the Abbey's website.

Tours: The included audioguide is excellent. Vergers (docents) give informative 90-minute guided tours (£5, schedule posted outside and inside entry, up to 6/day in summer, 2-4/day in winter).

○ Self-Guided Tour: You'll have no choice but to follow the steady flow of tourists through the church, along the route laid out for the audioguide. Here are the Abbey's top stops.

• *Walk straight through the north transept. Follow the crowd flow to the right, passing through a number of...*

❶ Memorials: Westminster Abbey has become a place where the nation comes to remember its own. You'll pass by statues on tombs, stained glass on walls, and plaques in the floor, all honoring illustrious Brits, both famous and not so famous.

• *Now enter the spacious nave and take it all in.*

❷ Nave: Look down the long and narrow center aisle of the church. Lined with the praying hands of the Gothic arches, glowing with light from the stained glass, this is more than a museum. With saints in stained glass, heroes in carved stone, and the bodies

LONDON

Westminster Abbey Tour

30 Meters
30 Yards

To Parliament
Square &
Whitehall

HENRY VII
CHAPEL

SIDE
CHAPELS

WOODEN
STAIRCASE

HIGH
ALTAR

CHAPTER
HOUSE

QUEEN'S
GALLERIES

ENTER
(NORTH
DOOR)

PYX

CHOIR

To Little Cloister
& College Garden

SCIENTISTS'
CORNER

GREAT
CLOISTER

NAVE

ENTER
(CLOISTERS &
CAFÉ ONLY)

CAFÉ &
WC

EXIT
(WEST
DOOR)

GIFT
SHOP

DEAN'S
YARD

① Memorials
② Nave
③ Choir
④ Coronation Spot
⑤ Shrine of Edward the Confessor
⑥ Tomb of Elizabeth I & Mary I
⑦ Chapel of King Henry VII

⑧ Royal Air Force Chapel
⑨ Tomb of Mary, Queen of Scots
⑩ Queen's Diamond Jubilee Galleries
⑪ Poets' Corner
⑫ Great Cloister
⑬ Coronation Chair

of England's greatest citizens under the floor stones, Westminster Abbey is the religious heart of England.

The king who built the Abbey was Edward the Confessor. Find him in the stained glass windows on the left side of the nave (as you face the altar). He's in the third bay from the end (marked *S: Edwardus rex...*), dressed in white and blue, with his crown, scepter, and ring. The Abbey's 10-story nave is the tallest in England. The sleek chandeliers, 10 feet tall, look small in comparison (16 were given to the Abbey by the Guinness family).

On the floor near the west entrance of the Abbey is the flower-lined Grave of the Unknown Warrior, one ordinary WWI soldier buried in soil from France with lettering made from melted-down weapons from that war. Take time to contemplate the 800,000 men from the British Empire who gave their lives. Their memory is so revered that, when Kate Middleton walked up the aisle on her wedding day, by tradition she had to step around the tomb.

• *Now walk straight up the nave toward the altar. This is the same route every future monarch walks on the way to being crowned. Midway up the nave, you pass through the colorful screen of an enclosure known as the...*

❸ **Choir:** These elaborately carved wood and gilded seats are where monks once chanted their services in the "quire"—as it's known in British churchspeak. Today, it's where the Abbey's boys choir sings the evensong. Up ahead, the "high" (main) altar—which usually has a cross and candlesticks atop it—sits on the platform up the five stairs.

❹ **Coronation Spot:** The area immediately before the high altar is where every English coronation since 1066 has taken place. Royalty are also given funerals here, and it's where most of the last century's royal weddings have taken place, including the unions of Queen Elizabeth II and Prince Philip (1947) and Prince William and Kate Middleton (2011).

• *Now veer left and follow the crowd. Pause at the wooden staircase on your right. This is the royal tomb that started it all.*

❺ **Shrine of Edward the Confessor:** Step back and peek over the dark coffin of Edward I to see the tippy-top of the green-and-gold wedding-cake tomb of King Edward the Confessor—the man who built Westminster Abbey. It was finished just in time to bury Edward and to crown his foreign successor, William the Conqueror, in 1066. After Edward's death, people prayed at his tomb, and, after getting good results, he was made a saint. His personal renown began the tradition of burying royalty in this church. Edward's tall, central tomb (which unfortunately lost some of its luster when Henry VIII melted down the gold coffin case) is surrounded by the tombs of eight other kings and queens.

• *At the top of the stone staircase, veer left into the private burial chapel of Queen Elizabeth I.*

❻ Tomb of Queens Elizabeth I and Mary I: Although only one effigy is on the tomb (Elizabeth's), there are actually two queens buried beneath it, both daughters of Henry VIII (by different mothers). Bloody Mary—meek, pious, sickly, and Catholic—enforced Catholicism during her short reign (1553-1558) by burning "heretics" at the stake.

Elizabeth—strong, clever, and Protestant—steered England on an Anglican course. She holds a royal orb symbolizing that she's queen of the whole globe. When 26-year-old Elizabeth was crowned in the Abbey, her right to rule was questioned (especially by her Catholic subjects) because she was considered the bastard seed of Henry VIII's unsanctioned marriage to Anne Boleyn. But Elizabeth's long reign (1559-1603) was one of the greatest in English history, a time when England ruled the seas and Shakespeare explored human emotions. When she died, thousands turned out for her funeral in the Abbey. Elizabeth's face on the tomb, modeled after her death mask, is considered a very accurate take on this hook-nosed, imperious "Virgin Queen" (she never married).

• *Continue into the ornate, flag-draped room up a few more stairs (directly behind the main altar).*

❼ Chapel of King Henry VII (the Lady Chapel): The light from the stained-glass windows; the colorful banners overhead; and the elaborate tracery in stone, wood, and glass give this room the festive air of a medieval tournament. The prestigious Knights of the Bath meet here, under the magnificent ceiling studded with gold pendants. The ceiling—of carved stone, not plaster (1519)—is the finest English Perpendicular Gothic and fan vaulting you'll see (unless you're going to King's College Chapel in Cambridge). The ceiling was sculpted on the floor in pieces, then jigsaw-puzzled into place. It capped the Gothic period and signaled the vitality of the coming Renaissance.

• *Go to the far end of the chapel and stand at the banister in front of the modern set of stained-glass windows.*

❽ Royal Air Force Chapel: Saints in robes and halos mingle with pilots in parachutes and bomber jackets. This tribute to WWII flyers is for those who earned their angel wings in the Battle of Britain (July-Oct 1940). A bit of bomb damage has been preserved—the little glassed-over hole in the wall below the windows in the lower left-hand corner.

• *Exit the Chapel of Henry VII. Turn left into a side chapel with the tomb (the central one of three in the chapel).*

❾ Tomb of Mary, Queen of Scots: The beautiful, French-educated queen (1542-1587) was held under house arrest for 19 years by Queen Elizabeth I, who considered her a threat to her sovereignty. Elizabeth got wind of an assassination plot, suspected Mary was behind it, and had her first cousin (once removed) beheaded. When Elizabeth died childless, Mary's son—James VI, King of Scots—also became King James I of England and Ireland. James buried his mum here (with her head sewn back on) in the Abbey's most sumptuous tomb.

• *Exit Mary's chapel. Continue on, until you emerge in the south transept. Look for the doorway that leads to a stairway and elevator to the...*

❿ Queen's Diamond Jubilee Galleries: In 2018, the Abbey opened a space that had been closed off for 700 years—an internal gallery 70 feet above the main floor known as the triforium. This balcony—with stunning views over the nave—now houses a small museum of interesting objects related to the Abbey's construction, the monarchs who worshipped here, royal coronations, and more from its 1,000-year history. (Because of limited space, a timed-entry ticket is required.)

• *After touring the Queen's Galleries, return to the main floor. You're in...*

⓫ Poets' Corner: England's greatest artistic contributions are in the written word. Many writers (including Chaucer, Lewis Carroll, T. S. Eliot, and Charles Dickens) are honored with plaques and monuments; relatively few are actually buried here. Shakespeare is commemorated by a fine statue that stands near the end of the transept, overlooking the others.

• *Exit the church (temporarily) at the south door, which leads to the...*

⓬ Great Cloister: You're entering the inner sanctum of the Abbey's monastery. The buildings that adjoin the church housed the monks. Cloistered courtyards like this gave them a place to stroll in peace while meditating on God's creations.

• *Go back into the church for the last stop.*

⓭ Coronation Chair: A gold-painted oak chair waits here under a regal canopy for the next coronation. For every English coronation since 1308 (except two), it's been moved to its spot before the high altar to receive the royal buttocks. The chair's legs rest on lions, England's symbol.

▲▲Houses of Parliament (Palace of Westminster)

This Neo-Gothic icon of London, the site of the royal residence from 1042 to 1547, is now the meeting place of the legislative branch of government. Like the US Capitol in Washington, DC, the complex is open to visitors. You can view parliamentary sessions in either the bickering House of Commons or the sleepy House of Lords. Or you can simply wander on your own (through a few closely monitored rooms) to appreciate the historic building itself.

The Palace of Westminster has been the center of political power in England for nearly a thousand years. In 1834, a horrendous fire gutted the Palace. It was rebuilt in a retro, Neo-Gothic style that recalled England's medieval Christian roots—pointed arches, stained-glass windows, spires, and saint-like statues. At the same time, Britain was also retooling its government. Democracy was on the rise, the queen became  a constitutional monarch, and Parliament emerged as the nation's ruling body. The Palace of Westminster became a symbol—a kind of cathedral—of democracy. A visit here offers a chance to tour a piece of living history and see the British government in action.

Cost and Hours: Free when Parliament is in session, otherwise must visit with a paid tour; nonticketed entry generally Oct-late July, House of Commons—Mon 14:30-22:30, Tue-Wed 11:30-19:30, Thu 9:30-17:30; House of Lords—Mon-Tue 14:30-22:00, Wed 15:00-22:00, Thu 11:00-19:30; last entry depends on debates; exact day-by-day schedule at www.parliament.uk.

Tours: Audioguide-£19.50, guided tour-£26.50, tours available Sat year-round 9:00-16:30 and most weekdays during recess (late July-Sept), 1.5 hours. Confirm the tour schedule and book ahead at www.parliament.uk or by calling 020/7219-4114. The ticket office also sells tour tickets, but there's no guarantee same-day spaces will be available (ticket office open Mon-Fri 10:00-16:00, Sat 9:00-16:30, closed Sun, in Portcullis House next to Westminster Tube Station, entrance on Victoria Embankment). For either a guided tour or an audioguide, arrive at the visitors entrance on Cromwell Green 20 minutes before your tour time to clear security.

Choosing a House: The House of Lords is less important politically, but they meet in a more ornate room, and the wait time is shorter (likely less than 30 minutes). The House of Commons is where major policy is made, but the room is sparse, and wait times are longer (30-60 minutes or more).

Crowd-Beating Tips: For the public galleries, lines tend to be longest at the start of each session, particularly on Wednesdays; for the shortest wait, show up later in the afternoon (but don't push it, as things sometimes close down early).

⊙ Self-Guided Tour: Enter midway along the west side of the building (across the street from Westminster Abbey), where

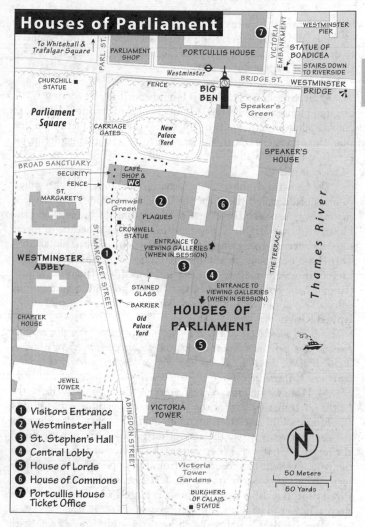

Houses of Parliament

To Whitehall & Trafalgar Square

PARL. ST.

PARLIAMENT SHOP

PORTCULLIS HOUSE

VICTORIA EMBANKMENT

WESTMINSTER PIER

❼

STATUE OF BOADICEA

STAIRS DOWN TO RIVERSIDE

CHURCHILL STATUE

FENCE

Westminster ⊖

BRIDGE ST.

BIG BEN

WESTMINSTER BRIDGE

Parliament Square

CARRIAGE GATES

New Palace Yard

Speaker's Green

SPEAKER'S HOUSE

BROAD SANCTUARY

SECURITY FENCE

CAFÉ, SHOP & **WC**

ST. MARGARET'S

Cromwell Green

❷

❻

PLAQUES

Thames River

CROMWELL STATUE

ENTRANCE TO VIEWING GALLERIES (WHEN IN SESSION)

WESTMINSTER ABBEY

❶

❸

❹

ENTRANCE TO VIEWING GALLERIES (WHEN IN SESSION)

THE TERRACE

CHAPTER HOUSE

STAINED GLASS

BARRIER

Old Palace Yard

HOUSES OF PARLIAMENT

❺

JEWEL TOWER

ABINGDON STREET

VICTORIA TOWER

❶ Visitors Entrance
❷ Westminster Hall
❸ St. Stephen's Hall
❹ Central Lobby
❺ House of Lords
❻ House of Commons
❼ Portcullis House Ticket Office

Victoria Tower Gardens

BURGHERS OF CALAIS STATUE

N

50 Meters

50 Yards

LONDON

a tourist ramp leads to the ❶ **visitors entrance.** Line up for the airport-style security check. You'll be given a visitor badge. If you have questions, the attendants are helpful.

• *First, take in the cavernous...*

❷ **Westminster Hall:** This vast hall—covering 16,000 square feet—survived the 1834 fire, and is one of the oldest and most important buildings in England. England's vaunted legal system was invented in this hall, as this was the major court of the land for 700 years. King Charles I was tried and sentenced to death here. Guy Fawkes was condemned for plotting to blow up the Halls of Parliament in 1605.

• *Continue up the stairs, and enter...*

❸ **St. Stephen's Hall:** This long, beautifully lit room was the original House of Commons. Members of Parliament (MPs) sat in church pews on either side of the hall—the ruling faction on one side, the opposition on the other. The room's murals depict major events in English history.

• *Continue into the...*

❹ **Central Lobby:** This ornate, octagonal, high-vaulted room is often called the "heart of British government," because it sits midway between the House of Commons (to the left) and the House of Lords (right). Video monitors list the schedule of meetings and events going on in this 1,100-room governmental hive. This is the best place to admire the Palace's interior decoration—carved wood, chandeliers, statues, and floor tiles. The room's decor trumpets the enlightenment of the British governing system. The colorful mosaics over the four doors represent the countries of the United Kingdom.

• *This lobby marks the end of the public space where you can wander freely. From here, you'll visit the House of Lords or the House of Commons. If either house is in session, you'll go through a series of narrow halls and staircases to reach the upper viewing galleries.*

❺ **House of Lords:** When you're called, you'll walk to the Lords Chamber by way of the long Peers' Corridor—referring to the House's 800 unelected members, called "Peers." Paintings on the corridor walls depict the antiauthoritarian spirit brewing under the reign of Charles I. When you reach the House of Lords Chamber, you'll watch the proceedings from the upper-level visitors gallery. Debate may occur among the few Lords who show up at any given time, but these days, their role is largely advisory—they have no real power to pass laws on their own.

The Lords Chamber is church-like and impressive, with stained glass and intricately carved walls. At the far end is the Queen's gilded throne, where she sits once a year to give a speech to open Parliament. In front of the throne sits the woolsack—a cushion stuffed with wool. Here the Lord Speaker presides, with a ceremonial mace behind the backrest. To the Lord Speaker's right are the members of the ruling party (a.k.a. "government") and to his left are the members of the opposition (the Labour Party). Unaffiliated Crossbenchers sit in between.

❻ **House of Commons:** The Commons Chamber may be much less grandiose than the Lords', but this is where the sausage gets made. The House of Commons is as powerful as the Lords, prime minister, and Queen combined. Of today's 650-plus MPs, only 450 can sit—the rest have to stand at the ends. As in the House of Lords, the ruling party sits to the right of the Speaker, opposition sits to the left.

Keep an eye out for two red lines on the floor, which must not be crossed when debating the other side. (They're supposedly two sword-lengths apart, to prevent a literal clashing of swords.) Between the benches is the canopied Speaker's Chair, for the chairman who keeps order and chooses who can speak next. A green bag on the back of the chair holds petitions from the public. The clerks sit at a central table that holds the ceremonial mace, a symbol of the power given Parliament by the monarch, who is not allowed in the Commons Chamber. When the prime minister visits, his ministers (or cabinet) join him on the front bench, while lesser MPs (the "backbenchers") sit behind. It's often a fiery spectacle, as the prime minister defends his policies, while the opposition grumbles and harrumphs in displeasure. It's not unheard-of for MPs to get out of line and be escorted out by the Serjeant at Arms and his Parliamentary bouncers.

Nearby: Across the street from the Parliament building's St. Stephen's Gate, the **Jewel Tower** is a rare remnant of the old Palace of Westminster, used by kings until Henry VIII. The crude stone tower (1365-1366) was a guard tower in the palace wall, overlooking a moat. It contains an exhibit on the medieval Westminster Palace and the tower (£5.70, daily 10:00-18:00, shorter hours and closed Mon-Fri in off-season; tel. 020/7222-2219). Next to the tower is a quiet courtyard with picnic-friendly benches.

Big Ben, the 315-foot-high clock tower at the north end of the Palace of Westminster, is named for its 13-ton bell, Ben. The light above the clock is lit when Parliament is in session. The face of the clock is huge—you can actually see the minute hand moving. For a good view of it, walk halfway over Westminster Bridge.

▲▲▲Churchill War Rooms

This excellent sight offers a fascinating walk through the underground headquarters of the British government's WWII fight against the Nazis in the darkest days of the Battle of Britain. It has two parts: the war rooms themselves, and a top-notch museum dedicated to the man who steered the war from here, Winston Churchill. Allow 1-2 hours for your visit.

Cost and Hours: £22 for timed-entry ticket (buy online in advance), includes essential audioguide; daily 9:30-18:00, July-Aug until 19:00, last entry one hour before closing; on King Charles Street, 200 yards off Whitehall—follow signs, Tube: Westminster; tel. 020/7930-6961, www.iwm.org.uk/churchill-war-rooms. The museum's gift shop is great for anyone nostalgic for the 1940s.

Affording London's Sights

London is one of Europe's most expensive cities, with the dubious distinction of having some of the world's steepest admission prices. But with its many free museums and affordable plays, this cosmopolitan, cultured city offers days of sightseeing thrills without requiring you to pinch your pennies (or your pounds).

Free Museums: Free sights include the British Museum, British Library, National Gallery, National Portrait Gallery, Tate Britain, Tate Modern, Wallace Collection, Imperial War Museum, Victoria and Albert Museum, Natural History Museum, Science Museum, Sir John Soane's Museum, the Museum of London, the Museum of the Home, and the Guildhall. About half of these museums request a donation of about £5, but whether you contribute is up to you. If you feel like supporting these museums, renting audioguides, using their café, and buying a few souvenirs all help.

Free Churches: Smaller churches let worshippers (and tourists) in free, although they may ask for a donation. The big sightseeing churches—Westminster Abbey and St. Paul's—charge higher admission fees, but offer free evensong services nearly daily (though you can't stick around afterward to sightsee). Westminster Abbey also offers free organ recitals most Sundays.

Other Freebies: London has plenty of free performances, such as lunch concerts at St. Martin-in-the-Fields (see page 83). For other freebies, check out www.whatsfreeinlondon.co.uk. There's no charge to enjoy the pageantry of the Changing of the Guard, rants at Speakers' Corner in Hyde Park (on Sun afternoon), displays at Harrods, the people-watching scene at Covent Garden, and the colorful streets of the East End. It's free to view the legal action at the Old Bailey and the legislature at work in the Houses of Parliament. You can get into the chapels at the Tower of London and Windsor Castle by attending Sunday services. And, Greenwich is an inexpensive outing. Many of its sights are free, and the DLR journey is cheap.

Good-Value Tours: The London Walks tours with professional guides (£12) are one of the best deals you can get. (Note that the guides for the "free" walking tours are unpaid by their companies, and they expect tips—I'd pay up front for an expertly guided tour instead.) Hop-on, hop-off big-bus tours, while expensive (around £30-40), provide a great overview and include free boat tours as well as city walks. (Or, for the price of a transit ticket, you could

Advance Tickets Recommended: While you can buy a ticket on-site, ticket-buying lines can be long (1-2 hours), so it's smart to buy a timed-entry ticket online in advance. You still may have to wait up to 30 minutes in the security line. Note: London Pass holders do not get to skip the line here—they wait along with ticket buyers.

get similar views from the top of a double-decker public bus.) A one-hour Thames ride to Greenwich costs about £12 one-way, but most boats come with entertaining commentary. A three-hour bicycle tour is about £27.

Buy Tickets Online: Tickets for many of London's most popular and expensive sights can be purchased online in advance, which will not only save you from standing in ticket-buying lines, but also will usually save you a few pounds per ticket.

Pricey...but Worth It? Big-ticket sights worth their hefty admission fees are the Tower of London, Kew Gardens, Shakespeare's Globe, and the Churchill War Rooms. The London Eye has become a London must-see—but you may feel differently when you see the price. St. Paul's Cathedral becomes more worthwhile if you climb the dome for the stunning view. Hampton Court Palace is well-presented and a reasonable value if you have an interest in royal history. The Queen charges royally for a peek inside Buckingham Palace and her fine art gallery and carriage museum. Madame Tussauds Waxworks is pricey but still hard for many to resist (see page 102 for info on discounts). Harry Potter fans gladly pay the Hagrid-size fee to see the sets and props at the Warner Bros. Studio Tour (but those who wouldn't know a wizard from a Muggle needn't bother).

Totally Pants (Brit-speak for Not Worth It): The London Dungeon is gimmicky, overpriced, and a terrible value...despite the long line. The cost of the wallet-bleeding ride to the top of The Shard is even more breathtaking than the view from Western Europe's tallest skyscraper.

Theater: Compared with Broadway's prices, London's theater can be a bargain. Seek out the freestanding TKTS booth at Leicester Square to get discounts from 25 to 50 percent on good seats (and full-price tickets to the hottest shows with no service charges). Buying directly at the theater box office can score you a great deal on same-day tickets, and even popular shows may have some seats under £20 (possibly with restricted views). A £5 "groundling" ticket for a play at Shakespeare's Globe is the best theater deal in town. Tickets to the Open Air Theatre at north London's Regent's Park start at £25. For more on all of these options, see "Entertainment in London," later.

Cabinet War Rooms: The 27-room, heavily fortified nerve center of the British war effort was used from 1939 to 1945. Churchill's room, the map room, and other rooms are just as they were in 1945. As you follow the one-way route, the audioguide explains each room and offers first-person accounts of wartime happenings here. Be patient—it's well worth it. While the rooms are spartan, you'll see how British gentility survived even as the city was bombarded—posted signs informed those working underground what the weather was like outside, and a cheery notice reminded them to turn off the lights to conserve electricity.

Churchill Museum: Don't bypass this museum, which occupies a large hall amid the war rooms. It dissects every aspect of the man behind the famous cigar, bowler hat, and V-for-victory sign. It's extremely well presented and engaging, using artifacts, quotes, political cartoons, clear explanations, and interactive exhibits to bring the colorful statesman to life. You'll get a taste of Winston's wit, irascibility, work ethic, passion for painting, American ties, writing talents, and drinking habits. The exhibit shows Winston's warts as well: It questions whether his party-switching was just political opportunism, examines the basis for his opposition to Indian self-rule, and reveals him to be an intense taskmaster who worked 18-hour days and was brutal to his staffers (who deeply respected him nevertheless).

A long touch-the-screen timeline lets you zero in on events in his life from birth (November 30, 1874) to his first appointment as prime minister in 1940. When World War II broke out, Prime Minister Chamberlain's appeasement policies were discredited, and—on the day that Germany invaded the Netherlands—the king appointed Churchill prime minister. Many of the items on display—such as a European map divvied up in permanent marker, which Churchill brought to England from the postwar Potsdam Conference—drive home the remarkable span of history this man influenced. Imagine: Churchill began his military career riding horses in the cavalry and ended it speaking out against nuclear proliferation. Churchill guided the nation through its darkest hour. His greatest contribution may have been his stirring radio speeches that galvanized the will of the British people. It's all the more amazing considering that, in the 1930s, the man I regard as the greatest statesman of the 20th century was seen as a washed-up loony ranting about the growing threat of fascist Germany.

Eating: Rations are available at the **$$ museum café** or, better, get a pub lunch at the nearby **$$ Westminster Arms** (food served downstairs, on Storey's Gate, a couple of blocks south of the museum).

Horse Guards

Mounted sentries change at the top of every hour, courtyard guards change Monday-Saturday at 11:00 (Sun at 10:00), and a colorful dismounting ceremony takes place daily at 16:00. The rest of the day, they just stand there—making for boring video (at Horse Guards Parade on Whitehall, directly across from the Banqueting House, between Trafalgar Square and 10 Downing Street, Tube: Westminster, www.changing-guard.com). Buckingham Palace pageantry is can-

celed when it rains, but the Horse Guards change regardless of the weather.

▲Banqueting House

England's first Renaissance building (1619-1622) is still standing. Designed by Inigo Jones, built by King James I, and decorated by his son Charles I, the Banqueting House came to symbolize the Stuart kings' "divine right" management style—the belief that God himself had anointed them to rule. The house is one of the few London landmarks spared by the 1698 fire and the only sur-viving part of the original Palace of Whitehall. Today it opens its doors to visitors, who enjoy a restful 10-minute audiovisual history, a 45-minute audioguide, and a look at the exquisite banqueting hall itself. As a tourist attraction, it's basically one big room, with sumptuous ceiling paintings by Peter Paul Rubens. At Charles I's request, these paintings drove home the doctrine of the legitimacy of the divine right of kings. Ironically, in 1649—divine right ig-nored—King Charles I was famously executed right here.

Cost and Hours: £7, includes audioguide, daily 10:00-17:00, may close for government functions—though it's always open at least until 13:00 (call ahead for recorded info), immediately across Whitehall from the Horse Guards, Tube: Westminster, tel. 020/3166-6155, www.hrp.org.uk.

ON TRAFALGAR SQUARE

Trafalgar Square, London's central square, worth ▲▲, is at the in-tersection of Westminster, The City, and the West End. It's the cli-max of most marches and demonstrations, and is a thrilling place to simply hang out. A remodeling of the square has rerouted car traffic, helping reclaim the area for London's citizens. At the top of Trafalgar Square (north) sits the domed National Gallery with its grand staircase, and to the right, the steeple of St. Martin-in-

LONDON

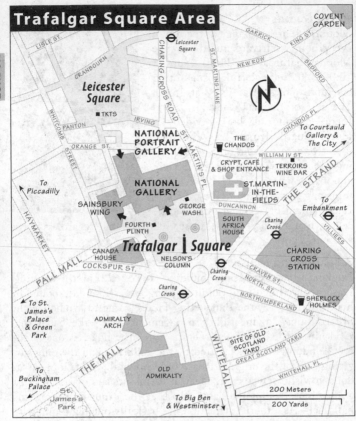

Trafalgar Square Area

COVENT GARDEN

Leicester Square

Leicester Square

■ TKTS

NATIONAL PORTRAIT GALLERY

NATIONAL GALLERY

SAINSBURY WING

FOURTH PLINTH

GEORGE WASH.

To Piccadilly

THE CHANDOS

CRYPT, CAFÉ & SHOP ENTRANCE

WILLIAM IV ST.

TERROIRS WINE BAR

ST.MARTIN-IN-THE-FIELDS

DUNCANNON

SOUTH AFRICA HOUSE

To Courtauld Gallery & The City

THE STRAND

To Embankment

VILLIERS

Trafalgar Square

CANADA HOUSE

COCKSPUR ST.

NELSON'S COLUMN

PALL MALL

Charing Cross

Charing Cross

CRAVEN ST.

NORTH ST.

NORTHUMBERLAND AVE.

CHARING CROSS STATION

SHERLOCK HOLMES

To St. James's Palace & Green Park

ADMIRALTY ARCH

WHITEHALL

SITE OF OLD SCOTLAND YARD

GREAT SCOTLAND YARD

WHITEHALL PL.

To Buckingham Palace

THE MALL

OLD ADMIRALTY

St. James's Park

To Big Ben & Westminster ↓

200 Meters

200 Yards

the-Fields, built in 1722, inspiring the steeple-over-the-entrance style of many town churches in New England. In the center of the square, Lord Nelson stands atop his 185-foot-tall fluted granite column, gazing out toward Trafalgar, where he lost his life but defeated the French fleet. Part of this 1842 memorial is made from his victims' melted-down cannons. He's surrounded by spraying fountains, giant lions, hordes of people, and—until recently—even more pigeons. A former London mayor decided that London's "flying rats" were a public nuisance and evicted Trafalgar Square's venerable seed salesmen (Tube: Charing Cross).

▲▲▲National Gallery

Displaying an unsurpassed collection of European paintings from 1250 to 1900—including works by Leonardo, Botticelli, Velázquez, Rembrandt, Turner, Van Gogh, and the Impressionists—this is one of Europe's great galleries. You'll peruse 700 years of art—from gold-backed Madonnas to Cubist bathers.

Cost and Hours: Free, £5 suggested donation, special exhibits extra; daily 10:00-18:00, Fri until 21:00, last entry to special exhibits 45 minutes before closing; floor plan-£2; on Trafalgar Square, Tube: Charing Cross or Leicester Square, tel. 020/7747-2885, www.nationalgallery.org.uk.

Tours: Free one-hour overview tours leave from the Sainsbury Wing info desk Mon-Fri at 14:00 (no tours Sat-Sun); excellent £5 audioguides—choose from one-hour highlights tour, several theme tours, or an option that lets you dial up info on any painting in the museum.

Eating: Consider splitting afternoon tea at the **$$$ National Dining Rooms,** on the first floor of the Sainsbury Wing (see page 190). The **$$$ National Café,** located near the Getty Entrance, has a table-service restaurant and café. Seek out the **$ Espresso Bar,** near the Portico and Getty entrances, for sandwiches and pastries.

Visiting the Museum: Enter through the Sainsbury Entrance (facing Trafalgar Square), in the modern annex to the left of the classic building, and climb the stairs.

Medieval: In Room 51 (and nearby rooms), shiny gold paintings of saints, angels, Madonnas, and crucifixions float in an ethereal gold never-never land. Art in the Middle Ages was religious, dominated by the Church. The illiterate faithful could meditate on an altarpiece and visualize heaven. It's as though they couldn't imagine saints and angels inhabiting the dreary world of rocks, trees, and sky they lived in.

One of the finest medieval altarpieces, *The Wilton Diptych,* is tucked in the small alcove in Room 51. Two saint/kings and St. John the Baptist present King Richard II (left panel) to the Virgin Mary and her rosy-cheeked baby (right panel), who are surrounded by angels with flame-like wings. Despite the gold-leaf background, the kings have distinct, down-to-earth faces.

Italian Renaissance: In painting, the Renaissance meant realism. Artists rediscovered the beauty of nature and the human body. In Room 63, find Van Eyck's *The Arnolfini Portrait* (1434), once thought to depict a wedding ceremony forced by the lady's

MEDIEVAL
1 ANONYMOUS – The Wilton Diptych

EARLY ITALIAN RENAISSANCE
2 UCCELLO – Battle of San Romano
3 BOTTICELLI – Venus and Mars
4 CRIVELLI – The Annunciation, with Saint Emidius
5 LEONARDO – The Virgin of the Rocks
6 LEONARDO – Virgin and Child with St. Anne and St. John the Baptist
7 VAN EYCK – The Arnolfini Portrait

HIGH RENAISSANCE
8 MICHELANGELO – The Entombment
9 RAPHAEL – Pope Julius II

MANNERISM
10 BRONZINO – An Allegory with Venus and Cupid
11 TINTORETTO – The Origin of the Milky Way

NORTHERN PROTESTANT ART
12 VERMEER – A Young Woman Standing at a Virginal

BAROQUE
13 RUBENS – The Judgment of Paris
14 REMBRANDT – Self-Portrait at the Age of 63
15 REMBRANDT – Belshazzar's Feast
16 VELÁZQUEZ – The Rokeby Venus
17 VAN DYCK – Equestrian Portrait of Charles I
18 CARAVAGGIO –The Supper at Emmaus

FRENCH ROCOCO
19 BOUCHER – Pan and Syrinx

BRITISH ROMANTIC ART
20 CONSTABLE – The Hay Wain
21 TURNER – The Fighting Téméraire

To Leicester Square ⊖ ↑
(5 min. walk)

SAINSBURY WING

ENTRANCE ON LEVEL 0

SELF-GUIDED TOUR
STARTS ON LEVEL 2

👣 TOUR BEGINS

SAINSBURY ENTRANCE

swelling belly. Today it's understood as a portrait of a solemn, well-dressed, well-heeled couple, the Arnolfinis of Bruges, Belgium (the woman likely is not pregnant—the fashion of the day was to gather up the folds of one's extremely full-skirted dress).

Michelangelo's (unfinished) *The Entombment* is inspired by ancient statues of balanced, anatomically perfect, nude Greek gods. Renaissance balance and symmetry reign. Christ is the center of the composition, flanked by two people leaning equally, who sup-

LONDON

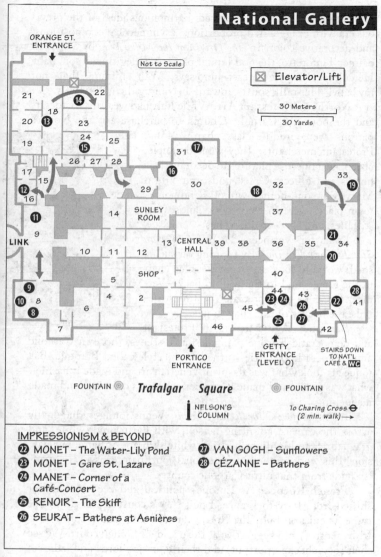

National Gallery

ORANGE ST. ENTRANCE

(Not to Scale)

⊠ Elevator/Lift

30 Meters
30 Yards

LINK

SUNLEY ROOM

CENTRAL HALL

SHOP

PORTICO ENTRANCE

GETTY ENTRANCE (LEVEL 0)

STAIRS DOWN TO NAT'L CAFÉ & WC

FOUNTAIN ◉ *Trafalgar Square* ◉ FOUNTAIN

NELSON'S COLUMN

To Charing Cross ⊖ (2 min. walk) →

IMPRESSIONISM & BEYOND

22 MONET – The Water-Lily Pond
23 MONET – Gare St. Lazare
24 MANET – Corner of a Café-Concert
25 RENOIR – The Skiff
26 SEURAT – Bathers at Asnières
27 VAN GOGH – Sunflowers
28 CÉZANNE – Bathers

port his body with strips of cloth. They, in turn, are flanked by two others.

Raphael's *Pope Julius II* gives a behind-the-scenes look at this complex leader. On the one hand, the pope is an imposing pyramid of power, with a velvet shawl, silk shirt, and fancy rings boasting of wealth and success. But at the same time, he's a bent and broken man, his throne backed into a corner, with an expression that seems to say, "Is this all there is?"

Mannerism: Developed in reaction to the High Renaissance,

Mannerism subverts the balanced, harmonious ideal of the previous era with exaggerated proportions, asymmetrical compositions, and decorative color. In *The Origin of the Milky Way* by Venetian painter Tintoretto, the god Jupiter places his illegitimate son, baby Hercules, at his wife's breast. Juno says, "Wait a minute. That's not my baby!" Her milk spurts upward, becoming the Milky Way.

Northern Protestant Art: While Italy had wealthy aristocrats and the powerful Catholic Church to purchase art, the North's patrons were middle-class, hardworking, Protestant merchants. They wanted simple, cheap, no-nonsense pictures to decorate their homes and offices. Greek gods and Virgin Marys were out, hometown folks and hometown places were in—portraits, landscapes, still lifes, and slice-of-life scenes.

Look for Vermeer's *A Young Woman Standing at a Virginal.* By framing off such a small world to look at—from the blue chair in the foreground to the wall in back—Vermeer forces us to appreciate the tiniest details, the beauty of everyday things.

Baroque: While artists in Protestant and democratic Europe painted simple scenes, those in Catholic and aristocratic countries turned to the style called Baroque. Baroque art took what was flashy in Venetian art and made it flashier, what was gaudy and made it gaudier, what was dramatic and made it shocking.

In Velázquez's *The Rokeby Venus*, Venus lounges diagonally across the canvas, admiring herself, with flaring red, white, and gray fabrics to highlight her rosy white skin and inflame our passion. This work by the king's personal court painter is a rare Spanish nude from that ultra-Catholic country.

French Rococo: As Europe's political and economic center shifted from Italy to France, Louis XIV's court at Versailles became its cultural hub. The Rococo art of Louis' successors was as frilly, sensual, and suggestive as the decadent French court. We see their rosy-cheeked portraits and their fantasies: lords and ladies at play in classical gardens, where mortals and gods cavort together. One of the finest examples is the tiny *Pan and Syrinx* by Boucher.

British Romantic Art: The reserved British were more comfortable cavorting with nature than with the lofty gods. Come-as-you-are poets like Wordsworth found the same ecstasy just in being outside. John Constable set up his easel out-of-doors, making quick sketches to capture the simple majesty of billowing clouds, spreading trees, and everyday rural life. Even British portraits (by Thomas Gainsborough and others) placed refined lords and ladies amid idealized greenery. The simple style of Constable's *The Hay Wain*—believe it or not—was considered shocking in its day.

Impressionism and Beyond: At the end of the 19th century, a new breed of artists burst out of the stuffy confines of the studio. They donned scarves and berets and set up their canvases in farmers' fields or carried their notebooks into crowded cafés, dashing off quick sketches in order to catch a momentary...impression. Check out Impressionist and Post-Impressionist masterpieces such as Van Gogh's *Sunflowers*. Van Gogh was the point man of his culture. He added emotion to Impressionism, infusing life even into inanimate objects. These sunflowers, painted with characteristic swirling brushstrokes, shimmer and writhe in either agony or ecstasy—depending on your own mood.

Cézanne's *Bathers* are arranged in strict triangles. He uses the Impressionist technique of building a figure with dabs of paint (though his "dabs" are often larger-sized "cube" shapes) to make solid, 3-D geometrical figures in the style of the Renaissance. In the process, his cube shapes helped inspire a radical new style—Cubism—bringing art into the 20th century.

▲▲National Portrait Gallery

A selective walk through this 500-year-long *Who's Who* of British history is quick and free, and puts faces on the story of England. The collection is well-described, not huge, and in historical sequence, from the 16th century on the second floor to today's royal family, usually housed on the ground floor. Some highlights: Henry VIII and wives; portraits of the "Virgin Queen" Elizabeth I, Sir Francis Drake, and Sir Walter Raleigh; the only real-life portrait of William Shakespeare; Oliver Cromwell and Charles I with his head on; portraits by Gainsborough and Reynolds; the Romantics (William Blake, Lord Byron, William Wordsworth, and company); Queen Victoria and her era; and the present royal family, including the late Princess Diana and the current Duchess of Cambridge—Kate.

Cost and Hours: Free, £5 suggested donation, special exhibits extra; daily 10:00-18:00, Fri until 21:00; excellent audioguide-£3, floor plan-£2; entry 100 yards off Trafalgar Square (around the corner from National Gallery, opposite Church of St. Martin-in-the-Fields), Tube: Charing Cross or Leicester Square, tel. 020/7306-0055, www.npg.org.uk.

▲St. Martin-in-the-Fields

The church, built in the 1720s with a Gothic spire atop a Greek-type temple, is an oasis of peace on wild and noisy Trafalgar Square. St. Martin cared for the poor. "In the fields" was where the first church stood on this spot (in the 13th century), between Westminster and The City. Stepping inside, you still feel a compassion for the needs of the people in this neighborhood—the church serves the homeless and houses a Chinese community center. The modern east window—with grillwork bent into the shape of a warped cross—was installed in 2008 to replace one damaged in World War II.

A freestanding glass pavilion to the left of the church serves as the entrance to the church's underground areas. There you'll find the concert ticket office, a gift shop, brass-rubbing center, and the recommended support-the-church Café in the Crypt.

Cost and Hours: Free, donations welcome; Mon-Fri 8:30-18:00, Sat-Sun from 9:00, closed to visitors during services—listed at the entrance and on the website; Tube: Charing Cross, tel. 020/7766-1100, www.stmartin-in-the-fields. org. The church is famous for its concerts, including a free lunchtime concert several days a week and evening concerts (for details, see "Entertainment in London," later, as well as the church's website).

THE WEST END AND NEARBY
▲Piccadilly Circus
Although this square is slathered with neon billboards and tacky attractions (think of it as the Times Square of London), the surrounding streets are packed with great shopping opportunities and swimming with youth on the rampage.

Nearby Shaftesbury Avenue and Leicester Square teem with fun-seekers, theaters, Chinese restaurants, and street singers. To the northeast is London's Chinatown and, beyond that, the funky Soho neighborhood. And curling to the northwest from Piccadilly Circus is genteel Regent Street, lined with exclusive shops.

▲Soho
North of Piccadilly, once-seedy Soho has become trendy—with many recommended restaurants—and is well worth a gawk. It's the epicenter of London's thriving, colorful youth scene, a fun and funky *Sesame Street* of urban diversity.

▲▲Covent Garden

This large square is filled with people and street performers—jugglers, sword swallowers, magicians, and guitar players. London's buskers (including those in the Tube) are auditioned, licensed, and assigned times and places where they are allowed to perform.

The square's centerpiece is a covered marketplace. A market has been here since medieval times, when it was the "convent"

garden owned by Westminster Abbey. In the 1600s, it became a housing development with this courtyard as its center, done in the Palladian style by Inigo Jones. Today's fine iron-and-glass structure was built in 1830 (when such buildings were all the Industrial Age rage) to house the stalls of what became London's chief produce market. Covent Garden remained a produce market until 1973, when its venerable arcades were converted to boutiques, cafés, and antique shops. A tourist market thrives here today (for details, see page 148).

The "Actors' Church" of St. Paul, the Royal Opera House, and the London Transport Museum (described next) all border the square, and theaters are nearby. The area is a people-watcher's delight, with cigarette eaters, Punch-and-Judy acts, food that's not good for you (or your wallet), trendy crafts, and row after row of boutique shops and market stalls. Better Covent Garden lunch deals can be found by walking a block or two away from the eye of this touristic hurricane (check out the places north of the Tube station, along Endell and Neal Streets).

▲London Transport Museum

This modern, well-presented museum is fun for kids and thought-provoking for adults (if a bit overpriced). Whether you're cursing or marveling at the buses and Tube, the growth of Europe's third-biggest city (after Istanbul and Moscow) has been made possible by its public transit system.

Cost and Hours: £18, kids under 18 free, daily 10:00-18:00, last entry 45 minutes before closing; pleasant upstairs café with Covent Garden view; in southeast corner of Covent Garden courtyard, Tube: Covent Garden, tel. 020/7379-6344, www.ltmuseum.co.uk.

Visiting the Museum: Take the elevator up to the top floor... and the year 1800, when horse-drawn vehicles ruled the road. Next, you descend to the first floor and the world's first underground Metro system, which used steam-powered locomotives (the Circle Line, c. 1865). On the ground floor, horses and trains are

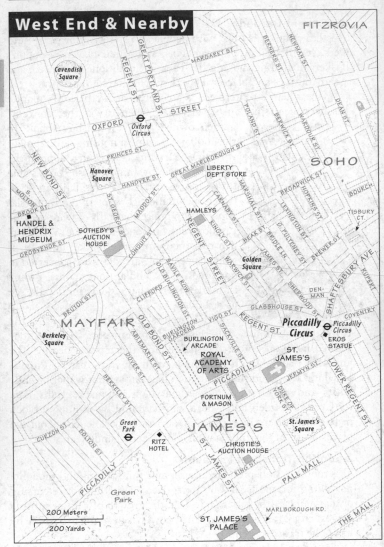

West End & Nearby

FITZROVIA

SOHO

MAYFAIR

ST. JAMES'S

Cavendish Square

Oxford Circus

Hanover Square

HANDEL & HENDRIX MUSEUM

SOTHEBY'S AUCTION HOUSE

HAMLEYS

LIBERTY DEP'T STORE

Golden Square

Berkeley Square

Green Park

BURLINGTON ARCADE

ROYAL ACADEMY OF ARTS

Piccadilly Circus

Piccadilly Circus

EROS STATUE

St. James's Square

FORTNUM & MASON

RITZ HOTEL

ST. JAMES'S

CHRISTIE'S AUCTION HOUSE

Green Park

200 Meters

200 Yards

MARLBOROUGH RD.

ST. JAMES'S PALACE

THE MALL

replaced by motorized vehicles (cars, taxis, double-decker buses, streetcars), resulting in 20th-century congestion. How to deal with it? In 2003, car drivers in London were slapped with a congestion charge, and today, a half-billion people ride the Tube every year.

▲Courtauld Gallery

This gallery, part of the Courtauld Institute of Art, may be closed for a multiyear renovation when you visit. If it is open, you'll see medieval European paintings and works by Rubens, the Impressionists

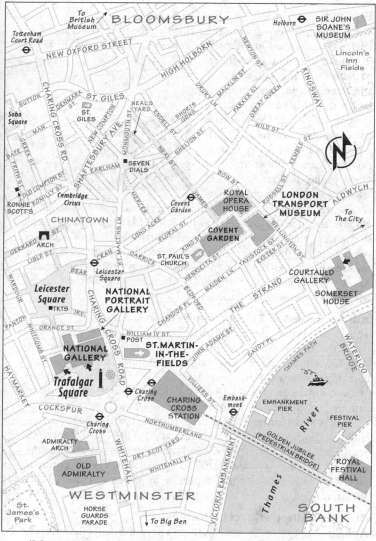

(Manet, Monet, and Degas), Post-Impressionists (Cézanne and an intense Van Gogh self-portrait), and more. The gallery is located within the grand Somerset House; enjoy the riverside eateries and the courtyard featuring a playful fountain.

Cost and Hours: £7, price can change with exhibit; generally daily 10:00-18:00 but may be closed for renovation; in Somerset House on the Strand, Tube: Temple or Covent Garden, recorded info tel. 020/7848-2526, www.courtauld.ac.uk.

BUCKINGHAM PALACE AREA

The working headquarters of the British monarchy, Buckingham Palace is where the Queen carries out her official duties as the head of state. She and other members of the royal family also maintain apartments here. The property hasn't always been this grand—James I (1603-1625) first brought the site under royal protection as a place for his mulberry plantation, for rearing silkworms.

Combo-Tickets: A £45 "Royal Day Out" combo-ticket covers the three palace sights that charge admission: the State Rooms, the Queen's Gallery, and the Royal Mews; the £20.70 version covers the Queen's Gallery and Royal Mews. You can also pay for each of these sights separately (prices listed later). For more information or to book online, see www.royalcollection.org.uk. Many tourists are more interested in the Changing of the Guard, which costs nothing at all to view.

▲State Rooms at Buckingham Palace

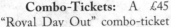

This lavish home has been Britain's royal residence since 1837, when the newly ascended Queen Victoria moved in. When today's Queen is at home, the royal standard flies (a red, yellow, and blue flag); otherwise, the Union Jack flaps in the wind. The Queen opens her palace to the public—but only for a couple of months in summer, when she's out of town.

Cost and Hours: £25 for State Rooms and throne room, includes audioguide; late July-Sept only, daily 9:30-19:30, Sept until 18:30, last entry 75 minutes before closing; limited to 8,000 visitors a day by timed entry; come early to the palace's Visitor Entrance (opens at 9:00), or book ahead in person, by phone, or online; Tube: Victoria, tel. 0303/123-7300—but Her Majesty rarely answers.

Queen's Gallery at Buckingham Palace

A small sampling of Queen Elizabeth's personal collection of art is on display in five rooms in a wing adjoining the palace. Her 7,000 paintings, one of the largest private art collections in the world, are actually a series of collections built upon by each successive monarch since the 16th century. The exhibits change two or three times a year and are lovingly described by the included audioguide. Because the gallery is small and security is tight (involving lines), visit this gallery only if you're a patient art lover interested in the current exhibit.

Cost and Hours: £12 but can change depending on exhibit, daily 10:00-17:30, from 9:30 late July-Sept, last entry 75 minutes before closing, Tube: Victoria, tel. 0303/123-7301. Men shouldn't miss the mahogany-trimmed urinals.

Royal Mews

A visit to the Queen's working stables is likely to be disappointing unless you follow the included audioguide or the hourly guided tour (April-Oct only, 45 minutes), in which case it's fairly entertaining—especially if you're interested in horses and/or royalty. You'll see only a few of the Queen's 30 horses (most active between 10:00 and 12:00), a fancy car, and a bunch of old carriages, finishing with the Gold State Coach (c. 1760, 4 tons, 4 mph). Queen Victoria said absolutely no cars. When she died, in 1901, the mews got its first Daimler. Today, along with the hay-eating transport, the stable is home to five Bentleys and Rolls-Royce Phantoms, with at least one on display.

Cost and Hours: £12; daily 10:00-17:00, off-season until 16:00, closed Sun in Nov and all of Dec-Jan; last entry 45 minutes before closing, generally busiest immediately after Changing of the Guard, guided tours on the hour in summer; Buckingham Palace Road, Tube: Victoria, tel. 0303/123-7302.

▲▲Changing of the Guard at Buckingham Palace

This is the spectacle every London visitor has to see at least once: stone-faced, bearskin-hatted guards changing posts with much

fanfare, accompanied by a brass band. (This is also where you'll see nearly every tourist in London gathered in one place at the same time.)

The most famous part takes place right in front of Buckingham Palace at 11:00. But before and after that, over the course of about an hour, several guard-changing ceremonies and parades converge within a few hundred yards of Buckingham Palace in a perfect storm of red-coated pageantry, more or less simultaneously. Most tourists just show up near the palace gate and get lost in the crowds, but if you're savvy, you can catch a satisfying glimpse from less crowded locations with much less wait than if you station yourself at the palace gate (see the "Changing of the Guard Timeline" sidebar). Once it's all over, unwind with a stroll through nearby St. James's Park.

Cost and Hours: Free, May-July daily at 11:00, Aug-April Sun-Mon, Wed, and Fri, no ceremony in very wet weather; exact schedule subject to change—call 020/7766-7300 for the day's plan, or check www.householddivision.org.uk (search "Changing the Guard"); Buckingham Palace, Tube: Victoria, St. James's Park, or

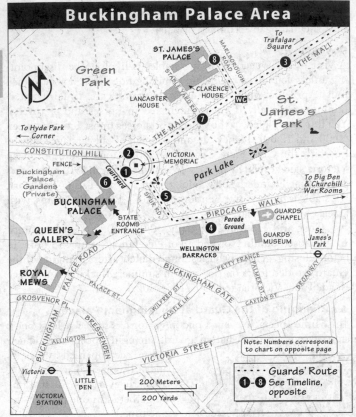

Green Park. Or hop into a big black taxi and say, "Buck House, please."

Tips: Download the official app for maps and background on the pageantry (www.rct.uk). The only public WC in the area is near St. James's Palace, just inside the gate to the park from Marlborough Road.

Viewing the Official Ceremony: The center of all this fanfare is the half-hour ceremony that takes place in the forecourt (between the palace and the fence) in front of Buckingham Palace. At 11:00 a batch of fresh guards meets the Old Guard in the courtyard, where the captain of the Old Guard hands over the keys. As the band plays, soldiers parade regimental flags (or "colours"), get counted and inspected—all with a lot of shouting—and finally exchange compliments before the tired guards return to Wellington Barracks, and a subset of the New Guard heads off to take over at St. James's Palace.

By the Palace Fence: If the actual changing of the Buckingham

Changing of the Guard Timeline

When	What
10:00	Tourists gather by the ❶ fence outside Buckingham Palace and the ❷ Victoria Memorial.
10:45	Cavalry guards, headed up ❸ The Mall back from their Green Park barracks, pass Buckingham Palace en route to the Horse Guards (except on Sundays).
10:57	❹ The New Guard, led by a band, marches in a short procession from Wellington Barracks down ❺ Spur Road to Buckingham Palace.
11:00	Guards converge around the Victoria Memorial before entering the ❻ fenced courtyard of Buckingham Palace for the main Changing of the Guard ceremony. (Meanwhile, farther away along Whitehall, the Horse Guard changes guard—except on Sundays, when it's at 10:00.)
11:10	Relief guards leave from Buckingham Palace along The Mall to Clarence House, via ❼ Stable Yard Road.
11:25	The remaining Old Guard leaves St. James's Palace for Buckingham Palace.
11:37	Cavalry guards, headed down The Mall back to their Green Park barracks from Horse Guards, pass Buckingham Palace.
11:40	The entire Old Guard, led by a band, leaves Buckingham Palace and heads up Spur Road for Wellington Barracks, while a detachment of the New Guard leaves Buckingham Palace to march up The Mall to take over at ❽ St. James's Palace (arriving around 11:45).

Palace guards is a must-see for you, show up at least an hour early to get a place front and center, next to the fence (shorter travelers should aim for two hours ahead in high season).

Near the Victoria Memorial: If you can't get a spot right by the gates, try the high ground on the circular Victoria Memorial, which can give you good (if more distant) views of the palace as well as the arriving and departing processions along The Mall and Spur Road. If grabbing an early spot, think about whether you'll still have a view once the crowds fill in—balustrades and other raised spots go quickly.

Following the Procession: If the main ceremony doesn't seem worth all the waiting and jostling, you can still enjoy plenty of fun fanfare—and the thrill of participating in the action—by planting yourself on the route of a string of processions that happen before, during, and after the official guard changing at Buckingham Palace.

To catch as much as possible, here's what I'd do:

Show up at St. James's Palace by 10:30 to see its soon-to-be-off-duty guards mobilizing in the courtyard (grab a spot just across Marlborough Road from the courtyard; people grouped on the palace side of the street will be asked to move when the inspection begins).

Just before they prepare to leave (at 10:43), march ahead of them down Marlborough Road to The Mall and pause at the corner to watch them parade past, possibly with a band, on their way to Buckingham Palace.

Then cut through the park and head to the Wellington Barracks—where a fresh batch of guards is undergoing inspection before they leave (at 10:57) for Buckingham Palace.

March along with the New Guard and their full military band, from the barracks to Buckingham Palace.

If it's too packed to see any of the action behind the palace gates, snap a few photos of the passing guards—and the crowds—before making your way back up The Mall, to where it meets Stable Yard Road, in time to watch several more processions: relief guards coming from Buckingham Palace at 11:10 for a switch of sentries at Clarence House (Prince Charles' official home), then other guards heading down The Mall *toward* Buckingham Palace at 11:25, and, at 11:37, a procession of cavalry guards en route from the Horse Guards to their barracks in Green Park.

Finally, at about 11:45, plant yourself back at the corner of The Mall and Marlborough Road for a great photo op as one last procession, the bulk of St. James's Palace New Guard, makes its way from Buckingham Palace to start its shift.

Join a Tour: Local tour companies such as **Fun London Tours** more or less follow the route above but add in history and facts about the guards, bands, and royal family to their already entertaining march. These walks add color and good value to what can otherwise seem like a stressful mess of tourists (£17, Changing of the Guard tour starts at Piccadilly Circus at 9:40, must book online in advance, www.funlondontours.com).

Sights in North London

▲▲▲British Museum

Simply put, this is the greatest chronicle of civilization...any-where. A visit here is like taking a long hike through *Encyclope-dia Britannica* National Park. The vast British Museum wraps around its Great Court (the huge entrance hall), with the

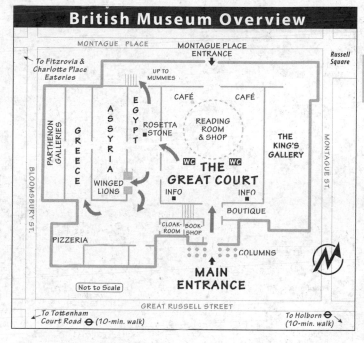

British Museum Overview

MONTAGUE PLACE

MONTAGUE PLACE ENTRANCE

Russell Square

To Fitzrovia & Charlotte Place Eateries

UP TO MUMMIES

CAFÉ   CAFÉ

PARTHENON GALLERIES

GREECE

ASSYRIA

EGYPT

ROSETTA STONE

READING ROOM & SHOP

THE KING'S GALLERY

BLOOMSBURY ST.

WINGED LIONS

WC   WC

THE GREAT COURT

INFO   INFO

BOUTIQUE

MONTAGUE ST.

PIZZERIA

CLOAK-ROOM   BOOK-SHOP

COLUMNS

Not to Scale

MAIN ENTRANCE

GREAT RUSSELL STREET

To Tottenham Court Road ⊖ (10-min. walk)

To Holborn ⊖ (10-min. walk)

LONDON

most popular sections filling the ground floor: Egyptian, Assyrian, and ancient Greek, with the famous frieze sculptures from the Parthenon in Athens. The museum's stately Reading Room—famous as the place where Karl Marx hung out while formulating his ideas on communism and writing *Das Kapital*—sometimes hosts special exhibits.

Cost and Hours: Free, £5 donation requested, special exhibits usually extra (and with timed ticket); daily 10:00-17:30, Fri until 20:30 (select galleries only), least crowded late on weekday afternoons, especially Fri; free guided tours offered, multimedia guide-£7; Great Russell Street, Tube: Tottenham Court Road, ticket desk tel. 020/7323-8181, www.britishmuseum.org.

Tours: Free 40-minute EyeOpener tours by volunteers focus on select rooms (daily 11:00-15:45, generally every 15 minutes). More in-depth 90-minute tours are offered Fri-Sun at 11:30 and 14:00. Ask about other specialty tours and lectures.

The £7 multimedia guide offers dial-up audio commentary and video on 200 objects, as well as several substantial and cerebral theme tours (must leave photo ID). There's also a fun family multimedia guide offering various themed routes.

🎧 Download my free British Museum audio tour.

Visiting the Museum: From the Great Court, doorways lead to all wings. To the left are the exhibits on Egypt, Assyria, and

LONDON

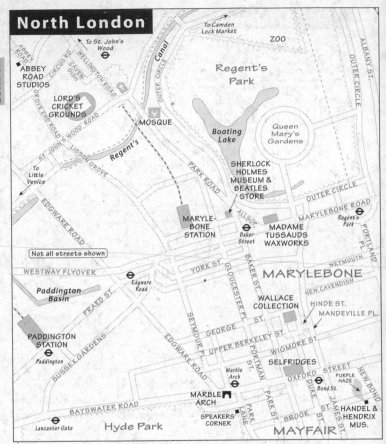

North London

To St. John's Wood

To Camden Lock Market

ZOO

Regent's Park

ABBEY ROAD STUDIOS

LORD'S CRICKET GROUNDS

MOSQUE

Regent's

To Little Venice

EDGWARE ROAD

Boating Lake

Queen Mary's Gardens

SHERLOCK HOLMES MUSEUM & BEATLES STORE

PARK ROAD

ALLSOP

OUTER CIRCLE

MARYLEBONE ROAD

Regent's Park

PORTLAND PL.

MARYLE-BONE STATION

Baker Street

MADAME TUSSAUDS WAXWORKS

Not all streets shown

WESTWAY FLYOVER

Paddington Basin

Edgware Road

PRAED ST.

PADDINGTON STATION

Paddington

SUSSEX GARDENS

BAYSWATER ROAD

Lancaster Gate

Hyde Park

YORK ST.

GLOUCESTER PL.

BAKER ST.

MARYLEBONE

WEYMOUTH

NEW CAVENDISH

WALLACE COLLECTION

HINDE ST.

MANDEVILLE PL.

SEYMOUR PL.

GEORGE ST.

UPPER BERKELEY ST.

WIGMORE ST.

PORTMAN ST.

SELFRIDGES

Marble Arch

OXFORD STREET

DUKE ST.

Bond St.

PURPLE HAZE

NEW BOND ST.

MARBLE ARCH

SPEAKERS' CORNER

PARK LANE

BROOK ST.

JAMES ST.

HANDEL & HENDRIX MUS.

MAYFAIR

EDGWARE ROAD

Greece—the highlights of your visit.

Egypt: Start with the Egyptian Gallery. Egypt was one of the world's first "civilizations"—a group of people with a government, religion, art, free time, and a written language. The Egypt we think of— pyramids, mummies, pharaohs,

and guys who walk funny—lasted from 3000 to 1000 BC with hardly any change in the government, religion, or arts.

The first thing you'll see in the Egypt section is the **Rosetta Stone.** When this rock was unearthed in the Egyptian desert in 1799, it was a sensation in Europe. This black slab, dating from 196 BC, caused a quantum leap in the study of ancient history.

LONDON

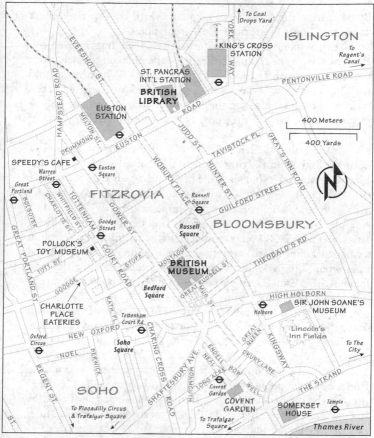

Finally, Egyptian writing could be decoded.

The hieroglyphic writing in the upper part of the stone was indecipherable for a thousand years. Did a picture of a bird mean "bird"? Or was it a sound, forming part of a larger word, like "burden"? As it turned out, hieroglyphics are a complex combination of the two, surprisingly more phonetic than symbolic. (For example, the hieroglyph that looks like a mouth or an eye is the letter "R.")

The Rosetta Stone allowed linguists to break the code. It contains a single inscription repeated in three languages. The bottom third is plain old Greek, while the middle is medieval Egyptian.

By comparing the two known languages with the one they didn't know, translators figured out the hieroglyphics.

Next, wander past the many **statues,** including a seven-ton Ramesses, with the traditional features of a pharaoh (goatee, cloth headdress, and cobra diadem on his forehead). When Moses told the king of Egypt, "Let my people go!" this was the stony-faced look he got. You'll also see the Egyptian gods as animals—these include Amun, king of the gods, as a ram, and Horus, the god of the living, as a falcon.

At the end of the hall, climb the stairs or take the elevator to **mummy** land. Mummifying a body is much like following a recipe. First, disembowel it (but leave the heart inside), then pack the cavities with pitch, and dry it with natron, a natural form of sodium carbonate (and, I believe, the active ingredient in Twinkies). Then carefully bandage it head to toe with hundreds of yards of linen strips. Let it sit 2,000 years, and...*voilà!* The mummy was placed in a wooden coffin, which was put in a stone coffin, which was placed in a tomb. (The pyramids were supersized tombs for the rich and famous.) The result is that we now have Egyptian bodies that are as well preserved as Larry King.

Many of the mummies here are from the time of the Roman occupation, when fine memorial portraits painted in wax became popular. X-ray photos in the display cases tell us more about these people.

Don't miss the animal mummies. Cats (near the entrance to Room 62) were popular pets. They were also considered incarnations of the cat-headed goddess Bastet. Worshipped in life as the sun god's allies, preserved in death, and memorialized with statues, cats were given the adulation they've come to expect ever since.

Assyria: Long before Saddam Hussein, Iraq was home to other palace-building, iron-fisted rulers—the Assyrians. They conquered their southern neighbors and dominated the Middle East for 300 years (c. 900-600 BC).

Their strength came from a superb army (chariots, mounted cavalry, and siege engines), a policy of terrorism against enemies ("I tied their heads to tree trunks all around the city," reads a royal inscription), ethnic cleansing and mass deportations of the vanquished, and efficient administration (roads and express postal service). They have been called the "Romans of the East."

The British Museum's valuable collection of Assyrian artifacts has become even more priceless since the recent destruction of ancient sites in the Middle East by ISIS terrorists.

Two human-headed winged stone lions guarded an Assyrian palace (11th-8th century BC). With the strength of a lion, the wings of an eagle, the brain of a man, and the beard of an ancient hipster, they protected the king from evil spirits and scared the

heck out of foreign ambassadors and
left-wing newspaper reporters. (What
has five legs and flies? Take a close
look. These winged quintupeds, which
appear complete from both the front
and the side, could guard both directions at once.)

Carved into the stone between the
bearded lions' loins, you can see one of
civilization's most impressive achievements—writing. This wedge-shaped
(cuneiform) script is the world's first
written language, invented 5,000
years ago by the Sumerians (of south-
ern Iraq) and passed down to their less-civilized descendants, the
Assyrians.

The **Nimrud Gallery** is a mini version of the throne room and
royal apartments of King Ashurnasirpal II's Northwest Palace at
Nimrud (9th century BC). It's filled with royal propaganda reliefs,
30-ton marble bulls, and panels depicting wounded lions (lion-
hunting was Assyria's sport of kings).

Greece: The history of ancient Greece (600 BC-AD 1) could
be subtitled "making order out of chaos." While Assyria was dominating the Middle East, "Greece"—a gaggle of warring tribes
roaming the Greek peninsula—was floundering in darkness. But
by about 700 BC, these tribes began settling down, experimenting
with democracy, forming self-governing city-states, and making
ties with other city-states.

During its Golden Age (500-430 BC), Greece set the tone for
all of Western civilization to follow. Democracy, theater, literature,
mathematics, philosophy, science, gyros, art, and architecture as
we know them, were virtually all invented by a single generation of
Greeks in a small town of maybe 80,000 citizens.

Your walk through Greek history starts with pottery—from
the earliest, with geometric patterns (8th century BC), to painted
black silhouettes on the natural orange clay, and then a few crudely
done red human figures on black backgrounds. Later, find a vase
painted with frisky figures **(Wine Cooler Signed by Douris as
Painter),** which shows a culture really into partying, as well as an
evolution into more realistic and three-dimensional figures.

The highlight is the **Parthenon Sculptures**—taken from the
temple dedicated to Athena, the crowning glory of an enormous
urban-renewal plan during Greece's Golden Age.

While the building itself remains in Athens, many of the Parthenon's best sculptures are right here in the British Museum—the
so-called Elgin Marbles, named for the shrewd British ambassador

who had his men hammer, chisel, and saw them off the Parthenon in the early 1800s.

These much-wrangled-over bits of the Parthenon (from about 450 BC) are indeed impressive. The marble panels you see lining the walls of this large hall are part of the frieze that originally ran around the exterior of the Parthenon, under the eaves. The statues at either end of the hall once filled the Parthenon's triangular-shaped pediments and showed the birth of Athena. The relief panels known as metopes tell the story of the struggle between the forces of human civilization and animal-like barbarism.

Rest of the Museum: Be sure to venture upstairs to see artifacts from Roman Britain that surpass anything you'll see at Hadrian's Wall or elsewhere in the country. Also look for the Sutton Hoo Ship Burial artifacts from a seventh-century royal burial on the east coast of England (Room 41). A rare Michelangelo cartoon (preliminary sketch) is in Room 90 (level 4).

▲Sir John Soane's Museum

Architects love this quirky place, as do fans of interior decor, eclectic knickknacks, and Back Door sights. Tour this furnished home on a bird-chirping square and see 19th-century chairs, lamps, wood-paneled nooks and crannies, sculptures, and stained-glass skylights just as they were when the owner lived here. As professor of architecture at the Royal Academy, Soane created his home to be a place of learning, cramming it floor to ceiling with ancient relics, curios, and famous paintings, including several excellent Canalettos and Hogarth's series on *The Rake's Progress* (which is hidden behind a panel in the Picture Room and opened randomly at the museum's discretion, usually twice an hour). Soane even purchased the Egyptian sarcophagus of King Seti I (Ramesses II's fa-

ther, on display in the basement) after the British Museum turned it down—at the time, they couldn't afford the £2,000 sticker price.

In 1833, just before his death, Soane established his house as a museum, stipulating that it be kept as nearly as possible in the state he left it. If he visited today, he'd be entirely satisfied by the diligence with which the staff safeguards his treasures. You'll leave wishing you'd known the man.

Cost and Hours: Free, but donations much appreciated; Wed-Sun 10:00-17:00, closed Mon-Tue; often long entry lines (especially Sat), knowledgeable volunteers in most rooms, guidebook-£5; free 30-minute tour of private apartment at 13:15 and 14:00, £15 one-hour highlights tour must be booked ahead online and runs Thu-Sun at 12:00 plus Sat-Sun at 11:00; 13 Lincoln's Inn Fields, quarter-mile southeast of British Museum, Tube: Holborn, tel. 020/7405-2107, www.soane.org.

▲▲▲British Library

Here, in just two rooms, are the literary treasures of Western civilization, from early Bibles to Shakespeare's *Hamlet* to Lewis Carroll's *Alice's Adventures in Wonderland* to the *Magna Carta*. The British Empire built its greatest monuments out of paper; it's through literature that England made her most lasting and significant contribution to civilization and the arts.

Cost and Hours: Free, £5 suggested donation, admission charged for special exhibits; Mon-Thu 9:30-20:00, Fri until 18:00, Sat until 17:00, Sun 11:00-17:00; 96 Euston Road, Tube: King's Cross St. Pancras or Euston, tel. 019/3754-6060, info tel. 020/7412-7676, www.bl.uk.

Tours: There are no guided tours or audioguides for the permanent collection. There are, however, guided tours of the building itself—the archives and reading rooms (for details, call 019/3754-6546 or see the website). Touch-screen computers in the permanent collection let you page virtually through some of the rare books. ∩ Download my free British Library audio tour.

Visiting the Library: Entering the library courtyard, you'll see a big statue of a naked Isaac Newton bending forward with a compass to measure the universe. The statue symbolizes the library's purpose: to gather all knowledge and promote humanity's endless search for truth.

Stepping inside, you'll find in the middle of the building a 50-foot-tall wall of 65,000 books teasingly exposing its shelves. In 1823 King George III gifted his collection to the people under the condition the books remain on display for all to see. The high-tech bookshelf—with moveable lifts to reach the highest titles—sits behind glass, inaccessible to commoners but ever-visible. Likewise, the reading rooms upstairs are not open to the public.

Everything that matters for your visit is in a tiny but exciting area variously called "The Sir John Ritblat Gallery," "Treasures of the British Library," or just "The Treasures." We'll concentrate on a handful of documents— literary and historical—that changed the course of history. Note that exhibits change often, and many of

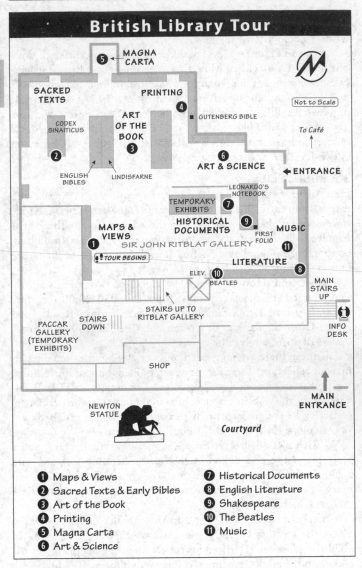

British Library Tour

5 → MAGNA CARTA

SACRED TEXTS

PRINTING

4

Not to Scale

CODEX SINAITICUS

ART OF THE BOOK 3

■ GUTENBERG BIBLE

To Café

2

6

ENGLISH BIBLES   LINDISFARNE

ART & SCIENCE

← ENTRANCE

LEONARDO'S NOTEBOOK

TEMPORARY EXHIBITS   7

MAPS & VIEWS

HISTORICAL DOCUMENTS   9

MUSIC

1   FIRST FOLIO

11

■ TOUR BEGINS   SIR JOHN RITBLAT GALLERY

LITERATURE   8

ELEV. 10

BEATLES

MAIN STAIRS UP

STAIRS DOWN

STAIRS UP TO RITBLAT GALLERY

i

INFO DESK

PACCAR GALLERY (TEMPORARY EXHIBITS)

SHOP

MAIN ENTRANCE

NEWTON STATUE

Courtyard

1 Maps & Views
2 Sacred Texts & Early Bibles
3 Art of the Book
4 Printing
5 Magna Carta
6 Art & Science

7 Historical Documents
8 English Literature
9 Shakespeare
10 The Beatles
11 Music

the museum's old, fragile manuscripts need to "rest" periodically in order to stay well-preserved. Upon entering the Ritblat Gallery, start at the far side of the room with the display case showing historic **1 maps and views,** illustrating humans' shifting perspective of the world. Next, move into the area dedicated to **2 sacred texts and early Bibles,** including the Codex Sinaiticus (or the Codex Alexandrinus that may be on display instead). This bound book from around AD 350 is one of the oldest complete Bibles in existence—

one of the first attempts to collect various books by different authors into one authoritative anthology.

In the display cases called ❸ **Art of the Book,** you'll find various medieval-era books, some beautifully illustrated or "illuminated." The lettering is immaculate, but all are penned by hand. The most magnificent of these medieval British "monk-uscripts" is the **Lindisfarne Gospels,** from AD 698. The text is in Latin, the language of scholars ever since the Roman Empire, but you can read an electronic copy of these manuscripts by using one of the touch-screen computers scattered around the room.

In the glass cases featuring early ❹ **printing,** you'll see the Gutenberg Bible—the first book printed in Europe using movable type (c. 1455). Suddenly, the Bible was available for anyone to read, fueling the Protestant Reformation.

Through a doorway is a small room with the ❺ **Magna Carta.** Though historians talk about *the* Magna Carta, several different versions of the document exist, some of which are kept in this room. The basis for England's constitutional system of government, this "Great Charter" listing rules about mundane administrative issues was radical because of the simple fact that the king had agreed to abide by them as law. Until then, kings had ruled by God-given authority, above the laws of men. Now, for the first time, there were limits—in writing—on how a king could treat his subjects.

Return to the main room to find display cases featuring trailblazing ❻ **art and science** documents by early scientists such as Galileo, Isaac Newton, and many more. Pages from Leonardo da Vinci's notebook show his powerful curiosity, his genius for invention, and his famous backward and inside-out handwriting. Nearby are many more ❼ **historical documents.** You may see letters by Henry VIII, Queen Elizabeth I, Darwin, Freud, Gandhi, and others.

Next, trace the evolution of ❽ **English literature.** Check out the AD 1000 manuscript of Beowulf, the first English literary masterpiece, and *The Canterbury Tales* (c. 1410), Geoffrey Chaucer's bawdy collection of stories. This display is often a greatest-hits sampling of literature in English, from Brontë to Kipling to Woolf to Joyce to Dickens. The most famous of England's writers— ❾ **Shakespeare**—generally gets his own display case. Look for the First Folio—one of the 750 copies of 36 of the 37 known Shakespeare plays, published in 1623. If the First Folio is not out for viewing, the library should have other Shakespeare items on display.

Now fast-forward a few centuries to ❿ **The Beatles.** Look for photos of John Lennon, Paul McCartney, George Harrison, and Ringo Starr. Among the displays, you may find manuscripts of song lyrics written by Lennon and McCartney. In the ⓫ **music** section, there are manuscripts by Mozart, Beethoven, Chopin, and others (kind of an anticlimax after the Fab Four, I know). George Frideric Handel's famous oratorio, the *Messiah* (1741), is often on display and marks the end of our tour. Hallelujah.

▲Wallace Collection

Sir Richard Wallace's fine collection of 17th-century Dutch Masters, 18th-century French Rococo, medieval armor, and assorted

aristocratic fancies fills the sumptuously furnished Hertford House on Manchester Square. From the rough and intimate Dutch lifescapes of Jan Steen to the pink-cheeked Rococo fantasies of François Boucher, a wander through this little-visited mansion makes you nostalgic for the days of the empire. This col-

lection would be a big deal in a midsize city, but here in London it gets pleasantly lost. Because this is a "closed collection" (nothing new is acquired and nothing permanent goes on loan), it feels more like visiting a classic English manor estate than a museum. It's thoroughly enjoyable.

Cost and Hours: Free, £5 suggested donation, daily 10:00-17:00, audioguide-£4, just north of Oxford Street on Manchester Square, Tube: Bond Street, tel. 020/7563-9500, www.wallacecollection.org.

▲Madame Tussauds Waxworks

This waxtravaganza is gimmicky, crass, and crazy expensive, but dang fun...a hit with the kind of tourists who skip the British Mu-

seum. The original Madame Tussaud did wax casts of heads lopped off during the French Revolution (such as Marie-Antoinette's). She took her show on the road and ended up in London in 1835. Now it's all about singing with Lady Gaga, and partying with The Beatles. In addition to posing with all the

eerily realistic wax dummies—from the Queen and Will and Kate to the Beckhams—you'll have the chance to learn how they created this waxy army; hop on a people-mover and cruise through a kid-pleasing "Spirit of London" time trip; and visit with Marvel superheroes. A nine-minute "4-D" show features a 3-D movie heightened by wind, "back ticklers," and other special effects.

LONDON

Beatles Sights

London's city center is surprisingly devoid of sights associated with the famous '60s rock band. To see much of anything, consider taking a guided walk (see page 55).

For a photo op, go to Abbey Road and walk the famous crosswalk pictured on the *Abbey Road* album cover (northwest of Regent's Park, Tube: St. John's Wood, get information and buy Beatles memorabilia at the small kiosk in the station). From the Tube station, it's a five-minute walk west down Grove End Road to the intersection with Abbey Road. The Abbey Road recording studio is the low-key white building to the right of Abbey House (it's still a working studio, so you can't go inside). Ponder the graffiti on the low wall outside, and...imagine. To re-create the famous cover photo, shoot the crosswalk from the roundabout as you face north up Abbey Road. Shoes are optional.

Nearby is **Paul McCartney's current home** (7 Cavendish Avenue): Continue down Grove End Road, turn left on Circus Road, and then right on Cavendish. Please be discreet.

The **Beatles Store** is at 231 Baker Street (Tube: Baker Street). It's small—some Beatles-logo T-shirts, mugs, pins, and old vinyl like you might have in your closet—and has nothing of historic value (open eight days a week, 10:00-18:30, tel. 020/7935-4464, www.beatlesstorelondon.co.uk; another rock memorabilia store is across the street).

Cost and Hours: £35, kids £30 (free for kids under 3), up to 25 percent cheaper online; combo-deal with the London Eye. Very flexible hours (check online), but roughly July-Aug and school holidays daily 8:30-18:00, Sept-June Mon-Fri 10:00-16:00, Sat-Sun 9:00-17:00, these are last entry times—it stays open roughly two hours later; Marylebone Road, Tube: Baker Street, tel. 0871-894-3000, www.madametussauds.com.

Crowd-Beating Tips: The ticket-buying line can be an hour or more (believe the posted signs about the wait). To avoid the ticket line, book a Priority Entrance ticket and reserve a time slot at least a day in advance. Or, pay royally for a Fast Track ticket in advance (available from souvenir stands and shops or at the TI), which gives you access to a dedicated entrance with shorter lines. The place is less crowded (for both buying tickets at the door and for simply enjoying the place) if you arrive after 15:00.

Sherlock Holmes Museum

Around the corner from Madame Tussauds, this meticulous re-creation of the (fictional) apartment of the (fictional) detective sits at the (real) address of 221b Baker Street. 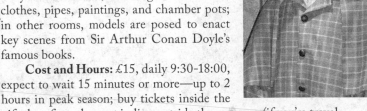 The first-floor replica (so to speak) of Sherlock's study delights fans with the opportunity to play Holmes and Watson while sitting in authentic 18th-century chairs. The second and third floors offer fine exhibits on daily Victorian life, showing off furniture, clothes, pipes, paintings, and chamber pots; in other rooms, models are posed to enact key scenes from Sir Arthur Conan Doyle's famous books.

Cost and Hours: £15, daily 9:30-18:00, expect to wait 15 minutes or more—up to 2 hours in peak season; buy tickets inside the gift shop first, then get in line outside the museum (if you're traveling with a partner, send one person in to buy tickets while the other waits in the entrance line); large gift shop for Holmes connoisseurs, including souvenirs from the BBC-TV series; Tube: Baker Street, tel. 020/7935-8866, www.sherlock-holmes.co.uk.

Nearby: Fans of BBC-TV's *Sherlock* series starring Benedict Cumberbatch—which this museum doesn't cover—may want to grab a bite or snap a photo at Speedy's Café, the filming location for the show's 221b exterior (located near Euston Station at 187 North Gower Street, Tube: Euston Square).

Sights in The City

When Londoners say "The City," they mean the one-square-mile business center in East London that 2,000 years ago was Roman Londinium. The outline of the Roman city walls can still be seen in the arc of roads from Blackfriars Bridge to Tower Bridge. Within The City are 23 churches designed by Sir Christopher Wren, mostly just ornamentation around St. Paul's Cathedral. Today, while home to only 10,000 residents, The City thrives with around 400,000 office workers coming and going daily. It's a fascinating district to wander on weekdays, but since almost nobody actually lives there, it's dull in the evening and on Saturday and Sunday.

You can 🎧 download my free audio tour of The City, which peels back the many layers of history in this oldest part of London.

▲▲▲St. Paul's Cathedral

Wren's most famous church is the great St. Paul's, its elaborate interior capped by a 365-foot dome. Since World War II, St. Paul's

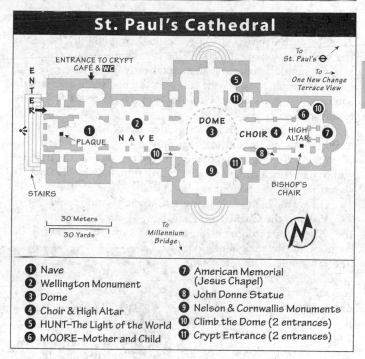

St. Paul's Cathedral

ENTRANCE TO CRYPT
CAFÉ & **WC**

ENTER

To
St. Paul's ⊖

To →
One New Change
Terrace View

5
11

6 **10**

DOME
3

1
PLAQUE **2** N A V E

CHOIR **4** HIGH
ALTAR **7**

10

8

9 **11**

BISHOP'S
CHAIR

STAIRS

30 Meters
30 Yards

To
Millennium
Bridge

- **1** Nave
- **2** Wellington Monument
- **3** Dome
- **4** Choir & High Altar
- **5** HUNT–The Light of the World
- **6** MOORE–Mother and Child
- **7** American Memorial (Jesus Chapel)
- **8** John Donne Statue
- **9** Nelson & Cornwallis Monuments
- **10** Climb the Dome (2 entrances)
- **11** Crypt Entrance (2 entrances)

has been Britain's symbol of resilience. Despite 57 nights of bombing, the Nazis failed to destroy the cathedral, thanks to St. Paul's volunteer fire watchmen, who stayed on the dome. Today you can climb the dome for a great city view. The crypt (included with admission) is a world of historic bones and memorials, including Admiral Nelson's tomb and interesting cathedral models.

Cost and Hours: £20, cheaper online, includes church entry, dome climb, crypt, tour, and audioguide; Mon-Sat 8:30-16:30 (dome opens at 9:30), closed Sun except for worship; Tube: St. Paul's, tel. 020/7246-8350, www.stpauls.co.uk.

Avoiding Lines: Purchasing online tickets in advance saves a little time (and a little money); otherwise the wait can be 15-45 minutes in summer and on weekends. To avoid crowds in general, arrive first thing in the morning.

Music and Church Services: Worship times are available on the church's website. Communion is generally Mon-Sat at 8:00

and 12:30. On Sunday, services are held at 8:00, 10:15 (Matins), 11:30 (sung Eucharist), 15:15 (evensong), and 18:00. The rest of the week, evensong is at 17:00 (Mon evensong is occasionally spoken, not sung). If you come 20 minutes early for evensong worship (under the dome), you may be able to grab a big wooden stall in the choir, next to the singers. On some Sundays, there's a free organ recital at 16:45.

Tours: There are 1.5-hour **guided tours** Mon-Sat at 10:00, 11:00, 13:00, and 14:00 (call to confirm or ask at church). Free 30-minute **"highlights" tours** are offered throughout the day. The **audioguide** (included with admission) contains video clips that show the church in action.

⌒ Download my free St. Paul's Cathedral **audio tour.**

Visiting the Cathedral: Even now, as skyscrapers encroach, the 365-foot-high dome of St. Paul's rises majestically above the rooftops of the neighborhood.

The tall dome is set on classical columns, capped with a lantern, topped by a six-foot ball, and iced with a cross. As the first Anglican cathedral built in London after the Reformation, it is Baroque: St. Peter's in Rome filtered through clear-eyed English reason. Though often the site of historic funerals (Queen Victoria and Winston Churchill), St. Paul's most famous ceremony was a wedding—when Prince Charles married Lady Diana Spencer in 1981.

Start at the far back of the ❶ **nave,** behind the font. This big church feels big. At 515 feet long and 250 feet wide, it's Europe's fourth largest, after those in Rome (St. Peter's), Sevilla, and Milan. The spaciousness is accentuated by the relative lack of decoration. The simple, cream-colored ceiling and the clear glass in the windows light everything evenly. Wren wanted this: a simple, open church with nothing to hide. Unfortunately, only this entrance area keeps his original vision—the rest was encrusted with 19th-century Victorian ornamentation.

Ahead and on the left is the towering, black-and-white ❷ **Wellington Monument.** Wren would have been appalled, but his church has become so central to England's soul that many national heroes are buried here (in the basement crypt). General Wellington, Napoleon's conqueror at Waterloo (1815) and the embodiment of British stiff-upper-lippedness, was honored here in a funeral packed with 13,000 fans.

The ❸ **dome** you see from here, painted with scenes from the life of St. Paul, is only the innermost of three. From the painted interior of the first dome, look up through the opening to see the light-filled lantern of the second dome. Finally, the whole thing is covered on the outside by the third and final dome, the shell of lead-covered wood that you see from the street. Wren's ingenious three-in-one design was psychological as well as functional—he wanted a low, shallow inner dome so worshippers wouldn't feel diminished.

The ❹ **choir** area blocks your way, but you can see the altar at the far end under a golden canopy. Do a quick clockwise spin around the church. In the north transept (to your left as you face the altar), find the big painting ❺ *The Light of the World* (1904), by the Pre-Raphaelite William Holman Hunt. Inspired by Hunt's own experience of finding Christ during a moment of spiritual crisis, the crowd-pleasing work was criticized by art highbrows for being "syrupy" and "simple"—even as it became the most famous painting in Victorian England.

Along the left side of the choir is the statue ❻ *Mother and Child* (1983), by the great modern sculptor Henry Moore. Typical of Moore's work, this Mary and Baby Jesus—inspired by the sight of British moms nursing babies in WWII bomb shelters—renders a traditional subject in an abstract, minimalist way.

The area behind the main altar, with three stained-glass windows, is the ❼ **American Memorial Chapel,** honoring the Americans who sacrificed their lives to save Britain in World War II. In brightly colored panes that arch around the big windows, spot the American eagle (center window, to the left of Christ), George Washington (right window, upper-right corner), and symbols of all 50 states (find your state seal). The Roll of Honor, a 500-page book under glass (immediately behind the altar), lists the names of 28,000 US servicemen and women based in Britain who gave their lives during the war.

Around the other side of the choir is a shrouded statue honoring ❽ **John Donne** (1573-1631), a passionate preacher in old St. Paul's, as well as a great poet ("never wonder for whom the bell tolls—it tolls for thee.") In the south transept are monuments to military greats ❾ **Horatio Nelson**, who fought Napoleon, and **Charles Cornwallis,** who was finished off by George Washington at Yorktown.

Climb the Dome: The 528-step climb is worthwhile, and each level (or gallery) offers something different. First you get to the Whispering Gallery (257 shallow steps, with views of the church interior). Whisper sweet nothings into the wall, and your partner (and anyone else) standing far away can hear you. For best effects, try whispering (not talking) with your mouth close to the wall, while your partner stands a few dozen yards away with his or her ear to the wall.

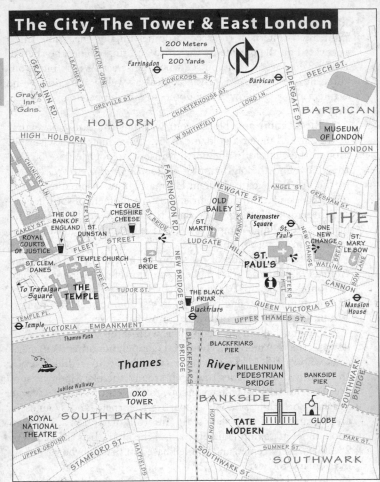

The City, The Tower & East London

After another set of (steeper, narrower) stairs, you're at the **Stone Gallery,** with views of London. Finally, a long, tight metal staircase takes you to the very top of the cupola, the **Golden Gallery,** with stunning, unobstructed views of the city. Looking west, you'll see the London Eye, and you might be able to make out the towers of Westminster Abbey. To the south, across the Thames, is the rectangular smokestack of the Tate Modern, with Shakespeare's Globe nestled nearby. To the east sprouts a glassy garden of skyscrapers, including the 600-foot-tall, black-topped Tower 42, the bullet-shaped 30 St. Mary Axe building (nicknamed "The Gherkin"), and two more buildings easily ID'd by their nicknames—"The Cheese Grater" and "The Walkie-Talkie." Farther

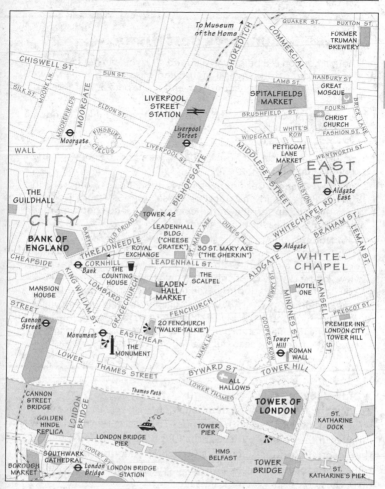

in the distance, the cluster of skyscrapers marks Canary Wharf. Just north of that was the site of the 2012 Olympic Games, now a pleasant park.

Crypt: The crypt is a world of historic bones and interesting cathedral models. Many legends are buried here—Horatio Nelson, who wore down Napoleon; the Duke of Wellington, who finished off Napoleon; and even Wren himself. Wren's actual tomb is marked by a simple black slab with no statue, though he considered this church to be his legacy. Back up in the nave, on the floor directly under the dome, is Christopher Wren's name and epitaph (written in Latin): "Reader, if you seek his monument, look around you."

London's Best Views

Though London is a height-challenged city, you can get lofty perspectives on it from several high-flying places. For some viewpoints, you need to pay admission, and at the bars or restaurants, you'll need to buy a drink.

London Eye: Ride the giant Ferris wheel for stunning London views. See page 119.

St. Paul's Dome: You'll earn a striking, unobstructed view by climbing hundreds of steps to the cramped balcony of the church's cupola. See page 107.

One New Change: Get fine, free views of St. Paul's Cathedral and surroundings—nearly as good as those from St. Paul's Dome—from the rooftop terrace of the One New Change shopping mall just behind and east of the church.

Tate Modern: One of the best, easiest, and cheapest views (free) is to head to the Tate Modern's annex—the Blavatnik Building—and ride the elevator to floor 10, where you'll enjoy sweeping views of the skyline (plus the Tate's own tower in the foreground). You can also ride to floor 6 of the main building. See page 122.

20 Fenchurch (a.k.a. "The Walkie-Talkie"): Get 360-degree views of London from the mostly enclosed Sky Garden, complete with a thoughtfully planned urban garden, bar, restaurants, and lots of locals. It's free to access but you'll need to make reservations in

▲Old Bailey

To view the British legal system in action—lawyers in little blond wigs speaking legalese with an upper-crust accent—spend a few minutes in the visitors' gallery at the Old Bailey courthouse, called the "Central Criminal Court." Don't enter under the dome; continue up the block about halfway to the modern part of the building—the entry is at Warwick Passage.

Cost and Hours: Free, generally Mon-Fri 10:00-13:00 & 14:00-17:00 depending on caseload, last entry at 12:40 and 15:40 but often closes an hour or so earlier, closed Sat-Sun, fewer cases in Aug; no kids under 14; 2 blocks northwest of St. Paul's on Old Bailey Street (down a tunnel called Warwick Passage, follow signs to public entrance), Tube: St. Paul's, tel. 020/7248-3277 www.cityoflondon.gov.uk.

Bag Check: Old Bailey has a strictly enforced policy of no bags, mobile phones, cameras, computers, or food. Small purses are OK (but no phones or cameras inside). You can check bags at many nearby businesses, including the Capable Travel agency just down the street at 4 Old Bailey (£5/bag).

advance and bring photo ID (Mon-Fri 10:00-18:00, Sat-Sun 11:00-21:00, 20 Fenchurch Street, Tube: Monument, https://skygarden.london/sky-garden). If you can't get a reservation, try arriving before 10:00 (or 11:00 on weekends) and ask to go up. Once in, you can stay as long as you like.

National Portrait Gallery: A mod top-floor restaurant peers over Trafalgar Square and the Westminster neighborhood. See page 83.

Waterstones Bookstore: Its hip, low-key, top-floor café/bar has reasonable prices and sweeping views of the London Eye, Big Ben, and the Houses of Parliament (see page 41, on Sun bar closes one hour before bookstore, www.5thview.co.uk).

The Shard: The observation decks that cap this 1,020-foot-tall skyscraper offer London's most commanding views, but at an outrageously high price. See page 125.

Primrose Hill: For dramatic 360-degree city views, head to the huge grassy expanse at the summit of Primrose Hill, just north of Regent's Park (off Prince Albert Road, Tube: Chalk Farm or Camden Town, www.royalparks.org.uk/parks/the-regents-park).

The Thames River: Various companies run boat trips on the Thames, offering a unique vantage point and unobstructed, ever-changing views of great landmarks (see page 57).

The Guildhall

Hiding out in The City, the Guildhall offers visitors a grand medieval hall and a delightful painting gallery for free (Mon-Sat 10:00-17:00, Sun 12:00-16:00). This served as the meeting spot for guilds in medieval times, and still hosts about 100 professional associations today. The **Guildhall Art Gallery** gives insight into old London society with mostly Victorian paintings.

▲Museum of London

This regular stop for local school kids gives the best overview of London history in town. Scale models and costumes help you visualize everyday life in the city through history—from Neanderthals, to Romans, to Elizabethans, to Victorians, to Mods, to today. The displays are chronological, spacious, and informative without being overwhelming, with enough whiz-bang multimedia displays (including the Plague and the Great Fire) to spice up otherwise humdrum artifacts.

   Cost and Hours: Free, daily 10:00-18:00, last entry one hour before closing, see the day's events board for special talks and tours, café, lockers, 150 London Wall at Aldersgate Street, Tube:

Barbican or St. Paul's plus a 5-minute walk, tel. 020/7001-9844, www.museumoflondon.org.uk.

▲▲▲Tower of London

The Tower has served as a castle in wartime, a king's residence in peacetime, and, most notoriously, as the prison and execution site of rebels. You can see the crown jewels, take a witty Beefeater tour, and ponder the executioner's block that dispensed with troublesome heirs to the throne and a couple of Henry VIII's wives.

Cost and Hours: £30.30, cheaper online, family ticket available; Tue-Sat 9:00-17:30, Sun-Mon from 10:00; Nov-Feb closes one hour earlier; free Beefeater tours available, skippable audioguide-£5, Tube: Tower Hill, tel. 0844-482-7788, www.hrp.org.uk.

Advance Tickets: To avoid the long ticket-buying lines, and save a few pounds off the gate price, buy tickets in advance for a specific day on the Tower website (print at home or collect on-site at group ticket office—see map on next page).

Alternatively, you can buy a voucher on your way to the Tower at the Trader's Gate gift shop, located down the steps from the Tower Hill Tube stop (look for the blue awning down in the stairway, between the Tube station and the busy street). The voucher is good any day and can be exchanged for a ticket at the group ticket office.

Visiting the Tower: Even an army the size of the ticket line couldn't storm this castle. The ❶ **entrance gate** where you'll show your ticket was just part of two concentric rings of complete defenses. As you enter, consult the daily event schedule, and consider catching a Beefeater tour.

When you're all set, go 50 yards straight ahead to the ❷ **traitors' gate.** This was the boat entrance to the Tower from the Thames. Princess Elizabeth, who was a prisoner here before she became Queen Elizabeth I, was carried down the Thames and through this gate on a barge, thinking about her mom, Anne Boleyn, who had been decapitated inside just a few years earlier. Many English leaders who fell from grace entered through here—Elizabeth was one of the lucky few to walk out.

Turn left to pass underneath the archway into the inner courtyard. The big, white tower in the middle is the ❸ **White Tower,** the original structure that gave this castle complex its name. William the Conqueror built it more than 950 years ago to put 15 feet of stone between himself and those he conquered. Over the centu-

Tower of London

50 Meters
50 Yards

To East End

DLR Gateway Tower

Tower Hill

ROMAN WALL

To The City

Trinity House Gardens

TRADER'S GATE SHOP Ⓔ

To Tower Bridge via road

BYWARD STREET

TOWER HILL

PEDESTRIAN WALKWAY

ALL HALLOWS-BY-THE-TOWER

EAT CAFÉ

GLOUCESTER COURT

TICKET KIOSKS

DRY MOAT

N

WC

PETTY WALES

GROUP TICKETS

Plaza

DRY MOAT

WC

Ⓐ

Ⓒ

TOWER WELCOME CENTRE

⓪

ⓧ

WHITE TOWER

Ⓒ

LOWER THAMES ST.

ENTER

❽

❼

❸

Ⓓ

BEEFEATER TOURS

TOWER GREEN

❻

TOWER SHOP

❶

❹

❾

Ⓑ

MOAT

❶❶

❿

⓬

❷

WC

TOWER PIER

EXIT

MOAT

VIEW OF TOWER BRIDGE

To St. Katharine's Pier

Thames River

TOWER BRIDGE

Main Sights

❶ Entrance Gate
❷ Traitors' Gate
❸ White Tower
❹ White Tower Museum
❺ Crown Jewels
❻ Tower Green
❼ Scaffold Site
❽ Beauchamp Tower
❾ Bloody Tower
❿ Medieval Palace
⓫ Walk the Wall (2)
⓬ Ravens

Other

Ⓐ Chapel Royal of St. Peter ad Vincula
Ⓑ Salt Tower
Ⓒ Fusilier Museum
Ⓓ Café
Ⓔ Trader's Gate Gift Shop (Tower Ticket Vouchers)

ries, the other walls and towers were built around it. Standing high above the rest of old London, the White Tower provided a gleaming reminder of the monarchy's absolute power over its subjects. If you made the wrong move here, you could be feasting on roast boar in the Banqueting Hall one night and chained to the walls of the prison the next. Torture ranged from stretching on the rack to the full monty: hanging by the neck until nearly dead, then "drawing"

Henry VIII (1491-1547)

The notorious king who single-handedly transformed England was a true Renaissance Man—six feet tall, handsome, charismatic, well-educated, and brilliant. He spoke English, Latin, French, and Spanish. A legendary athlete, he hunted, played tennis, and jousted with knights and kings. He played the lute and wrote folk songs; his "Pastime with Good Company" is still being performed. When 17-year-old Henry, the second monarch of the House of Tudor, was crowned king in Westminster Abbey, all of England rejoiced.

Henry left affairs of state in the hands of others, and filled his days with sports, war, dice, women, and the arts. But in 1529, Henry's personal life became a political atom bomb, and it changed the course of history. Henry wanted a divorce, partly because his wife had become too old to bear him a son, and partly because he'd fallen in love with Anne Boleyn, a younger woman who stubbornly refused to be just the king's mistress. Henry begged the pope for an annulment, but—for political reasons, not moral ones—the pope refused. Henry went ahead and divorced his wife anyway, and he was excommunicated.

The event sparked the English Reformation. With his defiance, Henry rejected papal authority in England. He forced monasteries to close, sold off some church land, and confiscated everything else for himself and the Crown. Within a decade, monastic institutions that had operated for centuries were left empty and gutted (many ruined sites can be visited today, including the abbeys of Glastonbury, St. Mary's at York, Rievaulx, and Lindisfarne). Meanwhile, the Catholic Church was reorganized into the (Anglican) Church of England, with Henry as its head. Though Henry himself basically adhered to Catholic doctrine, he discouraged the veneration of saints and relics, and commissioned an English translation of the Bible. Hard-core Catholics had to assume a low profile. Many English welcomed this break from Italian religious influence, but others rebelled. For the next few generations, England would suffer through bitter Catholic-Protestant differences.

Henry famously had six wives. The issue was not his love life (which could have been satisfied by his numerous mistresses), but the politics of royal succession. To guarantee the Tudor family's dominance, he needed a male heir born by a recognized queen.

Henry's first marriage, to Catherine of Aragon, had been arranged to cement an alliance with her parents, Ferdinand and

Isabel of Spain. Catherine bore Henry a daughter, but no sons. Next came Anne Boleyn, who also gave birth to a daughter. After a turbulent few years with Anne and several miscarriages, a frustrated Henry had her beheaded at the Tower of London. His next wife, Jane Seymour, finally had a son (but Jane died soon after giving birth). A blind marriage with Anne of Cleves ended quickly when she proved to be both politically useless and ugly—the "Flanders Mare." Next, teen bride Catherine Howard ended up cheating on Henry, so she was executed. Henry finally found comfort—but no children—in his later years with his final wife, Catherine Parr.

In 1536 Henry suffered a serious accident while jousting. His health would never be the same. Increasingly, he suffered from festering boils and violent mood swings, and he became morbidly obese, tipping the scales at 400 pounds with a 54-inch waist.

Henry's last years were marked by paranoia, sudden rages, and despotism. He gave his perceived enemies the pink slip in his signature way—charged with treason and beheaded. (Ironically, Henry's own heraldic motto was "Coeur Loyal"—true heart.) Once-wealthy England was becoming depleted, thanks to Henry's expensive habits, which included making war on France, building and acquiring palaces (he had 50), and collecting fine tapestries and archery bows.

Henry forged a large legacy. He expanded the power of the monarchy, making himself the focus of a rising, modern nation-state. Simultaneously, he strengthened Parliament—largely because it agreed with his policies. He annexed Wales, and imposed English rule on Ireland (provoking centuries of resentment). He expanded the navy, paving the way for Britannia to soon rule the waves. And—thanks to Henry's marital woes—England would forever be a Protestant nation.

When Henry died at age 55, he was succeeded by his nine-year-old son by Jane Seymour, Edward VI. Weak and sickly, Edward died six years later. Next to rule was Mary, Henry's daughter from his first marriage. A staunch Catholic, she tried to brutally reverse England's Protestant Reformation, earning the nickname "Bloody Mary." Finally came Henry's daughter with Anne Boleyn—Queen Elizabeth I, who ruled a prosperous, expanding England, seeing her father's seeds blossom into the English Renaissance.

London abounds with "Henry" sights. He was born in Greenwich (at today's Old Royal Naval College) and was crowned in Westminster Abbey. He built a palace along Whitehall and enjoyed another at Hampton Court. At the National Portrait Gallery, you can see portraits of some of Henry's wives, and at the Tower you can see where he executed them. Henry is buried alongside his third wife, Jane Seymour, at Windsor Castle.

LONDON

(cut open to be gutted), and finally quartering, with your giblets displayed on the walls as a warning.

Inside the White Tower is a ❹ **museum** with exhibits re-creating medieval life and the Tower's bloody history of torture and executions. The first suits of armor you see belonged to Henry VIII—on a horse, slender in his youth (c. 1515), then more heavy-set by 1540 (with his bigger-is-better codpiece). Upstairs, St. John's Chapel (1080) is the oldest surviving part of the original Tower—and the oldest church in London. On the top floor are the Tower's actual execution ax and chopping block.

Across from the White Tower is the entrance to the ❺ **crown jewels.** You'll pass through a series of rooms with videos and ex-hibits showing the actual coronation items in the order that they're used whenever a new king or queen is crowned. The Sovereign's Scepter is encrusted with the world's largest cut diamond—the 530-carat Star of Africa, beefy as a quarter-pounder. The orb symbolizes how Christianity rules over the earth, a reminder that even a "divine monarch" is not above God's law. The Crown of the Queen Mother (Elizabeth II's famous mum, who died in 2002) has the 106-carat Koh-I-Noor diamond glittering on the front (con-sidered unlucky for male rulers, it adorns the crown of the king's wife). The Imperial State Crown is what the Queen wears for offi-cial functions such as the State Opening of Parliament. Among its 3,733 jewels are Queen Elizabeth I's former earrings (the hanging pearls, top center), a stunning 13th-century ruby look-alike in the center, and Edward the Confessor's ring (the blue sapphire on top, in the center of the Maltese cross of diamonds).

Exiting the tower, turn right and walk past the White Tower, straight ahead to the grassy field called ❻ **Tower Green.** In me-dieval times, this was the "town square" for those who lived in the castle. Knights exercised and jousted here, and it was the last place of refuge in troubled times.

Near the middle of Tower Green is a granite-paved square, the ❼ **Scaffold Site.** It was here that enemies of the Crown would kneel before the king for the final time. On the left as you face the chapel, is the ❽ **Beauchamp Tower** (pronounced "BEECH-um"), one of several places in the complex that housed Very Important Prisoners.

Down toward the river, at the bottom corner of the green is ❾ **Bloody Tower,** where Sir Walter Raleigh was imprisoned for 13 years and wrote the first volume of his *History of the World.*

Walk under the Bloody Tower, cross the cobbled road, and bear right a few steps to find the stairs up onto the wall to reach the ❿ **Medieval Palace,** built around 1240 by Henry III, the king most responsible for the expansive Tower of London complex we see today. From the throne room, continue up the stairs to ⓫ **walk**

the wall for get a fine view of the Tower Bridge. Between the White Tower and the Thames are cages housing the ⑫ **ravens.** According to tradition, the Tower and the British throne are only safe as long as ravens are present here. Other sights at the Tower include the Salt Tower and the Fusilier Museum.

Tower Bridge

The iconic Tower Bridge (often mistakenly called London Bridge) was built in 1894 to accommodate the growing East End. While fully modern and hydraulically powered, the drawbridge was designed with a retro Neo-Gothic look.

The bridge is most interesting when the drawbridge lifts to let ships pass, as it does a thousand times a year (best viewed from the Tower side of the Thames). For the bridge-lifting schedule, check the website or call.

You can tour the bridge at the **Tower Bridge Exhibition,** with a history display and a peek at the Victorian-era engine room that lifts the span. Included in your entrance is the chance to cross the bridge—138 feet above the road along a partially see-through glass walkway. As an exhibit, it's overpriced, though the adrenaline rush and spectacular city views from the walkway may help justify the cost.

Cost and Hours: £9.80, daily 10:00-18:00 in summer, 9:30-17:30 in winter, enter at northwest tower, Tube: Tower Hill, tel. 020/7403-3761, www.towerbridge.org.uk.

Nearby: The best remaining bit of London's **Roman Wall** is just north of the Tower (at the Tower Hill Tube station). The chic **St. Katharine Dock,** just east of Tower Bridge, has private yachts and mod shops. Across the bridge, on the South Bank, is the upscale Butlers Wharf area, as well as City Hall, museums, the Jubilee Walkway, and, towering overhead, the Shard.

Sights in East London

▲The East End

Immediately east of The City (and Liverpool Street Station), London's East End is a vibrant neighborhood with great eateries, lively

markets, and interesting street art. It's also known as "Banglatown" for its Bangladeshi communities and curry houses along Brick Lane. Anchoring the area is Old Spitalfields Market, filled with merchants and creative food counters (see page 147 and page 187).

In medieval times, this was

Map legend:
1. Old Spitalfields Market Eateries
2. Ottolenghi Spitalfields
3. The English Restaurant
4. St. John Bread & Wine Restaurant
5. Gunpowder
6. Meraz Café
7. Old Truman Brewery & Café 1001
☠ Ripper murder site

the less desirable end, in part because it was downwind from the noxious hide-tanning district. London's east/west disparity was exacerbated in Victorian times, when the wind carried the pollution of a newly industrialized London. And it was during this time that Jack the Ripper terrorized this neighborhood.

This area has also long been the city's arrival point for new immigrants, from the French Protestant Huguenots (late 16th century), to Ashkenazi Jews (late 19th century), to Bangladeshi refugees (1970s). This mixing of cultures—along with a spirit of redevelopment—has given this area a wonderful energy that's well worth exploring.

▲Museum of the Home

This low-key museum (formerly the Geffrye Museum) is housed in an 18th-century almshouse north of Liverpool Street Station. Its rooms are furnished, themed to everyday life in different times and all very well described. It's an intimate peek at the middle class as its comforts evolved from 1600 to 2000. In summer, explore the fragrant herb garden. The museum has been closed for renovation but should be reopened by the time you visit; check locally.

Cost and Hours: Free, £3 suggested donation, Tue-Sun

LONDON

10:00-17:00, closed Mon, garden open April-Oct, 136 Kingsland Road, tel. 020/7739-9893, www.museumofthehome.org.uk.

Getting There: Take the Tube to Liverpool Street, then ride the bus 10 minutes north (bus #149 or #242—leave station through Bishopsgate exit and head left a few steps to find stop; hop off at the Pearson Street stop, just after passing the brick museum on the right). Or take the East London line on the Overground to the Hoxton stop, which is right next to the museum.

Sights on the South Bank

▲Jubilee Walkway

This riverside path is a popular pub-crawling pedestrian promenade that stretches all along the South Bank, offering grand views

of the Houses of Parliament and St. Paul's. On a sunny day, this is the place to see Londoners out strolling. The Walkway hugs the river except just east of London Bridge, where it cuts inland for a couple of blocks. It has been expanded into a 60-mile "Greenway" circling the city, including the 2012 Olympics site.

▲▲London Eye

This giant Ferris wheel, towering above London opposite Big Ben, is one of the world's highest observational wheels and London's answer to the Eiffel Tower. Riding it is a memorable experience, even though London doesn't have much of a skyline, and the price

is borderline outrageous. Whether you ride or not, the wheel is a sight to behold.

The experience starts with an engaging, four-minute show combining a 4-D movie with wind and water effects. Then it's time to spin around the Eye. Twenty-eight people ride in each of its 32 air-conditioned capsules (representing the boroughs of London) for the 30-minute rotation (you go around only once). From the top of this 443-foot-high wheel—the second-highest public viewpoint in the city—

even Big Ben looks small. Built to celebrate the new millennium, the Eye has become a permanent fixture on the London skyline and inspired countless other cities to build their own wheels.

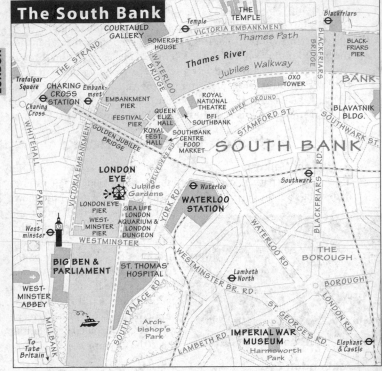

The South Bank

COURTAULD
GALLERY
THE STRAND
SOMERSET
HOUSE
Temple
THE
TEMPLE
VICTORIA EMBANKMENT
Blackfriars
BLACK-
FRIARS
PIER
Thames Path
Thames River
Jubilee Walkway
BLACKFRIARS BRIDGE
OXO
TOWER
BANK
Trafalgar
Square
CHARING
CROSS
STATION
Embank-
ment
Charing
Cross
WHITEHALL
EMBANKMENT
PIER
Festival
Pier
QUEEN
ELIZ.
HALL
ROYAL
NATIONAL
THEATRE
UPPER GROUND
BLAVATNIK
BLDG.
SOUTHWARK ST.
BFI
SOUTHBANK
STAMFORD ST.
GOLDEN JUBILEE
BRIDGE
ROYAL
FEST.
HALL
VICTORIA EMBANKMENT
BELVEDERE RD.
SOUTHBANK
CENTRE
FOOD
MARKET
SOUTH BANK
LONDON
EYE
Jubilee
Gardens
Waterloo
Southwark
BLACKFRIARS RD.
LONDON EYE
PIER
WEST-
MINSTER
PIER
SEA LIFE
LONDON
AQUARIUM &
LONDON
DUNGEON
YORK RD.
WATERLOO
STATION
WATERLOO RD.
West-
minster
PARL ST.
WESTMINSTER
THE
BOROUGH
BIG BEN &
PARLIAMENT
ST. THOMAS'
HOSPITAL
WESTMINSTER BR. RD.
Lambeth
North
BOROUGH
LONDON RD.
WEST-
MINSTER
ABBEY
MILLBANK
SOUTH PALACE RD.
Arch-
bishop's
Park
LAMBETH RD.
IMPERIAL WAR
MUSEUM
Harmsworth
Park
ST. GEORGE'S RD.
Elephant
& Castle
To Tate
Britain

Cost and Hours: £30, cheaper online, family ticket and combo-ticket with Madame Tussauds and other attractions available; daily 10:00-20:30 or later, Sept-May generally 11:00-18:00, check website for latest schedule, these are last-ascent times, Tube: Waterloo or Westminster. Thames boats come and go from London Eye Pier at the foot of the wheel.

Advance Tickets and Crowd-Beating Tips: The London Eye is busiest between 11:00 and 17:00, especially on weekends year-round and every day in July and August. For visits during these times, buy timed-entry tickets online in advance at www.londoneye.com or in person at the box office (in the corner of the County Hall building nearest the Eye); day-of tickets can sell out. You can present your advance ticket on your phone; otherwise print it at home, retrieve it from an onsite ticket machine (bring your payment card and confirmation code), or stand in the "Ticket Collection" line. Even if you buy in advance, you may wait 30-45 minutes to board your capsule. The Fast Track ticket may still entail a wait up to 30 minutes—it's probably not worth the expense.

LONDON

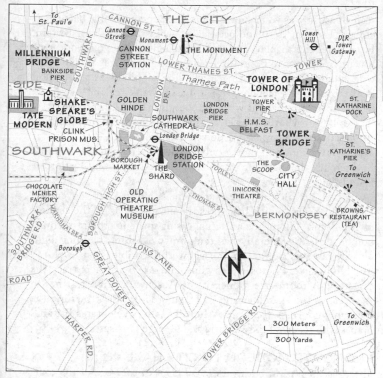

▲▲Imperial War Museum

This impressive museum covers the wars and conflicts of the 20th and 21st centuries. You can walk chronologically through World

War I, to the rise of fascism, World War II, the Cold War, The Troubles in Northern Ireland, the wars in Iraq and Afghanistan, and terrorism. Rather than glorify war, the museum explores the human side of the wartime experience and its effect on people back home. It raises thoughtful questions about one of civilization's more uncivilized, persistent traits. Allow plenty of time; lots of artifacts, interactive experiences, and multimedia exhibits can be engrossing.

Cost and Hours: Free, £5 suggested donation, special exhibits extra, daily 10:00-18:00, last entry one hour before closing, Tube: Lambeth North or Elephant and Castle; buses #3, #12, and #159 from Westminster area; tel. 020/7416-5000, www.iwm.org.uk.

Visiting the Museum: Start in the atrium to grasp the massive

scale of warfare as you wander among and under notable battle machines. The Spitfire plane overhead flew in the Battle of Britain.
From here, the displays unfold chronologically as you work your
way up from floor to floor. On level 0, enter **The First World War,**
with hundreds of fascinating items. The highlight of the exhibit
is a reconstructed trench, with a massive tank rearing overhead,
where you're bombarded with the sounds of war. Climb the stairs
for exhibits on **World War II.** A video clip shows the mesmerizing
Adolf Hitler, who roused a defeated Germany to rearm for war
again. At the museum shop, double back to see displays on Britain's
fight against the Nazis in North Africa and Operation Overlord—
i.e., D-Day.

Level 2, which may be under renovation in 2020, covers the
Post-War Years, which began (as the plaque says) "In the shadow
of The Bomb" (alongside an actual casing made for the Hiroshima
bomb). Level 3 generally has **temporary exhibits** shedding light
on why humans fight. The most powerful exhibit is on level 4—
The Holocaust. Photos, video clips, and a few artifacts trace the
sad story. A room-size model of the Auschwitz camp testifies to
the scale of the slaughter and its banal orderliness. Crowning the
museum on level 5, the **Lord Ashcroft Gallery** celebrates Britain's
heroes who received the Victoria and George Crosses.

FROM TATE MODERN TO CITY HALL

These sights are in Southwark (SUTH-uck), the core of the tourist's South Bank. Southwark was for centuries the place Londoners would go to escape the rules and decency of the city and let
their hair down. Bearbaiting, brothels, rollicking pubs, and theater—you name the dream, and it could be fulfilled just across the
Thames. A run-down warehouse district through the 20th century,
it's been gentrified with classy restaurants, office parks, pedestrian
promenades, major sights (such as the Tate Modern and Shakespeare's Globe), and a colorful collection of lesser sights. The area is
easy on foot and a scenic—though circuitous—way to connect the
Tower of London with St. Paul's.

▲▲Tate Modern

This striking museum fills a former power station across the river
from St. Paul's with a powerhouse collection including Dalí, Picasso, Warhol, and much more.

Cost and Hours: Free, £5 suggested donation, fee for special
exhibits; daily 10:00-18:00, Fri-Sat until 22:00, last entry to special
exhibits 45 minutes before closing, especially crowded on weekend
days (crowds thin out Fri and Sat evenings); view restaurant on top
floor, across the Millennium Bridge from St. Paul's; Tube: Southwark, London Bridge, St. Paul's, Mansion House, or Blackfriars

plus a 10- to 15-minute walk; or connect by Tate Boat museum ferry from Tate Britain—see page 59; tel. 020/7887-8888, www. tate.org.uk.

Tours: Free 45-minute guided tours are offered at the top of each hour between 11:00 and 16:00; free 10-minute gallery talks take place on occasion (see info desk for details).

Visiting the Museum: The permanent collection is generally on levels 2, 4, and part of level 3 of the Natalie Bell Building. Paint-

ings are arranged according to theme, not artist. Paintings by Picasso, for example, might be scattered in different rooms on different levels. To help you get started, find the "Start Display" room on level 2—highlighting a range of artworks.

Since 1960, London has ri-
valed New York as a center for the visual arts. You'll find British artists displayed here—look for work by David Hockney, Henry Moore, and Barbara Hepworth. American art is also prominently represented—keep an eye out for abstract expressionist works by Mark Rothko and Jackson Pollock, and the pop art of Andy Warhol and Roy Lichtenstein. After you see the Old Masters of Modernism (Matisse, Picasso, Kandinsky, and so on), push your mental envelope with works by Pollock, Miró, Bacon, Picabia, Beuys, Twombly, and beyond.

You'll find temporary exhibits throughout the museum—some free, some requiring a special admission. Additionally, the main hall features a different monumental installation by a prominent artist each year. The museum's newer twisted-pyramid, 10-story Blavatnik Building also hosts changing themed exhibitions, performance art, experimental film, and interactive sculpture incorporating light and sound.

▲Millennium Bridge
The pedestrian bridge links St. Paul's Cathedral and the Tate Modern across the Thames. This is London's first new bridge in a century. When it opened, the $25 million bridge wiggled when people walked on it, so it promptly closed for repairs; 20 months and $8 million later, it reopened. Nicknamed the "blade of light" for its sleek minimalist design (370 yards long, four yards wide, stainless steel with teak planks), its clever aerodynamic handrails deflect wind over the heads of pedestrians.

▲▲Shakespeare's Globe
This replica of the original Globe Theatre was built, half-timbered and thatched, as it was in Shakespeare's time. (This is the first

thatched roof constructed in London since they were outlawed after the Great Fire of 1666.) It serves as a working theater by night and offers tours by day. The original Globe opened in 1599, debuting Shakespeare's play *Julius Caesar.* The Globe originally accommodated 2,200 seated and another 1,000 standing. Today, slightly smaller and leaving space for reasonable aisles, the theater holds 800 seated and 600 groundlings.

Its promoters brag that the theater melds "the three A's"—actors, audience, and architecture—with each contributing to the play. The working theater hosts authentic performances of Shakespeare's plays with actors in period costumes, modern interpretations of his works, and some works by other playwrights. For details on attending a play, see page 151.

The complex's smaller Sam Wanamaker Playhouse—an indoor, horseshoe-shaped Jacobean theater—allows the show to go on in the winter, when it's too cold for performances in the outdoor Globe. Seating fewer than 350, the playhouse is more intimate and sometimes uses authentic candle lighting for period performances. While the Globe mainly presents Shakespeare's works, the playhouse tends to focus on the works of his contemporaries (Jonson, Marlow, Fletcher) and some new plays, though there's some crossover.

Touring the Globe: Tours depart from the box office every half-hour and last for 40 minutes (£17, £10 for kids 5-15; during

outdoor theater season—April-mid-Oct—last tours depart Mon at 17:00, Tue-Sat at 12:30, Sun at 11:30; off-season last tours at 17:00; Tube: Mansion House or London Bridge plus a 10-minute walk; tel. 020/7902-1400, www.shakespearesglobe.com).

Eating: The **$$$ Swan at the Globe** café offers a sit-down restaurant (for lunch and dinner, reservations recommended, tel. 020/7928-9444, www.swanlondon.co.uk), a drinks-and-plates bar, and a sandwich-and-coffee cart (Mon-Fri 8:00-closing, depends on performance times, Sat-Sun from 10:00).

▲Southwark Cathedral

While made a cathedral only in 1905, this has been the neighborhood church since the 13th century, and comes with some interesting history. The enthusiastic docents give impromptu tours if you ask.

Cost and Hours: Free, £1 map serves as photo permit, Mon-Fri 8:00-18:00, Sat-Sun from 8:30, Tube: London Bridge, tel. 020/7367-6700, www.cathedral.southwark.anglican.org.

Music: The cathedral hosts evensong Sun at 15:00, Tue-Fri at 17:30, and some Sat at 16:00; organ recitals are Mon at 13:15 and music recitals Tue at 15:15 (call or check website to confirm times).

▲Old Operating Theatre Museum and Herb Garret

Climb a tight and creaky wooden spiral staircase to a church attic where you'll find a garret used to dry medicinal herbs, a fascinating exhibit on Victorian surgery, cases of well-described 19th-century medical paraphernalia, and a special look at "anesthesia, the defeat of pain." Then you stumble upon Britain's oldest operating theater, where limbs were sawed off way back in 1821.

Cost and Hours: £6.50, Tue-Sun 10:30-17:00, Mon from 14:00, 9a St. Thomas Street, Tube: London Bridge, tel. 020/7188-2679, www.oldoperatingtheatre.com.

The Shard

Rocketing dramatically 1,020 feet above the south end of the London Bridge, this addition to London's skyline is by far the tallest building in Western Europe...for now. Designed by Renzo Piano (best known as the co-architect of Paris' Pompidou Center), the glass-clad pyramid shimmers in the sun and its prickly top glows like the city's nightlight after dark. Its uppermost floors are set aside as public viewing galleries, but the ticket price is as outrageously high as the building itself, especially given that it's a bit far from London's most exciting landmarks. (For cheaper view opportunities in London, see the sidebar on page 110.)

Cost and Hours: £39—book online in advance, advance ticket includes free return ticket in case of bad weather, otherwise pay 25 percent more on-site; family ticket available, least crowded on weekday mornings, but perhaps better photo opportunities in the early evening (less haze); daily 10:00-22:00, shorter hours Oct-March; Tube: London Bridge—use London Bridge exit and follow signs, tel. 0844-499-7111, www.theviewfromtheshard.com.

HMS *Belfast*

This former Royal Navy warship, a veteran of World War II that took part in the D-Day invasion, clogs the Thames just upstream from the Tower Bridge. The huge vessel—now manned with wax sailors—thrills kids who always dreamed of sitting in a turret shooting off their imaginary guns. If you're into WWII warships, this is the ultimate. Otherwise, it's just an expensive opportunity to get lots of exercise with a nice view of the Tower Bridge.

Cost and Hours: £18, cheaper online, kids 5-15—£9, kids under 5—free, family ticket available, includes audioguide; daily 10:00-18:00, Nov-Feb until 17:00, last entry one hour before closing; Tube: London Bridge, tel. 020/7940-6300, www.iwm.org.uk/visits/hms-belfast.

City Hall

The glassy, egg-shaped building near the south end of Tower Bridge is London's City Hall, designed by Sir Norman Foster, the architect who worked on London's Millennium Bridge and Berlin's Reichstag. Nicknamed "the Armadillo," City Hall houses the office of London's mayor—it's here that the mayor consults with the Assembly representatives of the city's 25 districts. An interior spiral ramp allows visitors to watch and hear the action below in the Assembly Chamber— ride the lift to floor 2 (the highest visitors can go) and spiral down. On the lower ground floor is a large aerial photograph of London and a handy cafeteria. Next to City Hall is the outdoor amphitheater called The Scoop (see page 154 for info on performances).

Cost and Hours: Free, open to visitors Mon-Thu 8:30-18:00, Fri until 17:30, closed Sat-Sun; Tube: London Bridge Station plus 10-minute walk, or Tower Hill Station plus 15-minute walk; tel. 020/7983-4000, www.london.gov.uk.

Sights in West London

▲▲Tate Britain

One of Europe's great art houses, Tate Britain specializes in British painting from the 16th century through modern times. The museum has a good representation of William Blake's religious sketches, the Pre-Raphaelites' naturalistic and detailed art, Gainsborough's aristocratic ladies, and the best collection anywhere of J. M. W. Turner's swirling works.

Cost and Hours: Free, £4 suggested donation, fee for special exhibits; daily 10:00-18:00, last entry 45 minutes before closing; free tours generally daily; on the Thames River, south of Big Ben and north of Vauxhall Bridge, Tube: Pimlico, Tate Boat museum ferry goes directly to the museum from Tate Modern—see page 59; tel. 020/7887-8888, www.tate.org.uk.

Tours: Free guided tours are generally offered daily at 11:00 (the best overview tour), with specialty tours at 12:00, 14:00, and 15:00.

Visiting the Museum: Works from the early centuries are located in the west half of the building (to your left), and 20th-century art is in the east half. Also to the east, in the adjacent Clore Gallery, are the works of J. M. W. Turner, John Constable, and William Blake. The Tate rotates its vast collection of paintings, so it's difficult to predict exactly which works will be on display. Pick up a map as you enter (£1 suggested donation) or download the museum's helpful app for a room-by-room guide.

1700-1800—Art Blossoms: With peace at home (under three King Georges), a strong overseas economy, and a growing urban center in London, England's artistic life began to bloom. As the English grew more sophisticated, so did their portraits. Painters branched out into other subjects, capturing slices of everyday life (find William Hogarth's unflinchingly honest portraits, and Thomas Gainsborough's elegant, educated women).

1800-1850—The Industrial Revolution: Newfangled inventions were everywhere, but along with technology came factories coating towns with soot, urban poverty, regimentation, and clock-punching. Many artists rebelled against "progress" and the modern world. They escaped the dirty cities to commune with nature. Or they found a new spirituality in intense human emotions, expressed in dramatic paintings of episodes from history. In rooms dedicated to the 1800s, you may see a number of big paintings devoted to the power of nature.

1837-1901—The Victorian Era: In the world's wealthiest nation, the prosperous middle class dictated taste in art. They admired paintings that were realistic (showcasing the artist's talent and work ethic), depicting slices of everyday life. Some paintings tug at the heartstrings, with scenes of parting couples, the grief of death, or the joy of families reuniting.

Overdosed with the gushy sentimentality of their day, a band of 20-year-old artists—including Sir John Everett Millais, Dante Gabriel Rossetti, and William Holman Hunt—said "Enough!" and dedicated themselves to creating less saccharine art (the Pre-Raphaelites). Like the Impressionists who followed them, they donned their scarves, barged out of the stuffy studio, and set up outdoors, painting trees, streams, and people, like scientists on a field trip. Still, they often captured nature with such a close-up clarity that it's downright unnatural.

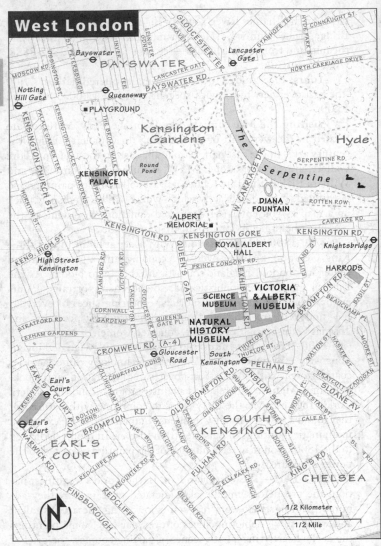

West London

BAYSWATER

Bayswater
Lancaster Gate
Notting Hill Gate
Queensway
PLAYGROUND

Kensington Gardens

Round Pond

KENSINGTON PALACE

Hyde

The Serpentine

SERPENTINE RD.

DIANA FOUNTAIN

ROTTEN ROW

ALBERT MEMORIAL

KENSINGTON RD.
KENSINGTON GORE
ROYAL ALBERT HALL

KENSINGTON RD.

Knightsbridge

KENS. HIGH ST.
High Street Kensington

PRINCE CONSORT RD.

HARRODS

SCIENCE MUSEUM

VICTORIA & ALBERT MUSEUM

CORNWALL GARDENS

NATURAL HISTORY MUSEUM

STRATFORD RD.

LEXHAM GARDENS

CROMWELL RD. (A-4)

Gloucester Road
South Kensington

PELHAM ST.

Earl's Court

EARL'S COURT

ONSLOW SQ.

SOUTH KENSINGTON

SLOANE AV.

CALE ST.

CHELSEA

FULHAM RD.

KING'S RD.

FINSBOROUGH

REDCLIFFE

1/2 Kilometer

1/2 Mile

N

LONDON

British Impressionism: Realistic British art stood apart from the modernist trends in France, but some influences drifted across the Channel (Rooms 1890 and 1900). John Singer Sargent (American-born) studied with Parisian Impressionists, learning the thick, messy brushwork and play of light at twilight. James Tissot used Degas' snapshot technique to capture a crowded scene from an odd angle. And James McNeill Whistler (born in America, trained in Paris, lived in London) composed his paintings like music—see some of his paintings' titles.

1900-1950—World Wars: As two world wars whittled down

the powerful British Empire, it still remained a major cultural force. British art mirrored many of the trends and "-isms" pioneered in Paris (Room 1930). You'll see Cubism like Picasso's, abstract art like Mondrian's, and so on. But British artists also continued the British tradition of realistic paintings of people and landscapes.

If British painters were less than avant-garde, their sculptors were cutting edge. Henry Moore's statues—mostly female, mostly reclining—capture the human body in a few simple curves, with minimal changes to the rock itself. Francis Bacon has become Britain's best-known 20th-century painter, exemplifying the angst of the early post-WWII years. His deformed half-humans/half-animals express the existential human predicament of being caught in a world not of your own making, isolated and helpless to change it.

1950-2000—Modern World: No longer a world power, Britain in the Swinging '60s became a major exporter of pop culture. British art's traditional strengths—realism, portraits, landscapes, and slice-of-life scenes—were redone in the modern style. Look for works by David Hockney, Lucian Freud, Bridget Riley, and Gilbert and George.

Clore Gallery: Walking through J. M. W. Turner's life's work, you can watch Turner's style evolve from clear-eyed realism to hazy proto-Impressionism (1775-1851). You'll also see how Turner dabbled in different subjects: landscapes, seascapes, Roman ruins, snapshots of Venice, and so on. The corner room of the Clore Gallery is dedicated to John Constable (1776-1837), who painted the English landscape realistically, without idealizing it.

▲National Army Museum

This museum tells the story of the British army from 1415 through the Bosnian conflict and Iraq, and how it influences today's society. The five well-signed galleries are neatly arranged by theme—"Army," "Battle," "Soldier," "Society," and "Insight"—with plenty of interactive exhibits for kids. History buffs appreciate the carefully displayed artifacts, from 17th-century uniforms to Wellington's battle cloak. Other highlights of the collection include the skeleton of Napoleon's horse, Lawrence of Arabia's silk robe, and Burberry's signature trench coat (originally designed for WWI soldiers).

Cost and Hours: Free, £5 suggested donation, daily 10:00-17:30; Royal Hospital Road, Chelsea, Tube: 10-minute walk from Sloane Square, exit the station and head south on Lower Sloane Street, turn right on Royal Hospital Road, the museum is two long blocks ahead on the left, tel. 020/7730-0717, www.nam.ac.uk.

HYDE PARK AND NEARBY

▲Apsley House (Wellington Museum)

Having beaten Napoleon at Waterloo, Arthur Wellesley, the First Duke of Wellington, was once the most famous man in Europe.

He was given a huge fortune, with which he purchased London's ultimate address, Number One London. His refurbished mansion offers a nice interior, a handful of world-class paintings, and a glimpse at the life of the great soldier and two-time prime minister. The highlight is the large ballroom, the Waterloo Gallery, decorated with Anthony van Dyck's *Charles I on Horseback* (over the main fireplace), Diego Velázquez's earthy *Water-Seller of Seville* (to the left of Van Dyck), and Jan Steen's playful *Dissolute Household* (to the right). Just outside the door, in the Portico Room, is a large portrait of the Duke of Wellington by Francisco Goya. The place is well described by the included audioguide, which has sound bites from the current Duke of Wellington (who still lives at Apsley).

Cost and Hours: £10.30, Wed-Sun 11:00-17:00, closed Mon-Tue, shorter hours Nov-March, open only Sat-Sun in Jan-March, 20 yards from Hyde Park Corner Tube station, tel. 020/7499-5676, www.english-heritage.org.uk.

▲Hyde Park and Speakers' Corner

London's "Central Park," originally Henry VIII's hunting grounds, has more than 600 acres of lush greenery, Santander Cycles rental stations, the huge man-made Serpentine Lake (with rental boats and a lakeside swimming pool), the royal Kensington Palace (described next), and the ornate Neo-Gothic Albert Memorial across from the Royal Albert Hall (for more about the park, see www.royalparks.org.uk/parks/hyde-park). The western half of the park is

known as Kensington Gardens. The park is huge—study a Tube map to choose the stop nearest to your destination.

On Sundays, from just after noon until early evening, **Speakers' Corner** offers soapbox oratory at its best (northeast corner of the park, Tube: Marble Arch). Characters climb their stepladders, wave their flags, pound emphatically on their sandwich boards, and share what they are convinced is their wisdom. Regulars have resident hecklers who know their lines and are always ready with a verbal jab or barb. "The grass roots of democracy" is actually a holdover from when the gallows stood here and the criminal was allowed to say just about anything he wanted to before he swung. I dare you to raise your voice and gather a crowd—it's easy to do.

The **Princess Diana Memorial Fountain** honors the "People's Princess," who once lived in nearby Kensington Palace. The low-key circular stream, great for cooling off your feet on a hot day, is in the south-central part of the park, near the Albert Memorial and Serpentine Gallery (Tube: Knightsbridge). A similarly named but different sight, the **Diana, Princess of Wales Memorial Playground,** in the park's northwest corner, is loads of fun for kids (Tube: Queensway).

Kensington Palace

For nearly 150 years (1689-1837), Kensington was the royal residence, before Buckingham Palace became the official home of the monarch. Sitting primly on its pleasant parkside grounds, the palace gives a barren yet regal glimpse into royal life—particularly that of Queen Victoria, who was born and raised here.

After Queen Victoria moved the monarchy to Buckingham Palace, lesser royals bedded down at Kensington. Princess Diana lived here both during and after her marriage to Prince Charles (1981-1997). More recently, Will and Kate moved in. However—as many disappointed visitors discover—none of these more recent apartments are open to the public. The palace hosts a revolving series of temporary exhibits, some great, others not so. To see what's on during your visit, check online.

Cost and Hours: £17.50; daily 10:00-18:00, Nov-Feb until 16:00, last entry one hour before closing; a long 10-minute stroll through Kensington Gardens from either High Street Kensington or Queensway Tube stations, tel. 0844-482-7788, www.hrp.org. uk.

Outside: Garden enthusiasts enjoy popping into the secluded Sunken Garden, 50 yards from the exit. Consider afternoon tea at the nearby Orangery (see page 190), built as a greenhouse for Queen Anne in 1704.

▲▲▲Victoria and Albert Museum

The world's top collection of decorative arts encompasses 2,000 years of art and design (ceramics, stained glass, fine furniture, clothing, jewelry, carpets, and more), displaying a surprisingly interesting and diverse assortment of crafts from the West, as well as from Asian and Islamic cultures. There's much to see, including Raphael's tapestry cartoons, Leonardo da Vinci's notebooks, the huge Islamic Ardabil Carpet (4,914 knots in every 10 square centimeters), a cast of Trajan's Column that depicts the emperor's conquests, and pop culture memorabilia, including the jumpsuit Mick Jagger wore for The Rolling Stones' 1972 world tour.

Cost and Hours: Free, £5 donation requested, fee for some special exhibits, daily 10:00-17:45, some galleries open Fri until 22:00, free tours daily, much-needed map—£1 donation; on Cromwell Road in South Kensington, Tube: South Kensington,

LONDON

from the Tube station a long tunnel leads directly to museum, tel. 020/7942-2000, www.vam.ac.uk.

Visiting the Museum: In the Grand Entrance lobby, look up into the rotunda to see the ❶ **Dale Chihuly chandelier,** epitomizing the spirit of the V&A's collection—beautiful manufactured objects that demonstrate technical skill and innovation, wedding the old with the new, and blurring the line between arts and crafts.

Now look up to the balcony (above the shop) and see the pointed arches of the ❷ **Hereford Screen,** a 35-by-35-foot, eight-ton rood screen (built for the Hereford Cathedral's sacred altar area). It looks medieval, but it was created with the most modern materials the Industrial Revolution could produce. George Gilbert Scott (1811-1878), who built the screen, redesigned much of London in the Neo-Gothic style, restoring old churches such as Westminster Abbey, renovating the Houses of Parliament, and building new structures like St. Pancras Station and the Albert Memorial—some 700 buildings in all.

The V&A has (arguably) the best collection of Italian Renaissance sculpture outside Italy. One prime example is

❸ *Samson Slaying a Philistine,* by Giambologna (c. 1562), carved from a single block of marble, which shows the testy Israelite warrior rearing back, brandishing the jawbone of an ass, preparing to decapitate a man who'd insulted him.

The ❹ **Medieval and Renaissance Galleries** display 1,200 years of decorative arts, showing how the mix of pagan Roman and medieval-Christian elements created modern Europe. In Room 8 is a glass case displaying the blue-and-gold, shoebox-sized ❺ **Becket Casket,** which contains the mortal remains (or relics) of St. Thomas Becket, who was brutally murdered. The enamel-and-metal workbox is a specialty of Limoges, France. In Room 10a, you'll run into the ❻ **Boar and Bear Hunt Tapestry.** Though most medieval art depicted the Madonna and saints, this colorful wool tapestry—woven in Belgium—provides a secular slice of life.

Two floors up, you'll see the tiny, pocket-size ❼ **notebook by Leonardo da Vinci** (Codex Forster III, 1490-1493), which dates from the years when he was living in Milan, shortly before undertaking his famous *Last Supper* fresco. The book's contents are all over the map: meticulous sketches of the human head, diagrams illustrating nature's geometrical perfection, a horse's leg for a huge equestrian statue, and even drawings of the latest ballroom

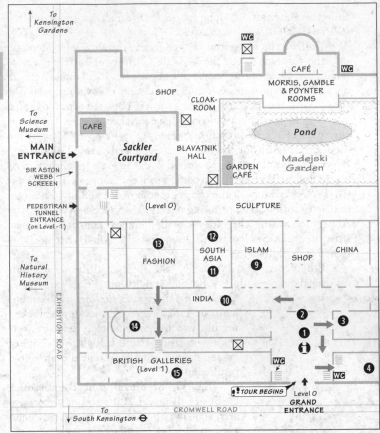

fashions. The adjacent computer lets you scroll through three of his notebooks and even flip his backwards handwriting to make it readable.

Back on level 0, enter Room 46b, and find **❽ Michelangelo casts** and other replica statues. These plaster-cast versions of famous Renaissance statues allowed 19th-century art students who couldn't afford a rail pass to study the classics. In Room 42, you'll see **❾ Islamic art,** reflecting both religious influences and a sophisticated secular culture. Many Islamic artists expressed themselves with beautiful but functional objects, such as the 630-square-foot Ardabil Carpet (1539-1540), which likely took a dozen workers years to complete. Also in the room are ceramics and glazed tile—all covered top to bottom in similarly complex patterns. The intricate interweaving, repetition, and unending lines suggest the complex, infinite nature of God (Allah).

In the hallway (technically "Room" 47b) is a glass case with a statue of **❿ Shiva Nataraja,** one of the hundreds, if not thousands,

Victoria & Albert Museum Tour

TEMPORARY EXHIBITS

WC

To 16

CAST COURT

ROOM

CAST COURT

JAPAN

8

46

STAIRS TO CAST COURTS VIEW

KOREA

7

5

6

1 Dale Chihuly Chandelier
2 Hereford Screen (above lobby)
3 GIAMBOLOGNA – Samson Slaying a Philistine
4 Medieval & Renaissance Galleries
5 Becket Casket
6 Boar & Bear Hunt Tapestry
7 Stairs to Leonardo Notebook
8 Michelangelo Casts
9 Islamic Art
10 Shiva Nataraja Statue
11 Possessions of Emperor Shah Jahan
12 Tipu's Tiger
13 Fashion Galleries
14 RAPHAEL – Tapestry Cartoons
15 British Galleries
16 Stairs up to Jewelry, Theater & British Silver

☒ ELEVATOR/LIFT

N

Not to Scale

To Harrods & Hyde Park Corner →

BROMPTON ROAD

of godlike incarnations of Hinduism's eternal being, Brahma. As long as Shiva keeps dancing, the universe will continue. In adjoining Room 41, a glass case in the center of the room contains **11 possessions of Emperor Shah Jahan,** including a cameo portrait, thumb ring, and wine cup (made of white nephrite jade, 1657). Shah Jahan—or "King of the World"—ruled the largest empire of the day, covering northern India, Pakistan, and Afghanistan. At the far end of Room 41 is the huge wood-carved **12 Tipu's Tiger,** a life-size robotic toy, once owned by an oppressed Indian sultan. When you turned the crank, the Brit's left arm would flail, and both he and the tiger would roar through organ pipes. (The mechanism still works.)

The **13 Fashion Galleries** display centuries of English fashion, from ladies' underwear, hoop skirts, and rain gear to high-society evening wear, men's suits, and more. Across the hall are **14 Raphael's tapestry cartoons.** The V&A owns seven of these full-size designs (approximately 13 by 17 feet, done in tempera on paper, now mounted on canvas). The cartoons were sent to factories in Brussels, cut into strips (see the lines), and placed on the looms.

Upstairs, Room 57 is the heart of the ⓯ **British Galleries,** which cover the era of Queen Elizabeth I. Find rare miniature portraits—a popular item of the day—including Hilliard's oft-reproduced *Young Man Among Roses* miniature, capturing the romance of a Shakespeare sonnet. Back in the Grand Entrance lobby, climb the staircase to level 2 to see ⓰ **jewelry, theater artifacts, silver,** and more.

▲▲Natural History Museum

Across the street from the Victoria and Albert, this mammoth museum is housed in a giant and wonderful Victorian, Neo-Romanesque building. It was built in the 1870s specifically for the huge collection (50 million specimens). Exhibits are wonderfully explained, with lots of creative, interactive displays. It covers everything from life ("creepy crawlies," human biology, our place in evolution, and awe-inspiring dinosaurs) to earth science (meteors, volcanoes, and earthquakes).

Cost and Hours: Free, £5 donation requested, fee for special exhibits, daily 10:00-18:00, helpful £1 map, long tunnel leads directly from South Kensington Tube station to museum (follow signs), tel. 020/7942-5000, exhibit info and reservations tel. 020/7942-5011, www.nhm.ac.uk. Free visitor app available via the "Visit" section of the website.

▲Science Museum

Next door to the Natural History Museum, this sprawling wonderland for curious minds is kid-perfect, with themes such as measuring time, exploring space, climate change, the evolution of modern medicine, and the Information Age. It offers hands-on fun, with trendy technology exhibits, a state-of-the-art IMAX theater (shows—£11, £9 for kids, family ticket available), the Garden—a cool play area for children up to age seven, plus several other pay-  to-enter attractions, including a virtual-reality spacecraft descent to Earth (£7) and Wonderlab kids area (£8, £6 for kids). Look for the family "What's On" brochure and ask about tours and demonstrations at the info desk.

Cost and Hours: Free, £5 donation requested, daily 10:00-18:00, last entry 45 minutes before closing, Exhibition Road, Tube: South Kensington, tel. 0333-241-4000, www.sciencemuseum.org.uk.

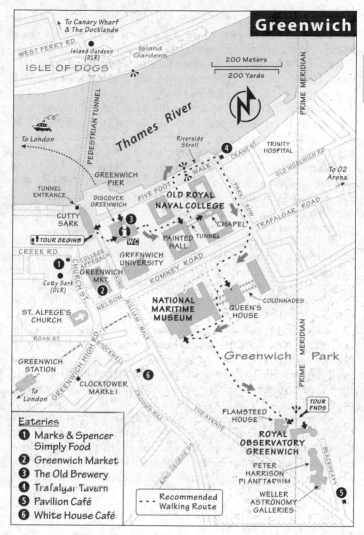

LONDON

Greenwich

To Canary Wharf
& The Docklands

WEST FERRY RD.

Island Gardens
(DLR)

Island
Gardens

ISLE OF DOGS

200 Meters

200 Yards

PRIME MERIDIAN

Thames River

To London

PEDESTRIAN TUNNEL

Riverside
Stroll

TRINITY
HOSPITAL

WALK

CRANE ST.

OLD WOOLWICH RD.

To O2
Arena

GREENWICH
PIER

FIVE FOOT

TUNNEL
ENTRANCE

DISCOVER
GREENWICH

OLD ROYAL
NAVAL COLLEGE

PARK ROW

TRAFALGAR ROAD

CUTTY
SARK

TOUR BEGINS

CREEK RD.

COLLEGE APPROACH

CHURCH ST.

Cutty Sark
(DLR)

WC

CHAPEL

PAINTED
HALL

TUNNEL
ENTRANCE

GREENWICH
UNIVERSITY

ROMNEY ROAD

GREENWICH
MKT.

NELSON

KING WILLIAM WALK

NATIONAL
MARITIME
MUSEUM

QUEEN'S
HOUSE

COLONNADES

ST. ALFEGE'S
CHURCH

ROAN ST.

Greenwich Park

STOCKWELL

GREENWICH
STATION

To
London

GREENWICH HIGH RD.

CLOCKTOWER
MARKET

CROOMS HILL

THE AVENUE

PRIME MERIDIAN

FLAMSTEED
HOUSE

TOUR
ENDS

Eateries

1. Marks & Spencer
   Simply Food
2. Greenwich Market
3. The Old Brewery
4. Trafalgar Tavern
5. Pavilion Café
6. White House Café

KING GEORGE ST.

ROYAL
OBSERVATORY
GREENWICH

PETER
HARRISON
PLANETARIUM

BLACKHEATH

WELLER
ASTRONOMY
GALLERIES

- - - Recommended
Walking Route

Sights in Greater London

EAST OF LONDON
▲▲Greenwich

This borough of London is an easy, affordable boat trip or DLR (Docklands Light Railway) journey from downtown. Along with majestic, picnic-perfect parks are the stately trappings of Britain's proud nautical heritage (the restored *Cutty Sark* clipper, the over-the-top-ornate retirement home for sailors at the Old Royal Naval College, and the comprehensive National Maritime Museum). It's also home to the Royal Observatory Greenwich, with a fine museum on how Greenwich Mean Time came to be and a chance to straddle the eastern and western hemispheres at the prime meridian. Boasting several top-notch museums (including some free ones), Greenwich is worth considering and easy to combine with a look at the Docklands (described later).

Getting There: For maximum efficiency and sightseeing, take the boat there for the scenery and commentary, and take the DLR back to avoid late-afternoon boat crowds (this plan also allows you to stop at the Docklands on the way home).

Various tour boats—with commentary and open-deck seating (2/hour, 30-75 minutes)—and faster Thames Clippers (every 20-30 minutes, 20-55 minutes) depart from several piers in central London. Thames Clippers also connects Greenwich to the Docklands' Canary Wharf Pier (2-3/hour, 15 minutes).

Docklands Light Railway (DLR) runs from the Bank-Monument Station to Cutty Sark Station in central Greenwich; it's one stop before the main—but less central—Greenwich Station (departs at least every 10 minutes, 20-minute ride, all in Zone 2).

Or, catch bus #188 from Russell Square near the British Museum (about 45 minutes to Greenwich).

Eating: Greenwich's parks are picnic-perfect, especially around the National Maritime Museum and Royal Observatory. Greenwich Market offers an international variety of tasty food stalls. Greenwich has almost 100 pubs. **$$$ The Old Brewery,** in the Discover Greenwich center, is a gastropub decorated with all things beer.

Markets: The Greenwich Market is an entertaining mini Covent Garden, located in the middle of the block between the Cutty Sark DLR station and the Old Royal Naval College (farmers market, arts and crafts, and food stands; daily 10:00-17:30; antiques Mon-Tue and Thu-Fri, www.greenwichmarketlondon.com).

▲▲Cutty Sark

When first launched in 1869, the Scottish-built *Cutty Sark* was the last of the great China tea clippers and the queen of the seas. She was among the fastest clippers ever built, the culmination of centuries of ship design. With 32,000 square feet of sail—and favorable winds—she could travel 300 miles in a day. But as a new century dawned, steamers began to outmatch sailing ships

LONDON

for speed, and by the mid-1920s the *Cutty Sark* was the world's last operating clipper ship.

In 2012, the ship was restored and reopened with a spectacular new glass-walled display space (though one critic groused that the ship now "looks like it has run aground in a giant greenhouse"). Displays explore the *Cutty Sark*'s 140-year history and the cargo she carried—everything from tea to wool to gunpowder—as she raced between London and ports all around the world.

Cost and Hours: £15, cheaper online, kids ages 4-15—£7.50, free for kids under age 4, family tickets available, combo-ticket with Royal Observatory—£26.25, kids combo-ticket—£17.60; daily 10:00-17:00; to skip the ticket-buying line reserve timed-entry tickets online or by phone, or show up around 13:00; unnecessary £6 guidebook, reservation tel. 020/8312-6608, www.rmg.co.uk.

Old Royal Naval College

Despite the name, these grand structures were built (1692) as a veterans' hospital to house disabled and retired sailors who'd served their country. In 1873, the hospital was transformed into one of the world's most prestigious universities for training naval officers. Today, the buildings host university students, music students, business conventions, concerts, and film crews drawn to the awe-inspiring space.

▲Painted Hall

Originally intended as a dining hall for pensioners, this sumptuously painted room was deemed too glorious (and, in the winter, too cold) for that purpose. So almost as

soon as it was completed, it became simply a showcase for visitors. Impressive as it is, the admission is quite steep to see gigantic paintings by an artist you've never heard of, featuring second-rate royals. But those who appreciate artistic spectacles and picking out lavish details will find it worthwhile.

Cost and Hours: £12, daily 10:00-17:00, sometimes closed for private events, www.ornc.org. Ticket includes audioguide and a 45-minute guided tour of the Old Royal Naval College grounds, not including the Painted Hall (departs from Discover Greenwich at the top of each hour).

▲National Maritime Museum

Great for anyone interested in the sea, this museum holds everything from a giant working paddlewheel to the uniform Admiral Horatio Nelson wore when he was killed at Trafalgar. A big glass roof tops three levels of slick, modern, kid-friendly exhibits about all things seafaring.

Cost and Hours: Free, daily 10:00-17:00, tel. 020/8858-4422, www.rmg.co.uk. The museum hosts frequent family-oriented events—singing, treasure hunts, and storytelling—particularly on weekends; ask at the desk. Listen for announcements alerting visitors to free tours on various topics.

▲▲Royal Observatory Greenwich

Located on the prime meridian (0° longitude), this observatory is famous as the point from which all time and distances on earth are measured. It was here that astronomers studied the heavens in order to help seafarers navigate. In the process, they used the constancy of the stars to establish standards of measurement for time and distance used by the whole world.

Cost and Hours: £16, includes audioguide, combo-ticket with *Cutty Sark*—£26.25; daily 10:00-17:00; tel. 020/8858-4422, reservations tel. 020/8312-6608, www.rmg.co.uk.

Visiting the Observatory: A visit here gives you a taste of the sciences of astronomy, timekeeping, and seafaring—and how they all meld together—along with great views over Greenwich and the distant London skyline. In the courtyard, snap a selfie straddling the famous prime meridian line in the pavement. In the museum, there's the original 1600s-era observatory and several early telescopes. You'll see the famous clocks from the 1700s that first set the standard of global time, as well as more recent timekeeping devices.

The **Weller Astronomy Galleries** has interactive, kid-pleasing displays allowing you to guide a space mission and touch a 4.5-billion-year-old meteorite (free, daily 10:00-17:00). And the state-of-the-art, 120-seat **Peter Harrison Planetarium** offers entertaining and informative shows several times a day where they project a view of the heavens onto the interior of the dome (£10, shows about every 45 minutes during the observatory's opening times, no morning shows on school days, check schedule online).

▲The Docklands

Nestled around a hairpin bend in the Thames, this area was London's harbor and warehouse district back in the 19th century, when Britannia ruled the waves. Today, glittering new skyscrapers rise from those historic canals and docks.

The heart of the Docklands is the Isle of Dogs, a marshy pen-

insula in the river's curve. But don't expect Jolly Olde England here. The Docklands is more about businesspeople in suits, creatively planned parks, art-filled plazas, and chain restaurants. Even so, traces of its rugged dockworker past survive. You'll see canals, former docks, brick warehouses, and a fine history museum. Most impressive of all, there's not a tourist in sight.

WEST OF LONDON

Because these two sights are in the same general direction, you can visit both in one day. Take the train from London Waterloo to Hampton Court Palace, then taxi to Kew Gardens (£20, about 30 minutes). If you're on a tight budget, the transit connection between Hampton Court and Kew is long but doable: Take bus #R68 from Hampton Court Station to the West Park Road stop (about one hour), then walk about a half-mile to the Kew Gardens gate (walk up West Park Road to, then through, the Kew Gardens train station).

▲▲Kew Gardens

For a fine riverside park and a palatial greenhouse jungle to swing through, take the Tube or the boat to every botanist's favorite escape, Kew Gardens. While to most visitors the Royal Botanic Gardens of Kew are simply a delightful opportunity to wander among 50,000 different types of plants, to the hardworking organization that runs them, the gardens are a way to promote the understanding and preservation of the botanical diversity of our planet.

Cost and Hours: £18, June-Aug £11 after 16:00, kids 4-16—£6, kids under 4—free; Mon-Thu 10:00-19:00, Fri-Sun until 20:00, closes earlier Sept-March—check schedule online, glasshouses close at 17:30 in high season—earlier off-season, free one-hour walking tours daily at 11:00 and 13:30, tel. 020/8332-5000, www.kew.org.

Getting There: By Tube, ride to Kew Gardens station, then cross the footbridge over the tracks, which drops you in a little community of plant-and-herb shops, a two-block walk from Victoria Gate (the main garden entrance). Boats also run to Kew Gardens from Westminster Pier (April-Oct; see page 59).

Eating: For a sun-dappled lunch or snack, walk 10 minutes from the Palm House to the **$$ Orangery Cafeteria** (Mon-Thu 10:00-17:30, Fri-Sun until 18:30, until 15:15 in winter, closes early for events).

Visiting the Gardens: Pick up a map brochure and check at the gate for a monthly listing of the best blooms. Garden lovers could spend days exploring Kew's 300 acres. For a quick visit, spend a fragrant hour wandering through three buildings: the Palm House, a humid·Victorian world of iron, glass, and tropical plants that was built in 1844; a Waterlily House that Monet would swim for; and the Princess of Wales Conservatory, a meandering modern greenhouse with many different climate zones growing countless cacti, bug-munching carnivorous plants, and more. Check out the Xstrata Treetop Walkway, a 200-yard-long scenic steel walkway that puts you high in the canopy 60 feet above the ground.

▲▲Hampton Court Palace

Fifteen miles up the Thames from downtown, the 500-year-old palace of Henry VIII, William and Mary, and other royals is worth ▲▲▲ for palace aficiona-

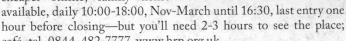

dos. The stately brick-and-stone palace stands overlooking the Thames and includes some fine Tudor halls and Georgian-era rooms, all made engaging by a sharp, well-produced, included audioguide.

Cost and Hours: £23.70, cheaper online, family ticket available, daily 10:00-18:00, Nov-March until 16:30, last entry one hour before closing—but you'll need 2-3 hours to see the place; café, tel. 0844-482-7777, www.hrp.org.uk.

Getting There: From London's Waterloo· Station, take a South West train. The train will drop you on the far side of the river from the palace—just walk across the bridge (2/hour, 35 minutes). Consider arriving at or departing from the palace by boat (connections with London's Westminster Pier, see page 59); it's a relaxing and scenic three- to four-hour cruise past two locks and a fun new/old riverside mix.

Background: Hampton Court was originally the palace of Henry VIII's minister and right-hand-man, Cardinal Thomas Wolsey. When Wolsey realized Henry VIII was experiencing a little palace envy, he gave the mansion to his king...clever guy. The Tudor palace was also home to Elizabeth I and Charles I. Later, when William and Mary moved in, they renovated about one-third of the palace (with help from Christopher Wren).

Visiting the Palace: Use the free map to find your way to the audioguide tour routes. Red-vested docents throughout the complex are happy to answer questions.

Henry VIII's apartments feature a breathtaking Great Hall,

with a marvelous hammerbeam ceiling, precious Abraham tap-estries that kept this huge room warm and cozy, and a portrait of Henry VIII's family. His private balcony looks down into the stunning Chapel Royal. His kitchens were capable of keeping 600 schmoozing courtiers well fed. At the end of the kitchens, dip into the Chapel Royal for a closer look at the wood-carved decor and the starry-sky-and-gold-beam ceiling.

The Young Henry VIII's Story exhibit introduces you to the dashing, athletic, young Henry VIII, from the perspective of Henry himself; his first wife, Catherine of Aragon; and his right-hand man, Thomas Wolsey. At the end of the Young Henry VIII section, stairs lead up to William III's apartments, from about 150 years after Henry's time.

Before leaving, stroll in the gardens. Don't miss the easy-to-overlook entrance (immediately on the right) to William and Mary's walled privy garden, like a mini-Versailles.

NORTH OF LONDON
The Making of Harry Potter:
Warner Bros. Studio Tour London

While you can visit several real-life locations where the Harry Potter movies were filmed, there's only one way to see imaginary places like Hogwarts' Great Hall, Diagon Alley, Dumbledore's office, and #4 Privet Drive: Visit the Warner Bros. Studio in Leavesden 20 miles north-west of London.

Attractions include the actual sets, costumes, and props used for the films; video interviews with the actors and filmmakers; and exhib-its about how the films' special effects were created.

The visit culminates with a stroll down Diagon Alley and a room-sized 1:24-scale model of Hogwarts.

Plan Ahead: It's essential to buy a ticket far in advance (entry possible only with reserved time slot). Allow about three hours at the studio, plus nearly three hours to get there and back.

Cost and Hours: £45—purchase timed-entry ticket online in advance, kids ages 5 to 15—£37, family ticket available; opening hours flex with season—first tour at 9:00 or 10:00, last tour as early as 14:30 or as late as 18:30, audio/videoguide-£5, café, tel. 0345-084-0900, www.wbstudiotour.co.uk.

Getting There: Take the frequent train from London Euston to Watford Junction (about 5/hour, 20 minutes), then catch the

Mullany's Coaches shuttle bus (instantly recognizable by its bright paint job) to the studio tour (2-4/hour, 15 minutes, £2.50 round-trip—cash only, buy ticket from driver).

More direct (and more expensive), Golden Tours runs multiple daily **buses** between their office near Victoria Station and the studio (price includes round-trip bus and studio entrance: adults—£75-90, kids—£70-85; reserve ahead at www.goldentours.com).

Shopping in London

Most stores are open Monday through Saturday from roughly 9:00 or 10:00 until 17:00 or 18:00, with a late night on Wednesday or Thursday (usually until 19:00 or 20:00). Many close on Sundays. Large department stores stay open later during the week (until about 21:00 Mon-Sat) with shorter hours on Sundays. If you're looking for bargains, visit one of the city's many street markets.

SHOPPING STREETS

The best and most convenient shopping streets are in the West End and West London (roughly between Soho and Hyde Park). You'll find midrange shops along **Oxford Street** (running east from Tube: Marble Arch), and fancier shops along **Regent Street** (stretching south from Tube: Oxford Circus to Piccadilly Circus) and **Knightsbridge** (where you'll find Harrods and Harvey Nichols; Tube: Knightsbridge). Other streets  are more specialized, such as **Jermyn Street** for old-fashioned men's clothing (just south of Piccadilly) and **Charing Cross Road** for books. **Floral Street,** connecting Leicester Square to Covent Garden, is lined with boutiques.

Another fine street, which runs between Oxford Street and Marylebone Road, is **Marylebone High Street** (ending near Regent's Park and Madame Tussauds). It feels more quaint and less ritzy than some of the streets described earlier, and it's fun to browse for its combination of high-end chain stores, local one-off shops, art concept stores, clothing boutiques, and sleek home decor...all under handsome red-brick turreted townhouses. Along this street is the unique **Daunts Books,** filling an old townhouse with titles organized geographically (for details, see page 41), and an outpost of **Emma Bridgewater,** a country-charming home decor store (sort of the English Martha Stewart, www.emmabridgewater. co.uk).

FANCY DEPARTMENT STORES

Harrods

Harrods is London's most famous and touristy department store. With more than four acres of retail space covering seven floors, it's a place where some shoppers could spend all day. (To me, it's still just a department store.) Big yet classy, Harrods has everything from elephants to toothbrushes (Mon-Sat 10:00-21:00, Sun 11:30-18:00, Brompton Road, Tube: Knightsbridge, tel. 020/7730-1234, www.harrods.com).

Harvey Nichols

Once Princess Diana's favorite and later Duchess Kate's, "Harvey Nick's" remains the department store *du jour* (Mon-Sat 10:00-20:00, Sun 11:30-18:00, near Harrods, 109 Knightsbridge, Tube: Knightsbridge, tel. 020/7235-5000, www.harveynichols.com). The store's fifth floor is a veritable food fest, with a gourmet grocery store, a fancy restaurant, a sushi bar, and a lively café.

Fortnum & Mason

The official department store of the Queen, Fortnum & Mason embodies old-fashioned, British upper-class taste. While some feel it is too stuffy, you won't find another store with the same storybook atmosphere. With rich displays and deep red carpet, Fortnum's feels classier and more relaxed than Harrods (Mon-Sat 10:00-21:00, Sun 11:30-18:00, elegant tea served in their Diamond Jubilee Tea Salon—see page 189, 181 Piccadilly, Tube: Green Park, tel. 020/7734-8040, www.fortnumandmason.com.

Liberty

Designed to make well-heeled shoppers feel at home, this half-timbered, mock-Tudor emporium is a 19th-century institution that thrives today. Known for its gorgeous "Liberty Print" floral fabrics, well-stocked crafts department, and castle-like interior, this iconic shop was a favorite of writer Oscar Wilde, who called it "the chosen resort of the artistic shopper" (Mon-Sat 10:00-20:00, Sun 11:30-18:00, Great Marlborough Street, Tube: Oxford Circus, tel. 020/7734-1234, www.liberty.co.uk.

STREET MARKETS

Those who appreciate antiques, artisan goods, and a fine bargain love London's street markets. There's good early-morning market activity somewhere any day of the week. The best markets—which combine lively stalls and a colorful neighborhood with cute and characteristic shops of their own—are Portobello Road and

Camden Lock Market. Hagglers will enjoy the no-holds-barred bargaining encouraged in London's street markets. **Greenwich** (a quick DLR ride from central London) also has its share of great markets, especially lively on weekends. **Warning:** Markets attract two kinds of people—tourists and pickpockets.

Portobello Road Market (Notting Hill)

Arguably London's best street market, Portobello Road stretches for several blocks through the delightful, colorful, funky-yet-quaint Notting Hill neighborhood. Charming streets lined with pastel-painted houses and offbeat antique shops are enlivened on Fridays and Saturdays with 2,000 additional stalls (9:00-19:00), plus food, live music, and more. (The best strategy is to come on Friday; most stalls are open, with half the crowds of Saturday.) If you start at Notting Hill Gate and work your way north, you'll find these general sections: antiques, new goods, produce, vintage clothing, more new goods, a flea market, and more food. While Portobello Road is best on Fridays and Saturdays, you can still enjoy this street's quirky shops on most other days as well (Tube: Notting Hill Gate, near recommended accommodations, tel. 020/7727-7684, www.portobelloroad.co.uk).

Camden Lock Market (Camden Town)

This huge, trendy arts-and-crafts market is divided into three areas, each with its own vibe (but all of them fresh and funky). The whole complex sprawls around an old-fashioned, still-functioning lock (used mostly for leisure boats) and its retro-chic, yellow-brick industrial buildings. The main market, set alongside the picturesque canal, features a mix of shops and stalls selling boutique crafts and artisanal foods.  The market on the opposite side of Chalk Farm Road is edgier, with cheap ethnic food stalls, lots of canalside seating, and punk crafts. The Stables, a sprawling, incense-scented complex, is decorated with fun statues of horses and squeezed into tunnels under the old rail bridge just behind the main market. It's a little lowbrow and wildly creative, with cheap clothes, junk jewelry, and loud music (daily 10:00-19:00, busiest on weekends, tel. 020/3763-9999, www.camdenmarket.com).

Leadenhall Market (The City)

One of London's oldest, Leadenhall Market stands on the original Roman center of town. Today, cheese and flower shops nestle between pubs, restaurants, and boutiques, all beneath a beautiful Victorian arcade (Harry Potter fans may recognize it as Diagon Alley). This is not a "street market" in the true sense, but more a hidden gem in the midst of London's financial grind (Mon-Fri 10:00-18:00, tel. 020/7332-1523, Tube: Monument or Liverpool; off Gracechurch Street near Leadenhall Street and Fenchurch).

East End Markets

These East End markets are busiest and most interesting on Sundays. See the map on page 118 for locations.

Petticoat Lane Market: Just a block from Spitalfields Market, this line of stalls sits on the otherwise dull, glass-skyscraper-filled Middlesex Street; adjoining Wentworth Street is grungier and more characteristic. Expect budget clothing, leather, shoes, watches, jewelry, and crowds (Sun 9:00-14:00, sometimes later; smaller market Mon-Fri on Wentworth Street only; no market Sat; Middlesex Street and Wentworth Street).

Spitalfields Market: This huge, mod-feeling market hall combines a shopping mall with old brick buildings and sleek modern ones, all covered by a giant glass roof. The shops, stalls, and a rainbow of restaurant options are open every day, tempting you with ethnic eateries, crafts, trendy clothes, bags, and an antiques-and-junk market (Mon-Fri 10:00-17:30—but vendors begin shutting down around 17:00, Sat from 11:00, Sun from 9:00; from the Tube stop, take Bishopsgate East exit, turn left, walk to Brushfield Street, and turn right; www.spitalfields.co.uk).

Truman Markets: Housed in the former Truman Brewery on Brick Lane, this cluster of markets is in the heart of the "Banglatown" Bangladeshi community. Of the East End market areas, these are the grittiest and most avant-garde. The markets are in full swing on Sundays, though you'll see some action on Saturdays and possibly other days (see hours below).

From Liverpool Street, head a few blocks east to Brick Lane and turn left. As you work your way north along Brick Lane through the Truman complex, you'll first come to the **Boiler House Food Hall** (on the left, filling an old warehouse with food stands and loud music), then the entrance to the **Vintage Market,** which occupies the basement with what claims to be London's largest assortment of vintage vendors (Mon-Sat 11:00-18:00, Sun from 10:00, www.vintage-market.co.uk). Just beyond, on the left, follow the crowds into the **Backyard Market,** with stylish clothing, arts, and crafts (Sat 11:00-18:00, Sun 10:00-17:00). Just beyond on the right, the **House of Vegan** fills yet another warehouse with exclusively vegetarian and vegan food stalls (Sat-Sun 11:00-18:00). Surrounding shops and eateries, including a fun courtyard of food trucks tucked off Brick Lane, are open all week.

Brick Lane Market: If you leave the Truman Brewery complex and continue north along Brick Lane, the action flows into a more casual assortment of food and arts stands and street performers called the Brick Lane Market. This spans several short blocks, from about Buxton Street to Bethnal Green Road—about a 10-minute walk. Continuing another 10 minutes north, then turning right onto Columbia Road, takes you to the next market.

Columbia Road Flower Market: This colorful shopping street is made even more lively by the Sunday-morning commotion of shouting flower vendors (Sun 8:00-15:00, www.columbiaroad. info). Halfway up Columbia Road, be sure to loop left up little Ezra Street, with characteristic eateries, boutiques, and antique vendors.

West End Markets

Covent Garden Market: Originally the convent garden for Westminster Abbey, the iron-and-glass market hall hosted a produce market until the 1970s (earning it the name "Apple Market"). Now it's a mix of fun shops, eateries, markets, and a more modern-day Apple Store on the corner. Mondays are for antiques, while arts and crafts dominate the rest of the week. Yesteryear's produce stalls are open daily 10:30-18:00, and on Thursdays, a food market brightens up the square (Tube: Covent Garden, tel. 020/7395-1350, www. coventgardenlondonuk.com).

Jubilee Market: This market features antiques on Mondays (5:00-17:00); a general market Tuesday through Friday (10:30-19:00); and arts and crafts on Saturdays and Sundays (10:00-18:00). It's located on the south side of Covent Garden (tel. 020/7379-4242, www.jubileemarket.co.uk).

Entertainment in London

For the best list of what's happening and a look at the latest London scene, check www.timeout.com/london. The free monthly *London Planner* covers sights, events, and plays, though generally not as well as the *Time Out* website.

THEATER (A.K.A. "THEATRE")

London's theater scene rivals Broadway's in quality and often beats it in price. Choose from 200 offerings—Shakespeare, musicals, comedies, thrillers, sex farces, cutting-edge fringe, revivals starring movie celebs, and more. London does it all well.

Seating Terminology: Just like at home, London's theaters sell seats in a range of levels—but the Brits use different terms: stalls (ground floor), dress circle (first balcony), upper circle (second balcony), balcony (sky-high third balcony), and slips (cheap seats on the fringes). Discounted tickets are called "concessions" (abbreviated as "conc" or "s"). "Restricted view" seats can be a bargain, but you won't be able to see all (or even most) of the stage. For floor plans of the various theaters, see www.theatremonkey.com.

Big West End Shows

Nearly all big-name shows are hosted in the theaters of the West End, clustering around Soho (especially along Shaftesbury Avenue) between Piccadilly and Covent Garden. With a centuries-old tradition of pleasing the masses, they present London theater at its grandest.

Well-known musicals may draw the biggest crowds, but the West End offers plenty of other crowd-pleasers, from revivals of classics to cutting-edge works by the hottest young playwrights. These productions tend to have shorter runs than famous musicals. Many productions star huge-name celebrities—London is a magnet for movie stars who want to stretch their acting chops.

You'll see the latest offerings advertised all over the city. The *Official London Theatre Guide,* a free booklet that's updated every two weeks, is a handy tool (find it at hotels, box offices, the City of London TI, and online at www.officiallondontheatre.co.uk). You can check reviews at www.timeout.com/london.

Most performances are nightly except Sunday, usually with two or three matinees a week. The few shows that run on Sundays are mostly family fare (such as *The Lion King*).

Buying Tickets for West End Shows

For most visitors, it makes sense to simply buy tickets in London. Most shows have tickets available on short notice—likely at a discount. But if your time in London is limited—and you have your heart set on a particular show that's likely to sell out (usually the newest shows, and especially on weekends)—you can buy peace of mind by booking tickets from home.

Advance Tickets: It's generally cheapest to buy your tickets directly from the theater, either through its website or by calling the theater box office. In most cases, a theater will reroute you to a third-party ticket vendor such as Ticketmaster (which usually comes with a booking fee of around £3/ticket). You can have your tickets emailed to you or pick them up before show time at Will Call. Note that many third-party websites sell all kinds of London theater tickets, but these generally charge higher prices and fees. It's best to try the theater's website or box office first.

Discount Tickets from the TKTS Booth: This famous outlet at Leicester Square sells discounted tickets (25-50 percent off) for many shows (£3/ticket service charge included, open Mon-Sat 10:00-19:00, Sun 11:00-16:30). TKTS offers a wide variety of shows on any given day, though they may not always have the hottest shows in town. You must buy in person at the kiosk, and the best deals are same-day only.

The list of shows and prices is continually updated and posted outside the booth and on their website (www.tkts.co.uk). For the best choice and prices, come early in the day—the line starts forming even before the booth opens (it moves quickly).

Take note: The real TKTS booth (with its prominent sign) is a freestanding kiosk at the south edge of Leicester Square. Several dishonest outfits nearby advertise "official half-price tickets"— avoid these, where you'll rarely pay anything close to half-price.

Tickets at the Theater Box Office: Even if a show is "sold out," there's usually a way to get a seat. Many theaters offer various discounts or "concessions": same-day tickets, cheap returned tickets, standing-room, matinee, senior or student standby deals, and more. Start by checking the show's website, then call the box office or simply drop by (many theaters are right in the tourist zone).

Same-day tickets (called **"day seats"**) can be an excellent deal. These generally go on sale *only in person* when the box office opens (typically at 10:00; for popular shows, people start lining up well before then). These tickets (£20 or less) tend to be single seats either in the nosebleed rows or with a restricted view—but sometimes they can be front-row seats.

Very popular shows don't bother with "day seats," but a few distribute tickets through a lottery (for instance, via the show's website or a drawing for hopefuls who show up in person during a certain time window on the day of the show). The more popular the show, the lower your chances are, but it's fun to give it a shot. Look up details on each show's website.

Another strategy is to show up at the box office shortly before show time (best on weekdays) and—before paying full price—ask about cheaper options. Last-minute return tickets are often sold at great prices as curtain time approaches.

For a helpful guide to "day seats"—including recent user reports on how early you need to show up—consult www.theatremonkey. com/dayseatfinder.htm; for tips on getting cheap and last-minute tickets, visit www.londontheatretickets.org and www.timeout. com/london/theatre.

Booking Through Other Agencies: Although booking through a middleman such as your hotel or a ticket agency is quick and easy (and may be your last resort for a sold-out show), prices are greatly inflated. Ticket agencies and third-party websites are often just scalpers with an address. If you do buy from an agency, choose one who is a member of the Society of Ticket Agents and Retailers (look for the STAR logo—short for "secure tickets from authorized retailers"). These legitimate resellers normally add a maximum 25 percent booking fee to tickets.

Scalpers (or "Touts"): As at any event, you'll find scalpers hawking tickets outside theaters. And, just like at home, those people may either be honest folk whose date just happened to cancel at the last minute...or they may be unscrupulous thieves selling forgeries. London has many of the latter.

Theater Beyond the West End

Tickets for lesser-known shows tend to be cheaper (figure £15-30), in part because most of the smaller theaters are government-subsidized. Remember that plays don't need a familiar title or famous actor to be a worthwhile experience—read up on the latest offerings online; *Time Out*'s website is a great place to start. Major noncommercial theaters include the National Theatre, Barbican Centre, Royal Court Theatre, Menier Chocolate Factory, and Bridge Theatre. The Royal Shakespeare Company performs at various theaters around London.

Shakespeare's Globe

To see Shakespeare in a replica of the theater for which he wrote his plays, attend a play at the Globe. In this round, thatched-roof, open-air theater, the plays are performed much as Shakespeare intended—under the sky, with no amplification.

The play's the thing from late April through mid-October (usually Tue-Sat 14:00 and 19:30, Sun either 13:00 and/or 18:30, tickets can be sold out months in advance). You'll pay £5 to stand and £23-47 to sit, usually on a backless bench (only a few rows and the pricier Gentlemen's Rooms have seats with backs, £2 cushions and £4 add-on backrests a good investment; dress for the weather).

The £5 "groundling" or "yard" tickets—which are open to rain—are most fun. Scurry in early to stake out a spot on the stage's edge, where the most interaction with the actors occurs. You're a crude peasant. You can lean your elbows on the stage, munch a snack (yes, you can bring in food—but bag size is limited), or walk around. I've never enjoyed Shakespeare as much as here, performed as it was meant to be in the "wooden O." If you can't get a ticket, consider waiting around. Plays can be long, and many groundlings leave before the end. Hang around outside and beg or buy a ticket from someone leaving early (groundlings are allowed to come and go). A few non-Shakespeare plays are also presented each year. If you can't attend a show, you can take a guided tour of the theater and museum by day (see page 123).

At the indoor Sam Wanamaker Playhouse, the season is designed to complement the Globe's summer season, though a few summer performances may take place here. In winter, the Playhouse hosts Shakespeare, Shakespearean-era plays, new works by up-and-coming playwrights, and early-music concerts. Many of the productions in this intimate venue (about 350 seats) are one-offs and can be more expensive.

To reserve tickets for plays at the Globe or Playhouse, drop by the box office (daily 10:00-18:00, open one hour later on performance days, New Globe Walk entrance, box office tel. 020/7401-9919; info tel. 020/7902-1400). You can also reserve online (www.shakespearesglobe.com, £2.50 booking fee). If the tickets are sold out, don't despair; a few often free up at the last minute. Try calling around noon the day of the performance to see if the box office expects any returned tickets. If so, they'll advise you to show up a little more than an hour before the show, when these tickets are sold (first-come, first-served).

The theater is on the South Bank, directly across the Thames over the Millennium Bridge from St. Paul's Cathedral (Tube: Mansion House or London Bridge). The Globe is inconvenient for public transport, but during theater season a regular supply of black cabs waits nearby, or you could try to order an Uber.

Outdoor and Fringe Theater

In summer, enjoy Shakespearean drama and other plays under the stars at the **Open Air Theatre,** in leafy Regent's Park in north London. You can bring your own picnic, order à la carte from the theater menu, or preorder a picnic supper from the theater at least 24 hours in advance (tickets from £25, available beginning in mid-Jan, season runs mid-May-mid-Sept; book at www.openairtheatre.org or—for an extra booking fee—by calling 0333-400-3562; grounds open 1.5 hours before performances; only one small bag permitted per person; 10-minute walk north of Baker Street Tube, near Queen Mary's Gardens within Regent's Park; detailed directions and more info at www.openairtheatre.org).

London's rougher evening-entertainment scene is thriving. Choose from a wide range of **fringe theater** and comedy acts (find posters in many Tube stations, or search for "fringe theater" on www.timeout.com; tickets can start as cheap as £5-10).

CONCERTS AT CHURCHES

For easy, cheap, or free concerts in historic churches, attend a **lunch concert,** especially:

- St. Bride's Church, with free half-hour lunch concerts twice a week at 13:15 (usually Tue and Fri—confirm in advance, church tel. 020/7427-0133, www.stbrides.com).

Evensong

One of my favorite experiences in Britain is to attend evensong at a great church. Evensong is an evening worship service that is typically sung rather than said (though some parts—including scripture readings, a few prayers, and a homily—are spoken). It follows the traditional Anglican service in the Book of Common Prayer, including prayers, scripture readings, canticles (sung responses), and hymns that are appropriate for the early evening—traditionally the end of the working day and before the evening meal. In major churches with resident choirs, this service is filled with quality, professional musical elements. A singing or chanting priest leads the service, and a choir—usually made up of both men's and boys' voices (to sing the lower and higher parts, respectively)—sings the responses. The choir usually sings a cappella, or is accompanied by an organ. While regular attendees follow the service from memory, visitors—who are welcome—are given an order of service or a prayer book to help them follow along.

The most impressive places for evensong include London (Westminster Abbey, St. Paul's, Southwark Cathedral, or St. Bride's Church), Cambridge (King's College Chapel), Canterbury Cathedral, Wells Cathedral, Oxford (Christ Church Cathedral), York Minster, and Durham Cathedral. While this list includes many of the grandest churches in England, be aware that evensong typically takes place in the small choir area—which is far more intimate than the main nave. (To see the full church in action, a concert is a better choice.) Evensong generally occurs daily between 17:00 and 18:00 (often two hours earlier on Sun)—check with individual churches for specifics. At smaller churches, evensong is sometimes spoken, not sung.

Note that evensong is not a performance—it's a somewhat somber worship service. If you enjoy worshipping in different churches, attending evensong can be a trip-capping highlight. Most major churches also offer organ or choral concerts—look for posted schedules or ask at the information desk or gift shop.

- Temple Church, also in The City, with free organ recitals weekly (Wed at 13:15, www.templechurch.com).
- St. James's at Piccadilly, with 50-minute concerts on Mon, Wed, and Fri at 13:10 (suggested £5 donation, info tel. 020/7734-4511, www.sjp.org.uk).
- St. Martin-in-the-Fields, offering concerts on Mon, Tue, and Fri at 13:00 (suggested £3.50 donation, church tel. 020/7766-1100, www.stmartin-in-the-fields.org).

St. Martin-in-the-Fields also hosts fine **evening concerts** by candlelight (£9-29, several nights a week at 19:30) and live jazz in its underground Café in the Crypt (£8-15, Wed at 20:00).

Evensong services are held at several churches, including St. Paul's Cathedral (see page 104), Westminster Abbey (see page 64), Southwark Cathedral (see page 125), and St. Bride's Church (Sun at 17:30).

Free **organ recitals** are usually held on Sunday at 17:45 in Westminster Abbey (30 minutes, tel. 020/7222-5152). Many other churches have free concerts; ask for the *London Organ Concerts Guide* at the TI.

SUMMER EVENINGS ALONG THE SOUTH BANK

If you're visiting London in summer, consider hitting the South Bank neighborhood after hours.

Take a trip around the **London Eye** while the sun sets over the city (the wheel spins until late—last ascent at 20:30 or later in summer). Then cap your night with an evening walk along the pedestrian-only **Jubilee Walkway,** which runs east-west along the river. It's where Londoners go to escape the heat. This pleasant stretch of the walkway—lined with pubs and casual eateries—goes from the London Eye past Shakespeare's Globe to Tower Bridge (you can walk in either direction).

If you're in the mood for a movie, take in a flick at the **BFI Southbank,** located just across the river, alongside Waterloo Bridge. Run by the British Film Institute, the state-of-the-art theater shows mostly classic films, as well as art cinema (Tube: Waterloo or Embankment, check www.bfi.org.uk for schedules and prices).

Farther east along the South Bank is **The Scoop**—an outdoor amphitheater next to City Hall. It's a good spot for movies, concerts, dance, and theater productions throughout the summer—with Tower Bridge as a scenic backdrop. These events are free, nearly nightly, and family-friendly. For the latest event schedule, see www.morelondon.com and click on "Events" (next to City Hall, Riverside, The Queen's Walkway, Tube: London Bridge).

SPORTING EVENTS

Tennis, cricket, rugby, football (soccer), and horse races all take place within an hour of the city. In summer Wimbledon draws a half-million spectators (www.wimbledon.com), while big-name English Premier League soccer clubs—including Chelsea, Arsenal, Tottenham Hotspur, and West Ham United—take the pitch in London to sell-out crowds (www.premierleague.com). The two biggest horse races of the year take place in June: the Royal Ascot Races (www.ascot.co.uk) near Windsor and the Epsom Derby (www.epsomderby.co.uk) in Surrey are both once-in-a-lifetime experiences.

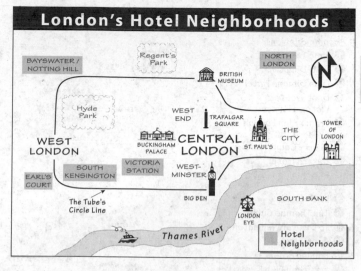

London's Hotel Neighborhoods

Securing tickets to anything sporting-related in London can be difficult—and expensive. Check the official team or event website several months in advance; tickets can sell out within minutes of going on sale to the general public. Third-party booking companies such as SportsEvents 365 (www.sportsevents365.com) and Ticketmaster (www.ticketmaster.co.uk) often have tickets to popular events at a premium price—a godsend for die-hard fans. Many teams also offer affordable, well-run stadium tours—check your favorite side's official website for details. Even if you can't attend a sports event in person, consider cheering on the action in a London pub.

Sleeping in London

London is an expensive city for lodging. Focus on choosing the right neighborhood, which is as important as selecting the right hotel. I've picked a handful of my favorite neighborhoods (Victoria Station, South Kensington, Earl's Court, Bayswater, and North London) and recommend a range of options for each, from £20 bunks to deluxe £300-plus doubles with all the comforts. Because such comforts (and charm) come at a price, I've also listed big, modern, good-value chain hotels scattered throughout the city, along with hostels, dorms, and apartment rental information.

I rank accommodations from **$** budget to **$$$$** splurge. For the best deal, contact my family-run places directly by phone or email. When you book direct, the owner avoids a commission and

LONDON

Victoria Station Neighborhood

Accommodations
1. Lime Tree Hotel
2. B&B Belgravia
3. Luna Simone Hotel
4. Best Western Victoria Palace
5. Premier Inn London Victoria
6. Cherry Court Hotel
7. Bakers Hotel

Eateries
8. La Bottega
9. The Thomas Cubitt
10. To Duke of Wellington
11. Grumbles
12. Pimlico Fresh
13. Seafresh Fish Rest.
14. The Jugged Hare
15. St. George's Tavern
16. Tachbrook Market

Services
17. Groceries (3)
18. To Launderette
19. Hop-On Bus Tours (3)
20. Tube, Taxis, City Buses
21. Buses to Windsor & Legoland
22. Buses to Luton & Stansted Airports

200 Meters

200 Yards

may be able to offer a discount. Book well in advance for peak season or if your trip coincides with a major holiday or festival (see the appendix). For more details on reservations, short-term rentals, and more, see the "Sleeping" section in the Practicalities chapter.

Looking for Hotel Deals Online: Given London's high hotel prices, it's worth searching for a deal. For more options, browse these accommodation discount sites: www.londontown. com (an informative site with a discount booking service), www. athomeinlondon.co.uk and www.londonbb.com (both list central B&Bs), www.lastminute.com, www.visitlondon.com, and www. eurocheapo.com.

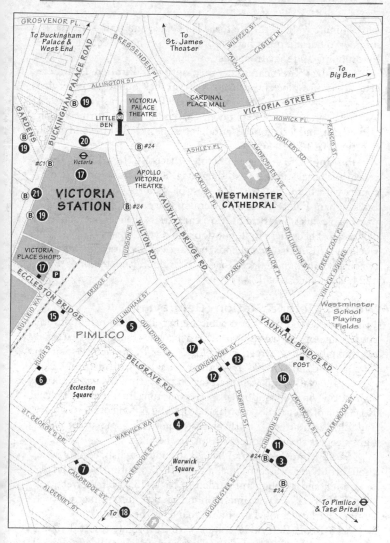

VICTORIA STATION NEIGHBORHOOD

The streets behind Victoria Station teem with little, moderately-priced-for-London B&Bs. It's a safe, surprisingly tidy, and decent area without a hint of the trashy, touristy glitz of the streets immediately surrounding the station. I've divided these accommodations into two broad categories: Belgravia, west of the station, feels particularly posh, while Pimlico, to the east, is still upscale and dotted with colorful eateries. While I wouldn't go out of my way just to dine here, each area has plenty of good restaurants (see "Eating in London," later). All of my recommended hotels are within a five-minute walk of the Victoria Tube, bus, and train stations. In summer, request a quiet back room; most of these B&Bs lack air-conditioning and may front busy streets.

Laundry: The nearest laundry option is **Pimlico Launderette,** about five blocks southwest of Warwick Square (self-service and same-day full-service, daily 8:00-19:00, last wash at 17:30; 3 Westmoreland Terrace—go down Clarendon Street, turn right on Sutherland, and look for the launderette on the left at the end of the street; tel. 020/7821-8692).

Parking: The 400-space Semley Place **NCP parking garage** is near the hotels on the west/Belgravia side (£42/day, possible discounts with hotel voucher, just west of Victoria Coach Station at Buckingham Palace Road and Semley Place, tel. 0845-050-7080, www.ncp.co.uk). **Victoria Station car park** is cheaper but a quarter of the size; check here first, but don't hold your breath (£30/day on weekdays, £15/day on weekends, entrance on Eccleston Bridge between Buckingham Palace Road and Bridge Place, tel. 0345-222-4224, www.apcoa.co.uk).

West of Victoria Station (Belgravia)

In Belgravia, the prices are a bit higher and your neighbors include some of the world's wealthiest people. These two places sit on tranquil Ebury Street, two blocks over from Victoria Station (or a slightly shorter walk from the Sloane Square Tube stop). You can cut the walk from Victoria Station to nearly nothing by taking a short ride on frequent bus #C1 (leaves from Buckingham Palace Road side of Victoria Station and drops you off on corner of Ebury and Elizabeth streets). Both places come with some street noise; light sleepers should request a room in the back.

$$$$ Lime Tree Hotel has 28 spacious, stylish, comfortable, thoughtfully decorated rooms, a helpful staff, a fun-loving breakfast room, and a delightful garden in back (135 Ebury Street, tel. 020/7730-8191, www.limetreehotel.co.uk, info@limetreehotel.co.uk, Charlotte and Matt, Laura manages the office).

$$$ B&B Belgravia comes with 26 bright, colorful rooms and high ceilings. It feels less than homey, but still offers good value for the location. Most of its rooms come with closets and larger-than-average space (family rooms, 66 Ebury Street, tel. 020/7259-8570, www.bb-belgravia.com, info@bb-belgravia.com).

East of Victoria Station (Pimlico)

This area feels a bit less genteel than Belgravia, but it's still plenty inviting, with eateries and grocery stores. Most of these hotels are on or near Warwick Way, the main drag through this area. Generally the best Tube stop for this neighborhood is Victoria (though the Pimlico stop works equally well for the Luna Simone). Bus

#24 runs right through the middle of Pimlico, connecting the Tate Britain to the south with Victoria Station, the Houses of Parliament, Trafalgar Square, the British Museum, and much more to the north.

$$$ Luna Simone Hotel rents 36 fresh, spacious, remodeled rooms with modern bathrooms. It's a smartly managed place, run for more than 50 years by twins Peter and Bernard—and Bernard's son Mark—and they still seem to enjoy their work (RS%, family rooms, 47 Belgrave Road near the corner of Charlwood Street, handy bus #24 stops out front, tel. 020/7834-5897, www.lunasimonehotel.com, stay@lunasimonehotel.com).

$$ Best Western Victoria Palace offers modern, if slightly worn, business-class comfort compared with some of the other creaky old guesthouses in the neighborhood. Choose from the 43 rooms in the main building (at 60 Warwick Way), or pay about 20 percent less by booking a nearly identical room in one of the annexes, each a half-block away—an excellent value for this neighborhood if you skip breakfast (air-con, elevator in main building only, 17 Belgrave Road and 1 Warwick Way, reception at main building, tel. 020/7821-7113, www.bestwesternvictoriapalace.co.uk, info@bestwesternvictoriapalace.co.uk).

$ Cherry Court Hotel, run by the friendly and industrious Patel family, rents 12 very small but bright and well-designed rooms with firm mattresses in a central location. Considering London's sky-high prices, this is an extraordinary budget choice (family rooms, fruit-basket breakfast in room, air-con, laundry, 23 Hugh Street, tel. 020/7828-2840, www.cherrycourthotel.co.uk, info@cherrycourthotel.co.uk, Neha answers emails and offers informed restaurant advice).

$$ OYO Hotels, an India-based chain that finances renovations for thousands of run-down budget hotels worldwide, has arrived in London. While they've salvaged some places that were at death's door, the standards are still pretty basic. If you're on a very tight budget, OYO hotels may be worth considering—including several in the Victoria Station area (www.oyorooms.com/gb). One of these is **Bakers Hotel,** which shoehorns 12 brightly painted rooms into a tight building (cheaper single rooms with shared bath, family rooms, 126 Warwick Way, tel. 020/7834-0729, www.bakershotel.co.uk, reservations@bakershotel.co.uk, Amin Jamani).

If considering chain hotels, there's also a fine **$$$ Premier Inn** in this area (82 Eccleston Square, www.premierinn.com).

"SOUTH KENSINGTON," SHE SAID, LOOSENING HIS CUMMERBUND

To stay on a quiet street so classy it doesn't allow hotel signs, make "South Ken" your London home. This upscale area has plenty of

South Kensington Neighborhood

To Kensington Palace

Kensington Gardens

ALBERT MEMORIAL

WEST CARRIAGE DRIVE

Hyde Park

SOUTH CARRIAGE DRIVE

To Knightsbridge

KENSINGTON

ROAD

ROYAL ALBERT HALL

N

ENNISMORE GARDENS

RUTLAND GATE

PRINCE CONSORT ROAD

PRINCE'S GARDENS

EXHIBITION ROAD

ALBERTOPOLIS

AYRTON ROAD

IMPERIAL COLLEGE ROAD

To Harrods

SCIENCE MUSEUM

BROMPTON ORATORY

BROMPTON RD.

VICTORIA & ALBERT MUSEUM

NATURAL HISTORY MUSEUM

BROMPTON ROAD

BROMPTON

CROMWELL ROAD

QUEENSBURY PL.

CROMWELL PLACE

THURLOE PLACE

Thurloe Square

WALTON ST.

QUEEN'S GATE

HARRINGTON ROAD

BUTE ST.

REECE MEWS

OWEN PL.

3

THURLOE STREET

4

5 South Kensington

PELHAM STREET

SLOANE AVE.

6

9

POST

2

7

1

Onslow Square

ONSLOW SQUARE

PELHAM CRESCENT

SYDNEY PL.

LUCAN PLACE

ELYSTAN STREET

OLD BROMPTON ROAD

9

ONSLOW MEWS E.

ONSLOW GARDENS

SUMNER PLACE

ROAD

IXWORTH PLACE

SOUTH KENSINGTON

ONSLOW

To Earl's Court

GARDENS

8

SELWOOD

FULHAM

CALE ST.

300 Meters

300 Yards

Accommodations
1 Aster House
2 Number Sixteen Hotel
3 The Pelham Hotel

Eateries & Other
4 Exhibition Road Food Circus

5 Daquise
6 Moti Mahal Indian Rest.
7 Old Brompton Road Eateries
8 The Anglesea Arms Pub
9 Groceries (2)

LONDON

colorful restaurants and easy access to the Victoria & Albert and Natural History museums; shoppers like being a short walk from Harrods and the designer shops of King's Road and Chelsea. When I splurge, I splurge here. The South Kensington Tube stop gives you access to both the handy Piccadilly and Circle/District lines, making it easy to get virtually anywhere in London; it's also easy to reach from Heathrow.

$$$$ Aster House, in a lovely Victorian town house, is run with care by friendly Simon and Leonie Tan, who've been welcoming my readers for years (I call it "my home in London"). It's a stately and sedate place, with 13 comfy rooms, a cheerful lobby, and lounge. Enjoy breakfast or just kicking back in the whisper-elegant Orangery, a glassy greenhouse (RS%, air-con, 3 Sumner Place, tel. 020/7581-5888, www.asterhouse.com, asterhouse@gmail.com).

$$$$ Number Sixteen, for well-heeled travelers, packs over-the-top class into its 41 artfully imagined rooms, plush designer-chic lounges, and tranquil garden. It's in a labyrinthine building, with boldly modern decor—perfect for an urban honeymoon (air-con, elevator, 16 Sumner Place, tel. 020/7589-5232, US tel. 1-888-559-5508, www.numbersixteenhotel.co.uk, sixteen@firmdale.com).

$$$$ The Pelham Hotel, a 52-room business-class hotel with crisp service and a pricey mix of pretense and style, is genteel, with low lighting and a pleasant drawing room and library among the many perks (air-con, elevator, fitness room, 15 Cromwell Place, tel. 020/7589-8288, US tel. 1-888-757-5587, www.pelhamhotel.co.uk, reservations.thepelham@starhotels.com).

NEAR EARL'S COURT

This neighborhood—a couple of Tube stops farther from South Kensington on the Piccadilly and Circle/District lines—is a nice compromise between local-feeling and accessible to travelers. It has a stately residential feel, and a high concentration of high-capacity, relatively expensive hotels. Solo travelers might consider one of the several quality chains here. The main drag that runs in front of the Tube station—Earl's Court Road—is lined with easy chain eateries.

$$$$ K+K Hotel George occupies a grand Georgian building on a quiet street just behind the Earl's Court Tube station. With spacious public areas, a wellness center, and 154 well-appointed rooms, it feels polished and professional (air-con, elevator, 1 Templeton Place, tel. 020/7598-8700, www.kkhotels.com, hotel.george@kkhotels.com).

$$$$ NH London Kensington, part of a Spanish hotel chain, has 121 business-style rooms offering reliable comfort and class. Bonuses include a pleasant garden patio, a fitness center, and

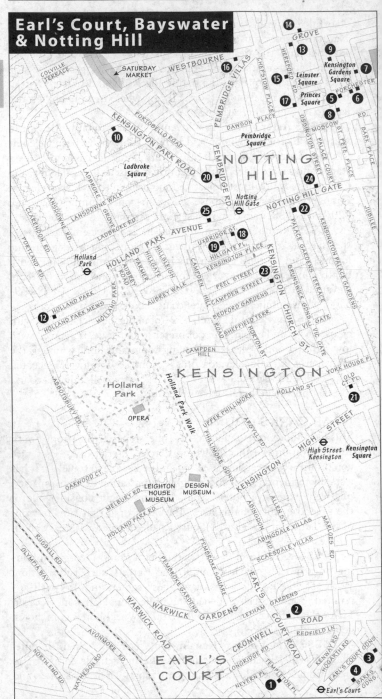

Earl's Court, Bayswater & Notting Hill

LONDON

SATURDAY Market

COLVILLE TERRACE

WESTBOURNE

PEMBRIDGE VILLAS

GROVE

14

HEREFORD RD

13

9

CHEPSTOW PLACE

16

Leinster Square

Kensington Gardens Square

7

15

Princes Square

5

PORCHESTER

17

8

6

DAWSON PLACE

MOSCOW RD

ST PETE RD

BARK PLACE

KENSINGTON PARK ROAD

10

PORTOBELLO ROAD

PEMBRIDGE RD

Pembridge Square

NOTTING HILL

PALACE COURT

PALACE PLACE

OSSINGTON STREET

Ladbroke Square

20

24

LADBROKE GROVE

LANSDOWNE WALK

LANSDOWNE RD

Notting Hill Gate

25

CLARENDON RD

PORTLAND RD

LADBROKE RD

HOLLAND PARK AVENUE

NOTTING HILL GATE

22

JUBILEE

HILLGATE

FARMER

HILLSLEIGH

UXBRIDGE ST

18

PALACE GARDENS TERRACE

KENSINGTON PALACE GARDENS

Holland Park

19

HILLGATE PL.

KENSINGTON PLACE

AUBREY RD

AUBREY WALK

CAMPDEN HILL

PEEL STREET

KENSINGTON CHURCH ST.

BRUNSWICK GDNS.

VIC. GATE

VIC. GDNS.

23

12

Holland Park Mews

HOLLAND PARK

CAMPDEN STREET

BEDFORD GARDENS

SHEFFIELD TERR.

HORTON ST.

CAMPDEN HILL

KENSINGTON

YORK HOUSE PL.

OLD CT. PL.

Holland Park

Holland Park Walk

HOLLAND ST.

21

OPERA

UPPER PHILLIMORE

PHILLIMORE GDNS.

ARGYLL RD

HIGH STREET

ABBOTSBURY RD

High Street Kensington

Kensington Square

OAKWOOD CT.

LEIGHTON HOUSE MUSEUM

DESIGN MUSEUM

MELBURY RD

KENSINGTON

ALLEN ST.

ABINGDON

HOLLAND PARK RD

HOLLAND PARK RD

ABINGDON VILLAS

SCARSDALE VILLAS

MARLOES RD

RUSSELL RD

PEMBROKE SQUARE

PEMBROKE GARDENS

OLYMPIA WAY

WARWICK GARDENS

EARL'S

LEXHAM GARDENS

COURT ROAD

ROAD

2

REDFIELD LN.

WARWICK ROAD

CROMWELL ROAD

KENWAY RD

HOGARTH RD

EARL'S COURT GDNS.

3

AVONMORE RD

NEVERN PL.

TEMPLETON PL.

LONGRIDGE RD

EARL'S

COURT

1

Earl's Court

4

BARKS. GDNS.

NORTH END RD

MATHESON RD

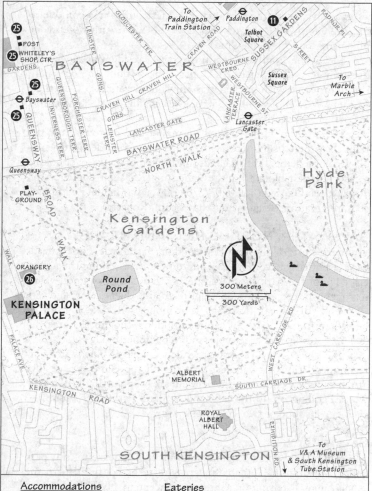

Accommodations
1. K+K Hotel George
2. NH London Kensington
3. Nadler Kensington
4. Henley House Hotel
5. Vancouver Studios
6. Phoenix & Kensington Gardens Hotels
7. London House Hotel
8. Princes Square Guest Accommodation
9. Garden Court Hotel
10. Portobello Hotel
11. Stylotel
12. Norwegian YWCA

Eateries
13. Cocotte
14. Farmacy
15. Hereford Road
16. Taqueria
17. The Prince Edward
18. Geales
19. Mazi
20. The Fish House of Notting Hill
21. Maggie Jones's
22. The Shed
23. The Churchill Arms Pub & Thai Kitchen
24. Café Diana
25. Groceries (5)
26. The Orangery (Afternoon Tea)

an extensive, tempting, optional breakfast buffet (air-con, elevator, 202 Cromwell Road, tel. 020/7244-1441, www.nh-hotels.com, nhkensington@nh-hotels.com).

$$$$ The **Nadler Kensington,** on a residential block, is a five-minute walk from Earl's Court Tube station. The 65 smallish rooms come with kitchenettes (air-con, elevator, 25 Courtfield Gardens, tel. 020/7244-2255, www.thenadler.com, kensington. info@thenadler.com).

$$$ Henley House Hotel is smaller and more warmly run than the others listed here, with 21 rooms in a modern, red-and-black color scheme. It fills a handsome brick townhouse overlooking a garden, a half-block from the Tube stop (RS%, air-con, elevator, 30 Barkston Gardens, tel. 020/7370-4111, www.henleyhousehotel. com, reservations@henleyhousehotel.com, Roberta).

BAYSWATER, NOTTING HILL, AND NEARBY

From the core of the tourist's London, vast Hyde Park spreads west, eventually becoming Kensington Gardens. Along the northern edge of the park sits Bayswater, with a cluster of good-value, reasonably priced accommodations in an area that's sleepy and very "homely" (Brit-speak for cozy). Your money will take you farther here than in most parts of central London—though the area can feel a bit sterile, and the hotels tend to be impersonal.

The Queensway Tube stop, while a couple of blocks from my recommendations, is handiest as it sits on the Central Line. I've also listed a few choices in the adjacent areas of Notting Hill (to the west), Paddington (to the east) and Holland Park (to the south)— each one just one or two Tube stops away.

Bayswater

Most of my Bayswater accommodations flank a peaceful, tidy park called Kensington Gardens Square (not to be confused with the much bigger Kensington Gardens adjacent to Hyde Park). One block east is the bustling street Queensway, a multicultural festival of commerce and eateries popular with young international travelers.

$$$ Vancouver Studios has 45 modern, tastefully furnished rooms that come with fully equipped kitchenettes, or you can pay for a continental breakfast. It's nestled between Kensington Gardens Square and Prince's Square and has its own tranquil garden patio out back (laundry, 30 Prince's Square, tel. 020/7243-1270, www.vancouverstudios.co.uk, info@vancouverstudios.co.uk).

$$$ Phoenix Hotel offers spacious, stately public spaces and 125 modern-feeling rooms with classy decor. While the rates can vary wildly, it's a good choice if you can get a deal (elevator, 1 Kensington Gardens Square, tel. 020/7229-2494, www.phoenixhotel. co.uk, reservations@phoenixhotel.co.uk).

$$$ London House Hotel has 103 spiffy, modern, cookie-cutter rooms at reasonable prices (family rooms, air-con, elevator, 81 Kensington Gardens Square, tel. 020/7243-1810, www. londonhousehotels.com, reservations@londonhousehotels.com).

$$$ Princes Square Guest Accommodation is a crisp (if impersonal) place renting 50 businesslike rooms with pleasant, modern decor. It's well located, practical, and a very good value, especially if you can score a good rate (elevator, 23 Prince's Square, tel. 020/7229-9876, www.princessquarehotel.co.uk, info@princessquarehotel.co.uk).

$$$ Garden Court Hotel is understated, with 40 simple, homey-but-tasteful rooms (family rooms, elevator, 30 Kensington Gardens Square, tel. 020/7229-2553, www.gardencourthotel. co.uk, info@gardencourthotel.co.uk).

$$ Kensington Gardens Hotel, with the same owners as the Phoenix Hotel, laces 17 rooms together in a tall, skinny building (breakfast served at Phoenix Hotel, 9 Kensington Gardens Square, tel. 020/7243-7600, www.kensingtongardenshotel.co.uk, info@ kensingtongardenshotel.co.uk).

Notting Hill

Just west of Bayswater (Tube: Notting Hill Gate), spreading out from the northwest tip of Kensington Gardens, this area is famous for two things: It's the site of the colorful Portobello Road Market (see page 146), and was the setting of the 1999 Hugh Grant/Julia Roberts film of the same name. The **$$$$ Portobello Hotel** is on a quiet residential street in the heart of the neighborhood. Its 21 rooms are funky yet elegant—both the style and location give it an urban-fresh feeling (elevator, 22 Stanley Gardens, tel. 020/7727-2777, www.portobellohotel.com, stay@portobellohotel.com).

Paddington

The streets and squares around Paddington Station teem with "budget" (but still overpriced) hotels handy to the Heathrow Express train and useful Tube lines. The well-run **$$ Stylotel** feels like the stylish, super-modern, aluminum-clad big sister of the EasyHotel chain. While the 42 rooms can be cramped, the beds have space for luggage underneath (RS%, family rooms, air-con, elevator, 160 Sussex Gardens, tel. 020/7723-1026, www.stylotel. com, info@stylotel.com, Andreas).

NORTH LONDON

These hotels are north of Regent Street, a long walk or quick Tube or bus ride from the lively Soho area and Hyde Park. These are

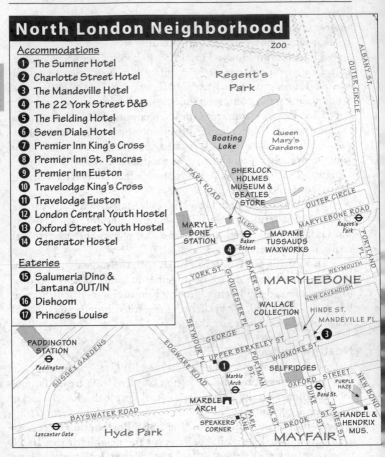

North London Neighborhood

Accommodations
1. The Sumner Hotel
2. Charlotte Street Hotel
3. The Mandeville Hotel
4. The 22 York Street B&B
5. The Fielding Hotel
6. Seven Dials Hotel
7. Premier Inn King's Cross
8. Premier Inn St. Pancras
9. Premier Inn Euston
10. Travelodge King's Cross
11. Travelodge Euston
12. London Central Youth Hostel
13. Oxford Street Youth Hostel
14. Generator Hostel

Eateries
15. Salumeria Dino & Lantana OUT/IN
16. Dishoom
17. Princess Louise

my closest hotels to the center of London, and some of my most expensive. The wide streets and grand homes (including Sherlock Holmes') gives this area an elegant aura...which is only slightly compromised by the hordes of tourists flocking through to reach Madame Tussauds.

$$$$ The Sumner Hotel rents 19 rooms in a 19th-century Georgian townhouse sporting large contemporary rooms and a lounge with fancy modern Italian furniture. This swanky place packs in all the amenities and is conveniently located north of Hyde Park and near Oxford Street, a busy shopping destination—close to Selfridges and a Marks & Spencer (RS%, air-con, elevator, 54 Upper Berkeley Street, a block-and-a-half off Edgware Road, Tube: Marble Arch, tel. 020/7723-2244, www.thesumner.com, hotel@thesumner.com).

$$$$ Charlotte Street Hotel, in the Fitzrovia neighborhood close to the British Museum, has inviting public spaces

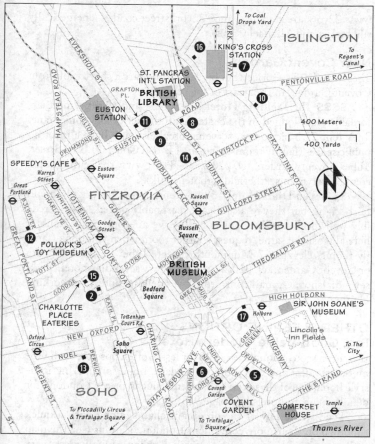

and 52 bright, elegant rooms (connecting family rooms, air-con, elevator, 15 Charlotte Street, Tube: Tottenham Court Road, tel. 020/7806-2000, www.charlottestreethotel.com, reservations@charlottestreethotel.com).

$$$$ The Mandeville Hotel, at the center of the action just one block from Bond Street Tube station, has a genteel British vibe, with high ceilings, tasteful art, just-vibrant-enough colors, and 142 rooms. It's a worthy splurge for its amenities and location, especially if you score a good deal (air-con, elevator, Mandeville Place, tel. 020/7935-5599, www.mandeville.co.uk, info@mandeville.co.uk).

$$$ The 22 York Street B&B offers a casual alternative in the city center, with an inviting lounge and 10 traditional, hardwood, comfortable rooms, each named for a notable London landmark (near Marylebone/Baker Street: From Baker Street Tube station, walk 2 blocks down Baker Street and take a right to 22 York Street—no sign, just look for #22; tel. 020/7224-2990, www.22yorkstreet.co.uk, mc@22yorkstreet.co.uk, energetically run by Liz and Michael Callis).

Near Covent Garden

These two hotels—pricey but oh so central—are a short walk from Covent Garden, in the heart of the action.

$$$$ The Fielding Hotel is a simple and slightly more affordable place lodged in the center of all the action on a quiet lane. They rent 25 basic rooms, serve no breakfast, and have almost no public spaces (family rooms, air-con, 4 Broad Court off Bow Street, Tube: Covent Garden, tel. 020/7836-8305, www.thefieldinghotel.co.uk, reservations@thefieldinghotel.co.uk).

$$ Seven Dials Hotel's 38 no-nonsense rooms are plain and fairly tight, but they're also clean, reasonably priced, and incredibly well located (some, but not all, have air-con). Since doubles here all cost the same, request a larger room when you book (family rooms, elevator, 7 Monmouth Street, Tube: Leicester Square or Covent Garden, tel. 020/240-0823, www.sevendialshotel.co.uk, sevendialshotel@gmail.com, run by friendly and hardworking Hanna).

OTHER SLEEPING OPTIONS
Big, Good-Value, Modern Hotels

If you can score a double for £100 (or less—often possible with promotional rates) and don't mind a modern, impersonal, American-style hotel, one of these can be a decent value in pricey London. (for details on chain hotels, see page 918).

I've listed a few of the dominant chains, along with a quick rundown on their more convenient London locations (see the map earlier to find chain hotels in North London). Quality can vary wildly so check online reviews. Some of these branches sit on busy streets in dreary train-station neighborhoods. While I wouldn't necessarily rule these out, ask for a quieter room, use common sense when exploring after dark, and wear a money belt.

I've focused on affordable options here. Pricier London hotel chains include Millennium/Copthorne, Grange, Firmdale, Thistle, InterContinental/Holiday Inn, Radisson, Hilton, and Red Carnation.

$$ Motel One, the German chain that specializes in affordable style, has a branch at Tower Hill, a 10-minute walk north of the Tower of London (24 Minories—see map on page 108, tel. 020/7481-6420, www.motel-one.com, london-towerhill@motel-one.com).

$$ Premier Inn has more than 70 hotels in greater London. Convenient locations include a branch inside London County Hall (next to the London Eye), at Southwark/Borough Market (near

Shakespeare's Globe, 34 Park Street), Southwark/Tate Modern (15 Great Suffolk Street), Kensington/Earl's Court (11 Knaresborough Place), Victoria (82 Eccleston Square), and Leicester Square (1 Leicester Place). In North London, the following branches cluster between King's Cross St. Pancras and the British Museum: King's Cross, St. Pancras, and Euston. Avoid the Tower Bridge location, south of the bridge and a long walk from the Tube—but London City Tower Hill, north of the bridge on Prescot Street (see map on page 108)—works fine (www.premierinn.com).

$$ Travelodge has close to 70 locations in London, including at King's Cross (200 yards in front of King's Cross Station, Gray's Inn Road) and Euston (1 Grafton Place). Other handy locations include King's Cross Royal Scot, Marylebone, Covent Garden, Liverpool Street, Southwark, and Farringdon; www.travelodge.co.uk.

$$ Ibis, the budget branch of the AccorHotels group, has a few dozen options across the city, with a handful of locations convenient to London's center, including London Blackfriars (49 Blackfriars Road) and London City Shoreditch (5 Commercial Street). The more design-focused Ibis Styles has branches near Earl's Court (15 Hogarth Road) and Southwark, with a theater theme (43 Southwark Bridge Road; https://ibis.accorhotels.com).

$ EasyHotel, with several branches in good neighborhoods, offers generally tiny, super-efficient, no-frills rooms that feel popped out of a plastic mold, down to the prefab ship's head-type "bathroom pod." Rates can be surprisingly low (with doubles as cheap as £30 if you book early enough)—but you'll pay à la carte for expensive add-ons, such as TV use, Wi-Fi, luggage storage, fresh towels, and daily cleaning (breakfast, if available, comes from a vending machine). If you go with the base rate, it's like hosteling with privacy—a hard-to-beat value. But you get what you pay for (thin walls, flimsy construction, noisy fellow guests, and so on). They're only a good deal if you book far enough ahead to get a good price and skip the many extras. Locations include Victoria (34 Belgrave Road), South Kensington (14 Lexham Gardens), and Paddington (10 Norfolk Place); www.easyhotel.com.

$ Hub by Premier Inn—the budget chain's no-frills, pod-style division—offers extremely small rooms (just a little bigger than the bed) in convenient locations for low prices (as affordable as £69; www.premierinn.com/gb/en/hub.html).

Hostels

Hostels can slash accommodation costs while meeting your basic needs. The following places are open 24 hours, have private rooms as well as dorms, and come with Wi-Fi.

¢ London Central Youth Hostel is the flagship of London's hostels, with all the latest in security and comfortable efficiency.

Families and travelers of any age will feel welcome in this wonderful facility. You'll pay the same price for any bed—so try to grab one with a bathroom (families welcome to book an entire room, book long in advance; between Oxford Circus and Great Portland Street Tube stations at 104 Bolsover Street—see map on page 166, tel. 0345-371-9154, www.yha.org.uk, londoncentral@yha.org.uk).

¢ **Oxford Street Youth Hostel** is right in the shopping and clubbing zone in Soho (14 Noel Street—see map on page 166, Tube: Oxford Street, tel. 0345-371-9133, www.yha.org.uk, oxfordst@yha.org.uk).

¢ **St. Paul's Youth Hostel,** near St. Paul's Cathedral, is modern, friendly, well-run, and a bit scruffy (36 Carter Lane, Tube: St. Paul's, tel. 0345-371-9012, www.yha.org.uk, stpauls@yha.org.uk).

¢ **Generator Hostel** is a brightly colored, hip hostel with a café and a DJ spinning the hits. It's in a renovated building tucked behind a busy street halfway between King's Cross and the British Museum (37 Tavistock Place—see map on page 166, Tube: Russell Square, tel. 020/7388-7666, http://staygenerator.com, ask.london@generatorhostels.com).

¢ **St. Christopher's Inn**, a cluster of three hostels, south of the Thames near London Bridge, has cheap dorm beds; one branch (the Oasis) is for women only. All have loud and friendly bars attached (must be over 18 years old, 161 Borough High Street, Tube: Borough or London Bridge, reservations tel. 020/8600-7500, www.st-christophers.co.uk).

¢ **Norwegian YWCA** (Norsk K.F.U.K.) is open to all Norwegian women and to non-Norwegian women under 30. (Men must be under 30 with a Norwegian passport.) On a quiet street near Holland Park in the Kensington area, it offers an open-face Norwegian ambience (private rooms available, 52 Holland Park—see map on page 162, Tube: Holland Park, tel. 020/7727-9346, www.kfukhjemmet.org.uk, kontor@kfukhjemmet.org.uk).

Apartment Rentals

Consider this option if you're traveling as a family, in a group, or staying several days. Websites such as Airbnb and VRBO let you correspond directly with property owners or managers, or consider one of the sites listed next. For more information on short-term rentals, see the Practicalities chapter.

LondonConnection.com rents several properties around London. **OneFineStay.com** offers stylish, contemporary flats (most of them part-time residences) in desirable London neighborhoods. **SuperCityUk.com** rents chic, comfortable aparthotels and serviced apartments in four buildings. Other options include **Cross-Pollinate.com, Coach House Rentals** (www.chsrentals.

com), VisitApartmentsLondon.co.uk, HomeFromHome.co.uk, and **APlaceLikeHome.co.uk.**

Eating in London

Far from the dated stereotypes of dreary British food, London is one of Europe's great food cities. Whether it's dining well with

the upper crust, sharing hearty pub fare with the blokes, or venturing to a fringe neighborhood to try the latest hotspot or street food at a market, eating out is an essential part of the London experience. The sheer variety of foods—from every corner of Britain's former empire and beyond—is astonishing.

I rank eateries from **$** budget to **$$$$** splurge. For more advice on eating in London, including ordering, tipping, and British cuisine and beverages, see the "Eating" section of the Practicalities chapter.

CENTRAL LONDON

Central London is absolutely packed—with both locals and tourists—and restaurants are overflowing, even on a "quiet" night. On weekends and later in the evenings, sidewalks and even the streets become congested with people out barhopping and clubbing. If you're looking for peace and quiet and a calm meal, avoid Friday and Saturday evenings here and go early on other nights.

Many popular chain restaurants permeate this area (for a description of some reliable chains, see page 929). There's no need to clutter up my listings and maps with these—like Starbucks or McDonald's, you can count on seeing them wherever you go.

Heart of Soho

With its many theaters, reputation as a rollicking nightspot, and status as *the* place where budding restaurateurs stake their claim on London's culinary map, the Soho neighborhood is a magnet for diners. As it's close to London's must-see's and do's, you could find yourself eating here a lot (convenient for dinner after a day of sightseeing, or before going to the theater). Even if Soho isn't otherwise on your radar, make a point to dine here at least once.

$$$ Andrew Edmunds Restaurant is a tiny candlelit space where you'll want to hide your guidebook and not act like a tourist. This little place—with a loyal clientele—is the closest I've found to Parisian quality in a cozy restaurant in London. The extensive wine

LONDON

Central London Restaurants

1. Andrew Edmunds Restaurant
2. Mildred's Vegetarian Rest. & Bao
3. Temper Soho
4. Kiln
5. Bocca di Lupo
6. Kricket Soho
7. Nopi
8. Hoppers
9. Princi
10. Yalla Yalla
11. Fernandez & Wells
12. Nordic Bakery
13. Ole & Steen
14. Gelupo Gelato
15. Kingly Court Eateries
16. Mother Mash & Dishoom
17. Four Seasons
18. Dumplings' Legend

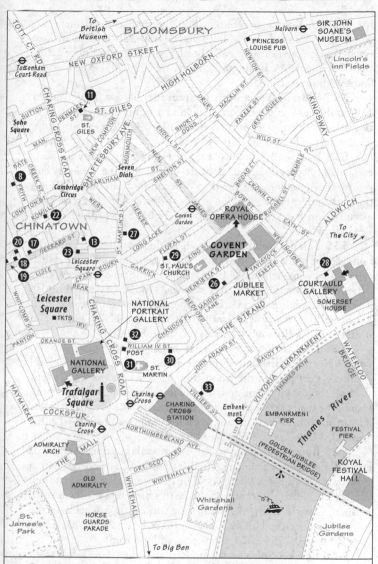

- ⑲ Viet Food
- ⑳ Rasa Sayang
- ㉑ XU Teahouse & Rest.; The Palomar
- ㉒ Y Ming Chinese Restaurant
- ㉓ Jen Café
- ㉔ The Wolseley
- ㉕ Brasserie Zédel
- ㉖ Rules Restaurant
- ㉗ Dishoom

- ㉘ Shapur Indian Restaurant
- ㉙ Lamb & Flag Pub
- ㉚ Terroirs Wine Bar
- ㉛ St. Martin-in-the-Fields Café in the Crypt
- ㉜ The Chandos Pub
- ㉝ Gordon's Wine Bar
- ㉞ Brown's Hotel Tea Room

list, modern European cooking, and creative seasonal menu are worth the splurge (daily 12:30-15:30 & 17:30-22:45, these are last-order times, come early or call ahead, request ground floor rather than basement, 46 Lexington Street, tel. 020/7437-5708, www.andrewedmunds.com).

$$ Mildred's Vegetarian Restaurant, across from Andrew Edmunds, has a creative, fun menu and a tight, high-energy interior filled with happy herbivores (daily 12:00-23:00, vegan options, 45 Lexington Street, tel. 020/7494-1634).

$$$ Bao is a minimalist eatery selling top-quality Taiwanese cuisine, specializing in delicate and delectable steamed-bun sandwiches (portions are small so order more than one). This is a popular spot, often with a line across the street; try to arrive early or late (Mon-Sat 12:00-15:00 & 17:30-22:00, Sun 12:00-17:00, 53 Lexington Street).

$$$ Temper Soho pleases well-heeled carnivores. From the nondescript office-block entrance, you'll descend to a cozy, stylish cellar filled with rich smoke from meat grilling on open fires. They carve off chunks for tacos and *parathas* (Indian-style flatbreads). The portions are small and pricey (order multiple courses), but meat lovers willing to pay leave satisfied (Mon-Sat 12:00-22:30, Sun until 21:00, 25 Broadwick Street, tel. 020/3879-3834).

$$$ Kiln invigorates the taste buds with the explosive flavors of Northern Thailand. Squeeze along the long, stainless-steel counter—peering into the wood-fired kilns where the frantic staff does all the cooking—or grab a table in the cramped cellar dining room. The menu skews slightly to the adventurous (i.e., organ meat and strong sauces and curries), with delicious results (daily 12:00-15:00 & 17:00-23:00, 58 Brewer Street).

$$$ Bocca di Lupo, a stylish and popular option, serves half and full portions of classic regional Italian food. Dressy but with a fun energy, it's a place where you'll be glad you made a reservation. The counter seating, on cushy stools with a view into the lively open kitchen, is particularly memorable, or you can take a table in the snug, casual back end (daily 12:30-15:00 & 17:15-23:00, 12 Archer Street, tel. 020/7734-2223, www.boccadilupo.com).

$$$ Kricket Soho serves upmarket Indian fare a few steps from Piccadilly Circus. Opt for the tight, stylish, unpretentious main floor (with counter seating surrounding an open kitchen) or the dining room in the cellar. The small-plates menu is an education in Indian cuisine beyond the corner curry house, with *kulchas* (miniature naan breads with toppings), *kheer* (rice pudding), and KFC—Keralan fried chicken (Mon-Sat 12:00-14:30 & 17:15-22:30, closed Sun, 12 Denman Street, tel. 020/7734-5612).

$$$$ Nopi is one of a handful of restaurants run by London celebrity chef Yotam Ottolenghi. The cellar features communal tables looking into the busy kitchen, and the cuisine is typical of Ottolenghi's masterful Eastern Mediterranean cooking, with an emphasis on seasonal produce. If you want to splurge in Soho, do it here (Mon-Sat 10:00-15:00 & 17:30-22:30, Sun until 16:00, 21 Warwick Street, tel. 020/7494-9584, www.ottolenghi.co.uk).

$$ Hoppers is an easy entry into Sri Lankan cuisine—reminiscent of Indian but with more tropical flourishes. You'll be glad the menu comes with a glossary of key terms—for example, hopper (a spongy yet firm rice-and-coconut pancake, shaped like a bowl), *kari* (Tamil for "curry"), and *roti* (flatbread). Be adventurous, and seek the waitstaff's advice (Mon-Sat 12:00-14:30 & 17:30-22:30, closed Sun, 49 Frith Street, tel. 020/3319-8110).

$$ Princi is a vast, bright, efficient, wildly popular Italian deli/bakery with Milanese flair. Along one wall is a long counter with display cases offering a tempting array of *pizza rustica,* panini, focaccia, pasta dishes, and desserts. Order your food at the counter, then find a space to share at a long table; or get it to go. They also have a classy restaurant section with reasonable prices if you'd rather have table service (daily 8:00-24:00, 135 Wardour Street, tel. 020/7478-8888).

$$ Yalla Yalla is a bohemian-chic hole-in-the-wall serving up high-quality Beirut street food—hummus, baba ghanoush, tabbouleh, and *shawarmas.* Eat in the cramped and cozy interior or at one of the few outdoor tables (daily 10:00-24:00, 1 Green's Court—just north of Brewer Street, tel. 020/7287-7663).

Between Soho and Covent Garden: Cozy and convivial, **$$ Fernandez & Wells** is a delightfully simple wine, cheese, and ham bar. Grab a stool as you belly up to the big wooden bar. Share a plate of tapas, top-quality cheeses, and/or Spanish, Italian, or French hams with fine bread and oil, all while sipping a nice glass of wine (generally Mon-Sat 10:00-22:00, Sun until 17:00, quality sandwiches at lunch, 1 Denmark Street, tel. 020/ 3302-9799).

Coffee and Pastries: Nordic Bakery is Scandinavian-sleek and faces the green and lovely Golden Square. They serve up good coffee, as well as delicious cinnamon buns and dark rye bread, among other light bites (Mon-Fri 7:30-20:00, Sat-Sun 9:00-19:00, 14A Golden Square, tel. 020/7487-5877). Similarly, keep an eye out for **Ole & Steen,** a chain of coffee shops with generous free samples of cinnamon buns (one location near Soho at 67 Charing Cross Road).

Gelato: Across the street from Bocca di Lupo (listed earlier) is its sister *gelateria,* **Gelupo,** with a wide array of ever-changing but always creative and delicious dessert favorites. Take away or enjoy their homey interior (daily 11:00-23:00, 7 Archer Street, tel. 020/7287-5555).

Near Carnaby Street

The area south of Oxford Circus between Regent Street and Soho Gardens entices hungry shoppers with attention-grabbing, gimmicky restaurants that fill the niche between chains and upscale eateries. Stroll along Ganton, Carnaby, Kingly, and Great Marlborough streets for something that fits your budget and appetite, or consider these.

Kingly Court, with three levels of international restaurants overlooking a convivial courtyard, is a handy place to comparison-shop for a meal. Favorites include **Le Bab,** serving elevated kebabs, and **Señor Ceviche,** with Peruvian raw fish fare (long hours daily, enter either at 9 Kingly Street or at 49 Carnaby Street).

$$$ Dishoom, the super-popular Indian restaurant (see full listing later, under "Near Covent Garden") also has a branch on Kingly Street, with the same top-notch fare and the same long lines (daily 8:00-23:00, 22 Kingly Street, tel. 020/7420-9322).

$$ Mother Mash is a bangers-and-mash version of a fish-and-chips shop. Choose your mash, meat, and gravy and enjoy this simple, satisfying, and thoroughly British meal (daily 10:00-22:00, 26 Ganton Street, tel. 020/7494-9644).

Chinatown

Chinatown is just next door to Soho. These listings straddle the two districts.

On the Main Drag, near the Archways: The intersecting main streets of Chinatown—Wardour Street and Gerrard Street, with the ornamental archways—are lined with touristy, interchangeable Chinese joints. **$$ Four Seasons** is a cheap, reliable, traditional standby (12 Gerrard Street; second location at 23 Wardour). A bit more appealing is **$$ Dumplings' Legend.** The draw here is their dumplings—particularly *siu long bao* (soup dumplings), which you can see being made fresh through the glassed-in kitchen as you enter (no reservations; on pedestrian main drag, 15 Gerrard Street). Other options worth considering include **$$$ Viet Food,** featuring tapas-style Vietnamese small plates with a busy chef in the window (34 Wardour Street); and **$ Rasa Sayang,** a hole-in-the-wall serving Malaysian wok dishes (5 Macclesfield Street).

On Rupert Street: These places are on easy-to-miss Rupert Street, one block over from Wardour. **$$$ XU Teahouse and Restaurant**—more sedate and sophisticated than the eateries in the heart of Chinatown—has a retro-feeling interior, genteel tea counter, and a short, well-curated Taiwanese menu. Come here to escape the bustle and enjoy a quality meal (daily 12:00-23:00, at #30, tel. 020/3319-8147). **$$$ The Palomar,** next door, serves well-respected Israeli and Middle Eastern small plates in a cozy atmosphere (daily 12:00-14:30 & 17:30-23:00, at #34, tel. 020/7439-8777).

On the Edge of Chinatown: $$ Y Ming Chinese Restaurant—across Shaftesbury Avenue from the ornate gates, clatter, and dim sum of Chinatown—has dressy, porcelain-blue European decor, serious but helpful service, and authentic Northern Chinese cooking. It's worth the short walk from the heart of Chinatown for food that's a notch above (good £15 meal deal offered 12:00-18:00, open Mon-Sat 12:00-23:30, closed Sun, 35 Greek Street, tel. 020/7734-2721, run for more than 20 years by William). **$ Jen Café,** across from the main Chinatown strip in the little square called Newport Place, is a humble Chinese corner eatery. Appreciated for its homemade dumplings, it only has stools and simple seating, but fast service, a fun and inexpensive menu, and a devoted following (Mon-Wed 11:00-20:30, Thu-Sun until 21:30, cash only, 4 Newport Place, tel. 020/7287-9708).

Swanky Splurges in Central London

$$$$ The Wolseley is the grand 1920s showroom of a long-defunct British car. The last Wolseley drove out with the Great Depression, but today this old-time

bistro bustles with formal waiters serving traditional Austrian and French dishes in an elegant black-marble-and-chandeliers setting fit for its location next to the Ritz. Although the food can be unexceptional, prices are reasonable considering the grand presentation and setting. Reservations are a must (cheaper soup, salad, and sandwich "café menu" available in all areas of restaurant, daily 11:30-23:00, 160 Piccadilly, tel. 020/7499-6996, www.thewolseley.com). They're popular for their fancy cream tea or afternoon tea (details later, under "Taking Tea in London").

$$$ Brasserie Zédel is the former dining hall of the old Regent Palace Hotel, the biggest hotel in the world when built in 1915. Climbing down the stairs from street level, you're surprised by a gilded grand hall that feels like a circa 1920 cruise ship, filled with a boisterous crowd enjoying big, rich French food—old-fashioned brasserie dishes. With vested waiters, fast service, and paper tablecloths, it's great for a group of friends. After 21:30, the lights dim, the candles are lit, and it gets more romantic with live jazz (nightly inexpensive *plats du jour*, daily 11:30-24:00, 20 Sherwood Street, tel. 020/7734-4888). Across the atrium is the hotel's original Bar Américain (which feels like the 1930s) and the Crazy Coqs venue—busy with "Live at Zédel" music, theater, comedy, and literary events (see www.brasseriezedel.com for schedule).

$$$$ Rules Restaurant, established in 1798, is as traditional as can be—extremely British, classy yet comfortable. It's a big, stuffy place, where you'll eat in a plush Edwardian atmosphere with formal service and plenty of game on the menu. (A warning reads, "Game birds may contain lead shot.") This is the place to dress up and splurge for classic English dishes (daily 12:00-23:00, between the Strand and Covent Garden at 34 Maiden Lane, tel. 020/7836-5314, www.rules.co.uk).

Near Covent Garden

Covent Garden bustles with people and touristy eateries. The area feels overrun, but if you must eat around here, you have some good choices.

$$$ Dishoom is London's hotspot for upscale Indian cuisine. The dishes seem familiar, but the flavors are a revelation. People line up early (starting around 17:00) for a seat, either on the bright, rollicking, brasserie-like ground floor or in the less appealing basement. Reservations are possible only until 17:45. With its oversized reputation, long lines of tourists, and multiple locations, it's easy to think it's overrated. But the food is simply phenomenal (daily 8:00-23:00, 12 Upper St. Martin's Lane, tel. 020/7420-9320, www.dishoom.com). Other locations include near King's Cross Station and Carnaby Street (listed earlier).

$$$ Shapur Indian Restaurant is a well-respected place serving classic Indian dishes from many regions, fine fish, and a
tasty and filling *thali* combination platter (including a vegetarian version). It's small, low energy, and dressy, with good service (Mon-Fri 12:00-14:30 & 17:30-23:30, Sat 15:00-23:30, closed Sun, next to Somerset House at 149 Strand, tel. 020/7836-3730, Syed Khan).

$$ Lamb and Flag Pub is
a survivor—a spit-and-sawdust pub serving traditional grub (like meat pies) two blocks off Covent Garden, yet seemingly a world away. Here since 1772, this pub was a favorite of Charles Dickens and is now a hit with local workers. At lunch, it's all food. In the evening, the ground floor is for drinking and the food service is upstairs (long hours daily, 33 Rose Street, go up the narrow alley from Floral Street, tel. 020/7497-9504).

Near Trafalgar Square

$$$ Terroirs Wine Bar is an enticing place with a casual but classy ambience that exudes happiness. It's a few steps below street level, with a long zinc bar that has a kitchen view and two levels of tables. The fun menu is mostly Mediterranean and designed to share. The meat and cheese plates complement the fine wines available by the glass (Mon-Sat 12:00-23:00, small bites only from 15:00-17:30, closed Sun, reservations smart, two blocks from Trafalgar Square but tucked away at 5 William IV Street, tel. 020/7036-0660, www. terroirswinebar.com).

$$ St. Martin-in-the-Fields Café in the Crypt is just right for a tasty meal on a monk's budget—maybe even on a monk's tomb. You'll dine sitting on somebody's gravestone in an ancient crypt. Their enticing buffet line is kept stocked all day, serving breakfast, lunch, and dinner (hearty traditional desserts, free jugs of water). They also serve a restful £11 afternoon tea (daily 12:00-18:00). You'll find the café directly under St. Martin-in-the-Fields, facing Trafalgar Square—enter through the glass pavilion next to the church (generally daily 10:00-19:30, profits go to the church, Tube: Charing Cross, tel. 020/7766-1158). On Wednesday evenings you can dine to the music of a live jazz band at 20:00 (food available until 21:00, band plays until 22:00, £8-15 tickets). While here, check out the concert schedule for the busy church upstairs (or visit www.stmartin-in-the-fields.org).

$$ The Chandos Pub's Opera Room floats amazingly apart from the tacky crush of tourism around Trafalgar Square. Look for it opposite the National Portrait Gallery (corner of William IV Street and St. Martin's Lane) and climb the stairs—to the left or right of the pub entrance—to the Opera Room. This is a fine Trafalgar rendezvous point and wonderfully local pub. They serve sandwiches and a better-than-average range of traditional pub meals for around £10—meat pies and fish-and-chips are their specialty. The ground-floor pub is stuffed with regulars and offers snugs (private booths) and more serious beer drinking. To eat on that level, you have to order upstairs and carry it down (kitchen open daily 11:30-21:00, Fri until 18:00, order and pay at the bar, 29 St. Martin's Lane, Tube: Leicester Square, tel. 020/7836-1401).

$$ Gordon's Wine Bar is a candlelit 15th-century wine cellar filled with dusty old bottles, faded British memorabilia, and nine-to-fivers. At the "English rustic" buffet, choose a hot meal or cold meat dish with a salad; the cheese plate comes with two big hunks of cheese (from your choice of 20), bread, and a pickle. Then step up to the wine bar and consider the many varieties of wine and port available by the glass (this place is passionate about port—even the house port is excellent). The low carbon-crusted vaulting deeper in the back seems to intensify the Hogarth-painting atmosphere.

London Pubs

Historic pubs still dot the London cityscape. The only place to see the very oldest-style tavern is at **$$ Ye Olde Cheshire Cheese,** which was rebuilt in 1667 (after the Great Fire) from a 16th-century tavern. Imagine this mazelike place, with three separate bars, in the pre-Victorian era: With no bar, drinkers gathered around the fireplaces, while tap boys shuttled tankards up from the cellar (pub grub, pricier meals in the restaurant, open daily, 145 Fleet Street, Tube: Blackfriars, tel. 020/7353-6170).

Late-Victorian pubs are more common, such as the lovingly restored **$$ Princess Louise,** dating from 1897 (open daily, no food Sat-Sun, 208 High Holborn, see map on page 166; Tube: Holborn, tel. 020/7405-8816). These places are fancy, often with heavily embossed wallpaper ceilings, decorative tile work, fine-etched glass, ornate carved stillions (the big central hutch for storing bottles and glass), and even urinals equipped with a place to set your glass.

London's best Art Nouveau pub is **$$ The Black Friar** (c. 1900-1915), with fine carved capitals, lamp holders, and quirky phrases worked into the decor. While now operated by a chain, it retains its period charm (open daily, outdoor seating, 174 Queen Victoria Street, Tube: Blackfriars, tel. 020/7236-5474).

These days, former banks are being repurposed as trendy, lavish pubs, with elegant bars and freestanding stillions, which provide a fine centerpiece. Three such places are **$$ The Old**

Although it's crowded—often downright packed with people sitting at shared tables—you can normally find a spot. When sunny, the crowd spills out onto the tight parkside patio (daily 11:00-22:30, 2 blocks from Trafalgar Square, bottom of Villiers Street at #47—the door is locked but it's just around the corner to the right, Tube: Embankment, tel. 020/7930-1408, manager Gerard Menan).

VICTORIA STATION NEIGHBORHOOD

These restaurants are within a few blocks of Victoria Station. As with the accommodations in this area, I've grouped them into east and west of the station (for locations, see the map on page 156).

Cheap Eats: For groceries, try the following places (all open long hours daily). Inside Victoria Station you'll find an **M&S Simply Food** (near the front, by the bus terminus) and a **Sainsbury's Local** (at rear entrance, on Eccleston Street). A larger **Sainsbury's**

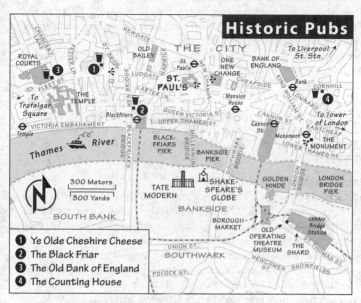

Historic Pubs

THE CITY

1 Ye Olde Cheshire Cheese
2 The Black Friar
3 The Old Bank of England
4 The Counting House

Bank of England (closed Sun, 194 Fleet Street, Tube: Temple, tel. 020/7430-2255), **$$ The Jugged Hare** (open daily, 172 Vauxhall Bridge Road—see map on page 156, Tube: Victoria, tel. 020/7614-0134), and **$$ The Counting House,** with great sandwiches, homemade meat pies, fish, and fresh vegetables (closed Sat-Sun; gets really busy with the buttoned-down 9-to-5 crowd after 12:15, especially Thu-Fri; 50 Cornhill, Tube: Bank, tel. 020/7283-7123).

---

is on Wilton Road near Warwick Way, a couple of blocks southeast of the station (closes early on Sun). A string of diverse restaurants lines Wilton Road. For affordable if forgettable meals, try the row of cheap little eateries on Elizabeth Street.

West of Victoria Station (Belgravia)

$ La Bottega is an Italian delicatessen that fits its upscale Belgravia neighborhood. It offers tasty, freshly cooked pastas, lasagnas, and salads, great sandwiches, and a good coffee bar with Italian pastries. It's fast (order at the counter). Grab your meal to go, or enjoy the Belgravia good life with locals, either sitting inside or at a sidewalk table (Mon-Fri 7:30-19:00, Sat-Sun 9:00-18:00, on corner of Ebury and Eccleston Streets, tel. 020/7730-2730).

$$$ The Thomas Cubitt, named for the urban planner who designed much of Belgravia, is a trendy neighborhood gastropub packed with young professionals. It's pricey, a pinch pretentious, and popular for its modern English cooking. With a bright but slightly cramped interior and fine sidewalk seating, it's great for a drink or meal. Upstairs is a more refined and pricier **restaurant** with the same kitchen (food served daily 12:00-22:00, reservations recommended, 44 Elizabeth Street, tel. 020/7730-6060, www. thethomascubitt.co.uk).

$$ Duke of Wellington pub is a classic neighborhood place with forgettable grub, sidewalk seating, and an inviting interior. A bit more lowbrow than my other Belgravia listings, this may be your best glimpse of ye olde London (food served Mon-Sat 12:00-15:00 & 18:00-21:00, Sun lunch only, 63 Eaton Terrace, tel. 020/7730-1782).

East of Victoria Station (Pimlico)

$$ Grumbles brags it's been serving "good food and wine at non-scary prices since 1964." Offering a delicious mix of "modern eclectic French and traditional English," this unpretentious little place with cozy booths inside (on two levels) and a few nice sidewalk tables is the best spot to eat well in this otherwise workaday neighborhood. Their traditional dishes are their forte (early-bird specials, open daily 12:00-14:30 & 18:00-23:00, reservations wise, a half-block north of Belgrave Road at 35 Churton Street, tel. 020/7834-0149, www.grumblesrestaurant.co.uk).

$ Pimlico Fresh's breakfasts and lunches feature fresh, organic ingredients, served up with good coffee and/or fresh-squeezed juices. This place is heaven if you need a break from your hotel's bacon-eggs-beans routine (takeout lunches, vegetarian options; Mon-Fri 7:30-18:00, breakfast served until 15:00; Sat-Sun 8:30-18:00; 86 Wilton Road, tel. 020/7932-0030).

$$$ Seafresh Fish Restaurant is the neighborhood place for plaice—and classic and creative fish-and-chips cuisine. You can either step up to the cheaper **takeout counter,** or eat in—enjoying a white-fish ambience. Though Mario's father started this place in 1965, it feels like the chippy of the 21st century (Mon-Sat 12:00-15:00 & 17:00-22:30, closed Sun, 80 Wilton Road, tel. 020/7828-0747).

$$ The Jugged Hare, a 10-minute walk from Victoria Station, fills a lavish old bank building, with vaults replaced by kegs of beer and a kitchen. They have a traditional menu and a plush, vivid pub scene good for a meal or just a drink (food served Mon-Fri 11:00-21:00, Sat-Sun until 20:00, 172 Vauxhall Bridge Road, tel. 020/7828-1543).

$$ St. George's Tavern is the neighborhood's best pub for a full meal. They serve dinner from the same menu in three zones: on the sidewalk to catch the sun and enjoy some people-watching (mostly travelers with wheelie bags), in the ground-floor pub, and in a classier downstairs dining room with full table service. The scene is inviting for just a beer, too (food served daily 12:00-22:00, corner of Hugh Street and Belgrave Road, tel. 020/7630-1116).

$ **Tachbrook Market,** filling a short traffic-free block near several recommended hotels, is a delightful place to browse a variety of food stalls. Sit on a nearby curb with the locals for a quick lunch. There's also a row of produce, fish, and meat vendors, making this more local-feeling than most London street markets (Mon-Sat 8:00-18:00, closed Sun, on Tachbrook Street just off Warwick Way).

SOUTH KENSINGTON

These places are close to several recommended hotels and just a couple of blocks from the Victoria and Albert Museum and Natural History Museum (Tube: South Kensington; for locations see the map on page 160). The Anglesea Arms pub is a bit farther, but well worth the walk.

Exhibition Road Food Circus: This one-block-long pedestrian zone (on the Victoria and Albert Museum side of the South Kensington Tube station) is lined with enticing little $-$$ eateries. Facing down Exhibition Road is the best-regarded place in the area, $$$ **Daquise**—serving elevated Polish cuisine in a sophisticated but unstuffy atmosphere. With so many chain restaurants in this area, Daquise is a rare "destination" restaurant (daily 12:00-23:00, 20 Thurloe Street, tel. 020/7589-6117).

Indian: $$ Moti Mahal, with minimalist-yet-upscale ambience and attentive service, serves delicious, mostly Bangladeshi cuisine. Consider chicken *jalfrezi* if you like spicy, and butter chicken if you don't (daily 12:00-14:30 & 17:30-23:30, 3 Glendower Place, tel. 020/7584-8428).

Old Brompton Road Eateries: This street, just one block from the South Kensington Tube station, is lined with a variety of good eateries. These two $ places are good for a quick bite: **Bosphorus Kebabs** (Turkish food, at #59) and **Beirut Express** (Lebanese, #65). $$ **Rocca,** at #73, is a bright and dressy Italian place with a heated terrace (daily 11:30-23:30, tel. 020/7225-3413).

Classic London Pub: $$ The Anglesea Arms, with a great terrace buried in a classy South Kensington residential area, is a destination pub that feels like the classic neighborhood favorite. It's a thriving and happy place, with a woody ambience. While the food is the main draw, this is also a fine place to just have a beer. Don't let the crowds here put you off. Behind all the drinkers, in back, is an elegant, mellow step-down dining room a world away from any tourism (meals served daily 12:00-15:00 & 18:00-22:00; heading west from Old Brompton Road, turn left at Onslow Gardens and go down a few blocks to 15 Selwood Terrace; tel. 020/7373-7960).

Supermarkets: Tesco Express (50 Old Brompton Road) and **Little Waitrose** (99 Old Brompton Road) are both open long hours daily.

BAYSWATER, NOTTING HILL, AND NEARBY

These are close to my recommended Bayswater and Notting Hill accommodations (for locations, see the map on page 162).

Near Bayswater Tube Station

$$ Cocotte is a "healthy rotisserie" restaurant specializing in delectable roast chicken, plus tempting sides and healthy salads (dine in or take away; daily 12:00-22:00, 95 Westbourne Grove, tel. 020/3220-0076).

$$$ Farmacy is focused on organic vegan fare...with a side of pretense. The menu includes earth bowls, meatless burgers and tacos, and superfood smoothies. With an all-natural, woodgrain vibe, it feels like a top-end health food store (daily 9:00-16:00 & 18:00-22:00, 74 Westbourne Grove, tel. 020/7221-0705).

$$$ Hereford Road is a cozy, mod eatery tucked away on Leinster Square, serving heavy, meaty English cuisine made with modern panache. Cozy two-person booths face the open kitchen up top; the main dining room is down below under skylights. There are also a few sidewalk tables (daily 18:00-22:00, also open for lunch Thu-Sun 12:00-14:30, reservations smart, 3 Hereford Road, tel. 020/7727-1144, www.herefordroad.org).

$$ Taqueria turns out tasty tacos, quesadillas, and other Mexican fare a short walk from my recommended Bayswater accommodations (daily 12:00-23:00, 141 Westbourne Grove, tel. 020/7229-4734).

$$ The Prince Edward serves good grub in a comfy, family-friendly, upscale-pub setting and at its sidewalk tables (Mon-Sat 10:30-23:00, Sun 12:00-22:30, 2 blocks north of Bayswater Road at the corner of Dawson Place and Hereford Road, 73 Prince's Square, tel. 020/7727-2221).

Supermarkets: Queensway is home to several supermarkets, including **Sainsbury's Local** and **Tesco Express** (both next to Bayswater Tube stop; a larger **Tesco** is near the post office farther along Queensway), and **Marks & Spencer** (inside Whiteleys Shopping Centre). All of these open early and close late (except on Sundays).

Notting Hill

$$$ Geales, which opened its doors in 1939 as a fish-and-chips shop, has been serving Notting Hill ever since. Today, while the menu is more varied, the emphasis is still on fish. The interior is casual, but the food is upscale. The crispy battered cod that put them on the map is still the best around (£15 two-course express menu for lunch and until 20:00 Tue-Fri; open Tue-Sun 12:00-15:00 & 18:00-22:00, closed Mon, reservations smart, 2 Farmer Street, just south of Notting Hill Gate Tube stop, tel. 020/7727-7528, www. geales.com).

$$$$ Mazi is a highly regarded Greek restaurant serving refined renditions of classic dishes, including Greek salad, grilled octopus, and *loukoumades* (doughnuts) in a contemporary, sophisticated setting. Since ordering several small plates can add up, the £15 two-course lunch is a good deal (daily 18:30-22:30, also Tue-Sun 12:00-15:00, 12 Hillgate Street, tel. 020/7229-3794).

$ The Fish House of Notting Hill is an old-fashioned and well-loved chippy, with takeaway on the ground floor and a more expensive **table service** section upstairs (daily 11:30-22:00, 29 Pembridge Road, tel. 020/7229-2626).

Supermarkets: Tesco Metro is a half-block from the Notting Hill Gate Tube stop (near intersection with Pembridge Road at 114 Notting Hill Gate).

Near Kensington Gardens

$$$$ Maggie Jones's has been feeding locals for over 50 years. Its countryside antique decor and candlelight make a visit a step back in time. It's a longer walk than most of my recommendations, but you'll get solid English cuisine. The portions are huge (especially the meat-and-fish pies, their specialty), and prices are a bargain at lunch. You're welcome to split your main course. The candlelit upstairs is the most romantic, while the basement is lively (daily 12:00-14:00 & 18:00-22:30, reservations recommended, 6 Old Court Place, east of Kensington Church Street, near High Street Kensington Tube stop, tel. 020/7937-6462, www.maggie-jones. co.uk).

$$$$ The Shed offers farm-to-table dishes in a rustic-chic setting. Owned by three brothers—a farmer, a chef, and a restaurateur—The Shed serves locally sourced modern English dishes. The portions are hearty, with big, meaty flavors—a change of pace from London's delicate high-end dining scene. It's tucked a block off busy Notting Hill Gate (Mon-Sat 18:00-24:00, also open for lunch Tue-Sat 12:00-15:00, closed Sun, reservations smart, 122 Palace Gardens Terrace, tel. 020/7229-4024, www.theshed-restaurant. com).

$$ The Churchill Arms Pub and Thai Kitchen is a combo establishment that's a hit in the neighborhood. It offers good beer and a thriving old-English ambience in front and hearty Thai dishes in an enclosed patio in the back. You can eat the Thai food in the tropical hideaway (table service) or in the atmospheric pub section (order at the counter). Bedecked with flowers on the exterior, it's festooned with Churchill memorabilia and chamber pots on the inside (including one with Hitler's mug on it—hanging from the ceiling farthest from Thai Kitchen—sure to cure the constipation of any Brit during World War II). Arrive by 18:00 or after 21:00 to avoid a line (food served daily 12:00-22:00, 119 Kensington Church Street, tel. 020/7727-4242 for the pub or 020/7792-1246 for restaurant, www.churchillarmskensington.co.uk).

$ Café Diana is a healthy little eatery serving sandwiches, salads, and Middle Eastern food. It's decorated—almost shrine-like—with photos of Princess Diana, who used to drop by for pita sandwiches (daily 8:00-23:00, cash only, 5 Wellington Terrace, on Bayswater Road, opposite Kensington Palace Garden gates, where Di once lived, tel. 020/7792-9606, Abdul).

NORTH LONDON

To avoid the touristy crush right around the British Museum, head a few blocks west to the Fitzrovia area. Here, tiny Charlotte Place is lined with small eateries (including my first two listings); nearby, the much bigger Charlotte Street has several more good options (Tube: Goodge Street). See the map on page 166 for locations.

$ Salumeria Dino serves up hearty £5 sandwiches, pasta, and Italian coffee. Dino, a native of Naples, has run his little shop for more than 30 years and has managed to create a classic-feeling Italian deli (cheap takeaway cappuccinos, Mon-Sat 7:30-18:00, closed Sun, 15 Charlotte Place, tel. 020/7580-3938).

$ Lantana OUT, next door to Salumeria Dino, is an Australian coffee shop that sells modern soups, sandwiches, and salads at their takeaway window (£8 daily hot dish). **Lantana IN** is an adjacent sit-down café that serves pricier meals (both Mon-Fri 8:00-18:00, Sat-Sun 9:00-17:00, 13 Charlotte Place, tel. 020/7637-3347).

Near the British Library: Farther north, in the Coal Drops Yard development just behind King's Cross Station, is a branch of the renowned Indian restaurant **$$$ Dishoom** (see description for Covent Garden branch, earlier). Not only is the food excellent, but it's a fun excuse to explore this development—a repurposing of an old industrial site on Regent's Canal.

EAST LONDON

Once known as *the* place to get authentic Indian and Bangladeshi food, the East End is now where lively restaurants, food trucks, and "pop-ups" come to get a toehold in an ever-evolving culinary scene. For locations, see the "East End" map on page 118.

Spitalfields Market Eateries

A few blocks east of Liverpool Street Station, this cavernous hall is filled with a festival of eateries. The modern part of the market—to the west, closer to the train station—has big, brassy outposts of all the predictable London chains. It's much better to focus on the historic, Victorian-age Old Spitalfields Market section, where you'll find a more interesting array of small, one-off **$-$$** eateries and pop-ups. Hours vary, but most places open around 10:00 (11:00 on Sat) and start closing down around 17:00. On weekdays, some stay open until 20:00, but selection is limited (www.oldspitalfieldsmarket.com).

Near Spitalfields Market

These places are burrowed in the tight streets near Spitalfields, a couple of blocks east of Liverpool Street Station.

$$$$ Ottolenghi Spitalfields showcases the big flavors of celebrity chef Yotam Ottolenghi's modern Israeli/Eastern Mediterranean dishes. It's squeezed along tiny Artillery Lane, one of the East End's narrowest and most atmospheric streets. Its little shop in front displays its appetizers and desserts, and sells a few Ottolenghi products, such as preserves, cookbooks, and so on (Mon-Sat 8:00-22:30, Sun 9:00-18:00, reservations recommended, 50 Artillery Lane, tel. 020/7247-1999, www.ottolenghi.co.uk).

$$$$ The English Restaurant, across from Spitalfields Market, started out as a Jewish bakery in the 17th century. It feels traditional for this trendy district, and is perhaps the best place to capture the ambience of the old East End. They serve up traditional British cuisine with a Belgian flair—like updated bread-and-butter pudding—in a snug dining room or a bistro-style bar area (Mon-Fri 8:00-23:00, Sat-Sun 9:30-18:00, 52 Brushfield Street, tel. 020/7247-4110).

$$$ St. John Bread and Wine Restaurant, with a "nose to tail" philosophy, is especially popular at breakfast—served until noon and featuring their award-winning bacon sandwich on thick bread with homemade ketchup (see if you can guess the special seasoning). They also have good lunches and dinners (daily 8:00-23:00, 94 Commercial Street, tel. 020/7251-0848).

$$$ Gunpowder—a modern alternative to the traditional curry houses on nearby Brick Lane—offers a short and carefully crafted menu of updated Indian fare in a tight, noisy, cozy brick space (Mon-Sat 12:00-15:00 & 17:30-22:30, closed Sun, 11 White's Row, www.gunpowderlondon.com).

On and near Brick Lane

Once synonymous with curry houses, historic Brick Lane now has many more options (though curry is still what many come here for).

$$ Brick Lane's Famous Curry Houses: This "Curry Row" comes with its own subculture—it's one of the only places in London where curbside hawkers pitch each eatery's "award-winning" pedigree and are eager to offer a discount. Ultimately, little distinguishes the options along here. Compare menus and deals, and take your pick. For something a notch above, head a half-block off Brick Lane to **Meraz Café,** offering a small, simple menu of Indian, Pakistani, and Bangladeshi dishes and homemade chutney (daily 11:00-23:00, 56 Hanbury Street, tel. 020/7247-6999).

Other Brick Lane Delights: The **Old Truman Brewery** hosts a fun courtyard of **$ food trucks** surrounded by prominent street art. Inside the brewery, **Café 1001** is a good place for coffee and cheap cafeteria fare.

FOOD MARKETS

In this expensive city, one of the most cost-effective ways to sample local dishes is to graze through a food market. You'll find English classics (meat pies, bangers and mash, grilled English cheddar cheese sandwiches) and cuisine from every corner of the globe. Most vendors accept credit cards. Keep track of which day of the week the various markets thrive, coordinate your sightseeing accordingly, and suddenly you're a temporary Londoner.

South London

Some of the best food markets in London are South of the Thames.

Borough Market: London's oldest fruit-and-vegetable market has been serving the Southwark community for more than 800 years. Today, it's the granddaddy of all London food halls. There are as many people taking photos as buying fruit, cheese, and beautiful breads, but it's still a fun carnival atmosphere with fantastic food stalls.

For maximum market and minimum crowds, join the locals on Thursdays (full market open Wed-Sat generally 10:00-17:00, surrounding food stalls also open Mon-Tue; south of London Bridge, where Southwark Street meets Borough High Street; Tube: London Bridge, tel. 020/7407-1002, www.boroughmarket.org.uk).

Southbank Centre Food Market: You'll find some of the city's most popular vendors in this paradise of street food near the London Eye. Food vendors are wedged between ugly concrete buildings and elevated train tracks, but the selection is enticing and the location is handy (Fri-Sat 12:00-20:00, Sun-Mon until 18:00, closed midweek; between the Royal Festival Hall and BFI Southbank at Hayward Gallery—from the river, go around behind the buildings to find it; Tube: Waterloo, or Embankment and cross the Jubilee Bridge; tel. 020/3879-9555, www.southbankcentre.co.uk).

The market also hosts various festivals throughout the year (German Christmas, coffee, and chocolate are among the favorites).

Ropewalk (Maltby Street Market): This short-but-sweet, completely untouristy food bazaar bustles on weekends under a nondescript rail bridge in the shadow of the Shard. Two-dozen vendors fill the narrow passage—about as long as a football field—with a festival of hipster/artisan carts selling a fun array of foods. Tucked among the carts are some good sit-down eateries, including The Walrus & The Carpenter for seafood and Spanish tapas bar Tozino (Sat 9:00-17:00, Sun 11:00-16:00, www.maltby.st). A short walk southeast of Tower Bridge, this youthful area has several rustic microbreweries tucked between self-storage shops and auto-repair garages.

TAKING TEA IN LONDON

While visiting London, consider partaking in this most British of traditions. While some tearooms—such as the wallet-draining tea service at Claridges and the finicky Fortnum & Mason—still require a jacket and tie, most others that I list happily welcome tourists in jeans and sneakers (and cost, on average, £35-50). Most tearooms are usually open for lunch and close about 17:00. At all the places listed next, it's perfectly acceptable for two people to order one afternoon tea and one cream tea and share the afternoon tea's goodies. At many places, you can spring an extra £10 or so to upgrade to a boozy "champagne tea." For details on afternoon tea, see page 931.

Traditional Tea Experiences

$$$ The Wolseley serves a good afternoon tea between their meal service. Split one with your companion and enjoy two light meals at a great price in classic elegance (generally served 15:00-18:30 daily, see full listing on page 177).

$$$$ The Capital Hotel, a luxury hotel a half-block from Harrods, caters to weary shoppers with its intimate five-table, linen-tablecloth tearoom. It's where the ladies-who-lunch meet to decide whether to buy that Versace gown they've been eyeing. Even so, casual clothes, kids, and sharing plates are all OK (daily 14:00-17:30, book ahead—especially on weekends, 22 Basil Street—see the "West London" color map at the back of this book, Tube: Knightsbridge, tel. 020/7591-1202, www.capitalhotel.co.uk).

$$$$ Fortnum & Mason department store offers tea at several different restaurants within its walls. You can "Take Tea in the Parlour" for a reasonably priced experience (including ice cream and scones; Mon-Sat 10:00-19:30, Sun 11:30-17:00). The pièce de resistance is their Diamond Jubilee Tea Salon, named in honor of the Queen's 60th year on the throne. At royal prices, consider it dinner (Mon-Sat 12:00-19:00, Sun until 18:00, dress up a bit—no shorts, "children must be behaved," 181 Piccadilly—see the "West London" color map at the back of this book, smart to reserve at least a week in advance, tel. 020/7734-8040, www.fortnumandmason.com).

$$$$ Brown's Hotel in Mayfair serves a fancy afternoon tea in its English tearoom (you're welcome to ask for second helpings of your favorite scones and sandwiches). Said to be the inspiration for Agatha Christie's *At Bertram's Hotel*, the wood-paneled walls and inviting fire set a scene that's more contemporary-cozy than pinky-raising classy (daily 12:00-18:00, reservations smart, no casual clothing, 33 Albemarle Street—see the "Central London Restaurants" map on page 172, Tube: Green Park, tel. 020/7518-4155, www.roccofortehotels.com).

$$$$ The Orangery at Kensington Palace may be closed for restoration when you visit. If so, you can take tea next door at the Kensington Palace Pavilion (daily 12:00-16:00, a 10-minute walk through Kensington Gardens from either Queensway or High Street Kensington Tube stations—see the map on page 162; tel. 020/3166-6113, www.hrp.org.uk).

Other Places to Sip Tea

Taking tea is not just for tourists and the wealthy—it's a true English tradition. If you want the teatime experience but are put off by the price, consider these options, more in the £15-30 range.

$$$ Browns Restaurant at Butler's Wharf serves an affordable afternoon tea with brioche sandwiches, traditional scones, and sophisticated desserts (daily 15:00-17:00, 26 Shad Thames facing Tower Bridge—see the map on page 172, tel. 020/7378-1700, www.browns-restaurants.co.uk).

$$ The Restaurant at Sotheby's, on the ground floor of the auction giant's headquarters, gives shoppers a break from fashionable New Bond Street (tea served Mon-Fri 15:00-16:45, reservations smart, 34 New Bond Street—see the map on page 172, Tube: Bond Street or Oxford Circus, tel. 020/7293-5077, www.sothebys.com).

At **$ Waterstones** bookstore you can put together a spread for less than £10 in their fifth-floor view café (203 Piccadilly).

Museum Cafés: Many museum restaurants offer a fine inexpensive tea service. The **$$$ National Dining Rooms,** within the Sainsbury Wing of the National Gallery on Trafalgar Square, serves a £7.50 cream tea and £22.50 afternoon tea with a great view from 14:30 to 16:30 (tea also served in National Café at the museum's Getty entrance, from 14:30 to 17:30; Tube: Charing Cross or Leicester Square, tel. 020/7747-2525). The **$$ Victoria and Albert Museum** café serves a classic cream tea in an elegant setting that won't break your budget, and the **$$$ Wallace Collection** serves reasonably priced afternoon tea and cream tea in its atrium (see page 102).

Shop Cafés: You'll find good-value teas at various cafés in shops and bookstores across London. Most department stores on Oxford Street (including those between Oxford Circus and Bond Street Tube stations) offer an afternoon tea.

London Connections

BY PLANE
London has six airports; I've focused my coverage on the two most widely used—Heathrow and Gatwick—with a few tips for using the others (Stansted, Luton, London City, and Southend). For more on flights within Europe, see the "Transportation" section of the Practicalities chapter.

Heathrow Airport
Heathrow Airport is one of the world's busiest airports. Consider this: 75 million passengers a year on 500,000 flights from

200 destinations traveling on 80 airlines, like some kind of global maypole dance. For Heathrow's airport, flight, and transfer information, call the switchboard at 0844-335-1801, or visit the helpful website www.heathrow.com (code: LHR).

Heathrow's terminals are numbered T-2 through T-5. Each terminal is served by different airlines and alliances; for example, T-5 is exclusively for British Air and Iberia Air flights, while T-2 serves mostly Star Alliance flights, such as United and Lufthansa.

You can walk between T-2 and T-3. From this central hub (called "Heathrow Central"), T-4 and T-5 split off in opposite directions (and are not walkable). The easiest way to travel between the T-2/T-3 cluster and either T-4 or T-5 is by Heathrow Express train (free to transfer between terminals, but tickets are required—hold onto your ticket even once you've passed through the turnstile—train departs every 15-20 minutes). You can also take a shuttle bus (free, serves all terminals), or the Tube (requires a ticket, serves all terminals).

If you're flying out of Heathrow, it's critical to confirm which terminal your flight will use (look at your ticket/boarding pass, check online, or call your airline in advance)—if it's T-4 or T-5,

LONDON

London's Airports

Luton •
✈ Luton
Stansted ✈

#757 & A1

Reading
St. PANCRAS
PADDINGTON
LIVERPOOL STREET
Southend
Southend ✈

Windsor #71 & 77
Tube →
D.L.R.

To Bath
Rail Air Link
✈
VICTORIA
VICTORIA COACH STN.
London City

Heathrow
EUROSTAR

Thames
London

Guildford

✈ Gatwick
Ashford
To Paris, Amsterdam & Brussels →

----- Rail
═══ Eurostar Rail
─── Tube & D.L.R.
- - - - Bus

ALL BUSES ARE NATIONAL EXPRESS
UNLESS NOTED

↓To Brighton

English Channel

allow extra time. Taxi drivers generally know which terminal you'll need based on the airline, but bus drivers may not.

Services: Each terminal has an airport information desk (open long hours daily), car-rental agencies, exchange bureaus, ATMs, a pharmacy, a VAT refund desk (tel. 0845-872-7627), and pay baggage storage (long hours daily, www.left-baggage.co.uk). Heathrow offers both free Wi-Fi and pay internet access points (in each terminal, check map for locations). You'll find a post office on the first floor of T-3 (departures area). Each terminal also has cheap eateries.

Heathrow's small **"TI"** (tourist info shop), even though it's a for-profit business, is worth a visit if you're nearby and want to pick up free information, including the *London Planner* visitors guide (long hours daily, 5-minute walk from T-3 in Tube station, follow signs to Underground; bypass queue for transit info to reach window for London questions).

Getting Between Heathrow and Downtown London

You have several options for traveling the 14 miles between Heathrow Airport and downtown London: Tube (about £6/person), bus (£8-10/person), express train with connecting Tube or taxi (£22-25, price does not include connecting Tube fare), or most expensive—taxi or car service. The one that works best for you will depend on

your arrival terminal, your destination in central London, and your budget.

By Tube (Subway): The Tube takes you from any Heathrow terminal to downtown London in 50-60 minutes on the Piccadilly Line (6/hour, buy ticket at Tube station self-service machine). Depending on your destination in London, you may need to transfer (for example, if headed to the Victoria Station neighborhood, transfer at Hammersmith to the District line and ride six more stops).

If you plan to use the Tube in London, it makes sense to buy a pay-as-you-go Oyster card (possibly adding a 7-Day Travelcard) at the airport's Tube station ticket machines. (For details on these passes, see page 41.) If you add a Travelcard that covers only Zones 1-2, you'll need to pay a small supplement for the initial trip from Heathrow (Zone 6) to downtown.

If you're taking the Tube from downtown London *to* the airport, note that Piccadilly Line trains don't stop at every terminal. Trains either stop at T-4, then T-2/T-3 (also called Heathrow Central), in that order; or T-2/T-3, then T-5. When leaving central London on the Tube, allow extra time if going to T-4 or T-5, and check the reader board in the station to make sure that the train goes to the right terminal before you board.

By Bus: Most buses depart from the outdoor common area called the Central Bus Station, a five-minute walk from the T-2/T-3 complex. To connect between T-4 or T-5 and the Central Bus Station, ride the free Heathrow Express train or the shuttle buses.

National Express has regular service from Heathrow's Central Bus Station to Victoria Coach Station in downtown London, near several of my recommended hotels. While slow, the bus is affordable and convenient for those staying near Victoria Station (£8-10, 1-2/hour, less frequent from Victoria Station to Heathrow, 45-75 minutes depending on time of day, tel. 0871-781-8181, www.nationalexpress.com). A less-frequent National Express bus goes from T-5 directly to Victoria Coach Station.

By Train: The **Heathrow Express** runs between Heathrow Airport and London's Paddington Station. At Paddington, you're in the thick of the Tube system, with easy access to any of my recommended neighborhoods—my Paddington hotels are just outside the front door, and Notting Hill Gate is just two Tube stops away.

The Heathrow Express is fast but pricey (£22-25 one-way, price depends on time of day, £37 round-trip, cheaper if purchased online in advance, covered by BritRail pass; 4/hour, Mon-Sat 5:00-

24:00, Sun from 6:00, 15 minutes to downtown from Heathrow Central Station serving T-2/T-3, 21 minutes from T-5; for T-4 take free transfer to Heathrow Central, tel. 0345-600-1515, www. heathrowexpress.co.uk).

All Heathrow Express stations have ticket barriers, which require a mobile or paper train ticket to pass through (required even for free transfers between terminals; well-marked machines located near barriers). Tickets can be purchased through the Heathrow Express website or app, or at ticket machines and windows at stations. You can also use funds on an Oyster card, but only for same-day fares (not for buying in advance).

A cheaper alternative to the Heathrow Express—the new **Crossrail Elizabeth line**—may not yet be operational by the time you visit, but when it opens, it will be faster (and more expensive) than the Tube; see www.tfl.gov.uk for updates.

By Car Service: Just Airports offers a private car service between five London airports and the city center (see website for price quote, tel. 020/8900-1666, www.justairports.com).

By Taxi or Uber: Taxis from the airport cost £45-75 to west and central London (one hour). For four people traveling together, this can be a reasonable option. Hotels can often line up a cab back to the airport for about £50. If running, Uber also offers London airport pickup and drop-off.

Gatwick Airport

Gatwick Airport is halfway between London and the south coast (code: LGW, tel. 0844-892-0322, www.gatwickairport.com). Gatwick has two terminals, North and South, which are easily connected by a free monorail (two-minute trip, runs 24 hours). Note that boarding passes say "Gatwick N" or "Gatwick S" to indicate your terminal. The Gatwick Express trains (described next) stop only at Gatwick South. Schedules in each terminal show only arrivals and departures from that terminal.

Getting Between Gatwick and Downtown London: Gatwick Express trains are the best way into London from this airport. They shuttle conveniently between Gatwick South and London's **Victoria Station,** with many of my recommended hotels close by (£20 one-way, £35 round-trip, at least 10 percent cheaper if purchased online, Oyster cards accepted but no discount offered, 4/hour, 30 minutes, runs 5:00-24:00 daily, a few trains as early as 3:30, tel. 0845-850-1530, www.gatwickexpress.com). If you buy your tickets at the station before boarding, ask about possible group deals. (If you see others in the ticket line, you could suggest buying your tickets together.) When going *to* the airport, at Victoria Station note that Gatwick Express has its own ticket windows right by the platform (tracks 13 and 14). You'll also find easy-to-use ticket machines nearby.

A train also runs between Gatwick South and **St. Pancras International Station** (£12.10, 3-5/hour, 45-60 minutes, www. thetrainline.com)—useful for travelers taking the Eurostar train (to Paris, Amsterdam, or Brussels) or staying in the St. Pancras/ King's Cross neighborhood.

While even slower, the **bus** is a cheap and handy option to the Victoria Station neighborhood. National Express runs a bus from Gatwick directly to Victoria Station (£10, at least hourly, 1.5 hours, tel. 0871-781-8181, www.nationalexpress.com); EasyBus has one that stops near the Earl's Court Tube stop (£4-10 depending on how far ahead you book, 2-3/hour, www.easybus.com).

London's Other Airports

Stansted Airport: From Stansted (code: STN, tel. 0844-335-1803, www.stanstedairport.com), you have several options for getting into or out of London. Two different **buses** connect the airport and London's Victoria Station neighborhood: National Express (£9-12, every 15 minutes, 2 hours, runs 24 hours a day, picks up and stops throughout London, ends at Victoria Coach Station or Liverpool Street Station, tel. 0871-781-8181, www.nationalexpress. com) and Airport Bus Express (£9, 2/hour, 1.5-2 hours). Or you can take the faster, pricier Stansted Express **train** (£19, cheaper if booked online, connects to London's Tube system at Tottenham Hale or Liverpool Street, 2-4/hour, 45 minutes, 4:30-23:00, www. stanstedexpress.com). Stansted is expensive by **cab**; figure £100-120 one-way from central London.

Luton Airport: For Luton (code: LTN, tel. 01582/405-100, www.london-luton.co.uk), the fastest way to get into London is by **train** to St. Pancras International Station (£14-17 one-way, 1-5/hour, 35-45 minutes—check schedule to avoid slower trains, tel. 0345-712-5678, www.eastmidlandstrains.co.uk); catch the 10-minute shuttle bus (every 10 minutes) from outside the terminal to the Luton Airport Parkway Station. You can purchase a shuttle bus and train combo-ticket from kiosks or ticket machines inside the airport. When buying your train ticket *to* Luton, make sure you select "Luton Airport" as your destination rather than "Parkway Station" to ensure the shuttle fare is included.

The **National Express bus** A1 runs from Luton to Victoria Coach Station (£7-11 one-way, 2/hour, 1-1.5 hours, runs 24 hours, tel. 0871-781-8181, www.nationalexpress.com). The **Green Line express bus** #757 runs to Buckingham Palace Road, just south of Victoria Station, and stops en route near the Baker Street Tube station—best if you're staying near Paddington Station or in North London (£10 one-way, 2-4/hour, 1-1.5 hours, runs 24 hours, tel.

0344-800-4411, www.greenline.co.uk). If you're sleeping at Luton, consider EasyHotel's Luton location.

London City and Southend Airports: To get into the city center from London City Airport (code: LCY, tel. 020/7646-0088, www.londoncityairport.com), take the Docklands Light Railway (DLR) to the Bank Tube station, which is one stop east of St. Paul's on the Central Line (less than £6 one-way, covered by Travelcard, a bit cheaper with an Oyster card, 20 minutes, www.tfl.gov.uk/dlr). Some EasyJet flights land farther out, at Southend Airport (code: SEN, tel. 01702/538-500, www.southendairport.com). Trains connect this airport to London's Liverpool Street Station (£16.20 one-way, 3-8/hour, 55 minutes, www.abelliogreateranglia.co.uk).

Connecting London's Airports by Bus

A handy **National Express bus** runs between Heathrow, Gatwick, Stansted, and Luton airports—easier than having to cut through the center of London—although traffic can be bad and can increase travel times (tel. 0871-781-8181, www.nationalexpress.com).

From Heathrow Airport to: Gatwick Airport (£25, 1-6/hour, about 1.5 hours—but allow at least three hours between flights), **Stansted Airport** (£27, 1-2/hour direct, 1.5 hours), **Luton Airport** (£27, roughly hourly, 1 hour).

BY TRAIN

London has a different train station for each region of Britain. There are nine main stations (see the map):

Euston: Serves northwest England, North Wales, and Scotland.

St. Pancras International: Serves north and south England, plus the Eurostar to Paris, Amsterdam, or Brussels (see "Crossing the Channel by Eurostar Train," later).

King's Cross: Serves northeast England and Scotland, including York and Edinburgh.

Liverpool Street: Serves east England, including Essex and Harwich.

London Bridge: Serves south England, including Brighton.

Waterloo: Serves south England, including Salisbury and Southampton.

Victoria: Serves Gatwick Airport, Canterbury, Dover, and Brighton.

Paddington: Serves south and southwest England, including Heathrow Airport, Windsor, Bath, Oxford, South Wales, and the Cotswolds.

Marylebone: Serves southwest and central England, including Stratford-upon-Avon.

In addition, London has several smaller train stations that

London's Major Train Stations

you're less likely to use, such as **Charing Cross** (serves southeast England, including Dover) and **Blackfriars** (serves Brighton).

Any train station has schedule information, can make reservations, and can sell tickets for any destination. Most stations offer a baggage-storage service (look for *left luggage* signs); because of long security lines, it can take a while to check or pick up your bag (www.left-baggage.co.uk). For more details on the services available at each station, see www.nationalrail.co.uk/stations. UK train and bus info is available at www.traveline.org.uk. For information on tickets and rail passes, see the Practicalities chapter.

Train Connections from London

To Points West

From Paddington Station to: Windsor (Windsor & Eton Central Station, 2/hour, 35 minutes, easy change at Slough), **Bath** (2/hour, 1.5 hours), **Oxford** (4/hour direct, 1 hour, more with transfer), **Moreton-in-Marsh** (hourly, 1.5 hours), **Penzance** (every 2 hours, 5 hours, more with change in Plymouth), **Cardiff** (2/hour, 2 hours).

To Points North

From King's Cross Station: York (3/hour, 2 hours), **Durham** (hourly, 3 hours), **Edinburgh** (2/hour, 4.5 hours). Trains to **Cambridge** also leave from here (4/hour, 1 hour).

From Euston Station to: Conwy (nearly hourly, 3.5 hours, transfer in Chester), Liverpool (hourly, 3 hours, transfer at Liverpool South Parkway), Blackpool (hourly, 3 hours, transfer at Preston), Keswick/Lake District (train to Penrith—hourly, 3.5 hours, then bus at Keswick), Glasgow (1-2/hour, 4.5 hours).

From London's Other Stations

Trains run between London and **Canterbury:** St. Pancras International Station to Canterbury West (hourly, 1 hour, more with transfer); Victoria Station to Canterbury East (hourly, 2 hours); Charing Cross Station—with stops at Waterloo East and London Bridge—to Canterbury West (hourly, 1.5 hours, more with transfers).

From Marylebone Station: Trains leave for **Stratford-upon-Avon** from this station, located near the southwest corner of Regent's Park (2/day direct, 2.5 hours; also 1-2/hour, 2 hours, transfer in Leamington Spa, Dorridge, or Birmingham Moor).

To Other Destinations: Greenwich (from Bank or Monument Tube stop take the DLR to Cutty Sark Station, 6/hour, 20 minutes), **Windsor** (to Windsor & Eton Riverside Station, 2/hour, 1 hour, from Waterloo Station), **Dover** (hourly, 1 hour, direct from St. Pancras International Station; also 1-2/hour, 2 hours, direct from Victoria Station; or hourly, 2 hours, direct from Charing Cross Station), **Brighton** (2/hour, 1 hour, direct from Victoria Station; 2/hour, 1.5 hours, direct from Blackfriars Station), **Portsmouth** (3/hour, 2 hours, direct from Waterloo Station, a few with change in Clapham Junction from Victoria Station), **Salisbury** (2/hour, 1.5 hours, from Waterloo Station).

BY BUS

Buses are slower but considerably cheaper than trains for reaching destinations around Britain and beyond. Most depart from **Victoria Coach Station,** which is one long block south of Victoria Station (near many recommended accommodations, Tube: Victoria). Inside the station, you'll find basic eateries, kiosks, and a helpful information desk stocked with schedules and staff ready to point you to your bus or answer any questions. Watch your bags carefully—thieves thrive at the station.

Ideally you'll buy your tickets online (for tips on buying tickets and taking buses, see page 944 of the Practicalities chapter). But if you must buy one at the station, arrive an hour before the bus departs, or drop by the day before. Ticketing machines are scattered

Public Transportation near London

LONDON

Rail
----- Bus
·········· Boat

Area covered by London Plus Pass

30 Kilometers

30 Miles (approx. scale)

Note: Bus Lines Follow Most Rail Lines

FRANCE

around the station (separate machines for National Express/Euro-lines and Megabus; you can buy either for today or for tomorrow); there's also a ticket counter near gate 21. For UK train and bus info, check www.travcline.info.

National Express buses go to: **Bath** (hourly, 3 hours), **Oxford** (2/hour, 2 hours), **Cambridge** (every 60-90 minutes, 2 hours), **Canterbury** (hourly, 2 hours), **Dover** (every 2 hours, 2.5 hours), **Brighton** (hourly, 2.5 hours), **Penzance** (5/day, 9 hours, overnight available), **Cardiff** (hourly, 3.5 hours), **Stratford-upon-Avon** (3/day, 3.5 hours), **Liverpool** (8/day direct, 5.5 hours, overnight available), **Blackpool** (1/day direct, more with transfer, 7 hours, overnight available), **York** (3/day direct, 6 hours), **Durham** (3/day direct, 7 hours, train is better), **Glasgow** (2-4/day direct, 10 hours, train is much better), **Edinburgh** (2/day direct, 10 hours, go by train instead).

To Dublin, Ireland: This bus/boat journey, operated by Eurolines, takes 10-12 hours (£45, 1/day, departs Victoria Coach Station at 18:00, check in with passport one hour before). Consider a cheap 1-hour Ryanair flight instead.

To the Continent: Especially in summer, buses run to destinations all over Europe, including Paris, Amsterdam, Brussels, and Germany (sometimes crossing the Channel by ferry, other times through the Chunnel). For any international connection, you need to check in with your passport one hour before departure. For details, call 0871-781-8181 or visit www.nationalexpress.com.

CROSSING THE CHANNEL BY EUROSTAR TRAIN

The Eurostar zips you (and up to 800 others in 18 sleek cars) from downtown London to downtown **Paris** (1-2/hour, 2.5 hours), **Brussels** (9/day, 2 hours), or **Amsterdam** (3/day, 4 hours; more with transfer in Brussels). The train travels at 190 mph, and the tunnel crossing is a 20-minute, silent, 100 mph nonevent. Your ears won't even pop.

Currently, trains only run direct from London to Amsterdam—those traveling *from* Amsterdam will need to change trains in Brussels and go through passport control. (Direct service from Amsterdam is in the works.)

Eurostar Tickets and Fares: A one-way ticket between London and Paris, Brussels, or Amsterdam can vary widely in price; for instance, $45-200 (Standard class), $160-310 (Standard Premier), and $400 (Business Premier). Fares depend on how far ahead you reserve and whether you're eligible for any discounts—available for children (under 12), youths (under 26), and adults booking months ahead or purchasing round-trip. You can book tickets 4-9 months in advance. Tickets can be exchanged before the scheduled departure for a fee (about $45 plus the cost of any price increase), but only Business Premier class allows any refund.

Buy tickets online using the print-at-home eticket option (see www.ricksteves.com/eurostar or www.eurostar.com). You can also order by phone through Rail Europe (US tel. 800-387-6782) for home delivery before you go, or through Eurostar (tel. 0843-218-6186, priced in euros) to pick up at the station. In Britain, tickets are issued only at the Eurostar office in St. Pancras. In continental Europe, you can buy tickets at any major train station in any country or at any travel agency that handles train tickets (expect a booking fee). If you have a Eurail Global Pass, seat reservations are available at Eurostar departure stations, through US agents, or by phone with Eurostar (generally harder to get at other train stations and travel agencies; $35 in Standard, $45 in Standard Premier, can sell out, no benefit with BritRail or other single-country pass).

Taking the Eurostar: Trains depart from and arrive at St.

Pancras International Station. Check in at least 30 minutes early (times listed on tickets are local; Britain is one hour earlier than continental Europe). Pass through airport-like security, show your passport to customs officials, and locate your departure gate. The waiting area has shops, newsstands, horrible snack bars and cafés (get food beforehand), free Wi-Fi, and a currency-exchange booth.

BY CRUISE SHIP

Many cruises begin, end, or call at one of several English ports offering easy access to London. Cruise lines favor two ports: Southampton, 80 miles southwest of London; and Dover, 80 miles southeast of London. If you don't want to bother with public transportation, most cruise lines offer transit-only excursion packages into London. For more details, see my *Rick Steves Scandinavian & Northern European Cruise Ports* guidebook.

Southampton Cruise Port

Within Southampton's sprawling port (www.cruisesouthampton. com), cruises use two separate dock areas, each with two terminals.

To reach London, it's about a 1.5-hour train ride. To get to Southampton Central Station from the cruise port, you can take a taxi or walk 10-15 minutes to the public ferry dock (Town Quay), where you can ride the QuayConnect bus to the train station. From there, trains depart at least every 30 minutes for London's Waterloo Station.

If you have time to kill in port, consider taking the train to Portsmouth (50-60 minutes), best known for its Historic Dockyard and many nautical sights, or stick around Southampton and visit the excellent SeaCity Museum, with a beautifully presented exhibit about the *Titanic*, which set sail from here on April 10, 1912.

Dover Cruise Port

Little Dover has a huge port. Cruises put in at the Western Docks, with two terminals.

Trains go hourly from Dover Priory Station to London. From either cruise terminal, the best way into town (or to the train station) is by taxi or shuttle bus (take it to Market Square, then walk 15 minutes to the train station). From Dover's station, a fast train leaves for London's St. Pancras International Station (hourly, 1 hour); slower, direct trains go to Victoria Station (1-2/hour, 2 hours) and Charing Cross Station (hourly, 2 hours).

If you have extra time in port, Dover Castle, perched upon chalk cliffs, is well worth a visit for its WWII-era Secret Wartime Tunnels. Or take the train to Canterbury (2/hour, less than 30 minutes), notable for its important cathedral and fine historic core.

WINDSOR & CAMBRIDGE

Windsor and Cambridge are two very different but equally enjoyable day-trip possibilities near London.

The primary residence of Her Majesty the Queen, Windsor hosts a castle that's regally lived-in, yet open to the public. This is simply a charming town to relax in—and its proximity to Heathrow Airport (60 minutes by train west of London) makes Windsor easy to combine with a flight into or out of London. Nearby is an oddball collection of intriguing sights, including Legoland Windsor, Eton College (Britain's most elite high school), Ascot Racecourse (for horse racing), and Highclere Castle, where *Downton Abbey* was filmed.

Britain's venerable University of Cambridge is mixed into the delightful town of Cambridge, north of London, which offers a mellow, fun-to-explore townscape with a big-league university.

Other destinations that make for a practical day trip from London include Stonehenge, Salisbury, Canterbury, Bath, and Oxford—all covered in other chapters.

GETTING AROUND

By Train: If day-tripping from London, take advantage of British Rail's discounts. The "off-peak day return" ticket is a round-trip fare that costs virtually the same as one-way, provided you depart London outside rush hour (usually after 9:30 on weekdays and anytime Sat-Sun). Be sure to get the "day return" ticket (round-trip within a single day) rather than the more expensive, standard "return" ticket. You can also save a little money if you purchase tickets before 18:00 the day before your trip.

By Train Tour: London Walks offers a variety of "Daytrips

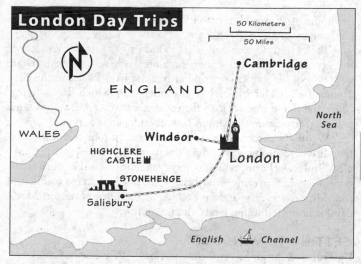

from London" tours year-round by train, including a Cambridge itinerary (see page 55 for more on London Walks).

Windsor

Windsor, a compact and easy walking town of about 30,000 people, originally grew up around the royal residence. In 1070, William the Conqueror continued his habit of kicking Saxons out of their various settlements, taking over what the locals called "Windlesora" (meaning "riverbank with a hoisting winch")—which eventually became "Windsor." William built the first fortified castle on a chalk hill above the Thames; later kings added on to his early designs, rebuilding and expanding the castle and surrounding gardens.

By setting up their primary residence here, modern monarchs increased Windsor's popularity and prosperity—most notably, Queen Victoria, whose stern statue glares at you as you approach the castle. After her death, Victoria rejoined her beloved husband, Albert, in the Royal Mausoleum at Frogmore House, a mile south of the castle in a private section of the Home Park (house and mausoleum rarely open). Within the grounds of Frogmore House is Frogmore Cottage—

the home of Prince Harry, the Duchess of Sussex (Meghan Markle), and wee Master Archie.

The current Queen considers Windsor her primary residence; she generally hangs her crown here on weekends, using it as an escape from her workaday grind at Buckingham Palace in the city. You can tell if Her Majesty is in residence by which flag is flying above the round tower: If it's the royal standard (a red, yellow, and blue flag) instead of the Union Jack, the Queen is at home.

While 99 percent of visitors just come to tour the castle and then leave, some enjoy spending the night. Daytime crowds trample Windsor's charm, which is most evident when the tourists are gone. Consider overnighting here—parking and access to Heathrow Airport are easy, and an evening at the horse races (on Mondays) is hoof-pounding, heart-thumping fun.

GETTING TO WINDSOR

By Train: Windsor has two train stations—Windsor & Eton Central and Windsor & Eton Riverside. London's Paddington Station connects with Windsor & Eton Central (2-3/hour, 35 minutes, easy change at Slough—typically just across the platform, www.gwr.com). London's Waterloo Station connects with Windsor & Eton Riverside (2/hour, no changes but slower—55 minutes, www.nationalrail.co.uk). Either trip costs about £11 one-way (a few pounds more for same-day return).

By Bus: Green Line buses #702 and #703 run—very slooooowly—from London's Victoria Colonnades (between the Victoria train and coach stations) to the Parish Church stop on Windsor's High Street, before continuing on to Legoland (1-2/hour, 1.5 hours to Windsor, prices typically £6-10 each way, tel. 0871-200-2233, www.firstgroup.com).

By Car: Windsor is about 20 miles from London. The town (and then the castle and Legoland) is well-signposted from the M-4 motorway. It's a convenient first stop if you're arriving at Heathrow and renting a car there.

From Heathrow Airport: You have two public transit options, both around £11. The train requires two changes (first take the Heathrow Express to Hayes & Harlington station, transfer to a train to Slough, then transfer again to Windsor, 50 minutes total). Or you can take First Bus Company's bus #8 or #9 from Terminal 5 (2/hour, 1 hour). London black cabs can (and do) charge whatever they like from Heathrow to Windsor; avoid them by calling a local cab company, such as Windsor Cars (tel. 01753/677-677, www.windsorcars.com).

Orientation to Windsor

Windsor's pleasant pe-
destrian shopping zone
litters the approach to its
famous palace with fun
temptations. You'll find
most shops and restau-
rants around the castle on
High and Thames streets,
and down the pedestrian
Peascod Street (PESS-
cot), which runs perpendicular to High Street.

TOURIST INFORMATION

The TI is in the Windsor Royal Shopping Centre's Old Booking Hall, immediately adjacent to Windsor & Eton Central Station (daily 10:00-16:00, sells discounted tickets to Legoland; tel.
01753/743-900, www.windsor.gov.uk).

ARRIVAL IN WINDSOR

By Train: Whichever train station you arrive at, you're only a five-
minute walk to the castle. From Windsor & Eton Central, walk
through the Windsor Royal Shopping Centre (which houses the
TI), and up the hill to the castle. From Windsor & Eton Riverside,
you'll see the castle as you exit—just follow the wall up and around
to the ticket office.

    By Car: Follow signs from the M-4 motorway for pay-and-
display parking in the center. River Street Car Park is closest to the
castle, but it's pricey and often full. The cheaper, bigger Alexandra
Car Park (near the riverside Alexandra Gardens) is farther west,
just below the central train station (find the stairs up to the station platform, and exit into the Windsor Royal Shopping Centre
with the TI). The cheapest parking option is the King Edward VII
Avenue car-park-and-ride, northeast of the castle on the B-470 (includes shuttle bus into town).

HELPFUL HINTS

Supermarkets: Pick up picnic supplies at **Marks & Spencer** (on
    the pedestrian shopping street near the TI, at 130 Peascod
    Street) or at **Waitrose** (bigger but a bit farther, buried in the
    King Edward Court Shopping Centre behind the central sta-
    tion). Just outside the castle, you'll find long benches near the
    statue of Queen Victoria—great for people-watching while
    you munch.
Hiking and Biking: Windsor and Eton occupy a lovely area on

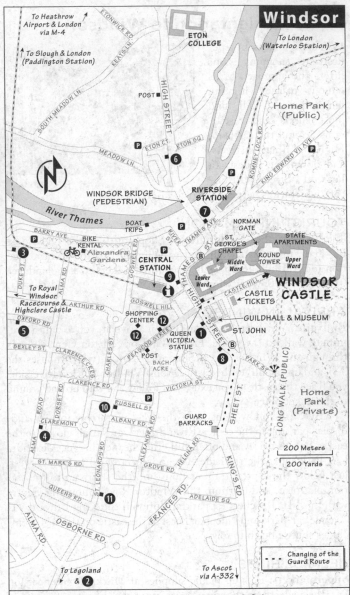

Windsor

To Heathrow Airport & London via M-4

To Slough & London (Paddington Station)

ETONWICK RD.

KEATS LN.

ETON COLLEGE

To London (Waterloo Station)

POST

HIGH STREET

SOUTH MEADOW LN.

Home Park (Public)

ETON CT.

ROMNEY LOCK RD.

KING EDWARD VII AVE

MEADOW LN.

ETON SQ.

6

P

P

N

WINDSOR BRIDGE (PEDESTRIAN)

RIVERSIDE STATION

7

River Thames

BOAT TRIPS

RIVER ST.

THAMES AVE.

NORMAN GATE

ST. GEORGE'S CHAPEL

STATE APARTMENTS

BARRY AVE.

BIKE RENTAL

Alexandra Gardens

GOSWELL RD.

THAMES ST.

B

Middle Ward

ROUND TOWER

Upper Ward

P

CENTRAL STATION

9

HIGH STREET

Lower Ward

WINDSOR CASTLE

DUKE ST.

ALMA RD.

To Royal Windsor Racecourse & Highclere Castle

ARTHUR RD.

GOSWELL HILL

i

CASTLE HILL

CASTLE TICKETS

OXFORD RD.

5

CHARLES ST.

SHOPPING CENTER

12

12

GUILDHALL & MUSEUM

ST. JOHN

BEXLEY ST.

CLARENCE CRES.

FEASOD STREET

QUEEN VICTORIA STATUE

1

B

DORSET RD.

CLARENCE RD.

POST

BACHELORS ACRE

8

PARK ST.

ROAD

ALEXANDRA RD.

VICTORIA ST.

SHEET ST.

Home Park (Private)

CLAREMONT

10

RUSSELL ST.

ALBANY RD.

LONG WALK (PUBLIC)

4

ST. MARK'S RD.

ST. LEONARDS RD.

GROVE RD.

HELENA RD.

GUARD BARRACKS

KING'S RD.

QUEENS RD.

11

OSBORNE RD.

FRANCES RD.

ADELAIDE SQ.

200 Meters

200 Yards

ALMA RD.

To Legoland & 2

To Ascot via A-332

- - - Changing of the Guard Route

Accommodations

1 Castle Hotel Windsor
2 To Park Farm B&B
3 76 Duke Street
4 Langton House B&B
5 Dee & Steve's B&B
6 Crown & Cushion

Eateries & Other

7 Bel & The Dragon
8 Cornucopia à la Russe
9 The Duchess of Cambridge
10 Al Fassia
11 Saffron
12 Grocery (2)

the Thames that's ideal for a pleasant walk or bike ride—get suggestions at the TI. You can rent bikes at **Extreme Motion,** near the river in Alexandra Gardens (summer daily 10:00-18:00, Sat-Sun only off-season, tel. 01753/830-220).

Sights in Windsor

▲▲WINDSOR CASTLE

Windsor Castle, the official home of England's royal family for 900 years, claims to be the largest and oldest occupied castle in the

world. Thankfully, touring it is simple. You'll see sprawling grounds, lavish staterooms, a crowd-pleasing dollhouse, and an exquisite Perpendicular Gothic chapel. Allow at least two hours for a complete visit.

Cost: £22.50, includes entry to castle grounds and all exhibits inside.

Hours: Grounds and most interiors open daily 10:00-17:15, Nov-Feb until 16:15, except St. George's Chapel, which is closed Sun to tourists (but open to worshippers; wait at the exit gate to be escorted in). Last entry to grounds and St. George's Chapel is 75 minutes before closing. Last entry to State Apartments and Queen Mary's Dolls' House is 45 minutes before closing.

Information: Tel. 020/7766-7324, www.rct.uk.

Crowd Control: Ticket lines can be quite long in summer. You can expect the worst crowds from opening until 13:00 any time of year. Avoid the wait by purchasing tickets in advance at www.rct.uk (collect them at the prepaid ticket window), or in person at the Buckingham Palace ticket office in London. (There's nowhere in Windsor to buy advance tickets.) All visitors must go through a security checkpoint, which can further slow entry at busy times.

Possible Closures: On rare occasions when the Queen is entertaining guests, the State Apartments close (and tickets are slightly reduced). Sometimes the entire castle closes. It's smart to call ahead or check the website (especially in mid-June) to make sure everything is open when you want to go. While you're at it, confirm the Changing of the Guard schedule.

Tours: An included **audioguide** (dry, reverent, informative) covers both the grounds and interiors. For a good overview—and an opportunity to ask questions—consider the free 30-minute **guided walk** around the grounds (about 5/day, schedule posted on path up to the main gate). The official £5 guidebook is full of gorgeous images and makes a fine souvenir but adds no information beyond what is covered in the audioguide and tour.

Changing of the Guard: The Changing of the Guard usually takes place Tuesday, Thursday, and Saturday at 11:00 (confirm schedule on website; canceled in very bad weather). The fresh guards, led by a marching band, leave their barracks on Sheet Street and march up High Street, hanging a right at Victoria, then a left into the castle's Lower Ward, arriving at about 11:00. After about a half-hour, the tired guards march back the

way the new ones came. If you want to view the ceremony from inside the castle, it's smart to arrive as early as possible (no later than 10:30 on quiet days) to have time to buy tickets, clear security, and stake out a spot with a clear view. If you arrive late, you could just wait for them to march by on High Street or on the lower half of Castle Hill.

Evensong: An evensong takes place in the chapel nightly at 17:15 (free for worshippers, line up at exit gate to be admitted).

Best View: While you can get great views of the castle from any direction, the classic views are from the wooded avenue called the Long Walk, which stretches south of the palace and is open to the public.

Eating: There are no real eateries inside (other than shops selling gifty boxes of chocolates and bottled water), so consider bringing a snack with you.

◑ Self-Guided Tour

After buying your ticket and going through security, pick up your audioguide and start strolling along the path through...

The Grounds

Head up the hill, enjoying the first of many fine castle views you'll see today. The tower-topped conical hill on your left represents the historical core of the castle. William the Conqueror built this motte (artificial mound) and bailey (fortified stockade around it) in 1080—his first castle in England. Among the later monarchs who spiffed up Windsor were Edward III (flush with French war booty, he made it a palace fit for a 14th-century king), Charles II (determined to restore the monarchy properly in the 1660s), and George IV (Britain's "Bling King," who financed many such vanity projects in the 1820s). On your right, the circular bandstand platform has a seal of the Order of the Garter, which has important

The Order of the Garter

In addition to being the royal residence, Windsor is the home of the Most Noble Order of the Garter—Britain's most prestigious chivalrous order. The castle's history is inexorably tied to this order.

Founded in 1348 by King Edward III and his son (the "Black Prince"), the Order of the Garter was designed to honor returning Crusaders. This was a time when the legends of King Arthur and the Knights of the Round Table were sweeping England, and Edward III fantasized that Windsor could be a real-life Camelot. (He even built the Round Tower as an homage to the Round Table.)

The order's seal illustrates the story of the order's founding and unusual name: a cross of St. George encircled with a belt and a French motto loosely translated as "Shame be upon he who thinks evil of it." Supposedly while the king was dancing with a fair maiden, her garter slipped off onto the floor; in an act of great chivalry, he rescued her from embarrassment by picking it up and uttering those words.

The Order of the Garter continues to the present day as the single most prestigious honor in the United Kingdom. There can be only 24 knights at one time (perfect numbers for splitting into two 12-man jousting teams), plus the sitting monarch and the Prince of Wales. Aside from royals and the nobility, past Knights of the Garter have included Winston Churchill, Bernard "Monty" Montgomery, and Ethiopian Emperor Haile Selassie. In 2008, Prince William became only the 1,000th knight in the order's history. Other current members include various ex-military officers, former British Prime Minister John Major, and a member of the Colman's Mustard family.

The patron of the order is St. George—the namesake of the State Apartments' most sumptuous hall and of the castle's own chapel. Both of these spaces—the grandest in Windsor—are designed to celebrate and honor the Order of the Garter.

ties to Windsor (see sidebar). This is where free guided tours depart (look for the posted schedule).

Passing through the small gate, you approach the stately St. George's Gate. Peek through here to the Upper Ward's **Quadrangle,** which is surrounded by the State Apartments (across the field) and the Queen's private apartments (to the right).

Turn left and follow the wall. Step into the long **exhibit** that traces the history of the castle, including models of how the structure evolved over time and illustrations of St. George's Hall in different historical periods.

Back outside, continue up the path. On your right-hand side, you enjoy great views of the **Round Tower** atop that original motte; running around the base of this artificial hill is the delightful, peaceful garden of the castle governor. The unusual design of this castle has not one "bailey" (castle yard), but three, which today make up Windsor's Upper Ward (where the Queen lives, which you just saw), Middle Ward (the ecclesiastical heart of the complex, with St. George's Chapel, which you'll soon pass on the left), and Lower Ward (residences for castle workers).

Continue all the way around this mini moat to the **Norman Gate,** which once held a prison. Carry on past the gate for even finer views of the Quadrangle.

Do a 180 and head back toward the Norman Gate, but before you reach it, go down the staircase on the right. You'll emerge onto a fine **terrace** overlooking the flat lands all around. It's easy to understand why this was a strategic place to build a castle. That's Eton College across the Thames. Imagine how handy it's been for royals to be able to ship off their teenagers to an elite prep school so close they could easily keep an eye on them... literally. The power-plant cooling towers in the distance mark the workaday burg of Slough (rhymes with "plow," immortalized as the setting for Britain's original version of *The Office*).

• *Note that this area may be torn up during your visit, as they are carrying out a years-long renovation of this part of the castle. Some of the items mentioned in the next part of the tour may be closed, and you may visit things in a different order than described.*

Turn right and wander along the terrace. You'll likely see two lines. The long one leads to Queen Mary's Dolls' House, then to the State Apartments. The short line skips the dollhouse and heads directly to the apartments. Read the following descriptions and decide if the dollhouse is worth the wait (or try again later in the day, when the line sometimes eases up).

Queen Mary's Dolls' House

This palace in miniature (1:12 scale, from 1924) is "the most famous dollhouse in the world." It was a gift for the adult Queen Mary (the wife of King George V, and the current Queen's grandmother), who greatly enjoyed miniatures. It's basically one big, dimly lit room with the large dollhouse in the middle, executed with an astonishing level of detail. Each fork, knife, and spoon on the expertly set banquet table is perfect and made of real silver—and the tiny pipes of its plumbing system actually have running water. But you're kept a few feet away by a glass wall, and constantly jostled by fellow sightseers in this crowded space, making it difficult to fully appreciate. Unless you're a dollhouse devotee, it's not worth waiting half an hour for a five-minute peek, but if the line is short it's worth a look.

State Apartments

Dripping with chandeliers, finely furnished, and strewn with history and the art of a long line of kings and queens, they're the best I've seen in Britain. This is where Henry VIII and Charles I once lived, and where the current Queen wows visiting dignitaries. Remember to take advantage of the talkative docents in each room, who are happy to answer your questions.

On your way in, you may pass through the **China Museum,** featuring items from the Queen's many exquisite settings for royal shindigs.

You'll climb the Grand Staircase up to the peach-colored **Grand Vestibule,** decorated with exotic items seized by British troops during their missions to colonize various corners of the world. Immediately to the left of the door into the next room, look for the bullet that killed Lord Nelson at Trafalgar.

In the next room, the magnificent wood-ceilinged **Waterloo Chamber** is wallpapered with portraits of figures from the pan-European alliance that defeated Napoleon. Find the Duke of Wellington (high on the far wall, in red) who outmaneuvered him at Waterloo, and Pope Pius VII (right wall, in red and white) whom Napoleon befriended...then imprisoned.

A highlight is **St. George's Hall,** decorated with emblems representing the knights of the prestigious Order of the Garter (see sidebar, earlier). This is the site of some of the most elaborate royal banquets—imagine one long table stretching from one end of the hall to the other and seating 160 VIPs. At the end of the hall, you enter the Queen's Guard Chamber, with more weapons and busts of English war heroes, from Nelson to Marlborough to Churchill.

At some point, you'll pass through a **series of living rooms**—bedchambers, dressing rooms, and drawing rooms of the king and queen (who traditionally maintained separate quarters). Many rooms are decorated with canvases by Rubens, Van Dyck, and Holbein. You may also tour some rooms that were restored after a fire in 1992, including the "Semi-State Apartments."

The **Garter Throne Room** is where new members of the Order of the Garter are invested (ceremonially granted their titles).

• *Exiting the State Apartments, you have one more major sight to see.*

Head back out the way you came in, but bear right/downhill toward (or follow signs to find)...

St. George's Chapel

This church is known for housing numerous royal tombs, and is an exquisite example of the Perpendicular Gothic style (dating from about 1500). More recent-

ly, it's where Prince Harry and Meghan Markle tied the knot in 2018. Enter at the bottom end, pick up a free map, and circle the interior clockwise, finding these highlights:

Stand at the back and look down the **nave,** with its classic fan-vaulting spreading out from each slender pillar and nearly every joint capped with an elaborate and colorful roof boss. Most of these emblems are associated with the Knights of the Garter, who consider St. George's their "mother church." Under the upper stained-glass windows, notice the continuous frieze of 250 angels, lovingly carved with great detail, ringing the church.

In the back-left corner (#4 on your church-issued map), take in the melodramatic monument to **Princess Charlotte of Wales,** the only child of King George IV. Heir to the throne, her death in 1817 (at 21, in childbirth) devastated the nation. Head up the left side of the nave and find the simple chapel (#6, just past the wooden gate) containing the tombs of the current Queen's parents, **King George VI and "Queen Mum" Elizabeth;** the ashes of her younger sister, Princess Margaret, are also kept here (see the marble slab against the wall). Farther up the aisle is the tomb of **Edward IV** (#8, past the door into the choir), who expanded St. George's Chapel.

Stepping into the **choir area** (#12), you're immediately aware that you are in the inner sanctum of the Order of the Garter. The banners lining the nave represent the knights, as do the fancy helmets and half-drawn swords topping the spire of each wood-carved seat. These symbols honor only living knights; on the seats are some 800 golden panels memorializing departed knights. Under your feet lies the **Royal Vault** (#13), burial spot of Mad King George III (nemesis of American revolutionaries). Strolling farther up the aisle, notice the marker in the floor: You're walking over the burial site of **King Henry VIII** (#14) and Jane Seymour, Henry's favorite wife (perhaps because she was the only one who died before he could behead her). The body of King Charles I, who was beheaded by Oliver Cromwell's forces at the Banqueting House, was also discovered here...with its head sewn back on.

Exiting the choir area at the far end, loop around to the left and head to the back of the church. Leaving the church proper in the far corner, you'll pass the gift shop. On your way out, pause at the door of the sumptuous 13th-century **Albert Memorial Chapel** (#28), redecorated in 1861 after the death of Queen Victoria's husband, Prince Albert, and dedicated to his memory.

• *After exiting the chapel, you come into the castle's...*

Lower Ward

This area is a living town where some 160 people who work for the Queen reside; they include clergy, military, and castle administrators. Just below the chapel, you may be able to enter a tranquil little horseshoe-shaped courtyard ringed with residential doorways—all of them with a spectacular view of the chapel's grand entrance.

MORE SIGHTS IN WINDSOR
Legoland Windsor

Paradise for Legomaniacs under age 12, this huge, kid-pleasing park has dozens of tame but fun rides (often with very long lines) scattered throughout its 150 acres. The impressive Miniland has 40 million Lego pieces glued together to create 800 tiny buildings and a mini tour of Europe. Several of the more exciting rides involve getting wet, so dress accordingly or buy a cheap  disposable poncho in the gift shop. While you may be tempted to hop on the Hill Train at the entrance, it's faster and more convenient to walk down into the park.

Cost: £64 but varies by day, significant savings when booked online at least 7 days in advance, 10 percent discount at Windsor TI, free for ages 3 and under, optional Q-Bot ride-reservation gadget allows you to bypass lines (£25-90 depending on when you go and how much time you want to save).

Hours: Generally Mon-Fri 10:00-17:00, until 18:00 in summer and on Sat-Sun; often closed Tue-Wed outside of summer; closed entirely in winter. Check website for exact schedule, tel. 0871-222-2001, www.legoland.co.uk.

Getting There: A £5 round-trip shuttle bus runs from the Parish Church stop on High Street (2/hour). If day-tripping from London, ask about rail/shuttle/park admission deals from Paddington or Waterloo train stations. For drivers, the park is on the B-3022 Windsor/Ascot road, two miles southwest of Windsor and

25 miles west of London. Legoland is clearly signposted from the M-3, M-4, and M-25 motorways (easy paid parking).

Eton College

Across the bridge from Windsor Castle is the most famous "public" (the equivalent of our "private") high school in Britain. Eton was founded in 1440 by King Henry VI; today it educates about 1,300 boys (ages 13-18), who live on campus. Eton has molded the characters of 19 prime ministers as well as members of the royal family—most recently princes William and Harry. Sparse on actual sights, the college is officially closed to visitors except via guided tour, where you may get a glimpse of the schoolyard, chapel, cloisters, and the Museum of Eton Life. However, curious and discreet visitors can often poke around the other grounds on their own—including the gardens, playing fields, and surrounding parks. For more information visit www.etoncollege.com or call 01753/370-100.

Eton High Street

Even if you're not touring the college, it's worth the few minutes it takes to cross the pedestrian bridge and wander straight up Eton's High Street. A bit more cutesy and authentic-feeling than Windsor (which is given over to shopping malls and chain stores), Eton has a charm that's fun to sample.

Windsor and Royal Borough Museum

Tucked into one room beneath the Guildhall (where Prince Charles remarried), this little museum does its best to give some insight into the history of Windsor and the surrounding area. They also have lots of special activities for kids. Ask at the desk whether tours are running to the Guildhall itself (visits only possible with a guide, leave sporadically, about 20-30 minutes); if not, it's probably not worth the admission—you can see most of the museum with a sweep of your head from the door.

Cost and Hours: £2, includes audioguide, Tue-Sat 10:00-16:00, Sun from 12:00, closed Mon, located in the Guildhall on High Street, tel. 01628/685-686, www.rbwm.gov.uk.

Boat Trips

Cruise up and down the Thames River for classic views of the castle, the village of Eton, Eton College, and the Royal Windsor Racecourse. Boats leave from the riverside promenade adjacent to Barry Avenue, and run from early spring through late fall.

Cost and Hours: 40-minute tour—£9.50, 1-2/hour daily 10:00-17:00; 2-hour tour—£14.55, 1-2/day; tel. 01753/851-900, www.frenchbrothers.co.uk.

Visiting Highclere Castle

If you're a fan of *Downton Abbey,* consider a day trip from London to Highclere Castle, the stately house where much of the show was filmed. Though the series was set in Yorkshire, the actual house is in Hampshire, about an hour's train ride west of London. Highclere has been home to the Earls of Carnarvon since 1679, but the present Jacobean-style house was rebuilt in the 1840s by Sir Charles Barry, who also designed London's Houses of Parliament. Noted landscape architect Capability Brown laid out the traditional gardens in the mid-18th century. The castle's Egyptian exhibit features artifacts collected by Highclere's fifth Earl, George Herbert, an amateur archaeologist. When Howard Carter discovered King Tut's tomb in 1922, he waited three weeks for his friend Herbert to join him before looking inside. The Earl died unexpectedly a few months later, prompting the legend of a "mummy's curse."

Cost and Hours: £23 for castle, garden, and Egyptian exhibit; £16 for garden plus either castle or Egyptian exhibit; £7 for garden only. Open in summer Sun-Thu 10:30-17:00, grounds open from 9:00, last entry one hour before closing, closed Fri-Sat; generally closed mid-Sept-mid-July except for special events. Reserve timed-entry tickets well in advance—tickets available several months ahead; 24-hour info tel. 01635/253-204, www.highclerecastle.co.uk.

Getting There: Highclere is 6 miles south of Newbury, about 70 miles west of London, off the A-34.

By Train and Taxi: Trains run from London's Paddington Station to Newbury (1-2/hour, 50-70 minutes, tel. 0345-7000-125, www.gwr.com). From Newbury train station, you can take a taxi (about £20 one-way) or reserve a car and driver (arrange in advance, £12.50/person round-trip; £25 minimum, tel. 07818/430-095, mapeng@msn.com).

By Tour: Brit Movie Tours offers an all-day bus tour of *Downton Abbey* filming locations, including Highclere Castle (sells out early, £80, includes castle/garden entry, £5 extra for Egyptian exhibit, depart London from outside Gloucester Road Tube Station, reservations required, tel. 0844-247-1007, from the US or Canada call 011-44-20-7118-1007, www.britmovietours.com).

Horse Racing

The horses race every Monday at the Royal Windsor Racecourse (£25 entry, online discounts, under age 18 free with an adult, April-Oct except no races in Sept and sporadic in Aug, off the A-308 between Windsor and Maidenhead, tel. 01753/498-400, www.windsor-racecourse.co.uk). The romantic way to get there from Windsor is by a 10-minute shuttle boat (£7.50 round-trip, www.frenchbrothers.co.uk). The famous Ascot Racecourse (described next) is also nearby.

NEAR WINDSOR
Ascot Racecourse

Located seven miles southwest of Windsor and just north· of the town of Ascot, this royally owned track is one of the most famous horse-racing venues in the world. The horses first ran here in 1711, and the course is best known for June's five-day Royal Ascot race meeting, attended by the Queen and 299,999 of her loyal subjects. For many, the outlandish hats worn on Ladies Day (Thu) are more interesting than the horses. Royal Ascot is usually the third week in June. The pricey tickets go on sale the preceding November; while the Friday and Saturday races tend to sell out far ahead, tickets for the other days are often available close to the date (check website). In addition to Royal Ascot, the racecourse runs the ponies year-round—funny hats strictly optional.

Cost: Regular tickets generally start from £20 and go as high as £80—may be available at a discount at TI, dress code enforced in some areas and on certain days, tel. 0844-346-3000, www.ascot.co.uk.

Sleeping in Windsor

$$$$ Castle Hotel Windsor, part of the boutique division of Accor Hotels, offers 108 rooms and elegant public spaces in a central location just down the street from Her Majesty's weekend retreat (air-con, elevator in main building, parking-£25/day, 18 High Street, tel. 01753/851-577, www.castlehotelwindsor.com, h6618@accor.com).

$$ Park Farm B&B, bright and cheery, is most convenient for drivers. But even if you're not driving, this beautiful place is such a good value, and the welcome is so warm, that you're unlikely to mind the bus ride into town (no kids under 12, cash only—credit card solely for reservations, shared fridge and microwave, free off-street parking, 1 mile from Legoland on St. Leonards Road near Imperial Road, 5-minute bus ride or 1-mile walk to castle, £5 taxi ride from station, tel. 01753/866-823, www.parkfarm.com, stay@parkfarm.com, Caroline and Drew Youds).

$$ 76 Duke Street has two nice rooms, but only hosts one set of guests at a time. While the bathroom is (just) outside your bedroom, you have it to yourself (15-minute walk from station at—you guessed it—76 Duke Street, tel. 01753/620-636 or 07884/222-225, www.76dukestreet.co.uk, bandb@76dukestreet.co.uk, Julia).

$$ Langton House B&B is a stately Victorian home with five spacious, well-appointed rooms (continental breakfast included but full English breakfast extra, family rooms, guest kitchen, 46 Alma Road, tel. 01753/858-299, www.langtonhouse.co.uk, bookings@langtonhouse.co.uk, Paul and Sonja Fogg with help from Chris).

$$ Dee and Steve's B&B is a friendly four-room place above a window shop on a quiet residential street about a 10-minute walk from the castle and station. The rooms are cozy, Dee and Steve are pleasant hosts, and breakfast is served in the contemporary kitchen/lounge, with bricks and beams. They have two affordable singles that share a bathroom (169 Oxford Road, tel. 01753/854-489, www.deeandsteve.com, dee@deeandsteve.com).

$$ Crown and Cushion is a good option on Eton's High Street, just across the pedestrian bridge from Windsor's waterfront (a short uphill walk to the castle). While the pub it's situated over is worn and drab, you're right in the heart of charming Eton, and the eight creaky rooms—with uneven floors and old-beam ceilings—are nicely furnished (free parking, 84 High Street in Eton, tel. 01753/861-531, www.thecrownandcushioneton.co.uk, info@thecrownandcushioneton.com).

Eating in Windsor

Elegant Spots with River Views: Several places flank Windsor Bridge, offering romantic dining after dark. The riverside promenade, with cheap takeaway stands scattered about, is a delightful place for a picnic lunch or dinner with the swans. If you don't see anything that appeals, continue up Eton's High Street, which is also lined with characteristic eateries.

In the Tourist Zone Around the Palace: Strolling the streets and lanes around the palace entrance—especially in the shopping zone near Windsor & Eton Station—you'll find countless inviting eateries. The central area also has a sampling of dependable British chains. Residents enjoy a wide selection of unpretentious little eateries just past the end of pedestrian Peascod Street, where it becomes St. Leonards Road. These include Saffron (recommended later) and a fire station turned pub-and-cultural center (The Old Court Artspace).

$$$ Bel & The Dragon is the place to splurge on high-quality classic British food in a charming half-timbered building with an upscale-rustic dining space (food served daily 12:00-15:00 & 18:00-22:00, afternoon tea served between lunch and dinner, bar open longer hours, on Thames Street near the bridge to Eton, tel. 01753/866-056).

$$$ Cornucopia à la Russe, with a cozy, woody atmosphere, serves elegant French and international dishes (two- and three-course lunch deals, open Mon 18:00-21:30, Tue-Sat 12:00-14:30 & 18:00-21:30, closed Sun, 6 High Street, tel. 01753/833-009).

$$ The Duchess of Cambridge's friendly staff serves up the normal grub in a pub that's right across from the castle walls. It feels big, modern, but tasteful, and with an open fireplace to boot. While the pub predates Kate, it was named in her honor following a recent remodel, and has the photos to prove her endorsement (daily 11:00-23:00 or later, 3 Thames Street, tel. 01753/864-405).

$$ Al Fassia—just beyond the end of the pedestrian zone— has authentic Moroccan cuisine, including tagines served in pottery (Mon-Fri 18:00-22:00, Sat-Sun from 12:00, 27 St. Leonards Road, tel. 01753/855-370).

$$ Saffron restaurant, while a fairly long walk from the castle, is the local choice for South Indian cuisine, with a modern interior and tasty dishes. Their vegetable *thali* is a treat (daily 12:00-14:30 & 17:30-23:30, 99 St. Leonards Road, tel. 01753/855-467).

Cambridge

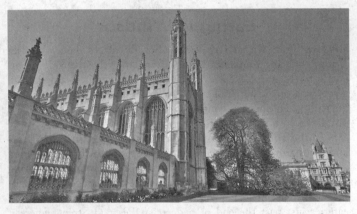

Cambridge, 60 miles north of London, is world-famous for its prestigious university. William Wordsworth, Isaac Newton, Charles Darwin, Alan Turing, Jane Goodall, and Prince Charles are only a few of its illustrious alumni. The university dominates— and owns—most of Cambridge, a historic town of about 125,000 people. Cambridge is the epitome of a university town, with busy bikers, stately residence halls, plenty of bookshops, and proud locals who can point out where DNA was originally modeled, the atom first split, and electrons discovered.

In medieval Europe, higher education was the domain of the Church and was limited to ecclesiastical schools. Scholars lived in "halls" on campus, which came to be known as "colleges." The first at Cambridge, Peterhouse, was founded in the 1280s. By 1350, Cambridge had eight separate colleges, each one a self-contained world in itself— enclosed behind walls, with a monastic-type courtyard, chapel, library, and lodgings. These colleges allied in a federation known as the University of Cambridge. That same arrangement survives to this day. Today, Cambridge has 31 colleges, totaling about 12,000 undergrads, scattered around the town center.

For travelers, Cambridge offers a pleasant medieval-era town, art-filled churches and museums, and—most of all—a chance to see some of the colleges (many are open to visitors—some free; others require a ticket at the gate). You can stroll the grounds and pop into a few public areas (mainly chapels and dining halls).

The town is easy to sort out. There's a small and youthful commercial center—quiet and traffic free (except for lots of bikes), one important museum (the Fitzwilliam), and lots of minor museums (all generally free). The River Cam has boat tours, three public bridges, and a strip of six colleges, whose gardens basically own the river through the center of town and make it feel like  an exclusive park. Trinity College has its famous Wren Library, and King's College has a famous ornate chapel. The city is filled with students year-round—scholars throughout the regular terms and visiting students enjoying summer programs.

PLANNING YOUR TIME

Cambridge can easily be seen as a day trip from London. A good five-hour plan is to follow my self-guided walk, spend an hour on a punt ride, tour the Fitzwilliam Museum (closed Mon), and see the Wren Library at Trinity College (open Mon-Sat for only two hours a day, so plan ahead). For a little extra color, consider joining a walk through town with a local guide from the TI (2 hours, repeats much of my self-guided walk but splices in local flavor). Confirm which sights are covered on the TI's walk, so you don't duplicate those on your own.

Your visit will be affected somewhat by the university schedule. Cambridge has three terms: Lent term from mid-January to mid-March, Easter term from mid-April to mid-June, and Michaelmas term from early October to early December. During exams (roughly the month of May), the colleges are closed to visitors, which can impede access to some of the town's picturesque little corners. When class is in session, Cambridge is a bustling town of students buzzing to class on bikes. Between terms there's less going on, but the main sights—King's College Chapel and the Wren Library at Trinity College—stay open, and Cambridge is never sleepy. On good-weather weekends, the town overflows with visitors—many of them trying their hand, unsuccessfully, at punting the Cam.

If you're in town for the evening, the evensong service at King's College Chapel (Mon-Sat at 17:30, Sun at 15:30) is a must. And if you like plays and music, events are always happening in this thriving cultural hub.

GETTING TO CAMBRIDGE

By Train: It's an easy 50-minute trip from London's King's Cross Station (hourly express trains). Cheaper direct trains also run from London's Liverpool Street Station, but take longer (2/hour, 1.5 hours). Rail information: tel. 0845-748-4950, www.nationalrail.co.uk.

By Bus: National Express X90 coaches run from London's Victoria Coach Station to the Parkside stop in Cambridge (every 60-90 minutes, 2 hours, tel. 0871-781-8181, www.nationalexpress.co.uk).

Orientation to Cambridge

Cambridge is small. Everything is within a pleasant walk. The main colleges form a north-south row, bordered on one side by the River Cam and on the other by the town. The town center, brimming with tearooms, has a TI and a colorful open-air market square. The train station is about a mile to the southeast.

TOURIST INFORMATION

Cambridge's TI is well run and well signposted, just off Market Hill Square in the town center. They offer walking tours and store bags (both described later), and sell bus tickets and an inexpensive map/guide (Mon-Sat 9:30-17:00, Sun 11:00-15:00, closed Sun in off-season, Peas Hill, tel. 01223/791-500, www.visitcambridge.org). In the same building as the TI, kids love the elaborate Harry Potter gift shop in a former courtroom.

ARRIVAL IN CAMBRIDGE

By Train: Cambridge's train station is about a mile southeast of the center. To get downtown, you can **walk** for about 25 minutes (exit straight ahead on Station Road, bear right at the war memorial onto Hills Road, and follow it into town); take public **bus** #1, #3, or #7 (referred to as "Citi 1," "Citi 3," and so on in schedules, but buses are marked only with the number; £1, pay driver, runs every 5-10 minutes, turn left when exiting station, cross the street, and

Cambridge

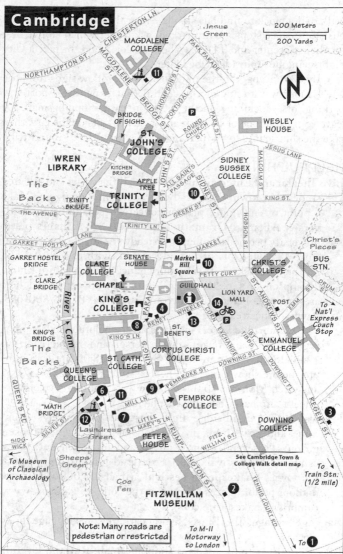

200 Meters

200 Yards

Note: Many roads are pedestrian or restricted

See Cambridge Town & College Walk detail map

Accommodations
1. To Lensfield Hotel
2. Hotel du Vin
3. Regent Hotel

Eateries
4. The Eagle Pub; Broad & Meat
5. Michaelhouse Café
6. The Anchor Pub
7. The Mill Pub
8. Agora at The Copper Kettle
9. Fitzbillies

Other
10. Grocery (2)
11. Scudamore's Punts (2)
12. Cambridge Chauffeur Punts
13. Cambridge Live Tickets
14. Bike Rental

walk half a block to find bus stands—near the far end of the many bus stops; since stops are unmarked, ask driver which stop is best for the city center and TI); pay about £6 for a **taxi;** or take a City Sightseeing **bus tour** (described later).

By Car: To park in the middle of town, follow signs from the M-11 motorway to any of the central (but expensive) short-stay parking lots—including one at the Lion Yard shopping mall. Or leave your car at one of six park-and-ride lots outside the city, then take the shuttle into town (parking-£1/day; shuttle-£3 round-trip).

HELPFUL HINTS

Live Theater and Entertainment: With all the smart and talented students in town, there is always something going on. Make a point of enjoying a play or concert. The **Cambridge University Amateur Dramatic Club (ADC)** is Britain's oldest university playhouse, offering a steady stream of performances since 1855. It's lots of fun and casual, with easy-to-get and inexpensive tickets. This is your chance to see a future Emma Thompson or Ian McKellen—alumni who performed here as students—before they become stars (tel. 01223/300-085, www.adctheatre.com).

> **Cambridge Live Tickets** is a very helpful service, offering event info and ticket sales in person and online (Mon-Fri 12:00-18:00, Sat from 10:00, Sun from 18:00 until 30 minutes before show time, 2 Wheeler Street, tel. 01223/357-851 answered Mon-Sat 10:00-18:00, www.cambridgelive.org.uk). The TI also has lists of what's playing.

Festivals: The **Cambridge Folk Festival** gets things humming and strumming in late July or early August (tickets go on sale several months ahead and often sell out; www.cambridgefolkfestival.co.uk). From mid-July through August, the town's **Shakespeare Festival** attracts 25,000 visitors for outdoor performances in some of the college's gardens (www.cambridgeshakespeare.com).

Baggage Storage: The TI (see listing earlier) stores luggage for £6 per bag.

Bike Rental: At the Lion Yard shopping mall, **Rutland Cycling** rents bikes (Mon-Fri 8:00-18:00, Sat from 9:00, Sun 10:00-17:00, look for it underground in the Grand Arcade, tel. 01223/307-655, www.rutlandcycling.com.

Cambridge and Oxford Colleges 101

Colleges, where students spend most of their time, are central to life at Cambridge and Oxford. Cambridge has 31 colleges, while Oxford has 38. Think of them less as schools and more as lodgings and social communities. They house, feed, and parent the students (including a "home professor" who coaches students), while the overall university offers formal teaching and lectures. Over the centuries, each college has developed a reputation: the rich elites, the partiers, the science nerds, the political progressives, and so on.

How to Visit: Some colleges are free to visit and welcoming to the public, some are closed off and very private, and others are famous and make money by charging for visits. Most are open only in the afternoons, and all have a similar design and etiquette. At their historic front gates, you'll find a porter's lodge where the porter delivers mail, monitors who comes and goes, and keeps people off the grass. Only fellows (senior professors) can walk on the grassy courts, which are the centerpiece of each college campus. Other than that, you can relax and roam freely, so long as an area is not locked or blocked with a "for members only" sign. Whether a college is open to visitors or private, you can usually at least pop in through the gate, chat with the porter, and enjoy the view of the court.

What You Will (and Won't) See: The court is ringed by venerable buildings, with a library, dormitories, a dining hall, and a chapel. The dining halls are easy to identify because they have big bay windows that mark the location of a "high table" where VIPs eat. A portrait of the college's founder usually hangs above the high table, and paintings of rectors and important alumni also decorate the walls. Students still eat in these halls, which is why they are rarely open to the public (but you can look in from the main door).

A college's chapel is the building that most often allows

visitors (including at evensong services, usually at 17:30 or 18:00). In the chapel, seating is usually arranged in several rows of pews that face each other to allow for antiphonal singing and chanting—where one side starts and the other responds. The chapels often contain memorials to students who died in World Wars I and II. Libraries are treasured and generally not open to the public. There's also a Senior Common Room (like a teachers' lounge but much fancier), where fellows share ideas in an exclusive social hall, creating a fertile intellectual garden. Student rooms are never open to the public during school terms, though some are available as vacation rentals when classes are not in session.

Tours in Cambridge

▲▲Walking Tour of the Colleges

A walking tour is the best way to understand Cambridge's mix of "town and gown." The walks can be more educational (read: dry) than entertaining, but they do provide a good rundown of the historic and scenic highlights of the university, some fun local gossip, and plenty of university trivia.

The TI offers **daily walking tours** of various lengths, subjects, and prices; Monday through Saturday, there's usually a tour at 11:00, 13:00 (also runs Sun), and 14:00. Check their website for the specific schedule (tel. 01223/791-500, www.visitcambridge. org). One good choice is the tour that includes King's College Chapel and Queens' College (£25, includes admission, 2 hours, usually Mon-Sat at 11:00). Groups are limited to 20, so it's smart to book online or drop in at the TI in advance to reserve a spot.

Private guides are available through the TI and affordable if you can assemble a group to share the cost (2-hour tour—£101; does not include individual college entrance fees, tel. 01223/791-500, tours@visitcambridge.org).

Walking Ghost Tour

If you're in Cambridge on the weekend, consider an £8 "ghost walk" to where spooky sightings have been reported (typically only in winter—when it's dark enough to be spooky, Fri-Sat at 18:00, organized by the TI, tel. 01223/791-500).

Bus Tours

City Sightseeing hop-on, hop-off bus tours are informative and cover the outskirts, including the American WWII Cemetery. But keep in mind that buses can't go where walking tours can—right into the center (£16.50, 80 minutes for full 19-stop circuit, 2-3/hour 10:00-17:30, recorded commentary, tel. 01223/433-250, www.city-sightseeing.com). If arriving by train, you can buy your ticket from the kiosk directly in front of the station, then ride the bus into town.

Cambridge Town and College Walk

This self-guided walk covers the essential sights. We start in the old market square, visit a couple of typical (if less-visited) colleges, pause at the dreamy River Cam, and finish at the glory of King's College Chapel. Although we won't go as far as Trinity College (Wren Library) or the Fitzwilliam Museum, they're close by and you can visit them on your own (covered in "Sights in Cambridge," later).

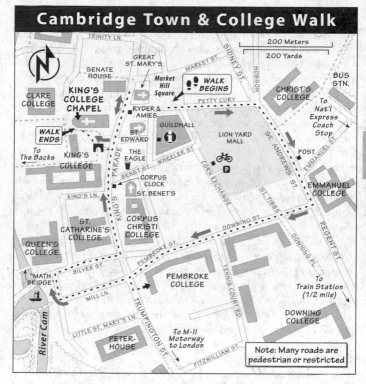

Cambridge Town & College Walk

• *Start on Market Hill Square in front of the Guildhall (the brick build-ing with a big clock up top).*

Market Hill Square

This square has been a center of commerce for more than a thou-sand years. At a glance, you can see the elements that combined to make Cambridge: church (Great St. Mary's rear end), univer-sity (those modern buildings are student lodgings), and trade (the open-air market and Guildhall).

Think of the history this place has seen: Romans first built a bridge over the Cam in AD 43, Anglo-Saxons and Danes estab-lished a market here in the Dark Ages, and Normans built a castle here (now gone) in the 11th century. The city's coat of arms (above the Guildhall door) shows medieval boats flocking to trade at the newly built bridge over the River Cam, which established "Cam-bridge."

But the big year was 1209. After scuffles in Oxford between its scholars and townsfolk, many of Oxford's academics fled here and started their own university. Where's "the university"? Every-

WINDSOR & CAMBRIDGE

where, mixed into the town, with the 31 individual colleges, university halls, and student dorms scattered about.

Cambridge suffered no bomb damage in World War II, so the older buildings you see are original. As you walk, notice how peaceful the town is, with almost no cars, but bikes everywhere. The Guildhall facing this square (the seat of the city council today) overlooks market stalls. The really big market is on Sunday (9:30-16:30) and features produce, arts, and crafts. On other days, you'll find mostly clothes and food stands (Mon-Sat generally 9:30-16:00).

• *Let's get started by exploring a bit of modern Cambridge. Facing the Guildhall, exit the square to your left down **Petty Cury Lane**, a modern pedestrian shopping street. At the end of the street, turn right, walking down St. Andrews Street (which connects the town center to the train station).*

*On the left side of the street is our first college: **Christ's College**. Its elaborate 16th-century gatehouse proudly displays the college's coat of arms and colors; look for others around town. Step inside to enjoy the classic court, next to a portrait of alum Charles Darwin (free, open daily 9:00-16:00). Don't linger—we'll see a better one in a minute.*

Continue down St. Andrews Street two long blocks toward the steeple, then pause at the college on the left...

Emmanuel College

This college offers a classic peek at a typical Cambridge college (free, open 9:00-18:00). Emmanuel was founded in 1584 as a Protestant college on land that had once been a Dominican friary. Like many monasteries and convents in the 16th century, the friary had been dissolved by the English king in an epic power struggle that left England with its own version of Christianity and the government with lots of land once owned by the Catholic Church.

Entering the courtyard, take in the layout. On the left is the dining hall, marked by its big bay window. Directly ahead (behind the big clock) is the Senior Common Room, a social hall for college fellows. Below the big clock is the entrance to the chapel. Go inside.

The **chapel** was designed by the famed architect Christopher Wren, who built many churches in the late 1600s; his work culminated with St. Paul's Cathedral. Wren gave this his typical two-toned treatment: white walls above and carved-wood below, all lit brilliantly. On the ceiling is a typical Wren design (all in white) of circles in squares, adorned with garlands. In the stained glass (left wall) find the portrait of John Harvard—the Emmanuel College student who went to America and founded a prestigious school of his own.

Explore more of the college grounds. You can look through the doorway into the dining hall (find it in the near-left corner of the courtyard, from where you came in); enjoy the garden behind the chapel, with its fish pond (dating back to monastic days when this was a source of their food); or chat with the porter.

• *Leaving Emmanuel College, walk straight ahead along Downing Street (which becomes Pembroke Street). Stop when you reach the intersection with King's Parade. Notice the recommended Fitzbillies Café on the right (famous for its local cinnamon roll, the Chelsea Bun), then turn left and walk a few steps to the entrance (on the left) to...*

Pembroke College

Founded in 1347, Pembroke is the third-oldest college in Cambridge. Step into the court, past the porter's lodge—it's polite to say hello and ask whether you can wander around. Survey the court. Ahead of you is the medieval dining hall. The fancy building with the pointed clock tower is the library (the statue in front is alumnus William Pitt the Younger—a great 18th-century

prime minister), with a charming garden beyond.

The highlight here is the chapel, to the right. It dates from about 1660 and is the first building (of any kind, anywhere) Christopher Wren completed. Before stepping inside to enjoy the interior, pause for a moment at the somber WWI and WWII memorial under the arcade. During the Great War, one in four students and faculty was killed.

• *From Pembroke College, cross King's Parade and follow Mill Lane directly down to the River Cam and its mill pond.*

River Cam, the Mill Pond, and Punting

From this perch you see the "harbor action" of Cambridge. The city was an important port in medieval times: Trading vessels from the North Sea (40 miles away) could navigate to here. Today a weir divides the River Cam from one of its tributaries, sometimes called the River Granta (on the left)—which leads through idyllic countryside from the town of Grantchester. Filling the mill pond

is a commotion of the iconic
Cambridge boats called punts.
Students hustle to take visitors
on a 45-minute trip with fun
commentary (see "Punting on
the Cam," later in this chapter).
Skilled residents rent boats for
themselves, as do not-so-skilled
tourists—much to the amusement of locals who sip their beer

while watching clumsy visitors fumble with the boats (which are
tougher to maneuver than they look). If you'd like a detour from
this sometimes-chaotic scene, simply cross the weir and walk along
the River Granta into the countryside—it quickly becomes sleepy
and idyllic.

But to continue this town walk, turn right and follow the narrow walkway along the harbor past the recommended Anchor Pub,
then up the stairs to the Silver Street Bridge. From the bridge,
you can watch more punt action and check out the famous "Math-
ematical Bridge," which links the old and new buildings of Queens'
College. This wooden bridge, although curved, is made entirely of
straight boards.

Gazing upstream past the wooden bridge, you see the start
of the park known as "the Backs"—the backs of six colleges that
line the river, with their fine architecture and most with bridges
connecting campus grounds or buildings on both sides of the river.
• *From the Silver Street Bridge, walk up Silver Street, back to King's
Parade, and turn left. You'll follow this about one block (passing the
stately Corpus Christi College on your right). At the first corner, find the
fancy gilded clock on your right.*

The Corpus Clock, Benet Street, and Eagle Pub

Designed and commissioned by Corpus Christi College alum
John Taylor, this **clock** was unveiled by Cambridge physicist Stephen Hawking in a 2008 ceremony. Perched on top is the Chro-
nophage—the "time eater"—a grotesque giant grasshopper that
keeps the clock moving and periodically winks at passersby. The
message? Time is passing, so live every moment to the fullest. It's
a real clock—one blue light marks the hour, the other the minutes.
At the top of the hour, it chimes with the sound of rattling chains.

The Eagle Pub, a venerable joint, is just down Benet Street
on the left. This is Cambridge's oldest pub and a sight in itself.
Poke into the courtyard and atmospheric rooms even if you don't
eat or drink here. From the courtyard, look up at the balcony of
second-floor guest rooms that date back to when this was a coach-
men's inn as well as a pub. (It's said that in Shakespeare's time,

plays were performed from this perch to entertain guests below.) Back inside the pub, find the fireplace with a photo and plaque that remember two esteemed regulars—Francis Crick and James Watson—the scientists who first described the structure of DNA. They announced their finding here in 1953.

At the back of the Eagle is an annex called the RAF Bar. During World War II, US Army Air Corps pilots famously hung out here before missions over Germany. The fun interior is plastered with stickers of air crews and WWII memorabilia.

St. Benet's Church, across the street from the pub, is the oldest surviving building in Cambridgeshire. The rough stone tower dates from 1020. The Saxons who built the church included circular holes in its bell tower to encourage owls to roost there and keep the mouse population under control.

• *Return to the creepy grasshopper clock and turn right, continuing down King's Parade past the regal front facade of King's College Chapel (we'll return here shortly) to the...*

Senate House

This stately classical building with triangular pediments is the ceremonial heart of the University of Cambridge. It's where the university's governing body meets. And it's where graduation ceremonies are held. In June, you might notice green boxes lining the front of this house. Traditionally, at the end of the term, students came to these boxes to see whether they had earned their de-

gree; those not listed knew they had flunked. Until 2010 this was the only notification students received about their status.

Looming across the street from the Senate House is **Great St. Mary's Church** (a.k.a. the University Church), with a climbable bell tower (£5, Mon-Sat 9:30-16:30, Sun 12:30-16:00, 123

stairs). On the corner nearby is **Ryder & Amies** (22 King's Parade), which has been the official university outfitter for 150 years. It's a great shop for college gear: sweaters, ties, and so on.

• *Backtrack to the entrance to King's College, buy your ticket, and enter through the grand gateway to the spacious grounds. In the courtyard, you're surrounded by buildings from every era of the college's long history. To the right is the famous chapel; straight ahead is the Neoclassical fellows hall; and to the left is the Neo-Gothic dining hall. The statue in the center is Henry VII, the man most responsible for the wonder we'll see next. Head for the chapel and step inside.*

▲▲King's College Chapel

Built from 1446 to 1515 by Henrys VI through VIII, this is England's best example of Perpendicular Gothic architecture and the most impressive building in Cambridge.

Cost and Hours: £9, erratic hours depending on school events; during academic term usually Mon-Fri 9:30-15:30, Sat until 15:15, Sun 13:15-14:30; during breaks (see page 219) usually daily 9:30-16:30; recorded info tel. 01223/331-1212. Buy tickets at the King's College visitors center at 13 Kings Parade, across the street from the main entrance gate.

Evensong: When school's in session, you're welcome to enjoy an evensong service in this glorious space, with a famous choir made up of men and boys (free, Mon-Sat at 17:30, Sun at 15:30; for

more on evensong, see page 153). Line up at the front entrance (on King's Parade) by 17:00 if you want prime seats in the choir.

Visiting the Chapel: Inside, stand and look down the nave, with its tunnel-like effect that accentuates both its length (290 feet) and height. It's exactly twice as tall (80 feet) as it is wide. Look up and marvel, as Christopher Wren did, at what was then the largest single span of **vaulted roof** anywhere. Built between 1512 and 1515, its 2,000 tons of incredible fan vaulting—held in place by the force of gravity—are a careful balancing act resting delicately on the buttresses visible outside the building. The round bosses in the center, each weighing nearly two tons, are what hold the structure together.

While Henry VI—who began work on the chapel—wanted it to be austere, his descendant Henry VII decided it should glorify the House of Tudor. So, lining the cream-colored walls are the personal symbols of Henry VII and his wife. There's the giant **Tudor coats-**

of-arms supported by a dragon (symbolizing Henry's dad) and greyhound (from his mom's side of the family). The Tudor double rose (of red and white roses) symbolizes the end of the bitter War of the Roses. The portcullis (the iron grate) honors the family of Henry VII's mother, Lady Margaret Beaufort. And the fleur-de-lis kept alive the fading hope that someday they might reclaim their place as rulers of France.

The 26 **stained-glass windows** date from the 16th century. It's the most Renaissance stained glass anywhere in one spot.

(Most of the stained glass in English churches dates from Victorian times, but this glass is three centuries older.) The lower panes show scenes from the New Testament, while the upper panes feature corresponding stories from the Old Testament. Consider-ing England's turbulent history, it's miraculous that these windows have survived for half a millennium in such a pristine state. After Henry VIII separated from the Catholic Church in 1534, many such windows and other Catholic features around England were destroyed. However, since Henry had just paid for these windows, he couldn't bear to destroy them. A century later, in the days of Oliver Cromwell, another wave of iconoclasm destroyed more win-dows around England. Though these windows were slated for re-moval, they stayed put. Finally, during World War II, the windows were taken out and hidden away for safekeeping, then painstak-ingly replaced after the war ended. The only nonmedieval windows are on the west wall (opposite the altar). These are in the Romantic style from the 1880s; when Nazi bombs threatened the church, all agreed they should be left in place.

The **choir screen** that bisects the church was added by Henry VII's son, King Henry VIII—see his "H.R." monogram carved into it, for Henry Rex. He commissioned the oak screen to com-memorate his marriage to Anne Boleyn. By the time it was fin-ished, so was she (beheaded). But it was too late to remove her initials, which were already carved into the screen (look on the far upper left and right for "R.A.," for Regina Anna—"Queen Anne"). Behind the screen is the **choir** area, elaborately carved with the crests of the college and university. This is where the renowned King's College Choir performs. There's a daily evensong (during school terms), with students in the front-row stalls, the choir in the middle, and fellows in back. On Christmas Eve, a special service is held here and broadcast around the world on the BBC—a tradition near and dear to British hearts.

At the far end of the church is Rubens' masterful *Adoration of the Magi* (1634). It's actually a family portrait: The admirer in the front (wearing red) is a self-portrait of Rubens, Mary looks an awful lot like his much-younger wife, and the Baby Jesus resembles their own newborn at the time. In typical Rubens style, there's a diagonal line (running from the lower left) throwing the focus onto the main figures: Jesus and Mary.

Finally, check out the long and fascinating **series of side rooms** that run the length of the nave. Dedicated to the history and art of the church, these are a great little King's College Chapel museum.

• *Exit the church opposite where you entered, into the college court. From here you can stroll the rich grounds all the way to the River Cam and then back, passing through the grand entry gate and onto King's Parade.*

Sights in Cambridge

My self-guided walk takes you to most of the main sights in Cambridge, but not all of them. Visiting the following places in and near town is also worthwhile.

▲▲Trinity College and Wren Library

Of the more than 100 Nobel Prize winners affiliated with Cambridge, about a third come from this richest and biggest of the

town's colleges, founded in 1546 by Henry VIII. The college has three sights to see: the entrance gate, the grounds, and the magnificent Wren Library.

Cost and Hours: Grounds—£3, daily 10:00-16:30, closes earlier off-season; library—free, Mon-Fri 12:00-14:00, during full term also Sat 10:30-12:30, closed Sun year-round; only 20 people allowed in at a time, tel. 01223/338-400, www.trin.cam.ac.uk.

Free Entrance to the Library: To see the Wren Library without paying for the grounds, access it from the riverside entrance (a long walk around the college via the Garret Hostel Bridge).

Trinity Gate: You'll notice gates like these adorning facades of colleges around town. Above the door is a statue of **King Henry VIII,** who founded Trinity because he feared that Cambridge's existing colleges were too cozy with the Church. Notice Henry's right hand holding a chair leg instead of the traditional scepter with the crown jewels. This is courtesy of Cambridge's Night Climbers, who first replaced the scepter a century ago. According to campus legend, decades ago some of the world's most talented mountaineers enrolled at Cambridge...in one of the flattest parts of England. (Cambridge was actually a seaport until Dutch engineers drained the surrounding swamps.) Lacking opportunities to practice their skill, they began scaling the frilly facades of Cambridge's college buildings under cover of darkness (if caught, they'd have been expelled). In the 1960s, climbers actually managed to haul an entire automobile onto the roof of the Senate House. The university had to bring in the army to cut it into pieces and remove it. Only 50 years later, at a class reunion, did the guilty parties finally fess up.

In the little park to the right, notice the lone **apple tree.** Supposedly, this tree is a descendant of the very one that once stood in the garden of Sir Isaac  Newton (who spent 30 years at Trinity). According to legend, Newton was inspired to investigate gravity when an apple fell from the tree onto his head. This tree stopped bearing fruit long ago; if you do see apples, they've been tied on by mischievous students.

Beyond the gate are the Trinity grounds. Note that there's often a fine and free view of Trinity College courtyard—if the gate is open—from Trinity Lane (leading, under a uniform row of old chimneys, around the school to the Wren Library).

Trinity Grounds: The grounds are enjoyable to explore. Inside the **Great Court,** the clock (on the tower on the right) double-rings at the top of each hour. It's  a college tradition to take off running from the clock when the high noon bells begin (it takes 43 seconds to clang 24 times), race around the courtyard, touching each of the four corners without setting foot on the cobbles, and try to return to the same spot before the ringing ends. Supposedly only one student (a young lord) ever managed the feat—a scene featured in *Chariots of Fire* (but filmed elsewhere).

The **chapel** (entrance to the right of the clock tower)—which pales in comparison to the stunning King's College Chapel—feels like a shrine to thinking, with statues honoring great Trinity minds both familiar (Isaac Newton, Alfred Tennyson, Francis Bacon) and unfamiliar. Who's missing? The poet Lord Byron, who was such a hell-raiser during his time at Trinity that a statue of him was deemed unfit for Church property; his statue stands in the library instead.

Wren Library: Don't miss the 1695 Christopher Wren-designed library, with its wonderful carving and fascinating original manuscripts. Just outside the library entrance, Sir Isaac Newton clapped his hands and timed the echo to measure the speed of sound as it raced down the side of the cloister and back. Inside, admire Wren's design—long, white, and aglow with the bright light of the Enlightenment. Wren designed the whole ensemble, including the bookshelves topped with busts of great thinkers. (The one thing he didn't design is the stained-glass window showing him being honored by George III.) Unlike the other libraries at Cambridge, Wren designed Trinity's on the upper floor, not the damp, dark ground floor. As a result, Wren's library is flooded with light, rather than water (and it's also brimming with students during exam times).

In the library's 12 display cases (covered with cloth that you flip back), you'll see a (rotating) display of medieval manuscripts, first editions, letters, and documents. You might see works by William Shakespeare, John Milton, Samuel Taylor Coleridge, and A. A. Milne's original *Winnie the Pooh* (the real Christopher Robin attended Trinity College). Don't miss the case with Newton's memorabilia—a lock of his hair, notebook, pocket watch, walking stick, a prism he used to see how light bent, and a 1687 edition of his landmark book *Principia Mathematica* that changed forever the way humans viewed the physical world.

▲Fitzwilliam Museum

One of Britain's best museums of antiquities and art outside London is the Fitzwilliam. Housed in a grand Neoclassical building a 10-minute walk south of Market Hill Square, it's a palatial celebration of beauty and humankind's ability to create it.

Cost and Hours: Free but £5 donation suggested; Tue-Sat 10:00-17:00, Sun from 12:00, closed Mon; lockers, Trumpington Street, tel. 01223/332-900, www.fitzmuseum.cam.ac.uk.

WINDSOR & CAMBRIDGE

Visiting the Museum: The Fitzwilliam's broad collection is like a mini-British Museum/National Gallery rolled into one. The ground floor features an extensive range of antiquities and applied arts—everything from Greek vases, Mesopotamian artifacts, and Egyptian sarcophagi to Roman statues, fine porcelain, and suits of armor.

Upstairs is the painting gallery, with works that span art history: Italian Venetian masters (such as Titian and Canaletto), a worthy English section (featuring Gainsborough, Reynolds, Hogarth, and others), a notable array of French Impressionist art (including Monet, Renoir, Pissarro, Degas, and Sisley), and even a few small Picassos. Rounding out the collection are old manuscripts, including some musical compositions from Handel.

Museum of Classical Archaeology

Although this museum contains no originals, it offers a unique chance to study accurate copies (19th-century casts) of virtually every famous ancient Greek and Roman statue. More than 450 statues are on display.

Cost and Hours: Free; Mon-Fri 10:00-17:00, Sat until 13:00 during term, closed Sun year-round; Sidgwick Avenue, tel. 01223/330-402, www.classics.cam.ac.uk/museum.

Getting There: The museum is a five-minute walk west of Silver Street Bridge; after crossing the bridge, continue straight until you reach a sign reading *Sidgwick Site.*

▲▲Punting on the Cam

For a little levity and probably more exercise than you really want, try renting one of the traditional flat-bottom punts at the river.

You'll use a giant pole to push yourself up and down (or around and around, more likely) the lazy Cam. The water's only about six or seven feet deep, so you move by literally pushing off from the river floor (someone in front can use a little paddle to help out).

This is one of the best memories the town has to offer, and once you get the hang of it, it's a fine way to enjoy the scenic side of Cambridge. It's less crowded in late afternoon (and less embarrassing).

Better yet, let someone else do the punting while you enjoy the ride. The 45-minute lazy punting trips are a delight—informatively narrated by your punter, who tries to avoid the clueless tourists creating a moving, aquatic obstacle course. Watching amateurs struggle with their massive poles, playing bumper cars in the busy river, you'll be happy someone else is at the helm. On a nice-weather day, there are few more relaxing activities.

Several companies rent punts and also offer tours. Both are open daily from about 9:00 until dusk when the weather's decent (typically March-Nov). **Scudamore's** has two locations: on Mill Lane, just south of the central Silver Street Bridge, and at the less convenient Quayside at Magdalene Bridge, at the north end of town (rental—£33/hour, 45-minute tour—£22/person, tel. 01223/359-750, www.scudamores.com). **Cambridge Chauffeur Punts,** just under the Silver Street Bridge, is a cheaper outfit (rental—£26/hour, 45-minute tour—£18/person, tel. 01223/354-164, www.punting-in-cambridge.co.uk). When it's not too busy, prices can be soft at either place for the guided tours—try asking for a discount.

If renting a punt in the Silver Street Bridge area, be clear on whether you're punting on the River Cam (the lovely but crowded stream that runs behind the pretty college campuses) or on the other side of the weir, at the River Granta (less crowded, it runs through idyllic countryside, but you won't see the famous landmarks). Most prefer the Cam.

NEAR CAMBRIDGE
Imperial War Museum Duxford

This former airfield, nine miles south of Cambridge, is popular with aviation fans and WWII history buffs. Wander through seven exhibition halls housing 200 vintage aircraft (including Spitfires, B-17 Flying Fortresses, a Concorde, and a Blackbird, some of which you can enter) as well as military land vehicles and special displays on Normandy and the Battle of Britain. The American Air wing thoughtfully portrays the achievements and controversies of British/US wartime collaboration, including the stories of American airmen based at Duxford.

Cost and Hours: £18, show local bus ticket for discount; daily 10:00-18:00, off-season until 16:00, last entry one hour before closing; tel. 01223/835-000, www.iwm.org.uk/visits/iwm-duxford.

Getting There: The museum is located off the A-505 in Duxford. On Sundays, direct Myalls bus #132 runs to the museum from the train station (4/day, 45 minutes, www.travelineeastanglia.org.uk). The rest of the week, it's best to take a taxi from Cambridge: Catch one at the taxi stand on St. Andrews Street next to the Lion Yard shopping mall (about £25 one-way).

Sleeping in Cambridge

While Cambridge is an easy side-trip from London (and you can enjoy an evening here before catching a late train back), its subtle charms might convince you to spend a night or two. Cambridge has few accommodations in the city center, and none in the tight maze of colleges and shops where you'll spend most of your time. These recommendations are about a 10- to 15-minute walk south of the town center, toward the train station.

$$$ Lensfield Hotel, popular with visiting professors, has 40 comfortable rooms—some old-fashioned, some refurbished (spa and fitness room, 53 Lensfield Road, tel. 01223/355-017, www.lensfieldhotel.co.uk, enquiries@lensfieldhotcl.co.uk).

$$$ Hotel du Vin is an upscale place that rents 41 spiffy rooms at a high price. It has a crooked-floors, duck-your-head historical character and a whiff of pretense (air-con, elevator to some rooms, light sleepers ask for quieter room in back, Trumpington Street 15, tel. 01223/928 991, www.hotelduvin.com, reception.cambridge@hotelduvin.com).

$$$ Regent Hotel has 22 modern, colorful rooms on the main road between the town center and train station. Half of the rooms overlook a giant park in back (air-con, elevator, 41 Regent Street, tel. 01223/351-470, www.regenthotel.co.uk, reservations@regenthotel.co.uk).

Eating in Cambridge

$$ The Eagle, near the TI and described earlier in my town walk, is the oldest pub in town. While the food is mediocre, the pub is a Cambridge institution—with a history so rich that a visit here practically qualifies as sightseeing (food served daily 11:00-22:00, 8 Benet Street, tel. 01223/505-020).

$ Michaelhouse Café is a heavenly respite from the crowds, tucked into the repurposed St. Michael's Church, just north of Great St. Mary's Church. At lunch, choose from salads and sandwiches, as well as a few hot dishes and a variety of tasty baked goods (Mon-Sat 8:00-17:00, breakfast served until 11:30, lunch served 11:30-15:50, closed Sun, occasional free lunchtime concerts, Trinity Street, tel. 01223/309-147). Between 15:00 and 17:00 whatever they have left from lunch is half-price.

$$ The Anchor Pub has a place in rock-and-roll history as a spot where Pink Floyd band members hung out in their early days. Today it's known for the best people-watching—and some locals say best food—in Cambridge. Choose from its outdoor riverside terrace, inside bar, or more romantic upstairs restaurant (all seating areas serve the same menu, but the upstairs menu has a few added specials; daily 12:00-21:30, on the riverfront at Silver Street, tel. 01224/353-554).

$$ The Mill Pub is a livelier, less formal alternative to The Anchor, but enjoys a similar location right on the river. The clientele is a mixture of students and tourists; the tipples are craft brews, local ales, and ciders; and the food is updated pub standards (daily 11:00-23:00, 14 Mill Lane, tel. 01223/311-829).

$ Bread & Meat serves simple soups and hearty sandwiches. Grab a signature *porchetta* sandwich to take away or snag a rustic table in the small dining room (Mon-Thu 11:30-20:00, Fri-Sat until 21:00, Sun until 17:00, 4 Benet Street, tel. 0791/808-3057).

$$ Agora at The Copper Kettle is a popular place for Greek and Turkish *meze*, beautifully situated facing King's College on King's Parade (also fish-and-chips at lunch, daily 8:00-20:30, later in summer, 4 King's Parade, tel. 01223/308-448).

$$ Fitzbillies, long a favorite for cakes (Chelsea buns) and coffee, offers inviting lunch and afternoon tea menus (daily, 51 Trumpington Street, tel. 01223/352-500).

$ Street Food on Market Hill Square: For an interesting lunch on the go, browse the many food carts tucked into the tight aisles of the open-air market that fills the historic old market square (daily 9:00-16:00). There's no real seating, but people squeeze along the wall around the stone fountain in the middle of the square.

$ Fast Food: For healthy fast-food chains, the corner of Petty Cury Lane and Sidney Street (a long block east of Market Hill Square) has several good options.

Supermarkets: There's a **Marks & Spencer Simply Food** at the train station (long hours daily) and a larger **Marks & Spencer Foodhall** on Market Hill Square (Mon 9:00-18:00, Tue-Sat 8:00-20:00, closed Sun). **Sainsbury's** supermarket is open later (Mon-Sat 8:00-23:30, Sun 11:00-17:00, 44 Sidney Street, at the corner of Green Street).

A good picnic spot is Laundress Green, a grassy park on the river, at the end of Mill Lane near the Silver Street Bridge punts. There are no benches, so bring something to sit on. Remember, the college lawns are private property, so walking or picnicking on the grass is generally not allowed. When in doubt, ask at the college's entrance.

Cambridge Connections

From Cambridge by Train to: York (hourly, 2.5 hours, transfer in Peterborough), **Oxford** (2-3/hour, 2.5 hours, change in London involves Tube transfer between train stations), **London** (King's Cross Station: 2/hour, 45 minutes; Liverpool Street Station: 2/hour, 1.5 hours). **Train info:** Tel. 0345-748-4950, www.nationalrail.co.uk.

    By Bus to: London (every 60-90 minutes, 2 hours), **Heathrow Airport** (1-2/hour, 3 hours), **Oxford** (2/hour, 4 hours). **Bus info:** Tel. 0871-781-8181, www.nationalexpress.com.

WINDSOR & CAMBRIDGE

CANTERBURY

Canterbury has long been one of England's most important religious destinations. For centuries, it welcomed crowds of pilgrims to its grand cathedral. While these days you'll see tourists rather than pilgrims, the town is rich in history and architectural splendor.

Pleasant, walkable Canterbury, like many cities in southern England, was founded by pagan Romans. Then along came St. Augustine, sent by the pope in AD 597 to convert England's King Ethelbert of Kent to Christianity. Ethelbert (who had a Christian wife) joined the Church and gave St. Augustine land to set up a monastery on the edge of town. As Christianity became more established in England, Canterbury became its center, and the Archbishop of Canterbury emerged as one of the country's most powerful men.

The famous pilgrimages to Canterbury increased in the 12th century, after the assassination of Archbishop Thomas Becket by followers of King Henry II. Becket was canonized as a martyr, rumors of miracles at the cathedral spread, and flocks of pilgrims showed up at its doorstep. Along the way, they'd stop off at inns and entertain each other with tales—sometimes bawdy and just for fun, sometimes devout and meaningful.

Today, the medieval city—heavily bombed during World War II—has been largely restored. The cathedral and surrounding streets are fairly well preserved. With its huge student population and thriving pedestrian-friendly zone in the center, Canterbury is a livable and fun-to-visit town. While the streets immediately surrounding the cathedral are quite touristy, beyond that core you'll discover a real, thriving town—with areas both gritty and genteel. It's a joy to simply wander the back streets, exploring fine gardens, sleepy canals, and student pubs. See the cathedral...then get lost in Canterbury.

PLANNING YOUR TIME

Because of its impressive cathedral, compact tourist zone, and relaxing ambience, Canterbury is an ideal day trip from London. With more time, it merits an overnight. (You could even come straight from the airport to Canterbury and sleep here for two nights, with a day of sightseeing.) If visiting for just a few hours, head straight for the cathedral, then spend the rest of your time strolling the town's pleasant pedestrian core (following my self-guided Canterbury Walk). If the cathedral is crowded, do the walk first and circle back later—then stick around for evensong in the ornate choir.

Orientation to Canterbury

With about 40,000 inhabitants (plus another 30,000 when its four universities are in session), Canterbury is big enough to be lively but small enough to be manageable.

Historic Canterbury lies within the remains of a medieval wall, which itself was built on top of an ancient Roman wall (you'll see fragments here and there, and the lone surviving gate is at the end of my Canterbury Walk). The old center, dominated by the towering cathedral, is cut down the middle by bustling High Street (which changes names to St. Peter's Street at one end and St. George's Street at the other). During the day, the action is on High Street and in the knot of medieval lanes surrounding the cathedral. At night, the city is quiet all around.

TOURIST INFORMATION

The TI is housed in the modern atrium at the back end of the Beaney House of Art and Knowledge. Pick up the free map and buy a ticket for the guided walk, described next (Mon-Sat 9:00-17:00, Thu until 19:00, Sun 10:00-17:00, 18 High Street—or enter directly to the TI around the corner on Best Lane, tel. 01227/862-162, www.canterbury.co.uk).

Guided Walk: Canterbury Tourist Guides offer a 1.5-hour walk departing from Buttermarket, the square opposite the cathedral entrance. While there's not a lot to see, there is a lot to talk about—and your guide is very good at that (£10, buy ticket at TI,

CANTERBURY

WEST STATION

● 15

To 5 →

To
Whitstable
via A-290 ←

ROPER RD.

STATION RD. W

NORTH LN.

THE CAUSEWAY

ST. DUNSTANS ST.

ST. RADIGUNDS

🚲 ● 16

POUND LN.

● 10

BLACKFRIARS

ST. PETER'S LN.

P

P

WALK ENDS

WEST GATE

MARLOWE THEATRE

THE FRIARS

KING ST.

ST. PETER'S ST.

CHAUCER STATUE

● 6

BEST LN.

ORANGE ST.

BEANEY HOUSE

ST. PETER'S PLACE

BLACK GRIFFIN LN.

ST. PETER'S GR.

River

i

HIGH STREET

GUILD-

To
London
via A-2 ←

RHEIMS WAY
(A2050)

● 13

Stour

● 17

THE CANTERBURY TALES

● 9

ST. MARGARET'S ST.

Marlowe Arcade

BEER CART LN.

WATLING ST.

Great

STOUR ST.

ROSEMARY LN.

CASTLE ST.

ST. JOHN'S ST.

MARLOWE AV.

CHURCH LN.

P

P

RHEIMS WAY

Dane John Garden

Fountain

● 3

MOUND

CITY WALLS

RHODAUS TOWN

PIN HILL

STATION

EAST STATION

ROAD E.

CANTERBURY

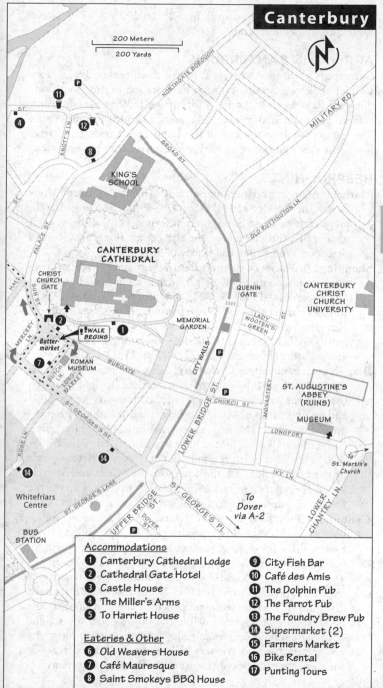

Canterbury

200 Meters
200 Yards

CANTERBURY CATHEDRAL

CHRIST CHURCH GATE

Buttermarket

WALK BEGINS

KING'S SCHOOL

MEMORIAL GARDEN

QUENIN GATE

LADY WOOTEN'S GREEN

CANTERBURY CHRIST CHURCH UNIVERSITY

ROMAN MUSEUM

CITY WALLS

ST. AUGUSTINE'S ABBEY (RUINS)

MUSEUM

To St. Martin's Church

To Dover via A-2

Whitefriars Centre

BUS STATION

Accommodations
1. Canterbury Cathedral Lodge
2. Cathedral Gate Hotel
3. Castle House
4. The Miller's Arms
5. To Harriet House

Eateries & Other
6. Old Weavers House
7. Café Mauresque
8. Saint Smokeys BBQ House
9. City Fish Bar
10. Café des Amis
11. The Dolphin Pub
12. The Parrot Pub
13. The Foundry Brew Pub
14. Supermarket (2)
15. Farmers Market
16. Bike Rental
17. Punting Tours

Streets: NORTHGATE BOROUGH, MILITARY RD., BROAD ST., OLD RUTTINGTON LN., KNOTT'S LN., PALACE ST., SUN ST., MERCERY LN., HALL, PUTH LN., LONG MARKET, BURGATE, ST. GEORGE'S ST., ROSE LN., CHURCH ST., LOWER BRIDGE ST., MONASTERY, LONGPORT, IVY LN., LOWER CHANTRY LN., ST. GEORGE'S LANE, UPPER BRIDGE ST., DOVER ST., ST. GEORGE'S PL.

daily at 11:00, April-Oct also at 14:00, tel. 01227/459-779, www.canterburyguidedtours.com).

ARRIVAL IN CANTERBURY

Canterbury's two train stations flank the town center. Trains from London's Victoria Station arrive at East Station; trains from London's St. Pancras and Charing Cross arrive at West Station. Both stations are about a 10-minute walk or £6 taxi ride from the center. The bus station is at the end of the High Street pedestrian area, inside the city walls just past the big Whitefriars shopping center.

HELPFUL HINTS

Markets: A modest **farmers market** is held every day except Monday at The Goods Shed (Tue-Sat 9:00-19:00, Sun until 16:00), just north of West Station. Another market, selling general goods, fills the east end of the city center along St. George's Street on Wednesday and Friday (8:00-17:00).

Shopping: A **Marks & Spencer** department store, with a supermarket on the ground floor, is near the east end of High Street (Mon-Sat 8:00-19:00, Sun 11:00-17:00, tel. 01227/462-281). Beyond that is the vast **Whitefriars Centre** shopping complex—sprawling over several blocks (most shops open Mon-Sat 9:00-18:30, Sun 11:00-17:00)—including a **Tesco Metro** grocery store (Mon-Sat 7:00-22:00, Sun 11:00-17:00).

Bike Rental: Canterbury Cycle Hire, a five-minute walk from the town center, rents bikes near West Station. To find them, go through the passage to the right of the House of Agnes B&B and around back (£24/day, one-way rental possible with pick-up or drop-off at their sister shops in Whitstable or Herne Bay, daily 10:00-18:00, 71 St. Dunstans Street, tel. 01227/388-058, www.kentcyclehire.com). For a pleasant daylong ride in the countryside, ask for a map of the "Crab and Winkle Way," a popular eight-mile biking trail from Canterbury to the charming fishing village of Whitstable.

Canterbury Punt and Rowboat Tours: For a leisurely, water-level view of Canterbury, consider a £9-15 cruise on the River Stour. Three fun-loving, student-run companies compete for your business. All have roughly the same cost for the simple, 45-minute route up and down the shallow creek; departures leave with demand from 10:00 to 17:00, and sometimes later. The punt trip (where you're propelled by the traditional single pole) is more of a joyride, while the big rowboat tours come with more serious narration. Enjoy the sales pitches along the bridge near the Old Weavers House, among other places. Of the three companies, only **Canterbury Punting Company** has a proper rental office (just off Stour Street on Water Lane, tel. 01227/464-797, www.canterburypunting.co.uk).

Theater: The **Marlowe Theatre** offers ballet performances, West End-style productions, speakers, and musicians in a cutting-edge space (book tickets online, by phone, or at the box office; The Friars, tel. 01227/787-787, www.marlowetheatre.com).

Canterbury Walk

This self-guided walk orients you to the old town center in about an hour (not including sightseeing stops).

• *Start just outside the cathedral gatehouse, at the square called...*

Buttermarket

Originally the dairy market, Buttermarket functioned as the center of medieval Canterbury. The buildings lining this charming square were built to house and feed pilgrims, whose business supported this town. When Archbishop Thomas Becket was brutally murdered inside his own cathedral in 1170 (see the sidebar later in this chapter), this already-holy place gained even more importance. Visitors began to report miraculous healings and other wondrous occurrences. Before long, pilgrims were coming from all over Europe to pay their respects and pray for miracles. Geoffrey Chaucer immortalized these pilgrims—and the tales they told while on the road—in *The Canterbury Tales* (see the sidebar later in this chapter).

The square's centerpiece is a **WWI memorial,** ravaged by a century of weather. Like many such monuments around Britain, it was later amended to also honor the local dead of World War II. On the monument, notice the shield with three black birds (called choughs, related to the crow—taken from the personal coat of arms of Thomas Becket). This is the symbol of Canterbury—watch for it all over town.

• *Face the entry to the cathedral grounds.*

Christ Church Gate

This fancy gate is packed with coats of arms that recognize leading families for their contributions. Its construction began in 1504

to commemorate the marriage of Prince Arthur of Wales (the heir to the English throne) to Catherine of Aragon. A year after their marriage, Arthur died without ever taking the throne, and Catherine went on to marry Arthur's brother, Henry—the first of Henry VIII's six wives. It was Henry's desire to divorce Catherine—and to marry her lady-in-waiting, Anne Boleyn—that caused the ecclesiastical split between England and Rome, which in turn boosted Canterbury Cathedral's status as simply the most important Catholic church in England to head of England's own Anglican Church.

Examine the gate's details. Above the high point of the arch are the royal Tudor coat of arms and the Tudor rose (the family seal of Arthur and Henry). To the right of the rose is the coat of arms of Catherine of Aragon (part of today's Spain—notice the red and yellow stripes). A modern bronze statue of Jesus welcomes all who enter. The Puritans pulled down the original statue in the 17th century, and the niche remained empty until this replacement was installed in 1990. Higher up is a strip of shields with symbols representing various biblical tales.

• You can either tour Canterbury Cathedral now (see my self-guided tour under "Sights in Canterbury"), or come back later. If you tour the cathedral now, you can rejoin this walk afterward by exiting through the gift shop, which is across from our next stop, Butchery Lane. Otherwise, face the cathedral gate and walk a block to the right to reach...

Butchery Lane

Walking down this historic lane, notice how the buildings jetty out with each floor. This was done to maximize usable square footage (and to reduce taxes) for each little plot of land. This lane is a reminder of how densely populated the town was within its protective walls. In later years it became fashionable to even out these old buildings with a flat front (though even then, these buildings often bulge with the original, top-heavy design in back).

Many such buildings were built as lodging for pilgrims. Walking down the lane, pause at the Happy Samurai restaurant (on the right). The passage just to its right leads into a courtyard. This was a classic "coaching inn," designed to provide horse carriages with safe off-street parking.

Just beyond on the left, the giant faux-columns mark the good **Canterbury Roman Museum** (described under "Sights in Canterbury"). Many of the museum's fascinating artifacts were discovered after WWII bombs exposed the city's ancient foundations as they destroyed a third of the town. While this entire street appears historic, only the right side is original. The buildings on the left, badly damaged or destroyed, were hastily replaced with ersatz "shoebox"-style buildings. But by the 1990s, Canterbury tore those down and rebuilt them in the old style.

A few doors farther down, look up on the right for the bull's head. Each street in a market town like Canterbury had a different specialty. Given its name, it's no surprise that this street was the location of the slaughterhouse.

• *Before moving on, look back for a fine view of the cathedral tower, framed by the houses along this street. Then carry on along Butchery Lane to where it opens up into...*

High Street (Part 1)

It's amazing to think that, until the 1960s, the A-2 highway ran through the center of town, bringing all the Dover-London traffic right down today's delightfully pedestrianized High Street.

Turn left and walk a half-block to where the street opens up into **St. George's Street** (filled with market stalls on Wednesdays and Fridays). Notice the modern architecture that predominates here—this part of town was hard-hit by WWII bombs. The modern Whitefriars shopping complex sprawls just beyond here and to the right. And St. George's Tower—straight ahead—marks the (approximate) location of the city's eastern St. George's Gate. A 10-minute walk beyond here takes you to the St. Augustine's Abbey complex, which put Canterbury on the map long before Becket or Chaucer (described later, under "Sights in Canterbury").

• *About-face and head back down High Street. Walk one block past Butchery Street to...*

Canterbury's Historic Main Intersection

This intersection marked the heart of the pilgrim's Canterbury. Pilgrims would enter through the West Gate, at the far end of High Street (where this walk ends). When they reached this point, they'd equip themselves with a pilgrim's badge and little vials of holy water—essentials for completing their pilgrimage. Then they'd turn up Mercery Lane (to the right) to the Christ Church Gate.

Before we follow their footsteps, look left, down **St. Margaret's Street**. This is where archaeologists have discovered ruins of Roman baths (now discreetly recovered and closed to the public). Partway down this street is an attraction called The Canterbury Tales, offering a hokey but educational re-creation of the Canterbury of Chaucer's time (described later, under "Sights in Canterbury").

Now turn around and begin strolling up the narrow alley called **Mercery Lane.** "Mercery" refers to the place where cloth was sold.

At the first house on the right, notice the gargoyles carved into the beams just overhead. This is likely an indication that plague victims died here; the gargoyles were meant to scare away evil spirits.

• *Soon you're back where we started, at Buttermarket. Facing the gate, turn left and follow the curve of Sun Street around the outside of the cathedral grounds for a stroll through...*

Back-Streets Canterbury

Away from touristy High Street and the knot of souvenir shops near the cathedral, this area feels untrampled, historic, and very English.

Following Sun Street, on the left is the Sun Hotel—described by Charles Dickens in *David Copperfield*. Continuing a short block to the next intersection, look right down Palace Street—better known around here as **"King's Street."** This was where, after Thomas Becket's assassination, King Henry II walked barefoot into town as an act of penance for his role in the accidental slaying. (For the full story, see the sidebar, later.) It's lined with historic buildings, and it leads to some delightful pubs. At the start of King's Street, on the right, look for Café Chambers. A plaque nearby identifies this as the place where the Pilgrims signed the papers to hire the *Mayflower* for their passage to the New World.

From this intersection, turn left down Orange Street. Follow this street for a couple of blocks toward the huge modern building. Pause at the bridge over the **River Stour** to enjoy the picturesque canals and consider a boat trip. Looking right down the river, you'll see the Blackfriars building sticking out over the canal. This was originally a dormitory for actual friars clad in back. In old buildings like this, the part hanging over the river was where the toilets were located—for easy disposal.

Just beyond the bridge is the massive **Marlowe Theatre**—a modern venue, named for Christopher Marlowe (Shakespeare's famous rival and a Canterbury native; for theater performance details, see "Helpful Hints," earlier). Just past the theater is a monument to Marlowe.

Backtrack across the river

and a short half-block, then turn right up **Best Lane.** You'll pass a classic Tudor home on the right (at #6), sided with roof shingles (in this case, painted white)—a typical architectural style in the county of Kent. Just beyond that, on the left, is the back door for the modern building that houses the TI, town library, and the free, worth-a-peek Beaney House museum (described under "Sights in Canterbury").

• *You'll reach a square marking High Street and the last stretch of this walk.*

High Street (Part 2)

In the little square is a recent statue honoring **Geoffrey Chaucer**. Around the base of the monument are characters from *The Can-*

terbury Tales—each one a portrait of a present-day resident who paid for the privilege of being depicted (see the list of donors on the back). On the scroll in Chaucer's hand are the opening lines of that work's prologue in Middle English:

> *Whan that Aprille with his*
> *shoures soote*
> *The droghte of Marche hath perced*
> *to the roote,*
> *And bathed every veyne in*
> *swich licour,*
> *Of which vertu engendred is*
> *the flour...*

Translation: After the March drought, April showers bathe every vine in "sweet liquor" to bring about spring renewal. (Springtime was also the time for pilgrims to make their journey to Canterbury.)

Head right down High Street (on the stretch called St. Peter's Street). On the left (at #25) is the 12th-century **Pilgrims' Hospital**—in this case, meaning "hospitality." This is where poor pilgrims could find free shelter in the undercroft. (Today, they charge tourists to visit; history buffs enjoy it, but for most it's skippable.)

Just beyond that, on the right, you'll get another look at the River Stour. The black-and-white, half-timbered **Old Weavers House** is the most atmospheric building in town, with its big windows for looms upstairs and its romantic setting over the river. Today it's a pricey but atmospheric recommended pub. After the pilgrim trade dried up, Canterbury fell on hard times. But French Huguenots (fleeing oppression in France) and Walloons (from today's Flanders, in Belgium) both settled here, importing a new skill: weaving.

Stationed here, you'll likely see students hawking their **boat tours** (both punting and big rowboats—see "Helpful Hints," earlier). Looking down the river, notice the kitschy "ducking stool"—used for dunking suspected witches in the river.

• *From here, you could simply explore. But to extend the walk, stroll down a more lowbrow stretch of the street a few short blocks to reach the...*

West Gate

Canterbury is ringed by walls—originally Roman, then medieval. Of the seven gates once leading into the medieval city, this is the last survivor (from 1380). Argu-

ably it was also the most important, as it led toward London and was where most pilgrims entered the town. To protect the town, gates were closed and locked after a certain time. Horseback pilgrims would pace themselves to get here just in time, prodding their horses at what they called a "Canterbury gallop"—also known as "cantering." Stroll around the gate, admiring its stout defenses (with slits for archers and square holes up high for cannons). Around the far side is a tranquil garden and a view of one of the river's tributaries.

• *Our walk is finished. From here, explore the area just outside the gate— called St. Dunstans, with some good eateries and the bustle of local life. Or backtrack through the gate and head up High Street. As you do, think of the many pilgrims who've gone before you—cementing Canterbury's place in English history.*

Sights in Canterbury

CANTERBURY CATHEDRAL

One of the most important churches in England, this cathedral, worth ▲▲▲, is the headquarters of the Anglican Church (that makes it akin to the English Vatican). There's been a church here ever since St. Augustine, the cathedral's first archbishop, broke ground in 597. In the 12th century, the cathedral's archbishop, Thomas Becket, was murdered in front of the altar. Just over two years later he was sainted, and Canterbury became a prime destination for religious pilgrims. When Henry VIII broke with the Roman Catholic Church 400 years later, this

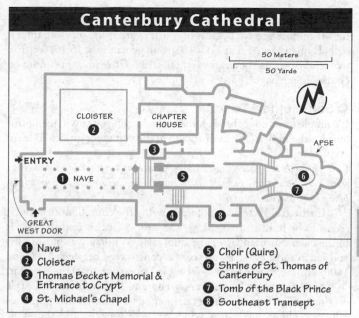

Canterbury Cathedral

50 Meters
50 Yards

CLOISTER ❷

CHAPTER HOUSE

❸

APSE

→ENTRY

❶ NAVE

❺

❻

❼

❹

❽

GREAT WEST DOOR

❶ Nave
❷ Cloister
❸ Thomas Becket Memorial & Entrance to Crypt
❹ St. Michael's Chapel
❺ Choir (Quire)
❻ Shrine of St. Thomas of Canterbury
❼ Tomb of the Black Prince
❽ Southeast Transept

CANTERBURY

cathedral became the Anglican version of St. Peter's Basilica. A visit here leaves you impressed by the resilience of this spot—so holy to so many for so long.

Cost and Hours: £12.50; Mon-Sat 9:00-17:30 (July-Aug until 18:00), Sun 12:30-17:00; slightly shorter hours Nov-Easter.

Information: Tel. 01227/762-862, www.canterbury-cathedral.org.

Renovation: A new welcome center (with a ticket office, information desk, and—up above—a gallery offering a free look into the close) is in the works. In the meantime, you may find things different than described here.

Tours: Knowledgeable guides wearing gold sashes are posted throughout the cathedral to answer questions. Guided £5 tours are offered Mon-Fri at 10:30, 12:00, and 14:30 (14:00 in winter); Sat at 10:30, 12:00, and 13:00; no tours Sun. At the shop inside the cathedral, you can rent an informative £4 audioguide. They also offer a handy brochure called "An American Trail," describing points of interest to Americans.

Evensong: The choral evensong is a beautiful opportunity to experience the church in action and filled with music—and at no cost. Arrive 15 minutes early—you'll be allowed through the gate for free when you say you're there for the service. Pick up a program as you enter, and take a seat in the choir—the intimate, central part of the church. The choral group (generally a local choir of men and boys, or a visiting choir in July and Aug) will then file in, and the 40-minute service begins. Stay afterward if the pipe organist is still playing (Mon-Fri at 17:30, Sat-Sun generally at 15:15, confirm weekend times as they can vary, tel. 01227/762-862). For more on evensong, see page 153.

⊘ Self-Guided Tour

It's simple to wander through the cathedral on your own, using this tour for the basics. Take advantage of the volunteer guides to learn even more.

• *Go through the gate into the courtyard that surrounds this massive church. As you enter, pick up a free map. A small café is to your right, beyond the welcome center.*

Cathedral Exterior: Before entering the church, notice that it seems to be built in two parts—the west is Gothic and the east is in the older Norman (Romanesque) style. While it was built in fits and starts, most of what you see was constructed between 1100 and 1400. For me, the interior is far more impressive than the exterior.

In many ways it's a French church: The architectural style originated in France; the craftsmen who created the precious 800-year-old stained-glass windows were French; and the stone was quarried in France and then shipped across the English Channel to this spot (more economical than getting stone from the nearest English quarry).

Circle around the left side of the cathedral to face its **Great West Door.** Look up at the life-size sculptures of English mon-  archs, including Queen Victoria, Prince Albert, Queen Elizbeth II, and the Duke of Edinburgh (both added quite recently)—a reminder that this church, while historic, is also a vital, living institution.

• *Enter either to the left of the Great West Door, or just around the corner to the right (facing the gate you used to enter the cathedral precinct). Take a seat at the back of the nave.*

❶ **Nave:** In the year 597, missionaries from Rome converted the king of Kent (this part of England) to Christianity. This was the king's seat of power; since they had his protection, the missionaries established Canterbury as the leading Christian church here in England. Its importance grew as Christianity spread, but the church really boomed after the murder of Thomas Becket in 1170—and his ensuing sainthood—put it on the pilgrimage trail. To accommodate the steady stream of pilgrims (so important to

Canterbury's medieval economy), the church grew bigger and bigger.

When Henry VIII broke with the Catholic Church during the Protestant Reformation, he seized or destroyed the Becket relics, and pilgrims stopped coming. But Henry made this cathedral the leading church of his independent Church of England. Today Canterbury Cathedral is the mother church of the worldwide Anglican Communion, and it remains the seat of its leading bishop, the Archbishop of Canterbury (a position currently held by the Most Reverend Justin Welby—number 105 in a very long line).

Today the church feels like two churches—the Gothic half (where you're sitting), which was for the common people, and the older Romanesque half (beyond the stone "screen," where you find the choir—or "quire" in British English), reserved exclusively for the community of Benedictine monks and church VIPs who ran the place.

The nave was once slathered in Catholic ornamentation—lots of ornate chapels, painted walls, and more stained glass. But with Henry VIII and the Reformation, the church's many chapels dedicated to various saints and wealthy families were cleared out. And then, after England's Civil War in the 1640s, came the more extreme Puritans. They were against music, color, festivals, and even Christmas. The Puritans made the building even more stern—whitewashing the paintings and purging the interior of its Gothic finery.

Behind you, notice the fine **West Window** portraying 13 of Christ's ancestors. The bottom two rows are mostly original, 12th-century stained glass. Looking ahead on the left side of the nave, notice also the **Victorian pulpit** carved and painted in the Gothic Revival style (1898). At the top of each hour a priest recites a welcome and a prayer from here, reminding all visitors that this is a holy and alive place of worship.

All of this could have been lost during World War II. The city was heavily bombed on several occasions, but heroic "fire-watchers" with long-handled shovels kept German incendiary bombs from destroying the building (like their counterparts on the rooftop of St. Paul's in London). A round **plaque** in the floor (center rear of nave) remembers these heroic men.

• *Exit the nave through the large wooden door to your left, and turn right into the...*

❷ **Cloister:** Although Henry VIII ended the Benedictine

order in England in 1540, you can still get a good sense of the old monastery complex by strolling through the cloister. Notice the ceiling, speckled with 800 family crests. Just as today we put names on bricks to recognize private contributions to a building project, these shields thanked wealthy medieval families for helping fund this amazing edifice.

• *Return to the nave and follow the route laid out by the map you picked up when you entered. Head up the left aisle. When you get to the choir (marked by a beautifully carved stone screen in the center of the nave), go down the stairs to your left (signs point to* The Martyrdom*). Immediately to your right is the...*

❸ **Thomas Becket Memorial:** This is where Thomas Becket was martyred. You'll see a humble plaque in the floor below a dramatic sculpture of two swords pointing to the place where he died (the shadows make it look like there are two more swords—fitting since there were four murderers). In 1982 Pope John Paul II knelt at the place of Becket's murder and prayed with the Archbishop of Canterbury—the first visit ever by a pope to England.

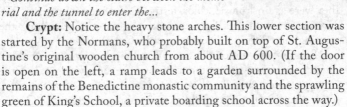

Notice the tunnel to your right. Built in the 15th century, this allowed for the steady flow of pilgrims to go under the altar to visit the site of the martyrdom without disturbing the worship service above.

• *Continue down the stairs between the memorial and the tunnel to enter the...*

Crypt: Notice the heavy stone arches. This lower section was started by the Normans, who probably built on top of St. Augustine's original wooden church from about AD 600. (If the door is open on the left, a ramp leads to a garden surrounded by the remains of the Benedictine monastic community and the sprawling green of King's School, a private boarding school across the way.)

The far end of the crypt is newer; it's Gothic rather than Romanesque and therefore has higher ceilings and more light. Hanging from the ceiling is a modern statue—a body made of rusty nails from the church's rooftop. Becket's tomb rested in the crypt from 1170 until 1220, and the spot became famous as a place of many miracles.

• *Continuing clockwise, circle back toward the stairway leading out of the crypt. While still down in the crypt, watch on the left for a small chapel marked* Église *Protestante Française.*

Huguenot Chapel: This space is literally a church within a church. For 300 years this chapel has been used by the French (Huguenot) Protestant community, who fled persecution in their

CANTERBURY

Thomas Becket and Canterbury Cathedral

In the 12th century, Canterbury Cathedral had already been a Christian church for more than 500 years. The king at the time, Henry II, was looking for a new archbishop, someone

who would act as a yes-man and allow him to gain control of the Church (and its followers). He found a candidate in his drinking buddy and royal chancellor: Thomas Becket (also called Thomas à Becket). In 1162, the king had his friend made a priest one day and consecrated as archbishop the next.

But Becket respected his holy office—surprising the king, and maybe even himself. Inspired by his new position, and wanting to be a true religious leader to his vast flock, he cleaned up his act, became dedicated to the religious tenets of the Church (dressing as a monk), and refused to bow to the king's wishes.

In December 1170, as tensions grew, Henry wondered aloud, "Will no one rid me of this turbulent priest?" Four knights took his words seriously, and assassinated Becket, cutting off the top of his head with their swords during vespers in the cathedral. The act shocked the medieval world. A furious yet regretful King Henry later submitted to walking barefoot through town and to being flogged by priests as an act of pious penitence.

Soon after Becket's death, word spread that miracles were occurring in the cathedral—prompting the pope to canonize Becket just over two years after his assassination. Soon the pilgrims came, hoping some of St. Thomas Becket's steadfast goodness would rub off (perhaps they also wanted to see the world—just like travelers today).

homeland for the more welcoming atmosphere in Protestant England. There's a service in French every Sunday at 15:00. The plaque declares that providing refuge against religious oppression and tyranny is just as important in the 21st century as it was 300 years ago.

• *Facing this chapel, turn right, walk to the end of the crypt, and climb up the stairs. Turn left to find...*

❹ **St. Michael's Chapel:** Also known as the Warrior's Chapel, this was built by Lady Margaret Holland to house family tombs. (She died in 1439 and lies in the middle between two of her husbands.) The chapel is also associated with the Royal East

Kent Regiment ("The Buffs"). Notice the fragile old military flags adorning the walls.

• *Turning to the center of the church, climb the seven steps ahead of you and stand directly under the bell tower.*

Bell Harry Tower: Built in 1503, this 190-foot tower is named for the church's biggest bell, cast in the early 1600s. Bend back and look way, way up at the fine fan vaulting at the highest point. The white cross in the center is called a "hatch." Five hundred years ago, above that hatch, a human-powered treadmill hoisted stones during construction. Spin 360 degrees and imagine the effort needed to build this fine stonework. Even though it was made of bricks rather than heavier stone, the columns supporting it weren't strong enough. Around you are several "strainer arches" retrofitted to give the tower extra support.

❺ **Choir:** Facing east, enjoy the impressive 15th-century **choir screen**—the finely carved wall that separated the public part of the church (behind you) from the monks' zone (the intimate central choir, through the arched doorway). Statues of six kings decorate the screen. Flanking the door are King Ethelbert (left) with the church in his hand—a reminder that he gave the land for this church in 597; and Edward the Confessor

(right)—who was both a saint and an English king. The stone chair to the right was for a guard who made sure the public stayed out of the monastic half.

If the chair's empty, step into the choir and the vast, older half of the church. Opening before you is the monk's world. (You can sit in these venerable chairs to enjoy a musical evensong service; see "Evensong," earlier.)

This part of the church is mostly Romanesque on the outside, but because a fire gutted the interior, the decoration you see is mostly Gothic. **St. Augustine's Chair,** which sits like a throne beyond the high altar, dates from the 13th century. It's a reminder that this church is the seat of the bishop—in fact, the leading bishop of all Anglican bishops.

• *Walk toward the high altar. Leave the choir through a gate on the left and turn right. Continue up the stairs to the far end (apse) behind the high altar, where you'll see a candle in the center of the floor. This was the site of the...*

❻ **Shrine of St. Thomas of Canterbury:** Beginning in the 12th century, hundreds of thousands of pilgrims came to worship the relics of Becket and to leave offerings. Originally, his tomb was in the crypt, but it was moved here in 1220 to improve access for the countless pilgrims. Imagine this site in the Middle Ages. You're surrounded by humble, devout travelers who've trudged miles upon miles to reach this spot. Now that they've finally arrived, they're hoping to soak up just a bit of the miraculous power that's supposed to reside here.

Then came King Henry VIII, who broke away from the pope so he could run his affairs without the Church's meddling. In 1538, he destroyed the original shrine. Dictatorial Henry VIII—no fan of a priest so loved for standing up to a king—had Thomas Becket's body removed. Legend says that to end the pilgrim traffic here, Henry had Becket's bones burned and the ashes scattered. It worked.

The chapel at the far east end of the church once held another Becket relic—his head. The chapel is now dedicated to "saints and martyrs of our own time"—people who have given their lives for their Christian faith, from Martin Luther King, Jr. to El Salvador's Óscar Romero. Page through the binders on either side of the entrance to review the stories of these inspirational pillars of faith. If so moved, light a candle.

• *Enjoy the 800-year-old windows—the best in the church—all around you. Then, follow the curve of the apse about 20 steps to a fancy tomb with a fancy set of armor (on your right).*

❼ Tomb of the Black Prince: Marked by a famous sculpture on his tomb, this is the final resting place of the Black Prince, Edward of Woodstock (d. 1376). The Prince of Wales and the eldest son of Edward III, the Black Prince was famous for his cunning in battle and his chivalry—the original "knight in shining armor."

• *Head downstairs, go straight, then turn left into the...*

❽ Southeast Transept: The stained-glass windows in the transept are refreshingly modern, created by Hungarian-born artist and refugee Ervin Bossányi, who was commissioned by the Dean of Canterbury to replace earlier windows damaged by WWII bombs. The themes are "Salvation" (left) and "Peace Among the Nations" (with Jesus blessing all different races, on the right).

• *Our cathedral tour is finished. If you have time, you can explore the grounds.*

Cathedral Precinct: Canterbury's mammoth church lies within a walled "precinct," a parklike complex of monastic buildings, church administration buildings, and a prestigious prep school. Past the far (apse) end of the cathedral (look up to see how its crenellations make it resemble a giant crown), a gate leads into the **Memorial Garden,** where the ashes of VIPs are scattered. This garden is built along a well-preserved stretch of Canterbury's city wall. Next, circle around the far/bottom side of the cathedral, where you'll find the ruins of other buildings from the abbey

The Canterbury Tales

The Canterbury Tales is one of the earliest and most influential works of English literature. In the late 14th century, author and diplomat Geoffrey Chaucer (c. 1343-1400) was so inspired by the cross-section of humanity undertaking the pilgrimage to Canterbury that he penned a collection of 24 engaging, sometimes bawdy tales told by fictional travelers.

The Canterbury Tales is arguably the oldest surviving travelogue, and the greatest work written in the Middle English vernacular—a bold move at a time when Latin and French were the literary languages of choice. (Chaucer's difficult-to-decipher Middle English is typically read today in a modern English translation.) But Chaucer lived on the cusp of a new age, which he helped bring to fruition: He was writing approximately 50 years after the Black Death had wiped out half of England's population, disproportionately killing French speakers (who tended to live in cities, where the plague spread quickly). He was also writing during the series of English-French conflicts that would come to be known as the Hundred Years' War—turning public opinion further against the French. His embrace of everyday English as a language worthy of literature was revolutionary (and later influenced Shakespeare, among other great English writers).

Chaucer demonstrates an impressive range of themes and genres within these tales, ranging from tragedy to romance to humor. Intensely relatable even hundreds of years later, *The Canterbury Tales* is a microcosm of human experience, featuring yarns spun by people from diverse walks of life: knight, miller, cook, lawyer, wife, merchant, squire, physician, monk, and nun. Despite their obvious differences, all of these travelers were drawn together by a shared faith and the desire to experience the power of the shrine of Thomas Becket...and by a mutual appreciation for a good story.

complex (a sanatorium and a chapel). Going through the easy-to-miss gate in the wall near these, you'll pop out into the quiet gardens and stately buildings that hide behind the giant structure. Much of this area belongs to the **King's School;** watch for high school students in their uniforms. Canterbury is very proud to have been home to Christopher Marlowe (1564-1593), who graduated from this school and later became a playwright who influenced his contemporary and rival, Shakespeare.

As you wrap up your visit, consider this: Even with all their power, wealth, and influence, two English kings were unable to successfully eradicate Thomas Becket's influence. A man of conscience—who once stood up to the most powerful ruler in England—continues to inspire visitors, nearly a thousand years after his death.

MORE SIGHTS IN THE OLD TOWN
▲The Canterbury Tales

This corny 40-minute audiovisual show offers a good review of English Lit class—or, if you're unfamiliar with Chaucer, a decent introduction. With live costumed actors, a lively audioguide, primitive lighting effects, and medieval smells, it dramatizes five of the tales in a series of amusement-park-style rooms. While more hokey than literary, the exhibit is rooted in a real appreciation for Chaucer's masterpiece. Kids (and adults) are welcome to dress up in the costume corner before beginning their pilgrimage.

Cost and Hours: £11; daily 10:00-17:00, Sept-March until 16:00 and closed Mon-Tue, these are last tour times; St. Margaret's Street, tel. 01227/696-002, www.canterburytales.org.uk.

CANTERBURY

▲Canterbury Roman Museum

The colorful displays in this impressive little museum illustrate Canterbury's Roman origins. The collection, which includes a helmet from Julius Caesar's 54 BC invasion, makes vivid the power and sophistication of the Romans in Britain.

Cost and Hours: £9, free for kids, daily 10:00-17:00, Butchery Lane, across from City Arms Inn, tel. 01227/785-575, www.canterburymuseums.co.uk.

Visiting the Museum: The subterranean one-way exhibit transports you back to Roman Canterbury, with illustrations and life-size models that capture a sense of the town called Durovernum Cantiacorum, circa AD 150. Exhibits re-create the Roman-era baths, theater, and forum, with explanations of the vendors who would have sold their wares here back then. You'll see games (with replicas you can actually play), ancient glass, religious artifacts, and more. Near the end, you'll walk past original underfloor heating, foundations, and mosaics—all displayed where they were found—plus a hands-on children's area.

Beaney House of Art and Knowledge

This museum is in the oversize, ornate town library building (with a modern annex in back that houses the TI). A big local personality from the Victorian age, surgeon Jim Beaney gave his eclectic personal collection of butterflies, stuffed animals, local paintings, and old armor to the city in 1899. He wanted all to enjoy his curiosities at no charge, and it's worth a quick visit. On the ground floor, the Garden Room displays paintings of bucolic country scenes and livestock by native son Thomas Sidney Cooper (1803-1902). The exhibit continues upstairs, with themed rooms covering explorers and collectors, as well as galleries devoted to paintings, decorative arts, and temporary exhibits.

Cost and Hours: Free; Tue-Sat 9:00-17:00 (Thu until 19:00),

Sun 10:00-17:00, closed Mon; 18 High Street, tel. 01227/862-162, www.canterburymuseums.co.uk.

EAST OF THE OLD TOWN

While historically significant, these two sights—about a 10-minute walk east of the Old Town center—aren't worth the trek unless you're interested in this area's early history.

St. Augustine's Abbey

The ruins of the original abbey—founded by the man himself, St. Augustine—sit right on the edge of town. At its peak, the abbey was a hive of activity, with a large church, cloister, and a cluster of service buildings for the monks. In the 16th century, King Henry VIII grew jealous of the wealth and influence held by England's monks, so he closed down the monasteries, retired the monks, and sold off the land and buildings to fill his own coffers. The abbey's buildings were converted to houses, while the large church was slowly dismantled and used as a building-material quarry for projects in the area.

Cost and Hours: £7.20, includes 45-minute audioguide; daily 10:00-18:00 (Oct until 17:00), Nov-March Sat-Sun only 10:00-16:00; tel. 01227/767-345, www.english-heritage.org.uk.

Getting There: Walk to the (southeast) end of St. George's Street, where it hits the ring road. Continue straight through the underpass; after you emerge, bear left along Ivy Lane, then turn left at the parking lot.

Visiting the Abbey: A modest museum sets up your visit. Virtual-reality headsets resurrect the site in its prime. Outside, the foundations and some fragments of the original structures (including a standing stone from the Neolithic period) are still visible in a grassy field, and the audioguide manages to bring the site to life. Pace the square of the cloister and imagine yourself as a monk in the early days of Christianity in England. On a sunny day, the abbey grounds are a fine place for a picnic.

St. Martin's Church

Set in the center of an old, slanted graveyard, humble little St. Martin's has the honor of being the oldest parish church in England. In continual use since 650, it sits on the foundations of a Roman temple and features an elegant Norman-era baptismal font (to the right of the entrance).

Cost and Hours: Free; sporadic hours, but usually Tue and Thu-Fri 11:00-15:00, Sat in summer only 11:00-17:00, Sun Eucharist at 9:00, churchyard always open; tel. 01227/768-072, www.martinpaul.org.

Getting There: Continue on the busy road 300 yards past St. Augustine's Abbey, and turn down the first real road to the left

(North Holmes Road); you'll see the churchyard's wooden entry gate from the main road.

Sleeping in Canterbury

Canterbury is a pleasant college town with loads of shops, restaurants, and pubs, making it a fine home base. There are relatively few accommodations within the old walls, but I've listed my favorites. The roads heading out of town, particularly New Dover Road, have clusters of B&Bs that are slim on charm but suitable for tired drivers.

$$$ Canterbury Cathedral Lodge, actually within the cathedral precinct, is a modern, bright, and comfy facility with 35 rooms—most with unbeatable cathedral views. Its sleek, simple-yet-elegant accommodations were designed for church guests but are open to all (rates include cathedral entry fee, elevator, private garden terrace and grounds are all yours after hours, limited on-site parking, tel. 01227/865-350, www.canterburycathedrallodge.org, stay@canterburycathedrallodge.org).

$$ Cathedral Gate Hotel, with 24 rooms spiraling through a treehouse floor plan, has old character (such as slanted floors) and modern amenities. It's as central as can be, on Buttermarket, just outside the church's gate (cheaper rooms with shared bath, 36 Burgate, tel. 01227/464-381, www.cathgate.co.uk, cathedralgatehotel@btconnect.com).

$$ Castle House, an eight-minute walk from the cathedral, has 15 spacious rooms and feels like a classic old guesthouse. Facing a big roundabout next to the city walls, it comes with castle views and an enclosed garden (family apartment, limited free parking, 28 Castle Street, tel. 01227/761-897, www.castlehousehotel.co.uk, info@castlehousehotel.co.uk).

$$ The Miller's Arms, on a quiet street across from the River Stour, rents 12 comfy, modern rooms that are an afterthought to the cozy pub and restaurant (pay parking, 2 Mill Lane, tel. 01227/456-057, www.millerscanterbury.co.uk, millersarms@shepherd-neame.co.uk).

$$ Harriet House offers tidy and comfortable rooms with sophisticated decor, a 15-minute walk along a scenic river footpath, north of the town center (free parking, 3 Broad Oak Road, enter around back on Market Way, tel. 01227/457-363, www.harriethouse.co.uk, enquiries@harriethouse.co.uk, Paul and Heidi).

Eating in Canterbury

As a student town, Canterbury is packed with eateries—especially along the pedestrianized shopping zone and around the cathedral.

$$$ Old Weavers House serves solid English food in a pleasant, historic building next to the river. Sit inside beneath sunny walls and creaky beams, or outside on their riverside patio under a leafy canopy. This is the most atmospheric of my listings, but it can feel touristy and gets very busy (daily 12:00-23:00, 1 St. Peter's Street, tel. 01227/464-660).

$$$ Café Mauresque is a tasty alternative to the pub scene. It offers a variety of Spanish and Moroccan tapas, platters, and *tagines* in an inviting setting with authentic Moroccan decor. If the place looks full, ask about additional seating upstairs (daily 12:00-21:30, reservations smart on weekends, 8 Butchery Lane, tel. 01227/464-300, www.cafemauresque.co.uk).

$$ Saint Smokeys BBQ House grills up delicious jerk-style barbecue chicken and sides. It's a short, pleasant walk away from the main tourist zone through a charming part of town where students and locals outnumber tourists. Order at the counter, then find a seat while your food is grilled to order (Mon-Sat 12:00-22:00, closed Sun, 17 Borough, tel. 01227/769-027).

$ City Fish Bar is your quintessential British chippy, serving several kinds of fried fish. Get yours for takeaway or grab a sidewalk table on this charming pedestrian street (Mon-Sat 10:00-19:00, Sun until 16:00, 30 St. Margaret's Street, tel. 01227/760-873).

$$$ Café des Amis, just outside the West Gate, is a local fixture for Mexican and Mediterranean fare in a crowded, convivial space with a Parisian-meets-Mexican-cantina vibe. Reservations are wise (daily 10:00-22:00, 95 St. Dunstans Street, tel. 01227/464-390, www.cafedez.com).

PUBS WITH CHARACTER

These pubs are popular for their atmosphere. The first two have better food and are within blocks of each other behind the cathedral in a quiet, cobbled, canalside neighborhood. The third is in the center and famous for its many microbrews.

$$ The Dolphin Pub, a local favorite, is a homey and relaxing 1930s pub with carefully chosen ales. While traditional, the food is a cut above typical pub grub and burgers, with quality local ingredients and daily specials. Sit in the main bar, in the sunroom, or at a picnic table in the grassy garden. It's easy to imagine local professors hanging out here (daily 12:00-14:00 & 18:00-21:00, bar open later; 17 St. Radigunds Street, tel. 01227/455-963).

$$$ The Parrot Pub claims to be the oldest pub in town. It feels that way, with a creaky ground floor and a kingly dining hall upstairs under lumbering timbers (same menu and cost). While it's less intimate and more formulaic than its neighbors, the food is highly regarded (daily 12:00-21:30, 1 Church Lane, tel. 01227/454-170).

$$ The Foundry Brew Pub offers up to 16 home brews on tap. Bartenders happily pour samples, serve beer flights, and explain the inspiration behind the name of their signature draft, Torpedo. The food—beer-inspired dishes like steak-and-ale pie and BBQ beer ribs—is forgettable; come here for the ale and the modern brewpub ambience (Mon-Thu 12:00-20:00, Fri-Sat until 21:00, Sun until 18:00, bar open later, 77 Stour Street, tel. 01227/455-899).

Canterbury Connections

Canterbury has two train stations, East and West, each about a 10-minute walk from the center.

From Canterbury by Train to: London (2/hour, 1 hour from Canterbury West Station to St. Pancras International Station; slower trains to Charing Cross station; also hourly, 1.5 hours from Canterbury East Station to Victoria Station), **Dover** (2/hour, 30 minutes, from Canterbury East to Dover Priory), **Rye** (hourly, 1 hour, from Canterbury West, transfer at Ashford International), **Hastings** (hourly, 1.5 hours, from Canterbury West, transfer at Ashford International), **Brighton** (hourly, 2.5 hours, 1-3 transfers, can be complicated—best connections through London's St. Pancras or Ashford International, from Canterbury West). **Train info:** Tel 0345-748-1950, www.nationalrail.co.uk.

By Bus to: London's Victoria Coach Station (about hourly, 2 hours), **Dover** (6/day, 45 minutes). **Bus info:** Tel. 0870-781-8181, www.nationalexpress.com.

DOVER & SOUTHEAST ENGLAND

Dover • Sissinghurst • Rye • Battle Abbey and 1066 Battlefield • Pevensey Castle

Dover guards the Straits of Dover, the narrowest part of the English Channel. For thousands of years it's overseen traffic between the Continent and Britain. Like much of southern England, Dover sits on a foundation of chalk. Miles of cliffs rise above the beaches, and perched above those cliffs is the impressive Dover Castle, England's primary defensive stronghold from Roman through modern times. From the nearby port, ferries, hydrofoils, and hovercrafts shuttle people and goods back and forth across the English Channel. France is only 23 miles away—on a clear day, you can easily see it from here.

Dover's castle is excellent, and well worth a side trip from either Canterbury (just 30 minutes away) or London (an hour away). The rest of the town, however, lacks charm—it's a hardscrabble port that was badly disfigured by WWII Nazi shelling (from the cliffs of France, just across the Channel). And the famed "White Cliffs of Dover" are marred by industrial sprawl—they can't hold a candle to the much more dramatic and bucolic white cliffs at Beachy Head (about a two-hour drive west, between Pevensey Castle and Brighton; see the Brighton chapter).

In the southeast English countryside near Dover, you can explore the quaint and fascinating garden at Sissinghurst, handcrafted by its larger-than-life creators; stroll the cobbles of the huggable hill town of Rye; visit the Battle of Hastings site—in the appropriately named town of Battle—where England's future course was charted in 1066; and see the evocative ruins of a Roman and Norman fort at Pevensey.

PLANNING YOUR TIME

On arrival in town (whether by car, train, or boat) head up to tour Dover Castle. Assuming you do both of the Secret Wartime Tunnel tours, plan for at least three hours. With additional time, stroll through the town center or view the White Cliffs before leaving town. If connecting Dover and towns west (such as Brighton), Battle and Rye can be visited en route (along with Pevensey Castle)— or you can take the inland route for Sissinghurst Garden.

Dover

Because of its easy access from the Continent, many travelers have a sentimental attachment to Dover as the first (or last) place they saw in England. But in recent decades—especially since the opening of the English Channel Tunnel in 1994—this workaday town has lost whatever luster it once had. Visitors should focus on a visit to the castle, standing sentry over Dover (and all of England) as it has for almost a thousand years.

Orientation to Dover

Gritty, urban-feeling Dover seems bigger than its population of 30,000. The town lies between two cliffs in a little valley carved out by its stream, the River Dour. While the streets stretch longingly toward the water, the core of the town is cut off from the harbor by the rumbling A-20 motorway and eyesore modern construction. The city center is anchored by Market Square and the mostly pedestrianized (but not particularly charming) main shopping drag. From here, an underpass leads to the beach and promenade with views of the port and the White Cliffs.

Tourist Information: Dover's TI, in the Dover Museum on Market Square, sells ferry and long-distance bus tickets (Mon-Sat 9:30-17:00, Sun 10:00-15:00 except closed Sun in winter, Market Square, tel. 01304/201-066, www.whitecliffscountry.org.uk).

Arrival in Dover: Trains arrive on the west side of town, a five-minute walk from the main pedestrian area and the TI. **Drivers** find plentiful parking close to the water—follow *P* signs. A couple of pay-and-display parking lots are a short walk from the TI and start of my town walk: One is tucked between St. Mary's Church and Pencester Gardens, and another is at the St. James Retail and Leisure Park (a big, modern strip mall with a handy M&S Foodhall). If you arrive by **boat** at the Eastern Docks, walk about 20-30 minutes along the base of the cliffs into town (with the sea on your left), or take a taxi (about £8). There is no public bus from

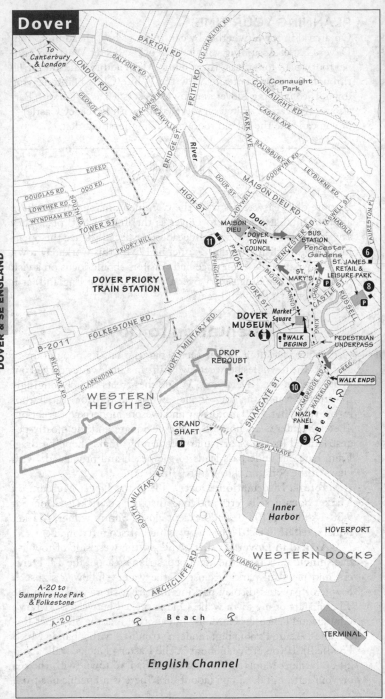

Dover

DOVER & SE ENGLAND

To Canterbury & London

BARTON RD.

LONDON RD.

BALFOUR RD.

GEORGE ST.

BEACONSFIELD

GRANVILLE ST.

BRIDGE ST.

FRITH RD.

OLD CHARLTON RD.

Connaught Park

CONNAUGHT RD.

CASTLE AVE.

PARK AVE.

SALISBURY RD.

GODWYNE RD.

LEYBURNE RD.

MAISON DIEU RD.

River

HIGH ST.

DOUR ST.

LADYWELL

EDRED

DOUGLAS RD.

ODO RD.

LOWTHER RD.

SOUTH RD.

WYNDHAM RD.

TOWER ST.

PRIORY HILL

EFFINGHAM

DOVER PRIORY TRAIN STATION

FOLKESTONE RD.

B-2011

BELGRAVE RD.

CLARENDON

NORTH MILITARY RD.

Dour

MAISON DIEU

DOVER TOWN COUNCIL

11

PRIORY

YORK ST.

BIGGIN

CANNON

ST. MARY'S

PENCESTER RD.

BUS STATION

Pencester Gardens

CHURCH

ST. JAMES RETAIL & LEISURE PARK

CASTLE ST.

KING ST.

RUSSELL

TASHAROLD

TASWELL RD.

LAURESTON PL.

6

P

8

P

DOVER MUSEUM & ℹ

Market Square

WALK BEGINS

PEDESTRIAN UNDERPASS

DROP REDOUBT

WESTERN HEIGHTS

GRAND SHAFT

P

SNARGATE ST.

CAMBRIDGE RD.

WATERLOO CRES.

10

WALK ENDS

Beach

NAZI PANEL

9

ESPLANADE

SOUTH MILITARY RD.

ARCHCLIFFE RD.

THE VIADUCT

Inner Harbor

HOVERPORT

WESTERN DOCKS

A-20 to Samphire Hoe Park & Folkestone

A-20

Beach

TERMINAL 1

English Channel

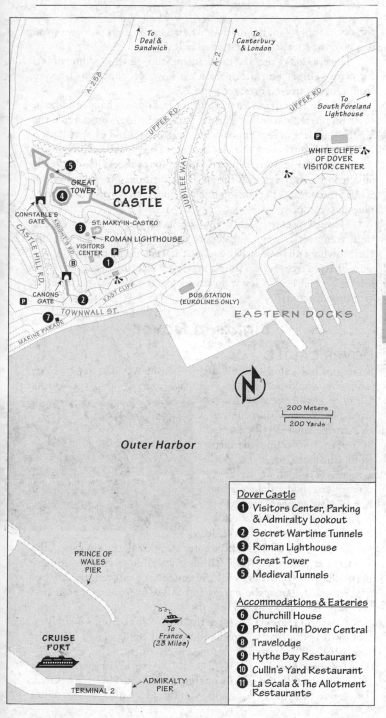

To Deal & Sandwich

To Canterbury & London

To South Foreland Lighthouse

UPPER RD.

A-258

A-2

UPPER RD.

JUBILEE WAY

WHITE CLIFFS OF DOVER VISITOR CENTER

5

GREAT TOWER

4

DOVER CASTLE

CONSTABLE'S GATE

3 ST. MARY-IN-CASTRO

ROMAN LIGHTHOUSE

KNIGHT'S RD

CASTLE HILL RD.

VISITORS CENTER

1

B

CANONS GATE

2 EAST CLIFF

7 TOWNWALL ST.

MARINE PARADE

BUS STATION (EUROLINES ONLY)

EASTERN DOCKS

N

200 Meters

200 Yards

Outer Harbor

PRINCE OF WALES PIER

CRUISE PORT

To France (23 Miles)

TERMINAL 2

ADMIRALTY PIER

DOVER & SE ENGLAND

<u>Dover Castle</u>
1 Visitors Center, Parking & Admiralty Lookout
2 Secret Wartime Tunnels
3 Roman Lighthouse
4 Great Tower
5 Medieval Tunnels

<u>Accommodations & Eateries</u>
6 Churchill House
7 Premier Inn Dover Central
8 Travelodge
9 Hythe Bay Restaurant
10 Cullin's Yard Restaurant
11 La Scala & The Allotment Restaurants

the docks into town, but on days when a cruise ship is docked, you can take the shuttle bus (described below).

Dover is also a popular destination (and starting/ending point) for **cruise ships.** For information on how to connect to London from Dover's cruise ports, see page 201.

Shuttle Bus: If you're without a car, and you happen to be in town on the same day that a cruise ship is visiting, you can ride the YMS Shuttle Bus—a Smurf-blue double-decker bus that does a handy loop connecting the city center, castle, White Cliffs visitor center, and cruise port. While designed for cruisers, it's also available to other travelers (£6 for an all-day ticket, bus departs from King Street near TI at the top of each hour, www.ymstravel.co.uk/blue-bus-company).

Dover Greeters: While the city has little meriting a guided tour, volunteer Dover Greeters are happy to walk guests through their town for an hour or two and give it a charming human dimension. This is a free service; simply arrange a meeting in advance (mobile 07712-581-557, www.dovergreeters.org.uk, dovergreeters@virginmedia.com).

Sights in Dover

DOVER CASTLE

Strategically located Dover Castle—considered "the key to England" by would-be invaders—perches grandly atop the White Cliffs of Dover. English troops were garrisoned within the castle's medieval walls for almost 900 years, protecting the coast from European invaders. With a medieval Great Tower as its centerpiece and battlements that survey 360 degrees of windswept coast, Dover Castle (worth ▲▲) has undeniable majesty. While  the historic parts of the castle are unexceptional, the exhibits in the WWII-era Secret Wartime Tunnels are unique and engaging—particularly the powerful, well-presented tour that tells the story of Operation Dynamo, the harrowing WWII rescue operation that saved the British Army at Dunkirk.

Cost and Hours: £20.90; daily 10:00-18:00, from 9:30 in Aug, Oct until 17:00; Nov-March Sat-Sun until 16:00, closed Mon-Fri; last entry and last tour departures one hour before closing.

Information: Tel. 01304/211-067, www.english-heritage.org.uk/dovercastle. In the middle of the complex, just below the Great Tower and near the parking lots, you'll find a handy visitors center (ask about special events such as falconry shows, especially on summer weekends).

Entrances: Two entry gates have kiosks where you can buy your ticket and pick up a map. The **Canons Gate** (for cars or those on foot) is closer to the Secret Wartime Tunnels, at the lower end of the castle. At the top of the castle, only pedestrians can enter through the **Constable's Gate,** near the Great Tower.

Crowd Alert: Summer weekends and holidays can be very crowded (especially around late morning). But the biggest potential headaches are lines for the two tours of the Secret Wartime Tunnels: the Operation Dynamo exhibit (with the longest wait) and the Underground Hospital. See "Planning Your Time," later, for more advice on timing your tunnel visits smartly.

Getting There: Drivers follow signs to the castle from the A-20 or the town center; approaching the castle, you'll enter the Canons Gate, buy your ticket at the booth, then loop around inside the castle grounds to reach parking lots near the visitors center. For those without a car, you can reach the castle by taxi (about £8); blue YMS Shuttle Bus, if it's running (described earlier); or on foot (steep but manageable hike). While it's a pretty long walk from the train station, from Market Square it's a brisk 15-20 minutes: Go up Castle Hill Road, and about 50 yards above St. Martin's Guesthouse look for an unmarked blacktop path on the right. As you walk in the woods, find a long set of stairs that leads to the Canons Gate ticket booth.

Planning Your Time: The key is timing the two Secret Wartime Tunnels tours—Operation Dynamo (often with a longer wait) and Underground Hospital. Each tour allows 30 people to enter at a time, with departures every 10-15 minutes. The two tours are next to each other; you'll see a line outside each door.

If you're early on a busy day, go directly to the Operation Dynamo tour to do it first, as it's a better tour, sets the historical stage to help you better appreciate the hospital tour, and ends nearby, making it easy to circle back for the hospital tour (which ends higher up the hill—more logically situated for hiking up to the Great Tower afterward).

Getting Around the Castle: The free "land train" loops around the castle's grounds about every 15 minutes, shuttling visitors between the Secret Wartime Tunnels, the entrance to the Great Tower, and the Medieval Tunnels (at the top end of the castle). Though handy for avoiding the ups and downs, nothing at the castle is more than a 10-minute walk from anything else—so you may spend more time waiting for the train than you would walking.

Background

Armies have kept a watchful eye on this strategic lump of land since Roman times (as evidenced by the still-standing ancient light-house). A linchpin for English defense starting in the Middle Ages, Dover Castle was heavily used in the time of Henry VIII and Elizabeth I. After a period of decline, the castle was rein-vigorated during the Napoleonic Wars and became a central command center in World War II (when naval headquarters were

buried deep in the cliffside). The tunnels were also used as a hospital and triage station for injured troops. After the war, in the 1960s, the tunnels were converted into a dramatic Cold War bunker—one of 12 designated sites in the UK that would house government officials and a BBC studio in the event of nuclear war. When it became clear that even the stout cliffs of Dover couldn't be guaranteed to stand up to a nuclear attack, Dover Castle was retired from active duty in 1984.

◑ Self-Guided Tour

The sights at Dover Castle basically cluster into two areas: the Secret Wartime Tunnels (with two, very different tunnel tours) and adjacent Admiralty Lookout (a WWI fire command post), both in the lower part of the castle (facing the sea); and the Great Tower and surrounding historical castle features (such as the old Roman lighthouse and the Medieval Tunnels), higher up at the hill's summit. The castle complex is sprawling and steep, but everything is well-signed.

Secret Wartime Tunnels

In the 1790s, with the threat of Napoleon looming, the castle's fortifications were beefed up again. So many troops were stationed here that they needed to tunnel into the chalk to provide sleeping areas for up to 2,000 men. These tunnels were vastly expanded during World War II, when operations for the war effort moved into a bomb-proof, underground air-raid shelter safe from Hitler's feared Luftwaffe. Winston Churchill watched air battles from here, while Allied commanders looked out over a battle zone nicknamed "Hellfire Corner." Two different tours take you into the tunnels: Operation Dynamo and Underground Hospital.

Operation Dynamo Tunnel Tour: From these tunnels in May 1940, Admiral Sir Bertram Ramsay oversaw the rescue mission wherein the British managed, in just 10 days, to evacuate some

Dover Castle and Operation Dynamo

It was during World War II that Dover Castle lived its most dramatic moments, most notably as the headquarters for the inspiring Operation Dynamo.

In May 1940, Germany attacked France and the Low Countries in a Blitzkrieg ("lightning war") strike that reached the English Channel in just 12 days. French, British, and Belgian forces were cut off when the Nazis flanked them to the west, pinning them into an ever-narrowing corner of northern France (around the port city of Dunkerque, which Brits call Dunkirk). As the Nazis closed in, it became clear that hundreds of thousands of British and other Allied troops being squeezed against the English Channel would soon be captured—or worse.

From the tunnels below Dover Castle, Admiral Sir Bertram Ramsay oversaw Operation Dynamo. In 10 days, using a variety of military and civilian ships, Ramsay staged a dramatic evacuation of 338,000 Allied soldiers from the beaches of Dunkirk (although in the end about 40,000 troops, mostly French, were captured).

Because so many were rescued under such desperate circumstances, the operation has been called a "victory in defeat." And although the Allies were forced to abandon northern France to Hitler, Operation Dynamo saved an untold number of lives and bolstered morale in a country just beginning the most devastating war it would ever face. On the day after the evacuation, Winston Churchill rallied the British people—and readied them for the coming conflict—with his most famous speech: "We shall defend our island, whatever the cost may be. We shall fight on the beaches, we shall fight on the landing grounds, we shall fight in the fields and in the streets, we shall fight in the hills; we shall never surrender."

This unlikely evacuation, often called the "Miracle at Dunkirk," has long loomed large in the British imagination—and it (finally) gained more international attention thanks to Christopher Nolan's award-winning 2017 film *Dunkirk*.

338,000 Allied soldiers from the beaches of Dunkirk in Nazi-occupied France (see the sidebar). In this 45-minute tour, you're led from room to room, where a series of well-produced audiovisual shows narrate, step-by-step, the lead-up to World War II and the exact conditions that led to the need for Operation Dynamo. You'll hear fateful radio addresses from Neville Chamberlain and King George VI announcing the declaration of war, and watch newsreel footage of Britain preparing its war effort. Imagine learning about war in this somber way (in the days before bombastic 24-hour cable news). Sitting around an animated map, you'll learn how Germany attacked Holland, Belgium, and France—and how the Allied troops tried to counterattack. You'll also see how the strategic tables turned, pinning the Allies down against the English Channel. Then you'll walk slowly down a long tunnel, as footage projected on the wall tells the stirring tale of the evacuation.

At the end of the guided portion, you're free to explore several rooms still outfitted as they were back in World War II—such as the mapping room, repeater station, and telephone exchange.

You'll exit onto a terrace, then enter the "Wartime Tunnels Uncovered" exhibit, which uses diaries, uniforms, archival films, and other artifacts to chart the development of the tunnels from the Napoleonic era to the Cold War.

Underground Hospital Tunnel Tour: Immediately next to the Operation Dynamo tour is the entrance to this shorter, lower-tech, 20-minute tour of the topmost levels of the tunnels, which were used during World War II as a hospital, then as a triage-type dressing station for wounded troops. Your guide leads you through the various parts of a re-created 1941 operating room and a narrow hospital ward as you listen to the story of an injured pilot of a Mosquito (a wooden bomber). Occasional smells and lighting effects enhance the tale. Finally, you'll climb a 78-step double-helix staircase and pop out next to the Admiralty Lookout. The Underground Hospital complements the Operation Dynamo tour well.

• *If you take the Underground Hospital tour, you'll surface right next to the Admiralty Lookout; otherwise, hike up the path overlooking the sea toward the visitors center and look for the statue of an admiral standing at attention. The lookout is near the grassy slope on the seaward side of the officers' barracks.*

Admiralty Lookout: Climbing around this WWI fire command post (the only bit of WWI history in the castle), you get a great sense of guarding the Channel. The threat of aerial bombardment was new in World War I—and it became devastating just a generation later in World War II. Climb to the rooftop for the best view possible (in the castle) of the famous White Cliffs, the huge ferry terminal, and the cruise port. While you can't see London... you can see France. The statue is of British Admiral Sir Bertram Ramsay, who heroically orchestrated Operation Dynamo.

• *Now follow the signs to get to the Great Tower and Roman Lighthouse.*

Great Tower Area

The oldest part of the vast castle complex still holds the high ground—the Great Tower and the Roman Lighthouse. Hiking up from the visitors center, you'll come through a gate, looking straight at the Great Tower. But first, turn your attention to the hill-capping buildings on your right.

Roman Lighthouse: The round, crenellated tower is a lighthouse *(pharos)* likely built during the second century AD, when the

Roman fleet for the colony of Britannia was based in the harbor below. To guide the boats, they burned wet wood by day (for maximum smoke), and dry wood by night (for maximum light). When the Romans finally left England 300 years later, the *pharos* is said to have burst into flames as the last ship departed.

The lighthouse stands within the scant remains of an 11th-century Anglo-Saxon fortress built to defend against Viking raids. Adjacent to the lighthouse is the unimpressive **St. Mary-in-Castro Church** (if it's open, step inside). A surviving example of Anglo-Saxon architecture, it was built around the year 1000 and substantially restored in the 19th century. The church used the lighthouse as its bell tower.

Henry II's Great Tower: A fortress was first built here shortly after the Battle of Hastings in 1066 (see the sidebar, later in the chapter). What you see today was finished in 1180 by King Henry II. For centuries, Dover Castle was the most secure fortress in all of England, and an important symbol of royal power on the coast.

The central building—reminiscent of the Tower of London— was the original tower (also called a "keep"). The walls are up to 20

feet thick. King Henry II slept on the top floor, surrounded by his best protection against an invading army. Imagine the attempt: As the thundering enemy cavalry makes its advance, the king's defenders throw caltrops (four-starred metal spikes meant to cut through the horses' hooves). His knights unsheathe their swords, and trained crossbow archers ring the tower, sending arrows into foreign armor. Later kings added buildings near the tower (along the inner bailey, which lines the keep yard) to garrison troops during wartime and to provide extra rooms for royal courtiers during peacetime. These are now filled with museum exhibits and a gift shop. On summer weekends, and for most of August, costumed actors wandering the grounds add to the fun.

Before going in the tower itself, check out some of the exhibits in the surrounding garrison buildings.

The Great Tower Story Exhibit, around to the right as you enter the courtyard, uses colorful displays and animated films to bring meaning to the place. You'll learn how Henry II married Eleanor of Aquitaine (creating an empire that encompassed much of today's England and France), how his heirs squandered it, and how they evolved into the Plantagenet dynasty that ruled England for some 300 years (including many of the famous Henrys and Richards).

The Princess of Wales's Royal Regiment and Queen's Regiment Museum (next door) collects military memorabilia and tells the story of these military units, which have fought in foreign conflicts for centuries—you'll see gritty helmet-cam footage from 21st-century deployments in Afghanistan.

Enter the **tower** itself (the door is a bit farther around the courtyard). The cellar, where you enter, holds the medieval kitchen and royal armory. From here, twist your way up the big spiral stairs to two more floors: a dining hall, throne room, kitchen, bedroom, and so on decorated with brightly colored furnishings. While there's no real exhibit, docents are standing by to answer questions, and the kid-friendly furnishings give a sense of what the castle was like in the Middle Ages. In the throne room (on the second floor up), face the throne and climb up the stairs on the left to find the well—which helped make the tower even more siege-resistant. Fans of Thomas Becket can look for his chapel, a tiny sacristy called the "upper chapel" (it's hiding down a forgotten hallway high in the building—go behind the throne, turn left, and look for the narrow hall). Climbing to the very top (about 120 stairs total) rewards you with a sweeping view of the town and sea beyond.

• *Exit the keep yard at the far end through the King's Gate. Cross a stone bridge and then descend a wooden staircase. Under these stairs is the entrance to the...*

Medieval Tunnels: This system of steep tunnels was originally built in case of a siege. While enjoyable for a kid-in-a-castle experience, there's little to see. From here, you can catch the tourist train or do the Battlements Walk. Much of Dover's success as a defendable castle came from these unique concentric walls—the battlements—which protected the inner keep.

• *Our tour of the castle is finished. For a fast return to town, exit out the Constable's Gate near the Medieval Tunnels and follow the path steeply down.*

WHITE CLIFFS OF DOVER

Chalky white cliffs surround Dover on both sides for miles. From the top of the cliff, you can get sweeping views over the town (and as far as France, in clear weather). Or you can see the cliffs themselves, either from below or from an adjacent viewpoint.

▲White Cliffs of Dover Visitor Centre

The best all-around experience is the National Trust visitor center, which is on a bluff just east of town (past Dover Castle—if you're

driving to the castle, it's an easy add-on, but non-drivers may find it's not worth the trouble). You'll pay a hefty parking fee to access this area, which has striking views down over Dover's busy port (and the white cliffs just beyond it). The visitor center is just a big shop/café, with WCs and a few interpretation panels. But it's a springboard for some enjoyable walks; see below.

Cost and Hours: Visitor Centre free; daily 10:00-17:00, off-season until 16:00; Upper Road, Langdon Cliffs, tel. 01304/207-326, www.nationaltrust.org.uk/white-cliffs-dover.

Getting There: If **driving,** head up the Castle Hill Road, pass the castle entrance, then take a sharp right turn onto Upper Road. After crossing over the A-2 motorway, look for the Visitor Centre entrance at the next hairpin turn (£5 parking). You can **walk** to the Visitor Centre from Dover, but it's pretty far (about 2.5 miles from the train station—walk along the base of the cliffs with the sea on your right, following footpath signs from the town center). Or, if the **YMS Shuttle** is running, you can take it to the Visitor Centre (for cruise ship passengers; described earlier).

Scenic Walks: It's well worth the 20-minute round-trip hike to follow the Viewpoint Walk. From the Visitor Centre, walk all

the way through the park-ing lot and keep going. After passing through a gate, take the left (upper) trail and hike a few minutes uphill, to a viewpoint just under several communication towers (at another gate). From here, you can look back over Dover and

its castle. Looking east, you'll get a fine view of the white cliffs just beyond. To extend your hike, you can continue two miles farther along the cliff top to the **South Foreland Lighthouse,** built in 1846, and enjoy the glorious view (£6, possible to enter only with 30-minute tour—confirm schedule at Visitor Centre before making the trip, generally closed Tue-Thu, tea room, tel. 01304/852-463, www.nationaltrust.org.uk/south-foreland-lighthouse).

Western Heights

This famous cliff—opposite Dover Castle, just southwest of town—provides a sweeping view of Dover (and occasionally of France). The trail along the cliff weaves around former gun posts that were originally installed during Napoleonic times, but were used most extensively during World War II. It was here that the British military amassed huge decoy forces designed to fool the Germans into thinking that the D-Day invasion would come from Dover—across the shortest stretch of water to Calais—rather than from ports farther west and across to Normandy. Today, the bunkers are abandoned, but in decent condition; you can usually crouch through a tunnel to get a closer look at the fortress. While this site is historic, the views are not quite as good as the White Cliffs of Dover Visitor Centre described earlier, and you don't see many white cliffs at all—just the port.

Cost and Hours: Free, open dawn until dusk, www.doverwesternheights.org.

Getting There: Drivers follow the A-20 west past the harbor to the Western Heights roundabout, take the Aycliff exit onto South Military Road, wind uphill for about a half-mile, then turn right at the small brown sign onto Drop Redoubt Road.

Samphire Hoe

This park, less than two miles south of Dover, is a good stop for those who wish to see more of the white cliffs—without the in-dustrial crush of the busy Dover docks. (It's also handy for drivers leaving town on the A-20 toward London, since it's an easy turn-off from the freeway.) Samphire Hoe, a chalk mead-owland beneath the cliffs, was created using more than six million cubic yards of chalk left over from the construction of the  Channel Tunnel in the early 1990s. What could have been a dumping ground is now a grassy expanse hosting a rich variety of plants and wildlife. The park has walking paths, an education building, and a tea kiosk, as well as a mile-long seawall that attracts anglers, wave watchers, and swimmers aiming for France. A plaque by the sea lists the names of 11 workers who died during the construction of the Channel Tunnel.

Cost and Hours: Free, pay parking, park open daily 7:00-dusk; tea kiosk daily Easter-Sept, weekends only in winter; tel. 01304/225-649, www.samphirehoe.co.uk.

Getting There: From Dover, drivers take the A-20 toward

London/Folkestone and watch for the Samphire Hoe exit. After waiting for the green light at the 007-style tunnel, you'll emerge at a pay-and-display parking lot. Walkers can follow the North Downs Way footpath, while cyclists can use the National Cycle Network Route 2; both are signposted from Dover—ask the TI for specifics.

Prince of Wales Pier

If it's a sunny day and you want a nice view of the cliffs and castle without heading out of town, stroll to the western end of the beachfront promenade (to the right, as you face the water), then hike out along the Prince of Wales Pier for perfect panoramas back toward the city (free, daily 8:00-dusk).

Boat Tours

The famous White Cliffs of Dover are almost impossible to appreciate from town. A 1.5-hour White Cliffs and Beyond boat tour around the bay gives you all the photo ops you need. You'll ride in a rigid inflatable boat that leaves from the Dover Sea Sports Centre (beach side), on the western end of the waterfront promenade (£35, 2 or more tours per day—smart to book ahead, max 12 people/boat, tel. 01304/212-880, www.doverseasafari.co.uk).

DOVER TOWN
▲Dover Museum

This modern and engaging museum, at the TI on Market Square, houses an amazing artifact (on the top floor): a large and well-preserved 3,500-year-old Bronze Age boat unearthed near Dover's shoreline. Museum officials claim this is the oldest seagoing boat in existence, underlining the extremely long trading history of Dover. The boat consists of oak planks lashed together with yew twine and stuffed with moss to be watertight.

You'll also see other finds from the archaeological site, an exhibit on boat construction techniques, and a 12-minute film. Across the hall, the Dover History Gallery tells the story of how this small but strategically located town has shaped history—from Tudor times to the Napoleonic era to World War II. And back down on the ground floor are exhibits covering the Roman and Anglo-Saxon periods.

Cost and Hours: Free, Mon-Sat 9:30-17:00, Sun 10:00-

DOVER & SE ENGLAND

15:00 except closed Sun in off-season; tel. 01304/201-066, www.
dovermuseum.co.uk.

Dover Town Walk

The center of Dover offers a dose of real-world England. After
visiting the castle and white cliffs, those with an hour to kill can
spend it taking this self-guided town walk. We'll begin on the
main square, venture up the main shopping street, and then circle
around through a riverside park to the beach and promenade.

• *Start in the square in front of the TI and Dover Museum.*

Market Square: This marks the site of the port in Roman
times. The ugly buildings all around are a reminder that the town
was rebuilt after suffering major bomb damage in World War II.
And the Dickens Corner building is a reminder that the great writer made many visits here. The old Georgian market building is now
filled by the TI and the Dover Museum, with its 3,500-year-old
Bronze Age boat (described earlier).

• *Head up the street to the left of the Dickens Corner building.*

Main Shopping Street (Cannon Street/Biggin Street): This
mostly traffic-free axis runs north from Market Square to the Town
Hall. As you walk, look up (above the dreary storefronts) to notice
fine Victorian architectural details. You'll pass St. Mary's Church,
which has a few surviving Norman parts but was largely rebuilt in
Victorian Neo-Gothic. Notice its flinty stone walls. There's plenty
of flint around here—which provided some sharp weapons that
helped the locals chase away the Romans when they first invaded.

Halfway down the next block on the left is the local **bingo
parlor** (Buzz Bingo). Soft and mesmerizing bingo parlors like this
make for a quirky geriatric scene nightly, and while restricted to
"members only," anyone can "join" for just the night. The regulars
would love to set you up for a few games—and perhaps offer you a
very cheap dinner.

Continue up a couple more blocks (through a section that permits car traffic). Re-entering the traffic-free zone of Biggin Street,
on your right is a **monument** to locals who were lost in the two
world wars (monuments like these are standard-issue in every British town). The historic buildings set back behind the monument are
elegant old council offices.

The huge, looming building straight ahead is the Town Hall—
also called **Maison Dieu.** The core of this building originated as
part of a Romanesque (or "Norman") 13th-century abbey complex,
which was later seized by the government during the Reformation
(16th century). For centuries it was used as a food warehouse for
the Royal Navy, until it became the Town Hall in 1834. Go up
the stairs facing High Street and peek into its cavernous main hall,
under a hammerbeam roof.

• *Walk between Maison Dieu and the war monument, and follow the walkway until you hit the little river. Then turn right again and follow the riverside path for a few blocks through the heart of the city.*

River Dour: Just seven miles long but famous for its trout, this river is part of a fine greenbelt and park that splits the center of Dover. The river powered the paper mills and breweries that once stoked the local economy. To this day, beer is big in Dover, which has multiple microbreweries.

• *Follow the river to, then through, a big city park (Pencester Gardens). At the end of the park, aim for the parking lot and WC, and then turn right on Church Street to circle back to Market Square. Continue downhill on King Street, through a pedestrian underpass. This "subway," which leads to the waterfront, is decorated with a crudely painted mural of boats that have used Dover's venerable port through the ages—from the Vikings' longship to the hovercraft. Climbing the stairs and exiting out the far side, walk straight ahead until you hit the water.*

Waterfront Promenade: Overlooking a pleasant, pebbly beach and a mighty port, this offers fine views of the castle and the white cliffs. Millions of pounds were spent to "uglify" the promenade (according to skeptical locals), but the history, memorials, and sea views make it a nice stroll anyway.

Far to the right, at the base of the pier, the clock tower with the Union Jack marks the Victorian-era customs station. This evokes the days before airplanes and undersea tunnels, when—for Brits—"going to Europe" generally meant going through Dover. Despite present-day alternatives, the English Channel still sees plenty of traffic. A ferry departs for France every hour. And more and more people are swimming the English Channel from here to Calais, 23 miles away. You can often see them training in the harbor.

Walk toward the clock tower. About two-thirds of the way there, keep a close eye along the walkway for an unusual **monument** displaying armored plating from Nazi gun emplacements at Calais. The Nazis shelled Dover between 1940 and 1944, discharging 84 rounds from those Calais guns. Just beyond that is a smaller monument to those lost in the evacuation from Dunkirk in 1940.

Sleeping and Eating in Dover

Sleeping: There's no reason to sleep in gritty Dover, with lovely Canterbury just 30 minutes away. But in a pinch, Dover has several **$$** chain hotels, including **Premier Inn Dover Central** and **Travelodge**—both near the harborfront promenade. While Dover has B&Bs, you won't find as many here as in other English towns. One place to consider is **$$ Churchill House,** a comfortable, traditional type of place. Neatly run by Alex Dimech and his parents, Alastair and Betty, it's perfectly situated, just at the base of the castle hill, with eight rooms plus a family-friendly flat (6 Castle Hill Road, tel. 01304/204-622, www.churchillguesthouse.co.uk, churchillguesthouse@gmail.com).

Eating: Your dining options in downtown Dover are few, and only a handful of places are open for dinner. My first two listings are on or near the beachfront promenade. The castle's cafés work fine for lunch.

$$$ Hythe Bay Restaurant is your best yacht club-style restaurant. It's literally built over the beach with a modern dining room, nice views, and a reputation for the best fish in town—including award-winning fish-and-chips (daily 12:00-21:30, The Esplanade, tel. 01304/207-740, www.hythebay.co.uk—if reserving, ask for window seat with a view).

$$$ Cullin's Yard Restaurant is a quirky, family-friendly microbrewery with a playful, international menu ranging from pasta, salads, and panini to fish-and-chips. Choose between picnic tables on the harbor or the shipwreck interior (daily 11:00-21:30, 11 Cambridge Road, tel. 01304/211-666).

$$ La Scala, tiny and romantic, serves a good variety of Italian dishes (Mon-Sat 12:00-14:00 & 18:00-22:00, closed Sun, 19 High Street, tel. 01304/208-044).

$$ The Allotment is trying to bring class to this ruddy town, with an emphasis on locally sourced ingredients (in Brit-speak, an "allotment" is like a community garden). The rustic-chic interior feels a bit like an upscale deli, and there's a charming patio out back. They serve a traditional afternoon tea on vintage crockery (Tue-Sat 9:00-21:30, closed Sun-Mon, 9 High Street, tel. 01304/214-467).

Dover Connections

While the train will get you to big destinations on the South Coast, the bus has better connections to smaller towns. Stagecoach offers good one-day "Dayrider" or one-week "Megarider" tickets covering anywhere they go in southeast England (tel. 0871-200-2233, www.stagecoachbus.com).

The Dover train station is called Dover Priory. Most buses stop at the "bus station" (it's more of a parking lot) on Pencester Road in the town center. Eurolines buses stop at the Eastern Docks, near the ferries to and from France.

From Dover by Train to: London (2/hour, 1 hour, direct to St. Pancras; also hourly, 2 hours, direct to Victoria Station or Charing Cross Station, more with transfers), **Canterbury** (2/hour, 30 minutes, arrives at Canterbury East Station), **Rye** (hourly, 1 hour, transfer at Ashford International), **Hastings** (hourly, 1.5 hours, transfer at Ashford International), **Brighton** (at least hourly, 2.5 hours, transfer at Ashford International or London Bridge Station). **Train info:** Tel. 0345-748-4950, www.nationalrail.co.uk.

By Bus: National Express (tel. 0871-781-8181, www.nationalexpress.com) goes to **London** (10/day, generally 3 hours) and **Canterbury** (6/day, 45 minutes). Stagecoach goes to **Rye** (hourly, 2 hours) and **Hastings** (hourly, 3 hours).

Ferries to France: In the mood for a glass of wine and some escargot? A day trip to France is only a short boat ride away (walk-on passengers generally £30 round-trip, car prices vary with demand). Two companies make the journey from Dover: P&O Ferries (1.5 hours to Calais, tel. 0800-130-0030, www.poferries.com), or DFDS Seaways (cars and bikes only, no foot passengers; 2 hours to Dunkirk or 1.5 hours to Calais, tel. 0871-574-7235, www.dfdsseaways.co.uk).

DOVER & SE ENGLAND

Southeast England

The following sights are in the countryside west of Dover, within an hour or two by train—less by car.

Sissinghurst Castle Garden

One of the most engaging gardens in southern England, Sissinghurst combines the fascinating story and personalities of its

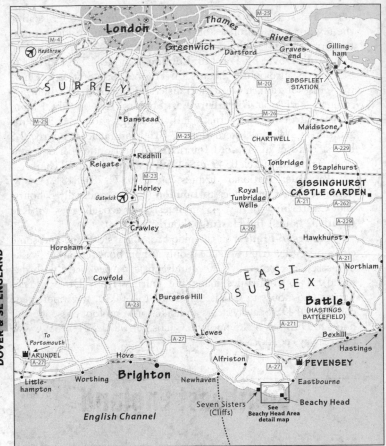

creators with an impeccably designed and maintained manor garden (worth ▲▲▲ for garden aficionados, and ▲▲ for anyone else).
Visitors enjoy climbing the surviving castle tower, learning about
the dynamic couple who created this place, sniffing around the
lovely plantings, and taking a tour of their private home. For an
English country estate, it's loaded with personality and blessedly
compact to tour.

Cost and Hours: £13.80, includes tour of South Cottage; garden open daily 11:00-17:30, typically closed Nov-mid-March—but
may be open weekends; shorter hours for tower, library, and South
Cottage; pay parking, café, plant shop.

Information: Tel. 01580/710-700, www.nationaltrust.org.
uk/sissinghurst-castle-garden.

Getting There: Sissinghurst is about 40 miles west of Dover,
off the A-262, near Cranbrook. **Trains** from London connect to
Staplehurst, about six miles away (2/hour, just over an hour from

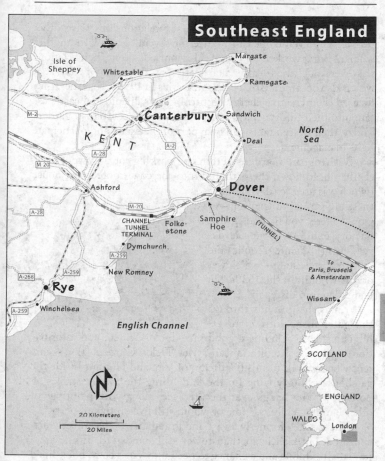

Southeast England

Isle of Sheppey

Margate

Whitstable

Ramsgate

M-2

Canterbury

Sandwich

K E N T

A-28

A-2

Deal

North Sea

M 20

Ashford

M-20

Dover

A-28

CHANNEL TUNNEL TERMINAL

Folke-stone

Samphire Hoe

(TUNNEL)

Dymchurch

A-259

To Paris, Brussels & Amsterdam

A-268

A-259

New Romney

Rye

English Channel

A-259

Winchelsea

Wissant

SCOTLAND

ENGLAND

WALES

London

20 Kilometers

20 Miles

DOVER & SE ENGLAND

Victoria Station, tel. 0345-748-4950, www.nationalrail.co.uk). From Staplehurst, take a **taxi** directly to the garden (£17 one-way, reserve at tel. 01580/890-003; return taxis can be busy in the afternoon—reserve ahead then as well), or a **bus** to the village of Sissinghurst, where you can **walk** along an idyllic footpath about a mile to the garden (path can be muddy; catch bus #5 from Staplehurst, hourly in the afternoon; for more info call 0871-200-2233 or use the journey planner at www.travelinesoutheast.org.uk).

Background: Sissinghurst is the work of writer Vita Sackville-West (1892-1962) and her husband, diplomat-author Harold Nicolson (1886-1968), who began creating their paradise here in 1930. Each was larger than life: Vita was a prizewinning author and poet, and a lover of Virginia Woolf, while Harold served in Parliament and was instrumental in writing the Balfour Declaration (a pivotal document in the creation of Israel). Their relationship was unconventional, particularly for their era: They had an open marriage, and both had same-sex relationships with other people. Vita even eloped to France for several years with another woman. But it worked for them. (Her journals about their relationship were published—after her death—as *Portrait of a Marriage*, which also became a BBC/PBS miniseries in 1990.) Together, they focused their creative energy on turning this dilapidated castle estate into their idiosyncratic version of the perfect English garden. Today, their descendants still own part of the estate and participate in its management.

Visiting the Gardens: From the parking lot, buy your ticket, then head down the path and into the cone-roofed oast house (which was used for drying hops; these are typical of the Kent region). Here you'll find introductory **exhibits** about the development, disintegration, and rebirth of the estate—which was originally built in the 1530s, but had fallen into disrepair.

Enter the grounds through the **gatehouse,** with more exhibits inside—including a good introductory video, and information about the Mediterranean-style "Delos Garden" that's currently being built to fulfill a dream of Vita and Harold. Inside the gatehouse's library wing (to the left, filling the former stables), a portrait of Vita hangs over the fireplace, along with paintings of other family members, some of whom still live on the property.

The castle—formerly a vast and grand affair—has mostly disappeared, but an Elizabethan **tower** still stands tall. Inside are a few small exhibits and a chance to peek into Vita's cozy, book-lined writing room. At the top of the tower (78 steps up), you can survey the garden and orchard from above, giving you an excellent orientation to the estate.

In every direction from the tower sprawls a series of interlocking **gardens.** Shaped entirely by Vita and Harold's personal whims, and still painstakingly maintained to their specifications, these are laid out in sections, each with a theme. Use your map to explore. Every section feels like a small outdoor room: the Herb Garden, fragrant and colorful; the White Garden, a two-tone masterpiece (all white and green); Harold's Lime Walk, beyond the cottage, with tidy rows of trees planted with tulips. There's always something blooming here, but the best show is in June, when the White Garden bursts with fragrant roses.

Tucked behind the tower, the postcard-perfect **South Cottage**—where Harold and Vita lived (and which is still owned and sometimes used by their descendants)—is typically open to a limited number of visitors on guided tours throughout the afternoon (first tour at 12:00). To secure a space on a guided tour, pick up a free, timed ticket at the cottage kitchen (these are available starting around 11:45—knock). A chatty docent will lead you on a fascinating, quirky, gossipy, intimate tour through the private quarters of this larger-than-life couple. Since the capacity is so small, the garden administration tries not to publicize the South Cottage tours, but they're worth planning for.

With more time, you can explore beyond the inner gardens, check out the estate's working farm, or stroll to the nearby lakes. Attendants in the gardens love to suggest how to spend your Sissinghurst time.

Rye

If you dream of half-timbered pubs and wisteria-covered stone churches, Rye is the photo op for you. A busy seaport village for

hundreds of years, Rye was frozen in time as silt built up and the sea retreated in the 16th and 17th centuries, leaving only a skinny waterway to remind it of better days. While shipbuilding and smuggling were the mainstays of the economy back then, antique shops, pricey restaurants, and expensive B&Bs drive business these days. Curdled in cobbled cuteness, Rye desperately tries to be southeast England's answer to a huggable Cotswolds village—and it nearly succeeds. But it feels a little artificial and greedy, packed with tourists trying to soak up some charm. Still, it's worth a stop and a stroll. There's no official **TI**, but you'll find visitor information at the Rye Heritage Centre.

Getting There: Trains connect to Rye from London (hourly, 1.5 hours from St. Pancras International Station, transfer at Ashford International) and Dover (hourly, 1 hour, transfer at Ashford International). Stagecoach **bus** #102 provides a direct connection to Dover (hourly, 2 hours, tel. 0871-200-2233, www.stagecoachbus. com). If coming by **car,** Rye is about 35 miles southwest of Dover off the A-259 (the route to Brighton). As you approach town, follow the canal to the old quays. The sea used to come up here, and the parking lot on Strand Quay would have been the wharf. I'd ignore the confusing *P* signs, which direct you to parking lots away from the town center—instead, navigate the one-way system, follow brown *Tour* signs, and try to squeeze into the small lot next to the Rye Heritage Centre (by the antique shops) across the street from the canal.

Visiting Rye: Rye's sights try to make too much of this little town, but a stroll along the cobbles is enjoyable. Here's an easy loop that will give you a sample of the town.

Start at the **Rye Heritage Centre,** with a visitor information center, a town audioguide (75 minutes), and an impressive scale model of the town, presented in a 20-minute sound-and-light show (if it's not running you can peek in at the model for free; Strand Quay/A-259, tel. 01797/226-696, www.ryeheritage.co.uk).

From near the Rye Heritage Centre, cobbled Mermaid Street leads straight up into the medieval heart of Rye. Along this street (on the left), look for the half-timbered, ivy-covered **Mermaid Inn,** rebuilt in 1420 after the original burned down (today it's an upscale hotel with plenty of four-poster beds). Step inside and have a peek into Rye's heyday, or splurge for an expensive lunch. Photos of recent celebrity customers are posted just inside the door.

Continuing up Mermaid Street, jog right up West Street, passing **Lamb House**—a tourable National Trust property where American novelist Henry James lived and worked (www.national-trust.org.uk/lamb-house).

Just beyond, you reach Church Square. The old **Church of St. Mary the Virgin** has a pleasant interior (described by a free pamphlet), an 84-step tower you can climb for a countryside view, and a red-brick water tower built in 1753 (tel. 01797/224-935).

Beyond the square is a miniature castle called the Ypres Tower, housing the **Rye Castle Museum,** with a modest collection of items

from the town's past. It's a fun excuse to twist through some tight stairways and corridors, see artifacts from the town's history (ships-in-bottles), and learn a bit about medieval crime and punishment. Don't miss the outdoor section: a prison exercise yard with downward-pointed jagged metal spikes to deter thoughts of escape. At the far end of the yard is a freestanding women's prison tower built in 1837. Before that, female prisoners—often prostitutes—were simply thrown in with male ones. Towers like this one gave female prisoners a safe space to serve out their sentences (tel. 01797/226-728, www.ryemuseum.co.uk). If you're visiting on a summer weekend, ask about the museum's second location—the East Street Museum—which features a 1745 fire engine and more about Rye's shipbuilding past.

Exiting the Castle Museum, turn right (walking with the

church on your left), then turn left at the paved street. You'll pass the town council hall (a popular wedding venue) on your right, then turn right to walk steeply downhill on shop-lined Lion Street. This takes you to **High Street** (and a record store filling an old brick grammar school). Turn left and browse your way down High Street, lined with pricey restaurants, twee coffee houses, and tourist-oriented boutiques. As it curves downhill, High Street becomes The Mint, eventually depositing you near the Rye Heritage Centre where we began.

Eating in Rye: The village seems designed to provide passing travelers with an expensive lunch. High Street is lined with a variety of restaurants, for every price range. The Mermaid Inn (described earlier) is historic, though the food is pricey and gets mixed reviews; locals prefer the Standard Inn, along The Mint near the bottom end of High Street.

Near Rye: Compared to sugary-sweet Rye, modest and medieval **Winchelsea** feels like an antacid. Small, inviting, and just far enough away from the maddening crowd, the town makes a good stop for a picnic lunch. The Little Shop on the square at 9 High Street sells all you need for a quiet meal on the village green. Winchelsea is about three miles southwest of Rye off the A-259, toward Hastings (www.winchelsea.com).

Battle Abbey and 1066 Battlefield

Located an hour southwest of Dover by car, the town of Battle commemorates the Battle of Hastings. In 1066, a Norman (French) nobleman—William, Duke of Normandy—was victorious in the Battle of Hastings and seized control of England, leading to a string of Norman kings and forever changing the course of English history. While the ▲▲ battlefield and adjoining ruined

abbey (built soon after the battle by William to atone for all the spilled blood) are worth ▲▲▲ to British-history buffs, anyone can appreciate the dramatic story behind the grassy field. Ignore the tourists and take a journey back in time...these fields would have looked almost the same a thousand years ago. Gaze across the unassuming little valley and imagine thousands of invading troops. Your visit can last from three minutes to three hours, depending on your imagination.

Getting There: If coming by **car,** the town of Battle is about 7 miles northwest of the town of Hastings. Though not on a major

The Battle of Hastings

The most epic of all of Europe's medieval *Game of Thrones*-style battles (minus the dragons and the ice zombies) took place on the most memorable date of the Middle Ages: October 14, 1066. The Battle of Hastings came about because England's celibate King Edward the Confessor had died without an heir, and three nobles claimed the throne.

An Anglo-Saxon noble named Harold Godwinson, Earl of Wessex, claimed that Edward gave him the throne on his deathbed. He was named king by the traditional council, but support for Harold was weak. A Viking king from Norway, Harald Hardrada, had a claim to the throne through his bloodline. And across the English Channel, French-born William, Duke of Normandy, claimed that Edward had per-

sonally selected *him* as his successor. As the descendant of Vikings who'd once settled in England, William also claimed to be of royal blood. (His enemies called him William the Bastard—his mother was the former Duke of Normandy's mistress.)

With the pope's blessing, William patiently gathered and trained a large Norman army. Meanwhile, Harold and the English army confronted Hardrada in the north of England. Harold's victory was decisive, but immediately he got word that William had sailed across the Channel and landed in the south. Harold and his army raced five days to meet William. Near the town of Hastings, Harold assembled his exhausted troops into a wall atop the highest hill (Senlac Hill).

Early in the morning on October 14, the Norman soldiers trudged up the hill. First, their archers rained arrows on the

road, it's well-signed from the busy A-259, whether you're coming from the east (Dover), the north (London), or the west (Brighton). There's a parking lot to the right of the abbey complex entrance (£4.50—purchase a token at the ticket desk inside, which you'll use to exit the parking lot). Battle can be reached by **train** from London's Charing Cross Station (hourly, 1.5 hours) or Cannon Street Station (2/hour, 1.5 hours), Hastings (2/hour, 15 minutes), or Dover (2/hour, 2 hours, 1-2 transfers). Follow signs from the train station to the abbey (about a 15-minute walk).

Cost and Hours: £12.30, includes essential audioguide; daily 10:00-18:00, Oct until 17:00, shorter hours in winter and closed certain days (check the website).

English. Next, foot soldiers on both sides fought hand-to-hand. The Normans' first attack was successfully deterred; at one point, William flipped up his helmet's visor to show his troops that he was still alive and fighting.

Then the tide turned. William's army began to retreat (a tactical maneuver, say the French). Seeing them flee, the English charged ahead, pursuing them down the hill. Suddenly, the Normans turned and attacked. Riding on horseback, the Norman soldiers utilized their stirrups as footholds to put force behind their lances.

The two sides fought a fierce 14-hour battle, with heavy casualties (7,000 dead in one day). In the battle's finale, Harold was killed (supposedly by an arrow through the eye). William—now "the Conqueror"—marched on to London, where he was crowned King of England in Westminster Abbey on Christmas Day, 1066. William commemorated the dead by building an abbey on the spot of the battle.

It's interesting to note that William's army of only 15,000 men proceeded to conquer a land of 1.5 million. The Norman conquest of England propelled the cultured yet isolated isle of Britain into the European mainstream of feudalism. William centralized the government and imported the Romanesque style of architecture—seen at places such as the White Tower at the Tower of London, and Durham Cathedral. The English call this style "Norman."

Historians speculate that, were it not for their secret weapon—the stirrup—England would have remained on the fringe of Europe (like Scandinavia), French culture and language would have prevailed in the New World...and you'd be reading this book today in French. *Sacré bleu!* William's conquest also muddied the political waters, setting in motion 400 years of conflict between England and France that would not be resolved until the end of the Hundred Years' War, in 1453.

Information: Tel. 01424/776-787, www.english-heritage.org.uk/battleabbey.

Eating: The abbey's visitor center has a **$** café serving light meals. And the main street of the town of Battle, right in front of the abbey complex, is lined with other eating options.

Visiting the Abbey and Battlefield: "Battle Abbey" is a sprawling complex that includes some buildings from the abbey monastic complex, the remains of others, a modern visitors center, and what's believed to be the actual battlefield site.

Enter and buy your ticket inside the towering gatehouse of the abbey complex, peering down the main street of Battle. Be sure to pick up the audioguide. Upstairs in the gatehouse is a (skippable) museum with a few items from the monks' era.

The audioguide leads you through the three main parts of the exhibit: the visitors center (with an informative movie); a walk through the battlefield itself; and a tour of the various buildings of the partly ruined abbey complex.

The **visitors center** has a café upstairs, while downstairs are modern, engaging exhibits that set the stage for the battle. The 15-minute film recounts with great drama the story of the battle, with animated scenes from the famous Bayeux Tapestry and live-action reenactments. You'll also see replicas of weapons used by the fighters that you can brandish—heavy metal.

Just beyond the visitors center is the **battlefield** site. Here you have two choices with your audioguide: Follow the short tour along a terrace overlooking the battlefield (about 20 minutes) or take the longer version out through the woods and across the fateful field (about 40 minutes, and well worth the extra time if the weather is decent). With sound effects and an engaging commentary that explains both the English and the Norman perspective, the audioguide really injects some life into the site. A few wood-carved figures help stoke your imagination as you walk through the big, empty field.

Regardless of which version of the audioguide tour you follow, you'll wind up at the remains of the **abbey.** Built by the victorious

William as an act of penance for the gruesome battle he helped cause, this grew into a sprawling Benedictine monastic complex. Today, some of its many buildings are entirely gone, others are ruined but still standing, and others are intact and being used by a local school (and therefore off-limits to visitors). Use the audioguide to chart your own path through the abbey, including some evocative pillared halls and a former dormitory that's now open to the sky. In the flat area near the top of the complex, find the big, flat stone in the middle of the church-shaped field of pebbles (marking the location of the long-gone Romanesque—or "Norman"—church). This is the Harold Stone, supposedly the place where an arrow pierced the eye of the English king—marking the site of the church's main altar.

Pevensey Castle

This massive, brooding fortress—in the one-street town of Pevensey—was used in Roman, Anglo-Saxon, medieval, and modern times. (Pevensey is part of the area dubbed "1066 Country," with ties to the Battle of Hastings.)

Pevensey Castle began as a Roman coastal fortification around AD 290. William the Conqueror made landfall very near here (at Norman's Bay) on September 28, 1066—just two-and-a-half weeks before the great battle. William and the Normans further fortified the castle, which is also now surrounded by an outer ring from the Middle Ages. The moat around the inner castle was probably flushed by the incoming tidewater (although the present coastline is now farther south). To enter the evocative, half-melted-sugar-cube ruins of the castle, you'll have to buy a ticket, but there's not much to see inside—just a small exhibition about its history, including the French Canadian and American troops who were stationed here in World War II. I'd skip the entry fee and just wander the scenic and grassy field around it. You can also step into the entrance terrace to get a sense of the interior.

Cost and Hours: Castle entry-£6.80, includes 45-minute audioguide; daily 10:00-18:00, shorter hours and closed Mon-Fri in winter; tel. 01323/762-604, www.english-heritage.org.uk/pevensey.

Getting There: Pevensey is less than a half-hour drive west of Battle, on the way to Brighton (where the A-259 coastal route and the faster A-27 inland route intersect). Drivers can park in the pay and display Castle Market Car Park tucked around behind the castle complex, just off the main road (with a pub and tearoom nearby).

DOVER & SE ENGLAND

BRIGHTON

Brighton—brash and flamboyant, with a carnival flair—is refreshing if you're suffering from an excess of doilies and museums. The city boasts a garish 19th-century Royal Pavilion, a loud and flashy pleasure pier, a proud heritage as England's most thriving gay community, and a long stretch of pebbly beach. It's no wonder that youthful bohemians and blue-collar Londoners alike make this town their holiday destination of choice.

In the 1790s, with Napoleon's armies running rampant on the Continent, aristocrats could no longer travel abroad on a traditional "Grand Tour" of Europe. King George IV chose the village of Brighthelmstone to build a vacation palace for himself, and royal followers began a frenzy of construction on the seashore. Soon this once-sleepy seaside village was transformed into an elegant resort town. With the rise of train travel, connections to London became quick and cheap, making Brighton an inviting getaway for working-class Londoners.

And just down the coast from Brighton—an easy add-on for drivers—are the finest white cliffs in England, at Beachy Head and the Seven Sisters.

PLANNING YOUR TIME

Brighton's main experiences—its Royal Pavilion, beach, pleasure pier, and strollable, colorful streets—can be done in just a few hours, making this an easy day trip from London (just one hour by train). If you've got a full day and a car, spend the rest of your day at Beachy Head and the Seven Sisters cliffs.

Debating between Brighton and Portsmouth? Travelers interested in arts, shopping, and restaurants are more likely to be turned on by lively Brighton, while those interested in maritime and WWII history might prefer traditional Portsmouth (see next chapter). Either destination works as a good day trip from London, but with more time, visiting both is a great plan—they complement each other well.

Orientation to Brighton

The city of "Brighton and Hove" is big, with over 270,000 people, about 35,000 of whom are students. It feels surprisingly urban for a seaside resort—like the Nice of England. Most tourists focus on the area near the waterfront. The heart of the tourist's Brighton is the Brighton Pier and, several blocks inland, the Royal Pavilion. Between these two landmarks is the twisty old center of town called The Lanes, jammed with restaurants and shops. North of The Lanes and past the Royal Pavilion is the popular bohemian neighborhood of North Laine, with funky shopping streets, grungy eateries, and street performers. The handiest B&B zone begins a 10-minute walk east of The Lanes, within a block of the seafront, in the colorful neighborhood called Kemptown.

TOURIST INFORMATION

Brighton has no brick-and-mortar TI, but volunteer-staffed points around town dispense maps and brochures. You'll find one on the pier (look for the kiosk on the left, just before the first big arcade hall) and one inside the Brighton Centre conference facility (on Kings Road). Other designated information points are at the gift shop at the Royal Pavilion and the ticket desk at the Toy and Model Museum (near the train station).

Otherwise, check www.visitbrighton.com, download the free Brighton Official Visitor City Guide app, or call or email the mildly helpful Visitor Information Contact Centre (daily 11:00-15:00 except closed Sun in Oct-March, tel. 01273/290-337, visitor.info@visitbrighton.com).

ARRIVAL IN BRIGHTON

Trains arrive at Brighton Station, a 15-minute walk from the city center. Exiting the station, you'll see bus stops in the little cul-de-sac straight ahead, at the top of Queens Road. If you're staying at one of my recommended B&Bs in Kemptown, hop on **bus #7** or **#27** (every 10-20 minutes, 10-minute ride; get off at either St. James's Street or Devonshire Place, depending on where you're staying—see the Brighton map in this chapter).

Drivers on the A-23 enter town on London Road, which becomes the heavily congested, tree-lined Grand Parade going straight to the water (ending near Brighton Pier). Parking is tricky

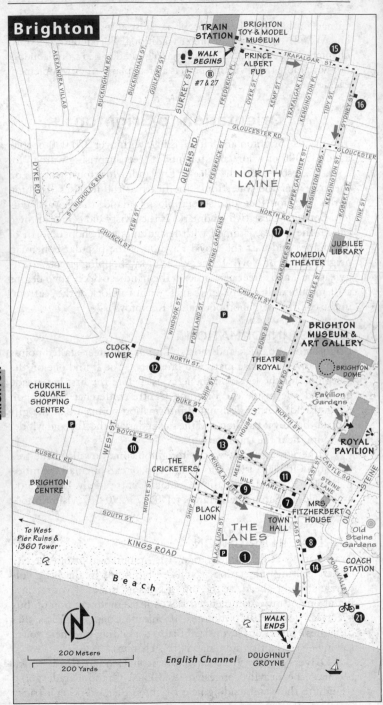

Brighton

BRIGHTON

- TRAIN STATION
- BRIGHTON TOY & MODEL MUSEUM
- WALK BEGINS
- PRINCE ALBERT PUB
- B #7 & 27
- ALEXANDRA VILLAS
- BUCKINGHAM ST.
- GUILFORD ST.
- SURREY ST.
- FREDERICK PL.
- OVER ST.
- KEMP ST.
- TRAFALGAR LN.
- TRAFALGAR ST.
- KENSINGTON PL.
- TIDY ST.
- SYDNEY ST.
- 15
- 16
- BUCKINGHAM RD.
- GLOUCESTER RD.
- DYKE RD.
- ST. NICHOLAS RD.
- KEW ST.
- QUEENS RD.
- FREDERICK ST.
- NORTH LAINE
- UPPER GARDNER ST.
- KENSINGTON GDNS.
- KENSINGTON ST.
- ROBERT ST.
- VINE ST.
- GLOUCESTER
- CHURCH ST.
- P
- SPRING GARDENS
- NORTH RD.
- GARDNER ST.
- JUBILEE LIBRARY
- 17
- KOMEDIA THEATER
- JUBILEE ST.
- WINDSOR ST.
- PORTLAND ST.
- P
- CHURCH ST.
- BOND ST.
- BRIGHTON MUSEUM & ART GALLERY
- CLOCK TOWER
- NORTH ST.
- 12
- SHIP ST.
- THEATRE ROYAL
- NEW RD.
- BRIGHTON DOME
- CHURCHILL SQUARE SHOPPING CENTER
- P
- WEST ST.
- BOYCE'S ST.
- DUKE ST.
- 14
- 13
- MEETING HOUSE LN.
- NORTH ST.
- Pavilion Gardens
- 10
- THE CRICKETERS
- PRINCE ALBERT ST.
- NILE ST.
- 9
- 11
- MARKET
- EAST ST.
- CASTLE SQ.
- STEINE LANE
- ROYAL PAVILION
- RUSSELL RD.
- MIDDLE ST.
- 7
- MRS. FITZHERBERT HOUSE
- OLD STEINE
- BRIGHTON CENTRE
- SOUTH ST.
- BLACK LION ST.
- SHIP ST.
- BLACK LION
- TOWN HALL
- 1
- THE LANES
- 8
- Old Steine Gardens
- To West Pier Ruins & i360 Tower
- KINGS ROAD
- P
- POOL VALLEY
- 14
- COACH STATION
- 21
- Beach
- WALK ENDS
- N
- 200 Meters
- 200 Yards
- English Channel
- DOUGHNUT GROYNE

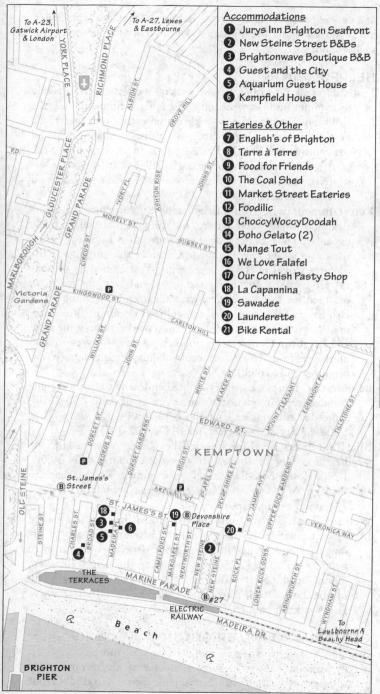

Accommodations
1. Jurys Inn Brighton Seafront
2. New Steine Street B&Bs
3. Brightonwave Boutique B&B
4. Guest and the City
5. Aquarium Guest House
6. Kempfield House

Eateries & Other
7. English's of Brighton
8. Terre à Terre
9. Food for Friends
10. The Coal Shed
11. Market Street Eateries
12. Foodilic
13. ChoccyWoccyDoodah
14. Boho Gelato (2)
15. Mange Tout
16. We Love Falafel
17. Our Cornish Pasty Shop
18. La Capannina
19. Sawadee
20. Launderette
21. Bike Rental

and very expensive: Signs lead to parking garages near the center, but if you're staying the night, ask your hotelier for the best place to leave your car.

HELPFUL HINTS

Festivals (and Crowds): Brighton can overflow with visitors in summer and on weekends. The busiest times include the Brighton Festival (May, www.brightonfestival.org; the Fringe Festival runs at the same time—www.brightonfringe.org) and the Summer LGBTQ+ Pride Festival (first or second week of Aug, www.brighton-pride.org). Off-season (roughly Oct-March), visitors may find more students, prices slashed, and attractions shuttered.

Entertainment in Brighton: Brighton hosts many concerts, theatrical performances, and more, and can be a more relaxed, less expensive place to get a dose of culture than London. Check what's on while you're in town. Consider the offerings at the **Theatre Royal** (a classic venue with West End-style theatrical productions, including the occasional test run for plays destined for London stages, www.theatreroyalbrighton.com); **Brighton Dome** (concerts and cultural events in three venues right next to the Royal Pavilion, www.brightondome.org); and **Brighton Centre,** a big, modern venue at the western end of the seafront (big-name contemporary music acts, www.brightoncentre.co.uk).

Laundry: St. James's Laundry is in Kemptown, near my recommended accommodations (self-service open daily 7:30-21:00, same-day full-service Tue-Thu 8:30-16:00—last drop-off at 14:00, 53 St. James's Street, tel. 01273/672-395).

Bike Rental: Try **Brighton Beach Bikes,** on the water next to the Brighton Pier (£6/hour, £16/4 or more hours, daily 10:00-17:00, closed Nov-Easter and when raining, on the beach to the right of the pier as you face the water, mobile 07917-753-794, www.brightonsports.co.uk).

Walking Tour: Julian from **The Brighton Story** offers casual yet informative 1.5-hour walks by request (contact to arrange or join a scheduled tour, price depends on number of people, tel. 07941/256-148, www.brightoncitywalks.com, julian@brightoncitywalks.com). There's also a **Ghost Walk of the Lanes** (£8, Wed-Sat at 19:30, 70 minutes, www.ghostwalkbrighton.co.uk).

GETTING AROUND BRIGHTON

Brighton is easy to cover by foot, but its well-run bus system is handy, especially if you're staying in one of my recommended guesthouses on Kemptown's New Steine Street (around £2/ride depending on how far you're going—ask driver, £5 CitySaver day pass, buy from driver, tel. 01273/886-200, www.buses.co.uk).

Brighton City Walk

This walk introduces you to Brighton's various personalities in about an hour and a half (without entering any sights). We'll cover Brighton's three distinct parts: contemporary Brighton; royal landmarks and the historic fishermen's quarter; and the fun-loving seafront. The walk begins at the train station.

Contemporary Brighton

The first part of our Brighton walk takes you along streets filled with interesting shops, fun pubs, and good coffee shops. This area is lively during the day, but sleepy after the shops close (around 18:00).

• *To reach the start of the walk, exit the train station, turn right, and walk out to the road. Do a sharp U-turn to the left, taking the steep, downhill street beneath the train station.*

Trafalgar Street: This road used to run past the main entrance of the train station. But when the tight curves required to reach the platforms became too challenging, Queens Road was built over your head. The brick structure on your left became warehouse space for the Bass brewery (founded in 1777). At the top of one of the arches is their red triangle logo—designed to be recognized even by illiterate drinkers.

Near the end of the underpass, on the left, is the **Toy and Model Museum**—a lovingly presented collection of historical toys from before the days of plastic (see listing later, under "Sights in Brighton").

Kitty-corner from the museum, you can't miss the vibrantly colorful **Prince Albert pub.** When a major music star dies, a graffiti portrait of them is added to the huge mural along its right side. Stroll along here for a closer look. The painting of the two "bobbies" (policemen) kissing (at street level, under glass) is a well-known piece by the famous street artist Banksy. (This is a Banksy-endorsed replica; the pub sold the original to an art collector.)

Now head downhill on Trafalgar Street past neighborhood stores, colorful street art, and several top-end, third wave coffee shops. After a few short blocks, look for Trafalgar Lane on the right—a skinny alley slathered with more murals.

• *A few short blocks beyond Trafalgar Lane, turn right down...*

Sydney Street: From this upper part of town, more shop-lined streets stairstep their way downhill to the seafront through an area called North Laine, with its "Soho by the Sea" vibe.

Browse down Sydney Street, passing boutiques, design shops,

more coffee shops (the Aussie-owned Pelicano is good), street eats (including the recommended We Love Falafel—good for lunch on the go), vintage stores, comics shops, bonsai tree vendors, and other all-around curiosities (need any crystals?). This street seems to specialize in clever names, like Posh Totty, Punker Bunker, and a pub called The Office.

• *At the bottom of Sydney Street, jog right one block, then left down the narrow, traffic-free...*

Kensington Gardens: This street is an artery of mostly local, one-off boutiques. The Resident Music record store, on your left, features live performances by up-and-coming bands. Neal's Yard Remedies at the bottom of the street represents a rare chain store along here. On Saturdays, Upper Gardner Street—one block over—hosts a thriving outdoor market.

• *At the bottom of Kensington Gardens, turn right for a few steps, then head left at the wider...*

Gardner Street: The quirky action continues along here (you'll pass the recommended Our Cornish Pasty Shop on the right). The landmark Komedia Brighton theater, on the left, is a popular venue for comedy acts and movie screenings.

• *At the bottom of Gardner Street, at busy Church Street, turn left for one block. Then turn right down the broad pedestrian New Road. You'll pass the yellow Neoclassical colonnade of the local Unitarian church on your right, followed by the painted-red-brick* **Theatre Royal** *(a popular venue for West End-type productions). Across the street from the theater is the entrance to the Pavilion Gardens and a taste of...*

Historic Brighton

• *Step into the Pavilion Gardens—the park surrounding the fanciful royal buildings of King George IV. Stand in the middle of the park—between the little café kiosk at the top of the garden, and the big Indian-style palace at the bottom.*

Pavilion Gardens: King George IV (r. 1820-1830) put Brighton on the map when he decided to build a vacation home here. Drawn by the healthy sea air, which he hoped would alleviate some of his health problems, he built the elaborate **Royal Pavilion** in a fanciful style that evoked Indian royal architecture. While George IV originally planned the palace as a holiday residence, it was used mainly as a party pad to entertain guests. The interior is well worth visiting (and described under "Sights in Brighton," later).

The building on your left (as you face the pavilion) was originally the royal stables. Today it holds the **Brighton Museum and Art Gallery,** a modest but eclectic collection that's worth a peek (described later, under "Sights in Brighton"). Part of that building contains **The Dome,** which hosts performances. The Concert Hall—its largest venue—was built to hold about 40 of the king's horses. Today it seats 1,700 in its Art Deco interior. It was in this hall that ABBA performed "Waterloo" at the 1974 Eurovision Song Contest. (They won the grand prize, vaulting them overnight to superstardom.)

Explore the **gardens,** where commoners enjoy lounging on the generous lawn, and where some of Brighton's top-notch street musicians often perform. For the best, unobstructed views of the king's creation, circle around to the back of the pavilion,

• *To continue our walk, make your way toward the pavilion's entrance, under the canopy. Turn right, walk around the Indian-style gateway, and you'll run into busy North Street—defining the northern edge of the historical center of town. Cross North Street and turn left along it, following it (as the street becomes Castle Square) toward the big parklike area. Bend right with the street, and pause at the bus stops around the corner. Face the park with the big fountain.*

Old Steine: While today it's just a grubby urban square, the Old Steine area has some interesting history. The name (pronounced "steen," or occasionally "stine") comes from old stones that were excavated here, and were likely used for prehistoric Druid ceremonies (Steine is related to the German word *Stein,* for "stone"). Back when Brighton was a humble fishing town in the 1500s, fishermen would fix their boats and mend their nets here, spreading them out on rocks in the sun to dry. When George IV first built his pavilion, this area was largely undeveloped, giving him access through parklike grounds to the seafront. But soon enough, other aristocrats sought their own royal vacations. With the construction of the train station in the 1840s, visitors flowed into town from London. The tall, skinny houses across the square popped up around this time. A few decades later, the row of grand hotels on your right was built.

With your back to the fountain, notice the grayish building with the *YMCA* at the top. To the right of its door (you may have to walk closer to see it) is a plaque identifying this as the home of one **Mrs. Fitzherbert,** the ill-fated lover of George IV (she lived here from 1801 to

1837). Because she was Catholic, and he was obligated to marry a fellow Protestant, they could not officially be together. (They married in secret, but the union was eventually annulled; George was forced to sham-marry his cousin instead.) Even so, her residence here—a stone's throw from the pavilion—suggests that they likely spent much time together.

• *Take the narrow lane on the right side of Mrs. Fitzherbert's house, called Little Steine Lane. You'll pop out at East Street—marking the eastern boundary of the original settlement here. Turn left for a few steps, then veer right through the little square with restaurant tables. Take the narrow lane between the recommended English's restaurant and the Sussex Arms pub. You're entering...*

The Lanes: This is Brighton's historic core, with an incredibly twisty street plan. Centuries ago, this was a motley collection of fishermen's cottages and their garden patches, woven together with meandering footpaths. While virtually none of those original buildings survive—most of them replaced as Brighton flourished in the 1800s—the street plan remains a spaghetti of narrow lanes.

Continuing on, you'll pop out at an area called Market Street, with a variety of eateries (see "Eating in Brighton," later). Keep going through this area, bearing right at the Pump House, then following the first tight lane on your left, Meeting House Lane. Soon you'll be surrounded by Brighton's famous **jewelry stores.** Eavesdrop on young couples window-shopping for an engagement ring.

Follow Meeting House Lane—under a comical number of jewelry store signs—until it dead-ends. Turn right, then immediately turn left (at The Lanes Armoury No. 26). On your left, ogle the over-the-top chocolate creations in the window of Brighton's famous **ChoccyWoccyDoodah** shop—a local landmark and Instagram mainstay (see "Eating in Brighton," later).

After the chocolate shop, bend right with the street, then take the next left on Union Street. When the lane opens out into the wider Ship Street, turn left and head a couple of blocks down Ship Street toward the water. Keep a close eye out, on the left, for **Black Lion Lane,** immediately before Ship Street Surgery. This is one of Brighton's super-narrow lanes, called "twittens" (from the Saxon word "twixt," meaning "between"). As you squeeze down the lane, notice (halfway down, on the right) three black-and-white houses. These are believed to be some of the oldest homes in Brighton (from the mid-1500s)—now rentable on Airbnb.

Continue all the way down the twitten, popping out 'twixt two pubs. Turn around to look at them: While **The Black Lion** on the left looks old, it's actually faux-historic, dating from 1974. The side of the building is distinct of Brighton, with cobbles from the seafront embedded in the outer walls. On the right, **The Cricketers** truly is historic, from 1547. The "Greene Room" upstairs is where the author Graham Greene supposedly stayed while writing his 1938 novel *Brighton Rock*. One of the main people suspected to be Jack the Ripper also rented a room here in 1888.

With that cheery thought, turn away from the pubs and head straight, then bear right down Price Albert Street. Partway down, on the right, are the cream-colored pillars of Brighton's **Town Hall**—which should technically be a *City* Hall. Even though Brighton lacks a cathedral (a key requirement for being a "city"), Queen Elizabeth II granted the adjoining communities of Brighton and Howe (collectively) with city status in 2000. Famously progressive Brighton is the only city in the UK governed by the Green Party—making it particularly environmentally friendly. If you arrived by car and found it difficult to drive and park here... that was the idea.

• *Carry on along Price Albert Street, passing Little East Street (with historic houses). Soon after, turn right down East Street and head to the water.*

Before crossing the busy seafront road, pause on the corner and look straight ahead at the monument (just to the right of the yellow-and-green pavilion). Titled **Kiss Wall**, it depicts various types of relationships: straight, gay, lesbian, and so on. It's a celebration of Brighton's famously LGBTQ-friendly culture and comes with an interesting optical illusion. Because the images are created by letting light through the back side, it becomes harder to see—and eventually invisible—as you get closer to the wall.

• *Cross the street, head behind the* Kiss Wall, *and continue straight down the stairs onto the small concrete pier.*

The Seafront

You're standing on "Doughnut Groyne" ("groyne" is the term for little concrete piers that delineate stretches of beach and break waves). This giant doughnut sculpture supposedly represents the universe, but it's never been a favorite of local residents. From this spot, do a quick spin and take in the scene—the pebbly beach, the pleasure pier, the weird silver tower, and the row of grand hotels facing the busy waterfront highway and promenade.

Seafront History: Brighton began as a humble fishing community (there's a small fishing museum to the right, below the promenade, with a collection of old boats out front). Back then, rather than the road and promenade, a cliff separated Brighton from its waterfront.

Facing the town, look a bit to the right, and try to pick out the words *Royal Albion* on a hotel between here and the pier. This was once the location of Dr. Richard Russell's surgery practice. Dr. Russell (1687-1759) was convinced that coming to Brighton and sipping the seawater was an ideal treatment for glandular ailments. His patients would stay here, then walk across the cliffs to hike down to the seafront for a drink. It was this perception of Brighton as a health resort that first drew George IV here for treatment.

The holidaygoers soon followed, but many Victorian London urbanites didn't know how to swim, and they were very modest about being seen in their bathing clothes. The solution was wooden cabins on wheels (called "bathing machines"), where they could change in privacy before being wheeled out to the water. When it was time to bathe, they were escorted by a burly local who would hold onto them, sometimes even dipping them into the sea. These helpers were called "dippers" (or, for men, "bathers"). Martha Gunn looms large in local lore as the "Queen of the Dippers."

Today's Seafront: While the days of chugging seawater and being dipped are long gone, Brighton remains a thriving holiday destination—mostly among working-class Londoners, but increasingly attractive to international travelers. Take in the Brighton of today.

To your right is the **Brighton Pier**—a pleasure pier lined with junk food, arcade games, carnival rides, and Brits on holiday (described later, under "Sights in Brighton").

Stretching in both directions is Brighton's **beach.** It's not quite Hawaii, but it's still enjoyable to walk along the large, flattened cobbles, called "shingles," and get your feet wet. Slingback chairs are available for rent, and the promenade along the beach is a lively place to stroll, or to linger for a drink or snack.

Facing town and looking left, you'll see two landmarks. First, out at sea, notice the skeleton of what was once the **West Pier**—a bookend to the surviving pleasure pier. It fell into disrepair, was damaged by a storm in the 1980s, and burned under uncertain

circumstances in the early
2000s.

Just beyond that, the
towering silver needle
is the i360 Tower. This
observation tower lifts
tourists up 450 feet in a
doughnut-like elevator
for a bird's-eye view over
Brighton. Designed by the
architects of the London Eye, the complex has struggled finan-
cially and isn't particularly beloved by locals (as it doesn't blend
well with the otherwise Regency-style historical architecture).
Ascending the tower is pricey and only worth considering on ex-
ceptionally clear days (£16.50, ride lasts about 20 minutes, www.
britishairwaysi360.com).

Just inland from the tower is **Brighton Centre,** a large concert
venue and convention center. In addition to being the venue where
Bing Crosby and The Jam both played their final performances
(not together), it also hosts political conventions—just another reminder that Brighton is a vital contemporary British city...not just
a seaside resort town.

Sights in Brighton

▲▲Brighton Royal Pavilion

Famous for his scandalous secret marriage to Catholic widow
Mrs. Fitzherbert, King George IV (r. 1820-1830) was lively, decadent, and trendsetting.

He loved to vacation by
the sea and host glamor-
ous dinner parties at this
palace. George was enam-
ored with Asian cultures
and styled his vacation
home with exotic decora-
tions from the East. The
exterior is Indian-style,
and the interior decor is predominantly Chinese-style. Some regard the palace itself as a work of art, adorned with gilded dragons
and carved palm trees. The result is colorful and exuberant...some
would say gaudy. Like Brighton itself, the place smacks of faded
elegance—but it's still fun to tour.

Cost and Hours: £15; daily 9:30-17:45, Oct-March 10:00-
17:15, last entry 45 minutes before closing; £2 audioguide, head

up East Street from The Lanes, bus stop on Old Steine Road, tel. 03000-290-902, www.brightonmuseums.org.uk.

Gardens: It's free to enter the restored Regency gardens surrounding the pavilion; the best viewpoint to take in the entire building is around back.

Visiting the Palace: Your palace visit follows a one-way route and hits the following highlights. Invest in the audioguide, as there's very little posted information (though docents are standing by to answer questions).

Entering the palace, King George IV's guests would be suitably greeted by the grand, pink-and-purple **long gallery.** Here and throughout the pavilion, examine the fine detail work—such as the "bamboo" stairway decoration that's actually carved from wood.

If guests were impressed by the long gallery, they were blown away by the **banqueting room.** Take a moment to appreciate the Chinese-inspired decor. Known as *chinoiserie,* this European interpretation of Chinese culture (often exaggerated and distorted as if in a funhouse mirror) was the height of fashion in those days. Imagine England's elite nibbling crumpets under the one-ton chandelier...with its dragons exhaling light through lotus-shaped shades. The ornate table is permanently set for the dessert course.

The elaborate **kitchen** was one of the most innovative of its time. Smoke from the fireplace rotated a huge rotisserie that could cook enough meat to feed a hundred hungry diners. The king was so particular about his food that he insisted his kitchen be attached to the dining room (unheard-of at the time). He also had a warming table built to keep food at the optimum temperature. Peruse the sample menu at the end of the kitchen, which represents an astonishing flaunting of culinary opulence. More than 100 courses were served to visiting aristocrats to symbolize British supremacy in Europe (George served as regent for his "mad king" father—George III—and regarded Napoleon's defeat at Waterloo as a personal triumph).

Head through the banqueting room gallery and two saloons into a room dedicated to George's true passion: music. In the massive **music room,** which goes toe-to-toe with the banqueting room, the royal band serenaded guests. The room's gilded, domed ceiling is made up of hundreds of plaster cockleshells, creating an illusion of height.

The **private apartments** were on the ground floor, to more easily accommodate the ailing king (who spent less and less time here near the end of his life). Note that this space is more intimate and cozy than the showpiece halls. (If you're intrigued by all this, dip into the dry but informative nine-minute film about the pavilion's history—which is partly a tour of areas that visitors don't see.) Here and in some other areas of the palace, you'll walk through austere tiled hallways where servants would scurry around, unseen, waiting on the royals.

Continuing upstairs, you're directed through one of many exhibits on the pavilion's ongoing renovation and upkeep regimen. A Chinese-wallpapered hall leads to the **tearoom** (where you can grab a bite on a terrace overlooking the park). Then, backtracking a bit, you'll stroll through the restored **Yellow Bow Rooms,** then **Queen Victoria's apartments,** where you'll learn the epilogue to the story of George's party palace. Queen Victoria first visited the Royal Pavilion in 1837 and felt it was a "strange, odd, Chinese place, both outside and inside." Uncle George was a big spender and had piled up huge debts. No expense was spared. Prudish Queen Victoria, who took the throne seven years after George's death, wanted more privacy than the pavilion provided and scorned the excesses in George's court—so she quickly off-loaded the decadent pavilion to the local town council (which still owns it today). Only recently did Queen Elizabeth II bring the original furniture out of storage and loan it to the pavilion.

Brighton Museum and Art Gallery

This museum—a sort of "every topic under one roof" collection—is worth a quick visit for its eclectic, thoughtfully presented exhibits on two concise floors. The core of the museum, similar to the Victoria and Albert Museum in London, displays decorative arts with a heavy focus on 20th-century art and design.

Cost and Hours: £6; Tue-Sun 10:00-17:00, closed Mon except holidays; just north of the Royal Pavilion, tel. 03000-290-902, www.brightonmuseums.org.uk.

Visiting the Museum: On the ground floor, head straight into the fine collection of furniture and design from the 20th century—including Gehry's *Wiggle* chair and the Dalí-inspired *Mae West Lips Sofa.* You'll go back through time as you approach the end of the hall, where you'll find somewhat out-of-place exhibits on Egyptology and archaeology.

The side wings feature a very good anthropology exhibit—featuring the stories and clothing of world cultures, thoughtfully told through the eyes of personal objects and stories; and "Mr. Willett's Popular Pottery," the museum founder's fun collection of colorful porcelain figurines.

Upstairs are a modest art gallery, an exhibit on town history, theatrical costumes and puppets, fashion, and good temporary exhibitions.

Brighton Pier

Glittering and shiny with amusement rides and carnival games, Brighton Pier is *the* place to go for a fix of "candy floss" (cotton candy), fortune-tellers, slot machines, and tacky souvenirs. The pier, opened in 1899 and long known as Palace Pier, has gone in and out of fashion; in recent years, it's come back to life, thanks to an expensive restoration.

Cost and Hours: Free entry to pier, most rides and arcade open daily 10:00-22:00, closing time depends on crowds and rain, tel. 01273/609-361, www. brightonpier.co.uk.

Visiting the Pier: The first stretch has stands selling candy floss, toffee apples, and slush drinks (plus a volunteer-staffed TI kiosk, on the left). The main pavilion is a 19th-century gem. If you ignore the garish arcade games, you might be able to imagine yourself as a Victorian Londoner out on holiday, seeing brilliant electric lights for the first time. From here, the pier continues, past doughnut, churro, and crêpe vendors, to the Palm Court restaurant, with its Sunset Garden out back.

Finally you'll reach the Funfair at the end, with carnival rides, such as bumper cars, roller coasters, and a haunted house (some rides covered by a wristband, others require separate tickets). Or, to really throw away your money, try your hand at games of skill—kick the football into the net, or knock over the stack of cans—for the chance to win a cheap stuffed animal. Is it tacky? Who cares? Look at how much fun everyone's having.

▲Brighton Toy and Model Museum

This joyful and endearing museum, located below the train station, proudly celebrates the "golden age of toymaking," from the late 1800s until the 1950s. Before the age of plastic and mass production, toys were lovingly hand-crafted and hand-painted. This extensive collection shows off rare or unique model railroads, toy planes and boats, Corgi brand matchbox cars, stuffed animals, miniature stoves and sewing machines that actually worked (to teach little girls housework), and much more. It's nostalgic for folks who recall playing with toys like these, and interesting for anyone.

Cost and Hours: £5.85, kids-£3.60; Tue-Fri 10:00-17:00, Sat from 11:00, closed Sun-Mon; 52 Trafalgar Street, tel. 01273/749-494, www.brightontoymuseum.co.uk.

Sleeping in Brighton

Brighton's bohemian character is fun during the day, but the town can be a little rough-and-tumble at night. In summer, prices jump on weekends, making otherwise good-value places suddenly overpriced. The price ranges noted here are for weekday stays—on summer weekends, they can go up a full price range. Summer also brings noisy partygoers roaming around until dawn—it's worth asking for a quieter room away from the street.

$$$ Jurys Inn Brighton Seafront, the only big hotel of my listings, is a worthwhile splurge for those who might not appreciate the idiosyncrasies of Brighton's B&Bs and guesthouses. It's perfectly located right in the middle of the seafront promenade, with The Lanes and its appealing restaurants right out the back door. With a snazzy atrium lobby, 210 cookie-cutter rooms, and business-class professionalism, it's a restful refuge from colorful and quirky Brighton (air-con, elevator, Kings Road, tel. 0127/320-6700, www.jurysinns.com).

KEMPTOWN B&BS AND GUESTHOUSES

Most of my recommended accommodations are in the eccentric Kemptown neighborhood, about a block from the beach and within a 10-minute walk of Brighton Pier and the Royal Pavilion. These tend to be guesthouses, which offer more rooms, professionalism, and anonymity than a B&B, but more character than a hotel. "Sea views" here are unimpressive and not worth the extra cost. None of these have air-conditioning or elevators. Several (Sea Spray, Marine View, and Strawberry Fields) face Kemptown's New Steine Street—essentially a long square with a park in the middle—which is lined with about a dozen guesthouses. The others are a couple of blocks closer to the center of town and the pier.

$$ Sea Spray has 16 fresh-feeling, stylish rooms and appealing, art-filled public spaces (some rooms with sea views, some with balconies, pricier suites including one with a private hot tub, sauna and massage, 26 New Steine Street, tel. 01273/680-332, www.seaspraybrighton.co.uk, seaspray@brighton.co.uk).

$$ Brightonwave Boutique B&B feels tasteful and grown-up, with eight comfortable rooms that lack the dated or borderline-tacky decor of other places nearby (10 Madeira Place, tel. 01273/676-794, www.brightonwave.com, info@brightonwave.com).

$$ Guest and the City is a stylish yet comfortable seven-room B&B close to the pier; some of the front-facing rooms come with stained-glass windows and historic tiled fireplaces (2 Broad

Street, tel. 01273/698-289, www.guestandthecity.co.uk, info@guestandthecity.co.uk, David and Eric).

$$ Aquarium Guest House rents seven crisp, minimalist rooms with plenty of natural light. Scott and Helen don't offer breakfast but provide fruit and snacks every morning (13 Madeira Place, tel. 01273/605-761, www.aquarium-guesthouse.co.uk, info@aquarium-guesthouse.co.uk).

$$ Kempfield House is tastefully run in a Georgian townhouse. The 13 rooms are elegantly simple and nicely appointed, though it's a lesser value than some (2-night minimum on weekends, 18 Madeira Place, tel. 01273/567-521, www.kempfieldhouse.co.uk, info@kempfieldhouse.co.uk).

$$ Marine View has 22 well-worn rooms (family room, some rooms with sea and pier views, 2-night minimum on weekends, 24 New Steine Street, tel. 01273/603-870, www.mvbrighton.co.uk, info@mvbrighton.co.uk).

$ Strawberry Fields Hotel is simple but efficient, renting 29 rooms with a fun strawberry theme; some rooms have shared bathrooms for lower rates (6 New Steine Street, tel. 01273/681-576, www.strawberry-fields-hotel.com, strawberryfields.brighton@gmail.com, Andrius and Amit). Skip their shabby sister property, Hamptons Hotel.

Eating in Brighton

If you haven't filled up with greasy boardwalk fare, you'll find plenty of good, affordable restaurants around town. Brighton offers an impressive variety of vegetarian restaurants and global cuisine, so it's easy to experiment.

THE LANES

Just up from the seafront, The Lanes is Brighton's historic old town, and has the best concentration of both trendy and traditional restaurants. It's smart to reserve at any of the first four listings, all of which have a loyal following.

$$$$ English's of Brighton, hiding on the side of the little square on East Street, is a venerable local institution that's been serving seafood specialties for more than 150 years to luminaries such as Charlie Chaplin and Laurence Olivier. The crisp, white-tablecloth-classy interior sprawls through several rooms on two floors, and there's seating out on the square (Mon-Fri 12:00-22:00, Sat-Sun from 17:00, 29 East Street, tel. 01273/327-980, www.englishs.co.uk).

$$$ Terre à Terre is a well-known, highly respected vegetarian restaurant. The eclectic menu is fun to peruse, and the food is top notch. While plain from the street, its interior is contemporary and welcoming, and the service is friendly (daily 12:00-22:30, closed Mon in winter, 71 East Street, tel. 01273/729-051).

$$$ Food for Friends is Brighton's other (and original) well-regarded, high-end vegetarian restaurant. Its menu of small and large plates, with an international bent, is designed to share (daily 9:00-22:00, 17 Prince Albert Street, tel. 01273/202-310, www.foodforfriends.com).

$$$$ The Coal Shed is for carnivores who scoff at the previous two listings. This place is all about meat—high-quality steaks, a short list of other (meaty) main courses, and hearty sides in a fun, rustic-chic interior (daily 12:00-16:00 & 18:00-22:00, 8 Boyce's Street, tel. 01273/322-998, www.coalshed-restaurant.co.uk).

On Market Street: This bustling area—more a long, wide square than a "street"—is packed with affordable eateries. Take a spin around to choose your favorite, but check out the following: **$$ Giggling Squid** serves up tasty Thai small plates in a simple, two-story interior (daily 12:00-22:00, at #11, tel. 01273/737-373). Next door, **$ Brighton Burger** is a cute little quasi-diner slinging good burgers. As there's no interior seating, you'll have to grab a table on the square (cash only, Mon-Sat 12:00-18:00, Sun until 16:00, at #11a, tel. 01273/205-979).

On North Street: Between the Lanes and North Laine is **$ Foodilic,** a buffet-style salad bar with healthy main courses and vegetarian options. It's a small and simple place wedged in bustling North Street; at lunch there's usually a line of hungry locals out the door (also serves breakfast; Mon-Sat 9:00-20:30, Sun until 18:00; 60 North Street, tel. 01273/774-138).

And for Dessert: ChoccyWoccyDoodah is as fun as its name, overwhelming the senses with extravagant chocolate sculptures and colorful candies. The charming café upstairs serves home-made cakes, specialty hot chocolates, and other decadent desserts (Mon-Sat 10:00-18:00, Sun from 11:00, 3 Meeting House Lane, tel. 01273/329-462). **Sugardough,** on Market Street, is a trendy place to pick up pastries, pies, and breads for a seafront picnic (daily 8:00-18:30, at #18, tel. 01273/739-973). **Boho Gelato** serves excellent homemade gelato at two locations in this area (6 Pool Valley and 31 Ship Street).

NORTH LAINE

Just north of The Lanes and the Royal Pavilion, this is Brighton's trendiest quarter—with creative new restaurants and fun, quirky shops popping up all the time. While this is a fast-changing scene, here are a few reliable options.

$$ Mange Tout ("Eat Everything") is a classic hipster café up on Trafalgar Street, near the train station. The delectable menu features French dishes, plus great coffee and good wines—all in a casual brasserie atmosphere with indoor and outdoor seating (Sun-Tue 9:00-17:00—kitchen until 15:00, Thu-Sat 9:00-15:00 & 18:00-22:00, 81 Trafalgar Street, tel. 01273/607-270, www.mangetoutbrighton.co.uk).

$ We Love Falafel is ideal for a healthy, memorable lunch right in the heart of colorful Sydney Street. In addition to traditional falafel, they have several other veggie fritter options. Seating is limited and it's often crowded, but the line moves fast and it's well worth the wait (Mon-Sat 11:00-18:00, closed Sun, 37 Sydney Street, tel. 01273/604-206).

$ Our Cornish Pasty Shop offers excellent versions of its namesake, including vegetarian and curry varieties. There are also delicious homemade desserts with gluten-free and vegan options. After 17:30, all pasties are sold two-for-one (daily 9:30-18:30, 24 Gardner Street, tel. 01273/688-063).

KEMPTOWN

To dine closer to home, simply wander the lively streets of Kemptown. St. James's Street, running parallel to the seafront a block inland, is lined with all types of cuisine: cheap burgers, fish-and-chips, Thai, Mediterranean, pub grub, and more. Ask your B&B host what's hot right now.

For Italian, try **$$ La Capannina,** a cozy restaurant with a run-by-an-Italian-family feel. If the woody main floor looks full, ask about additional seating downstairs (daily 12:00-14:30 & 18:00-23:00, just off St. James's Street at 15 Madeira Place, tel. 01273/680-839).

$$ Sawadee is a simple and welcoming family-run place serving Thai dishes on the main drag of Kemptown (daily 12:00-15:00 & 17:00-23:00, 87 St. James's Street, tel. 01273/624-233).

Brighton Connections

Brighton is well-connected to London and most coastal towns.

From Brighton by Train to: Gatwick Airport (6/hour, 30 minutes), **London**'s Victoria Station (2/hour direct, 1 hour; also to Blackfriars Station, 2/hour direct, 1.5 hours), **Portsmouth** (hourly direct, 1.5 hours, more with transfer), **Hastings** (2/hour direct, 1.5 hours), **Dover** (at least hourly, 2.5 hours, 1-3 transfers), **Canterbury** (hourly, 2.5 hours, 1-3 transfers). **Train info:** Tel. 0345-748-4950, www.nationalrail.co.uk.

By Bus: National Express (tel. 0871-781-8181, www.nationalexpress.com) runs buses to **Gatwick Airport** (at least hourly, 1 hour—train is better), **Heathrow Airport** (every two hours, 2.5 hours, more with transfer), **London**'s Victoria Coach Station (hourly, 2.5 hours), and **Portsmouth** (1/day direct, 2 hours).

Stagecoach buses (www.stagecoachbus.com) go to **Arundel** (hourly, fewer on Sun, 2.5 hours; see page 334).

South Downs Way and White Cliffs

Stretching east of Brighton is a coastline fringed with broad, rolling green downs, or hills—an area known as the South Downs Way. These hills are an excellent place to practice a favorite sport of the English: walking. Paths, well-tended by local walking clubs, weave through much of the English countryside, attracting weekend and holiday strollers, and anyone looking for fresh air and exercise. The highlights here are the dramatic chalk cliffs of the Seven Sisters and Beachy Head.

Planning Your Time: These sights make a good half-day side trip from Brighton, or you can visit them en route between Dover/Canterbury and Brighton (perhaps combined with Pevensey Castle and/or Battle Abbey, described in the previous chapter). The Beachy Head and Seven Sisters area can be enjoyed in about an hour—or longer if you take a hike.

BEACHY HEAD AND THE SEVEN SISTERS

Beachy Head and the Seven Sisters, worth ▲▲, is England's best "white cliff experience" and a highlight of any tour of England's south coast. A vast grassy field, wild yet pure as a putting green, reaches up to a dramatic, white-chalk cliff that stretches for miles with the open sea beyond and the crashing surf 500 feet below. Along the horizon stretches a line of seven lower, undulating cliffs.

While Beachy Head is the biggest of the cliffs, its neighbors are a bit more famous. Long ago, they were dubbed "The Seven Sisters" by groggy sailors who gazed lustily through the mist from their ships and imagined a can-can of seven maidens lifting their petticoats. While the chalk may look like lace, it's actually the shelly

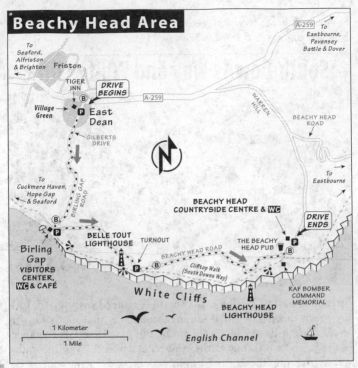

Beachy Head Area

To Seaford, Alfriston & Brighton

Friston

TIGER INN

DRIVE BEGINS

A-259

Village Green

East Dean

GILBERTS DRIVE

To Cuckmere Haven, Hope Gap & Seaford

BIRLING GAP ROAD

A-259

To Eastbourne, Pevensey Battle & Dover

WARREN HILL

BEACHY HEAD ROAD

To Eastbourne

BEACHY HEAD COUNTRYSIDE CENTRE & WC

DRIVE ENDS

BELLE TOUT LIGHTHOUSE

TURNOUT

BEACHY HEAD ROAD

Clifftop Walk (South Downs Way)

THE BEACHY HEAD PUB

Birling Gap

VISITORS CENTER, WC & CAFÉ

White Cliffs

BEACHY HEAD LIGHTHOUSE

RAF BOMBER COMMAND MEMORIAL

1 Kilometer

1 Mile

English Channel

BRIGHTON

ooze of a seabed formed about 100 million years ago, lifted high with the slow-motion collision of continents. The entire impressive, natural coastline is part of the South Downs National Park.

Dramatic as Beachy Head is, sadly, it's also a big draw for distraught people wanting to end their lives. About 20 people a year jump to their deaths from these cliffs, and you may see a comfort van in the parking lots with a chaplain at the ready, hoping to be able to intervene and prevent even more suicides.

Getting There: The area, just a 25-mile drive east of Brighton, is easy to visit by car: Simply loop south off the coastal A-259 between Seaford and Eastbourne (just after Friston). If you don't have a car, bus #13X runs three times daily between Brighton and Beachy Head from mid-June through August—but Sundays only off-season (www.buses.co.uk). If you're in a pinch, the more frequent buses #12, #12A, and #12X travel along the main road and stop at East Dean, just over a one-mile hike from Birling Gap. Another option is to take a train to Eastbourne, the big city just beyond Beachy Head. From there, you can take a taxi to Beachy Head or walk to Eastbourne Pier and ride a hop-on, hop-off bus to the cliffs (April-Sept only, see www.eastbournesightseeing.com).

Beachy Head Drive

This four-mile drive provides a good taste of this area. It starts in the village of East Dean, stops at viewpoints along the coast, and ends at the bluff with a visitors center and pub. With time, you can try to fit in one of the hikes described later. At the end of this drive, you can head back to Brighton or onward to the large town of Eastbourne (a mini-Brighton, with its own pleasure pier), then on to Pevensey or Battle.

• *Take the A-259 coastal road east from Brighton, which leads to the following four sights. For the first stop, drive to the village of East Dean: About three miles after leaving the town of Seaford, be ready to turn off on the right for Birling Gap. Just after turning off onto this road, immediately on your right is the delightful East Dean village green (Village Green Lane, free parking).*

East Dean: While a mile from the bluff, this is a very cute town for a meal or an overnight. Stone cottages made of flint, a fine church, and an inviting pub face the charming green. The **Tiger Inn** is the best place in the area for a reasonably-priced meal and great for an expensive overnight. It boasts a classic pub interior with fun walls to read, rustic picnic tables on the green, popular burgers and fish-and-chips, and five comfy but pricey rooms for rent (must book rooms online and pay in advance, tel. 01323/423-209, www.beachyhead.org.uk/the-tiger-inn).

• *From East Dean, continue south along the road toward Birling Gap (about a mile away).*

Birling Gap (Viewpoint and Beach Access): This handy settlement has the only access to the beach, the best views of the Seven Sisters, a fine National Trust visitors center/shop/café (daily 9:00-17:30), and easy pay-and-display parking.

First head down to the **beach.** The stairway, built like an Erector set, fits the cliff now, but with slow and steady erosion, the entire hamlet is doomed before too long. (Every few years, they have to move the entire staircase closer to the ever-receding cliff.) The staircase provides good views to the Seven Sisters and 51 steps down to the beach. As you stroll under the grand chalky walls,

marvel at the otherworldly whiteness of the cliff and the stones underfoot. Pick up a chunk of chalk to feel how soft and crumbly it is—the constant sloughing off is why these cliffs are so steep, dramatic, and pearly white (signs warn you to stay away from the immediate base of the cliffs). Stretching to your right (as you face

South Downs Way

The South Downs Way (often abbreviated SDW) runs for 100 miles along the chalk hills of England's south coast, from Winchester (25 miles inland in Hampshire) to Eastbourne (on the coast of East Sussex). This long, scenic ridge has attracted walkers for ages, and in 2011, the area surrounding the trail became England's 10th national park. Locals consider these trails a birthright.

The SDW is a bridleway, which means you can walk, bike, or ride a horse. To keep on course, look for the blue arrow signs with a white acorn in the middle or dots of blue paint on posts or trees. It's always a good idea to have a map; the UK Ordnance Survey Explorer maps are excellent and widely available (#123 covers the area around Beachy Head).

Walkers have priority over horses and bicycles, but it's polite to step aside and let them pass. While motorized vehicles are not allowed on the SDW itself, much of the path runs along farm tracks, so you may encounter fearsome tractors.

While you can walk along almost the entire southern coast, the best part for a day hike is the three-mile stretch out to Beachy Head from Birling Gap or from Eastbourne (find the path at the west end of King Edward's Parade, also called the B-2103; the small car park is often full, so you may need to park on a nearby street).

Many people walk the entire 100 miles, staying in B&Bs or hostels in towns along the way, or camping in designated areas. The SDW winds its way through or near many towns and villages, including Exton, Buriton, Arundel, Lewes, and Alfriston. Two good websites are www.southdowns.gov.uk and www.nationaltrail.co.uk. You can buy a guidebook at most UK bookshops or online through www.amazon.co.uk. Titles include *South Downs Way* by Jim Manthorpe, *South Downs Way National Trail Guide* by Paul Millmore, and *Walks in the South Downs National Park* by Kev Reynolds.

the sea) are the elegant Seven Sisters cliffs, offering chalky splendor as far as the eye can see. Hike along the beach as far as the weather—or your patience for walking slowly on monster pebbles—will allow. Walking along the base of England's famed white cliffs feels epic...almost cinematic.

Back up top, the **visitors center** has great displays on the local wildlife and geology (including erosion), fossils, the RAF Friston WWII air base that's nearby, and objects found in the many (at least 25) shipwrecks in this area. They enjoy giving advice on hiking from Birling Gap—a very good option. There are also WCs and a $ café serving light meals.

Before taking off, it's worth hiking about five minutes up the

bluff to the left (as you face the sea). Hike high enough that you can see the Belle Tout Lighthouse (described next), then look back. From up here, you enjoy even better views of the Seven Sisters. Stay back from the edge; not only are surprise wind gusts dangerous, but the cliffs are constantly sloughing off.

• *Back in the car, continue on the same road for about a mile. Just past the hill-capping Belle Tout Lighthouse is a small, skinny, pay-and-display parking lot. Stop here if only for a quick photo.*

Belle Tout Lighthouse Turnout: While there's no beach access here, this is your easiest "cliff access." Within a hundred yards of your car you'll enjoy the best view around of Beachy Head, views of the red-and-white lighthouse at the base of the cliff (150 feet tall and built in 1832), and a chance to get as close as you dare to the staggering cliff. Be careful—there are no guard railings. It's just putting green...and oblivion. From here you can hike in either or both directions: to the Belle Tout Lighthouse on the hill above (moved to its current location in 1999 to escape the cliffside erosion) or across the field, gradually up to Beachy Head itself.

• *A short drive farther east takes you to the top of Beachy Head Bluff. Look for the big pay-and-display parking lot on the left, as the road summits.*

Beachy Head Bluff: The physical high point of the road and the bluff is the main tourist stop (even though you can't see the white cliffs from here). There are commanding coastal views, a WWII Bomber Command Memorial, nice trails, and a chance to see hang gliders enjoying the coveted Beachy Head updrafts. Just downhill, adjoining the parking lot, the Beachy Head Countryside Centre features some good exhibits and an informative video playing on a loop in a little theater (free entry, daily 10:00-16:00, closed Nov-Easter, tel. 01323/737-273, www.beachyhead.org). Next door, **$$ The Beachy Head Pub** has lots of cozy seating overlooking the South Downs and so-so food.

• *If you continue along the same road past the bluff, you'll hit a T-intersection. A left turn (toward Seaford/A-259) takes you back to Brighton. A right turn (marked Town Centre/Seafront) drops you down into Eastbourne.*

Beachy Head Hikes

If you have time for a walk, these three routes are worthwhile. These trails are fairly steep, and it's important to watch your step: Long, windblown grass fields come to an abrupt end at the cliff edge, with no barrier between you and the sea crashing hundreds of feet below. For any hike in this area, get detailed advice locally before heading out. For more on Beachy Head hikes, see www.walkingclub.org.uk/book_2/walk_28.

For a **clifftop walk** with great sea views, but not the best vistas of the cliff face itself, hike between the Beachy Head Countryside Centre and the Belle Tout Lighthouse.

For head-on **views of the cliffs** as you walk, begin in the town of Seaford (between Brighton and Beachy Head) and hike to Hope Gap. Drivers can park at the trailhead at the east end of Seaford's waterfront. Or you can take the train to Seaford; from the train station, walk to the beach and turn left.

Another good option is to leave your car at Birling Gap and hike west along the **top of the Seven Sisters.** You can hike as far as the Cuckmere Valley, then return the way you came, or make your hike a loop by heading inland through the Friston Forest.

PORTSMOUTH

Portsmouth, the age-old home of the Royal Navy and Britain's second-busiest ferry port after Dover, is best known for its Historic Dockyard and many nautical sights. For centuries, Britain, a maritime superpower, relied on the fleets based in Portsmouth to expand and maintain its vast empire and guard against invaders. When sea power was needed, British leaders—from Henry VIII to Winston Churchill to Margaret Thatcher—have called upon Portsmouth to ready the ships.

As a major military target, the city of Portsmouth was flattened by WWII bombs (ironically, the Historic Dockyard was relatively unscathed). When the Allies gathered their forces in preparation for D-Day, the locals say there were so many ships in the harbor that it seemed you could walk deck to deck all the way to the Isle of Wight. Today, the town still feels deeply scarred by World War II. The cathedral survived because the Nazis used it as a beacon to help guide their bombs. The main drag—High Street—was mostly rebuilt since 1945 and is of almost no tourist interest. Postwar reconstruction was hasty and poorly planned, and the city became infamous for its bad architecture.

But an impressive gentrification is under way here. As the navy shrinks, tourism is moving in. Once the ultimate military town in Britain, today Portsmouth is changing. Efforts to rejuvenate tourism have included refurbishing Old Portsmouth, building a sprawling new waterfront shopping complex, and adding a sail-like monolith to the skyline. While Brighton rests on its holiday-making laurels—and revels in its shabby-chic—Portsmouth feels increasingly spiffy and contemporary.

The old nautical sights are impressive. Visitors can tour an

array of Royal Navy ships from
many eras, including the HMS
Victory, which played a key role
in Britain's battles with Napoleon's navy, and see the remains
of the *Mary Rose,* a 16th-century
warship that was a favorite of
Henry VIII. But the new spirit
of Portsmouth is equally worthwhile. Portsmouth seems to ex-

pertly balance its dual status as both a city of the past and one of
the future.

Near Portsmouth, on the road to Brighton, are two very different palaces: the ancient remains of Fishbourne Roman Palace, with
its striking mosaics; and thriving Arundel Castle, still the proud
home of an English duke.

PLANNING YOUR TIME

Portsmouth works well as a day trip from London, Bath, or Salisbury. The city's top sights—at the Historic Dockyard—can be seen
in a few hours. If you add the D-Day Story museum, bustling Gunwharf Quays and Spinnaker Tower, and a seaside-holiday atmosphere, you'll have no trouble filling a whole day. Consider spending the night.

Orientation to Portsmouth

Portsmouth, situated on an island, feels smaller than its population
of 200,000. Almost all of its visit-worthy sights line up along a
two-mile stretch of waterfront, from the Historic Dockyard in the
north to the Southsea neighborhood in the south. The walkable
core, in the north, contains the top sights: the Historic Dockyard,
Spinnaker Tower (views), Gunwharf Quays (shopping complex),
Millennium Promenade Walk, and Old Portsmouth; Southsea's
D-Day Story museum is a 10-minute bus ride or 30-minute walk
away.

TOURIST INFORMATION

The TI is located inside the Portsmouth Museum, about a mile
southeast of the Portsmouth Harbour train station; unless you're
going to the museum anyway, it's probably not worth a special trip
(daily 10:00-17:00, Oct-March until 16:30, Museum Road, tel.
023/9282-6722, www.visitportsmouth.co.uk, vis@portsmouthcc.
gov.uk). A more convenient tourist information point is at The
Hard Interchange bus station next to the Portsmouth Harbour
train station (daily 9:30-17:15).

Bus Tours: With vintage double-decker buses and live guides, **Local Haunts** does a 1.5-hour city tour during the tourist season (£11, buy tickets on the bus, June-Sept Thu and Sun at 14:00, leaves from Stand A at The Hard Interchange bus station near Historic Dockyard or 20 minutes earlier from the D-Day Story museum, www.localhaunts.com, info@localhaunts.com).

ARRIVAL IN PORTSMOUTH

Portsmouth has two **train** stations. Stay on the train until the final stop at the Portsmouth Harbour Station, conveniently located one long block from the entrance to the Historic Dockyard. The Hard Interchange bus station is just across from the train station.

Drivers approach Portsmouth on the M-27 motorway. First take the Portsmouth (W) exit, then follow signs for *Historic Waterfront*. As you get closer, individual parking lots are well-signposted (the one called "Historic Dockyard" is a garage just two blocks from the Dockyard).

Sights in Portsmouth

I've listed Portsmouth's sights from north to south.

HISTORIC DOCKYARD

When Britannia ruled the waves, it did so from Portsmouth's Historic Dockyard. Britain's great warships, known as the "Wooden Walls of England," were all that lay between the island nation and invaders from the Continent. Today, this harbor is still the base of the Royal Navy. (If you sneak a peek beyond the guard stations, you can see the British military at work.) The shipyard offers visitors a glimpse of maritime attractions new and old. Marvel at the modern-day warships anchored on the docks, then explore the fantastic collection of historic naval memorabilia and well-preserved ships. You can stroll around the Dockyard to see the exteriors of the HMS *Victory* and HMS *Warrior* for free, but going inside the attractions requires a ticket (and you must pass through bag security at the entrance whether you buy a ticket or not).

Planning Your Time: The Dockyard is a sprawling complex with about 10 different attractions (several are a shuttle-boat ride away). While the *Mary Rose* Museum has its own ticket, the rest of the sights are run by the Royal Dockyards and are covered by the same combo-ticket (though you can buy individual tickets, too). Save most of your time for the HMS *Victory*, the *Mary Rose* Museum, and the Museum of the Royal Navy. Visit the HMS *Warrior* and the HMS *M.33* briefly. If you have extra time, consider the harbor tour (departs from near the entry; drop by the dock to check

PORTSMOUTH

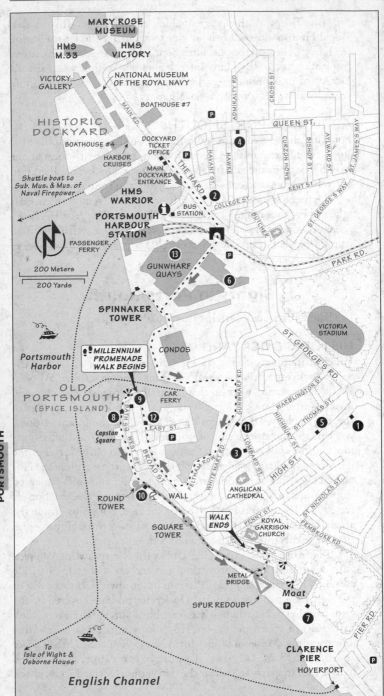

PORTSMOUTH

MARY ROSE MUSEUM

HMS M.33

HMS VICTORY

VICTORY GALLERY

NATIONAL MUSEUM OF THE ROYAL NAVY

BOATHOUSE #7

HISTORIC DOCKYARD

BOATHOUSE #4

DOCKYARD TICKET OFFICE

HARBOR CRUISES

Shuttle boat to Sub. Mus. & Mus. of Naval Firepower

MAIN DOCKYARD ENTRANCE

HMS WARRIOR

PORTSMOUTH HARBOUR STATION

PASSENGER FERRY

200 Meters
200 Yards

Portsmouth Harbor

OLD PORTSMOUTH (SPICE ISLAND)

Capstan Square

ROUND TOWER

SQUARE TOWER

To Isle of Wight & Osborne House

English Channel

ADMIRALTY RD.

QUEEN ST.

CROSS ST.

THE HARD

HAVANT ST.

HAWKE

COLLEGE ST.

BUTCHER

CURZON HOWE

BISHOP ST.

KENT ST.

AYLWARD ST.

ST. GEORGE'S WAY

ST. JAMES'S WAY

BUS STATION

PARK RD.

GUNWHARF QUAYS

SPINNAKER TOWER

CONDOS

MILLENNIUM PROMENADE WALK BEGINS

CAR FERRY

BATH SQ.

WEST ST.

EAST ST.

BROAD ST.

FELTHAM ROW

WHITE HART RD.

GUNWHARF RD.

TOWER RD.

ANGLICAN CATHEDRAL

WALL

VICTORIA STADIUM

ST. GEORGE'S RD.

WARBLINGTON ST.

HIGHBURY ST.

ST. THOMAS ST.

HIGH ST.

ST. NICHOLAS ST.

WALK ENDS

PENNY ST.

ROYAL GARRISON CHURCH

PEMBROKE RD.

METAL BRIDGE

Moat

SPUR REDOUBT

CLARENCE PIER

HOVERPORT

PIER RD.

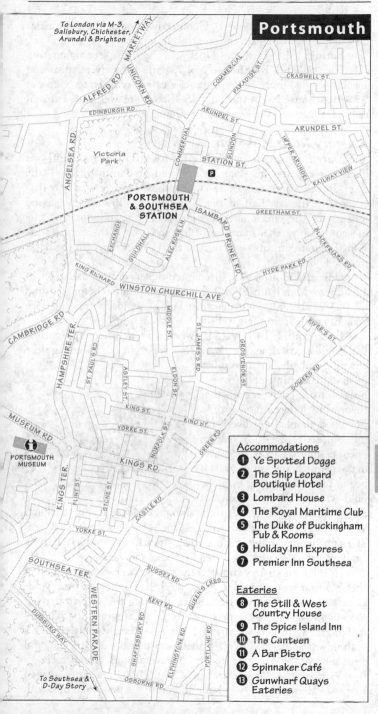

Portsmouth

To London via M-3,
Salisbury, Chichester,
Arundel & Brighton

ALFRED RD.

UNICORN RD.

MARKETWAY

COMMERCIAL RD.

PARADISE ST.

CRASWELL ST.

EDINBURGH RD.

ARUNDEL ST.

STANHOPE RD.

ARUNDEL ST.

ANGLESEA RD.

Victoria
Park

COMMERCIAL RD.

STATION ST.

UPPER ARUNDEL

RAILWAY VIEW

**PORTSMOUTH
& SOUTHSEA
STATION**

EXCHANGE RD.

GUILDHALL WALK

ALEC ROSE LN.

ISAMBARD BRUNEL RD.

GREETHAM ST.

BLACKFRIARS RD.

KING RICHARD

WINSTON CHURCHILL AVE.

HYDE PARK RD.

CAMBRIDGE RD.

HAMPSHIRE TER.

ST. PAUL'S RD.

ASTLEY ST.

MIDDLE ST.

ELDON ST.

ST. JAMES'S RD.

GROSVENOR ST.

RIVER'S ST.

SOMERS RD.

KING ST.

KING ST.

MUSEUM RD.

**PORTSMOUTH
MUSEUM**

KINGS TER.

FLINT ST.

YORKE ST.

NORFOLK ST.

KINGS RD.

GREEN RD.

STONE ST.

CASTLE RD.

YORKE ST.

SOUTHSEA TER.

WESTERN PARADE

SUSSEX RD.

QUEEN'S CRES.

DUISBURG WAY

KENT RD.

SHAFTESBURY RD.

ELPHINSTONE RD.

PORTLAND RD.

OSBORNE RD.

To Southsea &
D-Day Story

PORTSMOUTH

Accommodations

1 Ye Spotted Dogge
2 The Ship Leopard
  Boutique Hotel
3 Lombard House
4 The Royal Maritime Club
5 The Duke of Buckingham
  Pub & Rooms
6 Holiday Inn Express
7 Premier Inn Southsea

Eateries

8 The Still & West
  Country House
9 The Spice Island Inn
10 The Canteen
11 A Bar Bistro
12 Spinnaker Café
13 Gunwharf Quays
  Eateries

on times and availability first). Upon arrival, locate these priorities on a map to see things in the smartest order.

Eating: The Historic Dockyard has an accommodating cafeteria, called **$ Boathouse No. 7,** with a variety of meal and snack options. There is also a fancier eatery with water views at **$$$ Boathouse No. 4** (near HMS *Warrior*) as well as **$ cafés** at the *Mary Rose* and the Dockyard entrance.

▲▲*Mary Rose* Museum

The *Mary Rose* warship was King Henry VIII's favorite, and was likely named after his sister (Mary) and his family emblem (the rose). But the ship sank in 1545, and the wreckage was only discovered in the last half of the 20th century. The well-preserved remains of the wreck now provide the framework for this fine museum that gives a snapshot of life aboard a 16th-century warship. The museum sits right next to the HMS *Victory* (in the dark, rounded building).

Cost and Hours: £18, discounted tickets online; daily 10:00-17:30, Nov-March until 17:00, last entry 45 minutes before closing; tel. 023/9281-2931, www.maryrose.org. Download a free app with an audioguide from their website.

Background: In July 1545, when a French fleet approached the English coastline, the *Mary Rose* was sent out to engage the enemy. Suddenly, just two miles offshore, the ship tipped over—possibly from a stiff breeze; other theories include human error, a French cannonball, or overloading. Since all the gun bays were open, ready for battle, the water overwhelmed the ship and it began to sink. Netting over the hold was intended to keep out

enemy sailors trying to board the ship, but instead it trapped about 400 sailors as they scrambled to escape—only about 30 survived. The ship and its doomed crew settled, stuck in the mud in relatively shallow water, where they rested for about 450 years.

In 1982, about 15 years after the wreck was located, the half of the ship that was encased in mud—and thus protected from voracious shipworms—was raised. Since allowing the ship to dry out too quickly would cause the structure to disintegrate, for 20 years its remains were behind barriers, being constantly sprayed with a sealing wax solution. Officials finally started to let it dry out, and what's left of the *Mary Rose* is now uncovered and hard as rock.

Visiting the Museum: This £35 million museum—shaped like an oval jewel box—was built to reunite the preserved hull with thousands of its previously unseen contents. All sorts of Tudor-era items were found inside the wreck, such as clothes, dishes, weapons, a backgammon board, and an oboe-like instrument. There's even the skeletons of the crew and Hatch, the ship's dog. It's a fascinating look at everyday shipboard life from almost 500 years ago.

You'll walk down three levels of galleries with the *Mary Rose*'s hull on one side and exhibits containing artifacts on the other, mirroring the original hull to give you a better idea of the ship's scale. Items are showcased in relation to where they were found. Exhibits at either end focus on crew members' personal stories and their duties aboard ship. Recent DNA testing of the crew takes a closer look at how diverse Tudor England already was. There are re-creations of different parts of the ship such as the surgeon's cabin and the gun deck. Don't miss seeing the only surviving 16th-century crow's nest. Strategically placed high-tech information boards bring it all to life.

Royal Dockyards Sights

While the HMS *Victory* is the most important of the Royal Dockyards sights to see, several others are worth a look. Friendly and knowledgeable docents, many who were once seamen, are found throughout the complex, happily answering questions and telling tales of the sea.

Cost and Hours: £39 "Full Navy" ticket (good for a year) covers all Royal Dockyards sights. You can save by booking online (www.historicdockyard.co.uk/tickets), or by combining it with a day-trip train ticket from London (most trains depart from London's Waterloo Station, smart to buy at least one day ahead, tel. 0845/600-0650, www.southwesttrains.co.uk). Tickets are also sold for one, two, or three attractions (£18-36). All sights open daily 10:00-17:30, Nov-March until 17:00 (last tickets sold 1.5 hours before closing); tel. 023/9283-9766, www.historicdockyard.co.uk.

▲▲▲HMS *Victory*

This grand historic warship changed the course of world history. At the turn of the 19th century, Napoleon's forces were terrorizing the Continent. In 1805, Napoleon amassed a fleet of French and Spanish ships for the purpose of invading England. The Royal Navy managed to blockade the fleets, but some French ships broke through. Admiral Nelson, commander of the British fleet, pursued the ships aboard the HMS *Victory*, cornering them at Cape Trafalgar, off the coast of Spain (see sidebar). Today, the dry-docked HMS *Victory* is so well-preserved that it feels ready to haul anchor and pull out of the harbor at any moment. In fact, it's still a commissioned warship, the world's oldest. For the British, this ship is more a cathedral than a museum.

PORTSMOUTH

Visiting the Ship: Visitors follow a one-way route that spirals up and down through the ship's six decks, taking at least an hour (possibly longer if you linger with the free audioguide, which gives many details on the battle of Trafalgar). Though a 10-year restoration project is underway, the ship remains open. Here are the highlights.

Upper Deck: Following the designated path takes you upstairs, where you'll see Captain Thomas Hardy's cabin—not quite as posh as his boss Admiral Nelson's, but not bad. Up here, there's also access to the poop deck for more views. Before descending the stairs, notice the small golden plaque on the deck marking the spot where Nelson fell during the fateful Battle of Trafalgar—shot by a sniper. From here, the crew rushed him below deck to care for him during his dying hours.

Upper Gun Deck: This is filled with original cannons. To prevent the ship from tipping, the lightest were placed higher on the ship, with the heavy ones below. It took a well-trained British sailor two minutes to ready a cannon for firing, compared to the eight minutes French gunners needed to fire their cannons.

Great Cabin: This was Admiral Nelson's quarters. Imagine Nelson and his officers dining at the elegant table—or hunched over maps to plan an attack. While it looks like an officer's stately quarters, this space is also designed for action: All of the wood furniture was foldable and could be stowed quickly during battle. The black-and-white checkerboard "tile" flooring—inspired by Nelson's love of southern Italy (and its women)—is actually painted canvas, which could, like the carpets, be rolled up at a moment's notice. It took the crew less than 10 minutes to clear away all the upper-class trappings and turn this space into a fully functional cannon deck. Leaving the Great Cabin, you'll pass Nelson's hanging bunk—even the master of this ship slept on a glorified hammock rather than a bed.

Middle and Lower Gundecks: Climbing down, you can see how cramped the living conditions were for the sailors. When not in battle, they strung hammocks between the guns and ate at tables wedged under their strung-up beds. Sailors ate from square plates to save space. When a man died, his hammock was his burial cloth—his body was sewn up in the hammock, with a last stitch through the nose to ensure the man was really dead. (Since military service was obligatory, faking death was common.)

Orlop Deck: Explore the bowels of the ship, where the space becomes smaller and darker. Ask about the medical tools laid out on a table. During the battle nine sailors needed amputations, but the doctor was so good all nine survived (rare in those days). Guides are happy to give you an idea what the procedures involved. It's also down here that Nelson died, gasping his final words: "Thank God,

Nelson's Victory over Napoleon

Admiral Lord Horatio Nelson (1758-1805), a small man who suffered seasickness throughout his career, was a brilliant military strategist. He developed a new plan for taking on Napoleon's fleet: Instead of pulling parallel to the ships and firing broadside, he would drive a line of ships head-on, perpendicular to his opponent's fleet, cutting them into pieces. When the English attacked the French fleet off the southwest coast of Spain in 1805, they decimated their enemies, who were unable to return adequate fire. Victory was won, but Nelson, who courageously wore his bright uniform to inspire his men, was lost to a sniper's bullet. While sailors are usually buried at sea, Nelson's body was returned to London, where he was given a grand funeral and then entombed in St. Paul's Cathedral. The victory at Trafalgar solidified British dominance of the seas. Although Napoleon would menace Europe for another 10 years, he would never again challenge the British Royal Navy.

I have done my duty." The painting next to the spot of his death shows the admiral glowing like a saint as sailors look on in grief. (Whether this is an eyewitness account is suspect; check the size of the ship—either people were much smaller back then, or the painter had never been aboard the *Victory*.) After his death, Nelson was put in a cask filled with brandy to preserve his body. Legend has it that the cask was not quite as full by the time the sailors arrived in London.

▲National Museum of the Royal Navy

This museum, situated in three buildings, is packed with model ships, paintings, uniforms, and lots more Nelson hero-worship. There are several themed sections. The *Victory* Gallery includes a corny but informative 15-minute *Trafalgar Experience* multimedia show (with movies, mannequins, sound effects, and smoke) and offers a blow-by-blow account of the Battle of Trafalgar as you move through four rooms. It culminates with a viewing of a panoramic painting of the battle (*Panorama of the Battle of Trafalgar*, by W. L. Wyllie, 1931). If you want to see this, sign up for a time as you enter. The exhibit continues upstairs with figureheads and Nelson's funeral barge. The *HMS: Hear My Story* exhibit covers the experiences of ordinary sailors over the last 100 years, from the first days of World War I to recent conflicts in the Middle East.

▲HMS *Warrior*

This ship, while very impressive and fun to explore, never saw a day of battle...which explains why it's still intact, albeit fragile. The *Warrior* was the first ironclad warship, a huge technological

PORTSMOUTH

advance. Compare this ship, built in 1860, with the *Victory*, which was similar to the common warships at the time. The *Warrior* was unbeatable, and the enemy knew it. Its very existence was sufficient to keep the peace. It had about a 10-year window of technological invincibility. After 1870, with the advent of guns on turrets and stronger steam engines (so sails weren't needed at all), the HMS *Warrior* was mothballed.

Other Dockyard Sights

The **HMS *M.33*** is the last surviving WWI ship of the bloody Gallipoli Campaign, and the only WWI warship open to the public in Britain. Exploring this fascinating ship—with battle pockmarks showing under its paint—you see the crude yet state-of-the-art technology of 1915. Imagine it under attack and jammed with 67 sailors.

Boathouse #4 displays more historic boats in a re-creation of a working boatyard. Maritime history buffs will see D-Day ships, Falklands War vessels, and a replica of Ernest Shackleton's open lifeboat from his daring 1916 journey across the Antarctic Ocean.

An all-attraction ticket includes two interesting stops that require a quick shuttle-boat ride to reach: a WWII-era **Submarine Museum** and the **Museum of Naval Firepower.**

Harbor Cruise

You can scoot around the harbor and back to the Historic Dockyard in about 50 minutes by boat. The expansive view of the military complex is impressive, but you'll learn more about the ships from exploring the Dockyard sights on foot. As the boat also stops at Gunwharf Quays, taking this cruise at the very end of your Dockyard visit can be a smart way to eliminate the 10- to 15-minute walk to the Spinnaker Tower and surrounding mall (£10, included in Historic Dockyard combo-ticket, departs about hourly during the summer starting at 11:30, last cruise usually leaves at 16:30; 14:30 in winter, just inside Dockyard entrance, weather-dependent, tel. 01983/564-602).

SOUTH OF THE HISTORIC DOCKYARD

To reach the next sights from the Historic Dockyard, take the harbor cruise (described above) or walk south on the main road past Portsmouth Harbour train station, keeping the water on your right. Then turn right through the archway marked *Gunwharf Quays*, walking under the old brick rail bridge.

Gunwharf Quays

Part of the major (and successful) makeover of Portsmouth, the bustling Gunwharf Quays (pronounced "keys") is an American-style outdoor shopping center on steroids, with restaurants, shops, and entertainment. You'll find all the top shops here, as well as a casino, a bowling alley, a 14-screen cinema, trendy eateries with good views of the water, and a Holiday Inn Express. Shops are generally open daily 10:00-19:00.

Spinnaker Tower

Out at the far end of the shopping zone is this can't-miss-it edifice. Like Seattle's vaguely futuristic Space Needle, the 560-foot-tall Spinnaker Tower quickly became an icon of its city after its 2005 opening. You can ride to the 330-foot-high view deck for a panorama of the port and sea beyond, or court acrophobia with a stroll across "Europe's biggest glass floor" (£11.50, discounts available online or through TI, daily 10:00-18:00, book ahead in midsummer, booking tel. 023/9285-7520, www.spinnakertower.co.uk).

The tower is reminiscent of the billowing ships' sails that have played such a key role in the history of this city and country. This spinnaker has a sister on the Portsmouth skyline—another skyscraper designed to be its steam-funnel partner, making the harbor district skyline that of a massive ship. But the public didn't pick up on this and, for obvious reasons, dubbed the sister skyscraper "The Blue Lipstick." Filled with condos, it's part of an initiative to bring life back to the former military zone.

Old Portsmouth

Portsmouth's historic district—once known as "Spice Island" after the ships' precious cargo—is surprisingly quiet. For a long time, the old sea village was dilapidated and virtually empty. But successful revitalization efforts have brought a few inviting pubs and restaurants. From the Old Portsmouth promenade, you can watch a procession of 21st-century ferries as they navigate their way into and out of port. It's a pleasant place to stroll around and imagine how different this district was in the old days, when it was filled with salty fishermen and sailors who told tall tales and sang sea chanties in rough-and-tumble pubs.

Getting There: To walk to Old Portsmouth from the Historic Dockyard, first follow the earlier directions to Gunwharf Quays and the Spinnaker Tower. From the tower, head south along the plaza with the water on your right, following the decorative chain-link pattern in the sidewalk (see the Portsmouth map, earlier). Cross the bridge right in front of you, turn right and keep following the chain-link pattern to stay on the waterfront. Soon the chain becomes sandstone colored, and you will skirt around the ferry port and marina. Turn right on Feltham Row (which is a pedestrian path) to reach the old town. Eventually you emerge onto Broad Street, with the old defensive wall in front of you. Head to the right, and in a few blocks, you'll reach the small peninsula of Old Portsmouth. This is a favorite place, like a little park, where locals come for a meal or a drink at sunset.

Old Portsmouth Millennium Promenade Walk: The stylized chain links in the sidewalk mark the Millennium Promenade (also called the Renaissance Trail on some historical markers). The chain symbol recalls the great steel chain that once spanned the mouth of the harbor and was raised to block invading warships. For a pleasant (but often windy) hour-long after-dinner stroll, walk the portion of the well-marked trail south of Old Portsmouth along the oceanfront. Interpretive panels along the way give you insights into Portsmouth's fascinating history.

From the tip of Old Portsmouth, follow the trail around on the ocean side and turn right into small **Capstan Square,** where the harbor-spanning chain was raised to keep out enemy ships. Pass through a narrow arched doorway and climb up the stairs across the courtyard to the top of the 15th-century **Round Tower.** Up here, a plaque shows where the wreck of the *Mary Rose* was found. After taking in the view, follow the top of the old stone fortifications (which include the recommended Canteen restaurant) south to the Square Tower. With the notoriously blustery weather, local kids who hit the beach gather near the base of the wall, nicknamed the "Hot Walls," as it's out of the wind and collects warmth from the sun.

The 15th-century **Square Tower,** originally the residence of the governor of Portsmouth, was later used to store gunpowder. South of the Square Tower on the left is the small, roofless **Royal Garrison Church.** Founded in 1212 as a hospice, it was used as a shelter for overseas pilgrims traveling to Canterbury, Chichester, and Winchester. The church was later used by garrisoned troops before the nave lost its roof in a WWII bombing raid.

After walking south about 150 yards, you'll see a small moat on the left. You've reached the **Spur Redoubt,** part of the outer fortifications (see interpretive sign down by moat). Look for a plaque by the water that identifies the traffic that plies this harbor—from the hovercraft heading for the Isle of Wight to the big ferry sailing to Brittany.

To avoid the huge crowds that had gathered in town to see

him off, Admiral Nelson supposedly passed through this area on September 14, 1805, on his way to the Battle of Trafalgar. From the beach, he was rowed out to the *Victory*, waiting off the Isle of Wight. He didn't return to England alive.

The **Clarence Pier**, which is 200 yards beyond, kicks off a Coney Island-type, beach-party zone. Instead of going there, walk toward the pier until you reach the metal bridge that veers left from the chain-link path. Cross the bridge over the moat, pass through a tunnel under the earthen fortifications, and immediately turn right and climb up the short path to the top. Walk back along the top of the grassy fortifications. This is the end of our walk. Benches invite you to stop and watch the many passing ferries and other ships or to simply enjoy the sunset. If the weather's clear, you can see the Isle of Wight—if it's not too dear.

SOUTHSEA

Southsea gathers around the remains of beefy Southsea Castle, key to one of the world's most fortified harbors in the 19th century. On a sunny day, this appealing seafront neighborhood south of Old Portsmouth—with its long, broad, grassy park stretching for miles in front of fine old townhouses—bustles with locals enjoying their city. Just beyond is the entertaining South Parade Pier. While it's studded with some humdrum sights, the main reason to venture to Southsea is for its interesting D-Day museum.

▲▲The D-Day Story and Overlord Embroidery

This museum, worth ▲▲▲ to history buffs, was built to commemorate the 40th anniversary of the D-Day invasions during World War II, and was later refurbished in antici-pation of 75th-anniver-sary events. The museum features exhibits on the invasions and a tapestry commemorating the years leading up to D-Day.

Cost and Hours: £10; daily 10:00-17:30, Oct-March until 17:00; café on site—closed in off-season; on the waterfront about two miles south of the Spinnaker Tower, Clarence Esplanade, Southsea, tel. 023/9288-7261, https://thedday story.com.

Getting There: From the end of my "Old Portsmouth Mil-lennium Promenade Walk," it's a 20-minute stroll south. Or from Portsmouth's Hard Interchange bus station, take First Bus Company's bus #3 (#16 on Sundays), or Stagecoach bus #23 to the

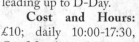

PORTSMOUTH

Southsea Shops stop on Osborne Road, then walk 10 minutes to the seafront (£2 one-way, £4.20 day pass, 2/hour, 10 minutes; ask at info booth about last return bus times). Drivers can park in the pay-and-display lot behind the museum.

Visiting the Museum: Along with items from D-Day and the Battle of Normandy, the museum shows how the Allies planned the invasion—how, for example, detailed maps emerged from vacation photos and postcards collected by civilians before the war. Touch screens help visitors connect their knowledge of espionage or battle tactics to the planning done before and during the landings, while displays incorporate first-person stories of those who took part, from both the Allied and German points of view.

The second half of the exhibit is the 272-foot-long **Overlord Embroidery** (named for the invasion's code name). The 34 appliquéd panels—stitched together over five years by a team of seamstresses, and originally displayed in a brewery's boardroom—were inspired by the Bayeux Tapestry that recorded William the Conqueror's battles during the Norman invasion of England a thousand years earlier. The panels chronologically trace the years from 1940 to 1944, from the first British men receiving their call-up papers in the mail to the successful implementation of D-Day. It celebrates everyone from famous WWII figures to unsung heroes of the home front.

ISLE OF WIGHT

Serious royal-family fans can consider a day trip from Portsmouth to the Isle of Wight to see **Osborne House,** a stunning Italianate palazzo that was Queen Victoria's beloved getaway for 50 years, until her death there in 1901. Today, the house has been lovingly restored and it seems as if she has just stepped away. Be sure to see the Durbar Room, decorated as an over-the-top homage to India, one of Victoria's most valued colonial prizes. The easiest way to day-trip to the house is to buy a combo-ticket that combines the round-trip boat ride, bus to and from the estate, and admission (£42, buy online at www.hovertravel.co.uk or at Hovertravel's Southsea terminal; Osborne House open daily 10:00-18:00, Oct until 17:00, erratic hours in winter—call first or check online; Osborne House tel. 01983/200-022, www.english-heritage.org.uk).

Getting There: Wightlink Ferries' high-speed, passenger-only catamarans to Ryde Pier on the Isle of Wight depart from the waterfront in front of the train station (1-2/hour, 22 minutes). Car ferries for the town of Fishbourne leave from south of Gunwharf Quays (1-2/hour, 45 minutes, cars and passengers; tel. 0333/999-7333, www.wightlink.co.uk). Hovertravel operates a passenger-only hovercraft from Southsea to Ryde (at least hourly, 10 minutes, tel. 01983/717-700, www.hovertravel.co.uk).

Sleeping in Portsmouth

If you just can't get enough of ships and sea air, Portsmouth is a charming and fairly quiet place to spend the night. Traditional B&Bs are becoming rare in Portsmouth but some private room and apartment options can be found on Airbnb.com. Most accommodations I list are within a few blocks of the waterfront.

$$$ Ye Spotted Dogge is a good splurge in a historical setting. The building dates to 1523 but most of the interior was updated in the 1700s, after a Duke of Buckingham was assassinated here (ask owner Ian for more history). Their six rooms differ in design but each has classical character. Guests can enjoy a large lounge area, garden, and a private bar (includes street parking with permit, 11 High Street, tel. 023/9242-7154, www.yespotteddogge. co.uk, mail@yespotteddogge.co.uk).

$$ The Ship Leopard Boutique Hotel offers 13 modern, clean rooms in a convenient location, just across from the Harbour train station and a short walk to the Historic Dockyard. Six rooms face the waterfront and offer great views (free parking, 15 The Hard, tel. 023/9287-6020, www.shipleopardboutiquehotel.co.uk, enquiries@shipleopardboutiquehotel.co.uk).

$$ Lombard House rents two rooms on a quiet residential street next to the cathedral, a 10-minute walk from the Historic Dockyard. The public areas are ornately decorated and feature original artwork. In 2005, as part of the bicentennial of the Battle of Trafalgar, the inn's historian-owners traveled around Europe as Admiral Nelson and his mistress, Lady Emma Hamilton. The hosts are happy to share the history of the 1602 home and will give short tours of Old Portsmouth, even if you aren't staying here (cash only, paid street parking, 9 Lombard Street, tel. 023/9286-2293, mobile 0743-5956-124, goldenfinni@gmail.com).

$$ The Royal Maritime Club offers a home away from home to sailors in town who don't want to bunk on the boat. Just two blocks up the road from the Historic Dockyard entrance, it also welcomes tourists, who share its grand public spaces, generous facilities (including a swimming pool, fitness center, game room, self-service laundry, even barbershop) and 100 comfortable, surprisingly newish rooms. The catch: They rent out their ballroom for parties, which can be noisy late—try requesting a quiet room. It's four blocks from the train station, opposite the oval-shaped Admiralty Tower (family suites, elevator, 16 first-come-first-served parking spots and discounts for parking in The Royal Dockyards lot, Queen Street, tel. 023/9282-4231 or 023/9283-7681, www. royalmaritimeclub.co.uk, info@royalmaritimeclub.co.uk).

$ The Duke of Buckingham pub, a few blocks inland from Old Portsmouth, is likely to have rooms when others are full.

While the accommodations take a backseat to the popular pub, the 18 basic rooms—some above the bar, some out back in separate cottages—are clean and comfortable (no breakfast, 119 High Street, tel. 023/9282-7067, www.dukeofbuckingham.co.uk, info@dukeofbuckingham.co.uk).

Chain Hotels: If other accommodations are full, consider a chain hotel, such as **Holiday Inn Express** (near Portsmouth Harbour train station and Historic Dockyard) or **Premier Inn Southsea** (half-mile south of Old Portsmouth along the waterfront, next to the kitschy, cotton-candy-carnival ambience of Clarence Pier).

Eating in Portsmouth

Dinnertime is the best time to head over to Old Portsmouth, eat at a pub, and then stroll along the Millennium Promenade (described earlier). The first two pubs listed serve overpriced pub grub with gorgeous views, right on the water—the busy maritime traffic makes for a fascinating backdrop.

$$ The Still & West Country House pub has dining in two appealing zones, both offering the same menu. Eat in the more casual main floor, or outside on the picnic benches with fantastic views of the harbor. Or head upstairs to the dining room with a gorgeous glassed-in conservatory that offers sea views and lovely window seats—especially enticing in cold weather (dining room open Mon-Sat 9:30-21:00, Sun 12:00-20:00, longer hours in the bar, 2 Bath Square, tel. 023/9282-1567).

$$ The Spice Island Inn, at the tip of the Old Portsmouth peninsula, has terrific outdoor seating, a family-friendly dining room upstairs, and many vegetarian offerings. This eatery is more down-and-dirty and less expensive (food served daily 11:00-22:00, bar open longer, 1 Bath Square, tel. 023/9287-0543). Their crowd spills into "The Point," the harborside square.

$$ The Canteen, located in the old stone fortification wall near the Round Tower, is a nice break from pub food. The views of the water are excellent and the dining areas are cozy. You can enjoy their contemporary dishes inside, on their "hidden deck," or as takeout (Sun-Wed 8:00-18:00, Thu-Sat until 21:00, Point Battery-Broad Street, tel. 023/9235-1935).

$$$ A Bar Bistro is a classy but relaxed seafood-and-wine kind of place, between Old Portsmouth and Gunwharf Quays (daily 12:00-22:00, 58 White Hart Road, tel. 023/9281-1585).

$ Spinnaker Café is great for a lunch or snack if you're in Old Portsmouth before dinner (breakfast served all day, daily 8:00-16:00, 96 Broad Street, mobile 0777-295-3143).

Gunwharf Quays: Eating options abound at this bustling mega-mall. Most restaurants line up along the waterfront by the

Spinnaker Tower. You'll pay too much in this high-rent district—and many of the places are chains selling mall food—but it's the most convenient one-stop neighborhood for dining and finding international options.

Portsmouth Connections

From Portsmouth by Train to: London (3/hour, 2 hours, direct to Waterloo Station, a few with change in Clapham Junction to Victoria Station), **Gatwick Airport** (hourly, 1.5 hours direct, more with transfer), **Bath** (hourly, 2 hours, more with transfer), **Salisbury** (hourly direct, 1.5 hours, more with transfer), **Oxford** (3/hour, 2.5 hours, 1 transfer), **Brighton** (direct trains hourly, 1.5 hours), **Exeter** (hourly, 3.5 hours, change in Salisbury). **Train info:** Tel. 0345-748-4950, www.nationalrail.co.uk.

By Bus: For most connections, the train is faster—take the bus only if you're on a tight budget. National Express buses go to **Brighton** (1 direct bus/day, 2 hours), **Salisbury** (1 direct bus/day, 1.5 hours), and **Bath** (1 direct bus/day, 3 hours; tel. 0871-781-8181, www.nationalexpress.com).

By International Ferry: Brittany Ferries (tel. 01752/648-000, www.brittanyferries.com) sails to France: **Caen** (2-4/day, 4 hours on high-speed boat, 7 hours on slower boat), **Cherbourg** (1-3/day, 4 hours), **St. Malo** (night crossing, 1/day, 11 hours), **Le Havre** (1/day, 8 hours). It also has overnight ferries to northern Spain. Condor Ferries (tel. 0845-609-1024, www.condorferries.co.uk) sails to the Channel Islands of **Guernsey** (daily, 7 hours) and **Jersey** (daily, 10 hours), and also to **Cherbourg**, France (1/week, 6 hours, summer only).

Near Portsmouth

These sights are very near the main A-27 road that connects Portsmouth with Brighton. They're worth considering for a stopover if you have time as you pass through.

Fishbourne Roman Palace

In the 1930s, a farmer just outside of Chichester found the remains of an early Roman palace on his land. Wary of archaeologists, he didn't disclose his find until 1960. The ensuing dig revealed a huge Roman-era villa, probably built around AD 50 by a local tribal chief who was loyal to the Roman Empire. In the main museum building, you'll find the collection's impressive centerpiece: well-preserved floor mosaics, which are on display in their original locations (visitors walk above them on an elevated walkway). Also in the main building is a museum telling the story of the palace and

Fishbourne's Roman era. The garden outside was reconstructed to resemble the original Roman plan. Across the parking lot, the Discovery Centre lets you peek into the offices and warehouses of the archaeologists at work—like a zoo for people in lab coats. You'll learn how the artifacts are handled on their long journey

from the ground to the display case. The palace is fairly interesting to most, but likely to fascinate true fans of Roman history. Go early to avoid the crush of field-tripping schoolchildren.

Cost and Hours: £9.80; daily 10:00-17:00, Nov-Feb until 16:00, mid-Dec-Jan Sat-Sun only; guidebook outlines very detailed tour, café, tel. 01243/785-859, www.sussexpast.co.uk/fishbourne.

Getting There: It's on the southwestern outskirts of the large town of Chichester, well-signed from the main A-27 motorway connecting Brighton and Portsmouth. First head for the town of Fishbourne, then follow *Roman Palace* signs through a very residential-feeling neighborhood to the museum. From the Fishbourne train station, the palace is a seven-minute walk.

▲Arundel Castle

This striking castle of Arundel (AIR-uhn-dull) graces the valley below with straight-out-of-a-storybook appeal. It feels relatively new because it is—a Neo-Gothic creation of the late 19th century. The Duke of Norfolk—the top dog among all English dukes—still lives here, in what amounts to a museum of his own family (the Fitzalan-Howards, who also own Castle Howard in Yorkshire). Pompous even for a castle, the self-aggrandizing exhibits, docents who speak in hushed awe of their employers, and opulent interiors offer a somehow off-putting taste of England's affection for its outmoded nobility. Still, castle buffs will find the gorgeous interior worth visiting, and the themed gardens are a delight—check out the Earl's Garden, which is based on 17th-century designs and contains an intriguing "stumpery."

Cost and Hours: Castle interior, chapel, and grounds-£20, private bedrooms-£2 more; grounds and chapel only-£13. The complex is closed most Mondays (except in May and Aug, check website); it's also closed Nov-March. While most castle stops are open 10:00-17:00, the main rooms—the reason for the steep entry fee—don't open until noon; last entry at 16:00. Parts of the castle can be unexpectedly closed for private events. Tel. 01903/882-173, www.arundelcastle.org. There's a lovely riverside café across the street.

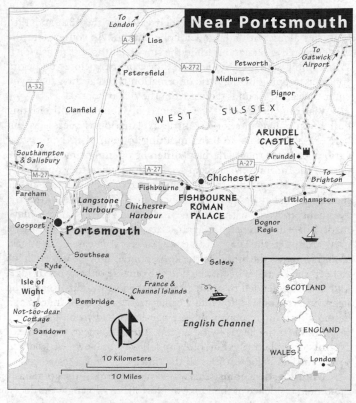

Near Portsmouth

To London

A-3 Liss

To Gatwick Airport

A-272 Petworth

Petersfield

Midhurst

A-32

Bignor

Clanfield

W E S T   S U S S E X

ARUNDEL CASTLE

To Southampton & Salisbury

A-27

Arundel

Chichester

A-27

To Brighton

M-27

Fareham

Fishbourne

FISHBOURNE ROMAN PALACE

Littlehampton

Langstone Harbour

Chichester Harbour

Gosport

Portsmouth

Bognor Regis

Southsea

Ryde

Selsey

Isle of Wight

To France & Channel Islands

To Not-too-dear Cottage

Bembridge

English Channel

Sandown

SCOTLAND

ENGLAND

WALES

London

10 Kilometers

10 Miles

Getting There: Arundel Castle is right on the A-27 between Brighton and Portsmouth—**drivers** just follow signs to the castle, and park at the pay lot across from the castle gate. The town of Arundel is connected by **train** from Portsmouth (2/hour, 1 hour, transfer in Barnham) and Brighton (1-2/hour, 1.5 hours, 1 transfer); Stagecoach **buses** also run from Brighton to Arundel (2/hour, fewer on Sun, 2.5 hours).

Background: The castle seems like the perfect medieval fortress. Well, almost. While the castle dates back to the 11th century, most of what you see today is actually a Victorian rebuild (1875-1900). The owners of the castle, the Catholic Dukes of Norfolk, weren't very popular in this Protestant country, and neither was their castle, which endured multiple sieges. The dukes

persevered, however, rebuilding their castle in the 18th and 19th centuries along with a large Catholic church. As you explore the castle, posted explanations fill in the story (such as an English Civil War exhibit with a Catholic spin). For a primer before you begin, consider stopping by the little information room at the gate as you enter the castle grounds (across from the ticket booth).

Visiting the Castle: The castle is all about its intimidating bulk and opulent interior—so little explanation is necessary. But here are a few tidbits to bring meaning to your visit. Notice that various parts of the castle have different opening times; if you're here in the morning, visit them according to when they open.

Castle Keep: This ancient centerpiece of the castle is a classic motte-and-bailey design (originally from 1067—the year after the Normans arrived), with a stout windowless fortress atop a man-made hill—double defense against attackers. Later, as the castle grew around it, the keep became the last resort in case of an attack. Walking across the bridge to the keep, ponder how easy it would be to keep the keep—it's connected to the outside only by one bridge, and is well-defended by strategically placed arrow slits. Inside the keep yard, stairs lead down to a cellar used as both a dungeon and a storehouse for resources in case the keep had to be used for a final stand. If the flag is flying up top, it used to mean the Duke of Norfolk or his heir (the Earl of Arundel) was in. Now—so as not to give terrorists a clue—it flies all the time.

Main Castle Rooms: This was—and remains—the gorgeously appointed residence of the Duke of Norfolk. As you ogle the decor, docents explain what you're looking at, and they are always eager to tell you about the lineage, heraldry, and personalities of their beloved dukes. Remember, this all dates from the late 1800s. You'll pass through an armory and a spectacular private **chapel** (19th-century "Catholic Revival") before entering the **Baron's Hall,** with a pair of giant fireplaces and some fine furniture (including a gorgeous inlaid-wood chest). This room is still used for functions... and, occasionally, for filming the British version of *Antiques Road-show*. Then you'll pass through a **picture gallery** displaying a *Who's Who* of the Dukes of Norfolk (no, really...who *are* these people?). (By the way, as you stroll, notice how nearly all the eyes in the paintings seem to follow you. Now, for the rest of your life, when some guide in some gallery brags about this stunt, you're allowed to not be impressed.) Enjoy strolling through the formal state dining room, bedrooms, and drawing rooms. Finally, you'll reach the highlight: a wonderful old **library** with rich mahogany woodwork and 10,000 musty leather-bound books on two levels.

Fitzalan Chapel: This family church—across a tree-filled garden from the main castle—is the final resting place of many of the Dukes of Norfolk. In the nave of the church, notice the grisly double-decker tomb of a 15th-century earl. Called a *memento mori*, or "reminder of death," this was carved during the earl's lifetime—with his virile, healthy self on the top level, and a rotting corpse on the bottom level—to remind him of his own mortality. Flanking the aisle, find the plaques dedicated to the most recent D.'s of N.: Bernard (who died in 1975) and his cousin Miles Francis (died in 2002). Today's Duke—Edward Fitzalan-Howard—is the 18th to hold the title...and you just walked through his house.

Earl's Garden: From the chapel, follow the signs and walk uphill into the Earl's Garden. Landscaped and maintained by a renowned gardener, the plantings intrigue and impress with their creativity. The stumpery (upturned oak trees), White Garden, and Italianate formal gardens are all lined with herbaceous borders, confirming England's obsession with all things green.

Arundel Town: If you have time to kill, check out the adjacent village of Arundel, where you'll find many fine pubs and shops. The little self-service **TI** is located inside the Arundel Museum, across from the castle entrance (daily in summer 10:00-16:00, Mill Road, tel. 01903/885-866, www.sussexbythesea.com).

DARTMOOR

Windswept and desolate, Dartmoor—one of England's best national parks—is one of the few truly wild places you'll find in this densely populated country. Dartmoor's vast medieval commons are still places where all can pass, anyone can graze their sheep, and ponies run wild. Old stone-slab clapper bridges remind hikers that for thousands of years, humans have trod these same paths. In other parts of England, stone circles, stone rows, and standing stones are cause for a tourist frenzy. In Dartmoor, where the terrain is littered with the highest concentration of prehistoric monuments in the UK, they're lonely and awaiting your visit.

Great literary minds, perhaps inspired by all that mystery and prehistory, have been drawn to Dartmoor for centuries: Sir Arthur Conan Doyle (his masterpiece, *The Hound of the Baskervilles*, was set here), Agatha Christie (who wrote her first mystery novel here), Evelyn Waugh (who wrote *Brideshead Revisited* here) to name a few. Even filmmaker Steven Spielberg (whose movie *War Horse* was filmed here) was inspired by Dartmoor's landscape.

Locals brag that Dartmoor is England as it was 50 years ago. Maybe that's why it's increasingly a retreat of the rich and famous. You'll find yourself sharing the narrow roads with luxury SUVs, as many retired CEOs and washed-up celebrities have resettled in this idyllic and remote countryside far from prying eyes. The area around Chagford has become known as the "Golden Triangle."

All that wealth aside, Dartmoor remains first and foremost the terrain of hikers. Dartmoor gives you a chance to be alone with England's history, jaded sheep, stately wild ponies, and seemingly endless moors. It's also a moody place: At sunset on a clear evening, the gold-tinged heather and rolling hills can be romantic; but on a gray and misty day, it's foreboding—and if you listen hard enough, you might just hear the howl of the hound of the Baskervilles.

PLANNING YOUR TIME

Dartmoor works well as a stopover between Cornwall (see next chapter) and the rest of England. While you could get a taste of Dartmoor with one overnight (after breakfast, do my "Dartmoor Drive" and/or visit Scorhill Stone Circle before moving on in the afternoon), it really deserves at least one full day and two overnights to fully appreciate its majesty and mystery. This is one of those places where time slows down...and puts a crimp in an ambitious itinerary.

GETTING AROUND DARTMOOR

By Car: Drivers have Dartmoor by the tail—but a good map or GPS device is essential...as is a fair amount of courage. Dartmoor's

narrow lanes are the most challenging in England: barely as wide as a single car, and often flanked by tall stone hedges covered in greenery. As most roads are too narrow for two cars to easily pass, you'll often have to pull up or reverse to the nearest wide spot in the road when encountering another car. Just follow the other driver's lead, fold in your mirrors as needed, and don't be shy to wave a thank you. For driving in Dartmoor, rent the smallest car you can tolerate, and you'll breathe easier. Secondary roads have less traffic on weekdays. The only places to buy gas on or near the moors are in Chagford and Bovey Tracey.

By Bus: Dartmoor is tricky for visitors without a car; bus connections are sparse on weekends and nearly nonexistent during the week (tel. 0871-200-2233, www.dartmoor.gov.uk or http://traveline.info). Newton Abbot, Okehampton, and Ivybridge are on minor rail lines, but the closest major city is Exeter.

During high season, the **Haytor Hoppa/#271** bus runs Saturdays only to cover the eastern side of Dartmoor (£5 hop-on/hop-off ticket, late May-mid-Sept 4/day), looping from Newton Abbot's train station to Bovey Tracey, up to Haytor and on to Widecombe-in-the-Moor and Hound Tor, before returning to Bovey Tracey and Newton Abbot. Two other bus routes from Exeter also connect to Dartmoor towns (Mon-Sat year-round, no buses Sun): Dartline **#173** to Chagford and Moretonhampstead (4/day), and Country Bus **#359** to Moretonhampstead (6/day).

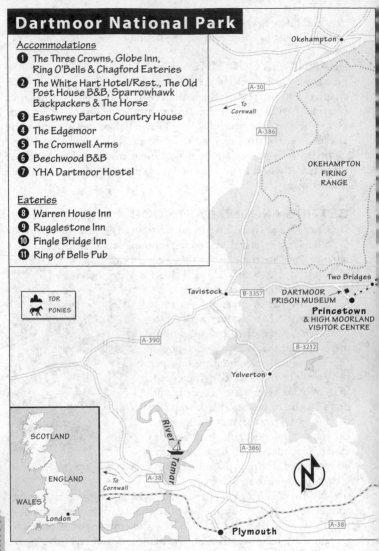

Dartmoor National Park

Accommodations

1. The Three Crowns, Globe Inn, Ring O'Bells & Chagford Eateries
2. The White Hart Hotel/Rest., The Old Post House B&B, Sparrowhawk Backpackers & The Horse
3. Eastwrey Barton Country House
4. The Edgemoor
5. The Cromwell Arms
6. Beechwood B&B
7. YHA Dartmoor Hostel

Eateries

8. Warren House Inn
9. Rugglestone Inn
10. Fingle Bridge Inn
11. Ring of Bells Pub

TOR
PONIES

Okehampton

A-30

To Cornwall

A-386

OKEHAMPTON FIRING RANGE

Two Bridges

Tavistock   B-3357   DARTMOOR PRISON MUSEUM

Princetown
& HIGH MOORLAND VISITOR CENTRE

A-390

B-3212

Yelverton

River Tamar

SCOTLAND

ENGLAND

WALES

London

To Cornwall

A-38

A-386

A-38

Plymouth

Orientation to Dartmoor

Devon, in which Dartmoor is located, is England's least densely populated and second-biggest county. Dartmoor National Park is vast (368 square miles), but I've focused on the most accessible chunk, at the northeastern end of the park between the A-30 and A-38 highways.

Throughout Dartmoor, there are more than 10,000 ancient monuments, all accessible to walkers. Park information offices are

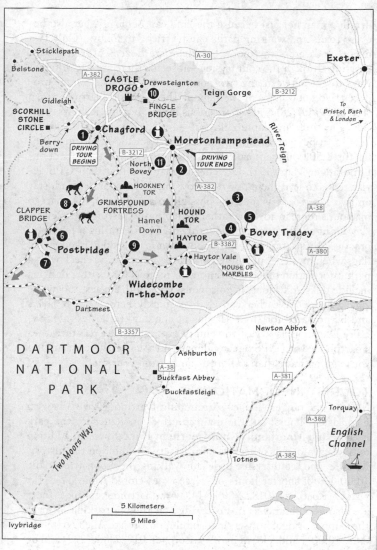

in Princetown, Postbridge, and Haytor (see "Tourist Information," later). The small villages that encroach on the park are charming. Towns of reasonable size (including Chagford, Moretonhampstead, Bovey Tracey, and Widecombe) have parking lots (free or cheap) and WCs (generally free). Moretonhampstead and Bovey Tracey also have TIs.

Two pieces of gear are essential: good shoes (you'll be slogging through mud and dodging "Dartmoor landmines"—wild-horse patties) and an Ordnance Survey map. You'll need this highly detailed map not just because the land can be boggy, but also because roads and walking paths can be tricky to follow. (Only two major roads cross the moor, but there are dozens of lesser roads twisting through the countryside—it seems there are five different ways to get between any two points.) The Ordnance Survey produces two good maps of the region. The 1:25,000 Dartmoor map (Explorer #OL28) is ideal for serious hikers, because it shows every ridge, feature, and landmark, but—until you get used to it—its detail can be overwhelming for drivers. Instead, drivers may prefer the 1:50,000 map (called "Okehampton & North Dartmoor," Landranger Map #191). Drivers also may find that their GPS device tends to lead them down narrow one-lane roads. Instead, stay on two-lane roads as much as possible to avoid stress; it's smart to map out a route in advance rather than blindly trusting your device.

Dangers: Parts of the moors are used by the military for target practice. These areas are clearly shown on maps, and marked by red flags when in use—but before going for a hike, always check with a park information office to ensure your route is OK. Other dangers include ticks and adders (a poisonous snake with a black-and-white zigzag stripe). Weather can change quickly here, so wear layers and be prepared for "four seasons in one day" (as locals say). Because Dartmoor is so vast and empty, getting lost is a real threat—a smartphone with GPS or a good map and a compass are essential if you're going more than a short distance from your car.

TOURIST INFORMATION

Most of the bigger villages surrounding Dartmoor have TIs with inconsistent hours, but the main information center for the park is the **High Moorland Visitor Centre** in Princetown. In addition to hiking info, this office has an interactive exhibit on the history, wildlife, and "countryside code" for walking the moors (free; daily 10:00-17:00, shorter hours off-season and closed Mon-Wed; Tavistock Road, tel. 01822/890-414, www.dartmoor.gov.uk). There are also good branches in **Postbridge** (at the big parking lot near the clapper bridge, hosts a small exhibit on Bronze Age Dartmoor; daily 10:00-17:00, closed in off-season; tel. 01822/880-272) and by **Haytor** (on the B-3387 3 miles west of Bovey Tracey, same hours as main branch, tel. 01364/661-520).

At any of these offices, you can buy your Ordnance Survey map and pick up the free information-packed *Enjoy Dartmoor* guide (also downloadable online). These offices are the best source of advice on hikes or driving routes, and each one sells an illustrated booklet with suggestions for self-guided walks in that area. The booklet on Haytor Rocks and Hound Tor (described later) comes with a fine foldout map and covers ancient, medieval, and early modern history. It lays out a circular seven-mile hike connecting landmarks with other neighboring sights. If you have a mobile device, you can download free, six-mile audio walks that start at each of the three park information centers (www.dartmoor.gov.uk; click on the magnifying glass to search for "audio walks").

The TIs in **Moretonhampstead** (daily 9:30-17:00, shorter hours and closed Mon-Wed off-season, New Street, tel. 01647/440-043, www.visitmoretonhampstead.co.uk) and **Bovey Tracey** (see "Sights in Dartmoor," later in this chapter) can also be helpful.

Guided Walks: Guided walks are offered by a local guiding collective called **Moorland Guides** (www.moorlandguides.co.uk). You can also go with your own guide for a hike of your choosing. **Tom Soby** offers a range of walks, including a popular one exploring the places featured in *The Hound of the Baskervilles* (4-hour private tours-£80, book 2 months in advance, mobile 07513-595-684, tomstors@hotmail.com). **Phil Page,** a former Dartmoor park manager, offers walks all year on topics from butterflies to literary works set in Dartmoor (£10/hour for up to 6 people, can pick you up and drive you to the hike, mobile 07858-421-148 or 07849-840-126, www.dartmoornaturetours.co.uk, enquiries@dartmoornaturetours.co.uk).

Dartmoor Drive

PONY, LAMB, AND MOOR JOYRIDE

This self-guided driving tour—worth ▲▲▲—is a convenient framework for your Dartmoor exploration. This route begins in Chagford and ends in nearby Moretonhampstead, but you can join or leave it wherever you like. The distances are short—the route is about 40 miles total—but the drive takes all day when you add in hikes and exploration. Linger at the desolate

viewpoints you find most appealing, and don't be afraid to venture off this plan for a walk to a secluded stone row or circle. If you have enough time, chase down leads suggested by locals—there are many hidden gems embedded in Dartmoor. If you're in a rush, you can squeeze this drive into three hours: Skip the detours (such as Grimspound and Princetown), choose just one tor to climb, and grab lunch on the go

• *Begin in the village of...*

▲Chagford

Perched on the edge of the moor, this tiny town is not only charming but actually feels like a real, normal slice of English life (www.visitchagford.com; park on the street for up to 2 hours or at the pay lot at the far end of town, past the church and Jubilee Hall—follow *P* signs). The small-town ambience here may make you feel like you've stepped into a time warp (or maybe a quaint BBC sitcom). Villages like this one (which was probably established in Saxon times) were built around Dartmoor as bases for the tin-mining industry. In 1305, Chagford became one of four Dartmoor stannary towns, a main center for "weighing and paying" the miners. The eight-sided **Market House** in the village square (known as the "pepper pot") is located on the site of the old stannary court/assayer's office.

St. Michael's Parish Church, at the upper end of town, mostly dates from the 15th century and is built out of the typical stone of the area, gray granite. The hard rock is tough to work, so most buildings here are fairly simple. An incident occurred here that is said to have inspired R. D. Blackmore's *Lorna Doone:* A bride named Mary Whiddon was shot dead by a former suitor as she left the church during her wedding in 1641. Look among the pews at the needlepoint cushions, a few of which bear a tinner's symbol: three rabbits in a circle, each with two ears, but they appear to share only three ears among them. (This motif also shows up in the stained-glass window over the door of the wine store on the town square.)

The little **village square**—named simply The Square—has all the essentials: bank, post office, small grocery store, pharmacy, butcher, delicatessen, and a few hardware shops that sell any hiking gear that you might have forgotten (including Ordnance Survey maps). Go gawk inside Bowden's hardware store and "Moorland Centre" to see how everything you could possibly ever need can be neatly crammed into one place. Don't

miss the glassed-in antique-hardware room way in the back, and the loft full of rain gear (Mon-Sat 9:00-17:30, closed Sun). Devonshire Dairy sells ice-cream cones, interesting cheeses from the area, and clotted cream by the pound (Mon-Sat 9:30-17:30, closed Sun, shorter hours off-season).

• *Hop in your car, drive past the church, and follow* Postbridge *signs directing you to the road south of Chagford (very skinny for a couple*

DARTMOOR

of miles), hit the B–3212, and turn right. Soon after you turn, you'll cross some...

Cattle Grates

Welcome to wild-pony country. The rumble of your tires over cattle grates—which you'll cross several times on our drive—tells you that you've entered an area without fences, where live-stock of all kinds can roam freely. It's also a reminder to slow down and watch the road closely, especially around blind corners—the animals find cars more in-teresting than scary, and you may well find some

sunning themselves in the middle of the road. I've had to lean on my horn several times to convince a dozing sheep to let me pass. As throughout England, you'll see sheep grazing and fluffy little lambs bounding through the heather. But Dartmoor adds its own unique touch: famously "wild," but remarkably tame, horses. (In fact, the horses are all owned by local farmers, who keep an eye on them as they graze the moors—notice that some horses are branded.) Horses have wandered here for centuries, and the brown ones are probably the most closely related to the ancestral Dartmoor breed. The park discourages people from feeding or even approaching the horses—they get used to mooching, so they often readily come up to people, but may bite or kick without warning.

• *After crossing the cattle grates, you're really into the heart of...*

The Moors

England's green, bucolic landscape is occasionally interrupted by brown, scrubby moorlands like these. A moor is characterized by its relative lack of vegetation, save for high grasses and heather—a dull-brown shrub that thrives here (and briefly turns a brilliant purple when it flowers in late summer). In the springtime, you may see splashes of vibrant yellow flowers on the plant called gorse (closely related to Scotch broom). The long, undulating expanses of open land, almost unbroken by trees but scattered with long-forgotten prehistoric stone monuments, make Dartmoor feel even more mysterious than other English moors.

• *On the left, you may notice the first of many tors—hilltop clusters of rocks—we'll see on this trip. This one overlooks the evocative remains of a Bronze Age settlement. If you're up for a hike, consider this optional de-tour to get a closer look: Turn left at the white and brown* Widecombe/Grimspound *sign, and follow the road for about a mile—keeping an eye*

*on those hilltop rocks above you on the left. The road reaches a steep bend
at a place where a mountain stream trickles down the hill; look for a tiny
sign and a three-car pullout on the right, and four stone steps on the left.
You can park and use these steps to start a 10-minute climb up to...*

Grimspound

As you face the hilltop pile of rocks, called Hookney Tor, look
right to the saddle between the two hills to find the huge, graceful
outer ring of Grimspound. Dating from 2000 BC, this late-Bronze
Age fortress was a settlement for 800 years. The outer stone wall
enclosed the smaller inner circles, which would have been stone
huts. In some of these footprints, the tall stones flanking the entryway are still visible. The outer wall was probably designed to
pen animals. Notice that the ring is designed to provide access to
the stream. Running water was both useful and (archaeologists believe) spiritually important to prehistoric peoples. Well-populated
in ancient times, the moors are thought to have become unlivable
in about 1200 BC because of climate change, and settlements like
these were abandoned. From the settlement, look across the valley;
on the left side of the adjacent ridge (to the left of the stone rabbit
fence that runs down to the valley), you'll see the faint remains of
hillside terraces, called lynchets, created by medieval farmers.

If you have time for a longer hike, consider huffing up to the
top of Hookney Tor for a better view down on Grimspound and
the surrounding hills. (A standing stone and a stone row are both
faintly visible—to those with excellent eyesight—on the top of the
ridge across the valley.) The flat hilltop above Grimspound (Hamel
Down) was covered with poles during World War II, to prevent
German gliders from landing there.

• *Back in your car, backtrack to the main road, and turn left to continue
south. After about a mile, on the left, just before the big parking lot, look
for the worn and weathered stub of a...*

Celtic Cross

All along the road, look for tall stone crosses like this one. These
marked the way for villagers to cross the moor, often for funeral
processions. Many of these began life as prehistoric pagan pillars,
and were carved into crosses later, after Christianization.

• *Soon after the cross, on the right, you'll see the...*

Warren House Inn

Named for a warrener (rabbit-raiser) who fed bunnies to hungry
miners, this pub comes with a fun history. This site has reputedly
been occupied by a travelers' rest stop for more than 900 years. In
1845, a pub across the road was falling down from disrepair, so
this "new" structure was built. Supposedly embers from the old fire

were used to light the fire in the new building—which has burned ever since. While the story is questionable, the **$$** food here is good—specializing in (of course) rabbit pie, as well as steak-and-ale pie. The glorious moorside seating, at picnic benches out front and across the road, make it an enticing stop for a meal or drink. If it's chilly, take advantage of the cozy interior, with that legendary fireplace still smoldering (daily 11:00-22:00, off-season closed for dinner Mon-Tue, tel. 01822/880-208, www.warrenhouseinn. co.uk).

• *There's a lot moor to see (sorry), so let's keep moving. Carry on along the same road into the town of...*

Postbridge

This functional village comes with one of Dartmoor's classic views. As you cross the bridge in the heart of town, on the left you'll see an

ancient bridge parallel to the road. Bridges like this one—essentially a post and a wide, flat stone lintel—dot the moor. Called clapper bridges, they date from the Middle Ages, if not earlier. For a closer look, pull over at the big parking lot on the right soon after the bridge, near the handy and very helpful national park office. If you have time, consider a hike—Postbridge is a good base for moor walks (pick up their booklet for walks from here).

• *Continue down to the village of Two Bridges, where you hit the B-3357. Our route turns left (east, follow sign to* Dartmeet*) on this road, but consider detouring to the right (west) to the town of* **Princetown**, *with its High Moorland Visitor Centre (see "Tourist Information," earlier). Princetown is also home to a historic high-security prison that held French prisoners during the Napoleonic Wars, and American POWs during the War of 1812; today it has a museum (see "Sights in Dartmoor," later). But if you've already gotten your fill of park info from the Postbridge office, and don't care about prison history, Princetown is skippable.*

Heading east on the B-3357, you'll cross more cattle grates and continue to enjoy moor scenery. Soon the straightforward highway disappears, and you'll have to use narrower back roads to reach our next stop. You'll feel lost, but use GPS or your map and track signs closely: Leaving the moor, cut through the forest and carry on straight through Dartmeet (worth a stop to see its clapper bridge and stroll up the stream), then veer uphill toward (but not all the way to) Ashburton. You'll go back up and down another mini moor; at this point, watch for the turnoff on the left

DARTMOOR

toward Sherril and Babeny; once on this road, continue straight (skipping the second Sherril/Babeny turnoff) into the village of Ponsworthy. From here signs direct you to our next stop (with a parking lot near the church).

▲Widecombe-in-the-Moor

Set in the center of the rolling hills, this adorable but often shopper-choked village is a scenic stop—and feels crowded after a drive on the empty moor. There's usually a farmers market on the fourth Saturday of every month, and generally a Thursday craft market during the summer at the 1537 Church House (mid-May-mid-Oct, www.widecombe-in-the-moor.com). Stroll through the tranquil churchyard—with views of hilltop tors on the horizon above—and dip into the Church of St. Pancras.

If you're ready for a meal, there are a few decent café options. Or drive on (turning right at the sign by the Church House)

down the country road to the **$$ Rugglestone Inn**—which is more likely to have local farmers than tourists drinking a pint. They serve up heaping plates of good, hearty food (meat and fish pies are the favorite)...but watch out for the high-powered local cider. Choose between the wonderfully claustrophobic interior, or stroll across the stream to the delightful garden (food served daily 12:00-14:00 & 18:30-21:00, tel. 01364/621-327, www. rugglestoneinn.co.uk).

• *Leave Widecombe, following signs for* Bovey Tracey *and enjoying the sky-high views. (On a clear day, you can see all the way to the English Channel.) Now we'll take a look at two of the better-known "tors" of Dartmoor. If you're tight on time, choose one: Haytor is famous and offers better views, but is more difficult to hike to, while Hound Tor is the more impressive formation.*

On the Bovey Tracey road, you'll spot a turnoff on the left toward Hound Tor and Merton, which we'll take later (or now, if you want to skip Haytor). To see Haytor, continue 1.5 miles farther on—you'll spot the rocky hilltop above you on the left. Park in the giant lot on the right (after a smaller one on the left; make sure to pay to park) and hike 15 minutes up to the grand...

▲Haytor

Dartmoor sits up on a granite plateau, and occasionally bare granite "peaks" poke up through the heather. (These are the crumbling craters of long-extinct volcanoes—covered by dirt and sediment that has since eroded away.) Like lonesome watchtowers looming above the barren landscape, these tors are Dartmoor's most distinctive landmarks—and Haytor is the most famous and popular, thanks to its easy access, great king-of-the-mountain feeling, and

excellent vantage point for panoramic views. Tors look like piles of boulders that you can imagine might have been dragged and dropped on hilltops by prehistoric developers, but they're all natural. This area is divided into two parts: Haytor itself, and

the adjacent Haytor Rocks. (The TI's little hiking guide describes a fine circular hike connecting Haytor Rocks and Hound Tor with a nearby quarry and a stone "tramway" from 1820.)

• *Yet another national park information office is on this same road, a minute beyond the parking lot. And if you'd like to detour into the town of* **Bovey Tracey** *(described under "Sights in Dartmoor," later), now's the time—it's 10 minutes away on the B-3387, down in the valley. En route are the gorgeous grounds of The Edgemoor, a recommended, picture-perfect place to enjoy a cream tea (described later, under "Eating in Dartmoor").*

Or, to continue our loop, backtrack to the Hound Tor/Merton turn-off (it's the next turnoff), which you'll now follow north through the moors. Soon you'll see another tor ahead and on the right. When you get to the little fork, follow the P signs to the right and park to walk up to...

▲▲Hound Tor

Perhaps the most striking tor in Dartmoor, and the inspiration for the Sherlock Holmes story *The Hound of the Baskervilles*, this

mighty clump of rocks impresses. According to legend, this stand of stones was once a pack of hunting dogs that had disrupted a witches' coven. As a punishment, the pooches were petrified. (The hunter who owned the dogs was turned into the nearby tor

called Bowerman's Nose, about a mile north of here.) Hike up and scramble over the many levels. In the valley beyond this ridge are the faint remains of some old Devon longhouses. These were situated at a gentle angle, with animals in the lower part and people in

Letterboxing

The local pastime of letterboxing began as a way to collect tourist postcards. What has evolved is a secret system of log-books hidden all over Dartmoor—inside metal boxes, squir-reled away under rocks, or stuffed in the brush. Your goal: Find the logbook and stamp, and add your name and stamp to as many books as possible (bring your own inkpad just in case). Since this practice is a bit under the radar, you'll need to enlist a local to help you get started. Ask at a local TI or at the YHA Dartmoor hostel (near Postbridge) or check out DartmoorLetterboxing.org.

the upper part—liquids and other waste would run downhill, while the heat generated by the livestock would warm its owners above.

• *Our tour is nearly finished. From the Hound Tor parking lot, back-track a few yards to the little fork and turn right, following signs to* M'hampstead. *You'll drive through the countryside before reaching the larger but still-charming town of* **Moretonhampstead.** *You'll find park-ing and free WCs on your left as you enter town (on Court Street). The town's tiny, thatched center is a busy traffic crossroads, with a few pubs and restaurants (including the recommended pub, The Horse), a Co-op grocery store, a pharmacy, a bakery, and a hardware store. What else could you need?*

Our drive is finished...but there's plenty more of Dartmoor to ex-plore. If you still have daylight left, consider heading north out of More-tonhampstead on the A-382 until the turnoff (to the right) for Drew-steignton and the **Fingle Bridge;** *or head back through Chagford and venture to the* **Scorhill Stone Circle** *(both described under "Sights in Dartmoor," next).*

Sights in Dartmoor

▲Walks on the Moors

Before you start walking, pick up an Ordnance Survey map (at any local shop or TI) or download one of the many hiking apps (Devon Walks is user friendly). The Princetown TI also has a map with suggestions for routes through the moors. Postbridge, in the heart of the moorlands, is a fine launch pad for good walks, and has a park information center that can suggest many well-outlined routes. Other good walking bases include Belstone in the north (for rugged scenery) and Ivybridge in the south (more forested). You can go almost anywhere—except the firing ranges. These are technically open for walking when not in use (you'll see red flags if they're closed), but it's probably best to avoid them entirely. For more pointers, read "Orientation to Dartmoor," earlier.

DARTMOOR

Here are a few ideas for popular, easy-to-moderate, two- to four-hour hikes in the region. Before attempting any of these, get details (and ideally maps) from a local TI or park office:

From **Scorhill Stone Circle** (described next), you can continue through Scorhill Down to the river, where you'll see a tolmen (a doughnut-shaped stone), then proceed through Chagford Common before hooking back up past Kestor Rock toward your car.

From **Postbridge,** consider the hike up to Bellever Tor, then circle around to the youth hostel and back to the bridge.

From **Haytor**'s park information office, circle around the base of Haytor Down to the village of Leighton, then hike back along the road.

From **Grimspound,** the Bronze Age settlement described on my "Dartmoor Drive," you can hike up to Hameldown Tor and along the summit of Hamel Down, then down into the valley and back to your car.

▲▲Scorhill Stone Circle

Hundreds of Neolithic ruins dot the landscape of Dartmoor, but the

Scorhill (SCO-rill) Stone Circle near Gidleigh may be the best. Stonehenge, *the* iconic stone circle, is much bigger—but it's also packed with crowds. Tranquil, forgotten Scorhill is yours alone—the way a stone circle should be. As it comes with a scenic stroll across a moor, it's a great sampling of what Dartmoor is all about—as much about the journey as about the destination.

Once there, you'll be alone with the heather, broom, ancient history...and, often, sheep and wild ponies. Enjoying the solitude at the circle, scan the horizon, noticing other formations all around you—some natural tors, others likely man-made like this one. Places like Scorhill are a rare case in our modern world where we simply don't know the who, what, why, or how.

Getting There: The trailhead, about a 15-minute drive west of Chagford, is tricky to find. (I wouldn't attempt it in a heavy fog—but if you do, take along a compass.) From Chagford, follow signs to *Gidleigh*—you'll drive west out of town, bear right (uphill) at the fork, then turn right at the next intersection; from there, cross over the very narrow bridge, then turn left to go through Murchington. Proceed straight, going up and down the hills through Gidleigh. Keep following the same off-the-beaten-path road through the mossy stone hamlet of Berrydown, until you dead-end at a little

DARTMOOR

parking lot (if in doubt, follow signs for *Scorhill*). Park, then walk through the gate and hike about 15 minutes straight ahead up and over the moor (with long stone fences on either side of you, which gradually widen—part of a system shepherds designed to funnel their sheep without the sheep realizing it). After cresting the hill (with 360-degree views), head down into the gentle valley and look for the circle below (when the wide, well-trod path through the heather forks, angle right). There is a clapper bridge about 200 yards to the left.

▲Teign Gorge and Fingle Bridge

In the town of Drewsteignton, a narrow road leads down into the Teign River Valley (from the B-3219, watch for the easy-to-miss *Fingle Bridge* signs to the right).

At the end of the road is the out-of-the-way but understandably popular **$$ Fingle Bridge Inn,** a pub set along a river and a picturesque old bridge. The food is good and reasonably priced, with daily specials and a hearty ploughman's lunch of open-face sandwiches. While the interior is cozy, on a nice day it can't match the delightful riverside picnic tables (lunch and cream tea served daily 12:00-15:00, dinner served Thu-Sat 18:00-21:00; tel. 01647/281-287, www.finglebridgeinn. co.uk). The bridge is a popular spot for weddings and fly-fishing. The trail across the road makes for an excellent post-meal amble along the river.

Castle Drogo

Just up the road from the Teign Gorge, you'll come across this elaborate country house—complete with a circular croquet lawn (you

can borrow balls and mallets at the ticket desk) and formal gardens—that has the honor of being the last castle built in England, finished in 1930.

Drogo's megalomaniacal owner, Julius Drewe, demanded a flat roof (to match the medieval castles he was imagining). But the modern building methods of the day couldn't support that unusual design, and the building leaked terribly even before it was completed. Consequently, the castle is undergoing extensive renovation. In the meantime, you can still visit the interior, but the collection of furnishings and noble bric-a-brac has been consolidated in one half of the complex, while the other half has cleverly been turned into a "work in progress" exhibit about the project itself—with knowledgeable docents who can explain exactly what went wrong and what's being done to fix it. The castle wasn't particularly worth visiting before the project, and even less so now; come here only if this is your best chance to see a noble estate.

Cost and Hours: £12.20; daily 11:00-17:00, grounds and visitors center open at 10:00, shorter hours off-season, closed late Dec-mid-Feb; café, tel. 01647/433-306, www.nationaltrust.org.uk/castledrogo. Some trails on the estate lead down to Fingle Bridge.

Dartmoor Prison Museum

It makes sense that a prison would be set upon the moors. To Victorian-age Londoners, this rugged and distant land must have felt like Siberia. Built in the early 1800s to house French military prisoners captured during the Napoleonic Wars (along with some American POWs from the War of 1812), Dartmoor Prison was later converted to incarcerate civilian criminals. Notorious until recently for housing some of the most unsavory convicts alive (sort of a British San Quentin), the prison was also briefly used in 1917 to hold conscientious objectors who refused to join in World War I. The museum, located in the former dairy across the street from the still-functioning prison, is well laid out and features historical exhibits and artifacts (from shackles to homemade items crafted by inmates) that offer insight into this infamous house of incarceration.

Cost and Hours: £4; daily 9:30-16:30, Fri and Sun until 16:00; just north of Princetown on the B-3357/Tavistock Road, tel. 01822/322-130, www.dartmoor-prison.co.uk.

Bovey Tracey

This town (pronounced "Buvvy Tracy") on the southeastern side of Dartmoor National Park is too big to be cute (pop. 7,000), but it does offer a few modest indoor options when the rains chase you off the moors (just 10 minutes' drive east of Haytor on the B-3387). The **TI** is located on the main street at the main pay-and-display lot on the right as you drive into town (Mon-Sat 10:00-16:00, Sun 9:30-15:30, sporadic hours off-season, Station Road, tel. 01626/832-047, www.boveytracey.gov.uk).

Bovey Tracey, a pottery town until the 1950s, is becoming known as a center for fine crafts. Clay was quarried nearby, and Josiah Wedgwood even nosed around here when deciding where to locate his china factory (he later chose Staffordshire). The **Devon Guild of Craftsmen** has an appealing gallery/museum and shop

DARTMOOR

in a restored riverside mill downtown. The bright, modern interior showcases items for sale by local artists; a few temporary exhibits also highlight local crafts (free, daily 10:00-17:30, café, immediately after crossing the river on Station Road, tel. 01626/832-223, www.crafts.org.uk).

The **House of Marbles,** on the outskirts of town, sounds goofy enough that you might want to visit. It's basically a giant gift shop inside a historic pottery with some interesting glassmaking displays. Check out the marble museum displaying antique marbles, ones made of odd materials, and fun, kinetic wire marble mazes in action that always draw a crowd (press the button to make them go). Nearby is a small pottery museum. The place is also home of the Teign Valley Glass Studios, and you can watch artisans at work creating contemporary glassware using traditional and modern techniques (free, artists in action generally Tue-Fri and sometimes also Sat 9:00-16:30, Sun 10:00-15:00, lunch and tea breaks posted). Outside in the courtyard, surrounded by café tables, are old, circa-1900 "muffle" kilns (signs describe their history). Beyond those is a sprawling children's area. In the gift shop, kids of all ages will love digging through the giant bins of multicolored marbles—they're actually made in Mexico, but big piles of them look really cool (free, Mon-Sat 9:00-17:00, Sun from 11:00, café, about 1.5 miles south of town toward Newton Abbot just off the A-382, at The Old Pottery on Pottery Road, tel. 01626/835-358, www. houseofmarbles.com).

NEAR DARTMOOR
▲Exeter Cathedral

The nearest large city to Dartmoor is Exeter, about 15 miles (a half-hour drive) east of the moor. A pleasant and bustling university city of 120,000, Exeter's claim to fame is its beautiful cathedral, which sits on a charming green facing the old town. With a Norman core later embellished in Decorated Gothic style, the cathedral could be worth a stop if you're passing through Exeter and have time to spare. Highlights of the grand interior include the ribbed vaulting; 400 colorful "bosses" (decorations at the intersection of vaulting spines, including the famous "Becket Boss," showing the execution of Thomas Becket); the unique minstrels' gallery (more commonly seen in palaces than churches); the colorful astronomical clock; and the quire, with its 50 fold-down, carved-wooden seats called misericords. A 300,000-piece LEGO model of the cathedral is slowly being constructed, brick-by-sponsored-brick to raise money for preservation. Donate £1 and place a brick yourself.

Cost and Hours: £7.50, includes audioguide and docent-led tour, look for discount coupon in *Visit Exeter* brochure, open to tourists Mon-Sat 9:00-17:00, Sun from 11:30, longer hours and free for worshippers, tel. 01392/285-983, www.exeter-cathedral. org.uk.

Sleeping in Dartmoor

Befitting such a mysterious destination, accommodations in Dartmoor tend to be quirkier than the English norm, with more character(s) than the staid, hotelesque accommodations in more mainline destinations. Sleeping here really feels like "going local." Given the confusing spaghetti of back roads, it's smart to call ahead for precise arrival instructions.

IN AND NEAR CHAGFORD

For a description of the handy home-base town of Chagford, see my "Dartmoor Drive," earlier. Along Chagford's main street, several pubs rent rooms upstairs.

$$$ The Three Crowns is trying to bring contemporary class to this traditional town, with 21 modern rooms across the street from the churchyard. Weekends can be noisier at this functioning pub (High Street, tel. 01647/433-444, www.threecrowns-chagford.co.uk, threecrowns@staustellbrewery.co.uk). This is also a good place to eat (see "Eating in Dartmoor," later).

$$ The Globe Inn, with seven decent rooms, is a lesser value (family room, parking lot nearby, 9 High Street, tel. 01647/433-485, www.theglobeinnchagford.co.uk, graham@theglobeinnchagford. co.uk, Graham and Mary). They're also open for **$$** meals (daily 12:00-14:30 & 18:00-21:00).

$$ Ring O'Bells, an old-school pub, has four simple but comfortable rooms that are worth considering if other options are booked (44 The Square, tel. 01647/432-466, www.ringobellschagford. co.uk, info@ringobellschagford.co.uk).

IN MORETONHAMPSTEAD

Moretonhampstead—larger and less quaint than Chagford or Widecombe-in-the-Moor—is a handy home base with its own share of half-timbered appeal. It feels more like a real working town and less like a backward cutesy village.

$$ The White Hart Hotel, which also hosts one of my recommended restaurants, rents 20 clean and modern rooms that lack character but are comfortable. The Mews, an eight-bedroom annex across the street, is a good option for large groups (The Square, tel. 01647/440-500, www.whitehartdartmoor.co.uk).

$ The Old Post House B&B, along the main road through Moretonhampstead, has five older, slightly musty rooms at an appealingly affordable price (spacious top-floor family room, 18

Court Street, tel. 01647/440-900, www.theoldposthouse.com, info@theoldposthouse.com, Steve and Zoe).

¢ **Sparrowhawk Backpackers,** with an easygoing hipster vibe, rents cheap beds in the Moretonhampstead town center, in the light-filled loft of a restored stone stable (private and family rooms, no breakfast, 45 Ford Street, tel. 01647/440-318, mobile 07870-513-570, www.sparrowhawkbackpackers.co.uk, ali@sparrowhawkbackpackers.co.uk, Alison).

IN AND NEAR BOVEY TRACEY

Sleep here if you want to be close to a real town on the edge of the national park, rather than the rustic villages inside Dartmoor. The town of Bovey Tracey is described earlier in this chapter.

$$$ Eastwrey Barton Country House is set on a terraced lawn halfway up the side of the Wray Valley between Moretonhampstead and Bovey Tracey. It has five warm and spacious rooms in a restored Georgian country house (countryside views, no children under 10, several nice lounges and an inviting garden, on the A-382 near Lustleigh, tel. 01647/277-338, www.eastwreybarton.co.uk, reservations@eastwreybarton.co.uk).

$$$ The Edgemoor screams "English countryside destination wedding" (and they do indeed host weddings and wedding parties on weekends). Filling a picturesque, ivy-draped 1879 schoolhouse (it's been taking guests since 1910), this family-run hotel has 17 rooms in an old shell, but with modern style. Aptly named, it sits right at the edge of the moor, just outside Bovey Tracey on the road to Haytor. It's a bit idiosyncratic, but memorable (free parking, Haytor Road, Lowerdown Cross—leave Bovey Tracey toward Haytor on the B-3387 and watch for the ivy-covered building on the right about a mile out of town, tel. 01626/832-466, www.edgemoor.co.uk, reservations@edgemoor.co.uk).

$ The Cromwell Arms, a 17th-century coaching inn right in the middle of Bovey Tracey, has 14 simple, comfortable rooms and is a good option if other listings are full (family room, minimum 2-night stay on weekends, Fore Street, tel. 01626/833-473, www.thecromwellarms.co.uk, info@thecromwellarms.co.uk, Gary and Julie). The pub serves good **$$$** meals in a traditional atmosphere (open daily).

NEAR POSTBRIDGE

Postbridge—more a wide spot in the road than a village—is a popular springboard for hikes. While there's not much here beyond a pub, a TI, and a gift shop, there are plenty of services in Princetown, about a 15-minute drive south.

DARTMOOR

$$ Beechwood B&B, right at the entrance to Postbridge (as you approach from Chagford), is energetically run by Sarah and Ian. This cozy guesthouse has five rooms, a comfy lounge, a fine garden, and a glassed-in breakfast area (family room, free parking, Postbridge, tel. 01822/880-332, www.beechwood-dartmoor. co.uk, enquiries@beechwood-dartmoor.co.uk).

¢ YHA Dartmoor on the moors is simple and institutional, but it comes with an impressive wildlife area out front so you can learn about the local terrain (private rooms available, breakfast extra, dinner available, open all year, reception open 8:00-10:00 & 17:00-21:00, free parking, kids' game room, tel. 0845-371-9622, www.yha.org.uk, dartmoor@yha.org.uk). It's about a mile south of Postbridge, well-signed from the main road.

Eating in Dartmoor

Like many borderline-touristy English holiday regions, Dartmoor has a surprising array of good-quality eateries—including a few "destination" restaurants that charge big prices to match their big reputations. I've focused my listings on pubs that emphasize their food and are located in charming villages or rustic countryside settings. Note that three of my favorites, all **$$**, are described earlier in this chapter: **Warren House Inn,** perched atop a moor south of Chagford; **Rugglestone Inn,** just outside the village of Widecombe-in-the-Moor; and the **Fingle Bridge Inn,** in the Teign Gorge.

IN AND NEAR CHAGFORD

In the charming town of Chagford, the main square is lined with practical eateries—both quick sandwich places and more traditional pub-like spots for dinner. All of my listings are near the square, each with a distinct character.

$$$ The Three Crowns, the best of the many pubs lining the main drag, is classy and modern, serving well-presented dishes more elegant than pub grub and with a respect for tradition. For seating, you have several options: traditional pub up front, modern glassed-in courtyard farther back, open-air interior courtyard, or a few outdoor tables (daily 12:00-14:30 & 18:00-21:00, High Street, tel. 01647/433-444).

$$ The Globe Inn offers the most classic pub scene in town, serving in three zones—the bar, the bar's lounge, and a classier restaurant. They are proud of their meat pies and fish-and-chips (food served daily 12:00-14:30 & 18:00-21:00, 9 High Street, tel. 01647/433-485).

$ Blacks Delicatessen is the perfect place to grab a quick

DARTMOOR

lunch. Peruse the options—quiches, pies, pasties, paninis, and soups—in their display case, and consider supplementing your choice with their carefully selected grocery items. You can sit out on The Square or—better yet—head for the hidden outdoor tables tucked behind the deli, in the churchyard around back (Mon-Sat 8:00-17:00, closed Sun, 28 The Square, tel. 01647/433-535).

$$ The Birdcage is a good lunch stop. It has a cozy, woody interior and a few tables out front, facing The Square. They specialize in pizzas (daily 9:00-15:00, 11 The Square, tel. 01647/433-883).

$$ 22 Mill Spice—an Indian restaurant serving large, tasty portions, including vegetarian dishes—is a rare opportunity to break away from hearty farm pub grub and sandwiches while in Dartmoor (daily 12:00-14:00 & 17:30-22:00, 22 Mill Street, 01647/432-900).

IN AND NEAR MORETONHAMPSTEAD

$$$ The Horse, with welcoming, lively decor and a well-respected chef, specializes in tasty, crispy wood-fired pizzas, along with other Mediterranean dishes and traditional pub fare. You can sit in the cozy and convivial pub up front, or a few steps down in the quieter, more modern dining room (dining room open Tue-Sat 12:30-14:30 & 18:30-21:00, Sun-Mon only pizzas 18:30-21:00, reservations recommended on weekends, 7 George Street, tel. 01647/440-242, http://thehorsedartmoor.co.uk).

In addition to The Horse, Moretonhampstead has two spit-and-sawdust pubs offering affordable food and drink, plus the upscale (almost pretentious) **$$$ White Hart Restaurant,** with a pleasantly traditional but spacious hunting-lodge feel (daily 12:30-14:15 & 18:00-20:30, The Square, tel. 01647/440-500, www.whitehartdartmoor.co.uk; also has rooms for rent—see "Sleeping in Dartmoor," earlier).

In North Bovey: This charming village—just a mile and a half (down narrow country lanes) from Moretonhampstead—has a triangular village green, more than its share of idyllic thatch, and a fine pub: **$$$ Ring of Bells** fills a 13th-century building with atmosphere, happy eaters, and good food. Choose between the various indoor dining spaces, or head out to the delightful yard, surrounded by thatched homes (daily 10:00-14:30 & 18:00-21:00, tel. 01647/440-375). They also have five **$$** rooms upstairs (www.ringofbells.net).

BETWEEN BOVEY TRACEY AND HAYTOR

The Edgemoor, about a mile outside of Bovey Tracey on the way to Haytor (B-3387), has a picture-perfect setting, filling an old ivy-covered schoolhouse. In good weather it's hard to resist the perfectly English garden out front, which seems made to order for a cream tea. Dinner portions are large and can be eaten in the old school pub, restaurant, or outside (daily 18:30-21:00). They also rent rooms (for directions and lodging details, see "Sleeping in Dartmoor," earlier).

CORNWALL

Penzance • St. Ives • Penwith Peninsula • East Cornwall

Set on a rocky peninsula at the southwest tip of England, Cornwall has a Celtic vibe. Its rugged scenery and wild, uncultivated appeal make you feel as if you're approaching the end of the world (and many natives would say it's exactly that). Harboring the remnants of an endangered Celtic culture (Cornish), an extinct tin-mining industry, and a gaggle of visit-worthy sights, this is one of England's most popular holiday regions—especially among the English.

Cornwall, as part of the "Celtic crescent" that nearly circles England, developed apart from the rest of the country, with its own Cornish language, which thrived for centuries. Fishing, shipping, and smuggling were the main businesses here for hundreds of years, but in the 18th century, tin mining became the major industry. The 20th century dealt a double blow to Cornwall: The local pilchard fishery became depleted, and cheap Asian and South American tin put an end to mining. Today's predominant trade is tourism, as evidenced by the many tourist traps littering the landscape.

But visitors flock here for good reason. The area is packed with ancient sites, adorable villages, and historic monuments, and the climate is unusually mild—making it perfect for gardening, walking, basking on the beach, and generally enjoying life. The region also exerts a pull on fans of British culture—the recent hit BBC series *Poldark* is set here, and the longtime favorite *Doc Martin* is shot in Port Isaac.

Venture to quaint seaside villages, a dramatic theater, a telegraph museum, a dead tin mine, the scant remains of an Iron Age village, and a thought-provoking stone circle. Cry "Land Ho!" at Land's End, and consider going by plane or ferry to the castaway Isles of Scilly. Farther northeast, the castle of a king named Arthur tickles travelers' imaginations, the harbor towns of Padstow and Port Isaac offer a taste of workaday (but still cute) Cornwall, and unusual gardens near Falmouth thrill those with green thumbs.

PLANNING YOUR TIME

Given that it takes so long to get to this edge of the world from the heart of England (figure a good half-day each way by car or train, not counting sightseeing stops), it makes sense to give yourself enough time here. Spending three nights and two days here allows you to slow down, see all the sights, and get a better feel for Cornish culture. Most of the noteworthy sights and villages wrap around the Penwith Peninsula, so you can line them up and see them on a handy circular route by car or bus. (With less time, a two-night stay based in Penzance, with one solid day rambling around the peninsula, offers a suitable first taste).

Set yourself up in a home base and spend most of your time venturing out on day trips. Romantic St. Ives has an artsy beach-bum ambience and is crowded with British holidaymakers in summer. Penzance, on the other hand, is a working-class shipping port with a weather-beaten, workaday main-street bustle, enthusiastic and welcoming natives, and many appealing eateries. Penzance's relative lack of tourist charm is actually an asset—it's much easier to drive into and out of, has better public-transportation connections, and enjoys a fine array of quality accommodations—making it my preferred home base.

The attractions farther east—Tintagel Castle, the coastal towns, and the gardens—are ideal for breaking up the long journey to or from Cornwall (en route to Bath or Dartmoor).

GETTING TO CORNWALL

By Car: To reach Penzance, figure about six hours from London, four hours from Bath or Salisbury, or two hours from Dartmoor. From London, the M-3 motorway speeds you as far as Exeter, where you'll pick up the A-30 the rest of the way (mostly four-lane, partly two-lane). If you're driving from Bristol or Bath, take the M-5 and consider a more scenic, less trafficked route: Partway down the M-5 from Bristol, near Tiverton, turn off onto the A-361 (a.k.a. the North Devon Link Road), which you can follow through North Devon before hopping on the A-39, which parallels

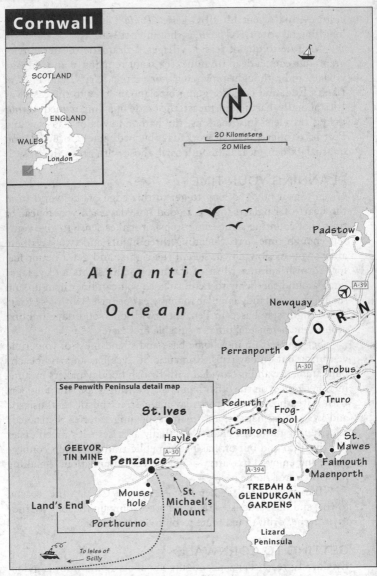

Cornwall

SCOTLAND

ENGLAND

WALES

London

20 Kilometers
20 Miles

Atlantic

Ocean

Padstow

Newquay

A-39

C O R N

Perranporth

A-30

Probus

Truro

See Penwith Peninsula detail map

St. Ives

Redruth

Frog-
pool

Hayle

Camborne

St.
Mawes

GEEVOR
TIN MINE

A-30

Penzance

A-394

Falmouth
Maenporth

Land's End

Mouse-
hole

St.
Michael's
Mount

TREBAH &
GLENDURGAN
GARDENS

Porthcurno

Lizard
Peninsula

To Isles of
Scilly

CORNWALL

the coastline (getting you close to Tintagel Castle, Port Isaac, and Padstow), rejoining the A-30 35 miles east of Penzance. This smaller road is more scenic and can be faster if traffic is heavy on the main road.

By Train: Train travelers arrive in Cornwall at Penzance, the most central and largest city on the coast (see "Penzance Connections," later).

By Plane: Cornwall's main airport is Newquay-Cornwall

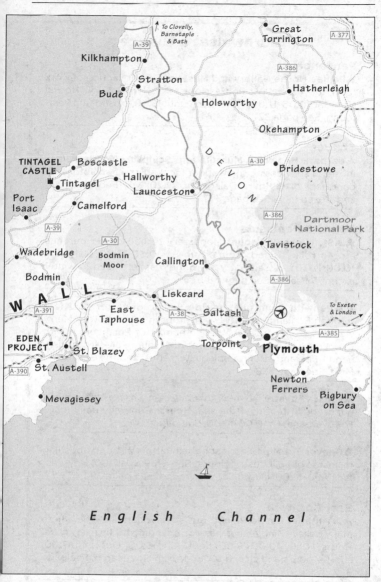

International (code: NQY, www.cornwallairportnewquay.com),
5 miles from Newquay and 35 miles northeast of Penzance.
Many rental car agencies operate at or near the airport. Public-
transportation connections into Penzance can be tricky—contact the Newquay TI for suggestions (tel. 01637/838-516, www.
visitnewquay.org). You'll likely find that it's easiest to spring for a
taxi (Newquay-based Coastline Travel, about £100, tel. 01637/860-
006, www.coastlinetravel.co.uk).

CORNWALL

Cornwall at a Glance

Penzance

▲**Penlee House Gallery and Museum** Fine collection of work from the local Post-Impressionist Newlyn School. **Hours:** Mon-Sat 10:00-17:00, Nov-March until 16:30, closed Sun year-round. See page 371.

St. Ives

▲**Barbara Hepworth Museum and Sculpture Garden** Small museum showcasing the work of local abstract sculptor Barbara Hepworth. **Hours:** Daily 10:00-17:20, Nov-Feb until 16:20 and closed Mon. See page 377.

Penwith Peninsula

▲▲**St. Michael's Mount** Monastery-turned-castle perched atop a rocky island. **Hours:** Sun-Fri 10:30-17:00 (July-Aug 10:00-17:30), closed Sat year-round; castle closed in winter except for tours. See page 382.

▲▲**Penwith Peninsula Joyride** Scenic drive (or bus ride) through England's far west, with stops in fishing towns, Merry Maidens stone circle, the beach hamlet of Porthcurno (with the Minack Theatre and Telegraph Museum), crassly touristy Land's End and its untrampled alternative, and the Geevor Tin Mine. See page 386.

▲**Minack Theatre** Open-air theater set in a rocky cliff perched hundreds of feet over the sea. **Hours:** Generally daily 9:30-17:30, off-season 10:00-16:00. See page 390.

▲**Geevor Tin Mine** Fascinating exhibit on this once-bustling mainstay of an industry. **Hours:** Sun-Fri 9:00-17:00, Nov-Easter 10:00-16:00, closed Sat year-round. See page 393.

East Cornwall

▲▲**Tintagel Castle** Ruined but still evocative castle where many believe King Arthur was born, clinging to the misty cliffs. **Hours:** Daily 10:00-19:00, Sept until 18:00, Oct until 17:00, shorter hours and closed some days in Nov-March. See page 397.

▲**Eden Project** Two huge greenhouses showcasing agriculture techniques of tomorrow. **Hours:** Daily 9:00-18:00, July-Aug until 18:30, Nov-March generally 10:00-16:30. See page 401.

▲**Trebah and Glendurgan Gardens** Pair of tropical gardens near Falmouth. **Hours:** Trebah—daily 10:00-17:00, until dusk in winter; Glendurgan—Tue-Sun 10:30-17:30, closed Mon except in Aug, closed Nov-mid-Feb. See page 403.

GETTING AROUND CORNWALL

This region is most satisfying by car, which allows you to pack a lot into each day. It's challenging but doable by public transportation, though you'll have to be selective.

By Car

Locals like to say, "Welcome to Cornwall, your car is not as wide as you think." You'll be navigating extremely narrow roads when you explore this corner of England.

A coastal road—B-3315 south of Penzance, and B-3306 to the west and north—links together almost all the best sights. Driving in Cornwall is generally easy, but parking is not, especially in summer, so it's a good idea to get an early start. Small villages often have tiny parking lots near the water and larger ones outside town; you'll do best to seek out pay-and-display lots rather than scrounging for free parking (keep a pile of coins in your car). Main roads (such as the A-30 and the A-38) can get very congested, especially on Bank Holiday weekends and in August, so allow extra time. Narrow, twisty Cornish lanes crisscross the spine of the peninsula, and can save time if the main routes are crowded—but you'll need a good map and navigator.

By Public Transportation

Note that most of these public-transit routes run less frequently off-season (mid-Sept-April).

By Bus: It's slow but possible to reach most Cornwall sights by bus (see "Penwith Peninsula by Bus" on page 396 for a recommended bus-trip day plan). Some double-deckers go topless May through September. Most regional buses are run by First Kernow, which sells passes that cover Penzance, St. Ives, Land's End, and the surrounding area (£15/1 day, £20/2 day, £25/3 day, 7-day and family passes available, pay driver or download their app; tel. 0345-602-0121, www.firstgroup.com). Another pass, called the Ride Cornwall Ranger, costs £18 for a full day of travel on all trains and most buses in Cornwall (www.nationalrail.co.uk).

The following bus routes are useful:

Bus **#A1** connects Penzance with Land's End, reaching destinations along the southern edge of the Penwith Peninsula (hourly Mon-Sat, 6/day Sun). It's about 10 minutes to Newlyn, 40 minutes to Porthcurno (stops near the Telegraph Museum and a steep uphill climb to the Minack Theatre), and 1 hour to Land's End. In summer, this route continues as bus #A3, from Land's End to St. Ives (hourly, 80 minutes), with stops at Land's End Airport (20 minutes) and Geevor Tin Mine (35 minutes from Land's End).

Buses **#A17** and **#A2** connect Penzance and St. Ives (#A17: 2/hour, 35 minutes; #A2: hourly, 50 minutes).

Cornish History

Throughout Cornwall, prehistoric huts, stone circles, and other mysterious structures stand witness to the region's long history. When the Romans arrived in Britain in the first century BC, the native Celtic inhabitants were forced to the farthest, most inhospitable corners of the island. To this day, a "Celtic crescent" still rings England, with several groups struggling to keep alive their fading languages, such as Welsh, Scottish Gaelic, Irish Gaelic, Manx (on the Isle of Man)...and Cornish.

This part of Britain—specifically Penzance—was ideally located for shipping, since boats could launch straight into the Atlantic, rather than having to tack from farther east all the way along the English Channel. It's no wonder that Penzance is best known as the namesake for a Gilbert and Sullivan musical about the high seas. Along with the sailors and pirates, artists love this scenic corner of Britain, which can change from sun-drenched to rainy and windblown in a matter of minutes. Dramatic clouds hit Cornwall like a hammer, and the sea changes color with the sky.

Rich deposits of metals—especially tin—have linked this rugged spit of land to the rest of the world. Cornish tin has been found in ancient plumbing as far away as Turkey and Pompeii (Italy). Cornwall wasn't conquered by the Romans, partly because of its remoteness, but also because the Cornish were already Roman trading partners. (You'll find no Roman forts in Cornwall, but you will find Roman goods.) With Cornish trading came an influx of exotic products—Cornish cooking is unique in England for its use of saffron, likely bartered with the Near East for metals.

In the 18th century, Cornwall's tin-mining industry enjoyed a boom (see sidebar on page 394). When the industry went bust in the late 19th century, mine owners from around the world began to recruit and relocate Cornwall's unemployed but highly skilled miners. This "Cornish diaspora" spread the culture from this

Bus #A2 also stops at Marazion near St. Michael's Mount (10 minutes from Penzance), as does bus #U4 from Penzance (hourly).

Bus #M6 connects Penzance with Newlyn and Mousehole (2/hour, 10 minutes to Newlyn, 20 minutes to Mousehole).

By Train: A scenic (read: slow) rail line connects Penzance and St. Ives, mostly running along the coast (roughly hourly with transfer in St. Erth, 30-60 minutes; tel. 0345-748-4950, www.nationalrail.co.uk).

By Guided Tour

To maximize your time and the number of sights you can see, consider a guided tour. **Tim Uff** offers a fine mix of expertise and teaching, enjoyable company, and great driving (£275-300/day for up to 8 people, mobile 07969-281-805, www.tourcornwall.com, corner of England across the face of the earth. For example, hundreds of Cornish miners went to California to get in on the Gold Rush. Locals brag, "Anywhere you find a deep hole in the ground, you'll find a Cornishman at the bottom of it." Similarly, Cornish graveyards read like a geography textbook, as headstones often list the places where the person lived.

The great migration of the late 19th century also left behind many ghost towns, which still dot the Cornish countryside. Today, many of these long-abandoned homes are being bought up by Londoners and converted into holiday villas.

The Cornish language—related to Welsh, and more distantly related to Scottish Gaelic and Irish Gaelic—was widely spoken here through the late 18th century. As the Industrial Revolution brought Britain together and Anglican church leaders refused to offer services in Cornish, the language became obsolete. Cornish survived only among a handful of speakers through the 19th and early 20th centuries. But, remarkably, Cornish held on, and—after a recent EU designation as an official minority language—it's now being taught in schools again. More people speak Cornish today than two centuries ago, and raising kids to be bilingual is in vogue.

Today, feisty Cornwall, with a half-million residents, is officially and for all practical purposes part of England (unlike Wales or Scotland). But native-born Cornishmen and Cornishwomen still cling to what makes them unique—they're Cornish first, British second. The fledgling Cornish independence movement has never really gotten anywhere, but that doesn't stop locals from displaying the flag of Cornwall: a black field (representing the earth) with a white cross (the tin flowing through the earth). Also look for bumper stickers boasting the Cornish word for "Cornwall": *Kernow.*

timuff@gmail.com). **Cornwall Discovery** offers a "Far West" tour that covers St. Ives, mining country, Land's End, and more on the Penwith Peninsula (£275-300/day for up to 6 people, mobile 07877-303-749, www.cornwalldiscovery.co.uk).

Penzance

Sure enough, Penzance had its share of pirates. Strategically situated near the very tip of Britain, the town was an ideal spot for pirates to hijack and plunder ships returning from the New World with untold treasures. But today's Penzance is less of a rough-and-tumble smuggler's cove and more of a blue-collar transportation hub. Penzance can't compete with the artsy vibe of St. Ives or the pre-

cious jewel-box quality of nearby
Mousehole, but it's cornered the
market on functionality: Well-
located B&Bs, good restaurants,
train and bus stations, and easy
parking make Penzance the
most practical home base for exploring the Cornish coast. And
its bustling main street, picturesque waterfront setting, and

agreeable natives make it an enjoyable place to "come home to" at
the end of a busy sightseeing day.

Orientation to Penzance

Penzance, with about 20,000 people, is situated on a small peninsula. The eastern part of the peninsula has the harbor and the
train and bus stations. The southern part has a broad and inviting
promenade, with most of the town's B&Bs nearby. Climbing uphill
from the water are various streets, including the busy Market Jew
Street (derived from the Cornish *Marghas Yow*, meaning "Thursday Market") and the atmospheric, restaurant-lined Chapel Street.
The hill is capped by the spire of the Church of St. Mary and the
grandly domed Market House, now a bank.

TOURIST INFORMATION

The **Welcome to West Cornwall Centre** is located between the
train and bus stations. They are generous with information on
the surrounding region, and also sell National Express long-distance bus tickets (Mon-Fri 10:00-17:00, Sat until 13:00, shorter
hours off-season, closed Sun year-round; Station Approach, tel.
01736/335-530, www.lovepenzance.co.uk).

HELPFUL HINTS

Festival: The annual **Golowan (Midsummer) Festival** engulfs
    Penzance for 10 days in mid- to late June. Things get espe-
    cially rowdy on Mazey Day, the last Saturday of the festi-
    val, with colorful parades and well-lubricated crowds (www.
    golowanfestival.org).

Art Pass: Art buffs can consider the £18 Art Pass, which provides
    unlimited access for seven days to the Penlee House Gallery
    and Museum in Penzance; the Tate Gallery, Barbara Hep-
    worth Museum, and Leach Pottery in St. Ives; and a discount
    at the shops in the Newlyn Art Gallery and the Exchange in
    Newlyn.

Baggage Storage: You can pay to stow your luggage at **Longboat**

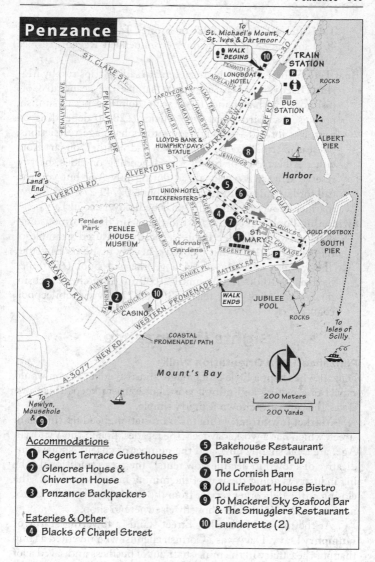

Penzance

To
St. Michael's Mount,
St. Ives & Dartmoor

WALK
BEGINS

TRAIN
STATION

ROCKS

ST. CLARE ST.

PENALVERNE AVE

PENALVERNE DR

PENWITH ST.
LONGBOAT
HOTEL

ADELAIDE ST.

BUS
STATION

ALBERT
PIER

TAROVEOR RD.

ALMA TER.

ST. JAMES ST.

BELGRAVIA ST.

HIGH ST.

CLARENCE ST.

LLOYDS BANK &
HUMPHRY DAVY
STATUE

MARKET JEW ST.

WHARF RD.

A-30

JENNINGS

Harbor

To
Land's
End

ALVERTON ST.

NEW ST.

ALVERTON RD.

UNION HOTEL
STECKFENSTERS

THE QUAY

Penlee
Park

PENLEE
HOUSE
MUSEUM

MORRAB RD.

ST. MARY'S TER.

QUEEN ST.

ST. MARY'S RD.

ABBEY

CHAPEL ST.

QUAY ST.

ST.
MARY'S

GOLD POSTBOX

SOUTH
PIER

Morrab
Gardens

REGENT TER.

CHAPEL

P

ALEXANDRA RD.

ALEX PL.

MENHAE

REDINNICK PL.

DANIEL PL.

BATTERY RD.

WALK
ENDS

JUBILEE
POOL

ROCKS

To
Isles of
Scilly

CASINO

WESTERN PROMENADE

COASTAL
PROMENADE/ PATH

A-3077 NEW RD.

Mount's Bay

200 Meters
200 Yards

To
Newlyn,
Mousehole
&

N

Accommodations
1 Regent Terrace Guesthouses
2 Glencree House &
Chiverton House
3 Penzance Backpackers

Eateries & Other
4 Blacks of Chapel Street

5 Bakehouse Restaurant
6 The Turks Head Pub
7 The Cornish Barn
8 Old Lifeboat House Bistro
9 To Mackerel Sky Seafood Bar
& The Smugglers Restaurant
10 Launderette (2)

Inn, across the street from the train station (daily 7:00-23:00, Market Jew Street, tel. 01736/364-137).

Laundry: Penzance's big waterfront **casino,** along the promenade past the Regent Terrace B&Bs, has a little launderette tucked around the right side (daily 7:30-20:00, tel. 01736/330-055). Next to the train station, **Suds & Surf** is another good option (daily 8:00-20:00, 4 East Terrace, tel. 01736/364-815). Both offer self- and full-service.

Taxis: Cabs line up at the train station. Or you can call **Anytime**

Taxis (tel. 01736/888-888) or **Stones Taxi** (tel. 01736/363-400) for the £5-6 fare to my recommended Regent Terrace accommodations.

Boat Tours: The 1.5- to 4-hour catamaran sailing trips run by **Marine Discovery** are a fun way to sample the beautiful Cornish coast, with a chance to see seals, dolphins, ocean sunfish, porpoises, seabirds, and even whales (£20-50 depending on tour, less for kids—though some tours have age restrictions, off-season trips may be canceled in bad weather, depart from either Albert Pier or South Pier depending on tides, best to reserve at least 3 weeks ahead during July-Aug but you can call for last-minute availability, mobile 07749-277-110, www.marinediscovery.co.uk, info@marinediscovery.co.uk).

Swimming Pool: Take a dip next to the sea in the enormous outdoor saltwater **Jubilee Pool**—a locally treasured example of the Art Deco lidos that enjoyed a heyday in 1930s England. They've also recently added a geothermal pool (£5, June-Sept daily 10:00-18:00—until 20:00 in Aug, check website for hours rest of year, tel. 01736/369-224, www.jubileepool.co.uk).

Sights in Penzance

Penzance Town Orientation Walk

Penzance has kept a little of its rough-and-real edge, as you would expect of a fishing and mining port, but tourism keeps this town alive. The core of the town is pretty simple.

Market Jew Street: From the train station, head up this main street, which has a workaday feel. The facades, fine in the Victorian Age, are a bit shabby now, and the number of charity shops is indicative of a town in decline (low rents). The area's traditional fishing industry is going the way of the mining industry before it. The closing of the helicopter service from the Isles of Scilly to Penzance means that 2,500 islanders now fly elsewhere to shop.

At the top of Market Jew Street stands a towering **statue of Humphry Davy.** Davy was a Cornish chemist who invented a lamp that put the canary in the mine shaft out of business and saved a lot of miners. Behind him, the towering Lloyd's Bank building looks stony and reliable.

Chapel Street: Just past the bank, take a left on The Greenmarket, and then veer left at the fork onto Chapel Street. On the left, the now-scruffy **Union Hotel** was one of England's great coaching inns until the train arrived in 1859. It was here in 1805 that Britons first heard the news of their country's victory over Napoleon's fleet at the Battle of Trafalgar and the death of Admiral Nelson. The Nelson Bar, inside, has a fine collection of Nelson prints. Just across the street is delightfully quirky Steckfensters Antiques. Continue downhill past recommended eateries and pubs: Bakehouse, Blacks of Chapel Street, The Turks Head, and The Cornish Barn.

Quay Street: After walking around the church veer left onto Quay Street *(Dolphin Tavern* sign is at end of street) and continue downhill until, just before the harbor, you strike gold—a **gold postbox.** London hosted the 2012 Summer Olympics and celebrated each gold medalist by painting a postbox in the winner's hometown gold. Rowing champ Helen Glover is from Penzance.

Harbor: Ahead is the harbor (and embarkation point for the ferry to the Isles of Scilly—described later, under "Peninsula Sights near Penzance"). Turn right, walk past the huge Art Deco 1935 public Jubilee Pool, which fills with the tide each day, and reach the promenade leading to the fishing port of Newlyn, a half-hour's stroll ahead (to take the stroll, see the listing below). Across the bay to the left is St. Michael's Mount (see "Peninsula Sights near Penzance," later). And now you've seen Penzance.

▲Penlee House Gallery and Museum

Filling a Victorian house in Penlee Park, the gallery hosts a fine collection from painters of the local Newlyn School. These Post-Impressionists, attracted to Cornwall in the late 1800s by the quality of light and the low cost of living, painted seascapes, portraits, and scenes of daily life. You'll enjoy bucolic, perfectly lit scenes from Cornwall's rocky coast and pasture-striped countryside. The ground floor shows off rotating exhibits, often from the museum's permanent collection. The upstairs has more paintings and a modest museum about Penzance's prehistoric and more recent history (learn how Penzance, Newlyn, and Mousehole were burned by Spanish raiders in 1595).

Cost and Hours: £5; Mon-Sat 10:00-17:00, Nov-March until 16:30, closed Sun year-round; smart to call ahead as the museum closes some or all of its galleries for a week several times a year to rearrange its collection, café with inviting garden terrace, Morrab Road, tel. 01736/363-625, www.penleehouse.org.uk.

Waterfront Stroll to Newlyn and Mousehole

A broad pedestrian promenade follows the coast around Mount's Bay, from Penzance to Newlyn—perfect for an early-morning or after-dinner stroll (about 30 minutes one-way). From Newlyn, a coastal footpath extends farther to Mousehole (another 30-minute walk; for more on these towns, see page 386). These days, any fishing that happens goes out of Newlyn.

Sleeping in Penzance

GUESTHOUSES ON REGENT TERRACE

Set just a block off the seashore, the upmarket guesthouses on this street are central and convenient. Rooms in front usually have views of the sea, while those in back overlook a churchyard. Most breakfast rooms are downstairs on the garden level. Though they're all run by friendly proprietors, these places feel more like small hotels than B&Bs. All offer free parking. Drivers should ask their hotelier for precise directions to the narrow and easy-to-miss Regent Terrace. Most places on this street require a three-night minimum stay in peak season.

$$ **Camilla House** is relaxed, traditional, and elegant, with contemporary class, neutral colors, an inviting lounge, made-to-order breakfasts, and lots of luxurious touches throughout. Fiona (who goes by "Fee") rents eight comfy, sunny rooms (at #12, tel. 01736/363-771, www.camillahouse.co.uk, enquiries@camillahouse.co.uk).

$$ **Warwick House** has seven fine rooms, sea views, a cozy lounge, and hosts happy to answer your questions (#17, tel. 01736/363-881, www.warwickhousepenzance.co.uk, enquiry@warwickhousepenzance.co.uk, Chris and Julie). They also rent a two-bedroom seafront cottage (www.tremorvahcottage.co.uk).

$$ **Chy-an-Mor Guest House** ("House of Sea") has nine rooms that try for elegance—some decorated in a vintage, French-traditional style. Tea and cakes may greet you upon arrival (no children under 10, closed Nov-mid-March, at #15, tel. 01736/363-441, www.chyanmor.co.uk, reception@chyanmor.co.uk, Louise and Richard).

$$ **Blue Seas Hotel** has eight simple, modern, cheerfully colorful rooms and serves a widely varied breakfast (closed mid-Dec-Jan, at #13, tel. 01736/364-744, www.blueseashotel-penzance.co.uk, info@blueseashotel-penzance.co.uk, Arnaud and Fiona).

$$ **Lombard House Hotel,** a lesser value, offers old-school chandeliered Georgian townhouse atmosphere. The nine rooms lack character, but most have sea views; the two top-floor attic rooms are cozy (at #16, tel. 01736/364-897, www.lombardhousehotel.com, rita.kruge@lombardhousehotel.com; Rita, Tom, and Phil).

CORNWALL

CHEAPER OPTIONS ON OR NEAR ALEXANDRA ROAD

Alexandra Road, about a five-minute walk down the promenade from Regent Terrace (and therefore a bit farther from the town center and restaurants), is lined with midrange accommodations and a hostel.

$$ Glencree House, with seven rooms in a beautiful granite Victorian townhouse, offers charming antique furniture, thoughtful little touches (such as packed lunches available), and comparable quality to the Regent Terrace guesthouses at a slightly lower price (just off Alexandra Road on quiet Mennaye Road at #2, tel. 01736/362-026, www.glencreehouse.co.uk, stay@glencreehouse. co.uk, Andrew and Lynsey).

$ Chiverton House is a stone Victorian home with six smallish rooms packed with wood furnishings (no children under 12, just off Alexandra Road at 9 Mennaye Road, tel. 01736/332-733, www.chivertonhousebedandbreakfast.co.uk, alan.waller@sky.com, Alan and Sally).

¢ Penzance Backpackers, with 30 beds in seven rooms, is situated in a townhouse on a B&B-studded stretch of Alexandra Road. This is your best bet for budget dorm beds (reception open 9:00-12:00 & 17:00-22:00, no lockout, tel. 01736/363-836, www. pzbackpack.com, info@pzbackpack.com).

Eating in Penzance

Wherever you eat, check the daily specials lists—most pubs serve fresh local fish and crab, along with the usual options. Many places also have early-bird specials on weekdays before 19:00. Most of my listings are on or near Chapel Street. This historic street runs up into town from the waterfront near Regent Terrace, toward Market Jew Street.

$$$ Blacks of Chapel Street is a black, sleek, and modern place serving British and Mediterranean dishes with a focus on seafood (fish specials, dinner salads, daily 12:00-14:30 & 16:30-22:00, 12 Chapel Street, tel. 01736/369-729, Susan).

$$$ Bakehouse Restaurant tries to keep things simple, featuring Cornish cuisine that highlights quality ingredients. The service is sharp and cheerful, the acoustics are noisy, and the decor is modern (good vegetarian options, steaks, open for dinner Mon-Sat from 17:30, closed Sun, on Chapel Street, set back on a little courtyard called Old Bakehouse Lane, tel. 01736/331-331).

$$ The Turks Head, the oldest pub in Penzance, is a dark, low-beamed gem. Serving basic pub grub and local ales, this is a popular spot—book ahead or arrive early. There are dining rooms in the back and downstairs, and a small terrace out back, but the pub in front is best for rubbing elbows with locals (food served daily 12:00-14:30 & 18:00-22:00, 49 Chapel Street, near intersection with Abbey Street, tel. 01736/363-093, www.turksheadpenzance.co.uk).

$$ The Cornish Barn is a modern-meets-traditional restaurant and smokehouse, focusing on fresh Cornish produce as well as local craft beers and wines. The interior balances rustic and modern, but on a nice day the garden is best. Open for breakfast, lunch, and dinner, this place offers good options from light snacks to heavy meals (food served daily 7:30-14:30 & 17:30-21:30, 20 Chapel Street, tel. 01736/339-414).

Along the Waterfront: $$ Old Lifeboat House Bistro offers the town's best-value waterfront meals, prepared with creativity and pride using local ingredients. Housed in a mid-1880s granite building—a former lifeboat station, complete with turret and bell—the bistro has comfy indoor and outdoor seating. They also offer nice lunch and coffee options on weekends (Mon-Thu 17:30-22:00, Fri-Sun from 12:00, Wharf Road near Jennings Street, tel. 01736/369-409).

IN NEWLYN

These restaurants are in nearby Newlyn, a pleasant 30-minute walk from Penzance.

$$$$ Mackerel Sky Seafood Bar is the foodie's best bet for a fun and creative menu featuring fresh local fish. The service is friendly, there's no pretense, and the tasty dishes are artfully presented (no reservations, daily 12:00-15:00 & 18:00-21:00, The Bridge, New Road, tel. 01736/444-444).

$$$ The Smugglers Restaurant is the best option for white-tablecloth dining (dinners only). This is where locals go to celebrate special occasions. Reservations are wise (daily 19:00-21:30, closed Sun-Tue in winter; facing the harbor along the main road, 12 Fore Street—pay to park near the harbor, then walk two minutes up the hill; tel. 01736/331-501, www.smugglersnewlyn.co.uk).

Penzance Connections

For connections within Cornwall, see "Getting Around Cornwall—By Public Transportation," earlier.

From Penzance by Train to: London's Paddington Station

(about hourly, 5-6 hours, possible transfer in Plymouth or Newton Abbot), **Salisbury** (about hourly, 5-6 hours, 1-2 transfers), **Bath** (1-2/hour, 4.5 hours, one direct, most 1-2 transfers), **Edinburgh** (every 1-2 hours, 10-17 hours, 1 direct, most transfer), **York** (every 1-2 hours, 8-10 hours, 1 direct, most transfer in Plymouth), **Exeter** (roughly hourly, 3 hours, possible transfer in Plymouth). **Train info:** Tel. 0345-748-4950, www.nationalrail.co.uk.

By Bus to: Exeter (1-4/day, 5-6 hours, possible transfer in Plymouth), **Brighton** (5/day, about 12 hours, transfers in Plymouth, Heathrow, or London), **Portsmouth** (2-5/day, 12 hours, transfer in Plymouth, Heathrow, or London), **London** (5/day direct, 9 hours, overnight available). **Bus info:** Tel. 0871-781-8181, www.nationalexpress.com.

St. Ives

Picturesque St. Ives is the closest thing to a Riviera resort in the region. And it is a zoo in peak times—absolutely mobbed by British families walking their dogs and endlessly licking ice-cream cones. A local told me, "You can smell the sweat and suntan oil for miles around."

With golden light reflecting off the aquamarine waves and twisty lanes, St. Ives began to attract artists in the early 20th century. The potter Bernard Leach practiced his craft here, as did sculptor Barbara Hepworth, and both have museums in town—along with dozens of other lesser-known artists. The Tate Gallery also has an unlikely branch here, which seems a bit too big-league for a little-league town. An annual music and arts festival keeps things humming in September (www.stivesseptemberfestival.co.uk).

While it's undeniably charming (especially before 10:00, when

CORNWALL

the day-tripping masses arrive), St. Ives sometimes feels like the worst of both worlds: tacky, overrun seaside resort meets self-important artist enclave oozing with pretense. Still, it's worth seeing—quickly.

Orientation to St. Ives

About half the size of Penzance, with 11,000 people, St. Ives occupies a few steep bits of land between sandy beaches. The town clusters around its sandy harbor, with a bulbous spit of land just beyond called The Island. From the quaint waterfront old town, newer development sprawls uphill toward the main road. Thanks to its warren of convoluted lanes, small St. Ives can be challenging to navigate.

Tourist Information: The TI, located in the library on Gabriel Street, sells town maps and has public computers (Mon-Sat 9:30-17:00, Sun 10:00-15:00, shorter hours off-season and closed on Sun, tel. 01736/796-297, www.stives-cornwall.co.uk).

ARRIVAL IN ST. IVES

By Car: St. Ives is a pain for drivers—parking is scarce and distant from town, and those who venture into the center find its streets congested with slow-moving pedestrians. As you approach town, you'll reach a roundabout with a "do not enter" sign (9:30-16:00, except for permitted vehicles). While this isn't usually enforced, driving past here is challenging enough that you'll probably prefer to go with the flow and park at one of the outlying pay lots (all with similar prices). The main option is the huge **Trenwith** car park above town, near the Leisure Centre—turn right just before the roundabout. From this lot, it's a steep downhill walk or easy £1 shuttle ride into town (drops off and picks up at the movie theater). You can also turn left at the roundabout and loop around to the **Barnoon** pay lot just above the Tate Gallery and Porthmeor Beach (the handiest lot if the Tate is your goal, but still a steep hike above the town center and harbor).

Yet another option—which lets you avoid driving in town entirely—is to leave your car at the park-and-ride lot at **St. Erth** on the way to St. Ives (affordable long-term parking, see map on page 382 for location), then ride the train from there into town.

By Train or Bus: If you are day-tripping from Penzance, the bus is your best option (see page 365). The train station and the bus station are both conveniently located near the waterfront; just exit and walk with the sea on your right into the heart of town.

CORNWALL

Sights in St. Ives

Art lovers can save money by buying the Art Pass, which includes the first three sights mentioned here, plus others in Cornwall (see page 368).

Tate Gallery

St. Ives very proudly hosts a branch of the prestigious London art museum. The modern building is big and outwardly impressive, but the ever-changing exhibits—focusing mostly on modern works by relatively obscure local artists—can be a letdown. Find out what's on before paying the entry price.

Cost and Hours: £10.50, £13 combo-ticket includes Barbara Hepworth Museum and Sculpture Garden, ask about art talk—likely at 13:00; daily 10:00-17:20, Nov-Feb until 16:20 and closed Mon, tel. 01736/796-226, www.tate.org.uk/stives.

▲Barbara Hepworth Museum and Sculpture Garden

Many visitors find this collection more accessible than the Tate's. Barbara Hepworth (1903-1975) was one of the first sculptors to create nonrepresentational art (that is, totally abstract works that didn't attempt to imitate the real world). She lived most of her life in St. Ives, and now her home and workshop—called Trewyn Studio—is a small museum, offering a chance to learn a bit about the artist and see her works: large, solid forms pierced by voids. These curvaceous, undulating works were inspired by, if not quite resembling, the sea, wind, clouds, sand, and light of St. Ives. While a few are inside, most of the pieces are sprinkled throughout the linger-worthy garden. While exploring, peek into her actual studio, with its dusty smocks and rusty chisels.

Cost and Hours: £7, £13 combo-ticket includes the Tate, ticket includes daily art talk—usually at 12:00 and 15:00, same hours and contact info as the Tate, at the corner of Ayr Lane and Barnoon Hill.

Leach Pottery Museum

This museum celebrates Bernard Leach, considered one of the founders of the mid-20th-century British studio-pottery movement. You'll walk through what was his actual studio, with its heavy-duty kilns, then tour a collection of works by Leach and his associates, as well as pieces by leading contemporary potters. The complex also includes an active workshop where potters still work (generally not viewable).

Cost and Hours: £6; Mon-Sat 10:00-17:00, Sun 11:00-16:00 except closed Sun Nov-Feb; Higher Stennack/B-3306, tel. 01736/799-703, www.leachpottery.com.

Getting There: The studio is well-marked from the upper

outskirts of St. Ives, on the road into town. It's a 15-minute walk from Royal Square in the center of town. Or, park at the Trenwith car park (described earlier); the studio is a six-minute uphill walk from there (disabled parking only at the studio, but you may find street parking nearby).

Stroll the Town

Besides gallery-hopping, the best way to enjoy St. Ives is by taking an ice-cream cone on a waterfront stroll. The slate-tile-clad High Street and pleasant waterfront have plenty of shops and ice-cream stands—though you'll have to squeeze through the crowds. Boats departing from the harbor can take you on trips around the cliffs and to the coves, a good way to appreciate why the Cornish coast was so popular with bootleggers and pirates.

Hit the Beach

St. Ives is popular with Brits on a "bucket-and-spade" holiday because it's surrounded by sandy beaches. In addition to the sandy central harbor—home to boats as well as swimmers—you'll find family-friendly Porthminster Beach (west) and surfer-friendly Porthmeor Beach (east). Tiny, secluded Porthgwidden Beach—hiding between the rocks under the high peninsula called The Island—is worth the hike.

If you enjoy water sports, find your inner dude by taking lessons from **St. Ives Surf School** on Porthmeor Beach. Choose between surfing, kayaking, and stand-up paddleboarding (£35/person includes equipment, equipment rentals also available, daily 9:00-18:00, tel. 01736/793-938, www.stivessurfschool.co.uk).

Sleeping in St. Ives

The town's charm wears thin with the hordes of tourists in high season, but the evenings are quiet enough to consider staying over. The first two options are in tight, twisty old buildings—climbing to your room can feel like spiraling up through a ship's hull.

$$ Cornerways rents six rooms (two overlook the harbor) with lots of grays, blacks, and exposed beams. It's got a smooth nautical-meets-contemporary vibe, with easygoing and helpful Tim at the helm (free Tate/Hepworth museum passes, 1 Bethesda Place, tel. 01736/796-706, mobile 07815-796-706, www.cornerwaysstives.co.uk, tim@cornerwaysstives.co.uk).

$$ The Anchorage has four cozy rooms and claustrophobic ceilings in a central location (may require multiple-night stay, 5 Bunkers Hill, tel. 01736/797-135, www.anchoragestives.co.uk, info@anchoragestives.co.uk, Sian—pronounced "Shawn").

$$ The Queens Hotel, with a recommended gastropub on the ground floor, has 10 bright and clean rooms on High Street just up

CORNWALL

from the harbor (tel. 01736/796-468, www.queenshotelstives.com, info@queenshotelstives.com).

Eating in St. Ives

While a few innovative chefs have tried their hand in St. Ives, in general the town sees a lot of turnover; most places are glitzy, emphasizing style over substance to lure in the one-time tourist trade. Ask locals what's good right now. Opening times for most St. Ives eateries can change from one day to the next, depending on weather and crowds.

Along the Harborfront: The main drag along the harbor has plenty of dining options—though most are tourist traps. Peruse the menus and views, and choose your favorite. **$$ The Rum & Crab Shack** serves about 40 types of rum, as well as locally sourced crab (delivered fresh each morning), but the "shack" is a misnomer—it's an appealingly modern space, with big windows looking out over the harbor (daily 10:30-24:00, The Wharf, tel. 01736/796-353). **$$ The Harbour St. Ives** prides itself on its fish selection and daily catch-of-the-day specials. Their upstairs seating area has a good harbor view (daily 11:00-22:00, far end of Wharf Road near Parish Church, tel. 01736/797-661).

Above Porthmeor Beach: For the best beach views in town—away from the worst of the tacky tourism—head to the **$$$ Porthmeor Beach Café**, across the street from the Tate Gallery. Classy but casual, its outdoor or enclosed seating overlooks Cornwall's most popular surfing beach (May-Oct daily 9:00-21:00, tel. 01736/793-366).

$ Pasties on Fore Street: Running parallel to the harbor one block inland, Fore Street is lined with tourist shops and some good budget eateries. It's hard to choose among the many Cornish pasty shops along here; I suggest following your nose to the best-looking option.

Gastropub: $$ The Queens Hotel is an appealingly scruffy-mod gastropub with a pinch of hipster and a whisper of indifferent service. Their well-priced fare appears on a handwritten chalkboard menu that changes regularly (daily 12:00-14:30 & 18:30-21:00 except no midday break on Sun, straight up High Street from the harbor, tel. 01736/796-468).

Fish-and-Chips: $ The Albatross, tucked away on Chapel

Street (uphill from the TI), serves tasty local fish-and-chips to take away (Mon-Sat 12:00-14:30 & 17:00-21:30, closed Sun, tel. 01736/798-492).

And for Dessert: You'll see places hawking "Cornish Ice Cream"—the frozen version of clotted cream, which means it's richer and creamier than the norm. For something deliciously different, try the lavender-and-honey flavor.

St. Ives Connections

The **bus** is more practical than the train for most connections. The most useful lines are #A17 to Penzance; #A2 to Penzance via Marazion (St. Michael's Mount); and #A3 to Land's End (via Geevor Tin Mine and Sennen Cove). For details, see page 365.

All **train** connections from St. Ives to points eastward go through St. Erth, where you'll switch from the cute little St. Ives Bay Line to the main line to Penzance (see "Penzance Connections," earlier).

Penwith Peninsula

Cornwall's Penwith Peninsula, at its western tip, is a pincushion of worthwhile stops. Literally meaning "headland," Penwith features rugged, rocky, windblown scenery; the best-preserved bits of traditional Cornish culture; and some of Britain's most ancient sites, to boot.

The first few destinations are easily accessible from Penzance, including the worthwhile St. Michael's Mount (east of—and visible from—Penzance), Chysauster Ancient Village (a few miles from Penzance, but only doable by car), and the Isles of Scilly (three-hour boat ride from Penzance or a plane ride from Land's End). For drivers, my "Penzance to St. Ives Drive" connects most of the highlights of the peninsula, heading west from Penzance, passing tiny port towns, prehistoric stone circles, a seaside theater, Land's End, historical tin mines, and miles of ruggedly beautiful coastline. (Many of these same sights are accessible by bus; see page 396 for a recommended itinerary.)

Hikers: If you have a hankering for a long hike in England, make it the Penwith Peninsula segment of the South West Coast Path. Distances are manageable (it's 17 miles from Penzance to Land's End), and you can coordinate with the local bus service to make a variety of walks fit your time and energy constraints. Inquire locally for information on taking advantage of the beloved coastal path (see sidebar).

CORNWALL

The South West Coast Path

England's longest hiking trail—and one of its most popular—the South West Coast Path runs 630 miles along the sea from Somerset to Dorset, including the coasts of Devon and Cornwall. Hiking the whole path takes up to two months, but there are many segments that make for great day hikes or leisurely nature walks. For interactive listings of the many options, see www.southwestcoastpath.org.uk.

Some of the path's most spectacular sections are along the Cornish coast. Cornwall has perhaps the mildest climate in the UK, and with the lack of snow and other extreme weather, the South West Coast Path appeals to hikers throughout the year. The trail frequently passes over high cliffs, allowing hikers to see for miles over the Celtic Sea and the English Channel. Wildlife is abundant here: Hikers often spot badgers, otters, butterflies, and birds such as warblers, marsh harriers, swifts, and starlings. The remains of foundries, engine houses, and heavy equipment dot the landscape—all that's left of the booming copper and tin mining operations that once dominated the Cornish countryside, the last of which closed in 1998.

Those looking for a full-day hike in Cornwall will enjoy the 11-mile Penzance to Porthcurno hike along Cornwall's western tip. Hikers will see the beautiful historic buildings of Penzance before a peaceful walk in the countryside, and finally land in the small town of Porthcurno, with its beautiful secluded beach and famous Minack Theatre. Buses run regularly from Porthcurno back to Penzance.

The Penzance-to-Marazion seafront walk, starting from Penzance's main parking lot, is an easy 4.2-mile out-and-back suitable for strollers and wheelchairs. You'll enjoy beautiful views across Mounts Bay to St Michael's Mount and Mousehole.

The Geevor Tin Mine loop, starting at the mine's parking lot, is ideal for families with kids. This 6.1-mile walk passes a beautiful lighthouse, a fort at Chun Castle, and a beach.

A short but scenic 1.5-mile one-way hike from Land's End to Sennen Cove is easily accessible by bus (described on page 397).

The Tintagel Circulars, a set of short loop hikes near the legendary Tintagel Castle in east Cornwall, also work well for kids. Start at the parking lot near the Old Post Office in the village of Tintagel and head out through farmland and along open clifftops.

Also in east Cornwall, the 5.3-mile Stay Café loop near Trebah and Glendurgan gardens is a pleasant meander full of coastal views, wildflowers, and riverside paths. Start at the parking lot in Maenporth—between Trebah Garden and Falmouth—and keep your eye out as you go for little paths leading down to tiny beaches.

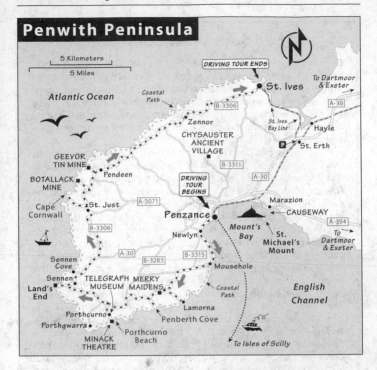

Peninsula Sights near Penzance

▲▲St. Michael's Mount

Bookending the English Channel along with France's Mont St-Michel (but on a smaller scale), this dramatic rock island has been inhabited for 1,500 years. Originally a Benedictine monastery, it was later turned into a fortified castle, and eventually a stately home, by the St. Aubyn family—who still own it today in partnership with the National Trust. If the tide is out, a pedestrian causeway connects the island to the town of Marazion (mah-rah-ZYE-on). Otherwise, a short ride in a motorboat (April-Oct only) will bring you up to the picturesque vest-pocket harbor just below the castle's lower gates. From there, a steep, uneven, rocky path curves its way up to the castle entrance.

Cost and Hours: Castle and garden-£16, castle only-£10.50, garden only-£8. Castle open Sun-Fri 10:30-17:00 (July-Aug 10:00-17:30), closed Sat year-round and all of winter except for tours; garden open Mon-Fri (Thu-Fri only in summer), closed off-season. Tours run from the mount's café "when tides and weather are favourable," usually Tue and Fri at 11:00 and 14:00—call to confirm. Tel. 01736/710-507, ferry and tide info tel. 01736/710-265, www.stmichaelsmount.co.uk.

CORNWALL

Getting There: Buses #U4 and #A2 run from Penzance to Marazion, while drivers can park in either of two waterfront parking lots in Marazion (£4.50, cash only). From there, it depends on the tide: At low tide (about four hours per day—most locals know the time or can show you a tide table), you can walk about a quarter-mile across the cobbled causeway to the island. At other times, you'll need to catch the boat (£2 one-way, runs continuously—or, in slow times, whenever 12 people show up, April-Oct only, 10 minutes, you'll be directed to one of three possible boarding sites, all near the causeway). Boats don't run on Saturdays, when the castle is closed.

Eating: For a convenient and good lunch option, try the mount's café or restaurant.

Visiting St. Michael's Mount: Most of England's castles are now owned by the state or by charities. The Great Depression bankrupted many noble English families, who were forced to sell off family estates and heirlooms. St. Michael's Mount is one of the few open to the public that has remained associated with the same family since the Middle Ages. Family portraits, some quite recent, adorn the walls.

After buying your ticket, head into the gated entry area. From here, you can enter the **garden** that curls most of the way around the base of the castle, with many tropical plants, a few prehistoric standing stones, and grand views.

The highlight is the **castle** itself, which you'll reach by hiking steeply upward. The castle interior is surprisingly petite. Docents posted in each room are eager to answer questions. You'll pass through an envy-inducing sea-view study and see some historic paintings of the place, before entering one of the building's highlights: the **Chevy Chase Room,** which was originally the refectory of the monastery that once stood here, and still has that long, somber dining-hall feel. It's named for the circa-1620 frieze that decorates the room, illustrating scenes from a beloved medieval ballad (not for the American comedic actor who knew how to choose a classy stage name). From there, proceed into the smoking room, where men would nurse cigars after dinner, *Downton Abbey* style. Hanging in the window is a weather gauge, filled with liquid that changes color as barometric conditions change. In the small frame is some nobleman's prized souvenir: a tiny blue scrap from the jacket that Napoleon wore at Waterloo.

CORNWALL

Step out onto the breathtaking **view terrace** (among the newest parts of the castle, it was built to take full advantage of this hilltop's scenic setting). Peer down to see the garden that wraps around the island—and keep an eye out for mysterious prehistoric standing stones, which were here before the castle.

Looping around to the landward side of the castle, you'll enter the **chapel,** built (as the core of that medieval monastery) in the 12th century, then rebuilt after an earthquake in the 13th by Bernard du Bec, the same abbot responsible for France's Mont St-Michel (locals affectionately call him "Bernard the Builder").

The genteel **Blue Drawing Room** has a vastly different style from what you've seen up to now. Ogling this room, it's easy to imagine the family that owns and lives in this complex hanging out here after-hours. (The painting over the fireplace flips around to reveal a flat-screen TV.) Passing through the map room (with historic maps of this place) and going down the stairs (peer over the bannister to parts of the castle reserved for the residents), you'll reach a small exhibit about the island's history and prehistory.

Before heading back down to the base of the mountain, look out to sea and ponder this: Locals claim that Jesus Christ visited Cornwall during his teen years. Supposedly he landed here at St. Michael's Mount, then traveled up to Glastonbury (near Bath). While this might seem patently bogus, natives persuasively insist that it could have happened: Joseph of Arimathea, who was a wealthy disciple of Jesus, was also a metal trader. He might have brought Jesus to this metal-rich peninsula on a business trip. All that we know of Jesus' life between his adolescence and age 30 is that he traveled in the "wilderness"...which Britain (and most of Europe) certainly was at that time.

Chysauster Ancient Village

Two millennia ago, the granite village of Chysauster (chih-ZOY-ster) was created high up on a windswept hillside of the Cornish moors. Today, anyone with an interest in prehistory will find it well worth the short drive from Penzance and quarter-mile uphill walk from the parking lot. While many such settlements are scattered around the Penwith Peninsula, Chysauster is relatively easy to find on your own and well set up for visitors.

Cost and Hours: £5; daily 10:00-17:00, July-Aug until 18:00, Oct until 16:00, closed Nov-Easter; mobile 07831-757-934, www.english-heritage.org.uk.

Getting There: The site is accessible only by car. It's tricky to find, hiding on backcountry roads a few miles north of Penzance: Leave town on the B-3311 (the back road to St. Ives); about 1.5 miles outside town, at Badgers Cross, turn left, following signs for *Trezelah* and *Newmill*. Follow that road for about a mile, watching for the parking lot (and WC building) on the left. Park and walk across the road, where a gravel trail leads you up through a field to the ticket kiosk.

Visiting Chysauster: For defensive reasons, the earliest settlements in Cornwall sat upon hilltops like this one. (Scanning the horizon virtually anywhere on the Penwith Peninsula, you'll notice that the summit of each hill is capped with the scant remains of an old house or fortress.) As life became more civilized and peaceful, people gradually moved down into valleys, and eventually to the coast—abandoning the difficult life at places like Chysauster.

This enigmatic ancient site encompasses nine cloverleaf-shaped homesteads, each one with circular rooms huddled around a central courtyard for protection and comfort. While the buildings were once roofed (most likely either with thatch or turf), it's unclear whether the central courtyard was also covered.

Information boards let you explore and understand each building and imagine how villages like this developed. From the first information board, bear right to #7, then do a counterclockwise loop to see the others. Linger in the two best-preserved houses, #6 and #4. The smaller rooms were used for storage, possibly for game (the people who lived here were hunter-gatherers); the larger rooms were dwellings. A unique feature of this community was an underground passage called a fogou, which may have been used for storage or as a place of refuge (one hides out about 135 yards southeast of house #7).

A place like Chysauster lets fertile imaginations run wild. Looking at the circular shape of each house, ponder the possibility that all of Britain's "mysterious" stone circles (such as Stonehenge)—which have been accounted for by a wide range of wildly creative explanations—may simply be the scant remains of a big round house. Or try this thought: If Jesus did visit Cornwall in his youth (as local legends suggest), these are the sorts of settlements he'd have seen.

Isles of Scilly

Just off the coast of Cornwall, this group of islands (pronounced "silly"), with a population of 2,500, sits right in the path of the Gulf Stream. The warm (or at least warmer) climate is perfect for growing a wide variety of exotic plants, so the islands boast a few gardens to visit. While enjoyable, the excursion takes the better part of a day.

Getting There: There are two ways to reach the islands. You can take a slow boat called the *Scillonian III* from Penzance (£48 same-day round-trip, £57 one-way, £115 round-trip, about 3 hours each way, sporadic schedule but generally departs Mon-Sat at 9:15 in summer from the Penzance Quay/Lighthouse Pier, no boats

CORNWALL

Nov-March, tel. 0845-710-5555, www.ios-travel.co.uk). Your other option is a **plane** from the Land's End airport (£125 same-day round-trip, £90 one-way, £180 round-trip, 15-minute flight). As the boat trip to the islands can be quite rough (fighting against the tide), consider flying over and sailing back (this "Air & Sea Day Trip" costs £95 for a same-day round-trip).

Penwith Peninsula Joyride

For me, exploring the Penwith Peninsula on a sunny day is the highlight of Cornwall and worth ▲▲. You'll see more by car, but I've also given directions to do the same general route by public bus—with a few sacrifices (see page 396). My driving route loops around the Penwith Peninsula clockwise, starting in Penzance and ending in St. Ives.

PENZANCE TO ST. IVES DRIVE

Though distances are short (the entire drive is less than 45 miles), plan on a full day to explore the region. Hedgerows are high, and the views are unforgettable: hidden coves, sweeping moorland, and vast seascapes. The friendly people you'll meet all along the way just add to this ultimate Cornish day out. But note that during peak summer season, traffic, parking, and crowds can be a problem. Generally expect to pay to park at nearly every stop.

• *Starting in Penzance, head south along the harbor promenade for less than a mile to get to...*

Newlyn

Newlyn is all about the fishing industry, with a hundred working boats and a busy fish market early each morning. Most of southwest England's fish comes from Cornwall, and most of Cornwall's fish is processed here in Newlyn.

Stop and survey the rugged little harbor. It's designed to handle the 20-foot tides. While the rough stones on the breakwater date from the 15th century, most of the harbor is 18th-century vintage. In the 19th century, trade here centered on tin and pilchards (sardines). All that crashed by 1900.

Tin mining was once a huge deal all along this coast, and if you believe that the tin trader Joseph of Arimathea (more famous as Jesus' uncle) traveled to Cornish tin mines from the Holy Land in the first century, consider that he very well could have landed here.

This harbor, along with much of the Penwith Peninsula, was seriously roughed up by the terrible storms of January 2014.

• *A short drive farther along the coast takes you to Mousehole. For a quick look at the little port, park in the pay-and-display lot on the Penzance side of Mousehole and walk in.*

Mousehole

Adorable little Mousehole (MOW-zle) is famous for smuggling, for fishing, and for being the last place where the pre-Roman language of Cornish was spoken. (A plaque on a wall marks the home of Dolly Pentreath, one of the last native Cornish speakers, who died in 1777.)

The wooden town was destroyed by a barrage of cannonballs from the Spanish Armada in 1595. (Spanish cannonballs decorate town gardens to this day.)
Today's stone town was rebuilt in the 17th century. The harbor has a tiny mouth to protect it from the wild sea (yes, like a mouse hole). Due to dramatic tides, the boats here are designed to be stranded in the mud—with either two keels or side supports so they stay upright until the water returns with the next high tide. At the Ship Inn Pub, the historic Fitzroy Barometer is embedded in the stone wall. This weather forecasting tool from 1854 saved many ships by predicting storms.

The colorful Mousehole Shop (on a nearby corner) is a fun spot for books and souvenirs. (*The Mousehole Cat* is a delightful children's book that tells and illustrates the legends of the town.) The ice cream shop next door is a convenient option to try the Cornish take on the dessert.

Mousehole has a few whitewashed homes, harkening back to Victorian times when the entire town would have been gleaming white. The lime wash helped waterproof the stone walls and was an excellent insulator. The beachside path from Newlyn makes an excellent 30-minute stroll (described on page 371).

At the parking lot is the inviting Rock Pool Café, with a shabby-chic vibe and a dramatic coastal setting. Just below it is a Victorian rock pool carved a century ago for kids to enjoy the sea life deposited there with each high tide. Chasing crabs and darting blennies (tiny fish able to survive in the air) is great fun.

Looking to the jagged ridge of rocks poking up from the deep just beyond the seawall, imagine how Mousehole (like many such Cornish towns) once specialized in a sort of reverse-piracy called "wrecking." During the rugged days of the late 18th century, townsfolk would place false lighthouse beacons high above town, misleading approaching ships into believing there was safe

CORNWALL

passage—and luring them right toward these hidden rocks. The ships would wreck, and the less scrupulous residents of Mousehole would rush out to salvage what they could.

• *Follow signs marked Outbound Traffic to make your way out of Mousehole and away from the coast. As you wind along this rural road, you'll find yourself dwarfed by centuries-old...*

Hedgerows

These are an icon of Cornwall, and while they may look soft like a bush, they are hard as rock (keep that in mind if you need to make room for an oncoming bus). Dating back to medieval times (when farmers cleaned up their fields to make them arable by stacking rocks to make walls lining the lanes), these have a stone frame, are filled with earth, and then overgrown with vegetation. They are not trimmed until July so the seeds can all fall, contributing to the "garden of England" feel of Cornwall. These roadside bouquets—of pink campions, bluebells, and white stitchwort—are more than pretty. They fight erosion.

• *Approaching Paul, the next hamlet up the road from Mousehole, turn left directly after the stony church. Continue on this road until its end at the B-3315, then turn left (west) toward Land's End. For a fun side trip, take the lane on the left after about two miles to...*

Lamorna Cove

About a mile down the tiny lane is the tough, tiny, and evocative port at Lamorna Cove, which was first used for smuggling contraband and then for the granite trade. Once there, drive delicately past the café to the pay-and-display parking lot. Like most of this coastline, this cove is still scarred by the violent storms of early 2014. Imagine the work involved in quarrying and shipping granite stones from here. The massive embankment of the River Thames in London didn't just happen—someone cut those big stones here and then shipped them. There are fine walks in either direction from here (including the South West Coast Path, which runs through here—see the sidebar, earlier).

Driving back to the main road, you'll pass the Lamorna Wink Pub, named for the winking code smugglers used when there was contraband for sale or a customs man was in town. Shortly after the pub, a tiny lane splits off to the right and goes down into a tangled Tolkien wonderland for adventurous drivers.

• *Back on the main road (B-3315), turn left and continue for almost a mile until you see a sign and a small parking pullout on the left for...*

Merry Maidens Stone Circle

In ancient times, stone circles had some sort of significant purpose—probably as a site for religious ceremonies, as a community

meeting place, or, most famously, as a celestial calendar. The Merry Maidens, very easy for drivers to reach, is far simpler than the famous circles at Stonehenge and Avebury. Still, it's a reminder that the Penwith Peninsula was inhabited in the Neolithic Age (roughly 2000 BC or earlier).

The story behind the name, most likely concocted in the Middle Ages, goes like this: A group of village women decided to go into the fields on Saturday night for some merriment and dancing. They lost track of time and danced into the Sabbath—neither remembering it nor keeping it holy. This displeased God, who turned the women to stone to serve as a warning to others.

This is just the beginning of a staggering variety of prehistoric monuments, settlements, and artifacts that still lie just beneath the surface of Cornwall. Penwith Peninsula is like an open-air archaeological museum dotted with stony souvenirs of prehistoric civilizations. About a hundred yards past the Merry Maidens is a burial mound, likely the tomb of a local chief dating from at least 2000 BC (left side of the road with a pullout and an info plaque).

At an intersection about a half-mile beyond the Merry Maidens, a weathered Celtic cross stands on the left side of the road. From the sixth to the tenth centuries, Celtic pilgrims traveled from Ireland through Wales and Cornwall to Galicia to visit Santiago de Compostela. And all along the route were Celtic crosses like this marking the way.

• *From the Merry Maidens, continue on the B-3315 west for three miles (following it left at the T-intersection, where a sign points you toward Land's End).*

Find a tiny road on the left with a sign for Penberth, which leads to another secret cove. This is Penberth Cove, an old pilchard fishing port where the capstan still hauls a few tough little boats up the cobbled landing. Notice the evocative skid marks in the stones, grooves worn by generations of hard fishing. Back on the main road, drive another two miles, then turn left to reach...

Porthcurno

The little hamlet of Porthcurno can be packed with visitors for three reasons: It's got the nicest beach in Cornwall, the famous Minack Theatre, and a fascinating telegraph museum. You can park for free by the theater or pay to park near the beach and museum; from here a steep lane leads to the theater.

Porthcurno Beach, just outside of town, is a secluded oasis of translucent blue water and soft sand cradled by striking granite cliffs. A great spot for a picnic and swim, the beach is a favorite of locals and visitors, as well as hikers on the South West Coast Path, which runs through the heathland up above.

▲Minack Theatre

This open-air theater—with 700 seats carved out of the rock—has the most spectacular setting of any theater in England. This gor-

geously landscaped theater is set in a rocky cliff with a terrace stage perched hundreds of feet over the sea. Imagine watching *The Tempest* with only the sunset and crashing waves for a background. While seeing a play is the best experience (tickets are inexpensive and easy to get), you can also simply visit to enjoy the garden-like setting and the wonderful story of the amazing woman who created it: Rowena Cade. A small exhibit on the history of the Minack includes a 10-minute video about Cade, a visionary theater lover who persevered to build this place. There's also a cliff-hanging coffeehouse (accessible only with admission).

If you're here at lunchtime on a sunny day, get a Cornish pasty and a bottle of elderflower *pressé* (a local herbal drink), and grab a grassy seat in a quiet corner at the high end of the theater for a dreamy picnic. Imagine the strategic value of telegraph cables emanating from this obscure port to places around the world (explained later). Watch the gannet birds dive for a fresh fish lunch. (They hit the water at 70 mph—locals say the bodies of young gannets often wash onto shore with broken necks after trying that stunt without experience.) You may even see a school of dolphins.

Cost and Hours: £5; theater generally open daily 9:30-17:30, off-season 10:00-16:00; also closes for sporadic events, such as children's matinees (several mornings each summer)—call ahead or check their website—tel. 01736/810-181, www.minack.com.

Performances: Shows cost £10-15 and are generally mid-May-mid-Sept, usually Mon-Fri at 20:00, and also Tue and Thu at 14:00. Bring a blanket and dress appropriately, as you'll be sitting on the grass, and plays are rarely cancelled because of weather.

Bus for Theater Performances: Round-trip bus service is available from Penzance and St. Ives for Tue-Thu evening shows; book online in advance with your theater ticket—seats fill up. You can also take the #A1 bus from Penzance to Porthcurno and walk 10 minutes uphill to the theater.

Telegraph Museum

In the 1920s, Porthcurno was the largest telegraph station in the world. At its peak, 180,000 miles of cable came together here. Imagine the importance of the telegraph: While it took six weeks to get a message from England to India in 1869, it took only nine minutes after the telegraph cable was laid from Porthcurno to India a year later. By the time World War II broke out, 14 cables tethered this village to the rest of the world. In 1940, defensive tunnels were built to protect the telegraph station and cables from the Nazis—who were then just 80 miles away in France.

Today, those tunnels and an adjacent building house a fascinating museum, tracing the history of the "Victorian Internet." The museum explains how underwater cables were made possible thanks to a new insulating material (a resin from a Malaysian tree called gutta-percha), how the cables were even more heavily armored in shallower water (where they could be damaged by the anchors of passing ships), and how ruptured cables were repaired in the briny deep. Ask about the worthwhile hourly presentation about underwater telegraphy, which helps bring the place to life. The tunnels are furnished as they would have been during wartime, when they protected England's very precious connection to the world. You can put on a helmet and escape via the stairs to the lookout high above.

Cost and Hours: £9; daily 10:00-17:00 except closed Tue-Fri in Nov-March, last entry one hour before closing; high above the main parking lot in Porthcurno on the road up to Minack Theatre—look for big white building marked *Museum,* tel. 01736/810-966, www.telegraphmuseum.org.

• *Once you're done touring Porthcurno, hop back in your car and backtrack to the B-3315, then turn left and drive three miles to...*

Land's End

The westernmost point in all of England should seem like a desolate, rugged place. In reality, it's a tacky tourist trap where greedy businesses have chewed up whatever small bit of charm or authen-

ticity this place might once have had. As you approach, you'll see endless signs bragging "the last"... everything: inn, hotel, refreshment stand, postal box, and so on. Come here only if you want to be able to say you've been to Land's End. (Consider

CORNWALL

lying.) You can get here directly from Penzance on the A-30 if you're not following this driving tour.

If you do visit, pay the £6 parking fee (enforced 24 hours/day; coins required 17:00-9:00) and walk straight from the parking lot through the low-budget theme park (stop at your own risk) out to the viewpoint. This was once considered the end of the civilized world, the last (or first) thing to be seen by departing (or arriving) ships. After gazing at the sea and guessing how far away from home you are, find out how close you were by checking your hometown at the picture stand on the right. For £11, they'll take your photo with a personalized signpost and mail it to you.

• *Head back inland and veer left (north) on the A-30. After about 2.5 miles, turn left on the B-3306, following signs to St. Just, the westernmost town in England, which used to support this area's tin-mining industry.*

In St. Just, follow the main street, lined with old workers' cottages, to the market square, where you can get authentic Cornish pasties at K&D McFadden and Sons Butchers (Mon-Sat 8:00-17:00, closed Sun, 11 Market Square, tel. 01736/788-136). Take the next left after the square, by the clock tower, and follow this road toward the coast until it ends at...

Cape Cornwall: "The Connoisseur's Land's End"

At this bluff with a memorial chimney capping it, you'll feel like you're at the end of England, all while escaping the commercialism of Land's End. Cape Cornwall offers a fine little walk and a strong memory. Pay to park, and for the most peaceful and evocative approach, go through the gate and across a grassy field to visit the ruins of the tiny sixth-century church of St. Helen's Oratory. Imagine a Celtic monk living here with just an altar, a fireplace, and a bed, dedicating his life to God. The trail then leads to the memorial capping the bluff. Just inland is a tin-mine captain's mansion, and in the distance is Land's End. Enjoy the perch.

From here the ground is honeycombed with mine tunnels. Since ancient times, this has been a center of tin mining. Mix tin and copper and you get bronze—great for weapons. (Around here, the Bronze Age was from 4000 BC to 800 BC.) Like West Virginia or North Wales, this area, reliant on mining in the Industrial Age, has had a tough time in the Information Age. Today all the working mines here are closed (the last one was shuttered in 1999), with just a few open for tourists. The buzz on the peninsula these days is about the BBC show *Poldark*, set in late 18th-century Cornwall.

• *From the center of St. Just, continue north on the B-3306 for almost a mile, then veer left at the road with a sign for Botallack. Follow this road to the coast to find the...*

Crown Mines of Botallack

This evocative coastal area is dotted with 19th-century Industrial Age ruins. In their 1860s heyday, the tin mines here employed more than 500 people. The desolate engine houses—which once pumped water out so they could mine a half-mile down and a half-mile out to sea—today invite hikers and photographers. You'll find free parking, a small, free information center about mining culture, and dramatic walks.

• *Continue along the coastal road for remarkable scenery and a peek at the historical Levant mine (with a working beam engine), then follow the road inland. At the T-intersection with the B-3306, turn left and go a quarter-mile to the...*

▲Geevor Tin Mine

Once 2,100 feet deep and extending half a mile under the ocean, the Geevor Mine closed in 1990. Tin mining here collapsed in the 1980s, and Marga-

ret Thatcher ended subsidies that were keeping it afloat—effectively prompting the closure of the mine (and earning lots of Cornish enemies). Geevor represents the last hurrah not only of Cornish tin mining, but, in a sense, of Britain's Industrial Age. Today, considered virtually a shrine by the local community, it's been converted into a museum, exhibiting most of its original buildings and machinery. Exploring the remnants of this recently defunct industry, you'll gain an appreciation for the simple, noble life of miners. Even if you're not into heavy metal, this unique look at tin mining is fascinating—and worth ▲▲▲ to those interested in engineering.

Cost and Hours: £14.90; Sun-Fri 9:00-17:00, Nov-Easter 10:00-16:00, closed Sat year-round, last entry one hour before closing; self-guided "free flow" visits in summer, guided tours go 3/day in winter—call or check online for exact times; wear good shoes, pick up free map at entry, café, tel. 01736/788-662, www.geevor. com.

Getting There from Penzance: If you're driving here directly from Penzance, take the A-30 Penzance bypass, then the A-3071 to St. Just and follow the brown *Historic Mining Area* signs. Take the right fork on the B-3318 to Pendeen, turn left at the crossroads to drive through Pendeen, and turn right at the Geevor entrance. You can also get here on bus #A17 from Penzance or St. Ives (2/hour; 40 minutes from Penzance, 80 minutes from St. Ives) or #A3

Cornwall's Tin-Mining Legacy

Cornwall's history is tied to its tin-mining industry. While Cornwall has always been known for its metal deposits, a major tin boom began here in the mid-1700s, as new steam-engine-powered pumps allowed tin to be mined below the water table. The industry peaked 200 years ago, when tin was the cutting edge of technology, and Cornwall was the Silicon Valley of Britain.

Miners would climb down into the narrow shafts, and use a hammer and a long bit to slowly drive deep, skinny holes into a vein of tin. Then they'd insert sticks of dynamite. Before safety fuses were invented, quills from bird feathers were used as fuses, so miners setting off gunpowder never knew how much time they had to reach safety before the explosion.

Deadly cave-ins were frequent. These were supposedly caused by mischievous Tommyknockers, Cornish pixies similar to leprechauns. But these mysterious creatures might simply have been a creation of the oxygen-starved imaginations of exhausted miners.

Mines employed the notorious "company store" system, where workers were paid in tokens that could only be redeemed at the store run by the mine (an obvious conflict of interest—which always worked to the company's advantage). To save money, miners made their own "hardhats." They'd take a felt hat and harden it by dipping it alternately in hot tree resin and soil. Then they'd stick a candle on the brim for light while they worked. Since miners had to buy their own candles (from the company store, of course), they'd extinguish them during their pitch-black lunch break to make them last longer.

After working all morning underground, Cornish tin miners looked forward to their traditional lunch of a pasty (PASS-tee). Basically a beef stew wrapped in a pastry crust, pasties had a

from St. Ives (summer only, 40 minutes). Check schedules at www.firstgroup.com.

Eating near the Mine: You can get hot, authentic, delicious Cornish pasties on the main square of the humble town of St. Just, at **K&D McFadden and Sons Butchers** (described earlier).

Visiting the Mine: Put on your hard hat and wander through the entrance building, keeping an eye out for a giant model (just before the exit) that once helped engineers keep track of the network of shafts—making it clear how extensive the mining industry was here. Then head outside, where you'll walk from shed to shed to see the various parts of the day-to-day workings of the mine.

The modern, well-presented **Hard Rock Museum** features exhibits for all ages about mining and the rocks that harbor valuable ores. On the ground floor, you'll find an extensive exhibit about geology (including a 220-pound chunk of tin-embedded stone), thick, crimped edge that miners could grab with dirty hands without contaminating their food. Because real flour was expensive, early miners skimped by using barley wheat—making for a very tough package. Leftover chunks of dough were often dropped into the mineshaft to appease the Tommyknockers.

Originally a pasty would be filled half with stew, and the rest with dessert, such as jam or apples. Nowadays there's a nice variety of flavors, like lamb and mint, but the full-meal deal is rare. The British government won trademark protection from the European Union for the Cornish pasty. That means the term "Cornish pasty" can only be applied to those pasties made in Cornwall using traditional techniques and recipes (www.cornishpastyassociation.co.uk). Look for pasties all over Cornwall (and throughout Britain). One of the best places is **K&D McFadden and Sons Butchers** in St. Just, near Geevor Tin Mine (see earlier).

Other than savory pasties, the crumbling smokestacks that dot the landscape today are the only remnants of Cornwall's now-dead tin-mining industry, which couldn't compete with cheap tin from Asia and South America. The ground underfoot is still honeycombed with forgotten tin mines. Older Cornish natives can still remember being in their houses and hearing the miners working underground.

display cases with items the miners took down into the shafts with them, and a very loud simulation of what it was like inside the mine shafts (press the button for sound effects). The *Geevor Voices* film (about 20 minutes) uses interviews and news clips to tell the story of the mine's operation, closure, and conversion to a museum. Upstairs are hands-on exhibits about the tin-making process, and a timeline of the mine's history.

"The Dry" is where the miners showered, changed, and dried their uniforms between shifts. Though it closed more than two decades ago, it feels as though the miners could show up at any time to clock in. Enjoy the old time-punch clock, the fun stickers on the miners' lockers, and graffiti showing their sense of humor (such as the *Ear Protection Must Be Worn* sign posted next to the toilets).

In **"The Mill,"** you'll see how a vast warehouse of "shaking

CORNWALL

tables"—like giant machines panning for gold—separated the miners' haul into its useable parts.

The finale is a 30-minute **underground tour** of an 18th-century mine (which predates the more recent mine that the current buildings supported, and was discovered by modern miners). A docent, often a former mine employee, gives you a coverall and leads you in. The mines—narrow and low (you'll be hunched for most of the tour, and claustrophobes will be miserable)—give you a sense of the difficult life of miners and the perilous conditions under which they worked. During very busy times in summer, you'll explore this area at your own pace, as docents posted throughout answer questions.

• *Back in your car, as you exit Geevor Tin Mine, turn left onto the B–3306. Enjoy the final stretch, the...*

Scenic Drive to St. Ives

For simple Cornwall beauty, drive the north shore of the Penwith Peninsula. In the 10 miles between Geevor Tin Mine and St. Ives, the little B–3306 is simply a joy as you ride through mining towns, farm hamlets, and pastoral fields. The winding hedgerows, built before motor traffic, make the road not quite two lanes wide. Hearty white-belted Galloway cows ignore the views, smokestacks mark old mines, and stony barns are just going through another century.

• *Our drive is over. Spend some time exploring St. Ives before heading back to Penzance along the B–3311.*

PENWITH PENINSULA BY BUS

If driving takes the joy out of a joyride for you, you can still visit many of the sights described in my "Penzance to St. Ives Drive" by bus. My recommended itinerary makes the best use of your time, but only works in summer, when bus service is regular.

Here's an overview:

Ride the #A1 bus from Penzance to Porthcurno (40 minutes), tour Porthcurno, then continue on the #A1 to Land's End (20 minutes). After a short hike in that area to Sennen Cove, ride bus #A3 from the cove to Geevor Tin Mine (30 minutes). After touring the mine, continue on #A3 to St. Ives (45 minutes). You can either hop off and explore St. Ives, or stay on the bus, which becomes the #A2 back to Penzance (and stops at Marazion near St. Michael's Mount en route if you want to tour that sight).

Be aware that some stops require walking up steep hills. Confirm bus schedules ahead of time, be selective about where you get off (as it's an hour between buses), and get an early start. For the best value, get a bus day pass (see page 365 for pass and schedule information for my recommended buses). See "Scenic Drive to St. Ives," earlier, for sight descriptions.

CORNWALL

Penzance to Porthcurno: From Penzance, take the bus in the direction of Land's End. On the way to Porthcurno, you'll see Merry Maidens Stone Circle from the left side of the bus. At Porthcurno, the bus exits the main road and eventually loops in front of the Telegraph Museum—get off at this stop.

Porthcurno: Visit the Minack Theatre first. From the bus, head to the main street (The Valley) and walk uphill 10 minutes, passing Porthcurno Beach Café. Follow signs for *Minack Theatre*. After your theater visit, walk back down the hill, visit the Telegraph Museum or Porthcurno Beach, and catch the next bus.

Land's End/Sennen Cove: Skip the town in favor of a 30-minute, 1.5-mile coastal hike to Sennen Cove. After getting off at the Land's End bus stop, walk toward the coast and veer right to reach the **First and Last House.** Continue north, with the water on your left. Along the way you'll enjoy great views, misleading *Maen Castle* signs (the "castle" is just a few rocks), a shipwreck, and a lookout house. Eventually the path drops you into the small beach community of Sennen Cove, with a large beach and a few cafés along the water. After your visit, head to the bus stop on Cove Hill Road across from Smart Surf School to catch the bus toward St. Ives.

Geevor Tin Mine: This stop can be difficult to identify; ask the driver to point it out. Walk about six minutes from the stop down to the mine.

St. Ives: After touring the mine, continue on toward St. Ives. Relax and take in the views as the bus winds around the north side of the peninsula. Once you arrive in St. Ives, you can either jump off and explore, or stay on the bus to return to Penzance.

Back to Penzance: On the way back to Penzance, the bus stops at Marazion near St. Michael's Mount. Get off to visit the sight, or continue back to Penzance.

East Cornwall

These destinations are a bit farther from Penzance, and closer to Dartmoor National Park. I've listed them from farthest to nearest to Penzance. Consider visiting them in this order as you head south, approaching the tip of Cornwall.

▲▲Tintagel Castle

Wild, rocky, remote, and romantic, Tintagel (tin-TAD-jell) is as dramatic as a castle can be. The real King Arthur—if he actually existed—was supposedly born here and ruled his lands from this rocky point. While the popular tales of Camelot are flights of fantasy, they may be based on a real person. Even though there's no physical record of King Arthur, the verbal tradition is strong enough that experts think a fifth- or sixth-century ruler by that name probably lived in this area, possibly basing himself in modern Camelford (which might be where "Camelot" comes from). Regardless of whether Arthur is fact or fiction, windblown Tintagel Castle is striking and one of England's more rewarding ruined-castle experiences. And, as a bonus, you get to enjoy a spectacularly scenic stretch of Cornish coastline. Bring a picnic to have lunch with a view, or eat at the on-site café.

Cost and Hours: £13—purchase timed-entry ticket in advance during peak times; daily 10:00-19:00, Sept until 18:00, Oct until 17:00, shorter hours and closed some days in Nov-March, last entry one hour before closing.

Advance Tickets Recommended: Buy a timed-entry ticket in advance online at their website to ensure entry. A limited number of same-day tickets (£14.50) are sold on-site, but they can sell out.

Information: Tel. 01840/770-328, www.english-heritage.org.uk.

Getting There: The castle clings to the coast below the tacky town of Tintagel (described later). If you're arriving by car, look for *Tintagel* signs from the A-39 as it passes through Camelford. Once you enter the village of Tintagel, take your pick of pay parking lots. Walk along the main street following brown castle signs, then hike down the steep road to the entrance (allow at least 30 minutes). To save a few minutes and avoid the nothing-special half-mile walk, hop the Land Rover shuttle (£2 each way), which runs continuously April-Oct between the top of the trail and the ticket office down at sea level. By public transportation from Penzance, it takes 3-4 hours, and involves one or more transfers (for specifics, call 0871-200-2233, or use the journey planner at www.travelinesw.com). For bus info, contact National Express (tel. 0871-781-8178, www.nationalexpress.com).

Visitor Information: Pick up the brochure that guides you to points of interest around the site. For the full story, invest in the £5 illustrated guidebook.

Visiting the Castle: A footbridge crosses the chasm between the main part of the castle on the island (actually a rocky peninsula attached by a narrow spit) and the mainland. The mainland and island were once joined by natural land bridge, which collapsed in the 15th or 16th century. Until 2019, visitors had to climb more than 100 steps to reach the cliff-top ruins. The **modern steel**

bridge re-creates the historic path (and the dramatic viewpoint), once again joining the divided castle sights. Your timed-entry ticket states the time you can cross the bridge and enter the castle.

You'll climb a path up to the mainland courtyard, then cross the footbridge to the island. In the **courtyard,** outdoor displays explain the sight's history. As you view intriguing historic objects, consider that more sixth-century artifacts are found here than anywhere else in Britain. Learn how this was an important center in the century after Rome abandoned Britain, a fact that lends credence to the hunch that a mighty King Arthur ruled from here. Arthur was first linked to this place in the 12th century, after the castle had been abandoned for six centuries. Geoffrey of Monmouth's not-entirely-factual 1136 tome, *The History of the Kings of Britain,* popularized the idea that Arthur had been conceived here. The exhibit explains how King Henry III's little brother, Richard, Earl of Cornwall, bought the castle in 1233 due to its association with Arthur and had it rebuilt. Another boost in its fame came in the Victorian Age, when many notable writers and artists came here for inspiration.

From the bridge, look down to the right to see the holes in the cliff below the ruins. One of these is supposedly **Merlin's cave.** (If the tide is out, you can climb down to explore the famous wizard's former home...and ponder how he managed to keep the carpet dry and prevent seals from climbing on the furniture.)

As you approach the rock-top castle, appreciate its naturally fortified, easily defensible position. Note the narrow and difficult approach to this hunk of land, and you can understand why Tintagel—meaning "fortress with narrow entrance"—is aptly named.

As you enter through the Victorian-era back door, you reach the **island courtyard**—castle remnants dating from the Middle Ages. Rather than belonging to Arthur (who would have lived centuries earlier), these structures were built for the brother of a 13th-century king. Notice that the walls are made of stacked sheets of slate, which was mined on this site for many years.

Continue through another evocative doorway, proceed straight along the cliff, and hike up to the viewpoint platform. All around you—including directly below—you'll see the foundations of ruined **Dark Age houses,** which actually date from around the time when Arthur most likely lived (the fifth century AD). Here archaeologists have found remains of items from as far away as North Africa and the Eastern Mediterranean—evidence of the wealth and status of this castle's owner. Notice that the farther you get out on the rock, the older the ruins are—Victorian, medieval, Dark Ages.

At the top of the island, the 360-degree views are spectacular. Circling around the site, you'll come across several interesting features: In the walled area straight ahead of where you summited the rock—called the **garden**—medieval residents could relax and entertain visitors in the summer. Just beyond that, the **well** was the source of water in the Middle Ages, and remains today's last resort in case of fire. The 11th-century **chapel** is recognizable for the altar at its far end. If you have time, linger up here. The craggy peaks across the tops of the cliffs make a perfect windblown picnic spot.

Near the Castle: Tintagel Town

This tacky town feels made for tourism—just a couple of streets around the trailhead to the castle. On my first visit I had a beer at the Excali Bar and kept looking for a menu with "the sword in the scone." The **Tintagel Visitor Centre,** at the first pay-and-display parking lot you come to, has a helpful info desk, a worthwhile history exhibit, and a WC (daily 10:00-17:00, Nov-Feb 10:30-16:00, tel. 01840/250-010). There are two overpriced "historic" sights in town: The **1380 Old Post Office** looks every bit its age (£4.80, 4 unimpressive rooms), and **King Arthur's Great Halls** boasts a Hall of Chivalry with pre-Raphaelite stained-glass windows and lots of romantic Knights-of-the-Round-Table-themed paintings (£5, closed Nov-Feb and Mon, at the roundabout).

Villages Just West of Tintagel

If you have some time between the Penwith Peninsula and Tintagel, consider stopping at one or both of these seafront villages.

Padstow

A little Cornish fishing port with a big culinary reputation, Padstow is the home of Michelin-starred chef Rick Stein and several of his fish restaurants. Although largely unknown stateside, this celebrity chef (who has hosted several cooking and travel series for BBC television) is famous in Britain, and has singlehandedly upped the culinary standards of Cornwall (spawning copycats eager to please foodies who pilgrimage here to dine at Stein's). Some people even call the town "Padstein."

Getting There: Padstow sits on a large estuary about 45 miles northeast of Penzance (roughly on the way to Tintagel Castle). From the main A-30 road, exit at the A-39 and follow *Padstow* signs for 12 miles (turning off onto the B-3274 about halfway there; total trip from the A-30 is about 20 minutes one-way). Entering town, follow *P* signs to the large pay lot along the wharf, a short walk from the harbor and town center.

CORNWALL

Visiting Padstow: Ideal for a lunchtime stopover, Padstow is still a working seaport, where local fisherman can sometimes be seen bringing in their daily catch. Tourists now browse the art galleries and enjoy their ice-cream cones, but the town has managed to retain a little of its gritty charm—particularly in the streets behind the harborfront.

Rick Stein's simply named **$$$$ Seafood Restaurant,** the flagship of his culinary empire, may be worth planning a meal around for curious foodies—but be sure to reserve ahead (£43 three-course lunch, daily 12:00-15:00 & 18:00-21:30, between the parking lot and the harbor, tel. 01841/532-700; for details on his eateries and accommodations, see www.rickstein.com).

There's more action along the wharf (near the parking lot), where a large building contains three less-upscale Rick Stein **eateries:** a fishmonger, a deli (with an *antipasti* counter, pasties, and pricey picnic fixin's), and expensive but very tasty fish-and-chips (if there's a long line for a table, look for the separate door for takeaway). Nearby, at the west end of the wharf, is the tourable **National Lobster Hatchery** (£4.50, daily 10:00-17:00, can close later in summer and earlier in winter, see website for exact times, www.nationallobsterhatchery.co.uk).

Port Isaac

While Port Isaac is a beautiful workaday fishing village tucked in a deep gash of rock just down the coast from Tintagel, it is trampled by devotees of *Doc Martin,* the popular British television series that's set and filmed here. It might as well be called Port Wenn—its fictional name in *Doc Martin*. Playing Port Wenn on TV has put this otherwise sleepy town on the map. Driving in from the A-389 highway, follow blue *P* signs to the triple-tiered pay parking lot with grand Atlantic Ocean panoramas (including distant views of Tintagel). Then hike back along the main road and climb steeply down into town, pausing periodically to enjoy the views of the deep gorge that protects the town's harbor. On the way into town, you'll pass *Doc Martin*'s old schoolhouse, now cleverly converted into a pub and hotel. (The small cottage where the good doctor resides is across the harbor from the schoolhouse.) Notice how boats are tethered by extremely long lines to the harbor; thanks to the dramatic tides, they're forced to gently beach themselves on sandbars at low tide.

▲Eden Project

Set in an abandoned china-clay mine, the Eden Project is an ambitious and futuristic work in progress—a theme park of global gardening with an environmental conscience. Exotic plants from all over the world are showcased in two giant biomes, reputedly the largest greenhouses in the world. The displays focus on sustainable farming and eco-conscious planting, but the most interesting thing here is the sheer audacity of the idea. If you're looking for a quaint English cottage garden, this isn't it. Rather than a flowery look at England's past, this "global garden" gives you a sense of how the shrinking of the world will affect us in the future.

Cost and Hours: £28.50, discounts online or if you arrive by bus; daily 9:00-18:00, July-Aug until 18:30, Nov-March generally 10:00-16:30, last entry 1.5 hours before closing. The domes can close as early as 15:00 for private events and off-season—check online or call first to confirm closing time, cafés, tel. 01726/811-911, www.edenproject.com.

Crowd Alert: The Eden Project can be crowded, especially on rainy days and weekdays June-Aug ("wet Wednesdays" are the worst). During peak-of-peak times, you may have to wait up to an hour to get in. To avoid this, consider arriving after 13:00.

Getting There: Drivers will find the Eden Project well-signposted from both the A-30 and the A-39—you'll be directed to the A-391, and follow signs from there. Park at one of the many outlying lots, note your parking lot's fruity symbol, then walk down into the Project (or take the free park-and-ride shuttle bus). By public transit, first take the train to St. Austell, where you'll meet bus #101 (hourly, tel. 0871-200-2233, www.firstgroup.com). Buses meet most arriving trains for the 20- to 30-minute run to the complex.

Visiting the Eden Project: While the site is multifaceted, it is dominated by two big biomes—the Rainforest and the Mediterranean. After buying your ticket, zigzag down into the pit and work your way through the various exhibits, including the enormous, hot, and hazy Rainforest Biome (where my camera completely fogged up; you can seek relief in an air-conditioned hut about halfway through); the smaller and more arid Mediter-

ranean Biome; an eatery-filled walkway connecting them called The Link; The Core, with educational exhibits; and lots of gardens. A land train and an elevator from The Core make it easier to get back up to the visitors center when you're done. Kid-oriented programs, rock and pop concerts, and other special events run throughout the year. Thrill seekers can pay extra to zipline over the biomes or ride a giant swing—see the website for all the hair-raising details.

It's an impressive concept, and the biomes are striking. But the educational exhibits are a bit too conceptual to be effective—leaving the whole expensive experience feeling somehow unmoored.

Gardens near Falmouth

Cornwall has many wonderful gardens, some with subtropical varieties of plants that thrive in this mild climate (www.greatgardensofcornwall.co.uk). These two gardens are a few miles apart on the same backcountry road, just south of Falmouth.

Getting There: If you're driving, take the A-39 or the A-394 into Falmouth until you see brown-and-white *Garden* signs—track these closely for four miles through the countryside to the gardens (Glendurgan is the better-signed of the two). If you're without a car, take bus #35 from Falmouth toward Helston (45-70 minutes, www.firstgroup.com).

▲Trebah Garden

The "Garden of Dreams" at Trebah (TREE-bah), set on 26 acres that bunny-hop down a ravine to the beach below, is a lush and tropical spectacle that makes for an unexpected treat. While most of England suffers from chilly arctic air, the Cornish peninsula is bathed in warmer air from the Gulf Stream—making average temperatures here much milder (the sea here never

drops below 50°F). Palms, succulents, bamboo, large azaleas, giant rhubarbs, and the prehistoric-looking gunnera might make you think that you're in the tropics (or wish that you were). The garden's exoticism impresses even nongardeners. While garden lovers wander in ecstasy, history buffs can ponder the fact that the beach below was used by some US troops in World War II to launch the D-Day attack on Omaha Beach.

Cost and Hours: £10.50, 50 percent off in winter or if you show bus ticket; daily 10:00-17:00, until dusk in winter, last entry one hour before closing; colorful year-round but flowers are best late March and April, café, tel. 01326/252-200, www.trebahgarden.co.uk.

Glendurgan Garden

Just up the road from Trebah, Glendurgan has a smaller collection of tropical plants mingled with more traditional English garden fare. Similarly set in a broad basin angled to the sea, Glendurgan is bigger but less striking than its neighbor. However, it comes with an extensive, kid-friendly hedge maze (about waist-high—but still entertaining—for an adult), built by the former owner to amuse his 12 children. Gardeners may appreciate its good orchids and its small "Holy Bank" of biblical-themed plants. And, down at the seashore, the fishing hamlet of Durgan makes it feel less like just an overblown backyard for aristocrats.

Cost and Hours: £10; Tue-Sun 10:30-17:30, closed Mon except in Aug, closed Nov-mid-Feb; best in spring, fee for worthwhile map/guide, pay parking, café, tel. 01326/252-020, www.nationaltrust.org.uk.

Sleeping near the Gardens: To maximize your time exploring the gardens, consider spending the night in or near salty Falmouth, a tidy harbor town nestled near the Tudor fortress of Pendennis Castle.

$$$ The Greenbank hotel is right on the water with a seagull's-eye view of the many boats moored in the Fal Estuary. Look near the hotel lobby for displays about Kenneth Grahame, who wrote parts of *The Wind in the Willows* while staying here (check for online deals, Harbourside, tel. 01326/312-440, www.greenbank-hotel.co.uk, reception@greenbank-hotel.co.uk).

$ Cornwall Plus rents double rooms with private bath at the joint campus of the University of Exeter and Falmouth University, located five miles from Falmouth along the A-39. The dorm rooms are only available July-August, when the college kids are on summer break (also rents apartments and cottages, café, grocery, launderette, Treliever Road, Penryn, tel. 01326/370-421, www.cornwall-plus.co.uk, booking@fxplus.ac.uk).

BATH

The best city to visit within easy striking distance of London is Bath—just a 1.5-hour train ride away. If ever a city enjoyed looking in the mirror, Bath's the one. Bath's narcissism is justified. It has more "government-listed" or protected historic buildings per capita than any other town in England. Built of the creamy warm-tone limestone called "Bath stone," it beams in its cover-girl complexion. Two hundred years ago, this city of 90,000 was the trendsetting Tinseltown of Britain. An architectural chorus line, it's a triumph of the Neoclassical style of the Georgian era—named for the four Georges who sat as England's kings from 1714 to 1830. Proud locals remind visitors that the town is routinely banned from the "Britain in Bloom" urban-beautification contest to give other towns a chance to win. Even with its mobs of tourists (2 million per year) and greedy prices, Bath is a joy to visit.

These days, a growing number of Bath-based professionals catch the 7:13 express train to London on their daily commute. And Bath's soothing hot springs are still around, attracting visitors as they have for thousands of years.

PLANNING YOUR TIME

Bath deserves two nights even on a quick trip. On a three-week England getaway, spend three nights in Bath, with one day for the city and one or two days for side trips to Bristol, Wells, Glastonbury, or your pick of stone circles. Ideally, use Bath as your jet-lag recovery pillow (easy access from Heathrow Airport), and do London at the end of your trip.

Consider starting your English vacation this way:

Day 1: Land at Heathrow. Connect to Bath either by train

A Quick Dip into the History of Bath

Bath's fame began with the allure of its hot springs—a rarity in Britain. Even in Celtic times, people made pilgrimages here to bathe in the (supposedly) curative waters. When the Romans conquered Britain, they built a large bathhouse around the spring and made Bath an important town. In medieval times, Bath's thriving wool trade and huge church (where the abbey stands today) made it the religious capital of Britain. Its influence peaked in 973 when King Edgar was crowned here.

Bath then declined, wasting away to a huddle of huts, with hot, smelly mud and 3,000 residents, oblivious to the Roman ruins 18 feet below their dirt floors. Then, in 1687, Queen Mary, fighting infertility, bathed here. Within 10 months, she gave birth to a son. A few years later, Queen Anne found the water eased her painful gout. Word of its miraculous waters spread, and Bath regained fame.

By the mid-1700s, Bath (population 30,000) was England's trendiest resort. Thousands of wealthy vacationers flocked here to soak in the mineral waters, socialize, flirt, see the latest plays, drink, dance, gamble, and party late into the night. It was the place to see and be seen in England.

Bath was rich, thriving on the wealth pouring into England from its overseas colonies in India, Africa, and America. The city built grand new buildings in the Georgian style that set the tone for all of England. Powdered-wig aristocrats rode in horse-drawn carriages or were carried through the town in sedan chairs. Streets were lined not with scrawny sidewalks but with wide "parades," upon which women in their stylishly wide dresses could spread their fashionable tails. Bath was a fantastic realm of frilly Baroque music by Handel (who performed here), lush paintings by Gainsborough (who lived here), and theater by famed actor David Garrick (who staged plays here).

It was all orchestrated by the charismatic party-thrower and bon vivant, Beau Nash. Although this was an era of strict class distinctions, at Bath the classes could mingle more freely—nobles, the rising middle class, bohemians, and even servants.

In the early 1800s, Bath's luster began to fade. Jane Austen (who lived here then) found all the pretentious trend-chasing, husband-hunting, and status-seeking "tiresome." Over the next century-and-a-half, Bath declined into exactly what Jane Austen had foreseen: a tacky touristy resort with run-down buildings.

Bath suffered considerable damage in World War II. After the Allies bombed the historic and well-preserved German city of Lübeck, the Germans picked up a Baedeker guide and chose a similarly lovely city to bomb: Bath.

But Bath has rebuilt to its former glory. It's still a major holiday destination for Brits, with much of the elegance, nightlife, and joie de vivre of the city in its prime.

via London Paddington, direct bus, or bus/train combination via Reading (for details, see page 191). You can also consider flying into Bristol, which has easy bus connections with Bath. While you don't need or want a car in Bath, those who land early and pick up their cars at the airport can visit Windsor Castle (near Heathrow) on their way to Bath. If you have the evening free in Bath, take a walking tour.

Day 2: 9:00—Tour the Roman Baths; 10:30—Catch the free city walking tour; 12:30—Picnic on the open deck of a tour bus; 14:00—Visit the abbey, then free time in the shopping center of old Bath; 15:30—Tour the No. 1 Royal Crescent Georgian house and Fashion Museum or Museum of Bath at Work. At night, consider seeing a play, take the evening walking tour (unless you did it last night), enjoy the Bizarre Bath comedy walk, or go for an evening soak in the Thermae Bath Spa.

Day 3 (and Possibly 4): Bath is a practical home base for visits to nearby sights. The port city of Bristol is just 15 minutes away by train and easily worth a day's sightseeing (see the end of this chapter). By car or bus, explore the mystical town of Glastonbury, the cathedral city of Wells, or the stone circles of Stonehenge and Avebury (see the next two chapters). Without a car or to go farther afield, consider a one-day Avebury/Stonehenge/cute towns minibus tour from Bath (Mad Max tours are best; see "Tours in and near Bath," later.

Orientation to Bath

Think of Bath as three sightseeing neighborhoods. In the center of town is the main cluster of sights: the Roman Baths, Pump Room, and Bath Abbey. A few blocks northeast is another group of sights around Pulteney Bridge. And, a 10-minute walk  to the northwest, are the Georgian-era sights: the Circus, Royal Crescent, Assembly Rooms, and several museums. Bath is hilly. In general, you'll gain elevation as you head north.

TOURIST INFORMATION

The TI is next to The Huntsman Inn pub and a block south of the abbey (Mon-Sat 9:30-17:30, Sun 10:00-16:00, Bridgwater House, 2 Terrace Walk, tel. 01225/614-420, www.visitbath.co.uk). It houses the Bath Box Office, where you can check for events going on all around town (see listing below, under "Helpful Hints").

ARRIVAL IN BATH

The Bath Spa **train station** has a staffed ticket desk and ticket machines. The **bus station** is immediately west of the train station, along Dorchester Street. Drivers can **park** at the Southgate shopping center near the train station. A handy luggage-check service is a half-block away (see "Helpful Hints," next).

The best route into the town center is the 10-minute walk up Southgate Street. Exiting the train station, turn left on Dorchester, then right onto pedestrian-only Southgate, Bath's main modern shopping street. Continue uphill as Southgate changes names to Stall Street, glance right at a photogenic arch, then keep going another block to a row of columns on the right. Stepping through the columns, you enter Abbey Churchyard—Bath's historic center—with Bath Abbey, the Roman Baths, and the Pump Room.

HELPFUL HINTS

Getting to Bath and Stonehenge by Tour: Several companies offer guided bus tours from London to Stonehenge, Salisbury, and Bath; you can abandon the tour in Bath, essentially using the tour as one-way transport; see page 493.

Festivals: In late May, the 10-day **Bath Festival** celebrates art, music, and literature (bathfestivals.org.uk/the-bath-festival/), overlapped by the eclectic **Bath Fringe Festival** (theater, walks, talks, bus trips; www.bathfringe.co.uk). The **Jane Austen Festival** unfolds genteelly in late September (www.janeausten.co.uk/festival). And for three weeks in December, the squares around the abbey are filled with a **Christmas market.**

The **Bath Box Office** sells tickets for festivals and most events (except those at the Theatre Royal), and can tell you exactly what's on tonight (inside the TI, tel. 01225/463-362, www.bathfestivals.org.uk). The city's weekly paper, the *Bath Chronicle*, publishes a "What's On" events listing each Thursday (www.thisisbath.com).

Bookstore: Topping & Company, an inviting bookshop, has frequent author readings, free coffee and tea, a good selection of maps, and tables filled with tidy stacks, including lots of books on the Bath region (daily 8:30-19:30, near the bottom of the street called "The Paragon"—where it meets George Street, tel. 01225/428-111, www.toppingbooks.co.uk).

Baggage Storage: @Internet & Luggage is a half-block in front of the train station (£2.50/bag per day, daily 8:00-22:00, 13 Manvers Street, tel. 01225/312-685).

Laundry: The **Spruce Goose Launderette** is between the Circus and the Royal Crescent, near several recommended restaurants on the pedestrian lane called Margaret's Buildings (bring coins, self-service, daily 8:00-20:00, last load at 19:00). **Speedy Wash** picks up your laundry anywhere in town on weekdays before 9:30 for same-day service (no pickup Sat, closed Sun, most hotels work with them, tel. 01225/427-616).

Bike Rental: You can rent a pricey bike or e-bike at **Green Park Bike Station** (£30/24 hours, includes lock and map, helmet extra; daily 10:00-16:00, Sept-April Tue-Sat only; must book in advance and leave cash security deposit and photo ID, at Green Park Station—enter through Sainsbury's on Lower Bristol Road, tel. 01225/920-148, www.greenparkbikestation.info).

Car Rental: Ideally, take the train or bus from downtown London to Bath, and rent a car as you leave Bath. Most offices close Saturday afternoon and all day Sunday, which complicates weekend pickups.

    Enterprise provides a pickup service for customers to and from their hotels (extra fee for one-way rentals, at Lower Bristol Road outside Bath, tel. 01225/443-311, www.enterprise.com). Others include **Thrifty** (pickup service and one-way rentals available, in the Burnett Business Park in Keynsham—between Bath and Bristol, tel. 01179/867-997, www.thrifty.co.uk), **Hertz** (one-way rentals possible, at Windsor Bridge, tel. 0843-309-3004, www.hertz.co.uk), and **National/Europcar** (one-way rentals available, about £15 by taxi from the train station, at Brassmill Lane—go west on Upper Bristol Road, tel. 0871-384-9985, www.europcar.co.uk). Skip **Avis**—it's a mile from the Bristol train station; you'd need to rent a car to get there.

Parking: As Bath becomes increasingly pedestrian-friendly, city-center street parking is disappearing. For a stress-free, time- and money-saving option, park for free at one of the big **Park & Ride lots** just outside of Bath at Newbridge, Lansdown, or Odd Down, and ride a shuttle bus 10 minutes into town (look for the *P&R* signs as you approach; shuttles run daily every 15 minutes, £3.40 round-trip, £6/group round-trip; tel. 0345-602-0121, www.firstgroup.com/bath-park-and-ride).

    If you drive into town, be aware that short-term lots fill up fast (£2/hour, 2- to 4-hour maximum). You'll find more spots in long-stay lots for about the same cost. The Southgate shopping center lot on the corner of Southgate and Dorchester streets is a five-minute walk from the abbey (£5/up to 3 hours, £14/24 hours, open 24/7); the Charlotte Street car park is the biggest and most convenient. For more info on parking

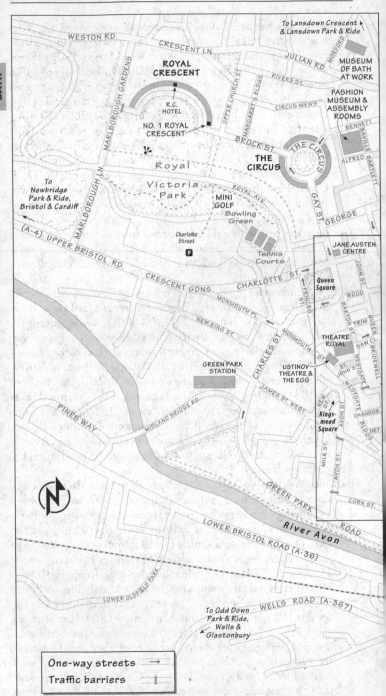

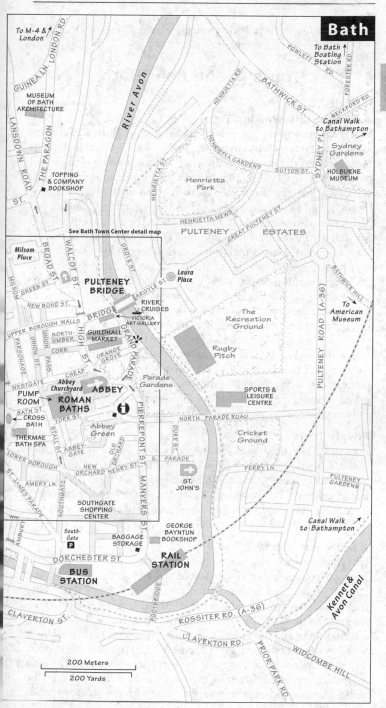

BATH

Bath

To M-4 & London

GUINEA LN. LONDON RD.

MUSEUM OF BATH ARCHITECTURE

THE PARAGON

LANSDOWN ROAD

ST.

TOPPING & COMPANY BOOKSHOP

River Avon

HENRIETTA RD.

BATHWICK ST.

POWLETT RD.

To Bath Boating Station

FORESTER RD.

BECKFORD RD.

Canal Walk to Bathampton

SYDNEY PL.

SUTTON ST.

Sydney Gardens

HOLBURNE MUSEUM

HENRIETTA ST.

HENRIETTA GARDENS

Henrietta Park

HENRIETTA MEWS

PULTENEY

GREAT PULTENEY ST.

ESTATES

See Bath Town Center detail map

Milsom Place

BROAD ST.

WALCOT ST.

GROVE ST.

Laura Place

BATHWICK HILL

PULTENEY ROAD (A-36)

To American Museum

PULTENEY BRIDGE

MILSOM ST.

GREEN ST.

NEW BOND ST.

EARGYLE ST.

BRIDGE

HIGH ST.

GRAND PARADE

River Cruises

VICTORIA ART GALLERY

UPPER BOROUGH WALLS

PARSONAGE

UNION ST.

NORTH-UMBER.

CORR.

GUILDHALL MARKET

ORANGE GROVE

The Recreation Ground

Rugby Pitch

WESTGATE

CHEAP ST.

Abbey Churchyard

ABBEY

Parade Gardens

SPORTS & LEISURE CENTRE

PUMP ROOM

ROMAN BATHS

BATH ST.

CROSS BATH

THERMAE BATH SPA

LOWER BOROUGH

ST. JAMES PARADE

AMERY LN.

STALL ST.

ABBEY-GATE

Abbey Green

NEW ORCHARD

YORK ST.

OLD ORCHARD

HENRY ST.

SOUTHGATE

PIERREPONT ST.

MANVERS ST.

DUKE ST.

S. PARADE

NORTH PARADE ROAD

Cricket Ground

FERRY LN.

PULTENEY GARDENS

ST. JOHN'S

Canal Walk to Bathampton

SOUTHGATE SHOPPING CENTER

South-Gate P

BAGGAGE STORAGE

GEORGE BAYNTUN BOOKSHOP

AMBURY

DORCHESTER ST.

RAIL STATION

BUS STATION

FOOTBRIDGE

Kennet & Avon Canal

CLAVERTON ST.

ROSSITER RD. (A-36)

LLAVEKTON RD.

PRIOR PARK RD.

WIDCOMBE HILL

200 Meters

200 Yards

(including Park & Ride service), see the "Maps and Guides" section of http://visitbath.co.uk.

Tours in and near Bath

IN THE CITY

▲▲▲Free City Walking Tours

Free two-hour tours are led by the **Mayor of Bath's Honorary Guides,** volunteers who share their love of Bath with its many visitors (as the city's mayor first did when he took a group on a guided walk back in the 1930s). These chatty, historical, and gossip-filled walks give you the lay of the land while you learn about the evolution of the city, its architecture, and its amazing Georgian social scene. How else would you learn that the old "chair ho" call for your sedan chair evolved into today's "cheerio" farewell? Tours leave from outside the Pump Room in the Abbey Churchyard (free, no tips, year-round Sun-Fri at 10:30 and 14:00, Sat at 10:30 only; additional evening walks May-Aug Tue and Thu at 18:00; www.bathguides.org.uk). Tip for theatergoers: When your guide stops to talk outside the Theatre Royal, skip out for a moment, pop into the box office, and see about snaring a great deal on a play for tonight.

The Honorary Guides also lead a free two-hour Pulteney Estate walk, including Great Pulteney Street and Sydney Gardens (May-Sept Tue and Thu at 11:00, departs from the Pump Room, no reservations necessary—just show up). It takes a look at the grand-if-unfinished 19th-century development of the city beyond Pulteney Bridge.

Private Tours

For a private tour, call the local guides' bureau, **Bath Parade Guides** (£100/2 hours, tel. 01225/337-111, www.bathparadeguides.co.uk, bathparadeguides@yahoo.com). **Mike James** is a good Blue Badge Bath guide (£150/half-day, £270/day, mike@mikejames.org). Mike also does food tours (see later) and Banksy street art walks in Bristol.

▲▲City Bus Tours

City Sightseeing's hop-on, hop-off bus tours zip through Bath. Jump on a bus at one of 17 signposted pickup points, pay the driver, climb upstairs, and hear recorded commentary about Bath. City Sightseeing has two 45-minute routes: the City Tour of Bath's center and the Skyline Tour outside town. On a sunny day, this is a multitasking tourist's dream come true: You can munch a sandwich, work on a tan, snap great photos, and learn a lot—all at once. Try to get one with a live guide (select tours only—confirm with driver); otherwise, bring your own earbuds if you've got 'em (the audio recording is sometimes hard to hear with the provided headsets). Save money by doing the bus tour first—your ticket gets you minor discounts at many sights (£16.50, ticket valid for 24 hours and both tour routes; City Tour generally 4/hour daily in summer 9:30-17:30, in winter 10:00-17:00, no buses Dec-Feb; Skyline Tour runs less frequently but year-round; tel. 01225/330-444, www.bathbuscompany.com).

Taxi Tours
Local taxis, driven by good talkers, go where big buses can't. A group of up to four can rent a cab for an hour (about £40; try to negotiate) and enjoy a fine, informative, and—with the right cabbie—entertaining private joyride. It's probably cheaper to let the meter run than to pay for an hourly rate but ask the cabbie for advice.

Food Tours
Savouring Bath Food Tour is worth considering for a three-hour movable feast with eight tasty stops (£55, most weekdays and Sat at 9:45 and 14:00, no Sun tours, book online, RS%—10 percent discount with code "ricksteves," www.savouringbath.com, tel. 01225/425-843, Mike James).

NEARBY SIGHTS
Bath is a good launchpad for visiting nearby Glastonbury, Wells, Avebury, Stonehenge, and more.

Mad Max Minibus Tours
Operating daily from Bath, Maddy offers thoughtfully organized, informative tours run with entertaining guides and limited to 16 people per group. Book as far ahead as possible in summer. The **Stonehenge, Avebury, and Villages** full-day tour covers 110 miles and visits Stonehenge, the Avebury Stone Circles, photogenic Lacock (LAY-cock), and the southernmost Cotswold village, Castle Combe (£42 plus £20 Stonehenge entry, tours depart daily at 8:30 and return at 17:30). Check their website for other tours: Stonehenge's inner circle, Cotswold villages (£38/half-day, £45/full day, daily at 8:30), and Wells, Glastonbury, and Cheddar Gorge (£45, Tue and Sat at 9:00).

All tours depart from downtown Bath near the abbey (outside the Abbey Hotel on 1 North Parade, arrive 15 minutes early, book at least 48 hours in advance; RS%—£10 rebate with online purchase of two separate tour itineraries, request when booking second tour, discount refunded to credit card; mobile 07990-505-970, phone answered daily 8:00-18:00, www.madmaxtours.co.uk, maddy@madmaxtours.co.uk).

Bath at a Glance

▲▲▲**Free City Walking Tours** Top-notch tours helping you make the most of your visit, led by the Mayor of Bath's Honorary Guides. **Hours:** Sun-Fri at 10:30 and 14:00, Sat at 10:30 only; additional evening walks offered May-Aug Tue and Thu at 18:00. See page 412.

▲▲▲**Roman Baths** Ancient baths that gave the city its name, tourable with good audioguide. **Hours:** Daily 9:00-18:00, July-Aug until 22:00, Nov-Feb 9:30-18:00. See page 416.

▲▲**Bath Abbey** 500-year-old Perpendicular Gothic church, graced with beautiful fan vaulting and stained glass. **Hours:** Mon-Sat 9:30-17:30, Sun 13:00-14:30 & 16:30-17:30. See page 422.

▲▲**The Circus and Royal Crescent** Stately Georgian (Neoclassical) buildings from Bath's 18th-century glory days. See pages 427 and 428.

▲▲**No. 1 Royal Crescent** Your best look at the interior of one of Bath's high-rent Georgian beauties. **Hours:** Daily 10:00-17:00. See page 429.

▲▲**Canalside Walk to Bathampton** This easy, hour-long stroll along an Industrial Age canal is a delightful escape from the busy town. See page 436.

▲**Pump Room** Swanky Georgian hall, ideal for a spot of tea or a taste of unforgettably "healthy" spa water. **Hours:** Daily 9:30-

Lion Tours

This well-run outfit runs full-day tours of Cotswold villages and "King Arthur's Realm" (£45 each), and gets you to Stonehenge with half- or full-day tours (Stonehenge and Lacock tour-£49; Stonehenge, Salisbury, and Cotswold villages-£61; Stonehenge inner circle access-£130; these prices include Stonehenge admission; RS%—£10/adult discount when you book any two full-day tours online, £5 discount for half-day tours—email after booking first tour for code; mobile 07769-668-668, www.liontours.co.uk, see website for details). If you ask in advance, you can bring your luggage along and use this tour to get to the Cotswolds (£5/person, minimum two people).

Other Tour Options

Scarper Tours runs four-hour narrated minibus tours to Stonehenge, giving you two hours at the site. This is basically a shuttle

16:00 for breakfast, lunch, and afternoon tea (open 18:00-21:00 for dinner July-Aug). See page 421.

▲**Pulteney Bridge and Parade Gardens** Shop-strewn bridge and relaxing riverside gardens. **Hours:** Bridge—always open; gardens—daily 10:00-18:00, Oct-April open 24 hours. See pages 424 and 425.

▲**Victoria Art Gallery** Paintings from the late 17th century to today. **Hours:** Daily 10:30-17:00. See page 425.

▲**Fashion Museum** 400 years of clothing under one roof, plus the opulent Assembly Rooms. **Hours:** Daily 10:30-18:00, Nov-Feb until 17:00. See page 432.

▲**Museum of Bath at Work** Gadget-ridden circa-1900 engineer's shop, foundry, factory, and office. **Hours:** Daily 10:30-17:00, Nov and Jan-March weekends only, closed Dec. See page 433.

▲**American Museum and Gardens** Insightful look primarily at colonial/early-American lifestyles, with 18 furnished rooms and eager-to-talk guides. **Hours:** Tue-Sun 10:00-17:00, late Nov-mid-Dec until 16:30, closed Mon, closed early Nov and mid-Dec-mid-March. See page 434.

▲**Thermae Bath Spa** Relaxation center that put the bath back in Bath. **Hours:** Daily 9:00-21:30. See page 435.

bus service from Bath with tickets (£25 transportation only, £40 including Stonehenge entry fee and reservation, departs from outside the Abbey Hotel on Terrace Walk, daily mid-March-Oct at 9:30 and 14:00, Nov-mid-March at 13:00, www.scarpertours.com, sally@scarpertours.com).

Celtic Horizons is a car service offering tours from Bath to destinations such as Stonehenge, Avebury, and Wells. They also provide a convenient transfer service (to or from London; Heathrow, Bristol, and other airports; the Cotswolds, and so on), with or without a tour itinerary en route. Allow about £35/hour for a group (comfortable minivans seat up to 8 people) and £150 for Heathrow-Bath transfers (1-3 people). Make arrangements and get pricing by email at info@celtichorizons.com (tel. 01373/800-500, US tel. 855-407-3200, www.celtichorizons.com).

Sights in Bath

IN THE TOWN CENTER
Abbey Churchyard

Ground zero for sightseeing is Abbey Churchyard, a vibrant square surrounded by the Roman Baths, Pump Room, and Bath Abbey. The Parade Gardens, Guildhall Market, Victoria Art Gallery, Pulteney Bridge, and River Avon are beyond the left corner of the abbey, a couple of minutes' walk away. Behind you, a block down Bath Street, is the Thermae Bath Spa.

Here in Abbey Churchyard, you can see the layers of Bath's history in a glance. The Roman Baths put the city on Europe's radar 2,000 years ago. The abbey made it an important medieval destination. The elegant Pump Room captures the city in its 18th-century heyday. And today's lively street performers show the city hasn't let up since.

The churchyard is also a showcase for Bath's distinctive Georgian architecture. The Pump Room's facade has a faux Greek-temple entrance: four tall columns support a triangular pediment with an inscription in Greek letters ("The greatest blessing is water"). Below that, the doorway is topped with a characteristic Georgian semicircular fanlight window. Five round windows and a fetching balustrade across the roofline complete the Neoclassical look.

Even the humble building opposite the Pump Room has some Georgian (if less fancy) elements. There's a triangular pediment on top. Doorways are topped with semicircles. The windows are symmetrically arranged, with some windows topped with cornices. The stonework is lightly adorned with classical garlands, and the sloped roof has dormer windows. You'll find Georgian features like these all over town.

▲▲▲Roman Baths

For thousands of years, humans have marveled at the hot water that bubbles out of the earth on this spot. In ancient Roman times, high society enjoyed soaking in the mineral springs, and they built a large bathhouse around it. From Londinium, Romans traveled so often to Aquae Sulis, as the city was called, to "take a bath" that finally it became known simply as Bath. Today, a fine museum surrounds the ancient bathhouse. With the help of a great audioguide, you'll wander past Roman artifacts, a temple pediment with an evocative bearded face, a bronze head of the god-

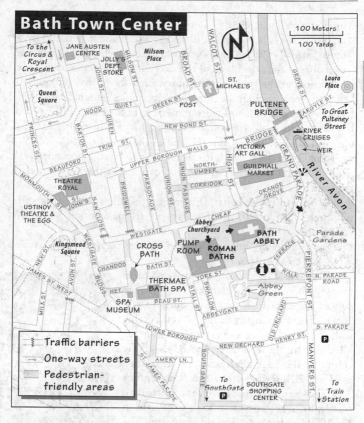

Bath Town Center

To the Circus & Royal Crescent

JANE AUSTEN CENTRE

JOLLY'S DEPT. STORE

Milsom Place

Queen Square

WALCOT ST.

BROAD ST.

ST. MICHAEL'S

GROVE ST.

Laura Place

BATH

JOHN ST.

MILSOM ST.

WOOD

QUIET

GREEN ST.

POST

PULTENEY BRIDGE

ARGYLE ST.

To Great Pulteney Street

QUEEN ST.

BARTON ST.

TRIM ST.

NEW BOND ST.

WALLS

UPPER BOROUGH

HIGH ST.

BRIDGE ST.

RIVER CRUISES

WEIR

PRINCES ST.

BEAUFORD

VICTORIA ART GALL.

GRAND PARADE

River Avon

MONMOUTH ST.

THEATRE ROYAL

PARSONAGE

UNION ST.

NORTH-UMBER.

CORRIDOR

GUILDHALL MARKET

ORANGE GROVE

USTINOV THEATRE & THE EGG

ST. JOHN'S

SAW CLOSE

BRIDEWELL

UNION PASSAGE

CHEAP

Abbey Churchyard

BATH ABBEY

Parade Gardens

Kingsmead Square

WESTGATE BLDGS.

WESTGATE

CHANDOS

BATH ST.

CROSS BATH

PUMP ROOM

ROMAN BATHS

TERRACE WALK

PIERREPONT ST.

AVON ST.

JAMES ST. WEST

MILK ST.

HET.

THERMAE BATH SPA

STALL ST.

YORK ST.

SWALLOW ST.

Abbey Green

N. PARADE ROAD

SPA MUSEUM

BEAU ST.

ABBEYGATE

S. PARADE

LOWER BOROUGH

OLD ORCHARD

ST. JAMES PARADE

AMERY LN.

SOUTH GATE

NEW ORCHARD

HENRY ST.

MANVERS ST.

To SouthGate

SOUTHGATE SHOPPING CENTER

To Train Station

100 Meters

100 Yards

Traffic barriers

One-way streets

Pedestrian-friendly areas

dess Sulis Minerva, excavated ancient foundations, and the actual mouth of the health-giving spring. At the end, you'll have a chance to walk around the big, steaming pool itself, where Romans once lounged, splished, splashed, and thanked the gods for the gift of therapeutic hot water.

Cost and Hours: £22, £20 off-peak days—see website, includes audioguide; daily 9:00-18:00, July-Aug until 22:00, Nov-Feb 9:30-18:00, last entry one hour before closing; tel. 01225/477-784, www.romanbaths.co.uk.

Combo-Ticket: If you plan to see both the Roman Baths and the Fashion Museum, you can save a little with the £25 Museums Saver combo-ticket, which also covers the temporary exhibit at the Victoria Art Gallery. If you buy the combo-ticket online, you'll save more—it's £22.50—and avoid ticket lines at both sights. Family Saver tickets are also available.

Crowd-Beating Tips: Long ticket lines are typical in the summer. You can use the "fast track" lane by buying a ticket online in advance, or by purchasing a combo-ticket at the Fashion

Museum or Victoria Art Gallery. On any day, try to visit early or late; peak time is between 13:00 and 15:00. If you're here in July or August, after 19:00 the baths are romantic, gas-lit, and all yours.

Tours: Take advantage of the excellent, included **audioguide.** In addition to the basic commentary, look for posted numbers to key into your audioguide for specialty topics—including a kid-friendly tour and musings from American expat writer Bill Bryson. For those with a big appetite for Roman history, in-depth 30-minute **guided tours** leave from the end of the museum at the edge of the actual bath (included with ticket, on the hour, a poolside clock shows the next departure time). You can revisit the museum after the tour.

Ɔ Self-Guided Tour: This brief tour follows the baths' one-way route; for more in-depth commentary, make ample use of the audioguide.

• *Begin by walking around the upper terrace, overlooking the swimming-pool–like Great Bath.*

Terrace: Lined with **statues** of VIRs (Very Important Romans), the terrace evokes ancient times but was built in the 1890s. The terrace sits atop the remarkably well-preserved lower story, which was actually built by the Romans: The bases of the columns, the pavement, and the lead-lined pool are all original from the first century AD. Those ancient ruins had sat undisturbed for centuries before finally being excavated in the 1870s and turned into this museum. The terrace statues help put a face on the baths' history: Julius Caesar first set foot in Britain (55 BC). Claudius conquered the Celts in

Bath (AD 43) and enclosed the first bathing pool with oak pilings. Hadrian (c. 120) enlarged the complex around it, and Constantine (c. 325) ruled when the baths were at their peak of grandeur. Enjoy the great **view** from the west end, looking back toward the abbey.

At the end of the terrace, before going downstairs, peer down into the **spring** (on the left through the window), where little air bubbles remind you that each day 240,000 gallons of water emerge from the earth—magically, it must have seemed to Romans—at a constant 115°F. It comes from rainwater that falls on the near-by hills, filters down through layers of limestone two miles deep, where it's heated by the earth's core, then rises back up through cracks to the surface. The water you see now first fell as rain about 10,000 years ago...making the Romans seem relatively recent.

• *Now you'll head downstairs to the...*

Museum: Start with its helpful **models.** The first model (of plexiglass) shows the humble baths that stood here around AD 70. It's just two buildings, with the spring in between, but it makes clear the complex's dual purpose: The bathhouse was for soaking in the healing waters, and the temple was for worshipping the goddess Sulis Minerva who gave mankind such a wondrous thermal spring.

The next model shows the baths at their peak, around AD 325. Get your bearings, because we'll soon be walking through the actual remains of this vast complex. The tallest building (with a barrel-arch roof) is the Great Bath you see today, with its big swimming pool. The smaller arched roofs alongside were other bathhouse buildings—dressing rooms, saunas, cold plunges, and so on. The red-tile-roofed section was the temple. You can make out the big rectangular temple courtyard enclosing the small temple. Also in the temple courtyard is a small altar where sacrifices were offered. Get a close look at the temple's colorful pediment (the triangular gable atop its four columns). Now, let's see that actual pediment, displayed nearby.

The fragments of the **temple pediment**—carved by indigenous Celtic craftsmen but with Roman themes—represent a remarkable cultural synthesis. Sit and watch for a while as a slide projection fills in historians' best guesses as to what once occupied the missing bits. The identity of the circular face in the middle puzzles researchers. (God? Santa Claus?) It could be the head of Medusa, the Gorgon monster, after it was slain by Perseus—are those snakes peeking through its hair and beard? And yet, the Gorgon was

traditionally depicted as female. Perhaps instead it's Neptune, the god of the sea—appropriate for this aquatic site.

The next exhibits examine every day **Roman life**—living, dying, and worshipping here in Aquae Sulis. You'll see vases, coins, and a stone head of a big-haired woman with her trendy first-century 'fro. The Beau Street Hoard—more than 17,500 Roman coins dating from 32 BC to AD 274 that were found near the Baths—emphasizes just how well-visited this area was.

Next up are a couple of rooms dedicated to **Roman worship.** You'll see some of the small but extremely heavy stone altars that pilgrims hauled here as an offering to the goddess. Nearby, take time to read some of the "curse tablets." These were small pewter pages that visitors would write a message on, roll up, and throw into the sacred spring, asking the goddess to grant their request. Many are comically spiteful and petty: "Curse whoever stole my clothes while I was bathing."

• *Next you'll walk through the ruins of the...*

Temple Courtyard: Imagine being a Roman arriving here to worship at the temple, which would have stood at the far end of the room. (That's made easy by the monitors, which recreate the scene from where you're standing.) You'd pause to sacrifice an animal atop the great **altar** (on the right); note the nicely carved statue of Hercules adorning the altar's left corner. Then you'd continue on to

the temple itself, where you'd come face-to-face with a gilded-bronze **statue** of the goddess Sulis Minerva (the surviving head is on display). The statue once wore a helmet (see the tiny holes for the rivets) and stood before a flaming cauldron. The goddess was a powerful multicultural hybrid of the Celtic goddess Sulis (who presided over the Aquae Sulis, or "waters of Sulis" in prehistoric times) and Minerva (a Roman life-giving mother-goddess),

with hints of the Greek warrior-goddess Athena. Downstairs, enjoy a close-up look at the spring **overflow,** part of the original drain system built two millennia ago that still carries excess water to the River Avon.

• *Now head down a hall (with more exhibits), until you emerge outside in the...*

Great Bath: Take a slow lap (by foot) around the perimeter, imagining the frolicking Romans who once immersed themselves in this five-foot-deep pool. (These days, the water has turned greenish because of algae—don't touch it.) Originally, this pool was housed in a spacious hall with a three-story-tall arched ceiling, and sunlight filtered in through vast windows.

Romans had bathhouses in all major cities and went to the baths almost daily. Besides a way to keep clean, baths were also fitness clubs for working out. Because the bathhouse was so large, it became the town's buzzing social center—a warm place to hang out on a rainy day. This bath had the added feature of a natural thermal spring, which had sulfurous content that purportedly leeched out impurities, cured arthritis, and restored vigor. Role-playing actors are generally lounging around happy to talk (in Latin or English).

• *Now explore more of the...*

Bath Complex: The **East Baths** is a series of rooms showing how Romans typically bathed (with naked bodies artfully and modestly projected). You'd undress in the first room, warm up in the next room, get a massage in another, then start the cool-down process in another room. The large **central hall** was a sauna, heated by the Romans' famed hypocaust system: Stubby brick columns

BATH

(which you can see) supported the floor, allowing the space in between to be filled with hot air to heat the room above.

Nearby is a giant red brick chunk of **roof span,** from when this was a cavernous covered swimming hall. At the corner, you'll see a length of original **lead pipe** (on the right, remarkably preserved since ancient times) and step over a small **canal** where hot water still trickles into the main pool. The water emerges from the spring at 115°F—about 10 degrees too hot for most people—but it quickly cools to a perfect hot-tub temperature. In modern times, Britons bathed in this swimming pool up until the 1970s, then opened the Thermae Spa a block away—fed by the same spring.

When you're ready to cool down, follow the route away from the big pool and into the **West Baths** with its big round *frigidarium,* or "cold plunge" pool sparkling with coins. Across the hall (up a few steps) you have a close-up look at the source of this entire complex—the **sacred spring.**

• *After returning your audioguide, pop over to the **fountain** for a free taste of the spa water, which purportedly has health benefits (see minerals listed on the wall). Then pass the WC, head up the stairs, go through the gift shop, and exit via (or stop for tea in) the Pump Room (described next).*

▲Pump Room

The Pump Room, an elegant Georgian hall just above the Roman Baths, offers visitors their best chance to raise a pinky in Neoclassical grandeur. Above the clock, a statue of Beau Nash—who promoted Bath as an aristocratic playground in the 1700s—sniffles down at you. Come for tea or a light meal (see hours in listing on page 451), or to try a famous (but forgettable) "Bath bun" with your spa water (the same water that's in the fountain at the end of the baths tour; also free in the Pump Room if you present your ticket). The spa water is served by an appropriately attired waiter, who will tell you the water is pumped up from nearly 100 yards deep and marinated in 43 wonderful minerals. Or for just the price of a coffee, drop in anytime—except during lunch—to enjoy live music (string trio or piano; times vary) and the atmosphere. Even if you don't eat here, you're welcome to enter the foyer for a view of the baths and dining room.

BATH

▲▲Bath Abbey

The town of Bath wasn't much in the Middle Ages, but an important church has stood on this spot since Anglo-Saxon times. King Edgar I was crowned here in 973, when the church was much bigger (before the bishop packed up and moved to Wells). Dominating the town center, today's abbey—the last great church built in medieval England—is 500 years old and a fine example of the Late Perpendicular Gothic style, with breezy fan vaulting  and enough stained glass to earn it the nickname "Lantern of the West."

Cost and Hours: £4 suggested donation, Mon-Sat 9:30-17:30, Sun 13:00-14:30 & 16:30-17:30, handy flier narrates a self-guided tour, ask about events—including concerts, services, and evensong, schedule also posted on the door and online, tel. 01225/422-462, www.bathabbey.org.

Evensong: Choral evensong generally takes place twice a week (Thu at 17:30 and Sun at 15:30, 45 minutes); spoken evening prayers on other days are also a beautiful 20 minutes of worship (17:30).

Tower Climb: If you've always wanted to witness the clanging of a huge church bell for all the town to hear, this is your chance—it's oddly satisfying. You can reach the top of the tower only with a worthwhile 50-minute guided tour. You'll hike up 212 steps for views across the rooftops of Bath and a peek down into the Roman Baths. In the rafters, you walk right up behind the clock face on the north transept, and get an inside-out look at the fan vaulting. Along the way, you'll hear a brief town history as you learn all about the tower's bells (£8, generally at the top of each hour when abbey is open, more often during busy times; Mon-Sat 10:00-16:00, no tours Sun, tour times usually posted outside abbey entrance, buy tickets in abbey gift shop).

Visiting the Abbey: This impressive church encapsulates Bath's long history in stone. It stands near the mineral springs where, even in pagan times, people came to worship. When Christianity arrived, a monastery was built here (8th century), then a larger church (11th century). The present church was begun in 1499.

The statues on the heavily ornamented **facade** relate the legend of how the present structure came about. It's 1499, and the energetic Bishop Oliver King was now in in charge. He's referenced by the statue at the far left, showing an olive tree (for "Oliver") with a crown in the middle (for "King"). The bishop had a dream of angels coming down from heaven—depicted in the sculpted ladders flanking the central tower (which shows angels climbing up and coming down head-first). Bishop King decided the dream meant he should tear down the old church of St. Peter (represented by the statue of Peter to the left of the central door) and build a completely new church that would unite heaven and earth.

No sooner was the church finished than it was stripped of its furnishings by King Henry VIII (1539), who dissolved the monastery and sold off its valuable lead roof and glass windows. (At the same time, the statue of Peter lost its head to mean-spirited iconoclasts; it was re-carved out of Peter's once supersized beard.)

For the next phase of the abbey's story, step inside and admire the **nave.** Queen Elizabeth I began repairing the abbey her father had plundered. In 1608, Bishop James Montague (see his large **tomb** on the left side of the nave) took over. One rainy day, he saw water dripping down inside the church, and vowed to finish the ceiling. Thanks to Montague we have one of the abbey's most splendid features—the fan vaulting. Montague's coat of arms, with three diamonds and eagles, are symbols found throughout the church. Next to the tomb, the stained-glass **window** depicts coats of arms of other donors who financed the church's windows. On the wall beneath the window are several **gravestones** honoring Bath's notable citizens, including Sir Isaac Pitman, who invented stenographer's shorthand. This is just one of more than 600 memorials to the deceased found in the church (on the walls or under your feet)—all part of the long history of Bath.

Cross to the opposite side of the nave toward the right transept. Just before entering the transept, find a gravestone on the wall for "Ricardi Nash"—better known as Beau Nash, Bath's 18th-century master of festivities. In the right transept is the 15-foot-tall stone **Waller Memorial.** It depicts the renowned English Civil War general Sir William Waller relaxing after liberating Bath from royalists. But the focus here is on his wife Jane, who died young. Now they gaze into each other's eyes for all eternity.

Before leaving the church, stand once again in the nave and appreciate the intricacy of the **fan vaulting** and brilliance of the windows. The glass, red-iron **lamps** and the **heating grates** on the floor are all remnants of the 19th century. (In a sustainable, 21st-century touch, the heat now comes from the baths' hot run-off water.) Note that a WWII bomb blast destroyed the medieval glass; what you see today is from the 1950s.

At the far end of the church (above the altar), the large **window** shows 52 scenes from Christ's life—good for weekly sermons for a year. The window to the left of the altar shows **King Edgar** being crowned. Edgar (in red) sits on a throne clutching the orb

and scepter while the Archbishop of Canterbury (in purple)
places the crown on his head.
Edgar was one of the first monarchs of what we now call England. His coronation in AD 973
established the protocols used by
all future English monarchs up
to the present—and it all started
here in Bath.

ALONG THE RIVER AND PULTENEY ESTATES

These pleasant, low-key sights are located along the River Avon
behind Bath Abbey. Taken together, they create an enjoyable scene
of shops, cafés, galleries, and people-watching.

Parade Gardens

Opposite the abbey, the Parade Gardens is a riverside park with
manicured lawns, knockout flowerbeds, a café, and good views of
the Pulteney Bridge. In season there's a small fee to enter the park,
which was designed by prolific 18th-century architect John Wood
the Elder (you'll read more about works in Bath by John and his
son—also John, also an architect—later). While the park is below
today's street level, it is at the ancient Roman street level. A great
way to enjoy a sunny day is to pack a picnic lunch and pay to enter
the gardens (£2, fee includes deck chairs, daily 10:00-18:00, Oct-
April free and open 24 hours, ask about summer concerts some Sun
at 15:00, entrance a block south of Pulteney Bridge).

Guildhall Market

The little old-school shopping mall just north of the Parade Gardens is a frumpy time warp in this affluent town. In the 12th century the king gave Bath the right to have a market and that market
moved from the abbey to here in the 18th century. Stand under the
central dome and feel the surviving character. The historic negoti-
ating table (or "nail") dates from 1768.

The Humbug shop sells traditional candy by the weight. Ste-
phane has been the cheesemonger here since 1975. The leather
goods shop offers Bath belts made to order. The yarn shop thrills
some. The modern café is trendy, but the deli is not—it hawks traditional meat pies and fresh cakes (including Bath buns). The old-
fashioned barber offers old-fashioned shaves. And the Market Café
has customers who've enjoyed it since the 1950s (opens at 9:00 for
breakfast).

▲Victoria Art Gallery

This small gallery, between the Guildhall Market and Pulteney Bridge, was opened in 1897 to celebrate the 60th anniversary of Queen Victoria's reign. Today it's a delightful space with two parts: The ground floor houses temporary exhibits, while the upstairs is filled with paintings from the late 15th century to the present, along with a small collection of decorative arts, including 187 porcelain and pottery dog figures.

Cost and Hours: Free, £2 suggested donation, temporary exhibits-£5, covered by combo-ticket with Roman Baths and Fashion Museum, daily 10:30-17:00, tel. 01225/477-233, www.victoriagal. org.uk.

Visiting the Gallery: The permanent painting collection, filling one grand room, presents an intimate world of portraiture and Bath-scapes. On the back wall, find Thomas Gainsborough's portrait of *Thomas Rumbold and Son*. During the 18th century, members of high society flocked to Bath and employed Gainsborough to paint their portraits as a souvenir. "Pick-pocketing by portraiture" he called it, as social climbers paid plenty to be featured on canvas. Thanks to this fad, Gainsborough found steady employment in Bath.

Nearby you can find cityscapes (18th century and now). *Bath from the East* offers a look at preindustrial Bath. Riffle through the white chests of drawers on the right to find even more scenes of Bath over the years.

As you exit the museum, a clever donation box on the staircase invites you to watch an artist at work; it's worth a small coin to see him in action.

▲Pulteney Bridge

Bath is inclined to compare its shop-lined Pulteney Bridge with Florence's Ponte Vecchio. That's pushing it. The bridge was commissioned by Frances Pulteney (more about her later) and designed in 1770 by Scottish architect Robert Adam in the same Georgian, or "Palladian," style that John Wood the Younger was applying to the row of townhouses known as Bath's Royal Crescent.

The best view of the bridge is from its downstream side. The most Palladian feature is the center of the bridge with the outline of a Greek temple seemingly stamped into the stone. The temple's

BATH

pediment is "broken"—that is, the triangle's base is purposely left incomplete. The bridge has grid windows, a few round medallions, and a central window that's bigger than the others, with an arched top. The view from the upstream side lets you see a few shops jutting out (cantilevered) from the bridge.

It's enjoyable to watch the meandering River Avon and listen as it cascades down the three-stairstep weir that controls the flow. By the way, "Avon" is the Celtic name for "river." When the Romans arrived and asked what's the name of this river, the Celts answered "Avon" (or "river"). So, the Romans named it "River River". That's why there are eight rivers in England named "Avon."

Across the bridge at Pulteney Weir, tour boat companies run **cruises**—see "Activities in Bath," later.

Pulteney Estates

Pulteney Estates, the section of Bath stretching from Pulteney Bridge across the river, was open farmland owned by the Earl of Bath until the 18th century. Inherited by Frances Pulteney (cousin to the earl) in 1762, she started a project to develop this land as a grand neighborhood in 1788. But with the French Revolution in 1789, England fell into an economic recession and construction ground to a halt. All that she built was the  Pulteney Bridge (a classy way to bridge the old town with this new zone over the river) and Great Pulteney Street—intended to be the central axis of this new Georgian Bath.

Looking at Great Pulteney Street and a Bath map, you can imagine what was planned. (The real estate taken up by the Henrietta Gardens and the Rugby Ground was slated to be part of the development.)

Georgian England was all about appearances. The grand, uniform facade was key—everything behind that was higgledy-piggledy (a great metaphor for social life in the 18th century). If Great Pulteney Street looks like a movie set to you, it did to the producers of the 2004 movie *Vanity Fair*, too, who used it as 18th-century London. The wide sidewalk was perfect for promenading a safe distance from splashing mud back when streets were unpaved.

In 1978 the UN established its UNESCO World Heritage listings, and Bath soon engaged in a major spiffing up of stately avenues like Great Pulteney Street. The city won the coveted listing in 1987.

The Mayor of Bath's Honorary Guides lead free two-hour

Pulteney Estate guided walks (for details, see "Tours in and near Bath," earlier).

NORTHWEST OF THE TOWN CENTER

Several worthwhile public spaces and museums can be found an uphill 10-minute walk to the northwest of the town center. If Bath is an architectural cancan, these are its knickers.

The entire area is a palatial housing development built during Bath's Golden Age of the 1700s. It's the masterpiece of the visionary father-and-son architects John Wood the Elder and John Wood the Younger. As visitors poured into the city, Bath was running out of suitable accommodations. The Woods bought large tracts of land northwest of downtown and built attractive vacation rentals for the rich and famous. In the process they helped forge the Georgian style of architecture soon found all over Britain.

Queen Square

This rectangular park surrounded by townhouses was Wood the Elder's first great real-estate development. He ringed the square with symmetrical facades in the classical style pioneered by the influential Italian architect Andrea Palladio. The north (uphill) side has a Greek-temple look to it, made of six columns topped with a triangular pediment. The windows are large, symmetrically placed, and topped with Palladian pediments and arches. The writer Jane Austen lived in the corner apartment to the right of the Francis Hotel (#13). Completing the square's classical look is a 70-foot-tall obelisk in the middle, generously donated by Beau Nash.

▲▲The Circus

True to its name, this is a circular housing complex. It was Wood the Elder's next great expansion, consisting of 30 symmetrical townhouses arranged in a perfect circle. The best views are from the middle of the Circus among the grand plane trees, on the capped old well. Imagine the days before indoor plumbing, when servant girls gathered here to fetch water—this was gossip central. If you stand on the well, your clap echoes three times around the circle—try it.

The circle of houses is broken into three segments, so that anyone approaching from the street has a great view of the crescent-shaped facades. Each residence has five stories. You'd enter at street level into the workaday public rooms. The entrances were made large enough that aristocrats

could be carried right through the door in their sedan chairs, and women could enter without disturbing their sky-high hairdos. The next floor up (with bigger windows) generally had ballrooms and dining rooms for hosting parties. The floor above that held bedrooms. The top floor (the tiny dormer windows in the roof) housed servant bedrooms, and the basement (below street level) held the kitchen and workrooms. Wood united it all with a symmetrical facade, but the arrangement of the actual rooms behind the facade was left to the owner's discretion. If you circled around, you'd see that the backs are a jumble, infamous for their "hanging loos" (bathrooms added years later).

Note the frieze—a continuous band of sculpted reliefs—located just above the ground floor. There are 525 different panels, each one unique, depicting everything from dogs to eagles to roses, scrolls, guitars, anchors, leaves, and roosters.

In its mid-1700s heyday, the Circus was home to Britain's elite. Prime Minister William Pitt the Elder (who oversaw the American colony's French and Indian War) lived at #11. Baron Robert Clive (who brought India under British control) vacationed here at #14 (on the sunny side of the Circus). Thomas Gainsborough set up shop at #17 to paint portraits of fashionable lords and ladies to take home as souvenirs. These days, the Circus has become home both to wealthy residents and businesses—you can get a cavity filled at #13.

Created at the height of Wood's creative powers, the Circus shows off the architect's mature style. There's Palladio's Greco-Roman classicism—Doric columns on the ground floor, Ionic in the middle, and Corinthian on top—like Rome's Colosseum. For more Georgian effects, Wood added a balustrade and ornamental acorns on the roofline. The circular shape was likely inspired by Stonehenge, representing Britain's Druid roots. And the symbolism in the frieze is distinctly Masonic. (When seen from a bird's-eye view, the Circus and its neighbor, the Royal Crescent, form the shape of a symbol dear to Freemasons—a key.) By combining the three styles—Roman, Celtic, and Masonic—Wood was creating his personal vision of Bath as the "new Rome."

▲▲Royal Crescent

This long, graceful arc of buildings evokes the wealth and gentility of Bath's glory days. The Royal Crescent was the majestic showpiece of John Wood the Younger. He took the Georgian style his father had pioneered and supersized it. The Crescent is a semicircular row of 30 townhouses 500 feet long and 50 feet tall. It's lined with 114 Ionic columns that span the middle two stories. A ground floor of large blocks and a balustrade across the roofline unites it all. In typical Georgian style, the only deviation from the sym-

metry is in the very center of the crescent, which has two pairs of columns and a taller arched window. The building's warm golden color is typical of the city, made of limestone from the surrounding hills, which began forming hundreds of millions of years ago when Bath was covered by an ocean.

Completed in 1774, the Royal Crescent quickly became the trendiest address in Bath. It offered stunning views of a park—a novel idea at the time that gave city dwellers a slice of the country. Like his father, Wood the Younger designed only the facade, allowing each resident to build whatever home they wanted behind it. Today many of the former five-story townhouses have been subdivided into single-floor apartments or offices.

Note the yellow door at #22. It caused a scandal when it was painted in the 1970s in violation of the housing covenants. But now the yellow door is practically a historical landmark itself. Although Jane Austen never lived here, you might think so given how often the Crescent has appeared as a backdrop in TV and movies.

As you cruise the Crescent, strut like an aristocrat. Now imagine you're poor: Notice the "ha ha fence," a drop-off in the front yard that acted as a barrier, invisible from the windows, for keeping out sheep and peasants. The refined and stylish **Royal Crescent Hotel** sits virtually unmarked in the center of the Crescent (with the giant magnolia growing up its wall). You're welcome to (politely) drop in to explore its fine ground-floor public spaces and back garden, where a gracious and traditional tea is served (see page 451).

If that makes you hungry, there are good, less expensive options on the small pedestrian lane midway between the Circus and the Crescent. The welcoming **$$ Green Bird Café** (at 11 Margaret's Buildings) serves an enticing soup, sandwich, and salad lunch menu.

▲▲No. 1 Royal Crescent

This former residence at the east end of the Crescent is now a museum, taking visitors behind the classy Georgian facade for a glimpse into the everyday life of wealthy residents during the mid-1700s. At the time, Britain was on the leading edge of global exploration and scientific discovery, and the period artifacts show the wide-ranging interests of the educated rich. Take the time to talk with the helpful docents (who almost give you no option but to learn), or you'll miss fascinating details like how high-class women shaved their eyebrows and pasted on carefully trimmed strips of mouse fur in their place.

Cost and Hours: £10.60, half price after 16:00, daily 10:00-17:00, tel. 01225/428-126, http://no1royalcrescent.org.uk.

Visiting the Museum: Start on the ground floor with the **Parlour,** the main room of the house used for breakfast in the mornings, business affairs in the afternoon, and various other everyday activities throughout the evening. The silver pot dispensed either coffee or tea—both of which were novel and expensive at the time. The Chippendale bookcase, with its octagonal woodwork, is typical, as is the (modern-looking but Georgian-era) design of the carpet.

The **Gentleman's Retreat**—an educated fellow's man-cave—has various proto-scientific objects, like a globe, telescope, and clock. You could turn the crank of one gadget to generate a spark—a shocking marvel to show party guests before the age of electricity.

In the **Dining Room,** refined 18th-century gentlemen ate with elegant dinnerware, drank, smoked, talked business, and relieved themselves behind the folding screen. The (fake) food displays suggest the abundance available to a nation whose colonial possessions spanned the globe. Before going upstairs, pause at the **Cabinet of Curiosities**—it's fine to open the drawers. This is a collection of odd and precious objects that a host would show his guests: fossils, tribal masks, and exotic weapons.

Heading upstairs, you enter more intimate rooms. The **Withdrawing Room** (later called simply a "drawing" room) is where the ladies would withdraw from the rude company of men to play the harpsichord and take tea on the sofa. Note the fake door, to maintain the Georgian symmetry of the room. In the **Lady's Bedroom,** you can picture her ladyship waking from her canopied bed, attended by her maid (who arrived through the hidden door), dressing at her table, and donning her big-hair wig. See the typical trinkets of a Georgian socialite, like a framed love letter and a wig scratcher. Up another flight is the **Gentleman's Bedroom,** with his wig, engravings of old cityscapes, and a great view out the window of the Royal Crescent.

The visit ends (down the servants' back stairs) in the basement with the **Servants Hall and Kitchen.** Find Fido on a treadmill. The wooden rack hanging from the ceiling kept the bread, herbs, and ham away from the mice. Notice also the "coal chute" adjacent to the kitchen. Remember, the servants lived way up in the attic, worked in the basement, and served the family on the middle floors—lots of upstairs and downstairs. The kind of English class system seen at the Royal Crescent reached its peak in the 1700s. But by the next century, a middle class was on the rise, and the era of harpsichords and linen doilies would soon be consigned to museums.

Assembly Rooms

Back when Bath was the liveliest city in Britain, festive partygoers would "assemble" here almost nightly to dance, drink, gamble, and mingle. The building was designed by John Wood the Younger as part of his real estate development. It came to replace the once-lively (but now passé) Assembly Rooms near the center of town. Some 200 years later, these lavish rooms are still used as a fashionable venue for parties and wedding receptions. You can tour the four rooms, which, though mostly empty, still retain echoes of 18th-century gaiety.

Cost and Hours: Free, same hours as the Fashion Museum (in the Assembly Rooms basement; see next).

Visiting the Assembly Rooms: The visit kicks off under the sunlit central cupola with two fine sedan chairs from the 1790s—the human-powered taxis of the day. Step into the largest and most important room—the **Ballroom.** It's huge—100 feet long and 40 feet high—with five glittering chandeliers. Picture the scene: The band plays from the balcony, while scores of dancers glide across the floor or warm themselves by the fireplaces. Women wear voluminous dresses and bouffant wigs. Men wear silk stockings, long coats, and powdered wigs. The master of ceremonies would announce a minuet—a slow, delicate dance in three-quarter time where each couple would take turns dancing in the middle while everyone else watched.

When the orchestra took a break, you might head into the **Octagon Room** for refreshments—tea, cakes, and cold cuts. You'd stand under the biggest of the Assembly Rooms' chandeliers, with 48 arms (which held candles in the 18th century). On the wall (high up) you'd find a portrait by Thomas Gainsborough of a man in a red suit. This is William Wade, the Assembly Rooms' master of ceremonies from 1769-1777, who filled the buckled shoes of legendary toastmaster, Beau Nash. Wade strikes a dandyish pose, showing off his ultra-chic outfit: red suit, gold waistcoat, ruffled sleeves, and George III-style powdered wig.

The adjoining room (now a café) was the **Card Room.** Men would adjourn here to drink, smoke, shoot billiards, and gamble at whist. The women would gravitate to the **Tea Room** for lighter beverages. This large room with a "stage" at one end could accommodate concerts—the music of Haydn and Handel was popular.

The social season at Bath lasted from October to May, and attracted fashionable people from across the country. The Assembly Rooms were a rare place in Britain where classes could mix and mingle—so long as they were properly dressed and observed etiquette. Social-climbing commoners with money could network with aristocrats down on their luck. Moms brought daughters here to find suitable husbands. Jane Austen came with her chaperone. Men and women who'd never met could touch hands as they did the minuet. People came to the Assembly Rooms for the thing Bath seemed to always have in good supply—fun.

The Assembly Rooms were gutted during the WWII bombing of Bath, but they were later restored to their original splendor. (Only the chandeliers are original.)

▲Fashion Museum

Housed underneath Bath's Assembly Rooms, this museum displays four centuries of fashion on one floor. The fact-filled audioguide can
stretch a visit to an informative and enjoyable hour. Like fashion itself, the exhibits change all the time, but there's always a section on historical trends. You'll see how fashion evolved—just like architecture and other arts—from Georgian to Regency, Victorian, the Swinging '60s, and so on. A major feature is the "Dress

of the Year" display: Since 1963 a fashion expert has anointed a new look to add to this collection. If you're intrigued by all those historic garments, go ahead and lace up your own trainer corset (which looks more like a life jacket) and try on a hoop underdress.

Cost and Hours: £9.50, includes audioguide; £25 combo-ticket includes Roman Baths and Victoria Art Gallery temporary exhibits, 10 percent cheaper online, family ticket available; daily 10:30-18:00, Nov-Feb until 17:00, last entry one hour before closing; free 30-minute guided tour in summer at 12:00 and 16:00, in winter at 12:00 and 13:00; self-service café, Bennett Street, tel. 01225/477-789, www.fashionmuseum.co.uk.

Nearby: Exiting the Assembly Rooms and Fashion Museum, turn left and walk 30 yards to **Alfred Street**—a typical street from the Woods' 18th-century housing expansion. At #14, notice the ironwork arch by the door that supports a gas lamp. "Link boys" carried torches through the dark streets, lighting the way for big shots in their sedan chairs as they traveled from one affair to the next. They extinguished their torches in the black conical "snuffers." The iron crank on the left was used to hoist bulky things downstairs to the servants' quarters. Few of these ironwork sets survived the dark days of the WWII Blitz, when most were collected to be melted down to make weapons. (Not long ago, Brits learned that their patriotic extra commitment to the national struggle had been for naught, as most of the metal ended up in junk heaps.)

Nearby, shoppers can head down **Bartlett Street,** just below the Fashion Museum, to browse boutique shops and the bric-a-brac filled antique center.

▲Museum of Bath at Work

This modest but informative museum north of the Assembly Rooms explains the industrial history of Bath. If you want to learn about the unglamorous workaday side of the spa town, this is the place.

Cost and Hours: £8, includes audioguide, daily 10:30-17:00, Nov and Jan-March weekends only, closed Dec, last entry one hour before closing, Julian Road, 2 steep blocks up Russell Street from Assembly Rooms, tel. 01225/318-348, www.bath-at-work.org.uk.

Visiting the Museum: The core of the museum is the well-preserved, circa-1900 fizzy-drink business of one Mr. Bowler. It

includes a Dickensian office, engineer's shop, brass foundry, essence room lined with bottled flavorings (see photo), and factory floor. It's just a pile of defunct gadgets—until the included audioguide resurrects Mr. Bowler's creative genius. Each item has its own story to tell.

Upstairs are display cases featuring other Bath creations through the years, including a 1914 Horstmann car, wheeled sedan chairs (this *is* Bath, after all), and versatile plasticine (colorful proto-Play-Doh—still the preferred medium of Aardman Studios, creators of the stop-motion animated Wallace & Gromit movies). On your way out, don't miss the intriguing exhibits on the ground floor, featuring cabinetmaking, the traditional methods for cutting the local "Bath stone," a locally produced six-stroke engine, and more.

Jane Austen Centre

This exhibition does a good job of illuminating the world of Bath's most famous writer. Jane Austen spent five tumultuous, sometimes troubled years in Bath (circa 1800, during which time her father died), where she bristled at the vapid social scene. Visitors are briefed on Austen's life and family history through a short film and docent talk, and then head downstairs where they are free to try on Regency-era costumes and sniff era-appropriate scents, taste Regency biscuits, play parlor games such as spillikins, and pen a note with a quill. You won't find any actual historic artifacts (except from the movie *Persuasion,* filmed in Bath), but none of that seems to bother the steady stream of happy Austen fans eager to take a photo with her overhyped waxwork likeness.

The gift shop—with "I love Mr. Darcy" tote bags and Colin Firth's visage emblazoned on pillowcases—is also well stocked with era-related items.

Cost and Hours: £12, family ticket available; the friendly doorman (Martin) welcomes you daily 9:45-17:30, July-Aug until 18:00; Nov-March Sun-Fri 11:00-16:30, Sat from 10:00; docent talks on the hour and at :20 and :40 past the hour, last entry one hour before closing; just northeast of Queen's Square at 40 Gay Street, tel. 01225/443-000, www.janeausten.co.uk. Austen fans appreciate an included pamphlet that locates a dozen "Jane Austen points" around town.

Tea: Upstairs, the **Regency Tea Rooms** (free entrance) hits the spot for Austen-ites with costumed waitstaff and themed teas (£8-12), including the all-out "Tea with Mr. Darcy" for £19.50 (same hours as museum, last order taken one hour before closing).

Museum of Bath Architecture

This humble but unique collection offers an intriguing look at the construction of this Georgian city, covering everything from the innovative town planning to the plasterwork. Near the entrance, an aerial map outlines Bath's expansion from its 17th-century origins to today's neighborhoods. In the back of the museum, an interactive model highlights town sights. Compare the 1694 Gilmore map—one of Bath's first tourist maps—with the one you're using today.

Cost and Hours: £6.70, Mon-Fri 14:00-17:00, Sat-Sun from 10:00, closed Nov-mid-Jan, last entry 45 minutes before closing, 10-minute intro film runs on a loop, a short walk east of the Fashion Museum/Assembly Rooms on a street called "The Paragon," tel. 01225/333-895, www.museumofbatharchitecture.org.uk.

SOUTH OF THE TOWN CENTER

George Bayntun Bindery and Bookshop

This high-end bookshop and working bindery near the train station is worth a peek. While the workshop is not open to the public, their bookshop—with a reverent, Oxford-library feel—welcomes visitors to browse through an impressive back-room collection of rare editions and old prints for sale (Mon-Fri 9:00-13:00 & 14:00-17:30, closed Sat-Sun, on Manvers Street, tel. 01225/466-000).

OUTER BATH

▲American Museum and Gardens

The UK's sole museum dedicated to American history has thoughtful exhibits on the history of Native Americans and the Civil War, but the museum's heart is with the decorative arts and cultural artifacts that reveal how Americans lived from colonial times to the mid-19th century. The 18 completely furnished rooms (from a bare-bones 1600s Mas-sachusetts dining/living room to a Rococo Revival explosion in a New Orleans bedroom) are hosted by eager guides waiting to fill you in on the everyday items that make domestic Yankee history surprisingly interesting. (In the Lee Room, look for the original mouse holes, strategically backlit in the floorboards.) The textile room is a quilter's nirvana. It's interesting to see your own country through British eyes—but on a nice day, the surrounding gardens (including a replica of George Washington's garden at Mount Vernon) and view of the hills might be the best reasons to visit. You could easily spend an afternoon here, enjoying the gardens, arboretum, and trails.

Cost and Hours: Museum and gardens-£13, gardens only-£7.50, Tue-Sun 10:00-17:00, late Nov-mid-Dec until 16:30, closed Mon, closed early Nov and mid-Dec-mid-March, last entry one hour before closing, at Claverton Manor, café, tel. 01225/460-503, www.americanmuseum.org.

Getting There: The museum is just east of town. From the city center take the #U1 bus to The Avenue stop (£2.90 one-way, £4.50 day ticket, 15-minute ride, 4/hour, stop is just before Bath University) and follow the tree-lined path (left of stone wall) 15 minutes. You could also hop a taxi for about £16. By car, it's well signed from A-36 and the city center.

Activities in Bath

▲Thermae Bath Spa

After simmering unused for a quarter-century, Bath's natural thermal springs once again offer R&R for the masses. The state-of-the-art spa is housed in a complex of three buildings that combine historic structures with new glass-and-steel architecture.

Is the Thermae Bath Spa worth the time and money? The experience is pricey and humble compared to similar German and Hungarian spas. The tall, modern building in the city center lacks any old-time elegance. Jets in the pools are limited, and the only water toys are big foam noodles. There's no cold plunge—the only way to cool off between steam rooms is to step onto a small, unglamorous balcony. The Royal Bath's two pools are essentially the same, and the water isn't particularly hot in either—in fact, the main attraction is the rooftop view from the top one.

All that said, this is the only natural thermal spa in the UK and your one chance to actually bathe in Bath. Consider an evening visit, when—on a chilly day—Bath's twilight glows through the steam from the rooftop pool.

Cost: The cheapest spa pass is £36 for two hours (£40 on weekends), which includes towel, robe, and slippers and gains you access to the Royal Bath's large, ground-floor "Minerva Bath"; four steam rooms and a waterfall shower; and the view-filled, open-air, rooftop thermal pool. Longer stays are £10 for each additional hour. The much-hyped £49 Twilight Package includes three hours and a meal (one plate, drink, robe, towel, and slippers). Bring your own swimsuit.

Thermae has all the "pamper thyself" extras (not included): massages, scrubs, and facials, including "watsu"—water shiatsu. Book treatments in advance by phone.

Hours: Daily 9:00-21:30, last entry at 19:00, pools close at 21:00. No kids under 16.

Information: It's 100 yards from the Roman Baths, on Beau Street (tel. 01225/331-234, www.thermaebathspa.com).

The Cross Bath: Operated by Thermae Bath Spa, this renovated circular Georgian structure across the street from the main spa provides a simpler and less-expensive bathing option. It has a hot-water fountain that taps directly into the spring, making its water hotter than the spa's (£20/1.5 hours, daily 10:00-19:30, last entry at 18:00, check in at Thermae Bath Spa's main entrance across the street—you'll be escorted to the Cross Bath, changing rooms, no access to Royal Bath, no kids under 12). If you're not comfortable playing footsie with strangers, it can feel cramped.

Spa Visitor Center: Also across the street, in the Hetling Pump Room, is a free one-room exhibit that explains the spring water's role in the founding of Bath (Mon-Sat 10:00-17:30, Sun 11:00-16:00, closed Oct-March). The visitor center rents a £2 audioguide for those wanting to explore the neighborhood around the baths.

▲▲Canalside Walk to Bathampton

An idyllic towpath leads three miles from Bath along the Kennet and Avon Canal to the sleepy village of Bathampton. For an unforgettable hour that gets you totally out of the city, don't miss this memorable little walk. You can do it as a round-trip or do it one-way, in either direction, with a taxi or boat connection. Or you can do it on a rental bike.

From Pulteney Bridge walk straight down Great Pulteney Street to the Holburne Museum with its fine modern café facing

Sydney Gardens. Continue straight a hundred yards through the gardens, over the train tracks (which put canals, built for industrial age cargo transport, out of business shortly after they were opened) to the Kennet and Avon Canal. At the canal, turn left and walk the towpath (being thankful you're not a horse pulling a barge) for about an hour to Bathampton. Consider the classic **George pub** there for a nice meal and a beer (reservations smart, tel. 01225/425-079, www.chefandbrewer.com). The canal, while pristine and idyllic, gives you a sense of the Industrial Age.

From The George you can hike back to Bath, or walk (on the left) along the road for five more minutes to the River Avon. There you'll find the bigger **Bathampton Mill pub,** with garden tables overlooking the Avon (tel. 01225/469-758, www.thebathamptonmill.co.uk) and the pier for the *Pulteney Princess* river cruise that glides back to Bath (see below). From here it's a £10 taxi back to Bath.

Other Walks: The Bath Skyline Walk is a six-mile wander around the hills surrounding Bath (leaflet at TI, or see www.nationaltrust.org.uk/bath-skyline). Plenty of other scenic paths are described in the TI's handouts.

River Cruise to Bathampton

The *Pulteney Princess* cruises to the neighboring village of Bathampton about hourly from Pulteney Weir. The river is like a Huck Finn dream—with trees encroaching on it, derelict old warehouses, and no riverside path. The cruise is a sleepy float with sporadic commentary, but it's certainly relaxing, and the boat has picnic-friendly sundecks. The Bathampton Mill pub awaits at the dock in Bathampton (£5 one-way, up to 12/day in good weather, one hour to Bathampton and back, WCs on board, mobile 07791-910-650, www.pulteneyprincess.co.uk). Consider combining the cruise with a walk along the parallel canal towpath (explained earlier). If stopping for a meal, between The Bathampton Mill (on the river) and The George (on the canal, a 5-minute walk from the river), I prefer The George.

Boating

The **Bath Boating Station,** in an old Victorian boathouse, rents rowboats, canoes, and punts (£8/person for first hour, then £4/hour; all day for £20; Wed-Sun 10:00-18:00, closed Mon-Tue and Oct-Easter, intersection of Forester and Rockcliffe roads, one mile northeast of center, tel. 01225/312-900, www.bathboating.co.uk).

Minigolf

Victoria Falls Adventure Golf, an 18-hole course set amid waterways, flowers, and trees in Royal Victoria Park, is scenic fun (£5.50, family ticket available, daily 10:00-dusk, between Royal

Avenue and Charlotte Street parking lot, tel. 01225/425-066, www.bathminigolf.com).

Swimming and Kids' Activities

The **Bath Sports and Leisure Centre** has a fine pool for laps as well as lots of waterslides. Kids will also enjoy the five-story play structure, bowling, and trampoline park (swimming-£4.90/adult, £3.40/kid, family discounts, Mon-Thu 6:30-22:30, Fri 7:30-19:00, Sat-Sun 8:00-21:00, kids' hours limited—check first, call for open-swim times, just across the bridge on North Parade Road, tel. 01225/486-905, www.better.org.uk—enter "Bath" under "By postcode/location").

Shopping

Shops in Bath close at about 17:30, and many are open on Sunday (11:00-16:00).

The Southgate area across from the train station hosts myriad chain stores. Guildhall Market is fun for old-school shopping. There's great browsing between the abbey and the Assembly Rooms. East of Queen Square, sprawling along Milsom Street is Jolly's (the UK's oldest department store), now home to upmarket boutiques. Explore the antique shops around Bartlett Street, below the Fashion Museum. The Bartlett Street Antique Centre is a collection of a dozen or so shops under one roof (Mon-Sat 10:00-16:30).

West of the town center, Green Park Station—with an Industrial Age, iron-and-glass roof—hosts a thriving farmers' market on Saturdays (9:00-13:00) and a flea market with antiques, collectibles, and curios the first Sunday of each month (8:00-16:00, on James Street West near Kingsmead Square, mobile 07946-430-338).

Nightlife in Bath

For an up-to-date list of events, pick up the local weekly newspaper, the *Bath Chronicle*, which includes a "What's On" schedule (www.bath.live).

▲▲Bizarre Bath Street Theater

For an entertaining walking-tour comedy act "with absolutely no history or culture," follow Toby or Noel on their creative and lively Bizarre Bath walk. This 1.5-hour "tour," which combines stand-up comedy with cleverly executed magic tricks, plays off unsuspecting passersby as well as tour members.

Cost and Hours: £10, RS%—£8 with this book, April-Oct nightly at 20:00, smaller groups Mon-Thu, promises to insult all nationalities and sensitivities, just racy enough but still good family fun, leaves from the Huntsman Inn, North Parade Passage, next to the TI, www.bizarrebath.co.uk.

▲Theatre Royal Performance

The restored 18th-century, 800-seat Theatre Royal, one of England's loveliest, offers a busy schedule of London West End-type plays, including many "pre-London" dress-rehearsal runs. The Theatre Royal also oversees performances at two other theaters around the corner from the main box office: Ustinov Studio (edgier, more obscure titles, many of which are premier runs in the UK) and "the egg" (for children, young people, and families).

Cost and Hours: £23-48; shows generally start at 19:30 or 20:00, matinees at 14:30, box office open Mon-Sat 10:00-20:00, Sun from 12:00 if there's a show; book in person, online, or by phone; on Saw Close, tel. 01225/448-844, www.theatreroyal.org.uk.

Ticket Deals: Forty nosebleed spots on a bench (misnamed "standbys") go on sale at noon Monday through Saturday for that day's evening performance in the main theater (£7.50, 2 tickets maximum). If the show is sold out, same-day "standing places" go on sale at 18:00 (12:00 for matinees) for £4 (cash only). Also at the box office, you can snatch up any "last minute" seats for £15-20 a half-hour before "curtain up." Shows in the Ustinov Theatre go for around £20, with no cheap-seat deals.

Sightseeing Tip: During the free Bath walking tour, your guide stops here. Pop into the box office, ask what's playing, and see if there are many seats left for that night. If plenty of seats remain unsold, you're fairly safe to come back 30 minutes before curtain time to buy a ticket at the cheaper price. Oh...and if you smell jasmine, it's the ghost of Lady Grey, a mistress of Beau Nash.

Evening Walks

Take your choice: comedy (Bizarro Bath, described earlier), history, or ghost tour. Free city walking tours are offered on some evenings in high season (described on page 412). Ghost Walks are a popular way to pass the after-dark hours (£8, cash only, 1.5 hours, year-round Thu-Sat at 20:00, leave from The Garrick's Head pub—to the left and behind Theatre Royal as you face it, tel. 01225/350-512, www.ghostwalksofbath.co.uk). The cities of York and Edinburgh—which have houses thought to be actually haunted—are better for ghost walks.

Pubs

Most pubs in the center are very noisy, catering to a rowdy twentysomething crowd. But on the top end of town, you can still find some classic old places with inviting ambience and live music. See the map on page 449 for locations.

The Old Green Tree, conveniently right in the town center, is a rare traditional pub offering a warm welcome (locally brewed real ales, no TVs, 12 Green Street, tel. 01225/448-259).

The Star Inn is much appreciated by locals for its fine ale and "no machines or music to distract from the chat." It's a throwback to the manly pubs of yesteryear, and its long bench, nicknamed "death row," still comes with a complimentary pinch of snuff on request. Try the Bellringer Ale, made just up the road (daily 12:00-14:30 & 17:30-late, no food served, 23 The Vineyards, top of The Paragon/A-4 Roman Road, tel. 01225/425-072, Jon). Guests are welcome to play the pub's piano.

The Bell has a jazzy, pierced-and-tattooed, bohemian feel, but with a mellow older crowd. Some kind of musical activity brews nearly nightly, such as jazz, blues, DJs, and open-mike (Mon-Sat 11:30-23:00, Sun 12:00-22:30, 103 Walcot Street, tel. 01225/460-426, www.thebellinnbath.co.uk). There's an inviting garden out back, often with a pizza oven fired up.

Summer Nights at the Baths or Along the Canal

In July and August, you can stretch your sightseeing day at the Roman Baths, open nightly until 22:00 (last entry 21:00), when the gas lamps flame and the baths are far less crowded and more atmospheric. To take a dip yourself, consider popping over to the Thermae Bath Spa (last entry at 19:00). And on long, warm summer evenings, the canal walk to Bathampton where a pub dinner awaits (described earlier) can be delightful.

Sleeping in Bath

Bath is a busy tourist town. Reserve in advance, and keep in mind B&Bs favor those lingering longer. Accommodations are expensive and can be about 25 percent more on Fridays and Saturdays. At B&Bs, it's worth asking for a weekday, three-nights-in-a-row, or off-season deal. If you're driving to Bath, stowing your car near the center will cost you (though some less-central B&Bs have parking): Take advantage of the Park & Ride lots outside of town or ask your hotelier for the best option.

NEAR THE ROYAL CRESCENT

These listings are all a 5- to 10-minute walk from the town center, and an easy 15-minute walk from the train station. With bags in tow you may want to either catch a taxi (£5-7) or (except for Brocks Guest House) hop on bus #4 (direction: Weston, catch bus inside bus station, pay driver £2.90, get off at the Comfortable Place stop—just after the park starts on the right, cross the street and backtrack 100 yards).

Except for Brocks, these B&Bs all face a busy arterial street (Upper Bristol Road, also known as Crescent Gardens); while the noise is minimal by urban standards and these B&Bs have well-insulated windows, light sleepers should request a rear- or side-facing room.

$$$ Marlborough House, exuberantly run by hands-on owner Peter, mixes modern style with antique furnishings and features a welcoming breakfast room with an open kitchen. Each of the six rooms comes with a sip of sherry (RS%, family room, air-con, minifridges, free parking, 1 Marlborough Lane, tel. 01225/318-175, www.marlborough-house.net, mars@manque.dircon.co.uk).

$$ Brocks Guest House rents six rooms in a Georgian townhouse built by John Wood in 1765. Located between the prestigious Royal Crescent and the courtly Circus, it's been redone in a way that would make the great architect proud. Each room has its own Bath-related theme (little top-floor library, 32 Brock Street, tel. 01225/338-374, www.brocksguesthouse.co.uk, brocks@brocksguesthouse.co.uk, Marta and Rafal).

$$ Brooks Guesthouse is the biggest and most polished of the bunch, albeit the least personal, with 22 modern rooms and classy public spaces, including an exceptionally pleasant breakfast room (limited pay parking, 1 Crescent Gardens, Upper Bristol Road, tel. 01225/425-543, www.brooksguesthouse.com, info@brooksguesthouse.com). They also rent two apartments.

$$ 2 Crescent Gardens, owner Giacomo's former family home, has six attractive rooms—some with views—and a bright, open breakfast room and homey living room (family room, limited free parking, closed Jan, 2 Crescent Gardens, tel. 01225/331-186, www.2crescentgardens.co.uk, 2crescentgardens@gmail.com, managed by Monika).

$$ Cornerways B&B is centrally located, simple, and pleasant, with three rooms and old-fashioned homey touches (RS%, cheaper without breakfast, DVD library, free parking, 47 Crescent Gardens, tel. 01225/422-382, www.cornerwaysbath.co.uk, info@cornerwaysbath.co.uk, Sue Black).

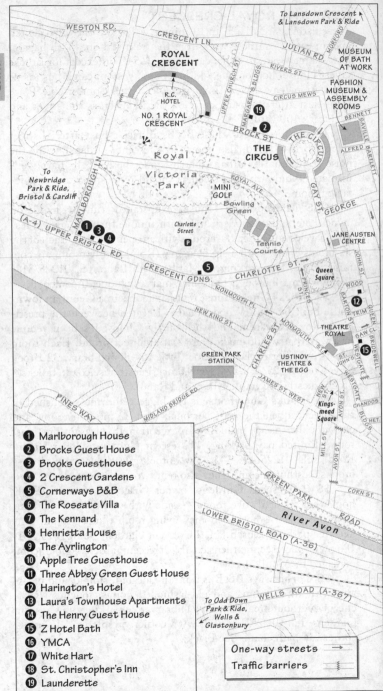

WESTON RD.

CRESCENT LN.

To Lansdown Crescent
& Lansdown Park & Ride

JULIAN RD.

MORFORD

MUSEUM
OF BATH
AT WORK

RIVERS ST.

UPPER CHURCH ST.

MARGARET'S BLDGS.

CIRCUS MEWS

FASHION
MUSEUM &
ASSEMBLY
ROOMS

ROYAL
CRESCENT

R.C.
HOTEL

NO. 1 ROYAL
CRESCENT

🅓🅙 **19**

2

BROCK ST.

THE
CIRCUS

BENNETT

ALFRED

BARTLETT

Royal

Victoria
Park

ROYAL AVE.

GAY ST.

GEORGE

To
Newbridge
Park & Ride,
Bristol & Cardiff

MARLBOROUGH LN.

MINI
GOLF

Bowling
Green

JANE AUSTEN
CENTRE

(A-4) UPPER BRISTOL RD.

Charlotte
Street

P

1 **3** **4**

Tennis
Courts

CRESCENT GDNS.

CHARLOTTE ST.

5

Queen
Square

WOOD

JOHN ST.

MONMOUTH PL.

PRINCES

BARTON ST.

TRIM

QUEEN

BRIDEWELL

12

NEW KING ST.

CHARLES ST.

MONMOUTH ST.

THEATRE
ROYAL

SAW CL.

15

WESTGATE

GREEN PARK
STATION

USTINOV
THEATRE &
THE EGG

ST. JOHN'S RD.

NEW ST.

WESTGATE BLDGS.

CHANDOS

PINES WAY

JAMES ST. WEST

Kings-
mead
Square

MILK ST.

AVON ST.

HET.

MIDLAND BRIDGE RD.

GREEN PARK

ROAD

CORN ST.

River Avon

LOWER BRISTOL ROAD (A-36)

WELLS ROAD (A-367)

To Odd Down
Park & Ride,
Wells &
Glastonbury

❶ Marlborough House
❷ Brocks Guest House
❸ Brooks Guesthouse
❹ 2 Crescent Gardens
❺ Cornerways B&B
❻ The Roseate Villa
❼ The Kennard
❽ Henrietta House
❾ The Ayrlington
❿ Apple Tree Guesthouse
⓫ Three Abbey Green Guest House
⓬ Harington's Hotel
⓭ Laura's Townhouse Apartments
⓮ The Henry Guest House
⓯ Z Hotel Bath
⓰ YMCA
⓱ White Hart
⓲ St. Christopher's Inn
⓳ Launderette

One-way streets ⟶
Traffic barriers ⫘⫘⫘

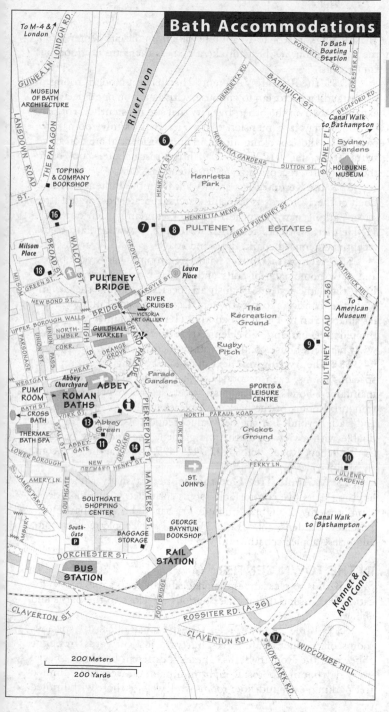

Bath Accommodations

To M-4 & London

GUINEA LN. LONDON RD.

GUINEA LN.

LANSDOWN ROAD

MUSEUM OF BATH ARCHITECTURE

THE PARAGON

TOPPING & COMPANY BOOKSHOP

ST.

BROAD ST.

16

WALCOT ST.

Milsom Place

GREEN ST.

18

MILSOM

NEW BOND ST.

UPPER BOROUGH WALLS

PARSONAGE

UNION PASS.

CORR.

NORTH-UMBER.

HIGH ST.

BRIDGE ST.

PULTENEY BRIDGE

GROVE ST.

River Avon

To Bath Boating Station

POWLETT RD.

FORESTER RD.

BECKFORD RD.

BATHWICK ST.

HENRIETTA RD.

SUTTON ST.

SYDNEY PL.

Canal Walk to Bathampton

Sydney Gardens

HOLBURNE MUSEUM

HENRIETTA GARDENS

6

HENRIETTA ST.

Henrietta Park

HENRIETTA MEWS

7 **8**

GREAT PULTENEY ST.

PULTENEY ESTATES

Laura Place

ARGYLE ST.

BATHWICK HILL

To American Museum

PULTENEY ROAD (A-36)

9

The Recreation Ground

Rugby Pitch

RIVER CRUISES

VICTORIA ART GALLERY

GUILDHALL MARKET

ORANGE GROVE

GRAND PARADE

Parade Gardens

SPORTS & LEISURE CENTRE

NORTH PARADE ROAD

PIERREPONT ST.

WESTGATE

CHEAP ST.

Abbey Churchyard

ABBEY

ROMAN BATHS

PUMP ROOM

BATH ST.

CROSS BATH

THERMAE BATH SPA

LOWER BOROUGH

S. JAMES PARADE

AMERY LN.

STALL'S

YORK ST.

ABBEY GATE

13

Abbey Green

11

OLD ORCHARD

14

NEW ORCHARD

HENRY ST.

DUKE ST.

ST. JOHN'S

FERRY LN.

Cricket Ground

10

PULTENEY GARDENS

Canal Walk to Bathampton

SOUTHGATE

SOUTHGATE SHOPPING CENTER

AMBURY

South-Gate P

DORCHESTER ST.

BUS STATION

MANVERS ST.

BAGGAGE STORAGE

GEORGE BAYNTUN BOOKSHOP

RAIL STATION

FOOTBRIDGE

CLAVERTON ST.

ROSSITER RD. (A-36)

CLAVERTON RD.

PRIOR PARK RD.

17

WIDCOMBE HILL

Kennet & Avon Canal

200 Meters

200 Yards

BATH

EAST OF THE RIVER

These listings are a 5- to 10-minute walk from the city center. From the train station, it's best to take a taxi, as there are no good bus connections.

$$$$ The Roseate Villa rents 21 stately yet modern rooms in a freestanding Victorian townhouse, with a park on one side and an extensive lawn on the other. In a city that's so insistently Georgian, it's fun to stay in a mansion that's Victorian (family rooms, free parking for those booking direct, in quiet residential area on Henrietta Street, tel. 01225/466-329, http://roseatehotels.com/bath/theroseatevilla, reception.trvb@roseatehotels.com).

$$$ The Kennard is a short walk from the Pulteney Bridge. Each of the 12 rooms is colorfully and elaborately decorated (free street parking permits, peaceful little Georgian garden out back, 11 Henrietta Street, tel. 01225/310-472, www.kennard.co.uk, reception@kennard.co.uk, Priya and Ajay).

$$$ Henrietta House, with large rooms, hardwood floors, and daily homemade biscuits and jam, is cloak-and-cravat cozy. Even the name reflects English aristocracy, honoring the daughter of the mansion's former owners, Lord and Lady Pulteney. Now it's smartly run by Peter and another Henrietta (family-size suites, limited free parking, 33 Henrietta Street, tel. 01225/632-632, www.henriettahouse.co.uk, reception@henriettahouse.co.uk).

$$$ The Ayrlington, next door to a bowling green, rents 19 spacious rooms, each decorated with panache. Though this well-maintained hotel fronts a busy street, it's reasonably quiet and tranquil. Rooms in the back have pleasant views of sports greens and Bath beyond. For the best value, request a standard top-floor double with a view of Bath (fine garden, free and easy parking, 24 Pulteney Road, tel. 01225/425-495, www.ayrlington.com, theayrlington@gmail.com).

$$ At Apple Tree Guesthouse, near a shady canal, hostess Ling rents five comfortable rooms sprinkled with Asian decor (family rooms, 2-night minimum Fri-Sat nights, free parking, 7 Pulteney Gardens, tel. 01225/337-642, www.appletreebath.com, enquiries@appletreebath.com).

IN THE TOWN CENTER

Since Bath is so pleasant and manageable by foot, a downtown location isn't essential, but these options are close to the baths and abbey.

$$$ Three Abbey Green Guest House offers 10 spacious rooms off a quiet, traffic-free courtyard just 50 yards from the abbey and the Roman Baths. There's a different breakfast special every day (family rooms, 2-night minimum on weekends, limited free parking, 2 ground-floor rooms work well for those with limited mobility, tel. 01225/428-558, https://threeabbeygreen.com, stay@threeabbeygreen.com, Sue, daughter Nicola, and son-in-law Alan). They also rent an apartment (2-night minimum).

$$ Harington's Hotel rents 13 fresh, modern rooms on a quiet street. This stylish place feels like a boutique hotel, but with a friendlier, laid-back vibe (pay parking, 8 Queen Street, tel. 01225/461-728, www.haringtonshotel.co.uk, post@haringtonshotel.co.uk, manager Julian). Owners Melissa and Peter rent nine apartments nearby (2-night minimum on weekends).

$$ Laura's Townhouse Apartments rents three flats on Abbey Green and others scattered around the city. The apartment called Abbey View comes with a washer/dryer and has views of the abbey from its nicely equipped kitchen. Laura provides a simple breakfast, but it's fun and cheap to stock the fridge. When Laura meets you to give you the keys, you become a local (2-night minimum, rooms can sleep four with Murphy and sofa beds, tel. 01225/464-238, www.laurastownhouseapartments.co.uk, bookings@laurastownhouseapartments.co.uk).

$$ The Henry Guest House is a simple, vertical place, renting seven clean rooms. It's friendly, well-run, and just two blocks from the train station (family room, 2-night minimum on weekends, 6 Henry Street, tel. 01225/424-052, www.thehenry.com, stay@thehenry.com, Christina).

BARGAIN ACCOMMODATIONS

$ Z Hotel Bath (the Brits say "zed") rents spare, modern rooms just big enough for the bed—your suitcase slides in a nook below. Though tight on space, hotel frills include organic linen and a daily wine-and-cheese buffet—and best of all, it's right in the center, just across from the Theatre Royal (breakfast extra, cheaper "inside" rooms lack windows, air-con, elevator, 7 Saw Close, tel. 01225/613 160, www.thezhotels.com, bath@thezhotels.com).

¢ The YMCA, centrally located on a leafy square, is safe, secure, quiet, and efficiently run with a youthful, dorm vibe (private en suite rooms and family rooms available, includes continental breakfast, laundry facilities, down a tiny alley off Broad Street on Broad Street Place, tel. 01225/325-900, www.bathymca.co.uk, stay@bathymca.co.uk).

¢ White Hart is a friendly and colorful place in need of a little updating, but offering good, cheap stays in a dorm or four private rooms (fine garden out back, 5-minute walk behind the train station at Widcombe—where Widcombe Hill hits Claverton Street, tel. 01225/338-053, www.whitehartbath.co.uk, enquiries@whitehartbath.co.uk). The White Hart also has a pub with a reputation for good food.

¢ St. Christopher's Inn, in a prime central location, is part of a chain of high-energy hubs for backpackers looking for beds and brews. Rooms are basic, clean, and cheap because they know you'll spend money on their beer. The inn sits above the lively, youthful Belushi's pub, which is where you'll find the reception (cheaper to book online, private rooms and family rooms available, laundry facilities, lounge, 9 Green Street, tel. 01225/481-444, www.st-christophers.co.uk, bath@st-christophers.co.uk).

Eating in Bath

Bath is bursting with eateries. There's something for every appetite and budget—just stroll around the center of town. A picnic dinner in the Royal Crescent Park or down by the river is ideal for aristocratic hoboes. The restaurants I recommend are mostly small and popular—reserve a table for dinner—especially on Friday and Saturday. Most pricey little bistros offer big savings with their two- and three-course lunches and "pretheatre" specials. Look for early-bird specials: If you order within the time window, you're in for a less-expensive meal. Vegetarianism is trendy here; any serious restaurant offers a veggie course.

UPSCALE ENGLISH
$$$$ **The Circus Restaurant** is a relaxing eatery serving well-executed seasonal dishes with European flair. Choose between the modern interior—with seating on the main floor or in the less-charming cellar—and a few tables on the peaceful street connecting the Circus and the Royal Crescent (Mon-Sat 12:00-late, closed Sun, 34 Brock Street, tel. 01225/466-020, www.thecircusrestaurant.co.uk).

$$$ **Eight Restaurant** looks simple—like a tidy living room with six tables crowded into it. But each dish is a beautifully presented work of edible art, the price is right, and the service is perfectly attentive. The eight seasonal Italian/French/English dishes (at around £14 each) are small, and while you can make it a light meal, a couple could enjoy trying three or four dishes family-style (daily 17:30-21:30, 3 North Parade Passage, tel. 01225/724-111, https://eightinbath.co.uk).

$$$$ **Clayton's Kitchen** is where Michelin-star chef Rob Clayton aims to offer affordable British cuisine without pretense. The food is artfully prepared and presented (daily from 12:00 and 18:00, a few outside tables, 15 George Street, tel. 01225/585-100, www.claytonskitchen.com).

$$$ **The Chequers** is so nice I raised it out of the pub category. It's pubby gourmet, serving a small menu of creative, beautifully presented British dishes to enjoy in their handsome bar on the ground floor or refined upstairs restaurant (with open kitchen).

Reasonable fixed-price lunches are available from 17:30-18:30 except Sunday (daily, just above the Royal Crescent at 50 Rivers Street, tel. 01225/360-017, www.thechequersbath.com). To enjoy the kitchen to the max, consider their seven-course tasting menu (£55, Mon-Fri only, request in advance with reservation).

PUB GRUB

$$$ The Garrick's Head, an elegantly simple gastropub around the corner from the Theatre Royal, serves traditional English dishes with a few Mediterranean options. There's a restaurant with table service on one side, a more casual bar on the other, and some tables outside great for people-watching—all with the same menu and prices (lunch and pretheater specials until 19:00, daily 12:00-23:00, 8 St. John's Place, tel. 01225/318-368).

$$ Crystal Palace, a casual and inviting standby a block from the abbey, faces the delightful little Abbey Green. With a

focus on food rather than drink, they serve "pub grub with a Continental flair" in three different spaces: a bar, a full-service restaurant, and an airy back patio (daily 11:00-23:00, 10 Abbey Green, tel. 01225/482-666). Their lunch menu, a simpler and cheaper option, is served until 17:00.

$$ The Raven attracts a boisterous local crowd. It empha-sizes beer—with an impressive selection of real ales—but serves some delicious savory pies for nourishment. The ground floor has a thick pub vibe while upstairs feels more like a restaurant (Mon-Fri 12:00-15:00 & 17:00-21:00, Sat-Sun 12:30-20:30, open longer for drinks; no kids under 10, 6 Queen Street, tel. 01225/425-045).

FISH

$$ The Scallop Shell is my top choice for fish in Bath. Hard-working Garry and his family offer grilled seafood along with fish-and-chips. Their £10 lunch special is served daily until 15:00. The ground floor is energized by the open kitchen while upstairs is qui-eter with a breezy terrace (Mon-Sat 12:00-21:30, Sun until 16:00, 22 Monmouth Place, tel. 01225/420-928).

$$$ Loch Fyne Fish Restaurant is an inviting outpost of this chain, serving fresh fish at reasonable prices. The big dining hall occupies what was once a lavish bank building and comes with a fun and family-friendly energy (two-course special until 18:00, daily 12:00-22:00, 24 Milsom Street, tel. 01225/750-120).

BATH

WESTON RD.

CRESCENT LN.

JULIAN RD.

CRESCENT LN.

ROYAL CRESCENT

18

R.C. HOTEL

NO. 1 ROYAL CRESCENT

RIVERS ST.

MOREFORD

MUSEUM OF BATH AT WORK

4

CIRCUS MEWS

FASHION MUSEUM & ASSEMBLY ROOMS

BENNETT

11 1

BROCK ST.

THE CIRCUS

SAVILLE

BARTLETT

Royal

Victoria Park

To Newbridge Park & Ride, Bristol & Cardiff

20

ALFRED ST.

ROYAL AVE.

GAY ST.

3

9

GEORGE

MARLBOROUGH LN.

MINI GOLF

Bowling Green

21

10

Charlotte Street

(A-4) UPPER BRISTOL RD.

P

Tennis Courts

JANE AUSTEN CENTRE

CHARLOTTE ST.

Queen Square

13

MONMOUTH PL.

8

PRINCES

JOHN ST.

WOOD

7

1 The Circus Restaurant
2 Eight Restaurant & Acorn Vegetarian Kitchen
3 Clayton's Kitchen
4 The Chequers
5 The Garrick's Head
6 Crystal Palace
7 The Raven
8 The Scallop Shell
9 Loch Fyne Fish Restaurant
10 Martini Restaurant
11 Rustico Bistro Italiano
12 Dough Pizza Restaurant
13 Olé Tapas
14 Eastern Eye
15 Thai Balcony Restaurant
16 Yak Yeti Yak
17 Hands Georgian Tearooms
18 Dower House
19 Market Café & Guildhall Market
20 Boston Tea Party
21 Chandos Deli
22 The Cornish Bakehouse
23 Gong Fu Noodle Bar; Seafoods Fish & Chips; Swoon
24 Chai Walla
25 Mission Burrito
26 Supermarket (3)
27 The Old Green Tree
28 The Star Inn
29 The Bell

NEW KING ST.

MONMOUTH ST.

CHARLES ST.

GREEN PARK STATION

THEATRE ROYAL

USTINOV THEATRE & THE EGG

23

5

JAMES ST. WEST

JOHN'S

BARTON ST.

TRIM

SAW CL.

QUEEN

BRIDEWELL

WESTGATE

24

25

15

CHANDOS

CHANDOS BLDGS.

HET.

Kingsmead Square

NEW

MILK ST.

AVON ST.

GREEN PARK ROAD

CORN ST.

River Avon

LOWER BRISTOL ROAD (A-36)

To Odd Down Park & Ride, Wells & Glastonbury

WELLS ROAD (A-367)

One-way streets →

Traffic barriers

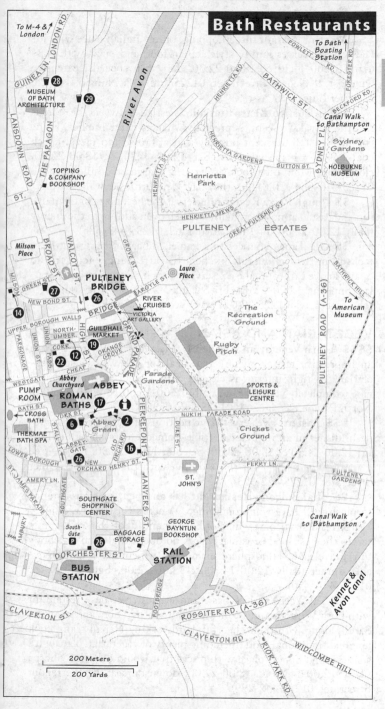

Bath Restaurants

To M-4 & London

GUINEA LN. LONDON RD.

FOWLETT RD.

To Bath Boating Station

FORESTER RD.

BECKFORD RD.

BATH

MUSEUM OF BATH ARCHITECTURE

28

29

River Avon

HENRIETTA RD.

BATHWICK ST.

SUTTON ST.

SYDNEY PL.

Canal Walk to Bathampton

Sydney Gardens

HOLBURNE MUSEUM

LANSDOWN ROAD

THE PARAGON

TOPPING & COMPANY BOOKSHOP

ST.

HENRIETTA GARDENS

Henrietta Park

HENRIETTA ST.

HENRIETTA MEWS

PULTENEY

GREAT PULTENEY ST.

ESTATES

Milsom Place

BROAD ST.

WALCOT ST.

GREEN ST.

27

GROVE ST.

Laura Place

BATHWICK HILL

MILSOM ST.

NEW BOND ST.

PULTENEY BRIDGE

26

ARGYLE ST.

To American Museum

PULTENEY ROAD (A-36)

14

UPPER BOROUGH WALLS

BRIDGE

HIGH ST.

RIVER CRUISES

VICTORIA ART GALLERY

The Recreation Ground

UNION ST.

PARSONAGE

NORTH-UMBER-

GUILDHALL MARKET

Rugby Pitch

22

CORK.

12

19

ORANGE GROVE

CHEAP.

WESTGATE

Abbey Churchyard

ABBEY

Parade Gardens

GRAND PARADE

PIERREPONT ST.

SPORTS & LEISURE CENTRE

PUMP ROOM

17

ROMAN BATHS

BATH ST.

CROSS BATH

YORK ST.

6

STALL ST.

2

Abbey Green

NORTH PARADE ROAD

Cricket Ground

DUKE ST.

THERMAE BATH SPA

ABBEY-GATE

16

OLD ORCHARD

HENRY ST.

FERRY LN.

PULTENEY GARDENS

LOWER BOROUGH

26

NEW ORCHARD

MANVERS ST.

AMERY LN.

ST. JAMES PARADE

SOUTHGATE

SOUTHGATE SHOPPING CENTER

ST. JOHN'S

Canal Walk to Bathampton

AMBURY

SouthGate P

26

BAGGAGE STORAGE

GEORGE BAYNTUN BOOKSHOP

DORCHESTER ST.

RAIL STATION

BUS STATION

FOOT BRIDGE

Kennet & Avon Canal

CLAVERTON ST.

ROSSITER RD. (A-36)

CLAVERTON RD.

RIOR PARK RD.

WIDCOMBE HILL

200 Meters

200 Yards

ITALIAN AND SPANISH

$$$ Martini Restaurant, a hopping, purely Italian place with jovial waiters, serves family-style Italian food and pizza with class (daily 12:00-14:30 & 18:00-22:30, daily fish specials, extensive wine list, 9 George Street, tel. 01225/460-818; Nunzio, Franco, and chef Luigi).

$$$$ Rustico Bistro Italiano, nestled between the Circus and the Royal Crescent, is precisely what its name implies. Franco and his staff are kept busy by a local crowd (no pizza, check chalkboard for specials, Tue-Sat 12:00-14:30 & 18:00-22:00, closed Sun-Mon, off Brock Street at 2 Margaret's Buildings, tel. 01225/310-064). If it's hot, they have delightful sidewalk seating.

$$ Dough Pizza Restaurant serves the best pizza in town in a fun and casual atmosphere with an open oven adding to the energy (daily 12:00-22:00, 14 The Corridor, tel. 01255/443-686).

$$ Olé Tapas bounces to a flamenco beat, turning out tasty tapas from their minuscule kitchen. If you're hungry for a trip to Spain, arrive early or make a reservation, as it's both tiny and popular (Sun-Thu 12:00-22:00, Fri-Sat until 23:00, up the stairs at 1 John Street, tel. 01225/424-274, www.oletapas.co.uk).

VEGETARIAN AND ASIAN

$$$$ Acorn Vegetarian Kitchen is pricey but highly rated (with an impressive tasting menu) and ideal for the well-heeled vegetarian. Its tight interior is elegant with a quiet and understated vibe (completely vegan menu, daily 12:00-15:00 & 17:30-21:30, 2 North Parade Passage, tel. 01225/446-059).

$$$ Eastern Eye serves large portions of Indian and Bangladeshi dishes in an impressive, triple-domed Georgian hall (Mon-Fri 12:00-14:30 & 18:00-23:30, Sat-Sun 12:00-23:30, RS%—free glass of wine or beer for those dining with this book, 8A Quiet Street, tel. 01225/422-323).

$$ Thai Balcony Restaurant has an open, spacious interior so plush, it'll have you wondering, "Where's the Thai wedding?" While residents debate which of Bath's handful of Thai restaurants serves the best food or value, there's no doubt that Thai Balcony's fun and elegant atmosphere makes for a memorable and enjoyable dinner (daily 12:00-14:30 & 18:00-22:00, Saw Close, tel. 01225/444-450).

$$ Yak Yeti Yak is a basic and earnest Nepalese restaurant with both Western and sit-on-the-floor seating. Sera and his wife, Sarah, along with their cheerful, hardworking Nepali team, cook up great traditional food (including plenty of vegetarian plates). It's a simple and honest place with prices that would delight a Sherpa (daily 12:00-14:00 & 18:00-22:00, downstairs at 12 Pierrepont Street, tel. 01225/442-299).

EVER SO ENGLISH AFTERNOON TEA

A tradition for anyone feeling both English and aristocratic is a formal "afternoon tea"—with a three-tiered trolley: delicate finger sandwiches, scones with clotted cream and jam, and cakes, accompanied by a fancy pot of tea. (A "cream tea" is just tea with scones, jam, and clotted cream.) While many places serve afternoon tea, the setting is critical for the experience.

$$$ The Pump Room sits above the Roman baths and for over two centuries has been Bath's iconic Georgian gathering place. The food comes with live music—piano or a string trio (£27 afternoon tea from noon; also open daily 9:30-16:00 for breakfast, tea/coffee and selection of pastries also available in the afternoon, dinner July-Aug 18:00-21:00 only; tel. 01225/444-477).

$ Hands Georgian Tearoom is an understated, family-run place a stone's throw from the abbey and the baths. With an elegant Georgian interior and traditional dishes, it's a good option for breakfast, lunch, or an economic afternoon tea in the center of the tourist bustle (cash only, Tue-Sat 9:30-17:00, Sun-Mon from 11:00, 1 Abbey Street, tel. 01225/463-928).

$$$ Dower House at the Royal Crescent Hotel is my choice on a sunny day as tea is served in an elegant garden—and they allow you to split one order, making the experience more affordable (£38 afternoon tea, daily 13:30-16:30, reserve a day ahead—a week ahead for Sat-Sun, 16 Royal Crescent, tel. 01225/823-333, www.royalcrescent.co.uk).

SIMPLE LUNCH AND BREAKFAST OPTIONS

For an olde tyme market experience, get breakfast at the Market Café. Chandos Deli is a more upscale foodie option. The Boston Tea Party is understandably packed with enthusiastic breakfasters. And bakeries and cafés all over town compete hard for the many Airbnb travelers that don't get that second "B" included.

$ Market Café, in the Guildhall Market, is where you can munch cheaply on a homemade meat pie or sip tea while surrounded by stacks of used books and old-time locals (traditional English meals including fried breakfasts all day, cash only, Mon-Sat 8:00-17:00, closed Sun, tel. 01225/461-593 a block north of the abbey, on High Street).

$ Boston Tea Party is what Starbucks aspires to be—the neighborhood coffeehouse and hangout. Its extensive breakfasts, bakery items, light lunches, and salads are fresh and healthy. They're popular with vegetarians and famously ethical in their business practices (daily 7:00-18:00, across from the Assembly Rooms at 8 Alfred Street, tel. 01225/476-465).

$ Chandos Deli has good coffee, breakfast pastries, and tasty £4 sandwiches made on artisan breads—plus meats, cheese, baguettes, and wine for assembling a gourmet picnic. Upscale yet casual, this place satisfies dedicated foodies who don't want to pay too much (Mon-Fri 8:00-17:30, Sat from 9:00, Sun from 10:00, 12 George Street, tel. 01225/314-418).

$ The Cornish Bakehouse has freshly baked takeaway pasties (Mon-Sat 7:30-18:00, Sun 9:00-17:30, off High Street at 11A The Corridor, tel. 01225/426-635). Munch your goodies at the nearby Parade Gardens or Abbey Churchyard.

$ Kingsmead Square is a shady space with a grand tree and inviting benches, surrounded by several ethnic joints where you can grab a bite and sit outside. **Gong Fu Noodle Bar** is a favorite with Chinese students studying in Bath (daily 11:00-23:00); **Chai Walla** serves up satisfying, simple Indian street food (no seating, Sun-Thu 12:00-17:00, Fri-Sat until late, Niraj); **Mission Burrito** is good if you crave Mexican (daily until 22:00); **Seafoods Fish & Chips** is a greasy standby but The Scallop Shell, described earlier, is a better value (daily until 21:00); and **Swoon** has the best gelato in town.

Supermarkets: Waitrose has a café upstairs and racks of inexpensive picnic-type meals to go on the ground level. There are some stools inside and a few tables on the street out front (Mon-Fri 7:30-21:00, Sat until 20:00, Sun 11:00-17:00, just west of Pulteney Bridge and across from post office on High Street). **Marks & Spencer,** near the bottom end of town, has a grocery at the back of its department store and the M&S Café on the top floor (Mon-Sat 8:30-19:00, Sun 11:00-17:00, 16 Stall Street). **Sainsbury's Local,** across the street from the bus station, has the longest hours (daily 7:00-23:00, 2 Dorchester Street).

Bath Connections

Bath's train station is called Bath Spa (tel. 0345-748-4959). The National Express bus station is just west of the train station (bus info tel. 0871-781-8181, www.nationalexpress.com). For all public bus services in southwestern England, see www.travelinesw.com.

From Bath to London: You can catch a **train** to London's Paddington Station (2/hour, 1.5 hours, best deals for travel after 9:30 and when purchased in advance, www.gwr.com), or save money—but not time—by taking the National Express **bus** to Victoria Coach Station (direct buses nearly hourly, 3.5 hours, avoid those with layover in Bristol, one-way-£7-12, cheapest to purchase online several days in advance).

Connecting Bath with London's Airports: To get to or from **Heathrow,** it's fastest and most pleasant to take the **train via London;** it takes about three hours total (airport to London Paddington-4/hour, Paddington to Bath-2/hour). With a rail pass, it's also the cheapest option, as the whole trip is covered. Without a rail pass, it's the most expensive way to go (£60 total for off-peak travel, cheaper bought in advance, up to £60 more for full-fare peak-time ticket; 2/hour, 2.25 hours depending on airport terminal, easy change between First Great Western train and Heathrow Express at London's Paddington Station).

The **National Express bus** is direct and often much cheaper for those without a rail pass, but it's less frequent and can take nearly twice as long as the train (nearly hourly, 3.5 hours, £24-40 one-way depending on time of day, tel. 0871-781-8181, www. nationalexpress.com). Doing a **train-and-bus combination** via the town of Reading can make sense for travelers without a rail pass, as it's more frequent, can take less time than the direct bus—allow 2.5 hours total—and can be much cheaper than the train via London (RailAir Link shuttle bus to Reading: 2-3/hour, 45 minutes; train from Reading to Bath: 2/hour, 1 hour; £31-41 for off-peak, nonrefundable travel booked in advance—but up to double for peak-time trains; tel. 0118-957-9425, buy bus ticket from www.railair.com, train ticket from www.gwr.com). Another option is the **minibus** operated by recommended tour company Celtic Horizons (see page 415).

You can get to or from **Gatwick** by train with a transfer in Reading (hourly, 3 hours, £55-75 one-way depending on time of day, cheaper in advance; avoid transfer in London, where you'll have to change stations; www.gwr.com) or by bus with a transfer at Heathrow (6/day, 4-5 hours, about £35 one-way, transfer at Heathrow Airport, www.nationalexpress.com).

Connecting Bath and Bristol Airport: Located about 20 miles west of Bath, this airport is closer than Heathrow and has good connections by bus. From Bristol Airport, your most convenient option is the Bristol Air Decker bus #A4 (£14, 2/hour, 1.25 hours, www.airdecker.com). Otherwise, you can take a taxi (£40) or call Celtic Horizons (see page 415).

From Bath by Train to: Bristol (Temple Meads station, 4/hour, 15 minutes), **Salisbury** (hourly direct, 1 hour), **Portsmouth** (hourly, 2.5 hours), **Exeter** (2/day direct, 1.5 hours, more with transfer in Bristol or Westbury), **Penzance** (1-2/hour, 5 hours, most 1-2 transfers), **Moreton-in-Marsh** (hourly, 2.5 hours, 1 transfer, more with additional transfers), **York** (hourly with transfer in Bristol, 4.5 hours, more with additional transfers), **Oxford** (hourly, 1.5 hours, transfer in Didcot), **Cardiff** (hourly, 1.5 hours), **Birmingham** (1/day direct, 2 hours, most with transfer in Bristol), and **points north** (from Birmingham, a major transportation hub, trains depart for Blackpool, Scotland, and North Wales; use a train/bus combination to reach Ironbridge Gorge and the Lake District).

From Bath by Bus to: **Salisbury** (hourly, 3 hours), **Avebury** (hourly, 2-2.5 hours, transfer in Devizes), **Portsmouth** (1/day direct, 6 hours), **Exeter** (6/day, 4 hours, most transfer in Bristol), **Penzance** (2/day, 8 hours, transfer in Bristol), **Cheltenham** or **Gloucester** (3/day, 3 hours, transfer in Bristol), **Stratford-upon-Avon** (1/day, 4 hours, transfer in Bristol), and **Oxford** (1/day direct, 2 hours, more with transfer). For bus connections to **Glastonbury** and **Wells**, see the next chapter.

Bristol

For an easy side trip from Bath, consider Bristol. This historic port city is the rugged, industrial (yet suddenly sassy and energized) counterpart to Bath—much like Glasgow's grit is the counterpart to Edinburgh's glam in Scotland. While Bath is refined and dressy, with an air that it's above everyday life, Bristol feels real. The city's sidewalks are fortified with metal edges to protect them  from the crush of barrels tumbling between ships and warehouses. So too, the city has an edge—both its people and its architecture seem weathered yet durable.

Bristol, sitting on the River Avon five miles from its mouth, was built on trade. The name means "place of the bridge," and it was born where the first Bristol Bridge crossed the river about a thousand years ago.

The river kinks and bends through town, giving the cityscape a lively ambience. It has Europe's highest tide (45 feet), which made the city a muddy mess until 1809, when a dam tamed the tides. The dam—with a lock and embankments—created Bristol's "Floating Harbour," which was a busy port until late in the 20th century.

Bristol really took off during the Age of Discovery and the rise of trade with the Americas. For a couple of centuries the city played a major role in the triangular shuttling of manufactured goods, rum, port, sherry, tobacco, sugar, and—most notoriously—

slaves between Africa, America, and Europe. It was a lose-win-win arrangement.

With the advent of the Industrial Age, while London continued to be the gateway to Europe, Bristol became England's port facing the west. It just made sense for goods to go by train from London to Bristol and then by ship westward. A big part of the city's story is the prolific work of a Victorian engineering genius with a crazy name—Isambard Kingdom Brunel—who designed railway stations, train lines (the Great Western Railway), and even an iron-hulled, propeller-driven steamship, all to expedite trade between London and New York City.

Because of its strategic and industrial importance, Bristol was heavily bombed in World War II. While much survived, much also was destroyed—you can tell by the haphazard mix of venerable old buildings and generally ugly development from the postwar era.

In modern times the port moved to the mouth of the Avon, and the old center of Bristol was redeveloped. Exploring the city, you feel a new vibe. While Bath protects its rowhouses and keeps them a uniform creamy tone, Bristol is known for its multicolored "painted terraces," coloring the surrounding hills like rainbows. The city of half a million is also energized by its sizable university with 50,000 students.

If Londoners were asked to describe the people of Bristol, they might consider them anti-Brexit, liberal, green—and a lot of old hippies. Vegan menus are the rage, hometown street artist Banksy decorates random walls...and look out for the cyclists.

GETTING TO BRISTOL

If you're staying in Bath, connect by commuter train (4/hour, 15 minutes). From Bath Spa Station, all trains on track 1 go to Bristol's Temple Meads Station (the main Bristol station). Don't worry about departure times as trains leave every 15 minutes. Just buy a ticket, go to track 1, and get on the next train. Don't drive here: Bristol is a pain for drivers. Bristol Airport, which is becoming more and more popular, is served by a cheap shuttle bus from the train station (6/hour, 30 minutes).

Orientation to Bristol

Bristol, while not as compact and charming as Bath, is reasonable on foot. You can easily connect everything in town from the train station (except for the Clifton Suspension Bridge) in under an hour. It's about 10 minutes to walk from the station into the old center. Bus #8 shuttles from the train station to the central College Green (at the cathedral and City Hall) and on to Clifton Village (near the Clifton Suspension Bridge) with departures every 10 minutes.

BATH

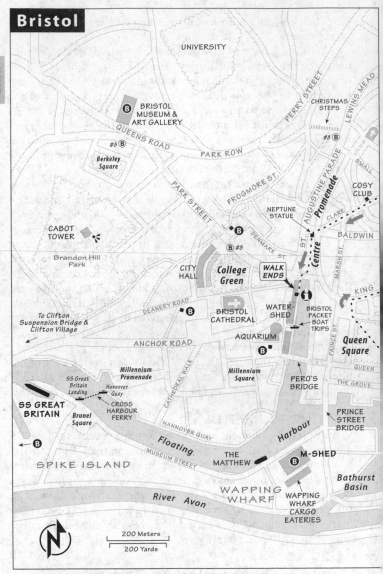

Bristol

UNIVERSITY

BRISTOL MUSEUM & ART GALLERY

CHRISTMAS STEPS

#8

PERRY STREET

LEWINS MEAD

QUEENS ROAD

PARK ROW

Berkeley Square

#8

PARK STREET

FROGMORE ST.

NEPTUNE STATUE

ST. AUGUSTINE PARADE

Promenade

COSY CLUB

CLARE

BALDWIN

CABOT TOWER

DENMARK ST.

#8

Centre

MARSH ST.

KING

Brandon Hill Park

CITY HALL

College Green

WALK ENDS

BRISTOL PACKET BOAT TRIPS

To Clifton Suspension Bridge & Clifton Village

DEANERY ROAD

BRISTOL CATHEDRAL

WATER-SHED

PRINCE ST.

Queen Square

ANCHOR ROAD

AQUARIUM

QUEEN

THE GROVE

Millennium Promenade

SS Great Britain Landing

Hannover Quay

Millennium Square

PERO'S BRIDGE

PRINCE STREET BRIDGE

SS GREAT BRITAIN

CROSS HARBOUR FERRY

CATHEDRAL WALK

Harbour

Brunel Square

HANNOVER QUAY

Floating

MUSEUM STREET

THE MATTHEW

M-SHED

Bathurst Basin

SPIKE ISLAND

WAPPING WHARF

WAPPING WHARF CARGO EATERIES

River Avon

N

200 Meters

200 Yards

Boats run like buses up and down the Floating Harbour. There's a handy ferry crossing from the SS *Great Britain* to Hanover Quay. And a fleet of "Bristol blue" taxis serves the town well.

On a day trip from Bath, plan for about three hours of sightseeing, an hour for my town walk, and about an hour for a harbor tour. You could also visit the famous Clifton Suspension Bridge just west of town, take a guided town and/or Banksy walking tour, and consider a lively evening with a late train back to Bath.

BATH

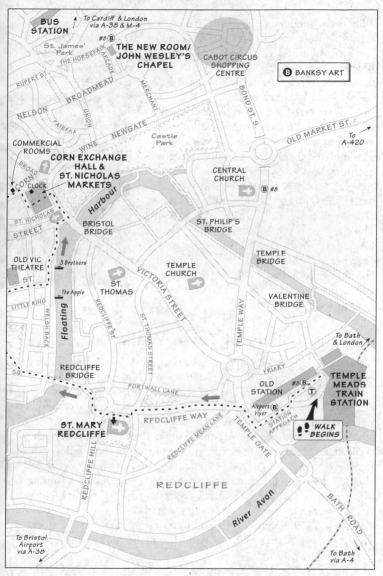

For a quick visit, I'd pick up a free "Visit Bristol" map at the train station and follow my town walk, described later, splicing in the main sights.

Tourist Information: The TI is on the riverfront at the head of the Centre Promenade (daily 10:00-17:00, 1 Canon's Road, www. visitbristol.co.uk; their toll phone number is as pricey as a phone-sex number—so I won't give it to you). The best thing about the

TI is their wonderful map (which you can also get at the Bath TI, at sights throughout Bristol, and at the main Bristol train station).

Local Guide: Liz Gamlin is a good guide who's earned her Blue Badge for Bristol and the West Country and can meet you at the station for a personalized tour (£120/half-day, mobile 07818-436-575, studytours@aol.com).

Street Art: The street artist known as Banksy was born here, and a handful of his legendary street paintings dot a scruffy part of town (see map). The TI sells a brochure outlining a do-it-yourself walking tour, or you can catch a street-art-themed guided tour. The "From Blackbeard to Banksy" walk is popular and reliable (£8, 2 hours, Thu-Sun at 11:30, departs from Bristol Cathedral, mobile 07811-975-275, www.blackbeard2banksy.com). If you search for "Banksy Bristol Trail" online, you'll find an app, printable maps, and several other walking tours worth considering.

Bristol Town Walk

This quick self-guided walk starts at Bath's main train station and ends at the TI. Along the way we'll see historic neighborhoods, a characteristic market, and one of the bridges that made this city famous. Allow about an hour. For details on specific sights, see the next section.

Main Station to the Bristol Bridge: From the station's exit, walk straight to a busy street, turn right, and then follow the main roadway as it curves to Redcliffe Way. Set your sights on the 300-foot-tall spire and walk to **St. Mary Redcliffe Church.** After visiting the church, continue on Redcliffe Way over Redcliffe Bridge (notice the houseboats lining the harbor). Imagine the town before its 1809 embankments and locks tamed the massive tides, creating the Floating Harbour. Check out the multicolored rowhouses on the hillside.

Just over the bridge, continue straight to the huge **Queen Square.** Walk diagonally through the square and then continue to King Street. Turn right and stroll the length of this characteristic street, passing historic pubs and the 18th-century Bristol Old Vic Theatre (which locals claim is England's oldest working theater). You can tell where WWII bombs fell (ugly new buildings) and where they didn't.

At the river, turn left, passing two permanently moored riverboats—floating temptations popular for alcoholic ciders and burgers: The **Apple** and **Three Brothers Burgers.** Ahead is the historic **Bristol Bridge** (with its 250-year-old stone arches reminding all that for a thousand years, a bridge at this spot was the reason for the town). From here, a network of canals connected much of Britain during the Industrial Age.

St. Nicolas Markets to the Watershed Building: At the bridge make a soft left and walk a couple blocks uphill on High Street toward the steeple of an old church. On the left find the arched entryway for **St. Nicolas Markets** and the **Corn Exchange Hall.** Wander through the market arcade (get lunch here if you're hungry) until your reach an alley. Turn right and come out on Corn Street, where you can study the Corn Exchange Hall facade before walking to your left down Corn Street.

The street ends at a wide brick plaza called the **Centre Promenade.** Cross at the statue of Neptune, turn left, and head for the red-brick **Watershed** building, where you'll find the TI and the departure point for Bristol Packet's **harbor tours.** Nearby is College Green with the City Hall, Bristol Cathedral, and a stop for bus #8 to the Clifton Suspension Bridge.

Sights in Bristol

In the City Center
The first four sights are in the order you'll see them on my self-guided walk, earlier. The New Room/John Wesley's Chapel is a short walk north.

St. Mary Redcliffe Church
Long the tallest structure in town, this church is marked by its elegant 300-foot-tall spire. Its 13th-century Gothic interior is worth a look. While its windows are mostly modern, the floors and walls are littered with the tombs and memorials of Bristol's leading citizens—including the father of William Penn, who founded Pennsylvania, and John Cabot, who sailed to America just after Columbus. If you wonder what a 500-year-old whale bone is doing hanging on the wall, ask a local about their favorite explorer.

Cost and Hours: Free, Mon-Sat 8:30-17:00, Sun 9:00-16:00, tel. 0117/231-0060, www.stmaryredcliffe.co.uk.

Queen Square
About 300 years ago, the rich merchant class built this square to get away from the commotion of Bristol's Old Town. Then, in the Industrial Age, they moved farther from the rabble a mile outside of town—establishing a "cliff town" or "Clifton"—and building aristocratic Georgian mansions there. The merchants left, but today the square remains elegant and people-friendly. Facing Queen Square are several historic addresses, including the home

of the first US-British consulate (a reminder of the importance of trade to Bristol back then).

▲▲Corn Exchange Hall and St. Nicholas Markets

This once formal and stately finance center feels as if it was overwhelmed by a rising tide of informal economy. The Corn Exchange Hall is now a commotion of  bric-a-brac dealers—like a permanent flea market under one grand Georgian roof. And this is just a small part of an entire block of stalls filling St. Nicholas Markets. Note the Victorian canopy of glass and iron in the center of the market. From lunchtime on, it's a thriving food circus with plenty of fun eateries and eclectic shops (see listing later, under "Eating in Bristol").

▲Corn Street

Home of England's first banks outside of London, Corn Street seems to celebrate the commerce that made Bristol an economic  powerhouse. Former palace-like banks and buildings of finance are now mostly grandiose pubs and restaurants. This pedestrianized stretch of Corn Street has an openair market (different days, different markets), which thrives around four historic "nail posts." These free-standing little brass pillars or platforms were where, back in the 17th century, deals were sealed and people would "pay on the nail." The clock on the Corn Exchange Hall facade famously tells both London time and Bristol time (11 minutes apart). It dates from the era before standard time. The advent of trains in the 1850s made having one standard time in Britain crucial, so "London time" (a.k.a. Greenwich Mean Time) became the unofficial standard. It finally became official throughout the realm in 1880 (eventually setting the world standard).

Nearby, the big **$$ Bristol Commercial Rooms** (once the domain of the merchant elite) is now a vast pub featuring craft beer. And another once-fancy Georgian bank is now another inviting pub, **$$ The Cozy Club.**

BATH

▲The New Room/John Wesley's Chapel
Featuring the world's oldest Methodist chapel (established in 1739), this exhibit tells the story of Methodism and the work of its founders, John and Charles Wesley. Its thoughtful little museum is particularly inspiring and fascinating—at least to Methodists.

Cost and Hours: Free, Mon-Sat 10:30-16:00, closed Sun, a 10-minute walk north of Bristol Bridge at 36 The Horsefair, tel. 0117/926-4740, www.newroombristol.org.uk.

Along the Harbor
An efficient plan for visiting this area is to catch a Bristol Packet boat at the TI, take 80 percent of the harbor tour, and get off at the SS *Great Britain*. After touring that ship, walk along the water 10 minutes to the M-Shed for its Bristol history exhibits. From there you can walk back to the station in about 20 minutes and catch your train to Bath.

▲Harbor Tour by Boat
Bristol Packet Boat Trips runs its "City Dock Tour" nearly hourly throughout the day in high season. You'll sit in an old, long, skinny canal boat on a relaxing loop around the Floating Harbour with light live narration (£6.75, 5/day, 45 minutes, tel. 0117/926-8157, www.bristolpacket.co.uk). Boats leave next to the TI at the Watershed building and from the dock at the SS *Great Britain*. Schedules are posted at both departure points (or call ahead).

▲▲▲Brunel's SS *Great Britain*
When built in 1843, the SS *Great Britain* laid the groundwork for modern shipping. It was by far the world's biggest ship, the first major iron-hulled vessel, and the first ship to cross the Atlantic powered by a propeller. More than 175 years later, it's drydocked a 10-minute walk west of Bristol's city center—marked by its towering old masts. Plan for a substantial visit that includes the  fine ship's museum, the well-restored ship itself, and an impressive exhibit devoted to its famous designer, Isambard Kingdom Brunel. If you walk here from the center, a fun little ferry crosses the harbor from Hannover Quay to the SS *Great Britain* (£1). Or you can get here by boat on the Bristol Packet harbor tour (described above).

Cost and Hours: £17, daily 10:00-18:00, Nov-March until 16:30, Great Western Dockyard, Gas Ferry Road, tel. 0117/926-0680, www.ssgreatbritain.org.

Visiting the Ship: Your SS *Great Britain* visit has three parts. First comes a one-way route of the dry dock and ship's museum. Start at the circa 1840s dry dock, where you'll walk under the ship (you feel like you're underwater, but it's just a shallow pool) for a close look at the iron hull and historic propeller. Then enter the museum, which takes you progressively back in time through the ship's fascinating history: 1970s salvaged and sailed to London; 1930s run aground and then scuttled in the Falklands; 1870s successful voyages sailing immigrants to Australia; 1860s economic failure as a luxury ship for the trip to New York; and 1843 launch.

Next cross the bridge onto the top deck of the actual ship. While onboard, be sure to talk with the role-playing docents; they're paid to chat with time travelers like you. Climb through the ship—wonderfully equipped as if sailing in the 1860s with a first-class zone, economy cabins, and massive engine room.

A free-standing building next to the ship—the "Being Brunel" exhibit—tells the story of the workaholic engineer and his amazing career. Brunel (1806-1859) was a dreamer who got things done—envisioning a fast and modern way to connect London and New York and then designing it: Paddington Station in London, the Great Western Railway to Bristol, the Temple Meads Station in Bristol, and the steam-powered ship that would finish the journey. He started the project in 1833...at the age of 27.

▲M-Shed and *The Matthew*

An old industrial shed (the port gave warehouses an address by lettering them) now tells Bristol's history with three galleries focusing on places, people, and lifestyles. You'll see lots of historic artifacts and an earnest attempt to deal with the city's slave-trade heritage. Historic ships are often moored just outside including a 1934 fireboat, *The Mayflower*—the oldest surviving steam-powered tugboat, and a modern replica of explorer John Cabot's good ship, *The Matthew*.

In 1497 John Cabot, sailing *The Matthew* across the North Atlantic, discovered a new-found land and cleverly called it just that. This modern replica of Cabot's ship, built to celebrate the 500th anniversary of his voyage, is usually moored at the M-Shed and (when in port) is free to climb through. A native of Italy (his real name was Giovanni Caboto), Cabot sailed from Bristol with a Bristol crew. Did the old fishermen here know something their captain didn't about that mysterious land just beyond the Atlantic's best cod banks?

Cost and Hours: M-Shed—Free, Tue-Sun 10:00-17:00, closed Mon, tel. 0177/352-6600, www.bristolmuseums.org.uk/m-shed; *The Matthew*—Free, March-Nov Tue-Sun 10:00-16:00, off-season weekends only, closed Mon year-round; Prince's Wharf, Wapping Road, tel. 0117/927-6868, https://matthew.co.uk.

Outer Bristol
▲Clifton Suspension Bridge and Clifton Village

A symbol of Bristol (a mile or so west of town), this bridge was completed in 1864 based on plans by engineer Isambard Kingdom Brunel. It's 700 feet long and rises 250 feet over the Avon Gorge, connecting Clifton Village and Leigh Woods. Bus #8 runs from the train station and from College Green to pleasant Clifton Village; from the bus stop it's a level walk to the bridge in a park-like setting. The free pedestrian walk across the bridge, with commanding views, leads to a visitors center (in Leigh Woods, free, open daily 10:00-17:00).

Clifton Village itself is a pleasant surprise. You can feel the escapism of the elites two centuries ago even today: The Georgian shops are upmarket boutiques and the Victorian Clifton Arcade is wonderfully shabby-chic. For extra credit, you can hike to Observatory Hill (with the remains of a historic windmill) and enjoy the high-wide view.

Eating in Bristol

For your day trip to Bristol, consider two festive food circuses for lunch.

$$ Wapping Wharf CARGO is a food festival of remodeled shipping containers behind the M-Shed (near SS *Great Britain)*. Part of a new community revitalizing a derelict harbor neighborhood, it's a thriving collection of about 50 containers that each function like food trucks, offering an eclectic world of creative and fun-loving eateries (generally open 11:00-20:00, most closed Mon).

$$ St. Nicholas Markets is the fun foodie zone in the city center described on my Bristol Town Walk. Under the iron-and-glass vaults of this Victorian market bustles another lively collection of colorful eateries offering an amazing variety of fast, fun, and inexpensive lunches (Mon-Sat 9:30-17:00, closed Sun).

GLASTONBURY & WELLS

The countryside surrounding Bath holds two particularly fine cathedral towns. Glastonbury (perhaps a.k.a. Avalon) is the ancient resting place of King Arthur, and home (maybe) to the Holy Grail. It can be covered well in two to three hours: See the abbey, climb the tor, and ponder your hippie past (and where you are now).

Nearby, medieval Wells gathers around its grand cathedral. Wells is simply a cute small town, much smaller and more medieval than Bath, with a uniquely beautiful cathedral that's best experienced at its evensong service.

GETTING AROUND THE REGION

By Car: Glastonbury and Wells are each about 20-25 miles from Bath and 140 miles from London. Drivers can do a 51-mile loop from Bath to Glastonbury (25 miles) to Wells (6 miles) and back to Bath (20 miles). Extend the trip to a 131-mile loop that includes two places covered in the next chapter: Drive from Bath to Avebury (25 miles) to Stonehenge (30 miles) to Glastonbury (50 miles) to Wells (6 miles) and back to Bath (20 miles).

By Bus and Train: The nearest train station is in Bath, served by regular trains from London's Paddington Station (2/hour, 1.5 hours). Wells and Glastonbury are both easily accessible by bus

Glastonbury & Wells Area

To Cardiff — M-49 — Patchway — Yate

River Severn — M-5

Portishead

Portbury

M5

Tickenham

Bristol

Kingswood

Pennsylvania

A-46

A-420

A-38

M-4

M-32

Bristol ✈

Keynsham

A-370

A-38

Congresbury

Banwell   A-368   Blagdon

CHEDDAR GORGE

M5   Axbridge

A-38   Cheddar

Wedmore

WILKINS CIDER FARM

Pensford

A-37   A-39

Clutton

Bishop Sutton

West Harptree

Farmborough

A-39

Peasdown St. John

Farington Gurney

Green Ore

A-39

A-371

Wells

GLASTONBURY TOR

Glastonbury

A-39   Ashcott

A-39   Walton

A-361

A-372

A-378

Langport   A-372

Ilchester

A-39   Pilton

A-361   West Pennard

Oakhill

Shepton Mallet

A-37

Prestleigh

A-371

A-359

A-37

Sparkford

A-303

To Stonehenge

Corston   **Bath**

Combe Down

A-367

Radstock   A-366

A-362

Buckland Dinham

Nunney

A-361   Cranmore   A-359

Wanstrow

SOMERSET

5 Kilometers

5 Miles

SCOTLAND

WALES   ENGLAND

London

GLASTONBURY & WELLS

from Bath. Bus #173 goes direct from Bath to **Wells** (nearly hourly, less frequent on Sun, 75 minutes), where you can continue on to **Glastonbury** by catching bus #376 (2/hour, 20 minutes, drops off directly in front of abbey entrance on Magdalene Street). To return to Bath, you'll likely go back through Wells (as direct bus service from Glastonbury to Bath is very limited). First Bus Company's

£11 day pass is a good deal if you plan on connecting Glastonbury and Wells from your Bath home base.

By Bike: A 10-mile path connects Wells and Glastonbury.

Glastonbury

Marked by its hill, or "tor," and located on England's most power-ful line of prehistoric sites, the town of Glastonbury gurgles with history and mystery.

In AD 37, Joseph of Ari-mathea—Jesus' wealthy uncle—reputedly brought vessels con-taining the blood of Jesus to Glastonbury, and with him, Christianity came to England. (Joseph's visit is plausible—long before Christ, locals traded lead and tin to merchants from the Levant.)

While this story is "proven" by fourth-century writings and accepted by the Church, the King-Arthur-and-the-Holy-Grail legends it inspired are not. Those medieval tales came when Eng-land needed a morale-boosting folk hero for inspiration during a war with France. They pointed to the ancient Celtic sanctuary at Glastonbury as proof enough of the greatness of the fifth-century warlord Arthur. In 1191, after a huge fire, Arthur's supposed re-mains (along with those of Queen Guinevere) were dug up from the abbey garden. Reburied in the abbey choir, Arthur and Guine-vere's gravesite is a shrine today. Many think the Grail trail ends at the bottom of the Chalice Well, a natural spring at the base of the Glastonbury Tor.

By the 10th century, Glastonbury Abbey was England's most powerful and wealthy, and was part of a nationwide network of monasteries that by 1500 owned one-quarter of all English land and had four times the income of the Crown. Then Henry VIII dis-solved the abbeys in 1536. He was particularly harsh on Glaston-bury—he not only destroyed the abbey but also hung and quartered the abbot, sending the parts of his body on four different national tours...at the same time. This was meant as a warning to other reli-gious clerics, and it worked.

But Glastonbury rebounded. In an 18th-century publicity campaign, thousands signed affidavits stating that they'd been healed by water from the Chalice Well, and once again Glaston-bury was on the tourist map. Today, Glastonbury and its tor are a center for "searchers"—too creepy for the mainstream Church but just right for those looking for a place to recharge their crystals. Glastonbury is also synonymous with its summer music-and-arts festival, a long-hair-and-mud Woodstock re-creation

that's a rite of passage for young music lovers in Britain.

Part of the fun of a visit to Glastonbury is just being in a town where every other shop and eatery is a New Age place. Locals who are not into this complain that on High Street, you can buy any kind of magic crystal or incense—but not a roll of TP. But, as this counterculture is their town's bread and butter, they do their best to sit in their pubs and go "Ommmmm."

Orientation to Glastonbury

TOURIST INFORMATION

The TI, located in St. Dunstan's House near the abbey, sells several booklets about area walks and bike rides, including the *Glastonbury and Street Town Guide,* and a £1.50 map (Mon-Sat 10:00-17:00, Sun until 16:00, shorter hours Oct-March, 1 Magdalene Street, tel. 01458/832-954, www.glastonburytic.co.uk). The TI also **rents bikes** (£20/day, £50 deposit).

HELPFUL HINTS

Market Day: Tuesday is market day for crafts, knickknacks, and local produce on the main street. There's also a country market Tuesday mornings in the Town Hall.

Glastonbury Festival: Nearly every summer (generally around the Summer solstice in June), the gigantic Glastonbury Festival—billing itself as the "largest music and performing arts festival in the world"—brings all manner of postmodern flower children to its notoriously muddy "Healing Fields." Music fans and London's beautiful people make the trek to see the hottest British and American bands. Anticipate increased traffic and crowds (especially on public transit; more than 165,000 tickets generally sell out), even though the actual music venue—practically a temporary city of its own—is six miles east of town (www.glastonburyfestivals.co.uk).

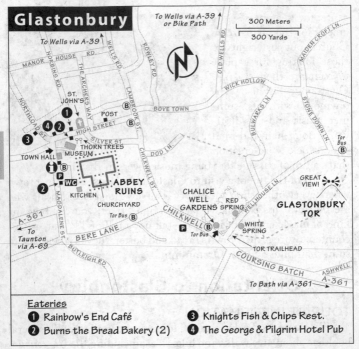

Glastonbury

To Wells via A-39 or Bike Path

300 Meters
300 Yards

Eateries
1 Rainbow's End Café
2 Burns the Bread Bakery (2)
3 Knights Fish & Chips Rest.
4 The George & Pilgrim Hotel Pub

Sights in Glastonbury

I've listed these sights in the order you'll reach them, moving from the town center to the tor.

Glastonbury Town

The tiny town itself is worth a pleasant stroll. The abbey came first, and Glastonbury grew up to serve it. For example, the George and Pilgrim Hotel was originally a freestanding structure built in the 15th century to house pilgrims. And St. John's Church, which dates from the same century, was constructed to give townsfolk a place to worship, as they weren't allowed in the abbey. The Market Cross at the base of High Street dates from around 1800.

Though Glastonbury is much older, its vibe dates to 1970, when the town hosted its first rock festival. Like Woodstock, it was held on a farm. Unlike Woodstock, the Glastonbury Festival had legs—it's been held on the same farm almost every year since. You'll still see many hippie and New Age shops in town.

▲▲Glastonbury Abbey

The massive and evocative ruins of the first Christian sanctuary in the British Isles stand mysteriously alive in a lush 36-acre park. Because it comes with a small museum, a dramatic history, and enthusiastic guides dressed in period costumes, this is one of the most engaging to visit of England's many ruined abbeys.

Cost and Hours: £8.25; daily 9:00-18:00, June-Aug until 20:00, Nov-Feb until 16:00.

Information: Tel. 01458/832-267, www.glastonburyabbey. com.

Getting There: Enter the abbey from Magdalene Street (around the corner from High Street, near the St. Dunstan's parking lot). Pay parking is nearby.

Tours and Demonstrations: Costumed guides offer 30-minute tours (generally daily March-Oct on the hour from 10:00). As you enter, confirm these times, and ask about other tour and show times.

Eating: Picnicking is encouraged—bring something from one of the shops in town (see "Eating in Glastonbury," later), or buy food at the small café on site (open May-Sept).

Background: The space that these ruins occupy has been sacred ground for centuries. The druids used it as a pagan holy site, and during Joseph of Arimathea's supposed visit here, he built a simple place of worship. In the 12th century—because of that legendary connection—Glastonbury was the leading Christian pilgrimage site in all of Britain. The popular abbey grew powerful and very wealthy, employing a thousand people to serve the needs of the pilgrims.

In 1184, there was a devastating fire in the monastery, and in 1191, the abbot here "discovered"—with the help of a divine dream—the tomb and bodies of King Arthur and Queen Guinevere. Of course, this discovery boosted the pilgrim trade in Glastonbury, and the new revenues helped to rebuild the abbey.

Then, in 1539, King Henry VIII ordered the abbey's destruction. When Glastonbury Abbot Richard Whiting questioned the king's decision, he was branded a traitor, hung at the top of Glastonbury Tor (after carrying up the plank that would support his noose), and his body cut into four pieces. His head was stuck over the gateway to the former abbey precinct. After this harsh example, the other abbots accepted the king's dissolution of England's abbeys, with many returning to monastic centers in France. Glastonbury Abbey was destroyed. With the roof removed, it fell into ruin and was used as a quarry.

Today, the abbey attracts both the curious and pious. Tie-dyed, starry-eyed pilgrims seem to float through the grounds, naturally high. Others lie on the grave of King Arthur, whose burial site is marked off in the center of the abbey ruins.

◯ Self-Guided Tour: After buying your ticket, pick up a map and tour the informative **museum** at the entrance building. A model shows the abbey in its pre-Henry VIII splendor, and exhibits tell the story of a place "grandly constructed to entice the dullest minds to prayer." Knowledgeable costumed guides are eager to share the site's story and might even offer an impromptu tour.

Next, head out to explore the green park, dotted with bits of the **ruined abbey.** You come face-to-face with the abbey's Lady Chapel, the site of the first wattle-and-daub church, possibly dating to the first century. Today, the crypt is dug out and exposed; posted information helps you imagine its 12th-century splendor.

The Lady Chapel became the abbey's west entry when the church expanded. The abbey was long and skinny, but vast. Measuring 580 feet, it was the longest in Britain (larger than York Minster is today) and Europe's largest building north of the Alps.

Before poking around the ruins, circle to the left behind the entrance building to find the two **thorn trees.** According to legend, when Joseph of Arimathea came here, he climbed nearby Wearyall Hill and stuck his staff into the soil. A thorn tree sprouted, and its descendant still stands there today; the trees here in the abbey are its offspring. In 2010, vandals hacked off the branches of the original tree on Wearyall Hill, but miraculously, the stump put out small green shoots the following spring. The trees inside the abbey grounds bloom twice a year, at Easter and at Christmas. If the story seems far-fetched to you, don't tell the Queen—a blossom from the abbey's trees sits proudly on her breakfast table every Christmas morning.

Ahead and to the left of the trees, inside what was the north wall, look for two trap doors in the ground. Lift up the doors to see surviving fragments of the abbey's original tiled floor.

Now hike through the remains of the ruined complex to the far end of the abbey. You can stand and, from what was the altar, look down at what was the gangly nave. Envision the longest church nave in England. In this area, you'll find the tombstone (formerly in the floor of the church's choir) marking the spot where the supposed relics of **Arthur and Guinevere** were interred.

Continue around the far side of the abbey ruins, feeling free to poke around the park. Imagine all of this green space—just a tiny part of the lands the abbey owned—bustling with the daily business of a powerful monastic community.

All those monks needed to eat. Take a look at the abbot's conical **kitchen,** the only surviving intact building on the grounds (see photo, previous page). Its size, and its simple exhibit about life in the abbey, gives you an idea of how big the community once was.

NEAR GLASTONBURY TOR

The tor is a steep hill at the southeastern edge of the town (it's visible from just about everywhere). The other two sights (the gardens and springs) are on your way to/from the tor.

Getting There: The garden and springs are about a 15-minute **walk** from the town center, toward the tor. The base of the tor is an additional five minutes. Climbing the tor is another 15-20 minutes.

If you don't want to walk, you have two options: The **Tor Bus** shuttles visitors from the town center to the base of the tor, stopping at the Chalice Well en route (£3.30 round-trip, 2/hour, departs on the half-hour from St. Dunstan's parking lot, near the TI and abbey, daily 10:00-12:30 & 14:00-17:00, doesn't run Oct-March). If you have a **car,** you won't find much parking nearby, so expect a bit of a hike (try the pay lot at the Draper sheepskin shop, near the Chalice Well on Chilkwell Street). A **taxi** to the tor trailhead costs about £7 one-way. Remember, these take you only to the bottom of the tor; to reach the top, you have to hike.

A good plan is to ride the shuttle bus to the tor, climb to the top, hike down, drop by Chalice Well Gardens, and stroll back into town from there.

Chalice Well Gardens

According to tradition, Joseph of Arimathea brought the chalice from the Last Supper to Glastonbury in AD 37. Supposedly it ended up in the bottom of a well, which is now the centerpiece of a peaceful and inviting garden. Even if the chalice is not at the bottom of the well (another legend says it made the trip to Wales), and the water is red from iron ore and not Jesus' blood, the tranquil setting attracts pilgrims still. If you're a fan of gardens—or want to say you've completed your grail quest—this place is worth a visit. To find the well itself, follow the well-marked path uphill alongside the gurgling stream, passing several places where you can drink from or wade in the healing water, as well as areas designated for

silent reflection. The stones of the well shaft date from the 12th century and are believed to have come from the church in Glastonbury Abbey (which was destroyed by fire). In the 18th century, pilgrims flocked to Glastonbury for the well's healing powers. Have a drink or take some of the precious water home—they sell empty bottles to fill.

Cost and Hours: £4.50, daily 10:00-18:00, Nov-March until 16:30, on Chilkwell Street/A-361, tel. 01458/831-154, www. chalicewell.org.uk.

Red and White Spring Waters
If you'd just like to sample the fabled water, two waterspouts are just around the corner from the Chalice Well Gardens entrance (just beyond the trailhead to the tor, where the bus drops off). The spout on the Chalice Well side comes from the Red Spring; the other spout's source is the White Spring. Try both and see which you prefer.

▲Glastonbury Tor
Seen by many as a Mother Goddess symbol, the Glastonbury Tor—a natural plug of sandstone on clay—has an undeniable geological charisma. Climbing the tor is the essential activity on a visit to Glastonbury. A fine Somerset view rewards those who hike to its 520-foot summit.

Climbing the Tor: From the base of the tor, a trail leads up to the top (about 15-20 uphill minutes, if you keep a brisk pace). While you can hike up the tor from either end, the less-steep approach (which most people take) starts next to the Chalice Well.

Hiking up to the top of the tor, survey the surrounding land—a former swamp, inhabited for 12,000 years, which is still below sea level at high tide. Up until the 11th century you could actually sail to the tower. The ribbon-like man-made drainage canals that glisten as they slice through the farmland are the work of engineers—Huguenot refugees who turned the marshy wasteland into something arable.

Looking out, find Glastonbury (at the base of the hill) and Wells (marked by its cathedral) to the right. Above Wells, a TV tower marks the 996-foot high point of the Mendip Hills. It was lead from these hills that attracted the ancient Romans (and, perhaps, Jesus' uncle Joe) so long ago. Stretching to the left, the Mendip Hills define what was the coastline before those Huguenot engineers arrived.

The tor-top tower is the remnant of a chapel dedicated to St. Michael. Early Christians often employed St. Michael, the warrior angel, to combat pagan gods. When a church was built upon a pagan holy ground like this, it was frequently dedicated to Michael.

But apparently those pagan gods fought back: St. Michael's Church was destroyed by an earthquake in 1275.

Eating in Glastonbury

$ Rainbow's End is one of several fine, healthy, vegetarian lunch cafés for hot meals (different every day), salads, herbal teas, soups, yummy homemade sweets, and New Age people-watching. If you're looking for a midwife or a male-bonding tribal meeting, check their notice board (vegan and gluten-free options, counter service, daily 10:00-16:00, 17 High Street, tel. 01458/833-896).

$ Burns the Bread has two convenient locations in town, making hearty pasties (savory meat pies) as well as fresh pies, sandwiches, delicious cookies, and pastries. Ask for a sample of the Torsy Moorsy Cake (a type of fruitcake made with cheddar), or try a gingerbread man made with real ginger. Grab a pasty and picnic with the ghosts of Arthur and Guinevere in the abbey ruins (Mon-Sat 7:00-17:00, Sun 10:00-16:00, main location at 14 High Street; smaller shop in St. Dunstan's parking lot next to the abbey, tel. 01458/831-532).

$ Knights Fish and Chips Restaurant has been in the same family since 1909 and is the town's top chippy. It's another fine option for a picnic at the abbey (more for table service, Mon-Sat 12:00-21:30, Sun until 19:30, closed Sun off-season, 5 Northload Street, tel. 01458/831-882, Kevin and Charlotte).

$$ The George & Pilgrim Hotel's wonderfully Old World pub might be exactly what the doctor ordered for visitors suffering a New Age overdose. The local owners serve up a traditional pub-grub menu (food served daily 12:00-14:45 & 18:00-20:45, 1 High Street, tel. 01458/831-146). They also rent **$$** rooms.

Glastonbury Connections

The nearest train station is in Bath. Local buses are run by First Bus Company (tel. 0845-602-0156, www.firstgroup.com).

From Glastonbury by Bus to: Wells (2/hour, 20 minutes, bus #376 headed to Bristol), **Bath** (nearly hourly, allow 2 hours, take bus to Wells, transfer to bus #173 to Bath, 1.5 hours between Wells and Bath). Buses are sparse on Sundays (generally one bus every other hour). If you're heading to points west, you'll likely connect through **Taunton** (which is a transfer point for westbound buses from Bristol).

Wells

Because this well-preserved little town has a cathedral, it can be called a city. It's England's smallest cathedral city (pop. just under 12,000), with one of its most interesting cathedrals and a wonderful evensong service (generally not offered July-Aug). Of all the towns you'll visit, Wells has the most buildings still operating as originally intended, and you'll spot a number of wells, water, and springs that helped give the town its name. Markets fill the town square on Wednesday (farmers market) and Saturday (general goods).

Orientation to Wells

TOURIST INFORMATION

The TI is in the lobby of the Wells & Mendip Museum, across the green from the cathedral. Consider picking up their free town map or buying the £1 *Wells City Trail* booklet (Mon-Sat 10:00-17:00, Nov-March until 16:00, closed Sun year-round, 8 Cathedral Green, tel. 01749/671-770, www.wellssomerset.com). The TI's attached museum houses displays on the archaeology and geology of nearby Mendip Hills and Wookey Caves, along with an exhibit on World War I (£3, same hours as TI).

Walking Tour: If you're here on a Wednesday, consider a town walking tour (£7, departs 11:00 in peak season, 1.5 hours, leaves from The Crown on Market Place, www.wellswalkingtours.co.uk).

ARRIVAL IN WELLS

If you're coming by **bus**, you can get off in the city center at the Sadler Street stop, around the corner from the cathedral (tell the driver that's your stop). Or you can disembark at the big, well-

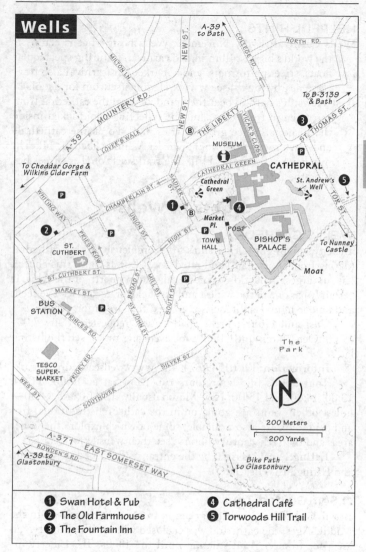

Wells

To Bath
A-39 to Bath
NORTH RD.
MILTON LN.
NEW ST.
MOUNTERY RD.
COLLEGE RD.
A-39
LOVER'S WALK
NEW ST.
THE LIBERTY
VICAR'S CLOSE
To B-3139 & Bath
ST. THOMAS ST.
③
To Cheddar Gorge & Wilkins Cider Farm
B
MUSEUM
CATHEDRAL GREEN
CATHEDRAL
St. Andrew's Well
⑤
Cathedral Green
TOR ST.
SADLER ST.
CHAMBERLAIN ST.
WHITING WAY
①
B
④
Market Pl.
POST
To Nunney Castle
②
UNION ST.
PRIEST ROW
HIGH ST.
TOWN HALL
P
BISHOP'S PALACE
ST. CUTHBERT
ST. CUTHBERT ST.
Moat
MARKET ST.
BROAD ST.
HILL ST.
SOUTH ST.
P
BUS STATION
PRINCES RD.
ST. JOHN ST.
TESCO SUPER-MARKET
PRIORY RD.
SILVER ST.
The Park
WEST ST.
SOUTHOVER
A-371
EAST SOMERSET WAY
ROWDEN'S RD.
A-39 to Glastonbury
200 Meters
200 Yards
Bike Path to Glastonbury

GLASTONBURY & WELLS

① Swan Hotel & Pub
② The Old Farmhouse
③ The Fountain Inn
④ Cathedral Café
⑤ Torwoods Hill Trail

organized bus station/parking lot (staffed Mon-Fri 9:30-13:30, closed Sat-Sun), about a five-minute walk from the town center at the south end of town. Find the Wells map at the head of the stalls to get oriented (the big church tower you see is *not* the cathedral); the signpost at the main pedestrian exit directs you downtown.

Drivers will find pay parking right on the main square, but because of confusing one-way streets, it's hard to reach; it's simpler to park at the Princes Road lot next to the bus station (enter on Priory Road) and walk five minutes to the cathedral.

HELPFUL HINTS

Wells Carnival: Every November Wells hosts what it claims is the world's biggest illuminated carnival, featuring spectacular floats, street performers, and a market fair (carnival also travels to nearby towns; see www.wellssomerset.com for details).

Best Views: It's hard to beat the grand views of the cathedral from the green in front of it...but the reflecting pool tucked inside the Bishop's Palace grounds tries hard. For a fine cathedral-and-town view from your own leafy hilltop bench, hike 10 minutes up Torwoods Hill. The trail starts on Tor Street behind the Bishop's Palace.

Sights in Wells

WELLS CATHEDRAL

The city's highlight is England's first completely Gothic cathedral (dating from about 1200 and rated ▲▲). Locals claim this church has the largest collection of medieval statuary north of the Alps. It certainly has one of the widest and most elaborate facades I've seen, and unique figure-eight "scissor arches" that are unforgettable.

Cost and Hours: Free, £6 donation requested; daily 7:00-19:00, Oct-March until 18:00; for evensong times, see the listing later.

Information: Tel. 01749/674-483, www.wellscathedral.org.uk.

Tours: Free one-hour tours run Mon-Sat at 10:00, 11:00, 13:00, 14:00, and 15:00; Nov-March usually at 12:00 and 14:00—unless other events are going on in the cathedral. Additional free and paid tours are also available, some of which explore the upper areas and the 17th-century library; see their website for details.

Eating: A café is right by the entrance (described in "Sleeping and Eating in Wells," later).

● Self-Guided Tour

Begin on the large, inviting **green** in front of the cathedral. In the Middle Ages, the cathedral was enclosed within "The Liberty," an area free from civil jurisdiction until the 1800s. The Liberty included the green on the west side of the cathedral, which, from the 13th to the 17th centuries, was a burial place for common folk, including 17th-century plague victims. The green became a cricket pitch, then a field for grazing animals and picnicking people. Today, it's the perfect spot to marvel at an impressive cathedral.

Peer up at the magnificent **facade.** The west front displays almost 300 original 13th-century carvings of kings and the Last Judgment. The bottom row of niches is empty, too easily reached by Cromwell's men, who were hell-bent on destroying "graven images." Stand back and imagine it as a grand Palm Sunday welcome with a cast of hundreds—all gaily painted back then, choristers singing boldly from holes above the doors and trumpets tooting through the holes up by the 12 apostles.

Now head **inside.** Visitors enter by going to the right, through the door under the small spire, into the lobby and welcome center.

At the **welcome center,** you'll be warmly greeted and reminded how expensive it is to maintain the cathedral. Pay the donation and pick up a map of the cathedral's highlights. Then head through the cloister and into the cathedral.

At your first glance down the nave, you're immediately struck by the general sense of light and the unique "scissors" or hourglass-shaped **double arch** (added in 1338 to transfer weight from the south—where the foundations were sinking under the tower's weight—to the east, where they were firm). Until Henry VIII and the Reformation, the interior was opulently painted in golds, reds, and greens. Later it was whitewashed. Then, in the 1840s, the church experienced the Victorian "great scrape," as locals peeled moldy whitewash off and revealed the bare stone we see today. The floral ceiling painting is based on the original medieval design: A single

pattern was discovered under the 17th-century whitewash and repeated throughout.

Small, ornate, 15th-century pavilion-like chapels flank the altar, carved in lacy Gothic for church VIPs. On the right, the **pulpit** features a post-Reformation, circa-1540 English script—rather than the standard Latin (see where the stonemason ran out of space

when carving the inscription—we've all been there). Since this was not a monastery church, the Reformation didn't destroy it as it did the Glastonbury Abbey church.

We'll do a quick clockwise spin around the cathedral's interior. First walk down the left aisle until you reach the north transept. The medieval **clock** does a silly but much-loved joust on the quarter-hour. If you get to watch the show, notice how like clockwork—the same rider gets clobbered, as he has for hundreds of years. The clock's face, which depicts the earth at the center of the universe, dates from 1390. The outer ring shows hours, the middle ring shows minutes, and the inner ring shows the dates of the month and phases of the moon. Above and to the right of the clock is Jack Blandiver, a chap carved out of wood in the 14th century. Beneath the clock, the fine **crucifix** (1947) was carved out of a yew tree. Also in the north transept is a door with well-worn steps leading up to the **Chapter House,** a grand space for huddles among church officials. Its sublime "tierce-ron" vaulting—a forerunner of the fan vaults you can see in later English Gothic style—make this one of the most impressive medieval ceilings in the country.

Now continue down the left aisle. On the right is the entrance to the **choir** (or "quire," the central zone where the daily services are sung). Go in and take a close look at the embroidery work on the cushions, which celebrate the hometowns of important local church leaders. Up above the east end of the choir is "Jesse's Window," depicting Jesus' family tree. It's also called the "Golden Window," because it's bathed in sunlight each morning.

Head back out to the aisle the way you came in, and continue to the end of the church. On the outside wall, on the left, is the entry to the undercroft, now a cathedral history exhibit worth a look. In the apse you'll find the **Lady Chapel.** Examine the medieval stained-glass windows. Do they look jumbled? In the 17th century, Puritan troops trashed the precious original glass. Much was repaired, but many of the broken panes were like a puzzle that was never solved. That's why today many of the windows are simply kaleidoscopes of colored glass.

Next to the chapel is the oldest known piece of wooden furniture in England: a **"cope chest,"** which is still used to store the clergy's garments. It is so large it can't be moved out through any of the cathedral's doors. Historians theorize that the chest is older than the existing building, and was originally installed around AD 800, in the Saxon church that predated the cathedral.

Now circle around and head up the other aisle. As you walk, notice that many of the black **tombstones** set in the floor have decorative recesses that aren't filled with brass (as they once were). After the Reformation in the 1530s, the church was short on cash, so they sold the brass lettering to raise money for roof repairs.

Once you reach the south transept, you'll find several items of interest. The **old Saxon font** survives from the previous church (AD 705) and has been the site of Wells baptisms for more than a thousand years. (Its carved arches were added by Normans in the

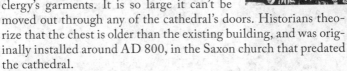

12th century, and the cover is from the 17th century.) In the far end of this transept (in the shade of the fancy chapels), a little of the original green and red wall painting, which wasn't whitewashed, survives.

Nearby, notice the **carvings** in the capitals of the freestanding pillars, with whimsical depictions of medieval life. On the first pillar, notice the man with a toothache and another man with a thorn in his foot. The second pillar tells a story of medieval justice: On the left, we see thieves stealing grapes; on the right, the woodcutter (with an ax) is warning the farmer (with the pitchfork) what's happening. Circle around to the back of the pillar for the rest of the story: On the left, the farmer chases one of the thieves, grabbing him by the ear. On the right, he clobbers the thief over the head with his pitchfork—so hard the farmer's hat falls off.

Also in the south transept, you'll find the entrance to the cathedral **Reading Room** and **Chained Library** (free, Mon-Fri 11:00-13:00 & 14:00-16:00, closed in winter; it's also often possible to step in for a quick look on Sat mornings). Housing a few old manuscripts, it offers a peek into a real 16th-century library. At the back of the Reading Room, peer through the doors and notice the irons chaining the books to the shelves—a reflection perhaps of the trust in the clergy at that time.

Head out into the cloister, then cross the courtyard back to the welcome center, shop, café, and exit. Go in peace.

MORE CATHEDRAL SIGHTS
▲▲Cathedral Evensong Service

The cathedral choir takes full advantage of heavenly acoustics with a nightly 45-minute evensong service. You'll sit right in the old "quire" as you listen to a great pipe organ and the world-famous Wells Cathedral choir.

Cost and Hours: Free, Mon-Sat at 17:15, Sun at 15:00, generally no service when school is out July-Aug unless a visiting choir performs, to check call 01749/674-483 or visit www.wellscathedral.org.uk. At 17:05 (Sun at 14:50), the verger ushers visitors to their seats. There's usually plenty of room.

Returning to Bath After the Evensong: Confirm the departure time for the last direct bus to Bath in advance—it's usually around 19:45; 19:20 on Sundays (10-minute walk from cathedral to station, bus may also depart from The Liberty stop—a 4-minute walk away).

Other Cathedral Concerts: The cathedral hosts several evening concerts each month (most £20-30, generally Thu-Sat at 19:00 or 19:30, buy tickets by phone or at box office in cathedral gift shop; Mon-Sat 10:30-16:30, Sun 11:30-16:30; tel. 01749/672-773). Concert tickets are also sometimes available at the TI, along with pamphlets listing what's on.

Vicars' Close

Lined with perfectly pickled 14th-century houses, this is the oldest continuously occupied complete street in Europe (since 1348; just a block north of the cathedral—go under the big arch and look left). It was built to house the vicar's choir, and it still houses church officials and choristers. These dwellings were bachelor pads until the Reformation allowed clerics to marry; they were then redesigned to accommodate families. Notice how the

close gets narrower at the top, creating the illusion that it is a longer lane than it is. Notice also the elevated passageway connecting these choristers' quarters with the church.

▲Bishop's Palace

Next to the cathedral stands the moated Bishop's Palace, built in the 13th century and still in use today as the residence of the bishop of Bath and Wells. While

the interior of the palace itself is dull, the grounds and gardens surrounding it are the most tranquil and scenic spot in Wells, with wonderful views of the cathedral. It's just the place for a relaxing walk in the park. Watch the swans ring the bell—hanging over the water just left of the entry gate—when they have an attack of the munchies.

Cost and Hours: £8; daily 10:00-18:00, Nov-March until 16:00, includes guided tour at set times, see schedule online or call; often closed on Sat for special events—call to confirm;

multimedia guide available for small fee; tel. 01749/988-111, www. bishopspalace.org.uk.

Visiting the Palace and Gardens: The palace's spring-fed moat was built in the 14th century to protect the bishop during squabbles with the borough. Bishops would generously release this potable water into the town during local festivals. Now the moat serves primarily as a pool for mute swans. The bridge was last drawn in 1831. Crossing that bridge, you'll buy your ticket and enter the grounds (past the old-timers playing a proper game of croquet—several times a week after 13:30). On your right, pass through the evocative ruins of the Great Hall (which was deserted and left to gradually deteriorate), and stroll through the chirpy south lawn. If you're feeling energetic, hike up to the top of the ramparts that encircle the property.

Circling around the far side of the mansion, walk through a door in the rampart wall, cross the wooden bridge, and follow a path to a smaller bridge and the wells (springs) that gave the city its name. Surrounding a reflecting pool with the cathedral towering overhead, these flower-bedecked pathways are idyllic. Nearby are an arboretum, picnic area, and sweet little pea-patch gardens.

After touring the gardens, the mansion's interior is a let-down—despite the borrowable descriptions that struggle to make the dusty old place meaningful. Have a spot of tea in the café (with outdoor garden seating—free access), or climb the creaky wooden staircase to wander long halls lined with portraits of bishops past.

SIGHTS NEAR WELLS

The following stops are best for drivers.

Cheddar Cheese

If you're in the mood for a picnic, drop by any local aromatic cheese shop for a great selection of tasty Somerset cheeses. Real farmhouse cheddar puts Velveeta to shame. The **Cheddar Gorge Cheese Company,** eight miles west of Wells, gives guests a chance to see the cheese-making process and enjoy a sample (£2, daily 10:00-15:00; take the A-39, then the A-371 to Cheddar Gorge; tel. 01934/742-810, www.cheddargorgecheeseco.co.uk).

Scrumpy Farms

Scrumpy is the wonderfully dangerous hard cider brewed in this part of England. You don't find it served in many pubs because of the unruly crowd it attracts. Scrumpy, at around 7 percent alcohol, will rot your socks—this is potent stuff. "Scrumpy Jack," carbonated mass-produced cider, is not real scrumpy. The real stuff is "rough farmhouse cider." It's said some farmers throw a side of beef into the vat, and when fermentation is done only the teeth remain. (Some use a pair of old boots, for the tannin from the leather.)

TIs list cider farms open to the public, such as **Wilkins Cider Farm** (also known as Land's End Farm)—a great Back Door travel experience (free, Mon-Sat 10:00-20:00, Sun until 13:00; west of Wells in Mudgley, take the B-3139 from Wells to Wedmore, then the B-3151 south for 2 miles, farm is a quarter-mile off the B-3151—tough to find, get close and ask locals; tel. 01934/712-385, www.wilkinscider.com).

Apples are pressed from August through December. Hard cider, while not quite scrumpy, is also typical of the West Country, but more fashionable, "decent," and accessible. You can get a pint of hard cider at nearly any pub, drawn straight from the barrel—dry, medium, or sweet.

Nunney Castle

The centerpiece of the charming and quintessentially English village of Nunney (between Bath and Glastonbury, off the A-361) is a striking 14th-century castle surrounded by a fairy-tale moat. Its rare, French-style design brings to mind the Paris Bastille. The year 1644 was a tumultuous one for Nunney. Its noble family was royalist (and likely closet Catholics). They defied Parliament, so Parliament ordered their castle "slighted" (deliberately destroyed) to ensure that it would threaten the order of the land no more. Looking at this castle, so daunting in the age of bows and arrows, you can see how it was no match for the modern cannon. The pretty Mendip village of Nunney, with its little brook, is also worth a wander.

Cost and Hours: Free, visitable at "any reasonable time," tel. 0370/333-1181, www.english-heritage.org.uk.

Sleeping and Eating in Wells

Sleeping: Wells is a pleasant overnight stop, with a few accommodation options.

$$$ Swan Hotel, a Best Western Plus facing the cathedral, is a big, comfortable, 50-room hotel. Prices for their Tudor-style rooms vary based on whether you want extras like a four-poster bed or a cathedral view. They also rent five apartments in the village

(Sadler Street, tel. 01749/836-300, www.swanhotelwells.co.uk, info@swanhotelwells.co.uk).

$$ The Old Farmhouse, a five-minute walk from the town center and cathedral, welcomes you with a secluded front garden and two tastefully decorated rooms (2-night minimum, secure parking, next to the gas station at 62 Chamberlain Street, tel. 01749/675-058, theoldfarmhousewells@hotmail.com, charming owners Felicity and Christopher Wilkes).

Eating: Downtown Wells is tiny. A fine variety of eating options are within a block or two of its market square, including classic pubs and little delis, bakeries, and takeaway places serving light meals.

$$ The Fountain Inn, on a quiet street 50 yards behind the cathedral, serves good pub grub (daily 12:00-14:00 & 18:00-21:00 except no dinner on Sun or lunch on Mon, pub open later, St. Thomas Street, tel. 01749/672-317).

$ The **café** in the cathedral welcome center offers a handy—if not heavenly—lunch (Mon-Sat 10:00-16:00, Sun from 11:00, may close earlier in winter, tel. 01749/676-543).

$$ The **Swan Hotel** has a pub that serves lunches in their garden across the street with a view over the green and cathedral (Sadler Street, tel. 01749/836-300).

Wells Connections

The nearest train station is in Bath. The bus station in Wells is at a well-organized bus parking lot at the intersection of Priory and Princes roads. Local buses are run by First Bus Company (for Wells, tel. 0845-602-0156, www.firstgroup.com), while buses to and from London are run by National Express (tel. 0871-781-8181, www.nationalexpress.com).

From Wells by Bus to: Bath (nearly hourly, less frequent on Sun, 75 minutes; if you miss the last direct bus to Bath, catch the bus to Bristol—runs hourly and takes one hour, then a 15-minute train ride to Bath), **Glastonbury** (2/hour, 20 minutes, take bus #376 toward the town of Street), **London**'s Victoria Coach Station (1/day direct, 4 hours; otherwise hourly with a change in Bristol).

GLASTONBURY & WELLS

AVEBURY, STONEHENGE & SALISBURY

Ooooh, mystery, history. England's southwest countryside holds some of the country's most goose-pimply prehistoric sites, as well as a particularly fine cathedral town. Get Neolithic at every druid's favorite stone circles, Avebury and Stonehenge. Then stop by Salisbury for its colorful markets and soaring cathedral.

PLANNING YOUR TIME

Avebury, Stonehenge, and Salisbury make a wonderful day out from Bath. With a car, you can do all three in a day if you're selective with your sightseeing.

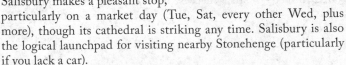

Everybody needs to see Stonehenge, but I'll tell you now: It looks just like it looks (though the visitors center makes it a well-worthwhile visit). Avebury is the connoisseur's stone circle: more subtle and welcoming.

Just an hour from Bath, Salisbury makes a pleasant stop, particularly on a market day (Tue, Sat, every other Wed, plus more), though its cathedral is striking any time. Salisbury is also the logical launchpad for visiting nearby Stonehenge (particularly if you lack a car).

GETTING AROUND THE REGION

By Car: Avebury, Stonehenge, and Salisbury are each about 35-40 miles from Bath and 85-90 miles from London. Drivers can do a 104-mile loop from Bath to Avebury (25 miles) to Stonehenge (30

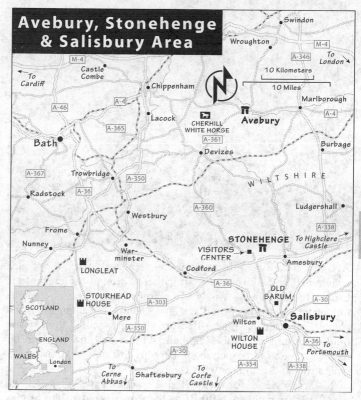

Avebury, Stonehenge & Salisbury Area

miles) to Salisbury (9 miles) and back to Bath (40 miles). For tips on incorporating Glastonbury and Wells, see the previous chapter.

By Bus and Train: The nearest train station is in Bath, with regular service from London's Paddington Station (2/hour, 1.5 hours). Many buses run between Bath and **Avebury,** all requiring one or two transfers (hourly, 2.5 hours, transfer at Trowbridge or Devizes). There's no bus between Avebury and Stonehenge.

A one-hour train trip connects Bath to **Salisbury** (hourly direct). With the best public transportation of all these towns, Salisbury is a good jumping-off point for **Stonehenge** or Avebury by bus or car. Stonehenge Tour buses run between Salisbury, Old Sarum, and Stonehenge (see "Getting to Stonehenge," later). Buses also run from Salisbury to **Avebury** (see "Salisbury Connections," later). For fares and schedules, check Traveline South West's easy-to-use website (www.travelinesw.com, tel. 0871-200-2233).

By Tour: From Bath, if you don't have a car, the most convenient and quickest way to see Avebury and Stonehenge is with a minibus tour. Mad Max is the liveliest of the tours leaving from Bath (see "Tours in and near Bath" on page 412).

Avebury

Avebury is an open-air museum of prehistory, with a complex of fascinating Neolithic sites all gathered around the great stone henge (circle). Among England's many stone circles, Avebury is unique for its vast size—a village is tucked into its center, and roads rumble between its stones. Because the surrounding area sports only a thin skin of topsoil over chalk, it is naturally treeless (similar to the area around Stonehenge). Perhaps this unique landscape—where the land connects with the big sky—made it the choice of prehistoric societies for their religious monuments. Whatever the case, Avebury dates to 2800 BC—six centuries older than Stonehenge. This complex, the St. Peter's Basilica of Neolithic civilization, makes for a fascinating visit. Some visitors enjoy it even more than Stonehenge.

Orientation to Avebury

Avebury is the name of a huge stone circle, as well as the tiny village that sits surrounded by its stones. It's easy to reach by car, but more difficult by public transportation (see "Getting Around the Region," earlier).

Tourist Information: There's no TI, but there's a National Trust information center in the Old Farmyard, and maps and booklets are sold in shops in the village. For more information on the Avebury sights, see www.nationaltrust.org.uk.

Parking: There's no public parking in the village center. Visitors park in a flat-fee National Trust lot along the A-4361—a five-minute walk from the village (£7, £4 after 15:00 and in winter, pay with coins or credit card at the machine, open summer 9:30-18:30, off-season until 16:30).

Stone Circles: The Riddle of the Rocks

Britain is home to roughly 800 stone circles, most of them rudimentary, jaggedly sparse boulder rings that lack the iconic

upright-and-lintel form of Stonehenge. But their misty, mossy settings provide curious travelers with an intimate and accessible glimpse of the mysterious people who lived in prehistoric Britain.

Bronze Age Britain (2000-600 BC) was populated by farming folk who had mastered the craft of smelting heated tin and copper together to produce bronze, which was used to make durable tools and weapons. Late in the Bronze Age, many of these clannish communities also put considerable effort into gathering huge rocks and arranging them into circles, perhaps for use in rituals with long-forgotten meanings. Some scholars believe the circles may have been used as solar observatories—used to calculate solstices and equinoxes to help plan life-sustaining seasonal crop-planting cycles. A few human remains have been discovered in the centers of some circles, but their primary use seems to have been for ceremonial purposes, not as burial sites. The superstitious people of the Middle Ages believed Stonehenge was arranged by giants (makes sense to me); nearby circles were thought to be petrified partiers who had dared to dance on the Sabbath.

Britain's stone circles generally lie in Scotland, Wales, and at the fringes of England. You'll find them marked in the Ordnance Survey atlas and signposted along rural roads. Ask a local farmer for directions—and savor the experience. I've highlighted my favorites in this book, and described each one in case you're being selective.

Stonehenge is by far the most famous, the only one with horizontal "lintels" connecting the monoliths, and comes with the most insightful visitors center.

Avebury is by far the biggest—so large that a small village was built inside it. Less crowded and easier to visit than Stonehenge, it's easy and fun to explore on your own.

Castlerigg is a pretty standard-issue stone circle, but it's handy for those going to the Lake District (just off the main road into Keswick; see page 738).

Scorhill, in Dartmoor, is the most remote, mysterious, and magical stone circle, requiring a long drive on rough roads, then a stroll across a moor. It's hard to reach but worth the effort (see page 351).

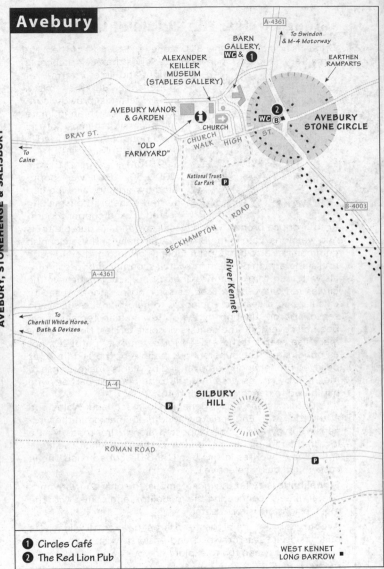

Avebury

ALEXANDER
KEILLER
MUSEUM
(STABLES GALLERY)

BARN
GALLERY,
WC & 1

EARTHEN
RAMPARTS

AVEBURY MANOR
& GARDEN

CHURCH

"OLD
FARMYARD"

BRAY ST.

CHURCH
WALK

HIGH

WC B 2

AVEBURY
STONE CIRCLE

ST.

To
Caine

To Swindon
& M-4 Motorway

A-4361

National Trust
Car Park P

BECKHAMPTON   ROAD

River Kennet

B-4003

A-4361

To
Cherhill White Horse,
Bath & Devizes

A-4

P

SILBURY
HILL

ROMAN ROAD

P

1 Circles Café
2 The Red Lion Pub

WEST KENNET
LONG BARROW

AVEBURY, STONEHENGE & SALISBURY

Sights in Avebury

All of Avebury's prehistoric sights—which spread over a wide
area—are free to visit and always open. The underwhelming museum and mansion charge admission and have limited hours. I've
linked the sights with directions for drivers who want to make a
targeted visit to all that Avebury has to offer.

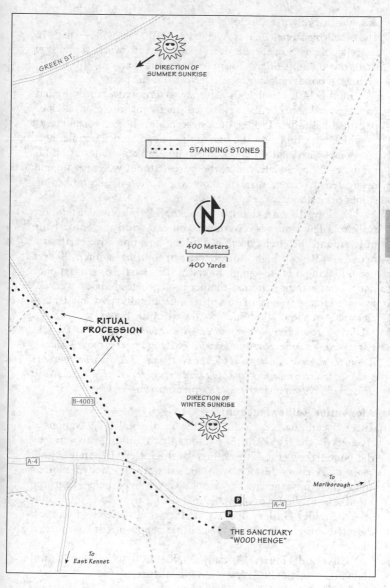

• *From the National Trust parking lot, follow the path five minutes through fields to the village center. On your right, you'll see the first access point to the big stone circle. (To pass through the gate, slide the handle sideways rather than lifting it.) Take some time exploring the remarkable...*

▲▲Avebury Stone Circle

The Neolithic stone circle at Avebury is 1,400 feet wide—that's 16 times as big as Stonehenge. It's so vast that it dwarfs the village that grew up in its midst. You're free to wander among 100 stones, ditches, mounds, and curious patterns from the past.

In the 14th century, in a frenzy of ignorance and religious paranoia, Avebury villagers buried many of these mysterious pagan stones. Their 18th-century descendants hosted social events in which they broke up the remaining pagan stones (topple, heat up, douse with cold water, and scavenge broken stones as building blocks). In modern times, the buried stones were dug up and re-erected. Concrete markers show where the missing broken-up stones once stood.

Explore. Touch a chunk of prehistory. While even just a short walk to a few stones is rewarding, you can stroll the entire half-mile around the circle, much of it along an impressive earthwork henge—a 30-foot-high outer bank surrounding a ditch 30 feet deep, making a 60-foot-high rampart. This earthen rampart once had stones standing around the perimeter, placed about every 30 feet, and four grand causeway entries. Originally, two smaller circles made of about 200 stones stood within the henge.

• *Directly across from the parking-lot trail, follow signs into the* Old Farmyard—*a little courtyard of rustic buildings near Avebury Manor. Today these house museums, WCs, the National Trust information center, a shop, a recommended café, and the two sights described next. (Note: These sights pale in comparison to the prehistoric sights.)*

Alexander Keiller Museum

This museum, named for the archaeologist who led excavations at Avebury in the late 1930s, is housed in two buildings (covered by the same ticket). The 17th-century **Barn Gallery** illustrates 6,000 years of Avebury history, with kid-friendly interactive exhibits about the landscape and the people who've lived here—from the Stone Age to Victorian times. Across the farmyard, the small, old-school **Stables Gallery** displays artifacts and skeletons from past digs and a re-creation of what Neolithic people might have looked like.

Cost and Hours: £5, daily 10:00-18:00, Nov-March until 16:00, tel. 01672/539-250, www.nationaltrust.org.uk.

• *Behind the Stables Gallery is the...*

Avebury Manor and Garden

Archaeologist Alexander Keiller's former home, a 500-year-old estate, was restored by a team of historians and craftspeople in collaboration with the BBC (for their 2011 documentary *The Manor Reborn*). Nine rooms were decorated in five different period styles showing the progression of design, from a Tudor wedding chapel to a Queen Anne-era bedroom to an early-20th-century billiards room. The grounds were also spruced up with a topiary and a Victorian kitchen garden. While it's fun to tour—and the docents enjoy explaining how each room was painstakingly researched and re-created—it's pricey and far from authentic...and it has nothing to do with Avebury's impressive circle.

Cost and Hours: £11, limited number of timed tickets sold per day; daily 11:00-17:00, shorter hours off-season, closed Jan-mid-Feb, last entry one hour before closing; buy tickets at Alexander Keiller Museum's Barn Gallery, tel. 01672/539-250, www.nationaltrust.org.uk.

• *The following sights are a long walk or a short drive from the center of Avebury.*

First, from the Avebury village center, the road southeast toward West Kennet and Malborough (B-4003, a.k.a. West Kennet Avenue) is evocatively lined with an "avenue" of stones. This is known as the...

▲Ritual Procession Way

This double line of stones provided a ritual procession way leading from Avebury to a long-gone wooden circle dubbed "The Sanctuary." This "wood henge," thought to have been 1,000 years older than everything else in the area, is considered to have been the genesis of Avebury and its big stone circle. (You can see the site of the former Sanctuary—turn left onto the A-4, look for the marked pullout on the left, and walk across the road—but all you'll see is an empty field with concrete blocks marking where the circle once stood.) Most of the stones standing along the procession way today were reconstructed in modern times.

• *From the end of the Ritual Procession Way, you can turn right (west) on the A-4. After a mile or so, look to the right for the dome-shaped green hill. Just beyond it is a handy parking lot. (Walkers can reach this in about 20 minutes from the National Trust parking lot.)*

▲Silbury Hill

This pyramid-shaped hill (reminiscent of Glastonbury Tor) is a 130-foot-high, yet-to-be-explained mound of chalk just outside of Avebury. More than 4,000 years old, this mound is considered the largest man-made object in pre-historic Europe (with the surface area of London's Trafalgar Square and the height of the Nelson Column). It's a reminder that we've only just scratched

the surface of England's mysterious and ancient religious landscape.

Inspired by a legend that the hill hid a gold statue in its center, locals tunneled through Silbury Hill in 1830, undermining the structure. Work is underway to restore the hill, which remains closed to the public. Archaeologists (who date things like this by carbon-dating snails and other little critters killed in its construction) figure Silbury Hill took only 60 years to build, in about 2200 BC. This makes Silbury Hill the last element built at Avebury and contemporaneous with Stonehenge. Some think it may have been an observation point for all the other bits of the Avebury site. You can still see evidence of a spiral path leading up the hill and a moat at its base.

The Roman road detoured around Silbury Hill. (Roman engineers often used features of the landscape as visual reference points when building roads. Their roads would commonly kink at the crest of hills or other landmarks, where they realigned with a new visual point.) Later, the hill sported a wooden Saxon fort, which likely acted as a lookout for marauding Vikings. And in World War II, the Royal Observer Corps stationed men up here to count and report Nazi bombers on raids.

Nearby: Across the road from Silbury Hill (a 15-minute walk through the fields) is **West Kennet Long Barrow.** This burial chamber, the best-preserved Stone Age chamber tomb in the UK, stands intact on a ridge. It lines up with the rising sun on the summer solstice. You can walk inside the barrow, or sit on its roof and survey the Neolithic landscape around you.

• *The final sight is about four miles west of Avebury, along the A-4 toward Calne (and Bath), just before the village of Cherhill. Pull over at the Avebury end of the village and look for the hill-capping obelisk; below it, carved into the hillside, is the...*

Cherhill White Horse

Throughout southern England, you'll see horses (and other objects) like this one carved into the downs (chalk hills). There is one genuinely prehistoric white horse in England (the Uffington White Horse); the Cherhill White Horse is an 18th-century creation. Prehistoric discoveries were all the rage in the 1700s, and it was a fad to make fake ones by cutting into the thin layer of topsoil to expose the chalk beneath. Nowadays, figures like this are cemented and painted white so that the design doesn't need to be weeded. Above the horse are the remains of an Iron Age hill fort known as Oldbury Castle—described on an information board at the pullout.

Eating in Avebury

$ Circles Café is practical and pleasant, serving healthy lunches, including vegan and gluten-free dishes, and cream teas on most days (daily 10:00-17:30, Nov-March until 16:00, no hot food after 14:30, in the Barn Gallery on the Old Farmyard, tel. 01672/539-250).

$$ The Red Lion—a classic thatched-roof pub right in the heart of Avebury village—has updated but unpretentious pub grub; a creaky, well-worn, dart-throwing ambience; a medieval well in its dining room; and ample outdoor seating (daily 10:00-22:00, High Street, tel. 01672/539-266).

Stonehenge

As old as the pyramids, and far older than the Acropolis and the Colosseum, this iconic stone circle amazed medieval Europeans, who figured it was built by a race of giants. And it still impresses visitors today. As one of Europe's most famous sights, Stonehenge, worth ▲▲▲, does a valiant job of retaining an air of mystery and majesty (partly because cordons, which keep hordes of tourists from trampling all over it, foster the illusion that it stands alone in a field). Although cynics manage to be underwhelmed by Stonehenge, most of its almost one million annual visitors agree that it's well worth the trip. At few sights in Europe will you overhear so many awe-filled comments.

GETTING TO STONEHENGE

Stonehenge is about 90 miles southwest of central London. To reach it from London, you can take a bus tour; go on a guided tour that uses public transportation; or do it on your own using public transit, connecting via Salisbury. It's not worth the hassle or expense to rent a car just for a Stonehenge day trip.

By Bus Tour from London: Several companies offer big-bus

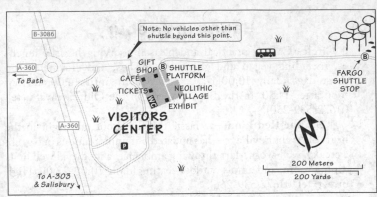

Note: No vehicles other than shuttle beyond this point.

day trips to Stonehenge from London, often with stops in Bath, Windsor, Salisbury, and/or Avebury. These generally cost about £50-100 (including Stonehenge admission), last 8-12 hours, and pack a 45-seat bus. Some include hotel pickup, admission fees, and meals; understand what's included before you book. The more destinations listed for a tour, the less time you'll have at any one stop. Well-known companies are **Evan Evans** (their bare-bones Stonehenge Express gets you there and back for £54, tel. 020/7950-1777 or US tel. 800-422-9022, www.evanevanstours.co.uk) and **Golden Tours** (£53, tel. 020/7630-2028 or US toll-free tel. 800-509-2507, www.goldentours.com). **International Friends** runs pricier but smaller 16-person tours that include Windsor and Bath (£145, tel. 01223/244-555, www.internationalfriends.co.uk).

By Bus Tour from Bath: I prefer **Mad Max**'s minibus tour and **Scarper Tours**' shuttle bus service. For details and additional options, see page 413.

By Guided Tour on Public Transport from London: The "Stonehenge and Salisbury Excursion" from **London Walks** travels by train and bus on Tuesdays from mid-May through early October (£93, includes all transportation, Salisbury walking tour, entry fees, and guided tours of Stonehenge and Salisbury Cathedral; pay guide, cash only, Tue at 8:45, meet at Waterloo Station's main ticket office, opposite Platform 16, verify price and schedule online, advance booking not required, tel. 020/7624-3978, www. walks.com).

On Your Own on Public Transport via Salisbury: From London, you can catch a train to Salisbury, then go by tour bus or taxi to Stonehenge. **Trains** to Salisbury run from London's Waterloo Station (around £42 for same-day return leaving weekdays after 9:30, 2/hour, 1.5 hours, tel. 0345-600-0650, www. southwesternrailway.com or tel. 03457-484-950, www.nationalrail.

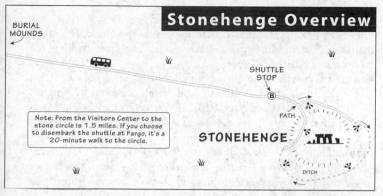

Stonehenge Overview

BURIAL MOUNDS

SHUTTLE STOP

Note: From the Visitors Center to the stone circle is 1.5 miles. If you choose to disembark the shuttle at Fargo, it's a 20-minute walk to the circle.

PATH

STONEHENGE

DITCH

AVEBURY, STONEHENGE & SALISBURY

co.uk). For details on trains to Salisbury from Bath, see "Getting Around the Region" at the beginning of this chapter.

From Salisbury, take the **Stonehenge Tour bus** to the site. These distinctive double-decker buses leave from the Salisbury train station, stop in Salisbury's center, then make a circuit to Stonehenge and Old Sarum, with lovely scenery and a decent light commentary along the way (£15, £30 includes Stonehenge as well as Old Sarum—whether you want it or not; tickets good all day, order online or pay driver; daily June-Aug 10:00-17:00, 2/hour; may not run June 21 because of solstice crowds, shorter hours and hourly departures off-season; 30 minutes from station to Stonehenge, tel. 01202/338-420, timetable at www.thestonehengetour. info).

A **taxi** from Salisbury to Stonehenge can make sense for groups (about £40-60). Try On Line City Cabs (tel. 01722/509-090, onlinecitycabs.co.uk) or Value Cars Taxis (tel. 01722/505-050, www.salisbury-valuecars.co.uk).

By Car: Stonehenge is well-signed just off the A-303, about 15 minutes north of Salisbury, an hour southeast of Bath, an hour east of Glastonbury, and an hour south of Avebury.

Stonehenge is about 70 miles and 1.5 hours west of **London Heathrow** (barring traffic). From the M-25 ring road, connect with the M-3 toward Southampton. Past Basingstoke, exit to the A-303. Continue west past Andover to Amesbury. In 3.5 miles, turn onto northbound A-360 at the roundabout, and follow "From Salisbury" directions from that point (see next).

From **Salisbury,** head north on the A-360 (at the St. Paul's roundabout, take the second exit, direction: Devizes). Continue for eight miles, crossing the A-303 roundabout. In one more mile you'll encounter another roundabout; follow it around to the exit for the well-marked visitors center.

ORIENTATION TO STONEHENGE

The visitors center, located 1.25 miles west of the circle, is a minimalist steel structure with a subtly curved roofline, evoking the landscape of Salisbury Plain.

Cost: £19, purchase timed-entry ticket in advance online, ticket includes shuttle-bus ride to stone circle, covered by English Heritage Pass (see page 910). If you neglect to buy a ticket in advance, you'll pay more and risk wasting time at the very crowded sight.

Hours: Daily 9:30-19:00, June-Aug 9:00-20:00, mid-Oct-March 9:30-17:00. Note that the last ticket is sold two hours before closing. Expect shorter hours and possible closures June 20-22 due to huge, raucous solstice crowds.

Information: Tel. 0370-333-1181, www.english-heritage.org.uk/stonehenge.

Advance Tickets Recommended: Up to 9,000 visitors are allowed to enter each day. While Stonehenge rarely sells out completely, you can avoid the long ticket-buying line by prebooking at least 24 hours in advance at www.english-heritage.org.uk/stonehenge. When prebooking, you'll be asked to select a 30-minute entry window. Try to be on time, but if you're late you can generally sweet talk your way in. Even those with a timed entry may have to wait in line for the shuttle bus to and from the stones.

Crowd-Beating Tips: For a less crowded, more mystical experience, come early or late. Things are pretty quiet before about 10:30 (head out to the stones first, then circle back to the exhibits); at the end of the day, aim to arrive just before the "last ticket" time (two hours before closing). Stonehenge is most crowded when school's out: summer weekends (especially holiday weekends) and anytime in August.

Tours: Worthwhile audioguides are available behind the ticket counter (included with Heritage Pass, otherwise £3). Or you can use the visitors center's free Wi-Fi to download the free "Stonehenge Audio Tour" app.

Visiting the Inner Stones: For the true Stonehenge fan, special one-hour access to the stones' inner circle is available early in the morning (times vary depending on sunrise; the earliest visit is at 5:00 in June and July) or after closing to the general public. Touching the stones is not allowed. Only 30 people are allowed at a time, so reserve well in advance (£45, allows you to revisit the site the same day at no extra charge, tel. 0370-333-0605). For details see the English Heritage website (select "Plan Your Visit," then "Stone Circle Access").

Length of This Tour: Allow at least two hours to see everything.

Services: The visitors center has WCs and a large gift shop. Services at the circle itself are limited to emergency WCs. Even in summer, carry a jacket, as there are no trees to act as a windbreak and there's a reason Salisbury Plain is so green.

Eating: A large **$ café** within the visitors center serves hot drinks, soup, sandwiches, and salads.

◐ SELF-GUIDED TOUR

This commentary is designed to supplement the sight's audioguide. Start by touring the visitors center, then take a shuttle (or walk) to the stone circle. If you arrive early in the day, do the stones first—before they get crowded—then circle back to the visitors center.

• *As you enter the complex, on the right is the...*

Permanent Exhibit

This excellent, state-of-the-art exhibit uses an artful combination of multimedia displays and actual artifacts to provide context for the stones.

You'll begin by standing in the center of a virtual Stonehenge, watching its evolution through 5,000 years—including simulated solstice sunrises and sunsets.

Then you'll head into the exhibits, where prehistoric bones, tools, and pottery shards tell the story of the people who built Stonehenge, how they lived, and why they might have built the stone circle. Find the forensic reconstruction of a Neolithic man, based on a skeleton unearthed in 1863. Small models illustrate how Stonehenge developed from a simple circle of short, stubby stones to the stout ring we know today. And a large screen shows the entire archaeological area surrounding Stonehenge (which is just one of many mysterious prehistoric landmarks near here). In 2010, within sight of Stonehenge, archaeologists discovered another 5,000-year-old henge, which they believe once encircled a wooden "twin" of the famous circle. Recent excavations revealed that people had been living on the site since around 3000 BC—about five centuries earlier than anyone had realized.

In the small side room, an exhibit examines the iconic status of Stonehenge, including its frequent appearances in popular culture (strangely, no Spinal Tap) and its history as a tourist destination. See the vintage Guinness ad showing smiling people having a picnic on the rocks.

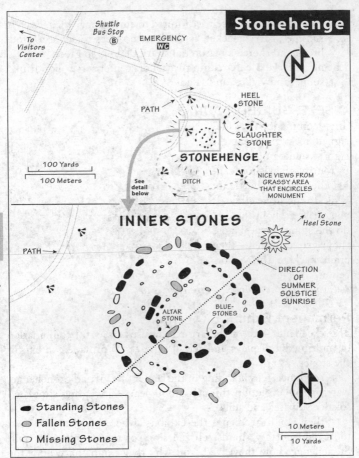

AVEBURY, STONEHENGE & SALISBURY

Then step outside and explore a village of reconstructed **Neo-lithic huts** modeled after the traces of a village discovered just northeast of Stonehenge. Step into the thatched-roof huts to see primitive "wicker" furniture and straw blankets. Docents demonstrate Neolithic tools—made of wood, flint, and antler. You'll also see a huge, life-size replica of the rolling wooden sledge thought to have been used to slo-o-owly roll the stones across Salisbury Plain. While you can't touch the stones at the site itself, you can touch the one loaded onto this sledge.

• Shuttle buses to the stone circle depart every 5-10 minutes from the platform behind the gift shop (there may be a wait). The trip takes six minutes. If you'd prefer, you can walk 1.5 miles through the fields to the site (use the map you receive with your ticket, or ask a staff member for directions).

Along the way, you have the option of stopping at **Fargo Plantation**, *where you can see several burial mounds (tell the shuttle attendant when you first get on if you want to disembark here). After wandering through the burial mounds, you'll need to walk the rest of the way to the stone circle (about 20 minutes).*

Stone Circle

As you approach the massive structure, walk right up to the knee-high cordon and let your fellow 21st-century tourists melt away. It's just you and the druids...

England has hundreds of stone circles, but Stonehenge—which literally means "hanging stones"—is unique. It's the only one that has horizontal cross-pieces (called lintels) spanning the vertical monoliths, and the only one with stones that have been made smooth and uniform. What you see here is a bit more than half the original structure—the rest was quarried centuries ago for other buildings.

Now do a slow **clockwise spin** around the monument, and ponder the following points. As you walk, mentally flesh out the missing pieces and re-erect the rubble. Knowledgeable guides posted around the site are happy to answer your questions.

It's now believed that Stonehenge, which was built in phases between 3000 and 1500 BC, was originally used as a cremation cemetery. But that's not the end of the story, as the monument was expanded over the millennia. This was a hugely significant location to prehistoric peoples. There are several hundred burial mounds within a three-mile radius of Stonehenge—some

likely belonging to kings or chieftains. Some of the human remains are of people from far away, and others show signs of injuries—evidence that Stonehenge may have been used as a place of medicine or healing.

Whatever its original purpose, Stonehenge still functions as a celestial calendar. As the sun rises on the summer solstice (June 21), the **"heel stone"**—the one set apart from the rest, near the road—lines up with the sun and the altar at the center of the stone circle. A study of more than 300 similar circles in Britain found that each was designed to calculate the movement of the sun, moon, and stars, and to predict eclipses in order to help early societies know when to plant, harvest, and party. Even in modern times, as the summer solstice sun sets in just the right slot at Stonehenge, pagans boogie.

Some believe that Stonehenge is built at the precise point where six **"ley lines"** intersect. Ley lines are theoretical lines of magnetic or spiritual power that crisscross the globe. Belief in the power of these lines has gone in and out of fashion over time. They are believed to have been very important to prehistoric peoples, but then were largely ignored until the early 20th century, when the English writer Alfred Watkins popularized them (to the scorn of serious scientists). More recently, the concept has been embraced by the New Age movement. Without realizing it, you follow these ley lines all the time: Many of England's modern highways follow prehistoric paths, and most churches are built over prehistoric monuments—placed where ley lines intersect. If you're a skeptic, ask one of the guides at Stonehenge to explain the mystique of this paranormal tradition that continued for centuries; it's creepy...and convincing.

Notice that two of the stones (facing the shuttle bus stop) are blemished. At the base of one monolith, it looks like someone has pulled back the stone to reveal a concrete skeleton. This is a clumsy **repair job** to fix damage done long ago by souvenir seekers, who actually rented hammers and chisels to take home a piece of Stonehenge. Look to the right of the repaired stone: The back of another stone is missing the same thin layer of protective lichen that covers the others. The lichen—and some of the stone itself—was sandblasted off to remove graffiti. (No wonder they've got Stonehenge roped off now.) The repairs were intentionally done in a different color, so as not to appear like the original stone.

Stonehenge's builders used two different types of stone. The tall, stout monoliths and lintels are sandstone blocks called **sarsen stones.** Most of the monoliths weigh about 25 tons (the largest is 45 tons), and the lintels are about 7 tons apiece. These sarsen stones were brought from "only" 20 miles away. Scientists have chemically matched the shorter stones in the middle—called **bluestones**—to outcrops on the south coast of Wales...240 miles away (close if you're taking a train, but far if you're packing a megalith). Imagine the logistical puzzle of floating six-ton stones across Wales' Severn Estuary and up the River Avon, then rolling them on logs about 20 miles to this position...an impressive feat, even in our era of skyscrapers.

Why didn't the builders of Stonehenge use what seem like perfectly adequate stones nearby? This, like many other questions about Stonehenge, remains shrouded in mystery. Think again about the ley lines. Ponder the fact that many experts accept none of the explanations of how these giant stones were transported. Then imagine congregations gathering here 5,000 years ago, raising thought levels, creating a powerful life force transmitted along the ley lines. Maybe a particular kind of stone was essential for maximum energy transmission. Maybe the stones were levitated here. Maybe psychics really do create powerful vibes. Maybe not. It's as unbelievable as electricity used to be.

Salisbury

Salisbury, an attractive small city set in the middle of the expansive Salisbury Plain, is the natural launch pad for visiting nearby Stonehenge. But it's also a fine destination in its own right, with a walkable core, a famously soaring cathedral (with England's tallest spire and largest green), and a thriving twice-weekly market (Tue and Sat). While well-cared-for, practical Salisbury isn't particularly cute or quaint. But that's part of its charm.

As the city most associated with Stonehenge, it's no surprise that Salisbury also has a very long history: It was originally settled during the Bronze Age—possibly as early as 600 BC—and later became a Roman town called Sarum (located on a hill above today's city). When the old settlement outgrew its boundaries, the townspeople relocated to the river valley below.

Today, sightseers flow through Salisbury on their way to Stonehenge. But if you have time to spare, spend some of it exploring this fine town.

Orientation to Salisbury

Salisbury (pop. 45,000) stretches along the River Avon in the shadow of its huge landmark cathedral. The heart of the city clusters around the vast Market Place. A few short blocks to the south is the walled complex of the Cathedral Close.

TOURIST INFORMATION

The TI is just off Market Place. If you're headed to Stonehenge, you can buy tickets here (Mon-Fri 9:00-17:00, Sat 10:00-16:00, Sun

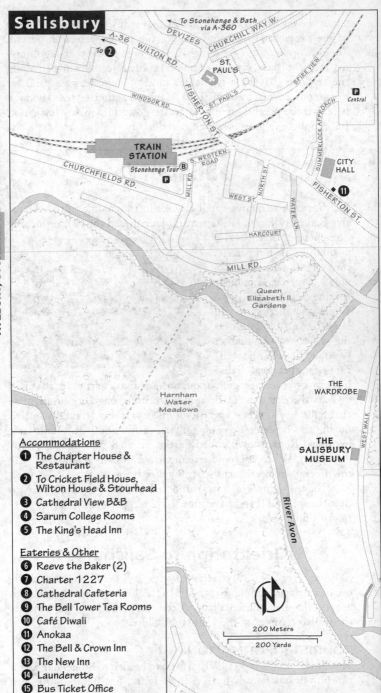

Salisbury

To Stonehenge & Bath
via A-360

DEVIZES

CHURCHILL WAY W.

A-36

WILTON RD.

To ②

ST. PAUL'S

SPIRE VIEW

WINDSOR RD.

FISHERTON ST.

ST. PAULS

P Central

SUMMERLOCK APPROACH

TRAIN STATION

CHURCHFIELDS RD.

Stonehenge Tour B

P

S. WESTERN ROAD

MILL RD.

WEST ST.

NORTH ST.

WATER LN.

CITY HALL

FISHERTON ST.

⑪

HARCOURT

MILL RD.

Queen Elizabeth II Gardens

Harnham Water Meadows

THE WARDROBE

WEST WALK

THE SALISBURY MUSEUM

River Avon

Accommodations

❶ The Chapter House & Restaurant
❷ To Cricket Field House, Wilton House & Stourhead
❸ Cathedral View B&B
❹ Sarum College Rooms
❺ The King's Head Inn

Eateries & Other

❻ Reeve the Baker (2)
❼ Charter 1227
❽ Cathedral Cafeteria
❾ The Bell Tower Tea Rooms
❿ Café Diwali
⑪ Anokaa
⑫ The Bell & Crown Inn
⑬ The New Inn
⑭ Launderette
⑮ Bus Ticket Office

N

200 Meters
200 Yards

AVEBURY, STONEHENGE & SALISBURY

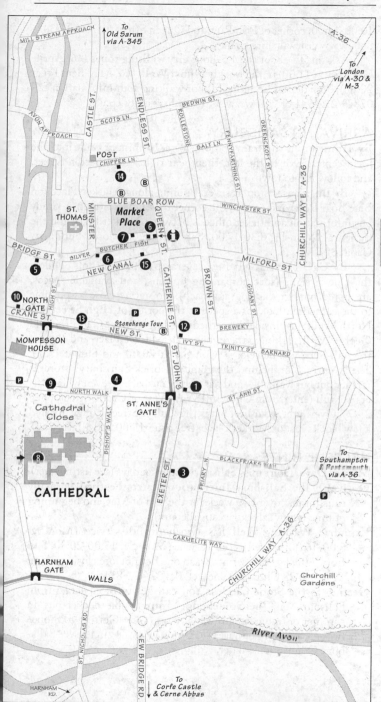

10:00-14:00, corner of Fish Row and Queen Street, tel. 01722/342-860, www.visitwiltshire.co.uk).

Ask the TI about the 1.5-hour **city walking tours** (£6, April-Oct daily at 11:00) or the weekly **Ghost Walk** (£6, May-Sept Fri at 20:00); both depart from the TI. For walking-tour information call 07873/212-941 or visit www.salisburycityguides.co.uk.

ARRIVAL IN SALISBURY

By Train: From the train station, it's a 10-minute walk into the town center: Exit to the left, then bear right on Fisherton Street, and follow it into town.

By Bus: Buses stop at several points along Market Place (on Blue Boar Row) and around the corner on Endless Street. A handy bus information and ticket office is between Market Place and the cathedral (Mon-Fri 8:30-17:00, Sat 9:00-15:00, closed Sun, New Canal 6).

By Car: Drivers will find several pay parking lots. Follow the blue *P* signs (specific parking options, and available spaces, are noted on signs as you approach). To get as close as possible to the cathedral, look for a space at the corner of High Street and North Walk, just inside the cathedral's High Street Gate. The Old George Mall parking garage, between Market Place and the cathedral, is handy, but closes Mon-Sat at 20:00 and Sun at 17:00. The "Central" lot, behind the giant red-brick Sainsbury's store, is farther out but walkable, and has plenty of spaces—even when others are full (enter from Churchill Way West or Castle Street, open 24/7). Overnight, your best bet is the Culver Street garage, located a few blocks east of Market Place (free after 15:00 and all day Sun).

HELPFUL HINTS

Market Days: Don't miss Salisbury's market days (see listing later).

Festivals: The **Salisbury International Arts Festival** normally runs for just over two weeks at the end of May and beginning of June (www.salisburyfestival.co.uk).

Laundry: Washing Well has two-hour full-service (Mon-Sat 8:00-16:00) as well as self-service (Mon-Sat 15:00-20:30, Sun from 7:00, last self-service wash one hour before closing; bring £1 coins, 28 Chipper Lane, tel. 01722/421-874).

Getting to the Stone Circles: You can get to Stonehenge from Salisbury on **The Stonehenge Tour** double-decker bus in summer or (more expensively) by **taxi** (see "Getting to Stonehenge," earlier). For buses to Avebury's stone circle, see "Salisbury Connections," later.

Sights in Salisbury

ON MARKET PLACE
▲Market Days

For centuries, Salisbury has been known for its lively markets. And today, the big "charter market" still fills the vast Market Place each Tuesday and Saturday (8:00-16:00). This all-purpose market has everything from butchers, fishmongers, and spices to hardware, clothes, and shoes. A little "food court" of international stands is in the center. While fun to browse, this is decidedly not a tourist-oriented market—but it's great for people-watching an age-old tradition still going on in a modern English city. At the top of the square is a handy row of bars and coffee shops with outdoor tables.

Every other Wednesday is the farmers market. And increasingly, the city council has been hosting a variety of other themed markets: Fridays alternate between vintage, French products, and "Foodie Friday" (typically once monthly each, 10:00-16:00). And if you brake for garage sales, you'll pull a U-turn for the occasional "Car Boot Sundays." For the latest schedule, see www.salisburycitycouncil.gov.uk.

▲St. Thomas's Church

This Gothic space—short and squat, but still airy and light-filled—boasts an unusual feature: A fully restored "Doom Painting" (illustration of the Last Judgment, c. 1475, over the choir). While these are commonplace in Continental churches, England's were whitewashed and forgotten during the Reformation. But St. Thomas's—long hidden behind the painted wooden coat-of-arms of Queen Elizabeth I, which is now displayed over the red door on the right—was uncovered and restored in the late 19th century. Examine the exquisite, Flemish-style details. Angels pulling the dead from their graves (on the left) to stand before the judgment of Jesus (at the top); some unfortunate souls are sent to the jaws of Hell (on the right)—past the Prince of Darkness, whose toe crosses the edge of the Gothic arch.

Cost and Hours: Free but donation requested, Mon-Sat 9:00-17:00, Sun from 12:00, just west of Market Place on St. Thomas's Square.

ON AND NEAR CATHEDERAL CLOSE
▲▲Salisbury Cathedral

This magnificent cathedral is visible for miles around because of its huge spire (the tallest in England at 404 feet). The surrounding enormous grassy field (called a "close") makes the Gothic master-piece look even larger. What's more impressive is that all this was built in a mere 38 years. When the old hill town of Sarum was moved down to the valley, its cathedral had to be replaced in a hurry. So, in 1220, the townspeople began building, and in 1258 their sparkling-new cathedral was ready for ribbon-cutting. Since the structure was built in just a few decades, its style is uniform, rather than the centuries-long patchwork common in cathedrals of the time. The cathedral also displays a remarkably well-preserved original copy of the Magna Carta (in the Chapter House).

Cost and Hours: £7.50 suggested donation, Mon-Sat 9:00-17:00, Sun 12:00-16:00, can be closed for special events. This working cathedral opens early for services: Be respectful if you arrive when one is in session.

Information: Tel. 01722/555-156, www.salisburycathedral.org.uk.

Tours: Free guided tours of the cathedral nave are offered every hour or so, when enough people assemble. Free stained glass tours run every Monday at 12:00.

Tower Tours: Imagine building a cathedral on this scale before the invention of cranes, bulldozers, or modern scaffolding. An excellent tower tour (1.5-2 hours) helps visitors understand how it was done. You'll climb in between the stone arches and the roof to inspect the vaulting and trussing; see a medieval winch that was used in the construction; and finish with the 332-step climb up the narrow tower for a sweeping view of the Wiltshire countryside. Because only 12 people are allowed on each tour, it's smart to reserve by phone or online a few days ahead—or even longer on summer weekends (£13.50; Mon-Sat hourly 10:15-15:15, Sun at 13:15 and 14:15, fewer tour times Oct-March; tel. 01722/555-156, www.salisburycathedral.org.uk/visit/tower-tours).

Evensong: Salisbury's daily choral evensong (Mon-Sat at 17:30, Sun at 16:30, about 45 minutes) is just as beautiful as the one in Wells Cathedral. Arrive up to 15 minutes early and enter through the north door. Spectators can sit in the nave, or you can ask to be seated in the wood-carved seats of the choir.

Eating: The cathedral has two fine eating options: a glassed-in cafeteria and an outdoor café with prime views (see "Eating in Salisbury," later).

Visiting the Cathedral: Enter through the cloister, around the west side of the building. Entering the church, you'll instantly feel the architectural harmony. Volunteer guides posted strategically throughout the church stand ready to answer your questions.

Step into the center of the **nave,** noticing how the stone col-

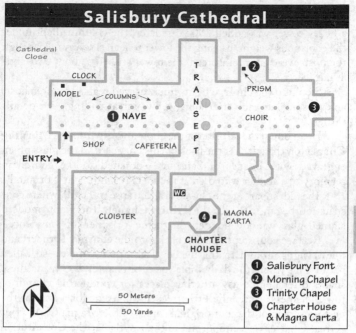

Salisbury Cathedral

Cathedral Close

CLOCK

MODEL

COLUMNS →

❶ NAVE

T R A N S E P T

PRISM

❷

CHOIR

❸

SHOP   CAFETERIA

ENTRY →

CLOISTER

WC

❹ MAGNA CARTA

CHAPTER HOUSE

50 Meters
50 Yards

N

❶ Salisbury Font
❷ Morning Chapel
❸ Trinity Chapel
❹ Chapter House
   & Magna Carta

umns march identically down the aisle—like a thick, gray forest of tree trunks. The arches overhead soar to grand heights, helping churchgoers appreciate the vast and amazing heavens. Now imagine the interior surfaces painted in red, blue, green, and gold, as they would have been prior to the whitewashing of the English Reformation.

Head to the far wall (the back-left corner), where an interesting **model** shows how this cathedral was built so quickly in the 13th century. A few steps toward the front of the church is the "oldest working clock in existence," dating from the 14th century (the hourly bell has been removed, so as not to interrupt worship services). On the wall by the clock is a bell from the decommissioned ship HMS *Salisbury*. Look closely inside the bell to see the engraved names of crew members' children who were baptized on the ship.

Wander down the aisle past monuments and knights' tombs, as well as tombstones set into the floor. About halfway down the nave, you'll see (and hear) the gurgling **Salisbury Font**—a modern, oxidized-bronze baptismal font dedicated in 2008 to honor the cathedral's 750th birthday. While it looks like a modern sculpture, it's also used for baptisms—one of many ways in which it's clear that this church is full of life.

When you reach the transept, gape up at the **columns.** These posts were supposed to support a more modest bell tower, but when a heavy tower was added 100 years later, the columns bent under the enormous weight, causing the tower to lean sideways. Although the posts were later reinforced, the tower still tilts about two-and-a-half feet.

Step into the **choir,** with its finely carved seats. This area hosts an evensong late each afternoon (well worth attending—see details earlier).

Head down the left side of the choir and dip into the **Morning Chapel** (on the left). At the back of this chapel, find the glass prism engraved with images of Salisbury—donated to the church in memory of a soldier who died at the D-Day landing at Normandy.

The oldest part of the church is at the apse (far end), where construction began in 1220: the **Trinity Chapel.** The giant, modern stained-glass window ponders the theme "prisoners of conscience."

Retrace your steps and exit back into the cloister. Turn left and follow signs around to the medieval **Chapter House**—so called because it's where the daily Bible verse, or chapter, was read. These spaces often served as gathering places for conducting church or town business. Enter the little freestanding tent for a look at the best preserved of the four original copies of the Magna Carta. This "Great Charter" is as important to the English as the Constitution is to Americans. Dating from 1215, the Magna Carta settled a dispute between England's King John and some powerful barons by guaranteeing that the monarch was not above the law. To this day, lawyers and political scientists admire this very early example of "checks and balances"—a major victory in the centuries-long tug-of-war between monarchs and nobles. Notice the smudge marks on the glass case, where historians have bumped their noses squinting at the minuscule script.

▲Cathedral Close

The enormous green surrounding the cathedral is the largest in England, and one of the loveliest. It's cradled in the elbow of the River Avon and ringed by row houses, cottages, and grand mansions. The church owns the houses on the green and rents them to lucky people with holy connec-  tions. A former prime minister, Edward Heath, lived on the green, not because of his political influence, but because he was once the church organist.

The benches scattered around the green are an excellent place for having a romantic moonlit picnic or for gazing thoughtfully at the leaning spire. Although you may be tempted to linger until it's late, don't—this is still private church property...and the heavy medieval gates of the close shut at about 22:00.

A few houses are open to the public, such as the overpriced Mompesson House and the medieval Wardrobe. The most interesting is...

▲The Salisbury Museum

Occupying the building just opposite the cathedral entry, this eclectic and sprawling collection was heralded by American expat travel writer Bill Bryson as one of England's best. While that's a stretch, the museum does offer a little something for everyone.

Cost and Hours: £8; Mon-Sat 10:00-17:00, Sun from 12:00 except closed Sun Oct-May; check with desk about occasional tours, 65 The Close, tel. 01722/332-151, www.salisburymuseum.org.uk.

Visiting the Museum: The highlight is the Wessex Gallery (to the left as you enter), with informative, interactive exhibits covering this area's rich prehistory—from Neanderthal ax heads to Iron Age cremation urns. Check out the ancient Roman mosaic floor and sarcophagus, and the sculpture fragments from the original Old Sarum cathedral. One exhibit details the excavation of Stonehenge, which began as early as 1620—back when it was believed to be Roman rather than druid.

The museum continues to the right of the entry, with a musty, dimly lit, but endearing collection of Salisbury's historic bric-a-brac—including the true-to-its-name "Salisbury Giant" puppet once used by the tailors' guild during parades, and some J. M. W. Turner paintings of the cathedral interior. Upstairs is a historical clothing exhibit and a collection of exquisite Wedgwood china and other ceramics.

JUST OUTSIDE SALISBURY

These two rewarding sights are practically on Salisbury's doorstep—within a 10-minute drive of Market Place. While neither is worth planning your day around, either can easily be combined with a trip to or from Stonehenge.

Old Sarum

Today, little remains of the original town of Old Sarum, but a little imagination can transport you back to *very* Olde England. The city was originally founded on a slope overlooking the plain below. Uniquely, it combined both a castle and a cathedral within an Iron Age fortification. Old Sarum was eventually abandoned, leaving only a few stone foundations. The grand views of Salisbury from here have in-"spired" painters for ages and provided countless picnickers with a scenic backdrop (bring lunch or snacks).

Cost and Hours: £5.40; daily 10:00-18:00, Oct until 17:00, Nov-March until 16:00; tel. 01722/335-398, www.english-heritage.org.uk.

Getting There: It's on the edge of Salisbury, two miles north of the city center off the A-345. The Stonehenge Tour bus stops here (see "Getting to Stonehenge," earlier), or you can take either bus #X5 or the Activ8 bus, both run by Salisbury Reds (www.salisburyreds.co.uk).

Background: Human settlement in this area stretches back to the Bronze Age, and the Romans, Saxons, and Normans all called this hilltop home. From about 500 BC through AD 1220, Old Sarum flourished, giving rise to a motte-and-bailey castle, a cathedral, and scores of wooden homes along the town's outer ring. The town grew so quickly that by the Middle Ages, it had outgrown its spot on the hill. In 1220, the local bishop successfully petitioned to move the entire city to the valley below, where space and water was plentiful. So, stone by stone, Old Sarum was packed up and shipped to New Sarum, where builders used nearly all the rubble from the old city to create a brand-new town with a magnificent cathedral.

Visiting the Site: From the parking lot or bus stop, you'll cross over the former moat to reach the core of Old Sarum. Inside you'll find a few scant walls and foundations. Colorful information plaques help resurrect the rubble. Additional ruins line the road between the site and the main road.

▲Wilton House and Garden

This sprawling estate, with a grand mansion and tidy gardens, has been owned by the Earls of Pembroke since King Henry VIII's time. The Pembrokes are a classy clan, and—unlike the many borderline-scruffy aristocratic homes in Britain—their home and garden are in exquisite repair and oozing with pride. Jane Austen fans particularly enjoy this stately home, where parts of 2005's Oscar-nominated *Pride and Prejudice* were filmed. But, alas, Mr. Darcy has checked out. Note the unusual weekend closure—the Pembrokes like to have the place to themselves on Fridays and Saturdays.

Cost and Hours: House and gardens-£15.50, gardens only-£6.50; open Easter weekend and Sun-Thu in May-Aug (house open 11:30-17:00, gardens 11:00-17:30), closed Fri-Sat and all of Sept-April; tel. 01722/746-728, www.wiltonhouse.co.uk.

Getting There: It's five miles west of Salisbury via the A-36, to Wilton's Minster Street. You can also reach it on Salisbury Reds bus #R3, park-and-ride bus #PR3, or—on Sundays—Salisbury Reds bus #3.

Visiting the Estate: The first stop is the **Old Riding School,**

which houses a faintly interesting (but skippable) 15-minute film about the family and their house, and a fine collection of luxury cars old and new.

Inside the **mansion,** you'll tour several gorgeous rooms decorated with classical sculpture and paintings by Rubens, Rembrandt, Van Dyck, and Brueghel. You'll also see plenty of family portraits and some quirky odds and ends, such as a series of paintings of the Spanish Riding School, and a lock of Queen Elizabeth I's hair. The perfectly proportioned Double Cube Room has served as everything from a 17th-century state dining room to a secret D-Day planning room during World War II...if only the portraits could talk. Fortunately, the docents posted in each room do—since there's no posted information, be sure to ask plenty of questions.

You'll exit to the garden—flat and perfectly tended, with pebbly paths and a golf course-quality lawn, stretching along the gurgling River Nadder and decorated with a few Neoclassical ornaments.

Nearby: The village of Wilton itself is a proud, workaday burg that's fun to explore. It boasts the Wilton House at one end of town, a cozy green at its center, and at the far end of town, the Italianate **Church of Sts. Mary and Nicholas**—dating from the Romantic period of the mid-19th century, when world travelers brought some of their favorite styles back home. The can't-miss-it church, along West Street, looks like it'd be more at home in the Veneto than on Salisbury Plain.

Sleeping in Salisbury

Salisbury's town center has very few accommodations. Noisy roads rumble past most of these places: Light sleepers can try asking for a quieter room in back (or pack earplugs). Drivers should ask about parking when reserving. The town gets particularly crowded during the arts festival (late May through early June). If you're in a pinch, there's a **Premier Inn** two miles outside of town.

$$$ The Chapter House is a boutique hotel with 17 stylish, modern rooms in a creaky old shell. The rooms are above their trendy restaurant, immediately across from the side entrance to the Cathedral Close (9 St. John's Street, tel. 01722/341-277, www.thechapterhouseuk.com).

$$$ Cricket Field House, a cozy little compound just outside of town on the A-36 toward Wilton, overlooks a cricket pitch and golf course. It has 10 large, comfortable rooms, its own gorgeous garden, and plenty of parking (Wilton Road, tel. 01722/322-595, www.cricketfieldhouse.co.uk, cricketfieldcottage@btinternet.com; Brian and Margaret James). While this place works best for drivers, it's a 20-minute walk from the train station or a five-minute bus ride from the city center.

$$ Cathedral View B&B is a classic, traditional B&B renting four rooms just off the Cathedral Close. Wenda and Steve are generous with travel tips, and Steve is an armchair town historian with lots of insights (cash only, 2-night minimum on weekends, no kids under age 10, 83 Exeter Street, tel. 01722/502-254, www.cathedral-viewbandb.co.uk, info@cathedral-viewbandb.co.uk).

$$ Sarum College is a theological college that rents 40 rooms in its building right on the peaceful Cathedral Close. Much of the year, it houses visitors to the college, but it usually has rooms for tourists as well. The well-worn, slightly institutional but clean rooms share hallways with libraries, bookstores, and offices; the five attic rooms come with dramatic cathedral views from their dormer windows (meals available, elevator, limited free parking, 19 The Close, tel. 01722/424-800, www.sarum.ac.uk, hospitality@sarum.ac.uk).

$$ The King's Head Inn rents 33 modern rooms above a chain Wetherspoon pub. While impersonal, it's a decent value and conveniently located—in a handsome old sandstone building between Market Place and the train station—and likely to have room when others are full (breakfast extra, deeply discounted Sun nights, aircon, elevator to some rooms, 1 Bridge Street, tel. 01722/438-400, www.jdwetherspoon.com, kingsheadinn@jdwetherspoon.co.uk).

Eating in Salisbury

There are plenty of atmospheric pubs all over town. For the best variety of restaurants, head to the Market Place area. Some places offer "early bird" specials before 19:00.

$ Reeve the Baker crafts an array of high-calorie delights and handy pick-me-ups for a fast and affordable lunch. Peruse the long cases of pastries and savory treats, and notice the locals waiting patiently at the fresh bread counter in back (Mon-Sat 7:30-17:30, Sun 10:00-16:00, tel. 01722/320-367). The main branch, on Market Place (at 2 Butcher Row), has seating both upstairs and out on the square—either with a nice view of the busy market. A much smaller second branch is at the corner of Market and Bridge streets at 61 Silver Street.

$$$ The Chapter House is a lively and popular restaurant with an enticing menu of British, South African, and international fare in a trendy setting (Mon-Sat 12:00-15:00 & 18:00-22:00, Sun until 20:00, 9 St. John's Street, tel. 01722/341-277).

$$$$ Charter 1227 is a high-end splurge (by Salisbury standards) filling a contemporary dining room upstairs, overlooking Market Place. The short, selective menu is much more affordable at lunch for their midweek "early bird" specials (open Tue-Sat 12:00-14:30 & 18:00-21:30, closed Sun-Mon, lunch specials Tue-Thu, reservations smart, 6 Ox Row, enter from Market Place, tel. 01722/333-118, www.charter1227.co.uk).

At the Cathedral: For lunch near the cathedral, you have two great choices. The **$ cafeteria** has a full menu and fills a winter garden squeezed between the buttresses and the cloister, with additional seating in the cloister itself (open same hours as cathedral). But on a sunny day, it's hard to imagine a nicer setting than **$ The Bell Tower Tea Rooms,** with outdoor tables on England's biggest close, peering up at its tallest cathedral tower (drinks, deli sandwiches, and affordable teas—£5.50 cream tea, afternoon tea is £24/2 people; choose a table, then order at the counter; daily 10:00-17:00).

Indian: If you're going to try Indian food, do it in Salisbury. These two excellent options both serve creative variations on the typical "curry house" fare: **$$$ Café Diwali** takes an "Indian street food" approach, with delicious, creative dishes served thali-style, on big silver platters (daily 12:00-14:00 & 18:00-22:30, 90 Crane Street, tel. 01722/329-700). And **$$$ Anokaa** serves up updated Indian cuisine in a dressy, contemporary setting (daily 12:00-14:00 & 17:30-23:00, 60 Fisherton Street, tel. 01722/414-142).

Pubs: $$ The Bell & Crown Inn is the best all-around choice, with reliable pub fare and atmosphere, and leather couches under heavy beams (daily 11:00-23:00, 83 Catherine Street, tel. 01722/338-102). **$$ The New Inn,** the local rugby pub, fills a creaky, atmospheric, 15th-century house rumored to have a tunnel leading directly into the cathedral—perhaps dug while the building housed a brothel? On a sunny day, their back garden is pleasant (daily 12:00-15:00 & 18:00-21:00, 41 New Street, tel. 01722/326-662).

Salisbury Connections

From Salisbury by Train to: London's Waterloo Station (2/hour, 1.5 hours), **Bath** (hourly direct, 1 hour). **Train info:** tel. 0345-748-4950, www.nationalrail.co.uk.

By Bus to: Bath (hourly, 3 hours, www.travelinesw.com), **Avebury** (hourly, 2 hours, transfer in Devizes, www.travelinesw.com). Many of Salisbury's long-distance buses are run by Salisbury Reds (tel. 01722/336-855 or 01202/338-420, www.salisburyreds.co.uk).

Near Salisbury

The most appealing sights in the Salisbury area are Stonehenge and Avebury. But if you have extra time here (or en route to your next stop), these attractions are worth considering. While best for drivers, and not worth going out of your way to see, they may appeal if you have a special interest in gardens, ruined castles, or cute villages.

Stourhead House and Gardens

Stourhead, designed by owner Henry Hoare II in the mid-18th century, is a sprawling 2,650-acre estate of rolling hills, meandering paths, placid lakes, and colorful trees, punctuated by classically inspired bridges and monuments. The creaky old mansion strains to make its obscure aristocratic owners interesting (with eager docents in each room), but the gardens are the real highlight: Take a two-mile loop hike around the lake.

Cost and Hours: £17.50 includes house and garden; house open daily 11:00-16:30, garden open daily 9:00-18:00, closes earlier off-season; parking-£4, tel. 01747/841-152, www.nationaltrust.org.uk. It's 28 miles (40 minutes) west of Salisbury in the village of Stourton.

Corfe Castle

Built by William the Conqueror in the 11th century, this castle was a favorite residence for medieval kings until it was destroyed by a massive gunpowder blast during a 17th-century siege. Today its jagged ruins cap a steep, conical hill, offering a fun excuse for a hike and sweeping views over the Dorset countryside. Park at the Castle View visitors center, then follow the path that curls around the back of the castle to the village (about 10 minutes). There you can buy your ticket, cross the drawbridge, and hike up. The castle is mostly an empty husk, with little to bring its dramatic history to life, but it's fun to scramble along its rocky remnants.

Cost and Hours: £10, daily 10:00-18:00, closes earlier off-season, tel. 01929/481-294, www.nationaltrust.org.uk. It's 44 miles (about one hour) south of Salisbury.

▲Cerne Abbas

Dorset County's most adorable village is cuddly, one-street Cerne Abbas (surn AB-iss)—about 45 miles (one hour) southwest of Salisbury. It's lined with half-timbered buildings and draped with ivy and wisteria. Park your car and go for a walk. Head up Abbey Street, passing the lovely St. Mary's Church on your way up to the village's namesake abbey. Let yourself in the gate and explore the mysterious, beautiful grounds. If you need a break, the town has some appealing pubs and the fine Abbots Tearoom (7 Long Street, tel. 01300/341-349).

The village is best known for the large chalk figure that's scraped into a nearby hillside: the famous **Cerne Abbas Giant.**

(To find it, head up the street just past Abbots Tearoom—by car or by foot; you can also follow brown road signs to *Giant Viewpoint*.) Chalk figures such as this one can be found in many parts of the region. Because the soil is only a few inches deep, the overlying grass and dirt can easily be removed to expose the bright white chalk bedrock beneath, creating the outlines. While nobody is sure exactly how old this figure is, or what its original purpose was, the giant is faithfully maintained by the locals, who mow and clear the fields at least once a year. This particular figure, possibly a fertility god, looks friendly...maybe a little too friendly. Locals claim that if a woman who's having trouble getting pregnant sleeps on the giant for one night, she will soon be able to conceive a child.

The area around Cerne Abbas can be fun to explore—with names seemingly invented on a bet by pub patrons on tuppence-ale night. Piddle Lane leads out of town to villages with names like Piddletrenthide, Piddlehinton (both on the aptly named River Piddle), Plush, Mappowder, Ansty, Lower Ansty, and, of course, Higher Ansty. More entertainment rewards careful map-readers in the surrounding hills: King's Stag, Fifehead Neville, Maiden Newton, Hazelbury Bryan, Poopton-upon-Piddle, Stock Gaylard, Bishop's Caundle, Alton Pancras, Melbury Bubb, Beer Hackett, Sturminster Newton, Nether Cerne, and Margaret Marsh. Believe it or not, only one of these names is made up.

OXFORD

Oxford • Blenheim Palace

Oxford, founded in the seventh century and home to the oldest university in the English-speaking world, originated as a simple trade crossroads at an ox ford...a convenient place for Anglo-Saxons to cross the river with their oxen. (Back then you could row to London from Oxford...in just five days.)

This humble town gained fame when the University of Oxford took root here. Ever since the first homework was assigned in 1167, its stellar graduates have influenced Western civilization. Its alumni include 27 British prime ministers, more than 60 Nobel Prize winners, well-known writers and actors, and even 11 saints.

Today's Oxford is a lively, globally minded city of 170,000. It's part university (with 60 percent of students from overseas), part industry (cranking out fashionable Mini cars and renowned craft beers), and part bedroom community for Londoners (with relatively affordable housing and an easy hour-long commute). Although you may see stodgy professors in their traditional black robes, this is a fun college town—with a quarter of the population between 18 and 23—filled with shopping, cheap eats, pranks, and rowdy, rollicking pubs.

For tourists, Oxford offers a pleasant town center plus historic colleges with literary connections. Never bombed in World War II, Oxford retains its rich honey-colored Cotswold limestone buildings. Many colleges allow visitors (for a small admission fee) to stroll their grounds and go inside a few historic buildings. Step off the busy, urban-feeling High Street into the hushed sanctuary of a grassy college quad. Stroll the garden where Lewis Carroll dreamed up his adventures for Alice, pop in to the dining hall that

Oxford or Cambridge?

England is home to two world-renowned universities: Oxford and Cambridge. Seeing one is usually enough. So the big question for many is, which one? Cambridge feels like a lazy, easygoing small town, and it's more approachable and charming, with lovely gardens along the River Cam. Oxford has more urban energy and stately buildings, with lots more to see and do. Cambridge is not really on the way to anything, making it better as a side-trip from London than as a stopover. Oxford sits near the Cotswolds, Stratford-upon-Avon, Warwick, and Blenheim Palace. Both are convenient to London (with an hour's train ride or an hour-and-a-half drive), but neither has an abundance of hotel options. If you can't choose, do both (there's a great bus connection between them—see "Oxford Connections," later).

inspired the one where Harry Potter eats, or grab a pint in the pub where J. R. R. Tolkien first spoke about hobbits.

Just half an hour outside of town is magnificent Blenheim Palace (described at the end of this chapter), England's finest countryside estate and the birthplace of Winston Churchill.

PLANNING YOUR TIME

Oxford is a convenient stop for people visiting the Cotswolds, Blenheim Palace, Stratford-upon-Avon, and Bath. In a single busy day, you could see the essential Oxford: my self-guided walk, Christ Church College, and the Ashmolean Museum.

Oxford's colleges are generally open to visitors, but each has its own visiting hours (which can be unpredictable). Your plans may be affected by whether school is in session (more atmospheric, though some sights may be closed to visitors) or on vacation (less lively but easier access). There are three terms: Michaelmas (Oct-Dec), Hilary (Jan-March), and Trinity (April-June). Summer sees an influx of foreign students on short-term programs, along with tour groups and Harry Potter fans, making the season a less stately time to visit.

Orientation to Oxford

While a typical American-style university has one self-contained campus with a town nearby, Oxford (like Cambridge) has colleges and buildings scattered throughout town. Roughly speaking, the university clusters around the building called the Radcliffe Camera, while the town's commercial center is near the Carfax Tower.

The main arteries are the north-south Cornmarket/St. Aldate's, and the east-west Queen Street/High Street. At the inter-

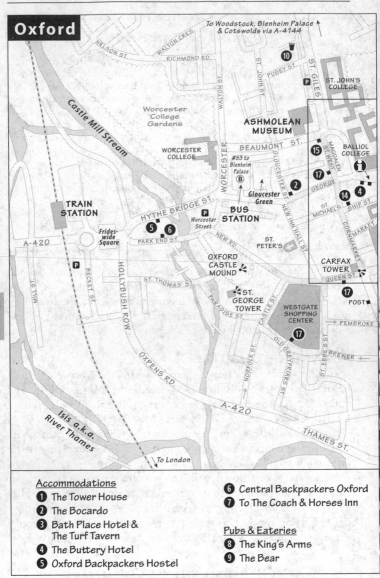

Oxford

To Woodstock, Blenheim Palace & Cotswolds via A-4144

NELSON ST.

WALTON CRES.

RICHMOND RD.

Castle Mill Stream

Worcester College Gardens

WORCESTER COLLEGE

WALTON ST.

PUSEY ST.

ST. JOHN'S COLLEGE

JOHN ST.

ASHMOLEAN MUSEUM

BEAUMONT ST.

WORCESTER ST.

#53 to Blenheim Palace

Gloucester Green

GLOUCESTER ST.

ST. GILES

BALLIOL COLLEGE

ST. MARY'S WEST

GEORGE

ST. MICHAEL'S

SHIP ST.

CORNMARKET

CARFAX TOWER

QUEEN ST.

POST

TRAIN STATION

Frideswide Square

A-420

HYTHE BRIDGE ST.

PARK END ST.

Worcester Street

BUS STATION

NEW INN HALL ST.

NEW RD.

ST. PETER'S

OXFORD CASTLE MOUND

ST. GEORGE TOWER

PARADISE ST.

CASTLE ST.

WESTGATE SHOPPING CENTER

OLD GREYFRIARS ST.

ST. EBBE'S ST.

PEMBROKE

BREWER ST.

MILL ST.

BECKET ST.

HOLLYBUSH ROW

ST. THOMAS' ST.

OXPENS RD.

NORFOLK ST.

A-420

THAMES ST.

Isis a.k.a. River Thames

To London

Accommodations
1 The Tower House
2 The Bocardo
3 Bath Place Hotel & The Turf Tavern
4 The Buttery Hotel
5 Oxford Backpackers Hostel
6 Central Backpackers Oxford
7 To The Coach & Horses Inn

Pubs & Eateries
8 The King's Arms
9 The Bear

section of these streets stands the stubby, 14th-century Carfax Tower (named for the French *carrefour*, or "crossroads")—the historic birthplace of the town. From here, pedestrianized Cornmarket—essentially an outdoor mall lined with shops and chain restaurants—heads north, where it intersects with another pedestrian zone at George Street/Broad Street.

The sightseers' Oxford is walkable and compact, and many streets are pedestrian-only. It's easy to get a feel for workaday

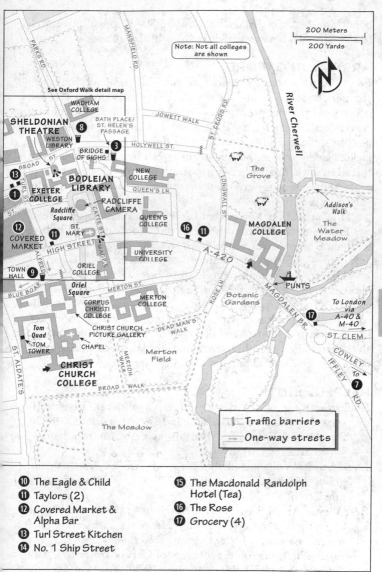

200 Meters

200 Yards

Note: Not all colleges are shown

N

See Oxford Walk detail map

WADHAM COLLEGE

SHELDONIAN THEATRE

WESTON LIBRARY

BATH PLACE/ ST. HELEN'S PASSAGE

BROAD ST.

BRIDGE OF SIGHS

HOLYWELL ST.

JOWETT WALK

ST. CROSS RD.

River Cherwell

The Grove

EXETER COLLEGE

TURL ST.

BODLEIAN LIBRARY

NEW COLLEGE

QUEEN'S LN.

RADCLIFFE CAMERA

Radcliffe Square

ST. MARY

QUEEN'S COLLEGE

Addison's Walk

The Water Meadow

CATTE ST.

LONGWALL ST.

MAGDALEN COLLEGE

COVERED MARKET

ALFRED ST.

HIGH STREET

UNIVERSITY COLLEGE

A-420

PUNTS

TOWN HALL

BLUE BOAR

ORIEL COLLEGE

Oriel Square

MERTON ST.

CORPUS CHRISTI COLLEGE

MERTON COLLEGE

ROSE LN.

Botanic Gardens

MAGDALEN BR.

To London via A-40 & M-40

ST. CLEM.

CHRIST CHURCH PICTURE GALLERY

DEAD MAN'S WALK

COWLEY RD.

IFFLEY RD.

To

Tom Quad

TOM TOWER

CHAPEL

MERTON WALK

Merton Field

ST. ALDATE'S

CHRIST CHURCH COLLEGE

BROAD WALK

The Meadow

Traffic barriers

One-way streets

OXFORD

10 The Eagle & Child
11 Taylors (2)
12 Covered Market & Alpha Bar
13 Turl Street Kitchen
14 No. 1 Ship Street
15 The Macdonald Randolph Hotel (Tea)
16 The Rose
17 Grocery (4)

Oxford, where knowledge is the town business—and procrastinating over a pint is the students' main hobby.

TOURIST INFORMATION

The TI offers walking tours, and sells a detailed town map and *A Quick Guide to Oxford*, which includes a basic map and do-it-yourself walking tour. They also offer baggage storage for a fee. If you're headed to Blenheim Palace, buy your tickets here at a discount (TI open Mon-Sat 9:30-17:00, Sun until 16:30, 15 Broad Street, tel. 01865/686-441, www.experienceoxfordshire.org).

ARRIVAL IN OXFORD

From the **train** station, the city center is a 10-minute walk (exit straight ahead and follow the signs). A taxi costs around £6—but because of many one-way streets, it may not be direct. The "tourism centre" desk in the train station is just a sales outlet for skippable bus tours; the real TI (see earlier) is in the city center. There are no lockers at the station, but day-trippers can leave their luggage at the TI in town, or at either of two youth hostels 400 yards in front of the train station toward the town center (see listings later, under "Sleeping in Oxford").

The **bus** station, a bit closer to downtown at Gloucester Green, is a five-minute walk from the heart of Oxford and the TI: Turn left onto George Street and follow it straight into town (no lockers at station—leave your bags at the TI or a hostel).

Drivers day-tripping into Oxford have several options. The cheapest is to use one of the outlying park-and-ride lots, which are about a 10-minute shuttle-bus ride from the town center. There are some pay parking lots closer to the center (including a handy one between the train station and downtown), but they're more expensive. There's also time-limited pay-and-display street parking north of the Ashmolean Museum, on St. Giles Street).

HELPFUL HINTS

Bookstore: One of the world's largest bookstores, **Blackwell's** started as a 12-foot-square shop in 1879 (Mon-Sat 9:00-18:30, Sun 11:00-17:00, coffee shop upstairs, WC on top floor, 48 Broad Street, tel. 01865/792-792).

Local Guide: William Underhill is a good Oxford-educated private guide (£55/hour, mobile 07802-328-956, williamunderhill@gmail.com).

Best Views: At the **University Church of St. Mary the Virgin,** climb the 127 narrow, twisting stairs of the 13th-century bell tower for views of Oxford's many spires and colleges. For an easier climb, skip up the 99 steps of **Carfax Tower** (£3, daily April-Sept 10:00-17:00, Oct until 16:00). Also consider the tower of the **Sheldonian Theatre.** The views from **Oxford Castle**'s tower are underwhelming and only accessible if you pay to join the tour. (For more on the church and theater, see my "Oxford Walk"; for details on the castle, see "Sights in Oxford.")

Harry Potter Sights: Christ Church College's atmospheric dining hall inspired the film sets used for Hogwarts' Great Hall. In the films, Christ Church's cloisters and Bodley Tower staircase were used as settings for a number of scenes. The **Divinity School** was the movie set for Hogwarts' infirmary (and Yule Ball), and **Duke Humfrey's Library** was Hogwarts' library (these are all described later). At **New College,** the cloisters and courtyard also hosted filmmakers. For more Harry Potter sights in England, see page 912, and consider taking a Harry Potter tour (see "Walking Tours," below).

Do-It-Yourself Tour: Information panels around town provide historical context and engaging facts about nearby sights. On the opposite side of each panel, you'll find a "you are here" map; use these to easily find your way around the maze of streets.

Tours in Oxford

▲Walking Tours
"University and City" walking tours from the TI, led by Blue or Green Badge guides, explain local history and traditions and take you inside one or two of the colleges. More informative than entertaining, these dry talks provide a solid historical background (£17, 2 hours, daily at 10:45, 11:15, 13:00, and 14:00; additional tours depending on demand—ask at TI for schedule).

They also offer themed £18 tours, including **Harry Potter** and **literary tours** about C. S. Lewis, J. R. R. Tolkien, and others. These tours often sell out, especially on Saturday; it's smart to book in advance (drop by, call, or go online, TI tel. 01865/686-441, www.experienceoxfordshire.org; tours depart from sidewalk in front of TI).

Walking Tours of Oxford offers themed group tours and private tours (Oxford University tour-£18, Fri-Sat at 11:30; £120 and up for 2-hour private tour; tel. 07833/176-196, www.walkingtoursofoxford.com).

Oxford Walking Tours leads more casual tours, departing hourly from the Trinity College gates, across from the TI (£12.95, daily 11:00-16:00, 1.5 hours, also evening ghost tours, call day before or morning of tour to confirm time, mobile 07790-734-387, www.oxfordwalkingtours.com, Stuart).

"Free tours"—which are not really free, as tips are expected at the end—are led by students (often expats) who memorize a script and are unlicensed. The tours are irreverent and can be fun (like a frat-party history class). They're aggressively pushed on the street (mostly in front of the TI, where more serious tours depart), and then tips are aggressively pushed when they're over.

Hop-On, Hop-Off Bus Tours

City Sightseeing Oxford runs double-decker buses around town (20 stops in all). Tickets include a 30-minute walking tour since much of Oxford is inaccessible by bus. Some buses have a live guide, others have recorded commentary—both are covered by the same ticket (£16; pay driver or buy tickets online, at the train station, TI, or Carfax Tower; runs every 10-15 minutes daily 9:30-18:00, less frequent and stops running earlier in winter, tel. 01865/790-522, www.citysightseeingoxford.com).

Oxford Walk

This stroll takes you through the heart of Oxford's sprawling collection of colleges and university buildings. Budget about 2.5 hours to do the walk while going inside some of the sights along the way.

• *Start at the intersection of Broad and Cornmarket streets.*

❶ Oxford's Birth: Town and Gown

Gazing down pedestrian-only Cornmarket with its modern shops, you see the historic town of Oxford. Looking east down Broad Street, you see the realm of the university. It's these two elements—"town and gown"—that combined to make the Oxford of today. Take a few steps down Cornmarket to see Oxford's oldest building—the tall, stone Saxon Tower, from around AD 1000. The town began as a fortified trading post with a "corn market." Then, in 1167, a university was founded—one of Europe's first—bringing a new and sometimes troublesome element: students. The university expanded outside the old town walls, including what is now Broad Street.

• *Walk east along Broad Street about 100 yards. Stop at a small patch of bricks embedded in the middle of the road. (Note that the helpful TI is just a few steps farther, on the right.)*

❷ Broad Street: Colleges

This street was originally the ditch that ran outside of the Anglo-Saxon town wall. By the 1200s, it became home to Oxford students. As the university grew, it became what you see today—a loose collection of university buildings mingled among shops and homes.

The **brick patch,** in the shape of a cross, marks the spot where three local bishops, known as the "Oxford Martyrs," were burned at the stake for heresy in 1555-56. Their crime: Protestantism. It's a reminder that Oxford, as a center of intellectual thought, has always been a major ideological battleground. In Oxford, ideas matter.

For now, turn your attention to the first of the university

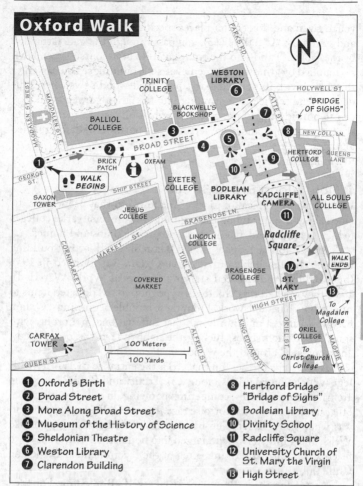

Oxford Walk

1. Oxford's Birth
2. Broad Street
3. More Along Broad Street
4. Museum of the History of Science
5. Sheldonian Theatre
6. Weston Library
7. Clarendon Building
8. Hertford Bridge "Bridge of Sighs"
9. Bodleian Library
10. Divinity School
11. Radcliffe Square
12. University Church of St. Mary the Virgin
13. High Street

buildings along our walk: **Balliol College** (on the left, with the cone-shaped turret). Founded in 1263, this is one of 38 colleges in the federation that composes Oxford University. Think of "colleges" as places where students live (eat, sleep, socialize, and get tutoring from faculty mentors) while they take classes in "university" buildings elsewhere in town. Each college is a self-contained community, with dorms, a dining hall, chapel, library, gardens, housing for faculty advisors, and a central quad. Each proudly has its own logo, colors, and reputation—the rich snobs, the partiers, the liberals. Balliol is known for producing politicians, but, like all colleges, it draws students from every major.

Most colleges allow visitors (for a small admission fee) to stroll the grounds and pop into a few select buildings. Just follow the map you're given and don't enter places specifically marked for students and staff only. At Balliol (£3), you pass through the gate (attended by the "porter") and into the front quad—a golf-course-green lawn surrounded by atmospheric medieval-style buildings. You can enter the chapel with its stained glass and carved-wood pews where students attend services. Continuing into the larger garden quad, you can step inside the impressive dining hall (unless it's mealtime) to see the long tables and place settings, and portraits of distinguished alumni.

• *Continue east, seeing...*

❸ More Along Broad Street

Broad Street is typical of most of the town, in that property is divided about evenly among three groups: the university, the colleges (which are independent entities), and private shops and homes.

At #17 (on the right) is an **Oxfam** shop. This tiny building is where the charitable organization Oxfam was founded in 1942 (by a Balliol grad) to feed starving victims of World War II. In 1947, they opened this Goodwill-type shop to sell donated items to fund more charitable work. From these humble beginnings, Oxfam has grown into a multimillion dollar international nonprofit, with some 1,200 such shops, fueling the fight to feed the poor, needy, and oppressed around the world.

A few steps farther (on the left) is the entrance to **Trinity College** (which you could also tour, £3). Trinity and Balliol have been archrivals for centuries, competing in rowing, in out-pranking each other, and in an annual tortoise race. **Exeter College** (on the right) was where J. R. R. Tolkien lived while an undergrad. He studied Welsh and Finnish (which merged into fictional elvish), went on to teach at Oxford, and drank often at the recommended Eagle and Child pub.

At #48 (on the left), step into **Blackwell's Bookshop.** Founded here in 1879, it has grown into a chain. This flagship store may not look that impressive initially, but make your way deep inside—beneath your feet in underground tunnels are an additional three miles of bookshelves in the 10,000-square-foot Norrington Room.

• *Directly across the street is the...*

❹ Museum of the History of Science

One of Europe's oldest museums, this place is worth ▲. It's an easily manageable display of scientific bric-a-brac (including Einstein's blackboard) that the scholars of Oxford used to change our world.

Cost and Hours: Free, £5 donation requested; Tue-Sun 12:00-17:00, closed Mon; borrow descriptions keyed to exhibit numbers.

Visiting the Museum: Upstairs, you'll find early globes, sundials, telescopes, and calculating machines. With a wedge-shaped quadrant, you could measure your position at sea in relation to the stars. A round astrolabe did the same but calculated the math for you.

In the basement, your eye will be drawn to a big crown. It adorns a huge lodestone—a natural magnet unearthed in the 1700s that could lift 160 pounds of iron. Exploring the other display cases, you'll see lots of flasks (including equipment used in developing penicillin), Marconi's early radios, and Lewis Carroll's photo-developing kit.

The museum's highlight is at the far end of the main room, hanging on the wall: Einstein's blackboard. Einstein personally scrawled this equation in chalk ($D = 1/c...$) during a lecture he gave at Oxford in 1931. Using the distance to a certain galaxy (D) as his starting point, he calculated the entire universe's density (p) and radius (P) in light years ("$L.J.$") to prove that the universe is indeed expanding.

By the way, university scientists once had the right to use the bodies of all executed criminals—and the dissecting was done right here in the basement.

• *We now begin diving into the university, starting with the big round Sheldonian Theatre next door.*

❺ Sheldonian Theatre

This ▲ venue for concerts and lectures is best known as the grand space for graduations and other important campus ceremonies.

This was the first major building designed by Sir Christopher Wren—a graduate of and astronomy professor at Oxford. It was such a success he went on to become England's best-known architect, including designing St. Paul's Cathedral in London. Wren's inspiration was ancient theaters—that is, curved on one end—but he added a roof. Wren placed 13 classical-looking stone heads out front, nicknamed "the emperors." (Some jokingly say they were carved to illustrate different styles of beards. Students occasionally prank them with funny hats or chalk lipstick.)

Cost and Hours: £3.50, hours posted on door but generally daily 10:00-16:00.

Visiting the Theater: Before entering the theater, make your way behind the Sheldonian (away from the street), to a Gothic-looking building with big windows and buttresses topped with prickly spires. This was the university's first purpose-built classroom (1427) and is its oldest surviving building—the **Divinity**

School (which we'll visit later). Admire the elaborately carved doorway, which was added later (1669) by Wren. Traditionally, graduating students would gather inside here, then walk out the Wren doorway and proceed grandly into the Sheldonian Theatre for the main ceremony. For now, let's go inside the Sheldonian Theatre (through the visitor's entrance).

The interior is basically one big round room ringed with seats. The construction is largely wood painted in pleasing red, white, and gold, and lit by the clear-glass windows. It's in this grand space that new students matriculate and graduates graduate. Picture the place on graduation day, filled with parents, with dignitaries seated at the end with the golden throne, and with students parading up to receive their degrees. Faculty members give speeches, the organ plays, and degrees are conferred in Latin. Think of the many famous grads over the years: Sir Walter Raleigh, Oscar Wilde, Stephen Hawking, Hugh Grant, and Bill Clinton.

The ceiling painting is made up of 32 separate panels, executed in the studio then pieced together with a grid of golden ropes. It depicts Truth—the radiant naked woman in the center—descending on a cloud to bless the university's Arts and Sciences (the robed women bearing harps, pens, quadrants, and telescopes). Most importantly, Truth banishes Ignorance—the Medusa near the pipe organ who tumbles down dramatically in defeat. (Also near the organ, on the wall, is a portrait of Wren.) Wren's domed ceiling was an engineering marvel, spanning a 70-by-80-foot hole. No beams were long enough to bridge that gap, so Wren had to construct a lattice of overlapping timbers.

You can climb 114 steps, walking among those big oak trusses, to a glass-covered cupola with great views. Looking southeast you'll see the heart of the university (where we'll soon be), with the prickly spires of the Bodleian Library and the dome in Radcliffe Square. Everywhere, you'll see why Oxford has been dubbed "the city of dreaming spires."

• *Exit the Sheldonian Theatre and cross Broad Street to the...*

❻ Weston Library

This building was constructed in the 1930s to house the overflow of university books when the venerable Bodleian Library began running out of space. Today, the Weston (worth ▲) welcomes visitors to enjoy its "Treasures"—an ever-changing selection of precious books, manuscripts, and letters from the vast collection. Nicknamed by locals "the best of the Bod," this is a literary treasure chest celebrating the genius of Oxford over the centuries. The two Treasures rooms are straight ahead as you enter. Items rotate in and out: You may see a Shakespeare First Folio, a copy of the Magna Carta, handwritten scores by Handel, or even a sixth-century scrap of birch bark with a recipe in Sanskrit to remove wrinkles and gray hair.

Cost and Hours: Free, suggested £5 donation, Mon-Sat 10:00-17:00, Sun from 11:00.

• *Now you're ready to enter the historic core of the university. From the Weston Library, cross Broad Street (keeping in mind there are miles of passages filled with books under your feet). Walk through the stately four-columned facade into the...*

❼ Clarendon Building

This building originally housed the Oxford University Press. Among the books printed here was the Lincoln Bible—used to inaugurate Presidents Lincoln and Obama. Exit the Clarendon out the other side.

• *Pause and look left for a glimpse of* ❽ *Hertford Bridge, known as the "Bridge of Sighs," after the one in Venice. This fanciful 19th-century skyway connects the two parts of Hertford College, and has become a popular symbol of Oxford, seen in many films. (The recommended Turf Tavern is nearby.)*

Keep going straight ahead, into the next building. You emerge in an open-air courtyard, surrounded by medieval-looking walls. You're in the center of the complex of buildings called the...

❾ Bodleian Library

As the university's main library (and one of the oldest in Europe), this is arguably the heart of Oxford's academic life, and worth

▲▲. The collection of books dates back to medieval times, and, as it expanded, various buildings were constructed to accommodate both the books and the students who studied them. The Schools Quadrangle (where you're standing) is the heart of the library, funded by Thomas Bodley in 1602. The statue in the courtyard honors William Pembroke, a friend of Shakespeare, founder of Pembroke College, and university chancellor when this part of the Bodleian was built. The doors branching off the courtyard led to the various university departments—the music school *(Schola Musica)*, astronomy *(Schola Astronomae)*, and so on—where classes were taught in Europe's universal language, Latin.

These days, the Bodleian is less about classrooms and more a research library for scholars. With some 11 million books and more than 100 miles of shelving in its underground stacks, "the Bod" is one of the world's largest and most famous libraries. By law, it's one of six "legal deposit" libraries in the UK—it must receive a copy of every book printed in the nation. The courtyard's main tower is called the Tower of the Five Orders, because of the five types of columns: Tuscan, Doric, Ionic, Corinthian, and Composite. The statue of King James I (ruler when the Bodleian was built) shows him handing out, what else? Books.

• *The ticket office for the Divinity School, our next stop, is directly beneath that tower. You can also book a guided tour for Duke Humfrey's Library (upstairs in the Divinity School—see description below). The entrance to the Divinity School is near the Pembroke statue.*

❿ Divinity School

The Divinity School, rated ▲▲, was the university's first purpose-built classroom—constructed in 1427 for teaching theology. The room, brilliantly lit by tall clear windows, is worth a look for its impressive fan-vaulted ceiling.

Cost and Hours: £2, Mon-Sat 9:00-17:00, Sun from 11:00. A tour of the Duke Humfrey's Library (described below) also includes a tour of the Divinity School.

Visiting the School: The room's ceiling is one of Britain's most intricate. It takes the traditional fan-vaulting another step, adding small ribs connecting the larger ribs, creating a net-like effect. The 455 bosses where the ribs join sport monograms of major donors. The lantern-like sculptures hanging down at the ends of the fans are what anchor the complex engineering forces in place. The windows are classic Perpendicular style—that is, very vertical, rising "perpendicular" to the ground.

Often on display is Sir Thomas Bodley's lockbox, with its intricate locking mechanism requiring several keys, turns, pushes, and pulls. Nearby, the chair is made of timbers from Sir Francis Drake's globe-circumnavigating ship. At the far end, note the stage—students stood here for oral exams, to be grilled by their profs.

At the height of the English Reformation (circa 1550), the room suffered damage from hardline Protestants. Notice the empty niche directly over the entry door where a crucifix once stood, and—just to the left—a defaced statue of St. Peter. The original colorful stained-glass windows were another casualty. And Protestants burned many of the university's Catholic-oriented books... prompting Bodley to re-energize the collection.

These days, students gather here to put on their gowns before walking to their graduation ceremony at the theater next door. A photo near the entry shows the university's first library. Before leaving, imagine hospital beds lining this hall...yes, it's the infirmary from the Harry Potter films.

Duke Humfrey's Library: Upstairs and only accessible on a guided tour, this historic library from 1488 is a world of musty, creaky old shelves of ancient-looking books, stacked neatly under a beautifully painted wooden ceiling (£9 one-hour tours generally run in the morning and early afternoon, £6 30-minute tours run later; check the schedule and buy your ticket at the kiosk, tel. 01865/287-400, www.tickets.ox.ac.uk). The tour, which also includes the Divinity School, shows you only a small section of the library, but tells much about its history and the huge stockpile of books below ground.

• *Return to the Schools Quadrangle courtyard. Turn right and exit the courtyard through the passageway (between "Schola Musicae" and "Naturalis Philosophiae"). You emerge in a vast square dominated by a big round building. You've reached...*

⓫ Radcliffe Square: The Historic Quad

The round, columned structure is Radcliffe Camera, probably Oxford's most iconic building.

Radcliffe Camera was built in the 1730s by major donor John Radcliffe (no relation to the Harry Potter actor) as an annex to the Bodleian Library. The architect, James Gibbs, was strongly influenced by Wren. Originally housing medical books, the building is a reading "room" (or "camera"). Only students and staff with special credentials can enter. They request books from the vast collection (including the thousands shelved in tunnels beneath the square), and study them at desks under the spacious rotunda.

Circle around the left side of the Radcliffe Camera and grab the bars of the fancy ironwork gate for a peek into **All Souls College.** It's named for the dead of the Hundred Years' War that England fought with France in the 14th and 15th centuries. The college is notorious for having the toughest entrance exam and is nicknamed "the school with no students" as its student body is composed entirely of research fellows. Famous alums include Lawrence of Arabia and Christopher Wren—who designed the ornate sundial on the far left.

• *Just past Radcliffe Camera is the most important church in town.*

⓬ University Church of St. Mary the Virgin

The University Church is where the university was born, and it remains the heart of Oxford's sprawling campus. A thousand years ago, this church stood at the center of the small, walled town. (The tower—the oldest part of this much-renovated church—dates from 1270.) As the embryonic university formed, this church was its only building: where scholars prayed, lectured, kept their books, administered affairs, and received graduation degrees with pomp and circumstance. As the university expanded and secularized, scholastic activities gravitated outward—to the Divinity School, Bodleian Library, and so on. By the 1600s, even graduation ceremonies were deemed too inappropriate for a church, and were moved to Wren's new Sheldonian Theatre. But the University Church has always remained the place to where the university's community goes for spiritual sustenance. In 1942, a small group of Oxford citizens met here to help desperate WWII victims in Greece, and founded what grew into the worldwide relief organization called Oxfam.

Cost and Hours: Free, £5 tower climb (127 steps) with great views; Mon-Sat 9:30-17:00, Sun from 11:30; garden café, crypt.

Visiting the Church: The church interior reflects the delicate balance Oxford keeps between various religious ideologies: Protestants, Catholics, and secularists. Once ornately decorated for Catholic worship, the interior was cleaned out after the Reformation for Protestant-style worship. A plaque on the wall memorializes a century of local martyrs in the fight between Catholics and Protestants. The reformer John Wesley, who founded the Methodist Church, preached from this pulpit. And through all of the church's history, the university chancellor has had a place—in the grand wood-carved stall at the far end of the nave.

There's no better symbol of Oxford's intellectual battles than "Cranmer's pillar" (located across the nave from the pulpit, marked with a small plaque of Cranmer). In 1556, the Protestant Reformer Thomas Cranmer was imprisoned in Oxford and ordered to recant his Protestant beliefs. He signed the recantation and also agreed to make a full confession of his heresy in public. A stage was erected for him against this pillar (resulting in damage to the stone near the base). Cranmer mounted the stage, and shocked the crowd by disavowing his (forced) recantation, while proudly asserting his Protestant beliefs. Knowing he'd be burned at the stake, he swore the first thing that would burn would be "that unworthy hand" that had signed the recantation. On March 21, 1556, Cranmer was tied to the stake and burned (at the spot two previous "Oxford Martyrs" also died, marked by the brick cross on Broad Street we saw earlier).

• *Circle around behind the church to...*

⓭ High Street

The central axis of Oxford, High Street has more colleges to the left (east) and the city center to the right (west, beyond the church tower a couple of blocks away). Traditionally, there's been tension between the privileged university population and the hardscrabble citizens of Oxford. In fact, it was a town-and-gown riot in 1209 that drove a group of professors and students out of Oxford to quieter Cambridge to found a rival university.

• *Your walk is over, but several sights are nearby. To the right is the lively* **Covered Market,** *a huge collection of characteristic shops and eateries. To the left is a pleasant walk past several colleges to the delightful*

*Magdalen College and the best place in town for a river trip on a **punt** (both described later, under "Sights in Oxford").*

*Directly ahead is a lane leading to the most important college in town, **Christ Church College** (described next). Cross High Street, head down Magpie Lane, and pass Kybald Street with the back entrance to Bill Clinton's school—University College. At the end of Magpie Lane, cross the street and go through a black iron gate, follow the hedge-lined lane, go through a kissing gate, and emerge in the vast Christ Church Meadows outside the city wall. Around to the right is the entrance to Christ Church College.*

Sights in Oxford

Note that some of the city's worthwhile sights are covered earlier, in my "Oxford Walk."

THE COLLEGES

You could spend a lot of time going from college to college here—but since they all have similar features, frankly, if you've seen a couple, that's enough. Still, each is unique—like individual works of art mixing architecture, gardens, and heritage. I've described just my three favorites: The dominant Christ Church College and the more intimate and welcoming Magdalen and Exeter Colleges. The entrance to each college is easy to spot—just look for a doorway with crests and a flagpole on the top. Each entry has an office with a porter (live-in caretaker). Inquire there to find out which buildings are open to visitors, and if any plays, music, evensong services, or lectures are scheduled.

▲Christ Church College

Of Oxford's colleges, Christ Church is the largest and most prestigious (and, some think, most pretentious). It's also the most popular (and most expensive) for tourists to visit—partly thanks to its historic fame, but mostly because scenes in the Harry Potter movies were filmed here.

The college was founded by Henry VIII's chancellor, Cardinal Thomas Wolsey, in 1524 on the site of an abbey dissolved by the king. The buildings survived the tumult of the Reformation because the abbey and its cathedral served as part of the king's new Church of England. It still has a close connection to the royal family. While all colleges boast of their esteemed alumni, none has a list as esteemed as Christ Church College: 13 of the 27 Oxford-educated prime ministers were Christ Church alums. William Penn (founder of Pennsylvania), John Wesley (influential Methodist leader), John Locke (English Enlightenment thinker), and Charles Dodgson (a.k.a. Lewis Carroll) also studied here. Its grounds include a grand old dining hall, a giant quad, and an impressive chapel that doubles as a cathedral.

Cost and Hours: £10—buy timed-entry ticket online in advance to bypass line, family ticket available; Mon-Sat 10:00-17:00, Sun from 14:00, last entry 45 minutes before closing; tel. 01865/276-492, www.chch.ox.ac.uk.

Dining Hall Closure: Note that the dining hall—the prime attraction for Harry Potter fans—is closed to outsiders when students are eating here. During the term, it's generally open to visitors Mon-Fri 10:00-11:30 & 14:00-17:00, Sat-Sun 14:00-17:00—but it can close on short notice. (Outside the school term, it's typically open daily 10:30-17:00.) Call ahead or check the website and plan your visit accordingly.

Evensong: Most days in Christ Church Cathedral, an excellent choir of students (sometimes accompanied by angelic-if-fidgety little boys) sings along to the church's pipe organ. This delightful service is open to anyone; linger after the service ends to hear the organist jam (free, Tue-Sun at 18:00, Mon service is spoken rather than sung, enter at Tom Tower, arrive 15-20 minutes early). For more on evensong, see page 153.

Getting There: The college is located on St. Aldate's; follow *Visitors' Entrance* signs (past the big tower and all the way to the end of the biggest building, toward the river). If visiting Christ Church after completing my self-guided walk, see the end of the walk for directions.

Visiting the College: As you enter the grounds through the visitors' entrance, you'll pass through a bit of countryside spreading out to the river. This huge park is actually part of the college. Called **Christ Church Meadow,** it was the setting Lewis Carroll used for the croquet scenes in *Alice's Adventures in Wonderland* (free, open dawn to dusk).

Your ticket comes with the essential self-guided tour booklet with map. "Custodians" wearing bowler hats are posted around the college to answer questions. You'll be sent along a one-way route with these main stops: dining hall, quadrangle, cathedral, and picture gallery.

Dining Hall: There's a commotion as you near the college's famous dining hall (passing a small cloister and a grand staircase where some Harry Potter scenes were filmed). The grand hall—with its splendid Gothic, hammer-beam ceiling and portraits of esteemed alumni looking down on its oh-so-old-English tables—is an amazing scene. The primary sponsor of the college is centered above the high table—Henry VIII in his younger, slimmer days—who took over after he deposed Cardinal Wosley. Below him is the bust of the current presiding royal (Queen Elizabeth II).

While Harry Potter scenes were filmed along the staircase with its fan-vaulted ceiling and mullion windows, the grand dining hall merely served as a model for set designers. Astute visitors immediately notice there are just three long rows of tables, not four as in Hogwarts.

Beyond the Harry Potter ties, there's also a strong Lewis Carroll connection. Carroll, a math professor in the college, was inspired by the dean's daughter Alice to create the adventures of *Alice in Wonderland*. The Alice in Wonderland window (above the fireplace, on the left) is rich with symbolic references to that book. In the upper half (on left in the yellow circle) is the real Alice (Alice Liddell) and opposite (on right in a similar circle) is the author.

Quadrangle: Now enter Tom Quad, a grassy field surrounded by college buildings. In the middle is a small fishpond with a statue of Mercury. Notice the outlines of archways ringing the quad; the architect wanted to create a giant cloister here, but funding ran out. (You can imagine the effect had the cloister been finished.)

The tall tower, designed by Christopher Wren, holds a six-ton bell called **Great Tom**. According to tradition, every night at 21:05 the bell clangs out 101 times—each chime calling the curfew for the 101 students who first boarded here. This gives the students four-and-a-half minutes to get from the pub through the gate by the last ring. Why not on the hour? When the tradition began, time zones had yet to be standardized—and since Oxford was 60 miles or five minutes of longitude west of Greenwich, clocks here were set five minutes earlier. That means 21:05 Greenwich Mean Time was 21:00 on the dot Oxford time. Although the UK standardized its time zone in the 1850s, Christ Church College has insisted on keeping Oxford time. (And that explains why the White Rabbit in *Alice in Wonderland* is always late.)

Cathedral: The college's 800-year-old chapel also serves as Christ Church Cathedral (the seat of an Anglican bishop). Built in the 12th century, it's one of oldest buildings in Oxford and one of England's smallest cathedrals. For 400 years, this was a monastery church. With the Reformation, England's monasteries were dissolved and most churches like this were destroyed, but this one survived. Through the centuries Bishop Berkeley (who inspired the founding of a great university in

Literary Oxford

Oxford's list of alumni is almost laughably impressive. A virtual factory for famous politicians—among them a couple dozen prime ministers (including the two most recent, Theresa May and Boris Johnson), Indira Gandhi, and Bill Clinton (who took classes here as a Rhodes scholar)—it's also the home of some of the most important scientists of the 20th century. Stephen Hawking (*A Brief History of Time*) went to Oxford, Richard Dawkins (*The Selfish Gene*) taught at Oxford, and Tim Berners-Lee—inventor of the World Wide Web—got in trouble for hacking into Oxford's computers. But Oxford may be most famous for its literary past.

J. R. R. Tolkien (1892-1973) graduated from the university and was a professor at Oxford, teaching the glories of Anglo-Saxon language and English literature through one of his favorite works, the epic poem *Beowulf*. He spent years in Oxford writing the books he's most famous for: *The Hobbit* and the three volumes of *The Lord of the Rings*, beloved by millions of readers.

C. S. Lewis (1898-1963), Tolkien's good friend, was a fellow at Oxford for almost 30 years. Lewis sent generations of children through the back of a wardrobe in his series *The Chronicles of Narnia*. At Oxford, Lewis was also the ringleader of a famous writing society called the Inklings, who met regularly at The Eagle and Child pub (which they called the "Bird and Baby"; see "Eating in Oxford," later). Picture these literary geniuses sitting in the pub's familiar confines. Lewis orders another round, while Tolkien tells Frodo's tale—with a pipe in hand—for the first time.

The Oxford-educated poet **W. H. Auden** (1907-1973) was a lifelong friend and correspondent of Tolkien's. (He was one of the first critics to publicly praise *The Lord of the Rings*.) Auden may be most familiar to Americans for the lines of his poem "Funeral Blues" that were quoted in the film *Four Weddings and a Funeral*: "He was my North, my South, my East and West, / My working week and my Sunday rest, / My noon, my midnight, my talk, my song; / I thought that love would last for ever: I was wrong."

Lewis Carroll (1832-1898), the pen name of Charles Lutwidge Dodgson, was a mathematician who taught at Oxford, where he met Alice Liddell, the dean's daughter and real-life inspiration for *Alice's Adventures in Wonderland*. The author lived at Christ Church College, and Carroll and Liddell would regularly play croquet—without the Queen of Hearts—in The Meadow.

California) and John Wesley (who founded the Methodist Church) both preached from the pulpit here. The church's highlights include a shrine to St. Frideswide—an obscure local saint who, in about the year 700, founded the first church in Oxford—in the northeast corner Latin Chapel. Vibrant Pre-Raphaelite windows from 1858 by Edward Burne-Jones tell the saint's story. In the south transept, a stained-glass window from 1320 shows the martyrdom of

Aldous Huxley (1894-1963), a prolific novelist and Oxford student, wrote the early science-fiction classic *Brave New World*, about a disturbing, mindless future. His later book, *The Doors of Perception*, was written under the influence of mescaline. (Jim Morrison, another fan of mind-altering experiences, named his band The Doors after the book.)

Literary great **Virginia Woolf** (1882-1941) was banned from using Oxford's library because she was a woman (Oxford didn't begin admitting women until 1920, though they could attend some classes before that). She later wrote her most important essay, "A Room of One's Own," where she parodied the university she nicknamed "Oxbridge," a combination of Oxford and Cambridge.

Oscar Wilde (1854-1900) did well at Oxford (graduating with the highest grade possible) and went on to become famous for his novels *(The Picture of Dorian Gray)*, plays *(The Importance of Being Earnest)*, homosexuality (his famous trial sent him to jail), and memorably witty quotes, such as "Men marry because they are tired; women, because they are curious: both are disappointed." Another of his quotes: "I can resist everything except temptation." And another: "We are all in the gutter, but some of us are looking at the stars."

Oxford's other notable literary stars include the poet **Percy Bysshe Shelley, Jonathan Swift** *(Gulliver's Travels)*, **T. S. Eliot** *(The Waste Land)*, **John le Carré** *(The Spy Who Came in from the Cold)*, **Philip Pullman** *(The Golden Compass*, part of his children's book series *His Dark Materials)*, **Martin Amis** *(Time's Arrow)*, **Helen Fielding** *(Bridget Jones's Diary)*, and—maybe most important of all to generations of children's book readers—Theodor Seuss Geisel (a.k.a. **Dr. Seuss**).

In addition to the **Harry Potter** connection, Brits are enthralled by locations relating to the Oxford-set **Inspector Morse** television series, an enormous UK hit from 1987 to 2000 (the equally popular sequels, **Inspector Lewis** and **Endeavour,** were also filmed here). Sort of the British Columbo or a modern-day Sherlock Holmes, this fictional police detective—having been trained as a scholar but opting for a real-world job—was quirky, cultured, and extremely effective.

Thomas Becket (whose face was blanked out to help him survive the Reformation).

To exit, you'll be steered through the Tom Quad again through Peckwater Quad (with not-very humble student accommodations facing the library). Note the graffiti on the walls here. This is the only allowable graffiti in Oxford: When rowing teams win, they can chalk their victory on the wall for all to see and celebrate.

(From March through June, only Picture Gallery ticket-holders can enter Peckwater Quad. During those months, go through the cloister and exit the college the way you entered.)

Picture Gallery: The sleepy Christ Church Picture Gallery rotates its collection of drawings and sketches by Albrecht Dürer, Michelangelo, Leonardo da Vinci, Raphael, and other Old Masters. There's also a permanent exhibit of oil paintings by the likes of Tintoretto, Veronese, Van Dyck, and Frans Hals (£4, £2 if you paid to enter the college; generally open Mon & Wed-Sat 10:30-17:00, Sun from 14:00, closed Tue. If visiting without touring the campus, enter at the Canterbury Gate, off Oriel Square).

Magdalen College

Sitting on the upper edge of town, this college (pronounced "maudlin")—where C. S. Lewis taught for 25 years—is my vote for the prettiest in Oxford. Pick up the self-guided walk brochure when you enter. Established in 1480, its cloister is a monastic-feeling square of stone and flowers, with narrow staircases leading to student rooms and gargoyles overhead—keeping an eye on things for more than 500 years. From the cloister, a sign for "Hall" directs you up some stairs to the dining hall (closed to public midday for student lunch). The chapel is gorgeous (with a fascinating black-and-white stained-glass window in the antechamber). Magdalen has the largest grounds of any of the Oxford colleges (big enough to include its own deer park, with actual deer browsing the grounds) and a peaceful café overlooking the sleepy river and lively punting scene.

Cost and Hours: £7, July-Sept daily 10:00-19:00, rest of the year open 13:00-18:00 or dusk—whichever is earlier, £10 guided tours sometimes offered in summer—ask at visitor desk, High Street next to Magdalen Bridge, tel. 01865/276-000.

Evensong: Evensong services in the exquisite chapel take place Tue-Sun at 18:00 (except July-Sept); while most days feature a mixed chorus of boys and men, Tuesday is generally the renowned boys choir, and Fridays is men only.

Exeter College

A smaller college, 700-year-old Exeter is centrally located, free to visit, and worth a peek. The highlight is its jewel-like Neo-Gothic chapel—oh-so Victorian from the 1860s and inspired by Paris' Sainte-Chapelle. It features William Morris' *The Adoration of the Magi* tapestry (on

the right). A bust of J. R. R. Tolkien, who studied here, is in the back.

Cost and Hours: Free, usually open daily 14:00-17:00, Turl Street, tel. 01865/279-600.

OTHER SIGHTS

▲▲Ashmolean Museum of Art and Archaeology

In 1683, celebrated antiquary Elias Ashmole insisted his collection of curiosities deserved its own building. Half of his trove originated with an even-more-eccentric royal gardener, John Tradescant, who loved to seek out interesting items while traveling in search of plants. Since its founding, this eclectic museum has expanded its reach across art forms, cultures, and centuries. Thanks to ongoing support, the huge collection continues to grow all these years later.

Cost and Hours: Free, suggested £5 donation, daily 10:00-17:00, basic café, rooftop restaurant open until 22:00 Thu-Sat, Beaumont Street, tel. 01865/278-000, www.ashmolean.org.

Visiting the Museum: While it doesn't rank with the big-league museums of London, the Ashmolean's vast holdings are

impressive for a small city. You won't see any particularly famous items, but will find intriguing and offbeat bits and pieces (such as Lawrence of Arabia's ceremonial dress, prehistoric Cycladic figurines from Greece, gorgeous Turkish and Middle Eastern tiles, a Stradivarius violin, and so on). The sheer volume of objects can be overwhelming, so check the sign across from the info desk for daily activities and current exhibits to zero in on your interests.

The museum is loosely organized geographically, with excellent displays of Chinese, Middle Eastern, Indian, Mediterranean, and other regional art and artifacts.

For an engaging introduction, head for the basement and peruse the "Exploring the Past" themed exhibits, which bring together eras of history and corners of the globe while examining a particular topic (such as money, textiles, and conservation). For example, the reading and writing section investigates translations of fragments of cuneiform from the ancient Near East, Linear B (early Greek), Scandinavian runes, and Egyptian papyrus.

As you browse your way up the floors, find your own favorites (I enjoyed the paintings of royal elephants from India). The Egyptian galleries feature various mummies, including a priest, a two-year-old boy, a cat, and even a baby crocodile. The Randolph

Student Life in Oxford Colleges

While we think of it as one big university, Oxford consists of 38 autonomous, self-funded colleges. Student life is centered around the particular college, where students eat, sleep, and make friends.

The college system really took off in 1167, when King Henry II banned English students from attending the University of Paris. The students—mostly poor peasant kids who'd been fortunate enough to be educated by monks—took refuge in Oxford. The teachers took them under their wing, renting out boarding houses and looking after them in an almost monastic environment. Each college had a particular  focus—for example, for 300 years Jesus College was exclusively for Welsh students, to produce that tribe's educated elite. Because colleges were behind walls, the townsfolk accused them of elitism, prompting "town-and-gown" clashes that occasionally turned violent. Nowadays, things are more relaxed. Each college may have a particular reputation (say, for science or literature), but students from any major can live there. Students must live there the first year, but might find accommodations elsewhere afterward. Even so, colleges are still very much their own world and many old traditions carry on for generations. Gowns (which

Sculpture Gallery, near the entrance, features Greek and Roman statues.

The museum's fine painting gallery showcases lesser-known pieces by Degas, Pissarro, Van Gogh, and others. It's fun to see artist J. M. W. Turner's view down High Street in Oxford...then walk a block to see today's version. If nothing else, the Ashmolean provides visitors to this university town a way to see a respectable range of English glass, Chinese porcelain, ancient sculpture, and tapestries without having to ride the train.

▲Oxford Castle

Originating as a classic Norman motte-and-bailey fort a millennium ago, Oxford's castle gradually evolved into a mighty fortress that was mostly destroyed after the English Civil War. Its surviving St. George Tower was used as a royalist prison, and—a century-and-a-half later—was expanded into a Victorian-era county jail, specializing in demoralizing prisoners with exhausting and humiliating punishments. The facility held prisoners up until 1996. Since used to be worn all the time) are still required for some formal dinners and functions.

Today, some 22,000 students attend Oxford (including 12,000 undergraduates, nearly all British, and 10,000 graduate students—mostly foreigners—whose higher fees help fund the university). Tuition runs about £10,000 a year for UK and EU residents; non-EU students pay double. The university is very exclusive—about 1 in 10 who apply get in.

Students enter the college in October and spend their first year preparing for preliminary exams. Once that hurdle is cleared, they study for two more years preparing for their final exams. If you visit in June, you might see students on their way to their finals wearing traditional academic robes and carnations on their lapels: white on the first

day, pink on the second day, and red on the final day. When students emerge from their final exam wearing a red carnation, they're greeted by friends and family who douse them with flour, glitter, and champagne or beer (a tradition called "trashing"). There's usually a happy ending: Among those who remain at Oxford all three years, the graduation rate is nearly 100 percent.

then, part of the complex was converted into a posh hotel, while the rest is now a tourist attraction. England has far bigger and better castles, but this is an entertaining and educational alternative to all of Oxford's academic sights.

Cost and Hours: £12.50 includes mandatory one-hour tour, daily 10:00-16:20, tours run every 20 minutes—book online in advance to avoid waiting during peak times; £1 if you only want to climb the motte and bailey; open daily 10:00-17:00; 44 Oxford Castle, tel. 01865/260-666, www.oxfordcastleandprison.co.uk.

Visiting the Castle: Although the surviving bits of the castle are small and sparse (basically, the original motte and bailey, one tall tower, and a few cells), this shell is brought to life by the one-hour tour led by a lively guide dressed in period garb.

The tour includes a climb to the top of the St. George Tower (for distant views over the town) and a visit to the crypt below, with an emphasis on grisly tales of prison life. You'll learn of cruel and unusual punishments and see the deep, circular grooves in the floor where prisoners were forced to work eight-hour shifts trudging around a capstan wheel in silence. The tour provides a strong historical basis—spinning the true tales of Empress Matilda (the usurped queen who dramatically escaped from here and went on to support her son in his quest to become King Henry II), Geoffrey of Monmouth (who first penned tales of King Arthur and Merlin in the 12th century), and other important figures connected to the castle. You'll also learn about everyday folks, like the two 17-year-old boys who served 21 days for stealing bread, and a 7-year-old girl, imprisoned for a week for borrowing a toy pram without permission. After the tour, you'll be set free to explore exhibits about prison history. Admission also includes access to the original motte (hill), where you can wind up the path to the scant remains of the bailey (fort).

Punting

Long, flat boats can be rented for punting (pushing with a long pole) along the River Cherwell. Chauffeurs are available, while the do-it-yourself crowd tends to get a little wet. Punting looks easier than it is, and you'll likely see first-timers creating log jams of incompetence. The guided ride includes a short lesson so you can actually learn how to do it right.

Cost and Hours: £22-24/hour per boat rental, £30 deposit if paying cash, leave ID with credit card; chauffeured punts-£30-32 per boat for 30 minutes and up to 4 people, higher prices for Sat-Sun; book ahead for weekends, rowboats and paddle boats available for the less adventurous, daily 9:30-dusk, closed Dec-Jan, Magdalen Bridge Boathouse, tel. 01865/202-643, www.oxfordpunting.co.uk.

Sleeping in Oxford

Sleeping cheaply in Oxford is not easy—you'll pay London-size prices for London-size rooms. The colleges and university own much of the town, so boarding space is at a premium. A few B&Bs line the main roads out of town, but they're less convenient for sightseeing; in the town center (where I've focused my listings), you'll find high-priced hotels and guesthouses in very old and poorly maintained buildings. Noise is an issue—mostly from students conversing or singing loudly in the streets on the way home from the pub. Try requesting a quiet room, but expect some noise regardless. Given the easy connections by train to the Cotswolds (Moreton-in-Marsh) and London, it's possible to make Oxford a day trip and sleep elsewhere. But if you're spending the night, here are some centrally located, reasonable options.

$$$$ The Tower House—with tight spaces, low ceilings, and small, worn-but-sweet rooms—couldn't be more central. Three of the eight rooms share a bathroom with a shower (reception and included breakfast around the corner at Turl Street Kitchen, no parking, request a quieter back room, 15 Ship Street, tel. 01865/246-828, www.towerhouseoxford.co.uk, info@towerhouseoxford.co.uk).

$$$ The Bocardo offers modern lodgings along bustling George Street, between the train station and the town center. Rare in this creaky old town, the 11 rooms come with urban style and lots of amenities. It's on a street with lots of nightclubs, so expect noise, and try asking for a quieter room (no breakfast, air-con, 24 George Street, tel. 01865/591-234, www.thebocardo.co.uk, reservations@thebocardo.co.uk).

$$$ Bath Place Hotel is a family-run place renting 16 humble rooms in a cluster of 17th century cottages tucked next to the bustling Turf Tavern courtyard. Rooms have modern en-suite bathrooms; the bedrooms are a bit worn but full of charm, with exposed beams and pitched ceilings (family rooms available, laundry service, off Holywell Street at 4 Bath Place, tel. 01865/791-812, www.bathplace.co.uk, info@bathplace.co.uk).

$$ The Buttery Hotel, up steep steps above a bakery (hence the name) and two doors down from the TI, rents 16 good-value rooms. The "deluxe" rooms are larger and have big windows overlooking bustling Broad Street—nice for views but not for noise; the cheaper "standard" rooms are quieter (family room available, no breakfast, no parking, 11 Broad Street, tel. 01865/811-950, www.thebutteryhotel.co.uk, enquiries@thebutteryhotel.co.uk, Sally).

$$ University Rooms offers budget-friendly en-suite rooms, many in the historic college buildings right in the center of Oxford. Like Booking.com, you choose from what's available based on your travel dates (family rooms available, some rooms do not include breakfast, better selection during school breaks, www.universityrooms.com).

¢ Hostels: This youthful town has two different hostels with "Backpackers" in their names, on parallel roads, both a 3-minute walk from the train station on the way to the town center. **Oxford Backpackers Hostel,** with ambience somewhere between grotty and funky, rents beds in single-sex and mixed dorms (includes continental breakfast, reception open 7:00-23:00, laundry service, 9A Hythe Bridge Street, tel. 01865/721-761, www.hostels.co.uk, oxford@hostels.co.uk). **Central Backpackers Oxford** is a Canadian- and Aussie-run place, with dorm rooms set around an inviting covered patio. It feels a bit tamer than Oxford Backpackers and has daily activities such as movie nights, BBQs, and pub crawls (no breakfast, laundry service, 13 Park End Street, tel. 01865/242-288, www.centralbackpackers.co.uk, oxford@centralbackpackers.co.uk).

Near Oxford: The charming 16th-century **$$ Coach & Horses Inn** is located seven miles southeast of Oxford in Chislehampton, across the street from a bus stop that connects the two towns (free parking, pub, tel. 01865/890-255, www.coachhorsesinn.co.uk, enquiries@coachhorsesinn.co.uk).

Eating in Oxford

PUBS

These pubs perfectly conform to what Americans imagine a British pub to be: a rambling series of cozy, well-worn rooms on sloping wooden floors filled with tight clusters of friends enjoying food and ale around ancient-feeling tables. The hours listed below are for when food is served—most stay open later to serve drinks.

$$ The King's Arms, across from the Clarendon Building, serves burgers and traditional English fare, including steak-and-ale pie and fish-and-chips in a convivial atmosphere (daily 11:00-21:30, 40 Holywell Street at corner of Parks Road, tel. 01865/242-369).

$$$ The Bear, hidden down a side street and close to the Christ Church Picture Gallery, is one of Oxford's oldest and most charming pubs. This teensy place proudly sports no right angles (go ahead—check) since 1242. Peruse the framed collections of amputated clothing on the walls and hold on to your tie if you're wearing one. If you're coming for lunch, arrive before the rush at 13:00 (daily 12:00-21:00, 6 Alfred Street at corner of Blue Boar Street, tel. 01865/728-164). There are a few picnic tables out back—leave through the pub's side door to find them, or walk to the left as you're facing the front.

$$$ The Turf Tavern—big, boisterous, and tucked into a short alley—is popular for its solid grub, outdoor beer garden, and warren of claustrophobic rooms nestled against the old city wall (daily 11:00-21:00, 4 Bath Place, tel. 01865/243-235). Advertising "an education in intoxication," this is reputedly the place where Bill Clinton didn't inhale. To find it from Holywell Street or the Bridge of Sighs on Queen's Lane, listen for the chatter of students enjoying a beer; otherwise, head for the gap marked *St. Helen's Passage*.

$$ The Eagle and Child, a long and thin series of rooms, is subdued, smaller, and more intimate than the other pubs listed. A five-minute walk from the city center, it's famous for its history and ambience. This was the gathering place of the writers known as the

Inklings (see sidebar on page 534), and a literary vibe still haunts the place. If you're a fan of Middle-earth and Narnia, stop in for a drink under photos of J. R. R. Tolkien and C. S. Lewis. The food is traditional, with a seasonal, modern twist (read the history above the door to the bar, Mon-Sat 11:00-21:00, Sun 12:00-20:00, 49 St. Giles Street, tel. 01865/302-925).

EATING CHEAPLY

$ Taylors is a student favorite for affordable high-quality panini and other deli items. There are a few tables, but most people get food to go and find a scenic spot for a picnic (daily 8:00-18:00, 19 High Street, tel. 01865/790-757). Other Taylors locations are in the Covered Market, and a block from Magdalen College at 58 High Street.

   $ Covered Market—a farmers market maze of shops, fruit stands, deli counters, and cafés—has a fine selection for breakfast, lunch, or a picnic (shops generally open around 8:00-10:00 and close around 16:30-17:30, on Sun generally open 10:00-16:00, between Market Street and High Street, near Carfax Tower). In particular, **$ Alpha Bar,** on the Market Street side, is known for its cheap but satisfying sandwich and salad offerings—the long lines at lunchtime speak for themselves (Mon-Sat 11:00-15:00).

   Chain Restaurants and Groceries: On Cornmarket, you'll find a slew of chain eateries with to-go food. George Street, which intersects Cornmarket on its way to the train station, has another string of reliable chains. For a picnic lunch, there's a **Marks & Spencer** at 18 Queen Street (near Carfax Tower), and **Sainsbury'**s at 21 Westgate (in the mall), St. Clement's Street (at the end of Magdalen bridge), and 7 Magdalen Street (near the Ashmolean Museum).

OTHER EATERIES

$$ Turl Street Kitchen, started by three Oxford grads, focuses on locally and ethically sourced ingredients. The menu changes daily, and good vegetarian options are always available. Their profits help support the charity Student Hubs, which connects students with various social causes. Service is thoughtful and unhurried (light breakfast also available; Sun-Wed 8:00-17:00, Thu-Sat until 23:00; 16 Turl Street, tel. 01865/264-171).

   $$$ No. 1 Ship Street, a modern British brasserie serving steak, lamb, and fish, and afternoon tea, is a nice break from the

OXFORD

student mobs and chain eateries on nearby Cornmarket (Mon-Sat 12:00-22:00, Sun until 16:30, 1 Ship Street, tel. 01865/806-637).

Afternoon Tea: $$$$ The Macdonald Randolph Hotel is a swanky place where proud parents take their graduating students for a fancy afternoon tea (reserve ahead, especially near the end of the term). You'll enjoy impeccable service and classic English afternoon tea under high ceilings and chandeliers (tea served daily 12:00-18:00, Beaumont Street, directly opposite Ashmolean Museum, tel. 0344/879-9132). **$$ The Rose,** a more affordable, less crowded alternative, offers good scones in a nondescript, modern atmosphere (daily 9:00-18:00, 51 High Street, tel. 01865/244-429).

Oxford Connections

From Oxford by Train to: London's Paddington Station (2/hour direct, 1 hour), **Bath** (2/hour, 1.5 hours, transfer in Didcot), **Moreton-in-Marsh** (hourly, 40 minutes), **Stratford-upon-Avon** (every 2 hours, 1.5 hours, transfer in Leamington Spa, Birmingham, or Banbury), **Salisbury** (1-2/hour, 2 hours, transfer in Basingstoke and sometimes also Reading), **Portsmouth** (3/hour, 2.5 hours, 1-2 transfers), **York** (hourly direct, 3.5 hours, more with transfers). **Train info:** tel. 0345-748-4950, www.nationalrail.co.uk.

By Bus to London: The Oxford Tube bus runs every 12-20 minutes during peak times to London's **Notting Hill Gate, Marble Arch,** and **Victoria Coach Station** (otherwise 2/hour, free Wi-Fi, tel. 01865/772-250, www.oxfordtube.com). The competing X90 bus runs every 15 minutes during peak times to **Baker Street, Marble Arch,** and **Victoria Coach Station** (otherwise 2-3/hour, free Wi-Fi, tel. 01865/785-400, www.oxfordbus.co.uk). The trip to London takes about 1.5 hours, and all buses depart from the Gloucester Green bus station—just show up and ask which bus is leaving first. National Express also runs buses to London (2/hour, 2.5 hours).

By Bus to Other Destinations: An independent bus service called The Airline shuttles students and visitors directly between Oxford and **Heathrow Airport** 24 hours a day (2/hour, 1.5 hours, £23) and to **Gatwick Airport** (hourly, 2.5 hours, £28; tel. 01865/785-400, www.theairline.info).

National Express runs buses to **Cambridge** (2/hour, 3.5 hours), **Stratford-upon-Avon** (1/day direct, 1 hour), and **Bath** (3/day direct, 2 hours, more with transfer). **Bus info:** Tel. 0871-781-8181, www.nationalexpress.com. For details on taking a public bus to **Blenheim Palace,** see the next section.

Blenheim Palace

Just 30 minutes' drive from Oxford (and convenient to combine with a drive through the Cotswolds), Blenheim Palace is one of England's best—worth ▲▲▲. Too many palaces can send you into a furniture-wax coma, but as a sightseeing experience and in simple visual grandeur, this palace is among Europe's finest. The Duke of Marlborough's home—one of the largest in England—is still lived in, which is wonderfully obvious as you prowl through it. The 2,000-acre yard, well-designed by Lancelot "Capability" Brown, is as majestic to some as the palace itself. Note: Americans who pronounce the place "blen-HEIM" are the butt of jokes. It's "BLEN-em."

John Churchill, first Duke of Marlborough, achieved Europe-wide renown with his stunning victory over Louis XIV of France's armies at the Battle of Blenheim in 1704. This was a major turning point in the War of the Spanish Succession—one of Louis' repeated attempts to gain hegemony over the continent. A thankful Queen Anne rewarded Churchill by building him this nice home, perhaps the finest Baroque building in England. Eleven dukes of Marlborough later, the palace is as impressive as ever. In 1874, a later John Churchill's American daughter-in-law, Jennie Jerome, gave birth at Blenheim to another historic baby in that line...and named him Winston.

GETTING TO BLENHEIM PALACE

Blenheim Palace sits at the edge of the cute cobbled town of Woodstock.

From Oxford by Bus: Take bus #S3 (2/hour, 40 minutes; bus tel. 01865/772-250, www.stagecoachbus.com). Catch it from the bus station at Gloucester Green or the train station. It stops twice near Blenheim Palace: the "Blenheim Palace Gates" stop is along the main road about a half-mile walk to the palace itself; the "Woodstock/Marlborough Arms" stop is in the village of Woodstock (handy if you want to poke around town before heading to the palace; this adds just a few more minutes' walking). The Woodstock stop also offers the most spectacular view of the palace and lake.

From the Cotswolds by Train: Your easiest train connection is from Moreton-in-Marsh to Hanborough—just 1.5 miles from the palace (£10, hourly, 30 minutes). From Hanborough station, take bus #233 (£3, buy on bus, 2/hour, 10 minutes, Mon-Sat only). Taxis don't wait at the station, but you can book one in advance (try A2B Taxis, tel. 07767/685-257; or Cabs 4U, tel. 07919/675-150).

By Car: Head for Woodstock (from the Cotswolds, follow signs for *Oxford* on the A-44); the palace is well-signposted once in town, just off the main road. Buy your ticket at the gate, then drive up the long driveway to park near the palace.

ORIENTATION TO BLENHEIM PALACE

Cost: £27, includes audioguide; park and gardens only-£17; 30% discount when you buy on site and show your train or bus ticket, discount palace tickets are available at TIs in surrounding towns—including Oxford and Moreton-in-Marsh—or on the #S3 bus from Oxford; family ticket available, £6.50 guidebook.

Hours: Daily 10:30-17:30, Nov-mid-Dec generally closed Mon-Tue, park open but palace closed mid-Dec-mid-Feb. Doors to the palace close at 16:45, it's "everyone out" at 17:30, and the park closes at 18:00. Late in the afternoon the palace is relaxed and quiet (even on the busiest of days).

Information: Tel. 0199/381-0530, www.blenheimpalace.com.

Tours: Audioguides are available for the **state rooms** (included in admission). Guided tours are available for the duke's **private apartment**—a.k.a. "Upstairs" Tour (£5, 2/hour, about 40 minutes, generally runs mid-Feb-Sept daily 11:00-16:30, tickets are limited), the **servants' quarters**—a.k.a. "Downstairs" Tour (£5, generally daily 10:30-16:00, about 40 minutes), and the **gardens** (included in admission).

Eating and Sleeping near the Palace: The **$$ Water Terrace Café** at the garden exit is delightful for basic lunch and teatime treats. The fancier **$$$ Orangery Restaurant,** serving afternoon tea and lunch, should be reserved in advance at the palace website (may be closed for renovation). There's also a **$** café with lighter fare in the East Courtyard Visitors Center and a **$** pizza café at the Pleasure Gardens.

In the pleasant, posh town of Woodstock just outside the palace gates, **$ Hampers Deli** is a good place to pick up provisions for a picnic on the palace grounds (31 Oxford Street, tel. 01993/811-535, www.hampersfoodandwine.co.uk). If you need a bed, consider a room in the characteristic old half-timbered **$$ Blenheim Buttery** (7 Market Place, tel. 01865/811-950, www.theblenheimbuttery.co.uk, info@theblenheimbuttery.co.uk).

VISITING THE PALACE

From the parking lot, you'll enter through the Visitors Center (shop, café, and WCs). Pick up a free map and daily tour program, consider signing up at the welcome desk for tours of the private apartment and the gardens, and head through the small courtyard. You'll emerge into a grand courtyard in front of the palace's columned yellow facade.

Facing the palace's steps, consider your six options: the state rooms, the Winston Churchill Exhibition, a skippable multimedia exhibit called The Untold Story, the private apartment tour, the gardens, and the Churchills' Destiny exhibit. The first three of these starts in the Great Hall, directly ahead. The palace state rooms and Winston Churchill Exhibition are substantial and most important (allow 1.5 hours total for both). The private apartment tour, an excellent behind-the-scenes peek at the palace, requires a special ticket and meets in the corner of the courtyard to the left. The gardens, through the wing on the right, are simply enchanting. And the Churchills' Destiny exhibit, worth a 15-minute walk-through, is in the stables (West Courtyard) farther to the right.

State Rooms: The state rooms are the fancy halls the dukes use to impress visiting dignitaries. These most sumptuous rooms in the palace are ornamented with fine porcelain, gilded ceilings, portraits of past dukes, photos of the present duke's family, and "chaperone" sofas designed to give courting couples just enough privacy...but not *too* much.

Enjoy the series of 10 Brussels tapestries that commemorate military victories of the First Duke of Marlborough, including the Battle of Blenheim. After winning that pivotal conflict, he scrawled a quick note on the back of a tavern bill notifying the queen of his victory (you'll see a replica). The tour offers insights into the quirky ways of England's fading nobility—for example, in exchange for this fine palace, the duke still pays "rent" to the Queen in the form of one ornamental flag per year.

Finish with the remarkable "long library"—with its tiers of books and stuccoed ceilings—before exiting through the chapel, near the entrance to the gardens.

Winston Churchill Exhibition: This is a fascinating display of letters, paintings, and other artifacts of the great statesman who was born here. You'll either be instructed to see this before touring the main state rooms or directed into this exhibition from the library—the last room of the state rooms tour—before leaving the palace.

A highlight of your visit, the exhibit gives you an appreciation for this amazing leader and how blessed Britain was to have him when it did. Along with lots of intimate artifacts from his life, you'll see the bed in which Sir Winston was born in 1874 (prematurely...his mother went into labor suddenly while attending a party here).

The Untold Story: Upstairs, to the left as you enter the Great Hall, is a modern, 40-minute multimedia program with stories covering 300 years of palace history (this is skippable).

Private Apartment ("Upstairs" Tour): For a more extensive visit, book a spot to tour the duke's private digs (see "Tours," earlier). You'll see the chummy billiards room, luxurious china, the servants quarters with 47 bells—one for each room to call the servants, private rooms, 18th-century Flemish tapestries, family photos, and so on.

Churchills' Destiny: In the "stables block" (under the gateway to the right as you face the main palace entrance) is an exhibit that traces the military leadership of two great men who shared the name Churchill: John, who defeated Louis XIV at the Battle of Blenheim in the 18th century, and in whose honor this palace was built; and Winston, who was born in this palace, and who won the Battle of Britain and helped defeat Hitler in the 20th century. It's remarkable that arguably two of the most important military victories in the nation's history were overseen by distant cousins. (Winston Churchill fans can visit his tomb, just over a mile away to the south in the Bladon town churchyard—the church is faintly visible from inside the palace. Look for the footpath across from the White House pub.)

Gardens: The palace's expansive gardens stretch nearly as far as the eye can see in every direction. From the main courtyard follow signs through a little door (to the right as you face the main palace entrance). You'll emerge into the **Water Terraces;** from there, you can loop around to the left, behind  the palace, to see (but not enter) the Italian Garden. Or, head down to the lake to walk along the waterfront trail; going left takes you to the rose gardens and arboretum, while turning right brings you to the Grand Bridge.

On the way out of the palace complex, stop in at **Pleasure Gardens,** where a lush and humid greenhouse flutters with butterflies. A kid zone with the "world's largest symbolic hedge maze" is worth a look if you haven't seen one and want some exercise. If driving, you'll pass these gardens on the way to the exit; otherwise, you can take the tiny train from the palace parking lot (2/hour).

THE COTSWOLDS

Chipping Campden • Stow-on-the-Wold • Moreton-in-Marsh

The Cotswold Hills, a 25-by-90-mile chunk of Gloucestershire, are dotted with enchanting villages. As with many fairy-tale regions of Europe, the present-day beauty of the Cotswolds is the result of an economic disaster. Wool was a huge industry in medieval England, and Cotswold sheep grew the best wool. (The famed Cotswold Lion breed goes back to ancient times when Romans bred one of their sheep with the indigenous breed to make a hybrid version that was big, bad for meat, and great for wool.) A 12th-century saying bragged, "In Europe the best wool is English. In England the best wool is Cotswold." The region prospered. Wool money built fine towns and houses. Local "wool" churches are called "cathedrals" for their scale and wealth. Stained-glass slogans say things like "I thank my God and ever shall, it is the sheep hath paid for all."

But with the rise of cotton and the Industrial Revolution, the woolen industry collapsed. The wealthy Cotswold towns fell into a depressed time warp; the homes of impoverished nobility became gracefully dilapidated. Today, visitors enjoy a harmonious blend of man and nature—the most pristine of English countrysides decorated with time-passed villages, rich wool churches, tell-me-a-story stone fences, and "kissing gates" you wouldn't want to experience alone. Appreciated by throngs of 21st-century Romantics, the Cotswolds are enjoying new

prosperity as rural-rooted citizens have been joined by wealthy re-
tirees, London executives who don't mind a lengthy commute, and
celebrities.

The north Cotswolds are best. Two of the region's coziest
towns, Chipping Campden and Stow-on-the-Wold, are eight and
four miles, respectively, from Moreton-in-Marsh, which has the
best public transportation connections. Any of these three towns
makes a fine home base for your exploration of the thatch-happiest
of Cotswold villages and walks.

PLANNING YOUR TIME

The Cotswolds are an absolute delight by car and, with a well-or-
ganized plan—and patience—are enjoyable even without one. Do
your homework in advance; read this chapter carefully. Then decide
if you want to rent a car, rely on public transportation (budgeting
for an inevitable taxi ride), or reserve a day with a tour company or
private driver. Whatever you choose, on a three-week countrywide
trip, I'd spend at least two nights and a day in the Cotswolds—its
charm has a softening effect on many uptight itineraries. You could
enjoy days of walking from a home base here.

Home Bases: Quaint without being overrun, **Chipping
Campden** and **Stow-on-the-Wold** both have good accommodations. Stow has a bit more character for an overnight stay and offers the widest range of choices. The plainer town of **Moreton-
in-Marsh** is the only one of the three with a train station, and
only worth visiting as a transit hub. While Moreton has the most
convenient connections, it's possible for nondrivers to home-base
in Chipping Campden or Stow—especially if you don't mind sort-
ing through bus schedules or springing for the occasional taxi to
connect towns. (This becomes even more challenging on Sundays,
when there is essentially no bus service.) These three towns are a
10- to 15-minute drive apart from each other.

Tourist Traps (Broadway, Bourton-on-the-Water, and Bibury): Mass tourism is channeled to a handful of towns that cater
to big buses and their groups. Known as "The Bs," this trio of village cuteness has invested in convenient coach lots (the *terra firma*
equivalent of cruise ship docks), and they're capitalizing on their
over-the-top quaintness and fame. Expect traffic congestion and
lots of crowds during the day as most visitors are day-tripping from
London or Stratford. If flexible, enjoy these towns at the end of the
day when they're relaxed and quiet.

Nearby Sights: If you want to take in some Shakespeare, note
that Stow, Chipping Campden, and Moreton are only a 30-minute
drive from **Stratford,** which offers a great evening of world-class
entertainment (see next chapter). And England's top countryside
palace, **Blenheim,** is located at the eastern edge of the Cotswolds,

between Moreton and Oxford (see previous chapter). For drivers, Blenheim fits well on the way into or out of the region.

One-Day Driver's Cotswold Blitz: Use a good map and re-shuffle this plan to fit your home base:

9:00	Browse through Chipping Campden, following my self-guided walk.
10:30	Joyride through Snowshill, Stanway, and Stanton, sightseeing at your choice of several worthwhile stops in the area.
13:00	Have lunch in Stow-on-the-Wold, then follow my self-guided walk there.
16:00	Drive to the Slaughters and Bourton-on-the-Water or Northleach; or, if you're up for a hike instead of a drive, walk from Stow to the Slaughters to Bourton, then catch the bus back to Stow.
19:00	Have dinner at a countryside gastropub (reserve in advance), then head home; or drive 30 minutes to Stratford-upon-Avon for a Shakespeare play.

Two-Day Plan by Public Transportation: This plan is best for any day except Sunday—when virtually no buses run—and assumes you're home-basing in Moreton-in-Marsh.

Day 1: Take the morning bus to Chipping Campden (likely departing around 9:30) to explore that town. Hike up Dover's Hill and back (about one-hour round-trip), or take the bus to Mickleton and walk (uphill, 45 minutes) to Hidcote Manor Garden for a visit there. Eat lunch in Chipping Campden, then squeeze in either Broad Campden or Broadway before returning directly from Broadway (bus #1 only) or Chipping Campden (bus #1 or #2) to Moreton.

Day 2: Take a morning bus to Stow. After poking around the town, hike from Stow through the Slaughters to Bourton-on-the-Water (about 3 hours at a relaxed pace), then return by bus or taxi to Moreton for dinner.

TOURIST INFORMATION

Local TIs stock a wide array of helpful resources and can tell you about any local events during your stay. Ask for the *Cotswold Lion* (or download the PDF from www.cotswoldsaonb.org.uk/about-us), the biannual magazine that includes listings for guided walks and hikes, events, and festivals. Each village also has its own assortment of brochures, often for a small fee. While being asked to pay for these items seems chintzy, realize that Cotswold TIs have lost much of their government funding and are struggling to make ends meet (some are run by volunteers). Most also sell Ordnance Survey maps prepared by the British government that are ideal for hiking. The "OS Maps" app has free basic maps of the region, and any purchase of a paper OS map comes with a code for a free digital version through the app.

GETTING AROUND THE COTSWOLDS
By Car

Joyriding here truly is a joy. Winding country roads seem designed to spring bucolic village-and-countryside scenes on the driver at every turn. Distances are wonderfully short, and easily navigable with GPS. As a backup, you could invest in the Ordnance Survey map of the Cotswolds, sold locally at TIs and newsstands (the £9 Explorer OL #45 map is excellent but geared toward hiking and is too detailed for drivers; a £5 tour map covers a wider area in less detail). Here are driving distances from Moreton: **Stow-on-the-Wold** (4 miles), **Chipping Campden** (8 miles), **Broadway** (10 miles), **Stratford-upon-Avon** (17 miles), **Warwick** (23 miles), **Blenheim Palace** (20 miles).

Car hiking is great. In this chapter, I cover the postcard-perfect (but discovered) villages. With a car and a good map (either GPS or the local Ordnance Survey), you can easily ramble about and find your own gems. The problem with having a car is that you are less likely to walk. Consider taking a taxi or bus somewhere, so that you can walk back to your car and enjoy the scenery (see suggestions next).

By Bus

The Cotswolds are so well-preserved, in part, because public transportation to and within this area has long been miserable. Fortunately, trains link the region to larger towns, and a few key buses connect the more interesting villages. Centrally located Moreton-in-Marsh is the region's transit hub—with the only train station and several bus lines.

To explore the towns, use the bus routes that hop through the Cotswolds about every 1.5 hours, lacing together main stops and ending at train stations. In each case, the entire trip takes about an hour. Individual fares are around £4. If you plan on taking more than two rides in a day, consider the Cotswolds Discoverer pass, which offers unlimited travel on most buses including those listed below (£10/day, www.escapetothecotswolds.org.uk/discoverer).

The TI hands out easy-to-read bus schedules for the key lines described here (or check www.traveline.info, or call the Traveline

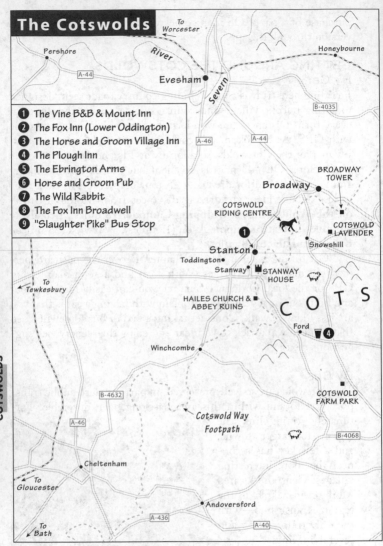

The Cotswolds

To Worcester

1. The Vine B&B & Mount Inn
2. The Fox Inn (Lower Oddington)
3. The Horse and Groom Village Inn
4. The Plough Inn
5. The Ebrington Arms
6. Horse and Groom Pub
7. The Wild Rabbit
8. The Fox Inn Broadwell
9. "Slaughter Pike" Bus Stop

Pershore

River Severn

Evesham

Honeybourne

A-44

B-4035

A-46

A-44

BROADWAY TOWER

Broadway

COTSWOLD RIDING CENTRE

COTSWOLD LAVENDER

Snowshill

1 Stanton

Toddington

Stanway

STANWAY HOUSE

C O T S

To Tewkesbury

HAILES CHURCH & ABBEY RUINS

Ford

4

Winchcombe

COTSWOLD FARM PARK

B-4632

A-46

Cotswold Way Footpath

B-4068

Cheltenham

To Gloucester

Andoversford

A-436

A-40

To Bath

info line, tel. 0871-200-2233). Put together a one-way or return trip by public transportation, making for a fine Cotswold day. If you're traveling one-way between two train stations, remember that the Cotswold villages—generally pretty clueless when it comes to the needs of travelers without a car—have no official baggage-check services. You'll need to improvise; ask sweetly at the nearest TI or business.

Note that no single bus connects the three major towns described in this chapter (Chipping Campden, Stow, and Moreton); to get between Chipping Campden and Stow, you'll have to change

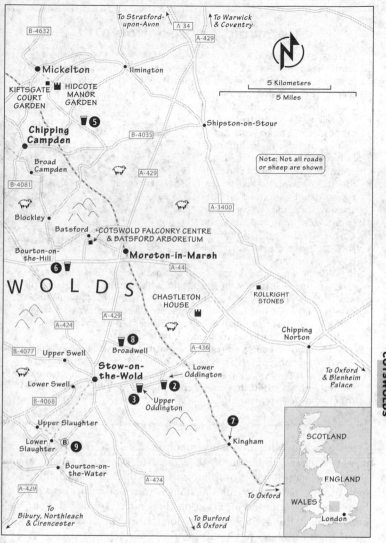

Note: Not all roads or sheep are shown

buses in Moreton. Since buses can be unreliable and connections aren't timed, it may be better to call a driver or taxi to go between Chipping Campden and Stow.

The following bus lines are operated by Johnsons Excelbus (tel. 01564/797-070, www.johnsonscoaches.co.uk): Buses **#1** and **#2** run from Moreton-in-Marsh to Blockley (#1 also stops in Broadway) on their way to Chipping Campden, and pass through Mickleton before ending at Stratford-upon-Avon.

The following buses are operated by Pulham & Sons Coaches (tel. 01451/820-369, www.pulhamscoaches.com): Bus **#801** goes

Cotswold Appreciation 101

History can be read into the names of the area. *Cotswold* could come from the Saxon phrase meaning "hills of sheep's cotes" (shelters for sheep). Or it could mean shelter ("cot" like cottage) on the open upland ("wold").

In the Cotswolds, a town's main street (called High Street) needed to be wide to accommodate the sheep and cattle being marched to market. Some of the most picturesque cottages were once humble row houses of weavers' cottages, usually located along a stream for their waterwheels (good examples in Bibury and Lower Slaughter). The towns run on slow clocks and yellowed calendars.

Fields of yellow (rapeseed) and pale blue (linseed) separate pastures dotted with black and white sheep. In just about any B&B, when you open your window in the morning, you'll hear sheep baa-ing. The decorative "toadstool" stones dotting front yards throughout the region are medieval staddle stones, which buildings were set upon to keep the rodents out.

Cotswold walls and roofs are made of the local limestone. The limestone roof tiles hang by pegs. To make the weight more bearable, smaller and lighter tiles are higher up. An extremely strict building code keeps towns looking what many locals call "overly quaint."

nearly hourly in both directions from Moreton-in-Marsh to Stow-on-the-Wold to Bourton-on-the-Water (connecting towns in about 15 minutes); most continue on to Northleach and Cheltenham (limited service on Sun in summer). Bus **#802** runs between Stow-on-the-Wold and Bourton-on-the-Water (4-5/day, 1 hour, none on Sun). Bus **#855** goes from Moreton-in-Marsh and Stow to Northleach to Bibury to Cirencester.

Warning: Leave yourself a sizeable cushion if using buses to make another connection (such as a train to London). Remember that bus service is essentially nonexistent on Sundays.

By Bike

Despite narrow roads, high hedgerows (blocking some views), and even higher hills, bikers enjoy the Cotswolds free from the constraints of bus schedules. For each area, TIs have fine route planners that indicate which peaceful, paved lanes are particularly

COTSWOLDS

While you'll still see lots of sheep, the commercial wool industry is essentially dead. It costs more to shear a sheep than the 50 pence the wool will fetch. In the old days, sheep lived long lives, producing lots of wool. When they were finally slaughtered, the meat was tough and eaten as "mutton." Today, you don't find mutton much because the sheep are raised primarily for their meat, and slaughtered younger. When it comes to Cotswold sheep these days, it's lamb (not mutton) for dinner (not sweaters).

Towns are small, and everyone seems to know everyone. The area is provincial yet ever-so-polite, and people commonly rescue themselves from a gossipy tangent by saying, "It's all very... mmm...yaaa."

In contrast to the village ambience are the giant manors and mansions that have private gated driveways you'll drive past. Many of these now belong to A-list celebrities, who have country homes here. If you live in the Cotswolds, you can call Madonna, Elizabeth Hurley, and Kate Moss your neighbors.

This is walking country. The English love their walks and vigorously defend their age-old right to free passage. Once a year the Ramblers, Britain's largest walking club, organizes a "Mass Trespass," when each of the country's 50,000 miles of public footpaths is walked. By assuring that each path is used at least once a year, they stop landlords from putting up fences. Any paths found blocked are unceremoniously unblocked.

Questions to ask locals: Do you think foxhunting should have been banned? Who are the Morris men? What's a kissing gate?

scenic for biking. In summer, it's smart to book your rental bike a couple of days ahead.

TY Cycles in Chipping Norton can deliver bikes to your hotel if it's within 15 miles of their shop (includes Stow, Chipping Campden, and Moreton-in-Marsh; hybrid bike—£25/first day, £15/additional day; ebike—£50/first day, £30/additional day; rates include pickup, delivery, helmet, lock, and map; Mon-Fri 8:30-17:00, Sat until 16:00, closed Sun, tel. 01608/238-150, www.tycycles.co.uk, enquiries@tycycles.co.uk, Tom and Rob Yeatman,). If you make it to **Bourton-on-the-Water,** you can rent bicycles through **Hartwells** on High Street (see page 594). In **Broadway,** ebikes are rentable at **Broadway Tower** (see page 572).

If you're interested in a biking vacation, **Cotswold Country Cycles** offers self-led bike tours of the Cotswolds and surrounding areas (tours last 3-7 days and include accommodations and luggage transfer, see www.cotswoldcountrycycles.com).

By Foot

Walking guidebooks and leaflets abound, giving you a world of choices for each of my recommended stops. If you're doing any hiking whatsoever, get the excellent Ordnance Survey Explorer OL #45 map, which shows every road, trail, and ridgeline (£9 at local TIs). Nearly every hotel and B&B offers hiking advice and has a box or shelf of local walking guides and maps, including Ordnance Survey #45. Don't hesitate to ask for a loaner. For a quick **circular hike** from a particular village, peruse the books and brochures offered by that village's TI, or search online for maps and route descriptions; one good website is www.nationaltrail.co.uk—select "Cotswold Way," then "Be Inspired," then "Circular Walks." Villages are generally no more than three miles apart, and most have pubs that would love to feed and water you.

For a list of **guided walks,** ask at any TI for the free *Cotswold Lion* magazine or visit www.cotswoldsaonb.org.uk. The walks range from 2 to 12 miles, and often involve a stop at a pub or tearoom.

Another option is to leave the planning to a company such as **Cotswold Walking Holidays,** which can help you design a walking vacation, provide route instructions and maps, transfer your bags, and even arrange lodging. They also offer six-night walking tours that come with a local guide. Walking through the towns allows you to slow down and enjoy the Cotswolds at their very best—experiencing open fields during the day and arriving into towns just as the day-trippers depart (www.cotswoldwalks.com).

There are many options for hikers, ranging from the "Cotswold Way" path that leads 100 miles from Chipping Campden all the way to Bath, to easy loop trips to the next village. Serious hikers enjoy doing a several-day loop, walking for several hours each day and sleeping in a different village each night.

One popular route is the **"Cotswold Ring":** Day 1—Moreton-in-Marsh to Stow-on-the-Wold to the Slaughters to Bourton-on-the-Water (12 miles); Day 2—Bourton-on-the-Water to Winchcombe (13 miles); Day 3—Winchcombe to Stanway to Stanton (7 miles), or all the way to Broadway (10.5 miles total); Day 4—On to Chipping Campden (just 5.5 miles); Day 5—Chipping Campden to Broad Campden, Blockley, Bourton-on-the-Hill, or Batsford, and back to Moreton (7 miles).

Realistically, on a short visit, you won't have time for that much hiking. But if you have a few hours to spare, consider venturing across the pretty hills and meadows of the Cotswolds. Each of the home-base villages I recommend has several options. Stow-on-the-Wold, immersed in pleasant but not-too-hilly terrain, is within easy walking distance of several interesting spots and is probably the best starting point. Chipping Campden sits along a ridge, which means that hikes from there are extremely scenic, but also more strenuous. Moreton—true to its name—sits on a marsh, offering flatter and less picturesque hikes.

Recommended Hikes

Here are a few hikes to consider, in order of difficulty (easiest first). I've selected these for their convenience to the home-base towns and because the start and/or end points are on bus lines, allowing you to hitch a ride back to where you started (or on to the next town) rather than backtracking by foot.

Stow, the Slaughters, and Bourton-on-the-Water: Walk from Stow to Upper and Lower Slaughter, then on to Bourton-on-the-Water (which has bus service back to Stow on #801 or #802). One big advantage of this walk is that it's mostly downhill (4 miles, about 2-3 hours one-way). For details, see page 586.

Chipping Campden, Broad Campden, Blockley, and Bourton-on-the-Hill: From Chipping Campden, it's an easy one-mile walk into charming Broad Campden, and from there, a more strenuous hike to Blockley and Bourton-on-the-Hill (Blockley is connected by buses #1 and #2 to Chipping Campden and Moreton). For more details, see page 563.

Winchcombe, Stanway, Stanton, and Broadway: You can reach the charming villages of Stanway and Stanton by foot, but it's tough going—lots of up and down. The start and end points (Winchcombe and Broadway) have limited bus connections, and in a pinch some buses do serve Stanton (but carefully check schedules before you set out).

Broadway to Chipping Campden: The hardiest hike of those I list here, this takes you along the Cotswold Ridge. Attempt it only if you're a serious hiker (5.5 miles).

Bibury and the Coln Valley are pretty, but limited bus access makes hiking there less appealing.

By Taxi or Private Driver

Two or three town-to-town taxi trips can make more sense than renting a car. While taking a cab cross-country seems extravagant, the distances are short (Stow to Moreton is 4 miles, Stow to Chipping Campden is 10), and one-way walks are lovely. If you call a cab, confirm that the meter will start only when you are actually picked up. Consider hiring a private driver at the hourly "touring rate" (generally around £35), rather than the meter rate. For a few more bucks than taking a taxi, you can have a joyride peppered with commentary. Whether you book a taxi or a private driver, expect to pay about £25 between Chipping Campden and Stow and about £20 between Chipping Campden and Moreton.

Note that the drivers listed here are not typical city taxi

The Cotswolds at a Glance

Chipping Campden and Nearby

▲▲**Chipping Campden** Picturesque market town with finest High Street in England, accented by a 17th-century Market Hall, wool-tycoon manors, and a characteristic Gothic church. See page 562.

▲▲**Stanway House** Grand, aristocratic home of the Earl of Wemyss, with the tallest fountain in Britain and a 14th-century tithe barn. **Hours:** June-Aug Tue and Thu only 14:00-17:00, closed Sept-May. See page 572.

▲**Stanton** Classic Cotswold village with flower-filled exteriors and 15th-century church. See page 575.

▲**Hidcote Manor Garden** Fragrant garden organized into color-themed "outdoor rooms" that set a trend in 20th-century garden design. **Hours:** Daily 10:00-18:00; Oct until 17:00; Nov-mid-Dec Sat-Sun 11:00-16:00, closed Mon-Fri; closed mid-Dec-Feb. See page 578.

▲**Broad Campden, Blockley, and Bourton-on-the-Hill** Trio of villages with sweeping views and quaint homes, far from the madding crowds. See page 578.

Stow-on-the-Wold and Nearby

▲▲**Stow-on-the-Wold** Convenient Cotswold home base with charming shops and pubs clustered around town square, plus popular day hikes. See page 579.

services (with many drivers on call), but are mostly individuals—it's smart to call ahead if you're arriving in high season, since they can be booked in advance on weekends.

To scare up a taxi in Moreton, try Stuart and Stephen at **ETC,** "Everything Taken Care of" (tel. 01608/650-343, www.cotswoldtravel.co.uk); see also the taxi phone numbers posted outside the Moreton train station office. In Stow, try **Tony Knight** (mobile 07887-714-047, anthonyknight205@btinternet.com). In Chipping Campden, call James at **Cotswold Private Hire** (mobile 07980-857-833), or **Les Proctor,** who offers village tours and station pick-ups (mobile 07580-993-492, Les also co-runs Cornerways B&B—see page 570). Tim Harrison at **Tour the Cotswolds** specializes in tours of the Cotswolds and its gardens, but will also do tours outside the area (mobile 07779-030-820, www.

▲**Lower and Upper Slaughter** Inaptly named historic villages—home to a working waterwheel, peaceful churches, and a folksy museum. See page 592.

▲**Bourton-on-the-Water** The "Venice of the Cotswolds," touristy yet undeniably striking, with petite canals and impressive Cotswold Motoring Museum. See page 593.

▲**Cotswold Farm Park** Kid-friendly park with endangered breeds of native British animals, farm demonstrations, and tractor rides. **Hours:** Daily 10:30-17:00, Nov-Dec until 16:00, closed Jan-Feb. See page 594.

▲**Bibury** Extremely touristy village of antique weavers' cottages, best for outdoor activities like fishing and picnicking. See page 598.

▲**Cirencester** Ancient 2,000-year-old city noteworthy for its crafts center and museum, showcasing artifacts from Roman and Saxon times. See page 598.

Moreton-in-Marsh and Nearby

▲**Moreton-in-Marsh** Relatively flat and functional home base with the best transportation links in the Cotswolds and a bustling Tuesday market. See page 600.

▲**Chastleton House** Lofty Jacobean-era home with a rich family history. **Hours:** Wed-Sun 13:00-17:00, closed Nov-mid-March and Mon-Tue year-round. See page 603.

COTSWOLDS

tourthecotswolds.co.uk). Peter Shelley at **Cotswolds by Car** offers custom tours in a comfy Range Rover (mobile 07968-330-485, www.cotswoldsbycar.com).

By Minibus Tour

Go Cotswolds offers a fast blitz of the most famous stops. It's an efficient way to see some of the Cotswold's most picturesque places (with seven stops in a 16-seat bus). Energetic Tom or Colin will pick you up from Stratford-upon-Avon, Chipping Campden, or Moreton-in-Marsh for a jam-packed day including about an hour each in Chipping Campden, Stow-on-the-Wold, and Bourton-on-the-Water (£40/person, Wed-Sun 9:45-17:00, tel. 07786-920-166, www.gocotswolds.co.uk, info@gocotswolds.co.uk). Handy option:

check out of your hotel, stow bag on bus, and catch the evening train in Moreton for your next stop.

Secret Cottage Cotswold Tours doesn't give you the famous stops; it's an intimate look at offbeat villages in a seven-seat minibus. You get short, guided visits to a selection of lesser-known villages, and tours include a cream tea served in a private cottage. Meet Becky at Moreton-in-Marsh's train station at 10:00 and you'll return to the station by 16:20 (£95/person, must reserve ahead online, tel. 01608/674-700, www.cotswoldtourismtours.co.uk).

Other Cotswold Tours

Lion Tours, which departs from Bath, offers a Cotswold Discovery full-day tour, and can drop you and your luggage off in Stow (see page 414 of the Bath chapter).

Town Walks: While none of the Cotswold towns offers regularly scheduled walks, many have voluntary **warden groups** who love to meet visitors and give walks for a small donation (see specific contact information later for Chipping Campden).

Chipping Campden

Just touristy enough to be convenient, the north Cotswold town of Chipping Campden (CAMden) is a ▲▲ sight. This market town, once the home of the richest Cotswold wool merchants, has some incredibly beautiful thatched roofs. Both the great British historian G. M. Trevelyan and I call Chipping Campden's High Street the finest in England.

Orientation to Chipping Campden

TOURIST INFORMATION

Chipping Campden's TI is tucked away in the old police station on High Street. Buy the cheap town guide with map, or the local *Footpath Guide* (daily 9:30-17:00; off-season Mon-Thu until 13:00, Fri-Sun until 16:00; tel. 01386/841-206, www.chippingcampdenonline.org).

HELPFUL HINTS

Festivals: The **Cotswold Olimpicks** are a series of tongue-in-cheek countryside games (such as competitive shin-kicking)

COTSWOLDS

held atop Dover's Hill, just above town (generally in late spring; check www.olimpickgames.co.uk). Chipping Campden also has a **music festival** in May.

Taxi: Try **Cotswold Private Hire, Les Proctor,** or **Tour the Cotswolds** (see page 559).

Parking: Find a spot anywhere along High Street and park for free with no time limit. There's also a pay-and-display lot on High Street, across from the TI (2-hour maximum). If those are full, there is free parking on the street called Back Ends. On weekends, you can also park for free at the school (see map).

Tours: The local members of the **Cotswold Voluntary Wardens** are happy to show you around town for a small donation to the Cotswold Conservation Fund (suggested donation-£4/person, 1.5-hour walks run May-Sept Tue at 14:00 and Thu at 10:00, meet at Market Hall; mobile 07761-565-661, Vin Kelly).

Walks and Hikes from Chipping Campden: Since this is a particularly hilly area, long-distance hikes are challenging. The easiest and most rewarding stroll is to the thatch-happy hobbit village of **Broad Campden** (about a mile, mostly level). From there, you can walk or take the bus (#2) back to Chipping Campden.

Or, if you have more energy, continue from Broad Campden up over the ridge and into picturesque **Blockley**—and, if your stamina holds out, all the way to **Bourton-on-the-Hill** (Blockley is connected by buses #1 and #2 to Chipping Campden and Moreton).

Alternatively, you can hike up to **Dover's Hill,** just north of the village. Ask locally about this easy, circular one-hour walk that takes you on the first mile of the 100-mile-long Cotswold Way (which goes from here to Bath).

For more about hiking, see "Getting Around the Cotswolds—By Foot," earlier.

Chipping Campden Walk

This self-guided stroll through "Campden" (as locals call their town) takes you from the Market Hall west to the old silk mill, and then back east the length of High Street to the church. It takes about an hour.

Market Hall: Begin at Campden's most famous monument—the Market Hall. It stands in front of

the TI, marking the town center. The Market Hall was built in 1627 by the 17th-century Lord of the Manor, Sir Baptist Hicks. (Look for the Hicks family coat of arms on the east end of the building's facade.) Back then, it was an elegant shopping hall for the townsfolk who'd come here to buy their produce. In the 1940s, it was almost sold to an American, but the townspeople heroically raised money to buy it first, then gave it to the National Trust for its preservation.

The timbers inside are true to the original. Study the classic Cotswold stone roof, still held together with wooden pegs nailed in from underneath. (Tiles were

cut and sold with peg holes, and stacked like waterproof scales.) Buildings all over the region still use these stone shingles. Today, the hall, which is rarely used, stands as a testimony to the importance of trade to medieval Campden.

Adjacent to the Market Hall is the sober WWI monument—a reminder of the huge price paid by nearly every little town. Walk around it, noticing how 1918 brought the greatest losses.

Between the Market Hall and the WWI monument you'll find a limestone disc embedded in the ground marking the ceremonial start of the Cotswold Way (you'll find its partner in front of the abbey in Bath—100 miles away—marking the southern end).

The TI is across the street, in the old police courthouse. If it's open, you're welcome to climb the stairs and peek into the **Magistrate's Court** (free, same hours as TI, ask at TI to go up). Under the open-beamed courtroom is a humble little exhibit on the town's history.

• *Walk west, passing the Town Hall (with the cute little bell tower) and the parking lot that was originally the sheep market, until you reach the Red Lion Inn. Across High Street (and a bit to the right), look for the house with a sundial and sign over the door reading...*

"Green Dragons": The house's decorative, black cast-iron fixtures (originally in the stables)

once held hay and functioned much like salad bowls for horses. Fine-cut stones define the door, but "rubble stones" make up the rest of the wall. The pink stones are the same limestone but have been heated, and likely were scavenged from a house that burned down.

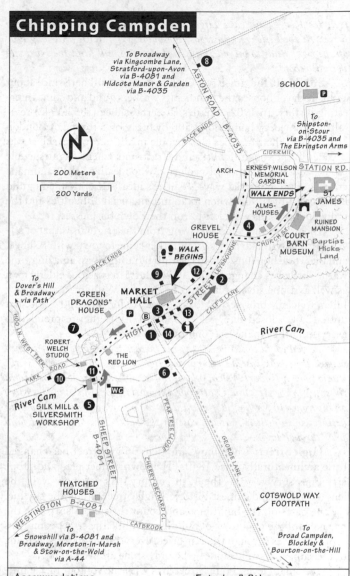

Chipping Campden

To Broadway
via Kingcombe Lane,
Stratford-upon-Avon
via B-4081 and
Hidcote Manor & Garden
via B-4035

SCHOOL

ASTON ROAD B-4035

To
Shipston-
on-Stour
via B-4035 and
The Ebrington Arms

BACK ENDS

CIDERMILL

STATION RD.

ARCH

ERNEST WILSON
MEMORIAL
GARDEN

WALK ENDS

ALMS-
HOUSES

ST.
JAMES

N

200 Meters

200 Yards

GREVEL
HOUSE

RUINED
MANSION

COURT
BARN
MUSEUM

Baptist
Hicks
Land

**WALK
BEGINS**

BACK ENDS

To
Dover's Hill
& Broadway
via Path

"GREEN
DRAGONS"
HOUSE

MARKET
HALL

HIGH STREET

LEYSBOURNE

CHURCH ST.

CALF'S LANE

River Cam

HOO LN. WEST TERR.

ROBERT
WELCH
STUDIO

PARK
ROAD

THE RED LION

WC

SILK MILL &
SILVERSMITH
WORKSHOP

River Cam

SHEEP STREET B-4081

PEAR TREE CLOSE

CHERRY ORCHARD CT.

GEORGE LANE

THATCHED
HOUSES

WESTINGTON B-4081

CATBROOK

COTSWOLD WAY
FOOTPATH

To
Snowshill via B-4081 and
Broadway, Moreton-in-Marsh
& Stow-on-the-Wold
via A-44

To
Broad Campden,
Blockley &
Bourton-on-the-Hill

COTSWOLDS

Accommodations

1. Noel Arms Hotel
2. The Lygon Arms Hotel & Pub
3. Badgers Hall B&B & Tea Room
4. Eight Bells Inn & Pub
5. Crafty Cottages
6. Cornerways & Stonecroft B&Bs
7. The Old Bakehouse & Butty's
8. Cherry Trees B&B

Eateries & Other

9. Michael's
10. Maharaja Indian Restaurant
11. Campden Coffee Company
12. Toko's
13. The Bantam Tea Rooms
14. Grocery

• *At the Red Lion, leave High Street and walk a block down Sheep Street. At the little creek just past the public WC, a 30-yard-long lane on the right leads to an old Industrial-Age silk mill (and the Hart silversmith shop).*

Silk Mill: The tiny River Cam powered a mill here since about 1790. Today it houses the handicraft workers guild and some interesting history. In 1902, Charles Robert Ashbee (1863-1942) revitalized this sleepy hamlet of 2,500 by bringing a troupe of London artisans and their families (160 people in all) to town. Ashbee was a leader in the romantic Arts and Crafts movement—craftspeople repulsed by the Industrial Revolution who idealized the handmade crafts and preindustrial ways. Ashbee's idealistic craftsmen's guild lasted only until 1908, when it ran into financial difficulties and the individual artisans were left to run their own businesses.

Today, the only shop surviving from the originals is that of **silversmith David Hart.** His grandfather came to town with Ashbee, and the workshop (upstairs in the mill building) is an amazing time warp—little has changed since 1902. Hart is a gracious elderly man as well as a fine silversmith, and he, his son William, and nephew Julian welcome browsers six days a week (Mon-Fri 9:00-17:00, Sat until 12:00, closed Sun, tel. 01386/841-100). They're proud that everything they make is a "one-off."

• *While you could continue 200 yards farther to see some fine thatched houses, this walk instead returns to High Street. On the corner is the studio shop of **Robert Welch**, a local industrial designer who worked in the spirit of the Arts and Crafts movement. His son and daughter carry on his legacy in the fine shop with sleek tableware, glassware, and bath fittings (with a little museum case in the back). Now turn right, and walk through town.*

High Street: Chipping Campden's High Street has changed little architecturally since 1840. (The town's street plan and property lines survive from the 12th century.) As you now walk the length of England's finest historic High Street, study the skyline, see the dates on the buildings, and count the sundials. Notice the harmony of the long rows of buildings. While the street comprises different styles through the centuries, everything you see was made of the same Cotswold stone—the only stone allowed today.

To remain level, High Street arcs with the contour of the hillside. Because it's so wide, you know this was a market town. In past centuries, livestock and packhorses laden with piles of freshly shorn fleece would fill the streets. Campden was a sales and distribution center for the wool industry, and merchants from as far away as Italy would come here for the prized raw wool.

High Street has no house numbers: Locals know the houses by their names. In the distance, you'll see the town church (where this walk ends). Notice that the power lines are buried underground, making the scene delightfully uncluttered.

As you stroll High Street, you'll find the finest houses on the uphill side. Decorative features (like the Ionic capitals near the TI) are added for nonstructural touches of class. Most High Street buildings are half-timbered, but with cosmetic stone facades. You may see some exposed half-timbered walls. Study the crudely beautiful framing, made of hand-hewn oak (you can see the adze marks) and held together by wooden pegs.

Peeking down alleys, you'll notice how the lots are narrow but very deep (33 x 330 feet). Called "burgage plots," this platting goes back to 1170. In medieval times, rooms were lined up long and skinny like train cars: Each building had a small storefront, followed by a workshop, living quarters, staff quarters, stables, and a garden at the very back. Now the private alleys that still define many of these old lots lead to comfy gardens. While some of today's buildings are wider, virtually all the widths are exact multiples of that basic first unit (for example, a modern building may be three times wider than its medieval counterpart).

• *Hike the length of High Street toward the church. After a couple hundred yards, just before Church Street, there's a fine mansion on the left.*

Grevel House: In 1367, William Grevel built what's considered Campden's first stone house. Sheep tycoons had big homes. Imagine back then, when this fine building was surrounded by humble wattle-and-daub huts. It had newfangled chimneys, rather than a crude hole in the roof. (No more rain inside!) Originally a "hall house" with just one big, tall room, it got its upper floor in the 16th century. The finely carved central bay window is a good early example of the Perpendicular Gothic style. The gargoyles scared away bad spirits—and served as rain spouts. The boot scrapers outside the door were fixtures in that muddy age—especially in market towns, where the streets were filled with animal dung.

• *Continue up High Street for about 100 yards. Go past Church Street (which we'll walk up later). On the right, at a big tree behind a low stone wall, you'll find a small Gothic arch leading into a garden.*

Ernest Wilson Memorial Garden: Once the church's vegetable patch, this small and secluded garden is a botanist's delight today. Pop inside if it's open. The garden is filled with well-labeled plants that the Victorian botanist Ernest Wilson brought back to England from his extensive travels in Asia. There's a complete history of the garden on the board to the left of the entry.

• *Backtrack to Church Street. Turn left, walk past the recommended Eight Bells pub, and hook left with the street. Along your right-hand side stretches...*

Baptist Hicks Land: Sprawling adjacent to the town church, the area known as Baptist Hicks Land held Hicks' huge estate and manor house. This influential Lord of the Manor was from "a family of substance," who were merchants of silk and fine clothing as well as money-lenders. Beyond the ornate gate (which you'll see ahead, near the church), only a few outbuildings and the charred corner of his **mansion** survive. The mansion

was burned by royalists in 1645 during the Civil War—notice how Cotswold stone turns red when burned. Hicks housed the poor, making a show of his generosity, adding a long row of almshouses (with his family coat of arms) for neighbors to see as they walked to church. These almshouses (lining Church Street on the left) house pensioners today, as they have since the 17th century. Across the street is a ditch built as a "cart wash"—it was filled with water to soak old cart wheels so they'd swell up and stop rattling.

On the right, filling the old **Court Barn**, is a small, fussy museum about crafts and designs from the Arts and Crafts movement, with works by Ashbee and his craftsmen (£5, Tue-Sun 10:00-17:00, Oct-March until 16:00, closed Mon, tel. 01386/841-951, www.courtbarn.org.uk).

• *Next to the Hicks gate, a scenic lane leads to the front door of the church. It's lined with 11 linden trees: Planted in about 1760, there used to be one for each of the apostles. But recently one of the trees died.*

St. James Church: One of the finest churches in the Cotswolds, St. James Church graces one of its leading towns. Both the town and the church were built by wool wealth. Go inside. The church is Perpendicular Gothic, with lots of light and strong verticality. Notice the fine vestments and altar hangings (intricate c. 1460 embroidery) behind protective blue curtains (near the back of the church). Tombstones pave the floor in the chancel (often under protective red carpeting)—memorializing great wool merchants through the ages.

At the altar is a brass relief of William Grevel, the first owner of the Grevel House (described earlier), and his wife. But it is Sir Baptist Hicks who dominates the church. His huge canopied tomb is the ornate final resting place for Hicks and his wife, Elizabeth. Study their faces, framed by fancy lace ruffs (trendy in the 1620s). Adjacent—as if in a closet—is a statue of their

daughter, Lady Juliana, and her husband, Lutheran Yokels. Juliana commissioned the statue in 1642, when her husband died, but had it closed up until *she* died in 1680. Then, the doors were opened, revealing these two people holding hands and living happily ever after—at least in marble. The hinges were likely used only once.

Just outside as you leave the church, look immediately around the corner to the right of the door. A small tombstone reads "Thank you Lord for Simon, a dearly loved cat who greeted everyone who entered this church. RIP 1986."

Sleeping in Chipping Campden

In Chipping Campden—as in any town in the Cotswolds—B&Bs offer a better value than hotels. Most of my listings are centrally located on the main street (or just off of it). Try to book well in advance, as rooms are snapped up early in the spring and summer by happy hikers heading for the nearby Cotswold Way. Rooms are also generally tight on Saturdays (when many charge a bit more and are reluctant to rent to one-nighters) and in September, another peak month. Parking is never a problem. Always ask for a discount if staying longer than one or two nights.

$$$ Noel Arms Hotel, the characteristic old hotel on the main square, has welcomed guests for 600 years. Its lobby was re-modeled in a medieval-meets-modern style, and its 27 rooms are well furnished with antiques (some ground-floor doubles, attached restaurant/bar and café, free parking, High Street, tel. 01386/840-317, www.noelarmshotel.com, reception@noelarmshotel.com).

$$$ The Lygon Arms Hotel (pronounced "lig-un"), attached to the popular pub of the same name, has small public areas and 10 cheery, open-beamed rooms (family rooms available, free parking, High Street, go through archway and look for hotel reception on the left, tel. 01386/840-318, www.lygonarms.co.uk, sandra@lygonarms.co.uk, Sandra Davenport).

$$$ Badgers Hall, above a tearoom, rents four somewhat overpriced rooms with antique furnishings beneath wooden beams (2-night minimum, no kids under 18, High Street, tel. 01386/840-839, www.badgershall.com, karen@badgershall.com, Karen). Their delightful half-timbered tearoom (open to guests only Thu-Sat) offers a selection of savory dishes, homemade cakes, tarts, and scones.

$$$ Eight Bells Inn rents six old-school rooms with modern en suite baths above a recommended pub (Church Street, tel. 01386/840-371, www.eightbellsinn.co.uk, info@eightbellsinn.co.uk).

$$$ Crafty Cottages, run by helpful lifelong Cotswolds residents Sally and Paul, supply home-away-from-home modern amenities in three cottages—two one-bedroom and one two-bedroom—right next to the silk mill (3-night minimum, Sheep Street, tel. 01386/849-079, www.craftycottages.com, enquiries@ craftycottages.com).

$$ Cornerways B&B is a fresh, bright, and comfy home a block off High Street. It's run by the delightful Carole Proctor, who can "look out the window and see the church where we were married." The two huge, light, airy loft rooms are great for families with children over 10 (2-night minimum, cash only, off-street parking, George Lane—walk through the arch beside Noel Arms Hotel, tel. 01386/841-307, www.cornerways.info, carole@cornerways. info). For a fee, Les can pick you up from the train station, or take you on village tours.

$$ Stonecroft B&B, next to Cornerways, has three polished, well-maintained rooms (one with low, slanted ceilings—unfriendly to tall people). The lovely garden with a patio and small stream is a tranquil place for meals or an early-evening drink (family rooms but no kids under 12, George Lane, tel. 01386/840-486, www.stonecroft-chippingcampden.co.uk, info@stonecroft-chippingcampden.co.uk, Roger and Lesley Yates).

$$ The Old Bakehouse, run by energetic young mom Zoe, rents two small-but-pleasant rooms in a 600-year-old home with exposed beams and cottage charm (cash only, Lower High Street, near intersection with Sheep Street, tel. 01386/840-979, mobile 07717-330-838, www.theoldbakehouse.org.uk, zoegabb@yahoo. co.uk).

$$ Cherry Trees B&B, set well off the road, is bubbly Angie's spacious, modern home, with three king rooms, one with balcony (2-night minimum, cash only, 10-minute walk from Market Hall or take bus to Aston Road, tel. 01386/840-873, www. cherrytreescampden.com, sclrksn7@tiscali.co.uk).

Eating in Chipping Campden

This town—filled with wealthy residents and tourists—comes with several good choices. I've listed some local favorites below. If you have a car, consider driving to one of the excellent countryside pubs mentioned in the sidebar on page 590.

$$$ Eight Bells pub is a charming 14th-century inn. It's the best deal going for top-end pub dining in town, with English dishes both classic and modern. They serve a daily special, summer salads, and always have a good vegetarian dish. The restaurant, classy pub, and terrace out back (lunch only) all have the same menu. Reservations are smart (daily 12:00-14:00 & 18:30-21:00, Church Street, tel. 01386/840-371, www.eightbellsinn.co.uk).

$$$ Michael's, a fun Mediterranean restaurant on High Street, serves hearty portions and breaks plates at closing every

Saturday night. Michael, who runs his place with a contagious love of life, is from Cyprus: The forte here is Greek, with plenty of *mezes*—small dishes. "The Meze" special gives you the works with a hearty selection of small plates (Tue-Sun 18:45-22:00, closed Mon, tel. 01386/840-826).

$$ Maharaja Indian Restaurant, filling the back end of the down-and-dirty Volunteer Inn pub, serves decent Indian standards (daily 18:00-22:30, grassy courtyard out back, Lower High Street, tel. 01386/849-281).

LIGHT MEALS

If you want a quick takeaway sandwich, consider these options. Munch your lunch on the benches on the little green near the Market Hall.

$ Butty's is a practical little eatery offering salads, tasty sandwiches, and wraps made to order (Mon-Fri 7:00-14:00, Sat 8:00-13:00, closed Sun, Lower High Street, tel. 01386/840-401).

$ Campden Coffee Company is a cozy little café with local goodies including salads, sandwiches, and homemade sweets (Sat-Mon 10:00-16:00, Tue-Fri from 9:00, on the ground floor of the Silk Mill, tel. 01386/849-251).

$ Toke's has a tempting selection of cheeses, meats, and wine for a make-your-own ploughman's lunch (Mon-Fri 9:00-18:00, Sat 10:00-17:00, Sun 10:00-16:00, just past the Market Hall, tel. 01386/849-345).

Afternoon Tea: The Bantam Tea Rooms (daily 9:30-17:00) and **Badgers Hall** (Thu-Sat 10:00-16:00), each a scone's throw from the Market Hall, are sweet and pastel places popular for their cakes, bakery goods, lunches, and afternoon tea.

Picnic and Groceries: The **Co-op grocery** (daily 7:00-22:00, next to TI on High Street) is handy for a picnic, with a good selection of sandwiches and takeaway items.

Near Chipping Campden

Because the countryside around Chipping Campden is particularly hilly, it's also especially scenic. This is a very rewarding area to poke around and discover little thatched villages.

WEST OF CHIPPING CAMPDEN

Due west of Chipping Campden lies the famous and touristy town of Broadway. Just south of that, you'll find my nominations for the cutest Cotswold villages. Like marshmallows in hot chocolate, Stanway, Stanton, and Snowshill nestle side by side, awaiting your arrival. (Note the Stanway House's limited hours when planning your visit.)

COTSWOLDS

Broadway

This postcard-pretty town, a couple of miles west of Chipping Campden, is filled with inviting shops and fancy teahouses. With a "broad way" indeed running through its middle, it's one of the bigger towns in the area. This means you'll likely pass through at some point if you're driving—but, since all the big bus tours seem to stop here, I usually give Broadway a miss. However, with a new road that allows traffic to skirt the town, Broadway has gotten cuter than ever. If driving, check out the top end of High Street (which is a dead end, residential, and a classic/modern Cotswolds neighborhood). Broadway has limited bus connections with Chipping Campden.

Ebike Rental and More: Follow *Tower Barn* signs from the Broadway Tower ticket office to a slick café and shop with fine Cotswolds goods and ebike rentals. From here, it's an easy pedal over country lanes to the nearby lavender fields (£9/hour, £35/day, daily 10:00-16:00, tel. 01386/852-390, https://broadwaytower.co.uk). There's also a nuclear bunker open on weekends (£4.50, closed Nov-March).

Broadway Tower ornaments a hill above Broadway. Just outside of town, on the road to Chipping Campden, signs direct you to the tower, which looks like a turreted castle fortification stranded in the countryside without a castle in sight. This 55-foot-tall observation tower is a "folly"—a uniquely English term for a quirky, outlandish novelty erected as a giant lawn ornament by some aristocrat with more money than taste. If you're also weighted down with too many pounds, you can relieve yourself of £5 to climb to its top for a view over the pastures. But the view from the tower's parklike perch is free, and almost as impressive (daily 10:00-17:00). A short hike beyond the tower just before sunset can be unforgettable.

Stanway

More of a humble crossroads community than a true village, sleepy Stanway is worth a visit mostly for its manor house, which offers an intriguing insight into the English aristocracy today. If you're in the area when it's open, it's well worth visiting.

▲▲Stanway House

The Earl of Wemyss (pronounced "Weemz"), whose family tree charts relatives back to 1202, opens his melancholy home and grounds to visitors two days a week in the summer. Walking through his house

offers a unique glimpse into the lifestyles of England's eccentric and fading nobility.

Cost and Hours: £9 ticket covers house and fountain, includes a wonderful and intimate audioguide narrated by the lordship himself; June-Aug Tue and Thu only 14:00-17:00, closed Sept-May, tel. 01386/584-469, www.stanwayfountain.co.uk.

Getting There: By car, leave the B-4077 at a statue of (the Christian) George slaying the dragon (of pagan superstition); you'll round the corner and see the manor's fine 17th-century Jacobean gatehouse. Park in the lot across the street. There's no public transportation to Stanway.

Visiting the Manor: The 14th-century **Tithe Barn** (near where you enter the grounds) predates the manor. It was originally where monks—in the days before money—would accept one-tenth of whatever the peasants produced. Peek inside: This is a great hall for village hoedowns. While the Tithe Barn is no longer used to greet motley peasants and collect their feudal "rents,"

the lord still gets rent from his vast landholdings, and hosts village fêtes in his barn.

Stepping into the obviously very lived-in **manor house,** you're free to wander around pretty much as you like, but keep in mind that a family does live here. His lordship is often roaming about as well. The place feels like a time warp. Ask a staff member to demonstrate the spinning rent-collection table. In the great hall, marvel at the one-piece oak shuffleboard table and the 1780 Chippendale exercise chair (a half-hour of bouncing on this was considered good for the liver).

The manor dogs have their own cutely painted "family tree," but the Earl admits that his last dog, C. J., was "all character and no breeding." Poke into the office. You can psychoanalyze the lord by the books that fill his library, the DVDs stacked in front of his bed (with the mink bedspread), and whatever's next to his toilet.

The place has a story to tell. And so do the docents stationed in each room—modern-day peasants who, even without family trees, probably have relatives going back just as far in this village. Talk to these people. Probe. Learn what you can about this side of England.

Wandering through the expansive backyard you'll see the earl's pet project: restoring "the tallest **fountain** in Britain"—300 feet tall, gravity-powered, and running for 30 minutes twice a day (at 14:45 and 16:00).

Signs lead to a working **watermill,** which produces flour from wheat grown on the estate (about 100 yards from the house, requires separate £4 ticket to enter).

Hailes Church and Abbey

A three-mile drive or pleasant two-and-a-half-mile walk from Stanway House along the Cotswold Way leads you to a fine Norman church and tranquil abbey ruins. There's also an adjacent museum displaying the abbey's surviving artifacts. While little remains of the abbey, just being here can be a moving experience.

Cost and Hours: Church-free, abbey and museum-£7, daily 10:00-17:00, until 18:00 in summer, closed Nov-March, free parking, tel. 01242/602-398, www.english-heritage.org.uk.

Visiting the Abbey: Richard, Earl of Cornwall (and younger brother of King Henry III) founded the abbey after surviving a shipwreck. His son Edmund turned it into a pilgrimage site after buying a vial of holy blood and bringing the relic to Hailes around 1270. Because of Henry VIII's dissolution of monasteries in the 16th century, not much remains of the abbey today.

The church—which predates the abbey by about a century—houses some of its original tiles and medieval stained glass. It's worth a look for its 800-year-old baptismal font and faded but evocative murals (including St. Christopher, patron saint of travelers, and a hunting scene attributed to a local knight). Check out the wooden screen added long after the original construction—notice how the arch had to be cut away in order for the screen to fit.

From Stanway to Stanton

These towns are separated by a row of oak trees and grazing land, with parallel waves echoing the furrows plowed by medieval farmers. Centuries ago, farmers were allotted long strips of land called "furlongs." The idea was to dole out good and bad land equitably. (One square furlong equals 10 acres.) Over centuries of plowing these, furrows were formed. Let someone else drive, so you can hang out the window under a canopy of oaks, passing stone walls and sheep. Leaving Stanway on the road to Stanton,

the first building you'll see (on the left, just outside Stanway) is a thatched cricket pavilion overlooking the village cricket green. Originally built for *Peter Pan* author J. M. Barrie, it dates from 1930 and is raised up (as medieval buildings were) on rodent-resistant staddle stones. Stanton is just ahead; follow the signs.

▲Stanton

Pristine Cotswold charm cheers you as you head up the main street of the village of Stanton, served by a scant few buses. Go on a photo safari for flower-bedecked doorways and windows.

Stanton's **Church of St. Michael** (with the pointy spire) betrays a pagan past. It's safe to assume any church dedicated to St. Michael (the archangel who fought the devil) sits upon a sacred pagan site. Stanton is actually at the intersection of two ley lines (a line connecting prehistoric or ancient sights). You'll see St. Michael's well-worn figure (and, above that, a sundial) over the door as you enter. Inside, above the capitals in the nave, find the

pagan symbols for the sun and the moon (see photo). While the church probably dates back to the ninth century, today's building is mostly from the 15th century, with 13th-century transepts. On the north transept (far side from entry), medieval frescoes show faintly through the 17th-century whitewash. (Once upon a time, these frescoes were considered too "papist.") Imagine the church interior colorfully decorated throughout. Original medieval glass is behind the altar. The list of rectors (at the very back of the church, under the organ loft) goes back to 1269. Finger the grooves in the back pews, worn away by sheepdog leashes. (A man's sheepdog accompanied him everywhere.)

Horse Riding: Jill Carenza's **Cotswolds Riding Centre**, set just outside Stanton village, is in the most scenic corner of the region. The facility's horses can take anyone from rank beginners to more experienced riders on a scenic "hack" through the village and into the high country (per-hour prices: £34/person on a group hack, £44/person semiprivate hack, £54 private one-person hack; lessons, longer/expert rides, and pub tours available; tel. 01386/584-250, www.

COTSWOLDS

cotswoldsriding.co.uk, info@cotswoldsriding.co.uk). From Stanton, head toward Broadway and watch for the riding center on your right after about a third of a mile.

Sleeping in Stanton: $$ The Vine B&B has four rooms in a lovingly worn family home near the center of town, next to the cricket pitch (ask if any matches are on if you're there on a Saturday in summer). While it suffers from absentee management, the Vine is convenient if you want to ride all day (most rooms share a WC but have a private shower, one room en suite, family room available, some stairs; for contact info, see listing for riding center, earlier).

Eating in Stanton: High on a hill at the far end of Stanton's main drag, nearest to Broadway, the aptly named **$$$ Mount Inn** serves upscale meals on its big, inviting terrace with grand views of Stanton rooftops and the Cotswold hills (daily 12:00-15:00 & 18:00-23:00, may be closed Mon-Tue off-season, Old Snowshill Road, tel. 01386/584-316).

Snowshill

Another nearly edible little bundle of cuteness, the village of Snowshill (SNAH-zul) has a photogenic triangular square with a characteristic pub at its base.

Snowshill Manor

Dark and mysterious, this old manor house is stuffed with the life-time collection of Charles Paget Wade (its management made me

promise not to promote it as an eccentric collector's pile of curi-osities). It's one big, musty cel-ebration of craftsmanship, from finely carved spinning wheels to frightening samurai armor to tiny elaborate figurines carved by prisoners from the bones of meat served at dinner. Taking seriously his family motto, "Let Nothing Perish," Wade dedicated his life and fortune to preserving things finely crafted.

Cost and Hours: £12.20; manor house open daily 11:00-17:30, closed Nov-March; gardens and ticket window open at 11:00, last entry one hour before closing, restaurant, tel. 01386/852-410, www.nationaltrust.org.uk/snowshillmanor.

Getting There: There's no direct access from the square; in-stead, the entrance and parking lot are about a half-mile up the road toward Broadway. Park there and follow the long walkway through the garden to get to the house. A golf-cart-type shuttle to the house is available for those who need assistance.

Getting In: This popular sight strictly limits the number of entering visitors by doling out entry times. No reservations are possible; to get a slot, you must report to the ticket desk. It can be up to an hour's wait—even more on busy days, especially weekends (when they can sell out for the day as early as 14:00). Tickets go on sale and the gardens open at 11:00. A good strategy is to arrive close to the opening time, and if there's a wait, enjoy the gardens (it's a 10-minute walk to the manor). If you have more time to kill, head into the village of Snowshill itself (a half-mile away) to wander and explore—or get a time slot for later in the day, and return in the afternoon.

Cotswold Lavender

In 2000, farmer Charlie Byrd realized that tourists love lavender. He planted his farm with 250,000 plants, and now visitors come to wander among his 53 acres, which burst with gorgeous lavender blossoms from mid-June through late August. His fragrant fantasy peaks late each July. Lavender—so famous in France's Provence—is not indigenous to this region, but it fits the climate and  soil just fine. A free flier in the shop explains the variations of blooming flowers. Farmer Byrd produces lavender oil (an herbal product valued since ancient times for its healing, calming, and fragrant qualities) and sells it in a delightful shop, along with many other lavender-themed items. In the café, enjoy a pot of lavender-flavored tea with a lavender scone.

Cost and Hours: Free to enter shop and café, £4 to walk through the fields and the distillery; generally open June-Aug daily 10:00-17:00, closed Sept-May, schedule changes annually depending on when the lavender blooms—call ahead or check their website; tel. 01386/854-821, www.cotswoldlavender.co.uk.

Getting There: It's a half-mile out of Snowshill on the road toward Chipping Campden (easy parking). Entering Snowshill from the road to the manor (described earlier), take the left fork, then turn left again at the end of the village.

EAST OF CHIPPING CAMPDEN

Hidcote Manor Garden is just northeast of Chipping Campden, while Broad Campden, Blockley, and Bourton-on-the-Hill lie roughly between Chipping Campden and Stow (or Moreton)—handy if you're connecting those towns.

▲Hidcote Manor Garden

This is less "on the way" between towns than the other sights in this section—but the grounds around this manor house are well worth a

detour if you like gardens. Hidcote is where garden designers pioneered the notion of creating a series of outdoor "rooms," each with a unique theme (such as maple room, red room, and so on) and separated by a yew-tree hedge. The garden's design, inspired by the Arts and Crafts movement, is most formal near the house and becomes more pastoral as it approaches the countryside. Follow your nose through a clever series of small gardens that lead delightfully from one to the next. Among the best in England, Hidcote Gardens are at their fragrant peak from May through August. But don't expect much indoors—the manor house has only a few rooms open to the public.

Cost and Hours: £13.50; daily 10:00-18:00, Oct until 17:00; Nov-mid-Dec Sat-Sun 11:00-16:00, closed Mon-Fri; closed mid-Dec-Feb; last entry one hour before closing, café, restaurant, tel. 01386/438-333, www.nationaltrust.org.uk/hidcote.

Getting There: If you're driving, it's four miles northeast of Chipping Campden—roughly toward Ilmington. The gardens are accessible by bus, then a 45-minute country walk uphill. Buses #1 and #2 take you to Mickleton (one stop past Chipping Campden), where a footpath begins next to the churchyard. Continuing more or less straight, the path leads through sheep pastures and ends at Hidcote's driveway.

Nearby: Gardening enthusiasts will also want to stop at **Kiftsgate Court Garden,** just across the road from Hidcote. While not as impressive, these private gardens are a fun contrast since they were designed at the same time and influenced by Hidcote (£9; May-July Sat-Wed 12:00-18:00, Aug from 14:00, closed Thu-Fri; April and Sept Sun-Mon and Wed only 14:00-18:00; closed Oct-March; tel. 01386/438-777, www.kiftsgate.co.uk).

▲Broad Campden, Blockley, and Bourton-on-the-Hill

This trio of pleasant villages lines up along an off-the-beaten-path road between Chipping Campden and Moreton or Stow. **Broad Campden,** just on the outskirts of Chipping Campden, has some of the cutest thatched-roof houses I've seen. **Blockley,** nestled higher in the picturesque hills, is a popular setting for films. The

same road continues on
to **Bourton-on-the-Hill**
(pictured), with fine views
looking down into a valley
and an excellent gastro-
pub (Horse and Groom,
described on page 590).
Blockley is connected to
Chipping Campden by bus
#1 and #2, or you can walk

(easy to Broad Campden, more challenging to the other two—see
page 559).

Stow-on-the-Wold

Located 10 miles south of Chipping Campden, Stow-on-the-
Wold—with a name that means "meeting place on the uplands"—
is the highest town in
the Cotswolds. Despite
its crowds, it retains its
charm, and it merits ▲▲.
Most of the tourists are
day-trippers, so nights—
even in the peak of sum-
mer—are peaceful. Stow
has no real sights other
than the town itself, some

good pubs, antiques stores, and cute shops draped seductively
around a big town square. Visit the church, with its evocative old
door guarded by ancient yew trees and the tombs of wool tycoons.
A visit to Stow is not complete until you've locked your partner in
the stocks on the village green.

Orientation to Stow-on-the-Wold

TOURIST INFORMATION
A small visitor information center—little more than a rack of brochures staffed by volunteers—is run out of the library in St. Edwards
Hall on the main square (hours generally Mon-Sat 10:00-14:00,
sometimes as late as 19:00, closed Sun; Oct-April Sat 10:00-14:00
only, tel. 01451/870-998). The TI in Moreton-in-Marsh is more
serious (see page 600).

HELPFUL HINTS

Services: Pay WCs are located at the north and south ends of town.

Taxi: See "Getting Around the Cotswolds—By Taxi or Private Driver," earlier in the chapter.

Parking: Park anywhere on Market Square free for two hours, and overnight between 18:00 and 9:00 (combining overnight plus daily 2-hour allowances means you can park free 16:00-11:00—they note your license, so you can't just move to another spot after your time is up; £50 tickets for offenders). You can also park for free on some streets farther from the center (such as Park Street and Well Lane) for an unlimited amount of time. A convenient pay-and-display lot is at the bottom of town (toward the Oddingtons), and there's free long-stay parking adjacent to the lot at Tesco Supermarket—an easy five-minute walk north of town (follow the signs).

Sunday Morning Town Walk: Volunteers give charming guided town walks once a week to raise a little money for community projects. It's fun to mix with English visitors as a local tells the town's story (£5, April-Sept Sun at 10:30, just show up at the stocks on Market Square).

Stow-on-the-Wold Walk

This six-stop self-guided walk covers about 500 yards and takes about 45 minutes. We'll start in the small park on the main square.

The Stocks on Market Square

Imagine this village during the 17th century when people were publicly ridiculed in stocks like this as a punishment. (Lock up your travel partner for a fun photo op.) Stow was born in pre-Roman times; it's where three trade routes crossed at a high point in the region (altitude: 800 feet). This square was the site of an Iron Age fort, and then a Roman garrison town. Starting in 1107, Stow was the site of an international fair, and people came from as far away as Italy to shop for wool fleeces on this vast, grassy expanse. Picture it in the Middle Ages (minus all the parked cars, and before the buildings in the center were added): a public commons and grazing ground, paths worn through the grass, and no well. Until the late 1800s, Stow had no running water; women fetched water from the "Roman Well" a quarter-mile down the hill.

With as many as 20,000 sheep sold in a single day, this square

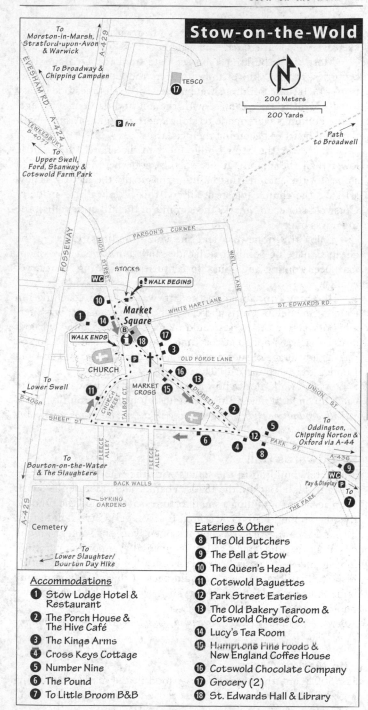

Stow-on-the-Wold

200 Meters
200 Yards

Path to Broadwell

To Moreton-in-Marsh, Stratford-upon-Avon & Warwick

To Broadway & Chipping Campden

TESCO

EVESHAM RD. • A-429

TEWKESBURY • B-4077

A-424

P Free

To Upper Swell, Ford, Stanway & Cotswold Farm Park

FOSSEWAY

HIGH STREET

PARSON'S CORNER

WELL LANE

ST. EDWARDS RD.

STOCKS

WALK BEGINS

WC

Market Square

WHITE HART LANE

WALK ENDS

B

CHURCH

OLD FORGE LANE

UNION ST.

To Lower Swell

B-4068

MARKET CROSS

CHURCH STREET CT.

TALBOT CT.

DIGBETH ST.

To Oddington, Chipping Norton & Oxford via A-44

SHEEP ST.

PARK ST.

A-436

WC

To Bourton-on-the-Water & The Slaughters

FLEECE ALLEY

FLEECE ALLEY

BACK WALLS

Pay & Display P

To

SPRING GARDENS

A-429

Cemetery

To Lower Slaughter/ Bourton Day Hike

THE PARK

COTSWOLDS

Accommodations

1. Stow Lodge Hotel & Restaurant
2. The Porch House & The Hive Café
3. The Kings Arms
4. Cross Keys Cottage
5. Number Nine
6. The Pound
7. To Little Broom B&B

Eateries & Other

8. The Old Butchers
9. The Bell at Stow
10. The Queen's Head
11. Cotswold Baguettes
12. Park Street Eateries
13. The Old Bakery Tearoom & Cotswold Cheese Co.
14. Lucy's Tea Room
15. Hamptons Fine Foods & New England Coffee House
16. Cotswold Chocolate Company
17. Grocery (2)
18. St. Edwards Hall & Library

was a thriving scene. And Stow was filled with inns and pubs to keep everyone housed, fed, and watered.

Most of the buildings you see date from the 17th and 18th centuries. A thin skin of topsoil covers the Cotswold limestone, from which these buildings were made. The local limestone is easy to cut, hardens after contact with the air, and darkens with age. Many buildings were made of stone quarried right on site—with the mini quarries becoming their cellars.

That's why the **Stow Lodge** (next to the church) lies a little lower than the church. It sits on the spot where locals quarried stones for the church. That building, originally the rectory, is now a hotel. The church (where we'll end this little walk) is made of Cotswold stone, and marks the summit of the hill upon which the town was built.

Enjoy the stonework and the crazy rooflines. Observe the cheap signage on solid stone facades and think about how shops have been coming and going for centuries in buildings that never change.

The **Stag Inn,** ahead on the left, was a typical coaching inn from a time before trains and cars, when land transport was literally horsepower. As horses could manage about 25 miles without a rest, coaches stopped at coaching inns to swap teams of horses. Taking advantage of such a relay of horses, travelers could go from London to Liverpool in 10 days.

As you walk, notice how locals stop to chat with each other to catch up on local news: This is a tight-knit little community.

• *Walk around the right of the building in the middle of the square and enter the library.*

St. Edwards Hall

The stately building in the square with the wooden steeple is St. Edwards Hall. Back in the 1870s, a bank couldn't locate the owner of an account containing a small fortune, so it donated the funds to the town to build this civic center. It serves as a City Hall, library, TI, and meeting place. When it's open, you can wander around upstairs to see the largest collection of Civil War portrait paintings in England—well described and an education in local 17th-century history. The library offers a candid peek at town life: community bulletin board, volunteers, history in a glass case, and historic town photos.

• *Beyond the library, at the far end of the square find the free-standing stone cross.*

The Market Cross

For 500 years, the Market Cross stood in the market reminding all Christian merchants to "trade fairly under the sight of God."

Notice the stubs of the iron fence in the stone base—a reminder of how countless wrought-iron fences were cut down and given to the government to be melted down during World War II. (Recently, it's been disclosed that all that iron ended up in junk heaps—frantic patriotism just wasted.) One of the plaques on the cross honors the Lord of the Manor, who donated money back to his tenants, allowing the town to finally finance running water in 1878. Panels at the top of the cross feature St. Edward, the Crucifixion, the wool trade, and a memorial to the Battle of Stow.

This is the site of the 1646 Battle of Stow. During the English Civil War, which pitted Parliamentarians against Royalists, Stow-on-the-Wold remained staunchly loyal to the king. The final battle of England's first Civil War was fought on this square as about 3,000 troops loyal to the king made their last stand. About 200 Royalist troops were killed (and survivors were locked up in the church). Ultimately, this cleared the way for the beheading of King Charles I and the rise of Oliver Cromwell.

Scan the square for **The Kings Arms,** with its great gables and spindly chimney. This square was where travelers parked their horses before spending the night at the inn. In the 1600s, this inn was considered the premium "posting house" between London and Birmingham. Because of its allegiance to the king, the town has an abundance of pubs with royal names (King's This and Queen's That).

Today, The Kings Arms cooks up pub grub and rents rooms upstairs. It's the opposite of a "free house"—it's part of a big chain owned by a national brewery and therefore does not offer any of the local beers on tap.

• *Walk down Digbeth Street.*

Digbeth Street

This street is lined with workaday shops, cute gift shops, many good little eateries, and beautiful Cotswold stone. It starts with a handy ATM. Then, from top to bottom you'll find: Hampton's Fine Foods (local gifty edibles), Cotswold Chocolate Company (pop in to watch Tony working in the back kitchen and his wife, Heidi, decorating his concoctions), the New England Coffee House (which feels like a village Starbucks with cozy lounge rooms upstairs), a "saddlery" for the many local horse enthusiasts, Lambournes (a traditional butcher), Cotswold Cheese Company (with old milk churns flanking the door), and the Old Bakery Tearoom (good for a cream tea or lunch; see "Eating in and near Stow," later).

Digbeth ends at a little triangular park in front of the former Methodist Church and across from the Porch House Hotel, with timbers that date from 947 (it claims—along with about 20 others—to be the oldest in England).

Just beyond the small grassy triangle was the place where locals gathered for bloody cockfights and bearbaiting (watching packs of hungry dogs tear at bears).

Today this is where—twice a year, in May and October—the Stow Horse Fair attracts thousands of nomadic Roma (called Gypsies by the less politically correct locals) and Travellers from far and wide. Thousands of people, who are determined not to be "miserable clock punchers," congregate down the street on the Maugersbury Road. Locals paint a colorful picture of the Roma, Travellers, and horses inundating the town. The young women dress up to distract the men because the horse fair—with its "grabbing" ritual—also functions as a marriage market. (It's a challenging time for the town, and many shops and pubs actually close up for the fair.)

• *Hook right and hike up the wide street.*

Sheep Street

As you head up Sheep Street, you'll pass a boutique-filled former brewery yard (on the left). Notice the old brewery's fancy street-front office, with its striking Welsh flint facade. This was the bad side of town (with the "smelly trades"). Across the street from the brewery was the slaughterhouse. And Sheep Street was originally not a street, but a staging place for medieval sheep markets. The sheep would be gathered here, then paraded into the market on the main square.

You'll notice narrow lanes on either side of the street. There are two explanations: one I like to believe (paths just wide enough for a single file of sheep to walk down, making it easier for merchants to count them) and another that's more likely true (practical walks between the long, narrow, medieval strips of land allotments). You'll see several of these so-called "fleece alleys" as you walk up the street.

• *Walk a couple blocks until you're one block from the traffic light and the highway, then make a right onto cute little Church Street, which leads to the church.*

St. Edwards Church

Before entering the church, circle it. On the back side, a wooden door is flanked by two ancient yew trees. While many see the door and think of the Christian scripture, "Behold, I stand at the door and knock," J. R. R. Tolkien fans see something quite different. Tolkien hiked the Cotswolds, and had a passion for sketching evocative trees such as this. *Lord of the Rings* enthusiasts are convinced this must be the inspiration for the Doors of Durin, leading into Moria.

Notice the two "bale tombs" (10 steps to the right of the door). Wool merchant gravestones were topped with a carved image of a tightly bound bale of wool.

Enter the church (usually open 9:00-17:00, except during services). While a wooden Saxon church stood here in the 10th century, today's structure is mostly from the 15th century. Its history is played up in leaflets and plaques just inside the door. The floor is paved with the tombs of big shots who made their money from wool and are still boastful in death. (Find the tombs crowned with the bales of wool.) Most of the windows are traditional Victorian (19th century) designs, but the two sets high up in the clerestory are from the dreamier Pre-Raphaelite school.

On the right wall, as you approach the altar, a monument remembers the many boys from this small town who were lost in World War I (50 out of a population of 2,000). There were far fewer in World War II. The biscuit-shaped plaque remembers an admiral from Stow who lost four sons defending the realm. It's sliced from an ancient fluted column (which locals believe is from Ephesus, Turkey).

During the English Civil War in the mid-1600s, the church was ransacked, and hundreds of soldiers were imprisoned here. The tombstone on the floor in front of the altar remembers the Royalist Captain Francis Keyt. His long hair, lace, and sash indicate he was a "cavalier," and true-blue to the king (Cromwellians were called "round heads"—named for their short hair). Study the crude provincial art—childlike skulls and (in the upper corners) symbols of his service to the king (armor, weapons).

Finally, don't miss the kneelers tucked in the pews. These are made by a committed band of women known as "the Kneeler Group." And with Reverend Martin Short for the pastor, the services could be pretty lively.

COTSWOLDS

Hiking from Stow

Stow/Lower Slaughter/Bourton Day Hike

Stow is made to order for day hikes. The most popular is the down-hill stroll to Lower Slaughter (3 miles), then on to Bourton-on-the-Water (about 1.5 miles more). It's a two-hour walk if you keep up a brisk pace and don't stop, but dawdlers should allow three to four hours. At the end, from Bourton-on-the-Water, a bus can bring you back to Stow. While those with keen eyes can follow this walk by spotting trail signs, it can't hurt to download or bring a map (ask to borrow one at your B&B). Note that these three towns are described in more detail starting on page 592.

To reach the trail from Stow, walk to the top of Sheep Street. At the busy A-429 highway, turn left. Head south of town on a foot-path alongside the busy highway, past the gas station for a couple hundred yards. Leave the highway on a well-marked trail (on the right) at Quarwood Cottage. You'll see a gravel lane with a green sign noting *Public Footpath/Gloucestershire Way/ Monarch's Way*).

Follow this trail for a delightful hour across farms, through romantic gates, across a fancy driveway, and past Gainsborough-painting vistas. You'll enjoy an intimate backyard look at local farm life. Although it seems like you could lose the trail, tiny easy-to-miss signs (yellow *Public Footpath* arrows—sometimes also marked *Gloucestershire Way* or *The Monarch's Way*—usually embedded in fence posts) keep you on target—watch for these very carefully to avoid getting lost. Finally, passing a cricket pitch, you reach **Lower Slaughter,** with its fine church and a mill creek leading up to its mill. (The people at the mill can call a taxi for a quick return to Stow.)

From Lower Slaughter, you can continue 30 minutes on Monarch's Way (follow green signs) into touristy Bourton-on-the-Water. Enjoy some time in Bourton itself and—when ready—catch the bus from in front of the Edinburgh Woolen Mill back to Stow (bus #801 departs roughly hourly, none on Sun, 10-minute ride; bus #802 also connects to Stow).

COTSWOLDS

Sleeping in Stow

$$$ Stow Lodge Hotel fills the historic church rectory with lots of old English charm. Facing the town square, with its own sprawling and peaceful garden, this lavish old place offers 21 large, thoughtfully appointed rooms with soft beds, stately public spaces, and a cushy-chair lounge (closed Jan, free parking, The Square, tel. 01451/830-485, www.stowlodge.co.uk, info@stowlodge.co.uk, helpful Hartley family).

$$ The Porch House rents 13 updated rooms with stone-wall and wood-beam accents (Digbeth Street, tel. 01451/870-048, www.porch-house.co.uk, info@porch-house.co.uk).

$$ The Kings Arms,
with 10 rooms above a
pub, manages to keep its
historic Cotswold charac-
ter while still feeling fresh
and modern in all the
right ways (steep stairs,
three slightly shabby "cot-
tages" out back, free park-
ing, Market Square, tel.

01451/830-364, www.kingsarmsstow.co.uk, info@kingsarmsstow.co.uk, Chris).

$$ Cross Keys Cottage offers four smallish but smartly up-dated rooms—some bright and floral, others classy white—with modern bathrooms. Kindly Margaret and Roger Welton take care of their guests in this 17th-century beamed cottage (RS%, call ahead to confirm arrival time, Park Street, tel. 01451/831-128, www.crosskeyscottage.co.uk, rogxmag@hotmail.com).

$ Number Nine has three large, bright, refurbished, and tastefully decorated rooms. This 200-year-old home comes with watch-your-head beamed ceilings and beautiful old wooden doors (9 Park Street, tel. 01451/870-333, mobile 07779-006-539, www.number-nine.info, enquiries@number-nine.info, James and Carol Brown).

$ The Pound is the quaint, centuries-old, slanty, cozy, and low-beamed home of Patricia Whitehead. She offers two bright, inviting rooms and a classic old fireplace lounge (cash only, down-town on Sheep Street next to the inn with the *Sheep* sign, tel. 01451/830-229, patwhitehead1@live.co.uk).

NEAR STOW

$ Little Broom B&B hides out in the neighboring hamlet of Maugersbury, which enjoys the peace Stow once had. It rents three cozy rooms and a studio apartment that share a lush garden and

pool (cash only, tel. 01451/830-510, www.cotswolds.info/webpage/
little-broom.htm, brendarussell1@hotmail.co.uk). Brenda has
racehorses, and her greenhouse keeps the pool warm throughout
the summer (guests welcome). It's a hilly half-mile walk from Stow:
Head east on Park Street and stay right toward Maugersbury. Turn
right into Chapel Street and take the first right uphill to the B&B.

Eating in and near Stow

While Stow has several good dining options, consider venturing out of town for a meal. You can walk to the pub in nearby
Broadwell, or—better yet—drive to one of several enticing gastropubs in the surrounding villages (see sidebar on page 590).

IN STOW
These places are all within a five-minute walk of each other, either on the main square or downhill on Queen and Park streets.
For good sit-down fish-and-chips, go to either pub on the main
square: The Queen's Head or The Kings Arms. For dessert, consider munching a locally made treat under the trees on the square's
benches and watching the sky darken, the lamps come on, and visitors having their photo fun in the stocks.

Restaurants and Pubs
$$$ The Old Butchers, named for its location rather than its
menu, specializes in fish. Serving oysters, scallops, and fish along
with steak and burgers, they offer both indoor and outdoor tables
and a good wine list (daily 12:00-14:30 & 18:30-21:30, 7 Park
Street, tel. 01451/831-700).

$$ Stow Lodge is *the* choice of the town's proper ladies. There
are two parts: The formal but friendly bar serves fine pub grub
(daily 12:00-14:00 & 19:00-20:30); the restaurant serves a popular
£30 three-course dinner (nightly, veggie options, good wines, just
off main square, tel. 01451/830-485, Val). On a sunny day, the pub
serves lunch in the well-manicured garden, where you'll feel quite
aristocratic.

$$$ The Bell at Stow, at the end of Park Street (on the edge
of town), has a youthful pub energy for a drink or for a full meal.
They serve up classic English dishes with seasonal, locally sourced
ingredients (daily 12:00-21:00, reservations recommended, tel.
01451/870-916, www.thebellatstow.com).

$$ The Queen's Head faces Market Square, near Stow
Lodge. With a classic pub vibe, it's a great place to bring your dog
and watch the eccentrics while you eat pub grub and drink the local
Cotswold brew, Donnington Ale. They have a meat pie of the day

and good fish-and-chips (beer garden out back, Mon-Sat 12:00-14:30 & 18:30-21:00, Sun 12:30-16:00, tel. 01451/830-563).

Cheaper Options

The grassy triangle where Digbeth hits Sheep Street has takeout fish-and-chips, Chinese, and Indian food. You can picnic at the triangle, or on the benches by the stocks on Market Street.

$ Cotswold Baguettes Take-Out has a line out the door for tasty takeout jacket potatoes, pasties, made-to-order sandwiches, and soup (Mon-Fri 9:00-16:00, Sat until 13:00, closed Sun, Church Street, tel. 01451/831-362).

$ Greedy's Fish and Chips, on Park Street, is the go-to place for takeout. There's no seating, but they have benches out front (Mon-Sat 12:00-14:00 & 16:30-20:30, closed Sun, tel. 01451/870-821).

$ Jade Garden Chinese Take-Away is appreciated by locals who don't want to cook (Wed-Mon 17:00-23:00, closed Tue, 15 Park Street, tel. 01451/870-288).

$$ The Prince of India, with a pleasant dining room, offers good Indian food to take out or eat in (nightly 18:00-23:00, 5 Park Street, tel. 01451/830-099).

$ The Old Bakery Tearoom is a local favorite hidden away in a tiny mall at the bottom of Digbeth Street with traditional cakes and light lunches (Mon-Wed & Fri-Sat 10:30-16:00, closed Thu and Sun, Digbeth Street, Alan and Jackie). Come here for soup, salad, sandwiches, and tea and scones (£6 cream tea is splittable).

$ The Hive is a quality modern café, where Jane and Sally offer breakfast, lunch, and tea with a warm welcome (Thu-Mon 9:00-17:00, closed Tue-Wed, Digbeth Street, tel. 01451/831-087).

$ Lucy's Tea Room is a nice option if you fancy a light lunch or cream tea on Market Square (daily 9:00-16:00, next to Stow Lodge).

Groceries: The **Co-op,** a small grocery store, faces the main square next to the Kings Arms (daily 7:00-22:00) and a big **Tesco** supermarket is 400 yards north of town.

PUB DINNER HIKE FROM STOW

From Stow, consider taking a half-hour countryside walk to the village of Broadwell, where you'll find a traditional old pub facing the village green that serves good basic grub in a convivial atmosphere.

$$ The Fox Inn Broadwell serves pub dinners (fish, meat pies, basic grub) and draws traditional ales—including the local Donnington ales. It's a classic, family-friendly pub (food served Mon-Sat 12:00-14:30 & 18:00-21:00, Sun 12:00-15:30 only, outdoor tables in garden out back, reservations smart, tel. 01451/870-909,

Great Country Gastropubs

These places—known for their high-quality meals and fine settings—are popular. Arrive early or phone in a reservation. (If you show up at 20:00, it's unlikely they'll be able to seat you for dinner if you haven't called first.) These pubs allow "well-behaved children," have overnight accommodations, and are practical only for those with a car. If you have wheels, make a point to dine at one of these—no matter where you're sleeping. For locations, see the map on page 554.

Near Stow

The first two (in Oddington, about three miles from Stow) are trendier and fresher, yet still in a traditional pub setting. The Plough (in Ford, a few miles farther away) is your jolly olde dark pub.

$$$$ The Fox Inn, a different Fox Inn than the one in Broadwell (see "Pub Dinner Hike from Stow"), has a long history but a fresh approach. It's a popular choice among local foodies for its updated pub classics and more creative, modern English dishes. They've perfected their upmarket rustic-chic vibe, with a genteelly Old World interior that's fresh and candle-lit and a delightful back terrace and garden (extensive wine list, Mon-Sat 12:00-14:30 & 18:30-21:30, Sun 12:00-19:00, in Lower Oddington, tel. 01451/870-555, http://thefoxatoddington.com).

$$$$ The Horse and Groom Village Inn in Upper Oddington is a smart place in a 16th-century inn, serving modern English and Continental food with plenty of vegetarian options, a good wine list (12 wines by the glass), and serious attention to beer. It boasts a wonderful fireplace and lots of meat on the menu (daily 12:30-14:30 & 18:00-21:00, tel. 01451/830-584, www.horseandgroomoddington.com).

Between Stow and Chipping Campden

$$$ The Plough Inn, in the hamlet of Ford, fills a fascinating 16th-century building—once a coaching inn, later a courthouse, and now a tribute to all things horse racing (it sits across from the Jackdaws Castle racehorse training facility). Eat from the same traditional English menu in the restaurant, bar, or garden. They are serious about their beer (owned by the local brewery), seasonal ingredients, and serving up heaping portions of stick-to-your-ribs pub-grub classics—a bit more traditional and less refined than others listed here (daily 12:00-14:00 & 18:00-21:00, all day Fri-Sun and June-Aug, 6 miles from Stow on the road to Tewkesbury, reservations smart, tel. 01386/584-215, www.theploughinnford.co.uk).

Near Chipping Campden
$$$$ The Ebrington Arms is a quintessential neighborhood pub with 21st-century amenities: modern British cuisine, home-brewed beer, an extensive wine list, and friendly (if occasionally slow) service. Rub elbows with locals in the crowded bar—energetic any day of the week. The restaurant and rotating menu are classy without being pretentious, and owners Jim and Claire make you feel welcome (daily 12:00-14:30 & 18:00-21:00, Sun until 15:30 and 20:30, 3 miles from Chipping Campden, reservations smart, tel. 01386/593-223, www.theebringtonarms.co.uk).

Near Moreton-in-Marsh, in Bourton-on-the-Hill
The hill-capping Bourton—about a five-minute drive (or two-mile uphill walk) above Moreton—offers sweeping views over the Cotswold countryside. Perched at the top of this steep, picturesque burg is an enticing destination pub.

$$$$ Horse and Groom Pub melds a warm welcome with a tempting menu of delicious modern English fare. They hit a good balance of old and new, combining unassumingly delicious food with a convivial spit-and-sawdust spirit. Choose between the lively, light, spacious interior or—in good weather—the terraced picnic-table garden out back (daily 12:00-15:00 & 18:00-21:00 except Sun until 20:30, tel. 01386/700-413, www.horseandgroom.info). Don't confuse this with The Horse and Groom Village Inn in Upper Oddington, near Stow (described earlier).

Other Gastropubs Worth a Drive
$$$ Eight Bells in Chipping Campden (described on page 570) and **$$$ The Mount Inn** in Stanton (described on page 576) are both up-scale options. **$$$$ The Wild Rabbit** in Kingham, five miles from Chipping Norton, is quiet, gourmet, and the most expensive of all. It's urbane-pub-meets-California, serving traditional British with a modern twist. The £65 tasting menu is a hit with foodies (on Church St. in Kingham, tel. 01608/658-389, www.thewildrabbit.co.uk).

COTSWOLDS

www.thefoxinnbroadwell.com). They'll happily drive diners back up to Stow when finished.

Getting There: It's 30 minutes downhill from Stow. While the walk is not particularly scenic (it's one-third paved lane, and the rest on an arrow-straight bridle path), it is peaceful, and the exercise is a good way to stoke your appetite. The trail is poorly marked, but it's hard to get lost: Leave Stow at Parson's Corner, continue downhill, pass the town well, follow the bridle path straight until you hit the next road, then turn right at the road and walk downhill into the village of Broadwell.

Near Stow-on-the-Wold

These sights are all south of Stow: Some are within walking distance (the Slaughters and Bourton-on-the-Water), and one is 20 miles away (Cirencester). The Slaughters and Bourton are tied together by the countryside walk described on page 586.

▲Lower and Upper Slaughter

"Slaughter" has nothing to do with lamb chops. It likely derives from an Old English word, perhaps meaning sloe tree (the one used to make sloe gin).

Lower Slaughter is a classic village, with ducks, a charming little church, a picturesque water mill, and usually an artist busy at her easel somewhere. The Old Mill Museum is a folksy ensemble with a tiny museum, shop, and café complete with a delightful terrace overlooking the millpond, enthusiastically run by Gerald and his daughter Laura, who just can't resist giving generous tastes of their homemade ice cream (£1 for museum, daily 10:00-18:00, Nov-Feb until dusk, tel. 01451/822-127, www.oldmill-lowerslaughter.com). Just behind the Old Mill, two kissing gates lead to the path that goes to nearby Upper Slaughter, a 15-minute walk or 2-minute drive away (leaving the Old Mill, take two lefts, then follow sign for *Wardens Way*). And if you follow the mill creek downstream, a bridle path leads to Bourton-on-the-Water (described next).

In **Upper Slaughter,** walk through the yew trees (sacred in pagan days) down a lane through the raised graveyard (a buildup of centuries of graves) to the peaceful church. In the far back of the fine cemetery, the statue of a wistful woman looks over the tomb of an 18th-century rector (sculpted by his son). Notice the town is missing a war memorial—that's because every soldier

who left Upper Slaughter for World War I and World War II survived the wars. As a so-called "Doubly Thankful Village" (one of only 13 in England and Wales), the town instead honors those who served in war with a simple wood plaque in the Town Hall.

Getting There: Though the stop is not listed on schedules, you should be able to reach these towns on bus #801 (from Moreton or Stow) by requesting the "Slaughter Pike" stop (along the main road, near the villages). Confirm with the driver before getting on. If driving, the small roads from Upper Slaughter to Ford and Kineton (and the Cotswold Farm Park, described later) are some of England's most scenic. Roll your window down and joyride slowly.

▲Bourton-on-the-Water

I can't figure out whether they call this "the Venice of the Cotswolds" because of its quaint canals or its miserable crowds. Either way, this town—four miles south of Stow and a mile from Lower Slaughter—is very pretty. But it can be mobbed with tour groups during the day: Sidewalks become jammed with disoriented tourists wearing nametags.

If you can avoid the crowds, it's worth a drive-through and maybe a short stop. It's pleasantly empty in the early evening and after dark.

Bourton's attractions are tacky tourist traps, but the three listed later might be worth considering. All are on High Street in the town center. In addition to these, consider Bourton's **leisure center** (big pool and sauna, a five-minute walk from town center off Station Road; Mon-Fri 6:30-22:00, Sat-Sun 8:00-20:00; shared with the school—which gets priority for use, tel. 01451/824-024).

Getting There: It's conveniently connected to Stow and Moreton by bus #801. Bus #802 also connects to Stow.

Parking: Finding a spot here can be tough. Even during the busy business day, rather than park in the pay-and-display parking lot a five-minute walk from the center, you can drive right into town and wait for a spot on High Street just past the village green. (Where the road swings left, turn a hard right [watch for signs for museums and TI] to go along the babbling brook and down High Street; there's a long row of free 1.5 hour spots starting just past the brook in front of the Edinburgh Woolen Mills Shop, on the right). After 18:00 you can park free just along the brook.

Tourist Information: The TI is tucked across the stream a short block off the main drag, on Victoria Street, behind The

Victoria Hall (Mon-Sat 9:30-17:00, Sun 10:00-14:00 except closed Sun Oct-April, tel. 01451/820-211).

Bike Rental: Hartwells on High Street rents bikes by half-day or day and includes a helmet, map, and lock (£11/3 hours; £16/day, Mon-Sat 9:00-18:00, Sun from 10:00, tel. 01451/820-405, www.hartwells.supanet.com).

▲Cotswold Motoring Museum

Lovingly presented, this good, jumbled museum shows off a life-time's accumulation of vintage cars, old lacquered signs, thread-bare toys, prewar memorabilia, and sundry British pop culture knick-knacks. If you appreciate old cars, this is nirvana. Wander the car-and-driver displays, which range from the automobile's early days to slick 1970s models, including period music to set the mood. Talk to an elderly Brit who's touring the place for some personal memories.

Cost and Hours: £6.25, daily 10:00-18:00, closed mid-Dec-mid-Feb, in the mill facing the town center, tel. 01451/821-255, www.cotswoldmotoringmuseum.co.uk.

Model Railway Exhibition

This exhibit of three model railway layouts is impressive only to train buffs (£3, June-Aug daily 11:00-17:00; closed Jan and Mon-Fri off-season; located in the back of a hobby shop, in the center of town, www.bourtonmodelrailway.co.uk).

Model Village

This light but fun display re-creates the town on a 1:9 scale in a tiny outdoor park, and has an attached room full of tiny models showing off various bits of British domestic life (£4.25, daily 10:00-18:00, until 16:00 in winter, at the edge of town, behind The Old New Inn, a few minutes' walk from the center, www.themodelvillage.com).

Walk to the Slaughters

From Bourton-on-the-Water, it's about a 30-minute walk (or a two-minute drive) to Upper and Lower Slaughter (described previously); taken together, they make for an easy two-hour round-trip walk from Bourton. (You could also walk from Stow through the Slaughters to Bourton—hike described on page 586.)

▲Cotswold Farm Park

Here's a delight for young and old alike. This park is the private venture of the Henson family, who are passionate about preserving rare and endangered breeds of native British animals. While it feels like a kids' zone (with all the family-friendly facilities you can imagine), it's a fascinating chance for anyone to get up  close and (very) personal with piles of mostly cute animals, including the sheep that made this region famous—the big and woolly Cotswold Lion. The "listening posts" deliver audio information on each rare breed.

Check the events board for seasonal demonstrations of farm life—such as milking, bottle-feeding, shearing, sheep shows (meet the seven local breeds), and more. Buy a bag of seed upon arrival, or have your map eaten by munchy goats as I did. Tykes love the "farm safari" tractor rides, maze, and zip line, and especially the "discovery barn"—where they can (carefully) handle wee chicks and bunnies.

Cost and Hours: £10.50, kids-£9, daily 10:30-17:00, Nov-Dec until 16:00, closed Jan-Feb, good guidebook (£5), restaurant and café, tel. 01451/850-307, www.cotswoldfarmpark.co.uk.

Getting There: It's well-signposted about halfway between Stow and Stanway (15 minutes from either). A visit here makes sense if you're traveling from Stow to Chipping Campden.

Northleach

While other towns may be cuter with more tourist-oriented sights, Northleach (nine miles south of Stow-on-the-Wold) is the best of the "untouched and untouristed" Cotswold villages. Officials made sure the main road didn't pass through town back in the 1980s, and today there's no TI and no place to park a big bus. It's invisible to mass tourism...and I like it.

The town's impressive main square (Market Place) and church attest to its position as a major wool center in the Middle Ages. Along with the Cotswolds Discovery Centre (on the big road at the edge of town), the town mostly consists of a main street leading to a fine old square facing a glorious church.

Drivers can park in the square called The Green or the adjoining Market Place. Bus #801 (with good Stow and Moreton connections) stops on the square, where there's an outdated map posted by the WC. For better information, find the nicely done Northleach map/guide (free at the church, post office, or Black Cat Community Café). Information is also online (www.northleach.gov.uk). Your best bet for a friendly and knowledgeable local might be the volunteer greeters at the church.

Eating: Three good options are all on or near Market Place. **$ Black Cat Community Café,** where the church lane hits the square, is run by the church and raises money for its charity work (Mon-Sat 9:00-16:30, closed Sun). Also facing the square is the **$$ Sherborne Arms** pub (long hours daily). It's a classic, family- and pet-friendly local, with a big fireplace, pool table, traditional ales and pub grub, outdoor seating, and a sloppy vibe.

$$$$ The Wheatsheaf Inn is the foodie's favorite for fine dining. With a pleasantly traditional dining room and a gorgeous sprawling garden, they offer modern English cuisine (long hours daily, on the main street into town one block before Market Place, tel. 01451/860-244, www.cotswoldswheatsheaf.com).

Market Place

Standing on the main square, you sense this was a fine medieval town. In fact, Northleach is a good example of a medieval "New Town." Hundreds of planned market towns like this were "planted" around England after the Norman conquest in 1066. Part of the Norman vision of creating a strong and centralized England was a land of logical towns, each with a triangular market place (likely symbolic of the Trinity) and a long High Street lined with standard and skinny "burgage plots"—parcels of land (from front-to-back: storefront, warehouse, living quarters, servants' quarters, stables, garden) all 33-feet-wide and reaching back to a service lane 330 feet behind the High Street. The Northleach economy got a boost in 1227 when it was granted a market charter by the king. Back then, traders came from far and wide...you could hear Italian-speaking wool importers in the streets. Nine centuries later, you can still see these skinny units (now either 33- or 66-feet wide) surviving.

While the market hall and the stocks may be gone, the square still has all the essentials of a town: bus stop, post office, pub, and so on, overseen by its church tower.

Church of Saints Peter and Paul

This fine Perpendicular Gothic church has been called the "cathedral of the Cotswolds." It's one of the Cotswolds' two finest "wool" churches (along with Chipping Campden's), paid for by 15th-century wool tycoons. And, with its enthusiastic corps of volunteer greeter/guides, it's the most welcoming place in town.

Pick up a flier and the fine town map/guide. Find the baptismal font with carved devils being crushed at its base (which dates from the 14th century and was part of the previous church). Ponder the brass plaques on the floor that memorialize big shots, showing sheep and sacks of wool at their long-dead feet, and inscriptions mixing Latin and Old English. Imagine the stained glass filling the windows before being destroyed—likely in the 17th century civil war. And don't miss the wonderful little exhibit about planned towns throughout medieval England in the north transept (daily 9:00-17:00 or until dusk, tel. 01451/861-132).

Cotswolds Discovery Centre at the Old Prison

This 18th-century building hosts displays about Cotswolds geology and history; pre-industrial farming including two shepherds' huts; and cell blocks and a courtroom from the building's previous uses. The on-site modern and glassy Cotswold Lion Café has indoor and outdoor seating (free, daily 9:30-16:30, on the A-429—Fosse Way—at the edge of Northleach, tel. 01451/862-000).

Coln Valley

Drivers will enjoy exploring the scenic Coln Valley, linking Northleach to Bibury as you pass through the enigmatic villages of Coln St. Dennis, Coln Rogers, Coln Powell, and Winson.

Chedworth Roman Villa

Secluded in thick woods in the Coln Valley are the remains of one of the finest aristocratic villas of fourth-century Roman Britain. Though well off the beaten path now, in its heyday of the late fourth century this wealthy farmstead was not far from a major Roman thoroughfare. You'll find a small museum and visitors center, and extensive, well-preserved floor mosaics. Rounding out the site are the remains of a small bath complex and a mossy spring once surrounded by an ostentatious water shrine. For history buffs with their own transportation, this is worth seeking out.

Cost and Hours: £11, daily 10:00-17:00, until 16:00 off-season, audioguide-£1, free guided tours daily, tel. 01242/890-256, www.nationaltrust.org.uk/chedworth.

Getting There: A half-mile beyond Northleach on the A-429, turn right and follow brown *Roman Villa* signs another four miles to the villa. Note: Don't follow *Chedworth* signs; these lead to Chedworth village.

▲Bibury

Six miles northeast of Cirencester, this village—long a favorite with British fond of strolling and fishing—is now so touristy I'd

only visit after hours. Bibury (BYE-bree) caters to tour buses, and lately has become a stop on the Instagram circuit and can be overwhelmed by selfie-stick tourists. After about 17:00, the light is warm and the masses are gone. The town offers some relaxing sights, including a row of very old weavers' cottages, a trout farm, a stream teeming with fat fish and proud ducks, and a church surrounded by rosebushes. A protected wetlands area on the far side of the stream hosts newts and water voles.

From the small parking lot, check out the posted map and information. Then walk the loop: up the main street (enjoying achingly beautiful homes with gardens and signs in Chinese that say keep out), then turn right along the old weavers' Arlington Row and back along the made-for-tour-groups paved path on the far side of the marsh, peeking into the rushes for wildlife.

For a closer look at the fish, cross the little bridge to the 15-acre **Trout Farm,** where you can feed them—or catch your own (£4.50 to walk the grounds, fish food-£0.60; daily 8:00-18:00, shorter hours off-season; catch-your-own only on weekends March-Oct 10:00-17:00, no fishing in winter, call or email to confirm fishing schedule, tel. 01285/740-215, www.biburytroutfarm.co.uk).

Getting There: Take bus #801 from Moreton-in-Marsh or Stow, then change to #855 in Northleach or Bourton-on-the-Water (3/day, 1 hour total).

Sleeping in Bibury: To spend the night in tiny Bibury, consider **$$ The William Morris B&B,** named for the 19th-century designer and writer (2 rooms, tearoom, 200 yards from the bridge toward the church at 11 The Street, tel. 01285/740-555, www. thewilliammorris.com, 11tearoom@gmail.com).

▲Cirencester

Almost 2,000 years ago, Cirencester (SIGH-ren-ses-ter) was the ancient Roman city of Corinium. Today it's the largest town of the Cotswold district. It's less cute and feels more bustling than

surrounding towns, but has a pleasant and pedestrianized historic center. It's 20 miles from Stow down the A-429, which was called Fosse Way in Roman times. The **TI**, in the shop at the Corinium Museum, answers questions and sells a town map and a town walking-tour brochure (same hours as museum, tel. 01285/654-180).

Getting There: By bus, take #801 from Moreton-in-Marsh or Stow, then change to #855 in Northleach or Bourton-on-the-Water for Cirencester (3/day, 1.5 hours total). Drivers follow *Town Centre* signs and find parking right on the market square; if it's full, retreat to the Waterloo pay-and-display lot (a 5-minute walk away).

Visiting Cirencester: Stop by the impressive **Corinium Museum** to find out why they say, "If you scratch Gloucestershire, you'll find Rome." The museum chronologically displays well-explained artifacts from the town's rich history, with a focus on Roman times—when Corinium was the second-biggest city in the British Isles (after Londinium). You'll see column capitals and fine mosaics before moving on to the Anglo-Saxon and Middle Ages exhibits (£6, Mon-Sat 10:00-17:00, Sun from 14:00,

COTSWOLDS

shorter hours off-season, Park Street, tel. 01285/655-611, www.coriniummuseum.org).

Cirencester's **church,** built in about 1490, is the largest of the Cotswold "wool" churches. The cutesy **New Brewery Arts** crafts center entertains visitors with traditional weaving and potting, workshops, an interesting gallery, and a good coffee shop (www.newbreweryarts.org.uk). Monday and Friday are general-**market** days, Friday features an antique market, and a crafts market is held every Saturday.

Moreton-in-Marsh

This workaday town—worth ▲—is like Stow or Chipping Campden without the touristy sugar. Rather than gift and antique shops, you'll find streets lined with real shops: ironmongers selling cottage name-plates and carpet shops strewn with the re-markable patterns that decorate B&B floors. A traditional market of 100-plus stalls fills High Street each Tuesday, as it has for the last 400 years (9:00-15:00, handicrafts, farm produce, clothing, books, and people-watch-ing; best if you go early). The Cotswolds has an economy aside from tourism, and you'll feel it here.

Orientation to Moreton-in-Marsh

Moreton has a tiny, sleepy train station two blocks from High Street, lots of bus connections, and the best **TI** in the region. Pe-ruse the racks of fliers, confirm rail and bus schedules, and consider the £0.50 *Town Trail* self-guided walking tour leaflet. Ask about discounted tickets for Blenheim Palace, easily visited between here and Oxford (TI open Mon-Fri 8:45-17:00, Sat 10:00-13:00, closed Sat Nov-Easter and Sun year-round, good public WC, tel. 01608/650-881).

HELPFUL HINTS

Laundry: The handy launderette is a block in front of the train station on New Road (daily 7:00-19:00, last self-service wash at 17:00, drop-off service options available—call ahead to ar-range, tel. 01608/650-888).

Bike Rental and Taxis: See "Getting Around the Cotswolds," earlier.

Parking: It's easy—anywhere on High Street is fine any time, as long as you want, for free (though there is a 2-hour parking limit for the small lot in the middle of the street). On Tues-days, when the market makes parking tricky, try the **Budgens** supermarket, where you can park for two hours.

Hikes and Walks from Moreton-in-Marsh: As its name implies, Moreton-in-Marsh sits on a flat, boggy landscape, making it a bit less appealing for hikes; I'd bus to Chipping Campden or to Stow, both described earlier, for a better hike (this is easy,

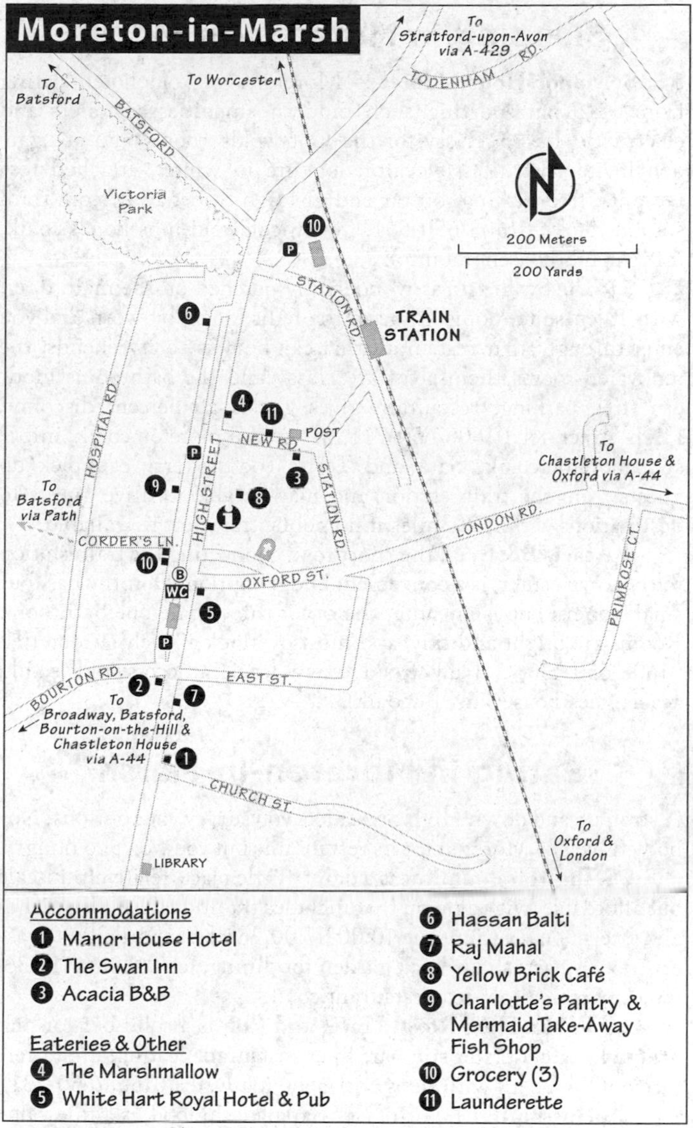
Moreton-in-Marsh
To Stratford-upon-Avon via A-429
To Worcester
To Batsford
BATSFORD
TODENHAM RD.
Victoria Park
200 Meters
200 Yards
STATION RD.
TRAIN STATION
HOSPITAL RD.
NEW RD.
POST
HIGH STREET
STATION RD.
To Chastleton House & Oxford via A-44
To Batsford via Path
LONDON RD.
CORDER'S LN.
OXFORD ST.
PRIMROSE CT.
WC
BOURTON RD.
EAST ST.
To Broadway, Batsford, Bourton-on-the-Hill & Chastleton House via A-44
CHURCH ST.
To Oxford & London
LIBRARY
Accommodations
1 Manor House Hotel
2 The Swan Inn
3 Acacia B&B
Eateries & Other
4 The Marshmallow
5 White Hart Royal Hotel & Pub
6 Hassan Balti
7 Raj Mahal
8 Yellow Brick Café
9 Charlotte's Pantry & Mermaid Take-Away Fish Shop
10 Grocery (3)
11 Launderette

since Moreton is a transit hub). If you do have just a bit of time to kill in Moreton, consider taking a fun and easy walk a mile out to the arboretum and falconry center in **Batsford** (described later).

Sleeping in Moreton-in-Marsh

$$$$ Manor House Hotel is Moreton's big old hotel, dating from 1545 but sporting such modern amenities as toilets and electricity. Its 35 classy-for-the-Cotswolds rooms and its garden invite relaxation (elevator, log fire in winter, attached restaurants, free parking, on far end of High Street away from train station, tel. 01608/650-501, www.cotswold-inns-hotels.co.uk, info@manorhousehotel.info).

$$ The Swan Inn is wonderfully perched on the main drag, with 10 en-suite rooms. Though the halls look a bit worn and you enter through a bar/restaurant that can be noisy on weekends, the renovated rooms themselves are classy and the bathrooms modern (free parking, restaurant gives guests 10 percent discount, High Street, tel. 01608/650-711, www.swanmoreton.co.uk, info@swanmoreton.co.uk, Sara and Terry Todd). Terry can pick up guests from the train station and may be able to drive guests to destinations within 20 miles if no public transport is available.

$ Acacia B&B, on the short road connecting the train station to the town center, is a convenient budget option. Dorothy has four small rooms: one is en suite, the other three share one bathroom. Rooms are bright and tidy, and most overlook a lovely garden (tel. 01608/650-130, 2 New Road, www.acaciainthecotswolds.co.uk, acacia.guesthouse@tiscali.co.uk).

Eating in Moreton-in-Marsh

A stroll up and down High Street lets you survey your options. Nobody travels to Moreton for its restaurants but you won't go hungry.

$$ The Marshmallow is a dainty little place, relatively upscale but affordable, with a menu that includes traditional English dishes and afternoon tea (Sun-Tue 10:00-17:00, Wed-Sat until 20:00, reservations smart, shady back garden for dining, tel. 01608/651-536, www.marshmallow-tea-restaurant.co.uk).

$$ White Hart Royal Hotel and Pub is a solid bet for pub grub with a characteristic bar, finer restaurant seating, and a terrace out back—all with the same menu (daily, tel. 01608/650-731).

$$ Hassan Balti, with tasty Bangladeshi food, is a fine value for sit-down or takeout (daily 12:00-14:00 & 17:30-23:30, tel. 01608/650-798). **Raj Mahal,** at the other end of town (on High Street, just past the White Hart), is also good.

$$ Yellow Brick Café, run by Tom and Nicola, has a delightful outdoor patio, cozy indoor seating, cheap and cheery menu, and a tempting display of homemade cakes (daily 9:00-17:00, just off High Street at 3 Old Market Way, tel. 01608/651-881).

$ Charlotte's Pantry serves fresh soups, salads, sandwiches, and pastries for lunch in a cheerful spot on High Street across from the TI (good cream tea, Mon-Sat 9:00-17:00, Sun from 10:00, tel. 01608/650-000).

$ Mermaid Take-Away Fish Shop is popular for its takeout fish and tasty selection of traditional savory pies (Mon-Sat 11:30-14:00 & 17:00-22:00, closed Sun, tel. 01608/651-391).

Picnic: There's a small **Co-op** grocery on High Street (daily 7:00-20:00), and a **Tesco Express** two doors down (Mon-Fri 6:00-23:00, Sat-Sun from 7:00). The big **Budgens** supermarket is at the far end of High Street (Mon-Sat 7:00-22:00, Sun 10:00-16:00). You can picnic across the street in pleasant Victoria Park (with a playground).

Nearby: The excellent **$$$$ Horse and Groom** gastropub in Bourton-on-the-Hill is two-miles away on the A-44 toward Chipping Campden (see page 590).

Moreton-in-Marsh Connections

Moreton, the only Cotswold town with a train station, is also the best base for exploring the region by bus (see "Getting Around the Cotswolds" on page 553).

From Moreton by Train to: London's Paddington Station (every 1-2 hours, 2 hours), **Bath** (hourly, 3 hours, 1-2 transfers), **Oxford** (hourly, 40 minutes), **Ironbridge Gorge** (hourly, 3 hours, 2 transfers; arrive Telford, then catch a bus or cab 5 miles to Ironbridge Gorge—see page 655), **Stratford-upon-Avon** (hourly, 3 hours, 2 transfers, slow and expensive, better by bus). **Train info:** Tel. 0345-748-4950, www.nationalrail.co.uk.

From Moreton by Bus to: Stratford-upon-Avon (#1 and #2 go via Chipping Campden: Mon-Sat 5/day, none on Sun, 1.5 hours, Johnsons Excelbus, tel. 01564/797 070, www.johnsonscoaches.co.uk).

Near Moreton-in-Marsh

▲Chastleton House

This stately home, located about five miles southeast of Moreton-in-Marsh, was lived in by the same family from 1607 until 1991. It offers a rare peek into a Jacobean gentry house. (Jacobean, which comes from the Latin for "James," indicates the style from the time of King James I—the early 1600s.) Built, like most Cotswold palaces, with wool money, it gradually declined with the fortunes of its aristocratic family, who lost much of their wealth in the war—not World War II, but the English Civil War in the 1640s. They stuck it out for centuries until, according to the last lady of the house, the place was "held together by cobwebs." It came to the National Trust on the condition that they would maintain its musty Jacobean ambience. It's so authentic that the BBC used it to film scenes

from its adaptation of *Wolf Hall* (a best-seller about Henry VIII's chief minister, Thomas Cromwell, who masterminded Henry's divorce, marriage to Anne Boleyn, and break with Rome). Wander on creaky floorboards, many of them original, chat with the knowledgeable volunteer guides, and understand this frozen-in-time relic revealing the lives of nobles who were land rich but cash poor. The docents are proud to play on one of the best croquet teams in the region (the rules of croquet were formalized in this house in 1868—if you fancy a round, the ticket counter can lend you a set). Page through the early 20th-century family photo albums in the room just off the entry.

Cost and Hours: £10.50; Wed-Sun 13:00-17:00, closed Nov-mid-March and Mon-Tue year-round; last entry one hour before closing, tel. 01608/674-355, www.nationaltrust.org.uk/chastleton. They let in 15 people every 10 minutes; when it's busy you may have a short wait.

Getting There: Chastleton House is well-signposted (be sure you follow signs to the house, not the town), about a 10-minute drive southeast of Moreton-in-Marsh off the A-44. It's a five-minute hike to the house from the free parking lot.

Batsford

This village has two side-by-side attractions that might appeal if you have a special interest or time to kill.

Getting There: Batsford is an easy 45-minute, 1.5-mile country walk west of Moreton-in-Marsh. By request, buses #1 and #2 will stop on the A-44, which is walking distance to Batsford Arboretum. You could also book a taxi in advance (see page 559).

Cotswold Falconry Centre

Along with the Cotswolds' hunting heritage comes falconry—and this place, with dozens of specimens of eagles, falcons, owls, and other birds, gives a sample of what these deadly birds of prey can do. You can peruse the cages to see all the different birds, but the demonstration, with vultures or falcons swooping inches over your head, is what makes it fun.

Cost and Hours: £10; daily mid-Feb-mid-Nov 10:30-17:30, closed rest of the year; flying displays at 11:30, 13:30, and 15:00,

plus in summer at 16:30; Batsford Park, tel. 01386/701-043, www.
cotswold-falconry.co.uk.

Batsford Arboretum and Garden Centre

This sleepy grove, with 2,800 trees from around the world, pales in
comparison to some of the Cotswolds' genteel manor gardens. But
it's next door to the Falconry Centre, and handy to visit if you'd
enjoy strolling through a diverse wood. The arboretum's café serves
lunch and tea on a terrace with sweeping views of the Gloucestershire countryside.

Cost and Hours: £9, Mon-Sat 9:00-17:00, Sun from 10:00,
Dec-Feb same hours but last entry at 15:00, tel. 01386/701-441,
www.batsarb.co.uk.

STRATFORD-UPON-AVON

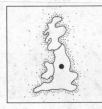

Stratford is Shakespeare's hometown. To see or not to see? Stratford is a must for every big bus tour in England, and one of the most popular side-trips from London. English majors and actors are in seventh heaven here. Sure, it's touristy, and nonliterary types might find it's much ado about nothing. But nobody back home would understand if you skipped Shakespeare's house.

Shakespeare connection aside, the town's riverside and half-timbered charm, coupled with its hardworking tourist industry, make Stratford a fun stop. But the play's the thing to bring the Bard to life—and you've arrived just in time to see the Royal Shakespeare Company (the world's best Shakespeare ensemble) making the most of their state-of-the-art theater

complex. If you'll ever enjoy a Shakespeare performance, it'll be here...even if you flunked English Lit.

PLANNING YOUR TIME

If you're just passing through Stratford, it's worth a half-day—stroll the charming core, visit your choice of Shakespeare sights (Shakespeare's Birthplace is best and easiest), and watch the swans along the river. But if you can squeeze it in, it's worth it to stick around to see a play; in this case, you'll need to spend the night here or drive in from the Cotswolds (just 30 minutes away; see previous chapter).

By Train or Bus: It's easy to stop in Stratford for a wander or an overnight. Stratford is well-connected by train to London and Oxford, and linked by bus and train to nearby towns (Warwick and Coventry to the north, and Moreton in the Cotswolds to the south).

By Car: Stratford, conveniently located at the northern edge of the Cotswolds, is made to order for drivers connecting the Cotswolds with points north (such as Ironbridge Gorge or North Wales). If you're driving north after you visit Stratford, you're within easy reach of two more worthwhile stop-offs: the impressive Warwick Castle and the evocative ruined cathedral at Coventry (both covered in the next chapter). Speedy travelers squeeze in all three of these towns (Stratford, Warwick, and Coventry) on a one-day drive-through: Leave the Cotswolds early, spend the morning exploring Stratford, have lunch and tour the castle in Warwick, visit Coventry's cathedral at the end of the day (last entry Mon-Sat at 16:00, Sun at 15:00; Sun evensong at 16:00), and drive in the evening to your next stop (you'll find driving tips at the end of this chapter). If you're more relaxed, see a play and stay in Stratford, then stop at Warwick and/or Coventry the following morning en route to your next destination.

Orientation to Stratford

Stratford, with around 30,000 people, has a compact old town, with the TI and theater along the riverbank, and Shakespeare's Birthplace a few blocks inland; you can easily walk to everything except Mary Arden's Farm. The core of the town is lined with half-timbered houses. The River Avon has an idyllic yet playful feel, with a park along both banks, rowboats, swans, and a fun old crank-powered ferry.

TOURIST INFORMATION

The TI is in a small brick building on Bridgefoot, where the main street hits the river (Mon-Sat 9:00-17:30, Sun 10:00-16:00, tel. 01789/264-293, www.shakespeare-country.co.uk). In addition to selling combo-tickets for the Shakespeare Birthplace Trust sights (cheaper here, see "Shakespearean Sights," later), the TI also sells discount tickets for Warwick Castle (£18 here, £29 on-site).

ARRIVAL IN STRATFORD

By Train: Don't get off at the Stratford Parkway train station—you want Stratford-upon-Avon. Once there, exit straight ahead from the train station, bear right up the stairs, then turn left and follow the main drag straight to the river. (For the Grove Road B&Bs, turn right at the first big intersection.)

By Car: If you're sleeping in Stratford, ask your B&B for

STRATFORD-UPON-AVON

Stratford-upon-Avon

STRATFORD-UPON-AVON

Accommodations
1. Adelphi, Ambleside & Salamander Guest Houses
2. Woodstock Guest House
3. Mercure Shakespeare Hotel
4. The Emsley Guest House
5. To Hemmingford House Hostel

Eateries
6. Le Bistro Pierre & Bear Free House
7. No. 9 Church Street
8. Edward Moon
9. Lambs & The Opposition
10. The Vintner Restaurant
11. Avon Spice
12. The Old Thatch Tavern
13. The Windmill Inn
14. The Garrick Inn
15. Grocery (2)
16. Barnaby's Fish & Chips
17. Kingfisher Fish & Chips
18. The Fourteas 1940s Tea Room
19. Bensons Restaurant & Tea Rooms

Other
20. Mailboxes Etc (Bag Storage)
21. Launderette (2)
22. Swan Fountain (Town Walks)
23. Jester Statue (Bard Walks)
24. City Bus Tours
25. Boat Rental (2)
26. River Cruises
27. Chain Ferry

Map labels: To Mary Arden's Farm, BIRMINGHAM RD., SHAKESPEARE ST., TRAIN STATION, P, To Worcester via A-46, STATION RD., ALCESTER RD., ARDEN ST., MANSELL ST., GREENHILL ST., WINDSOR ST., MEER ST., SHAKESPEARE'S BIRTHPLACE, AMERICAN FOUNTAIN, Market Place, ELY ST., GROVE RD., ROTHER ST., SCHOLARS LN., SHAKESPEARE'S SCHOOLROOM & GUILDHALL, CHURCH ST., CHESTNUT WALK, To Anne Hathaway's Cottage, BROAD WALK, NARROW LN., BROAD ST., BULL ST., SANCTUS ST., COLLEGE LN., OLD TOWN, HALL'S CROFT, COLLEGE ST.

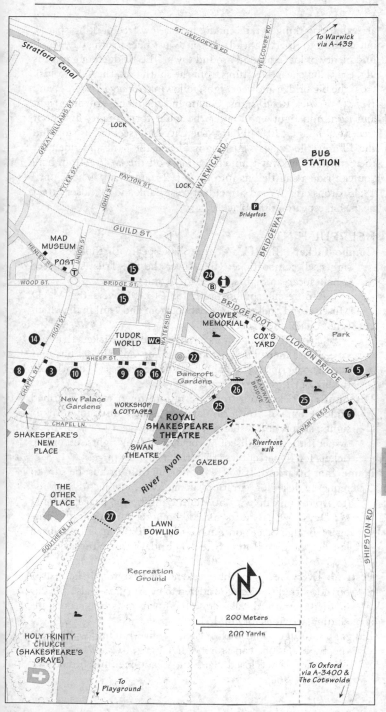

arrival and parking details (many have a few free parking spaces, but it's best to reserve ahead). If you're just here for the day, you'll find plenty of lots scattered around town. The Bridgefoot garage is big, easy, and cheap—coming from the south (i.e., the Cotswolds), cross the big bridge and veer right, following *Through Traffic, P,* and *Wark* (Warwick Road) signs. Go around the block—turning right and right and right—and enter the multistory garage; first hour free, £6/9 hours, £10/24 hours. The City Sightseeing bus stop and the TI are a block away. Parking is £1-3 at the park-and-ride near the Stratford Parkway train station, just off the A-46—from here you can ride a shuttle bus into town (£2 round-trip, 4/hour until 18:45, drops off at Wood Street NatWest Bank and Windsor Street near Shakespeare's Birthplace).

HELPFUL HINTS

Combo-Tickets: The TI and the Shakespeare Birthplace Trust sights sell combo-tickets that cover the five Trust sights (see "Shakespearean Sights," later, for details).

A different combo-ticket for £13.10 covers the MAD Museum and Shakespeare's Schoolroom and Guildhall (which is not one of the Trust sights).

City Sightseeing offers a range of combo-tickets that will save a little money if you combine a hop-on, hop-off bus tour with a boat cruise or rental, Shakespeare houses (3- or 5-house ticket), or the whole shebang.

Discounts: A ticket stub from a Stratford town walk (described under "Tours in Stratford," later) gets you a discount at many sights, shops, and restaurants. Also, ask the TI or your B&B owner if they have discount vouchers. Many sights sell online tickets for 10 percent less than the in-person price.

Name That Stratford: If you're coming by train or bus, be sure to request a ticket for "Stratford-upon-Avon," not just "Stratford" (to avoid a mix-up with Stratford Langthorne, near London.

Market Days: A local crafts and food market runs along the center of Bridge Street on Sundays from 10:00 to 17:00 (closed Jan-Feb), and on Rother Street on Fridays and Saturdays from 9:00 to 16:00.

Festival: Every year, on the weekend nearest to Shakespeare's birthday (traditionally considered to be April 23—also the day he died), Stratford celebrates. The town hosts free events, including activities for children.

Baggage Storage: Mailboxes Etc., a five-minute walk from the train station, can store your luggage (£2.50/bag, Mon-Fri hours vary, closed Sat-Sun, 12a Greenhill Street, tel. 01789/294-968).

Laundry: Laundry Quarter is on the road between the train station and the river (daily 8:00-20:00, 34 Greenhill Street, tel. 01789/417-766). The other option is **Sparklean,** a 10-minute walk from the city center, or about five minutes from the Grove Road B&Bs (daily 8:00-21:00, full-service option sometimes available—call, 74 Bull Street, tel. 01789/269-075).

Taxis: Try **007 Taxis** (tel. 01789/414-007) or the taxi stand on Woodbridge, near the intersection with High Street. To arrange for a private car and driver, contact **Platinum Cars** (£250/half-day tour, also does airport transfers from Heathrow and Birmingham, tel. 01789/264-626, www.platinumcars.co.uk).

Tours in Stratford

Stratford Town Walks

These entertaining, award-winning two-hour walks introduce you to the town and its famous playwright. Tours run daily year-round, rain or shine. Just show up at the Swan fountain (on the waterfront, opposite Sheep Street) in front of the Royal Shakespeare Theatre and pay the guide (£6, ticket stub offers discounts to some sights, shops, and restaurants; daily at 11:00, Sat also at  14:00, mobile 07855-760-377, www.stratfordtownwalk.co.uk). They also run an evening ghost walk (£7, Sat at 19:30, 1.5 hours, must book in advance).

Tudor World

This attraction offers 1.5-hour Shakespeare tours and one-hour ghost tours; see the listing under "Other Stratford Sights."

Bard Walks

A group of trained, costumed actors describe the city with Shakespearean flair, incorporating some of the Bard's most famous speeches and sonnets (£10, cash only, 1.5 hours, generally April-Oct Thu-Sun 14:00, book in advance, leaves from jester statue on Henley Street, mobile 07932-336-593, www.bardwalk.co.uk).

City Sightseeing Bus Tours

Open-top buses let you hop on and hop off at stops within the compact town, and head out to Anne Hathaway's Cottage and Mary Arden's Farm. The full 11-stop circuit takes about an hour and comes with entertaining and informative commentary (£15, ticket valid 24 hours, discount with town walk ticket stub, buy tickets on bus or at the TI; buses leave from the TI every 20 minutes, mid-April-Oct 9:30-17:00, no buses off-season, some weekend buses have live guides; tel. 01789/412-680, www.citysightseeing-stratford.com).

Shakespearean Sights

Stratford's five biggest Shakespeare sights are run by the Shakespeare Birthplace Trust (www.shakespeare.org.uk). While these sights are promoted like tacky tourist attractions—and designed to be crowd-pleasers rather than to tickle academics—they're well-run and genuinely interesting. Shakespeare's Birthplace, Shakespeare's New Place, and Hall's Croft are in town; Mary Arden's Farm and Anne Hathaway's Cottage are just outside Stratford. Each has a tranquil garden and helpful, eager docents who love to tell a story; and yet, each is quite different, so visiting all five gives you a well-rounded look at the Bard and his influences. (A sixth sight, Shakespeare's Schoolroom and Guildhall, is run by a separate organization, with a separate ticket.)

If you're here for Shakespeare sightseeing—and have time to venture to the countryside sights—you might as well buy a combo-ticket and drop into all five Shakespeare Birthplace Trust sights (described next). If your time is limited, visit only Shakespeare's Birthplace, which is the most convenient to reach (right in the town center) and offers the best historical introduction to the playwright.

Combo-Tickets: A combo-ticket that covers all five Shakespeare Birthplace Trust sights is called the **Full Story ticket**—a.k.a. the "five-house ticket"—and is sold at the TI and covered sights (£21 at the TI, £22.50 if purchased at a covered sight).

Another option is the £18 **any-three combo-ticket**. This ticket lets you choose three of the five Shakespeare Birthplace Trust sights—for instance, the birthplace, Anne Hathaway's Cottage, and Mary Arden's Farm (sold only at the TI; you'll get a receipt, then show it at the first sight you visit to receive your three-sight card).

Booking online saves you 10 percent; tickets are valid for one year.

IN STRATFORD
▲▲Shakespeare's Birthplace
While the birthplace itself is a bit underwhelming, it's rewarding to stand in the bedroom where Shakespeare was born, and helpful docents make this a good introduction to the Bard. A modern exhibit and live miniperformances emphasize how his work continues to inspire.

Cost and Hours: £17.50, covered by combo-tickets, daily 9:00-17:00, Nov-March 10:00-16:00, in town center on Henley Street, tel. 01789/204-016, www.shakespeare.org.uk.

Visiting Shakespeare's Birthplace: An introductory **exhibit** shows Shakespeare's enduring influence, with a video mash-up ranging from *The Simpsons* to the Hip-Hop Shakespeare Company. Check out the timeline of Shakespeare's plays, information about his upbringing and family life, and career in London. A few historical artifacts, including an original 1623 First Folio of Shakespeare's work, are also on display.

I find the **half-timbered Elizabethan building,** where young William grew up, a bit disappointing, as if millions of visitors have rubbed it clean of anything authentic. It was restored in the 1800s, and the furnishings are true to 1575, when William was 11. To liven up the otherwise dead-feeling house, chat up the well-versed, often-costumed attendants posted in many of the rooms, eager to engage with travelers and answer questions.

Shakespeare's father, John—who came from humble beginnings, but bettered himself by pursuing a career in glove-making (you'll see the window where he sold them to customers on the street)—provided his family with a comfortable upper-middle-class existence. The guest bed in the parlor was a major status symbol: They must have been rich to afford such a nice bed that wasn't used every day. This is also the house where Shakespeare and his bride, Anne Hathaway, began their married life together. Upstairs are the rooms where young Will, his siblings, and his parents slept (along with their servants). Look for the window etched with the names of important visitors, from Sir Walter Scott to actor Henry Irving. After Shakespeare's father died and William inherited the building, the thrifty playwright converted it into a pub to make a little money.

Exit into the fine **garden** where Shakespearean **actors** often perform brief scenes (they may even take requests). Pull up a bench and listen, imagining the playwright as a young boy stretching his imagination in this very place.

Shakespeare's New Place

While nothing remains of the house the Bard inhabited when he made it big (it was demolished in the 18th century), its manicured grounds are a tranquil spot to soak up some history. Today,

STRATFORD-UPON-AVON

William Shakespeare (1564-1616)

To many, William Shakespeare is the greatest author, in any language, period. In one fell swoop, he expanded and helped define modern English—the unrefined tongue of everyday people—and granted it a beauty and legitimacy that put it on par with Latin. In the process, he gave us phrases like "one fell swoop," which we quote without knowing that no one ever said it before Shakespeare wrote it.

Shakespeare was born in Stratford-upon-Avon in 1564 to John Shakespeare and Mary Arden. Though his parents were probably illiterate, Shakespeare is thought to have attended Stratford's grammar school, finishing his education at age 14. When he was 18, he married 26-year-old Anne Hathaway (she was three months pregnant with their daughter Susanna).

The very beginnings of Shakespeare's writing career are shrouded in mystery: Historians have been unable to unearth any record of what he was up to in his early 20s. We only know that seven years after his marriage, Shakespeare was living in London as a budding poet, playwright, and actor. He soon hit the big time, writing and performing for royalty, founding (along with his troupe) the Globe Theatre (a functioning replica of which now stands along the Thames' South Bank—see page 123), and raking in enough dough to buy New Place, a swanky mansion back in his hometown. Around 1611, the rich-and-famous playwright retired from the theater and moved back to Stratford, where he died at the age of 52.

With plots that entertained both the highest and the lowest minds, Shakespeare taught the play-going public about human nature. His tool was an unrivaled linguistic mastery of English. Using borrowed plots, outrageous puns, and poetic language, Shakespeare wrote comedies (c. 1590—*Taming of the Shrew, As You Like It*), tragedies (c. 1600—*Hamlet, Othello, Macbeth, King Lear*), and fanciful combinations (c. 1610—*The Tempest*), exploring the full range of human emotions and reinventing the English language.

Perhaps as important was his insight into humanity. His father was a glove-maker and wool merchant, and his mother was the daughter of a landowner from a Catholic family. Some scholars speculate that Shakespeare's parents were closet Catholics,

modern sculptures and traditional gardens adorn the grounds of the mansion Shakespeare called home for nearly 20 years. It's hard to imagine a house on this site, but vivid docent descriptions and visual aids bring the history to life. The expansive lawn is a pleasant respite from the hubbub of town, and the perfect place to sip a coffee or compose sonnets. Next door, Nash's House (which belonged practicing their faith during the rise of Protestantism. It is this tug-of-war between two worlds, some think, that helped enlighten Shakespeare's humanism. Think of his stock of great characters and great lines: Hamlet ("To be or not to be, that is the question"), Othello and his jealousy ("It is the green-eyed monster"), ambitious Mark Antony ("Friends, Romans, countrymen, lend me your ears"), rowdy Falstaff ("The better part of valor is discretion"), and the star-crossed lovers Romeo and Juliet ("But soft, what light through yonder window breaks"). Shakespeare probed the psychology of human beings 300 years before Freud. Even today, his characters strike a familiar chord.

The scope of his brilliant work, his humble beginnings, and the fact that no original Shakespeare manuscripts survive raise a few scholarly eyebrows. Some have wondered if Shakespeare had help on several of his plays. After all, they reasoned, how could a journeyman actor with little education have written so many masterpieces? And he was surrounded by other great writers, such as his friend and fellow poet, Ben Jonson. Most modern scholars, though, agree that Shakespeare did indeed write the plays and sonnets attributed to him.

His contemporaries had no doubts about Shakespeare—or his legacy. As Jonson wrote in the preface to the First Folio, "He was not of an age, but for all time!"

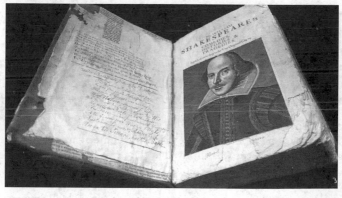

to Shakespeare's granddaughter and her husband) hosts a model of Shakespeare's house, domestic artifacts, period clothing, and a balcony view of the knot garden.

Cost and Hours: £12.50, covered by combo-tickets, daily 10:00-17:00, Nov-March until 16:00, 22 Chapel Street, tel. 01789/338-536.

Shakespearean Plays 101

Shakespeare's 38 plays span (and often intertwine) three genres: comedy, history, and tragedy. Brush up on some of the Bard's greatest hits before enjoying a performance in Stratford.

Comedy

As You Like It: Two brothers, a banished duke, noblemen, and a duke's daughter (Rosalind) fight and fall in love in the Forest of Arden, contemplating life, love, and death.

Much Ado About Nothing: Soldier Claudio and a nobleman's daughter, Hero, fall in love and play matchmakers to their unsuspecting friends. Trickery, slander, and heartbreak are overcome in an ultimately happy ending.

A Midsummer Night's Dream: Four Athenian lovers, two eloping, follow each other into the woods, where fairy King Oberon enchants them with a love potion. A mistaken identity leaves Lysander and Demetrius both pining after Helena, and Hermia without a groom.

The Tempest: Prospero, duke of Milan, is overthrown by his brother and Alonso (the king of Naples) and dwells on an enchanted island with daughter Miranda. When his old enemies wash ashore, Prospero enlists island spirits to seek his revenge—and Miranda falls in love with Alonso's son Ferdinand.

History

The Henriad: A series of four plays chronicles the demise of England's King Richard II, the rule of successor King Henry IV, and his relationship with rebellious son Prince Harry (eventually King

Hall's Croft

This former home of Shakespeare's eldest daughter, Susanna, gives a good idea of how the wealthy lived in the 17th century, with finer furnishings compared to the other Shakespeare properties. Since Susanna married a doctor, exhibits focus on Elizabethan-era medicine, leaving visitors grateful to live in modern times. Hall appears to have been a conscientious physician: He kept notes in Latin of all his cures. His treatment for scurvy—watercress and scurvy grass—are both now known to contain vitamin C.

Cost and Hours: £8.50, covered by combo-tickets, daily 10:00-17:00, Nov-March 11:00-16:00, on-site tearoom, between Church Street and the river on Old Town Street, tel. 01789/338-533.

Henry V). War across England and France forms the backdrop for Shakespeare's exploration of honor, nationalism, and power.

Tragedy

Romeo and Juliet: Lovers from rival families seek to marry, but are torn apart by their families. When Juliet fakes her death to avoid an arranged marriage, misunderstanding breeds heartbreak.

Macbeth: Three witches prophesize Macbeth's ascension from nobility to the throne of Scotland, leading Macbeth, aided by his ambitious wife, to embark on a violent mission to become king. Plagued by paranoia and hallucinations, he commits heinous crimes to gain—and maintain—power.

Othello: General Othello promotes Cassio to lieutenant over officer Iago. After Othello elopes with senator Brabantio's daughter Desdemona, a bitter Iago seeks revenge, manipulating the couple and Cassio by pitting one against another.

Hamlet: Haunted by his father's ghost, Prince Hamlet plots to kill his father's murderer, King Claudius. But when Hamlet inadvertently causes his lover Ophelia's death, her brother Laertes vows to kill Hamlet, with Claudius' help. A climactic duel between Laertes and Hamlet leads to a bloodbath.

King Lear: King Lear banishes daughter Cordelia to France, while daughters Regan and Goneril secretly plot his death. Lear's ally the Earl of Gloucester, at odds with his own sons, warns Lear of the vengeful plot, and Lear drifts into madness. Both men succumb to the political chaos created by their families' greed and betrayal.

Shakespeare's Grave (Holy Trinity Church)

Shakespeare was a rector for Holy Trinity Church when he died.

While the church is surrounded by an evocative graveyard, the Bard is entombed in a place of honor, right in front of the altar inside. The church marks the ninth-century birthplace of the town, which was once a religious settlement.

Cost and Hours: £4 donation, Mon-Sat 9:00-17:00 (Oct-March until 16:00), Sun from 12:30; no access to grave 13:00-14:30; 10-minute walk past the theater—see its graceful spire as you gaze down the river, tel. 01789/266-316, www.stratford-upon-avon.org.

Shakespeare's Schoolroom and Guildhall

The guildhall and the guild's schoolhouse help visitors imagine Shakespeare's childhood years. Built between 1418 and 1420, the guildhall was the headquarters for the Guild of the Holy Cross, where everyone from Stratford and nearby towns—from tradesmen to craftsmen to clergy and nobility—networked and struck deals. Anyone could join for a small fee; in return, the guild supported members' families, even employing priests to pray for their souls. It also provided social services, such as town infrastructure—and established Stratford's first school.

Cost and Hours: £8.50, £13.10 combo-ticket with MAD Museum, daily 11:00-17:00, Church Street, tel. 01789/203-170, www.shakespearesschoolroom.org.

Visiting the Guildhall and Schoolroom: The guildhall's priest's chapel and the Guild Chapel next door both contain fragments of medieval wall paintings that were probably whitewashed during Reformation efforts—during William's father's tenure as chamberlain here. (The paintings were uncovered when the chapel was restored in 1804 and are barely visible.)

In the very room where Shakespeare attended school for seven years, six days a week, you'll see a wood table with centuries-old student-carved graffiti, and you can try out a quill pen as you conjugate Latin. A costumed docent describes student life. Wood benches face each other so that kids could easily help each other learn. Since paper was so expensive, students were taught verbally, likely boosting young Will's flair for storytelling. Groups of traveling actors performed at the guildhall several times while Will attended school here. In the days before TV, movies, or social media, these productions were the pinnacle of entertainment, and likely inspired him.

JUST OUTSIDE STRATFORD

To reach either of these sights, it's best to drive or take the hop-on, hop-off bus tour (see "Tours in Stratford," earlier)—unless you're staying at one of the Grove Road B&Bs, which are an easy 20-minute walk from Anne Hathaway's Cottage. Both sights are well signposted (with brown signs) from the major streets and ring roads around Stratford. If driving between the sights, ask for directions at the sight you're leaving.

▲▲Mary Arden's Farm

Along with Shakespeare's Birthplace, this is my favorite of the Shakespearean sights. Famous as the girlhood home of William's mom, this homestead is in Wilmcote (about three miles from

Stratford). Built around two historic farmhouses, it's an open-air folk museum depicting 16th-century farm life...which happens to have ties to Shakespeare.

Cost and Hours: £15, covered by combo-tickets, daily 10:00-17:00, everyone's shooed out at 17:30, closed Nov-mid-March, on-site café and picnic tables, tel. 01789/338-535.

Getting There: It's most convenient by car (free parking) or hop-on, hop-off bus, but also easy to reach by train. The Wilmcote train station is a five-minute walk up the street (two stops from Stratford-upon-Avon on Birmingham- and London-bound trains, 1-2/hour, 5-minute trip, call London Midland to confirm departure time—tel. 0844-811-0133, www.londonmidland.com).

Visiting Mary Arden's Farm: The museum hosts many special events—check the board by the entry. There are always plenty of active, hands-on activities to engage kids. Save some time for a walk: There are 23 acres of bucolic trails, orchards, and meadows to explore.

Pick up a map (and handful of organic animal feed) at the entrance and wander the grounds and buildings. Throughout the complex, you'll see interpreters in Tudor costumes performing daily 16th-century chores, such as milking the sheep and cutting wood to do repairs on the house. They answer questions and provide fun, gossipy insight into what life was like at the time. Look out for heritage breeds of farmyard animals including goats, woolly pigs, and friendly donkeys.

The first building, **Palmer's farm** (mistaken for Mary Arden's home for hundreds of years, and correctly identified in 2000), holds

a kitchen where food is prepared over an open fire; at 13:00 each day the "servants" (employees) sit down in the adjacent dining room for a traditional dinner.

Mary Arden actually lived in the neighboring **farmhouse,** covered in brick facade and less impressive. The house is filled with kid-oriented activities, including period dress-up clothes, board games from Shakespeare's day, and a Tudor alphabet so kids can write their names in fancy lettering.

Of the many events here, the most enjoyable is the daily **bird of prey display,** with lots of mean-footed birds (call ahead for times). Chat with the falconers about their methods for earning the birds' trust: Like Katherine in *The Taming of the Shrew*—described as "my falcon" by husband Petruchio—the birds are motivated by food. Their hunger sets them to flight (a round-trip earns the bird a bit of food; the birds fly when hungry—but don't have the energy if they're *too* hungry). You may be given a bit of meat to feed the bird yourself.

▲Anne Hathaway's Cottage

Located 1.5 miles out of Stratford (in Shottery), this home is a 12-room farmhouse where the Bard's wife grew up. William courted Anne here—she was 26, he was only 18—and his tactics proved successful. (Maybe a little too much, as she was several months pregnant at their wedding.) Their 34-year marriage produced two more children, and lasted until his death in 1616 at age 52. The Hathaway family lived here from the 1500s until 1911, and much of the family's 92-acre farm remains part of the sight.

Cost and Hours: £12.50, covered by combo-tickets, daily 9:00-17:00, Nov-March 10:00-16:00, tearoom, tel. 01789/338-532.

Getting There: It's a 30-minute walk from central Stratford (20 minutes from the Grove Road B&Bs), a stop on the hop-on, hop-off tour bus, or a quick taxi ride from downtown Stratford (around £7). Drivers will find it well signposted entering Stratford from any direction, with easy cheap parking.

Visiting Anne Hathaway's Cottage: The thatched-roof **cottage** looks cute enough to eat, and it's fun to imagine the writer of some of the world's greatest romances wooing his favorite girl right here during his formative years. (If the place shakes, a tourist has thunked his or her head on the low beams.) The docent talks provide an intimate peek at life in Shakespeare's day.

Maybe even more interesting than the cottage are the **gardens,** which have several parts (including a prizewinning "traditional cottage garden"). Follow the signs to the "Woodland Walk" (look for the music-note willow sculpture on your way), along with a fun sculpture garden littered with modern interpretations of Shakespearean characters (such as Falstaff's mead gut, and a great photo-op statue of the British Isles sliced out of steel). From April through June, the gardens are at their best, with birds chirping, bulbs in bloom, and a large sweet-pea display. You'll also find a music trail, a butterfly trail, and various exhibits, like a teepee built

---

Stratford Thanks America

Residents of Stratford are thankful for the many contributions Americans have made to their city and its heritage. Along with pumping up the economy day in and day out with tourist visits, Americans paid for half the rebuilding of the Royal Shakespeare Theatre after it burned down in 1926. The Swan Theatre renovation was funded entirely by American aid. Harvard University inherited—you guessed it—the Harvard House, and it maintains the house today. London's much-loved theater, Shakespeare's Globe, was the dream (and gift) of an American. And there's even an odd but prominent "American Fountain" overlooking Stratford's market square on Rother Street, which was given in 1887 to celebrate the Golden Jubilee of the rule of Queen Victoria.

---

of sticks that is rigged up to play a selection of Shakespeare's love sonnets when you press a button.

THE ROYAL SHAKESPEARE COMPANY

The Royal Shakespeare Company (RSC), undoubtedly the best Shakespeare company on earth, performs year-round in Stratford and in London. Seeing a play here in the Bard's birthplace is a must for Shakespeare fans, and a memorable experience for anybody. Between its excellent acting and remarkable staging, the RSC makes Shakespeare as accessible and enjoyable as it gets.

The RSC makes it easy to take in a play, thanks to their very user-friendly website, painless ticket-booking system, and chock-a-block schedule that fills the summer with mostly big-name Shakespeare plays (plus a few more obscure titles to please the die-hard aficionados).

The RSC is enjoying renewed popularity after the update of its Royal Shakespeare Theatre. Even if you're not seeing a play, exploring this cleverly designed theater building is well worth your time. The smaller attached Swan Theatre hosts plays on a more intimate scale, with only about 400 seats.

▲▲▲Seeing a Play

Performances take place most days (Mon-Sat generally at 19:15 at the Royal Shakespeare Theatre or 19:30 at the Swan, matinees around 13:15 at the RST or 13:30 at the Swan, sporadic Sun shows). Shows generally last three hours or more, with one intermission; for an evening show, don't count on getting back to your B&B much before 23:00. There's no strict dress code—nice jeans and short-sleeve shirts are fine—but shorts are discouraged. If you're feeling bold, buy a £10 standing ticket and slip into an open seat as

The Look of Stratford

There's much more to Stratford than Shakespeare sights. Take time to appreciate the look of the town itself. While the main street goes back to Roman times, the key date for the city was 1196, when the king gave the town "market privileges." Stratford was shaped by its marketplace years. The market's many "departments" were located on logically named streets, whose names still remain: Sheep Street, Corn Street, and so on. Today's street plan—and even the 57' 9" width of the lots—survives from the 12th century. (Some of the modern storefronts in the town center are still that exact width.)

Starting in about 1600, three great fires gutted the town, leaving very few buildings older than that era. After those fires, tinderbox thatched roofs were prohibited—the Old Thatch Tavern on Greenhill Street is the only remaining thatched roof in town, predating the law and grandfathered in.

The town's main drag, Bridge Street, is the oldest street in town, but looks the youngest. It was built in the Regency style—a result of a rough little middle row of wattle-and-daub houses being torn down in the 1820s to double the street's width. Today's Bridge Street buildings retain that early 19th-century style.

Throughout Stratford, you'll see striking black-and-white half-timbered buildings, as well as half-timbered structures that were partially plastered over and covered up in the 19th century. During Victorian times, the half-timbered style was considered low-class, but in the 20th century—just as tourists came, preferring ye olde style—timbers came back into vogue, and the plaster was removed on many old buildings. But any black and white you see is likely to be modern paint. The original coloring was "biscuit yellow" and brown.

the lights dim—if nothing is available during the play's first half, something could open up after intermission.

Getting Tickets: Tickets range from £5 (standing) to £75, with most around £45 (discounts for families). Saturday-evening shows—the most popular—are the most expensive. You can book tickets as you like it: online (www.rsc.org.uk), by phone (tel. 01789/331-111, Mon-Sat 10:00-18:00, Sun until 17:00) or in person at the box office (Mon-Sat 10:00-20:00, until 18:00 on non-performance days, Sun until 17:00). Print tickets at home, pick them up at the theater 30 minutes before "curtain up," or just show them on your phone. Because it's so easy to get tickets online or by phone, it makes absolutely no sense to pay extra to book tickets through any other source.

Tickets go on sale 10 months in advance. Saturdays and very famous plays (such as *Romeo and Juliet* or *Hamlet*)—or any play with a well-known actor—sell out the fastest. Before your trip, check the website, and consider buying tickets if something strikes your fancy. But demand is difficult to predict, and some tickets do go unsold. On a past visit, on a sunny Friday in June, the riverbank was crawling with tourists. I stepped into the RSC on a lark to see if they had any tickets. An hour later, I was watching King Lear lose his marbles.

Even if there aren't any seats available, you may be able to buy a returned ticket on the same day of an otherwise sold-out show. Also, the few standing-room tickets in the main theater are sold only on the day of the show. While you can check at the box office anytime during the day, it's best to go either when it opens at 10:00 (daily) or between 17:30 and 18:00 (Mon-Sat). Be prepared to wait.

Visiting the Theaters
▲▲The Royal Shakespeare Theatre

The RSC's flagship theater is one of Stratford's most fascinating sights. If you're seeing a play here, come early to poke around the building and check out interesting tidbits of theater history. You need to take a guided tour (explained below) to see the back-stage areas, but you're welcome to wander the the-ater's public areas any time the building is open.

Cost and Hours: Free entry, £8.50 for *The Play's the Thing* exhibit; Mon-Sat 10:00-23:00, Sun until 17:00.

Information. Tel. 01789/331-111, www.rsc.org.uk.

Guided Tours: Well-informed RSC volunteers lead enter-taining, one-hour tours (£9; behind-the-scenes tour and front-of-the-house tours are at Royal Shakespeare Theatre; audition tours and From Page-to-Stage tours are at The Other Place—described later; tour schedule varies by day, depends on performances; call, check online, or go to box office to confirm schedule; best to book ahead).

Tour Combo-Ticket: The £15 Explorer Pass includes a the-ater tour of your choice, the tower climb, and *The Play's the Thing* exhibit (described later, book at box office or online).

Background: The original Victorian-style theater was built in 1879 to honor the Bard, but it burned down in 1926. The big Art Deco-style building you see today was erected in 1932 and out-fitted with a stodgy Edwardian "picture frame"-style stage, even though a more dynamic "thrust"-style stage—better for engaging the audience—was the actors' choice. (It would also have been closer in design to Shakespeare's original Globe stage, which jutted into the crowd.)

The latest renovation in 2011 addressed this ill-conceived design, adding an updated thrust-style stage. They've left the shell of the 1930s theater, but given it an unconventional deconstructed-industrial style, with the seats stacked at an extreme vertical pitch. Though smaller, the redesigned theater can seat about the same size audience as before (1,048 seats), and now there's not a bad seat in the house—no matter what, you're no more than 50 feet from the stage (the cheapest "gallery" seats look down right onto Othello's bald spot). Productions are staged to play to all of the seats throughout the show. Those sitting up high appreciate different details from those at stage level, and vice versa.

Visiting the Theater: From the main lobby and box office/gift shop area, there's plenty to see. First head left. In the circular **atrium** between the brick wall of the modern theater and fragments of the previous theater, notice the ratty old floorboards. These were pried up from the 1932 stage and laid down here—so as you wait for your play, you're treading on theater history. Upstairs on level 2, find the **Paccar Room,** with generally excellent temporary exhibits assembled from the RSC's substantial collection of historic costumes, props, manuscripts, and other theater memorabilia. Continue upstairs to level 3 to the Rooftop Restaurant (described later). High on the partition that runs through the restaurant, facing the brick theater wall, notice the four **chairs** affixed to the wall. These are original seats from the earlier theater, situated where the back row used to be (90 feet from the stage)—illustrating how much more audience-friendly the new design is.

Back downstairs, pass through the box office/gift shop area to find the **Swan Wing**—an old, Gothic-style Victorian space that survives from the original 1879 Memorial Theatre and hosts *The Play's the Thing*, an immersive exhibit that lets you digitally try on costumes, design sets, and grace a Shakespearean stage.

Back outside, across the street from the theater, notice the building with the steep gable and huge door (marked *CFE 1887*). This was built as a **workshop** for building sets, which could be moved in large pieces to the main theater. To this day, all the sets, costumes, and props are made here in Stratford. The row of **cottages** to the right is housing for actors. The RSC's reputation exerts enough pull to attract serious actors from all over the UK and beyond, who live here for the entire season. The RSC uses a repertory company approach, where the same actors appear in multiple shows concurrently. Today's Lady Macbeth may be tomorrow's Rosalind.

Tower View: For a God's-eye view of all of Shakespeare's houses, ride the elevator to the top of the RSC's tower (£3, £1 with tour ticket, buy ticket at box office or book online; tower open daily 10:00-17:00; Oct-March Sun-Fri 10:00-16:30, Sat until 12:15; closed 12:00-14:00 year-round during matinees). Aside from a few sparse exhibits, the main attraction here is the 360-degree view over the theater building, the Avon, and the lanes of Stratford.

The Food's the Thing: The main theater has a casual **$ café** with a terrace overlooking the river (sandwiches, daily 10:00-21:00), as well as the fancier **$$ Rooftop Restaurant**—though I'd dine elsewhere (Mon-Sat 11:30 until late, Sun 10:30-18:15, dinner reservations smart, tel. 01789/403-449, www.rsc.org.uk/rooftop).

The Swan Theatre

Adjacent to the RSC Theatre is the smaller (about 400 seats), Elizabethan-style Swan Theatre, named not for the birds that fill the park out front, but for the Bard's nickname—the "sweet swan of Avon." It has a vertical layout and a thrust stage similar to the RSC Theatre, but its wood trim and railings give it a cozier, more traditional feel. The Swan is used for lesser-known Shakespeare plays and alternative works. Occasionally, the lowest level of seats is removed to accommodate "groundling" (standing-only) tickets, much like at the Globe Theatre in London.

The Other Place (Former Courtyard Theatre)

A two-minute walk down Southern Lane from the original Royal Shakespeare Theatre, the Courtyard Theatre (affectionately called the "rusty shed" by locals) was built as a replacement venue while the RSC was being renovated. Now called The Other Place, it serves as a space for rehearsal, research, and development, and educates theater buffs about play production through its From Page-to-Stage tours, where you'll learn about everything from rehearsals to costumes to props. The venue also hosts a bar/café, plus monthly music nights, spoken-word nights, and family activities.

Cost and Hours: Music nights-free, tours-see Royal Shakespeare Theater guided tours earlier, café open Mon-Wed 9:30-18:00, Thu-Sat until 21:00, closed Sun, tel. 01789-403-493, www.rsc.org.uk.

The Dell

Summer open-air Shakespeare performances at Avonbank Gardens near Holy Trinity Church are easy, free, and fun: Just bring something to sit on and a picnic. These are not RSC productions; the company invites university and amateur groups to perform (June-Aug weekends, schedule posted on garden gates, www.rsc.org.uk/thedell)

Other Stratford Sights

Avon Riverfront

The River Avon is a playground of swans and canal boats. The swans have been the mascots of Stratford since 1623, when, seven years after the Bard's death, Ben Jonson's poem in the First Folio dubbed him "the sweet swan of Avon."

For a nice **riverfront walk,** consider crossing over the Tramway Footbridge and following the trail to the right (west) along the south bank of the Avon. To your left is the **Stratford Big Wheel,** not as big as the London Eye, but much cheaper (£5). From here, you'll get a great view of the Royal Shakespeare Theater across the river. Continuing down the path, you'll pass the local lawn bowling club (guest players welcome, £4, Tue and Thu 14:00-16:00) and Lucy's Mill Weir, an area popular with fishers and kayakers, where you can turn around. On the way back, cross the river by the chain ferry (described later) and return to the town center via the north bank for a full loop.

In the water you'll see colorful **canal boats.** These boats saw their workhorse days during the short window of time between the start of the Industrial Revolution and the establishment of the railways. Today they're mostly pleasure boats. The boats are long and narrow, so two can pass in the slim canals. There are 2,000 miles of canals in England's Midlands, built to connect centers of industry with seaports and provide vital transportation during the early days of the Industrial Revolution. Stratford was as far inland as you could sail on natural rivers from Bristol; it was the terminus of the man-made Birmingham Canal, built in 1816. Even today you can motor your canal boat all the way to London from here. Along the embankment,  look for the signs indicating how many hours it'll take—and how many locks you'll traverse—to go by boat to various English cities.

For a little bit of mellow river action, rent a **rowboat** (£7/hour per person) or, for more of a challenge, pole yourself around on a Cambridge-style **punt** (the canal is only 4-5 feet deep; same price as the rowboat and more memorable/embarrassing if you do the punting—don't pay £10 for a waterman to do the punting for you). You can rent boats at the Swan's Nest Boathouse across the Tramway Footbridge; another rental station, along the river next to the theater, has higher prices but is more conveniently located.

You can also try a sleepy 40-minute **river cruise** (£7, includes commentary, Avon Boating, board boat in Bancroft Gardens near the RSC Theater, tel. 01789/267-073, www. avon-boating.co.uk), or jump on the oldest surviving **chain ferry** in Britain (c. 1937, £0.50), which shuttles people across the river just beyond the theater.

The old **Cox's Yard,** a riverside timber yard until the 1990s, is a rare physical remnant of the days when Stratford was an industrial port. Today, Cox's has been taken over by a restaurant complex, with a café, lots of

outdoor seating, and occasional live music. Upstairs is the Attic Theatre, which puts on fringe theater acts (www. treadtheboardstheatre.co.uk).

In the riverfront park, roughly between Cox's Yard and the TI, the **Gower Memorial** honors the Bard and his creations. Named for Lord Ronald Gower, the man who paid for and sculpted the memorial, this 1888 work shows Shakespeare up top ringed by four of his most indelible creations, each representing a human pursuit: Hamlet (philosophy), Lady Macbeth (tragedy), Falstaff (comedy), and Prince Hal (history). Originally located next to the theater, it was moved here following the theater's destruction by fire in 1926.

▲MAD Museum

A refreshing change of pace in Bard-bonkers Stratford, this museum's name stands for "Mechanical Art and Design." It celebrates machines as art, showcasing a changing collection of skillfully constructed robots, gizmos, and Rube-Goldberg machines that spring to entertaining life with the push of a button. Engaging for anyone, riveting for engineers, it's pricey but conveniently located near Shakespeare's Birthplace.

Cost and Hours: £7.80, £13.10 combo-ticket also covers Shakespeare's Schoolroom and Guildhall, Mon-Fri 10:00-17:00, Sat-Sun until 17:30, last

STRATFORD-UPON-AVON

entry 45 minutes before closing, 4 Henley Street, tel. 01789/269-356, www.themadmuseum.co.uk.

Tudor World at the Falstaff Experience

This attraction is tacky, gimmicky, and more about entertainment than education. (And, while it's named for a Shakespeare character, the exhibit isn't about the Bard.) Filling Shrieve's House Barn with mostly kid-oriented exhibits (mannequins and descriptions, but few real artifacts), it sweeps through Tudor history from the plague to Henry VIII's privy chamber to a replica 16th-century tavern. If you're into ghost-spotting, their nightly ghost tours may be your best shot.

Cost and Hours: Museum-£6, daily 10:30-17:30; Shakespeare tour-£5, Sat at 14:00; ghost tours-£7.50, daily at 18:00, additional tours possible Fri-Sat; 40 Sheep Street, tel. 01789/298-070, www.tudorworld.com.

Sleeping in Stratford

Ye olde timbered hotels are scattered through the city center. Most B&Bs are a short walk away on the fringes of town, right on the busy ring roads that route traffic away from the center. (The recommended places below generally have double-paned windows for rooms in the front, but still get some traffic noise.)

In general, the weekend on or near Shakespeare's birthday (April 23) is particularly tight, but Fridays and Saturdays are always busy. This town is so reliant upon the theater for its business that some B&Bs have insurance covering their loss if the Royal Shakespeare Company ever stops performing in Stratford.

ON GROVE ROAD

These places are at the edge of town on busy Grove Road, across from a grassy square, and come with free parking when booked in advance. From here, it's about a 10-minute walk either to the town center or to the train station (opposite directions).

$$ Adelphi Guest House is run by Shakespeare buffs Sue and Simon, who pride themselves on providing a warm welcome, homemade gingerbread, and original art in every room (RS%, 39 Grove Road, tel. 01789/204-469, www.adelphi-guesthouse.com, info@adelphi-guesthouse.com).

$$ Ambleside Guest House is run with quiet efficiency and attentiveness by owners Peter and Ruth. The place has six rooms and a homey, airy feel with no B&B clutter (ground-floor room, family room, 41 Grove Road, tel. 01789/297-239, www.amblesideguesthouse.com, peter@amblesideguesthouse.com—include your phone number in your request, since they like to call you back to confirm with a personal touch).

$ Woodstock Guest House is a friendly, family-run, and classy place with five comfortable rooms (RS%, ground-floor room, 30 Grove Road, tel. 01789/299-881, www.woodstock-house.co.uk, jackie@woodstock-house.co.uk, bubbly Jackie).

$ Salamander Guest House, run by gregarious Frenchman Pascal and his wife, Anna, rents eight simple rooms that are a bit cheaper than their neighbors' (family room, free parking, 40 Grove Road, tel. 01789/205-728, www.salamanderguesthouse.co.uk, p.delin@btinternet.com).

ELSEWHERE IN STRATFORD

$$ Mercure Shakespeare Hotel, centrally located in a black-and-white building just up the street from Shakespeare's New Place, has 78 business-class rooms, each one named for a Shakespearean play or character. Some of the rooms are old-style Elizabethan higgledy-piggledy (with modern finishes), while others are contemporary style—note your preference when you reserve (breakfast extra, pay parking, Chapel Street, tel. 01789/294-997, www.mercure.com, h6630@accor.com).

$$ The Emsley Guest House, with Victorian style and modern comfort, holds five bright rooms named after different counties in England—plus a cozy guest library (family rooms, no kids under 5, free off-street parking, 5 minutes from train station at 4 Arden Street, tel. 01789/299 557, www.theemsley.co.uk, stay@theemsley.co.uk, Liz and Chris).

¢ Hostel: Family-friendly **Hemmingford House** has 32 rooms in a Georgian mansion, half of them en suite. It's a 10-minute bus ride from town (private rooms, family rooms, camping pods and tents, breakfast extra, take bus #X18 or #15 two miles to Alveston, hostel is on Wellesbourne Road, tel. 01789/297-093, www.yha.org.uk/hostel/stratford-upon-avon, stratford@yha.org.uk).

Eating in Stratford

RESTAURANTS

Stratford's numerous restaurants vie for your pretheater business, with special hours and meal deals. (Most offer light two- and three-course menus before 19:00.) You'll find many hardworking places on Sheep Street and Waterside. Unfortunately, post-theater dinners are more challenging, as most places close early.

$$$ Le Bistro Pierre, across the river near the boating station, is a French eatery that's been impressing Stratford residents and tourists alike. They have indoor or outdoor seating and French (read: slow) service (Mon-Fri 12:00-15:00 & 17:00-22:30, Sat until 16:00 & 23:00, Sun 12:30-16:30 & 18:00-22:00, Swan's Nest Hotel, Bridgefoot, tel. 01789/264-804). The pub next door, **Bear Free House,** is owned by the same people and shares the same kitchen, but offers a different menu.

$$$ No. 9 Church Street earns raves for its modern take on British classics, with an emphasis on seasonal and local ingredients, all served in a 400-year-old building with exposed beams and brick. Their tasting and pretheater menus are good deals; Saturday reservations are recommended (Tue-Sat 12:00-14:00 & 17:00-21:30, closed Sun-Mon, 9 Church Street, tel. 01789/415-522, www.no9churchst.com).

$$$ Edward Moon is an upscale English brasserie serving signature dishes like steak-and-ale pies and roasted lamb shank in a setting reminiscent of *Casablanca* (Mon-Fri 12:00-14:30 & 17:00-21:30, Sat until 15:00 & 22:00, Sun until 15:00 & 21:00, 9 Chapel Street, tel. 01789/267-069, www.edwardmoon.com).

$$$ Sheep Street Eateries: The next three places, part of the same chain, line up along Sheep Street, offering trendy ambience and modern English cuisine at relatively high prices (all three have good-value pretheater menus before 19:00). **Lambs** is intimate and serves meat, fish, and veggie dishes with panache. The upstairs feels dressy, under low half-timbered beams (daily 17:00-21:00, lunch served Tue-Sun, 12 Sheep Street, tel. 01789/292-554). **The Opposition,** next door, has a less formal "bistro" ambience (Mon-Thu 12:00-14:00 & 17:00-21:00, Fri-Sat until 22:30, closed Sun, tel. 01789/269-980; book in advance for post-theater dinner here Fri-Sat). **The Vintner,** just up the street, is known for their burgers (daily 9:30-22:00, Sun until 21:30, 4 Sheep Street, tel. 01789/297-259).

Indian: $$ Avon Spice has a good reputation and good prices for takeout or dine-in meals (daily 17:30-23:30, 7 Greenhill Street, tel. 01789/267-067).

PUBS

$$ The Old Thatch Tavern is, according to locals, the best place in town for beer, serving up London-based Fuller's brews. The atmosphere is cozy, and the food is a cut above what you'll get in other pubs; enjoy it either in the bar, in the tight, candlelit restaurant, or out on the quiet patio (daily 12:00-21:00, on Greenhill Street overlooking the market square, tel. 01789/295-216).

$$ The Windmill Inn serves decent, modestly priced fare in a 17th-century inn. It combines old and new styles, and—since it's a few steps beyond the heart of the tourist zone—actually attracts some locals as well. Order drinks and food at the bar, then either settle into a comfy chair or head out to the half-timbered courtyard to wait for your meal (daily 12:00-21:00, Church Street, tel. 01789/297-687).

$$ The Garrick Inn bills itself as the oldest pub in town, and comes with a cozy, dimly lit restaurant vibe. Choose between the pub or table-service section; either way, you'll dine on bland, pricey pub grub (daily 11:00-22:00, 25 High Street, tel. 01789/292-186).

PICNICS

With its sprawling and inviting riverfront park, Stratford is a particularly pleasant place to picnic. Choose a bench and enjoy views of the river and vacation houseboats while munching your meal. It's a fine way to spend a midsummer night's eve. For groceries or prepared foods, find **Marks & Spencer** on Bridge Street (Mon-Sat 8:00-18:00, Sun 10:30-16:30, small coffee-and-sandwiches café upstairs). Across the street, **Sainsbury's Local** stays open later than other supermarkets (daily 7:00-22:00).

For fish-and-chips, you have a couple of options: **$ Barnaby's** is a greasy fast-food joint near the waterfront—convenient if you want takeout for the riverside park just across the street (cash only, daily 11:00-19:30, at Sheep Street and Waterside). For better food (but a less convenient location—closer to my recommended B&Bs), queue up with the locals at **$ Kingfisher,** then ask for the freshly battered haddock (Mon-Sat 11:30-13:45 & 17:00-22:00, closed Sun, a long block up at 13 Ely Street, tel. 01789/292-513).

TEAROOMS

$$ The FourTeas 1940s Tea Room transports diners to another era, with period details ranging from the servers' housedresses to the ration-card menu to the Glenn Miller-era soundtrack. There's even an air-raid shelter beyond the terrace garden. Don't be fooled by the theme: This place eludes kitsch with high-quality pastry, classic sandwiches, all-day breakfast, and local ingredients (Mon-Sat 9:30-17:00, Sun 11:00-16:00, 24 Sheep Street, tel. 01789/293-908).

$$ Bensons Restaurant and Tea Rooms, across the street from Shakespeare's Birthplace, has outdoor tables right on the main pedestrian mall and friendly service (teas available all day, daily 9:00-17:30, 40 Henley Street, tel. 01789/415-572).

Stratford Connections

Remember: When buying tickets or checking schedules, ask for "Stratford-upon-Avon," not just "Stratford." Notice that a single train (running about every 2 hours) connects most of these destinations: Warwick, Leamington Spa (change for Coventry or Oxford), then London.

From Stratford-upon-Avon by Train to: London (3/day direct, more with transfers, 2-2.5 hours, to Marylebone Station), **Warwick** (8/day, 30 minutes, more with transfer), **Coventry** (at least hourly, 2 hours, change in Leamington Spa or Birmingham), **Oxford** (every 2 hours, 1.5 hours, change in Leamington Spa or Banbury), **Moreton-in-Marsh** (almost hourly, 3 hours, 2-3 transfers, slow and expensive, better by bus). **Train info:** tel. 0345-748-4950, www.nationalrail.co.uk.

By Bus to: Cotswolds towns (bus #1 or #2, Mon-Sat 5/day, none on Sun, 50 minutes to **Chipping Campden,** 1.5 hours to **Moreton-in-Marsh,** some also stop at Broadway and/or Blockley, Johnsons Excelbus, tel. 01564/797-070, www.johnsonscoaches. co.uk; on Sundays #606 provides service to Chipping Campden and Broadway, 2/day, 30 minutes, Marchants Coaches, tel. 01242/257-714, www.marchants-coaches.com), **Warwick** (#X18, hourly, 30 minutes, tel. 01604/676-060, www.stagecoachbus. com), **Coventry** (hourly, 1.25 hours, same bus as Warwick). A direct bus runs to **Oxford** once a day (National Express, tel. 0871-781-8181, www.nationalexpress.com, train is better). Most intercity buses stop on Stratford's Bridge Street (a block up from the TI). For bus info that covers all the region's companies, call Traveline at tel. 0871-200-2233 (www.travelinemidlands.co.uk).

By Car: Driving is easy and distances are short: **Chipping Campden** (12 miles), **Stow-on-the-Wold** (22 miles), **Warwick** (8 miles), **Coventry** (19 miles).

ROUTE TIPS FOR DRIVERS

These tips assume you're heading north from Stratford and considering visits to Warwick and/or Coventry (both described in the next chapter).

Stratford to Points North via Warwick and Coventry: Leaving the Bridgefoot garage in downtown Stratford, circle to the right around the same block, but stay on "the Wark" (Warwick Road, A-439). Warwick is eight miles away. The castle is just south of town on the right. (For parking advice, see "Arrival in Stratford," earlier.) When you're trying to decide whether to stop in Coventry, factor in Birmingham's rush hour—try to avoid driving through that city between 14:00-20:00, if you can (worst Fri-Sun; Mon-Thu it generally gets better earlier, around 18:30).

Including Coventry: After touring Warwick Castle, carry on through the center of Warwick town and follow signs to Coventry (still the A-439, then the A-46). If you're stopping in Coventry, follow signs painted on the road to the *City Centre,* and then to *Cathedral Parking.* Grab a place in the high-rise parking lot. Leaving Coventry, follow signs to *Nuneaton* and *M6 North* through lots of sprawl, and you're on your way.

Skirting Coventry: Take the M-69 (direction: Leicester) and follow the M-6 as it threads through giant Birmingham.

Once You're on the M-6: The highway divides into the free M-6 and an "M-6 Toll" road (designed to help drivers cut through the Birmingham traffic chaos). Take the toll road—£6.40 is a small price to pay to avoid all the nasty traffic (www.m6toll.co.uk).

When battling through sprawling Birmingham, keep your sights on the M-6. If you're heading for any points north—Ironbridge Gorge (Telford), North Wales, Liverpool, Blackpool, or the Lakes (Kendal for the South Lake District, Keswick for the North Lake District)—just stay relentlessly on the M-6 (direction: North West). Each destination is clearly signed directly from the M-6. For specifics on getting to Ironbridge Gorge, see page 666.

STRATFORD-UPON-AVON

WARWICK & COVENTRY

Just north of Stratford, you'll find England's single most spectacular castle: Warwick. This medieval masterpiece, which has been turned into a virtual theme park, is extremely touristy—but it's also historic and fun, and may well be Britain's most kid-friendly experience. The town of Warwick, huddled protectively against the castle walls, is a half-timbered delight—enjoyable for a lunch or dinner, or even for an overnight.

A bit farther north sits the decidedly *not* cute city of Coventry—a blue-collar burg that was notoriously obliterated by the Nazi Luftwaffe in World War II. While today's Coventry, having been rebuilt modern and drab, offers little charm, it does feature one of Britain's most poignant WWII sights: the charred husk of its once-grand cathedral, now left as a monument, with the inspiring new cathedral just next door. A few other intriguing museums round out Coventry's appeal.

PLANNING YOUR TIME

Warwick and Coventry are both ideal on-the-way destinations—lash them onto your itinerary as you head north from Stratford. Warwick Castle deserves at least three hours for a quick visit, but it can be an all-day outing for families. Coventry's cathedral can be seen quickly—in about an hour, if that's all the time you have—though the city's other sights could fill an additional couple of hours. If you're prioritizing, Warwick is (for most) the better stop, with its grand castle and charming town; Coventry is worthwhile primarily for its iconic cathedral ruins and for the chance to see a real, struggling, industrial Midlands city.

Warwick and Coventry are both reachable by public trans-

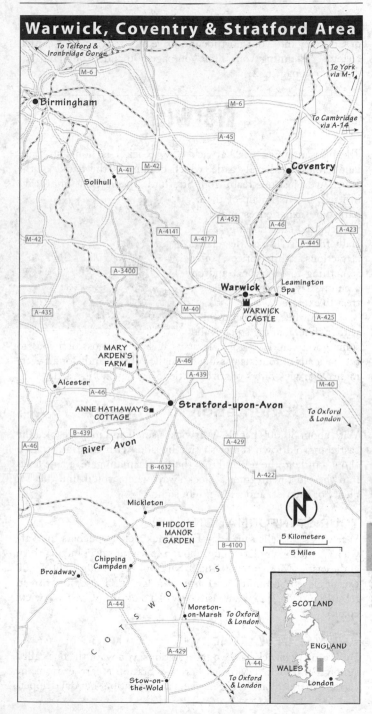

Warwick, Coventry & Stratford Area

To Telford & Ironbridge Gorge

M-6

Birmingham

M-6

To York via M-1

To Cambridge via A-14

A-45

Coventry

A-41

M-42

Solihull

A-452

A-46

A-423

A-4141

A-4177

A-445

M-42

A-3400

Warwick

Leamington Spa

A-435

M-40

WARWICK CASTLE

A-425

MARY ARDEN'S FARM

A-46

A-439

M-40

Alcester

A-46

ANNE HATHAWAY'S COTTAGE

Stratford-upon-Avon

To Oxford & London

B-439

A-46

River Avon

A-429

B-4632

A-422

Mickleton

N

HIDCOTE MANOR GARDEN

5 Kilometers

B-4100

5 Miles

Chipping Campden

Broadway

C O T S W O L D S

A-44

Moreton-on-Marsh

To Oxford & London

A-429

A-44

Stow-on-the-Wold

To Oxford & London

SCOTLAND

ENGLAND

WALES

London

portation, but easier for drivers. For tips on splicing Warwick and/or Coventry into your northbound drive out of Stratford, see that chapter's "Planning Your Time" on page 606 and "Route Tips for Drivers" on page 632.

Warwick

The pleasant town of Warwick ("WAR-ick") is home to England's finest medieval castle, which dominates the banks of the River Avon just upstream from Stratford. The castle is impressive in itself, but its lineup of theme park-type experiences makes it particularly entertaining, especially for kids. The castle-related attractions, while pricey, offer something for everyone, and on a sunny day, the grounds are a treat to explore.

Meanwhile, Warwick town—with a fine market square and some good eateries—goes about its business almost oblivious to the busloads of tourists passing through. While handy for an overnight, Warwick offers relatively little to see beyond its castle.

Orientation to Warwick

With about 30,000 people, Warwick is small and manageable. The castle and old town center sit side by side, with the train station about a mile to the north. From the castle's main gate, a lane leads into the old town center a block away, where you'll find the TI, plenty of eateries, and a few minor sights.

TOURIST INFORMATION

Warwick's TI sells same-day Fast Track ticket vouchers to Warwick Castle for a reduced rate, about a £5 savings over buying them at the castle (Mon-Fri 9:30-16:30, Sat from 10:00, Sun 10:00-16:00 except closed Sun mid-Dec-Easter, The Court House, Jury Street, tel. 01926/492-212, www.visitwarwick.co.uk, info@visitwarwick.co.uk).

ARRIVAL IN WARWICK

By Train: Warwick has two train stations; you want the one called simply "Warwick" (Warwick Parkway Station is farther from the castle). There are no luggage lockers at the station, but day-trippers

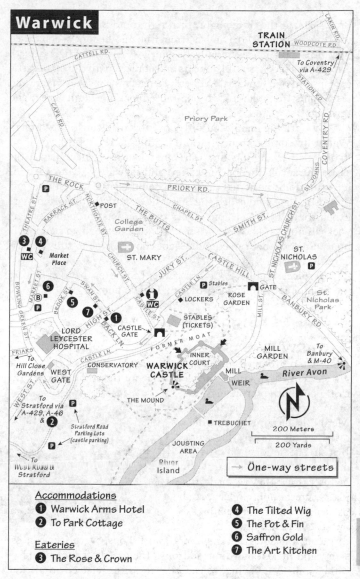

Warwick

TRAIN STATION

WOODCOTE RD.

LAKIN RD.

To Coventry via A-429

STATION RD.

CATTELL RD.

CAPE RD.

COVENTRY RD.

Priory Park

ST. JOHNS

THE ROCK

PRIORY RD.

THEATRE ST.

BARRACK ST.

POST

CHAPEL ST.

SMITH ST.

NICKNGATE ST.

College Garden

THE BUTTS

WC

Market Place

CHURCH ST.

ST. MARY

JURY ST.

CASTLE HILL

ST. NICHOLAS CHURCH ST.

ST. NICHOLAS

MARKET ST.

BROOK ST.

SWAN ST.

BOWLING GREEN ST.

St. Nicholas Park

CASTLE LN.

Stables

GATE

BANBURY RD.

LOCKERS

ROSE GARDEN

HIGH ST.

BACK LN.

WC

CASTLE ST.

STABLES (TICKETS)

MILL ST.

LORD LEYCESTER HOSPITAL

CASTLE GATE

FORMER MOAT

MILL GARDEN

To Banbury & M-40

FRIARS

CASTLE LN.

CONSERVATORY

INNER COURT

WARWICK CASTLE

MILL

WEIR

River Avon

To Hill Close Gardens

WEST GATE

THE MOUND

TREBUCHET

N

WEST ST.

To Stratford via A-429, A-46 &

Stratford Road Parking Lots (castle parking)

JOUSTING AREA

200 Meters

200 Yards

To West Road & Stratford

River Island

→ One-way streets

Accommodations
1 Warwick Arms Hotel
2 To Park Cottage

Eateries
3 The Rose & Crown

4 The Tilted Wig
5 The Pot & Fin
6 Saffron Gold
7 The Art Kitchen

can use the lockers near the castle (£2 coins only, at the entrance to the Stables Car Park; if lockers are all taken—or out of order—try asking at the castle info desk).

A **taxi** from the station to the castle or town center costs about £5. It's a 15-minute, one-mile **walk** from the station to the castle or town center: Exit straight ahead down the street, then bear right onto Coventry Road, where you'll start to see signs for the castle.

From here, at the traffic light, turn right onto St. John's Road. At the three-way fork, take Smith Street (the middle fork), soon called Jury Street (which eventually becomes Warwick's High Street). After a long block, the TI appears on your left, with the main castle gate just beyond (up Castle Street). To reach the market square and restaurants from the TI, go one more block on High Street and turn right.

By Car: The main Stratford-Coventry road cuts right through Warwick. Coming from Stratford (8 miles to the south), you'll hit two castle parking lots first (£6, buy token from machines at the castle entrance). The lots are pricey, and they are a 10- to 15-minute walk from the actual castle. You could try the closest one, just off Castle Lane and called the Stables Car Park, but it's even more expensive (£10). You'll find plenty of other lots throughout Warwick (around £4/4 hours) and street parking in the town center (£1/hour; often a 2-hour maximum—not enough time to fully experience the castle).

Services: Public WCs are at the TI and on Market Square (next to the recommended Rose and Crown pub).

Sights in Warwick

▲▲WARWICK CASTLE

Almost too groomed and organized, this theme park of a castle gives its crowds of visitors a decent value for the stiff entry fee. The cash-poor but enterprising Earl of Warwick hired the folks at Merlin Entertainments (which owns many other big-name British attractions) to wring maximum tourist dollars out of his castle. They've made the place entertaining indeed, and packed it with lively exhibits... but also watered down the history a bit, and added several layers of gift shops, overpriced concessions, and nickel-and-dime add-ons. The greedy feel of the place can be a little annoying, considering the already-steep admission. But—especially for kids—there just isn't a better medieval castle experience in England. With a lush, green, grassy moat and fairy-tale fortifications, Warwick Castle will entertain you from dungeon to lookout.

The castle is a 14th- and 15th-century fortified shell, holding an 18th- and 19th-century royal residence, surrounded by another one of dandy "Capability" Brown's landscape jobs (like at Blenheim Palace). You can tour the sumptuous staterooms, climb the towers and ramparts for the views, stroll through themed exhibits populated by aristocratic wax figures, explore the sprawling grounds and gardens, and—best of all—interact with costumed docents who explain the place and perform fantastic demonstrations of medieval weapons and other skills.

Cost: Steep £29 entry fee (see discount information below); entrance includes gardens and most castle attractions except for the gory Castle Dungeon (around £10 extra, cheaper if you purchase a combo-ticket).

Hours: Daily July-Sept 10:00-17:00, Oct-June generally until 16:00 or 17:00.

Information: Recorded info tel. 0871/265-2000, or call 01926/495-421 daily 9:00-17:00, www.warwick-castle.com.

Discounts: Booking online in advance saves money and time in the ticket line (discounts vary; see website for details). Or you can get a better deal, similar to that available online, by buying a Fast Track ticket (for the castle only; no combo-tickets) at the Warwick TI—these support a local travel business, let you avoid the line, and save you about £5. The Stratford TI also sells a discounted £18 ticket. English Heritage members get a 50 percent discount at the door.

Visitor Information: The guidebook (£4.75 at ticket office) guides you through the state rooms in souvenir-booklet form. If you tour the castle without the booklet's help, pick the brains of the earnest and talkative docents.

Demonstrations and Events: It's the well-presented demos and other events that make this castle particularly worthwhile.

These can include jousting competitions, archers showing off their longbow skills, sword fights, jester acts, falconry shows, and demonstrations of the trebuchet (like a catapult) and ballista (a type of giant slingshot). They're offered year-round, but most frequently in summer and on weekends and school holidays. When you buy your castle ticket, be sure to pick up the daily events flier and plan your day around these events.

Eating at the Castle: Consider bringing your own picnic to enjoy at the gorgeous grounds. Otherwise you're left with overpriced concessions stands scattered around the castle grounds (and marked on the map you get with your ticket), all serving variations on the same mass-produced food. **$ The Coach House** has cafeteria fare just before the turnstiles. Inside, **$$ The Undercroft** has a pizza, pasta, and salad buffet line (located in basement of palace). The **$ riverside pavilion** sells sandwiches and fish-and-chips, and has fine outdoor seating (in the park just before the bridge, behind the castle). **$$ The Conservatory** offers nobles-in-training a chance to sip tea and nibble on sandwiches with views of the peacock garden and pageant field. Fortunately, just 100 yards from the castle turnstiles—through a tiny gate in the wall—is Warwick town's workaday commercial district, with several better (and better-value) lunch options. It's worth the walk (see "Eating in Warwick," later), but be sure to get your hand stamped at the turnstiles before leaving so you can return after lunch.

◎ Self-Guided Tour

Buy your ticket and head through the turnstile into the moat area, where you'll get your first view of the dramatic castle. In good

weather, this lawn-like zone is filled with tents populated by costumed docents demonstrating everyday medieval lifestyles.

From the moat, two entrance gateways lead to the castle's **inner courtyard;** look for signs for where to enter each gate.

Within these mighty walls, there's something for every taste.

The bulge of land at the far right end of the courtyard, called **The Mound,** is where the original Norman castle of 1068 stood. Under this "motte," the wooden stockade (the "bailey") defined the courtyard in the way the castle walls do today. You can climb up to the top for a view down into the castle courtyard (do this at the end, since you can exit down the other side, toward the riverbank).

The main attractions are in the largest buildings along the side of the courtyard: the Great Hall, five lavish staterooms, and the chapel. Progressing through these rooms, you'll see how the castle complex evolved over the centuries, from the militarized Middle Ages to civilized Victorian times, from a formidable defensive fortress to a genteel manor home.

Enter through the cavernous **Great Hall,** decorated with suits of equestrian armor. Adjoining the Great Hall is the state dining room, with portraits of English kings and princes. Then follow the one-way route through the **staterooms,** keeping ever more esteemed company as you go—the rooms closest to the center of the complex were the most exclusive, reserved only for those especially close to the Earl of Warwick. You'll pass through a series of three drawing rooms (abbreviated from "withdrawing," from a time when these provided a retreat into a more intimate area after a to-do in the larger, more public rooms): first, one decorated in a deep burgundy; then the cedar drawing room, with intricately carved wood paneling, a Waterford crystal chandelier, and a Carrara marble fireplace; and the green drawing room, with a beautiful painted coffered ceiling and wax figures of Henry VIII and his six wives. The sumptuous Queen Anne Room was decorated in preparation for a planned 1704 visit by the monarch (unfortunately, Queen Anne never came—she got wind that one of her ladies-in-waiting, with whom she was fiercely competitive, was also coming, so she canceled at the last minute). Finally comes the blue boudoir, an oversized closet decorated in blue silk wallpaper. The portrait of King Henry VIII over the fireplace faces a clock once owned by Marie-Antoinette.

On your way out, you'll pass the earl's private **chapel.** The earl's family worshiped in the pews in front of the stone screen, while the servants would stand behind it. Notice the ornate wood-carved relief depicting a scene of the Greeks fighting the Amazons, based on a painting by Peter Paul Rubens. The organ in the back of the chapel was powered by a hand-pumped bellows.

Back out in the courtyard, to the left of the staterooms, are the entrances to two other, less impressive exhibits. The **Kingmaker**

exhibit (set in 1471) uses mannequins, sound effects, and smells to show how medieval townsfolk prepared for battle—from the blacksmiths and armory, to the wardrobe, to the final rallying cry, with costumed docents standing by. The **Royal Weekend Party** exhibit lets you explore staterooms staged as they appeared in 1898, but with an added narrative element: The philandering Daisy Maynard Greville, Countess of Warwick—

considered the most beautiful woman in Victorian England—is throwing a party, and big-name aristocrats are in attendance, including a young Winston Churchill. Among the guests is the Prince of Wales (the future King Edward VII), with whom Daisy had a long-time affair. Gossipy "servants" clue you in on who's flirting with whom. The rooms are populated by eerily convincing Madame Tussauds-style wax figures, and posted information and soundtracks loosely narrate the scandal.

You can climb up onto the **ramparts and tower**—a one-way, no-return route that leads you up and down the tallest tower (on very tight spiral stairs), leaving you at a fun perch from which to fire your imaginary longbow. The halls and stairs can be very crowded with young kids, and—as the signs warn—it takes 530 steep steps (both up and down) to follow the whole route; claustrophobes may want to skip it.

The **Princess Tower** offers children (ages 3-8) the chance to dress up as princesses and princes for a photo op. While it's included in the castle ticket, those interested must first sign up for a 15-minute time slot at the information tent in the middle of the courtyard, near the staterooms.

The other pricey and skippable add-on attraction can also be entered from the courtyard (if you didn't buy a combo-ticket at the entrance, you can buy individual tickets at the information tent near the staterooms). **The Castle Dungeon,** a gory, tacky knock-off of the London Dungeon, features a series of costumed hosts who entertain and spook visitors on a 50-minute tour.

Outside of the inner courtyard area are additional diversions. Surrounding everything is a lush, peacock-patrolled, picnic-perfect park, complete with a Victorian rose garden. The castle grounds are often enlivened by a knight in shining armor on a horse or a merry band of musical jesters. The grassy moat area is typically filled with costumed characters and demonstrations, including archery and falconry. Near the entrance to the complex is the  **Pageant Playground,** with medieval-themed slides and climbing areas for kids, and the **Horrible Histories Maze,** which includes six "history zones" that cover the Vikings to World War I. Down by the river is a bridge across to River Island, and—tucked around the back of the castle—a restored **mill and engine house,** with an exhibit that explains how the castle was electrified in 1894.

MORE SIGHTS IN WARWICK

While Warwick has a few attractions beyond the castle, most are not that exciting.

The most photogenic building in town (aside from the castle) is **Lord Leycester Hospital,** a gaggle of adjoining 14th-century

half-timbered houses next to the southern gate of High Street. Converted into a "hospital" (rest home for the elderly or ill) in 1571, it has a chapel, great hall, maze of old rooms, and pretty garden (overpriced at £8.50, garden only-£2; borrow self-guided tour brochure at entry, Tue-Sun 10:00-17:00, until 16:00 in winter, closed Mon year-round except Bank Holidays, 60 High Street, tel. 01926/491-422, www.lordleycester.com).

Garden fans will find three good ones in Warwick. Most appealing is the **Mill Garden,** down the quaint and half-timbered Mill Street; this small garden, which adjoins the castle property, has fantastic views of the River Avon and castle (£2.50, proceeds go to charity, daily 9:00-18:00, closed Nov-March, 55 Mill Street, tel. 01926/492-877). **Hill Close Gardens,** at the

other end of town near the racecourse, has 16 small Victorian garden plots (£4.50, daily 11:00-17:00, Nov-March until 16:00 and closed Sat-Sun, Bread and Meat Close, tel. 01926/493-339, www.hillclosegardens.com). The **Master's Garden** at Lord Leycester Hospital (described above) rounds out your options.

Sleeping in Warwick

If the following accommodations are full, several B&Bs line Emscote Road (A-445) northeast of the city center, about a mile from the castle.

$$ Warwick Arms Hotel, in the middle of the action on High Street, offers 40 modern rooms in a 300-year-old house. Narrow halls, wobbly floors, and creaking stairs add character to this charming, family-owned former coaching inn (family rooms, free parking, no elevator, 17 High Street, tel. 01926/492-759, www.warwickarmshotel.com, reception@warwickarmshotel.com).

$$ Park Cottage fills a creaky 1521 half-timbered house (once the dairy for the castle) with seven rooms and teddy-on-the-beddy touches. It's on the main road at the opposite end of town from the train station (near the racecourse and castle entrance), but Stuart and Janet will pick you up if their schedule allows (family room possible, free parking, 113 West Street/A-429, tel. 01926/410-319, www.parkcottagewarwick.co.uk, janet@parkcottagewarwick.co.uk).

Eating in Warwick

All of these are on or within a short stroll of Market Place.

$$$ The Rose and Crown is a popular gastropub serving English food with a modern twist. Enjoy the cozy but not claustrophobic interior—order food at the bar or dine in the table-service area—or sit outside (food served daily 7:30-22:00, open longer for drinks, 30 Market Place, tel. 01926/411-117).

$$$ The Tilted Wig does freshly prepared pub food in a rustic-chic setting on Market Place with indoor and outdoor seating (Sun-Thu 8:30-23:00, Fri-Sat until 24:00, 11 Market Place, tel. 01926/400-110).

$ The Pot & Fin serves up excellent fish-and-chips in a charming, rustic cottage setting a block off of Market Place (toward the castle). Everything is made fresh in-house. If you order takeaway, you can grab one of the tables; or head upstairs for the pricier table-service menu (Tue-Thu 12:00-15:00, Thu also 17:30-19:30, Fri-Sat 12:00-20:30, 48 Brook Street, tel. 01926/492-426).

$$ Saffron Gold is a well-regarded Indian restaurant serving tasty meals in an upscale setting with good service (Sun-Thu 17:30-23:30, Fri-Sat until 24:00, just a block off Market Square but tricky to find—in drab Westgate House building near the Marks & Spencer, on Westgate Close, tel. 01926/402-061).

$$$ The Art Kitchen, right on the main pedestrian shopping street, is a mod Thai bistro surrounding a bar (daily 11:00-22:00, 7 Swan Street, tel. 01926/494-303).

Warwick Connections

Warwick is on the train line between Birmingham's Moor Street Station and London's Marylebone Station; most other connections require a change in the adjacent town of Leamington Spa.

From Warwick by Train to: Leamington Spa (about 2/hour, 10 minutes), **Stratford** (8/day, 30 minutes, more with transfer in Birmingham—buses are better, see later), **Coventry** (2/hour, 30-60 minutes, transfer in Leamington Spa), **Oxford** (2/hour, 1 hour, transfer in Leamington Spa), **London**'s Marylebone Station

(1-2/hour direct, 1.5 hours, more with transfers in Leamington Spa). **Train info:** Tel. 0345-748-4950, www.nationalrail.co.uk.

By Bus to: Stratford-upon-Avon (hourly, 30 minutes, bus #X16, also slower #X18), **Coventry** (2-3/hour, 1 hour, bus #X17, also slower #X18, www.stagecoachbus.com).

Coventry

Coventry was bombed to smithereens in 1940 by the Nazi Luftwaffe (air force). From that point on, the German phrase for "to really blast the heck out of a place" was (roughly) "to coventrate" it. But Coventry rose from its ashes, and its message to our world is one of forgiveness, reconciliation, and the importance of peace.

Before it was infamous as a victim of World War II, Coventry had an illustrious history. According to legend, Coventry's most famous hometown girl, Lady Godiva, rode bareback and bare-naked through the town in the 11th century to convince her stubborn husband to lower taxes. You'll see her bronze statue on the market square a block from the cathedral, and a fun exhibit about her in the Herbert Art Gallery and Museum.

The cloth trade made Coventry one of England's leading cities in the Middle Ages. Its fortunes rose and fell over time, and by the 20th century it had become a major industrial center—first as Britain's main bicycle manufacturer, later as its top car-making city, and eventually as a major center of armaments and aircraft assembly (making it a key target for the Luftwaffe bombers). The city was utterly devastated by the Blitz; aside from the human toll, its greatest loss was its proud and famous St. Michael's Cathedral, which burned to the ground—the only English cathedral destroyed by the Nazis. Tellingly, Coventry's sister cities include two other places synonymous with horrific WWII destruction: Dresden, Germany, and Volgograd (formerly Stalingrad), Russia.

Today's Coventry isn't pretty. While many other WWII-damaged English towns were rebuilt quaint and cobbled, Coventry is all characterless modern concrete. But its cathedral—combining the still bombed-out shell of the old building, and a highly symbolic, starkly modern new one—is poignant and inspiring, and its other museums are quite good (and most are free). While

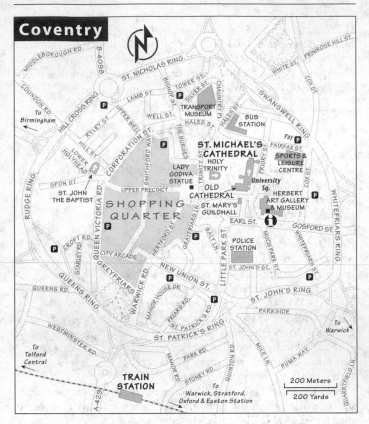

I wouldn't go out of my way to visit Coventry, if you're passing by, consider stopping off to browse through a bit of normal, everyday, urban England.

Orientation to Coventry

Coventry is a big city—with about 365,000 people—but everything of interest to visitors is in the small central core, which is bound by a busy ring road. You can walk from one end of the ring to the other in about 15 minutes. The train station is just south of the ring; the cathedral, St. Mary's Guildhall, and Herbert Art Gallery and Museum (with TI inside) are in the northeastern part of the ring; and the Transport Museum is about a 10-minute walk northwest of the cathedral.

TOURIST INFORMATION

The TI is located within the Herbert Art Gallery and Museum (Mon-Sat 10:00-16:00, Sun from 12:00, Jordan Well, tel.

WARWICK & COVENTRY

024/7623-4284, www.visitcoventry.co.uk, tic@culturecoventry.com).

ARRIVAL IN COVENTRY

If you're passing through Coventry by public transportation, baggage storage could be a problem—there's none at the train station, but you can use a baggage-storage website such as NannyBag.com to find storage nearby. The Transport Museum has lockers for use during a visit there.

By Train: From the train station (which sits just outside the ring road), it's about a 15-minute walk to the cathedral. Exit straight ahead and follow signs along the pedestrian route for the cathedral through the modern shopping district. The cathedral is the taller of the two pointy spires.

By Car: Use the pay parking lot on Cox Street (just off of Fairfax Street), near the cathedral. From the ring road, take junction (exit) 2. The parking lot is basically under the ring road, across from the Coventry Sports and Leisure Centre, and is a five-minute walk to the cathedral (turn left at the bus station and you'll see it ahead on your right).

Sights in Coventry

▲▲ST. MICHAEL'S CATHEDRAL

The symbol of Coventry is the bombed-out hulk of its old cathedral, with the huge new one adjoining it. This inspiring complex welcomes visitors.

Cost and Hours: The ruins of the old cathedral are free to enter (gates open daily roughly 9:00-17:00), though you'll pay to climb the tower and tour the small WWII museum (see later). Entering the new cathedral is also free, but consider making a donation to this worthwhile cause (Mon-Sat 10:00-17:00, Sun 12:00-16:00, last entry one hour before closing). To see the church in action, attend a service or afternoon evensong (Mon-Fri at 17:15, Sat-Sun at 16:00, evensong predictable only on Sun, otherwise service may be spoken) or the weekly organ recital (Mon at 13:00). The café is closed on Sundays.

Information: Tel. 024/7652-1200, www.coventrycathedral.org.uk.

Tours: Guided tours are offered of the ruins and the new cathedral (free, Mon-Sat 11:00, 12:15, and 14:00; Sun 13:00 only, subject to availability of volunteers so confirm in advance).

Tower Climb: You can walk 181 steps up to the top of the tower for views over the cathedral complex and city (£4, must be 8 or older, Mon-Sat 10:00-16:00, Sun 12:00-15:00, closed in bad weather).

Blitz Experience: Several rooms at the altar end of the old cathedral have been turned into a small "Blitz" museum. Volunteers tell the story of how Coventry endured and was shaped by the destruction of World War II (£1, generally daily 9:00-17:00, closed Nov-mid-Feb and when in use by school groups).

❍ Self-Guided Tour

A visit to the cathedral complex has two parts: First explore the ruins of the original building, then head into the new cathedral. You can pick up the free *Guide to the Ruined Cathedral* pamphlet at the TI; the new cathedral also hands out a floor plan that includes both the old and new churches.

Old Cathedral Ruins: Coventry's grand Perpendicular Gothic cathedral was the second to stand on this spot (built 1373-

1460). Its towering 303-foot-tall steeple—the third-highest in England—was a symbol for the city. On the night of November 14, 1940, Nazi Luftwaffe bombers filled the skies above Coventry. They dropped incendiary devices (firebombs) to light up the ground so they could see their targets. One of these hit the roof of the cathedral, which was quickly consumed in flames. (The tower survived.) Today the footprint and surviving walls stand as a testament to the travesty of war.

At the apse of the ruined structure (far end from tower) is a replica of the **charred cross;** the original is inside the new cathe-

dral. While surveying the wreckage after the bombing, workers found these beams lying on the ground in the shape of a cross—so they lashed them together and erected it here. The message "Father Forgive" (spoken by Christ on the cross) makes it clear that this is a symbol not of anger, but of reconciliation. Every Friday at 12:00, the Coventry Litany of Reconciliation is said in these ruins—asking forgiveness for the seven deadly sins.

Various **monuments** are scattered around the ruins. Directly to the left of the charred cross is the bronze memorial to an early 20th-century bishop. In a chilling bit of irony, there's a swastika on his headband—dating from a time when this was just a good-luck symbol, before it had been appropriated by Hitler and painted on the planes that destroyed this place. Closer to the tower, you'll see the modern *Ecce Homo* sculpture (depicting Christ before Pilate) and a reconciliation monument, showing two people embracing across a gulf.

Before going inside the new cathedral building, head out to the plaza just beyond the complex and look back at it: old and new cathedrals, set perpendicular to each other, creating a continuous ensemble of worship. The large sculpture on the side of the new cathedral depicts St. Michael triumphing over the devil, as foretold by the Book of Revelation.

The cathedral's visitors center is to the right; in this undercroft is a museum about the history of all three cathedrals that have stood on this site, with artifacts from each one. (Also notice, to your left, the glassy entrance to the Herbert Art Gallery and Museum—a good post-cathedral stop, described later.)

• *Now head into the new cathedral interior. If the main door (up the stairs) is open, head inside; otherwise, enter through the visitors center.*

New Cathedral: By the morning after the cathedral burned, the people of Coventry had already decided to rebuild it. Architect Basil Spence won the contest to design this reimagining of the important church: The ruined old cathedral represents death and sacrifice, while the new structure—part of the same continuum—represents resurrection. While at first the cold, gray walls inside the building make it feel gloomy and uninspired—almost (perhaps appropriately) like a giant bomb shelter—its highly symbolic design reveals itself to those who take the time to explore it.

Stand at the top of the main nave, on the giant letters that create a **gathering area** for the congregation. In the center of the nave near these letters, look for the maple leaf embedded in the floor—a

thank-you to Canadians whose donations helped fund this building. Looking down the nave, notice that the cathedral follows the same basic traditional layout of much older churches (long nave, choir area, high altar and apse at the far end) but features decidedly modern designs and decorations.

Turn right to take in the gigantic and gorgeous stained-glass window of the **baptistery**—a starburst with intensely warm colors at the center, cool colors at the perimeter. Beneath this is the baptismal font, which is carved into a chunk of rock from the hills near Bethlehem. Looking down the nave, notice that otherwise, the cathedral has relatively little stained glass...from here, at least.

Across the nave from the baptistery, walk up the stairs into the **Chapel of Unity.** With its circular shape and floor mosaics depicting the five continents, this chapel preaches understanding among all Christian faiths—an ecumenism that echoes the cathedral's mission of reconciliation.

Back out in the main nave, walk down the central aisle. Notice the well-worn **copper coins** embedded in the floor. Dating from 1962 (when the cathedral was consecrated), these help choir members keep a straight line as they process into the church.

Pause in front of the **choir,** with its modern, dramatically prickly canopy, designed to evoke Jesus' crown of thorns—or possibly birds in flight. The Christmas tree-shaped tower marks the seat of the bishop.

The green artwork that fills the far wall is not a fresco but a 74-foot-by-38-foot **tapestry** that depicts Jesus in a Byzantine Pantocrator ("creator of all") pose, surrounded by symbols of the Four Evangelists. Notice the faint outline of a small human being standing protected between Jesus' feet.

Turn around and look back down the **nave.** Remember how stained glass seemed in short supply from the far end of the church? From this direction, you can clearly see how the sawtooth-shaped design allows for row after row of colorful glass to be seen by worshippers as they return to their seats after taking communion. At the far end, notice that instead of a wall sealing off the church, there's a giant glass window—to emphasize the connection between this new cathedral and the old one just outside. Both buildings also use the same local red sandstone. This is intended to be one big, unified space.

Now circle around the left side of the choir to the back-left corner of the church, where stairs lead down to WCs, the church

WARWICK & COVENTRY

museum, and a café. Hanging at the top of the stairwell is the **original charred cross** that was found in the ruins of the cathedral after the bombing, shown on previous page.

Now cross toward the other side of the church. Right in the middle, you'll pass a misshapen cross above the main altar; in its center is a smaller cross consisting of three nails from the medieval church, which were also found in the wreckage. This **"cross of nails"** has become a symbol worldwide for postwar reconciliation. Several such crosses have been made, many of them given to other cities that were devastated by the war; one stands above the high altar of the rebuilt Frauenkirche in Dresden, Germany. (You can buy a small replica of the cross of nails in the cathedral shop, across from the main door.)

Continue to the far side of the church. You'll pass the **Chapel of Gethsemane,** with a crown of thorns-shaped screen around the window. Beyond that, walk down the hallway and into the **Chapel of Christ the Servant.** The clear (rather than stained-glass) windows remind worshippers to extend their faith and stewardship outside the walls of this building. Also displayed here are fragments of the old cathedral's original stained-glass windows.

NEAR THE CATHEDRAL
▲Herbert Art Gallery and Museum

This expanded, impressive museum complex and cultural center combines town history exhibits and art collections. Since it's free and directly behind the cathedral, it's well worth dropping in if you have some time to spare. As there are several exhibits—both permanent and temporary—be sure to explore the entire building (ask for a floor plan).

Cost and Hours: Free, Mon-Sat 10:00-16:00, Sun from 12:00, Jordan Well, tel. 024/7623-7521, www.theherbert.org.

Visiting the Museum: Near the entrance is the History Gallery, with enjoyable interactive exhibits that trace the city's story from its beginnings to the Blitz to today. You'll see actual artifacts from the Blitz and hear locals describe living through it. Beyond the information desk are small exhibits on peace and reconciliation (Coventry has understandably become a very pacifist city), and the small but entertaining Discover Godiva exhibit, which examines the legend (and possible fact) of Lady Godiva. Her husband, Earl Leofric, increased taxes dramatically on his subjects. She pleaded

with him for a tax cut, and he agreed—provided that she ride naked through town on horseback. A fun animated video shows how the legend evolved, with each generation of storytellers adding their own flourishes. One popular version says that the townspeople respectfully averted their eyes, except for one "Peeping Tom"—who was struck blind for his voyeurism. You'll also see paintings of the Lady, clips from movies about her, and companies that have appropriated her as a mascot. Upstairs is the museum's modest but enjoyable gallery of sculpture, Old Masters, modern and contemporary artwork, and temporary exhibits.

▲St. Mary's Guildhall

The story of this fine half-timbered building, sitting next to the cathedral and originally built for the merchant guild of St. Mary,

is rooted in the fascinating history of England's often-overlooked King Henry VI (r. 1422-1461). Afflicted with what today would be diagnosed as catatonic schizophrenia, Henry seemed to his medieval subjects to exist between our world and another—he'd drift into a trance and be unreachable for days or weeks at a time, then emerge reporting the vibrant visions he'd had. During the Wars of the Roses, Henry briefly moved the capital of England to Coventry, creating a special bond with the city. After his death, Henry's corpse reportedly bled in front of observers, leading them to conclude that he was miraculous. A cult of followers sprang up around Henry, centered here in Coventry. People began to pray for divine intervention from the man they came to call "Saint Henry." One young girl, who had been crushed under a wagon wheel, was miraculously healed when her mother prayed to Henry. (The pope sent delegates to verify some 300 reported miracles, and his half-nephew Henry VII unsuccessfully petitioned to have him canonized.) The local businessmen's guilds of Coventry built this fine hall to venerate their favorite king and unofficial saint.

Cost and Hours: Free, mid-March-early Oct Sun-Thu 10:00-16:00, closed Fri-Sat, during events, and off-season, tel. 024/7683-3328, www.coventry.gov.uk/stmarys.

Visiting the Hall: While it's fun and a bit spooky to explore the maze of tight old rooms, the highlight here is the great hall. The semicircular stained-glass window traces Henry VI's royal lineage—that's him in the center, flanked by his supposed ancestors, William the Conqueror, King Arthur, and the Roman emperor Constantine (notice that Constantine's cross is bigger than the others'—his mother, St. Helen, supposedly discovered Jesus' "true cross"). Below the window is a remarkable, if faded, 14th-century tapestry that also honors Henry (ask the attendants to briefly turn on the light to see it better). More than 500 years old, this tapestry is still in situ—in the location for which it was intended. The hall is staffed by knowledgeable attendants who love to explain its history. If you dare, also ask them about the constant ghost sightings in this building—so frequent they've become routine. Inexpensive handouts offer more details on the hall's history.

▲Coventry Transport Museum

A 10-minute walk from the cathedral, this good museum pays homage to Coventry's car-making heritage. For much of the 20th century, Coventry was the main auto production center of Britain, and in the 1950s and 1960s, more than a third of the city's population built cars. For car lovers, it's worth ▲▲.

Cost and Hours: £14, £1 lockers for use only while on the premises, daily 10:00-17:00, tel. 024/7623-4270, www.transport-museum.com.

Visiting the Museum: On two floors of a sprawling modern building, you can see the first, fastest, and most famous cars that came from this "British Detroit." The museum also shows off a collection of tractors, bicycles, motorcycles, and tanks...if it had wheels, they made it here.

The exhibit focuses on local production (Daimler, Standard, Triumph, and others), but a few famous non-Coventry cars are also included, such as Monty's staff car—a Humber Super Snipe—and a 1949 Land Rover. The collection also has the oldest surviving Standard car—the Roi de Beiges from 1907. Aside from the cars, you'll find interesting displays on how various modes of transportation changed the way people lived.

Coventry Connections

From Coventry by Train to: Warwick (hourly, 30 minutes, change in Leamington Spa), **Stratford-upon-Avon** (at least hourly, 1.5 hours, change in Leamington Spa or Birmingham), **Oxford** (hourly, 50 minutes), **London**'s Euston Station (6/hour, 1-2 hours), **Telford Central** (near Ironbridge Gorge; 2/hour, 1.5 hours, change in Birmingham). **Train info:** Tel. 0345-748-4950, www.nationalrail.co.uk.

IRONBRIDGE GORGE

The Industrial Revolution was born in the Severn River Valley. In its glory days, this valley—blessed with abundant deposits of iron ore and coal, and a river for transport—gave the world its first iron wheels, steam-powered locomotive, and cast-iron bridge (begun in 1779). Other industries flourished here, too—from mass-produced clay pipes to delicate porcelain and colorful decorative tiles. The museums in Ironbridge Gorge, which capture the essence of the Victorian Age, take you back into the days when Britain was racing into the modern era—and pulling the rest of the West with her.

Near the end of the 20th century, the valley went through a

second transformation: Photos taken just a few decades ago show an industrial wasteland. Today the Severn River Valley is lush and lined with walks and parkland. Even its bricks, while still smoke-stained, seem warmer and more inviting. Those who come for its "industrial" sights are pleasantly surprised to find an extremely charming corner of England—with wooded hillsides and tidy, time-warp brick villages.

PLANNING YOUR TIME

Without a car, Ironbridge Gorge isn't worth the headache for most (though I've included some tips at the end of this chapter). Drivers can slip it in between the Cotswolds/Stratford/Warwick and

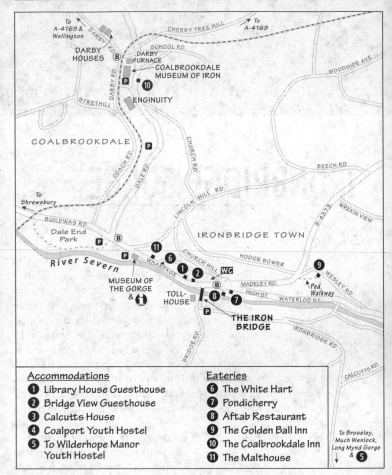

Accommodations
1. Library House Guesthouse
2. Bridge View Guesthouse
3. Calcutts House
4. Coalport Youth Hostel
5. To Wilderhope Manor Youth Hostel

Eateries
6. The White Hart
7. Pondicherry
8. Aftab Restaurant
9. The Golden Ball Inn
10. The Coalbrookdale Inn
11. The Malthouse

points north (such as the Lake District or North Wales). Speed demons zip in for a midday tour of the Blists Hill Victorian Town, look at the famous Iron Bridge and quaint Industrial Age town that sprawls around it, and head out. For an overnight visit, arrive in the early evening to browse the town, see the bridge, and walk along the river. Spend the morning touring the Blists Hill Victorian Town, have lunch there, and head to your next destination.

Those with more time (or a healthy interest in the Industrial Revolution) can spend two nights and a leisurely day strolling the town and exploring Blists Hill and the many museums, capped by dinner at one of my recommended restaurants.

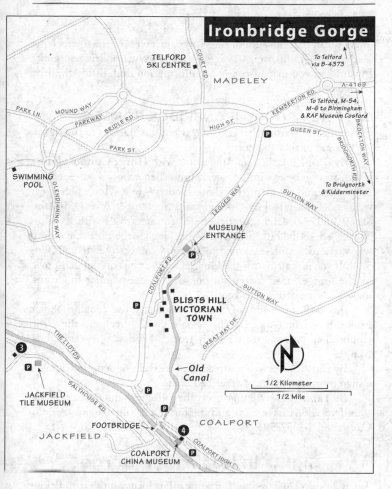

Orientation to Ironbridge Gorge

The village of Ironbridge is just a few blocks gathered around the Iron Bridge, which spans the peaceful, tree-lined River Severn. While the smoke-belching bustle is long gone, knowing that this wooded, sleepy river valley was the "Silicon Valley" of the 19th century makes wandering its brick streets almost a pilgrimage. Other villages—including Coalbrookdale, Jackfield, and Coalport—are scattered along the valley, all within a short drive or a long walk. The museum sights are scattered over three miles. The modern cooling towers (for coal, not nuclear energy) that you'll see west of town, looming ominously over these red-brick remnants, seem strangely appropriate.

TOURIST INFORMATION

The TI is in the Museum of the Gorge, just west of the town center (daily 10:00-16:00, tel. 01952/433-424, www.ironbridge.org.uk). In summer, you may also find an information desk inside the Iron Bridge tollbooth.

GETTING AROUND IRONBRIDGE GORGE

For connections from the Telford train or bus stations to the sights, see the end of this chapter.

By Bus: Link the area's museums with **Gorge Connect** buses, which run on busy summer weekends when school's out—including Easter and the two May Bank Holidays (Sat-Mon), plus every weekend from late July through mid-September (every 30 minutes 9:30-17:00, £2.50 day ticket—discounted to £1 with Passport Ticket—described in "Sights in Ironbridge Gorge"; see schedule at www.telford.gov.uk—search for "Gorge Connect"; tel. 01952/384-384). If you're waiting for the Gorge Connect bus on the main road by the bridge, or at a stop for one of the less-popular museums, make sure the driver sees you.

Bus **#19,** operated by Arriva, connects the Coalbrookdale Museum of Iron (stop: Coalbrookdale Post Office) and the TI in Ironbridge, but runs infrequently (roughly 7/day, www.arrivabus.co.uk).

By Car: Routes to the attractions are well-signed, so driving is a snap (museum parking described later).

By Taxi: Taxis will pick up at the museums and are a good option if you don't have a car and the bus is not convenient. Call Go Carz at tel. 01952/501-050.

Sights in Ironbridge Gorge

Ten museums clustered within a few miles focus on the Iron Bridge and all that it represents—but not all are worth your time. The Blists Hill Victorian Town is by far the best. The Museum of the Gorge attempts to give a historical overview, but the displays are humble—its most interesting feature is a short video that helps give context to other area sights. The Coalbrookdale Museum of Iron is interesting to metalheads. Enginuity is just for kids. The original Abraham Darby Furnace (free to view, located across from the Museum of Iron) is a shrine to 18th-century technology. And the Jackfield Tile Museum, Coalport China Museum, and Broseley Pipeworks delve into industries that picked up the slack when the iron industry shifted away from the Severn Valley in the 1850s.

Cost: Individual admission charges vary (£4.50-18.50); the £26.50 **Passport Ticket** covers admission to all area sights and gives a discount on the Gorge Connect bus. Even if you visit only the Blists Hill Victorian Town and the Coalbrookdale Museum of Iron, the Passport Ticket (which is good for a year) pays for itself.

Hours: All museums open daily 10:00-16:00 unless otherwise noted; closed Mon Oct-mid-March.

Information: Tel. 01952/433-424, www.ironbridge.org.uk.

Parking: To see the most significant sights by car, you'll park three times: once in town (either in the pay-and-display lot just over the bridge or at the Museum of the Gorge—the Iron Bridge and Gorge Museum are connected by an easy, flat walk); once at the Blists Hill parking lot; and once outside the Coalbrookdale Museum of Iron (Enginuity is across the lot, and the Darby Houses are a three-minute uphill hike away). While you'll pay separately to park at the Museum of the Gorge, a single £3 ticket is good for pay-and-display lots at all other sights.

IRONBRIDGE VILLAGE
▲▲Iron Bridge

While England was at war with her American colonies, this first cast-iron bridge was built in 1779 to show off a wonderful new building material. Lacking experience with cast iron, the builders erred on the side of sturdiness and constructed it as if it were made of wood. Notice that the original construction used traditional timber-jointing techniques rather than rivets. (Rivets are from later

repairs.) The valley's centerpiece is free, open all the time, and thought-provoking...cars still used it into the 1960s. Walk across the bridge to the tollhouse. Inside, read the fee schedule and notice the subtle slam against royalty. (England was not immune to the revolutionary sentiment inhabiting the colonies at this time.) Pedestrians paid half a penny to cross; poor people crossed cheaper by coracle—a crude tub-like wood-and-canvas shuttle ferry. Cross back to the town and enjoy a pleasant walk downstream along the towpath. Where horses once dragged boats laden with Industrial Age cargo, locals now walk their dogs.

Museum of the Gorge

Orient yourself to the valley at this simple museum, filling the Old Severn Warehouse. It's worthwhile merely for the 12-minute introductory video (on a continuous loop), which lays the groundwork for what you'll see in the other museums. You'll also see exhibits on local geology and ecology, some of the items that were produced here, and a well-explained, 30-foot model of the entire valley in its heyday.

Cost: £4.50, 500 yards upstream from the bridge, parking-£3 (3-hour maximum).

Nearby: Farther upstream from the museum parking lot is the fine riverside **Dale End Park,** with picnic areas and a playground.

COALPORT AND JACKFIELD
▲▲Blists Hill Victorian Town

This immersive open-air folk museum thrills kids and kids-at-heart by re-creating a fully formed society from the 1890s. You'll wander through 50 acres of commerce, industry, and chatty locals. It's particularly lively (with everything open and lots of docents— and engaged kids) on weekends and in summer; off-peak times can be sleepy. Compared to other open-air museums in Britain, it's refreshingly compact and manageable. Pick up the £5 Blists Hill guidebook for a good step-by-step rundown.

Cost and Hours: £18.50, daily until 16:30 mid-March-Sept.

Eating in Blists Hill: Several places serve lunch: a café near the entrance, the New Inn Pub for beer and pub snacks, a traditional fish-and-chips joint, and the Forest Glen cafeteria.

Visiting Blists Hill: The experience begins with a 360-degree movie showing Victorians at (noisy, hot, and difficult) work. Then you'll walk through a door and be transported back in time. The map you're given when entering is very important—it shows which stops in the big park are staffed with energetic docents in period clothes. Pop in to say hello to the banker, the post office clerk, the blacksmith, and the girl in the candy shop. Maybe the boys are singing in the pub. It's fine to take photos. Asking questions and chatting with the villagers is encouraged. How's the pay? What's a shilling? How about 1800s health care?

Stop by the pharmacy and check out the squirm-inducing setup of the dentist's chair—it'll make you appreciate modern dental care. Check the hands-on activities in the barn across the way. Down the street, kids like watching a candlemaker at work, as he explains the process and tells how candles were used back in the day. You'll find out what a "spinning donkey" is, why candles have two wicks, and why miners used green candles instead of white ones.

Just as it would've had in Victorian days, the village has a working pub, a greengrocer's shop, a fascinating squatter's cottage, and a snorty, slippery pigsty. On your way down to the ironworks, drop in on the high-end mine manager's house, with a doctor's surgery tucked in the back. Don't miss the explanation of the "winding engine" at the Blists Hill Mine (demos throughout the day).

At the back of the park, you can hop aboard a train and enter a clay mine, complete with a sound-and-light show illustrating the dangers of working in this type of environment (small charge, 15 minutes). Nearby, the Hay Inclined Plane was used to haul loaded tub boats between the river and the upper canal. Today, a passenger-operated lift hauls visitors instead (just press the button to call for it). At the top, you can walk along the canal back to the town.

Coalport China Museum

This museum fills an old porcelain factory directly downhill from Blists Hill, along the river. You'll see a few fine samples of china that was made here (the Caughley porcelain, at the end, is top-quality); walk through a long workshop, where workers demonstrate various aspects of porcelain production (molds, flowers, printing, glazing, painting, and gilding); peek into a working glassblower's shop; and walk around inside a cavernous "botte kiln." While a bit less engaging than most of Ironbridge's museums, it's informative and rounds out your look at the area.

Cost: £9.50.

▲Jackfield Tile Museum

While most area museums focus on the grit and brawn of the Industrial Revolution—iron, coal, that sort of thing—the Jackfield Tile Museum looks at the softer side of Severn Valley innovation. Located in the village of Jackfield (across the river from Ironbridge), here you can walk through several buildings in an old brick industrial complex where tiles are still produced. The highlight is seeing the wide range of uses and styles of tile—a material so versatile (and so beautiful) that it looks equally good in bathrooms and in churches, and even in London's Tube (much of the Underground tile came from right here). The modern Fusion facility next door suggests that tile's heyday isn't over.

Cost: £9.50.

COALBROOKDALE

Note that the Darby Houses close an hour before the other sights here; if visiting later in the day, go there first.

▲Coalbrookdale Museum of Iron and Abraham Darby's Old Furnace

The Coalbrookdale neighborhood is the birthplace of modern technology—locals like to claim it's where mass production was invented. The museum and furnace are located on either side of a

How to Smelt Iron...
and Change the World

The Severn Valley had an abundance of ingredients for big industry: iron ore, top-grade coal (processed into coke), and water for power and shipping. And the person who finally put all the pieces together was a clever Quaker brassmaker from Bristol named Abraham Darby.

Before Darby's time, iron ore was laboriously melted by charcoal—they couldn't use coal because sulfur made the iron brittle. Darby experimented with higher-carbon coke instead. With huge waterwheel-powered bellows, Darby burned coke at super-hot temperatures and dumped iron ore into the furnace. Impurities floated to the top, while the pure iron sank to the bottom of a clay tub in the bottom of the furnace.

Twice a day, the plugs were knocked off, allowing the "slag" to drain away on the top and the molten iron to drain out on the bottom. The low-grade slag was used locally on walls and paths. The high-grade iron trickled into molds formed in the sand below the furnace. It cooled into pig iron (named because the molds look like piglets suckling their mother). The pig-iron "planks" were broken off by sledgehammers and shipped away.

The River Severn became one of Europe's busiest, shipping pig iron to distant foundries, where it was melted again and made into cast iron (for projects such as the Iron Bridge), or to forges, where it was worked like toffee into wrought iron.

Once Darby cracked the coke code, iron became *the* go-to building material. Versatile and ubiquitous, iron became the plastic of the Victorian age. To this day, many of the icons of Britain—post boxes, frilly benches, fences in front of tidy houses—are made of iron. All thanks to the innovation that took place centuries ago, right here in the Severn Valley.

parking lot, tucked under a rail trestle. There's a café on-site, and the Coalbrookdale Inn—a classic pub—is just up the hill in front of the museum.

Cost: Museum—£9.50, £11.50 combo-ticket includes the Darby Houses; Furnace—free, volunteers sometimes lead free guided walks to the furnace (ask at museum info desk for times).

Visiting the Museum: The fresh, well-presented museum works hard to explain all facets of iron—which has been used to make tools since ancient times and makes up 95 percent of all industrial metal. You'll get a quick primer on the history of iron tools, then head up to the top floor and work your way down, chronologically, through the role iron played here in the Severn Valley. You'll see original items from Coalbrookdale's boom time (including a little three-legged pot created by Abraham Darby, c. 1714) and learn about the critical role Quakers (like Darby) played in the Industrial Revolution—several important individuals are profiled. You'll also see a detailed model of the Iron Bridge, and—on the middle floor—several Victorian Age items made possible by this innovation, from a gigantic cast-iron anchor to delicately crafted benches and sculptures.

Abraham Darby Furnace: Across from the museum, standing like a shrine to the Industrial Revolution, is Darby's blast fur-

nace, sitting inside a big glass pyramid and surrounded by evocative Industrial Age ruins. It was here that in 1709 Darby first smelted iron, using coke as fuel. To me, "coke" is a drink, and "smelt" is the past tense of smell... but around here, these words recall the event that kicked off the modern Industrial Age and changed the world (see the sidebar).

Enginuity

Enginuity is a hands-on funfest for kids. Riffing on Ironbridge's engineering roots, this converted 1709 foundry is full of entertaining-to-kids water contraptions, pumps, magnets, and laser games. Build a dam, try your hand at earthquake-proof construction, navigate a water maze, operate a remote-controlled robot, or power a turbine with your own steam. Mixed in among all this entertainment is a collection of vintage machines.

Cost: £9.50, across the parking lot from the Coalbrookdale Museum of Iron.

Darby Houses

Abraham Darby, who kicked off the Industrial Age when he figured out how to smelt iron in his big furnace, lived with his family in these two homes up on a ridge overlooking the Coalbrookdale Museum (go under the rail bridge and head uphill). Although Quakers, they were the area's wealthiest residents by far. Touring their homes, you'll learn a bit about their lifestyles, and about Quakers in general.

The 18th-century Darby mansion, **Rosehill House,** is decorated and furnished as the family home would have been in 1850. It features a collection of fine china, furniture, and trinkets from various family members. If the gilt-framed mirrors and fancy china seem a little ostentatious for wealth-shunning Quakers, keep in mind that these folks were rich beyond reason, and—as docents will assure you—considering their vast wealth, this was relatively modest. At the end of the tour is a collection of period clothes: You're welcome to dress up as a humble Quaker or a fashionable dandy.

Skip the adjacent **Dale House.** Dating from the 1710s, it's older than Rosehill, but almost completely devoid of furniture, and its exhibits are rarely open.

Cost and Hours: £5.95, £11.50 combo-ticket includes Coalbrookdale Museum of Iron, closes earlier than other museums—at 16:00—and closed entirely Oct-mid-March.

MORE SIGHTS AND EXPERIENCES IN AND NEAR IRONBRIDGE GORGE

Skiing and Swimming

A small brush-covered **ski and snowboarding slope** with two Poma lifts is at Telford Snowboard and Ski Centre in Madeley, two miles from Ironbridge Gorge; you'll see signs for it as you drive into Ironbridge Gorge (open practice times vary by day—schedule posted online, tel. 01952/382-621, www.telfordandwrekinleisure. co.uk). A public **swimming pool,** the Abraham Darby Sports and Leisure Centre, is near Madeley (5-minute drive from town on Ironbridge Road, tel. 01952/382-770).

Royal Air Force (RAF) Museum Cosford

This Red Baron magnet displays more than 80 aircraft, from warplanes to rockets. Get the background on ejection seats and a primer on the principles of propulsion (free, daily 10:00-17:00, Nov-Feb until 16:00, last entry one hour before closing, parking-£3/3 hours, Shifnal, Shropshire, on the A-41 near junction with the M-54, tel. 01902/376-200, www.rafmuseum.org.uk/cosford).

More Sights

If you're looking for reasons to linger in Ironbridge Gorge, these sights are all within a short drive: the **medieval town** of Shrewsbury, the **abbey village** of Much Wenlock, the **scenic Long Mynd gorge** at Church Stretton, the **castle** at Ludlow, and the **steam railway** at the river town of Bridgnorth. Shoppers like Chester (en route to points north). **Brosely Pipeworks,** in the town of Brosley Wood, offers a fascinating look at the mass-production of clay pipes, but its opening hours are limited (£5.95, open mid-May-Sept 10:30-16:00, tours required, at 10:30, 12:00, 13:30, and 15:00, closed off-season).

Sleeping in Ironbridge Gorge

$$ Library House Guesthouse is *Town and Country*-elegant. Located in the town center, a half-block downhill from the bridge, it's a classy, friendly gem that once served as the village library. Each of its three rooms is a delight, and the public spaces are decorated true to the Georgian period. The Chaucer Room, which includes a small garden, is the smallest and least expensive. Tim and Sarah will make you feel right at home (free parking just up the road, 11 Severn Bank, tel. 01952/432-299, www.libraryhouse.com, info@libraryhouse.com).

$$ Bridge View Guesthouse rents seven tidy but uninspired rooms over a tearoom directly at the Iron Bridge; true to its name, four rooms have bridge views. While less personal than Library House or Calcutts, they may have a room when those are full (free parking nearby, 10 Tontine Hill, tel. 01952/432-541, www.ironbridgeview.co.uk, bookings@ironbridgeview.co.uk).

OUTSIDE OF TOWN

$$ Calcutts House rents seven rooms in an 18th-century ironmaster's home and adjacent coach house. Rooms in the main house are elegant, while the coach-house rooms are bright, modern, and less expensive. Their inviting garden is a plus. Ask the owners, James and Sarah Pittam, how the rooms were named (free parking, Calcutts Road, tel. 01952/882-631, www.calcuttshouse.co.uk, info@calcuttshouse.co.uk). From Calcutts House, it's a delightful 15-minute stroll down a former train track into town.

¢ Coalport Youth Hostel, plush for a hostel, fills an old factory at the China Museum in Coalport (reception open 7:30-23:00, no lockout, High Street, tel. 0345-371-9325, www.yha.org.uk, coalport@yha.org.uk). Don't confuse this hostel with another area hostel, Coalbrookdale, which is only available for groups.

¢ Wilderhope Manor Youth Hostel, a beautifully remote Elizabethan manor house from 1586, is one of Europe's best hostels (it even has a bridal suite). On Sunday afternoons, tourists actually pay to see what hostelers get to sleep in (family rooms, reservations recommended, reception closed 10:00-15:00, restaurant open 18:00-20:30, tel. 0345-371-9149, www.yha.org.uk, wilderhope@yha.org.uk). It's in Longville-in-the-Dale, six miles from Much Wenlock, down the B-4371 toward Church Stretton.

Eating in Ironbridge Gorge

$$$$ The White Hart has a split personality—the woody pub section is Brit-rustic, while the two-level restaurant is white-tablecloth chic. Prices make this a splurge, but the food is creative and tasty

(Mon-Sat 11:00-21:30, Sun from 9:30, food served until 21:00, reservations smart on weekends, 10 Wharfage, tel. 01952/432-901, www.whitehartironbridge.com).

$$$ **Pondicherry,** in a former police station, serves Indian meals that gild the lily. The basement holding cells are now little plush lounges—a great option if you'd like your predinner drink "in prison" (daily 17:30-23:00, 57 Waterloo Street, tel. 01952/433-055). For cheaper (but still good) Indian food, look for $$ **Aftab,** a bit closer to the Iron Bridge.

$$ **The Golden Ball Inn** is a classic countryside pub high on the hill above Ironbridge. You can dine with the friendly local crowd in the "bar," eat in back with the 18th-century brewing gear in the quieter—and more formal—dining room, or munch out on the lush garden patio. This place is serious about beer, listing featured ales daily (food served Mon-Sat 12:00-21:00, Sun until 19:00, reservations smart on weekends, 10-minute hike up Madeley Road from the town roundabout, look for sign to pedestrian shortcut, 1 Newbridge Road, tel. 01952/432-179, www.goldenballironbridge.co.uk).

$$ **The Coalbrookdale Inn** is filled with locals enjoying excellent ales and simple pub grub—nothing fancy. This former "best pub in Britain" has a tradition of offering free samples from a lineup of featured beers. Ask which real ales are available (Mon-Fri 16:00-23:00, Sat-Sun from 12:00, lively ladies' loo, across street from Coalbrookdale Museum of Iron, 1 mile from Ironbridge, 12 Wellington Road, tel. 01952/432-166).

$$ **The Malthouse,** located in an 18th-century beer house, is popular with local twentysomethings. The menu includes pub standards, plus a few pricier, high-end dishes (food served daily 11:30-22:00, near Museum of the Gorge, 5-minute walk from center, The Wharfage, tel. 01952/433-712). For nighttime action, The Malthouse is *the* vibrant spot in town, with live rock music and a fun crowd (generally Fri-Sat).

Ironbridge Gorge Connections

Ironbridge Gorge is five miles southwest of Telford, which has the nearest train station.

Getting Between Telford and Ironbridge Gorge: It's easiest to take a **taxi** from Telford train station to Ironbridge Gorge (about £5.50 to Blists Hill, £9 to the Iron Bridge; call Go Carz at tel. 01952/501-050). If the Gorge Connect bus is running (described earlier, under "Getting Around Ironbridge Gorge"), you could take **bus #4** (2-5/hour) from the Telford train station to High Street in the town of Madeley. This is where the Gorge Connect bus originates and ends. Hop on it to ride to one of the museums, the TI, or the bridge.

By Train from Telford to: Birmingham (2/hour, 45 minutes), **Stratford-upon-Avon** (2/hour, 2.5 hours, 1-2 changes), **Moreton-in-Marsh** (hourly, 3 hours, 2 transfers), **Conwy** in North Wales (3/day direct, 2.5 hours, more with transfer), **Blackpool** (hourly, 2.5 hours, 2 changes), **Keswick/Lake District** (hourly, 4 hours total; 3 hours to Penrith with 1-2 changes, then catch a bus to Keswick—see page 754). **Train info:** Tel. 0345-748-4950, www.nationalrail.co.uk.

ROUTE TIPS FOR DRIVERS

Driving in from the Cotswolds and Stratford, take the M-40 to Birmingham, then the M-6 (direction northwest) through Birmingham. Be aware that traffic northbound through Birmingham is miserable from 14:00 to 20:00, especially on Fridays. Take one of two M-6 options: free with traffic through the city center; or the M-6 Toll, which, for around £7, skirts you north of the center with much less traffic—a very good bet during rush hour.

After Birmingham, follow signs to Telford via the M-54 (if on toll road, it'll be via the A-5). Leave the M-54 at the Telford/Ironbridge exit (Junction 4). Follow the brown Ironbridge signs through several roundabouts to Ironbridge Gorge. (Note: On maps, Ironbridge Gorge is often referred to as "Iron Bridge" or "Iron-Bridge.")

LIVERPOOL

Wedged between serene North Wales and the even-more-serene Lake District, Liverpool provides an opportunity to sample the "real" England. It's the best look at urban England outside of London.

Beatles fans flock to Liverpool to learn about the Fab Four's early days, but the city has much more to offer—most notably, a wealth of quality, free museums, a pair of striking cathedrals, a dramatic skyline mingling old red-brick maritime buildings and glassy new skyscrapers, and—most of all—the charm of the Liverpudlians.

Sitting at the mouth of the River Mersey in the metropolitan county of Merseyside, Liverpool has long been a major shipping center. Its port played a key role in several centuries of world history—as a point in the "triangular trade" of African slaves, a gateway for millions of New World-bound European emigrants, and a staging ground for the British Navy's Battle of the Atlantic against the Nazi's U-boat fleet. But Liverpool was devastated physically by WWII bombs, and then economically by the advent of container shipping in the 1960s. Liverpudlians looked on helplessly as postwar recovery resources were steered elsewhere, the city's substantial wartime contributions seemingly ignored.

Despite the pride and attention garnered in the 1960s by a certain quartet of favorite sons, Liverpool continued to decline through the 1970s and '80s. The Toxteth Riots of 1981, sparked by the city's dizzyingly high unemployment, brought worldwide attention to Liverpool's troubles.

But, finally, things started looking up. The city's status as the 2008 European Capital of Culture spurred major gentrification, EU funding, development of the "Liverpool ONE" commercial

On the Scouse

Nicknamed "Scousers" (after a traditional local stew, originally brought here by Norwegian immigrants), the people of Liverpool have a reputation for being relaxed, easygoing, and welcoming to visitors. The Scouse dialect comes with a distinctive lilt and quick wit (the latter likely a means of coping with long-term hardship)—think of the Beatles' familiar accents, and all their famously sarcastic off-the-cuff remarks, and you get the picture. Many Liverpudlians attribute these qualities to the Celtic influence here: Liverpool is a melting pot of not only English culture, but also loads of Irish and Welsh, as well as arrivals from all over Europe and beyond (Liverpool's diverse population includes many of African descent and the oldest Chinese community in Britain). Liverpudlians are also famous for their passion for football (soccer), and the Liverpool FC team—as locals will be quick to tell you—is one of England's best. And, along with the city, scouse stew is on the rise as well—you'll see it on menus all over town.

complex in the once bombed-out center, and a cultural renaissance. And, with some 50,000 students attending three universities in town, Liverpool is also a youthful city, with a pub or nightclub on every corner. Anyone who still thinks of Liverpool as a depressed industrial center is behind the times.

PLANNING YOUR TIME

Liverpool can easily fill a day of sightseeing. For the quickest visit, focus your time around the Albert Dock area, home to The Beatles Story, Merseyside Maritime Museum, Tate Gallery (for contemporary art lovers), Museum of Liverpool, and the British Music Experience. If time allows, consider a Beatles bus tour (departs from the Albert Dock).

A full day buys you time either to delve into the rest of the city (the rejuvenated urban core, the cathedrals, and the Walker Art Gallery near the train station), to binge on more Beatles sights (the Magical Beatles Museum or the boyhood homes of John and Paul), or a bit of both.

If you're here just for the Beatles, you can easily fill a day with Fab Four sights: Do the tour of John's and Paul's homes in the morning, then return to the Albert Dock area to visit the Beatles Story and/or the British Music Experience. Take an afternoon bus tour from the Albert Dock to the other Beatles' sights in town, winding up at the Cavern Quarter to tour the Magical Beatles Museum and enjoy a Beatles cover band in the reconstructed Cavern Club. (Beatles bus tours zip past the John and Paul houses from the outside, but visiting the interiors takes more time and should be reserved well in advance.)

International Beatles Week, celebrated in late August, is a very busy time in Liverpool, with lots of live musical performances.

Orientation to Liverpool

With nearly half a million people, Liverpool is Britain's fifth-biggest city. But for visitors, most points of interest are concentrated in the generally pedestrian-friendly downtown area. You can walk from one end of this zone to the other in half an hour. Since interesting sights and colorful neighborhoods are scattered throughout this area, it's enjoyable to connect your sightseeing on foot. (Beatles sights, however, are spread far and wide—it's most efficient to connect them with a tour.)

Tourist Information: Liverpool's TIs are just tiny desks freeloading in the Central Library (near the train station) and at the Magical Beatles Museum on Mathew Street (tel. 0151/707-0729, www.visitliverpool.com).

Private Guide: Paul Beesley, a local guide who runs the Liverpool Tour Guide Service with the help of others, is a good source for private guiding (£140/half-day, tel. 0151/374-2374, www.liverpooltgs.weebly.com, office@ltgs.co.uk).

ARRIVAL IN LIVERPOOL

By Train: The main **Lime Street train station** has eateries, shops, car rentals, and pay baggage storage (daily 7:00-21:00, weekends until 23:00, tel. 0151/909-3697, www.left-baggage.co.uk).

Getting to the Albert Dock: From Lime Street Station to the Albert Dock is about a 20-minute walk or a quick trip by subway or taxi.

To **walk,** exit straight out the front door. On your right,

you'll see the giant Neoclassical St. George's Hall; the Walker Art Gallery is just beyond it. To reach the Albert Dock, go straight ahead across the street, then head down the hill between St. George's Hall (on your right) and the big blob-shaped mall (on your left). Turn left onto Whitechapel Street and walk straight ahead all the way until you see the big red-brick warehouses of Albert Dock.

You can also take a **subway** from Lime Street Station to James Street Station, then walk about five minutes to the Albert Dock (£2.05, also covered by BritRail pass, www.merseyrail.org).

A **taxi** from Lime Street Station to the Albert Dock costs about £6. Taxis wait outside either of the side doors of the station.

By Plane: Liverpool John Lennon Airport (tel. 0871-521-8484, www.liverpoolairport.com, airport code: LPL) is about eight miles southeast of downtown, along the river. Buses to the airport depart regularly from Liverpool ONE Bus Station. Bus #500 is quickest (2/hour, 35 minutes, £2.30, covered by all-day ticket).

By Car: Most drivers approach Liverpool on the M-62 motorway, which dies at the edge of town. Just follow signs to *City Centre* and *Waterfront,* then brown signs to *Albert Dock,* where you'll find a huge pay parking lot. There's a bigger central garage at the Liverpool ONE commercial complex. If coming from Wales, take the toll tunnel under the River Mersey (£2) and follow signs for *Albert Dock.*

Tours in Liverpool

BEATLES BUS TOURS

If you want to see as many Beatles-related sights as possible in a short time, these tours are the way to go. Each drives by the houses where the Fab Four grew up (exteriors only), places they performed, and spots made famous by the lyrics of their hits ("Penny Lane," "Strawberry Fields," the Eleanor Rigby graveyard at St. Peter's Church, and so on). Even lukewarm fans will enjoy the commentary and seeing the shelter on the roundabout, the barber who shaves another customer, and the banker who never wears a mack in the pouring rain. (Very strange.)

LIVERPOOL

Liverpool

To Southport

PAISLEY
LEEDS ST.
A-565
MIDGHALL ST.
MARYBONE
VAUXHALL RD.
VAUXHALL ST.
HIGHFIELD ST.
COCKSPUR ST.
HATTON GARDEN
CHEAPSIDE
KING EDWARD ST.
EAST ST.
PALL MALL
BIXTETH ST.
EDMUND ST.
OLD HALL ST.
FAZAKER ST.
GEORGE
TITHEBARN ST.
VERNON ST.
CUNLIFFE ST.
DALE ST.
MOORFIELDS
M Moorfields
TUNNEL EXIT
NEW QUAY
CHAPEL ST.
RUMFORD
HACKINS HEY
EXCHANGE
PRINCES ST.
TEMPLE
STANLEY
CUMBER
VICTORIA

PRINCES DOCK

River Mersey

PRINCES PARADE

BATH ST.

TOWN HALL

MAGICAL BEATLES MUSEUM

ROYAL LIVER BLDG.
WATER ST.
CASTLE ST.
COOK ST.
MATHEW
HARR.
WALK ENDS
BRUNSWICK
N. JOHN ST.
LORD ST.
LIVERPOOL ONE MALL

PIER HEAD
CUNARD BLDG. & BRITISH MUSIC EXP.
CANADA BLVD.
James Street
M
JAMES ST.
Derby Square
QUEEN VICTORIA MONUMENT
S. JOHN ST.
PARADISE ST.

MERSEY FERRIES DOCK
PORT BLDG.
RED CROSS
STRAND ST.
P
Chavasse Park

Pier Head
BEATLES STATUE

Liverpool ONE Bus Station
B
CANNING PLACE
PARK LN.
LIVER ST.

QUEENSWAY BIRKENHEAD TUNNEL
MUSEUM OF LIVERPOOL

To Birkenhead

MARITIME & SLAVERY MUSEUMS
HARTLEY QUAY

200 Meters
200 Yards

TATE LIVERPOOL

ALBERT DOCK
Albert Dock
SALTHOUSE QUAY
WAPPING

N

THE BEATLES STORY
GOWER ST.
2
WHEEL OF LIVERPOOL

ARENA & CONVENTION CENTRE
1
KEEL WHARF

P
KINGS DOCK
KINGS PARADE

QUEENS WHARF

Pedestrian Shopping Zone

River Mersey

EXHIBITION CENTRE LIVERPOOL
HALFTIDE WHARF
Queen's Dock

- - - Victorian Liverpool Town Walk

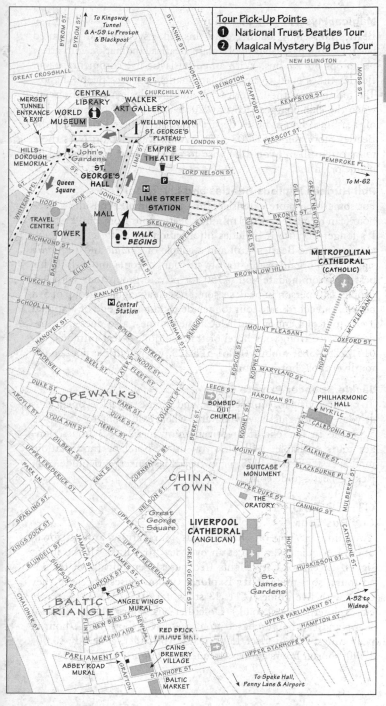

<u>Tour Pick-Up Points</u>
1 National Trust Beatles Tour
2 Magical Mystery Big Bus Tour

To Kingsway
Tunnel
& A-59 to Freston
& Blackpool

BYROM ST.

BYROM ST.

ST. ANNE ST.

NORTON ST.

ISLINGTON

NEW ISLINGTON

STAFFORD ST.

KEMPSTON ST.

MOSS ST.

GREAT CROSSHALL

HUNTER ST.

CHURCHILL WAY

PRESCOT ST.

MERSEY TUNNEL
ENTRANCE
& EXIT

CENTRAL
LIBRARY

WORLD
MUSEUM

WALKER
ART GALLERY

WELLINGTON MON.

ST. GEORGE'S
PLATEAU

LONDON RD.

PEMBROKE PL.

To M-62

HILLS-
BOROUGH
MEMORIAL

St.
John's
Gardens

EMPIRE
THEATER

LORD NELSON ST.

GILL ST.

GREAT NEWTON ST.

Queen
Square

ST. GEORGE'S HALL

LIME ST.

P

LIME STREET
STATION

BRONTE ST.

RUSSEL ST.

WHITECHAPEL

HOOD

FOE

JOHN'S ST.

MALL

SKELHORNE ST.

COPPERAS HILL

METROPOLITAN
CATHEDRAL
(CATHOLIC)

TRAVEL
CENTRE

TOWER

**WALK
BEGINS**

BROWNLOW HILL

RICHMOND ST.

BASNETT ST.

ELLIOT

LIME ST.

CHURCH ST.

SCHOOL LN.

RANLAGH ST.

M Central
Station

RENSHAW ST.

BENSON

MOUNT PLEASANT

OXFORD ST.

MT. PLEASANT

HANOVER ST.

GRADEWELL

SEEL ST.

BOLD
STREET

WOOD ST.

SLATER ST.

FLEET ST.

ROSCOE ST.

RODNEY ST.

MARYLAND ST.

HOPE ST.

DUKE ST.

ROPEWALKS

FARR ST.

COLQUITT ST.

LEECE ST.

HARDMAN ST.

PHILHARMONIC
HALL

MYRTLE

ARGYLE ST.

LYDIA ANN ST.

DUKE ST.

HENRY ST.

BERRY ST.

BOMBED-
OUT
CHURCH

RODNEY ST.

CALEDONIA ST.

GILBERT ST.

KENT ST.

CORNWALLIS ST.

MOUNT ST.

FALKNER ST.

BLACKBURNE PL.

MULBERRY ST.

UPPER FREDERICK ST.

PARK LN.

NELSON ST.

CHINA-
TOWN

SUITCASE
MONUMENT

UPPER DUKE ST.

THE
ORATORY

CANNING ST.

CATHARINE ST.

SPARLING ST.

UPPER PITT ST.

Great
George
Square

LIVERPOOL
CATHEDRAL
(ANGLICAN)

HOPE ST.

HUSKISSON ST.

KINGS DOCK ST.

BLUNDELL ST.

JAMAICA ST.

SIMPSON ST.

UPPER FREDERICK ST.

ST. JAMES ST.

GREAT GEORGE ST.

St.
James
Gardens

A-52 to
Widnes

CHALONER ST.

NORFOLK ST.

BRICK ST.

BALTIC
TRIANGLE

ANGEL WINGS
MURAL

NEW BIRD ST.

UPPER PARLIAMENT ST.

HAMPTON ST.

FLINT ST.

GREENLAND

RED BRICK
VINTAGE MKT.

ABBEY ROAD
MURAL

PARLIAMENT ST.

GRAFTON

CAINS
BREWERY
VILLAGE

STANHOPE ST.

UPPER STANHOPE ST.

BALTIC
MARKET

To Speke Hall,
Penny Lane & Airport

Magical Mystery Big Bus Tour

Beatles fans enjoy loading onto this old, psychedelically painted bus for a spin past Liverpool's main Beatles landmarks, with a few photo ops off the bus. With an enthusiastic live commentary and Beatles tunes cued to famous landmarks, it leaves people happy. The tour ends at the Cavern Club and includes general admission when the club charges a cover (£20, 5-8/day, fewer on Sun and in off-season, 2 hours, buses depart from the Albert Dock near the Beatles Story, tel. 0151/703-9100, www.cavernclub.org). As these tours often fill up, you'd be wise to book at least a day ahead by phone or online.

Phil Hughes Minibus Beatles and Liverpool Tours

For something more extensive, fun, and intimate, consider a five-hour (can be made shorter) minibus Beatles tour from Phil Hughes. It's longer because it includes information on historic Liverpool, along with the Beatles stuff and a couple of *Titanic* and *Lusitania* sights. Phil organizes his tour to fit your schedule and will do his best to accommodate you (£150 for private group tour with 1-5 people; £30/person in peak season if he can assemble a group of 5-8 people; can coordinate tour to include pickup from end of National Trust tour of Lennon and McCartney homes, also does door-to-door service from your hotel or train station, 8-seat minibus, tel. 0151/228-4565, mobile 07961-511-223, www.tourliverpool.co.uk, tourliverpool@hotmail.com).

Jackie Spencer Private Tours

To tailor a visit to your schedule and interests, Jackie Spencer is at your service...just say when and where you want to go (up to 5 people in her chauffeur-driven minivan-£240, 3 hours, longer tours available, will pick you up at hotel or train station, mobile 0799-076-1478, www.jackiespencerbeatleguide.com, jackie@beatleguide.com).

OTHER TOURS

City Bus Tour

Two different hop-on, hop-off bus tours cruise around town, offering a quick way to get an overview that links all the major sights. Liverpool City Sights (red buses) generally have recorded tours, so I prefer **City Explorer** (yellow buses), because they come with live guides (£11, 13 stops, tel. 0151/933-2324, www.cityexplorerliverpool.co.uk). On either bus, your ticket is valid 24 hours and can be purchased from the driver (both run 4/hour at peak times, 2/hour after 15:00, daily April-Oct, generally 10:00-17:00; shorter hours and less frequent in winter).

Liverpool at a Glance

▲▲**Museum of Liverpool** Three floors of intriguing exhibits, historical artifacts, and fun interactive displays tracing the port city's history, culture, and contributions to the world. **Hours:** Daily 10:00-17:00. See page 682.

▲▲**British Music Experience** Immersive and interactive museum on the history of British music from 1945 to current times. **Hours:** Daily 10:00-18:00. See page 684.

▲▲**Liverpool Cathedral** Huge Anglican house of worship—the largest cathedral in Great Britain—with cavernous interior and tower climb. **Hours:** Daily 8:00-18:00. See page 692.

▲▲**Magical Beatles Museum** Offers the best historic artifacts of the group with a special focus on the very early days. **Hours:** Daily 10:00-18:00. See page 688.

▲**The Beatles Story** Well-done if overpriced exhibit about the Fab Four, with a great audioguide narrated by John Lennon's sister, Julia Baird. **Hours:** Daily 9:00-19:00, Nov-March 10:00-18:00. See page 676.

▲**Merseyside Maritime Museum** and **International Slavery Museum** Duo of thought-provoking museums exploring Liverpool's seafaring heritage and the city's role in the African slave trade. **Hours:** Daily 10:00-17:00. See page 678.

▲**Walker Art Gallery** Enjoyable, easy-to-appreciate collection of European paintings, sculptures, and decorative arts. **Hours:** Daily 10:00-17:00. See page 686.

▲**Metropolitan Cathedral of Christ the King** Striking, daringly modern Catholic cathedral with a story as fascinating as the building itself. **Hours:** Daily 7:30-18:00. See page 690.

▲**Lennon and McCartney Homes** Guided visit to their 1950s boyhood homes, with restored interiors. **Hours:** Tours run three times daily in peak season. See page 694.

Ferry Cruise

Mersey Ferries offers cruises with recorded commentary that depart from the Pier Head ferry terminal, a 10-minute walk north of the Albert Dock. The 50-minute cruise makes two brief stops on the other side of the river. While you're welcome to hop off and on, there's little reason to get off across the river as city views are just as good from the boat (£10 round-trip, leaves Pier Head at top of

LIVERPOOL

hour, daily 10:00-15:00, Sat-Sun until 18:00 in April-Oct, café, WCs onboard, tel. 0151/330-1000, www.merseyferries.co.uk).

Sights in Liverpool

ON THE WATERFRONT

In its day, Liverpool was England's greatest seaport. It was along here (in front of the Cunard Building) that great ships embarked for America. For millions of people in the 19th century, this was their last stop before a new life in the New World.

But trade declined after 1890, as the port wasn't deep enough for the big new ships. The advent of mega container ships in the 1960s put the final nail in the port's coffin, and by 1972 the central port was closed entirely.

Today, it's once again full of energy and a busy hub of harbor traffic: the harbor tour boat, ferries to Belfast and the Isle of Man, and just beyond, in a tented structure, the Liverpool cruise port (each year about a hundred ships stop here).

Over the past couple of decades, this formerly derelict and dangerous area has been the focus of the city's rejuvenation efforts. Liverpool's waterfront is now a venue for some of the city's top attractions. Three zones interest tourists (from south to north): the Kings Dock, with Liverpool's futuristic arena, conference center, and adjacent Ferris wheel; the red-brick Albert Dock complex, with some of the city's top museums and lively restaurants and nightlife; and Pier Head, with the Museum of Liverpool, ferries across the River Mersey, and buildings both old/stately and new/glassy. Below are descriptions of the main sights at the Albert Dock and Pier Head.

At the Albert Dock

Opened in 1846 by Prince Albert and enclosing seven acres of water, the Albert Dock is surrounded by five-story brick warehouses. A half-dozen trendy eateries are lined up here, protected from the rain by arcades and padded by lots of shopping mall-type distractions. There's plenty of pay parking.

▲The Beatles Story

The Beatles seem like they're becoming a bigger and bigger attraction in Liverpool these days. This exhibit—while overpriced and a bit small—is well done. The story's a fascinating one, and even an avid fan will pick up some new information.

Cost and Hours: £17, includes audioguide; daily 9:00-19:00, Nov-March 10:00-18:00; tel. 0151/709-1969, www.beatlesstory.com.

Visiting the Museum: Start with a chronological stroll through the evolution of the Beatles, focusing on their Liverpool years: meeting as schoolboys, performing at (and helping decorate) the Casbah Coffee Club, making a name for themselves in Hamburg's red light district, meeting their manager Brian Epstein, and the advent of worldwide Beatlemania (with some help from Ed Sullivan). There are many actual artifacts (from George Harrison's first boyhood guitar to John Lennon's orange tinted "Imagine" glasses), as well as large dioramas celebrating landmarks in Beatles lore (a reconstruction of the Cavern Club, a life-size re-creation of the *Sgt. Pepper* album cover, and a walk-through yellow submarine). The last rooms trace the members' solo careers, and the reverence for John's peace work, including a replica of the white room he used while writing "Imagine." A separate room shows the history of the Beatles in India, where they practiced transcendental meditation (along with singer Donovan, actress Mia Farrow, and The Beach Boys' Mike Love) and worked on songs for *The White Album*. Rounding out the exhibits are a "Discovery Zone" for kids and (of course) the "Fab 4 Store," with an impressive pile of Beatles buyables.

The great audioguide, narrated by Julia Baird (John Lennon's little sister), captures the Beatles' charm and cheekiness in a way the stiff wax mannequins can't. You'll hear clips of interviews from the actual participants in the Beatles' story—their families, friends, and collaborators. Cynthia Lennon, John's first wife, still marvels at the manic power of Beatlemania,  while producer George Martin explains why he wanted their original drummer dumped for Ringo.

While this is a fairly sanitized look at the Fab Four (LSD and Yoko-related conflicts are glossed over), the exhibits remind listeners of all that made the group earth-shattering and even a little edgy—at the time. For example, performing before the Queen Mother, John Lennon famously quips: "Will the people in the cheaper seats clap your hands? And the rest of you, if you'll just rattle your jewelry." Surprisingly, there are no clips from the

Beatles' movies or performances—not even the epic *Ed Sullivan Show* broadcast. You'll find that it's strong on the Beatles' history, but you'll have to go elsewhere to understand why Beatlemania happened.

▲Merseyside Maritime Museum and International Slavery Museum

These museums tell the story of Liverpool, once the second city of the British Empire. The third floor covers slavery, while the first, second, and basement handle other maritime topics.

Cost and Hours: Free, donations accepted, daily 10:00-17:00, café, tel. 0151/478-4499, www.liverpoolmuseums.org.uk.

Background: Liverpool's port prospered in the 18th century as one corner of a commerce triangle with Africa and America. British shippers profited greatly through exploitation: About 1.5 million enslaved African people were taken to the Americas on Liverpool's ships (that's 10 percent of all African slaves). From Liverpool, the British exported manufactured goods to Africa in exchange for enslaved Africans; the slaves were then shipped to the Americas, where they were traded for raw material (cotton, sugar, and tobacco); and the goods were then brought back to Britain. While the merchants on all three sides made money, the big profit came home to England (which enjoyed substantial income from customs, duties, and a thriving smugglers' market). As Britain's economy boomed, so did Liverpool's.

After participation in the slave trade was outlawed in Britain in the early 1800s, Liverpool kept its port busy as a transfer point for emigrants. If your ancestors came from Scandinavia, Ukraine, or Ireland, they likely left Europe from this port. Between 1830 and 1930, nine million emigrants sailed from Liverpool to find their dreams in the New World.

Visiting the Museums: Begin by riding the elevator up to floor 3—we'll work our way back down.

On floor 3, three galleries make up the **International Slavery Museum.** First is a description of life in West Africa, which re-creates traditional domestic architecture and displays actual artifacts. Then comes a harrowing exhibit about enslavement and the Middle Passage (as the voyage to the Americas was called). The tools of the enslavers—chains, muzzles, and a branding iron—and the intense film about the Middle Passage drive home the horrifying experience of being abducted from your home and taken in life-threatening conditions thousands of miles away to toil for a wealthy stranger. The exhibits don't shy away from how Liverpool profited from slavery; you can turn local street signs around to find out how they were named after slave traders—even Penny Lane has slavery connections. Finally, the museum examines the legacy of slavery—both the persistence of racism in contemporary society and the substantial positive impact that people of African descent have had on European and American cultures. Walls of photos celebrate important people of African descent, and a music station lets you sample songs from a variety of African-influenced genres.

Continue down the stairs to the **Maritime Museum,** on floor 2. This celebrates Liverpool's shipbuilding heritage and displays actual ship components, model boats, and a gallery of nautical paintings. There's also good coverage of emigration. Part of that heritage is covered in an extensive exhibit on the *Titanic.* The shipping line and its captain were based in Liverpool, and 89 of the crew members who died were from the city. The informative panels allow you to follow real people as they set off on the voyage and debunk many *Titanic* myths (no one ever said it was unsinkable).

Floor 1 shows footage and artifacts from another maritime disaster—the 1915 sinking of the *Lusitania,* which was torpedoed by a German U-boat. She sank off the coast of Ireland in under 20 minutes; 1,191 people died in the tragedy, including 405 crew members from Liverpool. The attack on an unarmed passenger ship sparked riots in Liverpool and almost thrust the US into the war. Also on this floor, an extensive exhibit traces the **Battle of the Atlantic** (during World War II, Nazi U-boats attacked merchant ships bringing supplies to Britain, in an attempt to cripple this island nation). You'll see how crew members lived aboard merchant ships.

In the last room, three different exhibits overlap each other. *Carrying Passengers* covers Liverpool as a passenger port and gives an overview of passenger traffic in Britain today. *Carrying Cargos* focuses on cargo ships, imports and exports, and has an impressive figurehead from the HMS *Hastings. Life of a Seafarer* depicts life aboard ship, from leisure activities to diets and living conditions. From the early 1900s to the 1960s, most merchant fleet sailors came from towns like Liverpool.

A last section is dedicated to the MV *Derbyshire,* an oil tanker that disappeared in the South China Sea in 1980. The wreck was eventually found in 1994.

Make your way to the basement, where exhibits describe the tremendous wave of **emigration** through Liverpool's port. And the *Seized!* exhibit looks at the legal and illegal movement of goods through that same port, including thought-provoking displays on customs, taxation, and smuggling.

Tate Liverpool

This prestigious gallery of modern art is near the Maritime Museum. It won't entertain you as well as its London sister, the Tate Modern, but if you're into modern art, any Tate's great. Its two airy

The Beatles in Liverpool

The most iconic rock-and-roll band of all time was made up of four Liverpudlians who spent their formative years amid the bombed-out shell of WWII-era Liverpool. The city has become a pilgrimage site for Beatlemaniacs, but even those with just a passing interest in the Fab Four are likely to find themselves humming their favorite tunes around town. Most Beatles sights in Liverpool relate to their early days, before the psychedelia, transcendental meditation, Yoko, and solo careers. Because these sights are so spread out, the easiest way to connect all of them in one go is by tour (see "Tours in Liverpool," earlier).

All four of the Beatles were born in Liverpool, and any tour of town glides by the **home** most identified with each one's childhood: John Lennon at "Mendips," Paul McCartney at 20 Forthlin Road, George Harrison at 12 Arnold Grove, and Ringo Starr (a.k.a. Richard Starkey) at 10 Admiral Grove.

Behind John's house at Mendips is a wooded area called **Strawberry Field** (he added the "s" for the song). This surrounds a Victorian mansion that was, at various times, a Salvation Army home and an orphanage. John enjoyed sneaking into the trees around the mansion to play. Today visitors pose in front of Strawberry Field's red gate (a replica of the original).

During the Beatles' formative years in the mid-1950s, skiffle music (American-inspired rockabilly/folk) swept through Liverpool. As a teenager, John formed a skiffle band called the Quarrymen. Paul met John for the first time when he saw the Quarrymen on July 6, 1957, at **St. Peter's Church** in the suburb of Woolton. After the show, in the social hall across the street, Paul noted that John played only banjo chords (his mother had taught him to play on a banjo rather than a guitar—he didn't even know how to tune a guitar), and improvised many lyrics. John, two years older, realized he was a better improviser than a musician, so he was impressed when Paul borrowed a guitar, tuned it effortlessly, and played a note-perfect rendition of Eddie Cochran's "Twenty Flight Rock." Before long, Paul had joined the band.

The boys went to school on **Mount Street** in the center of Liverpool (near Hope Street, between the two cathedrals). John and his friend Stuart Sutcliffe attended the Liverpool College of Art, and Paul and his pal George Harrison went to Liverpool Institute High School for Boys. (When Paul introduced George to John as a possible new member for the band, John dismissed him as being too young...until he heard George play. He immediately became the lead guitarist.) Paul later bought his old school building and turned it into the Liverpool Institute for Performing Arts.

As young men, the boys rode the bus together to school—waiting at a bus stop in the **Penny Lane** neighborhood. Later they wrote a nostalgic song about the things they would observe while waiting there: the shelter by the roundabout, the barbershop, and the fireman with the clean machine.

By 1960 the group had officially become the Beatles: John Lennon, Paul McCartney, George Harrison, and. . . Pete Best and Stu Sutcliffe. The quintet grad-

ually built a name for themselves in Liverpool's "Mersey-beat" scene, performing at local clubs. While the famous **Cavern Club** is gone (the one you see advertised is a recon-struction, but does offer simi-lar ambience and good cover bands), the original **Casbah Coffee Club**—which the group felt more attached to—still ex-ists and is open for tours (3.5 miles northwest of downtown in Pete Best's former basement, prebook by calling the TI at tel. 0151/707-0729 or online at www.petebest.com).

The group went to Hamburg, Germany, to cut their teeth in the thriving music scene there. They wound up performing as the backing band for Tony Sheridan's single "My Bonny." When this caught on back in Liverpool, promoter Brian Epstein took note, and signed the act. His shrewd management would eventually propel the Beatles to superstardom.

Many people could be considered the "Fifth Beatle." John's friend Stu, who performed with the group in Hamburg, left to pur-sue his own artistic interests. Pete Best was the band's original drummer, but he was a loner and producers questioned his musi-cal chops, so he was replaced with Ringo Starr. (John later said, "Pete Best was a great drummer, but Ringo was a Beatle.") Brian Epstein, the manager who marketed the Beatles brilliantly before his untimely death, is another candidate. But—in terms of long-term musical influence—it's hard to ignore the case for George Martin, who produced all the Beatles' albums except *Let It Be*, and was instrumental in both forging and developing the Beatles sound.

By early 1964, the Beatles were already world-famous—but, as evidenced by their songs about Penny Lane and Strawberry Fields, they never forgot their Merseyside home.

floors dedicated to the rotating collection of statues and paintings from the 20th century are free; the top and ground floors are devoted to special exhibits. The Tate also has an inexpensive recommended café.

Cost and Hours: Free, donations accepted, £10 for special exhibits, daily 10:00-18:00, tel. 0151/702-7400, www.tate.org.uk/visit/tate-liverpool.

At Pier Head, North of the Albert Dock
A five-minute walk across the bridge north of the Albert Dock takes you to the Pier Head area, with a popular statue of the Beatles on the harborfront and the sights listed next.

▲▲Museum of Liverpool
This museum, in the blocky white building just across the bridge north of the Albert Dock, does a good job of fulfilling its goal to "capture Liverpool's vibrant character and demonstrate the city's unique contribution to the world." The museum is full of interesting items, fun interactive displays (great for kids), and fascinating facts that bring a whole new depth to your Liverpool experience.

Cost and Hours: Free, donations encouraged, daily 10:00-17:00, guidebook-£1, café, Mann Island, Pier Head, tel. 0151/478-4545, www.liverpoolmuseums.org.uk.

Visiting the Museum: First, stop by the information desk to check on the showtimes for the museum's various videos. If you have kids age six and under, ask about the hands-on *Little Liverpool* exhibit on the ground floor.

Ground Floor: On this level, *The Great Port* details the story of Liverpool's defining industry and how it developed through the Industrial Revolution. On display is an 1838 steam locomotive that was originally built for the Liverpool and Manchester Railway. The *Global City* exhibit focuses on how Liverpool's status as a major British shipping center made it the gateway to a global empire and features a 20-minute video, *Power and the Glory*, about Liverpool's role within the British Empire.

First Floor: Don't miss the *Liverpool Overhead Railway* exhibit, which features the only surviving car from this 19th-century elevated railway. You can actually jump aboard and take a seat to watch 1897 movie footage shot from the train line. A huge interactive model shows the railway's route. Also on this floor is the

History Detectives exhibit, which covers Liverpool's archaeology and history, including the story of the Liverpool Blitz (bombings by the German Luftwaffe in 1940-41—only London was bombed more than Liverpool during WWII raids over Britain).

Second Floor: If you're short on time, spend most of it here. The *People's Republic* exhibit examines what it means to be a Liverpudlian (a.k.a. "Scouser") and covers everything from housing and health issues to military and religious topics. As industrialized Liverpool has long been a hotbed of the labor movement, exhibits here also detail the political side of the city, including child labor issues and women's suffrage.

One fascinating display is the re-creation of Liverpool's 19th-century court housing, which consisted of a series of tiny dwellings bunched around a narrow courtyard. With more than 60 people sharing two toilets, this was some of the most overcrowded and unsanitary housing in Britain at the time.

On the other side of the floor, the *Wondrous Place* exhibit celebrates the arts, cultural, and sporting side of Liverpool. An exhibit on the city's famous passion for soccer features memorabilia and the 17-minute video *Kicking and Screaming,* about the rivalry between the Everton and Liverpool football teams and the sometimes tragic history of the sport (such as in 1989, when 96 Liverpool fans were crushed to death at a playoff match in Sheffield due to inept crowd control and an antiquated stadium).

Music is the other big focus here, with plenty of fun interactive stops that include quizzes, a karaoke booth, and listening stations featuring artists with ties to Liverpool (from Elvis Costello to Echo & the Bunnymen). And, of course, you'll see plenty of Beatles mania, including their famous suits, the original stage from St. Peter's Church (where John Lennon was performing the first time Paul McCartney laid eyes on him; located in the theater), and an eight-minute film on the band.

Finally, in the **Skylight Gallery,** look for Ben Johnson's painting *The Liverpool Cityscape, 2008,* a remarkable and fun-to-examine melding of old and new art styles. At first glance, it's a typical skyline painting, but Johnson used computer models to create perfect depictions of each building before he put brush to canvas. This method allows for a photorealistic, highly detailed, but completely sanitized portrait of a city. Notice there are no cars or people.

The Three Graces

Three towering buildings near the Museum of Liverpool, remnants of a time of great seafaring prosperity, are known collectively as Liverpool's Three Graces: the domed **Port of Liverpool Building** (which strains to evoke memories of St. Paul's Cathedral in London); the relatively dull and boxy **Cunard Building** (now

hosting the British Music Experience, described below); and the 1911 double-clock-towered **Royal Liver Building** (pronounced LIE-ver, Britain's first skyscraper—322 feet tall with spires topped by the city's mythical mascots, the "Liver birds").

The Royal Liver Building offers a tour to the top that is just an escorted walk through the working office building with an earnest guided spiel—it just isn't that interesting.

▲▲British Music Experience

This museum, located in the Cunard Building at Pier Head, goes beyond Liverpool's Beatlemania, immersing visitors in the history of British music of all genres from 1945 until today. The multimedia exhibits include costumes, instruments, recordings, and memorabilia from artists and bands such as David Bowie, Queen, Amy Winehouse, Coldplay, and Adele, plus the chance to play professional-grade instruments in a sound studio. You

could easily spend hours here, but plan for at least 90 minutes.

Cost and Hours: £14, daily 10:00-18:00, last entry 1.5 hours before closing, multimedia guide-£2; tel. 0344-335-0655, www.britishmusicexperience.com.

Visiting the Museum: The museum is one big room with a stage dominating the center that's flanked by eight zones covering different eras. Music videos and holographic performances play on the stage. You can work your way around the hall chronologically from 1945 (when, with the help of pop music culture, children began freeing themselves from being "little adults who dressed and acted like their parents").

Each section displays interesting facts about well-known artists, billboard art, costumes, instruments, and more. Your multimedia guide provides interviews, videos, and picture galleries. The first two sections (1945-1962, which covers jazz, skiffle, and rock-and-roll, and 1962-1966, covering R&B, Merseybeat, and the Beatles) have well-done interactive tables explaining the origin of these music genres and how the UK and US music scenes influenced each other. Timelines place the music in historical context, describing its relation to the politics and culture of each decade.

The final section is a studio where you can exercise your musical skills: take interactive instrument lessons (I learned to play a set of drums.); record your singing; or learn (and then record on video) dance moves that have been popular over the decades.

DOWNTOWN

Stepping away from the waterfront, you find Liverpool's workaday commercial center stretching east up to the train station and Walker Art Gallery and south past the massive Liverpool ONE shopping and residential complex. Take a moment with the map to get the lay of this easily walkable land: The older part of downtown stretches from Liverpool Town Hall down Castle Street to the huge Queen Victoria monument. Beyond the Victoria monument is Liverpool ONE. Next to that complex is the Ropewalks District stretching to Liverpool's "bombed-out church." Uphill from there you'll find the cathedral neighborhood, with the Catholic cathedral to the left and Chinatown and the Anglican cathedral to the right.

Victorian Liverpool Town Walk

If you're arriving at Lime Street Station, here's a stately way to get from the station into the city center. We'll start by walking through St. George's Plateau, past the Walker Art Gallery, and then downhill past St. John's Gardens to Beatles sights along Mathew Street. Along the way, the only sight of real importance is the Walker Gallery (free and well worth a look, see listing, later). But the walk gives you a feel for the grand side of 19th-century Liverpool.

St. George's Hall is the big, temple-like Neoclassical building facing the station. It originally contained courts and a concert hall; now it's a venue for conferences, civic events, and the performing arts. Between the hall and train station is **St. George's Plateau,** a gathering place for the community, with equestrian statues of Prince Albert and a youthful Queen Victoria that flank a somber memorial to the World Wars. Walk all around the memorial to appreciate the royal faces and the huge wartime losses Liverpool, like any British city, endured.

When John Lennon was shot, 25,000 gathered here for a candlelight vigil...probably recalling the last live Beatles' performance here in December 1965, in the **Empire Theatre** across the street. Take a look up Lord Nelson Street to the right of the theater to spot the recommended **Ma Egerton's Stage Door** pub, where many an artist went for a pint (and still do) after their performances.

The towering monumental column honors the Duke of Wellington, who beat Napoleon at the Battle of Waterloo in 1815.

Behind him is the **Walker Art Gallery,** which is like a mini version of London's National Gallery.

Now turn left and work your way downhill. The Neoclassical building adjacent to the Walker Gallery is the **Central Library,** containing a modern atrium (free, with TI open Mon-Sat 10:00-16:30) and, upstairs, the impressive Victorian Picton Reading Room. In front of the entrance, notice the long walkway engraved with famous book, movie, and music titles. Here and there you can see red letters sprinkled among the words, forming a puzzle to a secret code that the museum has yet to reveal.

The next grand building houses the **World Museum,** a catch-all family museum with five floors of kid-oriented exhibits. You'll see dinosaurs, an aquarium, artifacts from the ancient world, a planetarium, and theater (free, daily 10:00-17:00).

Continue strolling downhill along **St. John's Gardens** (across the street). Filled with statues, it celebrates influential locals—politicians and philanthropists. (With all the slave wealth, big shots here felt a need to be philanthropic.)

At the foot of the park, find a round bronze memorial to the Hillsborough Stadium tragedy when 96 local fans (most quite young) were crushed during a 1989 soccer game in Sheffield. That tragedy led to a big change in how stadium seating is built in Britain.

The gaping tunnel below (with statues of the king and queen flanking its entry) is the mouth to the **Mersey Tunnel,** the first road under the river, which was opened in 1934. Movie buffs might recognize it from a *Fast and Furious* car chase or from a Harry Potter flying-broom chase.

From here, head downhill to the left on Whitechapel for about six blocks. A block into the pedestrian zone you'll have entered the heart of Liverpool's commercial center. At Stanley Street go right and then left onto **Mathew Street**—historic for Beatles fans. Lined with bars and souvenir shops, it's super-touristy by day and sloppy and rowdy at night, often overrun with stag and hen parties on weekends (see listing, later).

▲Walker Art Gallery

Though it has few recognizable works, Liverpool's main art gallery offers an enjoyable walk through an easy-to-digest collection of European (mostly British) paintings, sculpture, and decorative arts. There's no audioguide, but many of the works are well explained by posted descriptions.

Cost and Hours: Free, donations accepted, daily 10:00-17:00, William Brown Street, tel. 0151/478-4199, www.liverpoolmuseums.org.uk.

Visiting the Museum: The ground floor has an information

desk, café, children's area, small decorative arts collection (with a fine selection of 18th-century fashion), and sculpture gallery focusing on 19th-century British Neoclassical works. The sculpture gallery has many works by John Gibson, a Welshman who grew up in Liverpool and later studied under the Italian master Antonio Canova. Gibson's *Tinted Venus* (in the case in the middle) was considered scandalous to Victorian mores because of the nude sculpture's lifelike pinkish tint. (Pinkish marble...yeow!)

Upstairs is a compact 15-room painting gallery. For a general chronological spin, from the top of the stairs head straight back through four rooms to find Room 1. (Paintings rotate in and out, so some mentioned here may not be on display.)

Room 1 (actually two adjoining rooms) has a famous Nicholas Hilliard portrait of Queen Elizabeth I (nicknamed "The Pelican," for her brooch) and a well-known royal portrait of Henry VIII by Hans Holbein. Room 3 has bombastic Baroque works by Rubens and Murillo (his Mary keeps her eyes on you as you cross the room), Room 4 features a Rembrandt self-portrait, while Room 5 focuses on 18th-century English painting, including canvases by Gainsborough, Hogarth (find the painting of the great actor David Garrick in the role of Richard III), and lots of horses by George Stubbs. Rooms 6-8 showcase a delightful array of Pre-Raphaelite works, among them Millais' evocative portrait of Isabella (Room 6). You'll find some Turners (a mushy landscape and a more sharp-focus Linlithgow Castle) in Room 7.

Room 10 makes the transition to the 20th century and Impressionism, while modern British art is displayed in Rooms 11-15. In Room 11, Bernard Fleetwood-Walker's *Amity* shows a pair of chaste but (apparently) sexually charged teenagers relaxing in the grass.

Mathew Street

The narrow, bar-lined Mathew Street, right in the heart of downtown, is ground zero for Beatles fans. The Beatles frequently performed in their early days together at the original Cavern Club,

LIVERPOOL

deep in a cellar along this street. While that's long gone, a mock-up of the historic nightspot (built with many of the original bricks) lives on a few doors down. Still billed as "the **Cavern Club**," this noisy bar is worth a visit to see the reconstructed cellar that's often filled by Beatles cover bands. While just a touristy pub draped in

memorabilia, dropping by in the afternoon for a live Beatles tribute act in the Cavern Club somehow just feels right. You'll have Beatles songs stuck in your head all day anyway, so you might as well see John and Paul wannabes strumming and harmonizing a close approximation of the original (open daily 10:00-24:00; live music daily from noon until late evening, free admission most of the time, small entry fee Thu-Sun evenings; tel. 0151/236-9091, www.cavernclub.org).

Across the street and run by the same owners, the **Cavern Pub** lacks its sibling's troglodyte aura, but makes up for it with walls lined with old photos and memorabilia from the Beatles and other bands who've performed here. Like the Cavern Club, the pub features frequent performances by Beatles cover bands and other acts (no cover, daily 11:00-24:00, tel. 0151/236-4041).

Out front is the Cavern's **Wall of Fame,** with a too-cool-for-school bronze John Lennon leaning up against a wall of bricks engraved with the names of musical acts that have graced the Cavern stage. Adjacent, notice the 57 number-one singles from 1953 to 2018 by Liverpool bands.

At the corner is the recommended **Hard Day's Night Hotel,** decorated inside and out to honor the Fab Four. Notice the statues of John, Paul, George, and Ringo on the second-story corners, and the Beatles gift shop (one of many in town) on the ground floor.

▲▲Magical Beatles Museum

Claiming to be "the world's most authentic Beatles museum," this fascinating-to-Beatles-fans collection is spread chronologically over three floors with thoughtful descriptions. Neil Aspinall, a roadie-hoarder, collected this memorabilia during the early years as if he knew the Beatles would make history. Filled with a trove of artifacts (letters, clothing, photos, and so on), each floor covers an era: before they were famous, the touring years, and the studio/psychedelic years. Beatle-geek staffers are standing by to tell stories and answer questions. It's strong on pre-Ringo days, because Neil was "a kind of stepfather" to Pete Best (the original drummer)...it's complicated.

Cost and Hours: £15, RS%—Roag Best (the owner and half-brother of Pete) promises 20 percent off with this book; daily 10:00-18:00, last entry one hour before closing, 50 yards from the Cavern Club at 23 Mathew Street, tel. 0151/236-1337, www. magicalbeatlesmuseum.com.

Other Sights in the City Center
Castle Street

One of the historic streets of Liverpool, Castle Street connected its medieval castle with its Town Hall. Today the Town Hall stands bold, the street is lined with bars and restaurants filling up the former offices of 19th-century banks, and the castle is long gone—replaced with a grand memorial to Queen Victoria. The monument seems fitting as the street is a parade of Victorian grandeur. Beyond Victoria (who somehow survived WWII bombing) is a zone that was obliterated by the bombing raids and was recently reborn.

Liverpool ONE

This sprawling shopping/residential/entertainment complex, opened in 2008, covers 42 acres. Liverpool was slow to rebuild after World War II, and this vast, once-derelict stretch of the city center symbolized the decades-long funk. But in the early 2000s, with the help of EU money to kickstart development, the city started its rejuvenation with this huge project. Back then it's said that half of all the construction cranes in Britain had been working here.

Liverpool ONE insists it is not a mall. It's designed as a modern complex with three stories of shops and an actual street plan so that it feels part of the neighboring zones. You can walk from the train station to Albert Docks crossing only two traffic streets thanks to Liverpool ONE. It has residential floors above the commercial floors, so it's also vibrant at night. With a world of famous-brand stores and restaurants, and lots of energy, the complex is worth a look. (Liverpool, with its trade heritage and successful Liverpool ONE development thanks to the EU, was one of the most anti-Brexit cities in the UK during the 2016 vote.)

Ropewalks District

Any big old-time port needed lots of rope, and that industry required long, straight lanes. Those long lanes now make up a happening zone of colorful, independent shops and restaurants. While the Ropewalks District sprawls several blocks wide, Bold Street is the most lively and fun place to explore.

Bombed-Out Church

In 1941, Nazi bombing raids gutted the fine Neo-Gothic St. Luke's Church, which was left in ruins as a memorial to those killed. It marks the gateway to both the Ropewalks District and Chinatown. (Liverpool has the oldest Chinatown and the biggest Chinese arch in Europe.)

CATHEDRALS NEIGHBORHOOD

Liverpool has not one but two notable cathedrals—one Anglican, the other Catholic. (As the Spinners song puts it, "If you want a cathedral, we've got one to spare.") Both are huge, architecturally significant, and well worth visiting. Near the eastern edge of downtown, they're connected by a 10-minute, half-mile walk on pleasant Hope Street, which is lined with theaters and good restaurants (see "Eating in Liverpool," later).

Liverpudlians enjoy pointing out that they have not only the world's only Catholic cathedral designed by a Protestant architect, but also the only Protestant one designed by a Catholic. With its large Irish-immigrant population, Liverpool suffered from tension between its Catholic and Protestant communities for much of its history. But during the city's darkest stretch of the depressed 1970s, the bishops of each church—Anglican Bishop David Sheppard and Catholic Archbishop Derek Worlock—came together and worked hard to reconcile the two communities for the betterment of Liverpool. (Liverpudlians nicknamed this dynamic duo "fish and chips" because they were "always together, and always in the newspaper.") It worked: Liverpool is a bold new cultural center, and relations between the two faiths remain healthy here. Join in this ecumenical spirit by visiting and appreciating the lively energy of both churches.

▲Metropolitan Cathedral of Christ the King (Catholic)

This daringly modern building, a cone topped with a crowned cylinder, seems almost out of place in its workaday Liverpool neighborhood. But the cathedral you see today bears no resemblance to Sir Edwin Lutyens' original 1930s plans for a stately Neo-Byzantine cathedral, which was to take 200 years to build and rival St. Peter's Basilica in Vatican City. (Lutyens was desperate to one-up the grandiose plans of Sir Giles Gilbert Scott, who was

building the Anglican Cathedral down the street.) The crypt for the ambitious church was excavated in the 1930s, but World War II (during which the crypt was used as an air-raid shelter) stalled progress for decades. In the 1960s, the plans were scaled back, and this smaller (but still impressive) house of worship was completed in 1967.

Cost and Hours: Cathedral—free entry but donations accepted, daily 7:30-18:00—but after 17:15 (during Mass), you won't be able to walk around; crypt—£3, Mon-Sat 10:00-16:00, closed Sun, last entry 45 minutes before closing, enter from inside church near organ; visitors center and an inviting café, Mount Pleasant, tel. 0151/709-9222, www.liverpoolmetrocathedral.org.uk.

Visiting the Cathedral: On the stepped plaza in front of the church, you'll see the entrance to the cathedral's visitors center and café (on your right). You're standing on a big concrete slab that provides a roof to the massive Lutyens Crypt underfoot. The existing cathedral occupies only a small part of the would-be cathedral's footprint. Because of the cathedral's tent-like appearance and ties to the local Irish community, some Liver-

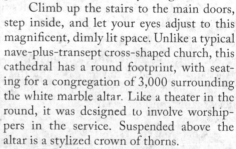

pudlians dubbed it "Paddy's Wigwam."

Climb up the stairs to the main doors, step inside, and let your eyes adjust to this magnificent, dimly lit space. Unlike a typical nave-plus-transept cross-shaped church, this cathedral has a round footprint, with seating for a congregation of 3,000 surrounding the white marble altar. Like a theater in the round, it was designed to involve worshippers in the service. Suspended above the altar is a stylized crown of thorns.

Spinning off from the round central sanctuary are 13 smaller chapels, many of them representing stages of Jesus' life. Each chapel is different. Explore, tuning into the symbolic details in each one. Also keep an eye out for the 14 exquisite bronze Stations of the Cross by local artist Sean Rice (on the wall).

The massive **Lutyens Crypt** (named for the ambitious original architect)—the only part of the originally planned cathedral to be completed—has huge vaults and vast halls lined with six million bricks. The crypt contains a chapel—with windows by Lutyens—that's still used for Sunday Mass, the tombs of three archbishops, a treasury, and an exhibit about the cathedral's construction.

Hope Street

The street connecting the cathedrals is the main artery of Liverpool's "uptown," a lively and fun-to-explore district loaded with

LIVERPOOL

dining and entertainment options. At the intersection with Mount Street is a monument consisting of concrete suitcases (explained by a nearby info plaque); just down this street is John's art school and Paul and George's high school—with the four grand columns. In addition to well-respected theaters, this street is home to the Liverpool Philharmonic and its namesake pub.

The **Philharmonic Dining Rooms,** kitty-corner from the Philharmonic Hall on Hope Street, must be the most flamboyantly Victorian pub in town. It's amazingly elaborate, the pink-marble urinals (while stinky) are downright genteel, and the cozy sitting areas on the ground floor will entice you to sip a pint. John Lennon said that his biggest regret about fame was "not being able to go to the Phil for a drink." And, if you saw Paul McCartney on *The Late Late Show* doing host James Corden's "Carpool Karaoke"—or watched it on YouTube—this was the site for Paul's surprise live concert (at the corner of Hope and Hardman streets, see the listing in "Eating in Liverpool," later).

▲▲Liverpool Cathedral (Anglican)

The largest cathedral in Great Britain, this gigantic house of worship hovers at the south end of downtown. Tour its cavernous interior and consider scaling its tower.

Cost and Hours: Free, £5 suggested donation, daily 8:00-18:00; £5.50 ticket includes tower climb (sold in the gift shop, 2 elevators and 108 steps), audioguide, and 10-minute *Great Space* film; tower—Mon-Sat 10:00-17:00 (Thu until sunset March-Oct), Sun 12:00-16:00 (changes possible depending on bell-ringing schedule); St. James Mount, tel. 0151/709-6271, www.liverpoolcathedral.org.uk.

Visiting the Cathedral: Over the main door is a modern *Risen Christ* statue by Elisabeth Frink. Liverpudlians, not thrilled with the featureless statue and always quick with a joke, have dubbed it **"Frinkenstein."**

Stepping inside, pick up a floor plan at the information desk, go into the main hall, and take in the size of the place. When

Liverpool was officially designated a "city" (seat of a bishop), they wanted to build a huge house of worship as a symbol of Liverpudlian pride. Built in bold Neo-Gothic style (like London's Parliament), it seems to trumpet with modern bombast the importance of this city on the Mersey. Begun in 1904, the cathedral's construction was interrupted by the tumultuous 20th century and not completed until 1978.

Go to the big circular tile in the very center of the cathedral, under the highest tower. This is a plaque for the building's architect, **Sir Giles Gilbert Scott** (1880-1960). While the church you're surrounded by may seem like his biggest legacy, he also designed an icon that's synonymous with Britain: the classic red telephone box. Notice the highly detailed sandstone carvings flanking this aisle.

Take a counterclockwise spin around the church interior. Head up the right aisle until you find the **model** of the original plan for the cathedral (press the button to light it up). Scott was a very young architect and received the commission with the agreement that he work closely under the wing of his more established mentor, George Bodley. These two architects' visions clashed, and Bodley usually won...until he died early in the planning stages, leaving Scott to pursue his own muse.

Nearby, the **"whispering arch"** spanning the monument has remarkable acoustics, carrying voices from one end to the other. Try it.

Continuing down the church, notice the very colorful, modern painting of *The Good Samaritan* (by Adrian Wiszniewski, 1995), high above on the right. The naked crime victim (who has been stabbed in his side, like the Crucifixion wound of Jesus) has been ignored by the well-dressed yuppies in the foreground, but the female Samaritan is finally taking notice. The canvas is packed with symbolism (for example, the Swiss Army knife, in a pool of blood in the left foreground, is open in the 3 o'clock position—the time that Jesus was crucified). This contemporary work of art demonstrates that this is a new, living church. But the congregation has its limits. This painting used to hang closer to the

front of the church, but now they've moved it here, to a lower profile spot.

Proceeding to the corner, you'll reach the entrance to the oldest part of the church (1910): the **Lady Chapel,** with stained-glass windows celebrating important women. (Sadly, the original windows were destroyed in World War II; these are replicas.)

Back up in the main part of the church, continue behind the main altar to the **Education Centre,** with a fun, sped-up video showing all of the daily work it takes to make this cathedral run.

Circling around the far corner of the church, you'll pass the children's chapel and chapterhouse, and then pass under another modern Wiszniewski painting *(The House Built on Rock).* Across from that painting, go into the choir to get a good look at the Last Supper altarpiece above the **main altar.**

Continuing back up the aisle, you'll come to the **war memorial transept.** At its entrance is a book listing Liverpudlians lost in war. Battle flags fly high on the wall above.

You'll wind up at the gift shop, where you can buy a ticket to climb to the top of the tower. The cathedral's café is up the stairs, above the gift shop.

Outside to the east of the cathedral, St. James Garden—once a sandstone quarry, then a spooky cemetery—is now a peaceful green space much appreciated by the community.

AWAY FROM THE CENTER
▲Lennon and McCartney Homes

John's and Paul's boyhood homes are now owned by the National Trust and have both been restored to how they looked during the lads' 1950s childhoods. While some Beatles bus tours stop here for photo ops, only the National Trust minibus tour gets you inside the homes. This isn't Graceland—you won't find an over-the-top rock-and-roll extravaganza here. If you don't know the difference between John and Paul, you'll likely be bored. But for die-hard Beatles fans who want to get a glimpse

The proud family home of the McCartney family; **Jim, Mary, Paul** and **Mike**

Accessible via The National Trust Tickets available from: **www.nationaltrust.org.uk/beatles** Telephone: **0151 427 7231** *(There is no direct access inside the house)*

into the time and place that created these musical masterminds, the National Trust tour is worth ▲▲▲.

Famous musicians who perform in Liverpool often make the pilgrimage to these homes—Bob Dylan turned up on one tour disguised in a hoodie—and Paul himself occasionally drops by. Ask the guides about recent memorable visitors.

Because the houses are in residential neighborhoods—and still share walls with neighbors—the National Trust runs only a few tours per day, limited to 15 or so Beatlemaniacs each.

Cost: £25, £31 includes a guidebook.

Reservations: Advance booking is strongly advised, especially in summer and on weekends or holidays. Book online or by phone as soon as you know your Liverpool plans—or at least two weeks ahead (tel. 0344-249-1895, www.nationaltrust.org.uk/beatles). If you haven't reserved ahead, you can try to book a same-day tour; the last tour of the day is least likely to be full.

Visitor Information: Tours run daily from the Albert Dock at 10:00, 11:00, and 14:10 (tours do not run Mon-Tue in mid-Feb-mid-March and Nov; no tours at all Dec-mid-Feb). They depart from the Jurys Inn (south across the bridge from The Beatles Story, near the Ferris wheel—meet in hotel lobby). The entire visit takes about 2.5 hours.

Visiting the Homes: A minibus takes you to the homes of John and Paul, with about 45 minutes inside each (no photos allowed inside either home). Each home has a caretaker who acts as your guide. These folks give an entertaining, insightful-to-fans talk that lasts about 30 minutes. You then have 10-15 minutes to wander through the house on your own. Ask lots of questions if their spiel peters out early—these docents are a wealth of information.

Mendips (John Lennon's Home): Even though he sang about being a working-class hero, John grew up in the suburbs of Liverpool, surrounded by doctors, lawyers, and—beyond the back fence—Strawberry Field.

This was the home of John's Aunt Mimi, who raised him in this house from the time he was five years old and once told him, "A guitar's all right, John, but you'll never earn a living by it." (John later bought Mimi a country cottage with those fateful words etched over the fireplace.) John moved out at age 23, but his first wife, Cynthia, bunked here for a while when John made his famous first trip to America. Yoko Ono bought the house in 2002 and gave it as a gift to the National

Trust (generating controversy among the neighbors). The house's stewards make this place come to life.

On the surface, it's just a 1930s house carefully restored to how it would have been in the past. But delve deeper. It's been lovingly cared for—restored to be the tidy, well-kept place Mimi would have recognized (down to dishtowels hanging in the kitchen). It's a lucky quirk of fate that the house's interior remained mostly unchanged after the Lennons left: The bachelor who owned it decades after them didn't upgrade much, so even the light switches are true to the time.

If you're a John Lennon fan, it's fun to picture him as a young boy drawing and imagining at his dining room table. His bedroom, with an Elvis poster and his favorite boyhood books, offers tantalizing hints at his later musical genius. Sing a song to yourself in the enclosed porch—John and Paul did this when they wanted an echo-chamber effect.

20 Forthlin Road (Paul McCartney's Home): In comparison to Aunt Mimi's house, the home where Paul grew up is simpler, much less "posh," and even a little ratty around the edges. Michael, Paul's brother, wanted it that way—their mother, Mary (famously mentioned in "Let It Be"), died when the boys were young, and it never had the tidiness of a woman's touch. It's been intentionally scuffed up around the edges to preserve the historical accuracy. Notice the differences—Paul has said that John's house was vastly different and more clearly middle class; at Mendips, there were books on the bookshelves—but Paul's father had an upright piano. He also rigged up wires and headphones that connected the boys' bed-

rooms to the living room radio so they could listen to rock-and-roll on Radio Luxembourg.

More than a hundred Beatles songs were written in this house (including "I Saw Her Standing There") during days Paul and John spent skipping school. The photos from Michael, taken in this house, help make the scene of what's mostly a barren interior much more interesting. Ask your guide how Paul would sneak into the house late at night without waking up his dad.

Nightlife in Liverpool

Liverpool hops after hours, especially on weekends. If you're out after dinner, here are a few suggestions.

Ropewalks and Nearby

A particularly lively zone is the area called Ropewalks, just east of the downtown shopping district and Albert Dock. Part of the protected historic area of Liverpool's docklands, the redeveloped Ropewalks area is now filled with pubs, nightclubs, and lounges— some of them rough around the edges, others posh and sleek. While this area is aimed primarily at the college-age crowd, it's still worth a stroll, and has a few eateries worth considering.

The Bridewell bar fills a circa-1850 police station with a lively pub atmosphere and a beer garden. Inside, past the bar, several jail cells have been converted into cozy seating areas (1 Campbell Square).

The Grapes, an artsy pub between Hope Street and Rope-walks, has a cracking atmosphere with a hard-working staff and a good selection of ales and cocktails. Upstairs is a cozy outdoor terrace (live music on Sun, 60 Roscoe Street).

Peter Kavanagh's, near the Anglican Cathedral, is worth the trek. It's a proper pub with no food but plenty of good ales, cocktails, and friendly locals. The interior is richly decorated with memorabilia from its various owners. Enjoy a pint on the outside terrace or in the comfy leather seating inside. There's a late-night quiz every Thursday at 22:00, and live music Tuesday and Saturday evenings (8 Egerton Street, cash only).

Downtown

The pubs listed here are best for serious drinkers and beer aficionados—the food is an afterthought.

Thomas Rigby's has hard-used wooden floors in the taproom that spill out into a rollicking garden courtyard. Its atmosphere is laid back, and chances are good you'll meet locals, especially after work hours (21 Dale Street).

Ye Hole in Ye Wall, around the corner and much more sedate, brags that it's Liverpool's oldest pub, from 1726. Notice the men's room on the ground floor—the women's room, required by law to be added in the 1970s, is upstairs (just off Dale Street on Hackins Hey).

The Globe, a few blocks over, right in the heart of downtown and surrounded by modern mega-malls, is a tight, cozy, local-feeling pub with five real ales and sloping floors (17 Cases Street).

The Cavern Quarter, with the Cavern Club and neighboring music bars, covers a one-block stretch of Mathew Street. Filled with Beatles bars and Beatles memories, it's packed with curious tourists by day and gets rowdier after dark—especially with hen and stag parties on weekend nights. You can always drink and dance to cover bands playing Beatles classics on Mathew Street.

LIVERPOOL

The Baltic Triangle

This area, just a short walk south from Albert Dock, is an up-and-coming, shabby-chic zone with street art, mod bars, trendy eateries, and an edgy night scene.

The most interesting part starts on **Jamaica Street** where Paul Curtis, "Liverpool's Banksy," (along with other local artists) has decorated the Baltic Triangle with creative murals. The main attractions are his fun-loving *Angel Wings* and *Abbey Road* (painted for the 50th anniversary of that album) on Grafton Street. Both are just waiting for you as photo ops. On Jordan Street, check out the rotating statue exhibition, always good for a selfie. Across the street is a mural of Liverpool's soccer coach Jürgen Klopp, a native of Germany who's made Liverpool a top contender in England's Premier League.

At the end of Jamaica Street is the popular **Camp and Furnace,** a cultural hub hosting events such as "Bongo's Bingo," singalongs, concerts, and a Beatles disco (67 Greenland Street, tel. 0151/708-2890, www.campandfurnace.com).

Across busy Parliament Street you'll find **Cains Brewery Village** with a surprisingly good secondhand mall called **Red Brick Vintage Market.** For food, head to the **Baltic Market,** a warehouse full of alternative pop-up eateries that has done a lot to put the neighborhood on the map (closed Mon-Wed, 107 Stanhope Street).

Sleeping in Liverpool

Your best budget options in this thriving city are the boring, predictable, and central chain hotels—though I've listed a couple of more colorful options also worth considering. Many hotels, including the ones listed below, charge more on weekends (particularly Sat), especially when the Liverpool FC soccer team plays a home game. Rates shoot up even higher two weekends a year: during the Grand National horse race (long weekend in April), and during Beatles Week in late August—avoid these times if you can. Prices plummet on Sunday nights.

$$ Hope Street Hotel is a class act that sets the bar for Liverpool's hotels. Located across from the Philharmonic on Hope Street (midway between the cathedrals, in a fun dining neighborhood), this stylish and contemporary hotel has 89 luxurious rooms with lots of hardwood, exposed brick, and elegant little extras. An extension, located in the former School for the Blind, has 50 additional rooms, a roof garden, a spa with a pool, and a cinema (breakfast extra—book ahead, elevator, some rooms handicap accessible, pay parking, 40 Hope Street, tel. 0151/709-3000, www.hopestreethotel.co.uk, sleep@hopestreethotel.co.uk).

$$ Hard Day's Night Hotel is ideal for Beatles pilgrims. Located in a carefully restored old building smack in the heart of the Cavern Quarter, its contemporary decor is purely Beatles, from its public spaces (lobby, lounge, bar, restaurant) to its 110 rooms, each with a different original Beatles portrait by New York artist Shannon. There's often live music in the afternoons in the lobby bar—and it's not all Beatles covers. What could have been a tacky travesty is instead tasteful, with a largely black-and-white color scheme

and subtle nods to the Fab Four (some rates include breakfast, elevator, internet-enabled TVs with music playlists, pay parking, Central Building, North John Street, tel. 0151/668-0479, www. harddaysnighthotel.com, enquiries@harddaysnighthotel.com).

$$ Sir Thomas Hotel is a centrally located hotel that was once a bank. The lobby has been redone in a trendy style, and the 39 rooms are comfortable. As windows are thin and it's a busy neighborhood, ask for a quieter room (some rates include breakfast, elevator, pay parking, 10-minute walk from station, 24 Sir Thomas Street at the corner of Victoria Street, tel. 0151/236-1366, www. thesirthomas.co.uk, reservations@thesirthomas.co.uk).

$ Aachen Guest Accommodations is a family-run hotel with 15 modern, straightforward rooms in an old Georgian townhouse. The hotel is situated on a pleasant street just uphill from the heart of downtown (includes breakfast, a few rooms have shared baths, 89 Mount Pleasant, tel. 0151/709-3477, www.aachenhotel.co.uk, aachenhotel@btconnect.com).

$ Hallmark Inn Liverpool, nearly next door in a stately old Georgian building, has tight hallways and 82 small rooms with mod decor and amenities (breakfast extra—prebook, no elevator and six floors, pay parking, 115 Mount Pleasant, tel. 0330-028-3426, www.hallmarkhotels.co.uk, liverpoolinn@hallmarkhotels. co.uk).

Other Chain Hotels: At the Albert Dock, you'll find a **Premier Inn** and **Holiday Inn Express.** Premier Inn has several other central branches, including downtown on Vernon Street and near the Liverpool ONE commercial complex on Hanover Street.

¢ Hostel: Run by the daughter of the Beatles' first manager, **International Inn Hostel** rents 100 budget beds in a former Victorian warehouse (includes sheets, all rooms have bathrooms, guest kitchen with free toast and tea/coffee available 24 hours, laundry room, game room/TV lounge, video library, 24-hour reception,

LIVERPOOL

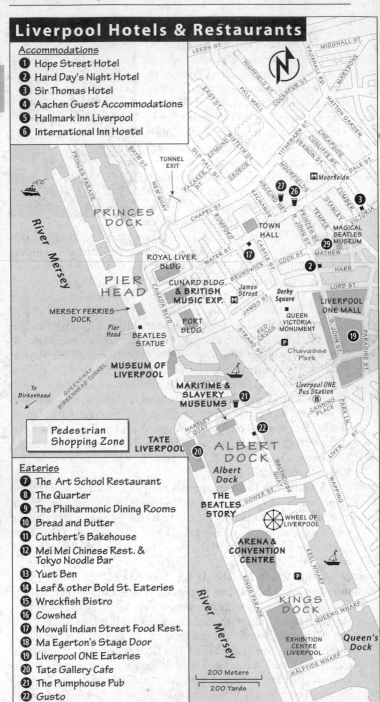

Liverpool Hotels & Restaurants

Accommodations
1. Hope Street Hotel
2. Hard Day's Night Hotel
3. Sir Thomas Hotel
4. Aachen Guest Accommodations
5. Hallmark Inn Liverpool
6. International Inn Hostel

Eateries
7. The Art School Restaurant
8. The Quarter
9. The Philharmonic Dining Rooms
10. Bread and Butter
11. Cuthbert's Bakehouse
12. Mei Mei Chinese Rest. & Tokyo Noodle Bar
13. Yuet Ben
14. Leaf & other Bold St. Eateries
15. Wreckfish Bistro
16. Cowshed
17. Mowgli Indian Street Food Rest.
18. Ma Egerton's Stage Door
19. Liverpool ONE Eateries
20. Tate Gallery Cafe
21. The Pumphouse Pub
22. Gusto

Pedestrian Shopping Zone

200 Meters
200 Yards

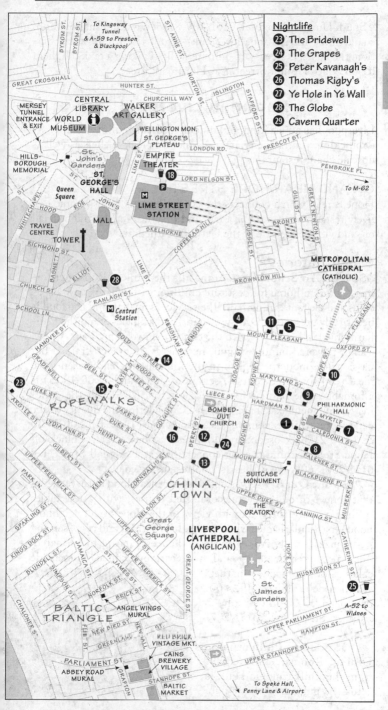

Nightlife
- 23 The Bridewell
- 24 The Grapes
- 25 Peter Kavanagh's
- 26 Thomas Rigby's
- 27 Ye Hole in Ye Wall
- 28 The Globe
- 29 Cavern Quarter

4 South Hunter Street, tel. 0151/709-8135, www.internationalinn. co.uk, info@internationalinn.co.uk). From the Lime Street Station, the hostel is an easy 15-minute walk; if taking a taxi, tell them it's on South Hunter Street near Hardman Street.

Eating in Liverpool

Liverpool has an exciting and quickly evolving culinary scene. As a rollicking, youthful city, it's a magnet for creative chefs as well as upscale chain restaurants.

ON AND NEAR HOPE STREET

Hope Street, which connects the two cathedrals, is also home to a lively restaurant scene. For a fast and practical lunch, grab a salad or sandwich at the café at the Catholic cathedral.

Classic Eateries

$$$$ The Art School Restaurant fills the Lantern Room of a former Victorian home for destitute children with what is now a spacious and elegant dining hall. The service is formal, and the food is beautifully presented. Dressy, elegant, and a block behind the Philharmonic Hall, it's a hit with the concert crowd. Chef Paul Askew, a high-powered bundle of gourmet energy, is French-trained but passionately modern English in the kitchen. The early fixed-price meal (£34 for three courses, served at lunch and 17:00-18:15) is affordable—the regular fixed-price offering (£75) and the enticing tasting menu (£95) are splurges. Considering the quality of the experience, while expensive, it's a good value (Tue-Sat 12:00-14:30 & 17:00-21:30, closed Sun-Mon, reservations smart, a block off Hope Street, behind the big concert hall at 1 Sugnall Street, tel. 0151/230-8600, www.theartschoolrestaurant.co.uk).

$$ The Quarter serves up Mediterranean food at rustic tables that sprawl through several connected houses, with a few tables spilling onto the sidewalk with views of the Hope Street neighborhood—particularly nice when sunny. It's youthful and cozy, serving pasta, pizza, and boards of meats and cheeses meant to be shared. They also offer breakfast and have carryout coffee, homemade cakes, and sandwiches in their attached deli (daily 8:00-23:00, deli open 12:00-15:00 only, 7 Falkner Street, tel. 0151/707-1965).

$$ The Philharmonic Dining Rooms, kitty-corner from the Philharmonic Hall, is actually a pub—but what a pub.

This place wins the "atmosphere award" for its old-time elegance. The bar is a work of art, and the three sitting areas on the ground floor (including the giant hall) are enticing places to tip back a pint. While primarily a drinking pub, I'd eat here for the atmosphere. The restaurant seating is upstairs, but the ambience is on the ground floor (food served daily 11:00-22:00, bar open until late, corner of Hope and Hardman streets, tel. 0151/707-2837).

$$ Bread and Butter is a cozy little restaurant serving a French-inspired menu. Look for daily specials and enjoy a cold pint in their beer garden (Tue-Sat 12:00-23:00, Sun 13:00-19:00, closed Mon, 23 Hope Street, tel. 0151/709-7612).

$$ Cuthbert's Bakehouse is a charming café and teahouse located two blocks down from the Liverpool Science Park. This is your best bet for an afternoon tea (£18 Cuthbert's classic, reserve in advance by phone). They also have an impressive range of tasty homemade cakes and sweets; check out their specialty—red velvet cake (Mon-Sat 10:00-18:00, Tue until 20:00, Sat until 19:00, Sun from 11:00, 103 Mount Pleasant, tel. 0151/709-9912).

Asian Cuisine

A few blocks southwest of Hope Street is Liverpool's thriving Chinatown neighborhood, with the world's biggest Chinese arch. Lots of enticing options dishing up Asian cuisine line up along Berry Street in front of the arch and Cornwallis Street behind it.

$$ Mei Mei Chinese Restaurant serves Cantonese to an enthusiastic local Chinese clientele. It's dressy, with a big enticing menu and a hardworking staff (daily 12:00-22:30, 9 Berry Street, tel. 0151/707-2888).

$$ Yuet Ben is one of Liverpool's most established Chinese restaurants (Wed-Sun 17:00-23:00, closed Mon-Tue, facing the arch at 1 Upper Duke Street, tel. 0151/709-5772).

$ Tokyo Noodle Bar is a cheap and simple diner featuring tasty noodle and rice dishes (Cantonese, Japanese, Malaysian, and so on) with service that's fast and furious (daily 12:00-22:45, 7 Berry Street, tel. 0151/708-6286).

ROPEWALKS

While primarily a nightlife zone, this gentrified area (between the pedestrian Liverpool ONE and the Hope Street neighborhood) also has a smattering of unique restaurants. Focus on Bold Street, lined with fun eateries.

$$ Leaf, with a wonderful energy, is my favorite on the street. Like Liverpool, it's a little bit of everything—sharing dishes, fresh bakery items, salads, vegetarian plates, soups, sandwiches, fun cocktails, and lots of tea—all driven by the simple philosophy: Where there's tea, there's hope. It's a chaotic, industrial-minimalist space with noisy acoustics. Grab a table and then order at the counter (daily 9:00-22:00, 65 Bold Street, tel. 0151/707-7747).

Other Bold Street Eateries: Along with trendy tapas, Middle Eastern, and Italian restaurants, look for these **$** places: **The Cat Café** (where you can actually munch and sip with a cuddly cat, #10 at the bottom of the street), **Johnny English** for traditional fish-and-chips (at #60), and the wildly popular **Mowgli Indian Street Food** (at #69 next to Leaf, also downtown location).

$$$ Wreckfish Bistro is dynamic and friendly with an open kitchen and a small, woody, and romantic dining area serving modern British cuisine. Despite its name, the menu is not particularly fishy. The food, while unpretentious, is beautiful in its fresh simplicity. The meals will entice you to come back—and back (daily 12:00-14:30 & 18:00-22:00, reservations smart, corner of Slater and Seel streets, tel. 0151/707-1960, www.wreckfish.co).

$$ Cowshed does char-grilled steaks and ice-cold cocktails in a rustic townhouse. You can eat at the bar or at a table in an inviting room in back. The service is refreshingly efficient (Tue-Thu 17:00-22:00, Fri until 22:30, Sat 12:00-22:30, Sun 12:00-22:00, 104 Seel Street, tel. 0151/708-7580).

DOWNTOWN

$ Mowgli Indian Street Food Restaurant, a phenom in town, hustles delicious traditional Indian dishes on little tin plates. Eat family-style, enjoying two or three plates per person. While it's trendy and set in an elegant location across from Town Hall, the prices are great—and the service is fun (daily 12:00-22:00, 3 Water Street, tel. 0151/236-6366). They have a second location in the Ropewalks District.

$ Ma Egerton's Stage Door is an enjoyable pub tucked away next to Lime Street Station. In addition to good ales, this place also serves well-priced pizzas and a tasty homemade beef scouse (the traditional stew brought to Liverpool by Norwegians, known as *lapskaus* in Norway). With its proximity to the Empire Theatre's stage door, the pub has been frequented by artists such as Tom Jones, Frank Sinatra, the Rolling Stones, and, of course, the Beatles (daily 11:00-late, 9 Pudsey Street, tel. 0151/345-3525).

Liverpool ONE: This huge modern shopping center, right in the heart of town, is filled with British chain restaurants. The upper

Leisure Terrace has a row of some popular chains, all with outdoor seating. If you want to dine on predictable mass-produced food, you'll have a wide selection here.

AT THE ALBERT DOCK

The eateries at the Albert Dock aren't high cuisine, but they're handy to your sightseeing. A slew of trendy restaurants come alive with club energy at night, but are sedate and pleasant in the afternoon and early evening. For lunch near the sights, consider the **$ Tate Gallery** café (daily 10:00-16:30). **$ The Pumphouse Pub,** with the tall brick chimney overlooking Canning Dock at the north edge of Albert Dock, is a touristy place for pub grub with a noisy interior and great harborside tables outside (£8 lunch deals, daily 11:00-21:00). **$$ Gusto** is a chain restaurant with a fancy and spacious interior, serving a wide selection of pasta, pizzas, steaks, and fish. Best seats on a warm day are on the back side overlooking the Albert Dock (Mon-Fri 12:00-23:00, Sat 10:00-23:30, Sun 10:00-23:00, Edward Pavilion).

Liverpool Connections

BY TRAIN

Note that many connections from Liverpool transfer at the Wigan North Western Station, which is on a major north-south train line.

From Liverpool by Train to: Blackpool (4-5/day direct, 1.5 hours; hourly with change in Wigan and/or Preston), **Keswick/Lake District** (train to Penrith—2/hour with change in Wigan or Lancaster, 2.5 hours; then bus to Keswick), **York** (hourly direct, 2 hours), **Edinburgh** (at least 2/hour, 4 hours, most change in Preston, Wigan, or York), **Glasgow** (1-2/hour, 4 hours, change in Preston and possibly elsewhere), **London**'s Euston Station (3/hour, 2.5 hours, more with changes), **Crewe** (3/hour, 45 minutes), **Chester** (4/hour, 45 minutes). **Train info:** Tel. 0345-748-4950, www.nationalrail.co.uk.

BY FERRY

By Ferry to Dublin, Republic of Ireland: P&O Irish Sea Ferries runs a car ferry only—no foot passengers (up to 5/day, 8.5-hour trip, prices vary widely—roughly £150 for car and 2 passengers, overnight ferry includes berth and meals—roughly £290, 20-minute drive north of the city center at Liverpool Freeport—Gladstone dock, check in 1-2 hours before departure, tel. 01304/448-888, www.poferries.com). Those without cars can take a ferry to Dublin via the Isle of Man (runs mid-June-Aug, www.steam-packet.com), or ride the train to North Wales and catch the Dublin ferry from Holyhead (www.stenaline.co.uk).

By Ferry to Belfast, Northern Ireland: Ferries sail from nearby Birkenhead roughly twice a day (8.5 hours, fares vary widely, tel. 0344-770-7070, www.stenaline.co.uk). Birkenhead's dock is a 15-minute walk from Hamilton Square Station on Merseyrail's Wirral Line.

ROUTE TIPS FOR DRIVERS

Leaving Liverpool, drive north along the waterfront, following signs to the M-58 (Preston). Once on the M-58 (and not before), follow signs to the M-6, and then the M-55 into Blackpool.

BLACKPOOL

Blackpool is Britain's tacky, laid-back under-belly. The private domain of its working class, the town is a faded and sticky mix of Coney Island, Las Vegas, and Denny's. Some people love it...others hate it. But it is, without a doubt, a spectacle. And it's real.

Blackpool grew up in the 1800s with the Industrial Revolution. Back then, it was a working-class vacation resort; entire mill towns would close down and take a two-week break here. Workers came to drink in the fresh air and, literally, the seawater (they figured it was healthy).

By the 1860s, little Blackpool (population 4,000) entertained 200,000 visitors a year. In the old days, conditioned by a world without central heating, people happily sat on Blackpool's sand even if the weather was cold and windy. Long piers were built to hold amusements and dance pavilions. From the ends of the jetties, excursion steamers took holiday-goers to North Wales and the Isle of Man.

These days Blackpool's blustery and cold beaches are generally empty. By the 1960s, cheap package tours were enticing working people to sunny and hot vacation spots outside England. Blackpool, overbuilt with too many hotels, began attracting low-end tourism ("stag" and "hen"—bachelor and bachelorette—parties), changing the character of the town. Nowadays, there are two Blackpools: the daytime Blackpool of kids riding roller coasters and grannies tucking into early-bird specials, and the drunken, debauched, late-night Blackpool of glass dance-floor clubs and bars. Even so, Blackpool remains an accessible and affordable fun zone for north Englanders—for them, the town is part of their DNA.

Be warned: Some will get to Blackpool and wonder, "Why

did Rick send me *here?*" Most Americans don't even consider a stop in Blackpool. Many won't like it. It's an ears-pierced-while-you-wait, tipsy-toupee kind of place. Huge arcade halls advertise free toilets and broadcast bingo numbers into the streets; the wind machine under a wax Marilyn Monroe blows at a steady gale; and the smell of fries, tobacco, and sugar is everywhere. Tacky, yes. Lowbrow, OK. More than a little run-down in parts, sure. If you're before or beyond kids, and not into kitsch and greasy spoons, skip it. But if you have kids, they'll enjoy Blackpool (hey, it's cheaper than Disneyland). And for those who are into nightlife, this town delivers. If you believe (as I do) that an itinerary should feature as many different facets of a culture as possible, consider a stop here. Blackpool is as English as the Queen—and considerably more fun.

PLANNING YOUR TIME

Ideally, get to Blackpool around lunchtime for an afternoon and evening of making the scene. Long-time fans of the city say the secret of Blackpool is to create family memories (like Disneyland does for Americans). It's a place to do something; dance, scream down a roller coaster, take in a show or amusement, succumb to a fortune-teller. A good overall plan is to ride the tram down to the Pleasure Beach amusement park, and then walk back along the waterfront to Blackpool Tower and the North Pier, dipping into whatever fun zones appeal. To find a more pristine beach, just keep walking north.

The evening light here is great, with the sun setting over the sea. Walk out along the peaceful North Pier at twilight. During the Blackpool Illuminations festival, much of the waterfront is decorated with lights, drawing crowds in fall, particularly on weekends (Sept through early Nov).

Blackpool is easy by car or train. Speed demons with a car can treat it as a midday break (it's just off the M-6, on the M-55) and continue north. If the weather's great and you love nature, the lakes are just two hours north. A visit to Blackpool sharpens the wonders of Windermere.

Orientation to Blackpool

Everything clusters along the Promenade, a tacky, glittering, six-mile-long, beachfront good-time strip mall punctuated by three

fun-filled piers reaching out into the sea. The Pleasure Beach rides are near the South Pier. Jutting up near the North Pier is Blackpool's stubby Eiffel-type tower. The most interesting shops, eateries, and theaters are inland from the North Pier. For a break from glitz, walk north along the Promenade beyond the commercial zone, following the sandy beach where a residential neighborhood stretches for miles. When you've had enough, just hop on the tram or a bus for a quick ride back.

TOURIST INFORMATION

The TI is in a building on the Promenade, across from Blackpool Tower (Mon-Sat 9:00-17:00, Sun 10:00-16:00; tel. 01253/478-222; www.visitblackpool.com). The free *Events Programme* lists local happenings; the TI staff can book shows and sells tickets to many of Blackpool's attractions—including Blackpool Tower and its various sights, Sandcastle Waterpark, and Madame Tussauds—often at a significant discount. If you're here with kids and going to the amusement parks, you may save money with the various combo-tickets; consider the **Resort Pass** (www.blackpoolresortpass.com) or the **Big Ticket** (www.theblackpooltower.com).

ARRIVAL IN BLACKPOOL

By Train: The main train station (Blackpool North) is three blocks from the town center. From the station, Talbot Road leads to the North Pier and the Promenade.

By Car: The motorway funnels you down Yeadon Way into a giant parking zone. Day-trippers can park here or head for one of the huge pay garages. If you're spending the night, my recommended accommodations are mostly north of the center, on the Promenade, and have easy parking.

HELPFUL HINTS

Markets: At the indoor **Abingdon Street Market,** vendors sell baked goods, fruit, bras, jewelry, eggs, and more (Mon-Sat 9:00-17:00, closed Sun).

Baggage Storage: Queen's Café across from the train station offers a left-luggage service (Wed-Mon 9:00-19:00, closed Tue,

24 High Street, tel. 01253/447-676). If that doesn't work, there's a checked luggage service at the bus station (National Express office at the corner of New Bonny Street and Central Drive).

Car Rental: If you decide to tour the Lake District by car, you'll find plenty of rental agencies in Blackpool, such as **Avis** (closed Sat afternoon and Sun, at the airport—just south of the South Pier, tel. 01253/209-188).

GETTING AROUND BLACKPOOL

By Public Transportation: Trams trundle up and down the waterfront, connecting all the sights. This electric tramway—the first in Europe—dates from 1885 (about £2/ride depending on length of trip, pay conductor, about 4/hour). You can purchase a day pass that covers both trams and buses (£5.50 from driver).

Many **buses** also run along the Promenade (similar prices to tram, buy on board, covered by day pass). Buses that run south to St. Annes and Lytham depart from Market Street, in front of the BHS store; buses going north toward Cleveleys leave from Clifton Street. For bus information, visit the Blackpool Transport office on Market Street (Mon-Sat 8:30-17:00, closed Sun, tel. 01253/473-001, www.blackpooltransport.com).

By Taxi: Cabs are easy to snare in Blackpool, and three to five people travel cheaper in a taxi than by tram. Hotels can get you a taxi by phone within a few minutes (no extra charge).

Sights in Blackpool

▲▲People-Watching

Blackpool's top sight is its people. You'll see England here as nowhere else. Grab someone's hand and a big baton of "rock" (hard candy), and stroll. Grown men walk around with huge teddy bears looking for places to play "bowlingo," a short-lane version of bowling. "Gypsy" psychics with celebrity photos in their windows promise to reveal your future. Kids ride donkeys on the beach. Ponder the thought of actually retiring here and spending your last years, day after day, wearing plaid pants and a bad toupee, surrounded by Blackpool. This place puts people in a talkative mood. Start up conversations. Ask a young couple on the street, "What's there to do here?" Find someone to explain the difference between tea and supper. Back at your hotel, join in the chat sessions in the lounge.

The Town and the Promenade

Stretching from the North Pier to Blackpool Tower, the **old town center** fills the area a few blocks inland from the beach. Wander this zone and do the promenade, and that's pretty much Blackpool. The streets feel a bit run-down and past their prime. The challenge is to grab snippets of the days when this was a thriving resort.

BLACKPOOL

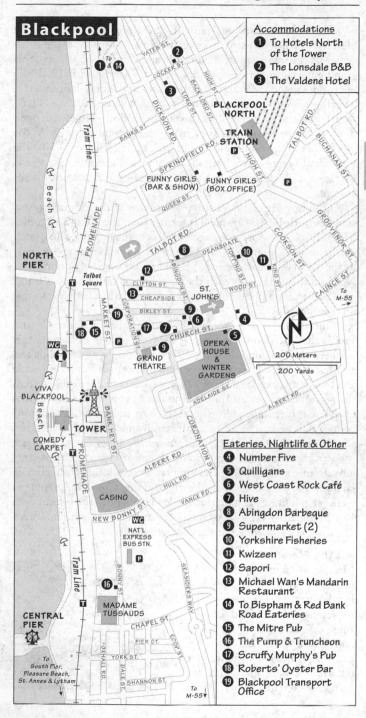

Blackpool

Accommodations
1. To Hotels North of the Tower
2. The Lonsdale B&B
3. The Valdene Hotel

YATES ST.
COCKER ST.
BACK LORD ST.
HIGH ST.
LORD ST.
DICKSON RD.
BANKS ST.
TALBOT RD.
BUCHANAN ST.

BLACKPOOL NORTH TRAIN STATION

SPRINGFIELD RD.
GROSVENOR ST.
CAUNCE ST.

FUNNY GIRLS (BAR & SHOW)
FUNNY GIRLS (BOX OFFICE)

QUEEN ST.

To M-55

TALBOT RD.
DEANSGATE
TOPPING ST.
WOOD ST.
KING ST.
COOKSON ST.

Talbot Square

CLIFTON ST.
CHEAPSIDE
BIRLEY ST.
ABINGDON ST.
CORPORATION ST.
CHURCH ST.

ST. JOHN'S

NORTH PIER

PROMENADE

Beach

Tram Line

Market St.

GRAND THEATRE

OPERA HOUSE & WINTER GARDENS

ADELAIDE ST.

ALBERT RD.

200 Meters
200 Yards

VIVA BLACKPOOL

TOWER

BANK HEY ST.

CORONATION ST.

COMEDY CARPET

ALBERT RD.
HULL RD.
VANCE RD.

CASINO

NEW BONNY ST.

NAT'L EXPRESS BUS STN.

BONNY ST.

SEASIDERS WAY

MADAME TUSSAUDS

CHAPEL ST.
PIER ST.
FOXHALL RD.
YORK ST.
DALE ST.
SHANNON ST.

CENTRAL PIER

To South Pier, Pleasure Beach, St. Annes & Lytham

To M-55

Eateries, Nightlife & Other
4. Number Five
5. Quilligans
6. West Coast Rock Café
7. Hive
8. Abingdon Barbeque
9. Supermarket (2)
10. Yorkshire Fisheries
11. Kwizeen
12. Sapori
13. Michael Wan's Mandarin Restaurant
14. To Bispham & Red Bank Road Eateries
15. The Mitre Pub
16. The Pump & Truncheon
17. Scruffy Murphy's Pub
18. Roberts' Oyster Bar
19. Blackpool Transport Office

The **Winter Gardens,** built in 1878, provided shelter when blustery weather drove visitors off the beach. Buried in the town center (at the intersection of Adelaide and Coronation streets), this grand entertainment complex includes a Victorian floral hall, an opera house, and cafés and bars that cater to the gray-haired set.

The **seaside promenade** has a certain draw. Classic "Heritage Trams" (some single deck, some double deck, some with open tops) stoke the nostalgia. They make the two-mile trip from the North Pier to the South Pier—and back again (3/hour, £3.50). The traditional horse-drawn wagons are now sugary pink Cinderella carriages, as little girls want to be princesses and demand drives change.

One tiny bit of the century-old charm of the original resort survives in **Roberts' Oyster Bar** (across from the TI at 90 Promenade). This little spot has served strollers in the mood for an oyster, whelk, or winkle since 1876. (Notice the actual building—it must be the oldest on the waterfront.) Explore your world of options with Neil and then fill a tub with the sampling of your choice. Or just grab a £5 seafood platter to take away or munch at a little view table on the sidewalk.

The stretch of the promenade from the Tower to the Central Pier is the "Golden Mile." While far from golden or a mile, this has been the fun zone since the 1970s. The origin of the shops and amusements here goes back to a day when unseemly salespeople and hustlers worked the beach. They were eventually expelled from the seafront and set up shop in the front yards of the hotels that once lined the promenade. The hotels have moved on, but the ancestors of those first tacky souvenir stands and amusements survive.

In front of the Tower, the promenade bulges out. This is a modern shoring-up of the beachfront embankment, part of Britain's defense system to fight a rising sea level resulting from climate change. The pavement hosts the entertaining **Comedy Carpet**—a walk-on, public-art installation made in homage to the hundreds of British comedians who've worked here at Blackpool, with hundreds of their jokes embedded in the concrete surface.

▲▲The Piers

Blackpool's famous piers were originally built for Victorian landlubbers who wanted to go to sea but were afraid of getting seasick. Each of the three amusement piers has its own personality and is a joy to wander (all are free and open with demand Easter-early Nov). Rides

operate on a token system (buy tokens from kiosks along the pier). Each pier has its own family-friendly bar, where kids are welcome all the time (typically open from about 12:00 until 17:00 or 18:00, but much later—about 23:00—in summer and on weekends).

The **North Pier** is my favorite. The oldest and longest of the piers, this was the birthplace of the resort in the 1860s. For 150 years (until just a few years ago), the pier charged admission. As you enter, on the left side, a series of information panels shows and tells the pier's interesting story. Stroll the sedate planked deck, which rests on the original cast-iron supports. As you walk, re-

member that Victorian resort-going was all about seeing and being seen. This is the most traditional and refreshingly uncluttered of the piers, and it's particularly nice at twilight. You can dance to piped-in early English rock as you make the scene. The Carousel Bar at the end has a free kids' DJ nightly in summer (parents drink beer while the kids bunny-hop and boogie). An old-time organist plays the Wurlitzer daily in the beer garden, with lounge chairs sheltered from the wind and aimed where the sun should be. At the very tip is a big theater offering corny kids' shows.

The **Central Pier,** with something for everyone, is lots of fun. Ride its Ferris wheel for the best view in Blackpool (rich photography at twilight; get the operator to spin you as you bottom out). The Family Bar at the end of the pier is a hit with kids.

The **South Pier** is the rollicking pier, with classic carnival rides, such as bumper cars and carousels. The two pricey adventure rides—Skycoaster and Skyscreamer—treat riders like rocks in a giant slingshot. This pier is also home to the Laughing Donkey Family Bar.

From the far end of any pier, look out at the horizon to see the natural-gas drilling platforms in the Irish Sea. In the distance, off the North Shore, castaway wind turbines capture energy.

▲Blackpool Tower

This mini Eiffel Tower, an 1894 vertical fun center, is the symbol of Blackpool. While you can roam around several floors of its core for free, its three main attractions—the view from the top, the circus, and the ballroom—charge admission. Other amusements include dinosaur minigolf (£5) and a view café on level 5.

Cost and Hours: Tickets are required to enter the attractions; see website for complete pricing options, kid and family tickets available, cheaper if you buy online or at TI. Open daily from 10:00, closing times vary per attraction and with the season, tel. 01253/622-242, www.theblackpooltower.com.

Visiting the Tower: An elevator zips up to the 518-foot-high **Blackpool Tower Eye** (£16). From here you can stroll across the "SkyWalk" glass floor and enjoy a smashing view, especially at sunset, and watch a "4-D" movie (3-D plus other startling effects).

The **Blackpool Tower Circus** is what you would expect but with no animals. There are generally several two-hour shows daily except Fridays, when the circus is closed (adults-£16.50, kids-£11.50, shows run Easter through Oct).

The **Blackpool Tower Ballroom** is an elegant spectacle with live organ music where golden oldies dance to golden oldies all day (organist plays daily 10:30-16:30). While you can watch from the balcony (£4), the real experience is to be on the old ballroom floor, dancing (£10). Seniors are happy to coach you in the WWII-era moves. The ballroom pub, serving basic grub, is a memorable place for lunch.

Madame Tussauds Blackpool

Just south of the Blackpool Tower, this sister to the famous waxworks in London features eerily realistic wax copies of famous people with whom you can pose for a hundred goofy photos. While the London Tussauds focuses on international stars, the one in Blackpool (understanding its target audience) focuses on British celebs: The average American likely won't be too excited by the figure of superstar competitive dart-thrower Phil Taylor.

Cost and Hours: £18, daily 10:00-17:00, near the Central Pier on the Promenade, tel. 0871-282-9200, www.madametussauds.com.

▲Pleasure Beach Amusement Park

Rated ▲▲▲ for roller-coaster enthusiasts, this 42-acre park attracts nearly six million visitors annually and is littered with rides galore, ice and illusion shows, and varied amusements. The Nickelodeon Land area features rides and characters tied into the popular children's TV network. Many rides are tame enough for the under-10 set, but the top few offer some of the best thrills in Europe: the Big One (with a

peak of 235 feet and reaching 85 mph, it's one of the world's fast-est, highest, and steepest roller coasters), the Infusion (a twisty, loopy speed rush), and the Ice Blast (which rockets you straight up before you bungee down). Also memorable is the Steeplechase—carousel horses stampeding down a roller-coaster track (a dream come true for *Mary Poppins* fans). The Revolution speeds you over a steep drop and upside down in a loop, then does it again back-ward, while the Valhalla ride zips you on a Viking boat in watery darkness past scary Nordic things like lutefisk. With two 80-foot drops and lots of hype, first you're scared, then you're soaked, and—finally—you're just glad you survived. Wallace and Gromit's Thrill-O-Matic zips you through some of the duo's most iconic ad-ventures. The park also offers several old wooden-framed rides full of historic charm—but brittle travelers will want to consider their necks and backs.

Cost: £10 admission includes a few attractions, then you can pay individually for rides with £1 tickets (2-15 tickets per ride). For unlimited rides, get a wristband (adults-£39, kids-£33, family ticket available, cheaper if purchased in advance online, covered by Resort Pass.

Hours: Daily Easter-early Nov, also open some weekends in Nov and Feb-Easter; opens at about 10:00 and closes as early as 17:00 or as late as 20:00 (and possibly later) depending on season, weather, and demand—check website; closed entirely Dec-Jan, tel. 0871-222-1234, www.blackpoolpleasurebeach.com.

Avoiding Lines: The park can be jam-packed in summer (July-Aug) and on school holidays; during these times, try to arrive early (ticket office opens at 9:30). If lines are horrendous, consider a Speedy Pass, which alerts you when it's your turn to board a ride—without having to wait in line (£15, more expensive VIP versions available, www.speedypassmobile.com).

Getting There: Pleasure Beach is on Ocean Boulevard, op-posite the South Pier. It's about two miles (a 45-minute walk) south of the North Pier, so consider taking the tram; there's a stop just outside the park entrance.

Sandcastle Waterpark

This popular indoor attraction, across the street from Pleasure Beach, has a big pool, long slides, a wave machine, and water, water, everywhere, at a constant temperature of 84 degrees. Fea-turing the longest tube waterslide in the world (called "Master Blaster"), this is a place where most kids could easily spend a day. It's not so bad for parents, either—thanks to the Sea Breeze Spa, which has a sauna, steam room, heated loungers, and other ameni-ties (extra fee applies).

Cost and Hours: Basic adult admission-£17, kids under age

12-£13.25; pay £6.75 extra for Hyperzone area with the best rides; family passes and discount tickets available online and at TI; daily April-Oct—hours vary with day and season—best to check your dates online, open weekends only Jan-March, closed or limited hours Nov-Dec; last admission one hour before closing, tel. 01253/343-602, www.sandcastle-waterpark.co.uk.

Blackpool Illuminations

Blackpool was the first town in England to "go electric" in 1879. Now, every fall, from September through early November, Blackpool stretches its tourist season by illuminating its six miles of waterfront with countless lights, all blinking and twinkling. People here speak with wonder about these lights. For many, it's a ritual that has been part of their family story for generations. The American in me kept saying, "I've seen bigger, and I've seen better," but I stuffed his mouth with cotton candy and just had some simple fun like everyone else on my specially decorated tram. If you're not here for the actual Illuminations season, you'll see the promenade still strung with countless light bulbs and can imagine the spectacle (for details, see www.visitblackpool.com).

St. Annes-on-Sea and Lytham

Had enough greasy food and flashing lights? The dual seaside villages of St. Annes and Lytham are an easy bus ride south of Blackpool and offer a welcome break (buses #7 and #11 run from Market Street in front of the BHS store every 15 minutes, 30 minutes to St. Annes, 45 minutes to Lytham, covered by the all-day tram/bus pass).

Get off at St. Annes Square, which is the first stop after the bus turns left following the long, dune-side straightaway. The town's promenade and the end of the simple Victorian pier (once you pass the noisy game arcade) feel like a breath of sanity. The broad sand beach is perfect for flying a kite, building a sandcastle, or watching happy dogs play in the surf. Consider strolling the beach northward all the way to the southern edge of the Promenade (about three miles—you can see the Pleasure Beach roller coasters from here); if you max out on sand and sea before that, simply cross the dunes back to the seaside road and find the nearest bus stop.

Little Lytham, a bit farther south (get off at Lytham Square), is best known for the Royal Lytham and St. Annes Golf Club—the site of several British Open tournaments. On the seafront, a seasonal museum at the Lytham Windmill explores the local history of mills and milling (seasonal TI on-site).

Nightlife in Blackpool

▲Live Theater in Blackpool

Blackpool always has a few razzle-dazzle music, dancing girl, racy humor, magic, and tumbling shows. Box offices around town can give you a rundown on what's available (£10-50 tickets). Your hotel has the latest. Blackpool is also a staging ground for some London West End plays—giving you a chance to enjoy a show for a fraction of the London cost.

You might try the **Opera House** at the Winter Gardens for musicals (tel. 01253/625-252, www.wintergardensblackpool.co.uk) and the **Grand Theatre,** a treasure built in 1894, for drama, ballet, and musicals (£15-40, tel. 01253/290-190, www.blackpoolgrand.co.uk). Both are on Church Street, a couple of blocks behind the Blackpool Tower. For the latest in evening entertainment, see the window displays at the TI on the Promenade or check VisitBlackpool.com.

Viva Blackpool is a newer venue with musicals and comedy shows alternating nightly at 19:30. Expect tribute shows to the Beatles, ABBA, or soul music. It's a very English scene, with cabaret seating for up to 600 (£17-£24, drinks and meals extra, on the Promenade just north of the Tower at 3 Church Street, tel. 01253/297-297, www.vivablackpool.com).

▲▲Funny Girls

Funny Girls puts on a "glam bam thank you ma'am" burlesque-in-drag show that delights footballers and grannies alike most

nights from 20:00 to 23:30 (with breaks and DJ music). A troupe of a dozen or so gorgeous guys go through an entire wardrobe, putting on skits and dances that range from the Charleston to Beyoncé to a very vampy *Sound of Music.* Between songs, the high-heeled MC entertains.

Get your drinks at the bar... unless the performers are dancing on it. The show, while racy, is not raunchy. The music is very loud. The crowd is young, old, straight, gay, very down-to-earth, and fun-loving. A weeknight is both a less expensive and less crushed experience; Fridays and Saturdays are jammed. While the area up front can be a mosh pit, there are more sedate tables in back, where service comes with a vampish smile. If you want to experience the show without standing, immersed in a bar crowd, pay extra to sit at a table (4- to 6-person shared tables, reservations smart Fri-Sat).

Getting Tickets: Admission is charged according to whether

BLACKPOOL

you're sitting or standing (£6-10 to stand, £15-26 to sit, dinner with the show from 19:00 for £25-35, price depends on day of the week, no shows Mon). Getting dinner in the adjacent restaurant before the show runs about £17 (dinner reservations required a couple of days in advance). You must be 18 to enter, and standing-room tickets are usually available at the door (doors open at 19:00, 5 Dickson Road). To reserve in advance, go online, buy from the TI, call 01253/649-194, or visit the box office (44 Queen Street, find door next to the Flying Handbag and go up the stairs—open Mon-Fri 9:30-17:30, closed Sat-Sun, www.funnygirlsshow.co.uk).

Other Nightspots
More than 100 years old, **The Mitre** pub serves beer in a cozy, truly rare, old-time Blackpool ambience. Drop in any time to survey the fun photos of old Blackpool and for the great people scene (real ales and cheap meals, daily 11:00-24:00, 3 West Street, tel. 01253/623-718). Other pubs in the center that are more traditional than rowdy (though admittedly touristy) are **The Pump and Truncheon** on Bonny Street behind Madame Tussauds (real ales and basic pub grub with exposed brick and a billiards table, tel. 01253/624-099), and **Scruffy Murphy's** Irish pub on Corporation Street (live music most weekends, tel. 01253/624-538).

Blackpool's clubs and discos are cheap, with live bands and an interesting crowd (nightly 22:00-late). With all the stag and hen parties, the late-night streets can be clotted with rude rowdies on Fridays and Saturdays.

Sleeping in Blackpool

Blackpool's 140,000 people provide 120,000 beds in 3,500 mostly dumpy, cheap, nondescript hotels and B&Bs. Remember, this town's in the business of accommodating the people who can't afford to go to Spain. Empty beds abound except summer weekends and from September through early November (during Illuminations, when everyone bumps up prices). With the huge number of hotels in town, prices get really soft off-season.

NORTH OF THE TOWER
These listings are on or near the waterfront in the quiet "posh end," a mile or two north of Blackpool Tower, with easy parking and access to the center by tram or bus. The first two listings have classy extras you wouldn't expect in Blackpool and aren't far from the North Pier. The last two are B&Bs with welcoming owners and lots of stairs, a short tram ride or approximately 35-minute walk from the North Pier.

$$$ **The Imperial Hotel** would like to brag that it's where

the Queen would stay in Blackpool. (They boast that every prime minister since they opened in 1867 has visited their #10 Bar.) With 180 rooms, it's the kind of grand, monumental hotel they don't make anymore, with a dark-paneled Old World elegance (some rates include breakfast, ask about dinner specials for guests, elevator, gym, spa, pool, pay parking, tram stop: Wilton Parade, North Promenade, tel. 01253/623-971, www.imperialhotelblackpool. co.uk, reception@imperialhotelblackpool.co.uk).

$$$ Grand Hotel Blackpool is good if you need a splurge, since it used to be a Hilton. Yes, I know, staying at a Hilton in Blackpool is like wearing a tux to eat a corndog. But this is a grand 274-room place with lots of views, a pool, sauna, gym, and comfortable rooms (breakfast extra, pay parking, tram stop: Wilton Parade, North Promenade, www.britanniahotels.com).

$$ The Fossil Tree Hotel has a mod Marriot vibe with a big welcoming breakfast room and nine spacious rooms with comfortable beds and some sea views. If you don't mind the stairs, ask for a top-floor room, which features great views over the beach and sea (no children, free parking, tram stop: Lowther Avenue, 30 yards north of hotel, 1.5 miles north of tower across from a peaceful stretch of beach, 100 Queens Promenade, North Shore, tel. 01253/351-599, https://fossiltree.co.uk, info@fossiltree.co.uk).

$ Beechcliffe Private Hotel has eight clean rooms run by friendly Lorraine and Bryan. The rooms are tight and simple, but this place has a homey touch—and since Bryan moved from IT to B&B, the Wi-Fi is speedy and reliable (no children, free parking, tram stop: Cabin—turn left from tram stop, then right at Shaftesbury Avenue, and walk a block away from the beach; 16 Shaftesbury Avenue, North Shore, tel. 01253/353-075, https:// thebeechcliffe.co.uk, info@thebeechcliffe.co.uk).

NEAR THE TRAIN STATION

These hotels are located on quiet Cocker Street, in a handy, if rough, neighborhood just a few short blocks from the train station. These family-run hotels cater to couples and families rather than to revelers. To reach them by tram, get off at the Pleasant Street stop, head right along the promenade (toward the tower), then turn left on Cocker Street.

$ The Lonsdale B&B offers four rooms in an oasis of peace behind a lush front porch garden. The plush lounge—with Edwardian paintings, furnishings, and a grand piano—takes you to another era. Steve has managed the place for 30 years, and his pride of ownership shows (2-night minimum on weekends, free parking, 25 Cocker Street—at the corner with Lord Street, tel. 01253/621-628, lonsdalehotel@hotmail.co.uk). His "Royal Edwardian Suite" is truly palatial.

$ The Valdene Hotel, with a small brick terrace facing the street, rents 10 slightly scruffy rooms above its generous lounge. This is about your cheapest option in Blackpool, but the rooms are tight (family room, 16 Cocker Street, tel. 01253/291-080, www.valdenehotelblackpool.com, valdenehotel@aol.com, Laura and Simon).

Eating in Blackpool

I wouldn't hope for great food in Blackpool. Generally, food in the Tower and along the Promenade is terrible. But if you explore the streets in the real town center, a few blocks up from the Promenade, you'll find some decent options.

NEAR ST. JOHN'S CHURCH

The pedestrianized area around St. John's Church is fronted by several popular eateries. Trendy cafés such as **$ Number Five** line the top of the square (open only until about 17:00). To fill the tank, head to **$ Quilligans,** a local favorite, across from the church. This kitschy, retro Blackpool diner suits the city's lowbrow aesthetic perfectly, with huge portions of comfort food (daily 9:00-18:00, tel. 01253/293-894). At the bottom of the square, **$ West Coast Rock Café** is popular with teens for its big portions and cheap prices. The **$ Hive** coffee shop is popular with locals for its soups, sandwiches, salads, and bakery items (daily 8:00-20:00, 80 Church Street, tel. 01253/296-686).

Carryout Options near St. John's Church: These places are good options for takeaway food; you can sit on a bench outside St. John's, or—better yet—head for the beach. **$ Abingdon Barbeque,** with its expansive deli counter, is mobbed with hungry locals at lunch, munching on cheap roasted chicken and meat pies (Mon-Sat 7:00-17:00, Sun 10:00-16:00 July-Dec only, takeaway only, 44 Abingdon Street, tel. 01253/621-817). **Marks & Spencer** has a big supermarket in its basement (Mon-Sat 8:00-18:00, Sun 10:30-16:30, just south of St. John's at 49 Church Street, tel. 01253/623-831). A **Co-op** supermarket is at the corner of Birley and Abingdon streets (daily 7:00-22:00).

TOPPING STREET AND NEARBY

This somewhat dingy street sits about halfway between the train station and the Promenade. But its lack of glitz helps keep some of the tourists away, making this a relatively local-feeling strip. Besides the listings below, your options here include a pair of Thai restaurants, two pubs with great old-fashioned ambience and passable food (The Washington and Churchills), and an Italian joint.

$ Yorkshire Fisheries is the locals' choice for fish-and-chips (better quality than the greasy joints on the Promenade). Eat in on the restaurant side, or order for takeaway from the counter next door (daily from 12:00, last order at 19:00, 18:00 on Sun, 16 Topping Street, tel. 01253/627-739).

$$ Kwizeen, located a block up from Topping Street, is a white-tablecloth bistro that serves Mediterranean and modern English dishes with a focus on locally sourced and creatively prepared food—a rarity in Blackpool (two- and three-course early-bird specials; open Mon-Fri 11:45-13:45 & 18:00-21:00, Sat 18:00-21:00, closed Sun; 47 King Street, tel. 01253/290-045, www.kwizeenrestaurant.co.uk).

CLIFTON STREET
Stretching up from the Promenade and the TI, this street has a few ethnic offerings, including Italian, Indian, and Chinese.

$$ Sapori offers good Italian food in a sophisticated atmosphere that makes you forget that the tackiness of Blackpool is just outside the front door (daily 17:00-23:00, 36 Clifton Street, tel. 01253/627-440).

$$ Michael Wan's Mandarin Restaurant is a local fixture that's been providing Blackpool with authentic Chinese cuisine since 1961 (Mon-Sat 12:00-14:00 & 17:30-23:00, Sun 17:30-22:30, 27 Clifton Street, tel. 01253/622-687).

IN THE NORTH END
If you're staying at the hotels at the north end of the Promenade and don't want to venture into the rowdy downtown for dinner, locals recommend riding the tram north to Bispham. From here, Red Bank Road has several acceptable eateries including Indian, Italian, fish-and-chips, and steakhouse choices. It's not high cuisine—but it's relatively convenient. The basic diner-style **$ Bispham Kitchen** has stick-to-your-ribs English comfort food, including good fish-and-chips (daily 8:30-20:30, open later late July-early Nov, at #14, tel. 01253/359-150).

Blackpool Connections

BY TRAIN
If you're heading to (or from) Blackpool by train, you'll usually need to transfer at **Preston** (4/hour, 25 minutes). The following trains leave from Blackpool's main (north) station.

From Blackpool to: Liverpool (4-5 direct, 1.5 hours, more with transfers), **Keswick/Lake District** (nearly hourly, allow 3 hours total for journey: 2-hour train to Penrith with transfer in Preston, then bus to Keswick; alternatively, you could take the train to Windermere—every 1-2 hours with a change in Preston and sometimes also Oxenholme, 2 hours—and ride the bus from there to Keswick), **Conwy** in North Wales (roughly hourly, 3 hours, 2-3 transfers), **York** (hourly direct, 3 hours, more with change in Manchester), **London**'s Euston Station (hourly, 3 hours, transfer in Preston), Telford near **Ironbridge Gorge** (hourly, 2.5 hours, 2 transfers). Train info: Tel. 0345-748-4950, www.nationalrail.co.uk.

ROUTE TIPS FOR DRIVERS

Leaving Blackpool to go anywhere, follow signs to the M-55, which starts at Blackpool and zips you to the M-6 (for points north or south).

THE LAKE DISTRICT

*Keswick and the North Lake District • Ullswater Lake •
South Lake District*

The Lake District is nature's lush green playground. Here, William Wordsworth's poems still shiver in trees and ripple on ponds. Nature rules this pristine land, and humanity keeps a wide-eyed but low profile. Relax, recharge, take a cruise or a hike, and maybe even write a poem. Renew your poetic license at Wordsworth's famous Dove Cottage.

Located in the northwestern county of Cumbria, the Lake District is about 30 miles long and 30 miles wide. Explore it by foot, bike, bus, or car. Locals are fond of declaring that their mountains are older than the Himalayas and once as tall, but have been worn down by the ages (Scafell Pike, the tallest peak in England, is only 3,206 feet). There's a walking-stick charm about the way nature and the culture mix here. Hiking along a windblown ridge or climbing over a rock fence to look into the eyes of a ragamuffin sheep, even tenderfeet get a chance to feel very outdoorsy. The tradition of staying close to the land remains true in the 21st century; restaurants serve organic food and you'll see stickers in home windows advocating for environmental causes.

Dress in layers, and expect rain mixed with "bright spells" (pubs offer atmospheric shelter at every turn). Drizzly days can be followed by delightful evenings.

Plan to spend the majority of your time in the unspoiled North Lake District. In this chapter, I focus on the town of Keswick, the lake called Derwentwater, and the vast, time-passed Newlands Valley. The North Lake District works great by car or by bus (with easy train access via Penrith), delights nature lovers, and has good accommodations to boot.

The South Lake District—slightly closer to London—is

known primarily for its sights related to Wordsworth and Beatrix Potter (of Peter Rabbit fame), and gets the promotion, tour crowds, and tackiness that comes with them. While the slate-colored towns (Ambleside, Windermere, Bowness-on-Windermere, and so on) are cute, they're also touristy—which means crowded and over-priced. I strongly recommend that you buck the trend and focus on the north.

Ideally, make your home base in or near Keswick, and side-trip from there into the South Lake District only if you're interested in the Wordsworth and Beatrix Potter sights. Dipping into the South Lake District also works well en route if you're driving between Keswick and points south.

PLANNING YOUR TIME

I'd suggest spending two days and two nights in this area. Penrith is the nearest train station, 45 minutes by bus or car from Keswick. Those without a car will use Keswick as a springboard: Cruise the lake and take a hike in the Catbells area, or hop on a minibus tour. If great scenery is commonplace in your life, the Lake District can be more soothing (and rainy) than exciting. If you're rushed, you could make this area a one-night stand—or even a quick drive-through. But since the towns themselves are unexceptional, a visit here isn't worth it unless you have time to head up into the hills at least once.

Two-Day Driving Plan: Here's the most exciting way for drivers coming from the south to max out their time here and see some South Lake District sights en route to the north:

Day 1: Leave the motorway at Kendal by 10:30; drive along Lake Windermere and through the town of Ambleside.

11:30	Tour Wordsworth Grasmere, the site of Dove Cottage.
13:00	Backtrack to Ambleside, where a small road (Kirkstone) leads up to the dramatic Kirkstone Pass and down (on route A-592) to Glenridding on Lake Ullswater.
15:00	Catch the next Ullswater boat and ride to Howtown. Depending on the available daylight, you can hike six miles (3-4 hours) from Howtown back to Glenridding. Or, with less time, ride the boat as far as Aira Force to hike up to the waterfall (1 hour) or skip the boat and walk to Lanty's Tarn (2 hours) right from the Glenridding parking lot.
19:00	Drive to your Keswick hotel or farmhouse B&B near Keswick, with a stop as the sun sets at Castlerigg Stone Circle.

Day 2: Spend the morning (3-4 hours) splicing the Catbells

high-ridge hike into a boat trip around Derwentwater. In the afternoon, make the circular drive from Keswick through the Newlands Valley, Buttermere, Honister Pass, and Borrowdale. You could tour the Honister Slate Mine en route (last tour at 15:30) and/or pitch-and-putt nine holes in Keswick before a late dinner.

GETTING AROUND THE LAKE DISTRICT
By Car

Nothing is very far from Keswick and Derwentwater. Pick up a good map (any hotel can loan you one), get off the big roads, and leave the car, at least occa-

sionally, for some walking. In summer, the Keswick-Ambleside-Windermere-Bowness corridor (A-591) suffers from congestion. Back lanes are far less trampled and lead you through forgotten villages, where sheep outnumber people.

To **rent a car** here, try Enterprise in Penrith. They'll transport you between Keswick and their office when you're picking up and dropping off the car (Mon-Fri 8:00-18:00, Sat 9:00-12:00, closed Sun, requires drivers license and second ID, reserve a day in advance, located at the David Hayton Peugeot dealer, Haweswater Road, tel. 01768/893-840). Larger outfits are more likely to have a branch in Carlisle, which is a bit to the north but well served by train (on the same Glasgow-Birmingham line as Penrith) and only a few minutes farther from the Keswick area.

Parking is tight throughout the region. It's easiest to park in the pay-and-display lots (generally about £1/hour; have coins on hand; most machines also take credit cards). If you're parking for free on the roadside, don't block vital turnouts. Never park on double yellow lines.

Without a Car

Those based in Keswick without a car manage fine. Because of the region's efforts to "green up" travel and cut down on car traffic, the bus service can be quite efficient for hiking and sightseeing. (Even with a car, consider leaving it in town and using the bus—that way you don't need to limit yourself to round-trip hikes.)

By Bus: Keswick has no real bus station; buses stop in front of the Booths supermarket where well-designed maps and posted schedules make your bus options very clear. Local buses take you quickly and easily (if not always frequently) to most nearby points

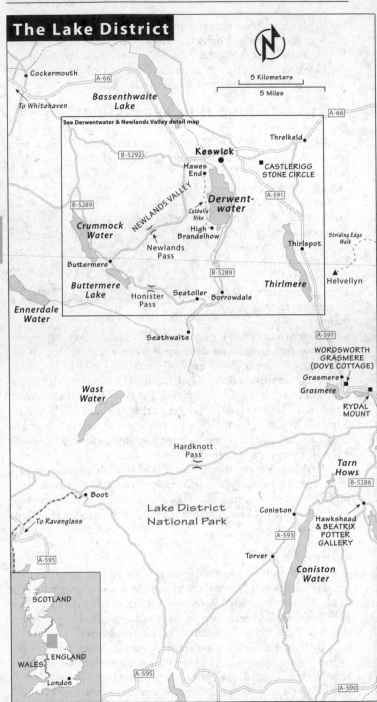

The Lake District

N

5 Kilometers

5 Miles

LAKE DISTRICT

Cockermouth

A-66

To Whitehaven

Bassenthwaite Lake

A-66

See Derwentwater & Newlands Valley detail map

B-5292

Keswick

Threlkeld

Hawes End

■ CASTLERIGG STONE CIRCLE

B-5289

Derwent-water

A-591

NEWLANDS VALLEY

Catbells Hike

High Brandelhow

Striding Edge Walk

Crummock Water

Newlands Pass

Thirlspot

Buttermere

B-5289

Thirlmere

▲ Helvellyn

Buttermere Lake

Honister Pass

Seatoller

Borrowdale

Ennerdale Water

Seathwaite

A-591

WORDSWORTH GRASMERE (DOVE COTTAGE)

Grasmere ●

Grasmere ■

Wast Water

RYDAL MOUNT

Hardknott Pass

Tarn Hows

B-5286

Coniston

Boot

Hawkshead & BEATRIX POTTER GALLERY

To Ravenglass

A-595

Lake District National Park

A-593

Torver

Coniston Water

SCOTLAND

ENGLAND

WALES

London

A-595

A-590

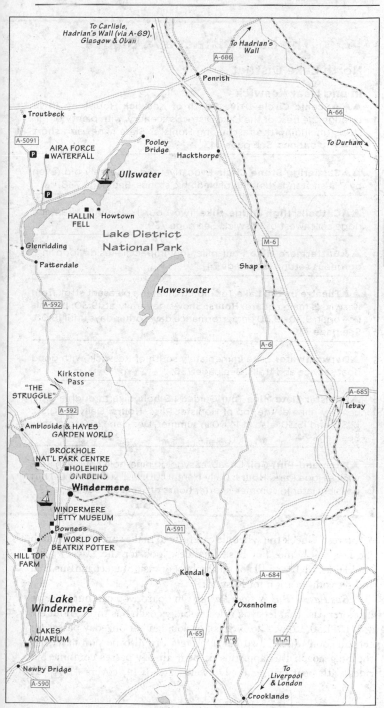

To Carlisle, Hadrian's Wall (via A-69), Glasgow & Oban

To Hadrian's Wall

A-686

Penrith

A-66

Troutbeck

A-5091

To Durham

AIRA FORCE WATERFALL

Pooley Bridge

Hackthorpe

Ullswater

M-6

HALLIN FELL

Howtown

Lake District National Park

Glenridding

Patterdale

Shap

A-592

Haweswater

A-6

Kirkstone Pass

A-685

"THE STRUGGLE"

A-592

Tebay

Ambleside & HAYES GARDEN WORLD

BROCKHOLE NAT'L PARK CENTRE

HOLEHIRD GARDENS

Windermere

WINDERMERE JETTY MUSEUM

Bowness

A-591

WORLD OF BEATRIX POTTER

HILL TOP FARM

Kendal

A-684

Lake Windermere

Oxenholme

LAKES AQUARIUM

A-65

M-6

Newby Bridge

To Liverpool & London

A-590

Crooklands

The Lake District at a Glance

North Lake District

In and Near Keswick

▲▲▲**Scenic Circle Drive South of Keswick** Hour-long drive through the best of the Lake District's scenery, with plenty of fun stops (including the fascinating Honister Slate Mine) and short side-trip options. See page 743.

▲▲**Castlerigg Stone Circle** Evocative and extremely old (even by British standards) ring of Neolithic stones. See page 738.

▲▲**Catbells High Ridge Hike** Two-hour hike along dramatic ridge southwest of Keswick. See page 739.

▲▲**Buttermere Hike** Four-mile, low-impact lakeside loop in a gorgeous setting. See page 741.

▲▲**Theatre by the Lake** Top-notch theater a pleasant stroll from Keswick's main square. **Hours:** Shows generally at 19:30; box office open 9:30-19:30 on performance days, other days until 18:00. See page 746.

▲**Derwentwater** Lake immediately south of Keswick, with good boat service and trails. See page 736.

▲**Honister Slate Mine Tour** Guided 1.5-hour hike through a 19th-century mine at the top of Honister Pass. **Hours:** Daily at 10:30, 12:30, and 15:30; also at 14:00 in summer; Dec-Jan 12:30 tour only. See page 744.

▲**Pitch-and-Putt Golf** Cheap, easygoing nine-hole course in Keswick's Hope Park. **Hours:** Daily from 10:00, last start at 18:00 but possibly later in summer, shorter hours off-season. See page 737.

of interest. Check the schedule carefully to make sure you can catch the last bus home. For bus schedules, look for the *Lakes by Bus* booklet (available at TIs or on any bus) or visit StagecoachBus.com and set your location for Keswick.

Bus Passes/Bus & Boat Passes: On board, you can purchase an Explorer pass that lets you ride any Stagecoach bus throughout the area (£11.50/1 day, £26/3 days), or you can get one-day passes for certain routes (described later); tickets can also be purchased via the Stagecoach Bus app. Bus & Boat all-day passes combine bus rides with boat cruises on Derwentwater (£14, covers #77/#77A

Ullswater Lake Area
▲▲Ullswater Hike and Boat Ride Long lake best enjoyed via steamer boat and seven-mile walk. **Hours:** Boats generally daily 9:45-16:55, 6-9/day April-Oct, fewer off-season. See page 755.

▲▲Lanty's Tarn and Keldas Hill Moderately challenging 2.5-mile loop hike from Glenridding with sweeping views of Ullswater. See page 755.

▲Aira Force Waterfall Easy uphill hike to picturesque waterfall. See page 756.

South Lake District
▲▲Dove Cottage at Wordsworth Grasmere The poet's humble home, with a museum that tells the story of his remarkable life. **Hours:** Daily 9:30-17:30, Nov-Feb 10:00-16:30 except closed Jan and for events in Dec and Feb (call ahead). See page 758.

▲Rydal Mount and Gardens Wordsworth's later, more upscale home. **Hours:** Daily 9:30-17:30; Nov-Dec and Feb 10:00-16:30 and closed Mon-Tue; closed Jan. See page 760.

▲Hill Top Farm Beatrix Potter's painstakingly preserved cottage. **Hours:** June-Aug daily 10:00-17:30; mid-Feb-May and Sept-Oct until 16:30 and closed Fri; house closed Nov-Dec but gardens and shop open Sat-Sun, closed Jan-mid-Feb; often a long wait to visit—call ahead. See page 762.

▲Beatrix Potter Gallery Collection of artwork by and background on the creator of Peter Rabbit. **Hours:** Daily 10:30-16:00, closed Nov-mid-Feb. See page 764.

bus and Derwentwater cruise) or Ullswater (£16, covers #508 bus and Ullswater cruise).

Bus routes: Buses **#X4** and **#X5** connect Penrith train station to Keswick (April-Oct hourly, every 2 hours on Sun, 45 minutes).

Bus **#77/#77A,** the Honister Rambler, makes the gorgeous circle from Keswick around Derwentwater, over Honister Pass, through Buttermere, and down the Whinlatter Valley (5-7/day clockwise, 4/day "anticlockwise," daily Easter-Oct, 1.75-hour loop). Bus **#78,** the Borrowdale Rambler, goes topless in the summer, affording a wonderful sightseeing experience in and of itself,

LAKE DISTRICT

heading from Keswick to Lodore Hotel, Grange Bridge, Rosthwaite, and Seatoller at the base of Honister Pass (hourly, daily Easter-Oct, 2/hour July-Sept, 30 minutes each way). Both of these routes are covered by the £8.50 Keswick and Honister Dayrider all-day pass.

Bus **#508,** the Kirkstone Rambler, runs between Penrith and Patterdale Hotel (near the bottom of Ullswater), stopping in Pooley Bridge (5/day, more frequent June-Aug with open-top buses, 50 minutes). Bus #508 also connects Glenridding and Windermere (1 hour).

Bus **#505,** the Coniston Rambler, connects Windermere with Hawkshead (about hourly, daily Easter-Oct, 35 minutes).

Bus **#555** connects Keswick with the south and Windermere (hourly, 2/hour July-Sept, 1 hour to Windermere).

Bus **#599,** the open-top Lakeland Experience, runs along the main Windermere corridor, connecting the big tourist attractions in the south: Grasmere and Dove Cottage, Rydal Mount, Ambleside, Brockhole (National Park Visitors Centre), Windermere, and lake cruises from Bowness Pier (3/hour June-Sept, 2/hour May and Oct, 50 minutes each way, £8.50 Central Lakes Dayrider all-day pass).

By Bike: Keswick works well as a springboard for several fine days out on a bike; consider a three-hour loop trip up Newlands Valley. Ask about routes at the TI or your bike rental shop. You cannot take bikes on local boats or buses. E-bikes are a boon for those who like biking but would enjoy a little help.

Several shops in Keswick rent road and mountain bikes (£20-25/day) and e-bikes (£30-50/day); rentals come with helmets and advice for good trips. Try **Whinlatter Bikes** (best prices, daily 10:00-17:00, free touring maps, 82 Main Street, tel. 017687/73940, www.whinlatterbikes.com); **E-Venture** (happy to store bags while you rent for no cost, daily 9:00-17:00, Elliot Park—facing the Keswick bus stop, tel. 017687/71363, www.e-venturebikes.co.uk); or **Keswick Bikes** (daily 9:00-17:30, 133 Main Street, tel. 017687/73355, www.keswickbikes.co.uk).

By Boat: A circular boat service glides you around Derwentwater, with several hiker-aiding stops along the way (for a cruise/hike option, see "Derwentwater Lakeside Walk" on page 737).

By Foot: Hiking information is available everywhere. Don't hike without a good, detailed map (wide selection at Keswick TI and at the many outdoor gear stores, or borrow one from your B&B). Helpful fliers at TIs and B&Bs describe the most popular routes. For an up-to-date weather report, check LakeDistrictWeatherLine.co.uk or call the local weather line: 0844-846-2444. Wear suitable clothing and footwear (you can rent boots in town), and plan for rain. Watch your footing—every year, several people die in hiking accidents in the area.

By Tour: For organized bus tours that run the roads of the Lake District, see "Tours in Keswick," later.

Keswick and the North Lake District

As far as touristy Lake District towns go, Keswick (KEZ-ick, population 5,000) is far more enjoyable than Windermere, Bowness, or Ambleside. Many of the place names around Keswick have Norse origins, inherited from the region's 10th-century settlers. Notice that most lakes in the region end in either *water* (e.g., Derwentwater) or *mere* (e.g., Windermere), which is related to the Dutch word for lake, *Meer*.

An important mining center for slate, copper, and lead through the Middle Ages, Keswick became a resort in the 19th century. Its fine Victorian buildings recall the days when city slickers first learned about "communing with nature," inspired by the Romantic poets (Wordsworth, Coleridge) who wandered the trails here. Today, the compact town is lined with tearooms, pubs, gift shops, and hiking-gear shops. The shore of the lake called Derwentwater is a pleasant 10-minute walk from the town center.

Orientation to Keswick

Keswick is an ideal home base, with plenty of good B&Bs, an easy bus connection to the nearest train station at Penrith, and a prime location near the best lake in the area, Derwentwater. In Keswick, everything is within a 10-minute walk of everything else: the pedestrian town square, the TI, recommended B&Bs, grocery stores, the wonderful municipal pitch-and-putt golf course, the main bus stop, a lakeside boat dock, and a central parking lot. Thursdays and Saturdays are market days in the town square, but the square is lively every day throughout the summer.

Keswick town is a delight for wandering. Its centerpiece, Moot Hall (meaning "meeting hall"), was a 16th-century copper warehouse upstairs with a market arcade below (it now houses the TI; most Lake District towns and villages have similar meeting halls). "Keswick" means "cheese farm"—a legacy from the time when the town square was the spot to sell cheese. When the town square went pedestrian-only, locals were all abuzz about people tripping over the curbs. (The English, seemingly thrilled by ever-present danger, are endlessly warning visitors to "watch your head," "duck or grouse," "watch the step," and "mind the gap.")

Keswick and the Lake District are popular with English holidaymakers who prefer to travel with their dogs. The town square in Keswick can look like the Westminster Dog Show, and the recommended Dog and Gun pub, where "well-behaved dogs are welcomed," is always full of patient pups. If you are shy about connecting with people, pal up to an English pooch—you'll often find they're happy to introduce you to their owners.

TOURIST INFORMATION

The National Park Visitors Centre/TI is in Moot Hall, right in the middle of the town square (daily 9:30-17:30, Nov-Easter until 16:30, tel. 0845-901-0845, www.keswick. org; you'll also find helpful planning info at www.lakedistrict.gov.uk, tel. 01539/724-555). Staffers are pros at advising you about hiking routes. They can also help you figure out public transportation to outlying sights and tell you about the region's various adventure activities.

The TI sells theater tickets, Keswick Launch tickets (at a £1 discount), fishing licenses, and brochures and maps that outline nearby hikes (including a series of *Lap Maps* featuring sights, walks, and driving/cycling tours). The TI and shops all over town also have books and maps for hikers, cyclists, and drivers.

The boards inside the TI's foyer are filled with posted information (about walks, talks, movies, theater, weather forecasts, and bus schedules). For information about the TI's guided walks, see "Tours in Keswick," later.

HELPFUL HINTS

Book in Advance: It's smart to book ahead if you'll be visiting during the summer or over a festival or bank-holiday weekend (see "Holidays and Festivals" in the appendix). If you have trouble finding a room (or a B&B that accepts small children), try www.keswick.org to search for available rooms.

Laundry: The town's launderette is on Bank Street, just up the

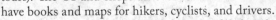

side street from the post office (full- and self-service; Mon-Fri
8:00-19:00, Sat-Sun 9:00-18:00, tel. 017687/75448).

Weather Info: Hikers should always check the daily fore-
cast by calling weather tel. 0844-846-2444 or visiting
LakeDistrictWeatherLine.co.uk.

Midges: Tiny biting insects called midges might bug you in this
region from late May through September, particularly at dawn
and dusk. The severity depends on the weather since wind and
sunshine can deter them, and insect repellant fends them off:
Ask the locals what works if you'll be hiking.

Local Candy: Be sure to try Kendal mint cakes, which are basically flat, mint-flavored sugar cubes. You'll find them in area
supermarkets and gift stores.

Groceries and More: Booths, a huge, modern supermarket (facing the Keswick bus stop), has a fine cafeteria (with inside and
outside seating), handy food to-go, a great book and map section, and a public WC (daily 7:00-22:00, shorter Sun hours,
Tithebarn Street, tel. 017684/73518).

Tours in Keswick

Walking Tours
The **Keswick TI** offer guided walks several times weekly, some free
and others £5-10, led by "Voluntary Rangers" in summer (depart
from Keswick TI; check the Events and Guided Walks page at
www.lakedistrict.gov.uk for schedule, descriptions, and advance
booking; optional contribution welcome at the end of a free walk).

Private Guides
Show Me Cumbria Private Tours, run by Andy, offers personalized tours all around the Lake District. He's based in Penrith
but can pick up in Keswick and other locations (£140/half-day
for 3-6 people, tel. 017688/64825, mobile 07809-026-357, www.
showmecumbria.co.uk, andy@showmecumbria.co.uk).

Discover Lakeland, led by friendly and experienced Blue
Badge guide Anna Grey, gives tours all over Cumbria and beyond.
She specializes in the Lake District but also gives tours at Hadrian's Wall (£160/half-day, £260/full day, mobile 07557-915-855,
www.discoverlakeland.uk, anna@discoverlakeland.co.uk).

Keswick Rambles Guided Walks, led by Pete and Lynn
Armstrong, offers private guided hikes of varying difficulty, including the popular Catbells trail. They'll meet you at your B&B
and ride with you on public transport (not included) to the trailhead (cost depends on hike but typically £90/day or £20-25/
person if more than 4, Easter-Oct, wear suitable clothing and
footwear, bring lunch and water, must book in advance, tel.

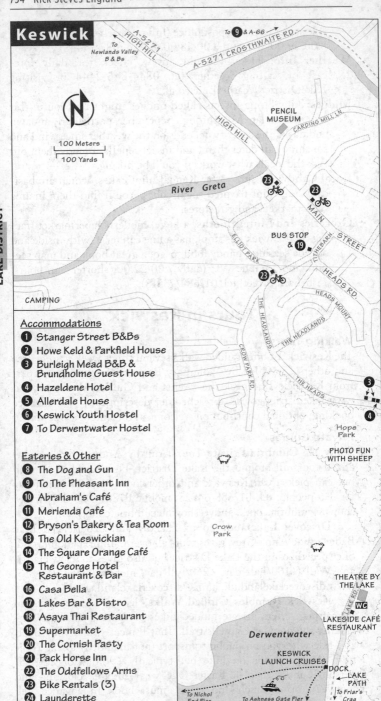

Keswick

To **9** & A-66

A-5271 CROSTHWAITE RD.

A-5271 HIGH HILL

To Newlands Valley B & Bs

HIGH HILL

N

100 Meters
100 Yards

River Greta

PENCIL MUSEUM

CARDING MILL LN.

MAIN STREET

BUS STOP & **19**

ELLIOT PARK

TITHEBARN STREET

HEADS RD.

HEADS MOUNT

THE HEADLANDS

THE HEADLANDS

THE HEADS

CROW PARK RD.

CAMPING

3
4

Hope Park

PHOTO FUN WITH SHEEP

Accommodations

1 Stanger Street B&Bs
2 Howe Keld & Parkfield House
3 Burleigh Mead B&B & Brundholme Guest House
4 Hazeldene Hotel
5 Allerdale House
6 Keswick Youth Hostel
7 To Derwentwater Hostel

Eateries & Other

8 The Dog and Gun
9 To The Pheasant Inn
10 Abraham's Café
11 Merienda Café
12 Bryson's Bakery & Tea Room
13 The Old Keswickian
14 The Square Orange Café
15 The George Hotel Restaurant & Bar
16 Casa Bella
17 Lakes Bar & Bistro
18 Asaya Thai Restaurant
19 Supermarket
20 The Cornish Pasty
21 Pack Horse Inn
22 The Oddfellows Arms
23 Bike Rentals (3)
24 Launderette

Crow Park

THEATRE BY THE LAKE

WC

LAKESIDE CAFÉ RESTAURANT

Derwentwater

KESWICK LAUNCH CRUISES

DOCK

LAKE PATH

To Friar's Crag

To Nichol End Pier

To Ashness Gate Pier

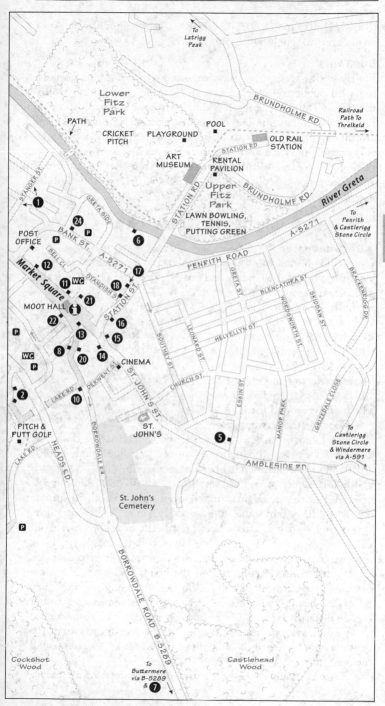

017687/71302, mobile 07342-637-813, keswickrambles.blogspot.co.uk, armstrongps1@gmx.com).

Bus Tours

For those who want to see the area without lots of hiking or messing with public transport, a bus tour can be the answer. **Mountain Goat Tours** is the region's dominant tour company and runs half- and full-day minibus excursions nearly every morning and afternoon from Keswick to all the scenic highlights. Customizable private tours are also available. For details, see their website (£22-40/half-day, £48/full day, tours run April-Oct, maximum of 16 persons, book in advance, tel. 015394/45161, www.mountaingoat.com, tours@mountain-goat.com).

Sights in Keswick

▲Derwentwater

One of Cumbria's most photographed and popular lakes, Derwentwater has four islands, good boat service, and plenty of trails.

The pleasant town of Keswick, near the lake's north end, is a short stroll from the shore. The roadside views aren't much, and while you can walk around the lake, much of the walk is boring. You're better off mixing a hike and boat ride, or simply enjoying a boat cruise around the lake.

Boating on Derwentwater:
Keswick Launch runs two **cruises** an hour, alternating clockwise and "anticlockwise" (boats depart on the half-hour, daily 10:00-16:30, July-Aug until 17:30, in winter 6/day generally weekends and holidays only, at end of Lake Road, tel. 017687/72263, www.keswick-launch.co.uk). Boats make seven stops on each 50-minute round-trip (may skip some stops or not run at all if the water level is very high—such as after a heavy rain). The boat trip costs about £2 per segment or £11 per round-trip circuit (£1 less if you book through TI) with free stopovers; you can get on and off all you want, but tickets are collected on the boat's last leg to Keswick, marking the end of your ride. If you want to hop on the scenic #77/#77A bus and also cruise Derwentwater, the Derwentwater Bus & Boat all-day pass covers both (see page 728). To be picked up at a certain stop, stand at the end of the pier and wave, or the boat may not stop. See the map on page 742 for an overview of all the boat stops.

Keswick Launch also rents **rowboats** for up to three people

(£10/30 minutes, £15/hour, open Easter-Oct, larger rowboats and motorboats available).

Derwentwater Lakeside Walk: A fine, marked trail runs all along Derwentwater (9 miles, 4 hours, floods after heavy rains), but much of it (especially the Keswick-to-Hawes End stretch) is not that interesting. The best hour-long section is the 1.5-mile path between the docks at High Brandelhow and Hawes End, where you'll stroll a level trail through peaceful trees. This walk works well with the lake boat described earlier.

For a very easy, paved stroll, walk 10 minutes from the Keswick dock clockwise to the Friar's Crag viewpoint. The Lakeside Café Restaurant overlooking the Keswick landing can be handy (daily 9:00-20:30).

Derwent Pencil Museum

Graphite was first discovered centuries ago in Keswick. A hunk of the stuff proved great for marking sheep in the 15th century. In 1832, the first crude Keswick pencil factory opened, and the rest is history (which is what you'll learn about here). While the factory that made the famous Derwent pencils is closed, a small modern building tells the story in a kid-friendly exhibit filling one small room.

Cost and Hours: £5, daily 9:30-17:00, last entry one hour before closing, humble café, 3-minute walk from town center, signposted off Main Street, tel. 017687/73626, www.pencilmuseum. co.uk.

Fitz Park

An inviting grassy park stretches alongside Keswick's tree-lined, duck-filled River Greta. There's a playground and plenty of room for kids to burn off energy. Consider an after-dinner stroll on the footpath. You may catch men in white (or frisky schoolboys in uniform) playing a game of cricket. There's the serious bowling green (where you're welcome to watch the experts play and enjoy the cheapest cuppa—i.e., tea—in town), and the public one where tourists are welcome to give lawn bowling a go. You can try tennis on a grass court or enjoy the putting green. Find the rental pavilion across the road from the art museum (open daily Easter-Sept 10:00-17:30, longer hours July-Aug, Station Road, mobile 07976-573-785).

Golf and Hope Park

A nine-hole ▲ pitch-and-putt golf course near the lush gardens in Hope Park separates the town from the lake and offers a classy, cheap, and convenient chance to golf near the birthplace of the sport. This is a fun and inexpensive experience—just right after a day of touring (£5 for pitch-and-putt, £3.50 for putting, £4.50 for

18 tame holes of "obstacle golf," £3 for *boules*, daily from 10:00, last round starts around 18:00, possibly later in summer, shorter hours off-season, café, tel. 017687/73445, www.hopeleisure.com).

Even if you're not a golfer, Hope Park is a fine place to walk among grazing sheep, with great photo ops.

Swimming

While the leisure center lacks a serious adult pool, it does have an indoor pool kids love, with a huge waterslide and wave machine (swim times vary by day and by season—call or check website, no towels or suits for rent, lockers-£1 deposit, 10-minute walk from town center, follow Station Road past Fitz Park and veer left, tel. 017687/72760, www.better.org.uk).

NEAR KESWICK
▲▲Castlerigg Stone Circle

For some reason, 70 percent of England's stone circles are here in Cumbria. Castlerigg is one of the best and oldest in Britain, and an easy stop for drivers. The circle—90 feet across and 5,000 years old—has 38 stones myste-riously laid out on a line between the two tallest peaks on the horizon. They may have served as a celestial calendar for ritual cel-ebrations. Imagine the ambience here, as ancient people filled this clearing in spring to celebrate

fertility, in late summer to commemorate the harvest, and in the winter to celebrate the winter solstice and the coming renewal of light. Festival dates may have been dictated by how the sun rose and set in relation to the stones. The more that modern academics study this circle, the more meaning they find in the placement of the stones. The two front stones face due north, toward a cut in the mountains. The rare-for-stone-circles "sanctuary" lines up with its center stone to mark certain celestial events. (Party!) For maximum "goose pimples" (as they say here), show up at sunset.

Cost and Hours: Free, always open, located 1.5 miles east of Keswick on Eleventrees Road—see map on page 742; about 30 minutes from town on foot; by car, follow brown signs—it's 3 min-utes off the A-66, limited but easy parking, www.english-heritage.org.uk.

Hikes and Drives
in the North Lake District

FROM KESWICK

For an easy, flat stroll, consider the trail that runs alongside Derwentwater (see "Sights in Keswick," earlier). More strenuous options are described next (for more detailed hike info, stop in at the Keswick TI).

▲▲Catbells High Ridge Hike

For a great "king of the mountain" feeling, 360-degree views, and a close-up look at the weather blowing over the ridge, take a two-hour hike above Derwentwater from Hawes End up along the ridge to Catbells (1,480 feet) and down to High Brandelhow. Because the mountaintop is basically treeless, you're treated to dramatic panoramas the entire way up. From High Brandelhow,

you can catch the boat back to Keswick or take the easy path along the Derwentwater shore to your Hawes End starting point. (Extending the hike farther around the lake to Lodore takes you to a waterfall, rock climbers, a fine café, and another boat dock for a convenient return to Keswick—for more about Lodore, see page 745). Note: When the water level is very high (for example, after a heavy rain), boats can't stop at Hawes End—ask at the TI or boat dock before setting out.

Catbells is probably the most dramatic family walk in the area (but wear sturdy shoes, bring a raincoat, and watch your footing). From Keswick, the lake, or your farmhouse B&B, you can see silhouetted figures—what locals call "crag rats"—hiking along this ridge.

Getting There: To reach the trailhead from Keswick, catch the "anticlockwise" boat (see "Boating on Derwentwater," earlier) and ride for 10 minutes to the second stop, Hawes End. (You can also ride to High Brandelhow and take this walk in the other direction, but I don't recommend it—two rocky scrambles along the way are easier and safer to navigate going uphill from Hawes End.) Note the schedule for your return boat ride. If driving, there's free but limited parking at Hawes End, and the road can be hard to find—get clear directions in town before heading out. (Hardcore hikers can walk to the foot of Catbells from Keswick via

LAKE DISTRICT

Portinscale, which takes about 40 minutes—ask your B&B or the TI for directions.)

The Route: The path is not signposted, but it's easy to follow, and you'll see plenty of other walkers. From Hawes End, walk away from the lake through a kissing gate to the turn just before the car park. Then turn left and go up, up, up. After about 20 minutes, you'll hit the first of two short scrambles (where the trail vanishes into a cluster of steep rocks), which leads to a bluff. From the first little summit (great for a picnic break),

and then along the ridge, you'll enjoy sweeping views of the lake on one side and of Newlands Valley on the other. The bald peak in the distance is Catbells. Broken stones crunch under each step, wind buffets your ears, clouds prowl overhead, and the sheep baa comically. To anyone looking up from the distant farmhouse B&Bs, you are but a stick figure on the ridge. Just below the summit, the trail disintegrates into another short, steep scramble. Your reward is just beyond: a magnificent hilltop perch.

After the Catbells summit, descend along the ridge to a saddle ahead. The ridge continues much higher, and while it may look like your only option, at its base a small, unmarked lane with comfortable steps leads left. Unless you're up for extending the hike (see "Longer Catbells Options," next), take this path down to the lake. To get to High Brandelhow Pier, take the first left fork you come across down through a forest to the lake. When you reach Abbot's Bay, go left through a swinging gate, following a lakeside trail around a gravelly bluff, to the idyllic High Brandelhow Pier, a peaceful place to wait for your boat back to Keswick. (You can pay your fare when you board.)

Note: after coming down from Catbells here, rather than return to the lake you can carry on to the charming little village of Grange, from where bus #78 travels back to Keswick (2/hour, the stop is over the Grange bridge on the main road).

Longer Catbells Options: Catbells is just the first of a series of peaks, all connected by a fine ridge trail. Hardier hikers can continue for nine miles along this same ridge, enjoying valley and lake views as they arc around the Newlands Valley toward (and even down to) Buttermere. After High Spy, you can descend an easy path into Newlands Valley. The ultimate, very full day-plan would be to take a bus to Buttermere, climb Robinson, and follow the ridge around to Catbells and back to Keswick.

Latrigg Peak

For the easiest mountain-climbing sensation around, take the short drive to the Latrigg Peak parking lot just north of Keswick, and hike 15 minutes to the top of the 1,200-foot-high hill, where you'll be rewarded with a commanding view of the town, lake, and valley, all the way to Bassenthwaite, the next lake over. At the traffic circle just outside Keswick, take the A-591 Carlisle exit, then an immediate right (direction: Ormathwaite/Underscar). Take the next right, a hard right, at the *Skiddaw* sign, where a long, steep, one-lane road leads to the Latrigg parking lot at the end of the lane. With more time, you can walk all the way from your Keswick B&B to Latrigg and back (it's a popular evening walk for locals).

Keswick to Threlkeld Railway Path

A four-mile railway path from downtown Keswick follows an old train track and the river to the village of Threlkeld (with two pubs). However, storm damage has closed the path, which is now being restored. For the latest, check at the TI or see www.lakedistrict. gov.uk.

Walla Crag

From your Keswick B&B, a fine two-hour walk to Walla Crag offers great fell (mountain) and ridge walking without the necessity of a bus or car. Start by strolling along the lake to the Great Wood parking lot (or drive to this lot), and head up Cat Ghyl (where "fell runners"—trail-running enthusiasts—practice) to Walla Crag. You'll be treated to great panoramic views over Derwentwater and surrounding peaks—especially beautiful when the heather blossoms in the summer. You can do a shorter version of this walk from the parking lot at Ashness Packhorse Bridge.

HIKES AND DRIVES OUTSIDE KESWICK

▲▲Buttermere Hike

The ideal little lake with a lovely circular four-mile stroll offers nonstop, no-sweat Lake District beauty. If you're not a hiker but wish you were, take this walk. If you're short on time, at least stop here and get your shoes dirty.

Buttermere is connected with Borrowdale and Derwentwater by a dramatic road that runs over rugged Honister Pass. Buses #77/#77A make a 1.75-hour round-trip loop between Keswick and Buttermere that includes a trip over this pass. The two-pub hamlet of Buttermere has two pay-and-display parking lots and free parking along the roadside by the church. There's also a pay parking lot at the Honister Pass end of the lake (at Gatesgarth Farm). The Syke Farm Tea Room in Buttermere is popular for its enticing farmmade ice cream (daily 11:30-17:00, light lunches, box lunches for hikers).

Derwentwater & Newlands Valley

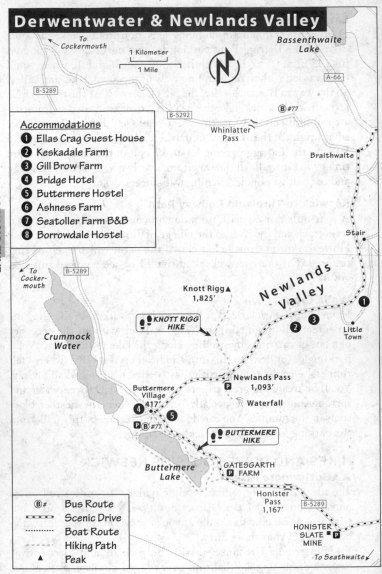

Accommodations
1. Ellas Crag Guest House
2. Keskadale Farm
3. Gill Brow Farm
4. Bridge Hotel
5. Buttermere Hostel
6. Ashness Farm
7. Seatoller Farm B&B
8. Borrowdale Hostel

Bassenthwaite Lake

To Cockermouth

1 Kilometer
1 Mile

B-5289
B-5292
Whinlatter Pass
ⓑ#77
A-66
Braithwaite
Stair

To Cockermouth
B-5289
Knott Rigg 1,825'
Newlands Valley
KNOTT RIGG HIKE
Crummock Water
Little Town
Newlands Pass 1,093'
Waterfall
Buttermere Village
417'
BUTTERMERE HIKE
Buttermere Lake
GATESGARTH FARM
Honister Pass 1,167'
B-5289
HONISTER SLATE MINE
To Seathwaite

ⓑ#   Bus Route
••••   Scenic Drive
········   Boat Route
– – –   Hiking Path
▲   Peak

See "Eating in the Newlands Valley," later, for more Buttermere eateries.

While you can circumnavigate the entire lake, the side opposite the road is nicest. You can walk from one end to the other—Buttermere to Gatesgarth Farm—in about an hour (using a pay and display lot at either end and/or bus #77). In Buttermere the trail starts at The Fish Hotel.

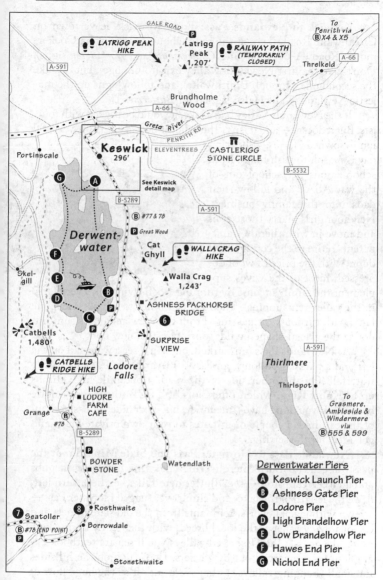

LAKE DISTRICT

Derwentwater Piers

- **A** Keswick Launch Pier
- **B** Ashness Gate Pier
- **C** Lodore Pier
- **D** High Brandelhow Pier
- **E** Low Brandelhow Pier
- **F** Hawes End Pier
- **G** Nichol End Pier

▲▲▲Scenic Circle Drive South of Keswick

This hour-long drive, which includes Newlands Valley, Buttermere, Honister Pass, and Borrowdale, offers the North Lake District's best scenery. (To do a similar route without a car from Keswick, take loop bus #77/#77A and use it as a do-it-yourself, hop-on, hop-off tour.) Distances are short, roads are narrow and have turnouts, and views are rewarding. Get a good map and ask your B&B host for advice. (For an overview of the route, see map.)

Keswick to Newlands Pass: From Keswick, leave town on Crosthwaite Road, then, at the roundabout, head west on Cockermouth Road (A-66, following *Cockermouth* and *Workington* signs). Don't take the first Newlands Valley exit (to Grange), but do take the second one (through Braithwaite), and follow signs up the majestic Newlands Valley (also signed for *Buttermere*).

If the **Newlands Valley** had a lake, it would be packed with tourists. But it doesn't—and it isn't. The valley is dotted with 500-year-old family-owned farms. Shearing day is reason to rush home from school. Sons get school out of the way ASAP and follow their dads into the family business. Neighbor girls marry those sons and move in with them. Grandparents retire to the cottage next door. With the price of wool depressed, most of the wives supplement the family income by running B&Bs (virtually every farm in the valley rents rooms). The road (six miles to the pass) has one lane, with turnouts for passing. From the Newlands Pass summit, notice the glacial-shaped wilds, once forested, now not.

At **Newlands Pass** (unmarked, but you'll see a waterfall on the left and a parking pullout), an easy 300-yard hike leads to a little waterfall. On the other side of the road, a one-mile hike climbs up to **Knott Rigg,** which offers lots of TPCB (thrills per calorie burned). If you don't have time for even a short hike, at least get out of the car, hike a couple of minutes to your own private bluff, and get a feel for the setting.

Newlands Pass to Honister Pass and Slate Mine: From the pass, descend to Buttermere (scenic lake, tiny hamlet with pubs and an ice-cream store—see "Buttermere Hike," earlier), turn left, drive the length of the lake, and climb over rugged Honister Pass—strewn with glacial debris, remnants from the old slate mines, and curious shaggy sheep (the local breed, with their curly horns, look more like goats). The U-shaped valleys you'll see are textbook examples of those carved out by glaciers. Look high on the hillsides for small "hanging valleys"—they were cut off by the huge flow of the much larger glacier that swept down the main valley floor.

The **Honister Slate Mine,** England's last still-functioning slate mine (and worth ▲), stands at the summit of Honister Pass. The youth hostel next to it was built to house miners in the 1920s. The mine offers worthwhile tours (perfect for when it's pouring outside): You'll put on a hard hat, load onto a bus for a short climb, then hike into a shaft to learn about the region's slate industry. It's

LAKE DISTRICT

a long, stooped hike into the mountain, made interesting by the guide and punctuated by the sound of your helmet scraping against low bits of the shaft. Standing deep in the mountain, surrounded by slate scrap and the beams of 30 headlamps

fluttering around like fireflies, you'll learn of the hardships of miners' lives and how "green gold" is trendy once again, making the mine viable. Even if you don't have time to take the tour, stop here for the slate-filled shop (£17.50, 1.5-hour tour; departs daily at 10:30, 12:30, and 15:30; additional tour at 14:00 in summer; Dec-Jan 12:30 tour only; reserve online or call ahead to confirm times and to book a spot, helmets and lamps provided, wear good walking shoes and bring warm clothing even in summer, café and nice WCs, tel. 017687/77230, www.honister.com, Roland).

The mine has a pay parking lot for hikers wanting access to nearby high-altitude trails. The slate mine also offers Via Ferrata adventures—where you climb/hike with a guide up a cliff clipped to a safety cable (£45/person, daily at 9:00, 12:00, and 15:00, 3 hours, see website for details).

From Honister Slate Mine to Lodore: From the mine, you'll drop into the sweet and homey **Borrowdale Valley,** with a few lonely hamlets. Circling past Borrowdale, you'll turn north onto the B-5289 (a.k.a. the Borrowdale Valley Road), which takes you past the following popular attractions:

The house-size **Bowder Stone,** thought to have cleaved from the top of a nearby cliff, sits about 15 minutes off the main road (signposted); a ladder lets you climb to the top. For a great lunch or snack, including tea and homemade quiche and cakes, drop in to the much-loved **$ High Lodore Farm Café** (daily 9:00-18:00, closed Nov-Easter, short drive uphill from the main road and over a tiny bridge, tel. 017687/77221).

Nearby is the village of **Grange,** which must be the cutest hamlet in the area. It's built of locally quarried Lakeland Green slate, and mostly by one builder, which adds to the tidy feel. Grange has a couple of inviting cafés and two tiny churches—one vibrant and welcoming; the other is home to the free "Borrowdale Story" history exhibit.

Farther along, **Lodore Falls** is a short walk from the road, behind the Lodore Hotel (a nice place to stop for tea and beautiful views). **Shepherds Crag,** a cliff overlooking Lodore, was made famous by pioneering rock climbers as far back as the 1890s. (Their descendants hang from little ridges on its face today.)

From Lodore, with a Detour, to Keswick: A very hard right off the B-5289 at the Ashness Gate Pier (signposted *Ashness Bridge, Watendlath*) and a steep half-mile climb on a narrow lane takes you to the postcard-pretty **Ashness Packhorse Bridge,** a quintessential Lake District scene (parking lot just above on right). A half-mile farther up, park the car and hop out (parking lot on left, no sign). You'll be startled by the "surprise view" of

Derwentwater—great for a lakes photo op. Continuing from here, the road gets extremely narrow en route to the hamlet of **Watendlath,** which has a tiny lake and lazy farm animals.

Return to the B-5289 and head back to Keswick. If you have yet to see it, cap your drive with a short detour from Keswick to the Castlerigg Stone Circle (described earlier).

Nightlife in Keswick

For a small and remote town, Keswick has lots going on in the evening. Remember, at this latitude it's light until 22:00 in midsummer.

▲▲Theatre by the Lake

Keswickians brag that they enjoy "London theater quality at Keswick prices." Their theater offers events year-round on two stages and a wonderful rotation of six plays from late May through October (plays vary throughout the week, with music concerts on Sun in summer). Attending a play here is a fine opportunity to enjoy a classy night out.

Cost and Hours: £10-36, discounts for those under 26; shows generally at 19:30; café, restaurant (pretheater dinners start at 17:30 and must be booked 24 hours ahead by calling 017687/81102), located off Lake Road with parking in adjacent lot. It's smart to buy tickets in advance—book at box office (daily 9:30-19:30 on performance days, other days until 18:00), by phone (tel. 017687/74411), at TI, or at www.theatrebythelake.com.

Pub Events

To socialize with locals, head to a pub for one of their special evenings. **Quiz nights** are popular at many local pubs, and tourists are more than welcome. Drop in, say you want to join a team, and you're in. If you like trivia, it's a great way to get to know people here (the Pack Horse Inn, on Packhorse Court, hosts quiz nights most Wed at 21:30).

The Oddfellows Arms has free **live music** (often classic rock) in summer (April-Oct Thu-Sun from 21:30, 19 Main Street). The Square Orange occasionally has live music on Wednesday evenings (20 St. John's Street) and the Pack Horse Inn on weekends.

Movies

The Lonsdale Alhambra Cinema, a restored, old-fashioned movie theater a few minutes' walk from the town center, plays block-busters and art films (St. Johns Street, tel. 017687/72195, www. keswickalhambra.co.uk).

Sleeping in Keswick

The Lake District abounds with attractive B&Bs, guesthouses, and hostels. It needs them all when the summer hordes threaten the serenity of this Romantic-era mecca.

Reserve your room in advance in high season. From November through March, you should have no trouble finding a room, but to get a particular place (especially on Saturdays), book ahead. If you're using public transportation, sleep in Keswick. Most of my recommended B&Bs and small hotels are within three blocks of the bus station and town square. If you're driving, staying outside Keswick is your best chance for a remote farmhouse experience.

Many Keswick listings charge extra for a one-night stay and most won't book one-night stays on weekends. Most don't welcome young children. None have elevators and all have lots of stairs—ask about a ground-floor unit if steps are a problem. Owners are enthusiastic about offering advice to get you on the right walking trail. Most accommodations have inviting lounges with libraries of books on the region and loaner maps.

This is still the countryside—expect huge breakfasts (often with a wide selection, including vegetarian options) and shower systems that might need to be switched on to get hot water. Parking is generally easy.

ON STANGER STREET

This street, quiet but just a block from Keswick's town center, is lined with B&Bs situated in Victorian slate townhouses. Each of these places is small and family-run. They all offer comfortably sized rooms, free parking, and a friendly welcome.

$$ Ellergill Guest House has four spic-and-span rooms with an airy, contemporary feel—several with views (2 percent surcharge for credit cards, 2-night minimum, no children under age 10, 22 Stanger Street, tel. 017687/73347, www.ellergill.co.uk, stay@ellergill.co.uk, Clare and Robin Pinkney).

$$ Badgers Wood B&B, at the top of the street, has six modern, bright, unfrilly view rooms, each named after a different tree (3 percent surcharge for credit cards, 2-night minimum, no children under age 12, special diets accommodated, 30 Stanger Street, tel. 017687/72621, www.badgers-wood.co.uk, enquiries@badgers-wood.co.uk, chatty Scotsman Andrew and his charming wife, Anne).

$$ Abacourt House, with a daisy-fresh breakfast room, has five pleasant doubles (2-night minimum on weekends, no children, sack lunches available, 26 Stanger Street, tel. 017687/72967, www.abacourt.co.uk, abacourt.keswick@btinternet.com, John and Heather).

$ Dunsford Guest House rents four updated rooms at bargain prices. Stained glass and wooden pews give the bright breakfast room a country-chapel vibe (RS%, cash only, 16 Stanger Street, tel. 017687/75059, www.dunsfordguesthouse.co.uk, info@dunsfordguesthouse.co.uk, Deb and Keith).

ON THE HEADS

The classy area known as The Heads has B&Bs with bigger and grander Victorian architecture and great views overlooking the pitch-and-putt range and out into the hilly distance. The golf-course side of The Heads has free parking, if you can snare a spot (easy at night). A single yellow line on the curb means

you're allowed to park for free, but only overnight (16:00-10:00).

$$$ Howe Keld has the polished feel of a boutique hotel, but offers all the friendliness of a B&B. Its 12 contemporary-posh rooms are spacious and tastefully decked out in native woods and slate. It's warm, welcoming, and family-run, with an à la carte breakfast cooked to order by chef Jerome (cash and 2-night minimum preferred, sack lunches available, tel. 017687/72417, www.howekeld.co.uk, laura@howekeld.co.uk, run with care by Laura and Jerome Bujard).

$$ Parkfield House, thoughtfully run and decorated by John and Susan Berry, is a big Victorian house with a homey lounge. Its six rooms, some with fine views, are bright and classy (RS%, 2-night minimum, no children under age 16, free parking, tel. 017687/72328, www.parkfieldkeswick.co.uk, parkfieldkeswick@hotmail.co.uk).

$$ Burleigh Mead B&B is a slate mansion from 1892. Gill (pronounced "Jill," short for Gillian) rents seven lovely rooms and offers a friendly welcome, as well as a lounge and peaceful front-yard sitting area that's perfect for enjoying the view (cash only, discount for longer stays, no children under age 8, tel. 017687/75935, www.burleighmead.co.uk, info@burleighmead.co.uk).

$$ Hazeldene Hotel, on the corner of The Heads, rents 10 spacious rooms, many with commanding views. There's even a "boot room" that doubles as a guest rec room with a ping-pong table. It's run with care by delightful Helen and Howard (ground-floor unit available, free parking, tel. 017687/72106, www.hazeldene-hotel.co.uk, info@hazeldene-hotel.co.uk).

$$ Brundholme Guest House has four bright and comfy rooms, most with sweeping views at no extra charge—especially from the front side—and a friendly and welcoming atmosphere (mini fridge, free parking, tel. 017687/73305, mobile 07739-435-401, www.brundholme.co.uk, bazaly@hotmail.co.uk, Barry and Allison Thompson).

ON ESKIN STREET

Just southeast of the town center, the area around Eskin Street is still within easy walking distance and has stress-free parking.

$$ Allerdale House, a classy, nicely decorated stone mansion with five rooms, is well run by Mat and Leigh Richards (RS%, 1.5 percent surcharge for credit cards, free parking, 1 Eskin Street, tel. 017687/73891, www.allerdale-house.co.uk, reception@allerdale-house.co.uk).

HOSTELS IN AND NEAR KESWICK

The Lake District's inexpensive hostels, mostly located in great old buildings, are handy sources of information and social fun.

¢ Keswick Youth Hostel, with a big lounge and a great riverside balcony, fills a converted mill. Travelers of all ages feel at home here, but book ahead—family rooms book up July through September (breakfast extra, café, bar, office open 7:00-23:00, center of town just off Station Road before river, tel. 017687/72484, www.yha.org.uk, keswick@yha.org.uk).

¢ Derwentwater Hostel, in a 220-year-old mansion on the shore of Derwentwater, is two miles south of Keswick (breakfast extra, family rooms; follow the B-5289 from Keswick—entrance is 2 miles along the Borrowdale Valley Road about 150 yards after Ashness exit—look for cottage and bus stop at bottom of the drive; tel. 017687/77246, www.derwentwater.org, contact@derwentwater.org).

LAKE DISTRICT

IN THE NEWLANDS VALLEY

If you have a car, drive 10 minutes west and south of Keswick into the majestic Newlands Valley (described earlier, under "Scenic Circle Drive South of Keswick") to find accommodations with easy parking, grand views, and perfect tranquility. Rooms here tend to be plainer and more dated than those in town and come with steep and gravelly roads, plenty of dogs, and an earthy charm. Don't expect mobile-phone service—even your B&B's satellite Wi-Fi can be spotty. Traditionally, farmhouses lacked central heating, and while they are now heated, you can still request a hot-water bottle to warm up your bed.

Getting to the Newlands Valley: Leave Keswick via the roundabout at the end of Crosthwaite Road, and then head west on Cockermouth Road (A-66). Take the Newlands Valley exit through Braithwaite (B-5292), and follow signs toward Buttermere and Newlands. All my recommended B&Bs are on this road, a 10- to 15-minute drive from Keswick. The one-lane road is tight but has turnouts for passing.

$$ Ellas Crag Guest House, with three rooms—each with a great view—is a comfortable stone house with a contemporary feel and tranquil terrace overlooking the valley. This homey B&B offers a good mix of modern and traditional decor, including beautifully tiled bathrooms (RS%, singles available Mon-Thu only, 2-night minimum, local free-range meats and eggs for breakfast, sack lunches available, huge DVD library, laundry, tel. 017687/78217, www.ellascrag.co.uk, info@ellascrag.co.uk, run by friendly Jane and Ed Ma).

$ Keskadale Farm is another good farmhouse experience, with Ponderosa hospitality. One of the valley's oldest, the house—with two guest rooms and a cozy lounge—is made from 500-year-old ship beams. This working farm is an authentic slice of Lake District life and is your chance to get to know lots of curly-horned sheep and the dogs that herd them. While her husband and sons work in the fields, Margaret Harryman runs the B&B (cash only, sack lunches available, closed Nov-May, tel. 017687/78544, www.keskadalefarm.co.uk, info@keskadalefarm.co.uk). They also rent a one-bedroom apartment that sleeps two (£450/week).

$ Gill Brow Farm is a rough-hewn working farmhouse more than 300 years old where Anne Wilson rents two simple but fine rooms, one with an en-suite bathroom, the other with a private bathroom down the hall (self-catering cottage that sleeps up to 6 also available, tel. 017687/78270, www.gillbrow-keswick.co.uk, info@gillbrow-keswick.co.uk).

IN BUTTERMERE

$$$$ Bridge Hotel, just beyond the Newlands Valley at Buttermere, offers 21 beautiful rooms—most of them quite spacious—and a classic Old World countryside-hotel experience. On Fridays and Saturdays, dinner is required (apartments available, minimum 2-night stay on weekends, tel. 017687/70252, www.bridge-hotel.com, enquiries@bridge-hotel.com). There are no shops within 10 miles—only peace and quiet a stone's throw from one of the region's most beautiful lakes. The hotel has a dark-wood pub/restaurant on the ground floor.

¢ **Buttermere Hostel,** a quarter-mile south of Buttermere village on Honister Pass Road, has good food and a peacefully rural setting (private and family rooms, breakfast extra, inexpensive dinners and packed lunches, office open 8:30-10:00 & 17:00-22:00, reservation tel. 0345-371-9508, www.yha.org.uk, buttermere@yha.org.uk).

NEAR BORROWDALE

$$ Ashness Farm, ruling its valley high above Derwentwater, immerses guests in farm sounds and lakeland beauty. On this 750-acre working farm, now owned by the National Trust, people have raised sheep and cattle for centuries. Today, Anne and her family are "tenant farmers," keeping this farm operating and renting five rooms to boot (cozy lounge, farm-fresh eggs and sausage for breakfast, sack lunches available, just above Ashness Packhorse Bridge, tel. 017687/77361, www.ashnessfarm.co.uk, enquiries@ashnessfarm.co.uk).

$$ Seatoller Farm B&B is a rustic 16th-century house on another working farm owned by the National Trust. Ruby rents three rooms in her B&B, one of five buildings in this hamlet. The lounge has a toasty fireplace, and while the old windows are small, the abundant flower boxes keep things bright (closed Dec-mid-Jan, tel. 017687/77232, www.seatollerfarm.co.uk, info@seatollerfarm.co.uk). There's also a farm cottage for rent by the week.

¢ **Borrowdale Hostel,** in the secluded Borrowdale Valley just south of Rosthwaite, is a well-run place surrounded by many ways to immerse yourself in nature. The hostel offers cheap dinners and sack lunches (private and family rooms, breakfast extra, office open 7:30-23:00, game room, reservation tel. 0845-371-9624, hostel tel. 017687/77257, www.yha.org.uk, borrowdale@yha.org.uk). To reach this hostel from Keswick by bus, take #78, the Borrowdale Rambler. Note that the last bus from Keswick departs around 18:00 most of year (see page 725 for bus details).

Eating in Keswick

Keswick has a variety of good, basic eateries, but nothing particularly outstanding. Most places stop serving by 21:00.

$$ The Dog and Gun serves good pub food (their rump of lamb is a hit) with great pub ambience. Upon arrival, muscle up to the bar to order your beer or meal. Then snag a table as soon as one opens up. Mind your head and tread carefully: Low ceilings and wooden beams loom overhead, while paws poke out from under tables below, as Keswick's canines wait patiently for their masters to finish their beer (food served daily 12:00-21:00,

famous goulash, dog treats, 2 Lake Road, tel. 017687/73463).

$$ The Pheasant Inn is a walk outside town, but locals trek here regularly for the food. The menu offers Lake District pub standards (fish pie, Cumberland sausage, guinea fowl) as well as more inventive choices. Check the walls for caricatures of pub regulars, sketched at these tables by a Keswick artist. There's a small restaurant section, but I much prefer eating in the bar (food served daily 12:00-14:00 & 18:00-21:00, bar open until 23:00, Crosthwaite Road, tel. 017687/72219). From the town square, walk past the Pencil Museum, hang a right onto Crosthwaite Road, and walk 10 minutes. For a more scenic route, cross the river into Fitz Park, go left along the riverside path until it ends at the gate to Crosthwaite Road, turn right, and walk five minutes.

$ Abraham's Café, popular with townspeople, is a fine value for lunch. It's tucked away on the upper floor of the giant George Fisher outdoor store (Mon-Sat 10:00-17:00, Sun 10:30-16:30, on the corner of Borrowdale and Lake streets, tel. 017687/71811).

$$ Merienda Café, with a friendly staff and a contemporary space, can be a welcome break from pub grub, serving up an inviting menu of international, North African, and vegetarian dishes (daily 9:00-21:00, 10 Main Street, tel. 017687/72024).

$$ Bryson's Bakery and Tea Room has an enticing ground-floor bakery, with sandwiches and light lunches. The upstairs is a popular tearoom. Order lunch to-go from the bakery, or for a few pence more, eat in, either sitting on stools or at a sidewalk table. Upstairs, consider their Cream Tea made with local ingredients; it's a good deal for what most would consider "afternoon tea," with sandwiches, scones, and little cakes served on a three-tiered platter (daily 9:00-17:00, 42 Main Street, tel. 017687/72257).

$ The Old Keswickian, a fish-and-chips shop, is a fixture on the main square, with an old-fashioned take-away bar on the ground floor and 70 seats upstairs in a proper dining room (£10 plates and meat pies, daily 11:00-19:30, takeaway until 20:00, on Market Square, tel. 017687/73861).

$$ The Square Orange Café—small and very orange—is a quirky place that just makes you want to smile. It's popular—and they take no reservations, so grab one of their eight little tables when you can and then order at the bar. The eclectic menu features Spanish tapas, Neapolitan pizzas, fun cocktails, and fine European beers (daily 12:00-15:00 & 17:00-21:00, 20 St. John's Street, tel. 017687/73888).

$$ The George Hotel Restaurant and Bar, with a good solid pub and a large hotel dining room adjacent, is a warm and cozy Old World place. They offer the same extensive and very English menu in both the restaurant and bar (order at the pub's bar or wait to be served in the restaurant, tel. 017687/72076, St. John's Street, reservations in dining room only).

Eateries on Station Street: The street leading from the town square to the leisure center has several restaurants, including **$$ Casa Bella,** a popular and well-priced Italian place that's good for families—reserve ahead (daily 12:00-15:30 & 17:00-21:00, 24 Station Street, tel. 017687/75575, www.casabellakeswick.co.uk). **$$ Lakes Bar and Bistro** is popular for its burgers, meat pies, and good fixed-price meal deals (daily 10:00-23:00, 25 Station Street, tel. 017687/74080). **$ Asaya Thai Restaurant,** a hard-working, bright-and-mellow place, is a solid, inexpensive bet (daily 17:00-22:00, 21 Station Street, tel. 017687/75111).

Picnic Food: $ The Cornish Pasty offers an enticing variety of fresh meat pies to-go (daily 9:00-17:00 or until the pasties are all gone, across from The Dog and Gun on Borrowdale Road, tel. 017687/72205). Or stop by the huge **Booths** grocery store (see "Helpful Hints," earlier).

EATING IN THE NEWLANDS VALLEY

The farmhouse B&Bs of Newlands Valley don't serve dinner, but guests have two good options for an evening meal: Go into Keswick, or take the lovely 10-minute drive to Buttermere. In Buttermere you have three choices: **$$ The Fish** pub has fine indoor and outdoor seating, but takes no reservations (food served daily 12:00-14:00 & 18:00-21:00, family-friendly, good fish and daily

LAKE DISTRICT

specials with fresh vegetables, tel. 017687/70253). The neighboring **$$ Bridge Hotel Pub,** a bit cozier and more expensive, takes a modern approach to classic pub grub. If you want fancy service, you can eat in the more formal hotel restaurant (food served daily 9:00-21:30, tel. 017687/70252). For lunch, also consider the **$ Croft House Farm Café,** which serves freshly made soups and sandwiches to eat on their sunny deck or to take away (daily 10:00-16:00, tel. 017687/70235).

Keswick Connections

The nearest train station to Keswick is in Penrith (no lockers). For train and bus info, check at a TI, visit Traveline.info, or call 0345-748-4950 (for train). Most routes run less frequently on Sundays.

From Keswick by Bus: For bus routes and connections, see "Getting Around the Lake District—Without a Car," earlier.

From Penrith by Bus to: Keswick (hourly, every 2 hours on Sun in Nov-April, 45 minutes, pay driver, Stagecoach bus #X4 or #X5), **Ullswater** and **Glenridding** (5/day, more frequent June-Aug with open-top buses, 50 minutes, bus #508). The Penrith bus stop is just outside the train station (bus schedules posted inside and outside station).

From Penrith by Train to: Blackpool (nearly hourly, 2 hours, change in Preston), **Liverpool** (2/hour, 2.5 hours, change in Wigan or Preston), **Birmingham**'s New Street Station (4/day direct, more with transfer, 3 hours), **Durham** (hourly, 3 hours, 1-2 transfers), **York** (roughly 2/hour, 4 hours, 1-2 transfers), **London**'s Euston Station (hourly, 3.5 hours), **Edinburgh** (8/day direct, more with transfer, 1.5 hours), **Glasgow** (hourly direct, 1.5 hours), **Oban** (5/day, 6 hours, transfer in Glasgow).

ROUTE TIPS FOR DRIVERS

From Points South to the Lake District: From Blackpool, Liverpool, or North Wales, the direct, easy way to Keswick is to leave the M-6 at Penrith and take the A-66 motorway for 16 miles to Keswick. For a scenic sightseeing drive through the south lakes to Keswick, exit the M-6 on the A-590/A-591 through the towns of Kendal and Windermere to reach Brockhole National Park Visitors Centre. From Brockhole, the A-road to Keswick is fastest, but the high road—the tiny road over Kirkstone Pass to Glenridding and lovely Ullswater—is much more dramatic.

Coming to or from the West: Only 1,300 feet above sea level, Hardknott Pass is still a thriller, with a narrow, winding, steeply graded road. Just over the pass are the scant but evocative remains of the Hardknott Roman fortress. It can be slow and frustrating when the one-lane road is clogged by traffic. Avoid it on summer weekends.

Ullswater Lake Area

Long, narrow Ullswater, which some consider the loveliest lake in the area, offers miles of diverse and grand Lake District scenery. The main town on Ullswater is the stony village of **Glenridding,** which is little more than a few pubs and shops along the bank of a spritely stream. Visit the **TI** there for advice on the Ullswater area (daily 9:30-17:30, Nov-March weekends only until 15:30, located in the village's pay parking lot, tel. 017684/82414, www.visiteden. co.uk). For locations of Ullswater sights, see the "Lake District" map earlier in this chapter.

▲▲Ullswater Hike and Boat Ride

While you can drive it or cruise the lake, I'd ride the boat from the south tip halfway up (to Howtown—which is nothing more than a dock) and hike back. Or walk first, then enjoy an easy boat ride back.

An old-fashioned **"steamer" boat** (actually diesel-powered) leaves Glenridding regularly for Howtown (departs daily generally 9:45-16:55, 6-9/day April-Oct, fewer off-season, 40 minutes; £7.30 one-way, £12 round-trip, £17 round-the-lake ticket lets you hop on and off, covered by Ullswater Bus & Boat day pass, family rates, drivers can use safe pay-and-display parking lot, by public transit take bus #508 from Penrith, café at dock, tel. 017684/82229, www.ullswater-steamers.co.uk).

From Howtown, spend three to four hours hiking and dawdling along the well-marked path by the lake south to Patterdale, and then along the road back to Glenridding. This is a serious seven-mile walk with good views, varied terrain, and a few bridges and farms along the way. For a shorter hike from the Howtown pier, consider a three-mile loop around Hallin Fell. A rainy-day plan is to ride the covered boat up and down the lake to Howtown and Pooley Bridge at the northern tip of the lake (2 hours). Boats don't run in bad weather—call ahead if it looks iffy.

If you'd rather get out on the water on your own, you can rent **canoes and kayaks** just south of Glenridding—ask locally for details.

▲▲Lanty's Tarn and Keldas Hill

If you like the idea of an Ullswater-area hike but aren't up for the long huff from Howtown, consider this shorter (but still moderately challenging and plenty scenic) loop that leaves right from the TI's pay parking lot in Glenridding (about 2.5 miles, allow 2 hours; before embarking, buy the leaflet at the TI that describes this walk).

From the parking lot, head to the main road, turn right to cross the Glenridding Beck river, then turn right again immediately and follow the river up into the hills. After passing a row of cottages, turn left, cross the wooden bridge, and proceed up the hill through the swing gate. Just before the next swing gate (set in a stone wall—do not go through this gate), turn left (following *Grisedale* signs) and head to yet another gate. From here you can see the small lake called Lanty's Tarn.

While you'll eventually go through this gate and walk along the lake to finish the loop, first you can detour to the top of the adjacent hill, called Keldas, for sweeping views over the near side of Ullswater (to reach the summit, climb over the step gate and follow the faint path up the hill). Returning to—and passing through—the swing gate, you'll walk along Lanty's Tarn on your left, then begin your slow, steep, and scenic descent into the Grisedale Valley. Reaching the valley floor (and passing a noisy dog breeder's farm), cross the stone bridge, then turn left and follow the road all the way back to the lakefront, where a left turn returns you to Glenridding.

▲Aira Force Waterfall

On the north bank of Ullswater, there's a delightful little park with parking, a ranger trailer, and easy trails leading a half-mile uphill to a powerful 60-foot-tall waterfall. At the falls a little loop trail takes you over two romantic stone arched bridges. Wordsworth was inspired to write three poems here...and after taking this little walk, you'll know why. Park at the pay-and-display lot just where the A-5091 from Troutbeck hits the lake and the A-592. To get to the falls with a much shorter walk (10 minutes), drivers can find the Park Brow pay & display lot above the lake on A-5091 (direction Troutbeck).

Helvellyn

Considered by many the best high-mountain hike in the Lake District, this breathtaking 7.5-mile round-trip route from Glenridding includes the spectacular Striding Edge—about a half-mile knife's edge along the ridge. (If this is too scary, there is a detour trail.) Be careful; this is a demanding six-hour hike with some scrambling, and should be done only in good weather, since the wind can be fierce. While it's not the shortest route, the Glenridding ascent is best. Get advice from the Ullswater TI in Glenridding or look for various books on this hike at any area TI.

▲Kirkstone Pass

Heading south from Ullswater to Windermere, you drive over the 1500-foot Kirkstone Pass. The stark Ullswater Valley is famous for its old, dry stone walls, built without mortar. Back in the 18th century, the British parliament passed a series of "enclosures acts," which allowed private ownership of what had been communal farmland. Landowners began squabbling about boundaries and set about establishing clear property lines with stone walls. But because the walls were expensive, the feuding landowners began collaborating and sharing the cost...and they began getting along. To this day, these fine walls still define the valley's family farms. If you look carefully, you can see "sheep creeps"—small holes in the walls to allow sheep to be moved conveniently from one field to the next.

At the summit, stop to enjoy the view and check out the Kirkstone Pass Inn, a 500-year-old coaching stop. The steep road just across from the inn is called "The Struggle" for the work it took for those long-ago coaches to climb it.

▲Holehird Gardens

South of Kirkstone Pass on the Ullswater-Windermere road, Holehird is a haven for gardeners. Run by Lakeland Horticultural Society volunteers for 50 years, it's one of the most enjoyable gardens in England. Stop first at the reception to take advantage of the info desk and pick up a map. Adjacent are the walled garden and several greenhouses. Of particular interest are several National Plant Collections, a scheme to systematically collect and preserve particular plant families cultivated in the UK. The Holehird examples are well worth seeking out.

Cost and Hours: Free, donations welcome, open dawn to dusk, car park, WC, on the A-592 one mile north of Windermere, tel. 105394/46008, www.holehirdgardens.org.uk.

South Lake District

The South Lake District has a cheesiness that's similar to other popular English resort destinations. Here, piles of low-end vacationers suffer through terrible traffic, slurp ice cream, and get candy floss caught in their hair. The area around Windermere is worth a drive-through if you're a fan of Wordsworth or Beatrix Potter, but you'll still want to spend the majority of your Lake District time (and book your accommodations) up north.

GETTING AROUND THE SOUTH LAKE DISTRICT

By Car: Driving is your best option to see the small towns and sights clustered here; consider combining your drive with the bus trip mentioned next. If you're coming to or leaving the South Lake District from the west, you could take the Hardknott Pass for a scenic introduction to the area (see "Keswick Connections", earlier, for route tips).

By Bus: Buses #599 and #555 are a fine and stress-free way to lace together the gauntlet of sights in the congested Lake Windermere area. Consider leaving your car at Grasmere and enjoying the breezy and extremely scenic bus #599, hopping off and on as you like (see page 725 for details).

By Boat: Windermere Lake Cruises run from Bowness to Ambleside and other points on the lake all year (several itineraries offered, some are seasonal; tel. 015394/43360, www.windermere-lakecruises.co.uk).

Sights in the South Lake District

WORDSWORTH SIGHTS

William Wordsworth was one of the first writers to reject fast-paced city life. During England's Industrial Age, hearts were muzzled and brains ruled. Science was in, machines were taming nature, and factory hours were taming humans. In reaction to these brainy ideals, a rare few—dubbed Romantics—began to embrace untamed nature and undomesticated emotions.

Back then, nobody climbed a mountain just because it was there—but Wordsworth did. He'd "wander lonely as a cloud" through the countryside, finding inspiration in "plain living and high thinking." He soon attracted a circle of like-minded creative friends.

The emotional highs the Romantics felt weren't all natural. Wordsworth's poet friends Samuel Taylor Coleridge and Thomas de Quincey got stoned on opium and wrote poetry, combining their generation's over-the-counter painkiller drug with their tree-hugging passions (Coleridge's opium scale is on view in Dove Cottage). Today, opium is out of vogue, but the Romantic appreciation of the natural world thrives as visitors continue to inundate the region.

▲▲Dove Cottage at Wordsworth Grasmere

Following a year-long renovation, Dove Cottage reopens in the spring of 2020 with a new name (Wordsworth Grasmere) and new galleries and displays to celebrate the 250th anniversary of Wordsworth's birth. For literary types, this visit is the top sight of the

Wordsworth at Dove Cottage

William Wordsworth (1770-1850) was a Lake District home-boy. Born in Cockermouth (in a house now open to the public), he was schooled in Hawkshead. In adulthood, he married a local girl, settled down in Grasmere and Ambleside, and was buried in Grasmere's St. Oswald's churchyard.

But the 30-year-old man who moved into Dove Cottage in 1799 was not the carefree lad who'd once roamed the district's lakes and fields. At Cambridge University, he'd been a C student, graduating with no job skills and no interest in a nine-to-five career. Instead, he and a buddy hiked through Europe, where Wordsworth had an epiphany of the "sublime" atop Switzerland's Alps. He lived a year in France, watching the Revolution rage. It stirred his soul. He fell in love with a Frenchwoman who bore his daughter, Caroline. But lack of money forced him to return to England, and the outbreak of war with France kept them apart.

Pining away in London, William hung out in the pubs and coffeehouses with fellow radicals, where he met poet Samuel Taylor Coleridge. They inspired each other to write, edited each other's work, and jointly published a groundbreaking book of poetry.

In 1799, his head buzzing with words and ideas, William and his sister (and soul mate), Dorothy, moved into the white-washed, slate-tiled former inn now known as Dove Cottage. He came into a small inheritance, and dedicated himself to poetry full time. In 1802, during a break in the war with France, William returned there to finally meet his daughter. (He wrote of the rich experience: "It is a beauteous evening, calm and free... / Dear child! Dear Girl! that walkest with me here, / If thou appear untouched by solemn thought, / Thy nature is not therefore less divine.")

Having achieved closure, Wordsworth returned home to marry a former kindergarten classmate, Mary. She moved into Dove Cottage, along with an initially jealous Dorothy. Three of their five children were born here, and the cottage was also home to Mary's sister, the family dog Pepper (a gift from Sir Walter Scott; see Pepper's portrait), and frequent houseguests who bedded down in the pantry: Scott, Coleridge, and Thomas de Quincey, the Timothy Leary of opium.

The time at Dove Cottage was Wordsworth's "Golden Decade," when he penned his masterpieces. But after almost nine years here, Wordsworth's family and social status had outgrown the humble cottage. They moved first to a house in Grasmere before settling down in Rydal Hall. Wordsworth was changing. After the Dove years, he would write less, settle into a regular government job, quarrel with Coleridge, drift to the right politically, and endure criticism from old friends who branded him a sellout. Still, his poetry—most of it written at Dove—became increasingly famous, and he died honored as England's Poet Laureate.

Lake District. Take a short tour of William Wordsworth's humble cottage; get inspired in its excellent museum, which displays original writings, sketches, personal items, and fine paintings; and wander the garden/orchard.

The poet whose appreciation of nature and a back-to-basics lifestyle put this area on the map spent his most productive years (1799-1808) in this well-preserved stone cottage on the edge of Grasmere. After functioning as the Dove and Olive Bow pub for almost 200 years, it was bought by his family. This is where Wordsworth got married, had kids, and wrote much of his best poetry. The place comes with some amazing artifacts, including the poet's passport and suitcase (he packed light) and his own furniture. Even during his lifetime, Wordsworth was famous, and Dove Cottage was turned into a museum in 1891—it's now protected by the Wordsworth Trust.

Cost and Hours: £9, daily 9:30-17:30, Nov-Feb 10:00-16:30 except closed Jan and for events in Dec and Feb (call ahead), café, bus #555 from Keswick, bus #555 or #599 from Windermere, tel. 015394/35544, www.wordsworth.org.uk. Pay parking in the Dove Cottage lot off the main road (A-591), 50 yards from the site.

Visiting the Cottage and Museum: Wordsworth's appreciation of nature, his Romanticism, and the ways his friends unleashed their creative talents with such abandon are appealing. The cottage tour and adjoining museum, with lots of actual manuscripts handwritten by Wordsworth and his illustrious friends, are both excellent. In dry weather, the garden where the poet was much inspired is lovely. (Visit this after leaving the cottage tour and pick up the description at the back door. The garden is closed when wet.) Allow 1.5 hours for this visit.

Poetry Readings: The Wordsworth Trust puts on poetry readings of Wordsworth's works written at Dove Cottage. Readings are held in the museum library in a relaxed and friendly setting (£5, confirm schedule in advance, same contact info as above).

▲Rydal Mount and Gardens

Located just down the road from Dove Cottage, this sight is worthwhile for Wordsworth fans. The poet's final, higher-class home, with a lovely garden and view, lacks the humble charm of Dove Cottage, but still evokes the creative spirit of the literary giant who lived here for 37 years. His family repurchased it in 1969 (after a 100-year gap), and his great-great-great-granddaughter still calls

Wordsworth's Poetry

At Dove Cottage, Wordsworth was immersed in the beauty of nature and the simple joy of his young, growing family. It was here that he reflected on both his idyllic childhood and his troubled 20s. The following are select lines from two well-known poems from this fertile time.

Ode: Intimations of Immortality

> There was a time when meadow, grove, and stream,
> The earth, and every common sight, to me did seem
> Apparelled in celestial light,
> The glory and the freshness of a dream.
> It is not now as it hath been of yore;—
> Turn wheresoe'er I may,
> By night or day,
> The things which I have seen I now can see no more.

I Wandered Lonely as a Cloud (Daffodils)

> I wandered lonely as a cloud
> That floats on high o'er vales and hills,
> When all at once I saw a crowd,
> A host, of golden daffodils;
> Beside the lake, beneath the trees,
> Fluttering and dancing in the breeze...
> . . . .
> For oft, when on my couch I lie
> In vacant or in pensive mood,
> They flash upon that inward eye
> Which is the bliss of solitude,
> And then my heart with pleasure fills,
> And dances with the daffodils.

LAKE DISTRICT

it home on occasion, as shown by recent family photos sprinkled throughout the house. After a short intro by the attendant, you are free to roam. Wander through the garden William himself designed, which has changed little since then. Surrounded by his nature, you can imagine the poet enjoying them with you. "O happy garden! Whose seclusion deep hath been so friendly to industrious hours; and to soft slumbers, that did gently steep our spirits, carrying with them dreams of flowers, and wild notes warbled among leafy bowers."

Cost and Hours: £7.50; daily 9:30-17:30, Nov-Dec and Feb 11:00-16:30 and closed Mon-Tue, closed Jan; occasionally closed for private functions—check website; tearoom, 1.5 miles north of Ambleside, well-signed, free and easy parking, bus #555 from Keswick, tel. 015394/33002, www.rydalmount.co.uk.

BEATRIX POTTER SIGHTS

Author and illustrator Beatrix Potter, of Peter Rabbit fame, lived and worked in the Lake District for years. Of the many attractions in the area that claim a connection to her, there are two serious sights: Hill Top, her farm, and the Beatrix Potter Gallery, filled with her sketches and paintings. The sights are two miles apart: Beatrix Potter Gallery is in Hawkshead, an extremely cute but extremely touristy town that's a 20-minute drive south of Ambleside; Hill Top Farm is south of Hawkshead, in Near Sawrey village.

On busy summer days, the wait to get into Hill Top Farm can last several hours. If you like quaint towns engulfed in Potter tourism (Hawkshead), this extra waiting time can be a blessing. Otherwise, you'll wish you were in the woods somewhere with Wordsworth.

To reach Hawkshead from Windermere, take bus #505 or catch the little 15-car ferry from Bowness (runs continually except when it's extremely windy, 10-minute trip, £5 car fare includes all passengers). If going straight to the farm, it's a 5-minute drive or 40-minute walk from the ferry landing. If you have questions, visit the Hawkshead TI inside the Ooh-La-La gift shop across from the parking lot (tel. 015394/36946). To reach Hill Top Farm from Hawkshead, see the directions later.

▲Hill Top Farm

A hit with Beatrix Potter fans (and skippable for others), this dark and intimate cottage, swallowed up in the inspirational and rough nature around it, provides an enjoyable if quick experience. The six-room farm was left just as it was when Potter died in 1943. At her request, the house is set as if she had just stepped out—flowers on the tables, fire on, low lights. While there's no printed information here, guides in  each room are eager to explain things. Fans of the classic *Tale of Samuel Whiskers* will recognize the home's rooms, furniture, and views—the book and its illustrations were inspired by an invasion of rats when Potter bought this place. If exasperated by long lines, remember you can enjoy the garden and see the house from outside for free at any time.

Beatrix Potter (1866-1943)

As a girl growing up in London, Beatrix Potter vacationed in the Lake District, where she became inspired to write her popular children's books. Unable to get a publisher, she self-published the first two editions of *The Tale of Peter Rabbit* in 1901 and 1902. When she finally landed a publisher, sales of her books were phenomenal. With the money she made, she bought Hill Top Farm, a 17th-century cottage, and fixed it up, living there sporadically from 1905 until she married in 1913. Potter was more than a children's book writer; she was a fine artist, an avid gardener, and a successful farmer. She married a lawyer and put her knack for business to use, amassing a 4,000-acre estate. An early conservationist, she used the garden-cradled cottage as a place to study nature. She willed it—along with the rest of her vast estate—to the National Trust, which she enthusiastically supported.

Cost and Hours: Farmhouse-£12, gardens-free; June-Aug daily 10:00-17:30; mid-Feb-May and Sept-Oct until 16:30 and closed Fri; house closed Nov-Dec but gardens and shop open Sat-Sun; closed Jan-mid-Feb; tel. 015394/36269, www.nationaltrust.org.uk/hill-top.

Getting In: Admission is by timed tickets, which cannot be booked in advance (only eight people are let in every five minutes). To beat the lines, get to the ticket office 15 minutes before it opens. Otherwise, call the farm for the current wait times (if no one answers, leave a message for the administrator; if the office is attended, someone will call you back). Big bus or student groups (common in late July and Aug) can book up several hours of entries at any moment if you're unlucky.

Getting There: Mountain Goat Tours runs a shuttle bus (Mountain Goat #525) from across the Hawkshead TI to the farm every 20-40 minutes (tel. 015394/45161). Drivers can take the B-5286 and B-5285 from Ambleside or the B-5285 from Coniston—be prepared for extremely narrow roads with no shoulders that are often lined with stone walls. You'll find the museum parking lot and ticket office about 150 yards down the road from the farm.

▲Beatrix Potter Gallery

Located in the cute town of Hawkshead, this gallery fills the one-time law office of Potter's husband with the wonderful and intimate drawings and watercolors she made to illustrate her books. Each year the museum highlights a new theme and brings out a different set of Potter's paintings, drawings, and other items. Unlike Hill Top, the gallery has plenty of explanation about her life and work, including touchscreen displays and information panels. Anyone will find this museum rather charming and her art surprisingly interesting.

Cost and Hours: £6.80, daily 10:30-16:00, closed Nov-mid-Feb, Main Street, drivers use the nearby Hawkshead pay-and-display lot and walk 200 yards to the town center, tel. 015394/36355, www.nationaltrust.org.uk/beatrix-potter-gallery.

Hawkshead Grammar School Museum

This interesting museum, just across from the pay-and-display parking lot, was founded in 1585 and is where William Words-worth studied from 1779 to 1787. It shows off old school benches and desks whittled with penknife graffiti.

Cost and Hours: £2.50 includes guided tour on the hour; Mon-Sat 10:00-13:00 & 14:00-17:00, closed Sun and Nov-March; tel. 015394/36735, www.hawksheadgrammar.org.uk.

The World of Beatrix Potter

This exhibit, a hit with children, is gimmicky, with all the historical value of a Disney ride. The 45-minute experience begins with a five-minute film introducing Potter and her characters. From there, you'll tour through a series of Lake District tableaux starring Mrs. Tiggy-winkle, Peter Rabbit, Mr. Jeremy Fisher, and company. In July and August, there's often a daily theater show ("Where is Peter Rabbit?")—check event schedule online and reserve ahead.

Cost and Hours: £8, kids-£4, daily 10:00-17:30, last entry one hour before closing, tearoom, on Crag Brow in Bowness-on-Windermere, tel. 015394/88444, www.hop-skip-jump.com.

MORE SIGHTS AT LAKE WINDERMERE

Brockhole National Park Visitors Centre

This visitors center (between Ambleside and Windermere on the A-591) is set in a lakeside park and surrounded by lots of touristic kitsch. It offers a free video on life in the Lake District, an information desk, exhibits, a shop (with maps and guidebooks), gardens, and nature walks. It's a popular place to bring kids for its adventure playground with slides, swings, nets, and swinging bridges. Other family activities include an aerial treetop trek, a zip line, and mini golf. Boat and bike rentals are also available.

Cost and Hours: Free entry but you'll pay to park; daily 10:00-17:00, Nov-March until 16:00; tel. 015394/46601, www.lakedistrict.gov.uk.

Cruise: For a joyride around famous Lake Windermere, you can catch the Brockhole "Green" cruise here (£9, runs daily April-Oct 10:20-17:45, hourly, 2/hour in summer, 50-minute circuit, scant narration, passengers can hop on and off on one ticket, tel. 015394/43360, www.windermere-lakecruises.co.uk).

Windermere Jetty Museum

On the east shore of Windermere, this museum offers a fun opportunity to learn about the boating history of the lake over the past 200 years. Brush up on your maritime vocabulary with the display of mooring warps, splicing fids, fenders, and more. Then view the museum's collection of 40 boats (about half are exhibited at any one time). You'll find rowing skiffs (including one belonging to Beatrix Potter), motorboats, and steam launches, including *Dolly,* a 19th-century example salvaged from the bottom of the lake in 1962. At the adjacent conservation workshop, watch the ongoing restoration of the old boats (there's a "conservation conversation" daily at 11:00); other vintage boats are berthed in the lakeside boathouse (daily presentation at 14:00). Kids will enjoy the model boat pond.

Cost and Hours: £9, £19 includes trip on the steam launch *Osprey,* daily 10:00-17:30; Nov-Feb 10:30-16:00; last entry one hour before closing, free parking, view café, tel. 01539/637-940, www.windermerejetty.org.

Getting There: The museum is just off the A-592, near Bowness Pier. Bus #599 from Ambleside (daily mid-July-Aug) stops at Bowness Pier (8-minute walk), where Windermere Lake Cruises also stop (www.windermere-lakecruises.co.uk).

Lakes Aquarium

Get a glimpse of the natural history of Cumbria via exhibits describing the local wildlife living in lake and coastal environments, including otters, eels, pike, and sharks. A rainforest exhibit features reptiles and marmoset monkeys. Experts give various talks throughout the day.

Cost and Hours: £9, £6 for kids under age 16, cheaper online, family deals, daily 10:00-18:00, until 17:00 in winter, last entry one hour before closing, in Lakeside, one mile north of Newby Bridge, at south end of Lake Windermere, tel. 015395/30153, www.lakesaquarium.co.uk.

Hayes Garden World

This extensive gardening center, a popular weekend excursion for locals, offers garden supplies, a bookstore, a playground, and gorgeous grounds. Gardeners could wander this place all afternoon. Upstairs is a fine cafeteria-style restaurant (open Mon-Sat 9:00-18:00, Sun 10:00-17:00, at south end of Ambleside on main drag, see *Garden Centre* signs, located at north end of Lake Windermere, tel. 015394/33434, www.hayesgardenworld.co.uk).

LAKE DISTRICT

YORK

Historic York is loaded with world-class sights. Marvel at the York Minster, England's finest Gothic church. Ramble The Shambles, York's wonderfully preserved medieval quarter. Enjoy a walking tour led by an old Yorker. Hop a train at one of the world's greatest railway museums, travel to the 1800s in the York Castle Museum, head back 1,000 years to Viking times at the Jorvik Viking Centre, or dig into the city's buried past at the Yorkshire Museum.

York has a rich history. In AD 71 it was Eboracum, a Roman provincial capital—the northernmost city in the empire. Constantine was proclaimed emperor here in AD 306. In the fifth century, as Rome was toppling, the Roman emperor sent a letter telling England it was on its own, and York—now called Eoforwic—became the capital of the Anglo-Saxon kingdom of Northumbria.

The city's first church was built in 627, and the town became an early Christian center of learning. The Vikings later took the town, and from the 9th through the 11th century, it was a Danish trading center called Jorvik. The invading and conquering Normans destroyed and then rebuilt the city, fortifying it with a castle and the walls you see today.

Medieval York, with 9,000 inhabitants, grew rich on the wool trade and became England's second city. Henry VIII used the city's fine Minster as the northern capital of his Anglican Church. (In today's Anglican Church, the Archbishop of York is second only to the Archbishop of Canterbury.)

In the Industrial Age, York was the railway hub of northern England. When it was built in 1877, York's train station was the world's largest. During World War II, the station suffered an aerial bombardment. (In response to Allied bombing of historic German towns, the Nazis unleashed the "Baedeker raids," bombing English cities—including York—that were described as the most historic and beautiful in the leading German guidebook of the day.)

Today, York feels like a big, traffic-free amusement park for adults. Its leading industry is tourism. It seems like everything that's great about Britain finds its best expression in this manageable town. While the city has no single claim to fame, York is more than the sum of its parts. With its strollable cobbles and half-timbered buildings, grand cathedral and excellent museums, thriving restaurant scene and welcoming locals, York delights.

PLANNING YOUR TIME

After London, York is the best sightseeing city in England. On even a 10-day trip through England, it deserves two nights and a day. For the best 36 hours, follow this plan: Arrive early enough to catch the 17:15 evensong service at the Minster, then take the free city walking tour at 18:15 (evening tours offered June-Aug only). Enjoy dinner (which you reserved in advance) at one of the city's bistros. The next morning at 9:00, take my self-guided walk, interrupting it midway with a tour of the Minster. Finish the walk and grab lunch. To fill your afternoon, choose among the town's many important sights (such as the York Castle Museum or the Railway Museum). Spend the evening enjoying a ghost walk of your choice and another memorable dinner.

This is a packed day; as you review this chapter, you'll see that there are easily two days of sightseeing fun in York.

Orientation to York

There are roughly 200,000 people in York and its surrounding area; about one in ten is a student. But despite the city's size, the sightseer's York is small. Virtually everything is within a few minutes' walk: sights, train station, TI, and B&Bs. The longest walk a visitor could take (from a B&B across the old town to the York Castle Museum) is about half an hour.

Bootham Bar, a gate in the medieval town wall, is the hub of your York visit. (In York, a "bar" is a gate and a "gate" is a street. Blame the Vikings.) At Bootham Bar and on Exhibition Square, you'll find the starting points for most walking tours and bus tours, handy access to the medieval town wall, a public WC, and

Bootham Street (which leads to my recommended B&Bs). To find your way around York, use the Minster's towers as a navigational landmark, or follow the strategically placed signposts, which point out all places of interest to tourists.

TOURIST INFORMATION

York's TI is a block in front of the Minster (Mon-Sat 9:00-17:00, Sun 10:00-16:00, 1 Museum Street, tel. 01904/550-099, www. visityork.org). They sell a quality £1 map.

York Pass: The TI sells a £45 one-day pass that covers all the sights in York, the City Sightseeing bus, riverboat ride, and a few regional sights. You'd have to be a very busy sightseer to make this pass worth the cost (it's good for a calendar day, not 24 hours; multiday options available, www.yorkpass.com).

ARRIVAL IN YORK

By Train: The train station is a 10-minute walk from downtown. Day-trippers can pay to store baggage at the small hut next to the Europcar office just off Queen Street—as you exit the station, turn right and walk along a bridge to the first intersection, then turn right (daily 8:00-20:00). Baggage storage is also available near Bootham Bar—see "Helpful Hints," later.

Recommended B&Bs are a 5- to 15-minute walk or a £7-9 taxi ride from the station. For walking directions to the B&Bs, see page 805.

To walk downtown from the station, exit straight, crossing the street through the bus stops, and turn left down Station Road, keeping the wall on your right. At the first intersection, turn right through the gap in the wall and then left across the river, and follow the crowd toward the Gothic towers of the Minster. After the bridge, a block before the Minster, you'll see the TI on your right.

By Car: Driving and parking in York is maddening. Those day-tripping here should follow signs to one of several park-and-ride lots ringing the perimeter. At these lots, parking is free, and cheap shuttle buses go every 10 minutes into the center. (But, oddly, they generally don't allow overnight parking.)

If you're sleeping here, park your car where your B&B advises and walk. As you near York (and your B&B), you'll hit the A-1237 ring road. Follow this to the A-19/Thirsk roundabout (next to river on northwest side of town). From the roundabout, follow signs for *York*, traveling through Clifton into Bootham. All recommended B&Bs are four or five blocks before you hit the medieval city gate (see the map on page 807). If you're approaching York from the south, take the M-1 until it becomes the A-1M, exit at junction 45 onto the A-64, and follow it for 10 miles until you reach York's

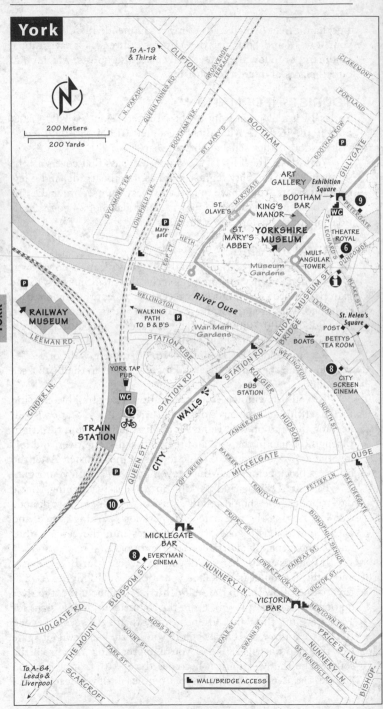

York

200 Meters
200 Yards

To A-19
& Thirsk

CLIFTON

GROSVENOR TERRACE

CLAREMONT

PORTLAND

N. PARADE

QUEEN ANNES RD.

BOOTHAM TER.

ST. MARY'S

MARYGATE

BOOTHAM

BOOTHAM ROW

GILLYGATE

SYCAMORE TER.

LONGFIELD TER.

ESP. CT.

HETH

FRED

Marygate

ART
GALLERY

Exhibition
Square

BOOTHAM
BAR

PETERGATE

9

WC

ST. OLAVE'S

KING'S
MANOR

ST. LEONARD'S

THEATRE
ROYAL

6

ST.
MARY'S
ABBEY

YORKSHIRE
MUSEUM

DUNCOMBE

MULT-
ANGULAR
TOWER

BLAKE ST.

Museum
Gardens

i

RAILWAY
MUSEUM

WELLINGTON

River Ouse

LENDAL
BRIDGE

MUSEUM ST.

LENDAL

St. Helen's
Square

POST

BETTYS
TEA ROOM

P

LEEMAN RD.

CINDER LN.

WALKING
PATH
TO B & B'S

STATION RISE

War Mem.
Gardens

STATION RD.

STATION RD.

BOATS

WELLINGTON

CITY
SCREEN
CINEMA

8

YORK TAP
PUB

WC

12

TRAIN
STATION

WALLS

ROUGIER

BUS
STATION

NORTH ST.

HUDSON

OUSE

QUEEN ST.

CITY

TANNER ROW

BARKER

TOFT GREEN

MICKELGATE

FETTER LN.

SKELDERGATE

10

TRINITY LN.

PRIORY ST.

BISHOPHILL SENIOR

MICKLEGATE
BAR

8 Everyman
Cinema

BLOSSOM ST.

NUNNERY LN.

LOWER PRIORY ST.

FAIRFAX ST.

VICTOR ST.

VICTORIA
BAR

NEWTOWN TER.

HOLGATE RD.

THE MOUNT

MOSS ST.

MOUNT ST.

PARK ST.

DALE ST.

SWANN ST.

PRICE'S LN.

ST. BENEDICT RD.

NUNNERY LN.

BISHOP

To A-64,
Leeds &
Liverpool

SCARCROFT

WALL/BRIDGE ACCESS

YORK

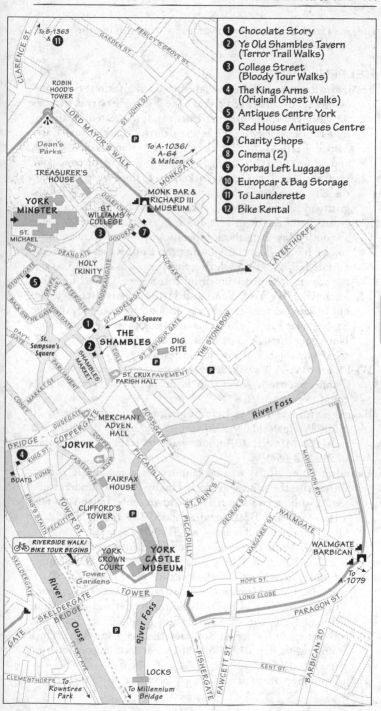

1 Chocolate Story
2 Ye Old Shambles Tavern (Terror Trail Walks)
3 College Street (Bloody Tour Walks)
4 The Kings Arms (Original Ghost Walks)
5 Antiques Centre York
6 Red House Antiques Centre
7 Charity Shops
8 Cinema (2)
9 Yorbag Left Luggage
10 Europcar & Bag Storage
11 To Launderette
12 Bike Rental

ring road (A-1237), which allows you to avoid driving through the city center.

HELPFUL HINTS

Festivals: Book a room well in advance during festival times and on weekends any time of year. The **Viking Festival** features *lur* horn-blowing, warrior drills, and re-created battles in mid-February (www.jorvikvikingfestival.co.uk). The **Early Music Festival** (medieval minstrels, Renaissance dance, and so on) zings its strings in early July (www.ncem.co.uk/yemf.shtml). The **Great Yorkshire Fringe Festival** keeps the city entertained the last two weeks of each July (www.greatyorkshirefringe.com). York claims to be the "Ascot of the North," and the town fills up on horse-race weekends (once a month May-Oct, check schedules at www.yorkracecourse.co.uk); it's especially busy during the **Ebor Races** in mid-August. (Many avoid York during this period, as prices go up and the streets are filled with drunken revelers. Others find that attractive.) The **York Food and Drink Festival** takes a bite out of late September (www.yorkfoodfestival.com). And the St. Nicholas Fair Christmas market jingles its bells from mid-November through Christmas. For a complete list of festivals, see www.visityork.org/whats-on/festivals.

Wi-Fi: Free Wi-Fi is available in the city center using York's City Connect network (select the "form" option and create an account to gain access).

Baggage Storage: Yorbag Left Luggage has a tiny office at 20 High Petergate (daily 9:00-19:00, just inside Bootham Bar near the Minster, 10-minute walk to train station, mobile 07561-852-654).

Laundry: Some B&Bs will do laundry for a reasonable charge. Otherwise the nearest place is **Haxby Road Launderette,** a long 15-minute walk north of the town center (or you can take a bus—ask your B&B for directions, 124 Haxby Road, call ahead for prices and hours—tel. 01904/623-379).

Bike Rental: With the exception of the pedestrian center, the town's not great for biking. But there are several fine countryside rides from York, and the riverside New Walk bike path is pleasant. **Cycle Heaven** is at the train station (£10/2 hours, £15/5 hours, £20/24 hours, includes helmet and lock, Mon-Fri 8:30-17:30, Sat 9:00-17:00, Sun 11:00-16:00, closed Sun off-season, to the left as you face the main station entrance from outside, tel. 01904/622-701). For location, see map on page 770.

Taxi: From the train station, taxis zip new arrivals to their B&Bs

for £7-9. Queue up at the taxi stand, or call 01904/623-332; cabbies don't start the meter until you get in.

Car Rental: If you're nearing the end of your trip, consider dropping your car upon arrival in York. The money saved by turning it in early just about pays for the train ticket that whisks you effortlessly to London. In York, you'll find these agencies: **Avis** (3 Layerthorpe, tel. 0844-544-6117); **Hertz** (at train station, tel. 0843-653-503); **Budget** (near the National Railway Museum behind the train station at 75 Leeman Road, tel. 01904/644-919); and **Europcar** (off Queen Street near train station, tel. 0371-384-3458). Beware: Car-rental agencies close early on Saturday afternoons and all day Sunday. This is OK when dropping off, but picking up at these times is possible only by prior arrangement (and for an extra fee).

Tours in York

WALKING TOURS
A walking tour in York is worth ▲▲▲.

Free Walks with Volunteer Guides
Charming locals give energetic, entertaining, and free two-hour walks through York (daily at 10:15 and 13:15, June-Aug also at 18:15; depart from Exhibition Square in front of the art gallery, tel. 01904/550-098, www.avgyork.co.uk). These tours often go long because the guides love to teach and tell stories. You're welcome to cut out early—but let them know, or they'll worry that they've lost you.

York Tour
York Tour offers two different, more intellectually demanding walks with a history focus (£18, daily at 14.00, 90 minutes; £15, daily at 18:00, 1 hour; meet at Exhibition Square, must book online, mobile 07963-791-937, www.yorktour.com). The evening walk is a nice option for those who appreciate history over ghost stories. **Alfred Hickling,** who runs York Tour, has a passion for York's history and also gives private tours (£90/half-day, mobile 07963-791-937 www.yorktour.com).

Ghost Walks
Each evening, the old center of York is crawling with creepy ghost walks. (York lays claim to being the most haunted city in Europe.) These walks are generally 1.5 hours long, cost £5-7, and go rain or shine. Reservations are usually not necessary. You simply show up at the advertised time and place, your black-clad guide appears, and you follow him or her to the first stop. Your guide gives a sample of

the entertainment you have in store, humorously collects the "toll," and you're off.

You'll see fliers and signboards all over town advertising the many ghost walks. Companies come and go, but I find there are three general styles of walks: street theater, historic, and storytelling. Here are three reliably good walks, one for each style (discount for children under 14).

The **Terror Trail Walk** has entertaining guides with backgrounds in the performing arts. The tours are both thought-provoking and historic. A good mix of horrifying stories, historical (fun) facts, humor, and role-play makes the tour playful and engaging (£5, daily at 18:45, meet in front of Ye Old Shambles Tavern on The Shambles, www.yorkterrortrail.co.uk).

The **Bloody Tour of York,** led by Mad Alice (an infamous figure in York lore), is an engaging walk with captivating descriptions about the plague, martyred saints, the torturing of regicide-wannabe Guy Fawkes, and other bloody tales. Alice may be mad, but she provides a fine blend of history, violence, and mayhem (£7, Thu-Sat at 18:00, also at 20:00 in April-Oct, no tours Sun-Wed, Dec-Jan by reservation only, meet outside St. Williams College behind the Minster on College Street, www.thebloodytourofyork.co.uk).

The **Original Ghost Walk,** said to be the first of its kind, dates to the 1970s. The walk covers some of the supposedly haunted places in York, where old dukes, Vikings, and Roman soldiers are still seen at night. The walk has more classic spooky storytelling than comedy, and you may learn that your B&B is haunted—or that sits atop an old graveyard (£5, daily at 20:00, meet outside The Kings Arms at Ouse Bridge, www.theoriginalghostwalkofyork.co.uk).

OTHER TOURS IN YORK
Food Tour
Tours in a Dish, led by Marion Martinez, makes five stops in three hours that can also serve as lunch. The tour visits small eateries offering both savory and sweet cuisine, mostly modern and eclectic rather than traditional English, where you meet the artisan (£50/person, 2-8 people, departs at 11:30 from the Minster, book online, mobile 07588-773-647, www.toursinadish.com).

Hop-on, Hop-off Bus Tour
City Sightseeing's half-enclosed, double-decker, hop-on, hop-off buses circle York, taking tourists past secondary sights that the city walking tours skip—the mundane perimeter of town. While you can hop on and off all day, York is so compact that these have no real transportation value. If taking a bus tour, I'd catch either one at Exhibition Square (near Bootham Bar) and ride it for an ori-

York at a Glance

▲▲▲**York Minster** York's pride and joy, and one of England's finest churches, with stunning stained-glass windows, text-book Decorated Gothic design, and glorious evensong services. **Hours:** Mon-Sat 9:00-18:30, Sun 12:30-15:00; shorter hours for tower and undercroft; evensong services Tue-Sat and some Mon at 17:15, Sun at 16:00. See page 784.

▲▲▲**Walking Tours** Variety of guided town walks and evening ghost walks covering York's history. **Hours:** Various times daily; fewer off-season. See page 773.

▲▲**York Castle Museum** Far-ranging collection displaying everyday objects from Victorian times to the present. **Hours:** Daily 9:30-17:00. See page 798.

▲▲**National Railway Museum** Train buff's nirvana, tracing the history of all manner of rail-bound transport. **Hours:** Daily 10:00-18:00. See page 799.

▲**Yorkshire Museum** Archaeology and natural history museum with York's best Viking exhibit, plus Roman, Saxon, Norman, and Gothic artifacts. **Hours:** Daily 10:00-17:00. See page 792.

▲**Merchant Adventurers' Hall** Vast medieval guildhall with displays recounting life and commerce in the Middle Ages. **Hours:** Sun-Fri 10:00-16:30, Sat until 13:30. See page 795.

▲**Jorvik Viking Centre** Entertaining and informative Disney-style exhibit/ride exploring Viking lifestyles and artifacts. **Hours:** Daily 10:00-17:00, Nov-March until 16:00. See page 796.

▲**Fairfax House** Glimpse into an 18th-century Georgian family house, with enjoyably chatty docents. **Hours:** Tue-Sat 10:00-17:00, Sun 11:00-16:00, Mon by tour only at 11:00 and 14:00, closed Jan-mid-Feb. See page 797.

▲**The Shambles** Atmospheric old butchers' quarter, with colorful, tipsy medieval buildings. See page 783.

▲**Ouse Riverside Walk or Bike Ride** Bucolic path along river to a mod pedestrian bridge. See page 801.

entation all the way around. Consider getting off at the National Railway Museum and skipping the last five minutes. In the summer, several departures come with a live guide (£15, pay driver, cash only, ticket valid 24 hours, Easter-Oct departs every 10-15 minutes, daily 9:00-17:30, less frequent off-season, about 1 hour, tel. 01904/633-990, www.yorkbus.co.uk).

Boat Cruise

City Cruise York does a lazy, narrated, 45-minute lap along the River Ouse (£10, April-Sept daily 10:30-16:30, runs every 30 minutes, off-season 4/day, no cruises Dec-Jan; leaves from Lendal Bridge, also 1-hour evening cruise at 19:30 and 21:15 for £12, leaves from King's Staith near Skeldergate Bridge; tel. 01904/628-324, www.citycruisesyork.com).

Yorkshire Day Trips

Two reliable companies run all-day minibus (16 passenger) tours with various routes covering the nearby North York Moors, Yorkshire Dales, and Whitby on the coast. Tours cost around £40 and are an efficient way to get a taste of this scenic and charming region without the headache and expense of a rental car (**Mountain Goat Tours**, tel. 01904/405-341, www.mountain-goat.com; and **Bob Holiday's Day Trips from York**, tel. 01609/779-933, www.bobholidays.com).

York Walk

Get a taste of Roman and medieval York on this easy, self-guided stroll. The walk begins in the gardens just in front of the Yorkshire Museum, covers a stretch of the medieval city walls, and then cuts through the middle of the old town. Start at the ruins of St. Mary's Abbey in the Museum Gardens (see the "York Walk" map).

❶ St. Mary's Abbey

This abbey dates to the age of William the Conqueror—whose harsh policies (called the "Harrowing of the North") consisted of massacres and destruction, including the burning of York's main church. His son Rufus, who tried to improve relations in the 11th century, established a great church here. The church became an abbey that thrived from the 13th century until the Dissolution of the Monasteries in the 16th century. The Dissolution, which accompanied the Protestant Reformation and break with Rome, was a power play by Henry VIII. The king wanted much more than just a divorce: He wanted the land and riches of the monasteries. Upset with the pope, he demanded that his subjects pay him taxes rather than give the Church tithes. (For more information, see the sidebar on page 788.)

As you gaze at this ruin, imagine magnificent abbeys like this scattered throughout the realm. Henry VIII destroyed most of them, taking the lead from their roofs and leav- ing the stones to scaveng- ing townsfolk. Scant as they are today, these ruins still evoke a time of im- mense monastic power. The one surviving wall was the west half of a very long, skinny nave. The tall

arch marked the start of the transept. Stand on the nearby plaque that reads *Crossing beneath central tower*, and look up at the air that now fills the space where a huge tower once stood. (Fine carved stonework from the ruined abbey is on display in a basement room of the adjacent Yorkshire Museum.)

• *With your back to the abbey, see the fine Neoclassical building hous- ing the* **Yorkshire Museum** *(worth a visit and described later, under "Sights in York"). Walk in front of this building and circle left down a tree-covered lane. On your right is a corner of the* **Roman Wall** *with the* **Multangular Tower.** *After 30 yards, a lane on the right leads through a garden, past yew trees (York means "place of the yew trees"), and through a small gated arch in the wall. Step through the wall and look right for a peek into the ruined tower.*

❷ Multangular Tower

This 12-sided tower (c. AD 300) was likely a catapult station built to protect the town from enemy river traffic. The red ribbon of bricks was a Roman trademark—both structural and decora- tive. The lower stones are Roman, while the upper (and bigger) stones are medieval. After Rome fell, York suffered through two centuries of a Dark Age. Then, in the ninth century, the Vikings ruled. They built with wood, so almost nothing from that period remains. The Normans came in 1066 and built in stone, generally atop Roman structures (like this wall). The wall that defined the ancient Roman garrison town worked for the Norman town, too. But after the English Civil War in the 1600s and Jacobite rebel- lions in the 1700s (Britain's last internal conflicts), fortified walls were no longer needed in the country's interior.

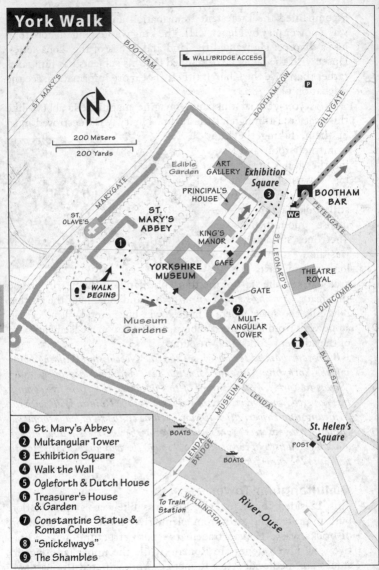

York Walk

WALL/BRIDGE ACCESS

BOOTHAM

ST. MARY'S

MARYGATE

Edible Garden

ART GALLERY

Exhibition Square

BOOTHAM ROW

GILLYGATE

200 Meters
200 Yards

PRINCIPAL'S HOUSE

ST. OLAVE'S

ST. MARY'S ABBEY

KING'S MANOR

❸

BOOTHAM BAR

PETERGATE

WC

①

YORKSHIRE MUSEUM

CAFÉ

ST. LEONARD'S

THEATRE ROYAL

DUNCOMBE

WALK BEGINS

GATE

② MULT- ANGULAR TOWER

Museum Gardens

BLAKE ST.

𝑖

① St. Mary's Abbey
② Multangular Tower
③ Exhibition Square
④ Walk the Wall
⑤ Ogleforth & Dutch House
⑥ Treasurer's House & Garden
⑦ Constantine Statue & Roman Column
⑧ "Snickelways"
⑨ The Shambles

BOATS

MUSEUM ST.

LENDAL

LENDAL BRIDGE

BOATS

St. Helen's Square

POST

To Train Station

WELLINGTON

River Ouse

YORK

• *Now, return to the tree-covered lane and turn right, walking between the museum and the Roman wall. Continuing straight, the lane goes between the abbot's palace and the town wall. This is a "snickelway"—a small, characteristic York lane or footpath. The snickelway pops out on...*

❸ Exhibition Square

With Henry VIII's Dissolution of the Monasteries, the abbey was destroyed and the Abbot's Palace became the **King's Manor** (from

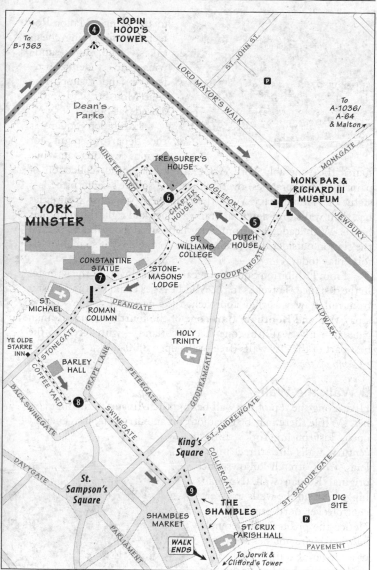

the snickelway, make a U-turn to the left and through the gate).
Enter the building under the coat of arms of Charles I, who stayed
here during the English Civil War in the 1640s. Today, the building is part of the University of York. Because the northerners were
slow to embrace the king's reforms, Henry VIII came here to personally enforce the Dissolution. He stayed 17 days in this mansion
and brought along 1,000 troops to make his determination clear.
You can wander into the grounds and building. A few stairs lead

to the King's Manor Refectory café serving cheap cakes, soup, and sandwiches to students, professors, and visitors like you (Mon-Fri 9:30-15:00, closed Sat-Sun).

Exhibition Square is the departure point for various walking and bus tours. The venerable York Art Gallery (£8, minor collection of paintings and ceramics) overlooks it. The square's centerpiece is a statue of William Etty. With the Industrial Age most great cities had their walls torn down and railway lines laid right through their hearts. With leadership from Etty, York saved its walls and parked the station outside, thus retaining the character that so many visitors enjoy today.

From Exhibition Square you can see the towers of the Minster in the distance. Travelers in the Middle Ages could see the Minster from miles away as they approached the city. Across the street is a pay WC and **Bootham Bar**—one of the fourth-century Roman gates in York's wall (this one faced Scotland)—with access to the best part of the city walls (free, walls open 8:00-dusk).

• *Climb up the bar.*

❹ Walk the Wall

Hike along the top of the wall behind the Minster to the first corner. (While there may be a padlock on an entry gate, it's generally open. Just push.) York's 13th-century walls are three miles long. This stretch follows the original Roman wall. Norman kings built up the walls to assert control over northern England. Notice the pivots in the crenellations (square notches at the top of a medieval wall), which once held wooden hatches to provide

cover for archers. The wall was extensively renovated in the 19th century. (Victorians may have saved the walls, but the fortifications were not "medieval" enough for their taste, so they ornamented them with fanciful extras, adding little touches such as Romantic arrow slits.)

At the corner with the benches—**Robin Hood's Tower**—you can lean out and see the moat outside. This was originally the Roman ditch that surrounded the fortified garrison town. (Looking at a town map, you can still make out the rectangular footprint of that original occupiers' green zone.) Continue walking for a fine view of the Minster, with its truncated main tower and the pointy rooftop of its chapter house.

Continue on to the next gate, **Monk Bar.** This fine medieval gatehouse is the home of the little **Richard III Museum** (described later, under "Sights in York").

• *Descend the wall at Monk Bar, and step outside the city's protective wall. Pass the portcullis (last lowered in 1953 for the Queen's coronation). Take 10 paces and gaze up at the tower. Imagine 10 archers behind the arrow slits. Keep an eye on the 17th-century guards, with their stones raised and primed to protect the town.*

Return through the city wall. After a short block, turn right on Ogleforth. ("Ogle" is the Norse word for owl, hence our word "ogle"—to look at something fiercely.)

York's Old Town

Walking down ❺ **Ogleforth,** ogle (on your left) a charming little brick house from the 17th century called the **Dutch House.** It was designed by an apprentice architect who was trying to show off for his master, and was the first entirely brick house in town—a sign of opulence. Next, also of brick, is a former brewery, with a 19th-century industrial feel.

Ogleforth jogs left and becomes **Chapter House Street** which leads on to the Minster. On your way you'll pass the ❻ **Treasurer's House** on the right, where a short detour to a tranquil garden awaits. While admission is charged to visit the stately house (daily 11:00-16:30), it's free to visit its garden and café. Pass through the ornate iron gate into the hallway and take a sharp left into the garden. Find a bench and pause to enjoy this pint-sized walled oasis before exiting onto Minster Yard with the pointed tower of the octagonal Chapter House looming in front of you.

Then, circle left around the back side of the Minster, past the stonemasons' lodge (where craftsmen are chiseling local limestone for the church, as has been done here since the 13th century), to the statue of Roman Emperor Constantine and an ancient Roman column.

Step up to lounging ❼ **Constantine.** Five emperors visited York when it was the Roman city of Eboracum. Constantine was here when his father died. The troops declared him the Roman emperor in AD 306 at this site, and

YORK

six years later, he went to Rome to claim his throne. In AD 312, Constantine legalized Christianity, and in AD 314, York got its first bishop.

The **ancient column,** across the street from Constantine, is a reminder that the Minster sits upon the site of the Roman head-quarters, or *principia.* The city placed this column here in 1971, just before celebrating the 1,900th anniversary of the founding of Eboracum—a.k.a. York.

• *If you want to visit the* **York Minster** *now, find the entrance on its west side, ahead and around the corner (see description on page 784). Otherwise, head into the town center. From opposite the Minster's south transept door (the door by Constantine), take a narrow pedestrian walk-way—which becomes Stonegate—into the tangled commercial center of medieval York. Walk straight down Stonegate, a street lined with fun and inviting cafés, pubs, and restaurants. Just before the Ye Old Starre Inne banner hanging over the street, turn left down the snickelway called Coffee Yard. (It's marked by a red devil.) Enjoy strolling another of York's...*

❽ "Snickelways"

This is a made-up York word combining "snicket" (a passageway between walls or fences), "ginnel" (a narrow passageway between buildings), and "alleyway" (any narrow passage)—snickelway. York—with its popu-lation packed densely inside its protective walls—has about 50 of these public pas-sages. In general, when exploring the city, you should duck into these—both for the adventure and to take a shortcut. While some of York's history has been bulldozed by modernity, bits of it hide and survive in the snickelways.

Coffee Yard leads past Barley Hall (look through the big window on the left to see its fine old interior), popping out at the corner of Grape Lane and Swinegate. Medieval towns named streets for the business done there. Swinegate, a lane of pig farmers, leads to the market. Grape Lane is a polite version of that street's original crude name, Gropec*nt Lane. If you were here a thousand years ago, you'd find it lined by brothels. Through-out England, streets for prostitutes (rife with men groping women) were called by this graphic name. Today, if you see a street named Grape Lane, that's usually its heritage.

Skip Grape Lane and turn right down Swinegate to a mar-ket (which you can see in the distance). The **Shambles Market,** popular for cheap produce and clothing, was created in the 1960s with the demolition of a bunch of colorful medieval lanes. Despite the rise of suburban shopping malls, it's good to see a bit of the old commercial zone with its medieval heritage thriving after all those centuries in the heart of York. (The collection of food trucks at the far end is a popular place for a fast, cheap, and memorable little lunch.)

• *In the center of the market, tiny "Little Shambles" lane (on the left) dead-ends into the most famous lane in York.*

❾ The Shambles

This colorful old street (rated ▲) was once the "street of the butchers." The name was derived from "shammell"—a butcher's bench upon which he'd cut and display his meat. In the 16th century, this lane was dripping with red meat. You can still see the hooks—once used to hang rabbit, pheasant, beef, lamb, and pigs' heads—under the eaves. Fresh slabs were displayed

on the fat sills, while people lived above the shops. All the garbage and sewage flushed down the street to a mucky pond at the end—a favorite hangout for the town's cats and dogs. Tourist shops now fill these fine, half-timbered Tudor buildings. Look above the modern crowds and storefronts to appreciate the classic old English architecture. While fires gutted most old English town centers, York's old town survives intact. (London would have looked like this before its devastating fire in 1666.) The soil here isn't great for building; notice how the structures have settled in the absence of a solid foundation.

Turn right and slalom down The Shambles. Just past the tiny sandwich shop at #37, pop in to the snickelway and look for very old **woodwork.** Study the 16th-century carpentry: mortise-and-tenon joints with wooden plugs rather than nails, and the wattle-and-daub construction (timber frames filled in with rubble and plastered over).

Next door (back on The Shambles) is the **shrine of St. Margaret Clitherow,** a 16th-century Catholic crushed by Protestants under her own door (as was the humiliating custom when a city wanted to teach someone a lesson). She was killed for refusing to testify about hiding priests in her home. Step into the tiny shrine for a peaceful moment to ponder Margaret, who in 1970 was sainted for her faith.

The Shambles reminds many of Diagon Alley in Harry Potter

films. While this lane inspired the set design (and the establishment of several Harry Potter shops at the bottom end of the lane), no filming was ever done here.

At the bottom of The Shambles is the cute, tiny **St. Crux Parish Hall,** which charities use to raise funds by selling light meals (see "Eating in York," later). Take some time to chat with the volunteers.

With blood and guts from The Shambles' 20 butchers all draining down the lane, it's no wonder The Golden Fleece, just below, is considered the most haunted pub in town.

• *Your town walk is finished. From here, you're just a few minutes from plenty of fun: street entertainment and lots of cheap eating options on King's Square, good restaurants on Fossgate, the York Castle Museum (a few blocks farther downhill), and the starting point for my Ouse Riverside Walk (see page 801).*

Sights in York

▲▲▲YORK MINSTER

The pride of York, this largest Gothic church north of the Alps (540 feet long, 200 feet tall) brilliantly shows that the High Middle Ages were far from dark. The word "minster" means an important church chartered with a mission to evangelize. As it's the seat of a bishop, York Minster is also a cathedral. While Henry VIII destroyed England's great abbeys, this was not part of a monastery (and Henry needed an ecclesiastical center for his  Anglican Church in the north), so it was left standing. It seats 2,000 comfortably; on Christmas and Easter, at least 4,000 worshippers pack the place. Today, more than 250 employees and 500 volunteers work to preserve its heritage and welcome more than a million visitors each year. It costs £11,000 a day to maintain the great church, and they just about break even with the revenue generated by tourism.

Cost: £12, includes guided tour, Undercroft Museum, and crypt; free for kids under age 16. If you buy your ticket online in advance, you can skip the ticket line. Ask a staff member where to enter.

Hours: The cathedral is open for sightseeing Mon-Sat 9:00-18:30, Sun 12:30-15:00. It opens for worship daily at 7:30. Closing time flexes with activities, but last entry is generally at 16:30. Sights within the Minster have shorter hours (listed later). The Minster may close for special events (check calendar on website).

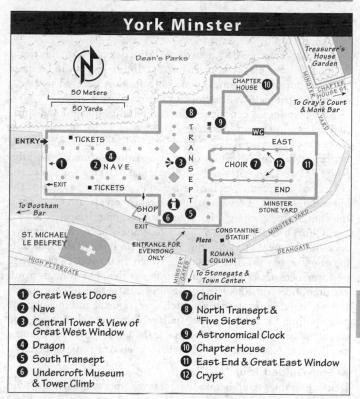

York Minster

Dean's Parks

CHAPTER HOUSE ❿

Treasurer's House Garden

50 Meters

50 Yards

To Gray's Court & Monk Bar

❽

❾

ENTRY ▸

■ TICKETS

WC

EAST

❶ ❷ **N A V E** ❹

➤➤ ❸

CHOIR ❼ ⓬ ⓫

T R A N S E P T

◂ EXIT

■ TICKETS

END

To Bootham Bar

SHOP ❻ ❺

MINSTER STONE YARD

EXIT

ST. MICHAEL LE BELFREY ✚

ENTRANCE FOR EVENSONG ONLY

CONSTANTINE STATUE

Plaza

ROMAN COLUMN

MINSTER YARD

DEANGATE

HIGH PETERGATE

To Stonegate & Town Center

❶ Great West Doors
❷ Nave
❸ Central Tower & View of Great West Window
❹ Dragon
❺ South Transept
❻ Undercroft Museum & Tower Climb

❼ Choir
❽ North Transept & "Five Sisters"
❾ Astronomical Clock
❿ Chapter House
⓫ East End & Great East Window
⓬ Crypt

YORK

Information: Tel. 01904/557-217 or 0844-393-0011, www. yorkminster.org.

Visitor Information: You'll get a free map with your ticket. For more information, pick up the inexpensive *York Minster Short Guide*. Helpful Minster guides stationed throughout are happy to answer your questions (but not on Sundays).

Tower Climb: It costs £5 for 30 minutes of exercise (275 steps) and forgettable views. The tower opens at 9:30 (13:15 on Sun), with ascents every 45 minutes; the last ascent is generally at 17:00, earlier in winter (no children under 8, not good for acrophobes, closes in extreme weather). Get your timed-entry ticket upon arrival, as only 50 visitors are allowed up at once. It's a tight, spiraling, claustrophobic staircase with an iron handrail. You'll climb about 150 steps to the top of the transept, step outside to cross a narrow walkway, then go back inside for more than 100 steps to the top of the central tower. From here, you'll have caged-in views of rooftops and the flat countryside.

Undercroft Museum: This museum focuses on the history of the site and its origins as a Roman fortress (Mon-Sat 10:00-17:00, Sun 13:00-16:00).

Tours: Free, guided hour-long tours depart from the ticket desk every hour on the hour (Mon-Sat 10:00-15:00, can be more frequent during busy times, none on Sun, they go even with just one or two people). You can join a tour in progress.

Evensong: To experience the cathedral in musical and spiritual action, attend an evensong (Tue-Sat at 17:15, Sun at 16:00, Mon spoken service at 17:15, enter at south door). Visiting choirs perform when the Minster's choir is on summer break (mid-July-Aug). Arrive 15 minutes early and wait just outside the choir in the center of the church. You'll be ushered in and can sit in one of the big wooden stalls. As evensong is a worship service, attendees enter the church free of charge. For more on evensong, see page 153.

Church Bells: If you're a fan of church bells, you'll experience ding-dong ecstasy Sunday morning at about 10:00 and during the Tuesday practice session between 19:00 and 22:00. These performances are especially impressive, as the church holds a full carillon of 35 bells (it's the only English cathedral to have such a range). Stand in front of the church's west portal and imagine the gang pulling on a dozen ropes (halfway up the right tower—you can actually see the ropes through a little window) while a talented carillonneur plays 22 more bells with a keyboard and foot pedals.

◉ Self-Guided Tour

Before entering, stand before the great west portal (under the twin towers). You'll notice this facade has lots of empty niches. These were potential "advertising" spaces, built to entice rich donors, but were never filled. An exception is in the center, where a bishop stands flanked by two wealthy dukes—one who gave stone (on the left, holding a stone) and another who gave timber (on the right, holding a beam).

Upon entering, decide whether you're climbing the tower. If so, get a ticket (with an assigned time). Also consider visiting the Undercroft Museum (described later) if you want to get a comprehensive history and overview of the Minster before touring the church.

• *Entering the church, turn 180 degrees and look back at the...*

❶ Great West Doors: These are used only on special occasions. Flanking the doors is a list of archbishops (and other church officials) that goes unbroken back to the 600s. The statue of Peter with the key and

Bible (between the doors) is a reminder that the church is dedicated to St. Peter, and the key to heaven is found through the word of God. While the Minster sits on the remains of a Romanesque church (c. 1100), today's church was begun in 1220 and took 250 years to complete. Up above, look for the female, headless "semaphore saints" (from 2004), using semaphore flag code to spell out a message with golden discs: "Christ is here".

• *Grab a chair and enjoy the view down the...*

❷ **Nave:** Your first impression might be of its spaciousness and brightness. One of the widest Gothic naves in Europe, it was built between 1280 and 1360—the middle period of the Gothic style, called "Decorated Gothic." Rather than risk a stone roof, builders spanned the space with wood. Colorful shields on the arcades are the coats of arms of nobles who helped tall and formidable Edward I, known as "Longshanks," fight the Scots in the 13th century.

The coats of arms in the clerestory (upper-level) glass represent the nobles who helped Edward I's son, Edward II, in the same fight. There's more medieval glass in this building than in the rest of England combined. This precious glass (including the Great East Window) survived World War II—hidden in stately homes throughout Yorkshire.

While originally a Roman Catholic church, it has been a Protestant church for 500 years—ever since the Reformation. Thankfully, rather than destroying the church, the practical Anglicans just purged it of its Roman Catholic iconography. You'll find no hint of the original pope-celebrating elements that ornamented it before the days of Henry VIII.

Walk to the very center of the church, under the ❸ **central tower.** Look up. An exhibit in the undercroft explains how gifts and skill saved this 197-foot tower from collapse. Use the neck-saving mirror to marvel at it.

Look back at the west end to marvel at the **Great West Window,** especially the stone tracery. While its nickname is the "Heart of Yorkshire," it represents the sacred heart of Christ, meant to remind people of his love for the world

Find the ❹ **dragon** on the right of the nave (two-thirds of the way up the wall, affixed to the top of a pillar). While no one is sure of its purpose, it pivots and has a hole through its neck—so it was likely a mechanism designed to raise a lid of a saint's coffin. Carved

England's Anglican Church

The Anglican Church (a.k.a. the Church of England) came into existence in 1534, when Henry VIII declared that he, and not Pope Clement VII, was the head of England's Catholics. The pope had refused to allow Henry to divorce his wife to marry his mistress Anne Boleyn (which Henry did anyway, resulting in the birth of Elizabeth I). Still, Henry regarded himself as a faithful Catholic—just not a *Roman* Catholic—and made relatively few changes in how and what Anglicans worshipped.

It's interesting to think of the Dissolution of the Monasteries in 1534 as "the first Brexit." It was spearheaded by a much-married, arrogant, overweight, egomaniacal Henry VIII—matched today by the Conservative Party's Boris Johnson. Henry (like Boris) wanted "to be free" from European meddling (the pope then, the EU today). The local sentiment (then as now) was no more money to Europe (tithes to the pope then, taxes to Brussels today) and no more intrusions into English life from the Continent.

Henry's son, Edward VI, later instituted many of the changes that Reformation Protestants were bringing about in continental Europe: an emphasis on preaching, people in the pews actually reading the Bible, clergy being allowed to marry, and a more "Protestant" liturgy in English from the revised Book of Common Prayer (1549). The next monarch, Edward's sister Mary I, returned England to the Roman Catholic Church (1553), earning the nickname "Bloody Mary" for her brutal suppression of Protestant elements. When Elizabeth I succeeded Mary (1558), she soon broke from Rome again. Today, many regard the Anglican Church as a compromise between the Catholic and Protestant traditions. In the US, Anglicans split off from the Church in England after the American Revolution, creating the Episcopal Church.

Ever since Henry VIII's time, the York Minster has held a special status within the Anglican hierarchy. After a long feud over which was the leading church, the archbishops of Canterbury and York agreed that York's bishop would have the title "Primate of England" and Canterbury's would be the "Primate of All England," directing all Anglicans and Episcopalians throughout the world.

out of a piece of Scandinavian oak, it's considered part of the earlier church built during Viking times. The statue, directly across the nave, is likely of St. George—the slayer of dragons and protector against pagan religious malpractice.

• *Facing the altar, turn right and head into the...*

❺ **South Transept:** Look up. The new "bosses" (carved medallions decorating the point where the ribs meet on the ceiling) are a reminder that the roof of this wing of the church was destroyed by fire in 1984, caused when lightning hit an electricity box. Some believe the lightning was God's angry response to a new bishop, David Jenkins, who questioned the literal truth of Jesus' miracles. (Jenkins had been interviewed at a nearby TV studio the night before, leading locals to joke that the lightning occurred "12 hours too late, and 17 miles off-target.") Regardless, the entire country came to York's aid. *Blue Peter* (England's top kids' show at the time) conducted a competition among its young viewers to design new bosses. Out of 30,000 entries, there were six winners (the blue ones—e.g., man on the moon, feed the children, save the whales).

Two other sights can be accessed through the south transept: the ❻ **Undercroft Museum** (explained later) and the **tower climb** (explained earlier). But for now, stick with this tour; we'll circle back to the south transept at the end, before exiting the church.

• *Head back into the middle of the nave and face the front of the church. You're looking at the...*

YORK

❼ **Choir:** Examine the choir screen—the ornate wall of carvings separating the nave from the choir. It's lined with all the English kings from William I (the Conqueror) to Henry VI (during whose reign it was carved, in 1461). Numbers indicate the years each reigned. It is literally covered in gold leaf, which

sounds impressive, but the gold is very thin...a nugget the size of a sugar cube can be pounded into a foil-like sheet the size of a driveway.

Step into the choir, where a service is held daily. All the carving was redone after an 1829 fire, but its tradition of glorious evensong services (sung by choristers from the Minster School) goes all the way back to the eighth century.

• *To the left as you face the choir is the...*

❽ **North Transept:** In this transept, the grisaille windows—dubbed the **"Five Sisters"**—are dedicated to British servicewomen who died in war. They were made in 1260, before colored glass was produced in England. Notice that the design has no figures, perhaps inspired by Islamic art seen by Christian Crusaders in the 13th century. The windows were originally much lighter but became darker after countless cracked panes were fixed over the centuries by added leading.

The 18th-century ❾ **astronomical clock** is worth a look (the sign helps you make sense of it). It's dedicated to the heroic Allied aircrews from bases here in northern England who died in World

War II. The Book of Remembrance below the clock contains 18,000 names.

• *A corridor leads to the Gothic, octagonal...*

🔟 **Chapter House:** This was the traditional meeting place of the governing body (or chapter) of the Minster. On the pillar in the middle of the doorway, the Virgin holds Baby Jesus while standing on the devilish serpent. The Chapter House, without an interior support, is remarkable (almost frightening) for its breadth. A model of the wooden construction (in the hallway just outside the door) illustrates the impressive 1285 engineering: with a wooden frame from which the ceiling actually hangs.

The fanciful carvings decorating the canopies above the stalls date from 1280 (80 percent are originals) and are some of the Minster's finest. Stroll slowly around the entire room and imagine that the tiny sculpted heads are a 14th-century parade—a fun glimpse

of medieval society. Grates still send hot air up robes of attendees on cold winter mornings.

The Chapter House was the site of an important moment in England's parliamentary history. In the late 1200s, the Scots under William Wallace and Robert the Bruce were threatening London. Fighting the Scots in 1295, Edward I (the "Longshanks" we met earlier) convened his parliament (a war cabinet) here, rather than down south in London. The government met here through the 20-year reign of Edward II, before moving to London during Edward III's rule in the 14th century (as then foreign policy was focused on fighting the French—in the Hundred Years' War—rather than the Scots).

• *Return to the main part of the church, turn left, and continue all the way down the nave (behind the choir) to the...*

🔟 **East End and Great East Window:** This part of the church is square, lacking a semicircular apse, typical of England's Perpendicular Gothic style (15th century). Monuments (almost no graves) were once strewn throughout the church, but in the Victorian Age, they were gathered into the east end, where you see them today.

The Great East Window, the size of a tennis court, is one of the great treasures of medieval art in Europe. It's completely original and recently cleaned and restored with its stone tracery, lead-ings, and painted glass (not stained) looking today as it did when finished in 1408.

Imagine being a worshipper here the day it was unveiled—mesmerized by this sweeping story told in more than 300 panels of painted glass climaxing with the Apocalypse. It's a medieval disaster movie—a blockbuster back in 1408—showing the end of the world in fire and flood and pestilence...vivid scenes from the book of Revelation. Angels trumpet disaster against blood-red skies. And there it is, the fifth panel up on the far left side...the devil giving power to the Beast of the Apocalypse, a seven-headed, ten-crowned lion, just as it was written in the Bible.

This must have terrified worshippers. A hundred years before Michelangelo frescoed the story of the beginning and end of time at the Sistine Chapel in Rome, this was unprecedented in its epic scale, and done by one man: John Thornton of Coventry.

Because of the Great East Window's immense size, the east end has an extra layer of supportive stonework, parts of it wide enough to walk along. In fact, for special occasions, the church choir has been known to actually sing from the walkway halfway up the window.

• *Looking under the central altar and choir (or going down a flight of steps) you can see the...*

⑫ Crypt: Here you can view the boundary of the much smaller, but still huge, Norman church from 1100 that stood on this spot (look for the red dots, marking where the Norman church ended, and note how thick the wall was). You can also see some of the old columns and additional remains from the Roman fortress that once stood here, the tomb of St. William of York (actually a Roman sarcophagus that was reused), and the modern concrete save-the-church foundations (much of this church history is covered in the Undercroft Museum).

• *You'll exit the church through the gift shop in the south transept. If you've yet to climb the* **tower***, the entrance is in the south transept before the exit. Also before leaving, look for the entrance to the...*

Undercroft Museum: Well-described exhibits follow the history of the site from its origins as a Roman fortress to the founding of an Anglo-Saxon/Viking church, the shift to a Norman place of worship, and finally the construction of the Gothic structure that stands today. The museum fills a space that was excavated following the near collapse of the central tower in 1967.

Videos re-create how the fortress and Norman structure would have been laid out, and various artifacts provide an insight into each period. Highlights include:

• The actual remains of the Roman fort's basilica (its hall of justice), which are viewable through a see-through floor including

YORK

patches of Roman frescoes from what was the basilica's ante-room.

- The Horn of Ulf, the finest Viking treasure in York. This intricately carved elephant's tusk was presented to the Minster in 1030 by Ulf, a Viking nobleman, as a symbol that he was dedicating his land to God and the Church. Consider the horn's travels: From Indian elephant, to Islamic carvers in southern Italy, to a Viking lord, to this church.

- The personal effects of Archbishop Walter de Gray who, in the 13th century, started the current church.

- The York Gospels manuscript, a thousand-year-old text containing the four gospels. Made by Anglo-Saxon monks at Canterbury, it's the only book in the Minster's collection that dates prior to the Norman Conquest. It is still used to this day to swear in archbishops.

• *This finishes your visit. Before leaving, take a moment to just be in this amazing building. Then, go in peace.*

Nearby: As you leave through the south transept, notice the people-friendly plaza created here and how effectively it ties the church in with the city that stretches before you. To your left are the Roman column from the ancient headquarters, which stood where the Minster stands today (and from where Rome administered the northern reaches of Britannia 1,800 years ago); a statue of Emperor Constantine (for more details, see page 781); and the York Minster Stone Yard, where masons are chiseling stone—as they have for centuries—to keep the religious pride and joy of York standing strong and looking good.

OTHER SIGHTS INSIDE YORK'S WALLS

I've listed these roughly in geographical order, from near the Minster at the northwest end of town to the York Castle Museum at the southeast end.

Note that several of York's glitzier and most heavily promoted sights (including Jorvik Viking Centre, Dig, and Barley Hall) are run by the York Archaeological Trust (YAT). While rooted in real history, YAT attractions are geared primarily toward kids and work hard (some say too hard) to make the history entertaining. If you like their approach and plan to visit several, ask about the various combo-ticket options.

▲Yorkshire Museum

Located in a lush, picnic-perfect park next to the stately ruins of St. Mary's Abbey (described in my "York Walk," earlier), the Yorkshire Museum is the city's serious "archaeology of York" museum. You can't dig a hole in York without hitting some remnant of the city's long past, and most of what's found ends up here. While the hordes line up at Jorvik Viking Centre, this museum has no crowds and provides a broader historical context, with more real artifacts. The three main collections—Roman, medieval, and natural history—are well described, bright, and kid-friendly.

Cost and Hours: £8, kids under 16 free with paying adult, daily 10:00-17:00, within Museum Gardens, tel. 01904/687-687, www.yorkshiremuseum.org.uk.

Visiting the Museum: At the entrance, you're greeted by an original, early fourth-century Roman statue of the god Mars. If he could talk, he'd say, "Hear me, mortals". There are three sections here: Roman (on this floor), medieval (downstairs), and natural history (a kid-friendly, fossil-based archaeology wing on this floor opposite the Roman stuff).

The **Roman** collection starts with a large map of the Roman Empire, set on the floor. Then, in a series of rooms, you'll see slice-of-life exhibits about Roman baths, a huge floor mosaic, and skulls accompanied by artists' renderings of how the people originally looked. (One man was apparently killed by a sword blow to the head—making it graphically clear that the struggle between Romans and barbarians was a violent one.) These artifacts are particularly interesting when you consider that you're standing in one of the farthest reaches of the Roman Empire.

The **medieval** collection is in the basement. During the Middle Ages, York was England's second city. One large room is dominated by ruins of the St. Mary's Abbey complex (described on page 776; one wall of the abbey still stands just out front—be sure to see it before leaving). In the center of the rooms is the Vale of York Hoard, displaying a silver cup and the accompanying treasures it held—more than 600 silver coins as well as silver bars and jewelry. A father and son team discovered the hoard (thought to have  been buried by Vikings in 927) while out for a day of metal detecting in 2007. You'll also see old weapons, glazed vessels, and a well-preserved 13th-century leather box.

The museum's prized pieces, a helmet and a pendant, are housed in this section. The eighth-century Anglo-Saxon helmet (known as the York Helmet or the Coppergate Helmet) shows a bit of barbarian refinement. Examine the delicate carving on its brass trim. The exquisitely etched 15th-century pendant—called the Middleham Jewel—is considered the finest piece of Gothic jewelry in Britain. The noble lady who wore this on a necklace believed that it helped her worship and protected her from illness. The back of the pendant, which rested near her heart, shows the Nativity. The front shows the Holy Trinity crowned by a sapphire (which people believed put their prayers at the top of God's to-do list).

In addition to the Anglo-Saxon pieces, the Viking collection is one of the best in England. Looking over the artifacts, you'll find that the Vikings (who conquered most of the Anglo-Saxon lands) wore some pretty decent shoes and actually combed their hair. The Cawood Sword, nearly 1,000 years old, is one of the finest surviving swords from that era.

Barley Hall

Uncovered behind a derelict office block in the 1980s, this medieval house has been restored to replicate a 1483 dwelling. It's designed to resurrect the Tudor age for visiting school groups—but with no historic artifacts other than its half-timbered wall, it feels soulless to adults.

Cost and Hours: £6, combo-tickets with Jorvik Viking Centre and/or Dig, daily 10:00-17:00, Nov-March until 16:00, 2 Coffee Yard off Stonegate, tel. 01904/615-505, www.barleyhall.co.uk.

Holy Trinity Church

Built in the late Perpendicular Gothic style, this church has windows made of precious clear and stained glass from the 13th to 15th century. It holds rare box pews, which rest atop a floor that is sinking as bodies of "the stinking rich" rot and coffins collapse. Enjoy its peaceful picnic-friendly gardens.

Cost and Hours: Free, daily 11:00-15:30, 70 Goodramgate, www.holytrinityyork.org.

Richard III Museum

The last king of England's Plantagenet dynasty got a bad rap from Shakespeare (the Tudors took over after Richard was killed in 1485, so Shakespeare followed the party line and demonized him as a hunchbacked monster). With the discovery of Richard's remains in Leicester in 2013, interest in him has skyrocketed, and this exhibit tries to excite visitors with all the blood and gore of that era, but it lacks any historic artifacts. Richard III groupies find it worth the time and money.

Cost and Hours: £3.50, daily 10:00-17:00, Monk Bar, tel. 01904/615-505, http://richardiiiexperience.com.

King's Square

This lively people-watching zone, with its inviting benches, once hosted a church. Then it was the site for the town's gallows. Today, it's prime real estate for buskers and street performers. Just hanging out here can be entertaining. Beyond is the most characteristic and touristy street in old York: The Shambles. Within sight of this lively square are plenty of cheap eating options (for tips, see "Eating in York," later).

York's Chocolate Story

Though known mainly for its Roman, Viking, and medieval past, York also has a rich history in chocolate. Throughout the 1800s and 1900s, York was home to three major confectionaries—including Rowntree's, originators of the venerable Kit Kat. This chocolate "museum" is childish and overpriced, with no historic artifacts and in a building with no significance. If you visit, you'll join a tour, which pairs generous samples with the history of York's confectionary connections—and you'll have a chance to make your own chocolate lolly.

Cost and Hours: £13, one-hour tours run every 15 minutes daily starting at 10:00, last tour at 16:00, King's Square, tel. 01904-527-765, www.yorkchocolatestory.com.

Dig

This hands-on, kid-oriented archaeological site gives young visitors an idea of what York looked like during Roman, Viking, medieval, and Victorian eras. Sift through "dirt" (actually shredded tires), dig up reconstructed Roman wall plaster, and take a look at what archaeologists have found recently. Entry is possible only with a one-hour guided tour (departures every 30 minutes); pass waiting time by looking at the exhibits near the entry. The exhibits fill the haunted old St. Saviour's Church.

Cost and Hours: £6.50, combo-tickets with Jorvik Viking Centre and/or Barley Hall, daily 10:00-17:00, Saviourgate, tel. 01904/615-505, www.digyork.com.

▲Merchant Adventurers' Hall

The word "adventurers" refers to investors of the day, and this

was a kind of merchants' corporate headquarters/early stock exchange. Claiming to be the finest surviving medieval guildhall in Britain (built from 1357 to 1361), the vast half-timbered building with marvelous exposed beams contains interesting displays about life and commerce in the Middle Ages when the economy revolved around guilds. You'll see three original, large rooms that are still intact: the great hall itself, where meetings took place; the undercroft, which housed a hospital and almshouse; and a chapel. Several smaller rooms are filled with exhibits about guilds in this 14th-century world trade center. Sitting by itself in its own little picnic-friendly park, the classic old building is worth a stop even just to see it from the outside. Remarkably, the hall is still owned by the same Merchant Adventurers society that built it 660 years ago (now a modern charitable organization).

Cost and Hours: £7, includes audioguide, Sun-Fri 10:00-16:30, Sat until 13:30, inviting café, south of The Shambles between Fossgate and Piccadilly, tel. 01904/654-818, www.merchantshallyork.org.

▲Jorvik Viking Centre

Take the "Pirates of the Caribbean," sail them northeast and back in time 1,000 years, sprinkle in some real artifacts, and you get Jorvik (YOR-vik). In the late 1970s, more than 40,000 artifacts were dug out of the peat bog right here in downtown York—the UK's largest archaeological dig of Viking-era artifacts. When the archaeologists were finished, developers were allowed to build the big Fenwick Department store next door, and the dig site was converted into this attraction, opened in 1984.

Jorvik blends museum exhibits with a 16-minute ride on theme-park-esque "time capsules" that glide through the re-created Viking street of Coppergate as it looked circa the year 975. Animatronic characters and modern-day interpreters bring the scenes to life. Innovative when it first opened, the commercial success of Jorvik inspired copycat rides/museums all over England. Some love Jorvik, while others call it gimmicky and overpriced. If you think of it as Disneyland with a splash of history, Jorvik's fun. To me, Jorvik is a commercial venture designed for kids, with too much emphasis on its gift shop. But it's also undeniably entertaining, and—if you take the time to peruse its exhibits and substantial museum with a rich trove of Viking artifacts—it can be quite informative.

Cost and Hours: £13, daily 10:00-17:00, Nov-March until 16:00, these are last-entry times, tel. 01904/615-505, www.jorvik-viking-centre.co.uk.

Crowd-Beating Tips: This popular attraction can come with long lines—especially during school breaks and mid-July through

YORK

August. At the busiest times (roughly 11:00-15:00), you may have to wait an hour or more. For £2 extra, you can book a slot in advance, either over the phone or on their website. Or avoid the worst lines by coming early or late in the day.

▲Fairfax House

This well-furnished home, one of the first Georgian townhouses in England, is perfectly Neoclassical inside. Its seven rooms on two floors are each staffed by pleasant docents eager to talk with you. They'll explain how the circa-1760 home was built as the dowry for an aristocrat's daughter. The house is compact and bursting with stunning period furniture (the personal collection of a local chocolate magnate), gorgeously restored woodwork, and lavish stucco ceilings that offer clues as to each room's purpose. For example, stuccoed philosophers look down on the library, while the goddess of friendship presides over the drawing room. Taken together, this house provides fine insights into aristocratic life in 18th-century England.

Cost and Hours: £7.50, Tue-Sat 10:00-17:00, Sun 11:00-16:00, Mon by one-hour guided tour only at 11:00 and 14:00, closed Jan-mid-Feb, near Jorvik Viking Centre at 29 Castlegate, tel. 01904/655-543, www.fairfaxhouse.co.uk.

Clifford's Tower

Perched high on a knoll across from the York Castle Museum, this ruin is all that's left of York's 13th-century castle. It's a textbook example of the basic Nor-
man castle "motte-and-bailey" design: a manmade hill with a fort (motte) with a circular stockade (bailey) at its foot. The bailey's footprint can be seen today, nearly a thousand years later, in the grassy, circular Eye of York court-
yard across from Clifford's Tower (and surrounded by Georgian buildings).

Cost and Hours: £5, daily 10:00-18:00, closes earlier off-season, tel. 01904/646-940, www.english-heritage.org.uk.

Background: Clifford's Tower is a memorial to medieval anti-Semitism. Throughout European history, moneylenders were often Jews. During bad times, frustrated Christians vented (and wiped clean their debts) by massacring those they called "Christ-killers" in their town.

In 1190, after the coronation of Richard I, anti-Semitism was considered patriotic. (Nobles encouraged angry racism—calling

England's Jews something akin to "rapists and murderers"—to stoke their base.) Taking the convenient cue, the angry mobs of York chased local Jews into the tower. An estimated 150 Jews locked themselves inside and, rather than face forced conversion or death at the hands of the bloodthirsty mob, they committed ritual suicide. The crowd then set the tower ablaze. (Read the whole story on the sign at the base of the hill.) Today, daffodils, with their six-pointed flowers recalling the Star of David, are planted as a memorial on the slopes leading to the tower.

The present tower was built 60 years after the massacre, but historians think the earthen mound may still hold evidence from the tragedy. If you go inside, you'll see a model of the original castle complex as it looked in the Middle Ages, and you can climb up to enjoy fine city views from the top of the ramparts—but neither is worth the cost of admission.

▲▲York Castle Museum

This fascinating social-history museum is a Victorian home show, one of the closest things to a time-tunnel experience England has

to offer. The one-way plan ensures that you'll see everything, including remakes of rooms from the 17th to 20th century, a re-creation of a Victorian street, a heartfelt WWI exhibit, and eerie prison cells.

Cost and Hours: £10, kids under 16 free with adult, daily 9:30-17:00, roaming guides happily answer your questions (no audioguide), cafeteria at entrance, tel. 01904/687-687, www.yorkcastlemuseum.org.uk. It's at the bottom of the hop-on, hop-off bus route. The museum can call you a taxi (worthwhile if you're hurrying to the National Railway Museum, across town).

Visiting the Museum: The exhibits are divided between two wings: the North Building (the former women's prison, to the left as you enter) and the South Building (former debtors' prison, to the right).

Follow the one-way route, starting in the **North Building.** You'll first visit the Period Rooms, illuminating Yorkshire lifestyles during different time periods (1600s-1950s) and among various walks of life. Toy Stories is an enchanting review of toys through the ages. Next is the Shaping the Body exhibit, detailing diet and fashion trends over the last 400 years. Check out the codpieces, bustles, and corsets that used to "enhance" the human form, and ponder some of the odd diet fads that make today's craziest diets seem normal. For foodies and chefs, the exhibit showcasing fireplaces and kitchens from the 1600s to the 1980s is especially tasty.

Next, stroll down the museum's re-created Kirkgate, a street from the Victorian era (1890s), when Britain was at the peak of its

power. It features old-time shops and storefronts, including a pharmacist, sweet shop, school, and grocer for the working class, along with roaming live guides in period dress. Around the back is a slum area depicting how the poor lived in those times.

Circle back to the entry and cross over to the **South Building.** In the WWI exhibit you can follow the lives of five York citizens as they experience the horrors and triumphs of the war years. One room plunges you into the gruesome world of trench warfare, where the average life expectancy was six weeks (and if you fell asleep during sentry duty, you'd be shot). A display about the home front notes that York suffered from Zeppelin attacks in which six died. At the end you're encouraged to share your thoughts in a room lined with chalkboards.

Exit outside and cross the castle yard. A detour to the left leads to a flour mill (open sporadically). Otherwise, your tour continues through the door on the right, where you'll

find another reconstructed historical street, this one capturing the spirit of the swinging 1960s—"a time when the cultural changes were massive but the cars and skirts were mini." Slathered with DayGlo colors, this street scene examines fashion, music, and television (including clips of beloved kids' shows and period news reports).

Finally, head into the York Castle Prison, which recounts the experiences of actual people who were thrown into the clink here. Videos, eerily projected onto the walls of individual cells, show actors telling tragic stories about the cells' one-time inhabitants.

ACROSS THE RIVER
▲▲National Railway Museum

If you like model railways, this is train-car heaven. The thunderous museum—displaying 200 illustrious years of British railroad history—is one of the biggest and best railroad museums anywhere.

Cost and Hours: Free but £5 suggested donation, daily 10:00-18:00, lockers-£3, café, restaurant, tel. 0333-016-1010, www.railwaymuseum.org.uk.

Getting There: It's about a 15-minute walk from the Minster (southwest of town, behind the train station). From the TI walk down Museum Street and cross the Lendal Bridge, then take a right and follow the signs. To skip the walk, a cute little "road train" shuttles you more quickly between the Minster and the Railway Museum (£3 one-way, runs daily Easter-Oct, leaves museum every 30 minutes 11:00-16:00 at :00 and :30 past each hour; leaves town—from Duncombe Place, 100 yards in front of the Minster—at :15 and :45 past each hour).

Visiting the Museum: Pick up the floor plan to locate the various exhibits, which sprawl through several gigantic buildings on both sides of the street. Throughout the complex are info stands with staff eager to talk trains and give directions.

The museum's most impressive room is the **Great Hall** (head right from the entrance area and take the stairs to the underground passage). Fanning out from this grand

roundhouse is an array of historic cars and engines, starting with the very first "stagecoaches on rails," with a crude steam engine from 1830. You'll trace the evolution of steam-powered transportation, from a replica of the Rocket (one of the first successful steam locomotives) to the era of the aerodynamic Mallard (famous as the first train to travel at a startling two miles per minute—a marvel back in 1938) and the striking Art Deco-style Duchess of Hamilton. The collection spans to the present day, with a replica of the Eurostar (Chunnel) train and the Shinkansen Japanese bullet train. Other exhibits include a steam engine that's been sliced open to show its cylinders, driving wheels, and smoke box, as well as a working turntable that's put into action twice a day. The Mallard Experience simulates a ride on the Mallard.

In the **North Shed** you find **The Works**—an actual workshop where engineers scurry about, fixing old trains. Live train switchboards show real-time rail traffic on the East Coast Main Line. Next to the diagrammed screens, you can look out to see the actual trains moving up and down the line. **The Warehouse** is loaded with more than 10,000 items relating to train travel (including dinnerware, signage, and actual trains). Exhibits feature dining cars, post cars, sleeping cars, train posters, and info on the Flying Scotsman (the first London-Edinburgh express rail service, now running all over Britain in private tours).

Crossing back to the entrance side, continue to the Station Hall, with a collection of older trains, including ones that the royals have used to ride the rails. One of these includes Queen Victoria's lavish royal car and a WWII royal carriage reinforced with armor. Behind the hall are the South Yard and the Depot, with actual working trains in storage. Families and die-hard train fans can hop on a steam train for a 10-minute ride (£4, daily 11:30-16:00, every 30 minutes).

OUTSIDE TOWN
▲Ouse Riverside Walk or Bike Ride
The New Walk is a mile-long, tree-lined riverside lane created in the 1730s as a promenade for York's dandy class to stroll, see, and be seen—and is a fine place for today's visitors to walk or bike. This hour-long walk is a delightful way to enjoy a dose of countryside away from York. It's paved, illuminated in the evening, and a popular jogging route any time of day.

Start from the riverside under Skeldergate Bridge (near the York Castle Museum) and walk south away from town for a mile. Notice modern buildings across the river, with their floodwalls. Shortly afterward, you cross the tiny River Foss on Blue Bridge, originally built in 1738. The easily defended confluence of the Foss and the Ouse is the reason the Romans founded York in AD 71. Look back to see the modern floodgate (built after a flood in 1979) designed to stop the flooding Ouse from oozing up the Foss. At the bridge, a history panel describes this walk to the Millennium Bridge.

Stroll until you hit the striking, modern **Millennium Bridge.** Sit a bit on its reclining-lounge-chair fence and enjoy the vibrations of bikes and joggers as they pass. There's a strong biking trend in Britain. The British have won many Olympic gold medals in cycling. In 2012, Bradley Wiggins became Sir Bradley Wiggins by winning the Tour de France; his countryman Chris Froome won it in several subsequent years, and Mark Cavendish has won 30 Tour de France stages. You'll see lots of locals riding fancy bikes and wearing high-tech gear while getting into better shape. (Energetic bikers can continue past the Millennium Bridge 14 miles to the market town of Selby.)

Cross the river and take a right to walk back home. Continue along the river until you come to the skateboard court. Here you can enter **Rowntree Park** through its fine old gate. This park was financed by Joseph Rowntree, a wealthy chocolate baron with a Quaker ethic of contributing to his community. In the 19th century, life for the poor was a Charles Dickens-like struggle. A rich man building a park for the working class, which even had a swimming pool, was quite progressive. Victorian England had a laissez-faire approach to social issues. Then, like now, many wealthy people believed things would work out for the poor if the government just stayed out of it. However, others, such as the Rowntree family, felt differently. Their altruism contributed to the establishment of a society that now takes care of its workers and poor much better.

Walk directly into the park toward the evocative Industrial Age housing complex capping the hill beyond the central fountain. In the park's brick gazebo are touching memorial plaques to WWI and WWII deaths. Rowntree also gave this park to York to remember those lost in the "Great War." Stroll along the delightful, duck-filled pond near the Rowntree Park Café, return to the riverside lane, and continue back into York. You're almost home.

Shopping in York

With its medieval lanes lined with classy as well as tacky little shops, York is a hit with shoppers. I find two kinds of shopping in York particularly interesting: antique malls and charity shops.

Antique Malls: Two places within a few blocks of each other are filled with stalls and cases owned by antique dealers from the countryside (all open daily). The malls, a warren of rooms on three floors with cafés buried deep inside, sell the dealers' bygones on commission. Serious shoppers do better heading for the country, but if you brake for garage sales you'll love these: The **Antiques Centre York** (41 Stonegate, www.theantiquescentreyork.co.uk), and the **Red House Antiques Centre** (a block from the Minster at Duncombe Place, www.redhouseyork.co.uk).

Charity Shops: In towns all over Britain, it seems one low-rent street is lined with charity shops, allowing locals to both donate their junk and buy the junk of others in the name of a good cause. (Talk about a win-win.) It's great for random shopping. And, as the people working there are often volunteers involved in that cause, it can lead to some interesting conversations. In York, on Goodramgate (stretching a block or so in from the town wall), you'll find "thrift shops" run by the British Heart Foundation,

Mind, and Oxfam. Good deals abound on clothing, purses, accessories, children's toys, books, CDs, and maybe even a guitar. If you buy something, you're getting a bargain and at the same time helping the poor, mentally ill, elderly, or even a pet in need of a vet (stores generally open between 9:00 and 10:00 and close between 16:00 and 17:00, with shorter hours on Sun).

Nightlife in York

PUBS

Even more than chocolate, York likes its beer. Many pubs serve inexpensive plates at lunch, then focus on selling beer in the evening. Others offer lunch and early dinner. You can tell by their marketing how enthusiastic they are about cooking versus drawing pints. While I've listed good eating pubs under "Eating in York," later, here are a few pubs I'd recommend to give your beer drinking an atmospheric kick:

The Maltings, just over Lendal Bridge, has classic pub ambience. While local beer purists swear by this place, the owners don't

allow swearing or music... which shapes the clientele. The pub's fine local and international beers and light-and-mellow vibe are conducive to drinking and talking. They do serve light lunches (simple salads and sandwiches only 12:00-14:00; cross the bridge and look down and left to Tanners Moat, tel. 01904/655-387).

The Blue Bell is one of my favorites for old-school York vibes. This tiny, traditional establishment with a time-warp Edwardian interior is the smallest pub in York. It has two distinct and inviting little rooms (no music, east end of town at 53 Fossgate, tel. 01904/654-904).

The House of the Trembling Madness is another fine watering hole with a cozy atmosphere; it sits above a "bottle shop" that sells a stunning variety of beers by the bottle to go (48 Stonegate).

Evil Eye Lounge, a hit with York's young crowd, is a creaky, funky, hip space famous for its strong cocktails and edgy ambience. There are even beds to lay in while you drink. You can order downstairs at the bar (with a small terrace out back) or head upstairs (42 Stonegate, tel. 01904/640-002).

The Golden Fleece claims to be the oldest and most haunted coaching inn in York (music nightly at 21:00, 16 Pavement, see listing in "Eating in York," later).

Riverside Eating and Drinking: On sunny days, there are several pubs with riverside tables just below Ouse Bridge, starting with **The King's Arms,** which boasts flood marks inside its door and has a rougher local crowd than other recommended pubs. For a cheap thrill, grab a pint indoors and sit outside at their rustic picnic tables (3 King's Staith, tel. 01904/659-435).

ENTERTAINMENT
Theatre Royal
This spiffed-up theater sporting an 18th-century facade offers a full variety of dramas, comedies, and works by Shakespeare. The locals are proud of the state-of-the-art main theater and little 100-seat theater-in-the-round (tickets £15-35, shows usually Tue-Sat at 19:30, tickets easy to get, on St. Leonard's Place near Bootham Bar and a 5- to 10-minute walk from recommended B&Bs, booking tel. 01904/623-568, www.yorktheatreroyal.co.uk). Those under 18 and students of any age can get tickets for £10-15.

Ghost Tours
You'll see fliers, signs, and promoters hawking a variety of entertaining after-dark tours. For a rundown on this scene, see page 773.

Movies
The centrally located **City Screen Cinema,** right on the river, plays both art-house and mainstream flicks. They also have an enticing café/bar overlooking the river that serves good food (13 Coney Street, tel. 0871-902-5726). The Art Deco **Everyman Cinema** is another good option (near the train station on Blossom Street, tel. 0872-436-9060).

Sleeping in York

July through October are the busiest (and usually most expensive) months. B&Bs often charge more for weekends and sometimes turn away one-night bookings, particularly for peak-season Saturdays. (York is worth two nights anyway.) Prices may spike for horse races and Bank Holidays (about 20 nights a season). Remember to book ahead during festival times (see "Helpful Hints" on page 772) and weekends year-round.

B&BS AND GUESTHOUSES
These places are all small and family-run. They come with plenty of steep stairs (and no elevators) but no traffic noise. Rooms can be tight; if maneuverability is important, say so when booking. For a

good selection, contact them well in advance. Most have permits to lend for street parking.

The handiest B&B neighborhood is the quiet residential area just outside the old town wall's Bootham Bar, along the road called Bootham. All of these are within a 10-minute walk of the Minster and TI, and a 5- to 15-minute walk from the station. If driving, head for the cathedral and follow the medieval wall to Bootham Bar. The street called Bootham leads away from Bootham Bar.

Getting There: From the train station it's an easy five-minute walk to the B&B neighborhood: Head to the north end of the station along track 2 (past the York Tap pub and racks of bicycles) and into the short-stay parking lot. You'll continue essentially straight along the tracks, never taking any stairs, over the river and along a footpath ultimately to a short stairway (on the right) that leads to the base of St. Mary's Street.

On or near Bootham Terrace

$$ St. Raphael Guesthouse, run by Fran and Jamie, has seven comfy rooms. Each is themed after a different York street, and lovingly accented with a fresh rose and home-baked banana bread. For more space, ask for their small apartment with a private entrance and courtyard (RS%, family rooms, 44 Queen Annes Road, tel. 01904/645-028, www.straphaelguesthouse.co.uk, info@straphaelguesthouse.co.uk).

$$ Alcuin Lodge, run by welcoming Darren and Mark, is a cozy place, with five rooms that feel personal (look for Darren's grandmother's vase and dresser) yet up to date (one room with private WC in the hallway just outside; 15 Sycamore Place, tel. 01904/629-837, www.alcuinlodge.com, darren@alcuinlodge.com).

$$ Bronte Guesthouse is a modern B&B with five airy, bright rooms and a lovely back garden. Little extras like a communal fridge stocked with water, ice, and milk and a room for playing cards make it easy to relax (family room available, 22 Grosvenor Terrace, tel. 01904/621-066, www.bronte-guesthouse.com, enquiries@bronte-guesthouse.com, Mick and Mandy).

$$ Arnot House, run by a hardworking daughter-and-mother team, is old-fashioned, homey, and lushly decorated with Victorian memorabilia. The three well-furnished rooms even have little libraries (2-night minimum preferred, no children, huge DVD library, 17 Grosvenor Terrace, tel. 01904/641-966, www.arnothouseyork.co.uk, kim.robbins@virgin.net, Kim and her cats Pickle and Tabitha).

$$ Bootham Guest House features creamy walls and contemporary furniture that are a break from more traditional York B&B decor. Of the eight rooms, six are en suite, while two share a bath (RS%, 56 Bootham Crescent, tel. 01904/672-123,

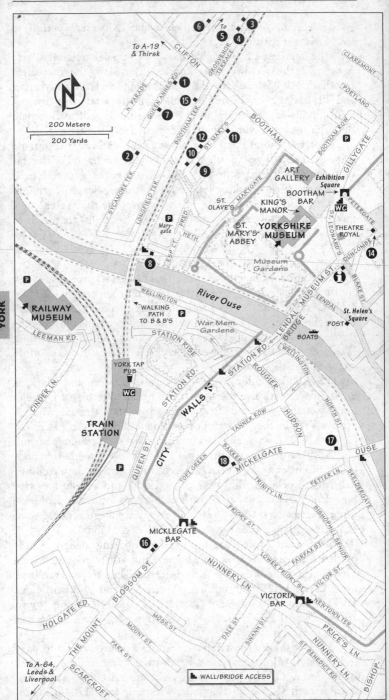

YORK

To A-19
& Thirsk

CLIFTON

6
To
5
4
3

N. PARADE
QUEEN ANNE'S RD.
GROSVENOR TERRACE

1
15
7

200 Meters
200 Yards

BOOTHAM TER.

12
11
ST. MARY'S
10
9

BOOTHAM

BOOTHAM ROW
GILLYGATE
P

CLAREMONT
PORTLAND

2

SYCAMORE TER.
LONGFIELD TER.

MARYGATE

ST. OLAVE'S

ST.
MARY'S
ABBEY

KING'S
MANOR

ART
GALLERY

Exhibition
Square

BOOTHAM
BAR
WC

PETERGATE
ST. LEONARD'S

THEATRE
ROYAL

DUNCOMBE
14

P
Marygate
LESS CT.
HETH.
FRED.

YORKSHIRE
MUSEUM

Museum
Gardens

LENDAL MUSEUM ST.

BLAKE ST.
LENDAL

i

St. Helen's
Square
POST

RAILWAY
MUSEUM

P

LEEMAN RD.

River Ouse

WELLINGTON

WALKING
PATH
TO B & B'S

P
War Mem.
Gardens

STATION RISE

STATION RD.

LENDAL
BRIDGE

BOATS

WELLINGTON

ROUGIER

HUDSON

NORTH ST.

OUSE

CINDER LN.

York Tap
Pub
WC

STATION RD.

STATION RD.

WALLS

CITY

QUEEN ST.

P

TRAIN
STATION

TANNER ROW

BARKER

18

MICKELGATE

TOFT GREEN

TRINITY LN.

PRIORY ST.

FETTER LN.
SKELDERGATE

17

BISHOPHILL SENIOR

MICKLEGATE
BAR

16

BLOSSOM ST.

NUNNERY LN.

LOWER PRIORY ST.
FAIRFAX ST.

VICTOR ST.
NEWTOWN TER.

VICTORIA
BAR

HOLGATE RD.

THE MOUNT

PARK ST.

MOSS ST.

MOUNT ST.

DALE ST.

SWANN ST.

PRICE'S LN.

NUNNERY LN.

ST. BENEDICT RD.

BISHOP.

To A-64,
Leeds &
Liverpool

SCARCROFT

WALL/BRIDGE ACCESS

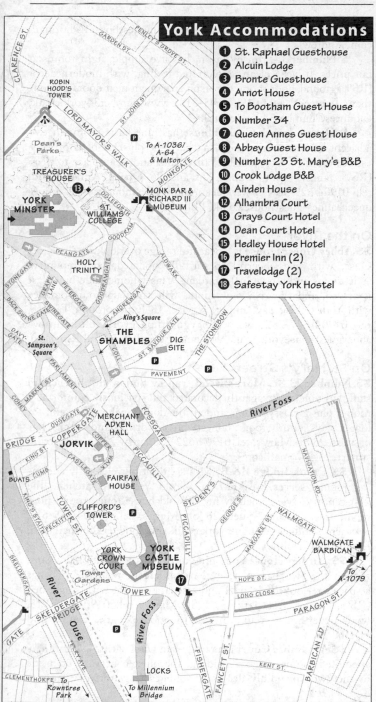

York Accommodations

1. St. Raphael Guesthouse
2. Alcuin Lodge
3. Bronte Guesthouse
4. Arnot House
5. To Bootham Guest House
6. Number 34
7. Queen Annes Guest House
8. Abbey Guest House
9. Number 23 St. Mary's B&B
10. Crook Lodge B&B
11. Airden House
12. Alhambra Court
13. Grays Court Hotel
14. Dean Court Hotel
15. Hedley House Hotel
16. Premier Inn (2)
17. Travelodge (2)
18. Safestay York Hostel

YORK

www.boothamguesthouse.co.uk, boothamguesthouse1@hotmail.com, Andrew).

$ Number 34, run by Jason, has five simple, light rooms at fair prices. It has a clean, uncluttered feeling, with modern decor (RS%, ground-floor room, 5-person apartment next door, 34 Bootham Crescent, tel. 01904/645-818, www.number34york.co.uk, enquiries@number34york.co.uk).

$ Queen Annes Guest House has nine basic rooms in two adjacent houses. While it doesn't have the plushest beds or richest decor, this is a respectable, affordable, and clean place to sleep (RS%, family room, lounge, 24 and 26 Queen Annes Road, tel. 01904/629-389, www.queen-annes-guesthouse.co.uk, info@queen-annes-guesthouse.co.uk, Phil).

On the River

$$ Abbey Guest House is a peaceful refuge overlooking the River Ouse, with five cheerful, beautifully updated, contemporary-style rooms and a cute little garden. A tasty homemade breakfast is served, and the riverview rooms will ramp up your romance with York (RS%, pay laundry service, 13 Earlsborough Terrace, tel. 01904/627-782, www.abbeyguesthouseyork.co.uk, info@abbeyguesthouseyork.co.uk, welcoming couple Jane and Kingsley).

On St. Mary's Street

$$ Number 23 St. Mary's B&B, run by Simon and his helpful staff, has nine extravagantly decorated and spaciously comfortable rooms, plus a classy lounge and all the doily touches (discount for longer stays, family room, honesty box for drinks and snacks, lots of stairs, 23 St. Mary's, tel. 01904/622-738, www.23stmarys.co.uk, stmarys23@hotmail.com).

$$ Crook Lodge B&B, with six tight but elegantly charming rooms, serves breakfast in an old Victorian kitchen. The 21st-century style somehow fits this old house (one ground-floor room, free parking, quiet, 26 St. Mary's, tel. 01904/655-614, www.crooklodgeguesthouseyork.co.uk, crooklodge@hotmail.com, David and Caroline).

$$ Airden House rents nine nice, mostly traditional rooms, though the two basement-level rooms are more mod—one has a space age-looking Jacuzzi and a separate room with single bed (RS%, lounge, free parking, 1 St. Mary's, tel. 01904/638-915, www.airdenhouse.co.uk, info@airdenhouse.co.uk, Emma and Heather).

$$ Alhambra Court is a family-run hotel with 24 charmingly appointed rooms. Relax outside in the quiet courtyard or inside in the two splendidly decorated lounges (elevator, pay laundry

service, free parking, 31 St. Mary's, tel. 01904/628-474, www.
alhambracourt.co.uk, stay@alhambracourt.co.uk)

HOTELS

$$$$ Grays Court Hotel is a historic mansion—the home of dukes
and archbishops since 1091—that now rents 12 rooms to travelers.
While its public spaces and gardens are lavish, its rooms are elegant
yet modest. The creaky, historic nature of the place makes for a
memorable stay. If it's too pricey for lodging, consider coming here
for its fine-dining **$$$$ Bow Room Restaurant** serving modern
English cuisine (Chapter House Street, tel. 01904/612-613, www.
grayscourtyork.com).

$$$ Dean Court Hotel, a Best Western facing the Minster, is
a big stately hotel with classy lounges and 37 comfortable rooms. It
has a great location and friendly vibe for a business-class establish-
ment. A few rooms have views for no extra charge—try requesting
one (elevator, restaurant, Duncombe Place, tel. 01904/625-082,
www.deancourt-york.co.uk, sales@deancourt-york.co.uk).

$$$ Hedley House Hotel, well run by a wonderful family,
has 30 clean and spacious rooms. The outdoor hot tub/sauna is a
fine way to end your day, or you can sign up for yoga or Pilates
(ask for a deal with stay of three or more nights, family rooms,
good two-course evening meals, in-house massage and beauty
services, free parking, 3 Bootham Terrace, tel. 01904/637-404,
www.hedleyhouse.com, greg@hedleyhouse.com, Greg and Louise Harrand). They also have three luxury studio apartments—see
their website for details.

Budget Chain Hotels: If looking for something a little less
spendy than the hotels listed earlier, consider several chains, with
central locations in town. These include **Premier Inn** (two branches side-by-side) and **Travelodge** (one location near the York Castle
Museum at 90 Piccadilly; second location on Micklegate).

HOSTEL

¢ **Safestay York** is a boutique hostel on a rowdy street (especially
on Fridays and Saturdays). Located in a big old Georgian house,
they rent 158 beds in 4- to 12-bed rooms, with great views, private prefab "pod" bathrooms, and reading lights for each bed. They
also offer fancier, hotel-quality doubles (family room for up to four,
continental breakfast extra, 4 floors, no elevator, air-con, Wi-Fi in
public areas only, self-service laundry, TV lounge, game room, bar,
lockers, no curfew, 5-minute walk from train station at 88 Micklegate, tel. 01904/627-720, www.safestay.com/ss-york-micklegate.
html, reception-yk@safestay.com).

Eating in York

York is a great food city, with a wide range of ethnic options and foodie bistros. Thanks to the local high-tech industry, the university, and tourism, there's a demand that sustains lots of creative and fun eateries.

If you're in a hurry or on a tight budget, picnic and light-meals-to-go options abound, and it's easy to find a churchyard, bench, or riverside perch where you can munch. On a sunny day, perhaps the best picnic spots in town are under the evocative 12th-century ruins of St. Mary's Abbey in the Museum Gardens (near Bootham Bar), in the park surrounding the Minster, or in the yard of little Holy Trinity Church (on Goodramgate).

Most bistros have good-quality, creative vegetarian options and offer economical lunch specials and early dinners (generally order by 18:30). After 19:00 or so, main courses cost £16-26 and fixed-price meals (two or three courses) go for around £25. If you're set on a particular place for dinner, reservations are often smart.

IN THE CITY CENTER
Fine Dining
$$$$ Skosh serves a smart local clientele gourmet tapas—modern, creative, and sharable small dishes that are a fusion of English and international cuisine. Its bright dining room is loud and fun, with an open kitchen adding energy to the mix. It's top quality with no pretense. The four stools at the bar are nice if you like watching the chef at work (£10 plates—three or four per person makes a meal, Wed-Sat 12:00-14:00 & 17:30-22:00, closed Sun-Tue, 98 Micklegate, tel. 01904/634-849).

Cheap Eats Around King's Square
King's Square is about as central as can be for sightseers. And from here, you can actually see several fine quick-and-cheap lunch options. After buying your takeout food, sit on the square and enjoy the street entertainers. Or, for a peaceful place to eat more prayerfully, find the Holy Trinity Church yard, with benches amid the old tombstones on Goodramgate (half a block to the right of York Roast Company).

$ York Roast Company is a local fixture, serving their Yorkshire pudding wrap (a kind of old English burrito) and hearty pork sandwiches with applesauce, stuffing, and "crackling" (roasted bits of fat and skin). If Henry VIII wanted fast food, he'd have eaten here (daily 10:00-23:00, order at counter then eat upstairs or take away for the same price, 74 Low Petergate, tel. 01904/629-197, second location at 4 Stonegate).

$ Drakes Fish & Chips across the street from York Roast

Company, is a local favorite chippy. While it's mostly takeout, for £3 extra you can sit and eat in their simple backroom dining area (daily 11:00-22:30, 97 Low Petergate, tel. 01904/624-788).

$ The Cornish Bakery, facing King's Square, cooks up pasties to eat in or take away (30 Colliergate, tel. 01904/671-177).

$ Shambles Market and Food Court has many food stalls and street-food vendors—like a corral of food trucks—offering fun, nutritious, and ethnic light meals. The Moros stand is particularly popular for its North African plates. This lively scene is wedged between The Shambles and Parliament Street (daily 7:00-17:00, until 16:00 in winter).

$ St. Crux Parish Hall is a medieval church now used by a medley of charities that sell tea, homemade cakes, and light meals (Tue-Sat 10:00-16:00, closed Sun-Mon, at bottom of The Shambles at its intersection with Pavement, tel. 01904/621-756).

$ Harlequin Café, a charming place, is appreciated for its good coffee and homemade cakes, as well as its light meals. It's up a creaky staircase overlooking King's Square. On weekend nights it morphs into a gin bar (Mon-Sat 10:00-16:00, Sun 11:00-15:00, 2 King's Square, tel. 01904/630-631).

$$ The Golden Fleece is a sloppy, dingy place with tilty floors that make you feel drunk even if you aren't. It's a good bet for casual pub grub in a characteristic setting, with music nightly at 21:00 (16 Pavement, across the street from the southern end of The Shambles, tel. 01904/625-171).

Groceries: A **Marks & Spencer Food Hall** is a block away from Shambles Market on Parliament Street (Mon-Sat 8:00-18:30, Sun 10:30-17:00).

On or near Stonegate and Swinegate

$$ Ask Italian Restaurant is part of a cheap and cheery Italian chain, but the food's fine, the price is right, and you'll slurp

your pasta in the majestic Neo-classical hall of York's Grand Assembly Rooms, lined with Corinthian marble columns (daily 11:00-22:00, weekends until 23:00; Blake Street, tel. 01904/637-254). Even if you're just walking past, peek inside to gape at the interior.

$$ Swinegate Bars and Eateries: Strolling this touristy street, you can simply take your pick of the various tempting restaurants and watering holes. Some are trendy, with thumping music, while others are tranquil; some

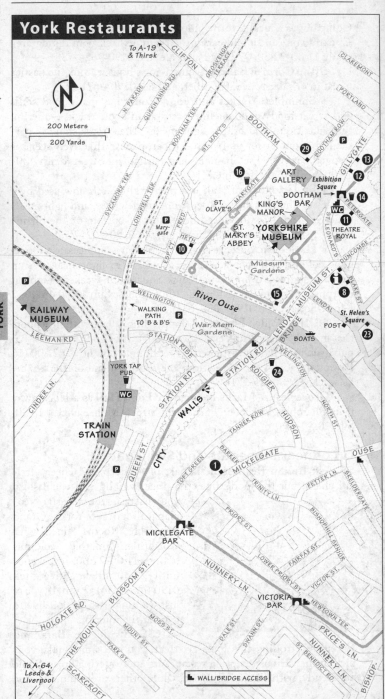

York Restaurants

To A-19 & Thirsk

CLIFTON

GROSVENOR TERRACE

CLAREMONT

PORTLAND

N. PARADE

QUEEN ANNE'S RD.

BOOTHAM TER.

ST. MARY'S

BOOTHAM

BOOTHAM ROW

GILLYGATE

29

13

12

200 Meters

200 Yards

SYCAMORE TER.

LONGFIELD TER.

16

MARYGATE

ART GALLERY

Exhibition Square

BOOTHAM BAR

PETERGATE

14

11

WC

ST. OLAVE'S

KING'S MANOR

THEATRE ROYAL

ESP. CT.

HETH.

Mary-gate

FRED.

10

ST. MARY'S ABBEY

YORKSHIRE MUSEUM

ST. LEONARD'S

DUNCOMBE

P

Museum Gardens

15

MUSEUM ST.

LENDAL

i

8

BLAKE ST.

River Ouse

LENDAL BRIDGE

St. Helen's Square

POST

23

P

RAILWAY MUSEUM

WALKING PATH TO B & B'S

War Mem. Gardens

STATION RD.

STATION RISE

BOATS

WELLINGTON

24

ROUGIER

NORTH ST.

OUSE

LEEMAN RD.

CINDER LN.

YORK TAP PUB

WC

STATION RD.

WELLINGTON

CITY WALLS

TANNER ROW

HUDSON

FETTER LN.

SKELDERGATE

BISHOPHILL SENIOR

TRAIN STATION

QUEEN ST.

TOFT GREEN

BARKER LN.

1

MICKELGATE

P

TRINITY LN.

PRIORY ST.

FAIRFAX ST.

VICTOR ST.

MICKLEGATE BAR

LOWER PRIORY ST.

NUNNERY LN.

BLOSSOM ST.

VICTORIA BAR

NEWTOWN TER.

HOLGATE RD.

THE MOUNT

PARK ST.

MOUNT ST.

MOSS ST.

DALE ST.

SWANN ST.

ST. BENEDICT RD.

PRICE'S LN.

NUNNERY LN.

BISHOP.

To A-64, Leeds & Liverpool

WALL/BRIDGE ACCESS

YORK

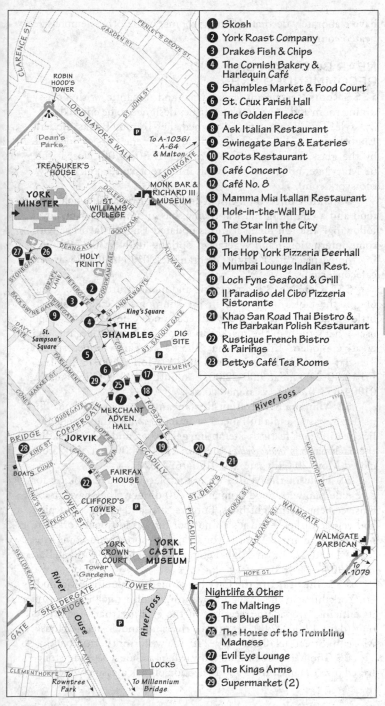

1. Skosh
2. York Roast Company
3. Drakes Fish & Chips
4. The Cornish Bakery & Harlequin Café
5. Shambles Market & Food Court
6. St. Crux Parish Hall
7. The Golden Fleece
8. Ask Italian Restaurant
9. Swinegate Bars & Eateries
10. Roots Restaurant
11. Café Concerto
12. Café No. 8
13. Mamma Mia Italian Restaurant
14. Hole-in-the-Wall Pub
15. The Star Inn the City
16. The Minster Inn
17. The Hop York Pizzeria Beerhall
18. Mumbai Lounge Indian Rest.
19. Loch Fyne Seafood & Grill
20. Il Paradiso del Cibo Pizzeria Ristorante
21. Khao San Road Thai Bistro & The Barbakan Polish Restaurant
22. Rustique French Bistro & Pairings
23. Bettys Café Tea Rooms

YORK

Nightlife & Other
24. The Maltings
25. The Blue Bell
26. The House of the Trembling Madness
27. Evil Eye Lounge
28. The Kings Arms
29. Supermarket (2)

have elaborately decorated dining rooms, while others emphasize heated courtyards.

NEAR BOOTHAM BAR AND RECOMMENDED B&BS

$$$$ Roots Restaurant feels formal and romantic, with a classy dining room and small gourmet dishes designed to be enjoyed family-style. To fully appreciate esteemed chef Tommy Banks' modern English cuisine, I'd opt for the £55 tasting menu (lots of fine wine by the glass, lunch from noon, dinner 17:30-21:00, closed Tue, 68 Marygate, no phone, reserve at info@rootsyork.co.uk or www.rootsyork.com).

$$ Café Concerto, a casual and cozy bistro with wholesome food and a charming musical theme, has an understandably loyal following. The fun menu features updated English favorites with some international and vegetarian options (daily 9:30-17:00, facing the Minster at 21 High Petergate, tel. 01904/610-478, www.cafeconcerto.biz).

$$$ Café No. 8 is a romantic and modern little bistro. Grab one of the tables in front or in the sunroom, or enjoy a shaded little garden out back if the weather's good. Chef Chris Pragnell uses what's fresh in the market to shape his simple, elegant, and creative modern British menu. There's an early dinner special Tuesday through Thursday until 18:30 (Mon 12:00-16:00, Tue-Fri 12:00-22:00, Sat 9:00-22:00, Sun until 16:00, 8 Gillygate, tel. 01904/653-074, www.cafeno8.co.uk).

$$ Mamma Mia Italian Restaurant is a popular choice for its pizza, pasta, and a full menu of Italian *secondi*. The casual, garlicky eating area features a tempting gelato bar, and in nice weather the back patio is *molto bello* (Tue-Sun 11:30-14:00 & 17:30-23:00, closed Mon, 20 Gillygate, tel. 01904/622-020).

$$ Hole-in-the-Wall Pub is the place if you're looking for a ye olde pub with good grub and a £10 dinner. They have an extensive menu with light bites, burgers, fish-and-chips, meat pies, and veggie dishes—and it's a fine spot for a traditional Yorkshire pudding. The atmosphere is your English pub dream come true (daily 11:30-22:00, on High Petergate just inside Bootham Bar, tel. 01904/634-468).

$$$ The Star Inn the City has a quality reputation for modern Yorkshire cuisine and a dressy dining hall. Lunch is served on its enticing riverside terrace, but in the evening that's for drinks only (daily 12:00-22:00, next to the river in Lendal Engine House, Museum Street, tel. 01904/619-208, www.starinnthecity.co.uk).

$$ The Minster Inn, an Edwardian alehouse serving stone-baked pizzas, tapas, and a good selection of cask ales and wines, is a friendly neighborhood hangout with an open courtyard that's fun in the summer (daily 12:00-23:00, 24 Marygate, tel. 01904/849-240).

Groceries: Sainsbury is handy for picnic provisions or a simple cheap dinner in your B&B room (daily 6:00-24:00, 50 yards outside Bootham Bar, on Bootham).

AT THE EAST END OF TOWN

This neighborhood is across town from my recommended B&Bs, but still central (and a short walk from the York Castle Museum). These places are all hits with local foodies; reservations are smart for all. The emerging bohemian-chic axis of Fossgate/Walmgate is lined with quality restaurants and has an inviting, untouristy energy.

$$ The Hop York Pizzeria Beerhall is a favorite for its simple approach and winning combo: pizza and beer. The pub pulls real ales in the front, serves wood-fired pies in an inviting space in the back, and offers live music featuring rock and pop covers (daily 12:00-23:00, food served until 21:00—Sun until 20:00, music Wed-Sun at 21:00; 11 Fossgate, tel. 01904/541-466).

$$ Mumbai Lounge Indian Restaurant (named for its top-floor lounge) is a local choice for Indian food (daily 12:00-14:00 & 17:30-23:30, 47 Fossgate, tel. 01904/654-155, www.mumbailoungeyork.co.uk).

$$ Loch Fyne Seafood and Grill is a fine fish value with an inviting and affordable menu served in a classic and spacious old hall. While a national chain, it still feels smart and has a caring waitstaff. Their three-course, £13 lunch special is served until 18:00 (daily 12:00-22:30, Foss Bridge House, Walmgate, tel. 01904/650-910).

$$$ Il Paradiso del Cibo Pizzeria Ristorante, with its adorable chaos, just feels special. It's an eccentric little place with tight seating, few tourists, and a fun bustle, run by a Sardinian with attitude (cash only, daily 12:00-15:00 & 18:00-22:00, 40 Walmgate, tel. 01904/611-444, www.ilparadisodelciboyork.com).

$$ Khao San Road Thai Bistro hits the spot if you need a Thai fix (daily from 17:00, 52 Walmgate, tel. 01904/635-599).

$$ The Barbakan Polish Restaurant is run by a Krakow family offering an inviting little Polish dining room with a passion for homemade cakes (Mon-Sat 9:00-13:00 & 18:00-22:00, Sun 10:00-21:00, 58 Walmgate, tel. 01904/672-474, www.deli-barbakan.co.uk).

$$$ Rustique French Bistro has one big room of tight tables and walls decorated with simple posters. The place has good prices (£20 three-course meal) and is straight French—right down to the welcome (daily 12:00-22:00, across from Fairfax House at 28 Castlegate, tel. 01904/612-744, www.rustiqueyork.co.uk).

$$ Pairings is a stylish wine bar with small bites, an extensive list of drinks, and a patient and helpful waitstaff. Two travelers can make a meal out of the £23 deli platter (which includes the fun of choosing any three meats or cheeses) and their £14 white or red pairing boards (daily 12:00-23:00, 28 Castlegate, tel. 01904/848-909). For wine lovers, this place can also be a fun stop before or after dinner.

TEAROOM

$$ Bettys Café Tea Rooms is a destination restaurant for many. Choose between a Yorkshire Cream Tea (tea and scones with clot-

ted Yorkshire cream and strawberry jam) or a full traditional English afternoon tea (tea, delicate sandwiches, scones, and sweets). With the afternoon tea, your table is so full of doily niceties that the food is served on a little three-tray tower. While you'll pay a little extra here, the ambience and people-watching are hard to beat. There's generally a line, but it moves quickly except at dinnertime. (Those just wanting to buy a takeaway pastry can skip the line and go directly to the bakery counter.) They'll offer to seat you sooner in the bigger and less atmospheric basement, but I'd be patient and wait for a place upstairs—ideally by the window. It's permissible for travel partners on a budget to enjoy the experience for about half the price by one ordering a "full tea"—£20, with enough little sandwiches and sweets for two to share—and the other a simple cup of tea (daily 9:00-21:00, tel. 01904/659-142, www.bettys.co.uk, St. Helen's Square). During World War II, Bettys was a drinking hangout for Allied airmen based nearby. Downstairs near the WC is a mirror signed by bomber pilots—read the story.

York Connections

From York by Train to: Durham (4/hour, 50 minutes), **London**'s King's Cross Station (3/hour, 2 hours), **Bath** (hourly with change in Bristol, 4.5 hours, more with additional transfers), **Oxford** (hourly direct, 3.5 hours, more with transfers), **Cambridge** (hourly, 2.5 hours, transfer in Stevenage or Peterborough), **Birmingham** (2/hour, 2.5 hours), **Keswick/Lake District** (train to Penrith: roughly 2/hour, 4 hours, 1-2 transfers; then bus, allow about 5 hours total), **Manchester Airport** (2/hour, 2 hours), **Edinburgh** (2/hour, 2.5 hours). **Train info:** Tel. 0345-748-4950, www.nationalrail.co.uk.

Connections with London's Airports: Heathrow (allow 4 hours minimum; from airport take Heathrow Express train to London's Paddington Station, transfer by Tube to King's Cross, then take train to York; for details on cheaper but slower Tube or bus option from airport to London King's Cross, see page 192), **Gatwick** (allow 4 hours minimum; from Gatwick South, catch Thameslink train to London's St. Pancras International Station; from there, walk to neighboring King's Cross Station, and catch train to York).

YORK

NORTH YORKSHIRE

Near York • North York Moors •
The North Yorkshire Coast

The countryside to the north of York—dubbed "North Yorkshire"—is speckled with pleasant attractions: the house and office of the "real" rural vet James Herriot, the desolately beautiful North York Moors, an eclectic mansion often used in movies, an engaging folk museum, a quirky WWII museum at a former POW camp, a kitschy scenic steam train, and several looming skeletons of destroyed abbeys. On the Yorkshire coast, you'll find an appealing pair of salty seaside towns. None of these is a top-tier sight in itself, but connecting several by car makes for a fine day of sightseeing.

GETTING AROUND NORTH YORKSHIRE

By Car: Driving is the best option—distances are short, the towns are small and easy to navigate, and there are plenty of tempting stopovers along the way. Map out an efficient itinerary before you go. As you drive, watch out for "wild" pheasants absentmindedly crossing the road. These birds are bred and fed by locals, and left to range freely through the woods...until autumn, when hunting season begins, and the fat, tame, and naive pheasants become easy prey.

By Public Transportation: You can reach most of these destinations by public transportation, but it requires patience (and, in some cases, a long walk from where the bus or train drops you off). York has decent bus connections to Thirsk, Castle Howard, Eden Camp, Pickering, and Whitby. A fun old steam train chugs through the middle of the North York Moors, from Pickering to Grosmont, with some continuing on to Whitby. I've listed the

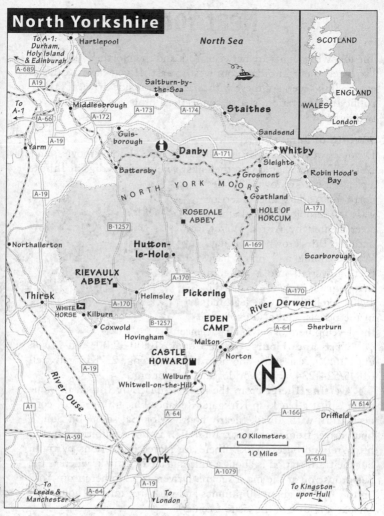

major bus and train connections (see sight listings for specifics), but as schedules change frequently, always confirm details (the York TI can help). For most connections, you can use the route planner at www.yorkshiretravel.net.

By Tour: Various tour companies offer guided bus excursions from York, focusing on Yorkshire Dales/James Herriot country, the North York Moors, Castle Howard, and more (ask at the York TI).

Near York

The following sights are between York and the North York Moors. I've listed them in order from west to east. If you have a car, it's easy to link several of these with a lazy countryside drive. If taking public transportation, sparse connections limit you to just one or two sights.

▲World of James Herriot

Devotees of the *All Creatures Great and Small* books, movies, and BBC TV series should visit the folksy veterinarian's digs in Thirsk,

a pleasant market town 23 miles north of York. James Herriot was an autobiographical character created by Alfred Wight, once the Thirsk town vet. Today, Wight's home and office have been converted into a museum that painstakingly re-creates the 1940s Skeldale House featured in the novels, and also explores the development of veterinary science.

Cost and Hours: £8.50, daily 10:00-17:00, off-season until 16:00, last entry one hour before closing, 23 Kirkgate, tel. 01845/524-234, www.worldofjamesherriot.org.

Getting There: From the market square in Thirsk, the museum is just a block up Kirkgate. Reliance bus #30 or #30X connects York with Thirsk (nearly hourly Mon-Sat, none on Sun, 1 hour, leaves from near York train station and/or Exhibition Square, http://reliancebuses.co.uk). There are more connections by train, but the train station is about a mile outside of Thirsk, whereas the bus drops you at the main square. Drivers can zip here from York on the A-19 in about 40 minutes and park free for two hours (get the parking disc in the visitors center).

Visiting the Museum: The museum holds the world's largest James Herriot memorabilia collection, including the original Austin 7 car from the TV show. Even nonfans will find the slice-of-1940s-life decor fascinating and the trivia intriguing. (For example, Alf Wight couldn't use his own name for his autobiographical protagonist without violating an antiadvertising law...so instead he named "himself" for his favorite Scottish soccer goalie, James Herriot.) Fans will be tickled by the museum's reverence for all things Herriot.

In the barn, watch the 15-minute documentary about the TV series; even the studio sets from the show have been re-created. The interactive children's section is particularly engaging, even for adults: Try your hand at horse dentistry and find out if you're strong enough to calve a cow.

Nearby: Die-hard Herriot fans might enjoy exploring the **Yorkshire Dales,** westward from and much tamer than the North York Moors. Get details about the region—and information about guided tours—at the York TI. Approaching Thirsk, keep an eye out on the right side of the road for the **White Horse**—a gigantic image in the hillside that overlooks the town of Kilburn. The figure was created by a schoolmaster and his students in 1857, who removed the soil to expose the light-colored bedrock.

▲Rievaulx Abbey

Rievaulx (ree-VOH) is the sprawling ruins of a 12th-century abbey. Since it's not near any major towns, its precut stones were less sus-

ceptible to plunder—so it's been left a bit more intact than many other ruined abbeys. Its beautiful and secluded setting—tucked away in a gentle, sheep-speckled valley—is appealing, but if you've seen other fine old abbeys, this is a rerun. Start with the little museum, then follow the included audioguide through the ruins. You'll learn how monastic life changed during the four centuries between its founding and its destruction by Henry VIII.

Cost and Hours: £8.50, includes audioguide; generally April-Sept daily 10:00-18:00, Oct until 17:00, off-season Sat-Sun only until 16:00; café, picnic tables, parking fee refunded when you buy abbey ticket, tel. 01439/798-228, www.english-heritage.org.uk.

Getting There: By car, it's just a short detour from the A-170. It's possible, but complicated, to get there by public transportation—ask for advice at the York TI. From York, first catch bus #31X to Helmsley (2/day Mon-Sat, none on Sun, 1 hour, leaves from York Exhibition Square, confirm bus goes all the way to Helmsley, www.traveline.info). From Helmsley, you can get to the abbey on foot (3 miles) or by taxi (the information center at Helmsley Castle, a short walk from Market Place, can help you with a taxi).

▲▲Castle Howard

Made popular by the filming of the *Brideshead Revisited* TV miniseries here, this fine, palatial 300-year-old home (more a manor than a "castle") is impressive. Taking more than 100 years to complete, it was commissioned in 1699 by Charles Howard, 3rd Earl of Carlisle. Howard chose John Vanbrugh, a playwright with no previous architectural training whatsoever, to design the house. This may explain some of the home's unique flourishes (like the grand, domed Great Hall—once the main entryway—which might be more at home in a Baroque church). Vanbrugh went on to build the even grander Blenheim Palace near Oxford (which is at least twice as interesting, if you're choosing between them—see page 545).

After being damaged in a 1940 fire, Castle Howard lay in ruins for years before being refurbished in the 1960s and opened to the public. The Howard family, whose precocious daughters are pictured throughout the place, still lives in one wing—and in winter, when the place is closed to the public, they use the rooms that are normally on the tour route. Fancy houses run in the family: Another branch of Howards currently resides at Arundel Castle, near the south coast (see page 334). Castle Howard's adventure playground for families, Skelf Island, has rope bridges, slides, zip lines, and food options on an island accessed by boat ride across the castle lake.

Cost and Hours: £19.50 for manor and grounds (including Skelf Island), £12 for grounds only (less in winter—grounds only, as the manor is closed); grounds open daily 10:00-17:00, until 15:30 in winter; manor open daily late March-Oct 10:30-17:00, last entry at 16:00 or even earlier on wedding days, closed Nov-late March except late Nov-late Dec—when it's decorated for Christmas; cafés and fresh produce store, tel. 01653/648-333, www.castlehoward.co.uk.

Getting There: It's in the countryside, 15 miles northeast of York, near Malton, off the A-64. It's ideal by car. You can also get here from York via the CastleLine bus (£10 round-trip, Mon-Sat 6/day, none Sun except July-Aug; 50-75 minutes, leaves from Station Avenue in York; get a voucher on the bus for discounted admission at Castle Howard; www.yorkbus.co.uk).

Visiting the Manor: As you follow the one-way tour route, read the English descriptions in each room. Chatty docents posted in key rooms explain what you're seeing. Many of the decorations are "souvenirs" from the Howards' travels—such as replicas of Roman busts and Greek statues, or paintings that attempt to jam several of a Grand Tour city's landmarks onto a single canvas, much like a collage postcard.

Visitors enter the house through the **West Wing.** After climbing the Grand Staircase, you'll veer into a series of bedrooms built in the mid-1700s in the Palladian style (constructed later than the other wings, and more staid and subdued than the flashy Baroque you'll see later). Starting in the 1830s, these bedrooms became the private apartments of George Howard and Lady Georgiana, whose marriage marked the union of two powerful families—the Howards and the Chatsworths. These days, the bedrooms are still used by guests when the house is closed to visitors. From here stretches the **Antique Passage,** lined with busts, sculptures, tables, and other items collected from Italy during the 4th Earl's visit there in the 1730s.

The passage leads from the West Wing into the **Great Hall,** the centerpiece of the house. The gigantic columns and tall arches draw your eye straight up to the highlight of the hall: the 70-foot-tall dome adorned with the work of the Venetian artist Pellegrini. Above the columns are paintings of the four elements (Earth, Fire, Air, and Water). The dome depicts the tale of Apollo's son Phaeton as he falls from his father's chariot and plummets to earth. The Great Hall and dome were destroyed in the 1940 fire, so what you see here has been rebuilt (which explains why the colors in the paintings are so vivid).

Now head upstairs to view **exhibits** on the manor's restoration after the fire and the filming of *Brideshead Revisited* (both the original TV miniseries and the later big-screen version, starring Emma Thompson and Michael Gambon).

Once back downstairs, you'll continue on to the **South Front,** with an impressive string of rooms built in the early 1700s in the Baroque style. Look up and notice the carved wood molding in these rooms, made from pine trees straight from the grounds. The Music Room features two pianos dating back to 1796 and 1805. The Crimson Dining Room's highlight is a large Canaletto painting depicting a view of Venice. The Turquoise Drawing Room showcases numerous paintings, including Thomas Gainsborough's *Girl with Pigs* and his portrait of Isabella Byron, mother of the 5th Earl and great aunt of the poet Lord Byron. In the Museum Room, look for the elaborate, multistory, blue Delft porcelain tulip vase—dating from the "Tulip Fever" era of the late 17th century, when a single flower could cost £1,000. Imagine the extravagance of filling this whole vase.

From the Museum Room, the Long Gallery leads back through the West Wing and to the **chapel.** The chapel was renovated in 1870-1875, when the floor was lowered and the ceiling and pillars redone to resemble those in the Royal Chapel at St. James's Palace in London. The stained-glass

windows, showing scenes from the life of Christ, were produced in 1872 by Morris & Co. (founded by the artist and designer William Morris). The chapel is still used for services and ceremonies, such as weddings and baptisms.

The chapel marks the end of the manor tour. From here, feel free to roam the sprawling grounds. The mini pyramid on the horizon—behind the big Atlas Fountain—was inspired by a trip to Egypt. The grounds also include several pools, lakes, and fountains, a rose garden, and a quiet wood.

Eden Camp

Once an internment camp for German and Italian POWs during World War II, this is now a theme museum on Britain's war experience. Sprawling, cluttered, pleasantly low-tech, and a bit hokey, the exhibit works best for Brits who want to help their kids (or grandkids) understand the war years. But even though it's overpromoted, its earnestness will win over WWII buffs, as it energetically tries to convey the spirit of a country Hitler couldn't conquer.

Cost and Hours: £10.50, daily 10:00-17:00, last entry at 16:00, closed late Dec-mid-Jan, cash only, mess-kitchen cafeteria, tel. 01653/697-777, www.edencamp.co.uk.

Getting There: It's near Malton, 18 miles northeast of York (notice its proximity to Castle Howard—it's easy to combine these two and more on a day's drive). Or, from York, you can catch Coastliner bus #840 (every 1-2 hours Mon-Sat, limited on Sun, 1 hour, leaves from York train station or Stonebow, www.yorkbus.co.uk).

Visiting Eden Camp: The comprehensive exhibits investigate a wide range of WWII and postwar topics. Various barracks detail the rise of Hitler, the fury of the Blitz, and the efforts on the home front—such as rationing and the Local Defense Volunteers, affectionately dubbed "Dad's Army." A detailed map and ample posted information are helpful, if a bit overwhelming.

An intense exhibit on the Blitz comes with the sound of bombs, the acrid smell of burning, and wartime mottos such as, "Hitler will send no warning—so always carry your gas mask." Don't miss hut #10, which details the actual purpose of the camp—a prison for captured Nazis and Italians during World War II. Enjoy the quirky handmade items—such as a miniature pair of shoes carved out of bread—created by bored POWs who were killing time. Consider the relative delight of being in the care of the gentlemanly English rather than in a Russian camp. It's no wonder the Germans and Italians settled right in.

North York Moors

In the lonesome North York Moors, sheep seem to outnumber people. Upon this high, desolate-feeling plateau, with spongy and inhospitable soil, bleating flocks jockey against scrubby heather for control of the terrain. Although the 1847 novel *Wuthering Heights* was set 60 miles to the southwest, you can almost imagine the mysterious Heathcliff plodding across this countryside. As you pass through this haunting landscape, crisscrossed by only a few roads, notice how the gloomy brown heather—which blooms briefly with purple flowers at summer's end—is burned back by wardens to clear the way for new growth. The vast undulating expanses of nothingness are punctuated by greener, sparsely populated valleys called dales. Park your car and take a hike across the moors on any small road. You'll come upon a few tidy villages and maybe even old Roman roads.

For information on the moors, visit www.northyorkmoors.org. uk. Most villages have at least one general store where you can buy a basic brochure suggesting local hikes. The Moors National Park Centre (near Danby, at the north end) has hiking tips and sells essential maps. Popular walks include a 5.5-mile loop near the Hole of Horcum, the 4.5-mile walk between Goathland and Grosmont, or the brief stroll to the waterfall near Goathland.

GETTING AROUND THE NORTH YORK MOORS

If you're **driving,** the easiest route across the moors is the A-169, which roughly parallels the steam-train line north to Grosmont; it passes the Hole of Horcum and comes close to Grosmont, before heading northeast to Whitby. To the west, smaller roads head north through Hutton-le-Hole (with its folk museum) and the village of Rosedale Abbey. While less straightforward—you'll need a good map and an even better navigator—this western zone really gets you deep into the moors.

Those relying on **public transportation** will primarily use the North Yorkshire Moors Railway (explained below).

Sights on the Moors

These locations are listed roughly from south to north (as you'd approach them coming from York).

Pickering

This functional town, the southern gateway to the North York Moors, is a major crossroads and a proud hub for this region's meager public transit.

The main reason to visit Pickering is to catch the **North York-shire Moors Railway** steam train into the moors. Otherwise, you can browse its Monday market (produce, knickknacks) and consider its rural-life museum (Hutton-le-Hole's is better)—but don't bother visiting Pickering unless you're passing through anyway.

With more time, consider stopping by Pickering's ruined 13th-century Norman **castle,** built on the site of a wooden castle from William the Conqueror's 11th-century heyday. Appreciate its textbook motte-and-bailey (stone fort on a grassy hilltop) design, and climb to the top to understand its strategic location (£5.70; daily 10:00-18:00, Oct until 17:00, closed Nov-March; on the ridge above town, tel. 01751/474-989, www.english-heritage.org.uk).

Getting There: Drivers find Pickering right on the A-169, 25 miles north of York (en route to the coast). Two-hour parking is across from the library, where Ropery Street meets Southgate; an all-day parking lot is on Vivis Lane, a couple of blocks south (£5/6 hours, £6 for over 6 hours). Those relying on public transportation can catch Coastliner bus #840 from York (every 1-2 hours Mon-Sat, limited on Sun, 1.5 hours, leaves from York train station, www.coastliner.co.uk); alternatively, you can shave a few minutes off the trip by taking the train to Malton, then catching bus #840 from there.

▲North Yorkshire Moors Railway

This 18-mile, one-hour steam-engine ride between Pickering and Grosmont (GROW-mont) runs through some of the best parts of the moors. Some trains continue from Grosmont on to the seaside town of Whitby; otherwise, you might be able to transfer in Grosmont to another train to reach Whitby (check schedules as you plan your trip). Once in Whitby, you can use the bus to connect to other towns along the coast (such as to Staithes) or to return to York.

Even with the small windows and the track situated mostly in a scenic gully, it's a good ride. You can stop along the way for a walk on the moors (or at the appealing village of Goathland) and catch the next train (£24-26 round-trip to Grosmont, £29-31 round-trip to Whitby, includes hop-on, hop-off privileges; runs daily late March-Oct, may run on some weekends in winter—check time-table online, schedule flexes with season but first train generally departs Pickering at 9:25, last train departs Grosmont between 17:00 and 18:30; trip takes about 1 hour one-way to Grosmont, about 2 hours to Whitby; tel. 01751/472-508—press 1 for 24-hour timetable info, www.nymr.co.uk).

▲Hutton-le-Hole

This postcard-pretty town, lining up along a river as if posing for its close-up, is an ideal springboard for a trip into the North York Moors. It has some touristy shops and invit-ing picnic benches, but Hutton-le-Hole's biggest attraction is the engaging **Ryedale Folk Museum.** This open-air complex il-lustrates farm life in the moors through recon-structed and furnished

historic buildings. The line of shops includes a village store, which served as one-stop shopping (the original Costco) to save locals the long trek into the closest market town. A humble cluster of tradi-tional thatched-roof cottages has a genuine lived-in feeling. If the beds are unmade, notice the "mattress" is made of rope stretched across a frame, which could be tightened for a firmer night's sleep (giving us the phrase "sleep tight"). A small-scale model of a tra-ditional Yorkshire village features adorable miniature houses. The Harrison Collection holds items representing English domestic life through the centuries, such as an early 1900s gramophone, a late Victorian sewing machine, a two-foot-tall gingerbread mold, and a blanket smoother (like a giant rolling pin). The museum is most worthwhile during frequent special weekends, when lively costumed docents explain what you're seeing along the way—check the online schedule or call ahead (£8.25; daily 10:00-17:00, off-season until 16:00, closed Dec-Jan; tel. 01751/417-367, www.ryedalefolkmuseum.co.uk).

Getting There: Drivers find it just north of the A-170. From Hutton-le-Hole, you can plunge northward directly into the North York Moors (which begin suddenly as you leave town). Without a car, you may be out of luck, as public transportation is limited—call the museum or check its website for the latest options.

NORTH YORKSHIRE

The Hole of Horcum

This huge sinkhole was supposedly scooped out by a giant. While not too exciting, it offers a good excuse to get out of your car and appreciate the moorland scenery (at the Saltergate car park).

Rosedale Abbey

A tranquil village on the west side of the moors (north of Hutton-le-Hole and far from the Hole of Horcum and Goathland), Rosedale Abbey offers a good dose of small-town moor life. Nestled between hills, it also provides pleasing moor views.

Goathland

This village, huddled along a babbling brook, is worth considering for a sleepy stopover, either on the steam-train trip or for drivers (it's an easy detour from the A-169).

Movie buffs enjoy Goathland's train station, which was used to film scenes at "Hogsmeade Station" for the early Harry Potter movies (for more on Harry Potter sights, see page 912). Brits also know and love Goathland as the setting for the long-running TV series *Heartbeat*, about a small Yorkshire town in the 1960s. You'll see TV sets intermingled with real buildings, and some shops are even labeled "Aidensfield," for the TV town's fictional name.

▲The Moors National Park Centre

This visitors center near Danby provides the best orientation for exploring the North York Moors National Park. (Unfortunately, it's at the northern end of the park—not as convenient if you're coming from York.) The grand old lodge offers excellent exhibits on various moorland topics, informative films about the landscape, an art gallery showcasing works by local artists inspired by these surroundings, a children's play area, an information desk, plenty of books and maps, guided nature walks, brass rubbing, a cheery cafeteria, and brochures on several good walks that start right outside the front door.

Cost and Hours: Free entry; daily 10:00-17:00, off-season until 16:00, Jan-Feb Sat-Sun only; café, pay parking, tel. 01439/772-737, www.northyorkmoors.org.uk.

Getting There: The Moors National Park Centre is nearly a mile from Danby in Esk Valley, in the northern part of the park (follow signs from Danby, which is a short drive from the A-171, running along the northern edge of the park). Danby is on the Esk Valley rail line, with connections to Grosmont and Whitby (4/day,

20 minutes from Danby to Grosmont, 40 minutes from Danby to Whitby, www.cskvalleyrailway.co.uk). From the Danby train station, it's a 1.5-mile walk to the visitors center.

North Yorkshire Coast

Two salty Yorkshire towns—one big (Whitby) and one small (Staithes)—are seaside escapes worth a stop for the seagulls, surf, and Captain Cook lore. If you're not seeing the English coast anywhere else on your trip, and you have an extra day in York, sidetripping here is worthwhile.

GETTING TO AND AROUND THE NORTH YORKSHIRE COAST

Yorkshire Coastliner bus #840 connects **York** to Whitby (2.5 hours, leaves from York train station, www.coastliner.co.uk). Alternatively, you can ride the train to Scarborough (hourly, 50 minutes), then catch bus #93 or #X93 to Whitby (1 hour).

To connect Whitby to the **North York Moors,** you can take the historic steam train from Pickering to Grosmont, with some trains continuing into Whitby (otherwise you may be able to transfer in Grosmont to a Whitby-bound train).

From **Durham,** you can get to Whitby by train with transfers in Darlington and Middlesbrough (3 hours, Middlesbrough-Whitby leg also stops at Grosmont, where you can catch the Moors steam train south to Pickering and Danby, near The Moors National Park Centre).

From **Whitby,** Arriva bus #X4 runs up and down the coast north of town, connecting you to Sandsend and Staithes en route to Middlesbrough; south of Whitby, buses #93 and #X93 run to Robin Hood's Bay (20 minutes, www.arrivabus.co.uk).

WHITBY

An important port since the 12th century, Whitby is a fun coastal resort town with about 14,000 people, a gaggle of steep and salty old streets, and enjoyable nauti-

cal ambience. Its busy harbor, bristling with ships' masts, is squeezed into a narrow canyon flanked on one side by the state-ly skeleton of its 11th-century abbey, and on the other by the bluff-topping West Cliff neigh-borhood. The harborfront zone is a carousel of Coney Island-type amusements and city dwellers from inland Yorkshire whoop-ing it up. Rounding out Whitby's claim to fame are its connections to Captain Cook and Bram Stoker (whose *Dracula* was partly writ-ten here).

If driving, consider first stopping by the hilltop sights (the abbey on one side of town, and West Cliff on the other). Then drive down into the old town center and drop your car in the pay-and-display parking lot across the street from the TI and near the train and bus stations. Walk about 200 yards toward the harbor—and the lone bridge spanning it—to get oriented.

From the bridge, face the sea to consider your options (de-scribed in more detail below): On the left is the waterfront prom-enade called Pier Road/Fish Quay, lined with tacky carnival dis-tractions, as well as the Magpie Café (popular fish-and-chips) and a tacky Dracula exhibit (skip it); above this scene is the West Cliff area, with fine views over town. On the right (across the bridge) is a warren of touristy lanes filled with hard-candy stores, knick-knack shops, and the Captain Cook Memorial Museum; overhead (but not quite visible from here) is the ruined abbey. The **TI** is on the harbor next to the train and bus stations (tel. 01723/383-636, www.discoveryorkshirecoast.com).

Hop-On, Hop-Off Bus: The double-decker, open-top Whit-by Town Tour bus starts near the whalebone arch (on the water-front promenade, near the Bay Royal Hotel) and makes an hour-long circuit to local attractions including Whitby Abbey (£7, ticket good for 24 hours, runs April-Sept, tel. 01947/602-922, www.coastalandcountry.co.uk).

Visiting Whitby: Whitby's main landmark is its ▲ **ruined abbey,** set on a bluff overlooking the harbor. Legend holds that a nun named Hilda found a snake-infested headland and drove

out the serpents, turning them into flat, spiral stones (actually the stones are fossils of extinct sea creatures called ammonites). Built on the site of Hilda's monastic settlement, the remains of this 11th-century version echo with the chants of ages past...enough to raise goose bumps even on a vampire *(Dracula* was partly set here). An app-based interactive tour, the Ammonite Quest, leads visitors around the ruins and explains the artifacts. Many of the stones from this formerly grand abbey were used to build houses in the town (£9, daily 10:00-18:00, shorter hours or closed off-season, Ammonite Quest tour included with admission, coffee shop, tel. 01947/603 568, www.english-heritage.org.uk). The abbey is connected to the streets below by a **staircase** of 199 steps at the end of the old town. In the olden days, poor people would carry the coffins of the departed up these steps, resting occasionally on broader steps called "coffin rests"...which, for practical reasons, are more frequent near the top. An alternate route up is via the path called Caedmon's Trod.

The small **Captain Cook Memorial Museum,** in an old ship-owner's house where Cook lodged for a few years, offers a dull look at the famous hometown sailor and his exotic voyages (£6, daily 10:00-17:00, by appointment off-season, tel. 01947/601-900, www.cookmuseumwhitby.co.uk). Two of Cook's boats *(Resolution* and *Endeavour)* were built in the Whitby shipyards; a full-size replica of the *Endeavour,* which has been used in many swashbuckling films, is often moored in Whitby.

Across the harbor from the abbey is **West Cliff,** a fun little hilltop park, with inviting benches and a lively kids' area. Supposedly it was from this vantage point that Bram Stoker contemplated Whitby's abbey...and inspiration bit him in the neck. In *Dracula,* a boat docks at the long pier, and a black dog—the Count in disguise—jumps off the boat and runs up the 199 steps to the abbey (where he hides out for the next three chapters, until he takes to the sea again). Nearby, the replica whale bones forming an archway over the path recall Whitby's former status as a major whaling city. When whalers returned to port, they'd prop up bones like these on their ships, as a sign to their wives and mothers (who were anxiously waiting ashore) that the trip had gone safely.

The hop-on, hop-off bus noted earlier leaves from the whale-bone arch. Or to go for a **walk along the beach,** consider strolling to nearby villages, then walking or catching an Arriva bus back:

Sandsend to the north is closer than Robin Hood's Bay to the south (check schedules at www.arrivabus.co.uk). Before heading out, check the tide tables (ask at TI).

Sleeping in Whitby: Consider the **$$ Crescent Lodge B&B** (atop the plateau behind West Cliff, 27 Crescent Avenue, tel. 01947/820-073, www.crescentlodgewhitby.com, info@crescentlodgewhitby.com) or the **¢ YHA Whitby** (one of England's most impressive hostels, right on the abbey grounds above town—and literally built with bits and pieces of that abbey, reservation tel. 0845-371-9049, www.yha.org.uk).

Eating in Whitby: In this nautical town, fish-and-chips are on everybody's mind. Options include **$$ Magpie Café** (a local institution, so expect lines, 14 Pier Road, tel. 01947/602-058), **$$ Quayside** (nearly next door to the Magpie, tel. 01947/825-346), and **$$ Mister Chips** (across the harbor and simpler, 68 Church Street, tel. 01947/604-683).

STAITHES

A ragamuffin village where the boy who became Captain James Cook got his first taste of the sea, Staithes (pronounced "staythz,"

about 10 miles north of Whitby) is a salty jumble of cottages bunny-hopping down a ravine into a tiny harbor. About a tenth the size of its big sister down the coast, Staithes is the yang to Whitby's yin. This refreshingly unpretentious town is gloriously stubborn about not wooing tourists (www.staithes-town.info).

Getting There: Staithes is an easy drive north of Whitby. Parking is tough—generally, you can drive in only to unload. A pay-and-display lot is at the top of the town. While you can take a bus from Whitby to Staithes, there's not much in low-key Staithes to justify the trip (40 minutes, www.arrivabus.co.uk).

Visiting Staithes: While dead as a doornail today, in 1816 Staithes was home to 70 boats and the busiest fishing station on

the northeast coast of England. Decades ago, the town supported 20 fishing boats—today, only three. But fishermen (who pronounce their town's name "steers" in the local dialect) still outnumber tourists here. The out-oftowners who do come here rent cottages in the old center and settle in for a long stay as temporary locals. The town has changed little since Captain Cook's days. Lots of flies and seagulls seem to have picked the barren cliffs raw. There's nothing to do but stroll the beach and enjoy a harborside beer or ice cream. As you gaze out at the scenery and rich light, imagine Staithes in the early 20th century, when a small artists' colony called the "Staithes Group" enjoyed painting this same scene.

For a bit more activity, drop by the **lifeboat station,** operated by the Royal National Lifeboat Institution (RNLI)—Britain's entirely volunteer answer to the Coast Guard. As this organization—England's sole method for responding to maritime emergencies—is entirely funded by donations, consider supporting the cause with a coin or two (tel. 01947/840-001, www.rnli.org.uk).

Eating in Staithes: Staithes has a couple of lowbrow pubs, including **$ The Royal George** (with well-worn, basic decor, along the main drag, tel. 01947/841-432) and **$ The Cod & Lobster** (scenic outdoor seating, cozy indoor space, and old-time Staithes photos, overlooking the harbor, tel. 01947/840-330). Or try the **$ Seadrift Café** (sweets and basic grub at outdoor tables fronting the harbor, tel. 01947/841-345).

DURHAM & NORTHEAST ENGLAND

Durham • Beamish Museum • Hadrian's Wall •
Holy Island and Bamburgh Castle

Northeast England harbors some of the country's best historical sights. Go for a Roman ramble at Hadrian's Wall, a reminder that Britain was an important Roman colony 2,000 years ago. Make a pilgrimage to Holy Island, where Christianity gained its first toehold in Britain. Marvel at England's greatest Norman church—Durham's cathedral—and enjoy an evensong service there. At the excellent Beamish Museum, travel back in time to the 19th and 20th centuries.

PLANNING YOUR TIME

For **train** travelers, Durham is the most convenient overnight stop in this region. But it can be problematic to see en route to another destination since there's limited baggage storage in Durham: Either stay overnight, check a baggage storage website like Stasher. com, or do Durham as a day trip from York. If you like Roman ruins, visit Hadrian's Wall (tricky but doable by public transportation). The Beamish Museum is an easy day trip from Durham (less than an hour by bus).

By **car,** you can easily visit everything in this chapter. Spend a night in Durham and a night near Hadrian's Wall, stopping at the Beamish Museum on your way to Hadrian's Wall.

For the best quick visit to Durham, arrive by midafternoon, in time to tour the cathedral and enjoy the evensong service (Tue-Sat at 17:15, Sun at 15:30; limited access and no tours during June graduation ceremonies). Sleep in Durham. Visit Beamish the next morning before continuing on to your next destination.

Durham

Without its cathedral, Durham would hardly be noticed. But this magnificently situated structure is hard to miss (even if you're zooming by on the train). Seemingly happy to go nowhere, Durham sits along the tight curve of its river, snug below its castle and famous church. It has a medieval, cobbled atmosphere and a scraggly peasant's indoor market just off the main square. Durham is home to England's third-oldest university, with a student vibe jostling against its lingering working-class mining-town feel. You'll see tattooed and pierced people in search of job security and a good karaoke bar. Yet Durham has a youthful liveliness and a small-town warmth that shines—especially on sunny days, when most everyone is out licking ice-cream cones.

Orientation to Durham

As it has for a thousand years, tidy little Durham (pop. 65,000) clusters everything safely under its castle, within the protective

hairpin bend of the River Wear. Because of the town's hilly topography, going just about anywhere involves a lot of up and down...and back up again. The main spine through the middle of town (Framwellgate Bridge, Silver Street, and Market Place) is level to moderately steep, but walking in any direction from that area involves some serious uphill climbing. Take advantage of the handy Cathedral Bus to avoid the tiring elevation changes—especially up to the cathedral and castle area, or to the train station (perched high on a separate hill).

TOURIST INFORMATION

Durham does not have a physical TI, but the town does maintain a call center and a useful website (calls answered Mon-Fri 9:00-17:00, tel. 03000-262-626, www.thisisdurham.com, visitor@thisisdurham.com).

During the summer, a group of 70 volunteers called **Durham Pointers** staff a tourist information cart in Market Place near the equestrian statue. They hand out free maps of the city and offer unbiased advice on Durham attractions—tell them Rick Steves sent you (late May-early Oct Mon-Fri 9:30-15:00, Sat 10:00-14:30, Sun 11:00-15:00, mobile 0758-233-2621, www.durhampointers.co.uk).

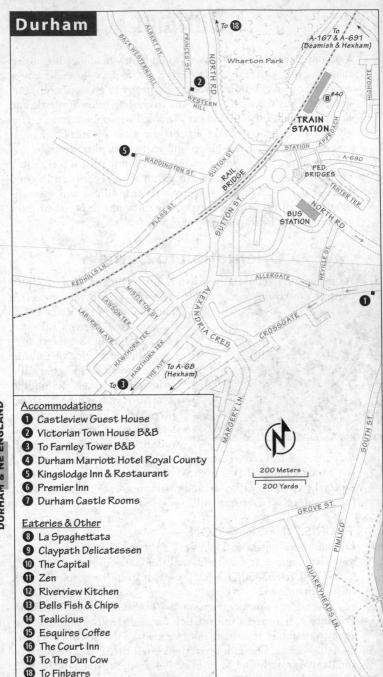

Durham

To 18

To A-167 & A-691 (Beamish & Hexham)

Wharton Park

HIGHGATE

2

BACK WESTERN HILL

ALBERT ST.

PRINCES' ST.

NORTH RD.

WESTERN HILL

B #40

TRAIN STATION

5

WADDINGTON ST.

SUTTON ST.

STATION APPROACH

A-690

RAIL BRIDGE

PED. BRIDGES

TENTER TER.

FLASS ST.

SUTTON ST.

BUS STATION

NORTH RD.

REDHILLS LN.

NEVILLE ST.

ALLERGATE

1

MISTLETOE ST.

LAWSON TER.

LABURNUM AVE.

HAWTHORN TER.

HAWTHORN TER.

ALEXANDRIA CRES.

CROSSGATE

THE AVE.

To A-68 (Hexham)

MARGERY LN.

To 3

N

200 Meters

200 Yards

GROVE ST.

SOUTH ST.

PIMLICO

QUARRYHEADS LN.

Accommodations

1. Castleview Guest House
2. Victorian Town House B&B
3. To Farnley Tower B&B
4. Durham Marriott Hotel Royal County
5. Kingslodge Inn & Restaurant
6. Premier Inn
7. Durham Castle Rooms

Eateries & Other

8. La Spaghettata
9. Claypath Delicatessen
10. The Capital
11. Zen
12. Riverview Kitchen
13. Bells Fish & Chips
14. Tealicious
15. Esquires Coffee
16. The Court Inn
17. To The Dun Cow
18. To Finbarrs
19. Grocery

DURHAM & NE ENGLAND

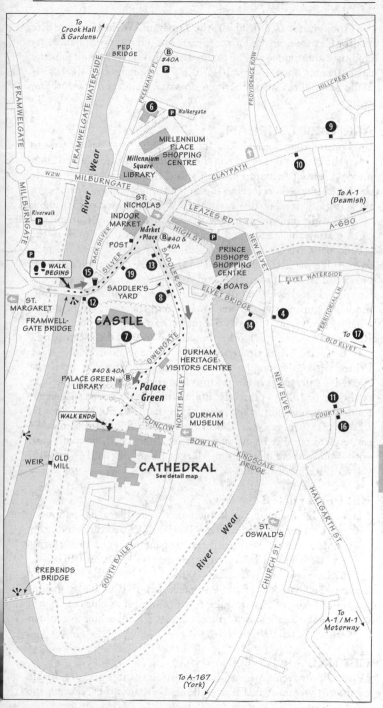

To Crook Hall & Gardens

PED. BRIDGE

FREEMAN'S PL.

B #40A
P

HILLCREST

PROVIDENCE ROW

6
P Walkergate

9

MILLENNIUM PLACE SHOPPING CENTRE

10

CLAYPATH

Millennium Square
LIBRARY

W2W

MILBURNGATE

To A-1 (Beamish)

A-690

FRAMWELGATE

FRAMWELGATE WATERSIDE

River Wear

MILBURNGATE

Riverwalk
P

P

ST. NICHOLAS

LEAZES RD.

INDOOR MARKET

Market Place

HIGH ST.

B #40 & 40A

P

POST

BACK SILVER ST.

SILVER ST.

15

19

13

SADDLER ST.

PRINCE BISHOPS SHOPPING CENTRE

WALK BEGINS

SADDLER'S YARD

8

BOATS

NEW ELVET

ELVET WATERSIDE

12

ST. MARGARET

FRAMWELLGATE BRIDGE

CASTLE

7

OWENGATE

ELVET BRIDGE

14

4

TERRITORIAL LN.

To 17

OLD ELVET

DURHAM HERITAGE VISITORS CENTRE

#40 & 40A
B

PALACE GREEN LIBRARY

Palace Green

NORTH BAILEY

DUNCOW

BOW LN.

DURHAM MUSEUM

NEW ELVET

11

COURT LN.

16

WALK ENDS

WEIR

OLD MILL

CATHEDRAL
See detail map

KINGSGATE BRIDGE

HALLGARTH ST.

ST. OSWALD'S

SOUTH BAILEY

River Wear

CHURCH ST.

To A-1 / M-1 Motorway

PREBENDS BRIDGE

To A-167 (York)

DURHAM & NE ENGLAND

Though not an official TI, the **Durham World Heritage Site Visitor Centre** near the Palace Green can offer some guidance, including a short video on the town. They also sell tickets to tour the castle (center open daily 9:30-17:00, 7 Owengate, tel. 0191/334-3805, www.durhamworldheritagesite.com, visitor.centre@durham.ac.uk).

ARRIVAL IN DURHAM

By Train: From the train station, the fastest and easiest way to reach the cathedral is to hop on the **Cathedral Bus** (described later, under "Getting Around Durham"). But the town's setting—while steep in places—is enjoyable to stroll through (and you can begin my self-guided walk halfway through, at the Framwellgate Bridge).

To **walk** into town, follow the *walkway route to Durham city* signs exiting the station and head along the road downhill to the second pedestrian turnoff (the spiral one within sight of the railway bridge), which leads almost immediately over a bridge above busy road A-690. From here, you can bypass the bridge and continue straight down the hill to some of my recommended accommodations (using this chapter's map—and the giant rail bridge as a handy landmark). Or cross the pedestrian bridge and take North Road into town to reach other hotels, the river, and the cathedral.

By Car: Drivers simply surrender to the wonderful 400-space Prince Bishops Shopping Centre parking lot (coming from the A-1/M-1 exit, you'll run right into it at the roundabout at the base of the old town). It's perfectly safe, with 24-hour access. An elevator deposits you right in the heart of Durham (£3.30/up to 4 hours, £11.50/over 6 hours, £1.50/overnight 18:00-8:00, must enter license plate number to use payment machines, cash or credit card with chip, a short block from Market Place, tel. 0191/375-0416, www.princebishops.co.uk).

HELPFUL HINTS

Markets: The main square, known as Market Place, has an indoor market (generally Mon-Sat 9:00-17:00, closed Sun) and hosts outdoor markets (Sat retail market generally 9:30-16:30, farmers' market third Thu of each month 9:30-15:30, tel. 0191/384-6153, www.durhammarkets.co.uk).

Tours: Each Saturday at 14:00 in peak season, **Blue Badge guides** offer 1.5-hour city walking tours (£4, meet at Durham World Heritage Site Visitor Centre, contact TI call center to confirm schedule, tel. 03000-262-626).

GETTING AROUND DURHAM

While all my recommended hotels, eateries, and sights are doable by foot, if you don't feel like walking Durham's hills, hop on the convenient **Cathedral Bus.** Bus #40 runs between the train station, Market Place, and the Palace Green (£1 all-day ticket, 3/hour Mon-Sat about 9:00-17:00, none on Sun; tel. 0191/372-5386, www.thisisdurham.com). A different bus (#40A) goes from Freeman's Place (near the Premier Inn) to Market Place and the Palace Green (2/hour Mon-Sat about 10:00-15:45). Confirm the route when you board.

Taxis zip tired tourists to their B&Bs or back up to the train station (about £5 from city center, wait on west side of Framwellgate Bridge at the bottom of North Road or on the east side of Elvet Bridge). If you need to call a taxi, try Polly's Taxis, mobile 07910-179-397.

Durham Walk

• *Begin this self-guided walk at Framwellgate Bridge (down in the center of town, halfway between the train station and the cathedral).*

Framwellgate Bridge was a wonder when it was built in the 12th century—much longer than the river is wide and higher than seemingly necessary. It was designed to connect stretches of solid high ground and to avoid steep descents toward the

marshy river. Note how elegantly today's Silver Street (which leads toward town) slopes into the Framwellgate Bridge. (Imagine that until the 1970s, this people-friendly lane was congested with traffic and buses.)

• *Follow Silver Street up the hill to the town's main square.*

Durham's **Market Place** retains the same plotting the prince bishop gave it when he moved villagers here in about 1100. Each

long and skinny plot of land was the same width (about eight yards), maximizing the number of shops that could have a piece of the Market Place action. Find today's distinctly narrow buildings (Whittard and TUI)—they still fit the 900-year-old plan. The widths of the other buildings fronting the square are multiples of that original shop width.

Examine the square's **statues.** Coal has long been the basis

DURHAM & NE ENGLAND

of this region's economy. The statue of Neptune was part of an ill-fated attempt by a coal baron to bribe the townsfolk into embracing a canal project that would make the shipment of his coal more efficient. The statue of the fancy guy on the horse is of Charles Stewart Vane, the Third Marquess of Londonderry. He was an Irish aristocrat and a general in Wellington's army who married a local coal heiress. A clever and aggressive businessman, he managed to create a vast business empire by controlling every link in the coal business chain—mines, railroads, boats, harbors, and so on.

In the 1850s throughout England, towns were moving their markets off squares and into Industrial Age iron-and-glass market halls. Durham was no exception, and today its funky 19th-century **indoor market** (which faces Market Place) is a delight to explore (closed Sun). There are also outdoor markets here on Saturdays and the third Thursday of each month.

Do you enjoy the sparse traffic in Durham's old town? It was the first city in England to institute a "congestion fee." When drivers enter the town Monday through Saturday, a camera snaps a photo of their car's license plate, and the driver must pay £2 that day or face a £50 fine by mail. This has cut downtown traffic by more than 50 percent. Locals brag that London (which now has a similar congestion fee) was inspired by Durham's success.

• *Head up the hill on Saddler Street toward the cathedral, stopping where you reach the chunk of wall at the top of a stairway. On the left, you'll see a bridge.*

A 12th-century construction, **Elvet Bridge** led to a town market over the river. Like Framwellgate, it's very long (17 arches) and designed to avoid riverside muck and steep inclines. Even today, Elvet Bridge leads to an unusually wide road—once swollen to accommodate the market action. Shops lined the right-hand side of Elvet Bridge in the 12th century, as they do today. An alley separated the bridge from the buildings on the left. When the bridge was widened, it met the upper stories of the buildings on the left, which became "street level."

Turn back to look at the chunk of **wall** by the top of the stairs—a reminder of a once-formidable fortification. The Scots, living just 50 miles from here, were on the rampage in the 14th century. After their victory at Bannockburn in 1314, they pushed farther south and actually burned part of Durham. Wary of this new threat, Durham built thick city walls. As people settled within the walls, the population density soared. Soon, open lanes were covered by residences and became tunnels (called "vennels"). A classic vennel leads to Saddlers Yard, a fine little 16th-century courtyard (opposite the wall, look for the yellow Vennels Café sign). While the vennels are cute today, centuries ago they were Dickensian nightmares—the filthiest of hovels.

• *Continue up Saddler Street. Just before the fork at the top of the street, duck through the blue door next to the Georgian Window sign. You'll see a bit of the medieval wall incorporated into the brickwork of a newer building and a turret from an earlier wall. Back on Saddler Street, you can see the ghost of the old wall (picture it standing exactly the width of the building now housing the Salvation Army). Veer right at Owengate as you continue uphill to the Palace Green. (The* **Durham World Heritage Site Visitor Centre** *is near the top of the hill, on the left.)*

The **Palace Green** was the site of the original 11th-century Saxon town, filling this green between the castle and an earlier church. Later, the town made way for 12th-century Durham's defenses, which now enclose the green. With the threat presented by the Vikings, it's no wonder people found comfort in a spot like this.

The **castle** still stands—as it has for a thousand years—on its motte (man-made mound). Like Oxford and Cambridge, Durham

University is a collection of colleges scattered throughout the town, and even this castle is now part of the school. Look into the old courtyard from the castle gate. It traces the very first and smallest bailey (protected area). As future bishops expanded the castle, they left their coats of arms as a way of "signing" the wing they built. Because the Norman kings appointed prince bishops here to rule this part of their realm, Durham was the seat of power for much of northern England. The bishops had their own army and even minted their own coins. The castle is accessible with a 45-minute guided tour, which includes the courtyard, kitchens, great hall, and chapel (£5, open most days when school is in session—but schedule varies so call ahead, buy tickets at Durham World Heritage Site Visitor Centre or Palace Green Library—described next, ask about possible self-guided tour in summer only, tel. 0191/334-2932, www.dur.ac.uk/durham.castle).

DURHAM & NE ENGLAND

Durham's Early Years

Durham's location, tucked inside a tight bend in the River Wear, was practically custom-made for easy fortifications. But it wasn't settled until 995, with the arrival of St. Cuthbert's body (buried in Durham Cathedral). Shortly after that, a small church and fortification were built upon the site of today's castle and church to house the relic. The castle was a classic "motte-and-bailey" design (with the "motte," or mound, providing a lookout tower for the stockade encircling the protected area, or "bailey"). By 1100, the prince bishop's bailey was filled with villagers—and he wanted everyone out. This was *his* place! He provided a wider protective wall, and had the town resettle below (around today's Market Place). But this displaced the townsfolk's cows, so the prince bishop constructed a fine stone bridge (today's Framwellgate) to connect the new town to grazing land he established across the river. The bridge had a defensive gate, with a wall circling the peninsula and the river serving as a moat.

• *Turning your back to the castle and facing the cathedral, on the right is the university's Palace Green Library.*

The **Palace Green Library** has a free permanent exhibit—*Living on the Hills*—that chronicles 10,000 years of human history on the site of Durham. It also hosts temporary exhibits in both its Wolfson Gallery and Dennyson Stoddart Gallery on everything from rare books to robots. Pop in or check online for current exhibits (temporary exhibits—generally £5, Tue-Sun 10:00-16:30, Mon 12:00-17:00, Palace Green, tel. 0191/334-2932, www.dur.ac.uk/library/asc).

• *This walk ends at Durham's stunning cathedral, described next.*

Sights in Durham

▲▲▲DURHAM'S CATHEDRAL

Built to house the much-venerated bones of St. Cuthbert from Lindisfarne (known today as Holy Island), Durham's cathedral offers the best look at Norman architecture in England. ("Norman" is British for "Romanesque.") In addition to touring the cathedral, try to fit in an evensong service.

Cost: Entry to the cathedral itself is free, though a £3 donation is suggested. You must pay to climb the tower and to enter the *Open Treasure* exhibit.

Hours: The cathedral is open to visitors Mon-Sat 9:00-18:00, Sun 12:30-17:00, daily until 20:00 mid-July-Aug, sometimes closes for special services, opens daily at 7:15 for worship and prayer. Access is limited for a few days in June, when the cathedral is used for graduation ceremonies (check online).

Information: Tel. 0191/386-4266, www.durhamcathedral. co.uk.

Visitor Information: A shop, café, and WC are tucked away in the cloister. Their pamphlet, *A Short Guide to Durham Cathedral*, is inexpensive and informative but dull.

Evensong: For a thousand years, this cradle of English Christianity has been praising God. To really experience the cathedral, attend an evensong service. Arrive early and ask to be seated in the choir. It's a spiritual Oz, as the choristers (12 men and 40 youngsters—now girls as well as boys) sing psalms—a red-and-white-robed pillow of praise, raised up by the powerful pipe organ. If you're lucky and the service goes well, the organist will run a spiritual musical victory lap as the congregation breaks up (Tue-Sat at 17:15, Sun at 15:30, 1 hour, sometimes sung on Mon; visiting choirs nearly always fill in when choir is off on school break mid-July-Aug; tel. 0191/386-4266). For more on evensong, see page 153.

Organ Recitals: Noted organists play most Wednesday evenings from July to early September (£10, 19:30, advance tickets available on the cathedral website under "What's On").

Tours: Regular tours run Monday through Saturday. If one is already in session, you're welcome to join (£5; tours at 10:30, 11:00, and 14:00; fewer in winter, call or check website to confirm schedule; £10 combo-ticket for guided tour and the *Open Treasure* exhibit).

Tower Climb: The view from the tower will cost you 325 steps and £5 (Mon-Sat 10:00-16:00, closes at 15:00 in winter, sometimes open Sun outside of services; closed during services, events, and bad weather; must be at least eight years old, no high heels or backless shoes; enter through south transept).

***Open Treasure* Exhibit:** This collection of the church's rare artifacts is housed in the former monks' quarters (£7.50, Mon-Sat 10:00-17:00, Sun from 12:30, last entry one hour before closing).

❍ Self-Guided Tour

Begin your visit outside the cathedral. From the Palace Green, notice how this fortress of God stands boldly opposite the Norman keep of Durham's fortress of man.

Look closely: The **exterior** of this awe-inspiring cathedral has a serious skin problem. In the 1770s, as the stone was crumbling, they crudely peeled it back a few inches. The scrape marks give

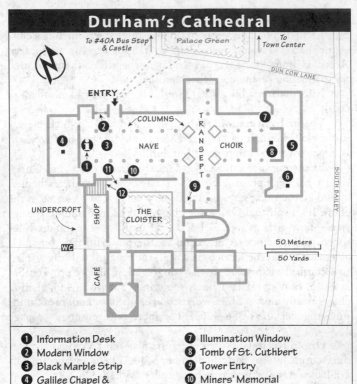

Durham's Cathedral

To #40A Bus Stop & Castle
Palace Green
To Town Center

DUN COW LANE

ENTRY

COLUMNS

TRANSEPT

NAVE

CHOIR

④
ⓘ
③
②
①
⑪
⑩
⑫
⑦
⑧
⑤
⑥
⑨

UNDERCROFT

SHOP

THE CLOISTER

WC

CAFÉ

SOUTH BAILEY

50 Meters
50 Yards

① Information Desk
② Modern Window
③ Black Marble Strip
④ Galilee Chapel & Tomb of the Venerable Bede
⑤ Chapel of the Nine Altars
⑥ LAWSON - Pietà
⑦ Illumination Window
⑧ Tomb of St. Cuthbert
⑨ Tower Entry
⑩ Miners' Memorial
⑪ Cloister Entry
⑫ Stairs to Open Treasure Exhibit

the cathedral a bad complexion to this day. For proof of this odd "restoration," study the masonry 10 yards to the right of the door. The L-shaped stones in the corner would normally never be found in a church like this—they only became L-shaped when the surface was cut back.

At the cathedral **door,** check out the big, bronze, lion-faced knocker (this is a replica of the 12th-century original, which is in the *Open Treasure* exhibit). The knocker was used by criminals seeking sanctuary (read the explanation).

Inside, purple-robed church attendants are standing by to happily answer questions. The handy **①** **information desk** at the back (right) end of the nave sells tickets for guided tours.

Notice the **②** **modern window** with the

novel depiction of the Last Supper (above and to the left of the entry door). It was given to the church by a local department store. The shapes of the apostles represent worlds and persons of every kind, from the shadowy Judas to the brightness of Jesus. This window is a good reminder that the cathedral remains a living part of the community.

Spanning the nave (toward the altar from the info desk), the ❸ **black marble strip** on the floor was as close to the altar as women were allowed in the days when this was a Benedictine church (until 1540). Sit down (ignoring the black line) and let the fine proportions of England's best Norman nave—and arguably Europe's best Romanesque nave—stir you. All the frilly woodwork and stonework were added in later centuries.

The architecture of the **nave** is particularly harmonious because it was built in a mere 40 years (1093-1133). The round

arches and zigzag-carved decorations are textbook Norman. The church was also proto-Gothic, built by well-traveled French masons and architects who knew the latest innovations from Europe. Its stone and ribbed roof, pointed arches, and flying buttresses were revolutionary in England. Notice the clean lines and simplicity. It's not as cluttered as other churches for several reasons: For centuries—out of respect for St. Cuthbert—no one else was buried here (so it's not filled with tombs). During Reformation times, sumptuous Catholic decor was removed. Subsequent fires and wars destroyed what Protestants didn't.

Head to the back of the nave and enter the ❹ **Galilee Chapel** (late Norman, from 1175). Find the smaller altar just to the left of the main altar. The paintings of St. Cuthbert and St. Oswald (seventh-century king of Northumbria) on the side walls of the niche are rare examples of Romanesque (Norman) paintings. Facing this altar, look above to your right to see more faint paintings on the upper walls above the columns. On the right side of the chapel, the upraised tomb topped with a black slab contains the remains of the **Venerable Bede,** an eighth-century Christian scholar who wrote the first history of England. We know this because the Latin reads, "In this tomb are the bones of the Venerable Bede."

Back in the main church, stroll down the nave to the center, under the highest **bell tower** in Europe (218 feet). Gaze up. The ropes turn wheels upon which bells are mounted. If you're stirred by the cheery ringing of church bells, tune in to the cathedral on Sunday (9:15-10:00 & 14:30-15:30) or Thursday (19:30-21:00

practice, trained bell ringers welcome, www.durhambellringers. org.uk), when the resounding notes tumble merrily through the entire town.

Continuing east (all medieval churches faced east), enter the **choir.** Monks worshipped many times a day, and the choir in the center of the church provided a cozy place to gather in this vast, dark, and chilly building. Mass has been said daily here in the heart of the cathedral for 900 years. The fancy wooden benches are from the 17th century. Behind the altar is the delicately carved Neville Screen from 1380 (made of Normandy stone in London, shipped to Newcastle by sea, then brought here by wagon). Until the Reformation, the niches contained statues of 107 saints. Exit the choir from the far-right side (south). Look for the stained-glass window (to your right) that commemorated the church's 1,000th anniversary in 1995. The colorful scenes depict England's history, from coal miners to cows to computers.

Step down behind the high altar into the east end of the church, which contains the 13th-century ❺ **Chapel of the Nine Altars.** Built later than the rest of the church, this is Gothic— taller, lighter, and relatively more extravagant than the Norman nave—but look up to see if you can spot an error in the symmetry. On the right, see the powerful modern ❻ **pietà** made of driftwood, with brass accents by local sculptor Fenwick Lawson.

Walk through the chapel to the north end where you will find an ❼ **illumination window** to your left. Designed by the glass artist Mel Howse, the window is a memorial to Sara Pilkington, a Durham University student who tragically died from a cardiac-related condition in 2012. The window casts vibrant colors onto the ❽ **tomb of St. Cuthbert.** Climb a few steps up to enter.

An inspirational leader of the early Christian Church in north England, St. Cuthbert lived in the Lindisfarne monastery (100 miles north of Durham, today called Holy Island and described later in this chapter). He died in 687. Eleven years later, his body was exhumed and found to be miraculously preserved. This stoked the popularity of his shrine, and pilgrims came in growing numbers. When Vikings raided Lindisfarne in 875, the monks fled with his body (and the famous illuminated Lindisfarne Gospels, now in the British Library in London). In 995, after 120 years of roaming, the monks settled in Durham on an easy-to-defend tight bend in the River Wear. This cathedral was built over Cuthbert's tomb.

Throughout the Middle Ages, a shrine stood here and was visited by countless pilgrims. In 1539, during the Reformation— whose proponents advocated focusing on God rather than saints— the shrine was destroyed. But pilgrims still come, especially on St. Cuthbert's feast day (March 20).

Continue through the chapel and exit down the stairs. Walk

down the **south transept** (to your left) to the ❾ **tower entry** (tower described earlier), as well as an astronomical clock and the Chapel of the Durham Light Infantry, a regiment of the British Army (1881-1968). The old flags and banners hanging above were actually carried into battle. On the right-hand side over the black door, look for a banner for the Durham Miners Association, one of many miners associations that existed—and still exist—in Durham today.

Return along the left side of the nave toward the entrance. Across from the entry is the door to the cloister. Along the wall by the cloister door, notice the ❿ **memorial honoring coal miners** who died, and those who "work in darkness and danger in those pits today." (This message is a bit dated. Durham's coal mines closed down in the 1980s.) The nearby book of remembrance lists mine victims. As an ecclesiastical center, a major university town, and a gritty, blue-collar coal-mining town, Durham's population has long been a complicated mix: priests, academics, and the working class.

After exiting the church, act like a monk and make a circuit of the Gothic ⓫ **cloister** (made briefly famous in a scene from the film *Harry Potter and the Sorcerer's Stone* in which Harry walks with his owl through a snowy courtyard). This area provides a fine view back up to the church towers.

Enter the ⓬ *Open Treasure* **exhibit** from the cloister, going upstairs to the Monks' Dormitory, a long, impressive room that stretches out under an original 14th-century timber roof. Formerly the monks' sleeping quarters, the room now holds artifacts from the cathedral treasury and monks' library. At the far end of the hall you'll find a door leading to the Collections Gallery. The double set of glass doors allows the cathedral to display more of its treasures in a climate-controlled environment—sometimes including a copy of the *Magna Carta* from 1216—as well as items from the Norman/medieval period (when the monks of Durham busily copied manuscripts), the Reformation, and the 17th century. The exhibit continues through the cloister's Great Kitchen, where the actual relics from St. Cuthbert's tomb are on view—his coffin, vestments, and cross—and ends in the undercroft, where you'll find a **shop** and a **café.**

MORE SIGHTS IN DURHAM

There's little to see in Durham beyond its cathedral, but it's a pleasant place to go for a stroll and enjoy its riverside setting.

Durham Museum

Situated in the old Church of St. Mary-le-Bow near the cathedral, this modest, somewhat hokey little museum does its best to illuminate the city's history, but it's worthwhile only on a rainy day. The

DURHAM & NE ENGLAND

exhibits, which are scattered willy-nilly throughout the old nave, include a reconstructed Victorian-era prison cell; a look at Durham industries past and present, especially coal mining (in Victorian times, the river was literally black from coal); and a 10-minute movie about 20th-century Durham. In the garden on the side of the church are two modern sculptures by local artist Fenwick Lawson, whose work is also in the cathedral.

Cost and Hours: £2.50; July-Sept daily 11:00-16:30, weekend afternoons only in off-season, closed Nov-March; corner of North Bailey and Bow Lane, tel. 0191/384-5589, www.durhammuseum. co.uk.

Riverside Path
For a 20-minute woodsy escape, walk Durham's riverside path from busy Framwellgate Bridge to sleepy Prebends Bridge.

Boat Cruise and Rental
Hop on the *Prince Bishop* for a relaxing one-hour narrated cruise of the river that nearly surrounds Durham (£10, Easter-Oct; for schedule, call 24-hour info line at 0191/386-9525, check their website, or go down to the dock at Brown's Boat House at Elvet Bridge, just east of old town; www.princebishoprc.co.uk). Sailings vary based on weather and tides. For some exercise with identical scenery, you can rent a rowboat at the same pier (£6.50/hour per person, £10 deposit, late-March-Oct daily 10:00-18:00, last rental at 17:00, tel. 0191/386-3779).

Crook Hall and Gardens
While most English gardens are in the countryside, Crook Hall is only a 10-minute walk from the city center, making it a convenient sight for travelers without a car. It has all the elements you'd expect in a classic English garden—walled "secret" gardens, a maze, a pool, and plenty of moss-covered statues. A map and witty signs take you on a self-guided tour.

Cost and Hours: £8, £6 off-season, March-Oct Sun-Wed 10:00-17:00, shorter hours off-season, closed Thu-Sat for weddings; café open daily 9:30-17:00, pay parking; from the city center, walk across the river and head north along the riverside path—it's on Frankland Lane, just past the Radisson Blu Hotel; tel. 0191/384-8028, www.crookhallgardens.co.uk.

Sleeping in Durham

Close-in pickings are slim in Durham. Because much of the housing is rented to students, there are only a handful of B&Bs. Otherwise, there are a few hotels within easy walking distance of the town center. During graduation (typically the last two weeks of June), everything is booked well in advance, and prices increase dramatically. Rooms can be tight on weekends any time of year.

B&BS

$$$ Castleview Guest House rents five airy, restful rooms in a well-located, 250-year-old guesthouse next door to a little church. If it's sunny, guests relax in the Eden-like backyard. Located on a charming cobbled street, it's just above Silver Street and the Framwellgate Bridge—take the stairs just after the church (free street-parking permit, 4 Crossgate, tel. 0191/386-8852, www.castle-view.co.uk, castle_view@hotmail.com, Anne).

$$ Victorian Town House B&B offers three spacious, boutique-like rooms in an 1853 townhouse. It's in a tidy residential area just down the hill from the train station and is handy to the town center. This is your best B&B option in Durham (family room, cash only, 2-night minimum preferred April-Oct, some view rooms, check-in 16:00-19:00 or by prior arrangement, 2 Victoria Terrace, 10-minute walk from train or bus station, tel. 0191/370-9963, www.durhambedandbreakfast.com, stay@durhambedandbreakfast.com, friendly Jill and Andy).

$$ Farnley Tower, a decent but impersonal B&B, has 16 large rooms and a quirky staff. On a quiet street at the top of a hill, it's a 15-minute hike up from the town center. Though you won't find the standard B&B warmth and service, this is a suitable alternative when the central hotels are booked (some rooms with cathedral view, family room, easy free parking, inviting yard, The Avenue—hike up this steep street and look for the sign on the right, tel. 0191/375-0011, www.farnley-tower.co.uk, enquiries@farnley-tower.co.uk, Raj and Roopal Naik). The Naiks also run the inventive Indian restaurant in the same building.

HOTELS

If the B&Bs are full, Durham could be a good place to resort to a bigger chain hotel, such as the Marriott (listed next) or the centrally located **Premier Inn** (on Freemans Place).

$$ Durham Marriott Hotel Royal County scatters its 150 posh, four-star but slightly scruffy rooms among several buildings sprawling across the river from the city center. The Leisure Club has a pool, sauna, hot tub, spa, and fitness equipment (breakfast included in some rates, elevator, free Wi-Fi in public areas, pay Wi-Fi in rooms, restaurant, pay parking, Old Elvet, tel. 0191/386-6821 or tel. 0870-400-7286, www.marriott.co.uk).

$$ Kingslodge Inn & Restaurant is a slightly worn but comfortable 23-room place with charming terraces, an attached restaurant, and a pub. Located in a pleasantly wooded setting, it's convenient for train travelers (family room, free parking, Waddington Street, Flass Vale, tel. 0191/370-9977, http://kingslodgeinn.co.uk, enquiries@kingslodgeinn.co.uk).

STUDENT HOUSING OPEN TO ANYONE

$$ Durham Castle, a student residence actually on the castle grounds facing the cathedral, rents rooms during the summer break (generally July-Sept). Request a room in the stylish main building, which is more appealing than the modern dorm rooms (includes breakfast in an elegant dining hall, Palace Green, tel. 0191/334-4106, www.dur. ac.uk/event.durham/tourism, durham.castle@durham.ac.uk). Note that the same office also rents rooms in other university buildings, but most are far less convenient to the city center—make sure to request the Durham Castle location when booking.

Eating in Durham

Durham is a university town with plenty of lively, inexpensive eateries. Especially on weekends, the places downtown are crowded with noisy college kids and rowdy townies, but as tourism increases, more good restaurants are popping up. Stroll down North Road, across Framwellgate Bridge, up through Market Place, and up Saddler Street, and consider the options suggested below. Some of the better choices are about a five-minute walk from this main artery—or a long hike to the suburbs—and worth the trek.

$$ La Spaghettata has some of the best Italian food in town. The hard-working staff serves pasta, pizza, and daily specials to hungry locals and tourists (Mon-Thu 17:00-22:30, Fri-Sun 11:30-14:00 & 17:00-22:30, 66 Saddler Street, tel. 0191/383-9290).

$ Claypath Delicatessen is worth the five-minute uphill walk above Market Place for lunch. Not just any old deli, this place assembles fresh ingredients and homemade bread into tasty sandwiches, salads, sampler platters, and more. They pride themselves on their killer espresso. While carryout is possible, most people eat in the casual, comfortable café setting (Tue-Fri 10:00-17:00, Sat until 16:00, closed Sun-Mon; from Market Place, cross the bridge and walk up Claypath to #57; tel. 0191/340-7209).

$$ The Capital, on the same stretch of road as Claypath Deli, has well-executed Indian food in a contemporary setting (daily 18:00-23:30, 69 Claypath, tel. 0191/386-8803).

$$ Zen is a modern, dark-wood place serving curries, noodles, fried rice, and other Asian fare. It's popular with students, so it's best to book a table or go early and sit in the bar (daily 11:00-22:00, Court Lane, tel. 0191/384-9588, www.zendurham.co.uk).

$$ Riverview Kitchen is a cozy place with a friendly staff and tables overlooking the river. They serve a wide variety of burgers, sandwiches, pancakes, salads, cakes, and more (Mon-Fri 9:30-17:00, Sat Sun 9:00-17:00, 21 Silver Street, tel. 0191/384-5777).

$ Bells is a standby for carryout fish-and-chips just off Market Place toward the cathedral. I'd skip their fancier dining room (generally Mon-Thu 11:00-21:00, Fri-Sat 11:00-24:00, Sun 12:00-16:00, 11 Market Place, tel. 0191/384-8974).

$ Tealicious is run by mother-and-daughter team Alison and Jenny, who bake homemade cakes and scones for their all-day tea. They also offer fresh soups and sandwiches. Look for a tall, skinny teahouse at the end of Elvet Bridge (Tue-Sat 10:00-16:00, Sun from 12:00, closed Mon, 88 Elvet Bridge, tel. 0191/340-1393).

$ Esquires Coffee offers breakfast all day, tasty cakes, and good coffee. Outside seats are great for people-watching, and there are a few tables overlooking the river (daily 9:15-18:45, by the Framwellgate Bridge at 22 Silver Street, tel. 0191/375-7578).

Pubs Across the Elvet Bridge: Two good options are within a five-minute walk of the Elvet Bridge (just east of the old town). **$$ The Court Inn** offers an eclectic menu of pub grub and an open, lively atmosphere (food served daily 11:00-22:00; cross the Elvet Bridge, turn right, walk several blocks, and then look left; Court Lane, tel. 0191/384-7350). **$ The Dun Cow** is popular with locals and good for beer and ales. There's a cozy "snug bar" up front and a more spacious lounge in the back. Read the legend behind the pub's name on the wall along the outside corridor. More sedate than the student-oriented places in the town center, this pub serves only snacks and light meals—come here to drink and nibble, not to feast (daily 11:00-23:00; from the Elvet Bridge, walk five minutes straight ahead to Old Elvet 37; tel. 0191/386-9219).

Splurge Outside the Town Center: One of Durham's top restaurants, **$$$$ Finbarrs** is an untouristy splurge serving sophisticated meat and seafood dishes. You'll find inventive twists on regional standards—such as roasted venison or duck breast—and daily fish selections. More than a mile from the city center, it's practical only for drivers or hardy walkers staying near the train station who don't mind a 20-minute hike. The evening fixed-price

DURHAM & NE ENGLAND

meals are one of the best deals in town, but they're not offered on the weekend (lunch and dinner specials available, Tue-Sun 12:00-14:30 & 18:00-21:30, closed Mon, reservations smart on weekends, northwest of town, Aykley Heads, tel. 0191/307-7033, www.finbarrsrestaurant.co.uk).

Supermarket: Look for **Tesco Metro** in the old town, just off Market Place (Mon-Sat 7:00-22:00, Sun 11:00-17:00). You can **picnic** on Market Place, or on the benches and grass outside the cathedral entrance (but not on the Palace Green, unless the park police have gone home).

Durham Connections

From Durham by Train to: York (4/hour, 50 minutes), **Keswick/Lake District** (train to Penrith—hourly, 3 hours, 1-2 transfers, then bus to Keswick), **London** (hourly direct, 3 hours, more with transfers), **Hadrian's Wall** (take train to Newcastle—4/hour, 20 minutes, then a train/bus or train/taxi combination to Hadrian's Wall—see "Getting Around Hadrian's Wall" later in this chapter), **Edinburgh** (hourly direct, 2 hours, more with changes, less frequent in winter). **Train info:** Tel. 0345-748-4950, www.nationalrail.co.uk.

ROUTE TIPS FOR DRIVERS

As you head north from Durham on the A-1 motorway (beyond the junction for the Beamish Museum, described next), you'll pass a famous bit of public art: **The Angel of the North,** a modern, rusted-metal angel standing 65 feet tall with a wingspan of 175 feet (wider than a Boeing 757). While initially controversial when it was erected in 1998, it has since become synonymous with Northeast England, and is a beloved local fixture.

Beamish Museum

This huge, 300-acre open-air museum, which re-creates life in northeast England during the 19th and 20th centuries, is England's best museum of its type. It takes at least three hours to explore its five sections: Pit Village (a coal-mining settlement with an actual mine); The Town (a 1913 street lined with

DURHAM & NE ENGLAND

actual shops); Pockerley Old Hall (the manor house of a "gentle-man farmer"); Home Farm (a preserved farm and farmhouse); and the newest section, 1950s Town (mid-century street still under development). This isn't a wax museum. If you touch the exhibits, they may smack you. Attendants at each stop happily explain everything. In fact, the place is only really interesting if you talk to the attendants—who make it worth ▲▲▲.

GETTING THERE

By **car,** the museum is five minutes off the A-1/M-1 motorway (one exit north of Durham at Chester-le-Street/Junction 63, well-signposted; it's a 12-mile, 25-minute drive northwest of Durham). You'll find free parking in the hills leading down to the main entrance.

Getting to Beamish from Durham by **bus** is an uncomplicated affair. Catch bus #21, #X21, or #50 from the Durham bus station (3-4/hour, 25 minutes) and transfer at Chester-le-Street to bus #8, #78A, #28, or #28A, which takes you right to the museum entrance (2/hour Mon-Sat, hourly Sun, 15 minutes, leaves from South Burns Stand L at the central bus kiosk, tel. 0191/420-5050, www.simplygo.com). Show your bus ticket for a 25 percent museum discount.

ORIENTATION TO BEAMISH MUSEUM

Cost and Hours: £19.50, children 5-16—£11.50, under 5-free; open Easter-Oct daily 10:00-17:00; off-season until 16:00, weekends only Dec-mid-Feb, and only The Town and Pit Village are open with vintage trams still running, last entry one hour before closing; check events schedule on chalkboard as you enter, tel. 0191/370-4000, www.beamish.org.uk.

Getting Around the Museum:
Pick up a free map at the entry to help navigate the five zones; while some are side-by-side, others are up to a 15-minute walk apart. Vintage trams and cool, circa-1910 double-decker buses shuttle visitors around the grounds,  and their attendants are helpful and knowledgeable. Signs on the trams advertise a variety of 19th-century products, from "Borax, for washing everything" to "Murton's Reliable Travelling Trunks."

Eating: Several eateries are scattered around Beamish, including a pub and tearooms (in The Town), a fish-and-chips stand (in the Pit Village), and various cafeterias and snack stands. Or bring a picnic.

VISITING THE MUSEUM

I've described the five areas in counterclockwise order from the entrance.

From the entrance building, bear left along the road, then watch for the turnoff on the right to the **Pit Village & Colliery.**

This is a company town built around a coal mine, with a schoolhouse, a Methodist chapel, and a row of miners' homes with long, skinny pea-patch gardens out front. Poke into some of the homes to see their modest interiors. In the Board School, explore the different classrooms, and look for the interesting poster with instructions for avoiding consumption (a.k.a. tuberculosis, a huge public-health crisis back then).

Next, cross to the adjacent colliery (coal mine), where you can take a fascinating—if claustrophobic—20-minute tour into the drift mine (check in at the "lamp cabin"—tours depart when enough people gather, generally every 5-10 minutes). Your guide will tell you stories about beams collapsing, gas exploding, and flooding; after that cheerful speech, you'll don a hard hat as you're led into the mine.

Notice in the lamp cabin how each lamp has a number. Miners arriving for work would yell out their number and be given a lamp and two tokens—one brass, one zinc—with that number. A "bankman" would collect each miner's zinc token as he entered the mine, returning it to the number board in the lamp cabin. When the miner exited at the end of the day, he would hang his brass token over the zinc one, signifying he'd safely left the mine. You'll also see a sign discouraging spitting. Miners would salivate a lot, primarily because of tuberculosis, but also from chewing tobacco.

Nearby (across the tram tracks) is the fascinating **mine elevator,** where you can see the actual steam-powered winding engine used to operate it. The "winderman" demonstrates how he skillfully eases both coal and miners up and down the tight mine shaft. This delicate, high-stakes job was one of the most sought-after at the entire colliery—passed down from father to son—and the winderman had to stay in this building for his entire shift (the seat of his chair flips up to reveal a built-in WC).

A path leads through the woods to Georgian-era **Pockerley,** which has two parts. First you'll see the **Waggonway,** a big barn filled with steam engines, including the re-created, first-ever passenger train from 1825. (Occasionally this train takes modern-day visitors for a spin on 1825 tracks—a hit with railway buffs.)

Then, walk back and climb the hill to **Pockerley Old Hall,** the manor house of a gentleman farmer and his family. The house dates from the 1820s, and—along with the farmhouse described later—is Beamish's only vintage building still on its original site (other buildings at Beamish were relocated from elsewhere

and reconstructed here). While not extremely wealthy, the farmer who lived here owned large tracts of land and could afford to hire help to farm it for him. This rustic home is no palace, but it was comfortable for the period. Costumed do-cents in the kitchen often bake delicious cookies from old reci-pes...and hand out samples.

The small garden terrace out front provides beautiful views across the pastures. From the garden, turn left and locate the nar-row stairs up to the "old house." Actually under the same roof as the gentleman farmer's home, this space consists of a few small rooms that were rented by some of the higher-up workers to shelter their entire families of up to 15 children (young boys worked on the farm, while girls were married off early). While the parents had their own bedroom, the children all slept in the loft up above (notice the ladder in the hall).

From the manor house, hop on a vintage tram or bus or walk 10 minutes to the **1950s Town,** a new zone where the mid-cen-tury buildings include a replica of a local welfare hall and com-munity center. Visit the clinic tucked in the back to talk with a midwife who would offer advice to new parents and do pediatric check-ups. Next, move into the assembly hall to experience card games, dances, and crafts.

From here, a short tram ride or five-minute walk takes you back to the Edwardian-era in **The Town** (c. 1913). This bustling street features several working shops and other buildings that are a delight to explore. In the Masonic Hall at the beginning of the town, ogle the grand high-ceilinged meeting room. Farther on, check out the fun, old metal signs in-side the garage. Across the street, poke into the courtyard to find the stables, which are full of carriages (and sometimes horses). The heavenly-smelling candy store sells old-timey sweets and has an actual workshop in back with trays of free samples. The newsagent sells stationery, cards, and old toys, while in the grocery, you can see old packaging and the scales used for weighing out products. Other buildings include a clothing store, a working pub (The Sun

Inn; don't expect 1913 prices), Barclays Bank, and a hardware store featuring a variety of "toilet sets" (not what you think).

For lunch, try the Tea Rooms cafeteria (upstairs); or, if the weather is good, picnic in the grassy park with the gazebo next to the tram stop. The row of townhouses includes both homes and offices (if the dentist is in, chat with him to hear some harrowing stories about pre-Novocain tooth extraction). At the circa-1913 railway station at the far end of The Town, you can stand on the bridge over the tracks to watch old steam engines go back and forth—along with a carousel of "steam gallopers."

Finally, walk or ride a tram or bus to the **Home Farm.** (This is the least interesting section—if you're running short on time, it's skippable.) Here you'll get to experience a petting zoo and see a

"horse gin" (a.k.a. "gin gan")—where a horse walking in a circle turned a crank on a gear to amplify its "horsepower," helping to replace human hand labor. Near the cafeteria, you can cross a busy road to the old farmhouse, still on its original site, where attendants sometimes bake goodies on a coal fire.

Hadrian's Wall

Cutting across the width of the Isle of Britain, this ruined Roman wall is one of England's most thought-provoking sights. Once a towering 20-foot-tall fortification, these days "Hadrian's Shelf," as some cynics call it, is only about three feet wide and three to six feet high. (The conveniently precut stones of the wall were carried away by peasants during the post-Rome Dark Ages and now form the foundations of many local churches, farmhouses, and other structures.) In most places, what's left of the wall has been covered over by centuries of sod, making it effectively disappear into the landscape. But for those intrigued by Roman history, Hadrian's Wall provides a fine excuse to take your imagination for a stroll. These are the most impressive Roman ruins in Britain. Pretend you're a legionnaire on patrol in dangerous and distant Britannia, at the empire's northernmost frontier...with nothing but this wall protecting you from the terrifying, bloodthirsty Picts just to the north.

Today, several restored chunks of the wall, ruined forts, and museums thrill history buffs. While a dozen Roman sights cling along the wall's route, I've focused my coverage on an easily digestible six-mile stretch right in the middle, where you'll find the best museums and some of the most enjoyable-to-hike stretches of the wall. Three top sights are worth visiting: From east to west, Housesteads Roman Fort shows you where the Romans lived; Vindolanda's museum shows you how they lived; and the Roman Army Museum explains the empire-wide military organization that brought them here. If you plan to visit all three, the Roman Army Museum is an ideal place to start, as it sets the stage for what you're about to see; it's also next to the Walltown Visitor Centre, where you can get your bearings for the region.

A breeze for drivers, this area can also be seen fairly easily in summer by bus for those good at studying timetables (see "Getting Around Hadrian's Wall," later).

Hadrian's Wall is in vogue as a destination for multiday hikes through the pastoral English countryside. The Hadrian's Wall National Trail runs 84 miles, following the wall's route from coast to coast (for details, go to www.nationaltrail.co.uk/HadriansWall). Through-hikers (mostly British) can walk the wall's entire length in four to ten days. You'll see them bobbing along the ridgeline, drying out their socks in your B&B's mudroom, and recharging at local pubs in the evening. For those with less time, the brief ridge walk next to the wall from Steel Rigg to Sycamore Gap to Housesteads Roman Fort gives you a perfect taste of the scenery and history.

Orientation to Hadrian's Wall

The area described in this section is roughly between the midsize towns of Bardon Mill and Haltwhistle, which are located along the busy A-69 highway. Each town has a train station and some handy B&Bs, restaurants, and services. However, to get right up close to the wall, you'll need to head a couple of miles north to the adjacent villages of Once Brewed and Twice Brewed (along the B-6318 road).

TOURIST INFORMATION

For an overview of your options, visit the helpful website at HadriansWallCountry.co.uk.

Portions of the wall are in Northumberland National Park. The **Walltown Visitor Centre** lies along the Hadrian's Wall bus #AD122 route and has information on the area, including walking guides to the wall (Easter-Oct daily 10:00-17:00, closed Nov-Easter, just off the B-6318 next to the Roman Army Museum, follow signs to *Walltown Quarry,* pay parking, tel. 01434/344-396, www. northumberlandnationalpark.org.uk).

Visitor information may also be found at **The Sill National Landscape Discovery Centre,** next to the recommended Twice Brewed Inn and about a half-mile from the Steel Rigg trailhead. The Sill, with its unique grassland roof, also features interactive exhibits about the surrounding landscape and includes an 86-bed hostel, a local crafts shop, and a café (daily April-Oct 9:30-18:00, Nov-March 10:00-16:00, pay parking, served by bus #AD122, on the B-6318 near Bardon Mill, tel. 01434/341-200, www.thesill. org.uk).

The helpful TI in **Haltwhistle,** a block from the train station inside the library, has a good selection of maps and guidebooks and schedule information for Hadrian's Wall bus #AD122 (year-round Mon-Fri 10:00-13:00 & 13:30-16:30, Sat 10:00-13:00, closed Sun, The Library, Westgate, tel. 01434/321-863, www. visitnorthumberland.com).

GETTING AROUND HADRIAN'S WALL

Hadrian's Wall is anchored by the big cities of Newcastle to the east and Carlisle to the west. Driving is the most convenient way to see Hadrian's Wall. If you're coming by train, consider renting a car for the day at either Newcastle or Carlisle; otherwise, you'll need to rely on trains and a bus to connect the sights, hire taxis, or book a private guide with a car. If you're just passing through for the day using public transportation, it's challenging to stop and see more than just one or two of the sights—study the schedules carefully and prioritize. Nondrivers who want to see everything—or even hike part of the wall—will need to stay one or two nights along the bus route.

By Car

Zip to this "best of Hadrian's Wall" zone on the speedy A-69; when you get close, head a few miles north and follow the B-6318, which parallels the wall and passes several viewpoints, minor sights, and

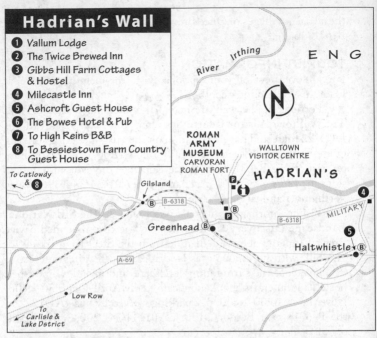

Hadrian's Wall

1 Vallum Lodge
2 The Twice Brewed Inn
3 Gibbs Hill Farm Cottages & Hostel
4 Milecastle Inn
5 Ashcroft Guest House
6 The Bowes Hotel & Pub
7 To High Reins B&B
8 To Bessiestown Farm Country Guest House

"severe dips." (These road signs add a lot to a photo portrait.) Buy a good local map to help you explore this interesting area more easily and thoroughly. Official Hadrian's Wall parking lots (including at the Walltown Visitor Centre, The Sill, Housesteads Roman Fort, and the trailhead at Steel Rigg) have pay-and-display machines.

Without a Car

To reach the Roman sights without a car, take the made-for-tourists Hadrian's Wall **bus #AD122** (named for the year the wall was built; runs only in peak season—see below). Essential resources for navigating the wall by public transit include the *Hadrian's Wall Country Map*, the bus #AD122 schedule, and a local train timetable for Northern Line #4—all available at local visitors centers and train stations (also see www.hadrianswallcountry.co.uk). If you arrive by train when the bus isn't running, you'll need to rely on taxis, a private guide, or long walks to visit the wall (see "Off-Season Options," later).

By Bus: Bus #AD122 connects the Roman sights (and several recommended accommodations) with train stations in **Haltwhistle** and **Hexham** (from £2/ride, £12.50 unlimited Day Rover ticket, buy tickets on board).

The bus runs between Haltwhistle and Hexham (8/day in each direction Easter-Sept, no service Oct-Easter). If you're coming from Carlisle or Newcastle, you'll need to take the train to

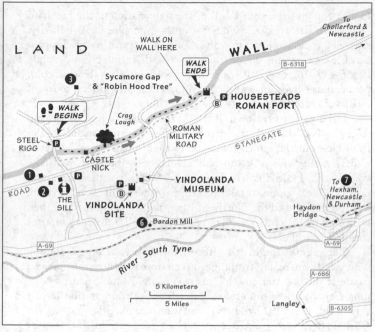

Haltwhistle or Hexham and pick up the bus there (tel. 01434/322-002, www.gonortheast.co.uk/ad122).

By Train: Northern Line's train route #4 runs parallel to and a few miles south of the wall much more frequently than the bus. While the train stops at stations in larger towns—including (west to east) **Carlisle, Haltwhistle, Hexham** and **Newcastle**—it doesn't take you near the actual Roman sights. You can catch bus #AD122 at Hexham and Haltwhistle (no bus service Oct-Easter; train runs hourly; Carlisle to Haltwhistle—30 minutes; Haltwhistle to Hexham—20 minutes; Hexham to Newcastle—40 minutes; www.northernrail.org).

By Taxi: These Haltwhistle-based taxi companies can help you connect the dots: Sprouls (tel. 01434/321-064, mobile 07712-321-064) or Diamond (mobile 07597-641-222). It costs about £14 one-way from Haltwhistle to Housesteads Roman Fort (arrange for return pickup or have museum staff call a taxi). Note that on school days, all of these taxis are busy shuttling rural kids to class in the morning (about 8:00-10:00) and afternoon (about 14:30-16:30), so you may have to wait.

By Private Tour: Peter Carney, a former history teacher who waxes eloquently on all things Roman, offers tours with his car and also leads guided walks around Hadrian's Wall, including the Roman Army Museum, Vindolanda, and Housesteads. He customizes the tour to suit your time frame and interests and is happy to pick you up from your B&B or the train station in the Hexham or Haltwhistle area (£200/day for up to 4 people, £150/half-day, does not include museum admission, £100 extra for pick-up at Carlisle or Durham, £75 extra at Newcastle train station, mobile 07585-139-016 or 07810-665-733, www.hadrianswall-walk.com, petercarney@hadrianswall-walk.com). Peter also offers tours of medieval Durham.

Off-Season Options: Bus #AD122 doesn't run off-season (Oct-Easter). The only alternative for bus transportation is #185 from Haltwhistle, which takes you to the Roman Army Museum (3/day). Otherwise, you can only get as far as the train will take you (that is, Haltwhistle)—from there, you'll have to take a taxi or hire a local guide to take you to the other sights. Or, if you're a hardy hiker, take the Northern Line train to Bardon Mill, then walk about 2 miles to Vindolanda and another 2.5 miles to Housesteads Roman Fort.

Baggage Storage: It's difficult to bring your luggage along with you. If you're day-tripping, you can store your luggage in **Newcastle** at the bus station which is part of the Eldon Square Shopping Center, a five-minute walk north of the train station (credit card only, tel. 01912/611-891, www.intu.co.uk/eldonsquare). In **Carlisle** try a web-based service such as Stasher.com. If you must travel with luggage, Housesteads Roman Fort and Vindolanda will most likely let you leave your bags at the sight entrance while you're inside. If you want to walk the wall, a baggage-courier service will send your luggage ahead to your next B&B in the region for about £7 per bag (contact Hadrian's Haul, mobile 07967-564-823, www.hadrianshaul.com).

Sights at Hadrian's Wall

▲▲Hiking the Wall

It's enjoyable to hike along the wall speaking Latin, even if only for a little while. Note that park rangers forbid anyone from actually walking on top of the wall, except along a very short stretch at Housesteads. On the following hike, you'll walk alongside the wall.

For a good, craggy, three-mile, one-way, up-and-down walk along the wall, hike between Steel Rigg and Housesteads Roman Fort. For a shorter hike, begin at Steel Rigg (where there's a pay parking lot) and walk a mile to Sycamore Gap, then back again (described next;

the Sill and Walltown visitors centers hand out a free description of this walk). These hikes are moderately strenuous and are best for those in good shape. You'll need sturdy shoes and a windbreaker to comfortably overcome the often-blustery environment. As you would while driving in Britain, stay on the left side of the path when you meet other hikers.

To reach the trailhead for the short hike from **Steel Rigg to Sycamore Gap,** take the little road off the B-6318 near the Twice Brewed Inn and park in the pay-and-display parking lot on the right at the crest of the hill. Walk through the gate to the shoulder-high stretch of wall, go to the left, and follow the wall running steeply down the valley below you. Ahead of you

are dramatic cliffs, creating a natural boundary made to order for this Roman fortification. Walk down the steep slope into the valley, then back up the other side (watch your footing on the stone stairs). Following the wall, you'll do a similar up-and-down routine three more times, like a slow-motion human roller coaster.

In the second gap is one of the best-preserved milecastles, #39 (called Castle Nick because it sits in a nick in a crag). Each milecastle controlled a gate, and the gates meant income since the Roman Empire would take a cut every time goods passed through them. That may explain why Hadrian wanted so many gates, even when there were rugged hills and cliffs in the way.

Soon after Castle Nick, you'll reach the third gap, called Sycamore Gap for the large symmetrical tree in the middle. (Do you

remember the 1991 Kevin Costner movie *Robin Hood: Prince of Thieves*? Locals certainly do—this tree was featured in it, and tourists frequently ask for directions to the "Robin Hood Tree.") You can either hike back the way you came or walk down a short stretch toward the main road to find a less strenuous path, which skirts lower down on the ridge (rather than following the wall up and down). The lower path leads back to the base of the Steel Rigg hill, where you can huff back up to your car.

If you continue on to Housesteads, you'll pass a traditional Northumbrian sheep farm, windswept lakes, and more ups and

The History of Hadrian's Wall

In about AD 122, during the reign of Emperor Hadrian, the Romans constructed this great stone wall. Stretching 73 miles coast to coast across the narrowest stretch of northern England, it was built and defended by some 20,000 troops. Not just a wall, it was a military complex with forts, ditches, settlements, and roads. At every mile of the wall, a castle guarded a gate, and two turrets stood between each castle. The milecastles are numbered (80 covering 73 miles, because a Roman mile was shorter than our mile).

In cross-section, Hadrian's Wall consisted of a stone wall—around 15 to 20 feet tall—with a ditch on either side. The flat-bottomed ditch on the south side of the wall, called the vallum, was flanked by earthen ramparts and likely demarcated the "no-man's land" beyond which civilians were not allowed to pass. Between the vallum and the wall ran a service road called the Military Way. Another less-elaborate ditch ran along the north side of the wall. In some areas—including the region that I describe—the wall was built upon a volcanic ridgeline that provided a natural fortification.

The wall's actual purpose is still debated. While Rome ruled Britain for 400 years, it never quite ruled its people. The wall may have been used for any number of reasons: to protect Roman Britain from invading Pict tribes from the north (or at least cut down on pesky border raids); to monitor the movement of people as a show of Roman strength and superiority; or to simply give an otherwise bored army something to do. (Emperors understood that nothing was more dangerous than a bored army.) Or perhaps the wall represented Hadrian's tacit admission that the empire had reached its maximum extent; Hadrian was known for consolidating his territory, in some cases giving up chunks of land that had been conquered by his predecessor, Trajan, to create an easier-to-defend (if slightly smaller) empire. His philosophy of "defense before expansion" is embodied by the impressive wall that still bears his name.

downs. The farther you go, the fewer people you'll encounter, making this hike even more magical. As you close in on Housesteads, you'll be able to actually walk on top of the wall.

▲▲Housesteads Roman Fort

With its respectable museum, powerful scenery, and the best-preserved segment of the wall, this is your best single stop at Hadrian's

Wall. It requires a steep hike up from the parking lot, but once there it's just you, the bleating sheep, and memories of ancient Rome.

Cost and Hours: £8 for site and museum, discount with bus ticket; if the main entrance line is long, you can pay admission fee at the museum; daily April-Sept 10:00-18:00, Oct until 17:00, Nov-March until 16:00; last entry 45 minutes before closing, pay parking, bus #AD122 stops here; museum tel. 01434/344-363, info tel. 0870-333-1181, www.english-heritage.org.uk/housesteads.

Visitor Information: The parking lot has a visitors center with WCs, a snack bar, and a gift shop. They sell a low-cost guidebook about the fort and another one covering the entire wall. If you're traveling by bus and want to leave your luggage, ask at the visitors center if they'll stow it for a bit.

Visiting the Museum and Fort: From the visitors center, head outside and hike about a half-mile uphill to the fort. At the top of the hill, duck into the **museum** (on the left) before touring the site. While smaller and housing fewer artifacts than the museum at Vindolanda, it's interesting nonetheless. Look for the giant Victory statue, which once adorned the fort's East Gate; her  foot is stepping on a globe, serving as an intimidating reminder to outsiders of the Romans' success in battle. A good seven-minute film shows how Housesteads (known back then as Vercovicium) would have operated.

Artifacts offer more insights into those who lived here. A cooking pot from Frisia (Northern Holland) indicates the presence of women, showing that soldiers came with their families in tow. A tweezer, probe, spoons, and votive foot (that would have been offered to the gods in exchange for a cure for a foot ailment) reveal the type of medical care you could expect. And a weighted die and a coin mold—perhaps used to make counterfeit money—show what may have been the less-than-savory side of life at the fort.

After exploring the museum, head out to the sprawling ruins of the **fort.** Interpretive signs and illustrations explain what you're seeing. All Roman forts were the same rectangular shape and design, containing a commander's headquarters, barracks, and latrines (Housesteads has the best-preserved Roman toilets found anywhere—look for them at the lower-right corner). This fort also had a hospital, granary, and a bakery where the soldiers would bake bread and cook meals. The fort was built right up to the wall, which runs along its upper end.

Even if you're not a hiker, take some time to walk the wall here. (This is the one place along the wall where you're actually allowed to get up and walk on top of it for a photo op.) Visually trace the wall to the left to see how it disappears into a bank of overgrown turf. *Game of Thrones* fans may enjoy visualizing how author George R. R. Martin was inspired by Hadrian's Wall to create the famous ice wall in his books.

▲▲Vindolanda

This larger Roman fort (which actually predates the wall by 40 years) and museum are just south of the wall. Although Housesteads has better ruins and the wall, Vindolanda has the more impressive museum, packed with artifacts that reveal intimate details of Roman life.

There are two entrances, an east entrance and the west main entrance. I recommend the main entrance for easy access. To get there, follow the signs to Vindolanda from the A-69 or the B-6318. (If you see a steep hill from the parking lot, you are at the east entrance.)

Cost and Hours: £8.25, £12.20 combo-ticket includes Roman Army Museum, discount with bus ticket; daily April-Sept 10:00-18:00, mid-Feb-March and Oct-Nov until 17:00, winter hours variable, last entry one hour before closing, call first during bad weather, free parking with entry, bus #AD122 stops here, café; tel. 01434/344-277, www.vindolanda.com.

Visitor Information: A free map and low-cost guidebook are available at the entrance.

Tours: Free guided tours are offered in high season (July-Aug Sat-Sun 10:30, 11:00, 13:00, and 14:00; Mon-Fri 11:00 and 13:00; Apr-June and Sept Sat-Sun 11:00 and 13:00 only, call to confirm). Archaeological talks and tours may be offered on weekdays as well. Both are included in your ticket.

Archaeological Dig: The Vindolanda site is an active dig—from Easter through September, you'll see the excavation work in progress (usually Mon-Fri, weather permitting). Much of the work is done by volunteers, including armchair archaeologists from the US.

Visiting the Site and Museum: After entering, stop at the model of the entire site as it was in Roman times (c. AD 213-276). Notice that the site had two parts: the fort itself, and the *vicus* (town) just outside that helped to supply it.

Head out to the **site,** walk-

ing through 500 yards of grassy parkland decorated by the foundation stones of the Roman fort and a full-size replica chunk of the
wall. Over the course of 400 years, at least nine forts were built on
this spot. The Romans, by lazily sealing the foundations from each
successive fort, left modern-day archaeologists with a 20-foot-deep
treasure trove of remarkably well-preserved artifacts: keys, coins,
brooches, scales, pottery, glass, tools, leather shoes, bits of cloth,
and even a wig. Many of these are now displayed in the museum,
well-described in English, German, French, and...Latin.

At the far side of the site, pass through the pleasant riverside
garden area on the way to the museum. The well-presented **museum** pairs actual artifacts with insightful explanations—such as a
collection of Roman shoes with a description about what each one
tells us about its wearer. The weapons (including arrowheads and
spearheads) and fragments of armor are a reminder that Vindolanda was an important outpost on Rome's northern boundary—look
for the Scottish skull stuck on a pike to discourage rebellion.

Thanks to Vindolanda's boggy grounds, trash tossed away by
the Romans was preserved in an airless environment. You'll see the
world's largest collection of Roman leather; tools that were used
for building and expanding the fort; locks and keys (the fort had
a password that changed daily—jotting it on a Post-It note wasn't
allowed); a large coin collection; items imported here from the far
corners of the vast empire (such as fragments of French pottery and
amphora jugs from the Mediterranean); beauty aids such as combs,
tools for applying makeup, and hairpins; and religious pillars and
steles.

But the museum's main attraction is its collection of writing
tablets. A good video explains how these impressively well-preserved examples of early Roman cursive were discovered here in
1973. Displays show some of the actual letters—written on thin
pieces of wood—alongside the translations. These letters bring Romans to life in a way that ruins alone can't. The most famous piece
(described but not displayed here) is the first known example of a
woman writing to a woman (an invitation to a birthday party). A
large interactive screen lets you choose and read tablets selected
by Robin Birley, a British archaeologist and former leader of the
excavations.

A separate room hosts the *Wooden Underworld* gallery. Although the Romans built in stone, many of their everyday personal
objects were made of wood, and this gallery hosts a collection of
2,000 items. See if you can find the wooden toilet seat and the toy
sword.

Finally, you'll pass through an exhibit about the history of the
excavations, including a case featuring the latest discoveries, on
your way to the shop and cafeteria.

DURHAM & NE ENGLAND

▲▲Roman Army Museum

This museum, a few miles farther west at Greenhead (near the site of the Carvoran Roman fort), has cutting-edge, interactive exhibits illustrating the structure of the Roman Army that built and monitored this wall, with a focus on the everyday lifestyles of the Roman soldiers stationed here. Bombastic displays, life-size figures, and several different films—but few actual artifacts—make this entertaining museum a good complement to the archaeological emphasis of Vindolanda.

Cost and Hours: £7, £12.20 combo-ticket includes Vindolanda, discount with bus ticket; April-Sept daily 10:00-18:00, mid-Feb-March and Oct daily until 17:00, Nov-Dec Sat-Sun only until 16:00, closed Jan-mid-Feb; free parking with entry, bus #AD122 stops here. Tel. 01697/747-485; if no answer, call Vindolanda tel. 01434/344-277; www.vindolanda.com.

Visiting the Museum: In the first room, a video explains the complicated structure of the Roman Army—legions, cohorts, centuries, and so on. While a "legionnaire" was a Roman citizen, an "auxiliary" was a noncitizen specialist recruited for their unique skills (such as horsemen and archers). A video of an army-recruiting officer delivers an "Uncle Caesar wants YOU!" speech to prospective soldiers. A timeline traces the history of the Roman Empire, especially as it related to the British Isles.

The good 20-minute *Edge of Empire* 3-D movie offers an evocative look at what life was like for a Roman soldier marking time on the wall, and digital models show reconstructions of the wall and forts. In the exhibit on weapons, shields, and armor (mostly replicas), you'll learn how Roman soldiers trained with lead-filled wooden swords, so that when they went into battle, their metal swords felt light by comparison. Another exhibit explains the story of Hadrian, the man behind the wall, who stopped the expansion of the Roman Empire, declaring that the age of conquest was over.

Sleeping and Eating near Hadrian's Wall

If you want to spend the night near Hadrian's Wall, set your sights on the area of Once Brewed and Twice Brewed, with a few accommodations options, a good pub, and easy access to the most important sights. I've also listed some other accommodations scattered around the region.

IN AND NEAR ONCE BREWED AND TWICE BREWED

Although the use of these two names can be slightly confusing, they simply describe a handful of houses that sit at the base of the ridge along the B-6318. Many locals just refer to the area as "The Sill." The Twice Brewed Inn and Milecastle Inn are reachable with Hadrian's Wall bus #AD122. Bus drivers can drop you off at Vallum Lodge by request (but they won't pick you up).

$$ Vallum Lodge is a cushy, comfortable, nicely renovated base situated near the vallum (the ditch that forms part of the fortification a half-mile from the wall itself). Its six cheery rooms are all on the ground floor, along with a guest lounge, and a separate guesthouse called the Snug has one bedroom and a kitchen. It's just up the road from The Twice Brewed Inn—a handy dinner option (pay laundry service, evening meal on request, Military Road, tel. 01434/344-248, www.vallum-lodge.co.uk, stay@vallum-lodge.co.uk, Samantha).

$$ The Twice Brewed Inn, two miles west of Housesteads and a half-mile from the wall, rents 19 basic, workable rooms, all en-suite (ask for a room away from the road, Military Road, tel. 01434/344-534, www.twicebrewedinn.co.uk, info@twicebrewedinn.co.uk). The inn's friendly **$$ brewpub** serves as the community gathering place and is a hangout for hikers and the archaeologists digging at the nearby sites. It serves real ales and large portions of good pub grub (vegetarian options, fancier restaurant in back with same menu, food served daily 12:00-21:00, Sun until 20:00).

Rural and Remote, North of the Wall: A practical choice for drivers, **$$ Gibbs Hill Farm Cottages and Hostel** is a friendly working sheep-and-cattle farm set on 700 acres in the stunning valley on the far side of the wall. The three, six-bed dorm rooms are in a restored hay barn (no breakfast, coin-op laundry facilities, 5-minute drive from Twice Brewed Inn or 30-minute walk from Steel Rigg trailhead, tel. 01434/344-030, www.gibbshillfarm.co.uk, val@gibbshillfarm.co.uk, warm Val). They also rent two self-catering cottages for two to four people by the week or occasionally shorter periods.

West of Once/Twice Brewed: $$ Milecastle Inn cooks up all sorts of exotic game and offers the best dinner around, according to hungry national park rangers. You can order food at the counter and sit in the pub, or take a seat in the table-service area. Make sure to finish off with their sticky toffee pudding with custard (food served daily Easter-Sept 12:00-20:45, Oct-Easter 12:00-14:30 & 18:00-20:30, smart to reserve in summer, North Road, tel. 01434/321-372, www.milecastle-inn.co.uk).

IN HALTWHISTLE

The larger town of Haltwhistle has a train station, along with stops for Hadrian's Wall bus #AD122 (at the train station and a few blocks east, at Market Place). It also has a helpful TI (see "Tourist

DURHAM & NE ENGLAND

Information," earlier), a launderette, several eateries, and a handful of B&Bs, including this one.

$$ Ashcroft Guest House, a large Victorian former vicarage, is 400 yards from the Haltwhistle train station and 200 yards from the Market Place bus stop. It has seven big, luxurious rooms, huge terraced gardens, and views from the comfy lounge, along with a two-bedroom apartment with kitchen, and ample free parking. If you want to indulge yourself after hiking the wall, this is the place (2-night minimum for apartment, family room, 1.5 miles from the wall, Lanty's Lonnen, tel. 01434/320-213, www. ashcroftguesthouse.co.uk, info@ashcroftguesthouse.co.uk, helpful Geoff and Christine James).

IN BARDON MILL

$$ The Bowes Hotel, with its friendly staff, is just a two-minute walk from the train station and has six attractive, shipshape rooms. The **$$ pub** downstairs has a good selection of ales and serves dinner Wed-Sat 12:00-20:00, Sun until 16:00 (tel. 01434/344-237, www.theboweshotel.uk, ian@theboweshotel.uk, Ian & Sar).

NEAR HEXHAM

$ High Reins offers four rooms in a stone house built by a shipping tycoon in the 1920s. The rooms are cushy and comfortable—there's a cozy feeling all over the place (cash only, 2-bedroom apartment also available in the house, lounge, 1 mile south of train station on the western outskirts of Hexham, Leazes Lane, tel. 01434/603-590, www.highreins.uk, bookings@highreins.uk, Jan and Peter Walton). They also rent an apartment in the town center; ask for details.

NEAR CARLISLE

$$ Bessiestown Farm Country Guest House, located far northwest of the Hadrian sights, is convenient for drivers connecting the Lake District and Scotland. It's a quiet and soothing stop in the middle of sheep pastures, with four bedrooms in the main house, a pair of two-bedroom apartments, and a honeymoon suite in the former stables. One apartment is on the ground floor, with an accessible bathroom (discount with 3-night stay, serves afternoon tea and an evening meal; in Catlowdy, midway between Gretna Green and Hadrian's Wall, a 30-minute drive north of Carlisle; tel. 01228/577-219, www.bessiestown.co.uk, info@bessiestown.co.uk, gracious Margaret and Jack Sisson).

Holy Island and Bamburgh Castle

This remote area is worthwhile only for those with a car. It's out of the way for most itineraries—unless you're driving between Durham and Edinburgh on the A-1 highway, in which case Holy Island and Bamburgh Castle (and Beamish Museum, described earlier) are easy stop-offs. It's also possible (but a hassle) to reach these sights by public transportation via Newcastle.

Holy Island (Lindisfarne)

Twelve hundred years ago, this "Holy Island"—then known as Lindisfarne—was Christianity's tenuous toehold on England. In  the AD 680s, Holy Island was the home and original burial ground of St. Cuthbert (he's now in Durham). We know it as the source of the magnificent Lindisfarne Gospels (AD 698; now in London's British Library), decorated by monks with some of the finest art from Europe's "Dark Ages." By the ninth century, Viking raids forced the monks to take shelter in Durham, but they returned centuries later to reestablish a church on this holy site.

Today Holy Island—worth ▲▲—makes a pleasant stop for modern-day pilgrims. You'll cross a causeway to a quiet town with a striking castle and the ruins of an evocative priory that was originally founded in 635.

GETTING TO HOLY ISLAND

Holy Island is reached by a two-mile causeway that's cut off twice a day by high tides. Safe crossing times are posted at each end of the causeway (and at www.lindisfarne.org.uk), warning **drivers** when this holy place becomes Holy Island—and you become stranded. Once on the island, signs direct you to a well-marked, mandatory pay parking lot at the entrance to town.

It's also possible to reach Holy Island by **public transit**, but it's not worth the effort unless you're a determined pilgrim. From Newcastle, take Arriva bus #X15 to Beal (5/day Mon-Sat, none on Sun, 2 hours, www.arrivabus.co.uk), then from Beal, ride Borders bus #477 (2/day Mon-Sat July-Aug, Wed and Sat only late May-

June & Sept-Oct, carefully confirm schedule for the complete connection before you head out, www.bordersbuses.co.uk). Or take a train from Newcastle to Berwick-upon-Tweed and catch #477 from there.

GETTING AROUND HOLY ISLAND
From the parking lot, it's an easy 10-minute **walk** into town and to the priory; the castle is about a 20-minute walk away. To save time, ride the convenient **shuttle bus,** which makes a circuit from the parking lot to the village green (next to the priory entrance), then out to the castle, and back again (£1.50, 3/hour, runs only when castle is open).

Sights on Holy Island

The three main attractions on Holy Island are the ruins of the old priory, the lookout tower, and the castle outside of town. The town itself is a charming little community of about 150 residents.

Holy Island Town
The town has B&Bs and cafés catering to tourists, a tiny post office, a fire station (with no firefighters—they're helicoptered in when the need arises), a six-student schoolhouse, and a tiny winery offering free tastes of their Lindisfarne mead. There's no official TI, but the **Lindisfarne Centre**—with a well-presented, kid-friendly history exhibit—acts as an unofficial information point and is proudly staffed by native Holy Islanders (£4 to tour the exhibit, daily April-Oct 10:00-16:00, open sporadically Nov-March, Marygate, tel. 01289/389-004, www.lindisfarne.org.uk).

Lindisfarne Priory
The priory has an evocative field of ruined church walls and a tiny but instructive museum. (A priory—run by a prior rather than an abbot—is similar to an abbey but smaller.)

Cost and Hours: £8, includes both museum and priory ruins; April-Sept daily 10:00-18:00, Oct daily until 17:00, Nov-March Wed-Sun until 16:00, closed Mon-Tue; low-cost guidebook available, tel. 01289/389-200, www.english-heritage.org.uk/lindisfarne.

Visiting the Priory: In the **museum,** you'll see exhibits about Holy Island's Anglo-Saxon culture, from stonework to manuscripts—including the famous Lindisfarne Gospels. The Gospels' text was in Latin, the language of scholars ever since the Roman Empire, but the illustrations—with elaborate tracery and interwoven decoration—are a mix of Irish, classical, and even Byzantine forms. These Gospels are a reminder that Christianity almost didn't make it in Europe. After the fall of Rome (which had established

Christianity as the Empire's official religion), much of Europe reverted to its pagan ways. In that chaotic era, Lindisfarne—an obscure monastery of Irish monks on a remote island—was one of the few beacons of light, tending the embers of civilization through the long night of the Dark Ages.

You can visit the adjacent church and churchyard without paying, but you need a ticket to get into the actual **priory ruins.**

The Lindisfarne monks fled the island in AD 875 to escape Viking raids. They made their way to Durham, and built a cathedral to hold the tomb of St. Cuthbert (see "Sights in Durham," earlier). Centuries later, in 1082, the monks returned to Holy Island to re-found the priory and build a fine church in a Norman (Romanesque) style similar to the one in Durham. They fended off invasions by Picts and Scots throughout the 14th century, and fortified the great church. But when Henry VIII "dissolved" (destroyed) the monasteries in the 1530s, the priory was one of his victims. The forgotten ruins were later excavated in the 1850s as an important example of early English (Anglo-Saxon) history.

As you walk through this site, you're stepping on several layers of history: a ruined Norman church sitting on the ruins of an earlier Anglo-Saxon one (where Cuthbert served as bishop), next to the still-standing Parish Church of St. Mary's, where Holy Islanders worship today. The priory ruins are well-explained by posted plaques and floor plans that help resurrect the rubble.

Lookout Tower

Situated on the "Heugh" (a stone ridge protecting the eastern harbor), this former coast guard tower has been turned into a 360-degree viewpoint open to the public. Climb up and enjoy the view. On a clear day you can see Bamburgh Castle in the distance. Notice the two stone obelisks in the water; these served as early 19th-century navigation beacons. To get to the tower from the priory entrance, head toward The Crown and Anchor pub and follow the small path to the right.

Lindisfarne Castle

Faintly visible from the priory ruins, the dramatically situated Lindisfarne Castle is enticing from afar. It makes for a fine photo op, but there's little of interest inside. Built in 1549—many centuries after the heyday of Cuthbert and the monks—the castle never really saw much action, and it was converted into a holiday home for an aristocratic publisher in the early 1900s. If you do visit, you'll wander through sparsely furnished rooms and stroll out onto the upper battery—an outdoor terrace with views of the priory ruins.

Cost and Hours: £9, daily mid-Feb-Oct generally 10:00-16:00; hours depend on tides—confirm times on website or at the National Trust shop on Marygate in town before heading out, tel. 01289/389-244, www.nationaltrust.org.uk/lindisfarne.

Bamburgh Castle

About 10 miles south of Holy Island, this grand castle—worth ▲—dominates the Northumbrian countryside and overlooks Britain's loveliest beach. Bamburgh (BOMB-ruh) was bought and passionately refurbished by Lord William George Armstrong, a wealthy industrialist, in the 1890s. While it's one of England's most dramatic castles from the outside, the interior (a 19th-century rebuild) lacks soul, barely cracking the country's top 10. But if you're passing by or visiting nearby Holy Island, Bamburgh may be worth a stop.

Cost and Hours: £11.25 includes staterooms and grounds, daily mid-Feb-Oct 10:00-17:00, winter Sat-Sun only 11:00-16:30, last entry one hour before closing, audioguide and guidebook available, parking-£2, also reachable by public transportation—consult www.traveline.info for specifics, tel. 01668/214-515, www.bamburghcastle.com.

Visiting the Castle: Bamburgh's main attraction is its staterooms; as you explore the rest of the grounds, you'll also have the chance to see several smaller exhibits. If arriving late in the day, go directly to the staterooms, which may close early. There's virtually no information inside the castle, aside from a few docents; to give meaning to your visit, either rent the inexpensive audioguide (with two hours of commentary) or buy the guidebook.

The **staterooms** feel lived-in because they still are—with Armstrong family portraits and aristocratic-yet-homey knick-knacks hanging everywhere. You'll enter through the medieval kitchen, with its three giant fireplaces, and work your way through smaller storage rooms to the King's Hall, with a fantastic teak ceiling and a J. M. W. Turner painting. At the far end of the great hall is a smaller (but still grand) alcove separated by an archway, which could be sealed off by gigantic folding doors. Continuing through the stairwell, notice the *private apartment* signs.

The armory once had a very different purpose—you can still see the apse of what was once a chapel. In the keep is a 145-foot-deep Anglo-Saxon well. The scullery (a medieval utility room) includes a long row of sinks and an alcove where they make fresh fudge. You'll wind up in the gift shop; before leaving, check out the archaeology room, with exhibits about the castle's history; and the dungeon, with cheesy mannequins being tortured.

Exploring the **grounds,** you can enjoy fine views over the sea and beach and get a good look at the stout 12th-century keep that's the castle's centerpiece. In the former stables is an art gallery displaying works by local artists. The Armstrong and Aviation Artefacts Museum features the inventions of the family that has owned the castle through modern times. Lord William George

Armstrong (1810-1900) was an engineer, scientist, and businessman who perfected hydraulic machinery and revolutionized gun making. His company later became Armstrong Whitworth, a pioneer in British aviation. You'll see several of his inventions, along with exhibits on planes, cars, shipbuilding, and more. While the museum is fun for aviation-history buffs, it may be dull to others.

Nearby: The village of Bamburgh is pleasant enough, with tourist-oriented cafés and fine views over a manicured cricket pitch of the looming castle. Better yet, go for a walk on the beach: Crisscrossed by walking paths, rolling dunes lead to a vast sandy beach and lots of families on holiday.

BRITAIN:
PAST & PRESENT

To fully appreciate the many fascinating sights you'll encounter in your travels, learn the basics of the sweeping story of this land and its people. (Generally speaking, the fascinating stories you'll hear from tour guides are not true...and the boring ones are.)

Regardless of the revolution we had more than 240 years ago, many American travelers feel that they "go home" to Britain. This most popular tourist destination has a strange influence and power over us. The more you know of Britain's roots, the better you'll get in touch with your own.

This chapter starts with a once-over of Britain's illustrious history. It's speckled throughout with more in-depth information about current issues and this great country's future.

British History

ORIGINS (2000 BC-AD 500)

When Julius Caesar landed on the misty and mysterious isle of Britain in 55 BC, England entered the history books. He was met by primitive Celtic tribes whose druid priests made human sacrifices and worshipped trees. (Those Celts were themselves immigrants, who had earlier conquered the even more mysterious people who built Stonehenge.) The Romans eventually settled in England (AD 43) and set about building towns and roads and establishing their capital at Londinium (today's London).

But the Celtic natives—consisting of Gaels, Picts, and Scots—were not easily subdued. Around AD 60, Boadicea, a queen of the Isle's indigenous people, defied the Romans and burned Londinium before the revolt was squelched. Some decades later, the Romans built Hadrian's Wall near the Scottish border as protection against their troublesome northern neighbors. Even today, the Celtic language and influence are strongest in these far reaches of Britain.

Londinium became a bustling Roman river-and-sea trading port. The Romans built the original London Bridge and a city wall, encompassing one square mile, which set the city boundaries for 1,500 years. By AD 200, London was a thriving, Latin-speaking capital of Roman-dominated England.

DARK AGES (500-1000)

As Rome fell, so fell Roman Britain—a victim of invaders and internal troubles. Barbarian tribes from Germany, Denmark, and northern Holland, called Angles, Saxons, and Jutes, swept through the southern part of the island, establishing Angle-land. These were the days of the real King Arthur, possibly a Christianized Roman general who fought valiantly—but in vain—against invading barbarians.

In 793, England was hit with the first of two centuries of savage invasions by barbarians from Norway, called the Vikings or Norsemen. King Alfred the Great (849-899) liberated London from Danish Vikings, reunited England, reestablished Christianity, and fostered learning. Nevertheless, for most of this 500-year period, the island was plunged into a dark age—wars, plagues, and poverty—lit only by the dim candle of a few learned Christian monks and missionaries trying to convert the barbarians. Today, visitors see little from this Anglo-Saxon period.

WARS WITH FRANCE, WARS OF THE ROSES (1000-1500)

Modern England began with yet another invasion. In 1066, William the Conqueror and his Norman troops crossed the English Channel from France. William crowned himself king in Westminster Abbey (where all subsequent coronations would take place). He began building the Tower of London, as well as Windsor Castle,

which would become the residence of many monarchs to come.

Over the succeeding centuries, French-speaking kings would rule England, and English-speaking kings invaded France as the two budding nations

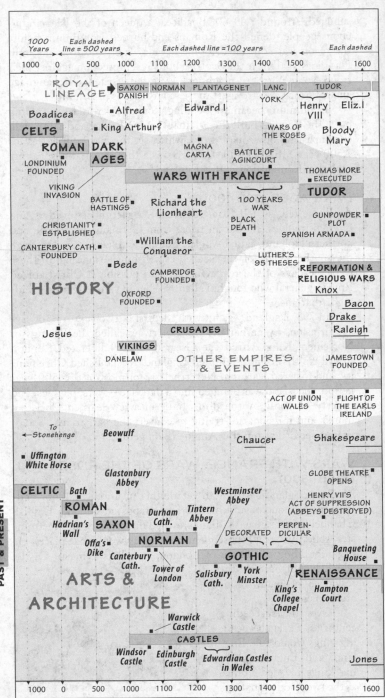

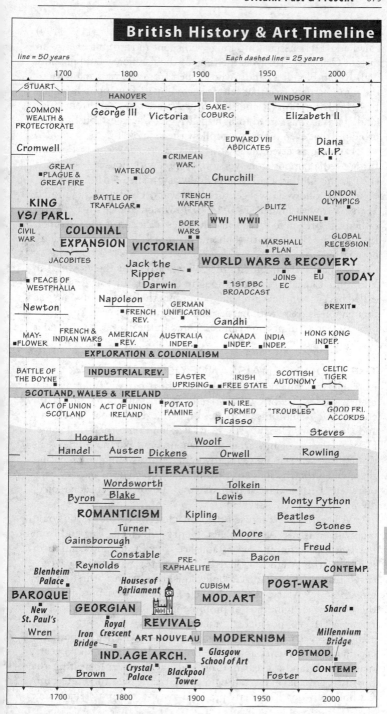

British History & Art Timeline

line = 50 years   Each dashed line = 25 years

1700   1800   1900   1950   2000

STUART

HANOVER   WINDSOR

COMMON-WEALTH & PROTECTORATE   George III   Victoria   SAXE-COBURG   Elizabeth II

Cromwell

GREAT PLAGUE & GREAT FIRE   WATERLOO   CRIMEAN WAR.   EDWARD VIII ABDICATES   Diana R.I.P.

Churchill

BATTLE OF TRAFALGAR   TRENCH WARFARE   BLITZ   LONDON OLYMPICS

KING VS/ PARL.   WWI   WWII   CHUNNEL

BOER WARS

CIVIL WAR   COLONIAL EXPANSION   VICTORIAN   MARSHALL PLAN   GLOBAL RECESSION

JACOBITES   Jack the Ripper   WORLD WARS & RECOVERY

PEACE OF WESTPHALIA   Darwin   JOINS EC   EU   TODAY

1ST BBC BROADCAST

Newton   Napoleon   GERMAN UNIFICATION   BREXIT

FRENCH REV.   Gandhi

MAYFLOWER   FRENCH & INDIAN WARS   AMERICAN REV.   AUSTRALIA INDEP.   CANADA INDEP.   INDIA INDEP.   HONG KONG INDEP.

EXPLORATION & COLONIALISM

BATTLE OF THE BOYNE   INDUSTRIAL REV.   EASTER UPRISING   IRISH FREE STATE   SCOTTISH AUTONOMY   CELTIC TIGER

SCOTLAND, WALES & IRELAND

ACT OF UNION SCOTLAND   ACT OF UNION IRELAND   POTATO FAMINE   N. IRE. FORMED   "TROUBLES"   GOOD FRI. ACCORDS

Picasso

Steves

Hogarth   Woolf

Handel   Austen   Dickens   Orwell   Rowling

LITERATURE

Wordsworth   Tolkein

Byron   Blake   Lewis   Monty Python

ROMANTICISM   Kipling   Beatles

Turner   Stones

Gainsborough   Moore

Constable   Freud

Reynolds   PRE-RAPHAELITE   Bacon   CONTEMP.

Blenheim Palace   Houses of Parliament   CUBISM   POST-WAR

BAROQUE   MOD.ART

New St. Paul's   GEORGIAN   Shard

Wren   Royal Crescent   REVIVALS   Millennium Bridge

Iron Bridge   ART NOUVEAU   MODERNISM

IND.AGE ARCH.   Glasgow School of Art   POSTMOD.

Brown   Crystal Palace   Blackpool Tower   Foster   CONTEMP.

1700   1800   1900   1950   2000

defined their modern borders. Richard the Lionheart (1157-1199) ruled as a French-speaking king who spent most of his energy on distant Crusades. This was the time of the legendary (and possibly real) Robin Hood, a bandit who robbed from the rich and gave to the poor—a populace that felt neglected by its francophone rulers. In 1215, King John (Richard's brother), under pressure from England's barons, was forced to sign the Magna Carta, establishing the principle that even kings must follow the rule of law.

London asserted itself as England's trade center. London Bridge—the famous stone version, topped with houses—was built (1209), and Old St. Paul's Cathedral was finished (1314).

Then followed two centuries of wars, chiefly the Hundred Years' War with France (1337-1443), in which France's Joan of Arc rallied the French to drive English forces back across the Channel. In 1348, the Black Death (bubonic plague) killed half of London's population.

In the 1400s, noble families duked it out for the crown. The York and Lancaster families fought the Wars of the Roses, so-called because of the white and red flowers the combatants chose as their symbols. Rife with battles and intrigues, and with kings, nobles, and ladies imprisoned and executed in the Tower, it's a wonder the country survived its rulers.

THE TUDOR RENAISSANCE (1500s)

England was finally united by the "third-party" Tudor family. Henry VIII, a Tudor, was England's Renaissance king. Powerful, charismatic, handsome, athletic, highly sexed, a poet, a scholar, and a musician, Henry VIII thrust England onto the world stage. He was also arrogant, cruel, gluttonous, and paranoid. He went through six wives in 40 years, divorcing, imprisoning, or executing them when they no longer suited his needs. (To keep track of each one's fate, British kids learn this rhyme: "Divorced, beheaded, died; divorced, beheaded, survived.")

When the Pope refused to grant Henry a divorce so he could marry his mistress Anne Boleyn, Henry "divorced" England from the Catholic Church. He established the Protestant Church of England (the Anglican Church), thus setting in motion a century of bitter Protestant/Catholic squabbles. Henry's first daughter, "Bloody" Mary, was a staunch Catholic who presided over the burning of hundreds of prominent Protestants. (For more on Henry VIII, see the sidebar on page 114.)

Mary was followed by her half-sister—Queen Elizabeth I—the daughter of Henry and Anne Boleyn. She reigned for 45 years, making England a great trading and naval power (defeating the Spanish Armada) and treading diplomatically over the Protestant/Catholic divide. Elizabeth presided over a cultural renaissance

known (not surprisingly) as the "Elizabethan Age." Playwright William
Shakespeare moved from Stratford-
upon-Avon to London, beginning a remarkable career as the earth's greatest
playwright. Sir Francis Drake circum-
navigated the globe. Sir Walter Raleigh explored the Americas, and Sir
Francis Bacon pioneered the scientific
method. London's population swelled.

But Elizabeth—the "Virgin
Queen"—never married or produced
an heir. So the English Parliament
invited Scotland's King James (Eliza-
beth's first cousin twice removed) to inherit the English throne.
The two nations have been tied together ever since, however fitfully.

KINGS VS. PARLIAMENT (1600s)

The enduring quarrel between England's kings and Parliament's
nobles finally erupted into the Civil War (1642). The war pitted
(roughly speaking) the Protestant Puritan Parliament against the
Catholic aristocracy. Parliament forces under Oliver Cromwell
defeated—and beheaded—King Charles I. After Cromwell died,

Parliament invited Charles' son to take the
throne—the "restoration of the monarchy."
To emphasize the point, Cromwell's corpse
was subsequently exhumed and posthu-
mously beheaded.

This turbulent era was followed by back-
to-back disasters—the Great Plague of 1665
(which killed 100,000) and the Great Fire
of 1666 (which incinerated London). London was completely rebuilt in stone, centered
around New St. Paul's Cathedral, which was
built by Christopher Wren. With a population over 200,000, London was now Europe's largest city. At home, Isaac Newton
watched an apple fall from a tree, leading him to explain the mysterious force of gravity.

In the war between kings and Parliament, Parliament finally
got the last word, when it deposed Catholic James II and imported
the Dutch monarchs William and Mary in 1688, guaranteeing a
Protestant succession.

PAST & PRESENT

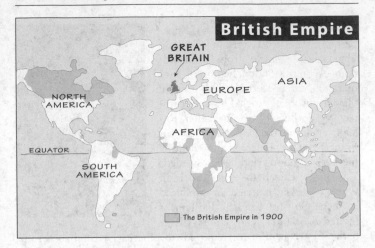

British Empire

GREAT BRITAIN

NORTH AMERICA

EUROPE

ASIA

AFRICA

EQUATOR

SOUTH AMERICA

☐ The British Empire in 1900

COLONIAL EXPANSION (1700s)

Britain grew as a naval superpower, colonizing and trading with all parts of the globe. Eventually, Britannia ruled the waves, exploiting the wealth of India, Africa, and Australia. (And America...at least until they lost their most important colony when those ungrateful Yanks revolted in 1776 in the "American War.") Throughout the century, the country was ruled by the German Hanover family, including four kings named George.

The "Georgian Era" was one of great wealth. London's population was now half a million, and one in seven Brits lived in London. The nation's first daily newspapers hit the streets. The cultural scene was refined: painters (like William Hogarth, Joshua Reynolds, and Thomas Gainsborough), the-ater (with actors like David Garrick), music (Handel's *Messiah*), and literature (Samuel Johnson's dictionary). Scientist James Watt's steam engines laid the groundwork for a coming Industrial Revolution.

In 1789, the French Revolution erupted, sparking decades of war between France and Britain. Britain finally prevailed in the early 1800s, when Admiral Horatio Nelson defeated Napoleon's fleet at the Battle of Trafalgar and the Duke of Wellington stomped Napoleon at Waterloo. (Nelson and Wellington are memorialized by many arches, columns, and squares throughout England.)

By war's end, Britain had emerged as Europe's top power.

PAST & PRESENT

VICTORIAN GENTILITY AND THE INDUSTRIAL REVOLUTION (1800s)

Britain reigned supreme, steaming into the Industrial Age with her mills, factories, coal mines, gas lights, and trains. By century's end, there was electricity, telephones, and the first Underground.

In 1837, eighteen-year-old Victoria became queen. She ruled for 64 years, presiding over an era of unprecedented wealth, peace, and middle-class ("Victorian") values. Britain was at its zenith of power, with a colonial empire that covered one-fifth of the world (for more on Victoria and her Age, see the sidebar on the next page).

Meanwhile, there was another side to Britain's era of superiority and industrial might. A generation of Romantic poets (William Wordsworth, John Keats, Percy Shelley, and Lord Byron) longed for the innocence of nature. Jane Austen and the Brontë sisters wrote romantic tales about the landed gentry. Painters like J. M. W. Turner and John Constable immersed themselves in nature to paint moody landscapes.

The gritty modern world was emerging. Popular novelist Charles Dickens brought literature to the masses, educating them about Britain's harsh social and economic realities. Rudyard Kipling critiqued the colonial system. Charles Darwin questioned the very nature of humanity when he articulated the principles of natural selection and evolution. Jack the Ripper, a serial killer of prostitutes, terrorized east London and was never caught. Not even by Sherlock Holmes—a fictional detective living at 221B Baker Street who solved fictional crimes that the real Scotland Yard couldn't.

WORLD WARS AND RECOVERY (20th Century)

The 20th century was not kind to Britain. Two world wars and economic struggles whittled Britain down from a world empire to an island chain struggling to compete in a global economy.

In World War I, Britain joined France and other allies to battle Germany in trench warfare. A million British men died. Meanwhile, after decades of rebellion, Ireland finally gained its independence—except for the Protestant-leaning Northern Ireland, which remained tied to Britain. This division of the Emerald Isle would result in decades of bitter strife, protests, and terrorist attacks known as "The Troubles."

In the 1920s, London was home to a flourishing literary scene, including T. S. Eliot (American-turned-British), Virginia Woolf, and E. M. Forster. In

Queen Victoria (1819-1901)

Plump, pleasant, and not quite five feet tall, Queen Victoria, with her regal demeanor and 64-year reign, came to symbolize the global dominance of the British Empire during its greatest era.

Born in Kensington Palace, Victoria was the granddaughter of "Mad" King George III, the tyrant who sparked the American Revolution. Her domineering mother raised her in sheltered seclusion, drilling into her the strict morality that would come to be known as "Victorian." At 18, she was crowned queen. Victoria soon fell deeply in love with Prince Albert, a handsome German nobleman. They married and set up house in Buckingham Palace (the first monarchs to do so) and at Windsor Castle. Over the next 17 years, she and Albert had nine children, whom they married off to Europe's crowned heads. Victoria's descendants include Kaiser Wilhelm II of Germany (who started World War I); the current monarchs of Spain, Norway, Sweden, and Denmark; and England's Queen Elizabeth II, who is Victoria's great-great-granddaughter.

Victoria and Albert promoted the arts and sciences, organizing a world's fair in Hyde Park (1851) that showed off London as *the* global capital. Just as important, they were role models for an entire nation; this loving couple influenced several generations with their wholesome middle-class values and devoted parenting. Though Victoria is often depicted as dour and stuffy—she supposedly coined the phrase "We are not amused"—in private she was warm, easy to laugh, plainspoken, thrifty, and modest, with a talent for sketching and journal writing.

In 1861, Victoria's happy domestic life ended. Her mother's death was soon followed by the sudden loss of her beloved Albert to typhoid fever. A devastated Victoria dressed in black for the funeral—and for her remaining 40 years. She hunkered down at Windsor with her family. Critics complained she was an absentee monarch. Rumors swirled that her kilt-wearing servant, John Brown, was not only her close friend but also her lover. For two decades, she rarely appeared in public.

1936, the country was rocked and scandalized when King Edward VIII abdicated to marry a divorced American commoner, Wallis Simpson. He was succeeded by his brother, George VI—"Bertie" of *The King's Speech* fame, and father of Queen Elizabeth II.

In World War II, the Nazi Blitz (aerial bombing campaign) reduced much of London to rubble, sending residents into Tube

Over time, Victoria emerged from mourning to assume her role as one of history's first constitutional monarchs. She had inherited a crown with little real power. But beyond her ribbon-cutting ceremonial duties, Victoria influenced events behind the scenes. She studiously learned politics from powerful mentors (especially Prince Albert and two influential prime ministers) and kept well informed on what Parliament was doing. Thanks to Victoria's personal modesty and honesty, the British public never came to disdain the monarchy, as happened in other countries.

Victoria gracefully oversaw the peaceful transfer of power from the nobles to the people. The secret ballot was introduced during her reign, and ordinary workers acquired voting rights (though this applied only to men—Victoria opposed women's suffrage). The traditional Whigs and Tories morphed into today's Liberal and Conservative parties. Victoria personally promoted progressive charities, and even paid for her own crown.

Most of all, Victoria became the symbol of the British Empire, which she saw as a way to protect and civilize poorer peoples. Britain enjoyed peace at home, while its colonial possessions included India, Australia, Canada, and much of Africa. Because it was always daytime someplace under Victoria's rule, it was often said that "the sun never sets on the British Empire."

The Victorian era saw great changes. The Industrial Revolution was in full swing. When Victoria was born, there were no trains. By 1842, when she took her first train trip (with much fanfare), railroads crisscrossed Europe. The telegraph, telephone, and newspapers further laced the world together. The popular arts flourished—it was the era of Dickens novels, Tennyson poems, Sherlock Holmes stories, Gilbert and Sullivan operettas, and Pre-Raphaelite paintings. Economically, Britain saw the rise of the middle class. Middle-class morality dominated—family, hard work, honor, duty, and sexual modesty.

By the end of her reign, Victoria was wildly popular, both for her personality and as a focus for British patriotism. At her Golden Jubilee (1887), she paraded past adoring throngs to Westminster Abbey. For her Diamond Jubilee (1897), she did the same at St. Paul's Cathedral. Cities, lakes, and military medals were named for her. When she passed away in 1901, it was literally the end of an era.

stations for shelter and the government into a fortified bunker (now the Churchill War Rooms). Britain was rallied through its darkest hour by two leaders: Prime Minister Winston Churchill, a remarkable orator, and King George VI, who overcame a persistent stutter. Amid the chaos of war, the colonial empire began to dwindle to almost nothing, and Britain emerged from the war as a shell of its former superpower self.

The postwar recovery began, aided by the United States. Many cheap, concrete (ugly) buildings rose from the rubble.

Culturally, Britain remained world-class. Oxford professor J. R. R. Tolkien wrote *The Lord of the Rings* and his friend C. S. Lewis wrote *The Chronicles of Narnia*. In the 1960s, "Swinging London" became a center for rock music, film, theater, youth culture, and Austin Powers-style joie de vivre. America was conquered by a "British Invasion" of rock bands (The Beatles, The Rolling Stones, and The Who, followed later by Led Zeppelin, Elton John, David Bowie, and others), and James Bond ruled the box office.

Britain joined the European Common Market, an economic precursor to the European Union, in 1973. The decade brought massive unemployment, labor strikes, and recession. A conservative reaction followed in the 1980s and 90s, led by Prime Minister and Eurosceptic Margaret Thatcher—the "Iron Lady." As proponents of traditional Victorian values—community, family, hard work, thrift, and trickle-down economics—the Conservatives took a Reaganesque approach to Britain's serious social and economic problems. They cut government subsidies to old-fashioned heavy industries (closing many factories, earning working-class ire), as they tried to nudge Britain toward a more modern economy.

In 1981, the world was captivated by the spectacle of Prince Charles marrying Lady Diana in St. Paul's Cathedral. Their children, Princes William and Harry, grew up in the media spotlight, and when Diana died in a car crash (1997), the nation—and the world—mourned.

The 1990s saw Britain finally emerging from decades of economic stagnation and social turmoil. An energized nation prepared for the new millennium.

EARLY 2000s

London celebrated the millennium with a new Ferris wheel (the London Eye), the Millennium Bridge, and an exhibition hall dubbed "The O2." Britain was ruled by left-of-center Prime Minister Tony Blair, until his popularity plummeted when he supported the US invasion of Iraq. On "7/7" in 2005, London was rocked by a terrorist attack—a harbinger of others to come.

Britain suffered mightily in the global recession of 2008. Voters turned to the Conservative Prime Minister David Cameron, who introduced austerity measures, but Britain was slow to recover.

Thankfully, one hot spot—Northern Ireland—was healed. In 2007, ultra-nationalists and ultra-unionists reached an agreement, ending almost 40 years of The Troubles.

In 2011, Prince William married commoner Kate Middleton

Get It Right

Americans tend to use "England," "Britain," and the "United Kingdom" (or "UK") interchangeably, but they're not quite the same.

- **England** is the country occupying the center and south-east part of the island.
- **Britain** is the name of the island.
- **Great Britain** is the political union of the island's three countries: England, Scotland, and Wales.
- The **United Kingdom** (UK) adds a fourth country, Northern Ireland.
- The **British Isles** (not a political entity) also includes the independent Republic of Ireland.
- The **British Commonwealth** is a loose association of possessions and former colonies (including Canada, Australia, and India) that profess at least symbolic loyalty to the Crown.

You can call the modern nation either the United Kingdom ("the UK"), "Great Britain," or simply "Britain."

in a lavish ceremony. And in 2018, William's younger brother Harry married American TV star Meghan Markle. The two couples, along with their children, have stirred renewed enthusiasm for the monarchy.

In 2012, in a one-two punch of festivity, the Brits hosted both the Olympic Games and the Queen's 60th year on the throne. A flurry of renovation turned former urban wastelands into hip, thriving people zones, and the country's future was looking rosier than ever.

Then came Brexit...

Britain Today

Without a doubt, Britain is one of the richest, freest, best-educated, and culturally powerful nations on earth. But it also has its challenges. To understand the British people today, it's helpful to survey the divided political landscape and global trends that they're dealing with. This includes the most vexing issue Brits have grappled with since World War II—Brexit.

POLITICAL LANDSCAPE

Britain is ruled by the House of Commons, with some guidance from the mostly figurehead Queen and House of Lords. The prime minister is the chief executive but is not elected directly by voters; rather, he or she assumes power as the head of the party that wins a majority in parliamentary elections. Elections are held every five years.

Britain's Parliament has traditionally been dominated by two parties: left-leaning Labour (currently led by Jeremy Corbyn) and right-leaning Conservative ("Tories," led by Boris Johnson). The dividing lines between them are familiar: Should government nurture the economy through spending on social programs (Labour's platform), or cut programs and taxes to allow businesses to thrive (as Conservatives say)?

In recent elections, third parties have made gains, including the Scottish National Party (SNP, led by Nicola Sturgeon) and the center-left Liberal Democrats). If no single party wins an outright majority, whoever rules must form a coalition. Because Britain does not have a single "constitution" clearly outlining the system of checks and balances, the British body politic relies more on a tradition of civility and mutual respect to make government work.

CHALLENGES

The biggest challenge facing Britain at the moment is, of course, Brexit—figuring out how to enact the 2016 referendum in which Britain voted to leave the European Union. But Brexit is inextricably tangled up with other issues that have long divided the nation, including the changing economy, immigration, terrorism, the country's place on the world stage, and the role of royalty.

Although prosperous, Britain faces a deepening gap of wealth inequality. The disposable income of the richest households ($85,000) is five times larger than that of the poorest ($16,500). This has ratcheted up the class consciousness that has always divided British society. And it's raised the question of whether the global economy that generates so much wealth has benefitted everyone equally.

Another divisive issue is the impact of immigration. Britain has long been home to immigrants from its former colonies (India, Pakistan, Bangladesh, Africa, the Caribbean), but it's a different story today. The number of people born abroad is now about 14 percent, up from 5 percent two decades ago. And today's newcomers are more likely to be from EU countries, especially Eastern Europe or poorer Mediterranean countries. These transplants can make a lot more money working here than back home. For the most part, Britain has assimilated these immigrants well. But some argue that they're taking British jobs and diluting its culture, all while receiving overgenerous financial aid.

Whenever terrorist attacks occur, the question arises about whether immigration might be to blame. Brits are stunned that many terrorists speak the Queen's English and were born and raised in Britain. It raises larger issues: How well is the nation

PAST & PRESENT

assimilating its immigrants? Does negativity toward immigrants fuel violence? Whatever the cause, the threat of terrorism has challenged the nation with how to balance security with privacy concerns. You'll see surveillance cameras everywhere.

As Britain ponders whether to remain in the EU, it faces a similar issue in its own backyard. In 2014, Scotland voted to remain a part of the UK, but Scottish nationalists continue to insist that Scotland would be better off free from the shackles of London-based problems.

Finally, Brits are divided on the eternal question of the royals. Is having a monarch and a royal family worth it? In decades past, many Brits wanted to toss the whole lot of them. But with the popularity of William, Kate, Harry, and Meghan, four out of five Brits now want to let the tradition live on. With Harry and Meghan's move to step back from royal duties, though, all bets are off.

BREXIT: BREAKING UP IS HARD TO DO

Since 2016, Brits have hotly debated its most momentous decision in generations: whether or not to exit the EU. Britain has been a member of Europe's customs union since as far back as 1973. But it never fully bought into the European Union, shunning the euro currency and resisting EU regulations and integration. Eurosceptics complained about being "ruled" from Brussels, and being "invaded" by immigrants from the EU.

It came to a head in 2016, when Prime Minister David Cameron decided to settle the question once and for all with a nationwide referendum: to stay in the EU and enjoy its trade benefits, or to leave and restore full national sovereignty. Both sides campaigned fiercely. The "Remain" (or anti-Brexit) camp had most of the high-profile supporters—including Cameron himself. The "Leave" (pro-Brexit) side was led by Nigel Farage (a rabble-rousing politician and TV personality with anti-immigration ties) and Boris Johnson (the flamboyant former mayor of London).

The debate was spirited and nasty. Many pro-Brexiteers, with their anti-immigration and rah-rah patriotism, drew charges of racism. The "Remain"-ers were called elitist and privileged.

The pollsters put "Remain" comfortably ahead. But "Leave" shocked the world by winning with 51.9 percent of the vote. It threw Britain (and the EU) into uncharted territory with no clear path forward. The British pound dropped by 10 percent, and David Cameron resigned. His Conservative successor, Theresa May (also a "Remain" supporter), was left with the thankless task of trying to carry out the will of the voters against a hostile EU and a reluctant establishment.

May gave the EU two year's notice that Britain was leaving. But by 2019, there was no agreement in sight, and the deadline was extended. The main debate was: hard or soft? The "Leave" camp lobbied for a clean and decisive break from the EU. This would require renegotiating trade deals, likely resulting in higher tariffs and higher prices all around. Others pushed for a "soft Brexit": keeping in place many of the favored EU trade relationships they enjoy today, without being a full member—similar to what Norway and Switzerland do with the EU. Still others lobby for a whole new referendum that would cancel Brexit altogether.

The issue has split the nation. Business leaders fear a Brexit will hamper London's position as a gateway to European business. Young British people fear losing the world they grew up in, where they can travel freely and live anywhere in Europe. England's industrialized North, which has struggled economically for decades, voted strongly to "Leave" while the "Soft South" of multinational business voted strongly to "Remain." (Think disaffected Rust Belt voters versus latte-sipping Coastal Elites.)

Voters in Scotland voted heavily against Brexit, and now there are murmurs of another Scottish independence vote. The stakes are even higher in Northern Ireland: The fragile peace that ended The Troubles works in part because of the EU's open border between Northern Ireland (part of the UK) and the Republic of Ireland (a separate country and EU member). A hard Brexit would create a hard border, potentially inflaming tensions in these divided communities.

Brexit has even divided the traditional political order. In the past, the Labour Party was always pro-EU while many Conservatives were Eurosceptics. Now both parties have factions in favor of staying in the EU, while other factions want to leave. Prime Minister Boris Johnson is in an unenviable position of trying to negotiate a deal with both a bickering Parliament and with the EU.

And so the question remains (as The Clash put it so eloquently): "Should I stay or should I go?"

The Brexit deadline was pushed back to fall of 2019—and could be pushed back further. By the time you read this, there will likely be new wrinkles and complications.

NOTABLE BRITS OF TODAY AND TOMORROW

Only history can judge which British names will stand the test of time, but many Brits stand large on the world stage.

There are well-known politicians, like Theresa May, Boris Johnson, and Jeremy Corbyn.

The list of British actors reads like a roll-call of Oscar and Emmy winners: Helen Mirren, Emma Thompson, Daniel Day-Lewis, Gary Oldman, Helena Bonham Carter, Jude Law, Ricky Gervais, James Corden, Daniel Radcliffe, Kate Winslet, Benedict

Cumberbatch, John Oliver, Tilda Swinton, Colin Firth, Eddie Redmayne, etc.

Of course, ever since the "British Invasion" of the '60s, Brits have dominated the pop music scene: Adele, Chris Martin of Coldplay, Jessie J, Ellie Goulding, Ed Sheeran, Sam Smith, Florence Welch of Florence and the Machine, etc.

In the literary field, Britain scoops up major awards, including Britain's own Man Booker Prize. There's J. K. Rowling, E. L. James, Hilary Mantel, Tom Stoppard, Nick Hornby, Ian McEwan, Zadie Smith.

There are well-known visual artists (Damien Hirst, Rachel Whiteread, Tracey Emin, Anish Kapoor), athletes (David Beckham, Bradley Wiggins, Andy Murray), and entrepreneurs (Sir Richard Branson, Lord Alan Sugar, James Dyson).

And, of course, there are Britain's biggest tabloid sensations in years, the new generation of royals: William, Kate, Harry, Meghan, and their cute little kids.

BRITISH TV

For many Americans, their first view of the British lifestyle came through British TV programs beamed into American homes. And no wonder. Although it has its share of lowbrow reality programming, much British television is still so good—and so British—that it deserves a mention as a sightseeing treat. After a hard day of castle climbing, watch the telly over tea in your B&B.

For many years there were only five free channels, but now nearly every British television can receive a couple dozen. BBC television is government-regulated and commercial-free. Broadcasting of its eight channels (and of the five BBC radio stations) is funded by a mandatory £154.50-per-year-per-household television and radio license (hmmm, 50 cents per day to escape commercials and public-broadcasting pledge drives...not bad). Channels 3, 4, and 5 are privately owned, are a little more lowbrow, and have commercials—but those "adverts" are often clever and sophisticated, providing a fun look at British life. About 60 percent of households pay for cable or satellite television.

Whereas California "accents" fill US airwaves 24 hours a day, homogenizing the way our country speaks, Britain protects and promotes its regional accents by its choice of TV and radio announcers. See if you can tell where each is from (or ask a local for help).

Commercial-free British TV, while looser than it used to be, is still careful about what it airs and when. But after the 21:00 "watershed" hour, when children are expected to be in bed, some nudity and profanity are allowed, and may cause you to spill your tea.

American programs (such as *Game of Thrones*, *CSI*, *Family Guy*,

Royal Families: Past and Present

Royal Lineage

802-1066	Saxon and Danish kings
1066-1154	William the Conqueror and Norman kings
1154-1399	Plantagenet (kings with French roots)
1399-1461	Lancaster
1462-1485	York
1485-1603	Tudor (Henry VIII, Elizabeth I)
1603-1649	Stuart (civil war and beheading of Charles I)
1649-1653	Commonwealth, no royal head of state
1653-1659	Protectorate, with Cromwell as Lord Protector
1660-1714	Restoration of Stuart dynasty
1714-1901	Hanover (four Georges, William IV, Victoria)
1901-1910	Saxe-Coburg (Edward VII)
1910-present	Windsor (George V to Elizabeth II)

The Royal Family Today

It seems you can't pick up a British newspaper without some mention of the latest event, scandal, or oddity involving the royal family. Here is the cast of characters:

Queen Elizabeth II wears the traditional crown of her great-great grandmother Victoria, who ruled for 63 years, 7 months, and 2 days. In September 2015, Queen Elizabeth officially over-took Victoria as England's longest-reigning monarch, and in April 2016 she became the first UK sovereign to reach 90 years old. Elizabeth's husband is Prince Philip, who's not considered king.

Their son, Prince Charles (the Prince of Wales), is next in line to become king—and already holds the title as the longest "heir in waiting." For years, Charles' love life was fodder for the British press. There was his fairytale 1981 marriage to Princess Di, then their bitter divorce, Diana's dramatic death in 1997, and the ongoing drama with Charles' longtime girlfriend—and now wife—Camilla Parker Bowles. (Camilla, the Duchess of Cornwall, would not become "Queen Camilla" if Charles becomes king—she'll be the "Princess Consort.")

These days it's Prince Charles' sons who generate the tabloid buzz. The older son, Prince William (b. 1982), is a graduate of Scotland's St. Andrews University and served as a search-and-rescue helicopter pilot with the Royal Air Force. In 2011, when William married Catherine "Kate" Middleton, the TV audience was estimated at one-quarter of the world's population—more than two billion people. Kate—a commoner William met at university—is now the

Duchess of Cambridge and will eventually become Britain's queen.

Their son, Prince George Alexander Louis, born in 2013—and later voted the most powerful and influential person in London by a poll in the *Evening Standard*—will ultimately succeed William as sovereign. (A conveniently timed change in the law ensured that William and Kate's firstborn would inherit the throne, regardless of gender.) In 2015, the couple welcomed the arrival of their second child, Princess Charlotte Elizabeth Diana, and in 2018, Prince Louis Arthur Charles.

William's brother, redheaded Prince Harry (b. 1984), has shaken his earlier reputation as a bad boy: He's proved his mettle as a career soldier, completing a tour in Afghanistan, doing charity work in Africa, and serving as an Apache aircraft commander pilot with the Army Air Corps. His marriage to American actress Meghan Markle—and the birth of their son Archie—added sparkle to the once-musty royals—at least until they stepped back from their royal duties.

Royal Sightseeing

You can see the trappings of royalty at Buckingham Palace (the Queen's London residence) with its Changing of the Guard; Kensington Palace—with a wing that's home to Will, Kate, and kids; Clarence House, the London home of Prince Charles and Camilla; Althorp Estate (80 miles from London), the childhood home and burial place of Princess  Diana; Windsor Castle, a royal country home near London that includes Frogmore Cottage where Harry and Meghan live; and the crown jewels in the Tower of London.

Your best chances to see the Queen are on three public occasions: State Opening of Parliament (on the first day of a new parliamentary session), Remembrance Sunday (early November, at the Cenotaph), or Trooping the Colour (one Saturday in mid-June, parading down Whitehall and at Buckingham Palace).

Otherwise, check www.royal.uk, where you can search for royal events.

Frasier, The Big Bang Theory, and trash-talk shows) are very popular. But the visiting viewer should be sure to tune the TV to more typically British shows, including a dose of British situation- and political-comedy fun, and the top-notch BBC evening news. British comedies have tickled the American funny bone for years, from sketch comedy *(Monty Python's Flying Circus)* to sitcoms (*Fawlty Towers, Blackadder, Red Dwarf, Absolutely Fabulous,* and *The Office*). Quiz shows and reality shows are taken very seriously here (*American Idol, America's Got Talent, Dancing with the Stars, Who Wants to Be a Millionaire?,* and *The X Factor* are all based on British shows). Jonathan Ross is the Jimmy Fallon of Britain for sometimes-edgy late-night talk. Other popular late-night "chat show" hosts include Graham Norton and Alan Carr. For a tear-filled, slice-of-life taste of British soaps dealing in all the controversial issues, see the popular and remarkably long-running *Emmerdale, Coronation Street,* or *EastEnders.* The costume drama *Downton Abbey,* the sci-fi serial *Doctor Who,* the small-town dramedy *Doc Martin,* and the modern crime series *Sherlock* have all become hits on both sides of the Atlantic.

WHAT'S SO GREAT ABOUT BRITAIN?

Brexit is the biggest challenge to the British way of life since the days of the Blitz. But it makes Britain no less Great. The Britain you visit today is vibrant and alive. It's smaller, and no longer the superpower it once was, but it's still a cultural and economic powerhouse.

Think of it. At its peak in the mid-1800s, Britain owned one-fifth of the world and accounted for more than half the planet's industrial output. Today, the Empire is down to the Isle of Britain itself and a few token scraps (the Falklands, Gibraltar, Northern Ireland) and a loose association of former colonies (Canada, Australia) called the "British Commonwealth."

Geographically, the Isle of Britain is small—smaller than the state of Oregon—and its highest mountain (Ben Nevis in Scotland at 4,411 feet) is a foothill by US standards. The population is a fifth that of the United States. Despite its size, Britain is the world's fifth-biggest economy, sixth-biggest manufacturer, and largest financial center (London). Twenty-six of the world's 500 largest companies are headquartered here.

The Britain you visit today remains a global superpower of heritage, culture, and tradition. It's a major exporter of actors, movies, and theater; of rock and classical music; and of writers, painters, and sculptors. It's the perfect place for you to visit and make your own history.

Architecture in Britain

From Stonehenge to Big Ben, travelers are storming castle walls, climbing spiral staircases, and snapping the pictures of 5,000 years of architecture. Let's sort it out.

The oldest ruins—mysterious and prehistoric—date from before Roman times back to 3000 BC The earliest sites, such as Stonehenge and Avebury, were built during the Stone and Bronze ages. The remains from these periods are made of huge stones or mounds of earth, even man-made hills, and were created as celestial calendars and for worship or burial. Britain is crisscrossed with imaginary lines said to connect these mysterious sights (ley lines). Iron Age people (600 BC-AD 50) left desolate stone forts. The Romans thrived in Britain from AD 50 to 400, building cities, walls, and roads. Evidence of Roman greatness can be seen in lavish villas with ornate mosaic floors, temples uncovered beneath great English churches, and Roman stones in medieval city walls. Roman roads sliced across the island in straight lines. Today, unusually straight rural roads are very likely laid directly on these ancient roads.

As Rome crumbled in the fifth century, so did Roman Britain. Little architecture survives from Dark Ages England, the Saxon period from 500 to 1000. Architecturally, the light was switched on with the Norman Conquest in 1066. As William earned his title "the Conqueror," his French architects built churches and castles in the European Romanesque style.

English Romanesque is called Norman (1066-1200). Norman churches had round arches, thick walls, and small windows; Durham Cathedral and the Chapel of St. John in the Tower of London are prime examples. The Tower of London, with its square keep, small windows, and spiral stone stairways, is a typical Norman castle. You can see plenty of Norman castles around England—all built to secure the conquest of these invaders from Normandy.

Typical Church Architecture

History comes to life when you visit a centuries-old church. Even if you wouldn't know your apse from a hole in the ground, learning a few simple terms will enrich your experience. Note that not every church has every feature, and that a "cathedral" isn't a type of church architecture, but rather a designation for a church that's a governing center for a local bishop.

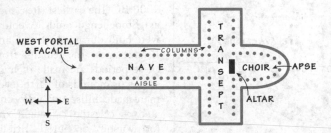

Aisles: The long, generally low-ceilinged arcades that flank the nave.

Altar: The raised area with a ceremonial table (often adorned with candles or a crucifix), where the priest prepares and serves the bread and wine for Communion.

Apse: The space beyond the altar, often bordered with small chapels.

Barrel Vault: A continuous round-arched ceiling that resembles an extended upside-down U.

Choir ("quire" in British English): A cozy area, often screened off, located within the church nave and near the high altar where services are sung in a more intimate setting.

Cloister: Covered hallways bordering a square or rectangular open-air courtyard, traditionally where monks and nuns got fresh air.

Facade: The exterior surface of the church's main (west) entrance, viewable from outside and usually highly decorated.

Groin Vault: An arched ceiling formed where two equal barrel vaults meet at right angles. Less common usage: term for a medieval jock strap.

Narthex: The area (portico or foyer) between the main entry and the nave.

Nave: The long, central section of the church (running west to east, from the entrance to the altar) where the congregation sits or stands through the service.

Transept: In a traditional cross-shaped floor plan, the transept is one of the two parts forming the "arms" of the cross. The transepts run north-south, perpendicularly crossing the east-west nave.

West Portal: The main entry to the church (on the west end, opposite the main altar).

Typical Castle Architecture

Castles were fortified residences for medieval nobles. Castles come in all shapes and sizes, but knowing a few general terms will help you understand them.

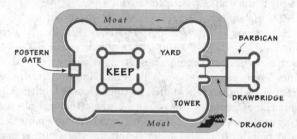

Barbican: A fortified gatehouse, sometimes a stand-alone building located outside the main walls.

Crenellation: A gap-toothed pattern of stones atop the parapet.

Drawbridge: A bridge that could be raised or lowered using counterweights or a chain and winch.

Great Hall: The largest room in the castle, serving as throne room, conference center, and dining hall.

Hoardings (or Gallery or Brattice): Wooden huts built onto the upper parts of the stone walls. They served as watchtowers, living quarters, and fighting platforms.

The Keep (or Donjon): A high, strong stone tower in the center of the castle complex; the lord's home and refuge of last resort.

Loopholes (or Embrasures): Narrow wall slits through which soldiers could shoot arrows.

Machicolation: A stone ledge jutting out from the wall, with holes through which soldiers could drop rocks or boiling oil onto wall-scaling enemies below.

Moat: A ditch encircling the wall, often filled with water.

Motte-and-Bailey: A type of early English castle, with a hilltop fort (motte) and an enclosed, fortified yard (bailey).

Parapet: Outer railing of the wall walk.

Portcullis: A heavy iron grille that could be lowered across the entrance.

Postern Gate: A small, unfortified side or rear entrance from which to launch attacks or escape.

Towers: Tall structures with crenellated tops or conical roofs serving as lookouts, chapels, living quarters, or dungeons.

Turret: A small lookout tower rising up from the top of the wall.

Wall Walk (or Allure): A pathway atop the wall where guards could patrol and where soldiers stood to fire at the enemy.

The Yard (or Bailey): An open courtyard inside the castle walls.

Gothic architecture (1200-1600) replaced the heavy Norman style with light, vertical buildings, pointed arches, soaring spires, and bigger windows. English Gothic is divided into three stages. Early English Gothic (1200-1300) features tall, simple spires; beautifully carved capitals; and elaborate chapter houses (such as the Wells Cathedral). Decorated Gothic (1300-1400) gets fancier, with more elaborate tracery, bigger windows, and ornately carved pinnacles, as you see at Westminster Abbey. Finally, the Perpendicular Gothic style (1400-1600, also called "rectilinear") returns to square towers and emphasizes straight, uninterrupted vertical lines from ceiling to floor, with vast windows and exuberant decoration, including fan-vaulted ceilings (King's College Chapel at Cambridge). Through this evolution, the structural ribs (arches meeting at the top of the ceilings) became more and more decorative and fanciful (the most fancy being the star vaulting and fan vaulting of the Perpendicular style).

As you tour the great medieval churches of Britain, remember that almost everything is symbolic. For instance, on the tombs of knights, if the figure has crossed legs, he was a Crusader. If his feet rest on a dog, he died at home; but if his legs rest on a lion, he died in battle. Local guides and books help us modern pilgrims understand at least a little of what we see.

Wales is particularly rich in English castles, which were needed to subdue the stubborn Welsh. Edward I built a ring of powerful castles in North Wales, including Conwy and Caernarfon.

Gothic houses were a simple mix of woven strips of thin wood, rubble, and plaster called wattle and daub. The famous black-and-white Tudor (or "half-timbered") look came simply from filling in heavy oak frames with wattle and daub.

The Tudor period (1485-1560) was a time of relative peace (the Wars of the Roses were finally over), prosperity, and renaissance. But when Henry VIII broke with the Catholic Church and disbanded its monasteries, scores of Britain's greatest churches were left as gutted shells. These hauntingly beautiful abbey ruins (Glastonbury, Tintern, Whitby, Rievaulx, Battle, St. Augustine's in Canterbury, St. Mary's in York, and lots more), surrounded by lush lawns, are now pleasant city parks.

Although few churches were built during the Tudor period, this was a time of house and mansion construction. Heating a home was becoming popular and affordable, and Tudor buildings featured small square windows and many chimneys. In towns, where land was scarce, many Tudor houses grew up and out, getting wider with each overhanging floor.

The Elizabethan and Jacobean periods (1560-1620) were followed by the English Renaissance style (1620-1720). English architects mixed Gothic and classical styles, then Baroque and classical styles. Although the ornate Baroque never really grabbed Britain, the classical style of the Italian architect Andrea Palladio did. Inigo Jones (1573-1652), Christopher Wren (1632-1723), and those they inspired plastered Britain with enough columns, domes, and symmetry to please a Caesar. The Great Fire of London (1666) cleared the way for an ambitious young Wren to put his mark on London forever with a grand rebuilding scheme, including the great St. Paul's Cathedral and more than 50 other churches.

The celebrants of the Boston Tea Party remember Britain's Georgian period (1720-1840) for its lousy German kings. But in architectural terms, "Georgian" is English for "Neoclassical." Its architecture was rich and showed off by being very classical. Grand ornamental doorways, fine cast-ironwork on balconies and railings, Chippendale furniture, and white-on-blue Wedgwood ceramics graced rich homes everywhere. John Wood Sr. and Jr. led the way, giving the trendsetting city of Bath its crescents and circles of aristocratic Georgian row houses.

The Industrial Revolution shaped the Victorian period (1840-1890) with glass, steel, and iron. Britain had a huge new erector set (so did France's Mr. Eiffel). This was also a Romantic period, reviving the "more Christian" Gothic style. London's Houses of Parliament are Neo-Gothic—they're just 140 years old but look 700, except for the telltale modern precision and craftsmanship. Whereas Gothic was stone or concrete, Neo-Gothic was often red brick. These were Britain's glory days, and there was more building in this period than in all previous ages combined.

The architecture of the mid-20th century obeyed the formula "form follows function"—it worried more about your needs than your eyes. But more recently, the dull "international style" has been nudged aside by a more playful style, thanks to cutting-edge architects such as Lord Norman Foster and Renzo Piano. In the last several years, London has made a point

of adding several creative buildings to its skyline: the City Hall (nicknamed "The Armadillo"), 30 St. Mary Axe ("The Gherkin"), 20 Fenchurch ("The Walkie-Talkie"), and the tallest building in

Western Europe, the pointy Shard London Bridge (called simply, "The Shard").

Even as it sets trends for the 21st century, Britain treasures its heritage and takes great pains to build tastefully in historic districts and to preserve its many "listed" (government-protected) buildings. With a booming tourist trade, these quaint reminders of its past— and ours—are becoming a valuable part of the British economy.

For more about British history, consider Europe 101: History and Art for the Traveler *by Rick Steves and Gene Openshaw, available at* www.ricksteves.com.

PRACTICALITIES

This chapter covers the practical skills of European travel: how to get tourist information, pay for things, sightsee efficiently, find good-value accommodations, eat affordably but well, use technology wisely, and get between destinations smoothly. For more information on these topics, see www.ricksteves.com/travel-tips.

Tourist Information

Before your trip, start with the Visit Britain website, which contains a wealth of knowledge on destinations, activities, accommodations, and transport in Great Britain (www.visitbritain.com). Transportation, sightseeing, and theater tickets can also be purchased (www.visitbritainshop.com/usa).

In Britain, a good first stop is generally the tourist information office (abbreviated **TI** in this book and locally as **TIC,** for "tourist information centre"). In London, the **City of London Information Centre,** near St. Paul's Cathedral, is helpful (see page 38).

TIs are in business to help you enjoy spending money in their town, but even so, I still make a point to swing by to pick up a city map and get information on public transit, walking tours, special events, and nightlife. Anticipating a harried front-line staffer, prepare a list of questions and a proposed plan to double-check. Some TIs have information on the entire country or at least the region, so try to pick up maps and printed information for destinations you'll be visiting later in your trip.

Due to funding constraints, some of Britain's TIs are struggling; village TIs may be staffed by volunteers who need to charge you for maps and informational brochures.

Travel Tips

Emergency and Medical Help: For any emergency service—ambulance, police, or fire—call **112** from a mobile phone or landline. Operators will deal with your request or route you to the right emergency service. If you get sick, do as the locals do and go to a pharmacy and see a "chemist" (pharmacist) for advice. Or ask at your hotel for help—they'll know of the nearest medical and emergency services.

ETIAS Registration: Beginning in 2021, US and Canadian citizens may be required to register online with the European Travel Information and Authorization System (ETIAS) before entering certain European countries (quick and easy process, $8 fee, valid 3 years). A useful private website with more details is www.schengenvisainfo.com/etias.

Theft or Loss: To replace a passport, you'll need to go in person to an embassy (see next). If your credit and debit cards disappear, cancel and replace them (see "Damage Control for Lost Cards" on page 907). File a police report, either on the spot or within a day or two; you'll need it to submit an insurance claim for lost or stolen rail passes or electronics, and it can help with replacing your passport or credit and debit cards. For more information, see www.ricksteves.com/help.

US Consulate and Embassy: Tel. 020/7499-9000 (all services), no walk-in passport services; for emergency two-day passport service, schedule an appointment or fill out the online Emergency Passport Contact Form, 24 Grosvenor Square, London, Tube: Bond Street, uk.usembassy.gov.

High Commission of Canada in London: Tel. 020/7004-6000, passport services available Mon-Fri 9:30-12:30, Canada House, Trafalgar Square, London, Tube: Charing Cross, www.unitedkingdom.gc.ca.

Time Zones: Britain is five/eight hours ahead of the East/West Coasts of the US—and one hour earlier than most of continental Europe. The exceptions are the beginning and end of Daylight Saving Time: Europe "springs forward" the last Sunday in March (two weeks after most of North America), and "falls back" the last Sunday in October (one week before North America). For a handy time converter, use the world clock app on your phone or download one (see www.timeanddate.com/worldclock).

Business Hours: Most stores are open Monday through Saturday (roughly 9:00 or 10:00 to 17:00 or 18:00). In cities, some stores stay open later on Wednesday or Thursday (until 19:00 or 20:00). Some big-city department stores are open later throughout the week (Mon-Sat until about 21:00). Sundays have the same pros and cons as they do for travelers in the US: Sightseeing attractions are generally open, many street markets are lively with shoppers, banks and many shops are closed, public transportation options are fewer (for example, no bus service to or from smaller towns), and there's no rush hour.

Watt's Up? Britain's electrical system is 220 volts, instead of North America's 110 volts. Most electronics (laptops, smartphones, cameras) and newer hair dryers convert automatically, so you won't need a converter, but you will need an adapter plug with three square prongs, sold inexpensively at travel stores in the US. Avoid bringing older appliances that don't automatically convert voltage; instead, buy a cheap substitute in Britain.

Discounts: Discounts (called "concessions" or "concs" in Britain) for sights are generally not listed in this book. However, seniors (age 65 and over), youths under 18, and students and teachers with proper identification cards (obtain from www.isic.org) can get discounts at many sights—always ask. Some discounts are available only for British citizens.

Money

Here's my basic strategy for using money in Europe:

- Upon arrival, head for a cash machine (ATM) at the airport and withdraw some local currency, using a debit card with low international transaction fees.
- In general, pay for bigger expenses with a credit card and use cash for smaller purchases. Use a debit card only for cash withdrawals.
- Keep your cash safe in a money belt.

PLASTIC VERSUS CASH

Although credit cards are widely accepted in Europe, cash is sometimes the only way to pay for cheap food, taxis, tips, and local

Exchange Rate

1 British pound (£1) = about $1.30

Britain uses the pound sterling. The British pound (£), also called a "quid," is broken into 100 pence (p). Pence means "cents." You'll find coins ranging from 1p to £2 and bills from £5 to £50.

To convert prices from pounds to dollars, add about 30 percent: £20=about $26, £50=about $65. (Check www.oanda.com for the latest exchange rates.)

guides. Some businesses (especially smaller ones, such as B&Bs and mom-and-pop cafés and shops) may charge you extra for using a credit card—or might not accept credit cards at all. Having cash on hand helps you out of a jam if your card randomly doesn't work.

I use my credit card to book and pay for hotel reservations, to buy advance tickets for events or sights, and to cover most other expenses. It can also be smart to use plastic near the end of your trip, to avoid another visit to the ATM.

WHAT TO BRING

I pack the following and keep it all safe in my money belt.

Debit Card: Use this at ATMs to withdraw local cash.

Credit Card: Handy for bigger transactions (at hotels, shops, restaurants, travel agencies, car-rental agencies, and so on), payment machines, and online purchases.

Backup Card: Some travelers carry a third card (debit or credit; ideally from a different bank), in case one gets lost, demagnetized, eaten by a temperamental machine, or simply doesn't work.

Stash of Cash: I carry $100-200 in US dollars as a cash backup, which comes in handy in an emergency (such as when banks go on strike or if your ATM card gets eaten by the machine).

What NOT to Bring: Resist the urge to buy pounds before your trip or you'll pay the price in bad stateside exchange rates. Wait until you arrive to withdraw money. I've yet to see a European airport that didn't have plenty of ATMs.

BEFORE YOU GO

Use this pre-trip checklist.

Know your cards. Debit cards from any major US bank will work in any standard European bank's ATM (ideally, use a debit card with a Visa or MasterCard logo). As for credit cards, Visa and MasterCard are universal, American Express is less common, and Discover is unknown in Europe.

PRACTICALITIES

Know your PIN. Make sure you know the numeric, four-digit PIN for all of your cards, both debit and credit. Request it if you don't have one, as it may be required for some purchases in Europe (see "Using Credit Cards," later), and allow time to receive the information by mail.

Report your travel dates. Let your bank know that you'll be using your debit and credit cards in Europe, and when and where you're headed.

Adjust your ATM withdrawal limit. Find out how much you can take out daily and ask for a higher daily withdrawal limit if you want to get more cash at once. Note that European ATMs will withdraw funds only from checking accounts; you're unlikely to have access to your savings account.

Ask about fees. For any purchase or withdrawal made with a card, you may be charged a currency conversion fee (1-3 percent) and/or a Visa or MasterCard international transaction fee (less than 1 percent). If you're getting a bad deal, consider getting a new debit or credit card. Reputable no-fee cards include those from Capital One, as well as Charles Schwab debit cards. Most credit unions and some airline loyalty cards have low or no international transaction fees.

IN EUROPE
Using Cash Machines

European cash machines work just like they do at home—except they spit out local currency instead of dollars, calculated at the day's standard bank-to-bank rate.

In most places, ATMs are easy to locate—in Britain ask for a "cashpoint." When possible, withdraw cash from a bank-run ATM located just outside that bank. Ideally, use the machine during the bank's opening hours, so you can go inside for help if your card is munched.

If your debit card doesn't work, try a lower amount—your request may have exceeded your withdrawal limit or the ATM's limit. If you still have a problem, try a different ATM or come back later—your bank's network may be temporarily down.

Avoid "independent" ATMs, such as Travelex, Euronet, Moneybox, Your Cash, Cardpoint, and Cashzone. These have high fees, can be less secure than a bank ATM, and may try to trick users with "dynamic currency conversion" (see later).

Exchanging Cash

Avoid exchanging money in Europe; it's a big rip-off. In a pinch you can always find exchange desks at major train stations or airports—convenient but with crummy rates. Anything over 5 percent for a transaction is piracy. Banks generally do not exchange money unless you have an account with them.

Using Credit Cards

Despite some differences between European and US cards, there's little to worry about: US credit cards generally work fine in Europe. I've been inconvenienced a few times by self-service payment machines that wouldn't accept my card, but it's never caused me serious trouble (I carry cash just in case).

European cards use chip-and-PIN technology; most chip cards issued in the US instead have a signature option. Some European card readers will accept your card as-is while others may generate a receipt for you to sign or prompt you to enter your PIN (so it's important to know the code for each of your cards). If a cashier is present, you should have no problems.

At self-service payment machines (transit-ticket kiosks, parking, etc.), results are mixed, as US cards may not work in some unattended transactions. If your card won't work, look for a cashier who can process your card manually—or pay in cash.

Drivers Beware: Be aware of potential problems using a US credit card to fill up at an unattended gas station, enter a parking garage, or exit a toll road. Always carry cash as a back-up and be prepared to move on to the next gas station if necessary. When approaching a toll plaza, use the "cash" lane.

Dynamic Currency Conversion

If merchants offer to convert your purchase price into dollars (called dynamic currency conversion, or DCC), refuse this "service." You'll pay extra for the expensive convenience of seeing your charge in dollars. If an ATM offers to "lock in" or "guarantee" your conversion rate, choose "proceed without conversion." Other prompts might state, "You can be charged in dollars: Press YES for dollars, NO for pounds." Always choose the local currency.

Security Tips

Even in "Jollie Olde Britain," pickpockets target tourists. Keep your cash, credit cards, and passport secure in your money belt, and carry only a day's spending money in your front pocket or wallet.

Before inserting your card into an ATM, inspect the front. If anything looks crooked, loose, or damaged, it could be a sign of a card-skimming device. When entering your PIN, carefully block other people's view of the keypad.

Don't use a debit card for purchases. Because a debit card pulls funds directly from your bank account, potential charges incurred by a thief will stay on your account while the fraudulent use is investigated by your bank.

While traveling, to access your accounts online, be sure to use a secure connection (see the "Tips on Internet Security" sidebar, later).

Damage Control for Lost Cards

If you lose your credit or debit card, report the loss immediately to the respective global customer-assistance centers. With a mobile phone, call these 24-hour US numbers: Visa (tel. +1 303/967-1096), MasterCard (tel. +1 636/722-7111), and American Express (tel. +1 336/393-1111). From a landline, you can call these US numbers collect by going through a local operator. European toll-free numbers can be found at the websites for Visa and MasterCard.

You'll need to provide the primary cardholder's identification-verification details (such as birth date, mother's maiden name, or Social Security number). You can generally receive a temporary card within two or three business days in Europe (see www. ricksteves.com/help for more).

If you report your loss within two days, you typically won't be responsible for unauthorized transactions on your account, although many banks charge a liability fee.

TIPPING

Tipping in Britain isn't as automatic and generous as it is in the US. For special service, tips are appreciated, but not expected. As in the US, the proper amount depends on your resources, tipping philosophy, and the circumstances, but some general guidelines apply.

Restaurants: It's not necessary to tip if a service charge is included in the bill (common in London—usually 12.5 percent). Otherwise, it's appropriate to tip about 10-12 percent for good service. For details on tipping in restaurants, see page 925.

Taxis: For a typical ride, round up your fare a bit (maximum 10 percent; for instance, if the fare is £7.40, pay £8). If the cabbie hauls your bags and zips you to the airport to help you catch your flight, you may want to toss in a little more. But if you feel like you're being driven in circles or otherwise ripped off, skip the tip.

Services: In general, if someone in the tourism or service industry does a super job for you, a small tip of a pound or two is appropriate...but not required. If you're not sure whether (or how much) to tip, ask a local for advice.

GETTING A VAT REFUND

Wrapped into the purchase price of your British souvenirs is a value-added tax (VAT) of about 20 percent. You're entitled to get most of that tax back if you purchase more than £30 (about $40) worth of goods at a store that participates in the VAT-refund scheme (although individual stores can require that you spend more—Harrods, for example, won't process a refund unless you spend £50). Typically, you must ring up the minimum at a single retailer—you can't add up your purchases from various shops to reach the required amount. (If the store ships the goods to your US home, VAT is not assessed on your purchase.)

Getting your refund is straightforward...and worthwhile if you spend a significant amount on souvenirs.

Get the paperwork. Have the merchant completely fill out the necessary refund document (either an official VAT customs form, or the shop or refund company's own version of it). You'll have to present your passport. Get the paperwork done before you leave the shop to ensure you'll have everything you need (including your original sales receipt).

Get your stamp at the border or airport. Process your VAT document at your last stop in the European Union (such as at the airport) with the customs agent who deals with VAT refunds. Arrive an additional hour before you need to check in to allow time to find the customs office—and wait. Some customs desks are positioned before airport security; confirm the location before going through security.

It's best to keep your purchases in your carry-on. If your item (such as a knife) isn't allowed as carry-on, pack it in your checked bag and alert the check-in agent. You'll be sent (with your tagged bag) to a customs desk outside security; someone will examine your bag, stamp your paperwork, and put your bag on the belt. You're not supposed to use your purchased goods before you leave. If you show up at customs wearing your new Wellingtons, officials might look the other way—or deny you a refund.

Collect your refund. You can claim your VAT refund from refund companies, such as Global Blue or Planet, with offices at major airports, ports, or border crossings (either before or after security, probably strategically located near a duty-free shop). These services (which extract a 4 percent fee) can refund your money in cash immediately or credit your card. Otherwise, mail the stamped refund documents to the address given by the shop where you made your purchase.

CUSTOMS FOR AMERICAN SHOPPERS

You can take home $800 worth of items per person duty-free, once every 31 days. Many processed and packaged foods are allowed, including vacuum-packed cheeses, dried herbs, jams, baked goods, candy, chocolate, oil, vinegar, mustard, and honey. Fresh fruits and vegetables and most meats are not allowed, with exceptions for some canned items. As for alcohol, you can bring in one liter duty-free (it can be packed securely in your checked luggage, along with any other liquid-containing items).

To bring alcohol (or liquid-packed foods) in your carry-on bag on your flight home, buy it at a duty-free shop at the airport. You'll increase your odds of getting it onto a connecting flight if it's packaged in a "STEB"—a secure, tamper-evident bag. But stay away from liquids in opaque, ceramic, or metallic containers, which usually cannot be successfully screened (STEB or no STEB).

For details on allowable goods, customs rules, and duty rates, visit www.help.cbp.gov.

Sightseeing

Sightseeing can be hard work. Use these tips to make your visits to England's finest sights meaningful, fun, efficient, and painless.

MAPS AND NAVIGATION TOOLS

A good map is essential for efficient navigation while sightseeing. The maps in this book are concise and simple, designed to help you locate recommended destinations, sights, and local TIs, where you can pick up more in-depth maps. Maps with even more detail are sold at newsstands and bookstores.

The *Rick Steves Britain, Ireland & London City Map* is useful for planning ($9, www.ricksteves.com). For those visiting London, *Bensons London Street Map* is my favorite for efficient sightseeing and might be the best £4 you'll spend. I also like the *Handy London Map and Guide* version, which shows every little lane and all the sights, and comes with a transit map. Many Londoners, along with obsessive-compulsive tourists, rely on the highly detailed *London A-Z* map book (generally £5-7, called "A to Zed" by locals, available at newsstands).

You can also use a mapping app on your mobile device. Be aware that pulling up maps or looking up turn-by-turn walking directions on the fly requires a data connection: To use this feature, it's smart to get an international data plan. With Google Maps or City Maps 2Go, it's possible to download a map while online, then go offline and navigate without incurring data-roaming charges, though you can't search for an address or get real-time walking directions. A handful of other apps—including Apple Maps and Navmii—also allow you to use maps offline.

PLAN AHEAD

Set up an itinerary that allows you to fit in all your must-see sights. For a one-stop look at opening hours, see the "At a Glance" sidebars for London, Cornwall, Bath, the Cotswolds, Liverpool, the Lake District, and York. Most sights keep stable hours, but you can easily confirm the latest by checking with the TI or visiting museum websites.

PRACTICALITIES

Don't put off visiting a must-see sight—you never know when a place will close unexpectedly for a holiday, strike, or royal audience. Many museums are closed or have reduced hours at least a few days a year, especially on holidays such as Christmas, New Year's, and Bank Holiday Mondays in May and August. A list of holidays is in the appendix; check for possible closures during your trip. In summer, some sights may stay open late. In the off-season, hours may be shorter.

Going at the right time helps avoid crowds. This book offers tips on the best times to see specific sights. Try visiting popular sights very early or very late. Evening visits (when possible) are usually peaceful, with fewer crowds. Late morning is usually the worst time to visit a popular sight.

If you plan to hire a local guide, reserve ahead by email. Popular guides can get booked up.

Study up. To get the most out of the self-guided tours and sight descriptions in this book, read them before you visit. The British Museum rocks if you understand the significance of the Rosetta Stone.

RESERVATIONS AND ADVANCE TICKETS

Given how precious your vacation time is, I recommend getting reservations for any must-see sight that offers them (see page 29).

To deal with lines, many popular sights sell advance tickets that guarantee admission at a certain time of day, or that allow you to skip entry lines. Either way, it's worth giving up some spontaneity to book in advance. While hundreds of tourists sweat in long ticket-buying lines, those who've booked ahead can get in quicker. In some cases, getting a ticket in advance simply means buying your ticket earlier on the same day. But for other sights, you may need to book weeks or even months in advance. As soon as you're ready to commit to a certain date, book it.

The advance-purchase price is often less expensive than what you would pay on-site. And many museums offer convenient mobile ticketing. Simply buy your ticket online and send it to your phone, eliminating the need for a paper ticket.

SIGHTSEEING PASSES

Many sights in England are managed by either English Heritage or the National Trust. Each organization has a combo-deal that can save some money for busy sightseers.

Membership in **English Heritage** includes free entry to more than 400 sights in England and discounted or free admission to about 100 more sights in Scotland and Wales. For most travelers, the **Overseas Visitor Pass** is a better choice than the pricier one-year membership (Visitor Pass: £35/9 days, £42/16 days, discounts for couples and families; membership: £56 for one person, £99 for two, discounts for families, seniors, and students, children under 19 free, www.english-heritage.org.uk/membership; tel. 0370-333-1181).

Membership in the **National Trust** is best suited for garden-and-estate enthusiasts, ideally those traveling by car. It covers more than 350 historic houses, manors, and gardens throughout Great Britain, including 100 properties in Scotland. From the US, it's easy to join online through the Royal Oak Foundation, the National Trust's American affiliate (one-year membership: $80 for one person, $125 for two, family and student memberships, www.royal-oak.org). For more on National Trust properties, see www.nationaltrust.org.uk.

Factors to Consider: An advantage to these deals is that you'll feel free to dip into lesser sights without considering the cost of admission. But remember that your kids already get in free or cheaply at most places, and people over 60 get discounted prices at many sights. If you're traveling by car and can get to the remote sights, you're more likely to get your money's worth out of a pass or membership, especially during peak season (Easter-Oct), when all the sights are open.

AT SIGHTS

Here's what you can typically expect:

Entering: You may not be allowed to enter if you arrive too close to closing time. And guards start ushering people out well before the actual closing time, so don't save the best for last.

Many sights have a security check. Allow extra time for these lines. Some sights require you to check daypacks and coats. (If you'd rather not check your daypack, try carrying it tucked under your arm like a purse as you enter.)

At ticket desks, you may see references to "Gift Aid"—a tax-deduction scheme that benefits museums—but this only concerns UK taxpayers.

Photography: If the museum's photo policy isn't clearly posted, ask a guard. Generally, taking photos without a flash or tripod is allowed. Some sights ban selfie sticks; others ban photos altogether.

Audioguides and Apps: Many sights rent audioguides with excellent recorded descriptions (about £5). If you bring your own earbuds, you can often enjoy better sound. If you don't mind being tethered to your travel partner, you'll save money by bringing a Y-jack and sharing one audioguide. Museums and sights often offer free apps that you can download to your mobile device (check their websites). And, I've produced free, downloadable audio tours for my Westminster Walk, the British Museum, the British Library,

Harry Potter Sights

Harry Potter's story is set in a magical, largely fictional Britain, but you can visit many real locations used in the film series. Other settings, like Diagon Alley, exist only at Leavesden Film Studios (north of London; see page 143).

London

Harry first realizes his wizard powers in *The Sorcerer's Stone* (2001) when talking with a snake at the **London Zoo**'s Reptile House. Later, Harry shops for school supplies in the glass-roofed **Leadenhall Market.**

In *The Chamber of Secrets* (2002), Harry catches the train to Hogwarts wizarding school at **King's Cross Station** from the fictional Platform 9¾. (For a fun photo-op, head to King's Cross Station's track 9 to find the *Platform 9¾* sign, the luggage cart that looks like it's disappearing into the wall, a Harry Potter gift shop...and a 30-minute wait in line to snap a photo.)

In *The Prisoner of Azkaban* (2004), a three-decker bus dumps Harry at the Leaky Cauldron pub, shot on rough-looking

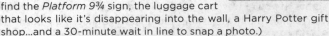

St. Paul's Cathedral, and Historic London: The City Walk; look for the 𝛀 symbol in this book. For more on my audio tours, see page 30.

Guided tours are most likely to occur during peak season (either for free or a small fee—figure £5-10—and widely ranging in quality). Some sights also run short introductory videos featuring their highlights and history. These are generally well worth your time and a great place to start your visit.

Temporary Exhibits: Museums may show special exhibits in addition to their permanent collection. Some exhibits are included in the entry price, while others come at an extra cost (which you may have to pay even if you don't want to see the exhibit).

Expect Changes: Artwork can be on tour, on loan, out sick, or shifted at the whim of the curator. Pick up a floor plan as you enter, and ask museum staff if you can't find a particular item.

Services: Important sights and cathedrals usually have a reasonably priced on-site café or cafeteria (handy places to rejuvenate during a long visit—try a cheap "cream tea" to pick up your energy in midafternoon, like Brits do). The WCs at sights are free and generally clean.

Before Leaving: At the gift shop, scan the postcard rack or thumb through a guidebook to be sure that you haven't overlooked

Stoney Street at the southeast edge of **Borough Market.**

When the Order takes to the night sky on broomsticks in *The Order of the Phoenix* (2007), they pass over plenty of identifiable landmarks, including the **London Eye, Big Ben,** and **Buckingham Palace.** The **Millennium Bridge** collapses into the Thames in the dramatic finale to *The Half-Blood Prince* (2009). The real government offices of **Whitehall** serve as exteriors for the Ministry of Magic.

Elsewhere in England

Near Bath: In *The Sorcerer's Stone,* Harry is chosen for Gryffindor's Quidditch team in the halls of the 13th-century **Lacock Abbey.** Harry attends Professor Snape's class in one of the abbey's peeling-plaster rooms.

Oxford: Christ Church College provided the model for Hogwarts' Great Hall. In *The Sorcerer's Stone,* Harry sneaks under a cloak of invisibility into the Hogwarts Library (really Duke Humfrey's Library), and he awakens in the Hogwarts infirmary (the big-windowed Divinity School of the Bodleian Library).

Northeast England: In *The Sorcerer's Stone,* Harry walks with his white owl, Hedwig, through a snowy courtyard in Durham's Cathedral.

something that you'd like to see. Every sight or museum offers more than what is covered in this book. Use the information I provide as an introduction—not the final word.

Sleeping

Extensive and opinionated listings of good-value rooms are a major feature of this book's Sleeping sections. Rather than list accommodations scattered throughout a town, I choose places in my favorite neighborhoods that are convenient to your sightseeing.

My recommendations run the gamut, from dorm beds to fancy rooms with all the comforts. I like places that are clean, central, relatively quiet at night, reasonably priced, friendly, small enough to have a hands-on owner or manager, and run with a respect for British traditions. I'm more impressed by a handy location and fun-loving philosophy than flat-screen TVs and a

PRACTICALITIES

Sleep Code

Hotels in this book are categorized according to the average price of a standard double room with breakfast in high season.

$$$$	**Splurge:** Most rooms over £160
$$$	**Pricier:** £120-160
$$	**Moderate:** £80-120
$	**Budget:** £40-80
¢	**Backpacker:** Under £40
RS%	**Rick Steves discount**

Unless otherwise noted, credit cards are accepted and free Wi-Fi is available. Comparison-shop by checking prices at several hotels (on each hotel's own website, on a booking site, or by email). For the best deal, *book directly with the hotel*. Ask for a discount if paying in cash; if the listing includes **RS%**, request a Rick Steves discount.

---

fancy gym. Most of my recommendations fall short of perfection. But if I can find a place with most of these features, it's a keeper.

Book your accommodations as soon as your itinerary is set, especially if you want to stay at one of my top listings or if you'll be traveling during busy times. See the appendix for a list of major holidays and festivals in Great Britain.

Some people make reservations as they travel, calling or emailing ahead a few days to a week before their arrival. If you're trying for a same-day reservation, it's best to call hotels at about 9:00 or 10:00, when the receptionist knows which rooms will be available. Some apps—such as HotelTonight.com—specialize in last-minute rooms, often at boutique or business-class hotels in big cities.

RATES AND DEALS

I've categorized my recommended accommodations based on price, indicated with a dollar-sign rating (see sidebar). The price ranges suggest an estimated cost for a one-night stay in high season in a standard double room with a private toilet and shower, and assume you're booking directly with the hotel (not through a booking site, which extracts a commission). Room prices can fluctuate significantly with demand and amenities (size, views, room class, and so on), but relative price categories remain constant. In London, breakfast is often not included in quoted hotel rates; you can opt out of the pricey hotel breakfast and get it on your own for less.

In Britain, small bed-and-breakfast places (B&Bs) generally provide the best value, though I also include some bigger hotels. Britain has a rating system for hotels and B&Bs. Its stars are supposed to imply quality, but I find they mean only that the place is paying dues to the tourist board. Rating systems often have little to do with value.

Room rates can be volatile at larger hotels that use "dynamic pricing" to set rates. Prices can skyrocket during festivals and conventions, while business hotels can have deep discounts on weekends when demand plummets. Of the many hotels I recommend, it's difficult to say which will be the best value on a given day—until you do your homework.

Booking Direct: Once your dates are set, compare prices at several hotels. You can do this by checking Hotels.com or Booking.com, and hotel websites. Then book directly with the hotel itself. Contact small family-run hotels directly by phone or email. When you go direct, the owner avoids the commission paid to booking sites, thereby leaving enough wiggle room to offer you a discount, a nicer room, or a free breakfast (if it's not already included). If you prefer to book online or are considering a hotel chain, it's to your advantage to use the hotel's website. When establishing prices, confirm if the charge is per person or per room (if a price is too good to be true, it's probably per person).

Booking directly also increases the chances that the hotelier will be able to accommodate any special needs or requests (such as shifting your reservation). Going through a middleman makes it more difficult for the hotel to adjust your booking.

Getting a Discount: Some hotels extend a discount to those who pay cash or stay longer than three nights. And some accommodations offer a special discount for Rick Steves readers, indicated in this guidebook by the abbreviation **RS%**. Discounts vary: Ask for details when you reserve. Generally, to qualify for this discount, you must book direct (not through a booking site), mention this book when you reserve, show this book upon arrival, and sometimes pay cash or stay a certain number of nights. In some cases, you may need to enter a discount code (which I've provided in the listing) in the booking form on the hotel's website. Rick Steves discounts apply to readers with either print or digital books. Understandably, discounts do not apply to promotional rates.

Staying in B&Bs and small hotels can save money over sleeping in big hotels. Chain hotels can be even cheaper, but they don't include breakfast. When comparing prices between chain hotels and B&Bs, remember you're getting two breakfasts (about a £25 value) for each double room at a B&B.

TYPES OF ACCOMMODATIONS
Hotels
In cities, you'll find big, Old-World elegant hotels with modern amenities, as well as familiar-feeling business-class and boutique

Using Online Services to Your Advantage

From booking services to user reviews, online businesses play a greater role in travelers' planning than ever before. Take advantage of their pluses—and be wise to their downsides.

Booking Sites

Booking websites such as Booking.com and Hotels.com offer one-stop shopping for hotels. While convenient for travelers, they present a real problem for independent, family-run hotels. Without a presence on these sites, small hotels become almost invisible. But to be listed, a hotel must pay a sizeable commission... and promise that its own website won't undercut the price on the booking-service site.

Here's the work-around: Use the big sites to research what's out there, then book direct with the hotel by email or phone, in which case hotel owners are free to give you whatever price they like. Ask for a room without the commission mark-up (or ask for a free breakfast if not included, or a free upgrade). If you do book online, be sure to use the hotel's website. The price will likely be the same as via a booking site, but your money goes to the hotel, not agency commissions.

As a savvy consumer, remember: When you book with an online booking service, you're adding a middleman who takes roughly 20 percent. To support small, family-run hotels whose world is more difficult than ever, book direct.

Short-Term Rental Sites

Rental juggernaut Airbnb (along with other short-term rental sites) allows travelers to rent rooms and apartments directly from locals, often providing more value than a cookie-cutter hotel. Airbnb fans appreciate feeling part of a real neighborhood and getting into a daily routine as "temporary Europeans." Depending on the host, Airbnb can provide an opportunity to get

hotels no different from what you may experience at home. But you'll also find hotels that are more uniquely European.

Outside of pricey big cities, you can expect to find good doubles for £80-120 (about $105-155), including cooked breakfasts and tax. Bigger cities, swanky B&Bs, and big hotels generally cost significantly more.

A "twin" room has two single beds; a "double" has one double bed. If you'll take either, let the hotel know, or you might be needlessly turned away. Some hotels can add an extra bed (for a small charge) to turn a double into a triple; some offer larger rooms for four or more people (I call these "family rooms" in the listings). If there's space for an extra cot, they'll cram it in for you. In general, a

PRACTICALITIES

to know a local person, while keeping the money spent on your accommodations in the community.

Critics view Airbnb as a threat to "traditional Europe," saying it creates unfair, unqualified competition for established guesthouse owners. In some places, the lucrative Airbnb market has forced traditional guesthouses out of business and is driving property values out of range for locals. Some cities have cracked down, requiring owners to occupy rental properties part of the year (and staging disruptive "inspections" that inconvenience guests).

As a lover of Europe, I share the worry of those who see residents nudged aside by tourists. But as an advocate for travelers, I appreciate the value and cultural intimacy Airbnb provides.

User Reviews

User-generated review sites and apps such as Yelp and TripAdvisor can give you a consensus of opinions about everything from hotels and restaurants to sights and nightlife. If you scan reviews of a restaurant or hotel and see several complaints about noise or a rotten location, you've gained insight that can help in your decision-making.

But as a guidebook writer, my sense is that there is a big difference between the uncurated information on a review site and the vetted listings in a guidebook. A user-generated review is based on the limited experience of one person, who stayed at just one hotel in a given city and ate at a few restaurants there. A guidebook is the work of a trained researcher who forms a well-developed basis for comparison by visiting many restaurants and hotels year after year.

Both types of information have their place, and in many ways, they're complementary. If something is well reviewed in a guidebook and also gets good online reviews, it's likely a winner.

triple room is cheaper than the cost of a double and a single. Three or four people can economize by requesting one big room.

An "en suite" room has a bathroom (toilet and shower/tub) attached to the room; a room with a "private bathroom" can mean that the bathroom is all yours, but it's across the hall. If you want your own bathroom inside the room, request "en suite." If money's tight, ask about a room with a shared bathroom. You'll almost always have a sink in your room, and as more rooms go en suite, the hallway bathroom is shared with fewer guests.

Note that to be called a "hotel," a place technically must have certain amenities, including a 24-hour reception (though this rule is loosely applied).

Modern Hotel Chains: Chain hotels—common in bigger cities all over Great Britain—can be a great value (£60-100, depending on location and season; more expensive in London). These hotels are about as cozy as a Motel 6, but they come with private showers/WCs, elevators, good security, and often an attached restaurant. Branches are often located near the train station, on major highways, or outside the city center.

This option is especially worth considering for families, as kids often stay for free. While most of these hotels have 24-hour reception and elevators, breakfast and Wi-Fi generally cost extra, and the service lacks a personal touch (at some, you'll check in at a self-service kiosk). When comparing your options, keep in mind that for about the same price, you can get a basic room at a B&B that has less predictable comfort but more funkiness and friendliness in a more enjoyable neighborhood.

Room rates change from day to day with volume and vary depending on how far ahead you book. The best deals generally must be prepaid a few weeks ahead and may not be refundable—read the fine print carefully.

The biggest chains are **Premier Inn** (www.premierinn.com) and **Travelodge** (www.travelodge.co.uk). Both have attractive deals for prepaid or advance bookings. Other chains operating in Britain include the Irish **Jurys Inn** (www.jurysinns.com) and the French-owned **Ibis** (www.ibishotel.com). Couples can consider **Holiday Inn Express,** which generally allows only two people per room. It's like a Holiday Inn lite, with cheaper prices and no restaurant (make sure Express is part of the name or you'll be paying more for a regular Holiday Inn, www.hiexpress.co.uk).

Arrival and Check-In: Hotels and B&Bs are sometimes located on the higher floors of a multipurpose building with a secured door. In that case, look for your hotel's name on the buttons by the main entrance. When you ring the bell, you'll be buzzed in.

Hotel elevators are common, though some older buildings still lack them. You may have to climb a flight of stairs to reach the elevator (if so, you can ask the front desk for help carrying your bags up). Elevators are typically very small—pack light, or you may need to send your bags up without you.

The EU requires that hotels collect your name, nationality, and ID number. When you check in, the receptionist will normally ask for your passport and may keep it for anywhere from a couple of minutes to a couple of hours. If you're not comfortable leaving your passport at the desk for a long time, ask when you can pick it up. Or, if you packed a color photocopy of your passport, you can generally leave that rather than the original.

If you're arriving in the morning, your room probably won't

be ready. Check your bag safely at the hotel and dive right into sightseeing.

In Your Room: Most hotel rooms have a TV, telephone, and free Wi-Fi (although in old buildings with thick walls, the Wi-Fi signal might be available only in the lobby). Simpler places rarely have a room phone.

More pillows and blankets are usually in the closet or available on request. Towels and linens aren't always replaced every day.

Air-conditioning isn't a given (I've noted which of my listings have it), but most places have fans.

Electrical outlets may have switches that turn the current on or off; if your appliance isn't working, flip the switch at the outlet.

Breakfast and Meals: Your room cost usually includes a traditional full cooked breakfast (fry-up) or a lighter, healthier continental breakfast.

Checking Out: While it's customary to pay for your room upon departure, it can be a good idea to settle your bill the day before, when you're not in a hurry and while the manager's in.

Hotelier Help: Hoteliers can be a good source of advice. Most know their city well, and can assist you with everything from public transit and airport connections to finding a good restaurant, the nearest launderette, or a late-night pharmacy.

Hotel Hassles: Even at the best places, mechanical breakdowns occur: Sinks leak, hot water turns cold, toilets may gurgle or smell, the Wi-Fi goes out, or the air-conditioning dies when you need it most. Report your concerns clearly and calmly at the front desk.

If you find that night noise is a problem (if, for instance, your room is over a noisy pub or facing a busy street), ask for a quieter room in the back or on an upper floor. To guard against theft in your room, keep valuables out of sight. Some rooms come with a safe, and other hotels have safes at the front desk. I've never bothered using one and in a lifetime of travel, I've never had anything stolen from my room.

For more complicated problems, don't expect instant results. Above all, keep a positive attitude. Remember, you're on vacation. If your hotel is a disappointment, spend more time out enjoying the place you came to see.

B&Bs and Small Hotels

B&Bs and small hotels are generally family-run places with fewer amenities but more character than a conventional hotel. They range from large inns with 15-20 rooms to small homes renting out a spare bedroom. Places named "guesthouse" or "B&B" typically have eight or fewer rooms. The philosophy of the management determines the character of a place more than its size and amenities.

Making Hotel Reservations

Reserve your rooms as soon as you've pinned down your travel dates. For busy national holidays, it's wise to reserve far in advance (see the appendix).

Requesting a Reservation: For family-run hotels, it's generally best to book your room directly via email or phone. For business-class and chain hotels, or if you'd rather book online, reserve directly through the hotel's official website (not a booking website).

Here's what the hotelier wants to know:
- Type(s) of rooms you want and size of your party
- Number of nights you'll stay
- Your arrival and departure dates, written European-style as day/month/year (for example, 18/06/21 or 18 June 2021)
- Special requests (such as en suite bathroom, cheapest room, twin beds vs. double bed, quiet room)
- Applicable discounts (such as a Rick Steves reader discount, cash discount, or promotional rate)

Confirming a Reservation: Most places will request a credit-card number to hold your room. If you're using an online reservation form, make sure it's secure by looking for the *https* or a lock icon at the top of your browser. If the hotel's website doesn't have a secure form where you can enter the number directly, it's best to share that confidential info via a phone call.

Canceling a Reservation: If you must cancel, it's courteous—and smart—to do so with as much notice as possible, especially for smaller family-run places. Cancellation policies can be strict; read

I avoid places run as a business by absentee owners. My top listings are run by people who enjoy welcoming the world to their breakfast table.

Compared to hotels, B&Bs and guesthouses give you double the cultural intimacy for half the price. While you may lose some of the conveniences of a hotel—such as fancy lobbies, in-room phones, and frequent bedsheet changes—I happily make the trade-off for the personal touches, whether it's joining my hosts for afternoon tea or relaxing by a common fireplace at the end of the day. If you have a reasonable but limited budget, skip hotels and go the B&B way.

B&B proprietors are selective about the guests they invite in for the night. Many do not welcome children. If you'll be staying for more than one night, you are a "desirable." In popular weekend-getaway spots, you're unlikely to find a place to take you for Saturday night only. If my listings are full, ask for guidance. Mentioning this book can help. Owners usually work together and can call up

From:	rick@ricksteves.com
Sent:	Today
To:	info@hotelcentral.com
Subject:	Reservation request for 19-22 July

Dear Hotel Central,

I would like to stay at your hotel. Please let me know if you have a room available and the price for:
• 2 people
• Double bed and en suite bathroom in a quiet room
• Arriving 19 July, departing 22 July (3 nights)

Thank you!
Rick Steves

the fine print before you book. Many discount deals require pre-payment, with no cancellation refunds.

Reconfirming a Reservation: Always call or email to reconfirm your room reservation a few days in advance. For B&Bs or very small hotels, I call again on my day of arrival to tell my host what time to expect me (especially important if arriving late—after 17:00).

Phoning: For tips on calling hotels overseas, see page 936.

an ally to land you a bed. Many B&B owners are also pet owners. If you're allergic, ask about resident pets when you reserve.

Rules and Etiquette: B&Bs and small hotels come with their own etiquette and quirks. Keep in mind that owners are at the whim of their guests—if you're getting up early, so are they; if you check in late, they'll wait up for you. Most B&Bs have set check-in times (usually in the late afternoon). If arriving outside that time, they will want to know when to expect you (call or email ahead). Most will let you check in earlier if the room is available (or they'll at least let you drop off your bag).

Most B&Bs and guesthouses serve a hearty cooked breakfast of eggs and much more (for details on breakfast, see the "Eating" section, later). Because the owner is often also the cook, breakfast hours are usually abbreviated. Typically the breakfast window lasts for 1-1.5 hours (make sure you know when it is before you turn in for the night). Some B&Bs ask you to fill in your breakfast order the night before. It's an unwritten rule that guests shouldn't show up at the very end of the breakfast period and expect a full cooked breakfast. If you do arrive late (or need to leave before breakfast is served), most establishments are happy to let you help yourself to cereal, fruit, juice, and coffee.

B&Bs and small hotels often come with thin walls and doors, and sometimes creaky floorboards, which can make for a noisy night. If you're a light sleeper, bring earplugs. And please be quiet in the halls and in your rooms at night...those of us getting up early will thank you for it.

Treat these lovingly maintained homes as you would a friend's house. Be careful maneuvering your bag up narrow staircases with fragile walls and banisters. And once in the room, use the luggage rack—putting bags on the bed can damage nice comforters.

In the Room: Most B&Bs offer "tea service" in the room—an electric kettle, cups, tea bags, coffee packets, and a pack of biscuits.

Your bedroom probably won't include a phone, but nearly every B&B has free Wi-Fi. However, the signal may not reach all rooms; you may need to sit in the lounge to access it.

You're likely to encounter unusual bathroom fixtures. The "pump toilet" has a flushing handle or button that doesn't kick in unless you push it just right: too hard or too soft, and it won't go. (Be decisive but not ruthless.) Most B&B baths have an instant water heater. This looks like an electronic box under the shower-head with dials and buttons: One control adjusts the heat, while another turns the flow off and on (let the water run for a bit to moderate the temperature before you hop in). If the hot water doesn't work, you may need to flip a red switch (often located just outside the bathroom). If the shower looks mysterious, ask your B&B host for help...*before* you take off your clothes.

Paying: Many B&Bs take credit cards, but may add the card service fee to your bill (about 3 percent). If you do need to pay cash for your room, plan ahead to have enough on hand when you check out.

Short-Term Rentals

A short-term rental—whether an apartment (or "flat"), house, or room in a local's home—is an increasingly popular alternative, especially if you plan to settle in one location for several nights. For stays longer than a few days, you can usually find a rental that's comparable to—and cheaper than—a hotel room with similar amenities. Plus, you'll get a behind-the-scenes peek into how locals live.

Many places require a minimum night stay and have strict cancellation policies. And you're generally on your own: There's no hotel reception desk, breakfast, or daily cleaning service.

Finding Accommodations: Websites such as Airbnb, FlipKey, Booking.com, and the HomeAway family of sites (HomeAway,

VRBO, and VacationRentals) let you browse a wide range of properties. Alternatively, rental agencies such as InterhomeUSA.com or RentaVilla.com, which list more carefully selected accommodations that might cost more, can provide more personalized service. For a list of rental agencies for London, see page 170.

Before you commit, be clear on the location. I like to virtually "explore" the neighborhood using the Street View feature on Google Maps. Also consider the proximity to public transportation and how well-connected the property is with the rest of the city. Ask about amenities (elevator, air-conditioning, laundry, Wi-Fi, parking, etc.). Reviews from previous guests can help identify trouble spots.

Think about the kind of experience you want: Just a key and an affordable bed...or a chance to get to know a local? There are typically two kinds of hosts: those who want minimal interaction with their guests, and hosts who are friendly and may want to interact with you. Read the promotional text and online reviews to help shape your decision.

Confirming and Paying: Many places require you to pay the entire balance before your trip. It's easiest and safest to pay through the site where you found the listing. Be wary of owners who want to take your transaction offline; this gives you no recourse if things go awry. Never agree to wire money (a key indicator of a fraudulent transaction).

Apartments or Houses: If you're staying in one place for four or more nights, it's worth considering an apartment or rental house (shorter stays aren't worth the hassle of arranging key pickup, buying groceries, etc.). Apartment or house rentals can be especially cost-effective for groups and families. European apartments, like hotel rooms, tend to be small by US standards. But they often come with laundry machines and small, equipped kitchens, making it easier and cheaper to dine in.

Rooms in Private Homes: Renting a room in someone's home is a good option for those traveling alone, as you're more likely to find true single rooms—with just one single bed, and a price to match. These can range from air-mattress-in-living-room basic to plush-B&B-suite posh. Some places allow you to book for a single night; if staying for several nights, you can buy groceries just as you would in a rental house. While you can't expect your host to also be your tour guide—or even to provide you with much info— some may be interested in getting to know the travelers who come through their home.

Other Options: Swapping homes with a local works for people with an appealing place to offer (don't assume where you live is not interesting to Europeans). Good places to start are www.homeexchange.com and LoveHomeSwap.com. To sleep for free,

Couchsurfing.com is a vagabond's alternative to Airbnb. It lists millions of outgoing members, who host fellow "surfers" in their homes.

Hostels

Britain has hundreds of hostels of all shapes and sizes. Choose your hostel selectively. Hostels can be historic castles or depressing tenements, serene and comfy or overrun by noisy school groups.

A hostel provides cheap beds in dorms where you sleep alongside strangers for about £20-30 per night. Travelers of any age are welcome if they don't mind dorm-style accommodations and meeting other travelers. Most hostels offer kitchen facilities, guest computers, Wi-Fi, and a self-service laundry. Hostels almost always provide bedding, but the towel's up to you (though you can usually rent one for a small fee). Family and private rooms are often available.

Independent hostels tend to be easygoing, colorful, and informal (no membership required; www.hostelworld.com). You may pay slightly less by booking direct with the hostel. **Official hostels** are part of Hostelling International (HI) and share an online booking site (www.hihostels.com). HI hostels typically require that you be a member or else pay a bit more per night. In Britain, these official hostels are run by the Youth Hostel Association (YHA, www.yha.org.uk).

Eating

These days, the stereotype of "bad food in Britain" is woefully dated. Britain has caught up with the foodie revolution—in fact, they're right there, leading the vanguard—and I find it's easy to eat very well here. London, in particular, is one of Europe's best food destinations.

British cooking has embraced international influences and local, seasonal ingredients, making "modern British" food quite delicious. While some dreary pub food still exists, you'll generally find the cuisine scene here innovative and delicious (but expensive). Basic pubs are more likely to dish up homemade, creative dishes than microwaved pies, soggy fries, and mushy peas. Even traditional pub grub has gone upmarket, with gastropubs that serve locally sourced meats and fresh vegetables.

All of Britain is smoke-free. Expect restaurants and pubs to be nonsmoking indoors, with smokers occupying patios and doorways outside. You'll find the Brits eat at about the same time of day as Americans do.

For listings in this guidebook, I look for restaurants that are convenient to your hotel and sightseeing. When restaurant-hunting,

Restaurant Code

Eateries in this book are categorized according to the average cost of a typical main course. Drinks, desserts, and splurge items can raise the price considerably.

$$$$	**Splurge:**	Most main courses over £20
$$$	**Pricier:**	£15-20
$$	**Moderate:**	£10-15
$	**Budget:**	Under £10

In Great Britain, carryout fish-and-chips and other takeout food is **$**; a basic pub or sit-down eatery is **$$**; a gastropub or casual but more upscale restaurant is **$$$**; and a swanky splurge is **$$$$**.

choose a spot filled with locals, not tourists. Venturing even a block or two off the main drag leads to higher-quality food for a better price.

Tipping: At pubs and places where you order at the counter, you don't have to tip. Regular customers ordering a round sometimes say, "Add one for yourself" as a tip for drinks ordered at the bar—but this isn't expected. At restaurants and fancy pubs with waitstaff, it's not necessary to tip if a service charge is already included in the bill (common in London—usually 12.5 percent). Otherwise, it's appropriate to tip about 10-12 percent; you can add a bit more for finer dining or extra good service. Tip only what you think the service warrants (if it isn't already added to your bill), and be careful not to tip double.

RESTAURANT PRICING

I've categorized my recommended eateries based on the average price of a typical main course, indicated with a dollar-sign rating (see sidebar). Obviously, expensive specialties, fine wine, appetizers, and dessert can significantly increase your final bill.

The categories also indicate the personality of a place: **Budget** eateries include street food, takeaway, order-at-the-counter shops, basic cafeterias, and bakeries selling sandwiches. **Moderate** eateries are nice (but not fancy) sit-down restaurants, ideal for a straightforward, fill-the-tank meal. Most of my listings fall in this category—great for getting a good taste of the local cuisine at a reasonable price.

Pricier eateries are a notch up, with more attention paid to the setting, presentation, and (often inventive) cuisine. **Splurge** eateries are dress-up-for-a-special-occasion-swanky—typically with an elegant setting, polished service, intricate cuisine, and an expansive (and expensive) wine list.

PRACTICALITIES

BREAKFAST (Fry-Up)

The traditional fry-up or full English breakfast—generally included in the cost of your room—is famous as a hearty way to start the day. Also known as a "heart attack on a plate," your standard fry-up is a heated plate with eggs, Canadian-style bacon and/or sausage, a grilled tomato, sautéed mushrooms, baked beans, and sometimes potatoes, kippers (herring), or fried bread (sizzled in a greasy skillet). Toast comes in a rack (to cool quickly and

crisply) with butter and marmalade. The meal is typically topped off with tea or coffee. At a B&B or hotel, it may start with juice and cereal or porridge. Many progressive B&B owners offer vegetarian, organic, gluten-free, or other creative variations on the traditional breakfast.

As much as the full breakfast fry-up is a traditional way to start the morning, these days most places serve a healthier continental breakfast as well—with a buffet of yogurt, cereal, fruit, and pastries. At some hotels, the buffet may also include hot items, such as eggs and sausage.

LUNCH AND DINNER ON A BUDGET

Even in pricey cities, plenty of inexpensive choices are available: pub grub, daily lunch and early-bird dinner specials, global cuisine, cafeterias, fast food, picnics, greasy-spoon cafés, cheap chain restaurants, and pizza.

I've found that portions are huge, and **sharing plates** is generally just fine. Ordering two drinks, a soup or side salad, and splitting a £10 meat pie can make a good, filling meal. If you're on a limited budget, share a main course in a more expensive place for a nicer eating experience.

Pub grub is the most atmospheric budget option. You'll usually get hearty lunches and dinners priced reasonably at £8-15 under ancient timbers (see "Pubs," later). Gastropubs, with better food, are more expensive.

Classier restaurants have some affordable deals. Lunch is usually cheaper than dinner; a top-end, £30-for-dinner-type restaurant often serves the same quality two-course lunch deals for about half the price.

Many restaurants have **early-bird** or **pre-theater specials** of two or three courses, often for a significant savings. They are usually available only before 18:30 or 19:00 (and sometimes on weekdays only).

Global cuisine adds spice to Britain's food scene. Eating Indian, Bangladeshi, Chinese, or Thai is cheap (even cheaper if you do takeout). Middle Eastern shops sell gyro sandwiches, falafel, and *shwarmas* (grilled meat in pita bread). An Indian samosa (greasy, flaky meat-and-vegetable turnover) costs about £2 and makes a very cheap, if small, meal. (For more, see "Indian Cuisine," later.) You'll find inexpensive, quick Asian options (often Chinese), such as all-you-can-eat buffets and takeaway places serving up standard dishes in to-go boxes.

Fish-and-chips are a heavy, greasy, but tasty British classic. Every town has at least one "chippy" selling takeaway fish-and-chips in a cardboard box or (more traditionally) wrapped in paper for about £5-7. You can dip your fries in ketchup, American-style, or "go British" and drizzle the whole thing with malt vinegar and fresh lemon.

Most large **museums** (and many historic **churches**) have handy, moderately priced cafeterias with forgettably decent food.

Picnicking saves time and money. Fine park benches and polite pigeons abound in most towns and city neighborhoods. You can easily get prepared food to go. The modern chain eateries on nearly every corner often have simple seating but are designed for takeout. Bakeries serve a wonderful array of fresh sandwiches and pasties (savory meat pastries). Street markets, generally parked in pedestrian-friendly zones, are fun and colorful places to stock up for a picnic.

Open-air markets and supermarkets sell produce in small quantities. The corner grocery store has fruit, drinks, fresh bread, tasty British cheese, meat, and local specialties. Supermarkets often have good deli sections, even offering Indian dishes, and sometimes salad bars. Decent packaged sandwiches (£3-4) are sold everywhere. Munch a relaxed "meal on wheels" picnic during your open-top bus tour or river cruise to save 30 precious minutes for sightseeing.

PUBS

Pubs are a fundamental part of the British social scene, and whether you're a teetotaler or a beer guzzler, they should be a part of your travel here. "Pub" is short for "public house." It's an extended common room where, if you don't mind the stickiness, you can feel the local pulse. Smart travelers use pubs to eat, drink, get out of the rain, watch sporting events, and make new friends. Unfortunately, many city pubs have been afflicted with an excess of brass, ferns, and video slot machines. The most traditional atmospheric pubs are in the countryside and in smaller towns.

It's interesting to consider the role pubs filled for Britain's working class in more modest times: For workers with humble domestic quarters and no money for a vacation, a beer at the corner pub was the closest they'd get to a comfortable living room, a place to entertain, and a getaway. And locals could meet people from far away in a pub—today, that's you!

Though hours vary, pubs generally serve beer daily from 11:00 to 23:00, though many are open later, particularly on Friday and Saturday. (Children are served food and soft drinks in pubs, but you must be 18 to order a beer.) As it nears closing time, you'll hear shouts of "last orders." Then comes the 10-minute warning bell. Finally, they'll call "Time!" to pick up your glass, finished or not, when the pub closes.

A cup of darts is free for the asking. People go to a public house to be social. They want to talk. Get vocal with a local. This is easiest at the bar, where people assume you're in the mood to talk (rather than at a table, where you're allowed a bit of privacy). The pub is the next best thing to having relatives in town. Cheers!

Pub Grub: For £8-15, you'll get a basic budget hot lunch or dinner in friendly surroundings. In high-priced London, this is your best indoor eating value. (For something more refined, try a **gastropub,** which serves higher-quality meals for £12-20.) The *Good Pub Guide* is an excellent resource (www.thegoodpubguide.co.uk). Pubs that are attached to restaurants, advertise their food, and are crowded with locals are more likely to have fresh food and a chef—and less likely to sell only lousy microwaved snacks.

Pubs generally serve traditional dishes, such as fish-and-chips, roast beef with Yorkshire pudding (batter-baked in the oven), and assorted meat pies, such as steak-and-kidney pie or shepherd's pie (stewed lamb topped with mashed potatoes) with cooked vegetables. Side dishes include salads, vegetables, and—invariably—"chips" (French fries). "Crisps" are potato chips. A "jacket potato" (baked potato stuffed with fillings of your choice) can almost be a meal in itself. A "ploughman's lunch" is a traditional British meal of bread, cheese, and sweet pickles. These days, you'll likely find more pasta, curried dishes, and quiche on the menu than traditional fare.

Meals are usually served from 12:00 to 14:00 and again from 18:00 to 20:00—with a break in the middle (rather than serving straight through the day). Since they make more money selling beer, many pubs stop food service early in the evening—especially on weekends. There's generally no table service. Order at the bar, and then take a seat. Either they'll bring the food when it's ready or you'll pick it up at the bar. Pay at the bar (sometimes when you order, sometimes after you eat). It's not necessary to tip unless it's a place with full table service. Servings are hearty, and service is quick. A beer, cider, or dram of whisky adds another couple of pounds. Free tap water is always available. For details on ordering beer and other drinks, see the "Beverages" section, later. For a list of recommended historic pubs in London, see page 180.

GOOD CHAIN RESTAURANTS

I know—you're going to Britain to enjoy characteristic little hole-in-the-wall pubs, so mass-produced food is the furthest thing from your mind. But several excellent chains with branches across the UK offer long hours, reasonable prices, reliable quality, and a nice break from pub grub. My favorites are Pret, Wasabi, and Eat. Expect to see these familiar names wherever you go:

$ Pret (a.k.a. Pret à Manger) is perhaps the most pervasive of these modern convenience eateries. Some are takeout only, and others have seating ranging from simple stools to restaurant-quality tables. The service is fast, the price is great, and the food is healthy and fresh. Their slogan: "Made today. Gone today. No 'sell-by' date, no nightlife."

$$ Côte Brasserie is a contemporary French chain serving good-value French cuisine in pleasant settings (early dinner specials).

Two **$** chains have reliably good coffee and pastries: **Paul** (French-style, with croissants, other pastries, and baguette sandwiches) and **Ole & Steen** (Scandinavian, with generous samples of cinnamon rolls). The coffee at either place is typically better than the ubiquitous British chains Costa and Nero.

$$ Le Pain Quotidien is a Belgian chain serving fresh-baked bread and hearty meals in a thoughtfully designed modern-rustic atmosphere.

$$ Byron Hamburgers, an upscale-hamburger chain with hip interiors, is worth seeking out if you need a burger fix. While British burgers tend to be a bit overcooked by American standards, Byron's burgers are your best bet.

$$ Wagamama Noodle Bar, serving pan-Asian cuisine (udon noodles, fried rice, and curry dishes), is a noisy, organic slurpathon. Portions are huge and splittable. There's one in almost every mid-size city in Britain, usually located in sprawling halls filled with long shared tables and busy servers who scrawl your order on the placemat.

$$$ Loch Fyne Fish Restaurant is a Scottish chain that raises its own oysters and mussels. Its branches offer an inviting, lively atmosphere with a fine fishy energy and no pretense (early-bird specials).

$ Marks & Spencer department stores have inviting deli sections with cheery sit-down eating (along with their popular sandwiches-to-go section). M&S food halls are also handy if you're renting a city flat and want to prepare your own meals.

$$ Busaba Eathai is a hit in several cities for its snappy (sometimes rushed) service, boisterous ambience, and good, inexpensive Thai cuisine.

$$ Thai Square is a dependable Thai option with a nice atmosphere (salads, noodle dishes, curries, meat dishes, and daily lunch box specials). Most branches are in London.

$$ Masala Zone is a London chain providing a good, predictable alternative to the many one-off, hole-in-the-wall Indian joints around town. Try a curry-and-rice dish, a *thali* (platter with several small dishes), or their street food specials. Each branch has its own personality.

$$ Franco Manca is a taverna-inspired pizzeria serving Neapolitan-style pies using organic ingredients and boasting typical Italian charm. If you skip the pricey drinks, you can feast very cheaply here.

$$ Ask and **Pizza Express** serve quality pasta and pizza in a pleasant, sit-down atmosphere that's family-friendly.

$$ Japanese: Three popular chains serve fresh and inexpensive Japanese food. **Itsu** and **Wasabi** are two bright and competitive chains that let you assemble your own plate in a fun and efficient way, while **Yo! Sushi** lets you pick your dish off a conveyor belt and pay according to the color of your plate.

Carry-Out Chains: While the following may have some seating, they're best as places to grab prepackaged food on the run.

Major supermarket chains have smaller, offshoot branches that specialize in sandwiches, salads, and other prepared foods to go. These can be a picnicker's dream come true. Some shops are stand-alone, while others are located inside a larger store. The most prevalent—and best—is **M&S Simply Food** (an offshoot of Marks & Spencer; there's one in every major train station). **Sainsbury's Local** grocery stores also offer decent prepared food; **Tesco Express** and **Tesco Metro** run a distant third.

Some "cheap and cheery" chains provide office workers with good, healthful sandwiches, salads, and pastries to go. These include **Pod** and **Eat** (with slightly higher-quality food and higher prices).

INDIAN CUISINE

Eating Indian food is "going local" in cosmopolitan, multiethnic Britain. You'll find Indian restaurants in most cities, and even in small towns. Take the opportunity to sample food from Britain's former colony. Indian cuisine is as varied as the country itself. In general, it uses more exotic spices than British or American cuisine—some hot, some sweet. Indian food is very vegetarian-friendly, offering many meatless dishes.

For a simple meal that costs about £10-12, order one dish with rice and naan (Indian flatbread). Generally, one order is plenty for two people to share. Many Indian restaurants offer a fixed-price combination that offers more variety, and is simpler and cheaper than ordering à la carte. For about £20, you can make a mix-and-match platter out of several shareable dishes, including dal (simmered lentils) as a starter, one or two meat or vegetable dishes with sauce (for example, chicken curry, chicken *tikka masala* in a creamy tomato sauce, grilled fish tandoori, or chickpea *chana masala*), *raita* (a cooling yogurt that comes on the side—it helps extinguish your mouth if eating spicy dishes), rice, naan, and an Indian beer (wine and Indian food don't really mix) or spiced chai tea (usually served with milk). An easy way to taste a variety of dishes is to order a *thali*—a sampler plate of various specialties.

AFTERNOON TEA

Once the sole province of genteel ladies in fancy hats, afternoon tea has become more democratic in the 21st century. These days, people of leisure punctuate their day with an afternoon tea at a tearoom. Tearooms, which often serve appealing light meals, are usually open for lunch and close at about 17:00, just before dinner.

The cheapest "tea" on the menu is generally a "cream tea"; the most expensive is the "champagne tea." **Cream tea** is simply a pot of tea and a homemade scone or two with jam and thick clotted cream. (For maximum pinkie-waving taste per calorie, slice your scone thin like a miniature loaf of bread.) **Afternoon tea**—what many Americans would call "high tea"—is a pot of tea, small finger foods (such as sandwiches with the crusts cut off), scones, an assortment of small pastries, jam, and thick clotted cream. **Champagne tea** includes all of the goodies, plus a glass of bubbly. **High tea** to the English generally means a more substantial late afternoon or early evening meal, often served with meat or eggs.

British Chocolate

My chocoholic readers are enthusiastic about British chocolates. As with other dairy products, chocolate seems richer and creamier here than it does in the US, so even standbys such as Mars, Kit Kat (which was actually invented in York—see page 795), and Twix have a different taste. Some favorites include Cadbury Gold bars (filled with liquid caramel), Cadbury Crunchie bars, Nestlé's Lion bars (layered wafers covered in caramel and chocolate), Cadbury's Boost bars (a shortcake biscuit with caramel in milk chocolate), Cadbury Flake (crumbly folds of melt-in-your-mouth chocolate), Aero bars (with "aerated" chocolate filling), and Galaxy chocolate bars (especially the ones with hazelnuts). Thornton shops (in larger train stations) sell a box of sweets called the Continental Assortment, which comes with a tasting guide. (The highlight is the mocha white-chocolate truffle.) British M&Ms, called Smarties, are better than American ones. Many Brits feel that the ultimate treat is a box of either Nestlé Quality Street or Cadbury Roses—assortments of filled chocolates in colorful wrappers. (But don't mention the Kraft takeover of Cadbury in 2010—many Brits believe the American company changed the recipe for their beloved Dairy Milk bars, and they're not happy about it). At ice-cream vans, look for the beloved traditional "99p"—a vanilla soft-serve cone with a small Flake bar stuck right into the middle.

DESSERTS (SWEETS)

To the British, the traditional word for dessert is "pudding," although it's also referred to as "sweets" these days. Sponge cake, cream, fruitcake, and meringue are key players.

Trifle is the best-known British concoction, consisting of sponge cake soaked in brandy or sherry (or orange juice for children), then covered with jam and/or fruit and custard cream. Whipped cream can sometimes put the final touch on this "light" treat.

The British version of custard is a smooth, yellow liquid. Cream tops most everything that custard does not. There's single cream for coffee. Double cream is really thick. Clotted cream is the consistency of whipped butter.

Fool is a dessert with sweetened pureed fruit (such as rhubarb, gooseberries, or black currants) mixed with cream or custard and chilled. Elderflower is a popular flavoring for sorbet.

Flapjacks here aren't pancakes, but are dense, sweet oatmeal cakes (a little like a cross between a granola bar and a brownie). They come with toppings such as toffee and chocolate.

Scones are tops, and many inns and restaurants have their

secret recipes. Whether made with fruit or topped with clotted cream, scones take the cake.

BEVERAGES

Beer: The British take great pride in their beer. Many locals think that drinking beer cold and carbonated, as Americans do, ruins the taste. Most pubs will have **lagers** (cold, refreshing, American-style beer), **ales** (amber-colored, cellar-temperature beer), **bitters** (hop-flavored ale, perhaps the most typical British beer), and **stouts** (dark and somewhat bitter, like Guinness).

At pubs, long-handled pulls (or taps) are used to draw the traditional, rich-flavored "real ales" up from the cellar. These are the connoisseur's favorites and often come with fun names. Served straight from the brewer's cask at cellar temperature, real ales finish fermenting naturally and are not pasteurized or filtered, so they must be consumed within two or three days after the cask is tapped. Naturally carbonated, real ales have less gassiness and head; they vary from sweet to bitter, often with a hoppy or nutty flavor.

Short-handled pulls mean colder, fizzier, mass-produced, and less interesting keg beers. Mild beers are sweeter, with a creamy malt flavoring. Irish cream ale is a smooth, sweet experience. Try the draft cider (sweet or dry)...carefully.

Order your beer at the bar and pay as you go, with no need to tip. An average beer costs about £4. Part of the experience is standing before a line of hand pulls, and wondering which beer to choose.

As dictated by British law, draft beer and cider are served by the pint (20-ounce imperial size) or the half-pint (9.6 ounces). In 2011, the government sanctioned an in-between serving size—the schooner, or two-thirds pint (it's become a popular size for higher alcohol-content craft beers). A popular summer drink is a **shandy** (half beer and half British "lemonade," similar to 7-Up).

Whisky: While bar-hopping tourists generally think in terms of beer, many pubs are just as enthusiastic about serving whisky. If you are unfamiliar with whisky (what Americans call "Scotch" and the Irish call "whiskey"), it's a great conversation starter. Many pubs have dozens of whiskies available. Lists describe their personalities (peaty, heavy iodine finish, and so on), which are much easier to discern than most wine flavors.

A glass of basic whisky generally costs around £2.50. Let a

The British Accent

In the olden days, a British person's accent indicated his or her social standing. Eliza Doolittle had the right idea—elocution could make or break you. Wealthier families would send their kids to fancy private schools to learn proper pronunciation. But these days, in a sort of reverse snobbery that has gripped the nation, accents are back. Politicians, newscasters, and movie stars are favoring deep accents over the Queen's English. While it's hard for American ears to pick out the variations, most Brits can determine where a person is from based on their accent...not just the region, but often the village, and even the part of town.

local teach you how to drink it "neat," then add a little water. Make a friend, buy a few drams, and learn by drinking. Keep experimenting until you discover the right taste for you.

Other Alcoholic Drinks: Many pubs also have a good selection of wines by the glass and a fully stocked bar for the gentleman's "G and T" (gin and tonic). **Pimm's** is a refreshing and fruity summer liqueur, traditionally popular during Wimbledon. It's an upper-class drink—a rough bloke might insult a pub by claiming it sells more Pimm's than beer.

Non-Alcoholic Drinks: Teetotalers can order from a wide variety of soft drinks—both the predictable American sodas and other more interesting bottled drinks, such as ginger beer (similar to ginger ale but with more bite), root beers, or other flavors (Fentimans brews some unusual options that are stocked in many pubs).

Staying Connected

One of the most common questions I hear from travelers is, "How can I stay connected in Europe?" The short answer is: more easily and cheaply than you might think.

The simplest solution is to bring your own device—mobile phone, tablet, or laptop—and use it just as you would at home (following the money-saving tips later such as getting an international plan or connecting to free Wi-Fi whenever possible). Another option is to buy a European SIM card for your US mobile phone. Or you can use European landlines and computers to connect. Each of these options is described next, and more details are at www. ricksteves.com/phoning. For a practical one-hour talk covering tech issues for travelers, see www.ricksteves.com/mobile-travel-skills.

USING A MOBILE PHONE IN EUROPE

Here are some budget tips and options.

Sign up for an international plan. To stay connected at a lower cost, sign up for an international service plan through your carrier. Most providers offer a simple bundle that includes calling, messaging, and data. Your normal plan may already include international coverage (T-Mobile's does).

Before your trip, call your provider or check online to confirm that your phone will work in Europe, and research your provider's international rates. Activate the plan a day or two before you leave, then remember to cancel it when your trip's over.

Use free Wi-Fi whenever possible. Unless you have an un-limited-data plan, you're best off saving most of your online tasks for Wi-Fi. You can access the internet, send texts, and even make voice calls over Wi-Fi.

Most accommodations in Europe offer free Wi-Fi, but some—especially expensive hotels—charge a fee. Many cafés (including Starbucks and McDonald's) have free hotspots for customers; look for signs offering it and ask for the Wi-Fi password when you buy something. You'll also often find Wi-Fi at TIs, city squares, major museums, public-transit hubs, airports, and aboard trains and buses. In Britain, another option is to sign up for Wi-Fi access through a company such as BT (one hour-£4, one day-£10, www.btwifi.co.uk) or The Cloud (free though sometimes slow, www.skywifi.cloud).

Minimize the use of your cellular network. The best way to make sure you're not accidentally burning through data is to put your device in "airplane" mode (which also disables phone calls and texts), turn your Wi-Fi back on, and connect to networks as needed. When you need to get online but can't find Wi-Fi, simply turn on your cellular network (or turn off airplane mode) just long enough for the task at hand.

Even with an international data plan, wait until you're on Wi-Fi to Skype, download apps, stream videos, or do other mega-byte-greedy tasks. Using a navigation app such as Google Maps over a cellular network can take lots of data, so do this sparingly or offline.

Limit automatic updates. By default, your device constantly checks for a data connection and updates apps. It's smart to disable these features so your apps will only update when you're on Wi-Fi. Also change your device's email settings from "auto-retrieve" to "manual" (or from "push" to "fetch").

Use Wi-Fi calling and messaging apps. Skype, WhatsApp, FaceTime, and Google Hangouts are great for making free or low-cost calls or sending texts over Wi-Fi worldwide. Just log on to a Wi-Fi network, then connect with any of your friends or family

How to Dial

International Calls
Whether phoning from a US landline or mobile phone, or from a number in another European country, here's how to make an international call. I've used one of my recommended London hotels as an example (tel. 020/7730-8191).
Initial Zero: Drop the initial zero from international phone numbers—except when calling Italy.
Mobile Tip: If using a mobile phone, the "+" sign can replace the international access code (for a "+" sign, press and hold "0").

US/Canada to Europe
Dial 011 (US/Canada international access code), country code (44 for Britain), and phone number.
▶ To call the London hotel from home, dial 011-44-20/7730-8191.

Country to Country Within Europe
Dial 00 (Europe international access code), country code, and phone number.
▶ To call the London hotel from Spain, dial 00-44-20/7730-8191.

Europe to the US/Canada
Dial 00, country code (1 for US/Canada), and phone number.
▶ To call from Europe to my office in Edmonds, Washington, dial 00-1-425-771-8303.

Domestic Calls
To call within Britain (from one British landline or mobile phone to another), simply dial the phone number, including the initial 0 if there is one.
▶ To call the London hotel from Edinburgh, dial 020/7730-8191.

members who use the same service. If you buy credit in advance, with some of these services you can call or text anywhere for just pennies.

Some apps, such as Apple's iMessage, will use the cellular network for texts if Wi-Fi isn't available: To avoid this possibility, turn off the "Send as SMS" feature.

Buy a European SIM card. If you anticipate making a lot of local calls or need a local phone number, or if your provider's international data rates are expensive, consider buying a SIM card in Europe to replace the one in your (unlocked) US phone or tablet. SIM cards are sold at department-store electronics counters, some newsstands, and vending machines. If you need help setting it up, buy one at a mobile-phone shop (you may need to show your passport).

PRACTICALITIES

More Dialing Tips

Toll and Toll-Free Numbers: It's generally not possible to dial British toll or toll-free numbers from a US mobile or landline (although you can sometimes get through using Skype). Look for a direct-dial number instead.

More Phoning Help: See HowToCallAbroad.com.

European Country Codes		Ireland & N. Ireland	353 / 44
Austria	43	Italy	39
Belgium	32	Latvia	371
Bosnia-Herzegovina	387	Montenegro	382
Croatia	385	Morocco	212
Czech Republic	420	Netherlands	31
Denmark	45	Norway	47
Estonia	372	Poland	48
Finland	358	Portugal	351
France	33	Russia	7
Germany	49	Slovakia	421
Gibraltar	350	Slovenia	386
Great Britain	44	Spain	34
Greece	30	Sweden	46
Hungary	36	Switzerland	41
Iceland	354	Turkey	90

There are no roaming charges when using a European SIM card in other EU countries, though to be sure you get this "roam-like-at-home" pricing, buy your SIM card at a mobile-phone shop and ask if this feature is included.

WITHOUT A MOBILE PHONE

It's less convenient but possible to travel in Europe without a mobile device. You can make calls from your hotel and check email or get online using public computers.

Most **hotels** charge a fee for placing calls—ask for rates before you dial. You can use a prepaid international phone card (usually available at newsstands, tobacco shops, and train stations) to call out from your hotel. Dial the toll-free access number, enter the card's PIN code, then dial the number.

PRACTICALITIES

Tips on Internet Security

Make sure that your device is running the latest versions of its operating system, security software, and apps. Next, ensure that your device and key programs (like email) are password-protected. On the road, use only secure, password-protected Wi-Fi hotspots. Ask the hotel or café staff for the specific name of their Wi-Fi network, and make sure you log on to that exact one.

If you must access your financial info online, use a banking app rather than accessing your account via a browser. A cellular connection is more secure than Wi-Fi. Avoid logging onto personal finance sites on a public computer.

Never share your credit-card number (or any other sensitive information) online unless you know that the site is secure. A secure site displays a little padlock icon, and the URL begins with *https* (instead of the usual *http*).

If there's no phone in your **B&B** room, and you have an important, brief call to make, politely ask your hosts if you can use their personal phone. Use a cheap international phone card with a toll-free access number, or offer to pay your host for the call.

Public pay phones are hard to find in Britain, and they're expensive. To use one, you'll pay with a major credit card (minimum charge-£1.20) or coins (minimum charge-£0.60).

Some hotels have **public computers** in their lobbies for guests to use; otherwise you may find them at public libraries (ask your hotelier or the TI for the nearest location). On a European keyboard, use the "Alt Gr" key to the right of the space bar to insert the extra symbol that appears on some keys. If you can't locate a special character (such as @), simply copy and paste it from a web page.

MAIL

You can mail one package per day to yourself worth up to $200 duty-free from Europe to the US (mark it "personal purchases"). If you're sending a gift to someone, mark it "unsolicited gift." For details, visit www.cbp.gov, select "Travel," and search for "Know Before You Visit." The British postal service works fine, but for quick transatlantic delivery (in either direction), consider services such as DHL (www.dhl.com). For postcards, get stamps at the neighborhood post office, newsstands within fancy hotels, and some minimarts and card shops.

PRACTICALITIES

Transportation

Figuring out how to get around in Europe is one of your biggest trip decisions. **Cars** work well for two or more traveling together (especially families with small kids), those packing heavy, and those delving into the countryside. **Trains** and **buses** are best for solo travelers, blitz tourists, city-to-city travelers, and those who want to leave the driving to others. Smart travelers can use short hop **flights** within Europe to creatively connect the dots on their itineraries. Just be aware of the potential downside of each option: A car is an expensive headache in any major city; with trains and buses you're at the mercy of a timetable; and flying entails a trek to and from a usually distant airport.

If your itinerary mixes cities and countryside, my advice is to connect cities by train (or bus) and to explore rural areas by rental car. Arrange to pick up your car in the last big city you'll visit, then use it to lace together small towns and explore the countryside. For more detailed information on transportation throughout Europe, see www.ricksteves.com/transportation.

TRAINS

Regular tickets on Britain's great train system (15,000 departures from 2,400 stations daily) are the most expensive per mile in all of Europe. For the greatest savings, book online in advance and leave after rush hour (after 9:30 weekdays).

Since Britain's railways have been privatized, a single train route can be operated by multiple companies. However, one website covers all train lines (www.nationalrail.co.uk), and another covers all bus and train routes (www.traveline.org.uk for information, not ticket sales). Another good resource, which also has schedules for trains throughout Europe, is German Rail's timetable (www.bahn.com).

As with airline tickets, British train tickets can come at many different prices for the same journey. A clerk at any station can figure out the cheapest fare for your trip.

While generally not required, reservations are free and can normally be made well in advance. They are an especially good idea for long journeys or for travel on Sundays or holidays. Make reservations at any train station, by phone, or online when you buy your ticket. With a point-to-point ticket, you can reserve as late as two hours before train time, but rail-pass holders should book seats at least 24 hours in advance (see later for more on rail passes). You must reserve in advance for Caledonian Sleeper overnight trains between London and Scotland (www.sleeper.scot).

For information on the high-speed Eurostar train through the "Chunnel" to Paris, Brussels, or Amsterdam, see page 200.

Great Britain's Public Transportation

Legend:
- ----- Rail
- ——— Eurostar
- - - - Bus
- ····· (8H) Ferry with crossing time

N

50 Kilometers
50 Miles

Orkney Islands · Stromness
Scrabster · Gill
· John O' Groats
Thurso
Lewis

Skye · Inverness · Elgin
· Portree · Culloden
Kyle   Loch   Aviemore · Aberdeen
Mallaig   Ness
Fort William   SCOTLAND
Pitlochry
Mull   Perth · Dundee
Oban · Leuchars
Stirling · St. Andrews
Edinburgh

North Sea

Glasgow   Berwick
Holy Island

(2H)   Cairnryan   Hexham
Larne (2.5H)   Stranraer   Newcastle   To Amsterdam (15H)
Belfast   Carlisle   Durham
N. IRE.   Penrith
(8H)   Keswick · Whitby
Irish Sea   Windermere · Danby
Isle   Settle · Scarborough
of Man   ENGLAND
Dublin (7H)   Preston   York
(2-3H)   Blackpool   Leeds · Hull   To Zeebrugge (10H)
Holyhead · Conwy   Liverpool   Grimsby
REP.   Bangor   Manchester
OF   Caernarfon   Betws-y-Coed   Chester   Lincoln
IRE.   Bed.   Blaenau   Stoke
Pwllheli   Ffest.   Derby   Peter-   King's
Harlech   Telford   Wolv.   borough   Lynn   Norwich
To   Aberystwyth   Ironbridge   Birmingham
Rosslare   Gorge   Coventry   Ely   Cambridge
(3.5H)   Stratford   Warwick   Harwich
Fishguard   WALES   Chelt.   Moreton   Oxford   To Hoek (6H)
Carmarthen   Stow   London   Ebbs-
Swansea   Newport   Reading   Windsor   fleet   Canter-
Cardiff   Bath   STONE-   bury
Bristol   HENGE   Salisbury   Ashford   Dover
Atlantic   Wells   West-   1.5H To Calais
Ocean   Glastonbury   bury   Brighton   EUROSTAR (2.5H)
Exeter   Southampton   Newhaven   (4H)
Dartmoor   Portsmouth   To Dieppe
Truro   English Channel   To Paris, Brussels & Amsterdam
St. Ives · Plymouth
Penzance · Falmouth   To Roscoff (6H)   To St-Malo (11H)   To Caen (Ouistreham) (6H)   FRANCE

Rail Passes

Since Britain's pay-as-you-go train tickets are some of the most expensive in Europe, BritRail passes can pay for themselves quickly, especially if you ride a long-distance train (for example, between London and Scotland). A rail pass offers hop-on flexibility and no need to lock in reservations, except for overnight sleeper cars.

The BritRail pass (covering England, Scotland, and Wales) and the BritRail England-only pass come in "consecutive day" and "flexi" versions, with price breaks for youths (under age 26), seniors (60 and up), off-season travelers, and groups of three or more. Most allow one child under 16 to travel free with a paying adult or senior. If you're exploring the backcountry with a BritRail pass, second class is a good choice since many of the smaller train lines don't even offer first-class cars.

Other BritRail options include Scotland-only passes, "London Plus" passes (good for travel in most of southeast England but not in London itself), and South West passes (good for the Cotswolds, Bath, Dorset, Devon, Cornwall, plus part of South Wales).

BritRail passes cannot be purchased locally; buy your pass through an agent before leaving the US. Make sleeper reservations in advance; you can also make optional, free seat reservations (recommended for busy weekends) at staffed train stations.

If your travels are taking you from Britain to the Continent, the Eurail Global Pass covers trains on both sides of the English Channel, and Eurostar trains beneath it (with a paid seat reservation). It's generally cheaper to buy one pass for your whole trip than separate, single-country passes. Global passes also come in "consecutive day" and "flexi" versions, with price breaks for youths (under age 28) and seniors (60 and up). Up to two kids under 12 travel free with you on an adult-rate pass.

For more detailed advice on figuring out the smartest rail-pass options for your train trip, visit www.ricksteves.com/rail.

Buying Tickets

In Advance: The best fares go to those who book their trips well in advance of their journey. Savings can be significant. For a London-York round-trip (standard class), the peak "anytime" fare is about £245 (usually paid by business travelers) and up to £106 for "off-peak." However, if you book online at least a week ahead, off-peak and advance-purchase discounts can combine for a rate closer to £50. An "advance" fare for the same ticket booked a couple of months out can cost as little as £30. If traveling longer distances, such as from Scotland to England, expect higher fares but greater advance discounts.

To book ahead, go in person to any station, look online at www.nationalrail.co.uk, or call 0345-748-4950 (from the US, dial

Rail Pass or Point-to-Point Tickets?

Will you be better off buying a rail pass or point-to-point tickets? It pays to know your options and choose what's best for your itinerary.

Rail Passes

A BritRail Pass lets you travel by train in Scotland, England, and Wales for two to eight days within a one-month period, 15 days within two months, or for continuous periods of up to one month. In addition, BritRail sells England-only and other regional passes. Britain is also covered (along with most of Europe) by the classic Eurail Global Pass. Discounted rates are offered for children, youths, and seniors.

Rail passes are best purchased outside Europe (through travel agents or Rick Steves' Europe). For more on rail passes, including current prices, visit RickSteves.com/rail.

Point-to-Point Tickets

If you're taking just a couple of train rides, buying individual point-to-point train tickets may save you money over a pass. Use this map to add up approximate pay-as-you-go fares for your itinerary, and compare that to the price of a rail pass. Keep in mind that significant discounts on point-to-point tickets may be available with advance purchase.

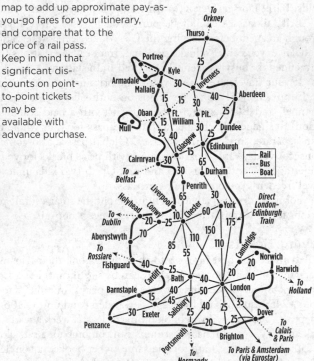

Map shows approximate costs, in US dollars, for one-way, second-class tickets at off-peak rates.

Sample Train Journey

Here is a typical example of a personalized train schedule printed out at a British train station (also online at www.
nationalrail.co.uk). At the Salisbury station, I told the clerk that
I wanted to leave after 16:15 for Moreton-in-Marsh in the Cotswolds. Even though the trip involved two transfers, this schedule allowed me to easily navigate the rails.

Travel by	Leaving	From	Platform	To	Arriving	Platform	Duration
Train	16:21	Salisbury [SAL]	2	Basingstoke [BSK]	16:55	3	0h 34m
		South West Trains service from Exeter St David's to London Waterloo					
Train	17:04	Basingstoke [BSK]	5	Reading [RDG]	17:28	2	0h 24m
		First Great Western service from Basingstoke to Reading					
Train	17:50	Reading [RDG]	9	Moreton-in-Marsh [MIM]	18:54	1	1h 04m
		First Great Western service from London Paddington to Hereford					

Often the conductor on your previous train can tell you
which platform your next train will depart from, but it's wise
to confirm. Scrolling overhead screens on the platforms often
show arrivals, departures, and intermediate stops; some list
train departures by their final destination only. If you are traveling to an intermediate stop and aren't sure which platform
you need, ask any conductor or at the info desk. For example,
after checking with the conductor, I know that I'll need to look
for *Oxford* to catch the train for Moreton-in-Marsh.

Britain's train system can experience delays, so don't
schedule your connections too tightly if you need to reach
your destination at a specific time.

011-44-20-7278-5240, phone answered 24 hours) to find out the
schedule and best fare for your journey; you'll then be referred to
the appropriate vendor—depending on the particular rail company—to book your ticket. If you order online, be sure you know
what you want; it's tough to reach a person who can change your
online reservation. You'll pick up your ticket at the station, or you
may be able to print it at home. (BritRail pass holders, however,
cannot make online seat reservations.)

A company called **Megabus** (through their subsidiary Mega-
train) sells some discounted train tickets well in advance on a few
specific routes, though their focus is mainly on selling bus tickets
(info tel. 0871-266-3333, www.megatrain.com).

Buying Train Tickets as You Travel: If you'd rather have the
flexibility of booking tickets as you go, you can save a few pounds
by buying a round-trip ticket, called a "return ticket" (a same-day
round-trip, called a "day return," is particularly cheap for short excursions); buying before 18:00 the day before you depart; traveling

after the morning rush hour (this usually means after 9:30 Mon-Fri); and going standard class instead of first class. Preview your options at www.nationalrail.co.uk.

Senior, Youth, Partner, and Family Deals: To get a third off the price of most point-to-point rail tickets, seniors can buy a Senior Railcard (ages 60 and up), younger travelers can buy a 16-25 Railcard (ages 16-25, or full-time students 26 and older), and two people traveling together can buy a Two Together Railcard (ages 16 and over). A Family and Friends Railcard gives adults about 33 percent off for most trips and 60 percent off for their kids age 5 to 15 (maximum 4 adults and 4 kids). Each Railcard costs £30; for non-UK citizens, it's best to purchase the pass at a staffed rail station in England, Scotland, or Wales upon arrival as you need a UK delivery address to buy it online (pass also sold at some London airports; some passes require passport-type photo; passport needed for proof of age; see www.railcard.co.uk). These cards are valid for a year on almost all trains, including special runs such as the Heathrow Express, but are not valid on the Eurostar to Paris, Amsterdam, or Brussels.

BUSES

Although buses are about a third slower than trains, they're also a lot cheaper. And buses go many places that trains don't. Most domestic buses are operated by **National Express** (tel. 0871-781-8181, www.nationalexpress.com); their international departures are called **Eurolines** (www.eurolines.co.uk). Note that Brits distinguish between "buses" (for in-city travel with lots of stops) and "coaches" (long-distance cross-country runs)—though for simplicity in this book, I call both "buses."

A smaller company called **Megabus** undersells National Express with deeply discounted promotional fares—the further ahead you buy, the less you pay (some trips for just £1.50, tel. 0141/352-4444, www.megabus.com). While Megabus can be much cheaper than National Express, they tend to be slower than their competitor and their routes mainly connect cities, not smaller towns. They also sell discounted train tickets on selected routes.

Try to avoid bus travel on Friday and Sunday evenings, when weekend travelers are more likely to make buses sell out.

To ensure getting a ticket—and to save money with special promotions—book your ticket in advance online or over the phone. The cheapest prepurchased tickets usually cannot be changed or refunded; other fare types charge a change fee. Check if the ticket is only "amendable" or also "refundable" when you buy. Round-trip bus tickets usually cost less than two one-way fares.

If you want to take a bus from your last destination to the nearest airport, you'll find that National Express often offers

airport buses. Bus stations are normally at or near train stations (in London, the main bus station is a block southwest of Victoria Station).

TAXIS AND RIDE-BOOKING SERVICES

Most British taxis are reliable and cheap. In many cities, two people can travel short distances by cab for little more than the cost of bus or subway tickets. If you like ride-booking services such as Uber, their apps usually work in Britain just like they do in the US: Request a car on your mobile phone (connected to Wi-Fi or data), and the fare is automatically charged to your credit card. London's Uber is facing a legal challenge; check ahead to confirm it is operating.

RENTING A CAR

It's cheaper to arrange most car rentals from the US, so research and compare rates before you go. Most of the major US rental agencies (including Avis, Budget, Enterprise, Hertz, and Thrifty) have offices throughout Europe. Also consider the two major Europe-based agencies, Europcar and Sixt. Consolidators such as Auto Europe (www.autoeurope.com—or the sometimes cheaper www.autoeurope.eu) compare rates at several companies to get you the best deal.

Wherever you book, always read the fine print. Check for add-on charges—such as one-way drop-off fees, airport surcharges, or mandatory insurance policies—that aren't included in the "total price."

Rental Costs and Considerations

Figure on paying roughly $250 for a one-week rental for a basic compact car. Allow extra for supplemental insurance, fuel, tolls, and parking.

Manual vs. Automatic: Almost all rental cars in Europe are manual by default—and cars with a stick shift are generally cheaper. If you need an automatic, request one in advance. An automatic makes sense for most American drivers: With a manual transmission in Britain, you'll be sitting on the right side of the car and shifting with your left hand...while driving on the left side of the road. When selecting a car, don't be tempted by a larger model, as it won't be as maneuverable on narrow, winding roads or when squeezing into tight parking lots.

Age Restrictions: Rental companies in Britain require you to be at least 21 years old and to have held your license for one year. Drivers under the age of 25 may incur a young-driver surcharge, and some rental companies will not rent to anyone 75 or older.

Choosing Pick-up/Drop-off Locations: Always check the hours of the locations you choose: Many rental offices close from

British Radio

Local radio broadcasts can be a treat for drivers sightseeing in Britain. Many British radio stations broadcast nationwide; your car radio automatically detects the local frequency a station plays on and displays its name.

The BBC has five nationwide stations, which you can pick up in most of the country. These government-subsidized stations have no ads.

BBC Radio 1: Pop music, with youthful DJs spinning top 40 hits and interviewing big-name bands.

BBC Radio 2: The highest-rated station nationwide, aimed at a more mature audience, with adult contemporary, retro pop, and other "middle of the road" music.

BBC Radio 3: Mostly classical music, with some jazz and world music.

BBC Radio 4: All talk—current events, entertaining chat shows, special-interest topics such as cooking and gardening, and lots of radio plays.

midday Saturday until Monday morning and, in smaller towns, at lunchtime. When selecting an office, plug the addresses into a mapping website to confirm the location. A downtown site is generally cheaper—and might seem more convenient than the airport. But pedestrianized and one-way streets can make navigation tricky when returning a car at a big-city office or urban train station. Wherever you select, get precise details on the location and allow ample time to find it.

Picking Up Your Car: Before driving off in your rental car, check it thoroughly and make sure any damage is noted on your rental agreement. Rental agencies in Europe tend to charge for even minor damage, so be sure to mark everything. Find out how your car's gearshift, lights, turn signals, wipers, radio, and fuel cap function, and know what kind of fuel the car takes (diesel vs. unleaded). When you return the car, make sure the agent verifies its condition with you. Some drivers take pictures of the returned vehicle as proof of its condition.

Be aware that Brits call it "hiring a car," and directional signs at airports and train stations will read *Car Hire*.

The AA: The services of Britain's Automobile Association are included with most rentals (www.theaa.com), but check for this when booking to be sure you understand its towing and emergency road-service benefits.

Car Insurance Options

When you rent a car in Europe, the price typically includes liability

BBC Radio 5 Live: Sporting events as well as news and sports talk programs.

You'll encounter regional variations of BBC stations, such as BBC London, Radio York, BBC Scotland, and BBC Gaelic. At the top of the hour, many BBC stations broadcast the famous "pips" (indicating Greenwich Mean Time) and a short roundup of the day's news.

Beyond the BBC offerings, several private stations broadcast music and other content with "adverts" (commercials). Some are nationwide, including **XFM** (alternative rock), **Classic FM** (classical), **Absolute Radio** (pop), and **Capital FM** (pop).

Traffic Alerts: Ask your rental-car company about turning on automatic traffic alerts that play on the car radio. Once these are enabled (look for the letters *TA* or *TP* on the radio readout), traffic reports for the area you are driving in will periodically interrupt programming.

insurance, which covers harm to other cars or motorists—but not the rental car itself. To limit your financial risk in case of damage to the rental, choose one of these three options: Buy a Collision Damage Waiver (CDW) with a low or zero deductible from the car-rental company (roughly 30-40 percent extra), get coverage through your credit card (free, but more complicated), or get collision insurance as part of a larger travel-insurance policy.

Basic **CDW** costs $15-30 a day and typically comes with a $1,000-2,000 deductible, reducing but not eliminating your financial responsibility. When you reserve or pick up the car, you'll be offered the chance to "buy down" the deductible to zero (for an additional $10-30/day; this is sometimes called "super CDW" or "zero-deductible coverage").

If you opt for **credit-card coverage,** you must decline all coverage offered by the car-rental company—which means they can place a hold on your card for up to the full value of the car. In case of damage, it can be time-consuming to resolve the charges. Before relying on this option, quiz your card company about how it works.

If you're already purchasing a **travel-insurance policy** for your trip, adding collision coverage can be an economical option. For example, Travel Guard (www.travelguard.com) sells affordable renter's collision insurance as an add-on to its other policies; it's valid everywhere in Europe except the Republic of Ireland, and some Italian car-rental companies refuse to honor it, as it doesn't cover you in case of theft.

For more on car-rental insurance, see www.ricksteves.com/cdw.

Navigation Options

If you'll be navigating using your phone or a GPS unit from home, remember to bring a car charger and device mount.

Your Mobile Phone: The mapping app on your phone works fine for navigating Europe's roads, but for real-time turn-by-turn directions and traffic updates, you'll need mobile data access. And driving all day can burn through a lot of very expensive data. The economical work-around is to use map apps that work offline. By downloading in advance from Google Maps, City Maps 2Go, Apple Maps, Here WeGo, or Navmii, you can still have turn-by-turn voice directions and maps that recalibrate even though they're offline.

You must download your maps before you go offline—and it's smart to select large regions. Then turn off your data connection so you're not charged for roaming. Call up the map, enter your destination, and you're on your way. Even if you don't have to pay extra for data roaming, this option is great for navigating in areas with poor connectivity.

GPS Devices: If you want the convenience of a dedicated GPS unit, known as a "satnav" in Britain, consider renting one with your car ($10-30/day). These units offer real-time turn-by-turn directions and traffic without the data requirements of an app. The unit may come loaded only with maps for its home country; if you need additional maps, ask.

A less-expensive option is to bring a GPS device from home. Be sure to buy and install the maps you'll need before your trip.

Paper Maps and Atlases: Even when navigating primarily with a mobile app or GPS, I always make it a point to have a paper map, ideally a big, detailed regional road map. It's invaluable for getting the big picture, understanding alternate routes, and filling in if my phone runs out of juice. The free maps you get from your car-rental company usually don't have enough detail. It's smart to buy a better map before you go, or pick one up at a local gas station, bookshop, newsstand, or tourist shop.

Several good road atlases cover all of Britain. Ordnance Survey, Collins, AA, and Bartholomew editions are all available at tourist information offices, gas stations, and bookstores. The tourist-oriented Collins Touring maps do a good job of highlighting the many roadside attractions you might otherwise drive right past. Before you buy a map, look at it to be sure it has the level of detail you want.

DRIVING IN BRITAIN

Driving here is basically wonderful—once you remember to stay on the left and after you've mastered the roundabouts. Every year, however, I get a few notes from traveling readers advising me that,

Driving in Great Britain

N

m = miles
h = hours

Note: Your times may vary based on traffic, sheep, construction & road conditions.

To Durness

To John O' Groats

Ullapool

Portree

Skye

35m · 1h

Kyle of Lochalsh

70m · 2.25h

85m · 2h

120m · 2.5h

60m · 1.25h

85m · 2h

20m · .5h

60m · 1.5h

105m · 2.75h

Inverness

Loch Ness (Urquhart Castle)

90m · 1.75h

Aberdeen

SCOTLAND

90m · 2.75h

Pitlochry

80m · 2h

Glencoe

Mull

35m · 1h

80m · 1.75h

70m · 1.5h

60m · 1.5h

Oban

85m · 1.75h

Fionn-phort

Craig-nure

100m · 2.5h

25m · .5h

Stirling

40m · 1h

50m · 1.5h

St. Andrews

Glasgow

50m · 1h

Edinburgh

135m · 2.5h

100m · 2.5h

130m · 3h

75m · 2h

125m · 2.75h

Holy Island

60m · 1.75h

90m · 2.25h

Cairnryan

145m · 3h

Hadrian's Wall (Housesteads Fort)

65m · 1.5h

50m · 1h

Keswick (N. Lake Dist.)

Durham

20m · .5h

120m · 3h

75m · 1.5h

85m · 2h

Windermere (S. Lake Dist.)

Whitby

50m · 1h

35m · 1h

100m · 2h

York

20m · .5h

Blackpool

Preston

40m · 1h

130m · 3.5h

40m · 2.5h

160m · 3h

40m · .75h

Holyhead

60m · 1.25h

Liverpool

30m · 1h

Conwy

25m · .5h

15m · .5h

Caernarfon

25m · .75h

Ruthin

30m · 1h

75m · 2h

Betws-y-Coed

ENGLAND

220m · 4h

170m · 4h

150m · 3.5h

Iron-bridge

10m · .25h

Coventry

70m · 1.5h

70m · 1.5h

Warwick

10m · .5h

10m · .5h

35m · 1.0h

Stratford

110m · 2h

Cambridge

WALES

Cotswolds (Stow)

70m · 2h

90m · 2h

60m · 1.25h

Tintern

50m · 1h

Oxford

60m · 1.5h

65m · 1.5h

65m · 1.5h

Cardiff

London

55m · 1.25h

20m · .75h

Bath

50m · 1h

Avebury

60m · 1.5h

Wells

Glastonbury

30m · 1h

85m · 1.75h

55m · 1h

Canterbury

10m · .25h

50m · 1.25h

100m · 2h

60m · 1.5h

To Land's End

80m · 2h

120m · 2.5h

Salisbury

45m · 1h

50m · 1.5h

85m · 3h

Dover

100m · 2h

Dartmoor Nat'l Park

50m · 1.5h

Corfe Castle

Brighton

Portsmouth

PRACTICALITIES

for them, trying to drive in Britain was a nerve-racking and regrettable mistake. If you want to get a little slack on the roads, drop by a gas station or auto shop and buy a green *P* (probationary driver with license) sign to put in your car window (don't get the red *L* sign, which means you're a learner driver without a license and thus prohibited from driving on motorways).

Many Yankee drivers find the hardest part isn't driving on the left, but steering from the right. Your instinct is to put yourself on the left side of your lane, which means you may spend your first day or two drifting into the left shoulder or curb. It helps to remember that the driver always stays close to the center line.

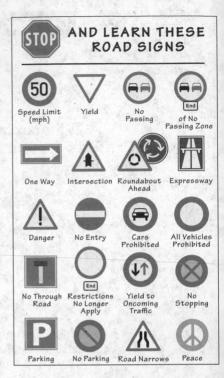

STOP AND LEARN THESE ROAD SIGNS

Speed Limit (mph) · Yield · No Passing · End of No Passing Zone

One Way · Intersection · Roundabout Ahead · Expressway

Danger · No Entry · Cars Prohibited · All Vehicles Prohibited

No Through Road · End Restrictions No Longer Apply · Yield to Oncoming Traffic · No Stopping

Parking · No Parking · Road Narrows · Peace

Road Rules: Be aware of Britain's rules of the road. Seat belts are mandatory for all, and kids under age 12 (or less than about 4.5 feet tall) must ride in an appropriate child-safety seat. It's illegal to use a mobile phone while driving—pull over or use a hands-free device. In Britain, you're not allowed to turn left on a red light unless a sign or signal specifically authorizes it, and on motorways it's illegal to pass drivers on the left. Ask your car-rental company about these rules, or check the "International Travel" section of the US State Department website (www.travel.state.gov, search for your country in the "Learn About Your Destination" box, then click "Travel and Transportation").

Speed Limits: Speed limits are in miles per hour: 30 mph in town, 70 mph on the motorways, and 60 or 70 mph elsewhere (though, as back home, many British drivers consider these limits advisory). The national sign for the maximum speed is a white circle with a black slash. Motorways have electronic speed limit signs; posted speeds can change depending on traffic or the weather. Follow them accordingly.

Note that road-surveillance cameras strictly enforce speed limits. Any driver (including foreigners renting cars) photographed speeding will get a nasty bill in the mail. (Cameras—in

foreboding gray boxes—
flash on rear license plates
to respect the privacy of
anyone sharing the front
seat with someone he or
she shouldn't.) Signs (an
image of an old-fashioned
camera) alert you when
you're entering a zone that
may be monitored by these
"camera cops." Heed them.

Roundabouts: Don't let a roundabout spook you. After all, you routinely merge into much faster traffic on American highways back home. Traffic flows clockwise, and cars already in the roundabout have the right-of-way; entering traffic yields (look to your right as you merge). You'll probably encounter "double-roundabouts"—figure-eights where you'll slingshot from one roundabout directly into another. Just go with the flow and track signs carefully. When approaching an especially complex roundabout, you'll first pass a diagram showing the layout and the various exits. And in many cases, the pavement is painted to indicate the lane you should be in for a particular road or town.

Freeways (Motorways): The shortest distance between any two points is usually the motorway (what we'd call a "freeway"). In Britain, the smaller the number, the bigger the road. For example, the M-4 is a freeway, while the B-4494 is a country road.

Motorway road signs can be confusing, too few, and too late. Miss a motorway exit and you can lose 30 minutes. Study your map before taking off. Know the cities you'll be lacing together, since road numbers are inconsistent. British road signs are never marked with compass directions (e.g., *A-4 West*); instead, you need to know what major town or city you're heading for *(A-4 Bath)*. The driving directions in this book are intended to be used with a good map. Get a road atlas, easily purchased at gas stations in Britain, or download digital maps before your trip (see page 948).

Unless you're passing, always drive in the "slow" lane on motorways (the lane farthest to the left). The British are very disciplined about this; ignoring this rule could get you a ticket (or into a road-rage incident). Remember to pass on the right, not the left.

Rest areas are called "services" and often have a number of useful amenities, such as restaurants, cafeterias, gas stations, shops, and motels.

Fuel: Gas (petrol) costs about $5.50 per gallon and is self-serve. Pump first and then pay. Diesel costs about the same. Diesel rental cars are common; make sure you know what kind of fuel your car takes before you fill up. Unleaded pumps are usually green.

How to Navigate a Roundabout

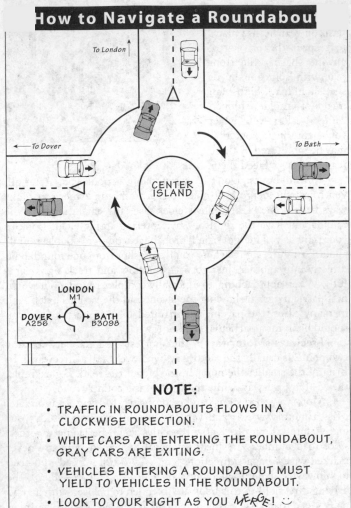

NOTE:

- TRAFFIC IN ROUNDABOUTS FLOWS IN A CLOCKWISE DIRECTION.
- WHITE CARS ARE ENTERING THE ROUNDABOUT, GRAY CARS ARE EXITING.
- VEHICLES ENTERING A ROUNDABOUT MUST YIELD TO VEHICLES IN THE ROUNDABOUT.
- LOOK TO YOUR RIGHT AS YOU MERGE! ☺

Note that self-service gas pumps and automated tollbooths and parking garages often accept only a chip-and-PIN credit card or cash. It might help if you know the PIN for your US credit and debit cards, but just in case a machine rejects them, be sure to carry sufficient cash. For more on chip and PIN, see page 906.

Driving in Cities: Whenever possible, avoid driving in cities. Be warned that London assesses a congestion charge (see page 51). Most cities have modern ring roads to skirt the congestion. Follow signs to the parking lots outside the city core—most are a 5- to 10-minute walk to the center—and avoid what can be an unpleasant grid of one-way streets (as in Bath) or roads that are only available to public transportation during the day (as in Oxford).

Driving in Rural Areas: Outside the big cities and except for the motorways, British roads tend to be narrow. In towns, you may have to cross over the center line just to get past parked cars. Adjust your perceptions of personal space: It's not "my side of the road" or "your side of the road," it's just "the road"—and it's shared as a cooperative adventure. If the road's wide enough, traffic in both directions can pass parked cars simultaneously, but frequently you'll have to take turns—follow the locals' lead and drive defensively.

Narrow country lanes are often lined with stone walls or woody hedges—and no shoulders. Some are barely wide enough for one car (one-lane roads are often referred to as "single-track" roads). Go slowly, and if you encounter an oncoming car, look for the nearest pullout (or "passing place")—the driver who's closest to one is expected to use it, even if it means backing up to reach it. If another car pulls over and blinks its headlights, that means, "Go ahead; I'll wait to let you pass." British drivers—arguably some of the most courteous on the planet—are quick to offer a friendly wave to thank you for letting them pass (and they appreciate it if you reciprocate). Pull over frequently—to let faster locals pass and to check the map.

Parking: Pay attention to pavement markings to figure out where to park. One yellow line marked on the pavement means no parking Monday through Saturday during work hours. Double yellow lines mean no parking at any time. Broken yellow lines mean short stops are OK, but you should always look for explicit signs or ask a passerby. White lines mean you're free to park.

In towns, rather than look for street parking, I generally just pull into the most central and handy pay-and-display parking lot I can find. To pay and display, feed change into a machine, receive a timed ticket, and display it on the dashboard or stick it to the driver's-side window. Rates are reasonable by US standards, and locals love to share stickers that have time remaining. If you stand by the machine, someone on their way out with time left on their sticker will probably give it to you. Most machines in larger towns accept credit cards with a chip, but it's smart to keep coins handy for machines that don't.

In some municipalities, drivers will see signs for "disc zone" parking. This is free, time-limited parking. But to use it, you must obtain a clock parking disc from a shop and display it on the dashboard (set the clock to show your time of arrival). Return within the signed time limit to avoid being ticketed.

Some parking garages (a.k.a. car parks) are automated and record your license plate with a camera when you enter. The Brits call a license plate a "number plate" or just "vehicle registration." The payment machine will use these terms when you pay before exiting.

FLIGHTS

To compare flight costs and times, begin with an online travel search engine: Kayak is the top site for flights to and within Europe, easy-to-use Google Flights has price alerts, and Skyscanner includes many inexpensive flights within Europe. To avoid unpleasant surprises, before you book be sure to read the small print about refunds, changes, and the costs for "extras" such as reserving a seat, checking a bag, or printing a boarding pass.

Flights to Europe: Start looking for international flights about four to six months before your trip, especially for peak-season travel. Depending on your itinerary, it can be efficient and no more expensive to fly into one city and out of another. If your flight requires a connection in Europe, see my hints on navigating Europe's top hub airports at www.ricksteves.com/hub-airports.

Flights Within Europe: Flying between European cities is surprisingly affordable. Before buying a long-distance train or bus ticket, check the cost of a flight on one of Europe's airlines, whether a major carrier or a no-frills outfit like **EasyJet** or **Ryanair**. Other airlines to consider include **CityJet** (based at London City Airport, www.cityjet.com), **TUI Airways** (www.tui.co.uk), **Flybe** (www.flybe.com), and **Brussels Airlines** (with frequent connections from Heathrow to its Brussels hub, www.brusselsairlines.com).

Be aware that flying with a discount airline can have drawbacks, such as minimal customer service and time-consuming treks to secondary airports.

Flying to the US and Canada: Because security is extra tight for flights to the US, be sure to give yourself plenty of time at the airport. Charge your electronic devices before you board in case security checks require you to turn them on (see www.tsa.gov for the latest rules).

Resources from Rick Steves

Begin Your Trip at RickSteves.com

My mobile-friendly **website** is *the* place to explore Europe in preparation for your trip. You'll find thousands of fun articles, videos, and radio interviews; a wealth of money-saving tips for planning your dream trip; travel news dispatches; a video library of my travel talks; my travel blog; my latest guidebook updates (www.ricksteves.com/update); and my free Rick Steves Audio Europe app. You can also follow me on Facebook, Instagram, and Twitter.

Our **Travel Forum** is a well-groomed collection of message boards, where our travel-savvy community answers questions and shares their personal travel experiences—and our well-traveled staff chimes in when they can be helpful (www.ricksteves.com/forums).

Our **online Travel Store** offers bags and accessories that I've designed to help you travel smarter and lighter. These include my popular carry-on bags (which I live out of four months a year), money belts, totes, toiletries kits, adapters, guidebooks, and planning maps (www.ricksteves.com/shop).

Our website can also help you find the perfect **rail pass** for your itinerary and your budget, with easy, one-stop shopping for rail passes, seat reservations, and point-to-point tickets (www.ricksteves.com/rail).

Rick Steves' Tours, Guidebooks, TV Shows, and More

Small Group Tours: Want to travel with greater efficiency and less stress? We offer more than 40 itineraries reaching the best destinations in this book...and beyond. Each year about 30,000 travelers join us on about 1,000 Rick Steves bus tours. You'll enjoy great guides and a fun bunch of travel partners (with small groups of 24 to 28 travelers). You'll find European adventures to fit every vacation length. For all the details, and to get our tour catalog, visit www.ricksteves.com/tours or call us at 425/608-4217.

Books: *Rick Steves England* is just one of many books in my series on European travel, which includes country and city guidebooks, Snapshots (excerpted chapters from bigger guides), Pocket guides (full-color little books on big cities), "Best Of" guidebooks (condensed, full-color country guides), and my budget-travel skills handbook, *Rick Steves Europe Through the Back Door*. A complete list of my titles—including phrase books; cruising guides; and travelogues on European art, history, and culture; and more—appears near the end of this book.

TV Shows and Travel Talks: My public television series, *Rick Steves' Europe*, covers Europe from top to bottom with over 100 half-hour episodes—and we're working on new shows every year (watch full episodes at my website for free). My free online video library, Rick Steves Classroom Europe, offers a searchable database of short video clips on European history, culture, and geography (classroom.ricksteves.com). And to raise your travel I.Q., check out the video versions of our popular classes (covering most European countries as well as travel skills, packing smart, cruising, tech for travelers,

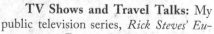

European art, and travel as a political act—www.ricksteves.com/travel-talks.

Radio: My weekly public radio show, *Travel with Rick Steves,* features interviews with travel experts from around the world. It airs on 400 public radio stations across the US, or you can hear it as a podcast. A complete archive of programs is available at www.ricksteves.com/radio.

Audio Tours on My Free App: I've produced dozens of free, self-guided audio tours of the top sights in Europe. For those tours and other audio content, get my free **Rick Steves Audio Europe app,** an extensive online library organized by destination. For more on my app, see page 30.

APPENDIX

Holidays and Festivals

This list includes selected festivals in England plus national holidays observed throughout Britain. Many sights and banks close on national holidays—keep this in mind when planning your itinerary. Throughout Britain, hotels get booked up during Easter week; over the Early May, Spring, and Summer Bank Holidays; and during Christmas, Boxing Day, and New Year's Day. On Christmas, virtually everything shuts down—even the Tube in London. Museums also generally close on December 24 and 26.

Many British towns have holiday festivals in late November and early December, with markets, music, and entertainment in the Christmas spirit (for instance, Keswick's Victorian Fayre).

Before planning a trip around a festival, verify the dates with the festival website, the Visit Britain website (www.visitbritain. com), or my "Upcoming Holidays and Festivals in England" web page (www.ricksteves.com/europe/england/festivals).

Jan 1	New Year's Day
Mid-Feb	London Fashion Week (www.londonfashionweek.co.uk)
Mid-Feb	Jorvik Viking Festival, York (costumed warriors, battles; www.jorvik-viking-festival.co.uk)

April	Easter Sunday-Monday: April 12-13, 2020; April 4-5, 2021
May	Early May Bank Holiday: May 8, 2020; May 3, 2021 Spring Bank Holiday: May 25, 2020; May 31, 2021
Early-mid-May	Jazz Festival, Keswick (www.keswickjazzfestival.co.uk)
Late May	Chelsea Flower Show, London (www.rhs.org.uk/chelsea)
Late May-early June	Bath Festival (www.bathfestivals.org.uk)
Late May-early June	Fringe Festival, Bath (alternative music, dance, and theater; www.bathfringe.co.uk)
Early June	Beer Festival, Keswick (music, shows; www.keswickbeerfestival.co.uk)
Early-mid June	Trooping the Colour, London (military bands and pageantry, Queen's birthday parade; www.qbp.army.mod.uk)
Late June	Royal Ascot Horse Race, Ascot (near Windsor; www.ascot.co.uk)
Mid-late June	Golowan (Midsummer) Festival, Penzance (www.golowanfestival.org)
Late June-mid-July	Wimbledon Tennis Championship, London (www.wimbledon.org)
Mid-July	Early Music Festival, York (www.ncem.co.uk)
Late July-early Aug	Cambridge Folk Festival (www.cambridgefolkfestival.co.uk)
Late Aug	Notting Hill Carnival, London (costumes, Caribbean music, www.thelondonnottinghillcarnival.com)
Late Aug	Bank Holiday: Aug 31, 2020; Aug 30, 2021 (England and Wales only)
Sept-early Nov	Illuminations, Blackpool (waterfront light festival, www.visitblackpool.com/illuminations)
Mid-Sept	London Fashion Week (www.londonfashionweek.co.uk)
Late Sept	Jane Austen Festival, Bath (www.janeausten.co.uk)
Late Sept	York Food and Drink Festival (www.yorkfoodfestival.com)
Nov 5	Bonfire Night (bonfires, fireworks, effigy burning of 1605 traitor Guy Fawkes)
Dec 24-26	Christmas holidays

Books and Films

To learn more about England's past and present, check out a few of these books and films.

Nonfiction

All Creatures Great and Small (James Herriot, 1972). Herriot's beloved semi-autobiographical tales of life as a Yorkshire veterinarian were made into a long-running BBC series (1978-1990).

The Anglo Files: A Field Guide to the British (Sarah Lyall, 2008). A *New York Times* reporter in London wittily recounts the eccentricities of life in the UK.

Cider with Rosie (Laurie Lee, 1959). This semi-autobiographical boyhood novel set in a Cotswolds village just after World War I has been adapted for TV three times, including once by the BBC in 2015.

Dead Wake (Erik Larson, 2015). Larson gives an evocative account of the doomed 1915 voyage of British luxury liner *Lusitania*, sunk by a German U-boat during World War I.

England: 1000 Things You Need to Know (Nicolas Hobbes, 2009). Hobbes presents a fun peek into the facts, fables, and foibles of English life.

Fever Pitch (Nick Hornby, 1992). Hornby's memoir illuminates the British obsession with soccer.

A History of Britain (Simon Schama, 2000-2002). The respected historian presents a comprehensive, thoroughly readable three-volume collection.

A History of Modern Britain (Andrew Marr, 2007). This searching look at the transformations in British life over the last few decades accompanies a BBC documentary series of the same name.

How England Made the English: From Hedgerows to Heathrow (Harry Mount, 2012). Mount offers a witty, engaging look at the symbiotic relationship between the English landscape and English culture.

The Kingdom by the Sea: A Journey Around the Coast of Great Britain (Paul Theroux, 1983). After 11 years as an American expatriate in London, travel writer Theroux takes a witty tour of his adopted homeland.

A Land (Jacquetta Hawkes, 1951). This postwar best-seller is a sweeping, poetic natural history of the British landscape and imagination.

The Last Lion (William Manchester, final book completed by Paul Reid; 1983, 1988, and 2012). This superb, three-volume biography recounts the amazing life of Winston Churchill from 1874 to 1965.

Literary Trails (Christina Hardyment, 2000). Hardyment reunites famous authors with the environments that inspired them.

My Love Affair with England (Susan Allen Toth, 1994). Toth brings England vividly to life in a captivating traveler's memoir recalling the country's charms and eccentricities.

Notes from a Small Island (Bill Bryson, 1995). In this irreverent and delightful memoir, US expat Bryson writes about his travels through Britain—his home for two decades.

A Traveller's History of England (Christopher Daniell, revised 2005). A British archaeologist and historian provides a comprehensive yet succinct overview of English history.

With Wings Like Eagles (Michael Korda, 2009). An English-born writer gives a historical analysis of Britain's pivotal WWII air battles versus the German Luftwaffe.

Fiction

For the classics of British drama and fiction, read anything—and everything—by William Shakespeare, Charles Dickens, Jane Austen, and the Brontës.

Atonement (Ian McEwan, 2001). This disquieting family saga set in upper-class England at the start of World War II dramatizes the consequences of a childhood lie. The 2007 motion picture starring James McAvoy and Keira Knightley is also excellent.

Behind the Scenes at the Museum (Kate Atkinson, 1995). Starting at her conception, this book's quirky narrator recounts the highs and lows of life in a middle-class English family.

Brideshead Revisited (Evelyn Waugh, 1945). This celebrated novel examines the intense entanglement of a young man with an aristocratic family.

Bridget Jones's Diary (Helen Fielding, 1996). A year in the life of a single 30-something woman in London is humorously chronicled in diary form (also a motion picture, with several sequels).

High Fidelity (Nick Hornby, 1995). This humorous novel traces the romantic misadventures and musical musings of a 30-something record-store owner. Another good read is Hornby's 1998 coming-of-age story, *About a Boy*. (Both books were also made into films.)

Macbeth (William Shakespeare, 1606). Shakespeare's "Scottish Play" depicts a guilt-wracked general who assassinates the king to take the throne.

Mapp and Lucia (E. F. Benson, 1931). A rural village in the 1930s becomes a social battlefield. In *Lucia in London* (1927), the protagonist attempts social climbing in the big city.

A Morbid Taste for Bones (Ellis Peters, 1977). Brother Cadfael, a

Benedictine monk-detective, tries to solve a murder in 12th-century Shropshire (first book in a series; also adapted for British TV in 1996).

The Murder at the Vicarage (Agatha Christie, 1930). The prolific mystery writer's inquisitive Miss Marple character is first introduced in this book.

The Paying Guests (Sarah Waters, 2014). This realistic and suspenseful tale of love, obsession, and murder plays out amid the shifting culture of post-WWII upper-class London.

The Pillars of the Earth (Ken Follett, 1990). This epic set in a fictional town in 12th-century England chronicles the birth of Gothic architecture.

Rebecca (Daphne du Maurier, 1938). This mysterious tale set on the Cornish coast examines upper-class English lives and their secrets.

Restoration (Rose Tremain, 1989). This evocative historical novel takes readers to the heights and depths of 17th-century English society.

The Strange Case of Dr. Jekyll and Mr. Hyde (Robert Louis Stevenson, 1886). This famous Gothic yarn by a Scottish author chronicles a fearful case of transformation in London, exploring Victorian ideas about conflict between good and evil.

SS-GB (Len Deighton, 1979). In a Nazi-occupied Great Britain, a Scotland Yard detective finds there's more to a murder than meets the eye.

A Study in Scarlet (Sir Arthur Conan Doyle, 1888). This mystery novel introduced the world to detective Sherlock Holmes and his trusty sidekick, Dr. Watson.

The Sunne in Splendour (Sharon Kay Penman, 2008). Penman's big entertaining book paints King Richard III as a rather decent chap (one in a series of historical novels).

The Unlikely Pilgrimage of Harold Fry (Rachel Joyce, 2012). A man impetuously sets off on a walk across Britain to visit an old friend—and sees his country as never before.

The Warden (Anthony Trollope, 1855). The first novel in the "Chronicles of Barsetshire" series addresses moral dilemmas in the 19th-century Anglican church.

White Teeth (Zadie Smith, 2000). The postwar lives of two army buddies, a native Englishman and a Bengali Muslim, are chronicled in this acclaimed debut novel.

Wolf Hall (Hilary Mantel, 2010). At the intrigue-laced Tudor court of Henry VIII, Thomas Cromwell becomes the king's right-hand man. The story continues in *Bring Up the Bodies* (2012) and concludes in *The Mirror and the Light*.

Film and TV

Austin Powers: International Man of Mystery (1997). Mike Myers stars in this loony send-up of midcentury English culture, the first film in a three-part series.

Battle of Britain (1969). An all-star cast and marvelous aerial combat scenes tell the story of Britain's "finest hour" of World War II.

Bend It Like Beckham (2003). A teenage girl of Punjabi descent plays soccer against her traditional parents' wishes in this lighthearted comedy-drama.

Billy Elliot (2000). A young boy pursues his dream to dance ballet amid a coal miners' strike in working-class northern England.

Blackadder (1983-1989). This wickedly funny BBC sitcom starring Rowan Atkinson skewers various periods of English history in the course of four series (also several TV specials).

Call the Midwife (2012-). London's poor East End comes to gritty, poignant life in this BBC drama tracing the lives of a team of nurse midwives in the late 1950s and early 1960s.

Chariots of Fire (1981). This Academy Award winner traces the lives of two British track stars competing in the 1924 Paris Olympics.

The Crown (2016-). The Netflix biographical drama explores the life of Elizabeth II—England's longest-reigning queen.

Doc Martin (2004-). A brilliant but socially inept London surgeon finds new challenges and opportunities when he opens a practice in a seaside village in Cornwall.

Downton Abbey (2010-2015). This popular aristocratic soap opera follows the travails of the Crawley family and their servants in early-20th-century Yorkshire (shot at Highclere Castle, about 70 miles west of London).

Elizabeth (1998). Cate Blanchett portrays Queen Elizabeth I as she learns the royal ropes during the early years of her reign, and reprises her role in the sequel, *Elizabeth: The Golden Age* (2007).

Elizabeth I (2005). In this BBC/HBO miniseries, the inimitable Helen Mirren chronicles the queen's later years with a focus on her court's intrigue and her yearning for love.

Foyle's War (2002-2015). This fine BBC series follows detective Christopher Foyle as he solves crimes in southern England during and shortly after World War II.

Goodbye, Mr. Chips (1939). The headmaster of a boys' boarding school in Victorian-era England recalls his life in this romantic drama.

Gosford Park (2001). This intriguing film is part comedy, part murder mystery, and part critique of England's class stratification in the 1930s.

A Hard Day's Night (1964). The Beatles star in their debut film, a comedy depicting several days in the life of the band.

Hope and Glory (1987). John Boorman directed this semi-autobiographical story of a boy growing up during World War II's London blitz.

Howards End (1992). This Academy Award winner, based on the E. M. Forster novel, captures the stifling societal pressure underneath the gracious manners in turn-of-the-century England.

The Imitation Game (2014). Cryptanalyst Alan Turing (Benedict Cumberbatch) is recruited by British intelligence agency MI6 to help crack the Nazis' Enigma code during World War II.

James Bond films (1962-). These classic films follow a dashing officer in Britain's Secret Intelligence Service, who likes his martinis "shaken, not stirred."

Jane Eyre (2011). Charlotte Brontë's 1847 gothic romance has been made into a movie at least nine times, most recently this one starring Mia Wasikowska and Michael Fassbender.

The King's Speech (2010). Colin Firth stars as the stuttering King George VI on the eve of World War II.

Lark Rise to Candleford (2008-2011). Based on Flora Thompson's memoirs, this evocative series chronicles life in a poor Victorian-era hamlet and its neighboring, more hoity market town.

A Man for All Seasons (1966). Lord Chancellor Sir Thomas More incurs the wrath of Henry VIII when he refuses to help annul the king's marriage to Catherine of Aragon.

Mr. Bean (1990-1995). Rubber-faced comedian Rowan Atkinson's iconic character bumbles through life barely uttering a word in this zany sitcom (that also spawned two motion pictures).

Monty Python and the Holy Grail (1975). This surreal take on Arthurian legend is a classic of British comedy.

Notting Hill (1999). Hugh Grant and Julia Roberts star in this romantic comedy set in the London neighborhood of...you guessed it.

Persuasion (1995). Set in 19th-century England, this Jane Austen tale of status was partially filmed in Bath.

Poldark (2015-). In this hit BBC series, Ross Poldark returns to Cornwall after fighting in the Revolutionary War to find his estate, tin mines, and relationship in ruins.

Pride and Prejudice (1995). Of the many versions of Jane Austen's classic, this BBC miniseries starring Colin Firth is the winner.

The Queen (2006). Helen Mirren expertly channels Elizabeth II at her Scottish Balmoral estate in the days after Princess Diana's death. Its prequel, *The Deal* (2003), probes the relationship between Tony Blair and Gordon Brown.

The Remains of the Day (1993). Anthony Hopkins stars as a butler

APPENDIX

doggedly loyal to his misguided, politically naive master in 1930s England.

Sammy and Rosie Get Laid (1987). An unconventional middle-class couple's promiscuous adventures expose racial tensions in multi-ethnic London.

Sense and Sensibility (1995). Star Emma Thompson wrote the screenplay for this adaptation of Jane Austen's 1811 novel of the Dashwood sisters, who seek financial security through marriage.

Shakespeare in Love (1999). Tudor-era London comes to life in this clever, romantic film set in the original Globe Theatre.

Sherlock (2010-). Holmes (Benedict Cumberbatch) and Watson (Martin Freeman) are excellent in this BBC update of the detective's story, set in present-day London.

Sherlock Holmes (2009). Robert Downey Jr. tackles the role of the world's most famous detective.

Sweeney Todd (2007). Johnny Depp stars as a wrongfully imprisoned barber who seeks revenge in this gritty Victorian-era musical.

Tinker, Tailor, Soldier, Spy (2011). There's a Soviet mole inside Britain's MI6 and retired agent George Smiley is summoned to ferret him out, in this adaptation of John le Carré's 1974 espionage thriller.

To Sir, with Love (1967). Sidney Poitier grapples with social and racial issues in an inner-city school in London's East End.

The Tudors (2007-2010). Showtime's racy, lavish series is a gripping, loosely accurate chronicle of the marriages of Henry VIII.

Upstairs, Downstairs (1971-1975). An aristocratic family and their servants make a new home at 165 Eaton Place in this TV series.

Waterloo Bridge (1940). This Academy Award-nominated romantic drama recalls the lost love between a ballerina (Vivien Leigh) and a WWI army officer.

Wolf Hall (2015). The exploits of Thomas Cromwell, the chief minister to King Henry VIII, are detailed in this excellent BBC historical miniseries.

Victoria (2017-). This PBS Masterpiece Theatre series chronicles the rise and reign of Queen Victoria (Jenna Coleman).

For Kids

A Bear Called Paddington (Michael Bond, 1958). A bear from Peru winds up in a London train station, where he's found and adopted by a human family. The 2014 *Paddington* film is also fun viewing.

B is for Big Ben (Pamela Duncan Edwards, 2008). Explore England from A to Z with rhymes, trivia, and bright illustrations.

The Chronicles of Narnia books (C.S. Lewis, 1950-1956) and movies (2005-2010). Four siblings escape from WWII London into a magical world. The first of the seven novels, *The Lion, the Witch & the Wardrobe,* was also a BBC miniseries (1988).

Harry Potter books (J. K. Rowling, 1997-2007) and films (2001-2011). After discovering he's a wizard, a young boy in England gets whisked off to a magical world of witchcraft and wizardry. There, he finds great friendships as well as grave evils, which he alone can destroy.

A Little Princess (1995). In this film adaptation of the classic novel, a young girl's fortunes fall and rise again in a Victorian London boarding school.

Mary Poppins (1964). Though filmed on a set in California, this beloved musical starring Julie Andrews and Dick Van Dyke is set in Edwardian London. In the sequel, *Mary Poppins Returns* (2018), the kids are grown and revisited by Mary (Emily Blunt) and her friend Jack (Lin-Manuel Miranda).

Peter Pan (2003). The latest in a long line of films adapting the classic 1902 novel *Peter and Wendy,* this live-action version flies real English children to Neverland.

Robin Hood and the Golden Arrow (Robert D. San Souci, 2010). This illustrated retelling is a good introduction for youngsters to the legend of Robin Hood and his merry men.

The Secret Garden (Frances Hodgson Burnett, 1911). Orphaned Mary discovers nature and love in a gloomy Yorkshire mansion on the edge of a moor in this beloved classic, which has been adapted for stage and screen.

Wallace & Gromit TV series and films (1990-2012). Absent-minded inventor Wallace and his dog, Gromit, may live in northwest England, but these unique characters are beloved by children around Great Britain and the rest of the world.

Winnie-the-Pooh and *The House at Pooh Corner* (A. A. Milne, 1926-1928). This two-volume classic children's tale, set in England, revolves around a bear and his friends in the Hundred Acre Wood. The success of Milne's books has led to numerous book, film, and TV adaptations.

Young Sherlock Holmes (1985). A young Sherlock and his sidekick, Watson, work to solve the mystery of a series of nonsensical suicides (some scenes may be frightening for younger children).

Conversions and Climate

Numbers and Stumblers

- Some British people write a few of their numbers differently than we do: 1 = *1*, 4 = *4*, 7 = *7*.
- In Europe, dates appear as day/month/year, so Christmas 2021 is 25/12/21.
- What Americans call the second floor of a building is the first floor in Britain.
- On escalators and moving sidewalks, Brits keep the left "lane" open for passing. Keep to the right.
- To avoid the British version of giving someone "the finger," don't hold up the first two fingers of your hand with your palm facing you. (It looks like a reversed victory sign.)

Metric Conversions

Britain uses the metric system for nearly everything. Weight and volume are typically calculated in metrics: A kilogram is 2.2 pounds, and one liter is about a quart (almost four to a gallon). Temperatures are given in Celsius, although some newspapers also list them in Fahrenheit.

1 foot = 0.3 meter	1 square yard = 0.8 square meter
1 yard = 0.9 meter	1 square mile = 2.6 square kilometers
1 mile = 1.6 kilometers	1 ounce = 28 grams
1 centimeter = 0.4 inch	1 quart = 0.95 liter
1 meter = 39.4 inches	1 kilogram = 2.2 pounds
1 kilometer = 0.62 mile	32°F = 0°C

Imperial Weights and Measures

Britain hasn't completely gone metric. Driving distances and speed limits are measured in miles. Beer is sold as pints (though milk can be measured in pints or liters), and a person's weight is measured in stone (a 168-pound person weighs 12 stone).

1 stone = 14 pounds
1 British pint = 1.2 US pints
1 imperial gallon = 1.2 US gallons or about 4.5 liters

Clothing Sizes

When shopping for clothing, use these US-to-UK comparisons as general guidelines (but note that no conversion is perfect).

Women: For pants and dresses, add 4 (US 10 = UK 14). For blouses and sweaters, add 2. For shoes, subtract 2½ (US size 8 = UK size 5½).

Men: For clothing, US and UK sizes are the same. For shoes, subtract about ½ (US size 9 = UK size 8½).

Children: Clothing is sized similarly to the US. UK kids' shoe sizes are about one size smaller (US size 6 = UK size 5).

Britain's Climate

First line, average daily high; second line, average low; third line, average days without rain. For more detailed weather statistics for destinations in this book (and elsewhere), check www.wunderground.com.

	J	F	M	A	M	J	J	A	S	O	N	D
LONDON												
	43°	44°	50°	56°	62°	69°	71°	71°	65°	58°	50°	45°
	36°	36°	38°	42°	47°	53°	56°	56°	52°	46°	42°	38°
	16	15	20	18	19	19	19	20	17	18	15	16
YORK												
	43°	44°	49°	55°	61°	67°	70°	69°	64°	57°	49°	45°
	33°	34°	36°	40°	44°	50°	54°	53°	50°	44°	39°	36°
	14	13	18	17	18	16	16	17	16	16	13	14

APPENDIX

Fahrenheit and Celsius Conversion

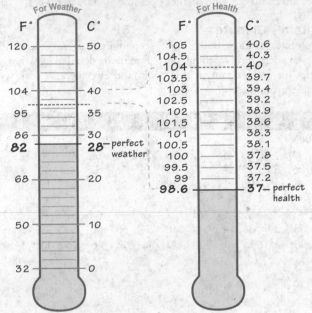

Europe takes its temperature using the Celsius scale, while we
opt for Fahrenheit. For a rough conversion from Celsius to
Fahrenheit, double the number and add 30. For weather, remember
that 28°C is 82°F—perfect. For health, 37°C is just right. At a
launderette, 30°C is cold, 40°C is warm (usually the default
setting), 60°C is hot, and 95°C is boiling. Your air-conditioner
should be set at about 20°C.

Packing Checklist

Whether you're traveling for five days or five weeks, you won't need more than this. Pack light to enjoy the sweet freedom of true mobility.

Clothing

- ❑ 5 shirts: long- & short-sleeve
- ❑ 2 pairs pants (or skirts/capris)
- ❑ 1 pair shorts
- ❑ 5 pairs underwear & socks
- ❑ 1 pair walking shoes
- ❑ Sweater or warm layer
- ❑ Rainproof jacket with hood
- ❑ Tie, scarf, belt, and/or hat
- ❑ Swimsuit
- ❑ Sleepwear/loungewear

Money

- ❑ Debit card(s)
- ❑ Credit card(s)
- ❑ Hard cash (US $100-200)
- ❑ Money belt

Documents

- ❑ Passport
- ❑ Tickets & confirmations: flights, hotels, trains, rail pass, car rental, sight entries
- ❑ Driver's license
- ❑ Student ID, hostel card, etc.
- ❑ Photocopies of important documents
- ❑ Insurance details
- ❑ Guidebooks & maps

Toiletries Kit

- ❑ Basics: soap, shampoo, toothbrush, toothpaste, floss, deodorant, sunscreen, brush/comb, etc.
- ❑ Medicines & vitamins
- ❑ First-aid kit
- ❑ Glasses/contacts/sunglasses
- ❑ Sewing kit
- ❑ Packet of tissues (for WC)
- ❑ Earplugs

Electronics

- ❑ Mobile phone
- ❑ Camera & related gear
- ❑ Tablet/ebook reader/laptop
- ❑ Headphones/earbuds
- ❑ Chargers & batteries
- ❑ Phone car charger & mount (or GPS device)
- ❑ Plug adapters

Miscellaneous

- ❑ Daypack
- ❑ Sealable plastic baggies
- ❑ Laundry supplies: soap, laundry bag, clothesline, spot remover
- ❑ Small umbrella
- ❑ Travel alarm/watch
- ❑ Notepad & pen
- ❑ Journal

Optional Extras

- ❑ Second pair of shoes (flip-flops, sandals, tennis shoes, boots)
- ❑ Travel hairdryer
- ❑ Picnic supplies
- ❑ Water bottle
- ❑ Fold-up tote bag
- ❑ Small flashlight
- ❑ Mini binoculars
- ❑ Small towel or washcloth
- ❑ Inflatable pillow/neck rest
- ❑ Tiny lock
- ❑ Address list (to mail postcards)
- ❑ Extra passport photos

British-Yankee Vocabulary

For a longer list, plus a dry-witted primer on British culture, see *The Septic's Companion* (Chris Rae). Note that instead of asking, "Can I help you?" many Brits offer a more casual "You alright?" or "You OK there?"

advert: advertisement

afters: dessert

Antipodean: an Australian or New Zealander

aubergine: eggplant

banger: sausage

bangers and mash: sausage and mashed potatoes

Bank Holiday: legal holiday

bap: small roll, roll sandwich

bespoke: custom-made

biro: ballpoint pen

biscuit: cookie

black pudding: sausage made with onions, pork fat, oatmeal, and pig blood

bloody: damn

bobby, rozzer: policeman ("the Bill" is more common)

Bob's your uncle: there you go, there you have it, (with a shrug), naturally

boffin: nerd, geek

bollocks: all-purpose expletive (a figurative use of testicles)

bolshy: argumentative, aggressive

bonnet: car hood

boot: car trunk

braces: suspenders

bridle way: path for walkers, bikers, and horse riders

brilliant: cool, awesome

brolly: umbrella

bubble and squeak: cabbage and potatoes fried together

bum: butt

candy floss: cotton candy

caravan: trailer

car-boot sale: temporary flea market, often for charity

car park: parking lot

cashpoint: ATM

casualty, infirmary: emergency room

cat's eyes: road reflectors

ceilidh (KAY-lee): informal evening of song and folk fun (Scottish and Irish)

cheap and cheerful: budget but adequate

cheap and nasty: cheap and bad quality

cheers: good-bye or thanks; also a toast

chemist: pharmacist

Chinese whispers: playing "telephone"

chippy: fish-and-chips shop; carpenter

chips: French fries

chock-a-block: jam-packed

chuffed: pleased

clearway: road where you can't stop

coach: long-distance bus

concession, concs: discounted admission

coronation chicken: curried chicken salad

cos: romaine lettuce

cot: baby crib

cotton buds: Q-tips

courgette: zucchini

craic (pronounced "crack"): fun, good conversation (Irish/Scottish and spreading to England)

crisps: potato chips

cuppa: cup of tea

dear: expensive

dicey: iffy, risky

digestives: round graham cookies

dinner: lunch or dinner

diversion: detour

dogsbody: menial worker, underappreciated staff

donkey's years: ages, long time

draughts: checkers

draw: marijuana

dual carriageway: divided highway (four lanes)

dummy: pacifier

elevenses: coffee-and-biscuits break before lunch

face flannel: washcloth

faggot: fried meatball

fancy: to like, to be attracted to (a person)

fell: hill or high plain (Lake District)

fiver: £5 bill

fizzy drink: pop or soda

flat: apartment

flutter: a bet

fly tipping: dumping garbage illegally

football, footie: soccer

fortnight: two weeks (shortened from "fourteen nights")

fringe: hair bangs

Frogs: French people

fruit machine: slot machine

full Monty: whole shebang, everything

gallery: balcony

gammon: ham; also an older person with right-wing views

gangway: aisle

ganja: marijuana

gaol: jail (same pronunciation)

gateau (or gateaux): cake

gear lever: stick shift

geezer: "dude"

goods wagon: freight truck

gormless: stupid

goujons: breaded and fried fish or chicken sticks

green fingers: green thumbs

grotty: unpleasant, lousy

half eight: 8:30 (not 7:30)

hard cheese: bad luck

hen night (or **hen do**): bachelorette party

homely: homey or cozy

hoover: vacuum cleaner

ice lolly: Popsicle

interval: intermission

ironmonger: hardware store

jacket potato: baked potato

jelly: Jell-O

jiggery-pokery: nonsense, shenanigans

Joe Bloggs: John Q. Public

jumble (sale): rummage sale

jumper: sweater

just a tick: just a second

kipper: smoked herring

kitchen roll: paper towels

knackered: exhausted (Cockney: cream crackered)

knickers: ladies' panties

knocking shop: brothel

ladybird: ladybug

lady fingers: flat, spongy cookie

lady's finger: okra

lay-by: stopping place on road

left luggage: baggage check

lemonade: lemon-lime soda

lemon squash: lemonade, not fizzy

let: rent

lift: elevator

loo: toilet or bathroom

lorry: truck

mack: mackintosh raincoat

made redundant: laid off

mangetout: snow peas

marrow: summer squash

mate: buddy (boy or girl)

mean: stingy

mental: crazy, wild, memorable

mobile (MOH-bile): cell phone

moggie: cat

naff: tacky or trashy

nappy: diaper

natter: talk on and on

newsagent: corner store

nought: zero

noughts & crosses: tic-tac-toe

off-licence: liquor store

on the pull: on the prowl

OTT: over the top, excessive

panto, pantomime: silly but fun play performed at Christmas

pants: (noun) underwear, briefs; (adj.) terrible, ridiculous

pear-shaped: messed up, gone wrong

petrol: gas

pillar box: mailbox

pissed (rude), **paralytic, bevvied, wellied, popped up, merry, trollied, ratted, rat-arsed, pissed as a newt:** drunk

pitch: playing field

plaster: Band-Aid

plonk: cheap, bad wine

plonker: one who drinks bad wine (a mild insult)

prat: idiot

press-on towel: panty liner

public school: private "prep" school (e.g., Eton)

publican: pub owner

pudding: dessert

pukka: first-class

punter: customer, especially in gambling

quid: pound (£1)

randy: horny

rasher: slice of bacon

read: study, as a college major

return ticket: round trip

revising; doing revisions: studying for exams

roundabout: traffic circle

rubber: eraser

rubbish: bad

satnav: satellite navigation, GPS

Scotch egg: hard-boiled egg wrapped in sausage meat and fried

self-catering: accommodation with kitchen

Sellotape: Scotch tape

services: freeway rest area

serviette: napkin

setee: couch

shag: intercourse (cruder than in the US)

shambolic: chaotic

shandy: lager and 7-Up

silencer: car muffler

single ticket: one-way ticket

single track: country road, often one lane

skip: dumpster

sleeping policeman: speed bumps

smalls: underwear

snap: photo (snapshot)

snogging: kissing, necking, making out

sod: mildly offensive insult

sod it, sod off: screw it, screw off

sod's law: Murphy's law

soda: soda water (not pop)

soldiers: toast sticks for dipping

solicitor: lawyer

spanner: wrench

spend a penny: urinate

spotted dick: raisin cake with custard

stag night (or **stag do**): bachelor party

starkers: buck naked

starters: appetizers

state school: public school

sticking plaster: Band-Aid

sticky tape: Scotch tape
stone: 14 pounds (weight)
stroppy: bad-tempered
subway: underground walkway
surgical spirit: rubbing alcohol
suspenders: garters
suss out: figure out
swede: rutabaga
ta: thank you
take the mickey/take the piss: tease
tatty: worn out or tacky
taxi rank: taxi stand
tenner: £10 bill
theatre: live stage
throw shapes: dance to pop music
tick: check mark
tight as a fish's bum: cheapskate (watertight)
tin: can
tip: public dump
tipper lorry: dump truck

toad in the hole: sausage dipped in batter and fried
top hole: first rate
torch: flashlight
towpath: path along a river
trainers: sneakers
treacle: golden syrup
twee: quaint, cutesy
twitcher: bird-watcher
verge: grassy edge of road
verger: church official
wee (verb): urinate
Wellingtons, wellies: rubber boots
whacked: exhausted
whinge (rhymes with hinge): whine
wind up: tease, irritate
witter on: gab and gab
wonky: weird, askew
yob, chav, ned: hooligan
zebra crossing: crosswalk
zed: the letter Z

INDEX

INDEX

INDEX

INDEX

INDEX

INDEX

MAP INDEX

MAP INDEX

Start your trip at

Our website enhances this book and turns

Explore Europe

At ricksteves.com you can browse through thousands of articles, videos, photos and radio interviews, plus find a wealth of money-saving travel tips for planning your dream trip. And with our mobile-friendly website, you can easily access all this great travel information anywhere you go.

TV Shows

Preview the places you'll visit by watching entire half-hour episodes of *Rick Steves' Europe* (choose from all 100 shows) on-demand, for free.

ricksteves.com

your travel dreams into affordable reality

Radio Interviews

Enjoy ready access to Rick's vast library of radio interviews covering travel tips and cultural insights that relate specifically to your Europe travel plans.

Travel Forums

Learn, ask, share! Our online community of savvy travelers is a great resource for first-time travelers to Europe, as well as seasoned pros.

Travel News

Subscribe to our free Travel News e-newsletter, and get monthly updates from Rick on what's happening in Europe.

Classroom Europe

Check out our free resource for educators with 400+ short video clips from the *Rick Steves' Europe* TV show.

Audio Europe™

Rick's Free Travel App

Get your FREE **Rick Steves Audio Europe**™ app to enjoy...

- Dozens of self-guided tours of Europe's top museums, sights and historic walks
- Hundreds of tracks filled with cultural insights and sightseeing tips from Rick's radio interviews
- All organized into handy geographic playlists
- For Apple and Android

With Rick whispering in your ear, Europe gets even better.

Find out more at ricksteves.com

Pack Light and Right

*Gear up for your
next adventure at
ricksteves.com*

Light Luggage

Pack light and right
with Rick Steves'
affordable, custom-
designed rolling carry-on
bags, backpacks, day
packs and shoulder bags.

Accessories

From packing cubes to
moneybelts and beyond,
Rick has personally
selected the travel
goodies that will
help your trip
go smoother.

Shop at ricksteves.com

Rick Steves has

Experience maximum Europe

Save time and energy

This guidebook is your independent-travel toolkit. But for all it delivers, it's still up to you to devote the time and energy it takes to manage the preparation and logistics that are essential for a happy trip. If that's a hassle, there's a solution.

Rick Steves Tours

A Rick Steves tour takes you to Europe's most interesting places with great

great tours, too!

with minimum stress

guides and small groups of 28 or less. We follow Rick's favorite itineraries, ride in comfy buses, stay in family-run hotels, and bring you intimately close to the Europe you've traveled so far to see. Most importantly, we take away the logistical headaches so you can focus on the fun.

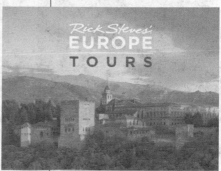

Join the fun

This year we'll take 33,000 free-spirited travelers— nearly half of them repeat customers—along with us on 50 different itineraries, from Athens to Istanbul. Is a Rick Steves tour the right fit for your travel dreams?

Find out at ricksteves.com, where you can also request Rick's latest tour catalog. Europe is best experienced with happy travel partners. We hope you can join us.

See our itineraries at ricksteves.com

A Guide for Every Trip

BEST OF GUIDES

Full-color guides in an easy-to-scan format. Focused on top sights and experiences in the most popular European destinations

Best of England
Best of Europe
Best of France
Best of Germany
Best of Ireland
Best of Italy
Best of Scotland
Best of Spain

COMPREHENSIVE GUIDES

City, country, and regional guides printed on Bible-thin paper. Packed with detailed coverage for a multi-week trip exploring iconic sights and venturing off the beaten path

Amsterdam & the Netherlands
Barcelona
Belgium: Bruges, Brussels, Antwerp & Ghent
Berlin
Budapest
Croatia & Slovenia
Eastern Europe
England
Florence & Tuscany
France
Germany
Great Britain
Greece: Athens & the Peloponnese
Iceland
Ireland
Istanbul
Italy
London
Paris
Portugal
Prague & the Czech Republic
Provence & the French Riviera
Rome
Scandinavia
Scotland
Sicily
Spain
Switzerland
Venice
Vienna, Salzburg & Tirol

HE BEST OF ROME

e, Italy's capital, is studded with
an remnants and floodlit-fountain
es. From the Vatican to the Colos-
, with crazy traffic in between, Rome
derful, huge, and exhausting. The
s, the heat, and the weighty history

of the Eternal City where Caesars walked
can make tourists wilt. Recharge by taking siestas, gelato breaks, and after-dark
walks, strolling from one atmospheric
square to another in the refreshing evening air.

ed *Pantheon*—which
est dome until the
ly 2,000 years old
ny over 1,500).

of Athens in the *Vat-
dies the humanistic
ce.

gladiators fought
another, entertaining

Rome *ristorante*

Rick Steves books are available from your favorite bookseller.
Many guides are available as ebooks.

POCKET GUIDES

Compact color guides for shorter trips

Amsterdam
Athens
Barcelona
Florence
Italy's Cinque Terre
London
Munich & Salzburg

Paris
Prague
Rome
Venice
Vienna

SNAPSHOT GUIDES

Focused single-destination coverage

Basque Country: Spain & France
Copenhagen & the Best of Denmark
Dublin
Dubrovnik
Edinburgh
Hill Towns of Central Italy
Krakow, Warsaw & Gdansk
Lisbon
Loire Valley
Madrid & Toledo
Milan & the Italian Lakes District
Naples & the Amalfi Coast
Nice & the French Riviera
Normandy
Northern Ireland
Norway
Reykjavík
Rothenburg & the Rhine
Sevilla, Granada & Southern Spain
St. Petersburg, Helsinki & Tallinn
Stockholm

CRUISE PORTS GUIDES

Reference for cruise ports of call

Mediterranean Cruise Ports
Scandinavian & Northern European
 Cruise Ports

Complete your library with...

TRAVEL SKILLS & CULTURE

*Study up on travel skills and gain
insight on history and culture*

Europe 101
Europe Through the Back Door
Europe's Top 100 Masterpieces
European Christmas
European Easter
European Festivals
For the Love of Europe
Travel as a Political Act

PHRASE BOOKS & DICTIONARIES

French
French, Italian & German
German
Italian
Portuguese
Spanish

PLANNING MAPS

Britain, Ireland & London
Europe
France & Paris
Germany, Austria & Switzerland
Iceland
Ireland
Italy
Spain & Portugal

Credits

RESEARCHERS
To help update this book, Rick relied on...

Cameron Hewitt

Born in Denver and raised in central Ohio, Cameron settled in Seattle in 2000. Ever since, he has spent three months each year in Europe, contributing to guidebooks, tours, radio and television shows, and other media for Rick Steves' Europe, where he serves as content manager. Cameron married his high school sweetheart (and favorite travel partner), Shawna, and enjoys taking pictures, trying new restaurants, and planning his next trip.

Pål Bjarne Johansen

A tour guide and guidebook researcher for Rick Steves' Europe (covering Scandinavia and Spain), Pål grew up in the Norwegian countryside near Oslo. He discovered his passion for travel and adventure at a young age and has backpacked much of the world. He first visited Spain with his family when he was four and has been back numerous times since, to this land that he considers his second home. When he's not working for Rick Steves, you'll find Pål skiing the Norwegian woods in winter and sailing the seven seas in summer.

Carrie Shepherd

After a childhood spent traipsing around New England, Carrie had a college semester in London, spurring her to explore and travel as much as her budget and employers allow. She's spent her career writing and editing arts and entertainment content, and now works as a guidebook editor and researcher for Rick Steves' Europe.

Kevin Williams

Kevin embarked on a European backpacking trip when he was 18, and he's been hooked on Europe ever since. He soon returned to study European history in England and spent his free time exploring the rest of the continent. He is a devoted soccer fan and will catch a match in Europe whenever he can. When he's not on the road, Kevin can be found cheering on the Seattle Sounders or taking in the beauty of Cascadia.

CONTRIBUTOR
Gene Openshaw

Gene has co-authored more than a dozen *Rick Steves* books, specializing in writing walks and tours of Europe's cities, museums, and cultural sights. He also contributes to Rick's public television series, produces audio tours on Europe, and is a regular guest on Rick's public radio show. Outside of the travel world, Gene has co-authored *The Seattle Joke Book*. As a composer, he has written a full-length opera called *Matter*, a violin sonata, and dozens of songs. He lives near Seattle with his daughter, enjoys giving presentations on art and history, and roots for the Mariners in good times and bad.

ACKNOWLEDGMENTS
Thanks to Roy and Jodi Nicholls for their research help, to Sarah Murdoch for writing the original version of the southern England chapters, to Melanie Jeschke for the original version of the Oxford chapter, and to friends listed in this book, who put the "Great" in Great Britain.

PHOTO CREDITS
Front Cover: Tintagel Castle, Cornwall © Justin Foulkes / Sime / eStock Photo
Back Cover (left to right): © Acceleratorhams, Dreamstime.com; © Ciro Amedeo Orabona, Dreamstime.com; © Boonlong Noragitt, Dreamstime.com
Title Page: Castle Combe, Cotswolds © Dominic Arizona Bonuccelli

Alamy: 82 © Ian Dagnall Computing, 126 bottom © Chronicle
Dreamstime: 8 top © Bhofack2
Public Domain via Wikimedia Commons: 114, 881 top, 884

Additional Photography: Dominic Arizona Bonuccelli, Orin Dubrow, Tom Griffin, Cameron Hewitt, Sandra Hundacker, Suzanne Kotz, Cathy Lu, Addie Mannan, Lauren Mills, Gene Openshaw, Carrie Shepherd, Robyn Stencil, Rick Steves, Gretchen Strauch, Kevin Williams. Photos are used by permission and are the property of the original copyright owners.

Avalon Travel
Hachette Book Group
1700 Fourth Street
Berkeley, CA 94710

Text © 2020 by Rick Steves' Europe, Inc. All rights reserved.
Maps © 2020 by Rick Steves' Europe, Inc. All rights reserved.
Underground Map © 2020 Transport for London. Registered User No. 19/S/3451/P
Used with permission.

Printed in Canada by Friesens.
Ninth Edition. First printing March 2020.

ISBN 978-1-64171-227-9

For the latest on Rick's talks, guidebooks, tours, public television series, and public radio
show, contact Rick Steves' Europe, 130 Fourth Avenue North, Edmonds, WA 98020,
425/771-8303, www.ricksteves.com, rick@ricksteves.com.

Hachette Book Group supports the right to free expression and the value of copyright. The
purpose of copyright is to encourage writers and artists to produce the creative works that
enrich our culture. The scanning, uploading, and distribution of this book without permission is a theft of the author's intellectual property. If you would like permission to use material from the book (other than for review purposes), please contact permissions@hbgusa.
com. Thank you for your support of the author's rights. The publisher is not responsible for
websites (or their content) that are not owned by the publisher.

Rick Steves' Europe

Managing Editor: Jennifer Madison Davis
Assistant Managing Editor: Cathy Lu
Special Publications Manager: Risa Laib
Editors: Glenn Eriksen, Julie Fanselow, Tom Griffin, Suzanne Kotz, Rosie Leutzinger,
  Jessica Shaw, Carrie Shepherd
Editorial & Production Assistant: Megan Simms
Editorial Interns: Maxwell Eberle, Amelia Benich
Researchers: Cameron Hewitt, Pål Bjarne Johansen, Carrie Shepherd, Kevin Williams
Graphic Content Director: Sandra Hundacker
Maps & Graphics: David C. Hoerlein, Lauren Mills, Mary Rostad
Digital Asset Coordinator: Orin Dubrow

Avalon Travel

Senior Editor and Series Manager: Madhu Prasher
Editors: Jamie Andrade, Sierra Machado
Copy Editor: Kelly Lydick
Proofreader: Elizabeth Jang
Indexer: Stephen Callahan
Production & Typesetting: Lisi Baldwin, Rue Flaherty, Jane Musser
Cover Design: Kimberly Glyder Design
Maps & Graphics: Kat Bennett, Mike Morgenfeld

*Although every effort was made to ensure that the information was correct at the time of going to
press, the author and publisher do not assume and hereby disclaim any liability to any party for any
loss or damage caused by errors, omissions, mushy peas, or any potential travel disruption due to
labor or financial difficulty, whether such errors or omissions result from negligence, accident, or any
other cause.*

COLOR MAPS

England • West London • East London
• London Underground • Bath

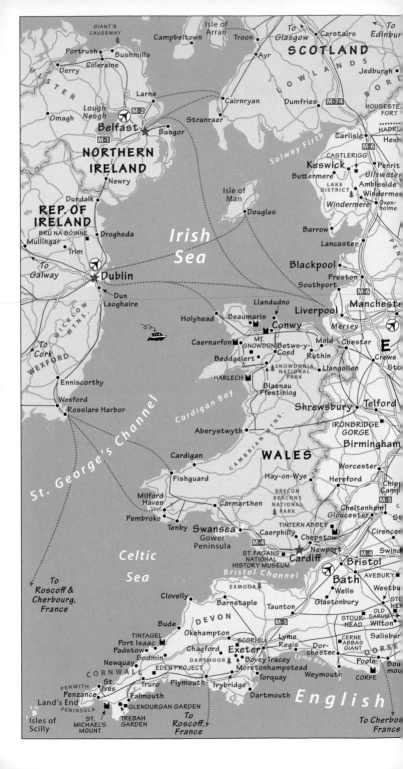

England

LEGEND

═══A-24═══	Freeway/Motorway
────	Major Rail Line
✈	Airport
♠	National Park/Natural Wonder
■	Ruin, Museum, Other Point of Interest
⌂	Castle/Monument/Palace

50 Kilometers
50 Miles

Berwick-upon-Tweed
Beal
Holy Island
BAMBURGH CASTLE
Alnwick
Newcastle-upon-Tyne
Durham
AMISH SEUM
Middlesbrough
Staithes
Grosmont
NORTH YORK MOORS
Whitby
Robin Hood's Bay
Goathland
ORK SHIRE ALES
EVAULX BBEY
Thirsk
Hutton-le-Hole
Pick
Scarborough
CASTLE HOWARD
EDEN CAMP
Bridlington
York
Doncaster
ds
Sheffield
M-1
Kingston-upon-Hull
Grimsby

North Sea

LAND
D L A N D S
Lincoln
Newark
rby
Nottingham
M-1
Boston
Skegness
The Wash
Cromer
cester
Stamford
Peter-borough
King's Lynn
Norwich
Great Yarmouth
Coventry
Warwick
ratford
Northampton
Ely
E A S T
reton
BLENHEIM PALACE
Luton
Cambridge
A N G L I A
Ipswich
Oxford
Hertford
Stansted
Harwich
M-40
Leavesden
M-11
Colchester
cot
Thames
London
eading
Windsor
Heathrow
City
Greenwich
Southend
Southend-on-Sea
M-3
M-23
M-20
M-2
Whitstable
Ramsgate
achester
Gatwick
K E N T
Canterbury
To Amsterdam, Netherlands
To Hoek van Holland, Netherlands
Zeebrugge
Ostende
Bruges
BELGIUM
E-40
E-17
uthampton
Portsmouth
ARUNDEL
SISSINGHURST GARDENS
Battle
PEVENSEY
Ashford
Folkestone
Dover
WHITE CLIFFS OF DOVER
Dunkirk
Calais
Channel Tunnel
FIGHBOURNE
LUREAN PALACE
Brighton
Newhaven
Alfriston
Hastings
Rye
Eastbourne
BEACHY HEAD
of ht
Lille
E-42
FRANCE
Channel
To St-Malo, France
To Caen (Ouistreham), France
To Dieppe, France
A-16
A-26
To Paris
To Paris
To Brussels

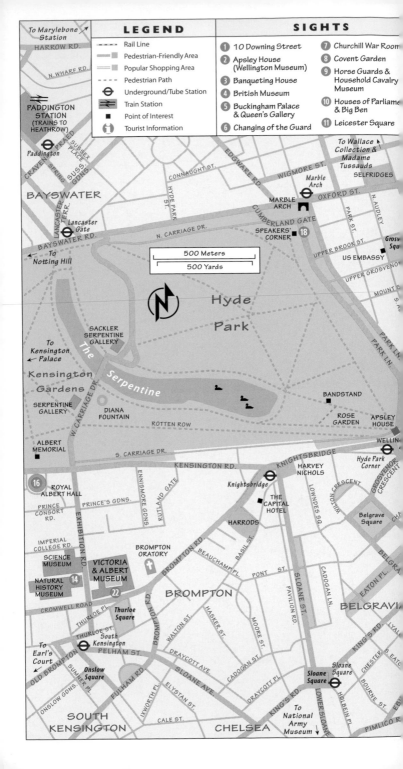

LEGEND

- ----- Rail Line
- Pedestrian-Friendly Area
- Popular Shopping Area
- ----- Pedestrian Path
- ⊖ Underground/Tube Station
- ⇌ Train Station
- ■ Point of Interest
- ⓘ Tourist Information

SIGHTS

1. 10 Downing Street
2. Apsley House (Wellington Museum)
3. Banqueting House
4. British Museum
5. Buckingham Palace & Queen's Gallery
6. Changing of the Guard
7. Churchill War Room
8. Covent Garden
9. Horse Guards & Household Cavalry Museum
10. Houses of Parliament & Big Ben
11. Leicester Square

To Marylebone Station

HARROW RD.

N. WHARF RD.

PADDINGTON STATION (TRAINS TO HEATHROW)

Paddington

CRAVEN RD. PRAED ST. SPRING ST. SUSSEX PLACE SUSS. GDNS. LANCASTER TERR.

BAYSWATER

Lancaster Gate

To Notting Hill

CONNAUGHT ST. EDGWARE RD.

HYDE PARK ST. N. CARRIAGE DR.

BAYSWATER RD.

WIGMORE ST. Marble Arch SELFRIDGES

MARBLE ARCH OXFORD ST.

CUMBERLAND GATE SPEAKERS' CORNER 18

To Wallace Collection & Madame Tussauds

N. AUDLEY ST.

PARK ST. UPPER BROOK ST. Grosv Squ

US EMBASSY

UPPER GROSVENO

MOUNT S

500 Meters

500 Yards

Hyde Park

SACKLER SERPENTINE GALLERY

To Kensington Palace

The Serpentine

Kensington Gardens

SERPENTINE GALLERY

DIANA FOUNTAIN

ROTTEN ROW

ALBERT MEMORIAL

S. CARRIAGE DR.

BANDSTAND

ROSE GARDEN

APSLEY HOUSE

WELLIN

PARK LN.

PARK LN.

KENSINGTON RD.

KNIGHTSBRIDGE

Hyde Park Corner

16 ROYAL ALBERT HALL

PRINCE CONSORT RD.

ENNISMORE GDNS.

PRINCE'S GDNS.

RUTLAND GATE

Knightsbridge

HARVEY NICHOLS

THE CAPITAL HOTEL

LOWNDES ST.

WILTON

GROSVENOR CRESCENT

CRESCENT

Belgrave Square

BELGRA

IMPERIAL COLLEGE RD.

SCIENCE MUSEUM

EXHIBITION RD.

NATURAL HISTORY MUSEUM 14

HARRODS

BROMPTON ORATORY BROMPTON RD. BEAUCHAMP PL.

BASIL ST.

PONT ST.

CADOGAN LN.

EATON PL.

CROMWELL ROAD

VICTORIA & ALBERT MUSEUM 22

Thurloe Square

BROMPTON

BELGRAVI

To Earl's Court

THURLOE PL.

THURLOE ST. South Kensington PELHAM ST.

OLD BROMPTON RD.

SUMNER PL.

Onslow Square

ONSLOW GDNS.

PELHAM ST.

WALTON ST.

HASKER ST.

DRAYCOTT AVE.

FULHAM RD.

IXWORTH PL.

ELYSTAN ST.

CALE ST.

SOUTH KENSINGTON

SLOANE AVE.

MOORE ST.

PAVILION RD.

SLOANE ST.

CADOGAN ST.

DRAYCOTT PL.

Sloane Square

To National Army Museum

CHELSEA

KING'S RD.

LOWER SLOANE

HOLBEIN PL.

PIMLICO P

KING'S RD. LYAL

CHESTER B FACE

BOURNE

Sloane Square

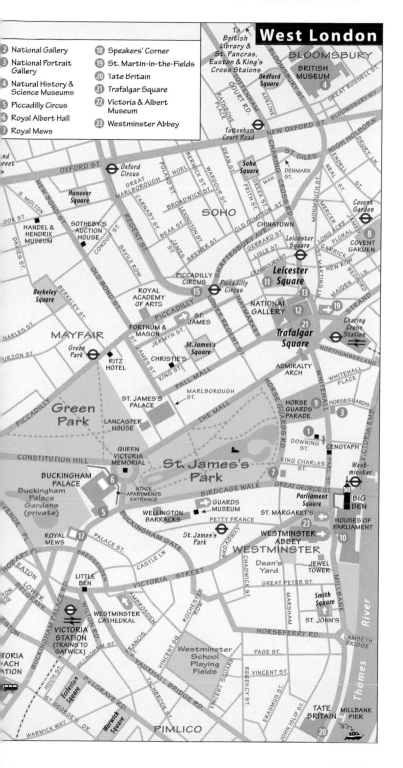

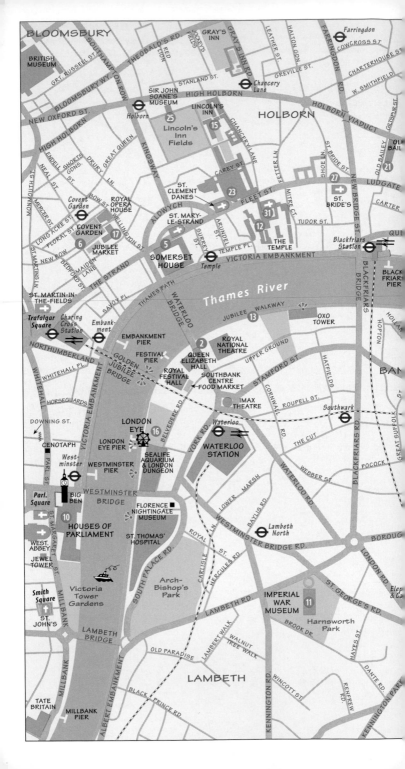

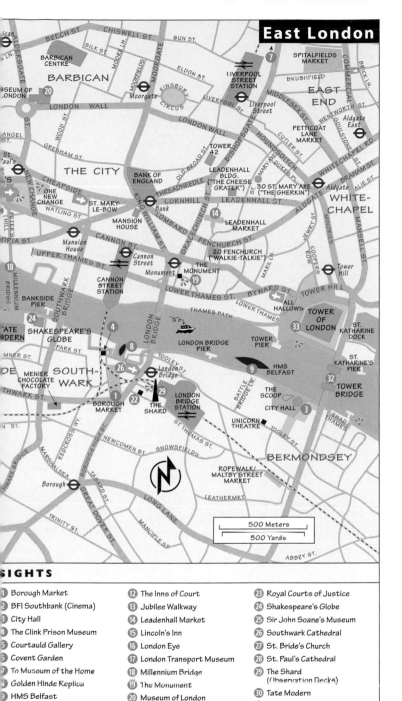

East London

SIGHTS

1. Borough Market
2. BFI Southbank (Cinema)
3. City Hall
4. The Clink Prison Museum
5. Courtauld Gallery
6. Covent Garden
7. To Museum of the Home
8. Golden Hinde Replica
9. HMS Belfast
10. Houses of Parliament & Big Ben
11. Imperial War Museum
12. The Inns of Court
13. Jubilee Walkway
14. Leadenhall Market
15. Lincoln's Inn
16. London Eye
17. London Transport Museum
18. Millennium Bridge
19. The Monument
20. Museum of London
21. Old Bailey
22. Old Operating Theatre Museum & Herb Garret
23. Royal Courts of Justice
24. Shakespeare's Globe
25. Sir John Soane's Museum
26. Southwark Cathedral
27. St. Bride's Church
28. St. Paul's Cathedral
29. The Shard (Observation Decks)
30. Tate Modern
31. Temple Church
32. Tower Bridge
33. Tower of London

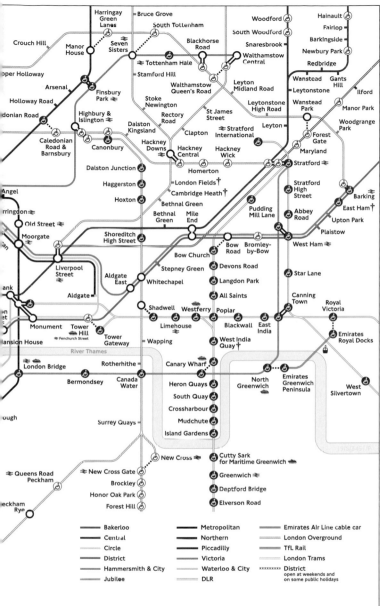

Bath

CRESCENT
LANE
JULIAN RD.
MOREFORD ST.

MUSEUM OF BATH AT WORK
8

ROYAL CRESCENT

RIVERS ST.

Catharine Place

CIRCUS MEWS

RUSSELL ST.

LANSDOWN

UPPER CHURCH ST.

MARLBOROUGH BLDGS.

14

NO. 1 ROYAL CRESCENT
9

MARGARETS BLDGS.

BROCK ST.

THE CIRCUS

BENNETT ST.

SAVILLE ROW

FASHION MUSEUM & ASSEMBLY ROOMS
4

ALFRED ST.

BARTLETT ST.

The Circus
3

GRAVEL WALK

MILES BLDGS.

Royal Victoria Park

ROYAL AVE.

GAY ST.

GEORGE ST.

MILSOM

MIL PL.

MINI GOLF

Bowling Green

Tennis Courts

JANE AUSTEN CENTRE
6

MARLBOROUGH LANE

P

← To A-4 & Bristol

UPPER BRISTOL RD.

NELSON PL. W.

CHARLOTTE ST.

QUEEN SQ. PL.

Queen Square
12

JOHN ST.

WOOD ST.

QUEEN ST.

QUIET

PALACE YARD

NEW KING ST.

POST

CHARLES ST.

PRINCESS ST.

MONMOUTH

THEATRE ROYAL
15

ST. JOHN'S PL.

UPPER BOR

SAW CLOSE

BRIDEWELL LN.

USTINOV THEATRE & THE EGG

WESTGA

NORFOLK BUILDINGS

P

Kingsmead Square

CR
B

CHANDO'S BLDGS.

JAMES ST.

WEST

HETLING CT.

GREEN PARK

Green Park

MILK ST.

AVON ST.

THERM
BATH S

LEGEND

- ▭▭▭ Rail Line
- ▬▬▬ ■ Pedestrian-Friendly Area
- ▬▬▬ ■ Popular Shopping Area
- - - - Footpath
- ■ Point of Interest/Landmark
- ✚ Tourist Information
- → One-Way Streets
- ∿∿∿ Traffic barriers

200 Meters
200 Yards

GREEN PARK RD.

CORN ST.

River
Avon

B

WELLS RD.

← To Wells via A-367

SIGHTS

1 Abbey		**9** No. 1 Royal Crescent
2 To American Museum & Gardens		**10** Parade Gardens
3 The Circus		**11** Pulteney Bridge
4 Fashion Museum & Assembly Rooms		**12** Queen Square
5 Guildhall Market		**13** Roman Baths & Pump Room
6 Jane Austen Centre		**14** Royal Crescent
7 Museum of Bath Architecture		**15** Theatre Royal
8 Museum of Bath at Work		**16** Thermae Bath Spa
		17 Victoria Art Gallery

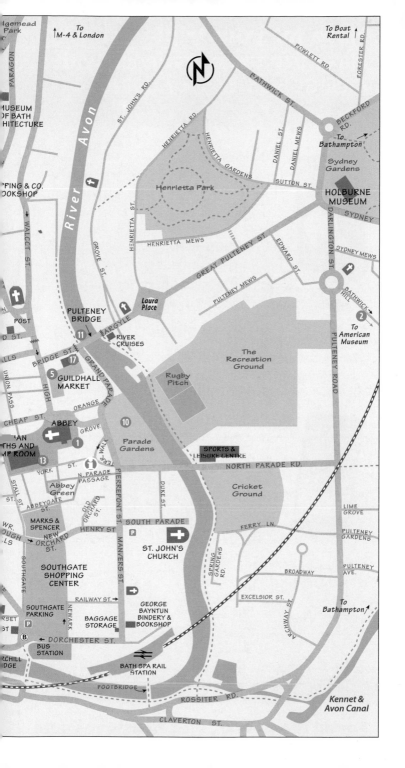

More for your trip!
Maximize the experience with Rick Steves as your guide

Guidebooks
Make side trips smooth and affordable with Rick's Britain and London guides

Planning Maps
Use the perfect pre-trip planning tool for mapping out your itinerary

Rick's TV Shows
Preview your destinations with a wide variety of shows covering England

Rick's Audio Europe™ App
Get free self-guided audio tours for London's top sights

Small Group Tours
Take a lively, low-stress Rick Steves tour through England

For all the details, visit ricksteves.com